INDIANA

PRENTICE HALL
LITERATURE

PENGUIN EDITION

PEARSON

Prentice
Hall

Upper Saddle River, New Jersey

Boston, Massachusetts

4 4690 00306589 9

13-digit ISBN 978-0-13-200804-4
10-digit ISBN 0-13-200804-1

3 4 5 6 7 8 9 10   10 09 08

Cover: *Cafe-terrace at Night (Place du forum in Arles)*, 1888. Oil on canvas, Vincent van Gogh, Erich Lessing/Art Resource, NY.

ACKNOWLEDGMENTS

Grateful acknowledgment is made to the following for copyrighted material:

Addison Wesley Longman Limited Excerpts from *Sundiata: An Epic of Old Mali* by D. T. Niane. © Longman Group Limited 1965, reprinted by permission of Pearson Education Limited. Translated by G.D. Pickett.

The Bancroft Library, Admin. Offices From *Desert Exile,* "The Uprooting of a Japanese Family," pp. 69–78 by Yoshiko Uchida. Copyright © 1982 by University of Washington Press: Seattle. Courtesy of the Bancroft Library, University of California, Berkeley.

Elizabeth Barnett, literary executor for the Edna St. Vincent Millay Society "Conscientious Objector" by Edna St. Vincent Millay from *Collected Poems,* Harper-Collins. Copyright © 1934, 1962 by Edna St. Vincent Millay and Norma Millay Ellis. All rights reserved. Used by permission of Elizabeth Barnett, literary executor.

Dave Barry From "What Baseball Means to Me" by Dave Barry from *What Baseball Means to Me: A Celebration of Our National Pastime.* Copyright © 2002 by Curt Smith and the National Baseball Hall of Fame and Museum, Inc. All rights reserved.

Alexandra Broyard "Books of the Times" feature by Anatole Broyard from *The New York Times,* November 9, 1983. Copyright © 1983 by Anatole Broyard. Used by permission of Alexandra Broyard.

Anchor Books/Doubleday "The Sun Parlor" from *The Richer, The Poorer* by Dorothy West, copyright © 1995 by Dorothy West. Used by permission of Doubleday, a division of Random House, Inc.

Susan Bergholz Literary Services From "In Commemoration: One Million Volumes" by Rudolfo A. Anaya from *A Million Stars by Anaya.* Copyright © by Rudolfo Anaya. "Tepeyac" by Sandra Cisneros from *Vintage Cisneros.* Copyright © 2004 by Sandra Cisneros. All rights reserved.

Chana Bloch "Pride" by Dahlia Ravikovitch, translated by Chana Bloch and Ariel Bloch, from *The Window.* Copyright © 1987 by Chana Bloch. All rights reserved. Reprinted by permission.

Brandt & Hochman Literary Agents, Inc. "By the Waters of Babylon" by Stephen Vincent Benét. Copyright © 1937 by Stephen Vincent Benét. Copyright renewed © 1965 by Thomas C. Benét, Stephanie Mahin, and Rachel B. Lewis. Used by permission of Brandt & Hochman Literary Agents, Inc.

Brooks Permissions "The Bean Eaters" by Gwendolyn Brooks from *Blacks.* Copyright © 1991 by Gwendolyn Brooks, published by Third World Press, Chicago. Reprinted by consent of Brooks Permissions.

Christo and Jeanne-Claude "Christo and Jeanne-Claude: *The Gates* Project for Central Park, New York" from *www.christojeanneclaude.net.*

City of Durham, NC—Human Resources Department Summer Employment Application by Staff of the City of Durham, NC—Human Resources Department. Reprinted by permission.

Don Congdon Associates, Inc. "There Will Come Soft Rains" by Ray Bradbury from *Collier's Weekly,* 1950. Copyright © 1950 by Crowell Collier Company, renewed 1977 by Ray Bradbury. Reprinted by permission. "Contents of the Dead Man's Pocket" by Jack Finney from *Collier's,* 1956. Copyright © 1957 by Crowell Collier Publishing, renewed 1984 by Jack Finney.

Crown Publishers, a division of Random House, Inc. "Damon and Pythias" from *Classic Myths to Read Aloud* by William F. Russell, copyright © 1988 by William F. Russell. Used by permission of Crown Publishers, a division of Random House, Inc.

Dial Books for Young Readers, a division of Penguin Young Readers Group, a member of Penguin Group (USA) Inc. "Cupid and Psyche" by Sally Benson from *Stories of the Gods and Heroes.* Copyright 1940, renewed © 1968 by Sally Benson. Used by permission of Dial Books for Young Readers, a division of Penguin Young Readers Group, a member of Penguin Group (USA) Inc., 345 Hudson Street, New York, NY 10014. All rights reserved.

Dorling Kindersley Ltd. "Mali" by Dorling Kindersley World from *Dorling Kindersley World Reference Atlas.*

(Continued on page R68, which is hereby considered an extension of this copyright page.)

CONTRIBUTING AUTHORS

The contributing authors guided the direction and philosophy of *Prentice Hall Literature: Penguin Edition.* Working with the development team, they helped to build the pedagogical integrity of the program and to ensure its relevance for today's teachers and students.

Kevin Feldman

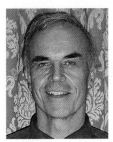

Kevin Feldman, Ed.D., is the Director of Reading and Intervention for the Sonoma County Office of Education and an independent educational consultant. He publishes and provides consultancy and training nationally, focusing upon improving school-wide literacy skills as well as targeted interventions for struggling readers, special needs students, and second language learners. Dr. Feldman is the co-author of the California Special Education Reading Task Force report and the lead program author for the 2002 Prentice Hall secondary language arts program *Timeless Voices, Timeless Themes.* He serves as technical consultant to the California Reading and Literature Project and the CalSTAT State Special Education Improvement Project. Dr. Feldman has taught for nineteen years at the university level in Special Education and Masters' level programs for University of California, Riverside, and Sonoma State University.

Dr. Feldman earned his undergraduate degree in Psychology from Washington State University and has a Master's Degree from UC Riverside in Special Education, Learning Disabilities, and Instructional Design. He has an Ed.D. from the University of San Francisco in Curriculum and Instruction.

Sharon Vaughn

Sharon Vaughn, Ph.D., is the H.E. Hartfelder/The Southland Corporation Regents Professor at the University of Texas and also director of the Vaughn Gross Center for Reading and Language Arts at the University of Texas (VGCRLA). As director of the VGCRLA, she leads more than five major initiatives, including The Central Regional Reading First Technical Assistance Center; the Three-Tier Reading Research Project; a bilingual-biliteracy (English/Spanish) intervention research study; the Grades 1–4 Teacher Reading Academies that have been used for teacher education throughout Texas and the nation; and the creation of online professional development in reading for teachers and other interested professionals.

Dr. Vaughn has published more than ten books and over one hundred research articles. She is Editor in Chief of the *Journal of Learning Disabilities* and serves on the editorial board of more than ten research journals, including the *Journal of Educational Psychology,* the *American Educational Research Journal,* and the *Journal of Special Education.*

Kate Kinsella

Kate Kinsella, Ed.D., is a teacher educator in the Department of Secondary Education at San Francisco State University. She teaches coursework addressing academic language and literacy development in linguistically and culturally diverse classrooms. Dr. Kinsella maintains secondary classroom involvement by teaching an academic literacy class for adolescent English learners through the University's Step to College Program. She publishes and provides consultancy and training nationally, focusing upon responsible instructional practices that provide second language learners and less proficient readers in grades 4–12 with the language and literacy skills vital to educational mobility.

Dr. Kinsella is the program author for *Reading in the Content Areas: Strategies for Reading Success,* published by Pearson Learning, and the lead program author for the 2002 Prentice Hall secondary language arts program *Timeless Voices, Timeless Themes.* She is the co-editor of the *CATESOL Journal* (California Association of Teachers of ESL) and serves on the editorial board for the *California Reader.* A former Fulbright scholar, Dr. Kinsella has received numerous awards, including the prestigious Marcus Foster Memorial Reading Award, offered by the California Reading Association in 2002 to a California educator who has made a significant statewide impact on both policy and pedagogy in the area of literacy.

Differentiated Instruction Advisor
Don Deshler

Don Deshler, Ph.D, is the Director of the Center for Research on Learning (CRL) at the University of Kansas. Dr. Deshler's expertise centers on adolescent literacy, learning strategic instruction, and instructional strategies for teaching content-area classes with academically diverse student bodies. He is the author of *Teaching Content to All: Evidence-Based Inclusive Practices in Middle and Secondary Schools,* a text which presents the instructional practices that have been tested and validated through his research at CRL.

UNIT AUTHORS

An award-winning contemporary author hosts each unit in each level of Prentice Hall Literature. *Serving as guides for your students, these authors introduce literary concepts, answer questions about their work, and discuss their own writing processes, using their works as models. Following are the featured unit authors for Grade 10.*

Susan **Vreeland (b. 1946)**

Unit 1: Fiction and Nonfiction Susan Vreeland has extensive experience in writing both fiction and nonfiction. Her book *Girl in Hyacinth Blue*, which describes the successive owners of an imaginary painting by Vermeer, received the San Diego Book Awards' Best Novel of the Year prize. Other novels include *The Forest Lover* and *The Passion of Artemisia*. Ms. Vreeland has also written about 250 nonfiction articles on a variety of subjects.

C. J. **Cherryh (b. 1942)**

Unit 2: Short Stories C. J. Cherryh is the ideal guide for the short-story unit. A popular and critically acclaimed fantasy and science-fiction writer, she has won numerous prizes for her short stories and for her more than forty novels. For example, she received the coveted Hugo Award for both her short story "Cassandra" and her novels *Downbelow Station* and *Cyteen*. Her hobbies include traveling, weaving, and ice skating, in addition to studying marine life, dinosaurs, and art.

Erik **Weihenmayer (b. 1968)**

Unit 3: Types of Nonfiction: Essays and Speeches As an athlete and motivational speaker, Erik Weihenmayer has experience in writing various types of nonfiction, including informal essays and an autobiography. On May 25, 2001, he became the first blind climber in history to reach the summit of Mt. Everest. He wrote about his life and the experience of climbing Everest in *Touch the Top of the World*, a bestseller that *Publishers Weekly* called "moving and adventure packed."

Cornelius **Eady (b. 1954)**

Unit 4: Poetry Cornelius Eady is a well-known poet and teacher of poetry, making him an ideal guide for this unit. His books include *Victims of the Latest Dance Craze*, which was named a Lamont Poetry Selection by the Academy of American Poets, and *The Gathering of My Name*, which was nominated for a Pulitzer Prize. A music-theater piece he collaborated on was a finalist for a Pulitzer Prize in Drama. In addition, his work frequently draws inspiration from African American musical traditions.

David Henry **Hwang (b. 1957)**

Unit 5: Drama As a dramatist, David Henry Hwang achieved early success in the theater with his first play, *FOB (Fresh Off the Boat)*. It won the 1981 Obie Award as the best new off-Broadway play of the season. He established himself as a major talent with *M. Butterfly*, which won a Tony Award for best play on Broadway. His recent work includes *Tibet Through the Red Box*, a play that appeals to both young people and adults.

John Phillip **Santos (b. 1957)**

Unit 6: Themes in Literature: Heroes and Dreamers
John Phillip Santos is well suited to serve as a guide for this unit by virtue of his memoir, *Places Left Unfinished at the Time of Creation*, a National Book Award Finalist. This lyrical book weaves together family history, literary references, and reflections to explore a variety of themes. Mr. Santos, the first Mexican American to win a Rhodes scholarship, has also written documentary films.

Program Advisors

Kathryn Leibrock Allison
English Department Chair
North Central High School
MSD Washington Township
Indianapolis, Indiana

Linda L. Doerr
Teacher, Language Arts,
Speech, Drama
Memorial Park Middle School
Fort Wayne, Indiana

Laura B. Eller
Grade 7 Language Arts Teacher
Noblesville Middle School
Noblesville, Indiana

Joyce Dudgeon
English Teacher/
Department Chair
Noblesville Middle School
Noblesville, Indiana

Pam Fischer
English Teacher, Lawrence
Central High School
Indianapolis, Indiana

Janet L. Garrett
Digital Age Literacy Coach
MSD of Lawrence Township
Indianapolis, Indiana

Pamala Griffin
8th Grade Language Arts
Teacher / AVID Leader
Belzer Middle School
Lawrence Township
Indianapolis, Indiana

Letitia Gustas
6th Grade English/
Reading Teacher
Department Chairperson
Grimmer Middle School
Schererville, Indiana

Donald Kopenec
English Department Chairman
Donald E Gavit HS

Jenny Leist
Teacher
Scribner Middle School
New Albany, Indiana

Nancy Mast
English Curriculum Coordinator
Hobart Middle School
Hobart, Indiana

Diane Messman
Teacher of Language Arts
Kesling Middle School
LaPorte, Indiana

Chandre Morgan
English Teacher
Indianapolis Public Schools
Indianapolis, Indiana

Rachel Nichols
Teacher/Department Chairperson
Bloomington High
School North
Bloomington, Indiana

Brenda G. Scheidler
Supervisor of Language Arts
District Resource/
Curriculum Supervisor
Evansville-Vanderburgh School
Corporation
Evansville, Indiana

Helen E. Shiffer
English Department Chairman
Carmel High School
Carmel, Indiana

Michelle Smith
8th Grade Reading Teacher
Brown I.C.
South Bend, Indiana

Sherelle M. Smith
Language Arts Teacher
George Washington Community
School
Indianapolis Public Schools
Indianapolis, Indiana

Cynthia Taylor
English Teacher
Warren Central High School
Indianapolis, Indiana

Penny Tokoly
English Department Chair
Lake Central High School
St. John, Indiana

Eileen M. Torrence
English Chair
Terre Haute South Vigo
High School
Terre Haute, Indiana

Charles R. Wells
Teacher
Emerson School for Visual
and Performing Arts
Gary, Indiana

Indiana
Academic Achievement Handbook

Unit 1

Fiction and Nonfiction

***All selections and workshops in this unit support your
Indiana standards.***

How does fact relate to fiction?

Short Stories

All selections and workshops in this unit support your Indiana standards.

How do we find solutions?

Types of Nonfiction: Essays and Speeches

Unit 3

 All selections and workshops in this unit support your Indiana standards.

How do we gather information?

Poetry

**All selections and workshops in this unit support your
Indiana standards.**

How do we respond to the world?

Unit 5 | Drama

All selections and workshops in this unit support your Indiana standards.

How do other people see us?

Unit 6

Themes in Literature
Heroes and Dreamers

 ***All selections and workshops in this unit support your
Indiana standards.***

How does our heritage help shape us?

SELECTIONS BY READING SKILL

All selections and workshops in this unit support your Indiana standards.

(Continued on next page)

SELECTIONS BY THEME

◼ On the Edge

◼ Striving for Success

Clashing Forces

Turning Points

■ Expanding Horizons

■ Joining Past and Future

INFORMATIONAL TEXTS AND OTHER NONFICTION

■ Reading Informational Materials—Instructional Workshops

■ Additional Nonfiction—Selections by Type

■ Literature in Context—Reading in the Content Areas

**A wealth of expository nonfiction is found throughout this program.
Nonfiction texts are highlighted in red in the Index.**

COMPARING LITERARY WORKS

SKILLS WORKSHOPS

▌ Writing Workshops

▌ Spelling Workshops

▌ Communications Workshops

Your Guide to Indiana
Standards and Testing

What's an Academic Standard?

Indiana's **Academic Standards** outline the skills and information you are expected to learn in major academic areas. Your English teachers are responsible for helping you master all of the Academic Standards in English/Language Arts. Here is a sample Academic Standard for tenth grade as well as a question that tests your understanding of the standard.

Standards Groupings

Indiana's Academic Standards for English/Language Arts are divided into seven standards that cover Reading, Writing, and Listening and Speaking. You can apply the skills in these areas to all of your academic classes.

Taking the Test

As a student in Indiana, you will be tested in language arts in grade 10. This test consists of multiple-choice, open-ended, and extended-response items. Extended-response items include an essay that you write in response to a prompt.

SAMPLE STANDARD

10.3.9 Explain how voice and the choice of a narrator affect characterization and the tone, plot, and credibility of a text.

SAMPLE QUESTION

1 This passage has a tone of

- O gentle appeal
- O political challenge
- O spontaneous rant
- O neutral observation

Soybean field in
Brownsburg, Indiana

Indiana's Academic Standards

Grade 10

The following pages list the Indiana Academic Standards for English/Language Arts.

Reading

Standard 1: <u>READING</u>: Word Recognition, Fluency, and Vocabulary Development

Structural Features of Informational and Technical Materials

10.1.1	Understand specific technical vocabulary.
10.1.2	Distinguish the meaning of words and their implication.
10.1.3	Use knowledge of ancient mythology to understand new words.
10.1.4	Understand literal and figurative meanings.

Standard 2: READING: Comprehension and Analysis of Nonfiction and Informational Texts

Structural Features of Informational and Technical Materials

10.2.1	Analyze formatting of informational documents.

Analysis of Grade-Level-Appropriate Nonfiction and Informational Text

10.2.2	Compare first-hand and second-hand accounts of an event.
10.2.3	Follow directions to use sophisticated technology.
10.2.4	Examine how the author's perspective influences the structure and tone of the text.

Expository (Informational) Critique

10.2.5	Make statements and draw conclusions about a text.

Standard 3: <u>READING</u>: Comprehension and Analysis of Literary Text

Structural Features of Literature

10.3.1	Analyze many different forms of dramatic literature.
10.3.2	Compare and contrast the presentation of a specific theme or topic across different genres.
10.3.3	Evaluate interactions between characters and how these affect the plot.
10.3.4	Analyze characters' traits through narration and dialogue.
10.3.5	Compare works that express a universal theme.
10.3.6	Evaluate an author's use of time and sequence.

Reading
(continued)

10.3.7	Evaluate the use of literary devices including figurative language, imagery, allegory, and symbolism.
10.3.8	Evaluate the impact of ambiguities, contradictions and ironies in the text.
10.3.9	Evaluate the use of voice and narrator.
10.3.10	Identify and evaluate dialogue, soliloquies, asides, character foils and stage designs in dramatic literature.
10.3.13	Explain how narrator's voice affects meaning.

Literary Criticism

10.3.11	Evaluate the aesthetic qualities of style.
10.3.12	Analyze how literature is related to the themes and issues of its historical period.

Standard 4: **WRITING**: Processes and Features

Writing

Organization and Focus

10.4.1	Brainstorm ideas with classmates, teachers and peers and develop a draft.
10.4.2	Establish a thesis and focus for the piece.
10.4.3	Use effective language (action verbs, active voice, sensory details).
10.4.13	Utilize techniques to write coherently.

Research Process and Technology

10.4.4	Use clear research questions and methods to compile evidence from many sources.
10.4.5	Use supporting evidence to develop main ideas within the body of the composition.
10.4.6	Synthesize information from multiple different sources.
10.4.7	Integrate quotations and citations into text.
10.4.8	Use appropriate conventions for documentation in text.
10.4.9	Use graphic software programs to design and publish documents.

Evaluation and Revision

10.4.10	Review and revise writing.
10.4.11	Revise writing based on specific criteria.
10.4.12	Provide constructive criticism to other writers.

Standard 5: **WRITING**: Applications (Different Types of Writing and Their Characteristics)

10.5.1	Write biographical or autobiographical narratives.
10.5.2	Write responses to literature.
10.5.3	Write expository compositions.
10.5.4	Write persuasive compositions.
10.5.5	Write business letters.
10.5.6	Write technical documents.
10.5.7	Use varied and expanded vocabulary.

| 10.5.8 | Write for different purposes and audiences. |

Writing
(continued)

Research Application

| 10.5.9 | Writer or deliver a research project that has been developed using a systematic research process. |

Standard 6: <u>WRITING</u>: English Language Conventions

Grammar and Mechanics of Writing

| 10.6.1 | Identify and correctly use clauses, phrases and punctuation. |
| 10.6.2 | Demonstrate an understanding of sentence construction. |

Manuscript Form

| 10.6.3 | Produce well-punctuated, legible work. |
| 10.6.4 | Apply appropriate manuscript conventions. |

Standard 7: <u>LISTENING AND SPEAKING</u>: Skills, Strategies, and Applications

Listening and
Speaking

Comprehension

| 10.7.1 | Summarize a speaker's purpose and point of view. |
| 10.7.2 | Correctly develop a speech and include quotations. |

Organization and Delivery of Oral Communication

10.7.3	Recognize and use elements of classical speech forms.
10.7.4	Use visual aids to enhance presentations.
10.7.5	Produce notes for extemporaneous speeches.
10.7.6	Select effective verbal and nonverbal techniques for presentations.

Analysis and Evaluation of Oral and Media Communications

10.7.7	Make judgments about the ideas being discussed.
10.7.8	Compare and contrast the ways in which media genres cover the same event.
10.7.9	Analyze historically significant speeches.
10.7.10	Assess how language and delivery affect mood of the speech.
10.7.11	Evaluate a speaker's presentation.
10.7.12	Analyze the types of arguments used by the speaker.
10.7.13	Identify and evaluate the artistic effects of a media presentation.

Speaking Applications

10.7.14	Deliver narrative presentations.
10.7.15	Deliver expository presentations.
10.7.16	Apply appropriate interviewing techniques.
10.7.17	Deliver oral responses to literature.
10.7.18	Deliver persuasive arguments.
10.7.19	Deliver descriptive presentations.

Writing Assessment Scoring Rubrics

The following rubrics are used to score student writing in Indiana. Use them to improve your writing and to check your work as you prepare for the test.

Writing Applications Overview

Score Level	Ideas and Content	Organization	Style	Voice
	Does the writing sample:			
6	• Fully accomplish the task? • Include thorough, relevant, and complete ideas?	• Organize ideas logically?	• Exhibit exceptional word usage? • Demonstrate exceptional writing technique?	• Demonstrate effective adjustment of language and tone to task and reader?
5	• Fully accomplish the task? • Include many relevant ideas?	• Organize ideas logically?	• Exhibit very good word usage? • Demonstrate very good writing technique?	• Demonstrate effective adjustment of language and tone to task and reader?
4	• Accomplish the task? • Include relevant details?	• Organize ideas logically?	• Exhibit good word usage? • Demonstrate good writing technique?	• Demonstrate an attempt to adjust language and tone to task and reader?
3	• Minimally accomplish the task? • Include some relvant details?	• Exhibit an attempt to organize ideas logically?	• Exhibit ordinary word usage? • Demonstrate average writing technique?	• Demonstrate an attempt to adjust language and tone to task and reader?
2	• Only partially accomplish the task? • Include few relevant details?	• Exhibit a minimal attempt to organize ideas logically?	• Exhibit minimal word usage? • Demonstrate minimal writing technique?	• Demonstrate language and tone that may be inappropriate to task and reader?
1	• Fail to accomplish the task? • Include very few relevant ideas?	• Organize ideas illogically?	• Exhibit less than minimal word usage? • Demonstrate less than minimal writing technique?	• Demonstrate language and tone that may be inappropriate to task and reader?

Language Conventions Rubric

Score	Does the writing sample exhibit a good command of language skills?
4	In a Score Point 4 paper, there are no errors that impair the flow of communication. Errors are infrequent and will generally be of the first-draft variety; they have a minor impact on the overall communication. • Do words have very few or no capitalization errors? • Do sentences have very few or no punctuation errors? • Do words have very few or no spelling errors? • Do sentences have very few or no grammar or word usage errors? • Writing has very few or no paragraphing errors. • Writing has very few or no run-on sentences or sentence fragments.

Score	Does the writing sample exhibit an adequate command of language skills?
3	In a Score Point 3 paper, errors are occasional but do not impede the flow of communication; the writer's meaning is not seriously obscured by errors in language conventions. • Do words have occasional capitalization errors? • Do sentences have occasional punctuation errors? • Do words have occasional spelling errors? • Do sentences have occasional grammar or word usage errors? • Writing may have occasional paragraphing errors. • Writing may have run-on sentences or sentence fragments.

Score	Does the writing sample exhibit a minimal command of language skills?
2	In a Score Point 2 paper, errors are typically frequent and may cause the reader to stop and reread part of the writing. While some aspects of the writing may be more consistently correct than others, the existing errors do impair communication. With a little extra effort on the reader's part, it is still possible to discern most, if not all, of what the writer is trying to communicate. • Do words have frequent capitalization errors? • Do sentences have frequent punctuation errors? • Do words have frequent spelling errors? • Do sentences have frequent grammar or word usage errors? • Writing may have errors in paragraphing, or paragraphing may be missing. • Writing is likely to have run-on sentences or sentence fragments.

Score	Does the writing sample exhibit a less than minimal command of language skills?
1	In a Score Point 1 paper, errors are serious and numerous; they often cause the reader to struggle to discern the writer's meaning. Errors are frequently of a wide variety. There may be sections where it is impossible to ascertain what the writer is attempting to communicate. • Do words have many capitalization errors? • Do sentences have many punctuation errors? • Do words have many spelling errors? • Do sentences have many grammar and word usage errors? • Writing may have errors in paragraphing, or paragraphing may be missing. • Writing is likely to have run-on sentences or sentence fragments.

Extended Response Practice

Writing Task 1

In our society, people are often rewarded for performing well. For example, hard work and discipline in school are usually rewarded with good grades, and some students find this recognition satisfying. Ralph Waldo Emerson, on the other hand, once wrote, "The reward of a thing well done is to have done it."

Write an essay in which you respond to Emerson's observation. Explain what he meant and whether you agree or disagree with him.

Be sure to include:

- an explanation of Emerson's observation in your own words
- an outline of your position on the subject
- examples from your experience and relevant details to support your argument
- an organization that is logical and coherent

Be sure to include:

- the purpose of your organization
- enough convincing details that will persuade the sponsor to make a pledge to your organization
- descriptive words that will appeal to the sponsor's emotions
- clear, well-constructed sentences

Writing Task 2

People like to belong to organizations that support worthwhile causes. Choose an organization that is devoted to a cause you believe is important.

Write a letter to persuade a sponsor to make a pledge to this organization. Use language that will appeal to your sponsor and provide concrete examples that show how your organization has helped others. Your letter should begin with a strong opening that catches the sponsor's attention and end with an appeal that states the action you want the sponsor to take.

Writing Task 3

Think about the various appliances in your home. Pick one. Consider what life would be like without this appliance. How has it made domestic life easier?

Write to inform someone about why this appliance is important in the home.

Be sure to include:

- a clear description of the appliance and how it has made life easier in the home
- details that are specific and relevant to the appliance
- ideas that are clearly and logically presented

Indiana Skills Review

Skills Review for the Indiana Reading Test

Your mastery of the Indiana Academic Standards in English/Language Arts is measured by the Indiana Reading Test. To do well on this exam, you'll need to practice the skills assessed.

The Indiana Skills Review provides six short tests with questions that assess skills tested on the Indiana Reading Test. Your teacher will set the pace for the review. As you work through the material, note the Academic Standards tested for each test and the types of questions that pose a struggle for you. For a full-length practice test, use the one in the *Indiana Test Preparation Workbook.*

Indiana Skills Review

Test	Use After Unit	Skill Focus	Skill Review
1	1	Make Predictions	27–104
		Cause and Effect	105–197
2	2	Make Inferences	215–302
		Draw Conclusions	303–403
3	3	Main Idea and Supportive Details	423–494
4	4	Persuasive Appeals	495–575
		Read Fluently	589–660
		Paraphrase	661–723
5	5	Summarize	743–814
		Reading Shakespeare	815–959
6	6	Cultural Context	977–1058
		Compare and Contrast	1059–1163

A Note to Parents

The Indiana Academic Standards outline the knowledge that your child needs to succeed on the Indiana Reading Test. Using the chart to the left, you can help your child review the skills covered in this textbook and monitor your child's progress toward mastering these concepts.

Indiana Skills Review

Test 1

The following selection is from a short story called "The Birthmark." In this passage, Aylmer, a scientist, becomes consumed with the idea of removing a small birthmark from his wife's cheek. Read the selection, and answer the questions that follow.

The Birthmark

Nathaniel Hawthorne

At all the seasons which should have been their happiest he invariably, and without intending it, nay, in spite of a purpose to the contrary, reverted to this one disastrous topic. Trifling as it at first appeared, it so connected itself with innumerable trains of thought and modes of feeling that it became the central point of all. With the morning twilight Aylmer opened his eyes upon his wife's face and recognized the symbol of imperfection; and when they sat together at the evening hearth his eyes wandered stealthily to her cheek, and beheld, flickering with the blaze of the wood-fire, the spectral hand that wrote mortality where he would fain have worshipped.

1 Which of the following BEST describes the conflict in this passage?

- o Aylmer is too interested in science to pay attention to his wife.
- o Aylmer is bored with his wife.
- o Aylmer is so obsessed with his wife's imperfection that he fights to concentrate on anything else.
- o Aylmer is obsessed with his own imperfections.

2 From this passage, you can MOST accurately predict that

- o Aylmer will forget about his wife's birthmark
- o Aylmer will attempt to remove the birthmark
- o Aylmer will stop practicing science forever
- o Aylmer will be driven to commit suicide

3 The author's mentioning that early on in the marriage, everything "reverted to this one disastrous topic" is an example of

- o foreshadowing
- o alliteration
- o dramatic irony
- o metaphor

4 Which of the following BEST describes the author's purpose?

- o to make the reader sympathize with Aylmer's wife
- o to amuse the reader
- o to explain Aylmer's obsession
- o to create a lighthearted setting

5 This passage PROBABLY comes from

- o an autobiography
- o an epistolary novel
- o a first-person narrative
- o a third-person narrative

6 Which of the following BEST describes the effect that the birthmark has on Aylmer?

- o It makes him love his wife more than ever.
- o It drives him to renounce science forever.
- o It makes him question his marriage.
- o It becomes the sole focus of his everyday life.

Academic Standards

Question 1: 10.3.3	*Question 2:* 10.3.3
Question 3: 10.3.6	*Question 4:* 10.3.1
Question 5: 10.3.1	*Question 6:* 10.3.3

Indiana Skills Review

This selection is from the opening paragraph of the short story "The Fall of the House of Usher." Read the selection, and answer the questions that follow.

THE FALL OF THE HOUSE OF USHER

Edgar Allan Poe

During the whole of a dull, dark, and soundless day in the autumn of the year, when the clouds hung oppressively low in the heavens, I had been passing alone, on horseback, through a singularly dreary tract of country; and at length found myself, as the shades of the evening drew on, within view of the melancholy House of Usher. I know not how it was; but, with the first glimpse of the building, a sense of insufferable gloom pervaded my spirit. I say insufferable; for the feeling was unrelieved by any of that half-pleasurable, because poetic, sentiment, with which the mind usually receives even the sternest natural images of the desolate or terrible.

1 Which of the following phrases helps you understand the setting of the passage?

- o "I had been passing alone"
- o "singularly dreary tract of country"
- o "I know not how it was"
- o "that half-pleasurable, because poetic, sentiment"

2 The author PROBABLY includes the house in this opening description

- o to make the reader feel at home
- o to show that the narrator notices everything
- o to suggest a connection between the house and one or more characters
- o to show where the narrator lives

3 Judging from the title, you can infer that

- o the story will involve some kind of collapse
- o the story has an unexpected ending
- o the narrator is extremely troubled
- o the narrator will be injured by the end of the story

4 What does the speaker reveal about him/herself when he/she says that the "sternest natural images of the desolate or terrible" are usually "half-pleasurable"?

- o He/She usually has an optimistic view of life.
- o He/She is a very lonely person.
- o He/She is looking forward to the end of his/her journey.
- o He/She finds some enjoyment in experiencing terrible things.

5 Which of the following themes is BEST demonstrated in this passage?

- o the relationship between characters and their surroundings
- o the struggle between people and nature
- o a person's attempt to control science
- o the relationship of storytelling to reality

6 From the narrator's description, you can infer that

- o he/she cannot see the house very well
- o the house has an eerie quality
- o he/she is eager to reach the house
- o the house is in very good condition

Academic Standards	
Question 1: 10.3.1	*Question 2:* 10.3.1
Question 3: 10.3.1	*Question 4:* 10.3.4
Question 5: 10.3.2	*Question 6:* 10.3.2

Indiana Skills Review

This selection is from a speech delivered by Susan Brownell Anthony in 1873 after she had been arrested for voting in the 1872 presidential election. Anthony was a lifelong advocate of civil rights for women. Read the selection, and answer the questions that follow.

INDIANA

On Woman's Right to the Suffrage

Susan Brownell Anthony

The only question left to be settled now is: Are women persons? And I hardly believe any of our opponents will have the hardihood to say they are not. Being persons, then, women are citizens; and no State has a right to make any law, or to enforce any old law, that shall abridge their privileges or immunities. Hence, every discrimination against women in the constitutions and laws of the several States is to-day null and void, precisely as in every one against negroes.

1 What is the author's MAIN purpose in this selection?

- o   to persuade
- o   to inform
- o   to entertain
- o   to satirize

2 What is the author's MAIN argument in favor of women's right to vote?

- o   States do not have the right to make laws.
- o   Married women should be allowed to vote only if their husbands agree.
- o   Women are citizens, and every citizen is entitled to the right to vote.
- o   The Constitution is null and void.

3 What phrase BEST describes the tone of this passage?

- o   gentle appeal
- o   political challenge
- o   spontaneous rant
- o   neutral observation

4 When the author says that "no State has a right to make any law ... that shall abridge their privileges or immunities," the word *abridge* means

- o   to shorten or condense, as a book
- o   to increase or expand
- o   to connect, as by a bridge
- o   to cut off or deprive

5 In this passage, the author encourages people to

- o   discriminate against women
- o   support women's right to vote
- o   ignore state laws
- o   oppose male citizenship

6 In addition to women, the author identifies what group of people as sharing in the struggle for civil rights?

- o   European immigrants
- o   Chinese
- o   American Indians
- o   African Americans

Academic Standards	
Question 1: 10.2.5	*Question 2:* 10.2.5
Question 3: 10.2.4	*Question 4:* 10.1.2
Question 5: 10.2.2	*Question 6:* 10.2.5
Question 7: 10.2.4	

Indiana Skills Review

The following selection is a sonnet written by William Shakespeare. Read the selection, and answer the questions that follow.

Sonnet 116

William Shakespeare

Let me not to the marriage of
  true minds
Admit impediments.
  Love is not love
Which alters when it
  alteration finds,
Or bends with the remover
  to remove:
Oh no! it is an ever-fixèd mark,
That looks on tempests and is
  never shaken;
It is the star to every wand'ring
  bark[1],
Whose worth's unknown, although
  his height be taken.[2]
Love's not Time's fool, though rosy
  lips and cheeks
Within his bending sickle's
  compass come;[3]
Love alters not with his brief hours
  and weeks,
But bears it out even to the edge
  of doom.
  If this be error and
    upon me proved,
  I never writ, nor no man
    ever loved.

---

[1] any small sailing vessel
[2] i.e., although its height may be measured.
[3] i.e., within the range of Time's sickle (an agricultural tool with a curved blade).

1 When the speaker says, "Love is not love / Which alters when it alteration finds," he means that

- o love changes when people change
- o true love endures in spite of changes
- o a love that endures is worthless
- o love can be altered to fit any situation

2 Which sentence BEST paraphrases the lines, "Love's not time's . . . compass come"?

- o Time and love claim many victims.
- o Although the appearance of youth may fade with time, love itself will not fade.
- o Love, like beauty, fades with time.
- o Time will test the strength of love.

3 The last two lines of the poem ("If this . . . ever loved") suggest that the speaker is PROBABLY

- o a poet or writer
- o an actor
- o Father Time
- o a broken-hearted lover

4 You can tell that this poem is a sonnet because

- o it is lyrical and uses figurative language
- o none of the lines rhyme
- o every line is part of a rhyming couplet
- o it consists of fourteen lines of iambic pentameter

5 What type of figurative language does the speaker use to describe love?

- o simile
- o metaphor
- o onomatopoeia
- o hyperbole

6 The phrase "compass come" is an example of what sound device?

- o consonance
- o slant rhyme
- o onomatopoeia
- o alliteration

Academic Standards

Question 1: 10.3.5	Question 2: 10.3.8
Question 3: 10.3.9	Question 4: 10.3.1
Question 5: 10.3.7	Question 6: 10.3.7

Indiana Skills Review

Juliet, of the Capulet family, has just met and fallen in love with Romeo Montague, whose family is feuding with the Capulets. Read the selection, and answer the questions that follow.

Romeo and Juliet

William Shakespeare

Juliet. 'Tis but thy name that is my enemy;
Thou art thyself though, not a Montague.
What's Montague? it is nor hand, nor foot,
Nor arm, nor face, nor any other part
Belonging to a man. O! be some other name:
What's in a name? that which we call a rose
By any other name would smell as sweet;
So Romeo would, were he not Romeo call'd,
Retain that dear perfection which he owes
Without that title[1]. Romeo, doff[2] thy name;
And for that name, which is no part of thee,
Take all myself.

---

[1] i.e., the perfection that is his regardless of the title "Montague."
[2] To rid oneself of.

1 Which sentence BEST summarizes the main idea of this selection?

- o Romeo plans to kidnap Juliet.
- o Juliet is in love with Romeo, but he does not love her in return.
- o It is not Romeo's name but his qualities that make him who he is.
- o Juliet hates Romeo because he is a Montague.

2 When Juliet says, "that which we call a rose / By any other name would smell as sweet," she means that

- o Romeo has given her a rose
- o many other flowers smell as sweet as roses
- o people call roses by many different names
- o even if a rose were called by another name, it would have the same scent

3 If Romeo cannot "doff" his name, Juliet will have to choose between

- o Romeo and one of his relatives
- o her family and Romeo
- o an education and an arranged marriage
- o living in a convent and living with her family

4 What universal tragic theme is reflected in the obstacles that Romeo and Juliet face?

- o conflict of individual against society
- o conflict of individual against himself or herself
- o conflict of individual against individual
- o conflict of individual against nature

5 Which phrase BEST describes the form of this passage?

- o Shakespearean sonnet
- o epic poetry
- o blank verse
- o rhyming couplets

6 What will MOST LIKELY happen to Romeo and Juliet at the end of the tragedy?

- o Their families will reconcile.
- o They will cease to love each other.
- o They will marry secretly and run away together.
- o Their families' feud will lead to their death.

Academic Standards	
Question 1: 10.3.8	*Question 2:* 10.3.4
Question 3: 10.3.3	*Question 4:* 10.3.2
Question 5: 10.3.1	*Question 6:* 10.3.3

Indiana Skills Review

The following is from Book VIII of The Odyssey. *In this selection, the main character, Odysseus, has been challenged to prove his strength in a stone-throwing competition. Read the selection, and answer the questions that follow.*

The Odyssey

Homer

He spake, and clad even as he was in his mantle leaped to his feet, and caught up a weight larger than the rest, a huge weight heavier far than those wherewith the Phaeacians contended in casting. With one whirl he sent it from his stout hand, and the stone flew hurtling: and the Phaeacians, of the long oars, those mariners renowned, crouched to earth beneath the rushing of the stone. Beyond all the marks it flew, so lightly it sped from his hand, and Athene in the fashion of a man marked the place, and spake and hailed him…

1 Judging from the selection, you can PROBABLY guess that

  o the stone did not fly very far

  o physical strength was considered important in Homer's time

  o Odysseus was surprised by how far he threw the stone

  o the Greeks thought that intelligence was more important than strength

2 The phrase "clad even as he was in his mantle" serves to illustrate that

  o Odysseus's throw is that much more impressive because he is wearing a cloak

  o Odysseus does not care very much about winning the contest

  o Odysseus's stone is much heavier than all of the others'

  o Odysseus had been preparing for the contest all along

3 Which of the following BEST explains why Odysseus is considered an epic hero?

o   He is smarter and stronger than most men.

o   He endures a long, difficult, and meaningful journey.

o   He has godlike powers.

o   He takes a very long time to return home.

4 Which of the following BEST defines the meaning of the word *renowned* in the fifth line?

o   cowardly   o   well-known

o   brave   o   angry

5 A modern-day humorous retelling of the story above would be considered a

o   tragedy   o   drama

o   romance   o   parody

6 The above passage is different from a myth because

o   you can prove that this story actually took place.

o   it does not explain natural phenomena.

o   it has a storylike quality, and myths are more factual.

o   myths do not usually involve contests.

Academic Standards	
Question 1: 10.3.3	*Question 2:* 10.3.11
Question 3: 10.3.1	*Question 4:* 10.1.4
Question 5: 10.3.2	*Question 6:* 10.3.2
Question 7: 10.3.1	

Fiction and Nonfiction

Unit 1 Overview

PART 1: Making and Revising Predictions
PART 2: Analyzing Cause and Effect

Academic Standards
In This Unit You Will

- Distinguish the meaning of words and their implication. (10.1.2)

- Examine how the author's perspective influences the structure and tone of the text. (10.2.4)

- Evaluate interactions between characters and how these affect the plot. (10.3.3)

- Evaluate an author's use of time and sequence. (10.3.6)

- Use varied and expanded vocabulary. (10.5.7)

- Write for different purposes and audiences. (10.5.8)

Introduction
Fiction and Nonfiction

From the Author's Desk

Susan Vreeland
Talks About the Forms

Susan
Vreeland

Y ou've probably heard that nonfiction is true and fiction is not true. More precisely, **nonfiction** reports on real people, events, and ideas, while **fiction** narrates an imagined story. Nonfiction aims to inform, while fiction aims to generate feeling. You read fiction to inhabit the world of another person; that is, to live the fictive dream and feel the emotions of the characters. Along the way, you might discover some truth about people or life.

▲ **Susan Vreeland** has written award-winning novels and has also published nonfiction in major newspapers and magazines.

Characters to Care About

What I look for in fiction is a character whom I care about, one who grows as a result of the conflicts and experiences narrated. I like to contemplate how I would have felt or acted in a similar situation. As a young reader, I came to love the characters in Harper Lee's novel *To Kill a Mockingbird*. Because of them, I began to think about issues of conscience and racial prejudice. It's important, then, to choose your reading wisely so its effect will be a deepening of your heart.

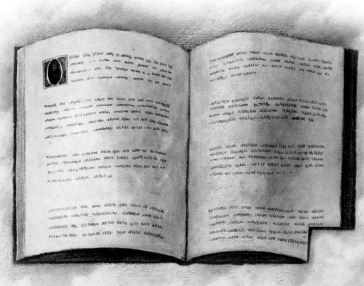

◄ **Critical Viewing**
Based on what Vreeland says about her own experiences as a reader, do you think she would identify with the figure in this illustration? Why or why not? **[Infer]**

Connecting Fiction and Nonfiction

I love **historical novels**—fictional stories with real historical settings—because they allow me to imagine what it was like to live in a culturally different time, or in a foreign setting. They give me a better understanding of the present by showing the stages society has gone through. Authors of historical fiction do research in nonfiction sources, so that characters play out their personal stories against an accurate picture of the time.

Such novels are not **biographies,** narratives of a person's life that include everything from birth to death, revealing these facts in an outsider's objective tone. Instead, a historical novel develops selected themes with invented scenes and dialogue delivered in what sounds like the subject's own voice.

The passage here is from a biography of the seventeenth-century Dutch painter Johannes Vermeer, a character in my story "Magdalena Looking." The biography reports a fact that I expanded into the plot of my story. When the historical record doesn't reveal an element I need, such as someone with whom my historic person can interact, I have to invent it. In this case, I chose one of Vermeer's daughters, named her Magdalena, and gave her characteristics that would develop my theme.

Catharina and Vermeer did well in that eleven of their fifteen children lived, and had to be cared for, fed, clothed, and schooled. . . . [H]ow Vermeer dealt with these interruptions we can only guess. His paintings reflect a turning-away from the messiness of life to a perfected state where there is no discordant clatter, crying or shouting. . . .

from *Vermeer, A View of Delft*
—*Anthony Bailey*

More About Susan Vreeland

Susan Vreeland (b. 1946) was a high school English teacher in California for thirty years. She got her start as a writer by publishing articles in magazines and newspapers. Then, she won acclaim for her novel *Girl in Hyacinth Blue.* This award-winning book was made into the Hallmark Hall of Fame movie *Brush with Fate,* starring Glenn Close.

Fast Facts

▶ To research one of her travel articles, Vreeland trekked in the Himalayas, near Mt. Everest.

▶ She believes that the experience of writing *Girl in Hyacinth Blue* helped her to recover from a serious illness.

▶ She and her husband, a software engineer, enjoy skiing, taking walks, visiting museums, and traveling.

Exploring Fiction and Nonfiction

Elements of Fiction

Fiction is narrative prose about characters and events from the author's imagination. All works of fiction share the following basic elements:

- **Setting** is the time and place in which a story takes place.
- **Plot** is the progression of related events in a work of fiction. Plot originates in a **conflict,** or problem, that sets off a sequence of actions, rises to a **climax,** or point of greatest intensity, and ends with a **resolution,** or conclusion.
- **Characters** are the individuals who take part in the story's action.
- **Dialogue** is conversation between or among characters. In some literary works, characters speak in an **idiom** or **dialect**, a way of speaking particular to a group or region. Characters may also use **idiomatic expressions**, phrases that mean something different from their individual words and help a writer to show a character's personality. For example, "raining cats and dogs" is an idiomatic expression.
- **Point of View** is the perspective from which a story is told.

    First-person point of view: the story is told by a character who participates in the action of the story.

    Third-person point of view: the story is told by a narrator outside the story.

- **Theme** is the underlying meaning or insight that an author conveys in a story. A **universal theme** is one that applies to all people in all cultures.

Types of Fiction

Novels are extended works of fiction that are usually organized into segments called *chapters*. Novels may include subplots in addition to the main story line and may explore a number of characters in depth.

Novellas are intermediate works of fiction that are longer than short stories but are more concise and focused than novels.

Short Stories are brief narratives, with carefully limited action that allows the writer to focus on one main plot complication.

Speed Bump

THAT'S HIS SUBPLOT...

JONATHON MILLER — AUTHOR

Elements of Nonfiction

In addition to conveying information, a nonfiction writer may offer a particular view of his or her subject, using elements such as the following:

- **Tone** expresses an author's attitude toward the subject and the readers. It is conveyed through choice of words and details.
- **Perspective** is the author's point of view on the subject, including the opinions that the author expresses and the source of the author's information—whether general research, for example, or personal experience.

Purposes of Nonfiction

Nonfiction is written for a variety of purposes, including those listed here:

- **To persuade:** Editorials, speeches, and reviews are often written to influence the opinions or actions of an audience.
- **To inform:** Articles, news reports, and instructions present facts to increase the knowledge and understanding of an audience.
- **To entertain:** Humor columns and many biographies and autobiographies are written for the enjoyment of an audience.

Check Your Understanding

Indicate whether each of the following written works is an example of fiction or nonfiction.

1. an account of the Lewis and Clark expedition
2. a review of a current movie
3. a report on a meteor impact in the year 2038
4. a conversation between a walrus and a carpenter
5. a report on a medical research study

▼ **Critical Viewing**
What questions about this image could nonfiction answer?
[Synthesize]

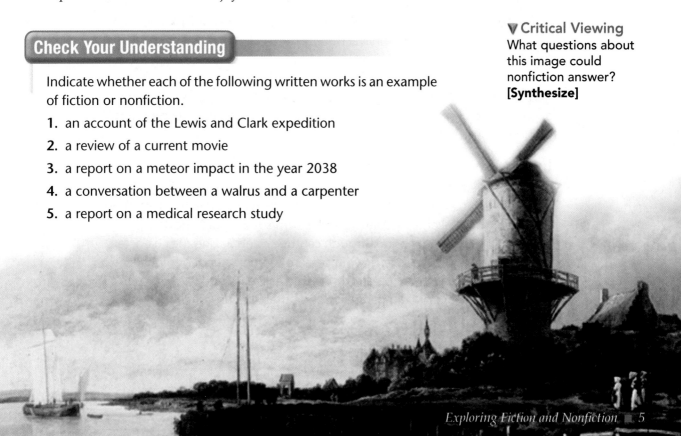

When I was nine, my great-grandfather, a painter, guided my hand holding a watercolor brush until a lily appeared on the paper before me. How many girls throughout history would have longed to be taught that, but had to do washing and mending instead?

Paintings Inspire Stories

Now, whenever I look at paintings of people, stories rise in my imagination. I wonder, What was the relationship between artist and model? Was the artist sick with dread over how he would feed his family? What did his children want from him the day he painted that? These questions, and my desire to explore my heritage, prompted me to create Magdalena, the fictional daughter of the seventeenth-century Dutch painter Johannes Vermeer.

Settings and Conflicts From Paintings

While looking through a book of his paintings, wondering who owned them and feeling moved by their survival through time, I felt I was seeing **settings** for stories. He had repeated items in several paintings—a wall map, a woman's blue silk jacket, a Turkish rug, a luminous window of pale yellow glass—that told me he had a reverence for beautiful things, as I do. The expressions on some of the faces suggested yearnings and inner **conflicts** that I could use for characters like Magdalena.

Inventing a Painting, Discovering a Theme

I felt compelled to invent a painting made by Vermeer, using elements from his real paintings, and to add objects from my own imagination—a glass of milk, a sewing basket, Magdalena's shoes with square gold buckles. I imagined tracing this painting through centuries, and having the characters who encountered it live their most important moments under its influence, ending with the day it was painted, in a story called "Magdalena Looking." The title of my novel would be the name of the painting, *Girl in Hyacinth Blue,* and the power of great art to offer a moving experience would be my **theme.**

Magdalena Looking

Susan Vreeland

Late one afternoon when Magdalena finished the clothes washing and her mother let her go out, she ran from their house by the Nieuwe Kerk across the market square, past van Buyten's bakery, over two cobbled bridges across the canals, past the blacksmith's all the way to Kethelstraat and the town wall where she climbed up and up the ochre stone steps, each one as high as her knee, to her favorite spot in all of Delft,[1] the round sentry post. From that great height, oh, what she could see. If only she could paint it. In one direction Schiedam Gate and beyond it the twin towers of Rotterdam Gate, and ships with odd-shaped sails the color of brown eggshells coming up the great Schie River from the sea, and in another direction strips of potato fields with wooden plows casting shadows over the soil like long fingers, and orchards, rows of rounded green as ordered as Mother wished their eleven young lives to be, and the smoke of the potteries and brickeries, and beyond that, she didn't know. She didn't know.

She stood there looking, looking, and behind her she heard the creak and thrum of the south windmill turning like her heart in the sea wind, and she breathed the brine[2] that had washed here from other shores. Below her the Schie lay like a pale yellow ribbon along

▲ Critical Viewing
This Vermeer portrait inspired the character of Magdalena. What impression of the character does it convey? **[Interpret]**

Fiction
Character and Setting
In her opening paragraph, Vreeland quickly establishes the setting of the story and gives the reader a strong first impression of the main character.

---

1. Nieuwe Kerk (nü´ e kärk) . . . **van Buyten's** (fän bī´ tens) . . . **Kethelstraat** (kā´ tel strät) . . . **Delft**
. . . *Nieuwe Kirk* means "New Church"; Kethelstraat is a street in the city; Delft is a manufacturing city on the Schie River in the Netherlands.
2. brine (brīn) saltwater.

the town wall. The longer she looked, the more it seemed to borrow its color from the sky. In the wind, the boats along the Schie docks with their fasteners clanking and their hollow bellies nudging one another made a kind of low rattling music she loved. It wasn't just today. She loved the sentry post in every kind of weather. To see rain pocking the gray sea and shimmering the stone bridge, to feel its cold strings of water on her face and hands, filled her to bursting.

She moved to a notch in the wall and just then a gust of wind lifted her skirts. The men on the bridge waiting with their bundles to go to sea shouted something in words she did not understand. She'd never tell Mother. Mother did not want her going there. The sentry post was full of guards smoking tobacco, Mother had said. There was some dark thing in her voice, as though she thought Magdalena should be afraid, but Magdalena did not know how to feel that then, or there.

Up there, high up above the town, she had longings no one in the family knew. No one would ever know them, she thought, unless perhaps a soul would read her face or she herself would have soul enough to speak of them. Wishes had the power to knock the breath out of her. Some were large and throbbing and persistent, some mere pinpricks of golden light, short-lived as fireflies but keenly felt. She wished for her chores to be done so she'd have time to race to the town wall every day before supper, or to the Oude Kerk[3] to lift the fallen leaves from her brother's grave. She wished her baby sisters wouldn't cry so, and the boys wouldn't quarrel and wrestle underfoot or run shouting through the house. Father wished that too, she knew. She wished there were not so many bowls to wash, thirteen each meal. She wished her hair shone flaxen in the sunlight of the market square like little Geertruida's.[4] She

▼ **Critical Viewing**
Magdalena is very aware of color. How many different colors can you identify in this painting by her father, Johannes Vermeer? **[Analyze]**

---

3. **Oude Kerk** (ou´ de kārk)
4. **Geertruida's** (kher trī´ das)

wished she could travel in a carriage across borders to all the lands drawn on her father's map.

She wished the grocer wouldn't treat her so gruffly when he saw her hand open out to offer four guilders,[5] all that her mother gave her to pay the grocery bill that was mounting into the hundreds, as far as she could tell. She wished he wouldn't shout; it sent his garlic breath straight into her nostrils. The baker, Hendrick van Buyten, was kinder. Two times so far he let Father pay with a painting so they could start over. Sometimes he gave her a still-warm bun to eat while walking home. And sometimes he put a curl of honey on it. She wished the grocer was like him.

She wished Father would take the iceboat to the Schie more often. He'd bought a fine one with a tall ivory sail. "Eighty guilders," Mother grumbled. "Better a winter's worth of bread and meat." On winter Sundays if the weather was clear, and if he was between paintings, it whisked them skimming across the white glass of the canal. She'd never known such speed. The sharp cold air blew life and hope and excitement into her ears and open mouth.

She remembered wishing, one particular morning when Father mixed lead white with the smallest dot of lead-tin yellow[6] for the goose quill in a painting of Mother writing a letter, that she might someday have someone to write to, that she could write at the end of a letter full of love and news, "As ever, your loving Magdalena Elisabeth."

He painted Mother often, and Maria he painted once, draped her head in a golden mantle and her shoulders in a white satin shawl. She was older, fifteen, though only by eleven months. It might be fun to dress up like Maria did, and wear pearl earrings and have Father position her just so, but the only part she really wished for was that he would look and look and pay attention.

More than all those wishes, she had one pulsing wish that outshone all the others. She wished to paint. Yes, me, she thought, leaning out over the stone wall. I want to paint. This and everything. The world from that vantage point stretched so grandly. Up there, beauty was more than color and shapes, but openness, light, the air itself, and because of that, it seemed untouchable. If only the act of wishing would make her able. Father only smiled queerly when she told him she wanted to paint, just as if she'd said she wanted to sail the seas, which, of course, she also wished, in order to paint what she would see. When she said so, that she wished to paint, Mother thrust into her hands the basket of mending to do.

Susan Vreeland
Author's Insight
With the list of Magdalena's wishes, I reveal her character, as well as giving a great deal of background needed to understand the story.

MODEL SELECTION

Susan Vreeland
Author's Insight
Important to my story is the fact that in the seventeenth century and earlier, it was extremely unlikely that a young woman could be trained as an artist.

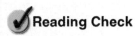

Reading Check

Name one thing Magdalena wishes her father would do.

---

5. **guilders** (gil′ dərz) The guilder is the basic unit of Dutch currency.
6. **lead white . . . lead-tin yellow** references to pigments made from lead and tin and mixed with oil to produce paints of various colors.

Often from the edge of the room, she'd watch him work. Because he was always asking for quiet, with the little ones running through the room laughing or shouting, she didn't ask him many questions. He rarely answered anyway. Still, she studied how much linseed oil he used to thin the ultramarine,[7] and watched him apply it over a glassy layer of reddish brown. By magic, it made the dress he painted warmer than the blue on the palette. He would not let her go with him to the attic where he ground lead-tin yellow to powder, but he did send her to the apothecary[8] for the small bricks of it, and for linseed oil. Always there was money for that, but she didn't know what to answer when the apothecary demanded the guilders for her brother's potions still owed after he died.

If only she could have colors of her own, and brushes. She wouldn't just paint pictures of women inside cramped little rooms. She'd paint them out in marketplaces, bending in the potato fields, talking in doorways in the sunlight, in boats on the Schie, or praying in the Oude Kerk. Or she'd paint people skating, fathers teaching their children on the frozen Schie.

---

7. linseed oil . . . ultramarine Linseed oil, made from the seed of the flax plant, can be used as the base for oil paint. Ultramarine is a rich blue.

8. apothecary (ə päth′ ə ker′ ē) historical term for a pharmacist; a dealer in medicines and various other preparations and chemicals.

▲ Critical Viewing Identify two differences between the scene in this painting and Magdalena's time posing for her father, as described on pages 11–13. [Contrast]

Fathers teaching their children. The thought stopped her.

Looking from the sentry tower at a cloud darkening the river, she knew, just as she knew she'd always have washing and mending to do, that it would not be so. She'd worn herself out with wishing, and turned to go. She had to be home to help with supper.

On a spring day that began in no special way, except that she had climbed the town wall the afternoon before, and all over Delft lime trees lining the canals had burst into chartreuse[9] leaves, and light shone through them and made them yellower except where one leaf crossed over another and so was darker—on that spring-certain day, out of some unknown, unborn place came that scream. "I hate to mend," she shouted to the walls, to Mother, to anyone. "It's not making anything."

Father stepped into the room, looked at Mother and then scowled at Magdalena. It had been her job to keep her little brothers quiet for him, or shoo them out of doors, and here she was, the noisy one. No one moved. Even the boys were still. At first she looked only at Father's hand smeared with ultramarine powder, not in his eyes, too surprised by the echo of her voice to fling out any additional defiance. She loved him, loved what he did with that hand, and even, she suspected, loved what he loved, though they had not spoken of it. When that thought lifted her face to his, she saw his cheeks grow softer, as if he noticed her in his house for the first time. He drew her over to the table by the window, brought the sewing basket, placed on her lap her brother's shirt that needed buttons, adjusted the chair, opened the window, a little more, then less, and discovered that at a certain angle, it reflected her face. "If you sit here mending, I will paint you, Magdalena. But only if you stop that shouting." He positioned her shoulders, and his hands resting a moment were warm through the muslin[10] of her smock and seemed to settle her.

Mother rushed over to take away Geertruida's glass of milk.

"No, leave it, Catharina. Right there in the light."

For days she sat there, still as she could for Father, and yet sewing a few stitches every so often to satisfy Mother. In that mood of stillness, all the things within her line of vision touched her deeply. The tapestry laid across the table, the sewing basket, the same glass repoured each day to the same level, the amber-toned map of the world on the wall—it plucked a lute string in her heart that these things she'd touched, grown as familiar to her as her own skin, would be looked at, marveled at, maybe even loved by viewers of his painting.

Fiction
Plot Here, Vreeland raises the tension in Magdalena's conflict with her own role in life. This conflict will move the plot, or sequence of events, along.

Vocabulary Builder
defiance (dē fī´əns) *n.* the act of defying; open resistance to authority

Reading Check

What is Magdalena's father's response to her tantrum?

---

9. **chartreuse** (shär trōoz´) pale, yellowish green.
10. **muslin** (muz´ lin) stong, plain cotton cloth.

On sunny days the panes of window glass glistened before her. Like jewels melted into flat squares, she thought. Each one was slightly different in its pale transparent color—ivory, parchment, the lightest of wines and the palest of tulips. She wondered how glass was made, but she didn't ask. It would disturb him.

Outside the window the market chattered with the selling of apples and lard and brooms and wooden buckets. She liked the cheese porters in their flat-brimmed red hats and stark white clothes. Their curved yellow carrying platforms stacked neatly with cheese rounds were suspended on ropes between pairs of them, casting brown shadows on the paving stones. Two platforms diagonally placed in the midground between their carriers would make a nice composition with the repeated shapes of those bulging cheese rounds. She'd put a delivery boy wheeling his cart of silver cod in the background against the guild hall, and maybe in the foreground a couple of lavender gray pigeons pecking crumbs. The carillon[11] from Nieuwe Kerk ringing out the hour sounded something profound in her chest. All of it is ordinary to everyone but me, she thought.

All that month she did not speak, the occasion too momentous to dislodge it with words. He said he'd paint her as long as she didn't shout, and so she did not speak a word. Her chest ached like a dull wound when she realized that her silence did not cause him a moment's reflection or curiosity. When she looked out the corner of her eye at him, she could not tell what she meant to him. Slowly, she came to understand that he looked at her with the same interest he gave to the glass of milk.

Maybe it was because she wasn't pretty like Maria. She knew her jaws protruded and her watery, pale eyes were too widely set. She had a mole on her forehead that she always tried to hide by tugging at her cap. What if no one would want the painting? What then? It might be her fault, because she wasn't pretty. She wished he'd say something about her, but all he said, not to her directly, more to himself, was how the sunlight whitened her cap at the forehead, how the shadow at the nape of her neck reflected blue from her collar, or how the sienna of her skirt deepened to Venetian red[12] in the folds. It was never her, she cried to herself, only something surrounding her that she did not make or even contribute to knowingly. Another wish that never would come true, she saw then, even if she lived forever, was that he, that someone, would look at her not as an artistic study, but with love. If two people love the same thing, she reasoned, then they

---

11. **carillon** (kar´ ə län´) a set of tuned church bells.
12. **sienna** (sē en´ ə) . . . **Venetian** (və nē´ shən) **red** colors; sienna is a reddish or yellowish brown, and Venetian red is a brownish red.

Vocabulary Builder
parchment
(parch´mənt) *adj.*
creamy or yellowish color of the paper used for special documents, letters, or artwork

Fiction
Character and Point of View Although Vreeland tells the story in the third person, the **narrator** sees deep into Magdalena and helps the reader understand her.

must love each other, at least a little, even if they never say it. Nevertheless, because he painted with such studied concentration, and because she held him in awe, she practiced looking calm for him as she looked out the window, but when she saw the canvas, what she intended as calm looked more like wistfulness.[13]

The painting was not bought by the brewer, Pieter Claesz van Ruijven,[14] who bought most of her father's work. He saw it, but passed over it for another. Disgrace seared her so that she could not speak that night. The painting hung without a frame in the outer kitchen where the younger children slept. Eventually the family had to give up their lodgings at Mechelen on the square, and take smaller rooms with Grandmother Maria on the Oude Langendijck.[15] Her father stopped taking the iceboat out to the Schie, sold it, in fact. He rarely painted, the rooms were so cramped and dark, the younger children boisterous, and a few years later, he died.

When she washed him in his bed that last time, his fingers already cold, she had a thought, the shame of which prevented her from uttering: It would make a fine painting, a memorial, the daughter with towel and blue-figured washing bowl at bedside, her hand covering his, the wife exhausted on the Spanish chair clutching a crucifix, the father-husband, eyes glazed, looking to another landscape. While he painted everyone else, no one was there to paint him, to make him remembered. She yearned to do it, but the task was too fearsome. She lacked the skill, and the one to teach her had never offered.

Even though she asked for them, Mother sold his paints and brushes to the Guild of St. Luke. It helped to pay a debt. When Mother became sick with worry, Magdalena had the idea to take the painting to Hendrick van Buyten, the baker, because she knew he liked her. And he accepted it, along with one of a lady playing a guitar, for the debt of six hundred seventeen guilders,

▼ **Critical Viewing**
In this painting by Vermeer, which details suggest the same care in arranging a scene that the character of Vermeer shows in the story? Explain. **[Connect]**

---

13. **wistfulness** a mood of wishfulness or vague longing.
14. **Pieter Claesz van Ruijven** (pē ter kläs fän rī fen)
15. **Mechelen** (me′ khe len) . . . **Oude Langendijck** (ou′ de läŋ en dīk) The Mechelen was an inn owned by the Vermeer family. The Oude Langendijck is a canal in Delft.

six stuivers,[16] more than two years' worth of bread. He smiled at her and gave her a bun.

Within a year, she married a saddlemaker named Nicolaes, the first man to notice her, a hard worker whose pores smelled of leather and grease, who taught her a pleasure not of the eyes, but, she soon realized, a man utterly without imagination. They moved to Amsterdam and she didn't see the painting again for twenty years.

In 1696, just after their only living child, Magritte, damp with fever, stopped breathing in her arms, Magdalena read in the *Amsterdamsche Courant* of a public auction of one hundred thirty-four paintings by various artists. "Several outstandingly artful paintings," the notice said, "including twenty-one works most powerfully and splendidly painted by the late J. Vermeer of Delft, will be auctioned May 16, 1:00, at the Oude Heeren Logement."[17] Only a week away. She thought of Hendrick. Of course he couldn't be expected to keep those paintings forever. Hers might be there. The possibility kept her awake nights.

Entering the auction gallery, she was struck again by that keenest of childhood wishes—to make a record not only of what she saw, but

---

16. **stuivers** (stī´ fers) coins worth a fraction of a guilder; roughly, a dime.
17. **Oude Heeren Logement** (ou´ de her´ en lōzh mōn)

Fiction
Character By filling in the sad events that have occurred between the death of Magdalena's father and the auction, Vreeland inspires compassion for the main character.

◄ **Critical Viewing** What details in this painting by Vermeer confirm the descriptions in the story of his love of color and light? Explain. **[Make Connections]**

how. The distance she'd come from that, and not even a child to show for it! She shocked herself by asking, involuntarily, what had been the point of having lived? Wishing had not been enough. Was it a mistake that she didn't beg him to teach her? Maybe not. If she'd seen that eventually, with help, she could paint, it might have made the years of birthing and dying harder. But then the birthing and dying would have been painted and the pain given. It would have served a purpose. Would that have been enough—to tell a truth in art?

She didn't know.

To see again so many of Father's paintings was like walking down an avenue of her childhood. The honey-colored window, the Spanish chair, the map she'd stared at, dreaming, hanging on the wall, Grandmother Maria's golden water pitcher, Mother's pearls and yellow satin jacket—they commanded such a reverence for her now that she felt they all had souls.

And suddenly there she was on canvas, framed. Her knees went weak.

Hendrick hadn't kept it. Even though he liked her, he hadn't kept it.

Almost a child she was, it seemed to her, gazing out the window instead of doing her mending, as if by the mere act of looking she could send her spirit out into the world. And those shoes! She had forgotten. How she loved the buckles, and thought they made her such a lady. Eventually she'd worn the soles right through, but now, brand-new, the buckles glinted on the canvas, each with a point of golden light. A bubble of joy surged upward right through her.

No, she wasn't beautiful, she owned, but there was a simplicity in her young face that she knew the years had eroded, a stilled longing in the forward lean of her body, a wishing in the intensity of her eyes. The painting showed she did not yet know that lives end abruptly, that much of living is repetition and separation, that buttons forever need resewing no matter how ferociously one works the thread, that nice things almost happen. Still a woman overcome with wishes, she wished Nicolaes would have come with her to see her in the days of her sentry post wonder when life and hope were new and full of possibility, but he had seen no reason to close up the shop on such a whim.

She stood on tiptoe and didn't breathe when her painting was announced. Her hand in her pocket closed tight around the twenty-four guilders, some of it borrowed from two neighbor women, some of it taken secretly from the box where Nicolaes kept money for leather supplies. It was all she could find, and she didn't dare ask for more. He would have thought it foolish.

"Twenty," said a man in front of her.

Susan Vreeland
Author's Insight
Here's what I wanted to convey about Magdalena: If it had been evident that she had talent, her limited life might have been more painful to her because she'd be conscious of unfulfilled possibility. Not knowing if she had talent made her life of sorrows more bearable.

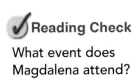

Reading Check

What event does Magdalena attend?

"Twenty-two," said another.

"Twenty-four," she said so loud and fast the auctioneer was startled. Did he see something similar in her face? He didn't call for another bid. The painting was hers!

"Twenty-five."

Her heart cracked.

The rest was a blur of sound. It finally went to a man who kept conferring with his wife, which she took as a good sign that it was going to a nice family. Forty-seven guilders. Most of the paintings sold for much more, but forty-seven was fine, she thought. In fact, it filled her momentarily with what she'd been taught was the sin of pride. Then she thought of Hendrick and a pain lashed through her. Forty-seven guilders minus the auctioneer's fee didn't come close to what her family had owed him.

She followed the couple out into the drizzle of Herengracht,[18] wanting to make herself known to them, just to have a few words, but then dropped back. She had such bad teeth now, and they were people of means. The woman wore stockings. What would she say to them? She didn't want them to think she wanted anything.

She walked away slowly along a wet stone wall that shone iridescent, and the wetness of the street reflected back the blue of her best dress. Water spots appeared fast, turning the cerulean[19] to deep ultramarine, Father's favorite blue. Light rain pricked the charcoal green canal water into delicate, dark lace, and she wondered if it had ever been painted just that way, or if the life of something as inconsequential as a water drop could be arrested and given to the world in a painting, or if the world would care.

She thought of all the people in all the paintings she had seen that day, not just Father's, in all the paintings of the world, in fact. Their eyes, the particular turn of a head, their loneliness or suffering or grief was borrowed by an artist to be seen by other people throughout the years who would never see them face to face. People who would be that close to her, she thought, a matter of a few arms' lengths, looking, looking, and they would never know her.

---

18. **Herengracht** (her´ en khräkht) the "Gentleman's Canal"; one of the three main canals in the center of the city of Amsterdam.
19. **cerulean** (sə roō´ lē ən) sky-blue.

Fiction
Plot In many stories, the resolution is a clear win or certain loss. Magdalena's concluding thoughts represent a little of both.

Susan Vreeland
Author's Insight
Magdalena has changed from a girl with many wishes, to a woman who didn't want the buyers "to think she wanted anything." Despite this fading of desire, she can still take quiet, private joy in the look of things.

Q. Why didn't you tell this story in the first person?

A. Magdalena has a natural intelligence, but she is not educated. Telling the story entirely from her point of view would limit my word choice and sentence complexity. In order to convey complex thoughts, it was sometimes necessary to write long sentences with embedded phrases and dependent clauses. Therefore, it was necessary to provide a third-person voice exterior to her, an invisible narrator, to deliver the complex thoughts as well as the shorter emotional sentences that seem to come directly from her.

Q. What is the meaning of the story's title, "Magdalena Looking"?

A. Although her father sees objects, light, color, and faces with great intensity of feeling, he is blind to his daughter's equally intense observations and to her deep longing to paint. Nevertheless, *her* vision is keen. She "sees" that her father looks upon her as only an object, a bearer of shape and color, and later she "sees" that her husband has no imagination. Ironically, the one thing she can't see is her own depth and spiritual beauty as revealed in the painting.

StudentCorner

Q. Why is Magdalena afraid of her own father?
—Neelaj Shah, Alexandria, Louisiana

A. What might appear as fear is probably just distance. Generally, children were more formal with their parents centuries ago. She knew her role— to keep the younger children quiet for him. Because of her love for paintings, she held him in awe, which contributes to distance. Also, Vermeer was so absorbed in his work, always thinking about painting, composition, color, as well as worrying about supporting his family, that he might have seemed cold or unapproachable to her. Nevertheless, as much as their roles and personalities allowed, they did love one another.

 Writing Workshop: *Work in Progress*

Autobiographical Narrative
For an autobiographical narrative you may write, list five favorite songs. Then, write the places and people you associate with each song. Save the Song List in your writing portfolio.

From the Author's Desk
Susan Vreeland Introduces "Artful Research"

I suppose I'll always be a teacher in one way or another. Even while writing, I'm teaching, whether I'm writing fiction which teaches about life, or nonfiction, which teaches by explaining something. In both cases, my "class" is invisible, so I have to fire up their curiosity and make the writing clear without me being there.

Expository Nonfiction: "teaching an invisible class"

In my **expository article**, "Artful Research," I'm teaching an invisible class of fiction writers, my **audience**. I want them to learn how they can make their own stories better by doing specific research.

Article versus Essay

An **article** differs from an **essay** in that its main intent is to provide useful information, while the main intent of an essay is to put forth an argument on an issue. There is some overlap, however. Both can use a **thesis** and examples. Among other **purposes,** an article can present the necessity or advantages of a certain course of action and can then provide methods to carry out that action.

Techniques of Nonfiction: The "Hook"

That's what "Artful Research" does. Because I'm not in the room with them, my audience might at any moment turn the page and ignore me. As a **hook** to catch their attention, I begin with a curious example of a writer needing to know something that might seem odd. Then, I tell them what I want them to remember: my thesis, followed by examples from the writing of *Girl in Hyacinth Blue,* the novel that includes "Magdalena Looking." Because the novel spans 350 years, I needed to do a lot of research, so it's a good example.

After I get readers to agree to the necessity and benefits of research, particularly for a historical novel but not exclusively, I offer them some research methods that I've discovered, including possible sources for information.

Artful Research

*I*s it possible for an ordinary person to climb over the area railings of #7 Eccles Street, either from the path or the steps, lower himself down from the lowest part of the railings till his feet are within two feet or three of the ground and drop unhurt? I saw it done myself but by a man of rather athletic build. I require this information in detail in order to determine the wording of a paragraph.

James Joyce[1] wrote this to his aunt once when he was out of Dublin. Can't you just imagine her muttering, "That boy! What will he think of next?" as she looks for her umbrella to go out in the rain and take the trolley to Eccles Street?

    Excessive? Unnecessary? Stalling from the act of writing? Joyce's letter is instructive and revealing.

Susan Vreeland
Author's Insight
I use this type of question, called a rhetorical question, to direct readers' thinking toward an answer I want them to have.

---

1. James Joyce (1882–1941) famed Irish writer noted for *Dubliners* (1914), a collection of short stories, and *Ulysses* (1922), a novel, among other works.

Similarly, I must admit that I sent my French translator on a mission to find out whether the carvings of heads on the façade of the Ministère de la Défense[2] on Boulevard Saint-Germain in Paris are repeats of the same face or different faces. Among other things, she told me I had the wrong street!

While some writers may be more cavalier, claiming that it's fiction, after all, I hold with the meticulous Joyce, not wholly out of allegiance to a recognized master, but for the sake of the richness of story that results. For me, research gives direction, depth, and authority to the writing; it doesn't just decorate a preconceived story with timely trivia.

Early research tends to be scattered, while one searches for the story, but later, usually during or after a first draft when one discovers in the work some needed information, it becomes pinpoint precise. At either time, an array of interesting material, some of it crucial, some merely useable, will emerge—and sometimes leap off

---

2. **Ministère de la Défense** (mēn i stär′ də lä dā fäns′) the Ministry of Defense building in Paris, France.

Susan Vreeland's
Historical Fiction Writer's Research Wish List

These are the types of books I hunt down in used bookstores:

- history of art by time period and country
- history of music
- history of costume
- history of transportation, manufacture, household devices
- books of names of things, including tools and architecture
- atlases with street maps of cities
- foreign-language dictionaries
- time-sequence histories
- field guides to birds, flowers, and trees

These are the reference books on my shelves that I turn to often:

- **The *Oxford English Dictionary*.** Crowning every historical fiction writer's wish list is the mother of all dictionaries, the *Oxford English Dictionary*, which indicates when individual words came into use and how and when their meanings changed. There are three versions that won't break the bank: *The New Shorter OED*, two volumes; *The Compact OED*, small print with magnifying glass; and the *OED* on CD-ROM.

- *Timetables of History: A Horizontal Linkage of People and Events,* by Bernard Grun (Touchstone Press). The entire book is an indexed grid, with years beginning at 5000 B.C. down the left column and categories across the top: History and Politics; Literature and Theater; Religion and Philosophy; Visual

the page. The results can be exciting. A single unexpected line can prompt a whole story. For example, the line in Jacob Presser's grim history, *Ashes in the Wind: The Destruction of Dutch Jewry*, indicating that in 1941, Jews were not allowed to keep pigeons, provided the genesis of my story "A Night Different from All Other Nights."

That story is one of eight linked narratives comprising my composite novel, *Girl in Hyacinth Blue*, which traces an alleged Vermeer[3] painting in reverse chronology through the centuries, showing how defining moments in people's lives are lived under its influence. Besides the present, six time periods and numerous locales in the Netherlands are evoked: 1942 in Amsterdam; 1896 in Vreeland (yes, a real village located between Amsterdam and Utrecht); 1798 in The Hague during French rule: 1717 in Oling, Delfzijl, Westerbork, and Groningen (which I learned had been a university town since 1614, prompting my focal character to be a student); 1665 in Delft; and 1685 in Amsterdam. Naive in understanding what such a project entailed, I found that by the end, I had consulted seventy-six books.

✓ **Reading Check**

What is Susan Vreeland's attitude about research?

---

3. **Vermeer** (ver mir´) Jan (yän) Vermeer (1632–1675), renowned Dutch painter.

Arts; Music; Science and Technology; Daily Life. If I'm looking for whether I can have a character turn on a water faucet in a Paris flat in 1883 (indexed under Plumbing), this is the first book I turn to.

- **Timelines: Day by Day and Trend by Trend from the Dawn of the Atomic Age to the Close of the Cold War,** by Paul Dickson (Addison Wesley). Besides news items by date, this book gives fads, innovations, hot topics, additions to the national lexicon, and phrases typical of the time.

- **The Writer's Digest Books reference series,** which includes
  - *Everyday Life in the 1800s*, Marc McCutcheon
  - *The Writer's Guide to Everyday Life in Renaissance England*, Kathy Lynn Emerson

- *The Writer's Guide to Everyday Life in the Middle Ages*, Sherrilyn Kenyon

- *English Through the Ages*, by William Brohaugh, gives approximate dates of the first recorded use of words, by category.

- *Roget's International Thesaurus*, edited by Barbara Ann Kipfer (HarperCollins). The index lists items of apparel, fabrics, furniture, hairstyles, tools and machinery, vehicles, vessels, musical instruments, animals, plants, stones, minerals, woods, colors, types of glass, manners of cooking, foods—all of which can be checked against historical references.

I'd been to the Netherlands only once, twenty-five years ago for three days, and I had never seen a Vermeer painting face to face. Blithely, I went ahead. I read books on Vermeer, Dutch art and social and cultural history, the Holocaust[4] as experienced in the Netherlands, the changing geography of the Netherlands as more land was reclaimed from the sea,[5] Erasmus' adages,[6] the history of costume, Passover and the practice of Jewish customs, Amsterdam's diamond trade, Dutch superstitions and treatment of witches, the French occupation, and the engineering of windmills and dikes.

Twenty printout pages from the Internet on the engineering of windmills (they vary regionally), on gears, wallowers, Archimedean screws, and drive shafts yielded one paragraph establishing the authority of my character the windmill engineer. More importantly, the research also suggested a metaphor appropriate for him:

> I had fancied love a casual adjunct and not the central turning shaft making all parts move. I had not stood astonished at the power of its turning.

I would not have arrived at his critical self-assessment and the epiphany of the story without meandering through gears and drive shafts.

Here are ten research sources and approaches, beginning with the most obvious and ending with the ultimate—travel—that I used for either *Girl in Hyacinth Blue* or my subsequent novel, *The Passion of Artemisia*, which takes place in seventeenth-century Italy.

▲ **Critical Viewing**
In what way does this illustration represent Vreeland's claim that research enriches fiction? [**Make Connections**]

---

4. **the Holocaust** (häl´ ə kôst´) the persecution, imprisonment, and mass murder of Jews by Nazi Germany before and during the Second World War (1939–1945).
5. **reclaimed from the sea** Significant portions of the Netherlands were originally covered by water. To drain water from this land, the Dutch built a system of dikes (dams) and canals.
6. **Erasmus' adages** (i raz´ məs əs a´ di jəz) the sayings or brief observations of Desiderius (des´ ə dir´ ē əs) Erasmus (1469–1536), an influential Dutch scholar.

1. **Works on history, politics, and social conditions** A couple of titles might serve to show how I approached possible narratives from different angles: on the one hand, *Daily Life in Rembrandt's Holland*; on the other, *The Embarrassment of Riches: An Interpretation of Dutch Culture in the Golden Age*. Some I used as browser books; others, for specific information. Their bibliographies proved to be good sources for characters' names.

2. **Biography, autobiography, personal narrative, and oral history** The mere memory of Anne Frank's *Diary of a Young Girl* suggested that I create a young character the antithesis of Anne in terms of self-expression, yet suffering similar revelations.

3. **Geography books** These can give information about weather, topography, crops, industry, indigenous plants, birds, and other animals.

4. **Maps** Besides those available in travel bookstores, universities often have historical map collections. This was essential for *Girl* because I had to know if certain villages and canals existed at the time of each of the stories.

5. **Travel books** Those of the descriptive sort, the older the better, provide visual and cultural detail.

6. **Novels** Novels written at the time, written about the time, or set in the same place can be helpful in revealing attitudes, concerns, expressions, syntax, and diction.

7. **Paintings** Paintings done in the same time and place as one's fiction are excellent sources of information about costume, hairstyles, jewelry, household furnishings, landscape, available foods, flowers typical of the region, even the quality of light in a region, Vermeer's "trademark."

8. **Children's and juvenile fiction and nonfiction** Works for younger readers are sufficient in some cases and have the advantages of providing evocative illustrations and simplifying complicated political histories.

9. **Interviews and phone calls** Don't neglect the importance of interviews and phone calls. People are intrigued by novelists and are usually delighted to be consulted. For *Girl in Hyacinth Blue*, I consulted a pigeon breeder to learn why the owning of pigeons was prohibited to Jews under the German occupation and how homing pigeons "worked."

10. **Going there!** While travel is not always practical (I wrote *Girl in Hyacinth Blue* entirely while undergoing cancer treatment and could not travel), it will yield unexpected insights.

Susan Vreeland
Author's Insight
While writing *Girl in Hyacinth Blue*, I had a serious illness. Unable to leave the house, I couldn't do necessary research on windmill engineering. A concerned former student, who knew that writing was the key to my survival, did the research for me without my asking. The love metaphor, which I quote on page 22, was the result.

Reading Check

Why does Vreeland think novels are useful for research?

So when does one stop researching and start writing? You write when the story comes to life, when it assumes some structure, when you can't help but start, not when you know everything you'll need to know. That's impossible to anticipate before you get into the heart of the writing. You might need to push yourself away from the safer act of research and leap into a first draft.

Don't get bogged down with fears of historical inaccuracy when writing a first draft. In one of the flood stories in *Girl in Hyacinth Blue*, the student needs to write a note. He's in a rowboat. He can't dip a pen in an inkwell. Did they have pencils in 1717? Look it up later. Keep writing. Keep the momentum going. If you don't know what they ate, leave it blank and get down the more important elements of the scene.

One caveat: Even if you put into your manuscript some fact delectable to you, recalling your delight in discovering it, if the story does not justify it, take it out. Type it up. Pin it on your wall. Use it elsewhere. But don't include it! The book is about characters, not about research.

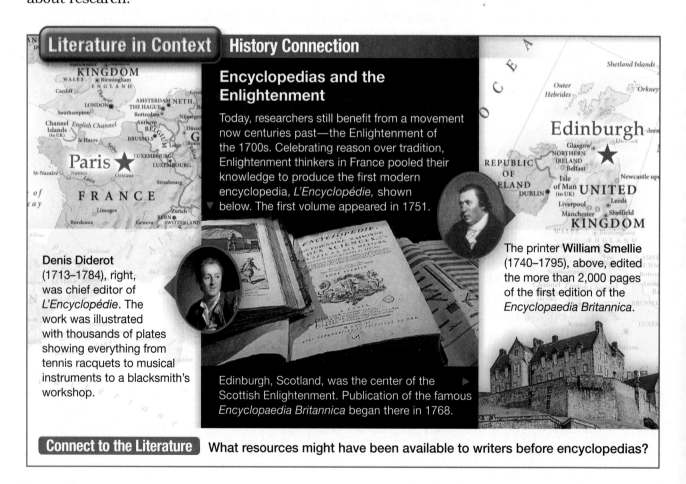

Literature in Context   History Connection

Encyclopedias and the Enlightenment

Today, researchers still benefit from a movement now centuries past—the Enlightenment of the 1700s. Celebrating reason over tradition, Enlightenment thinkers in France pooled their knowledge to produce the first modern encyclopedia, *L'Encyclopédie,* shown below. The first volume appeared in 1751.

Denis Diderot (1713–1784), right, was chief editor of *L'Encyclopédie*. The work was illustrated with thousands of plates showing everything from tennis racquets to musical instruments to a blacksmith's workshop.

The printer **William Smellie** (1740–1795), above, edited the more than 2,000 pages of the first edition of the *Encyclopaedia Britannica.*

Edinburgh, Scotland, was the center of the Scottish Enlightenment. Publication of the famous *Encyclopaedia Britannica* began there in 1768.

Connect to the Literature   What resources might have been available to writers before encyclopedias?

Q. Why do you include the request from James Joyce before you state your thesis?

A. This article appeared in a writer's magazine. No one was assigned to read it. Therefore, I had to stop the reader from turning pages by beginning with something curious or startling. A concrete example from a famous author might do this. Because Joyce's request is for such a small detail, the passage is surprising, and therefore it could work as a hook.

Q. How did your sense of the audience for this article influence choices you made in writing it?

A. First, I wanted to convince new writers that research rather than guesswork, even for small details, is what professional writers do, so I started with the Joyce quote. I also wanted to give practical methods, which I could do in a list. In it, I refer to my needs for information, hoping that they will recognize needs for researched information in their own stories. Prompting such a recognition was my main purpose.

StudentCorner

Q. How long does it typically take you to do research for a story or novel?

—**Amanda Hinzman, Appleton, Wisconsin**

A. For a historical novel centering on a real individual, I immerse myself for nearly half a year in that person's life and time period. With this much done, I can begin writing. For a short story, I may be able to find out all I need in a month. I love the research process because it gives me more than facts. It gives me attitudes. It's how I come to inhabit the characters' lives.

 Writing Workshop: *Work in Progress*

Autobiographical Narrative

Choose one song from the Song List in your writing portfolio. Write a few sentences explaining why this song is one of your favorites. Save this annotated Song List in your writing portfolio.

Fiction and Nonfiction

Thinking About the Selections

1. **Respond:** Do you sympathize with Magdalena? Why or why not?

2. **(a) Recall:** What is Magdalena's "one pulsing wish"?
   (b) Interpret: What obstacles prevent Magdalena from fulfilling her wish? **(c) Evaluate:** Are Magdalena's disappointments due more to her own character and behavior or to circumstances beyond her control? Explain.

3. **(a) Draw Conclusions:** Did Magdalena demonstrate artistic talent? Explain. **(b) Support:** Identify the characteristics that show Magdalena's artistic ability. Then, identify any opposing evidence that suggests that she does not have talent. **(c) Discuss:** In a small group, discuss your responses. Together, come to a final conclusion about Magdalena's potential as an artist.

4. **(a) Recall:** In "Artful Research," Vreeland writes "For me, research gives direction, depth, and authority to the writing. . . ." Complete a chart like the one shown by noting three passages from "Magdalena Looking" that demonstrate Vreeland's meaning.
   (b) Support: Explain your reason for choosing each one.

How Research Helps in Fiction

"Magdalena Looking" Passage	Why You Chose It

Fiction and Nonfiction Review

5. **(a)** How does the time and cultural **setting** of "Magdalena Looking" influence the **conflict** that she experiences? **(b)** Would she experience similar conflicts if she lived today? Explain.

6. Which aspect of **nonfiction** is more developed in "Artful Research," exploration of ideas or sharing information? Support your answer.

Research the Author

Using the Internet and library resources, identify other Vreeland works, both fiction and nonfiction, that focus on art. Present your findings as a **bulletin board display.**
- Provide summaries of Vreeland's works that relate to art and artists.
- Add quotations from Vreeland's interviews and writing.
- If possible, add images of paintings, artists, and Vreeland herself.

QuickReview

Selections at a Glance
In **Magdalena Looking,** an artist's daughter yearns to be seen for herself.

In **Artful Research,** the author discusses a writer's research techniques and resources.

Go Online
Assessment
For: Self-test
Visit: www.PHSchool.com
Web Code: eqa-6101

Fiction: literary narratives about imagined people and events

Nonfiction: literary works that present information about real people, events, or ideas

Setting: the time and place in which a literary work takes place

Conflict: the problem or struggle faced by a character in a literary work

Make Predictions

Reading and Vocabulary Skills Preview

Reading: Make Predictions

Academic Standards

- Evaluate an author's use of time and sequence. (10.3.6)
- Use varied and expanded vocabulary. (10.5.7)
- Write for different purposes and audiences. (10.5.8)

▶ **Predicting** means making a logical assumption about what will happen later. **Verifying** a prediction is checking its accuracy. When you **revise** a prediction, you adjust it to fit new information.

Skills and Strategies You Will Learn in Part 1

In Part 1, you will learn

- to **use your prior knowledge,** or what you already know, to help you **make predictions.** (p. 30)
- to **ask questions** to **make, verify, and revise predictions.** (p. 56)
- to identify the **purpose and structure** of informational materials to help you **make predictions** about content. (p. 82)

Using the Skills and Strategies in Part 1

In Part 1, you will learn to make, verify, and revise predictions. These skills help you organize and remember what you have read. They also keep you involved in your reading by leading you to make connections between events.

➤ **Example:** "Come see," she said excitedly, pulling me to the attic stairs. I had been up there once before to see her dad's paintings. "There was a sign up, 'Adopt Us.' I called the number . . . I took all three kittens, carried them home; I put them upstairs to keep them away from Tommy . . ." At the top of the stairs, she flung open the door. "See?" she said, turning to point. "Oh, no!" she cried.

Story Details		My Prior Knowledge		My Prediction
• Kittens are left alone in a painter's studio. • His daughter is horrified at the result.	+	• Kittens like to explore. • Art supplies are messy.	→	The kittens escaped and spilled some paint.

Additional Story Details		Prediction Verified?		Revised Prediction
"He's been working on it for over a year," she said.	=	Not entirely	→	The kittens escaped and damaged a painting.

Academic Vocabulary: Words for Responding to Literature

The following words will help you discuss the selections in this unit.

Word	Definition	Example sentence
eloquent *adj.*	expressing meaning clearly, forcefully, and memorably	The audience was deeply affected by her *eloquent* speech.
perceive *v.*	see; to understand	We do not *perceive* the character's true grief until the end of the story.
spontaneous *adj.*	seeming to occur without planning	She writes in a *spontaneous* style.
subjective *adj.*	of a person's thoughts and feelings; also a grammatical term	The essay is written from a *subjective* viewpoint.
innovative *adj.*	inventive; done in a new or unusual way	The novel contained *innovative* narrative techniques.

Vocabulary Skills You Will Learn in Part 1

▶ A **word root** is the part of the word that contains its basic meaning.

In Part 1 you will learn
- the root *-loqu-* (p. 54)   • the root *-nov-* (p. 80)   • the root *-spont(e)-* (p. 80)

Dictionary entries specify a word's root and origin.

The word comes originally from Latin.   *This prefix means "out."*

el•o•quent (el´ ō kwent) *adj.* [<L e-, out + *loqui,* speak] **1.** vivid, forceful, or fluent in speech or writing; *an eloquent speaker* **2.** characterized by clear and forceful expression: *an eloquent speech*

The root means "speak." Knowing this will help you remember the full meaning, "vivid, forceful, or fluent in speech."

Activity Look up the words from the chart in a dictionary. Use the information in each entry to identify the root of the word. Explain how knowing the root helps you to understand the word's meaning.

Practice these skills with either "The Monkey's Paw" (p. 32) or "The Leap" (p. 45).

Academic Standards

- Examine how the author's perspective influences the structure and tone of the text. (10.2.4)
- Evaluate interactions between characters and how these affect the plot. (10.3.3)
- Evaluate an author's use of time and sequence. (10.3.6)

Literary Analysis

A **plot** is the sequence of related events in a story. A typical plot concerns a **conflict**—a struggle between opposing forces—and follows a pattern like the one shown.

- **Exposition:** The writer gives background on the characters and situation.
- **Rising action:** Events intensify the conflict.
- **Climax:** The tension reaches its highest point because the outcome of the conflict is about to be revealed.
- **Falling action:** The tension lessens because the outcome is clear.
- **Resolution:** The final outcome. Often, the resolution involves a change or an insight.

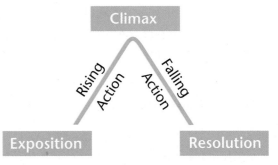

Writers use various techniques to add tension to a story. One technique is **foreshadowing**—giving details that hint at upcoming events.

Reading Skill

A **prediction** is a logical idea about what will happen. To make predictions, pay attention to story details and **use your prior knowledge.**

- Knowledge of stories with similar plots can help you predict events.
- Knowledge of human nature can help you predict how characters will act.

Vocabulary Builder

The Monkey's Paw

- **maligned** (mə līnd′) *adj.* spoken ill of (p. 36) *The CD, maligned by critics, was still a tremendous hit.*
- **furtively** (fur′ tiv lē) *adv.* secretively; sneakily; stealthily (p. 38) *She reached furtively for the last slice of pie.*
- **apathy** (ap′ ə thē) *n.* lack of interest or emotion (p. 39) *The bored audience looked at the speaker with apathy.*

The Leap

- **encroaching** (en krōch′ iŋ) *adj.* intruding on, especially in a gradual manner (p. 45) *The encroaching clouds dimmed the sun.*
- **extricating** (eks′ tri kāt′ iŋ) *n.* setting free; removing from a difficult situation (p. 48) *Extricating his kite from a tree is difficult.*
- **tentative** (ten′ tə tiv) *adj.* hesitant; not confident (p. 51) *I took a tentative bite of the unusual dessert.*

Background

The British View of India "The Monkey's Paw" tells of an eerie object that arrives in England from India. From the late 1700s until 1947, India was a British colony. In letters and visits back home, British soldiers passed on information and misinformation about India's culture. Before long, India came to represent the mysterious and supernatural, as this story shows.

Connecting to the Literature

Reading/Writing Connection The monkey's paw in this story is a mysterious object that can grant wishes and change events. However, the characters are warned that there will be "consequences." Write three reasons why you would or would not make a wish in this situation. Use at least three of the following words: *alter, complicate, evaluate, intervene.*

> **READ MORE**
>
> by W. W. Jacobs
> *The Monkey's Paw and Other Tales of Mystery and the Macabre*

Meet the Author

W. W. Jacobs (1863–1943)

As a boy, William Wymark Jacobs traveled far and wide in his imagination. He lived in London, England, in a house near the docks, and he listened eagerly to the tales of adventure told by sailors whom he met there. These tales shaped the stories he wrote as an adult—stories in which everyday life is disrupted by strange and fantastic events. "The Monkey's Paw" is his most famous tale of the supernatural.

More Than Horror Although today W. W. Jacobs is best known for this tale of suspense, in his own lifetime he was famous as a humorist. In fact, he wrote works of various kinds, and he wrote them in quantity. When a collection of his works was published in 1931, it contained seventeen books!

Fast Facts

▶ "The Monkey's Paw" made for spine-tingling theater. A one-act adaptation of the story played on Broadway in 1907 and was revived in 1923.

▶ Moviemakers have told the strange tale of "The Monkey's Paw" eight times! The first film version of the story was made in 1915. More recent remakes came out in 1996 and 2003.

Go Online
Author Link

For: More about the author
Visit: www.PHSchool.com
Web Code: eqe-9102

the Monkey's Paw

W.W. Jacobs

I

Without, the night was cold and wet, but in the small parlor of Laburnam Villa the blinds were drawn and the fire burned brightly. Father and son were at chess, the former, who possessed ideas about the game involving radical changes, putting his king into such sharp and unnecessary perils that it even provoked comment from the white-haired old lady knitting placidly by the fire.

"Hark at the wind," said Mr. White, who, having seen a fatal mistake after it was too late, was amiably desirous of preventing his son from seeing it.

"I'm listening," said the latter, grimly surveying the board as he stretched out his hand. "Check."

"I should hardly think that he'd come tonight," said his father, with his hand poised over the board.

"Mate,"[1] replied the son.

"That's the worst of living so far out," bawled Mr. White, with sudden and unlooked-for violence; "of all the beastly, slushy, out-of-the-way places to live in, this is the worst. Pathway's a bog, and the road's a torrent. I don't know what people are thinking about. I suppose because only two houses on the road are let, they think it doesn't matter."

"Never mind, dear," said his wife, soothingly; "perhaps you'll win the next one."

Mr. White looked up sharply, just in time to intercept a knowing glance between mother and son. The words died away on his lips, and he hid a guilty grin in his thin gray beard.

"There he is," said Herbert White, as the gate banged to loudly and heavy footsteps came toward the door.

The old man rose with hospitable haste, and opening the door, was heard condoling with the new arrival. The new arrival also condoled with himself, so that Mrs. White said, "Tut, tut!" and coughed gently as her husband entered the room, followed by a tall, burly man, beady of eye and rubicund of visage.[2]

"Sergeant Major Morris," he said, introducing him.

The sergeant major shook hands, and taking the proffered seat by the fire, watched contentedly while his host got out tumblers and stood a small copper kettle on the fire.

At the third glass his eyes got brighter, and he began to talk, the little family circle regarding with eager interest this visitor from distant parts, as he squared his broad shoulders in the chair and spoke of wild scenes and doughty[3] deeds; of wars and plagues and strange peoples.

Literary Analysis
Plot What important background information about the characters and their home is given in the exposition of this story?

✔ **Reading Check**

Who has arrived at the White's house?

---

1. **mate** *n.* checkmate, a chess move that prevents the opponent's king from escaping capture and so ends the game.
2. **rubicund** (roo′ bə kund′) **of visage** (viz′ ij) having a red face.
3. **doughty** (dou′ ē) *adj.* brave.

"Twenty-one years of it," said Mr. White, nodding at his wife and son. "When he went away he was a slip of a youth in the warehouse. Now look at him."

"He don't look to have taken much harm," said Mrs. White, politely.

"I'd like to go to India myself," said the old man, "just to look round a bit, you know."

"Better where you are," said the sergeant major, shaking his head. He put down the empty glass, and sighing softly, shook it again.

"I should like to see those old temples and fakirs and jugglers," said the old man. "What was that you started telling me the other day about a monkey's paw or something, Morris?"

"Nothing," said the soldier, hastily. "Leastways nothing worth hearing."

"Monkey's paw?" said Mrs. White, curiously.

"Well, it's just a bit of what you might call magic, perhaps," said the sergeant major, offhandedly.

His three listeners leaned forward eagerly. The visitor absent-mindedly put his empty glass to his lips and then set it down again. His host filled it for him.

"To look at," said the sergeant major, fumbling in his pocket, "it's just an ordinary little paw, dried to a mummy."

He took something out of his pocket and proffered it. Mrs. White drew back with a grimace, but her son, taking it, examined it curiously.

"And what is there special about it?" inquired Mr. White as he took it from his son, and having examined it, placed it upon the table.

"It had a spell put on it by an old fakir," said the sergeant major, "a very holy man. He wanted to show that fate ruled people's lives, and that those who interfered with it did so to their sorrow. He put a spell on it so that three separate men could each have three wishes from it."

His manner was so impressive that his hearers were conscious that their light laughter jarred somewhat.

"Well, why don't you have three, sir?" said Herbert White, cleverly.

The soldier regarded him in the way that middle age is wont to regard presumptuous youth. "I have," he said, quietly, and his blotchy face whitened.

"And did you really have the three wishes granted?" asked Mrs. White.

"I did," said the sergeant major, and his glass tapped against his strong teeth.

▼ **Critical Viewing**
Does the atmosphere, or mood, of this photograph fit the story? Explain. **[Connect]**

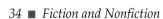

"And has anybody else wished?" persisted the old lady.

"The first man had his three wishes, yes," was the reply; "I don't know what the first two were, but the third was for death. That's how I got the paw."

His tones were so grave that a hush fell upon the group.

"If you've had your three wishes, it's no good to you now, then, Morris," said the old man at last. "What do you keep it for?"

The soldier shook his head. "Fancy, I suppose," he said, slowly. "I did have some idea of selling it, but I don't think I will. It has caused enough mischief already. Besides, people won't buy. They think it's a fairy tale, some of them, and those who do think anything of it want to try it first and pay me afterward."

"If you could have another three wishes," said the old man, eyeing him keenly, "would you have them?"

"I don't know," said the other. "I don't know."

He took the paw, and dangling it between his forefinger and thumb, suddenly threw it upon the fire. White, with a slight cry, stooped down and snatched it off.

"Better let it burn," said the soldier, solemnly.

"If you don't want it, Morris," said the other, "give it to me."

"I won't," said his friend doggedly. "I threw it on the fire. If you keep it, don't blame me for what happens. Pitch it on the fire again, like a sensible man."

The other shook his head and examined his new possession closely. "How do you do it?" he inquired.

"Hold it up in your right hand and wish aloud," said the sergeant major, "but I warn you of the consequences."

"Sounds like the *Arabian Nights*,"[4] said Mrs. White, as she rose and began to set the supper. "Don't you think you might wish for four pairs of hands for me?"

Her husband drew the talisman from his pocket, and then all three burst into laughter as the sergeant major, with a look of alarm on his face, caught him by the arm. "If you must wish," he said, gruffly, "wish for something sensible."

Mr. White dropped it back in his pocket, and placing chairs, motioned his friend to the table. In the business of supper the talisman was partly forgotten, and afterward the three sat listening in an enthralled fashion to a second installment of the soldier's adventures in India.

"If the tale about the monkey's paw is not more truthful than those he has been telling us," said Herbert, as the door closed behind their guest, just in time for him to catch the last train, "we shan't make much out of it."

---

4. **Arabian Nights** collection of stories from the ancient Near East telling of fantastical adventures and supernatural beings.

Literary Analysis
Plot How does the information about the previous wishers foreshadow danger for the Whites?

Reading Check

According to the sergeant major, what is special about the monkey's paw?

"Did you give him anything for it, Father?" inquired Mrs. White, regarding her husband closely.

"A trifle," said he, coloring slightly. "He didn't want it, but I made him take it. And he pressed me again to throw it away."

"Likely," said Herbert, with pretended horror. "Why, we're going to be rich, and famous and happy. Wish to be an emperor, Father, to begin with; then you can't be bossed around."

He darted round the table, pursued by the <u>maligned</u> Mrs. White armed with an antimacassar.[5]

Vocabulary Builder
maligned (mə līnd´)
adj. spoken ill of

Mr. White took the paw from his pocket and eyed it dubiously. "I don't know what to wish for, and that's a fact," he said, slowly. "It seems to me I've got all I want."

"If you only cleared the house, you'd be quite happy, wouldn't you?" said Herbert, with his hand on his shoulder. "Well, wish for two hundred pounds,[6] then; that'll just do it."

His father, smiling shamefacedly at his own credulity, held up the talisman, as his son, with a solemn face somewhat marred by a wink at his mother, sat down at the piano and struck a few impressive chords.

"I wish for two hundred pounds," said the old man distinctly.

A fine crash from the piano greeted the words, interrupted by a shuddering cry from the old man. His wife and son ran toward him.

"It moved," he cried, with a glance of disgust at the object as it lay on the floor. "As I wished it twisted in my hand like a snake."

"Well, I don't see the money," said his son as he picked it up and placed it on the table, "and I bet I never shall."

"It must have been your fancy, Father," said his wife, regarding him anxiously.

He shook his head. "Never mind, though; there's no harm done, but it gave me a shock all the same."

Reading Skill
Making Predictions
What do characters in stories about wishes usually learn? Predict the results of Mr. White's wish.

They sat down by the fire again while the two men finished their pipes. Outside, the wind was higher than ever, and the old man started nervously at the sound of a door banging upstairs. A silence unusual and depressing settled upon all three, which lasted until the old couple rose to retire for the night.

"I expect you'll find the cash tied up in a big bag in the middle of your bed," said Herbert, as he bade them good night, "and something horrible squatting up on top of the wardrobe watching you as you pocket your ill-gotten gains."

Herbert sat alone in the darkness, gazing at the dying fire, and seeing faces in it. The last face was so horrible and so simian[7] that he gazed at it in amazement. It got so vivid that, with a little uneasy

---

5. antimacassar (an´ ti mə kas´ ər) *n.* small cover for the arms or back of a chair or sofa.
6. pounds *n.* units of English currency, roughly comparable to dollars.
7. simian (sim´ ē ən) *adj.* monkeylike.

laugh, he felt on the table for a glass containing a little water to throw over it. His hand grasped the monkey's paw, and with a little shiver he wiped his hand on his coat and went up to bed.

II

In the brightness of the wintry sun next morning as it streamed over the breakfast table Herbert laughed at his fears. There was an air of prosaic wholesomeness about the room which it had lacked on the previous night, and the dirty, shriveled little paw was pitched on the sideboard with a carelessness which betokened no great belief in its virtues.

"I suppose all old soldiers are the same," said Mrs. White. "The idea of our listening to such nonsense! How could wishes be granted in these days? And if they could, how could two hundred pounds hurt you, Father?"

"Might drop on his head from the sky," said the frivolous Herbert.

"Morris said the things happened so naturally," said his father, "that you might if you so wished attribute it to coincidence."

"Well, don't break into the money before I come back," said Herbert, as he rose from the table. "I'm afraid it'll turn you into a mean, avaricious[8] man, and we shall have to disown you."

His mother laughed, and following him to the door, watched him down the road, and, returning to the breakfast table, was very happy at the expense of her husband's credulity. All of which did not prevent her from scurrying to the door at the postman's knock, nor prevent her from referring somewhat shortly to retired sergeant majors of bibulous habits when she found that the post brought a tailor's bill.

"Herbert will have some more of his funny remarks, I expect, when he comes home," she said, as they sat at dinner.

"I dare say," said Mr. White, "but for all that, the thing moved in my hand; that I'll swear to."

"You thought it did," said the old lady soothingly.

"I say it did," replied the other. "There was no thought about it; I had just—What's the matter?"

His wife made no reply. She was watching the mysterious movements of a man outside, who, peering in an undecided fashion at the house, appeared to be trying to make up his mind to enter. In mental connection with the two hundred pounds, she noticed that the stranger was well dressed, and wore a silk hat of glossy newness. Three times he paused at the gate, and then walked on again. The fourth time he stood with his hand upon it, and then with sudden resolution flung it open and walked up the path. Mrs. White at the same moment placed her hands behind her, and hurriedly

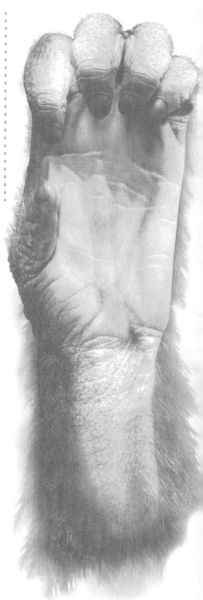

Literary Analysis
Plot How does the conversation about the money foreshadow a problem?

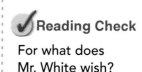 **Reading Check**

For what does Mr. White wish?

---

8. **avaricious** (av´ ə rish´ əs) *adj.* greedy for wealth.

unfastening the strings of her apron, put that useful article of apparel beneath the cushion of her chair.

She brought the stranger, who seemed ill at ease, into the room. He gazed at her <u>furtively</u>, and listened in a preoccupied fashion as the old lady apologized for the appearance of the room, and her husband's coat, a garment which he usually reserved for the garden. She then waited patiently for him to broach his business, but he was at first strangely silent.

"I—was asked to call," he said at last, and stooped and picked a piece of cotton from his trousers. "I come from 'Maw and Meggins.'"

The old lady started. "Is anything the matter?" she asked, breathlessly. "Has anything happened to Herbert? What is it? What is it?"

Her husband interposed. "There, there, mother," he said, hastily. "Sit down, and don't jump to conclusions. You've not brought bad news, I'm sure, sir," and he eyed the other wistfully.

"I'm sorry—" began the visitor.

"Is he hurt?" demanded the mother, wildly.

The visitor bowed in assent. "Badly hurt," he said quietly, "but he is not in any pain."

"Oh, thank God!" said the old woman, clasping her hands. "Thank God for that! Thank—"

She broke off suddenly as the sinister meaning of the assurance dawned upon her and she saw the awful confirmation of her fears in the other's averted face. She caught her breath, and turning to her husband, laid her trembling old hand upon his. There was a long silence.

"He was caught in the machinery," said the visitor at length, in a low voice.

"Caught in the machinery," repeated Mr. White, in a dazed fashion, "yes."

He sat staring blankly out at the window, and taking his wife's hand between his own, pressed it as he had been wont to do in their old courting days nearly forty years before.

"He was the only one left to us," he said, turning gently to the visitor. "It is hard."

The other coughed, and, rising, walked slowly to the window. "The firm wished me to convey their sincere sympathy with you in your great loss," he said, without looking round. "I beg that you will understand I am only their servant and merely obeying orders."

There was no reply; the old woman's face was white, her eyes staring, and her breath inaudible; on the husband's face was a look such as his friend the sergeant might have carried into his first action.

"I was to say that Maw and Meggins disclaim all responsibility," continued the other. "They admit no liability at all, but in

Vocabulary Builder
furtively (fʉr´ tiv lē) *adv.* secretively; sneakily; stealthily

consideration of your son's services they wish to present you with a certain sum as compensation."

Mr. White dropped his wife's hand, and rising to his feet, gazed with a look of horror at his visitor. His dry lips shaped the words, "How much?"

"Two hundred pounds," was the answer.

Unconscious of his wife's shriek, the old man smiled faintly, put out his hands like a sightless man, and dropped, a senseless heap, to the floor.

III

In the huge new cemetery, some two miles distant, the old people buried their dead, and came back to a house steeped in shadow and silence. It was all over so quickly that at first they could hardly realize it, and remained in a state of expectation as though of something else to happen—something else which was to lighten this load, too heavy for old hearts to bear.

But the days passed, and expectation gave place to resignation—the hopeless resignation of the old, sometimes miscalled <u>apathy</u>. Sometimes they hardly exchanged a word, for now they had nothing to talk about, and their days were long to weariness.

It was about a week after that the old man, waking suddenly in the night, stretched out his hand and found himself alone. The room was in darkness, and the sound of subdued weeping came from the window. He raised himself in bed and listened.

"Come back," he said, tenderly. "You will be cold."

"It is colder for my son," said the old woman, and wept afresh.

The sound of her sobs died away on his ears. The bed was warm, and his eyes heavy with sleep. He dozed fitfully, and then slept until a sudden wild cry from his wife awoke him with a start.

"The paw!" she cried wildly. "The monkey's paw!"

He started up in alarm. "Where? Where is it? What's the matter?"

She came stumbling across the room toward him. "I want it," she said quietly. "You've not destroyed it?"

"It's in the parlor, on the bracket," he replied, marveling. "Why?"

She cried and laughed together, and bending over, kissed his cheek.

"I only just thought of it," she said hysterically. "Why didn't I think of it before? Why didn't *you* think of it?"

"Think of what?" he questioned.

"The other two wishes," she replied rapidly. "We've only had one."

"Was not that enough?" he demanded, fiercely.

"No," she cried triumphantly; "we'll have one more. Go down and get it quickly, and wish our boy alive again."

The man sat up in bed and flung the bedclothes from his quaking limbs. "You are mad!" he cried, aghast.

Literary Analysis
Plot In what way does the stranger's answer increase the tension of the rising action?

Vocabulary Builder
apathy (ap´ə thē) *n.* lack of interest or emotion

Reading Skill
Making Predictions Do you think the Whites will make another wish? Why or why not?

Reading Check

How has the Whites' first wish been fulfilled?

"Get it," she panted; "get it quickly, and wish—Oh, my boy, my boy!"

Her husband struck a match and lit the candle. "Get back to bed," he said unsteadily. "You don't know what you are saying."

"We had the first wish granted," said the old woman feverishly; "why not the second?"

"A coincidence," stammered the old man.

"Go and get it and wish," cried his wife, quivering with excitement.

The old man turned and regarded her, and his voice shook. "He has been dead ten days, and besides he—I would not tell you else, but—I could only recognize him by his clothing. If he was too terrible for you to see then, how now?"

"Bring him back," cried the old woman, and dragged him toward the door. "Do you think I fear the child I have nursed?"

He went down in the darkness, and felt his way to the parlor, and then to the mantelpiece. The talisman was in its place, and a horrible fear that the unspoken wish might bring his mutilated son before him ere he could escape from the room seized upon him, and he caught his breath as he found that he had lost the direction of the door. His brow cold with sweat, he felt his way round the table, and groped along the wall until he found himself in the small passage with the unwholesome thing in his hand.

Even his wife's face seemed changed as he entered the room. It was white and expectant, and to his fears seemed to have an unnatural look upon it. He was afraid of her.

"*Wish!*" she cried, in a strong voice.

"It is foolish and wicked," he faltered.

"*Wish!*" repeated his wife.

He raised his hand. "I wish my son alive again."

The talisman fell to the floor, and he regarded it fearfully. Then he sank trembling into a chair as the old woman, with burning eyes, walked to the window and raised the blind.

He sat until he was chilled with the cold, glancing occasionally at the figure of the old woman peering through the window. The candle-end, which had burned below the rim of the china candle-stick, was throwing pulsating shadows on the ceiling and walls, until, with a flicker larger than the rest, it expired. The old man, with an unspeakable sense of relief at the failure of the talisman, crept back to his bed, and a minute or two afterward the old woman came silently and apathetically beside him.

Neither spoke, but lay silently listening to the ticking of the clock. A stair creaked, and a squeaky mouse scurried noisily through the wall. The darkness was oppressive, and after lying for some time screwing up his courage, he took the box of matches, and striking one, went downstairs for a candle.

Literary Analysis
Plot In what way does this new wish increase the tension of the story?

At the foot of the stairs the match went out, and he paused to strike another; and at the same moment a knock, so quiet and stealthy as to be scarcely audible, sounded on the front door.

The matches fell from his hand and spilled in the passage. He stood motionless, his breath suspended until the knock was repeated. Then he turned and fled swiftly back to his room, and closed the door behind him. A third knock sounded through the house.

"*What's that?*" cried the old woman, starting up.

"A rat," said the old man in shaking tones—"a rat. It passed me on the stairs."

His wife sat up in bed listening. A loud knock resounded through the house.

"It's Herbert!" she screamed. "It's Herbert!"

She ran to the door, but her husband was before her, and catching her by the arm, held her tightly.

"What are you going to do?" he whispered hoarsely.

"It's my boy; it's Herbert!" she cried, struggling mechanically. "I forgot it was two miles away. What are you holding me for? Let go. I must open the door."

"Don't let it in," cried the old man, trembling.

"You're afraid of your own son," she cried, struggling. "Let me go. I'm coming, Herbert, I'm coming."

There was another knock, and another. The old woman with a sudden wrench broke free and ran from the room. Her husband followed to the landing, and called after her appealingly as she hurried downstairs. He heard the chain rattle back and the bottom bolt drawn slowly and stiffly from the socket. Then the old woman's voice, strained and panting.

"The bolt," she cried, loudly. "Come down. I can't reach it."

But her husband was on his hands and knees groping wildly on the floor in search of the paw. If he could only find it before the thing outside got in. A perfect fusillade[9] of knocks reverberated through the house, and he heard the scraping of a chair as his wife put it down in the passage against the door. He heard the creaking of the bolt as it came slowly back, and at the same moment he found the monkey's paw, and frantically breathed his third and last wish.

The knocking ceased suddenly, although the echoes of it were still in the house. He heard the chair drawn back and the door opened. A cold wind rushed up the staircase, and a long loud wail of disappointment and misery from his wife gave him courage to run down to her side, and then to the gate beyond. The street lamp flickering opposite shone on a quiet and deserted road.

---

9. **fusillade** (fyo͞o′ sə lād′) *n.* rapid firing, as of gunshots.

Literary Analysis
Plot How does the difference between what Mr. and Mrs. White are trying to do bring events to a climax?

Apply the Skills

The Monkey's Paw

Thinking About the Selection

1. **Respond:** What is the most frightening moment in the story? Why?
2. **(a) Recall:** How does each of the Whites react when first hearing the legend of the monkey's paw? **(b) Contrast:** How do the reactions of the mother and the father change?
3. **(a) Recall:** What event fulfills Mr. White's first wish?
   (b) Make a Judgment: Do you think the first wish really "comes true," or is there just a coincidence of events? Explain.
4. **(a) Recall:** How does Mr. White word his first wish? **(b) Infer:** What painful outcome seems to follow from his wording?
   (c) Discuss: In a group, discuss the strengths and weaknesses of other ways the wish could have been worded. Decide whether any version is foolproof. Share your decision with the class.
5. **Draw Conclusions:** Explain whether you think the events of the story prove the fakir's point that "fate ruled people's lives, and that those who interfered with it did so to their sorrow."

Literary Analysis

6. What information about the paw is given in the **exposition**?
7. **(a)** Describe three events in the **rising action** that increase the tension in the **plot**. **(b)** Where does the story reach its **climax**?
8. Identify two details that **foreshadow** the tragic outcome of the first wish.

Reading Skill

9. **(a)** Using a chart like the one shown, indicate how you used your prior knowledge to **make a prediction** about one of the wishes.

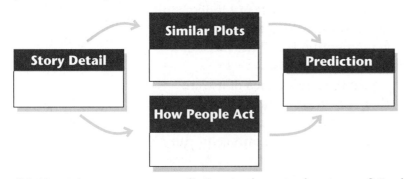

(b) How close was your prediction to the actual outcome? Explain your answer.

QuickReview

Who's Who in the Story

Mr. and Mrs. White: an older couple living in a remote area

Herbert: their son

Sergeant Major Morris: an old friend of Mr. White's who served in India

Go Online
—Assessment
For: Self-test
Visit: www.PHSchool.com
Web Code: eqa-6103

Plot: the sequence of related events in a story, including *exposition, rising action, climax, falling action,* and *resolution*

Foreshadowing: hints about future plot events

Prediction: a logical idea about what will happen

Vocabulary Builder

Practice **Analogies** show the relationships between pairs of words. Use a word from the vocabulary list for "The Monkey's Paw," on page 30, to complete each analogy. Your choice should create a word pair that matches the relationship between the first two words given. Explain the relationship in each analogy.

1. ran : rapidly :: crept : _____?_____
2. kindness : cruelty :: passion : _____?_____
3. nourished : starved :: praised : _____?_____

Adding Words to Your Vocabulary Use a dictionary to find the meanings of *malignant, furtive,* and *apathetic.* Explain how each word's meaning is related to the meaning of a vocabulary word on page 30. (For more about using a dictionary, see page R6.)

Writing

Write a brief **sequel** to this tale in which someone else finds the paw.
- Use a plot outline or map to plan the details for your story.
- As you draft and revise, try to capture Jacobs's writing style. Use descriptive words to create a spooky atmosphere of horror. Use foreshadowing to build suspense.

For *Grammar, Vocabulary,* and *Assessment,* see **Build Language Skills,** pages 54–55.

Extend Your Learning

Listening and Speaking In a small group, conduct an **interview** between a journalist and the Whites after the tragedy. Plan questions that will focus the Whites' retelling of the story. After the interview, discuss which questions and responses were most effective. Each team member should offer one suggestion to improve the interview.

Research and Technology Imagine you are the director of a film version of this story. Write a **scene proposal** for your movie. First, make a clear purpose statement, such as *I want my scene to make people think* or *I want to scare viewers.* Then, research film techniques you can use to meet your purpose, such as the use of cross-cutting. Combine your research with story details to outline your plan.

Build Understanding • *The Leap*

Background

Circus Families Circus families often develop their own acts and pass the specific skills involved, such as acrobatics or juggling, from one generation to the next. Many young circus performers, like the mother in "The Leap," miss traditional schooling to develop awesome physical talents.

Connecting to the Literature

Reading/Writing Connection In "The Leap," a mother draws on her past as a circus performer to give her daughter a heroic gift of love. Write a few sentences about an emotional gift you have given or received. Use at least three of these words: *demonstrate, devote, enrich, enlighten.*

Review

For **Literary Analysis, Reading Skill,** and **Vocabulary Builder,** see page 30.

READ MORE

by Louise Erdrich

The Beet Queen

Love Medicine

Meet the Author

Louise **Erdrich** (b. 1954)

Louise Erdrich's fiction and poetry celebrate life's richness. Born to a German American father and a French–Native American mother, Erdrich writes from the complex perspective of two distinct cultures.

A Family Tradition Erdrich grew up in North Dakota, where she often visited with her relatives in the Turtle Mountain Band of Chippewa, a Native American people. With little exposure to television or movies, Erdrich became fascinated by the story-telling tradition that surrounded her. "The people in our families made everything into a story," she explains. Her first published book, *Love Medicine,* a group of interrelated stories, brought Erdrich national acclaim.

Fast Facts

▶ *Love Medicine* was rejected by the first twenty-eight publishers to whom Erdrich sent it.

▶ When finally published, the book won rave reviews and the National Book Critics Circle Award.

Go Online
Author Link

For: More about the author
Visit: www.PHSchool.com
Web Code: eqe-9103

The LEAP

Louise Erdrich

My mother is the surviving half of a blindfold trapeze act, not a fact I think about much even now that she is sightless, the result of <u>encroaching</u> and stubborn cataracts. She walks slowly through her house here in New Hampshire, lightly touching her way along walls and running her hands over knickknacks, books, the drift of a grown child's belongings and castoffs. She has never upset an object or as much as brushed a magazine onto the floor. She has never lost her balance or bumped into a closet door left carelessly open.

It has occurred to me that the catlike precision of her movements in old age might be the result of her early training, but she shows so little of the drama or flair one might expect from a performer that I tend to forget the Flying Avalons. She has kept no sequined costume, no photographs, no fliers or posters from that part of her youth. I would, in fact, tend to think that all memory of double somersaults and heart-stopping catches had left her arms and legs were it not for the fact that sometimes, as I sit sewing in the room of the rebuilt house in which I slept as a child, I hear the crackle, catch a whiff of smoke from the stove downstairs, and suddenly the room goes dark, the stitches burn beneath my fingers, and I am sewing with a needle of hot silver, a thread of fire.

I owe her my existence three times. The first was when she saved herself. In the town square a replica tent pole, cracked and splintered, now stands cast in concrete. It commemorates the disaster

Vocabulary Builder
encroaching (en krōch´ iŋ) *adj.* intruding on, especially in a gradual manner

Reading Check

What was the narrator's mother's profession?

that put our town smack on the front page of the Boston and New York tabloids. It is from those old newspapers, now historical records, that I get my information. Not from my mother, Anna of the Flying Avalons, nor from any of her in-laws, nor certainly from the other half of her particular act, Harold Avalon, her first husband. In one news account it says, "The day was mildly overcast, but nothing in the air or temperature gave any hint of the sudden force with which the deadly gale would strike."

I have lived in the West, where you can see the weather coming for miles, and it is true that out here we are at something of a disadvantage. When extremes of temperature collide, a hot and cold front, winds generate instantaneously behind a hill and crash upon you without warning. That, I think, was the likely situation on that day in June. People probably commented on the pleasant air, grateful that no hot sun beat upon the striped tent that stretched over the entire center green. They bought their tickets and surrendered them in anticipation. They sat. They ate caramelized popcorn and roasted peanuts. There was time, before the storm, for three acts. The White Arabians[1] of Ali-Khazar rose on their hind legs and waltzed. The Mysterious Bernie folded himself into a painted cracker tin, and the Lady of the Mists made herself appear and disappear in surprising places. As the clouds gathered outside, unnoticed, the ringmaster cracked his whip, shouted his introduction, and pointed to the ceiling of the tent, where the Flying Avalons were perched.

They loved to drop gracefully from nowhere, like two sparkling birds, and blow kisses as they threw off their plumed helmets and high-collared capes. They laughed and flirted openly as they beat their way up again on the trapeze bars. In the final vignette of their act, they actually would kiss in midair, pausing, almost hovering as they swooped past one another. On the ground, between bows, Harry Avalon would skip quickly to the front rows and point out the smear of my mother's lipstick, just off the edge of his mouth. They made a romantic pair all right, especially in the blindfold sequence.

That afternoon, as the anticipation increased, as Mr. and Mrs. Avalon tied sparkling strips of cloth onto each other's face and as they puckered their lips in mock kisses, lips destined "never again to meet," as one long breathless article put it, the wind rose, miles off, wrapped itself into a cone, and howled. There came a rumble of

---

1. **Arabians** horses of the Arabian breed.

Literary Analysis
Plot How does the statement from the news account foreshadow a tragic event?

Reading Skill
Making Predictions What details help you predict that something will go wrong?

electrical energy, drowned out by the sudden roll of drums. One detail not mentioned by the press, perhaps unknown—Anna was pregnant at the time, seven months and hardly showing, her stomach muscles were that strong. It seems incredible that she would work high above the ground when any fall could be so dangerous, but the explanation—I know from watching her go blind—is that my mother lives comfortably in extreme elements. She is one with the constant dark now, just as the air was her home, familiar to her, safe, before the storm that afternoon.

From opposite ends of the tent they waved, blind and smiling, to the crowd below. The ringmaster removed his hat and called for silence, so that the two above could concentrate. They rubbed their hands in chalky powder, then Harry launched himself and swung, once, twice, in huge calibrated beats across space. He hung from his knees and on the third swing stretched wide his arms, held his hands out to receive his pregnant wife as she dove from her shining bar.

It was while the two were in midair, their hands about to meet, that lightning struck the main pole and sizzled down the guy wires, filling the air with a blue radiance that Harry Avalon must certainly have seen through the cloth of his blindfold as the tent buckled and the edifice[2] toppled him forward, the swing continuing and not returning in its sweep, and Harry going down, down into the crowd with his last thought, perhaps, just a prickle of surprise at his empty hands.

My mother once said that I'd be amazed at how many things a person can do within the act of falling. Perhaps, at the time, she was teaching me to dive off a board at the town pool, for I associate the idea with midair somersaults. But I also think she meant that even in that awful doomed second one could think, for she certainly did. When her hands did not meet her husband's, my mother tore her blindfold away. As he swept past her on the wrong side, she could have grasped his ankle, the toe-end of his tights, and gone down clutching him. Instead, she changed direction. Her body twisted toward a heavy wire and she managed to hang on to the braided metal, still hot from the lightning strike. Her palms were burned so terribly that once healed they bore no lines, only the blank scar tissue of a quieter future. She was lowered, gently, to the sawdust ring just underneath the dome of the canvas roof, which did not entirely settle but was held up on one end and jabbed through, torn, and

---

2. edifice (ed´ i fis) *n.* large structure or building.

Literary Analysis
Plot In what way do these descriptions of events increase the tension in the rising action?

✔ Reading Check
What happens to Harry on the day of the gale?

still on fire in places from the giant spark, though rain and men's jackets soon put that out.

Three people died, but except for her hands my mother was not seriously harmed until an overeager rescuer broke her arm in extricating her and also, in the process, collapsed a portion of the tent bearing a huge buckle that knocked her unconscious. She was taken to the town hospital, and there she must have hemorrhaged,[3] for they kept her, confined to her bed, a month and a half before her baby was born without life.

Harry Avalon had wanted to be buried in the circus cemetery next to the original Avalon, his uncle, so she sent him back with his brothers. The child, however, is buried around the corner, beyond this house and just down the highway. Sometimes I used to walk there just to sit. She was a girl, but I rarely thought of her as a sister or even as a separate person really. I suppose you could call it the egocentrism[4] of a child, of all young children, but I considered her a less finished version of myself.

When the snow falls, throwing shadows among the stones, I can easily pick hers out from the road, for it is bigger than the others and in the shape of a lamb at rest, its legs curled beneath. The carved lamb looms larger as the years pass, though it is probably only my eyes, the vision shifting, as what is close to me blurs and distances sharpen. In odd moments, I think it is the edge drawing near, the edge of everything, the unseen horizon we do not really speak of in the eastern woods. And it also seems to me, although this is probably an idle fantasy, that the statue is growing more sharply etched, as if, instead of weathering itself into a porous mass, it is hardening on the hillside with each snowfall, perfecting itself.

It was during her confinement in the hospital that my mother met my father. He was called in to look at the set of her arm, which was complicated. He stayed, sitting at her bedside, for he was something of an armchair traveler and had spent his war quietly, at an air force training grounds, where he became a specialist in arms and legs broken during parachute training exercises. Anna Avalon had been to many of the places he longed to visit—Venice, Rome, Mexico, all through France and Spain. She had no family of her own and was taken in by the Avalons, trained to perform from a very young age. They toured Europe before the war, then based themselves in New York. She was illiterate.

It was in the hospital that she finally learned to read and write, as a way of overcoming the boredom and depression of those weeks,

---

3. **hemorrhaged** (hem′ ər ij'd′) *v.* bled heavily.
4. **egocentrism** (ē′ gō sen′ triz əm) *n.* self-centeredness; inability to distinguish one's own needs and interests from those of others.

Vocabulary Builder
extricating (eks′ tri kāt′ iŋ) *n.* setting free; removing from a difficult situation (*verb used as a noun*)

Literary Analysis
Plot Which details in this paragraph provide additional exposition?

and it was my father who insisted on teaching her. In return for stories of her adventures, he graded her first exercises. He bought her her first book, and over her bold letters, which the pale guides of the penmanship pads could not contain, they fell in love.

I wonder if my father calculated the exchange he offered: one form of flight for another. For after that, and for as long as I can remember, my mother has never been without a book. Until now, that is, and it remains the greatest difficulty of her blindness. Since my father's recent death, there is no one to read to her, which is why I returned, in fact, from my failed life where the land is flat. I came home to read to my mother, to read out loud, to read long into the dark if I must, to read all night.

Once my father and mother married, they moved onto the old farm he had inherited but didn't care much for. Though he'd been thinking of moving to a larger city, he settled down and broadened his practice in this valley. It still seems odd to me, when they could have gone anywhere else, that they chose to stay in the town where the disaster had occurred, and which my father in the first place had found so constricting. It was my mother who insisted upon it, after her child did not survive. And then, too, she loved the sagging farmhouse with its scrap of what was left of a vast acreage of woods and hidden hay fields that stretched to the game park.

▲ **Critical Viewing**
What feelings might a scene like this inspire in an on-looker? **[Infer]**

 **Reading Check**

How do the narrator's mother and father first meet?

I owe my existence, the second time then, to the two of them and the hospital that brought them together. That is the debt we take for granted since none of us asks for life. It is only once we have it that we hang on so dearly.

I was seven the year the house caught fire, probably from standing ash. It can rekindle, and my father, forgetful around the house and perpetually exhausted from night hours on call, often emptied what he thought were ashes from cold stoves into wooden or cardboard containers. The fire could have started from a flaming box, or perhaps a buildup of creosote inside the chimney was the culprit. It started right around the stove, and the heart of the house was gutted. The babysitter, fallen asleep in my father's den on the first floor, woke to find the stairway to my upstairs room cut off by flames. She used the phone, then ran outside to stand beneath my window.

When my parents arrived, the town volunteers had drawn water from the fire pond and were spraying the outside of the house, preparing to go inside after me, not knowing at the time that there was only one staircase and that it was lost. On the other side of the house, the superannuated[5] extension ladder broke in half. Perhaps the clatter of it falling against the walls woke me, for I'd been asleep up to that point.

As soon as I awakened, in the small room that I now use for sewing, I smelled the smoke. I followed things by the letter then, was good at memorizing instructions, and so I did exactly what was taught in the second-grade home fire drill. I got up, I touched the back of my door before opening it. Finding it hot, I left it closed and stuffed my rolled-up rug beneath the crack. I did not hide under my bed or crawl into my closet. I put on my flannel robe, and then I sat down to wait.

Outside, my mother stood below my dark window and saw clearly that there was no rescue. Flames had pierced one side wall, and the glare of the fire lighted the massive limbs and trunk of the vigorous old elm that had probably been planted the year the house was built, a hundred years ago at least. No leaf touched the wall, and just one thin branch scraped the roof. From below, it looked as though even a squirrel would have had trouble jumping from the tree onto the house, for the breadth of that small branch was no bigger than my mother's wrist.

Standing there, beside Father, who was preparing to rush back around to the front of the house, my mother asked him to unzip her dress. When he wouldn't be bothered, she made him understand. He couldn't make his hands work, so she finally tore it off and stood there in her pearls and stockings. She directed one of the men to

Reading Skill
Making Predictions
Based on facts in the story about Anna's past, what do you predict she will do next?

---

5. **superannuated** (so͞o′ pər an′ yo͞o āt′'d) *adj.* too old to be usable.

lean the broken half of the extension ladder up against the trunk of the tree. In surprise, he complied. She ascended. She vanished. Then she could be seen among the leafless branches of late November as she made her way up and, along her stomach, inched the length of a bough that curved above the branch that brushed the roof.

Once there, swaying, she stood and balanced. There were plenty of people in the crowd and many who still remember, or think they do, my mother's leap through the ice-dark air toward that thinnest extension, and how she broke the branch falling so that it cracked in her hands, cracked louder than the flames as she vaulted with it toward the edge of the roof, and how it hurtled down end over end without her, and their eyes went up, again, to see where she had flown.

I didn't see her leap through air, only heard the sudden thump and looked out my window. She was hanging by the backs of her heels from the new gutter we had put in that year, and she was smiling. I was not surprised to see her, she was so matter-of-fact. She tapped on the window. I remember how she did it, too. It was the friendliest tap, a bit <u>tentative</u>, as if she was afraid she had arrived too early at a friend's house. Then she gestured at the latch, and when I opened the window she told me to raise it wider and prop it up with the stick so it wouldn't crush her fingers. She swung down, caught the ledge, and crawled through the opening. Once she was in my room, I realized she had on only underclothing, a bra of the heavy stitched cotton women used to wear and step-in, lace-trimmed drawers. I remember feeling light-headed, of course, terribly relieved, and then embarrassed for her to be seen by the crowd undressed.

I was still embarrassed as we flew out the window, toward earth, me in her lap, her toes pointed as we skimmed toward the painted target of the fire fighter's net.

I know that she's right. I knew it even then. As you fall there is time to think. Curled as I was, against her stomach, I was not startled by the cries of the crowd or the looming faces. The wind roared and beat its hot breath at our back, the flames whistled. I slowly wondered what would happen if we missed the circle or bounced out of it. Then I wrapped my hands around my mother's hands. I felt the brush of her lips and heard the beat of her heart in my ears, loud as thunder, long as the roll of drums.

Vocabulary Builder
tentative (ten´ tə tiv) *adj.* hesitant; not confident

Literary Analysis
Plot How is the conflict resolved?

Apply the Skills

The Leap

Thinking About the Selection

1. **Respond:** Which event in Anna's life surprised you the most? Why?
2. **(a) Recall:** What does Anna decide to do when the circus tent pole is struck by lightning? **(b) Interpret:** In what sense does the narrator owe her life to her mother's decision?
3. **(a) Recall:** Identify the two other ways in which the narrator owes her life to her mother. **(b) Compare and Contrast:** Compare the three ways in which the narrator owes her life to her mother. Identify at least one difference and one similarity among them.
4. **(a) Summarize:** Describe the scene at the end in which the mother leaps. **(b) Infer:** Why does the mother make the leap? **(c) Discuss:** In a group, discuss the qualities or ideas that the leap might represent. As a group, choose one idea to share with the class.

Literary Analysis

5. What information about the mother is given in the **exposition**?
6. **(a)** Describe three events in the **rising action** that increase the tension in the **plot**. **(b)** Where does the story reach its **climax**? Explain your answer.
7. What insight about the relationship between mother and daughter is presented in the **resolution** of the story?
8. Give two examples of **foreshadowing** in the story.

Reading Skill

9. **(a)** Using a chart like the one shown, indicate how you used prior knowledge to **make a prediction** about the outcome of the story.

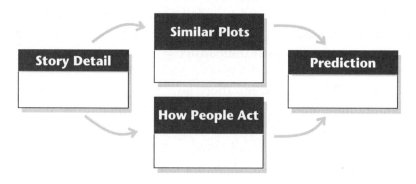

(b) How close was your prediction to the actual outcome of the story? Explain your answer.

Story at a Glance
A daughter describes three ways in which she owes her life to her mother.

For: Self-test
Visit: www.PHSchool.com
Web Code: eqa-6104

Plot: the sequence of related events in a story, including *exposition, rising action, climax, falling action,* and *resolution.*

Foreshadowing: hints about future plot events

Prediction: a logical idea about what will happen

Vocabulary Builder

Practice **Analogies** show the relationships between pairs of words. Use a word from the vocabulary list for "The Leap," on page 30, to complete each analogy. Your choice should create a word pair that matches the relationship between the first two words given. Explain the relationship in each analogy.

1. happiness : cheerful :: insecurity : _____?_____
2. knowledge : teaching :: freedom : _____?_____
3. receiving : giving :: retreating : _____?_____

Adding Words to Your Vocabulary Use a dictionary to find the meanings of *encroach, extricate,* and *tentatively.* Explain how each meaning is related to the definition of a vocabulary word on page 30. (For more on using a dictionary, see page R6.)

Writing

Write a brief **sequel** to this story in which you tell another exciting episode in which the narrator's mother uses her circus skills to rescue someone.

- Use a plot outline or map to plan the details for your story.
- As you draft and revise, try to capture Erdrich's writing style. Provide descriptive details that tell about fantastic events in a matter-of-fact way. Use foreshadowing to build suspense.

For *Grammar, Vocabulary,* and *Assessment,* see **Build Language Skills,** pages 54–55.

Extend Your Learning

Listening and Speaking In a small group, conduct an **interview** between a journalist writing about circus families and the narrator. Plan questions that help the narrator retell the main events of the story. After the interview, discuss which questions and responses were most effective. Each team member should offer a suggestion to improve the interview.

Research and Technology Imagine you are the director of a film version of this story. Write a **scene proposal** for your movie. First, make a clear purpose statement, such as *I want my scene to make people think about families* or *I want to keep viewers in suspense.* Then, research film techniques you can use to meet your purpose, such as the use of crosscutting. Combine your research with story details to outline your plan.

Build Language Skills

Vocabulary Skill

Word Roots The word *eloquent* is built from the prefix *e-,* meaning "out," and the Latin root *-loqu-,* meaning "speak." Knowing the meaning of the prefix and root helps you remember that *eloquent* means "speak out with force or clarity." Other words containing the root *-loqu-* will also refer to speech or speaking.

Practice In a dictionary, look up each of the words containing the root *-loqu-.* For each word, explain how the root's meaning contributes to the meaning of the word.

1. colloquial
2. eloquent
3. ventriloquist
4. soliloquy
5. loquacious

Grammar Lesson

Common Nouns and Proper Nouns A **common noun** refers to any one of a certain kind of person, place, or thing. A **proper noun** names a specific person, place, or thing. Proper nouns always begin with capital letters.

Common Nouns	Proper Nouns
writer	Louise Erdrich, W. W. Jacobs
city	St. Louis, Nairobi
athlete	Derek Jeter, Venus Williams

MorePractice

For more practice with common and proper nouns, see the Grammar Handbook, p. R39.

Practice Underline the common nouns in the following sentences. Then, substitute a proper noun if it is more precise and adds clarity.

1. Looking at the roads of our town, the engineer predicted that we would soon have problems with traffic.
2. The mountains beyond the school were already covered in snow.
3. The city was a unique blend of sophistication and small-town warmth.
4. That athlete scored many points in the last game.
5. The girl had a perception that the subject was very difficult.

W G Prentice Hall Writing and Grammar Connection: Chapter 16, Section 1

Reading: Make Predictions

Standards Assessed
- 10.2.4
- 10.3.3
- 10.3.6

Directions: *Read the following selection. Then, answer the questions.*

   The "Red Death" had long devastated the country. No pestilence had ever been so fatal, or so hideous. . . .

   But the Prince Prospero was happy and dauntless and sagacious. When his dominions were half depopulated, he summoned to his presence a thousand hale and lighthearted friends from among the knights and dames of his court, and with these retired to the deep seclusion of one of his castellated abbeys.

   —from "The Masque of the Red Death" by Edgar Allan Poe

1. Which detail is least significant in making a prediction about a plague you know is spread through contact?

   A Everyone invited is healthy.

   B The nobles will lock themselves away from sick peasants.

   C The Prince is rich.

   D The Prince is healthy.

2. What might lead you to revise a prediction that the Prince and his nobles will escape illness?

   A An unknown party guest arrives.

   B Everyone enjoys the party.

   C The peasants continue to die.

   D The castle is locked.

3. What information about the Red Death is most helpful for making a prediction about the Prince's fate?

   A All social classes were affected.

   B Poe made up the Red Death.

   C Victims bled heavily.

   D People were unprepared.

4. ". . . with these retired to the deep seclusion of one of his castellated abbeys" leads the reader to conclude:

   A The Prince's friends will meditate.

   B The Prince's friends will rest in a quiet, peaceful place.

   C The Prince and his friends will stay in the castle until the plague is over.

   D The Prince and his friends will try to save as many peasants as they can.

Timed Writing: Explanation [Connections]

Write a well-structured essay in which you explain the consequences of believing in superstition. Support your points with examples from both literature and experience. **(25 minutes)**

 ## Writing Workshop: *Work in Progress*

Autobiographical Narrative

Jot down a list of places that you have visited or where you have spent time. Next to each item, list three words or names you associate with the place. Keep this list in your writing portfolio.

Practice these skills with either the selection from *Swimming to Antarctica* (p. 58) or "Occupation: Conductorette" (p. 73).

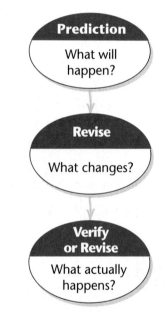

Academic Standards

- Examine how the author's perspective influences the structure and tone of the text. (10.2.4)
- Evaluate an author's use of time and sequence. (10.3.6)

Literary Analysis

The **author's perspective** in a literary work includes the judgments, attitudes, and experiences the author brings to the subject. An author's perspective determines which details he or she includes, as in these examples:

- A writer with firsthand experience of an event might report his or her own reactions as well as generally known facts.
- A writer with a positive view of a subject may emphasize its benefits.

A work may combine several perspectives. For example, a writer may tell what it felt like to live through an event. In addition, the writer may express his or her present views of the experience. As you read, look for details that suggest the author's perspective.

Prediction
What will happen?

Revise
What changes?

Verify or Revise
What actually happens?

Reading Skill

As you read, **make predictions,** or educated guesses, about what will happen next. Then, check your predictions as you read.

- **Revise,** or adjust, your predictions as you gather more information.
- **Verify,** or confirm, predictions by comparing the outcome you predicted to the actual outcome.

To help you make, verify, and revise predictions, **ask questions** like the ones shown on the chart.

Vocabulary Builder

from Swimming to Antarctica

- **prolonged** (prō lôṇ´´d) *adj.* extended; lengthy (p. 61) *His prolonged absence is due to serious illness.*
- **equilibrium** (ē´ kwi lib´ rē əm) *n.* a state of balance (p. 63) *See how well she keeps her equilibrium walking on the balance beam!*
- **buffer** (buf´ ər) *v.* lessen a shock; cushion (p. 68) *A helmet helps buffer the impact of a fall.*

Occupation: Conductorette

- **self-sufficiency** (self´ sə fish´ ən sē) *n.* independence (p. 73) *His self-sufficiency helped him survive being lost in the woods for three days.*
- **dingy** (din´ jē) *adj.* dirty-looking; shabby (p. 74) *The dark walls made the room dingy.*
- **supercilious** (sōō´ pər sil´ ē əs) *adj.* expressing an attitude of superiority; contemptuous (p. 74) *The queen gave the peasant a supercilious smile.*

Build Understanding • from *Swimming to Antarctica*

Autobiography

Background

Cold-Water Swimming Swimming in frigid water, as Lynne Cox does, puts great stress on the body. The body's core—the heart, lungs, and brain—must stay warm or normal muscle and brain function will be impaired, a condition called *hypothermia.* Water temperatures as "warm" as forty-four degrees Fahrenheit would kill most swimmers.

Connecting to the Literature

Reading/Writing Connection Preparing for a big event, such as a record-breaking swim, is half the battle. Make a list of ways you prepare mentally and physically to face a challenge. Use at least three of the following words: *attain, focus, maximize, minimize.* As you read, compare your plans to Cox's preparations for her swim.

READ MORE

by Lynne Cox

Swimming to Antarctica

Meet the Author

Lynne **Cox** (b. 1957)

Raised in California, Lynne Cox got started breaking records when she was young. At age fourteen, she swam twenty-six miles from Catalina Island to the California coast. The next year, she broke the men's and the women's records swimming the English Channel.

Made to Swim Cox has a high percentage of body fat, evenly distributed around her body. This fat helps her float and provides insulation. Her unique body has allowed her to swim in waters ranging from the Bering Strait to Antarctica. Today, Lynne Cox stands as the most successful cold-water long-distance swimmer ever.

Fast Facts

▶ Cox swims in only a bathing suit, swim cap, and goggles—whatever the temperature!
▶ During her swim around the Cape of Good Hope (the southern tip of Africa), she was chased by a shark.

Go **Online**
Author Link

For: More about the author
Visit: www.PHSchool.com
Web Code: eqe-9104

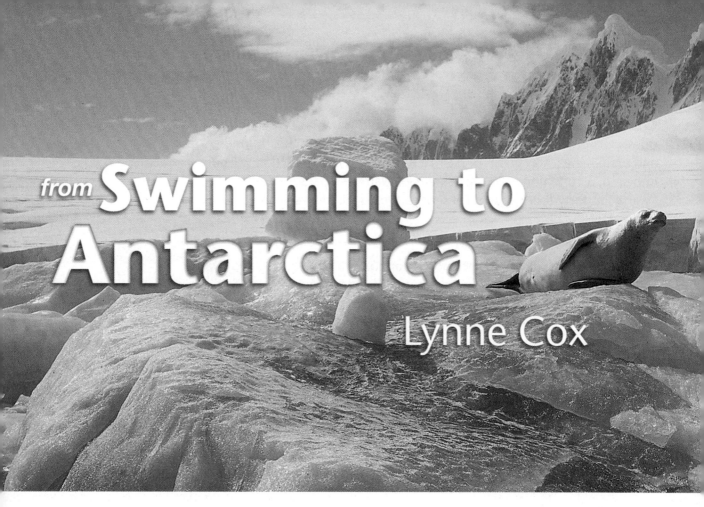

from **Swimming to Antarctica**

Lynne Cox

In 2002, swimmer Lynne Cox attempted an ambitious feat—swimming a mile in the frigid waters of Antarctica. Cox sailed on the ship Orlova with a team of seven friends, including team leader Barry Binder and her physicians, Susan Sklar, Gabriella Miotta, and Laura King. Bob Griffith and Martha Kaplan, Cox's agent, would scout for danger as Cox swam, while Dan Cohen stood by as a rescue swimmer. Scott Pelley, a television producer, also came. The ship's crew included Dr. Anthony Block and expedition leader Susan Adie. Before attempting a mile, Cox tested her reactions on a shorter swim.

When I returned to my cabin, I thought for a long time about what I was about to attempt.

I had mixed feelings about the test swim. In some ways, it had given me confidence; I now knew that I could swim for twenty-two minutes in thirty-three-degree water. But it had also made me feel uncertain. It had been the most difficult and probably the most dangerous swim I had ever done. Part of me wanted to be satisfied with it. Part of me didn't want to attempt the mile. I was

Literary Analysis
Author's Perspective
What do the opening sentences indicate about the author's attitude toward her swim?

afraid. The water temperature on the big swim would be a degree colder. Thirty-two degrees. That was a magic number, the temperature at which freshwater froze. I wondered if in thirty-two-degree water the water in my cells would freeze, if my body's tissues would become permanently damaged. I wondered if my mind would function better this time, if I would be able to be more aware of what was happening, or if it would be further dulled by the cold. Would my core temperature drop faster, more quickly than I could recognize? Would I be able to tell if I needed to get out? Did I really want to risk my life for this? Or did I want to risk failure?

The other part of me wanted to try, wanted to do what I had trained for, wanted to explore and reach beyond what I had done. That part of me was excited about venturing into the unknown. That part of me knew I would have felt a tremendous letdown if I didn't get a chance to try. I wanted to do it now.

The next morning, on December 15, 2002, Susan called me up to the bridge. She pointed out Water Boat Point. The tiny gray beach between steep glaciers was completely blocked by icebergs and brash ice.[1] There was no place to land.

---

1. brash ice *n.* floating fragments of ice.

Reading Skill
Verifying Predictions
Use details from the narrative to predict whether Cox will succeed or fail.

✓ **Reading Check**

What will Cox attempt to do?

We continued sailing south through the Gerlache Strait, past mountain-high glaciers and by ship-sized icebergs ranging in shades of blue from juniper berry to robin's-egg to light powder blue. In the protection of the Antarctic Peninsula, the wind dropped off and the sea grew calmer. When we reached Neko Harbor, about an hour later, Susan called me up to the bridge. She was excited. The beach was free of icebergs and brash ice. A landing was possible.

Now I would have a chance to swim the first Antarctic mile. I was thrilled and scared, but I tried to remain calm; I knew that the weather could suddenly change and the swim would be off. I met with Barry Binder, who said, "I'll get the crew into the Zodiacs² and come and get you when everything's set."

I walked to the ship's library, drank four eight-ounce cups of hot water, and ate two small croissants for breakfast—they were high in fat and carbohydrates, two sources of energy I would need for the swim. Then I started through the hallway to my cabin, where many of the *Orlova*'s passengers were waiting, eager to find out if I was going to swim. They wished me luck and said they would wait for me at the finish. I stopped by Dan's cabin to ask him if he would jump into the water with me at the end of the swim. He was already in his dry suit, prepared to go. Everyone was doing what we had practiced. All I could do was to go back to my room and wait. Gabriella came in to take a core temperature; it was up to 100.4 degrees. Knowing I was venturing into unknown waters, I must have psyched myself up so much that I increased my body temperature. Gabriella left me alone while I put on my swimsuit and sweats. I rubbed sunscreen on my face, but not on my arms or legs; it could make my skin slippery, and if my crew needed me to get out of the water quickly, that would create a problem. The night before, three of the crew had spotted a pod of eight killer whales swimming into the Gerlache Strait. They hadn't been moving fast. I hoped they were still north of us.

I stared out the window at the brown crescent-shaped beach. There were snow-covered hills directly above the beach, and massive glaciers on either side. I picked out landmarks, places I could aim for, so I'd know if I was on or off course.

Dr. Block caught me at the top of the stairs, just before we stepped out the door and onto the ramp, and asked if I would sit down on a step so he could trace two veins on my hands with a blue Magic Marker. It was just a precaution, he said, in case I needed emergency assistance; this way he would easily be able to find a vein to start an IV. I gave him my right hand and watched him draw the blue lines for the television camera. It gave me the creeps. Why

Literary Analysis
Author's Perspective
What details indicate that the writer's perspective before the swim includes fear and doubt?

---

2. **Zodiacs** *n.* speedboats.

did he have to do this now, right before I swam? Didn't he realize this kind of stuff psychs people out? *I know the swim is dangerous, but he could have done this hours ago, not just before I swam. Get over it,* I told myself. *Shake it off. Take a deep breath. Refocus. Take another breath. Good. Now think about the swim.* I smiled. *I'm so ready for this.*

Walking to the door, I peeked out and felt a blast of icy wind hit my face from the northwest. It was blowing in off the glaciers in gusts to twenty-five knots,[3] and the air temperature was thirty-two degrees. I felt the hair rising on my arms and my jaw tighten to suppress a shiver. I was much more nervous than I had been during my first swim. I had greater expectations of myself now. I wanted to swim the first Antarctic mile, and I knew I would be very disappointed if I didn't succeed.

I stared across the icy water at Neko Harbor's beach and felt excitement building within me. Quickly, before I could lose my chance, I pulled off my sweat suit and shoes and stuck them in a corner of the ship, climbed down the gangway, sat on the platform, and dangled my feet in the water. Surprisingly, it didn't feel any colder than it had two days before. I didn't realize then that the nerves on my skin's surface had been damaged from the first swim. I didn't know that the nerves that signaled danger weren't firing. I wasn't aware that my first line of defense was gone. I had no idea that <u>prolonged</u> exposure in thirty-two-degree water could cause permanent nerve and muscle damage. And I didn't know then that when an untrained person is immersed in water colder than forty degrees, their nerves are cooled down so they can't fire at the neuromuscular level. After only seven or eight minutes the person's body seizes up and [he or she] can't move. It was a good thing I didn't know any of this. All I knew was that I was ready. I took a deep breath, leaned back, and threw myself forward into the thirty-two-degree water.

When I hit the water, I went all the way under. I hadn't intended to do that; I hadn't wanted to immerse my head, which could over-stimulate my vagus nerve[4] and cause my heart to stop beating. Dog-paddling as quickly as I could, I popped up in the water, gasping for air. I couldn't catch my breath. I was swimming with my head up, hyperventilating.[5] I kept spinning my arms, trying to get warm, but I couldn't get enough air. I felt like I had a corset tightening around my chest. I told myself to relax, take a deep breath, but I couldn't slow my breath. And I couldn't get enough air in. I

---

3. **knots** (näts) *n.* a rate of speed. One knot equals one nautical mile (6,076.12 feet) per hour.
4. **vagus** (vāg′ əs) **nerve** *n.* either of a pair of nerves running from the brain to the heart that regulate the heartbeat.
5. **hyperventilating** *v.* breathing so rapidly or deeply as to cause dizziness or fainting.

Literary Analysis
Author's Perspective
How does this passage reflect both how it felt to live through the event and how it feels to look back on it?

Vocabulary Builder
prolonged (prō lôŋ′d)
adj. extended; lengthy

Reading Check

List two dangers Cox faces on her swim.

tried again. My body wanted air, and it wanted it now. I had to override that reaction of hyperventilating. I had to concentrate on my breath, to press my chest out against the cold water and draw the icy air into my lungs.

My body resisted it. The air was too cold. My body didn't want to draw the cold air deep into my lungs and cool myself from the inside. It wanted to take short breaths so the cold air would be warmed in my mouth before it reached my lungs. I was fighting against myself.

I noticed my arms. They were bright red, and I felt like I was swimming through slush. My arms were thirty-two degrees, as cold as the sea. They were going numb, and so were my legs. I pulled my hands right under my chest so that I was swimming on the upper inches of the sea, trying to minimize my contact with the water. I was swimming fast and it was hard to get enough air. I began to notice that the cold was pressurizing my body like a giant tourniquet. It was squeezing the blood from the exterior part of my body and pushing it into the core. Everything felt tight. *Focus on your breath,* I told myself. *Slow it down. Let it fill your lungs. You're not going to be able to make it if you keep going at this rate.*

It wasn't working. I was laboring for breath harder than on

the test swim. I was in oxygen debt,[6] panting, gasping. My breath was inefficient, and the oxygen debt was compounding. In an attempt to create heat, I was spinning my arms wildly, faster than I'd ever turned them over before. Laura later told me that I was swimming at a rate of ninety strokes per minute, thirty strokes per minute quicker than my normal rate. My body was demanding more oxygen, but I couldn't slow down. Not for a nanosecond. Or I would freeze up and the swim would be over.

An icy wave slapped my face: I choked and felt a wave of panic rise within me. My throat tightened. I tried to clear my throat and breathe. My breath didn't come out. I couldn't get enough air in to

Reading Skill
Verifying Predictions
Do these details verify your original prediction or lead you to revise it?

▲ **Critical Viewing**
Explain whether or not any of the dangers faced by Cox are represented in this photograph.
[Connect]

---

6. **oxygen debt** *n.* an increased need for oxygen in the body brought on by intensive activity.

clear my throat. I glanced at the crew. They couldn't tell I was in trouble. If I stopped, Dan would jump in and pull me out. I still couldn't get a good breath. I thought of rolling on my back to give myself time to breathe, but I couldn't. It was too cold. I closed my mouth, overrode everything my body was telling me to do, held my breath, and gasped, coughed, cleared my windpipe, and relaxed just a little, just enough to let my guard down and catch another wave in the face. I choked again. I put my face down into the water, hoping this time I could slow my heart rate down. I held my face in the water for two strokes and told myself, *Relax, just turn your head and breathe.*

It was easier to breathe in a more horizontal position. I thought it might be helping. I drew in a deep breath and put my face down again. I knew I couldn't do this for long. I was losing too much heat through my face. The intensity of the cold was as sharp as broken glass. I'd thought that swimming across the Bering Strait[7] in thirty-eight-degree water had been tough, but there was a world of difference between thirty-eight degrees and thirty-two. In a few seconds, the cold pierced my skin and penetrated into my muscles. It felt like freezer burn, like touching wet fingers to frozen metal.

Finally I was able to gain control of my breath. I was inhaling and exhaling so deeply I could hear the breath moving in and out of my mouth even though I was wearing earplugs. I kept thinking about breathing, working on keeping it deep and even; that way I didn't have time to think about the cold.

My brain wasn't working as it normally did. It wasn't flowing freely from one idea to another—it was moving mechanically, as if my awareness came from somewhere deep inside my brain. Maybe it was because my body was being assaulted with so many sensations, too different and too complex to recognize. Or maybe it was because my blood and oxygen were going out to the working muscles. I didn't know.

For the next five or six minutes, I continued swimming, telling myself that I was doing well, telling myself that this was what I had trained for. Then something clicked, as if my body had gained equilibrium. It had fully closed down the blood flow in my skin and fingers and toes. My arms and legs were as cold as the water, but I could feel the heat radiating deep within my torso and head, and this gave me confidence. I knew that my body was protecting my brain and vital organs. Staring through the clear, silver-blue water, I examined my fingers; they were red and swollen. They were different than when I'd been swimming in the Bering Strait, when they'd

---

7. **Bering Strait** (bā′ riŋ strāt) the body of water between Russia and Alaska, joining the Pacific and Arctic oceans.

Literary Analysis
Author's Perspective
Name one way in which the details in this paragraph might be different if presented by a crew member on the boat.

Vocabulary Builder
equilibrium (ē′ kwi lib′ rē əm) *n.* a state of balance

✓ Reading Check
List two effects of the cold water on Cox's mind and body.

looked like the fingers of a dead person. They looked healthy, and I thought their swollenness would give me more surface area, more to pull with.

I smiled and looked up at the crew, who were in the Zodiacs on either side of me. Each of them was leaning forward, willing me ahead. Their faces were filled with tension. Gabriella, Barry, Dan, and Scott were leaning so far over the Zodiac's pontoon I felt as if they were swimming right beside me. I was sprinting faster than I ever had before, moving faster than the Zodiac, and I was getting fatigued quickly. The water was thicker than on the test swim, and it took more force to pull through on each stroke. My arms ached. I didn't feel right; I couldn't seem to get into any kind of a rhythm. Then I sensed that something was wrong.

We were heading to the left, toward some glaciers. This didn't make sense; we couldn't land there. It was too dangerous. The glaciers could calve[8] and kill us.

"Barry, where are we going?" I shouted, using air I needed for breathing.

He pointed out our direction—right toward the glaciers. I didn't understand. I didn't want to go that way. I wanted to aim for the beach. I was confused. I was moving my arms as fast as they would go, and it was taking all I had. From each moment to the next, I had to tell myself to keep going. The water felt so much colder than on the test swim. It had already worked its way deep into my muscles. My arms and legs were stiff. My strokes were short and choppy. But I kept going, telling myself to trust the crew and focus on the glaciers to watch the outcropping of rocks that was growing larger. I couldn't get into any kind of pace.

Abruptly the Zodiacs zagged to the right. I looked up and thought, *Wow, okay; we're heading for the beach now.* For a moment, I started to feel better. I was able to extend my reach farther, and I could see passengers from the *Orlova* walking along the snowbanks. In the distance, their clothes lost their color and they looked black, like giant penguins. I saw smaller black figures, too—real penguins nesting near the edge of the shore. For a few moments, I felt like I was going to be okay, like I was going to make it in to shore, but then the Zodiacs abruptly turned farther to the right, and we were headed past the beach for another range of glaciers.

Finally, it occurred to me that the *Orlova* had anchored too close to shore for me to swim a mile, so Barry was adding distance by altering the course. And the ship's captain was on the bridge

---

8. calve (kăv) *v.* to give birth to young; used here to refer to the "birth" of a new ice mass when a piece of a glacier splits off.

Reading Skill
Verifying Predictions
Do the details in this paragraph verify or lead you to revise your prediction about whether Cox will succeed?

Antarctica: The Coldest Place on Earth

▲ The Amundsen–Scott South Pole Station was established by the United States in 1956.

Connect to the Literature What does this information suggest about the significance of Cox's endeavor?

- Antarctica is an ice-covered continent that covers the South Pole.
- Antarctica is the coldest place on Earth. Temperatures have reached a record 120 ° F below zero in the winter.
- Antarctica has no native population.
- The Antarctic icecap is the largest reserve of fresh water or snow in the world.

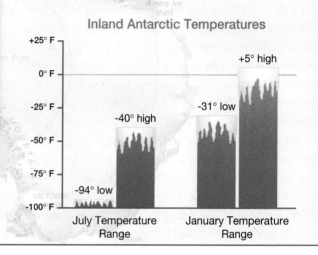

Inland Antarctic Temperatures

+25° F
0° F
-25° F   -40° high
-50° F
-75° F
-94° low
-100° F

-31° low   +5° high

July Temperature Range   January Temperature Range

---

monitoring our course on his GPS[9] and radioing our Zodiacs, updating them on the distance we had traveled. One of the passengers, Mrs. Stokie, who was on the bridge with him, told me later, "The captain was watching you and he was shaking his head. He was an older man, and he had experienced everything. And now he was seeing something new. It was good for him. Still, I think he couldn't believe it."

We continued on right past the beach, toward more glaciers.

"How long have I been swimming?" I asked.

"Fifteen minutes," Barry said.

I had swum a little more than half a mile. I looked up at the shore. If I turned left, I could make it in. I could reach the shore. This struggle could be over. But I wouldn't complete the mile. I had swum farther two days before. But I was tired now, and this was so much harder. I just didn't feel right. I couldn't figure out what the problem was. I kept talking to myself, coaching myself to keep going. Then I felt it; it was the water pressure, and it was increasing on my back. It meant there was a strong current behind me. I

Literary Analysis
Author's Perspective
Identify one detail in this paragraph that shows Cox's past perspective and one that comes from her present perspective.

✓**Reading Check**

What progress has Cox made on her swim?

---

9. GPS "Global Positioning System," referring here to a portable device that provides information about the bearer's location and speed.

looked at the glaciers onshore, using the fixed points to gauge how fast the current was flowing. It was flowing at over a knot. I wondered if I would have enough strength to fight it when we turned around and headed back for the beach. It would cut my speed by half and could cause me to lose heat more rapidly.

Barry and the crew in the Zodiacs couldn't feel what was happening. They had no idea we were moving into a risky area. If the current grew any stronger, it could cost us the swim. Barry motioned for me to swim past a peninsula and across a narrow channel. I lifted my head and pulled my hands directly under my chest, to gain more lift, so I could look across the bay and see if we had any other options for landing. There were no alternatives. This made me very uncomfortable. Chances were good that there would be a strong current flowing into or out of the narrow bay. And if we got caught in that current, all would be lost.

We started across the inlet, and within a moment I could feel that second current, slamming into our right side at two knots, pushing us into the inlet. Without any explanation, I spun around, put my head down, dug my arms into the water, and crabbed[10] into the current. I focused on repositioning myself so I could parallel shore again and head toward Neko Harbor. Barry knew I knew what I was doing. But the abrupt course change caught the Zodiac drivers by surprise. They scattered in different directions, trying to avoid ramming into each other and trying to catch up with me. The motor on the lead Zodiac on my left sputtered and stopped. The second Zodiac immediately pulled up beside me. I sprinted against the current.

"How long have I been swimming?"

"Twenty-one minutes," Barry said. He and all the crew were watching me intently, their faces filled with tension and concern.

I put my head down, and something suddenly clicked. Maybe it was because I knew shore was within reach, or maybe because I got a second wind; I don't know. But I was finally swimming strongly, stretching out and moving fluidly. My arms and legs were as cold as the sea, but I felt the heat within my head and contained in my torso and I thrilled to it, knowing my body had

---

10. crabbed *v.* moved sideways or diagonally.

carried me to places no one else had been in only a bathing suit. I looked down into the water; it was a bright blue-gray and so clear that it appeared as if I were swimming through air. The viscosity of the water was different, too; it was thicker than any I had ever swum in. It felt like I was swimming through gelato. And I got more push out of each arm stroke than I ever had before. I looked at the crew. They were leaning so far over the pontoons, as if they were right there with me. I needed to let them know I was okay.

I lifted my head, took a big breath, and shouted, "Barry, I'm swimming to Antarctica!"

I saw the smiles, heard the cheers and laughs, and I felt their energy lift me. They were as thrilled as I was. I swam faster, extending my arms, pulling more strongly, reaching for the shores of Antarctica. Now I knew we were almost there.

The crew was shouting warnings about ice. I swerved around two icebergs. Some chunks looked sharp, but I was too tired to care. I swam into whatever was in my path. It hurt, but all I wanted now was to finish.

As we neared shore, I lifted my head and saw the other passengers from the *Orlova*, in their bright red and yellow hats and parkas, tromping down the snowbanks, spreading their feet and arms wide for balance, racing to the water's edge to meet us. I lifted my foot and waved and saw my crew break into bigger smiles.

I'm almost done, I thought. *I feel okay. I feel strong. I feel warm inside. My arms and legs are thirty-two degrees. But I feel good. I can stretch out my strokes and put my face in the water. Maybe I can go a little farther. Maybe I can see what more I can do. Maybe I can swim five or ten more minutes. Or maybe I should be happy with what I've done. My skin is so cold I can't feel it, and when I stop swimming, I don't know how far my temperature's going to drop.* I looked at my watch. Twenty-three minutes. I'd been in a minute longer than two days before. *How much difference would a minute make?* I asked myself. *How much difference is there between thirty-two-degree and thirty-three-degree water? Remember what Dr. Keatinge[11] said: once your temperature starts to drop, it will drop very fast. If you continue swimming, you're going to cool down even more. Remember how hard you shivered last time? Remember how much work it was? Remember how uncomfortable you were? This is the place where people make mistakes, when they're tired and cold and they push too far into the unknown. You could really hurt yourself. Finish now. You've done a good job. Be satisfied with what you've done. Go celebrate with your friends.*

Literary Analysis
Author's Perspective
Explain in what way the author's perspective on her swim changes as she nears the shore.

✔ **Reading Check**

What changes for Cox after she shifts her course?

---

11. Dr. Keatinge Cox's doctor on her swim across the Bering Strait.

Turning in toward shore, I again lifted my foot and waved it, and my friends waved back and cheered. One hundred yards from shore, I saw chinstrap penguins sliding headfirst, like tiny black toboggans, down a steep snowbank. When they reached the base of the hill, they used their bristly tails like brakes, sticking them into the snow to stop their momentum. They waddled across the beach at full tilt, holding their wings out at their sides for balance. Reaching the water, they dove in headfirst, then porpoised across it, clearing it by one or two feet with each surface dive. They tucked their wings back by their sides so they would be more aerodynamic. When they neared the Zodiacs, they dove and flapped their wings under the water as if they were flying through air. It was amazing to think this was the only place they would fly. They zoomed under me in bursts of speed, and their bubbles exploded like white fireworks. More penguins joined in. One cannonballed off a ledge, another slipped on some ice and belly flopped, and three penguins swam within inches of my hands. I reached out to touch one, but he swerved and flapped his wings, so he moved just beyond my fingertips. I had no idea why they were swimming with me, but I knew it was a good sign; it meant there were no killer whales or leopard seals in the area.

When I reached knee-deep water, Dan jumped in, ran through the water, looped his arm through mine, and helped me stand. "Are you okay?" he asked.

"Yes. We made it!" I said.

Everyone around me was crying. Susan Adie helped Dan pull me up the incline. Martha wrapped a towel around my shoulders. Barry hugged me tightly. Laura and Susan began drying me off. I was so cold I was already starting to shiver hard. My legs were stiffer than after the other swim. The crew helped me into the Zodiac and I flopped onto the floor. Laura and Susan piled on top of me to protect me from the wind, and we pounded across the water, my head slamming into the Zodiac's floor. I managed to lift my head so that someone could place a hand under it to <u>buffer</u> the impact. I was so cold and stiff and shaking harder than before.

When we reached the *Orlova*, it took me a minute to stand, to gain my balance, and as I climbed the ramp's steps I clung to the railing and pulled myself up, shaking hard. By the time I reached the top of the ramp, my teeth were chattering and I was breathing harder and faster than when I had been swimming. I didn't like being so cold. I didn't like my body having to work so hard. My temperature had dropped to 95.5 degrees, and I couldn't control my shaking. I just let go, and my body bounced up and down with shakes and shivers.

Reading Skill
Verifying Predictions
How does this outcome match up with your predictions?

Vocabulary Builder
buffer (buf´ ər) v. lessen a shock; cushion

Quickly Martha and Dan and the three doctors huddled around me like emperor penguins, and their combined comfort and body heat began to warm me. It seemed as if I would never stop shaking, and I was completely exhausted. Within half an hour my shivering had subsided to small body shudders. Once I was able to stand and maintain my balance, the doctors helped me pull on a special top and pants that had been designed by a friend. She had sewn pockets under the arms, in the groin area, and into a scarf and had placed chemical packs that emitted heat inside the pockets. Their placement in the clothing warmed the major blood-flow areas of my body so that I was heated from the inside out. It was effective, and within an hour my temperature was back to normal.

That night we celebrated with everyone aboard the *Orlova*. I had swum the first Antarctic mile—a distance of 1.06 miles, in fact—in thirty-two-degree water in twenty-five minutes. I had been able to do what had seemed impossible because I'd had a crew who believed in me and in what we as human beings were capable of. It was a great dream, swimming to Antarctica.

▲ **Critical Viewing**
Does this Antarctic landscape match what you imagined based on Cox's descriptions? Explain. **[Connect]**

Literary Analysis
Author's Perspective
Which details show the difference between Cox's perspective before and after her swim?

Apply the Skills

from *Swimming to Antarctica*

Thinking About the Selection

1. **Respond:** Which part of Cox's story did you find the most exciting? Why?
2. **(a) Recall:** List three ways in which Cox prepares for her mile-long swim. **(b) Analyze Causes and Effects:** For each way, explain the effect it has or is intended to have.
3. **(a) Recall:** What physical challenge causes Cox to struggle at the start of her swim? **(b) Analyze:** What does Cox's ability to overcome this challenge reveal about her?
4. **(a) Recall:** Identify two instances in which Cox gives herself a pep talk. **(b) Summarize:** What is the main point Cox makes in each pep talk? **(c) Analyze:** Is each pep talk effective? Why?
5. **(a) Speculate:** Identify two reasons Cox may have had for making the swim. **(b) Summarize:** List the dangers that Cox faces. **(c) Evaluate:** Explain whether the swim was worth the effort.

Literary Analysis

6. **(a)** Using a chart like the one shown, analyze the **author's perspective** in the selection.

Author's Perspective	
Types of Details Included	Examples of Each
❏ researched facts ❏ personal experiences ❏ opinions ❏ attitudes	_____ _____ _____ _____

   (b) Referring to your chart, briefly describe Cox's perspective.
7. **(a)** List two ways in which Cox's story would be different if told by a news reporter. **(b)** Do you think Cox's firsthand perspective adds to the story's drama? Explain.

Reading Skill

8. Identify details in the selection that you used to **verify a prediction**.
9. **(a)** Identify one prediction you **revised** as you read. **(b)** In a small group, discuss your predictions and explain why you revised them.

QuickReview

Story at a Glance
Long-distance swimmer Lynne Cox tries to become the first person to swim in the freezing waters of Antarctica.

For: Self-test
Visit: www.PHSchool.com
Web Code: eqa-6105

Author's Perspective: an author's judgments, attitudes, and experiences concerning the topic on which he or she writes

Verifying and Revising Predictions: confirming and adjusting educated guesses about what will happen

Vocabulary Builder

Practice For each sentence, explain whether it makes sense given the meaning of the underlined word. If it does not make sense, write a new sentence using the word correctly.

1. After <u>prolonged</u> workouts at the gym, he is finally back in shape.
2. The best tightrope walkers have no sense of <u>equilibrium</u>.
3. Please turn off the stereo and open all the windows; I need to <u>buffer</u> myself from those loud jackhammers outside.

Adding Words to Your Vocabulary Use a dictionary to find the Latin origin of *equilibrium.* Then, find another word that includes the Latin word part *-equi-* and explain what this word part adds to its meaning. (For more about using a dictionary, see page R6.)

Writing

Using your prior knowledge and information you have learned from Cox's memoir, write a brief **description** of a scene in Antarctica. Identify the mood, or atmosphere, you want to create, whether it be awe, danger, beauty, or isolation. Use precise words to capture the scene and to create your chosen mood.

For *Grammar, Vocabulary,* and *Assessment,* see **Build Language Skills,** pages 80–81.

Extend Your Learning

Listening and Speaking Hold a **group discussion** about Cox's extraordinary endeavor. Consider these questions as they apply to Cox and to your own life:
- Was the outcome worth Cox's effort and the risks she took?
- Do all people have a need to seek out and conquer challenges?

Summarize and evaluate comments as the discussion unfolds. At the end of the discussion, formulate one or two possible conclusions.

Research and Technology Cox's success depends on research, including self-observation. Keep a **daily observation journal** charting your speed or accomplishments in some activity, such as the number of miles you run in a day or the number of sales you ring up in an hour. Include a graph or chart mapping how your skills develop. At the end of two weeks, write a brief paragraph based on your journal.

Autobiography

Background

Jobs and World War II During the 1940s, the time Maya Angelou recalls, millions of American men went overseas to fight World War II. Their absence created new opportunities at home. Six million women went to work in industry to aid the war effort, taking jobs from which they had formerly been excluded. Although African Americans still faced prejudice, some found—or made—new opportunities for themselves.

Connecting to the Literature

Reading/Writing Connection In her struggle to find work, Angelou seems strongest when the odds are toughest. Write a brief paragraph about a time when you faced a challenge. Use at least three of these words: *attain, aspire, challenge, persist.*

Review

For **Literary Analysis, Reading Skill,** and **Vocabulary Builder,** see page 56.

READ MORE

by Maya Angelou
Gather Together in My Names
The Heart of a Woman

Meet the Author

Maya **Angelou** (b. 1928)

Maya Angelou was born Marguerite Johnson in St. Louis, Missouri. *I Know Why the Caged Bird Sings,* the work from which this selection comes, is the first part of her autobiography.

Up From Hard Times Some of the communities in which Angelou grew up were segregated—African Americans were excluded from facilities, including schools, used by whites. Yet Angelou rejects bitterness, saying, "The honorary duty of a human being is to love."

Angelou has had diverse experiences in life. She worked with Dr. Martin Luther King, Jr., in the civil rights movement. Afterward, she moved to Africa, where she lived from 1961 to 1966. Her literary success came in the 1970s.

Fast Facts

▶ Angelou has written and directed films.
▶ Angelou read one of her poems at President William Jefferson Clinton's inauguration in 1993.

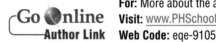

Go Online
Author Link

For: More about the author
Visit: www.PHSchool.com
Web Code: eqe-9105

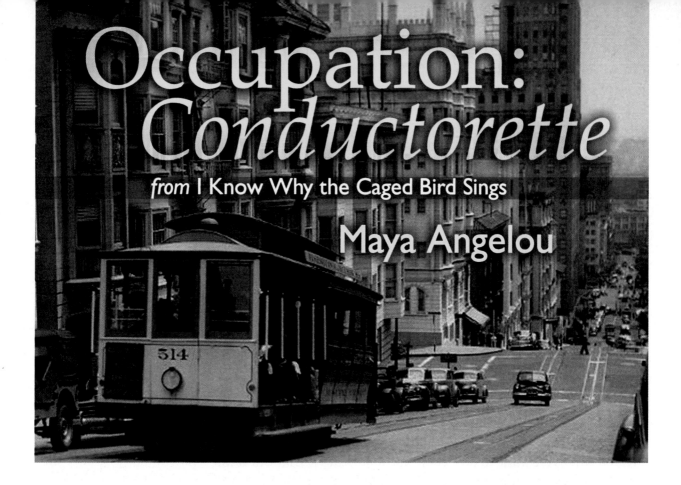

Occupation: Conductorette

from I Know Why the Caged Bird Sings

Maya Angelou

The young Angelou has just returned to San Francisco after an adventure-filled trip. Things are changing at home, she discovers, and her brother moves out soon after her return. Restless, discontent, Angelou ponders her next step.

I had it. The answer came to me with the suddenness of a collision. I would go to work. Mother wouldn't be difficult to convince; after all, in school I was a year ahead of my grade and Mother was a firm believer in <u>self-sufficiency</u>. In fact, she'd be pleased to think that I had that much gumption, that much of her in my character. (She liked to speak of herself as the original "do-it-yourself girl.")

Once I had settled on getting a job, all that remained was to decide which kind of job I was most fitted for. My intellectual pride had kept me from selecting typing, shorthand or filing as subjects in school, so office work was ruled out. War plants and shipyards demanded birth certificates, and mine would reveal me to be fifteen, and ineligible for work. So the well-paying defense jobs were also out. Women had replaced men on the streetcars as conductors and motormen, and the thought of sailing up and down the hills of San

Vocabulary Builder
self-sufficiency (self′ sə fish′ ən sē) *n.* independence

✔**Reading Check**
What is Angelou's goal?

Francisco in a dark-blue uniform, with a money changer at my belt, caught my fancy.

Mother was as easy as I had anticipated. The world was moving so fast, so much money was being made, so many people were dying in Guam, and Germany,[1] that hordes of strangers became good friends overnight. Life was cheap and death entirely free. How could she have the time to think about my academic career?

To her question of what I planned to do, I replied that I would get a job on the streetcars. She rejected the proposal with: "They don't accept colored people on the streetcars."

I would like to claim an immediate fury which was followed by the noble determination to break the restricting tradition. But the truth is, my first reaction was one of disappointment. I'd pictured myself, dressed in a neat blue serge suit, my money changer swinging jauntily at my waist, and a cheery smile for the passengers which would make their own work day brighter.

From disappointment, I gradually ascended the emotional ladder to haughty indignation, and finally to that state of stubbornness where the mind is locked like the jaws of an enraged bulldog.

I would go to work on the streetcars and wear a blue serge suit. Mother gave me her support with one of her usual terse asides, "That's what you want to do? Then nothing beats a trial but a failure. Give it everything you've got. I've told you many times, 'Can't Do is like Don't Care.' Neither of them have a home."

Translated, that meant there was nothing a person can't do, and there should be nothing a human being didn't care about. It was the most positive encouragement I could have hoped for.

In the offices of the Market Street Railway Company, the receptionist seemed as surprised to see me there as I was surprised to find the interior <u>dingy</u> and the décor drab. Somehow I had expected waxed surfaces and carpeted floors. If I had met no resistance, I might have decided against working for such a poor-mouth-looking concern. As it was, I explained that I had come to see about a job. She asked, was I sent by an agency, and when I replied that I was not, she told me they were only accepting applicants from agencies.

The classified pages of the morning papers had listed advertisements for motorettes and conductorettes and I reminded her of that. She gave me a face full of astonishment that my suspicious nature would not accept.

"I am applying for the job listed in this morning's *Chronicle* and I'd like to be presented to your personnel manager." While I spoke in <u>supercilious</u> accents, and looked at the room as if I had an oil well

Literary Analysis
Author's Perspective
Which details in this passage show Angelou's teenage personality? Which show her attitude as an adult?

Vocabulary Builder
dingy (din´ jē) *adj.* dirty-looking; shabby

Vocabulary Builder
supercilious (soo´ pər sil´ ē əs) *adj.* expressing an attitude of superiority; contemptuous

---

1. Guam (gwäm), **and Germany** places where World War II (1939–1945) was fought. Guam is an island in the Pacific Ocean.

in my own backyard, my armpits were being pricked by millions of hot pointed needles. She saw her escape and dived into it.

"He's out. He's out for the day. You might call tomorrow and if he's in, I'm sure you can see him." Then she swiveled her chair around on its rusty screws and with that I was supposed to be dismissed.

"May I ask his name?"

She half turned, acting surprised to find me still there.

"His name? Whose name?"

"Your personnel manager."

We were firmly joined in the hypocrisy to play out the scene.

"The personnel manager? Oh, he's Mr. Cooper, but I'm not sure you'll find him here tomorrow. He's . . . Oh, but you can try."

"Thank you."

"You're welcome."

And I was out of the musty room and into the even mustier lobby. In the street I saw the receptionist and myself going faithfully through paces that were stale with familiarity, although I had never encountered that kind of situation before and, probably, neither had she. We were like actors who, knowing the play by heart, were still able to cry afresh over the old tragedies and laugh spontaneously at the comic situations.

The miserable little encounter had nothing to do with me, the me of me, any more than it had to do with that silly clerk. The incident was a recurring dream, concocted years before by stupid whites and it eternally came back to haunt us all. The secretary and I were like Hamlet and Laertes[2] in the final scene, where, because of harm done by one ancestor to another, we were bound to duel to the death. Also because the play must end somewhere.

I went further than forgiving the clerk, I accepted her as a fellow victim of the same puppeteer.

On the streetcar, I put my fare into the box and the conductorette looked at me with the usual hard eyes of white contempt. "Move into the car, please move on in the car." She patted her money changer.

Her Southern nasal accent sliced my meditation and I looked deep into my thoughts. All lies, all comfortable lies. The receptionist was not innocent and neither was I. The whole charade we had played out in that crummy waiting room had directly to do with me, Black, and her, white.

I wouldn't move into the streetcar but stood on the ledge over the conductor, glaring. My mind shouted so energetically that the

---

2. **Hamlet and Laertes** (lā ur´ tēz) characters in William Shakespeare's tragedy *Hamlet* who duel at the end of the play.

▲ Critical Viewing
Based on this ticket, make an inference about one of the tasks of a conductorette. Explain. **[Infer]**

✓ Reading Check
What major obstacle does Angelou face in her job quest?

announcement made my veins stand out, and my mouth tighten into a prune.

I WOULD HAVE THE JOB. I WOULD BE A CONDUCTOR-ETTE AND SLING A FULL MONEY CHANGER FROM MY BELT. I WOULD.

The next three weeks were a honeycomb[3] of determination with apertures for the days to go in and out. The Negro organizations to whom I appealed for support bounced me back and forth like a shuttlecock on a badminton court. Why did I insist on that particular job? Openings were going begging that paid nearly twice the money. The minor officials with whom I was able to win an audience thought me mad. Possibly I was.

Downtown San Francisco became alien and cold, and the streets I had loved in a personal familiarity were unknown lanes that twisted with malicious intent. Old buildings, whose gray rococo façades[4] housed my memories of the Forty-Niners, and Diamond Lil, Robert Service, Sutter and Jack London, were then imposing structures viciously joined to keep me out. My trips to the streetcar office were of the frequency of a person on salary. The struggle expanded. I was no longer in conflict only with the Market Street Railway but with the marble lobby of the building which housed its offices, and elevators and their operators.

During this period of strain Mother and I began our first steps on the long path toward mutual adult admiration. She never asked for reports and I didn't offer any details. But every morning she made breakfast, gave me carfare and lunch money, as if I were going to work. She comprehended the perversity of life, that in the struggle lies the joy. That I was no glory seeker was obvious to her, and that I had to exhaust every possibility before giving in was also clear.

On my way out of the house one morning she said, "Life is going to give you just what you put in it. Put your whole heart in everything you do, and pray, then you can wait." Another time she reminded me that "God helps those who help themselves." She had a store of aphorisms which she dished out as the occasion demanded. Strangely, as bored as I was with clichés, her inflection gave them something new, and set me thinking for a little while at least. Later when asked how I got my job, I was never able to say exactly. I only knew that one day, which was tiresomely like all the others before it, I sat in the Railway office, ostensibly

---

3. **honeycomb** (hun´ ē kōm´) wax structure, filled with holes, that bees build to store honey.
4. **rococo façades** (rə kō´ kō fə sädz´) elaborately designed front sides.

Literature in Context

History Connection

San Francisco and the Gold Rushes
When she looks at the buildings of San Francisco, Angelou thinks of names associated with the gold rushes of the 1800s:

- **Forty-Niners** the prospectors who poured into the San Francisco area in the California Gold Rush of 1849. They transformed San Francisco from a small town of 800 to a rough-and-tumble city of 25,000.
- **Diamond Lil** a flamboyant entertainer
- **Robert Service** Canadian poet who portrayed the miners of the Yukon Gold Rush of the 1890s
- **Robert Sutter** owner of the land where gold was first discovered in California
- **Jack London** writer who re-created his experiences in the Yukon Gold Rush in stories and the novel *Call of the Wild* (1903)

Connect to the Literature

How does Angelou feel about the buildings she associates with these historical figures?

waiting to be interviewed. The receptionist called me to her desk and shuffled a bundle of papers to me. They were job application forms. She said they had to be filled in triplicate. I had little time to wonder if I had won or not, for the standard questions reminded me of the necessity for dexterous lying. How old was I? List my previous jobs, starting from the last held and go backward to the first. How much money did I earn, and why did I leave the position? Give two references (not relatives).

Sitting at a side table my mind and I wove a cat's ladder of near truths and total lies. I kept my face blank (an old art) and wrote quickly the fable of Marguerite Johnson, aged nineteen, former companion and driver for Mrs. Annie Henderson (a White Lady) in Stamps, Arkansas.

I was given blood tests, aptitude tests, physical coordination tests, and Rorschachs,[5] then on a blissful day I was hired as the first Negro on the San Francisco streetcars.

Mother gave me the money to have my blue serge suit tailored, and I learned to fill out work cards, operate the money changer and punch transfers. The time crowded together and at an End of Days I was swinging on the back of the rackety trolley, smiling sweetly and persuading my charges to "step forward in the car, please."

For one whole semester the street cars and I shimmied up and scooted down the sheer hills of San Francisco. I lost some of my need for the Black ghetto's shielding-sponge quality, as I clanged and cleared my way down Market Street, with its honky-tonk homes for homeless sailors, past the quiet retreat of Golden Gate Park and along closed undwelled-in-looking dwellings of the Sunset District.

My work shifts were split so haphazardly that it was easy to believe that my superiors had chosen them maliciously. Upon mentioning my suspicions to Mother, she said, "Don't worry about it. You ask for what you want, and you pay for what you get. And I'm going to show you that it ain't no trouble when you pack double."

She stayed awake to drive me out to the car barn at four thirty in the mornings, or to pick me up when I was relieved just before dawn. Her awareness of life's perils convinced her that while I would be safe on the public conveyances, she "wasn't about to trust a taxi driver with her baby."

When the spring classes began, I resumed my commitment with formal education. I was so much wiser and older, so much more independent, with a bank account and clothes that I had bought for myself, that I was sure that I had learned and earned the magic formula which would make me a part of the gay life my contemporaries led.

Reading Skill
Verifying Predictions
Explain whether the details in this paragraph verify or lead you to revise your prediction about whether Angelou will get the job.

---

5. **Rorschachs** (rôr´ shäks´) The Rorschach test is a method of analyzing an individual's personality using abstract images.

Apply the Skills

Occupation: Conductorette

Thinking About the Selection

1. **Respond:** Did you hope Angelou would get the conductorette job? Explain.
2. **(a) Recall:** To what does Angelou compare her first encounter with the secretary at the railway company?
   (b) Analyze Causes and Effects: Explain how the greeting of the streetcar conductorette changes Angelou's view of the meeting.
3. **Interpret:** Explain why Angelou insists on becoming a conductorette. List details supporting your answer.
4. **(a) Interpret:** Find two passages in which Angelou's mother reacts to her quest, and explain what each shows about the mother's view of life. **(b) Draw Conclusions:** In what ways does her mother contribute to Angelou's success?

Literary Analysis

5. **(a)** Using a chart like the one shown, analyze the **author's perspective** in the selection.

Author's Perspective	
Types of Details Included	Examples of Each
❏ researched facts	_____
❏ personal experiences	_____
❏ opinions	_____
❏ attitudes	_____

   (b) Referring to your chart, briefly describe Angelou's perspective.
6. What is Angelou's present attitude toward herself when young? In your answer, consider her use of phrases such as "haughty indignation" to describe her reactions at the time.

Reading Skill

7. Identify details in the selection that you used to **verify a prediction.**
8. **(a)** Identify one prediction you **revised** as you read. **(b)** In a small group, discuss your predictions and explain why you revised them.

QuickReview

Story at a Glance
Maya Angelou tells the story of her search for a job in the racially divided world of 1940s San Francisco.

Go Online
—Assessment
For: Self-test
Visit: www.PHSchool.com
Web Code: eqa-6106

Author's Perspective: an author's attitudes, judgments, and experiences concerning the topic on which he or she writes

Verifying and Revising Predictions: confirming and adjusting educated guesses about what will happen

Vocabulary Builder

Practice Explain whether each sentence makes sense given the meaning of the underlined word. If it does not make sense, write a new sentence using the word correctly.

1. She whines until her little brother makes her lunch for her—a clear sign of her <u>self-sufficiency</u>.
2. I painted the room a bright white to add to its <u>dingy</u> feeling.
3. When you ask him for help, give him a <u>supercilious</u> look.

Adding Words to Your Vocabulary Use a dictionary to find the Latin origin of the vocabulary word *supercilious.* Then, find another word that uses the prefix *super-*, and explain what the prefix adds to its meaning. (For more about using a dictionary, see page R6.)

Writing

Using your prior knowledge and what you have learned from Angelou's work, write a brief **description** of a 1940s streetcar ride. Identify the mood, or atmosphere, you want to create, whether it be one of bustle or of frustration. Use precise words to capture the scene and create the mood.

For *Grammar, Vocabulary,* and *Assessment,* see **Build Language Skills,** pages 80–81.

Extend Your Learning

Listening and Speaking Hold a **group discussion** about Angelou's experiences. Consider these questions as they apply to Angelou and to your own life:

- Was Angelou's effort worth the result?
- Should people insist on respect from others, or should they walk away from people who are disrespectful?

Summarize and evaluate comments as the discussion unfolds. At the end of the discussion, formulate one or two possible conclusions.

Research and Technology Observe or conduct interviews with someone who has a job you might be interested in some day. Keep a **daily observation journal** to chart the person's work, recording the important tasks of each day and the time each takes. After two weeks, write a paragraph drawing a conclusion based on your research.

Build Language Skills

Vocabulary Skill

Word Roots *Spontaneous* ideas are often *innovative*. The root *-sponte-* means "free will." The root *-nov-* means "new." It is sensible that something done freely would produce new results. *Spontaneous* is an adjective that describes free and impulsive activity. The noun that identifies the quality is *spontaneity*. To describe the way something was done, use the adverb *spontaneously*. Like *spontaneous*, *innovative* is an adjective. It describes something new and unusual. The noun for the new and unusual thing is *innovation*. The meaning of other words containing the roots *-nov-* and *-sponte-* also involve the ideas of freedom and newness.

Practice Using a dictionary, briefly explain what the root contributes to the meaning of each *-nov-* or *-sponte-* word used. Then, use each of the phrases in a sentence.

1. a *novel* suggestion

2. the *novelty* of being in another country

3. the children's *spontaneity*

4. just a *novice*

5. *spontaneous* combustion

Grammar Lesson

Abstract and Concrete Nouns **Concrete nouns** name specific things that can be directly experienced or perceived by the senses. **Abstract nouns** name ideas or concepts that cannot be seen, heard, felt, tasted, smelled, or directly experienced. For example, the word *airplane* is a concrete noun because it names something you can see, feel, and hear. *Justice,* on the other hand, is a concept that cannot be directly perceived by the senses.

Practice On your paper, label each noun as concrete or abstract. Use each word in a sentence.

1. marigolds

2. logic

3. breeze

4. dignity

5. sunrise

MorePractice

For more practice using abstract and concrete nouns, see the Grammar Handbook, p. R40.

W̶G Prentice Hall Writing and Grammar Connection: Chapter 16, Section 1

Reading: Making and Revising Predictions

Standards Assessed
- 10.4.4
- 10.5.5
- 10.7.16

Directions: *Read the selection. Then, answer the questions.*

As soon as the pound notes were placed in his palm Jonathan simply closed it tight over them and buried fist and money inside his trouser pocket. He had to be extra careful because he had seen a man a couple of days earlier collapse into near-madness in an instant before that oceanic crowd because no sooner had he got his twenty pounds than some heartless ruffian picked it off him.

—from "Civil Peace" by Chinua Achebe

1. Based on the passage, readers can reasonably predict that Jonathan will
   A give his money away to the needy.
   B steal money from one of the people.
   C have no further financial worries.
   D face some danger.

2. Based on the passage, readers can reasonably predict that Jonathan
   A will share his money with the man whose money was stolen.
   B will use the information others give him to make money.
   C will continue to be observant.
   D will find the man whose money was stolen.

3. What new information would verify a prediction that pickpockets will steal Jonathan's money?
   A A man asks for directions.
   B Jonathan realizes the money is gone.
   C The man Jonathan saw asks for help.
   D Jonathan puts the money in a safe place.

4. Which new information would lead you to revise a prediction that pickpockets will steal Jonathan's money?
   A Jonathan walks through a crowd.
   B Police discover that the man Jonathan had seen actually lost his money.
   C Police warn Jonathan to be very careful with his money.
   D A ruffian approaches Jonathan in the street.

Timed Writing: Persuasion [Critical Stance]

"I try to plant peace if I do not want discord; to plant loyalty and honesty if I want to avoid betrayal and lies." —*Maya Angelou*
In an essay, defend or refute this statement. Support your view with examples from "Swimming to Antarctica" or "I Know Why the Caged Bird Sings" and your experience. **(25 minutes)**

 Writing Workshop: *Work in Progress*

Autobiographical Narrative
Review the names and sentences that you associate with a place. Use your notes to write three to four lines about each item. Choose the one that is most meaningful to you and write a few sentences telling why.

Job Applications

In Part 1, you learned to make predictions while you read literature. Making predictions can also help you prepare to apply for a job. If you read "Occupation: Conductorette," you may be interested to learn more about job applications and how to prepare to fill one out.

About Job Applications

A **job application** is a form that an employer uses to gather information about a person seeking employment. This information helps the employer to evaluate applicants—to make predictions about whether or not the applicant will be good at the job. Most job applications ask for the following kinds of information:

- Name and address
- Social Security number
- Schools attended
- Work experience
- Useful skills
- References

Reading Skill

Before you go to fill out a job application, **predict** which information you will be asked to provide. **Use prior knowledge** from other applications, the type of job, and details from the job posting or ad.

Although you cannot predict every question you will be asked, predicting will help you prepare. Use a checklist like the one shown here:

Items for Completing a Job Application

- ☐ Driver's license and Social Security card (or another form of identification)

- ☐ Names, addresses, dates, and contact information for schools attended, previous employers, volunteer work, and references

- ☐ List of special skills, such as knowledge of foreign languages, typing ability, and knowledge of computer programs

Academic Standards

- Use clear research questions and methods to compile evidence from many sources. (10.4.4)
- Write business letters. (10.5.5)
- Apply appropriate interviewing techniques. (10.7.16)

Summer Employment
City of Durham, NC

DURHAM

1869

Mayor's Youth Works Summer Program
Are you between the ages of 14 and 21?
Yes____ No____

Please Print or Type - Use Blue or Black Ink

Check One (1) I am applying for:

☐ Impact Team   ☐ Parks & Recreation   ☐ Private Sector   ☐ OEED

Name _____
　　　　(Last)　　　　　　(First)　　　　　　(MI)

Address _____
　　　　(Street)　　　　(City/State)　　　　(Zip Code)

Driver's License #_____ Class _____

Telephone #_____ (Work) _____

Are you related by blood or marriage to any person now employed by the City? __No __Yes

If yes, give name/relationship/and work location of relatives(s) _____

EDUCATION

School Name and Location	From/to Attended	Completed # of Years	Diploma or Degree	Year Received
Middle School				
High School				
College/Other				

For ease of reading, each section of the application is introduced by a bold-faced title.

EMPLOYMENT HISTORY

May we contact your present or last employer regarding your experience and qualifications?
__Yes __No

Work History: List below all employment for the last 5 years; use an additional sheet if needed.

Job Title: _____ Dates Employed _____

Reason for Leaving: _____

Employer's Name _____ Address _____

Supervisor's Name _____ Describe Work Duties/Responsibilities _____

_____

_____

Applicants are given only limited space to describe responsibilities on previous jobs. Answers should be brief.

(Cont'd)

SKILLS INVENTORY

Check all certificates, skills, or experience which you possess and indicate the length of experience.

General

__ Record keeping _____
__ Working with Senior Citizens _____
__ Working with young children (5–12)_____
__ Working with adolescents (13–19)_____

Pool Positions

__ AED Certification _____
__ CPR Certification _____
__ Water Safety Instructor_____
__ Pool Supervision_____
__ Pool Maintenance _____
__ ARC-01 Lifeguard Certification _____
     (NM or Lifesaving Instructor)

Athletics

__ Volleyball_____
__ Soccer_____
__ Softball_____
__ Racquetball _____
__ Baseball_____
__ Basketball_____
__ Tennis_____
__ Other_____

Special Populations
(Working with Disabled Persons)

__ Physically Disabled _____
__ Hearing Impaired_____
__ Visually Impaired _____
__ Multi-Disabled _____
__ Developmentally Disabled_____
__ Adapted Aquatics Certificates _____

Programs/Day Camps
(Planned Activities as Group Leader or Instructor)

__ Sports_____
__ Gymnastics _____
__ Arts and Crafts _____
__ Drama_____
__ Music _____
__ Baton _____
__ Pre-Schoolers _____
__ Supervision _____

VOLUNTEER EXPERIENCE

Organization/Volunteer Site	Year Volunteered	# of Hours	Duties/Responsibilities

ADDITIONAL INFORMATION - List any additional skills or knowledge you possess which relate to this position

_____

CERTIFICATION AND RELEASE (PLEASE READ CAREFULLY BEFORE SIGNING BELOW)

I hereby certify that all statements on this application and applicant flow sheet are true and complete to the best of my knowledge and belief. I understand that falsification (including omission) regarding this record may be considered cause for immediate termination of employment or disqualification from the application process, if discovered before employment. I authorize the City to use the information provided and to review my background including but not limited to reference checks, education, driving record verification, and credit history. This information may also be used for internal data and record keeping. I authorize persons, schools, and current and previous employers to provide the City with any relevant information needed to consider me for employment.

_____

Signature/Date

> In this section, space is provided to add a brief explanation of additional skills.

> The applicant's signature is required on the form.

Monitor Your Progress

Reading: Preparing for and Reading Applications

Directions: *Choose the letter of the best answer to each question about the application.*

1. Which of the following items would you not anticipate needing to fill out the job application?

   A driver's license

   B credit card

   C Social Security card

   D list of schools attended

2. Which of the following experiences would you jot down to prepare to fill in the Volunteer Experience section of the form?

   A unpaid work shelving books at your local library

   B mowing your aunt's lawn for an hourly wage

   C helping your neighbor groom her dog as a favor

   D counterwork at a fast-food restaurant

3. Which of the following preparations could someone skip before filling out this application?

   A jotting notes on any training he or she has received

   B contacting any previous employers to ensure they will serve as references

   C writing a brief explanation of his or her personal beliefs

   D determining if any relatives are employed by the city

Reading: Comprehension and Interpretation

Directions: *Write your answers on a separate piece of paper.*

4. Propose two jobs for which this form could be used. Support your answer with application details. **[Integrating]**

5. Why do you think the employer requests information about volunteer experience, not just work history? **[Generating]**

Timed Writing: Persuasion

Write a letter in which you recommend yourself to the person hiring for the City of Durham. Organize your information based on the general categories on the form. (You may omit dates.) Include details that show you are a good candidate. **(20 minutes)**

Comparing Literary Works · Style

Style

A writer's **style** is made up of the features that make his or her expression of ideas distinctive. Two writers may write on the same topic, or even tell the same story, in very different styles. Here are two important elements of style:

- **Diction,** or word choice, involves the type of words the writer uses. Writers can choose to use words that are difficult or simple, abstract or concrete, old-fashioned or hip.
- **Syntax,** or sentence structure, is related to the way words are organized to express ideas. One writer may write a series of short, punchy sentences, driving home each new idea. Another may play with readers, putting a key idea at the end of a long, twisty sentence.

Academic Standards

- Examine how the author's perspective influences the structure and tone of the text. (10.2.4)
- Evaluate the aesthetic qualities of style. (10.3.11)
- Use effective language (action verbs, active voice, sensory details). (10.4.3)

Comparing Writers' Styles

Writers may use various styles, depending on their **purpose,** or reason for writing. A direct style—simple words and short sentences—might be suited for informing the general public. A complex, roundabout style might be suited for expressing a character's innermost thoughts.

Use a chart like the one shown to compare the writers' styles and purposes in "Marian Anderson, Famous Concert Singer" and "Tepeyac."

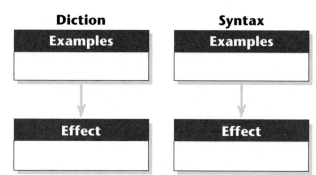

Vocabulary Builder

Marian Anderson . . .

- **staunch** (stônch) *adj.* steadfast; loyal (p. 89) *James is a <u>staunch</u> supporter of his family.*

- **lucrative** (loo′ krə tiv) *adj.* producing wealth; profitable (p. 90) *He closed the business when it was no longer <u>lucrative</u>.*

- **debut** (dā byoo′) *n.* first public appearance (p. 90) *The singer was nervous before her <u>debut</u>.*

- **repertoire** (rep′ ər twär′) *n.* a stock of works, such as songs, that a performer is prepared to present (p. 93) *The singer's <u>repertoire</u> was limited to show tunes.*

Tepeyac

- **canopied** (kan′ ə pēd) *adj.* covered by a cloth suspended from poles or a framework (p. 94) *If it rains, stay in the <u>canopied</u> area.*

- **dimpled** (dim′ pəld) *adj.* marked with small hollows or indentations (p. 95) *The baby's <u>dimpled</u> cheeks invited nonstop pinching.*

- **arabesques** (ar′ ə besks′) *n.* elaborate decorative designs of intertwined lines (p. 96) *When I doodle, I draw <u>arabesques</u>, not objects.*

- **irretrievable** (ir′ i trēv′ ə bəl) *adj.* impossible to regain or recover (p. 96) *After the computer crashed, the files were <u>irretrievable</u>.*

Build Understanding

Connecting to the Literature

Reading/Writing Connection Each of these selections focuses on an admirable person—a great concert singer in "Marian Anderson, Famous Concert Singer" and the narrator's grandfather in "Tepeyac." Jot down a few sentences about the special traits of a person whom you admire. Use at least three of the following words: *embody, innovate, participate, accomplish.*

Meet the Authors

Langston **Hughes** (1902–1967)

In the 1920s and 1930s, African American writers, artists, and musicians based in Harlem, a neighborhood in New York City, gave vivid, intense expression to the African American experience. The period is known as the Harlem Renaissance, and Langston Hughes is acknowledged as one of its dominant forces.

Jazz Rhythms on the Page Harlem Renaissance artists dedicated themselves to finding authentically African American styles. Hughes crafted a style, especially in his poetry, that reflected the rhythms and moods of jazz and blues music. (You can read one of Hughes's poems on page 682.)

Sandra **Cisneros** (b. 1954)

Born to a Mexican father and a Mexican American mother, Sandra Cisneros spent her childhood shuttling between Chicago and Mexico City. The only girl among seven children, Cisneros felt as if she had "seven fathers." Struggling to find her identity, she took refuge in reading and writing.

Winning Honors Although her family was not well-off, Cisneros managed to attend the prestigious Writers' Workshop at the University of Iowa. Her first novel, the autobiographical *The House on Mango Street* (1984), was a commercial and critical success, earning her the American Book Award from the Before Columbus Foundation in 1985.

Go Online
Author Link

For: More about the authors
Visit: www.PHSchool.com
Web Code: eqe-9106

Marian Anderson
FAMOUS CONCERT SINGER

Langston Hughes

Background   Marian Anderson (1897?–1993) was one of the first African American singers to gain widespread recognition as a performer of classical music, including opera.

When Marian Anderson was born in a little red brick house in Philadelphia, a famous group of Negro singers, the Fisk Jubilee Singers, had already carried the spirituals all over Europe. And a colored woman billed as "Black Patti" had become famous on variety programs as a singer of both folk songs and the classics. Both Negro and white minstrels had popularized American songs. The all-Negro

▲ **Critical Viewing**
Judging from this photograph, predict what you will learn about Marian Anderson's personality. **[Predict]**

musical comedies of Bert Williams and George Walker had been successful on Broadway. But no well-trained colored singers performing the great songs of Schubert, Handel, and the other masters, or the arias from famous operas, had become successful on the concert stage. And most people thought of Negro vocalists only in connection with spirituals. Roland Hayes[1] and Marian Anderson were the first to become famous enough to break this stereotype.

Marian Anderson's mother was a <u>staunch</u> church worker who loved to croon the hymns of her faith about the house, as did the aunt who came to live with them when Marian's father died. Both parents were from Virginia. Marian's mother had been a schoolteacher there, and her father a farm boy. Shortly after they moved to Philadelphia where three daughters were born, the father died, and the mother went to work at Wanamaker's department store. But she saw to it that her children attended school and church regularly. The father had been an usher in the Union Baptist Church, so the congregation took an interest in his three little girls. Marian was the oldest and, before she was eight, singing in the Sunday school choir, she had already learned a great many hymns and spirituals by heart.

One day Marian saw an old violin in a pawnshop window marked $3.45. She set her mind on that violin, and began to save the nickels and dimes neighbors would give her for scrubbing their white front steps—the kind of stone steps so characteristic of Philadelphia and Baltimore houses—until she had $3.00. The pawnshop man let her take the violin at a reduced price. Marian never became very good on the violin. A few years later her mother bought a piano, so the child forgot all about it in favor of their newer instrument. By that time, too, her unusual singing voice had attracted the attention of her choir master, and at the age of fourteen she was promoted to a place in the main church choir. There she learned all four parts of all the hymns and anthems and could easily fill in anywhere from bass to soprano.

Sensing that she had exceptional musical talent, some of the church members began to raise money so that she might have singing lessons. But her first teacher, a colored woman, refused to accept any pay for instructing so talented a child. So the church folks put their money into a trust fund called "Marian Anderson's Future," banking it until the time came for her to have advanced training. Meanwhile, Marian attended South Philadelphia High School for Girls and took part in various group concerts, usually doing the solo parts. When she was fifteen she sang a group of

---

1. Roland Hayes (1887–1977) famous African American tenor.

Vocabulary Builder
staunch (stônch) *adj.*
steadfast; loyal

Literary Analysis
Style Identify an example of a direct, down-to-earth word or phrase in this passage.

**Reading Check**

What organization supported the development of Anderson's talent?

songs alone at a Sunday School Convention in Harrisburg and word of her talent began to spread about the state. When she was graduated from high school, the Philadelphia Choral Society, a Negro group, sponsored her further study and secured for her one of the best local teachers. Then in 1925 she journeyed to New York to take part, with three hundred other young singers, in the New York Philharmonic Competitions, where she won first place, and appeared with the orchestra at Lewisohn Stadium.

This appearance was given wide publicity, but very few <u>lucrative</u> engagements came in, so Marian continued to study. A Town Hall concert was arranged for her in New York, but it was unsuccessful. Meanwhile, she kept on singing with various choral groups, and herself gave concerts in churches and at some of the Negro colleges until, in 1930, a Rosenwald Fellowship made European study possible. During her first year abroad she made her <u>debut</u> in Berlin. A prominent Scandinavian concert manager read of this concert, but was attracted more by the name, *Anderson,* than by what the critics said about her voice. "Ah," he said, "a Negro singer with a Swedish name! She is bound to be a success in Scandinavia." He sent two of his friends to Germany to hear her, one of them being Kosti Vehanen who shortly became her accompanist and remained with her for many years.

Sure enough, Marian Anderson did become a great success in the Scandinavian countries, where she learned to sing in both Finnish and Swedish, and her first concert tour of Europe became a critical triumph. When she came back home to America, she gave several programs and appeared as soloist with the famous Hall Johnson Choir, but without financial success. However, the Scandinavian people, who had fallen in love with her, kept asking her to come back there. So, in 1933, she went again to Europe for 142 concerts in Norway, Sweden, Denmark, and Finland. She was decorated by the King of Denmark and the King of Sweden. Sibelius[2] dedicated a song to her. And the following spring she made her debut in Paris where she was so well received that she had to give three concerts that season at the Salle Gaveau.[3] Great successes followed in all the European capitals. In 1935 the famous conductor, Arturo Toscanini, listened to her sing at Salzburg.[4] He said, "What I heard today one is privileged to hear only once in a hundred years." It was in Europe that Marian Anderson began to be acclaimed by critics as "the greatest singer in the world."

When Marian Anderson again returned to America, she was a seasoned artist. News of her tremendous European successes had

Vocabulary Builder
lucrative (lōō´ krə tiv) *adj.* producing wealth; profitable
debut (dā byōō´) *n.* first public appearance

Literary Analysis
Style How do the words *sure enough* contribute to the informal, conversational diction?

---

2. **Sibelius** (si bā´ lē oos) Jean Sibelius (1865–1957), a Finnish composer.
3. **Salle Gaveau** (sȧl ga vō´) concert hall in Paris, France.
4. **Salzburg** city in Austria noted for its music festivals.

preceded her, so a big New York concert was planned. But a few days before she arrived at New York, in a storm on the liner crossing the Atlantic, Marian fell and broke her ankle. She refused to allow this to interfere with her concert, however, nor did she even want people to know about it. She wore a very long evening gown that night so that no one could see the plaster cast on her leg. She propped herself in a curve of the piano before the curtains parted, and gave her New York concert standing on one foot! The next day Howard Taubman wrote enthusiastically in *The New York Times*:

> Marian Anderson has returned to her native land one of the great singers of our time. . . . There is no doubt of it, she was mistress of all she surveyed. . . . It was music making that probed too deep for words.

A coast-to-coast American tour followed. And, from that season on, Marian Anderson has been one of our country's favorite singers, rated, according to *Variety*,[5] among the top ten of the concert stage who earn over $100,000 a year. Miss Anderson has sung with the great symphony orchestras, and appeared on all the major radio and television networks many times, being a particular favorite with

5. *Variety* a show-business newspaper.

▲ Critical Viewing
Does this photograph of Anderson's concert in Washington, D.C., support Hughes's description of her success? Explain. **[Support]**

✓ Reading Check

In which region of the world did Anderson first find success?

the millions of listeners to the Ford Hour. During the years she has returned often to Europe for concerts, and among the numerous honors accorded her abroad was a request for a command performance before the King and Queen of England, and a decoration from the government of Finland. Her concerts in South America and Asia have been as successful as those elsewhere. Since 1935 she has averaged over one hundred programs a year in cities as far apart as Vienna, Buenos Aires, Moscow, and Tokyo. Her recordings have sold millions of copies around the world. She has been invited more than once to sing at the White House. She has appeared in concert at the Paris Opera and at the Metropolitan Opera House in New York. Several colleges have granted her honorary degrees, and in 1944 Smith College made her a Doctor of Music.

In spite of all this, as a Negro, Marian Anderson has not been immune from those aspects of racial segregation which affect most traveling artists of color in the United States. In his book, *Marian Anderson,* her longtime accompanist, Vehanen, tells of hotel accommodations being denied her, and service in dining rooms often refused. Once after a concert in a Southern city, Vehanen writes that some white friends drove Marian to the railroad station and took her into the main waiting room. But a policeman ran them out, since Negroes were not allowed in that part of the station. Then they went into the smaller waiting room marked, COLORED. But again they were ejected, because *white* people were not permitted in the cubby hole allotted to Negroes. So they all had to stand on the platform until the train arrived.

The most dramatic incident of prejudice in all Marian Anderson's career occurred in 1939 when the Daughters of the American Revolution, who own Constitution Hall in Washington, refused to allow her to sing there. The newspapers headlined this and many Americans were outraged. In protest a committee of prominent people,

▲ Critical Viewing
What feeling does this painting of Anderson's famous Washington, D.C., concert capture?
[Interpret]

including a number of great artists and distinguished figures in the government, was formed. Through the efforts of this committee, Marian Anderson sang in Washington, anyway—before the statue of Abraham Lincoln—to one of the largest crowds ever to hear a singer at one time in the history of the world. Seventy-five thousand people stood in the open air on a cold clear Easter Sunday afternoon to hear her. And millions more listened to Marian Anderson that day over the radio or heard her in the newsreels that recorded the event. Harold Ickes, then Secretary of the Interior, presented Miss Anderson to that enormous audience standing in the plaza to pay honor, as he said, not only to a great singer, but to the basic ideals of democracy and equality.

In 1943 Marian Anderson married Orpheus H. Fisher, an architect, and settled down—between tours—in a beautiful country house in Connecticut where she rehearses new songs to add to her already vast <u>repertoire</u>. Sometimes her neighbors across the fields can hear the rich warm voice that covers three octaves singing in English, French, Finnish, or German. And sometimes they hear in the New England air that old Negro spiritual, "Honor, honor unto the dying Lamb. . . ."

Friends say that Marian Anderson has invested her money in real estate and in government bonds. Certainly, throughout her career, she has lived very simply, traveled without a maid or secretary, and carried her own sewing machine along by train, ship, or plane to mend her gowns. When in 1941 in Philadelphia she was awarded the coveted Bok Award for outstanding public service, the $10,000 that came with the medallion she used to establish a trust fund for "talented American artists without regard to race or creed." Now, each year from this fund promising young musicians receive scholarships.

Vocabulary Builder
repertoire (rep´ ər twär´) *n.* a stock of works, such as songs, that a performer is prepared to present

Literary Analysis
Style Which words and phrases here give a direct illustration of Anderson's lifestyle?

Thinking About the Selection

1. **Respond:** What most impressed you about Anderson's life? Explain.
2. **(a) Recall:** According to Hughes, in what area had African American singers not received recognition before Anderson? **(b) Infer:** How can you explain this lack of recognition?
3. **(a) Recall:** Identify one action Anderson's congregation took to help her career. **(b) Infer:** What does their decision to help suggest about Anderson's talent as a young girl? Explain.
4. **(a) Summarize:** What type of difficulties did Anderson face when traveling in the United States? **(b) Infer:** What attitude led to these difficulties? **(c) Analyze:** In what sense was Anderson's outdoor concert in Washington, D.C., a response to this attitude?

TEPEYAC
SANDRA CISNEROS

When the sky of Tepeyac[1] opens its first thin stars and the dark comes down in an ink of Japanese blue above the bell towers of La Basílica de Nuestra Señora,[2] above the plaza photographers and their souvenir backdrops of La Virgen de Guadalupe, above the balloon vendors and their balloons wearing paper hats, above the red-<u>canopied</u> thrones of the shoeshine stands, above the wooden booths of the women frying lunch in vats of oil, above the *tlapalería*[3] on the corner of Misterios and Cinco de Mayo, when the photographers have toted up their tripods and big box cameras, have rolled away the wooden ponies I don't know where, when the balloon men have sold all but the ugliest balloons and herded these last few home, when the shoeshine men have grown tired of squatting on their little wooden boxes, and the women frying lunch have finished packing dishes, tablecloth, pots, in the big straw basket in which they came, then Abuelito[4] tells the boy with dusty hair, *Arturo, we are closed,* and in crooked shoes and purple elbows Arturo pulls down with a pole the corrugated metal curtains—first the one on Misterios, then the other on Cinco de Mayo—like an eyelid over each door, before Abuelito tells him he can go.

This is when I arrive, one shoe and then the next, over the sagging door stone, worn smooth in the middle from the huaraches of those who have come for tins of glue and to have their scissors sharpened, who have asked for candles and cans of boot polish, a half-kilo sack of nails, turpentine, blue-specked spoons, paintbrushes, photographic paper, a spool of picture wire, lamp oil, and string.

Abuelito under a bald light bulb, under a ceiling dusty with flies, puffs his cigar and counts money soft and wrinkled as old Kleenex,

---

1. **Tepeyac** (tep ā yäk´) Tepeyac Hill lies in the northern part of Mexico City.
2. **La Basílica de Nuestra Señora** (lä bä sil´ ē kä dā nwäs´ trä sen yō´ rä) the Basilica [Church] of Our Lady, lying at the foot of Tepeyac Hill on the site where, according to legend, Juan Diego had a vision in 1531.
3. *tlapalería* (tlä pä lä rē´ ä) *n.* the Mexican equivalent of a hardware store.
4. **Abuelito** (ä bwā lē´ tō) *n.* affectionate Spanish term for "grandfather."

money earned by the plaza women serving lunch on flat tin plates, by the souvenir photographers and their canvas Recuerdo[5] de Tepeyac backdrops, by the shoeshine men sheltered beneath their fringed and canopied kingdoms, by the blessed vendors of the holy cards, rosaries, scapulars, little plastic altars, by the good sisters who live in the convent across the street, counts and recounts in a whisper and puts the money in a paper sack we carry home.

I take Abuelito's hand, fat and <u>dimpled</u> in the center like a valentine, and we walk past the basilica, where each Sunday the Abuela[6] lights the candles for the soul of Abuelito. Past the very same spot where long ago Juan Diego brought down from the *cerro*[7] the miracle that has drawn everyone, except my Abuelito, on their knees, down the avenue one block past the bright lights of the *sastrería*[8] of

Señor Guzmán who is still at work at his sewing machine, past the candy store where I buy my milk-and-raisin gelatins, past La Providencia *tortillería* where every afternoon Luz María and I are sent for the basket of lunchtime tortillas, past the house of the widow Márquez whose husband died last winter of a tumor the size of her little white fist, past La Muñeca's mother watering her famous dahlias with a pink rubber hose and a skinny string of water, to the house on La Fortuna, number 12, that has always been our house. Green iron gates that arabesque[9] and scroll like the initials of my name, familiar whine and clang, familiar lacework of ivy growing

---

5. **Recuerdo** (rā kwer′ *tho*) Spanish for "souvenir."
6. **Abuela** (ä bwā′ lä) *n.* Spanish for "grandmother."
7. ***cerro*** (se′ rō) *n.* Spanish for "hill."
8. ***sastrería*** (säs tre rē′ ä) *n.* tailor's shop.
9. **arabesque** (ar′ ə besk′) *v.* branch out in complex, intertwining lines (usually a noun referring to such lines).

▲ **Critical Viewing**
Does this photograph capture the spirit of the market the narrator describes? Explain. **[Connect]**

Vocabulary Builder
dimpled (dim′ pəld) *adj.* marked with small hollows or indentations

✓ **Reading Check**
With whom does the narrator live in Tepeyac?

over and between except for one small clean square for the hand of the postman whose face I have never seen, up the twenty-two steps we count out loud together—*uno, dos, tres*—to the supper of *sopa de fideo* and *carne guisada*—*cuatro, cinco, seis*—the glass of *café con leche*—*siete, ocho, nueve*—shut the door against the mad parrot voice of the Abuela—*diez, once, doce*—fall asleep as we always do, with the television mumbling—*trece, catorce, quince*—the Abuelito snoring—*dieciséis, diecisiete, dieciocho*—the grandchild, the one who will leave soon for that borrowed country—*diecinueve, veinte, veintiuno*—the one he will not remember, the one he is least familiar with—*veintidós, veintitrés, veinticuatro*—years later when the house on La Fortuna, number 12, is sold, when the *tlapalería*, corner of Misterios and Cinco de Mayo, changes owners, when the courtyard gate of <u>arabesques</u> and scrolls is taken off its hinges and replaced with a corrugated sheet metal door instead, when the widow Márquez and La Muñeca's mother move away, when Abuelito falls asleep one last time—*veinticinco, veintiséis, veintisiete*—years afterward when I return to the shop on the corner of Misterios and Cinco de Mayo, repainted and redone as a pharmacy, to the basilica that is crumbling and closed, to the plaza photographers, the balloon vendors and shoeshine thrones, the women whose faces I do not recognize serving lunch in the wooden booths, to the house on La Fortuna, number 12, smaller and darker than when we lived there, with the rooms boarded shut and rented to strangers, the street suddenly dizzy with automobiles and diesel fumes, the house fronts scuffed and the gardens frayed, the children who played kickball all grown and moved away.

Who would've guessed, after all this time, it is me who will remember when everything else is forgotten, you who took with you to your stone bed something <u>irretrievable</u>, without a name.

Thinking About the Selection

1. **Respond:** Would you have liked to have visited Tepeyac with the narrator? Why or why not?

2. **(a) Recall:** List three details the narrator remembers about the market at Tepeyac. **(b) Synthesize:** What overall impression or feeling about the market do these details create? Explain your answer.

3. **Interpret:** To what event is the narrator referring when she says, "the grandchild, the one who will leave soon for that borrowed country"?

4. **(a) Analyze:** List two things that have changed in Tepeyac when the narrator returns. **(b) Draw a Conclusion:** Why is the narrator surprised to discover at the end that "it is me who will remember"?

Apply the Skills

Marian Anderson, Famous Concert Singer • Tepeyac

Comparing Styles

QuickReview

Style: the features that make a writer's expression of ideas distinctive. Style includes the writer's *diction* and *syntax*.

Purpose: the author's reason for writing

Go Online
——Assessment
For: Self-test
Visit: www.PHSchool.com
Web Code: eqa-6107

1. **(a)** Explain how Hughes's **style** helps make Anderson seem accessible or sympathetic to readers, despite her fame.
   (b) Explain how Cisneros's style helps re-create the rushing flow of memories.

2. **(a)** Using a chart like the one shown, compare each writer's style at the dramatic moment indicated.

Moment	Hughes Washington, D.C., Concert	Cisneros Concluding Realization
Type of words		
Type of sentences		
Similar to / different from rest of work?		

   (b) Based on your chart, explain the way in which each writer's style—or a shift in the writer's style—adds dramatic effect.

Writing to Compare Literary Works

An author's style is usually related to his or her **purpose,** or reason for writing. Evaluate each selection to decide which style is more effective in accomplishing the author's purpose. In an essay, support your opinion with relevant examples and quotations from the selections. Consider these questions before you draft:

- What is the writer trying to accomplish in each selection?
- How does the writer's style help achieve this purpose?
- Are there places in which the style gets in the way of the purpose?

Vocabulary Builder

Practice In each set of words, identify the word that does not belong. Explain how the meaning of the italicized word helped determine your answer.

1. *staunch* / courage / stain
2. *lucrative* / music / notes
3. *debut* / retirement / argument
4. *repertoire* / journal / book
5. *canopied* / dessert / cloth
6. *dimpled* / indented / dry
7. *arabesques* / patterns / horses
8. *irretrievable* / lost / unusual

Reading

Directions: *Questions 1–5 are based on the following selection.*

[Magdalena] stood on tiptoe and didn't breathe when her painting was announced. Her hand in her pocket closed tight around the twenty-four guilders, some of it borrowed from two neighbor women, some of it taken secretly from the box where [her husband] Nicolaes kept money for leather supplies. It was all she could find, and she didn't dare ask for more. He would have thought it foolish.

"Twenty," said a man in front of her.

"Twenty-two," said another.

"Twenty-four," she said so loud and fast the auctioneer was startled. Did he see something similar in her face? He didn't call for another bid. The painting was hers!

"Twenty-five."

—from *Girl in Hyacinth Blue,* by Susan Vreeland

1. **What prior knowledge could help you predict whether or not Magdalena will acquire the painting?**
   A knowing the true value of the painting
   B knowing the rules for bidding
   C knowing the value of a guilder
   D knowing what type of personality auctioneers generally have

2. **What detail in the passage helps you predict whether Magdalena will bid again?**
   A She wants the painting.
   B Nicolaes keeps money in a box.
   C She only has twenty-four guilders.
   D The man in front of her first bid twenty guilders.

3. **Which would not affect a prediction about her reaction to the outcome of the auction?**
   A details about who purchased the painting
   B details about who painted the painting
   C details about why she wants the painting
   D details about her husband's art

4. **Which sentence would verify a prediction that Magdalena was saddened when she was outbid?**
   A "Ladies and gentleman, there's been a terrible mistake."
   B Amid the excitement, no one noticed that the painting had vanished.
   C The painter slipped quietly out of the auction house.
   D As the gavel banged, a tear trickled down her face.

5. **From the passage, readers can reasonably predict that, if Nicolaes finds out about his wife's reason for taking the money, he will**
   A be angry with her.
   B share her enthusiasm for obtaining the painting.
   C encourage her to invest in other paintings.
   D be confused by her determination to buy the painting.

Vocabulary

Directions: *Choose the sentence in which the word is used correctly.*

6. **spontaneous**
   A As soon as he entered, there was a spontaneous outburst of applause.
   B I have practiced every day, so I will be able to give a spontaneous speech.
   C Most people are quite spontaneous at formal events.
   D The spontaneous of the choice surprised us.

7. **perceive**
   A They only perceive what is kept well hidden.
   B If I perceive the obstacle, I am likely to run right into it.
   C Although you say it is there, I do not perceive it.
   D They perceive hard to get what they want.

8. **subjective**
   A Scientists are expected to report their subjective views of nature.
   B The test will be graded on a subjective basis.
   C I chose the red one instead of the blue for subjective reasons.
   D Whether it is raining is subjective.

9. **innovate**
   A Computers innovate our new ideas.
   B We will innovate that idea.
   C To innovate in transportation takes years of testing.
   D To innovate is to be old-fashioned.

10. **eloquent**
    A That politician is known for eloquent, persuasive speeches.
    B The eloquent in his writing is his trademark.
    C The character's eloquent was a subject of discussion.
    D Despite her eloquent the audience was not impressed.

Directions: *Choose the definition that best fits each word.*

11. **eloquence**
    A fashionable prose
    B graceful speech
    C harsh speech
    D tactless comments

12. **loquacious**
    A tall
    B talkative
    C suffering
    D illuminated

13. **nova**
    A a planet that falls out of an old orbit
    B a star that takes on new brightness
    C a small asteroid
    D a meteor

14. **novelty**
    A instability
    B smallness
    C newness
    D largeness

Writing Workshop

Narration: Autobiographical Narrative

Autobiographical narratives can be as simple as a remembrance of a weekend vacation or as complex as the entire story of the writer's life. Use the steps outlined in this workshop to write your own autobiographical narrative.

Assignment Write an autobiographical narrative about an event in your life that changed your outlook or helped you grow.

What to Include Your autobiographical narrative should feature these elements:
- a clear sequence of events involving you, the writer
- a problem or conflict
- effective descriptions of people, places, and events
- use of dialogue to show character
- an insight you gained as a result of this experience
- error-free grammar, including correct use of possessive nouns

To preview the criteria on which your autobiographical narrative may be judged, see the rubric on page 104.

Prewriting

Choosing Your Topic

List events by category. Brainstorm for events from your life. First, create a four-column chart like the one shown. Then, list experiences that fit each category. Then, review your work to choose a topic.

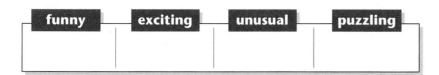

funny	exciting	unusual	puzzling

Gathering Details

Create character and setting cards. Once you have selected a story from your life, prepare to focus your narrative by identifying the main conflict or insight you want to explain. Write an index card for each important character or setting.
- For settings, jot down physical details to use in your descriptions.
- For characters, include facts like name, age, and appearance. Also note personality, habits, and the person's role in your story.

Academic Standards

- Analyze characters' traits through narration and dialogue. (10.3.4)
- Evaluate an author's use of time and sequence. (10.3.6)
- Write biographical or autobiographical narratives. (10.5.1)

Using the Form
You may use elements of this form in these types of writing:
- journals
- eyewitness accounts
- persuasive essays

Work in Progress
Review the work you did on page 17 and page 25.

Reading Writing Connection

To get a feel for narrative nonfiction, read the excerpt from *Swimming to Antarctica* by Lynne Cox on page 58.

Drafting

Shaping Your Writing

Devise a plan for telling your story. As you write, tell important events in logical order. Use this plot diagram to help structure your narrative.

Be sure to identify the climax, or point of highest interest, before you begin writing so you can build to this key moment.

Climax
—Build to the point of highest interest.

Develop the conflict.—

Rising Action

Falling Action

—Reduce the suspense and decrease the tension.

Resolution
Tie up the loose ends.

Exposition
Set the scene and introduce the characters.

Providing Elaboration

Use dialogue. *Dialogue*—the conversations among people in a narrative—can add interest to your writing. Use dialogue to advance the plot and show what characters are like. You might also create interior monologues: statements that reveal your exact thoughts at the time.

> **Narration:** She told me not to go into the cave.
> **Dialogue:** "Don't go in there without a flashlight," she warned.

Revising

Revising Your Overall Structure

Revise to strengthen unity. Review your draft to make sure that ideas flow logically. Identify paragraphs on the same topic and consider combining them. Divide paragraphs that discuss more than one topic.

Revising Your Paragraphs

Vary sentence length. Add interest by including both long and short sentences in your narrative. If you find a series of short, choppy sentences, combine some of them. Adding a short, energetic sentence can emphasize an exciting moment.

Reading Writing Connection

To see the complete student model from which this example is taken, see page 103.

Student Model: Varying Sentence Length

The "off-road" in question was to be our front and back yards. ~~The "off-road" area was close to the woods~~. I planned a fairly straightforward circuit around the house. . . .

(the latter of which happened, incidentally, to back up to the North Carolina woods)

> Combining two short sentences into one longer one adds interest.

Integrating Grammar Skills

Using Possessive Nouns Correctly

A **possessive noun** indicates possession or ownership. An apostrophe must be used to form a possessive noun.

Prentice Hall Writing and Grammar Connection: Chapter 28, Section 6

Identifying Incorrect Possessive Nouns You might find these three kinds of mistakes involving possessive nouns:

- nouns that are possessive but do not have an apostrophe
- possessive nouns that have an apostrophe in the wrong place
- nouns that are not possessive but include an apostrophe

Clarify Your Meaning Thinking about what you mean will help you choose the correct possessive noun.

The student's essays were due on Friday. *(one student, many essays)*
The students' essays were due on Friday. *(more than one student)*

In the following example, the plural noun is not possessive. It should not have an apostrophe.

Wrong: The student's laughed.
Right: The students laughed.

Fixing Incorrect Possessive Nouns To fix the possessive nouns in your writing, look for any nouns that show ownership.

1. **Ask yourself whether the noun is singular or plural.**

2. **Follow these rules to place the apostrophe correctly:**

A. Add an apostrophe and *s* to show the possessive case of most singular nouns.
     the ocean's roar   Julia's bicycle   James's poem

B. Add an apostrophe to show the possessive case of plural nouns ending in *s* or *es*.
     the branches' leaves   the Canadians' houses

C. Add an apostrophe and *s* to show the possessive case of plural nouns that do not end in *s* or *es*.
     the people's stories   the children's department

Apply It to Your Editing

Scan your writing for apostrophes. You might find some in abbreviations, but others will be used in possessive nouns. Check that each possessive noun is punctuated correctly. Then, review your writing for possessives that are missing their apostrophes.

Student Model: Alexandria Symonds
Royersford, PA

The Collision, or Hardly Extreme

Some people are simply not meant for extreme athletics, I thought to myself as I slowly regained consciousness. *I am one of those people. I will never compete in the X Games; I should just stick to my orderly world where "sports" include Scrabble.* I would have continued in this thought pattern, but a feeling like someone stabbing me in the eye with a dozen dull forks grabbed my attention instead.

I was bored that Saturday afternoon in May of 1998—so bored, in fact, that it seemed like a bright and creative idea to see if my old girly purple bike could be used for off-roading. The "off-road" in question was to be our front and back yards (the latter of which happened, incidentally, to back up to the North Carolina woods). I planned a fairly straightforward circuit around the house, complicated only slightly by the fact that our house sat on a hill.

It is prophesied that if the earth ever loses its gravitational pull, the moon will abandon its orbit and spin, instead, in a straight line into infinity. Something similar happened to me after a couple of laps around the house. I had reached a speed so high that I concentrated solely on pedaling to maintain it—forgetting, as it were, to turn at a pivotal point in the round. The difference, however, between the moon and me is that while the moon could spin into infinity unobstructed, there was a forest in my way.

I realized a split second too late that I hadn't made the turn and knew there was no use trying to do it now. In retrospect, I could have jumped off the bike, but logical thoughts rarely occur when one is hurtling toward a giant oak tree at 25 miles per hour. Instead, I stopped pedaling, closed my eyes, and braced myself for the impact.

I never actually felt it. When I opened my eyes, I was crumpled on the grass in a position I'm sure humans were never intended to take. My bike was tangled in my limbs, and a searing pain in my left eye was the only thing I could feel. After a bit of reflection about my "extreme" lack of foresight, I decided the best response was to scream as loudly as I could.

The events immediately following my ill-fated rendezvous with the tree are a blur; but I know that somehow I made it to the hospital, where I endured what seemed like endless tests and injections. I would be okay, but my recovery was a painful process. While the rest of me suffered only surface cuts and deep bruises, my left eye was swollen shut for a week. It was distended for months afterwards, and I still have some puffy scar tissue that causes my left eye to close more than the right when I smile.

Still, every time I get photos developed and notice this phenomenon, it serves as a reminder that I was simply not meant for any kind of physical activity more "extreme" than skipping.

Alexandria's thoughts provide an intriguing beginning for the narrative.

Specific details about Alexandria's state of mind and her bicycle add color and interest to the tale.

Her sense of humor gives a spark to the narrative.

Key details create a vivid picture and also keep the story moving.

Details here echo the beginning of the narrative and bring the story full circle.

Writing Workshop

Editing and Proofreading

Check your draft for errors in format, grammar, and punctuation.
Focus on Punctuating Dialogue: Check that you have punctuated dialogue correctly. Quotation marks should surround a character's exact words or thoughts. Make sure that there is a closing quotation mark for every opening quotation mark. (For more on punctuating dialogue, see Quotation Marks on page R48.)

Publishing and Presenting

Consider one of the following ways to share your writing:
Illustrate your narrative. Use photographs or drawings to illustrate people, places, or events in your narrative. Assemble a clean copy of your narrative, choosing an appropriate title and cover.
Give a dramatic reading. Rehearse reading your narrative aloud. Using a copy as a reading script, underline words that you will emphasize. Note places where you will vary your reading rate. Your goal is to sound like yourself while sharing an interesting personal event.

Reflecting on Your Writing

Writer's Journal Jot down your thoughts on the experience of writing an autobiographical narrative. Begin by answering these questions:
- Which part of your narrative changed the most when you revised it? Why?
- How did writing about this experience change your view of it?

> *Prentice Hall Writing and Grammar Connection: Chapter 4*

Rubric for Self-Assessment

To assess your own autobiographical narrative, use this rubric.

Criteria	Rating Scale
	not very *very*
Focus: How clearly do you explain the insight gained from this experience?	1 2 3 4 5
Organization: How clearly do you present the sequence of events?	1 2 3 4 5
Support/Elaboration: How effective are your descriptions of people, places, and events?	1 2 3 4 5
Style: How effective is your use of dialogue?	1 2 3 4 5
Conventions: How correct is your grammar, especially your use of possessive nouns?	1 2 3 4 5

Skills You Will Learn

Literature You Will Read

Reading and Vocabulary Skills Preview

Reading: Cause and Effect

> A **cause** is an event, an action, or a situation that makes something happen. An **effect** is the event that results from that cause.

(IN) Academic Standards

- Distinguish the meaning of words and their implication. (10.1.2)
- Compare and contrast the presentation of a specific theme or topic across different genres. (10.3.2)
- Evaluate an author's use of time and sequence. (10.3.6)

Skills and Strategies You Will Learn in Part 2

In Part 2, you will learn
- to **reflect on key details** to **find clues to cause and effect.** (p. 108)
- to **reread** to **analyze causes and effects.** (p. 142)
- to **use charts and diagrams** to **analyze cause and effect.** (p. 166)

Using the Skills and Strategies in Part 2

Cause-and-effect relationships exist when events lead to or are the result of other events. Thinking about the relationships between events and circumstances can help you recognize causes and effects.

The example shows how you can apply the skills and strategies in Part 2 to a work.

| **Reflecting** on this **detail** will help you see the real cause of the rise in sales. | When you **reread**, you will notice the writer explains that illness was not the cause of the rise in sales. |

This year, orange juice purchases in the city jumped during the months of February and March. At the same time, sales of aspirin and medical thermometers were up. Yet the Health Department reported no rise in complaints of colds, flu, or allergies for those months. One reason for the increase in sales is the epidemic of the year before. It was not that people were struck with illness this winter. Rather, they remembered last year. They wanted to make sure they were ready this time.

This word is a clue to help you **analyze** the cause of the surge in sales.

Academic Vocabulary: Words for Responding to Literature

The following words will help you to talk and write about the selections in this unit.

Word	Definition	Example Sentence
preliminary *adj.*	leading up to; preparing for	After a few *preliminary* scenes, the writer moves right into the action—an exciting car chase.
priority *n.*	something that is more important than other things	This writer's *priority* is revealing a complex character, not telling a suspenseful story.
fluent *adj.*	of writing or speech that is especially smooth and expressive	Her writing is *fluent*, yet she has surprisingly little to say.
intuitive *adj.*	perceived or understood immediately, without conscious thought	The reader makes an *intuitive* connection between the empty room and the family's unhappiness.
initial *adj.*	having to do with the beginning of something	My *initial* reaction was indifference, but I soon grew to love the characters.

Vocabulary Skills You Will Learn in Part 2

▶ The **origin of a word** is the history of how its meaning came to be.

The history of many English words can be traced to Latin—the language of the Roman Empire. As travelers and soldiers carried the language to new places, the requirements of different cultures, governments, climates, and native languages led to changes in pronunciation and meaning. Most dictionaries provide information about a word's origins. In Part 2, you will learn

- the origin and forms of *preliminary*

- the origin and forms of *fluent*

Activity Look up *initial* and *prior* in a dictionary. Use the information in each entry to identify the different languages and meanings in the word's history. Explain these changes for each word.

Practice these skills with either "Contents of the Dead Man's Pocket" (p. 110) or "Games at Twilight" (p. 129).

Literary Analysis

The **conflict** in a short story is a struggle between two forces.

- In an **external conflict,** a character struggles against an outside force, such as an element of nature or another character.
- In an **internal conflict,** a character struggles with his or her own opposing desires, beliefs, or needs.
- In many stories, the conflict intensifies until one force wins and a **resolution** of the conflict occurs.

To build interest in a conflict, writers may hint at events to come or "stretch out" episodes that lead up to a crucial moment. In these ways, they create **suspense,** a rising curiosity or anxiety in readers. As you read, use a chart like this one to record conflicts.

Reading Skill

A **cause** is an event, an action, or a situation that produces a result. An **effect** is the result produced. To better follow a story, **analyze causes and effects** as you read, determining which earlier events lead to which later events. Many stories are chains of cause and effect, in which one event leads to the next.

To analyze causes and effects, **reflect on key details** that the writer spends time explaining or describing. For example, a writer's description of a dangerous coastline prepares you to understand the cause-and-effect relationships leading to the sinking of a ship.

Academic Standards

- Distinguish the meaning of words and their implication. (10.1.2)
- Analyze many different forms of dramatic literature. (10.3.1)
- Evaluate interactions between characters and how these affect the plot. (10.3.3)

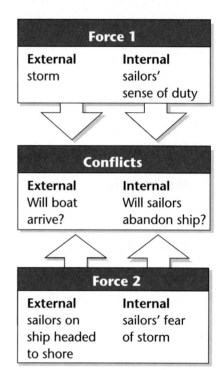

Force 1	
External	**Internal**
storm	sailors' sense of duty

Conflicts	
External	**Internal**
Will boat arrive?	Will sailors abandon ship?

Force 2	
External	**Internal**
sailors on ship headed to shore	sailors' fear of storm

Vocabulary Builder

Contents of the Dead Man's Pocket

- **convoluted** (kän´ və loot´ id) *adj.* intricate; twisted (p. 112) *The <u>convoluted</u> maze confused the mouse.*
- **deftness** (deft´ nis) *n.* skillfulness (p. 117) *She ascended the slope with the <u>deftness</u> of a goat.*
- **imperceptibly** (im´ pər sep´ tə blē) *adv.* so slowly or slightly as to be barely noticeable (p. 118) *Fish nibbled <u>imperceptibly</u> at my bait.*

Games at Twilight

- **livid** (liv´ id) *adj.* discolored, as by a bruise; red with anger (p. 130) *Today, the bruise around his eye turned <u>livid</u>.*
- **defunct** (dē fuŋkt´) *adj.* no longer in use or existence; dead (p. 133) *The <u>defunct</u> computer gathered cobwebs.*
- **dogged** (dôg´ id) *adj.* stubborn (p. 135) *It took a day of <u>dogged</u> efforts to solve the puzzle.*

Short Story

Background

Before Computers In the 1950s, when this story takes place, there were no computers or photocopiers. To make copies, people used carbon paper—black-coated sheets that transferred written or typed marks onto blank paper below. Without a carbon copy, a lost document might be gone forever—a possibility the main character in this story dreads.

Connecting to the Literature

Reading/Writing Connection Living sometimes means taking chances. Some we regret; others we relish. In order to avoid losing an important document, the man in this story takes a chance based on a moment's impulse. List a few chances you have taken, such as trying out for a team or speaking up in class. Indicate which worked out well and which you regret. Use three of these words: *anticipate, challenge, initiate, maximize, minimize.*

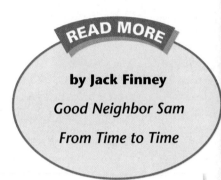

READ MORE

by Jack Finney

Good Neighbor Sam

From Time to Time

Meet the Author

Jack **Finney** (1911–1995)

While working at an advertising agency, Jack Finney dreamed of becoming a writer. He realized his dream when he entered his first short story in a contest sponsored by a magazine—and won!

Tales of Time Finney became especially well known for blending realistic and imaginary details into tales of time travel. In his popular works, the hero often escapes from the present into a simpler and calmer time in the past. However, Finney was happy to live in the present. "There's no past time I'd like to stay in," he said. "I want to stay here permanently."

Fast Facts

▶ Finney's novel *Invasion of the Body Snatchers* has been made into a movie three times.

▶ It took Finney twenty-five years to publish a sequel to his most popular work, *Time and Again.*

 **Go** ●**nline**
Author Link

For: More about the author
Visit: www.PHSchool.com
Web Code: eqe-9108

Contents of the Dead Man's Pocket

Jack Finney

At the little living-room desk Tom Benecke rolled two sheets of flimsy[1] and a heavier top sheet, carbon paper sandwiched between them, into his portable. *Interoffice Memo*, the top sheet was headed, and he typed tomorrow's date just below this; then he glanced at a creased yellow sheet, covered with his own handwriting, beside the typewriter. "Hot in here," he muttered to himself. Then, from the short hallway at his back, he heard the muffled clang of wire coat hangers in the bedroom closet, and at this reminder of what his wife was doing he thought: Hot, no— guilty conscience.

He got up, shoving his hands into the back pockets of his gray wash slacks, stepped to the living-room window beside the desk and stood breathing on the glass, watching the expanding circle of mist, staring down through the autumn night at Lexington Avenue, eleven stories below. He was a tall, lean, dark-haired young man in a pullover sweater, who looked as though he had played not foot-ball, probably, but basketball in college. Now he placed the heels of

---

1. flimsy (flimˊ zē) *n.* thin typing paper for making carbon copies. Carbon copies are created by placing carbon paper, a sheet coated with an inklike substance, between two pieces of typing paper.

his hands against the top edge of the lower window frame and shoved upward. But as usual the window didn't budge, and he had to lower his hands and then shoot them hard upward to jolt the window open a few inches. He dusted his hands, muttering.

But still he didn't begin his work. He crossed the room to the hallway entrance and, leaning against the doorjamb, hands shoved into his back pockets again, he called, "Clare?" When his wife answered, he said, "Sure you don't mind going alone?"

"No." Her voice was muffled, and he knew her head and shoulders were in the bedroom closet. Then the tap of her high heels sounded on the wood floor and she appeared at the end of the little hallway, wearing a slip, both hands raised to one ear, clipping on an earring. She smiled at him—a slender, very pretty girl with light brown, almost blonde, hair—her prettiness emphasized by the pleasant nature that showed in her face. "It's just that I hate you to miss this movie; you wanted to see it too."

"Yeah, I know." He ran his fingers through his hair. "Got to get this done though."

Literary Analysis
Conflict What internal conflict of Tom's does this paragraph show?

She nodded, accepting this. Then, glancing at the desk across the living room, she said, "You work too much, though, Tom—and too hard."

He smiled. "You won't mind though, will you, when the money comes rolling in and I'm known as the Boy Wizard of Wholesale Groceries?"

"I guess not." She smiled and turned back toward the bedroom.

At his desk again, Tom lighted a cigarette, then a few moments later as Clare appeared, dressed and ready to leave, he set it on the rim of the ash tray. "Just after seven," she said. "I can make the beginning of the first feature."

He walked to the front-door closet to help her on with her coat. He kissed her then and, for an instant, holding her close, smelling the perfume she had used, he was tempted to go with her; it was not actually true that he had to work tonight, though he very much wanted to. This was his own project, unannounced as yet in his office, and it could be postponed. But then they won't see it till Monday, he thought once again, and if I give it to the boss tomorrow he might read it over the weekend . . . "Have a good time," he said aloud. He gave his wife a little swat and opened the door for her, feeling the air from the building hallway, smelling faintly of floor wax, stream gently past his face.

He watched her walk down the hall, flicked a hand in response as she waved, and then he started to close the door, but it resisted for a moment. As the door opening narrowed, the current of warm

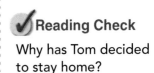

Reading Check

Why has Tom decided to stay home?

air from the hallway, channeled through this smaller opening now, suddenly rushed past him with accelerated force. Behind him he heard the slap of the window curtains against the wall and the sound of paper fluttering from his desk, and he had to push to close the door.

Turning, he saw a sheet of white paper drifting to the floor in a series of arcs, and another sheet, yellow, moving toward the window, caught in the dying current flowing through the narrow opening. As he watched, the paper struck the bottom edge of the window and hung there for an instant, plastered against the glass and wood. Then as the moving air stilled completely, the curtains swinging back from the wall to hang free again, he saw the yellow sheet drop to the window ledge and slide over out of sight.

He ran across the room, grasped the bottom edge of the window and tugged, staring through the glass. He saw the yellow sheet, dimly now in the darkness outside, lying on the ornamental ledge a yard below the window. Even as he watched, it was moving, scraping slowly along the ledge, pushed by the breeze that pressed steadily against the building wall. He heaved on the window with all his strength and it shot open with a bang, the window weight rattling in the casing. But the paper was past his reach and, leaning out into the night, he watched it scud steadily along the ledge to the south, half plastered against the building wall. Above the muffled sound of the street traffic far below, he could hear the dry scrape of its movement, like a leaf on the pavement.

The living room of the next apartment to the south projected a yard or more farther out toward the street than this one; because of this the Beneckes paid seven and a half dollars less rent than their neighbors. And now the yellow sheet, sliding along the stone ledge, nearly invisible in the night, was stopped by the projecting blank wall of the next apartment. It lay motionless, then, in the corner formed by the two walls—a good five yards away, pressed firmly against the ornate corner ornament of the ledge, by the breeze that moved past Tom Benecke's face.

He knelt at the window and stared at the yellow paper for a full minute or more, waiting for it to move, to slide off the ledge and fall, hoping he could follow its course to the street, and then hurry down in the elevator and retrieve it. But it didn't move, and then he saw that the paper was caught firmly between a projection of the <u>convoluted</u> corner ornament and the ledge. He thought about the poker from the fireplace, then the broom, then the mop—discarding each thought as it occurred to him. There was nothing in the apartment long enough to reach that paper.

It was hard for him to understand that he actually had to abandon it—it was ridiculous—and he began to curse. Of all the papers

---

Reading Skill
Analyzing Cause and Effect Which key details explain why the paper drops out the window?

Literary Analysis
Conflict Explain how an external conflict here helps create suspense.

Vocabulary Builder
convoluted (kän′ və lo͞ot′ id) *adj.* intricate; twisted

on his desk, why did it have to be this one in particular! On four long Saturday afternoons he had stood in supermarkets counting the people who passed certain displays, and the results were scribbled on that yellow sheet. From stacks of trade publications, gone over page by page in snatched half hours at work and during evenings at home, he had copied facts, quotations, and figures onto that sheet. And he had carried it with him to the Public Library on Fifth Avenue, where he'd spent a dozen lunch hours and early evenings adding more. All were needed to support and lend authority to his idea for a new grocery-store display method; without them his idea was a mere opinion. And there they all lay, in his own improvised shorthand—countless hours of work—out there on the ledge.

For many seconds he believed he was going to abandon the yellow sheet, that there was nothing else to do. The work could be duplicated. But it would take two months, and the time to present this idea . . . was *now*, for use in the spring displays. He struck his fist on the window ledge. Then he shrugged. Even if his plan were adopted, he told himself, it wouldn't bring him a raise in pay—not immediately, anyway, or as a direct result. It won't bring me a promotion either, he argued—not of itself.

But just the same, and he couldn't escape the thought, this and other independent projects, some already done and others planned for the future, would gradually mark him out from the score of other young men in his company. They were the way to change from a name on the payroll to a name in the minds of the company officials. They were the beginning of the long, long climb to where he

▲ **Critical Viewing**
What dangers in Tom's situation does this image capture? **[Connect]**

Reading Skill
Analyzing Cause and Effect What might cause Tom to go after the paper?

✓**Reading Check**
What problem does Tom face?

◀ **Critical Viewing**
Explain how this photograph helps you understand Tom's feelings in the story. **[Relate]**

was determined to be, at the very top. And he knew he was going out there in the darkness, after the yellow sheet fifteen feet beyond his reach.

By a kind of instinct, he instantly began making his intention acceptable to himself by laughing at it. The mental picture of himself sidling along the ledge outside was absurd—it was actually comical—and he smiled. He imagined himself describing it; it would make a good story at the office and, it occurred to him, would add a special interest and importance to his memorandum, which would do it no harm at all.

To simply go out and get his paper was an easy task—he could be back here with it in less than two minutes—and he knew he wasn't deceiving himself. The ledge, he saw, measuring it with his eye, was about as wide as the length of his shoe, and perfectly flat. And every fifth row of brick in the face of the building, he remembered—leaning out, he verified this—was indented half an inch, enough for the tips of his fingers, enough to maintain balance easily. It occurred to him that if this ledge and wall were only a yard aboveground—as he knelt at the window staring out, this thought was the final confirmation of his intention—he could move along the ledge indefinitely.

On a sudden impulse, he got to his feet, walked to the front closet and took out an old tweed jacket; it would be cold outside. He put it on and buttoned it as he crossed the room rapidly toward the

Reading Skill
Analyzing Cause and Effect What effect does Tom hope the story of his adventure will have on listeners?

open window. In the back of his mind he knew he'd better hurry and get this over with before he thought too much, and at the window he didn't allow himself to hesitate.

He swung a leg over the sill, then felt for and found the ledge a yard below the window with his foot. Gripping the bottom of the window frame very tightly and carefully, he slowly ducked his head under it, feeling on his face the sudden change from the warm air of the room to the chill outside. With infinite care he brought out his other leg, his mind concentrating on what he was doing. Then he slowly stood erect. Most of the putty, dried out and brittle, had dropped off the bottom edging of the window frame, he found, and the flat wooden edging provided a good gripping surface, a half inch or more deep, for the tips of his fingers.

Now, balanced easily and firmly, he stood on the ledge outside in the slight, chill breeze, eleven stories above the street, staring into his own lighted apartment, odd and different-seeming now.

First his right hand, then his left, he carefully shifted his fingertip grip from the puttyless window edging to an indented row of bricks directly to his right. It was hard to take the first shuffling sideways step then—to make himself move—and the fear stirred in his stomach, but he did it, again by not allowing himself time to think. And now—with his chest, stomach, and the left side of his face pressed against the rough cold brick—his lighted apartment was suddenly gone, and it was much darker out here than he had thought.

Without pause he continued—right foot, left foot, right foot, left—his shoe soles shuffling and scraping along the rough stone, never lifting from it, fingers sliding along the exposed edging of brick. He moved on the balls of his feet, heels lifted slightly; the ledge was not quite as wide as he'd expected. But leaning slightly inward toward the face of the building and pressed against it, he could feel his balance firm and secure, and moving along the ledge was quite as easy as he had thought it would be. He could hear the buttons of his jacket scraping steadily along the rough bricks and feel them catch momentarily, tugging a little, at each mortared crack. He simply did not permit himself to look down, though the compulsion to do so never left him; nor did he allow himself actually to think. Mechanically—right foot, left foot, over and again—he shuffled along crabwise, watching the projecting wall ahead loom steadily closer . . .

Then he reached it, and, at the corner—he'd decided how he was going to pick up the paper—he lifted his right foot and placed it carefully on the ledge that ran along the projecting wall at a right

Literary Analysis
Conflict Name one internal and one external conflict in Tom's new situation.

Reading Check

Describe Tom's progress on the first part of his journey.

angle to the ledge on which his other foot rested. And now, facing the building, he stood in the corner formed by the two walls, one foot on the ledging of each, a hand on the shoulder-high indentation of each wall. His forehead was pressed directly into the corner against the cold bricks, and now he carefully lowered first one hand, then the other, perhaps a foot farther down, to the next indentation in the rows of bricks.

Very slowly, sliding his forehead down the trough of the brick corner and bending his knees, he lowered his body toward the paper lying between his outstretched feet. Again he lowered his fingerholds another foot and bent his knees still more, thigh muscles taut, his forehead sliding and bumping down the brick V. Half squatting now, he dropped his left hand to the next indentation and then slowly reached with his right hand toward the paper between his feet.

He couldn't quite touch it, and his knees now were pressed against the wall; he could bend them no farther. But by ducking his head another inch lower, the top of his head now pressed against the bricks, he lowered his right shoulder and his fingers had the paper by a corner, pulling it loose. At the same instant he saw, between his legs and far below, Lexington Avenue stretched out for miles ahead.

He saw, in that instant, the Loew's theater sign, blocks ahead past Fiftieth Street; the miles of traffic signals, all green now; the lights of cars and street lamps; countless neon signs; and the moving black dots of people. And a violent instantaneous explosion of absolute terror roared through him. For a motionless instant he saw himself externally—bent practically double, balanced on this narrow ledge, nearly half his body projecting out above the street far below—and he began to tremble violently, panic flaring through his mind and muscles, and he felt the blood rush from the surface of his skin.

In the fractional moment before horror paralyzed him, as he stared between his legs at that terrible length of street far beneath him, a fragment of his mind raised his body in a spasmodic jerk to an upright position again, but so violently that his head scraped hard against the wall, bouncing off it, and his body swayed outward to the knife edge of balance, and he very nearly plunged backward and fell. Then he was leaning far into the corner again, squeezing

▲ Critical Viewing
Contrast the movement the man in this image is making with Tom's method of moving along the ledge. **[Contrast]**

Reading Skill
Analyzing Cause and Effect What is the effect of Tom's glimpse of the avenue below?

and pushing into it, not only his face but his chest and stomach, his back arching; and his fingertips clung with all the pressure of his pulling arms to the shoulder-high half-inch indentation in the bricks.

He was more than trembling now; his whole body was racked with a violent shuddering beyond control, his eyes squeezed so tightly shut it was painful, though he was past awareness of that. His teeth were exposed in a frozen grimace, the strength draining like water from his knees and calves. It was extremely likely, he knew, that he would faint, to slump down along the wall, his face scraping, and then drop backward, a limp weight, out into nothing. And to save his life he concentrated on holding onto consciousness, drawing deliberate deep breaths of cold air into his lungs, fighting to keep his senses aware.

Then he knew that he would not faint, but he could neither stop shaking nor open his eyes. He stood where he was, breathing deeply, trying to hold back the terror of the glimpse he had had of what lay below him; and he knew he had made a mistake in not making himself stare down at the street, getting used to it and accepting it, when he had first stepped out onto the ledge.

It was impossible to walk back. He simply could not do it. He couldn't bring himself to make the slightest movement. The strength was gone from his legs; his shivering hands—numb, cold and desperately rigid—had lost all <u>deftness</u>; his easy ability to move and balance was gone. Within a step or two, if he tried to move, he knew that he would stumble clumsily and fall.

Seconds passed, with the chill faint wind pressing the side of his face, and he could hear the toned-down volume of the street traffic far beneath him. Again and again it slowed and then stopped, almost to silence; then presently, even this high, he would hear the click of the traffic signals and the subdued roar of the cars starting up again. During a lull in the street sounds, he called out. Then he was shouting "*Help!*" so loudly it rasped his throat. But he felt the steady pressure of the wind, moving between his face and the blank wall, snatch up his cries as he uttered them, and he knew they must sound directionless and distant. And he remembered how habitually, here in New York, he himself heard and ignored shouts in the night. If anyone heard him, there was no sign of it, and presently Tom Benecke knew he had to try moving; there was nothing else he could do.

Eyes squeezed shut, he watched scenes in his mind like scraps of motion-picture film—he could not stop them. He saw himself stumbling suddenly sideways as he crept along the ledge and saw his upper body arc outward, arms flailing. He saw a dangling

Literary Analysis
Conflict What internal conflict does Tom's external conflict cause?

Vocabulary Builder
deftness (deft′ nis) *n.* skillfulness

✔️**Reading Check**

What event introduces a new obstacle in Tom's journey?

shoestring caught between the ledge and the sole of his other shoe, saw a foot start to move, to be stopped with a jerk, and felt his balance leaving him. He saw himself falling with a terrible speed as his body revolved in the air, knees clutched tight to his chest, eyes squeezed shut, moaning softly.

Out of utter necessity, knowing that any of these thoughts might be reality in the very next seconds, he was slowly able to shut his mind against every thought but what he now began to do. With fear-soaked slowness, he slid his left foot an inch or two toward his own impossibly distant window. Then he slid the fingers of his shivering left hand a corresponding distance. For a moment he could not bring himself to lift his right foot from one ledge to the other; then he did it, and became aware of the harsh exhalation of air from his throat and realized that he was panting. As his right hand, then, began to slide along the brick edging, he was astonished to feel the yellow paper pressed to the bricks underneath his stiff fingers, and he uttered a terrible, abrupt bark that might have been a laugh or a moan. He opened his mouth and took the paper in his teeth, pulling it out from under his fingers.

By a kind of trick—by concentrating his entire mind on first his left foot, then his left hand, then the other foot, then the other hand—he was able to move, almost <u>imperceptibly</u>, trembling steadily, very nearly without thought. But he could feel the terrible strength of the pent-up horror on just the other side of the flimsy barrier he had erected in his mind; and he knew that if it broke through he would lose this thin artificial control of his body.

During one slow step he tried keeping his eyes closed; it made him feel safer, shutting him off a little from the fearful reality of where he was. Then a sudden rush of giddiness swept over him and he had to open his eyes wide, staring sideways at the cold rough brick and angled lines of mortar, his cheek tight against the building. He kept his eyes open then, knowing that if he once let them flick outward, to stare for an instant at the lighted windows across the street, he would be past help.

He didn't know how many dozens of tiny sidling steps he had taken, his chest, belly, and face pressed to the wall; but he knew the slender hold he was keeping on his mind and body was going to break. He had a sudden mental picture of his apartment on just the other side of this wall—warm, cheerful, incredibly spacious. And he saw himself striding through it, lying down on the floor on his back, arms spread wide, reveling in its unbelievable security. The impossible remoteness of this utter safety, the contrast between it and where he now stood, was more than he could bear. And the barrier

Vocabulary Builder
imperceptibly (im´ pər sep´ tə blē) *adv.* so slowly or slightly as to be barely noticeable

broke then, and the fear of the awful height he stood on coursed through his nerves and muscles.

A fraction of his mind knew he was going to fall, and he began taking rapid blind steps with no feeling of what he was doing, sidling with a clumsy desperate swiftness, fingers scrabbling along the brick, almost hopelessly resigned to the sudden backward pull and swift motion outward and down. Then his moving left hand slid onto not brick but sheer emptiness, an impossible gap in the face of the wall, and he stumbled.

His right foot smashed into his left anklebone; he staggered sideways, began falling, and the claw of his hand cracked against glass and wood, slid down it, and his fingertips were pressed hard on the puttyless edging of his window. His right hand smacked gropingly beside it as he fell to his knees; and, under the full weight and direct downward pull of his sagging body, the open window dropped shudderingly in its frame till it closed and his wrists struck the sill and were jarred off.

For a single moment he knelt, knee bones against stone on the very edge of the ledge, body swaying and touching nowhere else, fighting for balance. Then he lost it, his shoulders plunging backward, and he flung his arms forward, his hands smashing against the window casing on either side; and—his body moving backward—his fingers clutched the narrow wood stripping of the upper pane.

For an instant he hung suspended between balance and falling, his fingertips pressed onto the quarter-inch wood strips. Then, with utmost delicacy, with a focused concentration of all his senses, he increased even further the strain on his fingertips hooked to these slim edgings of wood. Elbows slowly bending, he began to draw the full weight of his upper body forward, knowing that the instant his fingers slipped off these quarter-inch strips he'd plunge backward and be falling. Elbows imperceptibly bending, body shaking with the strain, the sweat starting from his forehead in great sudden drops, he pulled, his entire being and thought concentrated in his fingertips. Then suddenly, the strain slackened and ended, his chest touching the window sill, and he was kneeling on the ledge, his forehead pressed to the glass of the closed window.

Dropping his palms to the sill, he stared into his living room—at the red-brown davenport[2] across the room, and a magazine he had left there; at the pictures on the walls and the gray rug; the entrance to the hallway; and at his papers, typewriter and desk, not two feet from his nose. A movement from his desk caught his eye

---

2. **davenport** (dav´ ən pôrt´) *n.* large couch.

Literary Analysis
Conflict Why does this lengthy description at a moment of excitement add to the suspense?

✔ **Reading Check**

What happens when Tom reaches the window?

and he saw that it was a thin curl of blue smoke; his cigarette, the ash long, was still burning in the ash tray where he'd left it—this was past all belief—only a few minutes before.

His head moved, and in faint reflection from the glass before him he saw the yellow paper clenched in his front teeth. Lifting a hand from the sill he took it from his mouth; the moistened corner parted from the paper, and he spat it out.

For a moment, in the light from the living room, he stared wonderingly at the yellow sheet in his hand and then crushed it into the side pocket of his jacket.

He couldn't open the window. It had been pulled not completely closed, but its lower edge was below the level of the outside sill; there was no room to get his fingers underneath it. Between the upper sash and the lower was a gap not wide enough—reaching up, he tried—to get his fingers into; he couldn't push it open. The upper window panel, he knew from long experience, was impossible to move, frozen tight with dried paint.

Very carefully observing his balance, the fingertips of his left hand again hooked to the narrow stripping of the window casing, he drew back his right hand, palm facing the glass, and then struck the glass with the heel of his hand.

His arm rebounded from the pane, his body tottering, and he knew he didn't dare strike a harder blow.

But in the security and relief of his new position, he simply smiled; with only a sheet of glass between him and the room just before him, it was not possible that there wasn't a way past it. Eyes narrowing, he thought for a few moments about what to do. Then his eyes widened, for nothing occurred to him. But still he felt calm: the trembling, he realized, had stopped. At the back of his mind there still lay the thought that once he was again in his home, he could give release to his feelings. He actually *would* lie on the floor, rolling, clenching tufts of the rug in his hands. He would literally run across the room, free to move as he liked, jumping on the floor, testing and reveling in its absolute security, letting the relief flood through him, draining the fear from his mind and body. His yearning for this was astonishingly intense, and somehow he understood that he had better keep this feeling at bay.

He took a half dollar from his pocket and struck it against the pane, but without any hope that the glass would break and with very little disappointment when it did not. After a few moments of thought he drew his leg up onto the ledge and picked loose the knot of his shoelace. He slipped off the shoe and, holding it across the instep, drew back his arm as far as he dared and struck the leather

Reading Skill
Analyzing Cause and Effect What key detail from the beginning of the story helps you understand the cause of Tom's situation?

Literary Analysis
Conflict What new internal conflict does Tom experience?

heel against the glass. The pane rattled, but he knew he'd been a long way from breaking it. His foot was cold and he slipped the shoe back on. He shouted again experimentally, and then once more, but there was no answer.

The realization suddenly struck him that he might have to wait here till Clare came home, and for a moment the thought was funny. He could see Clare opening the front door, withdrawing her key from the lock, closing the door behind her, and then glancing up to see him crouched on the other side of the window. He could see her rush across the room, face astounded and frightened, and hear himself shouting instructions: "Never mind how I got here! Just open the wind—" She couldn't open it, he remembered, she'd never been able to; she'd always had to call him. She'd have to get the building superintendent or a neighbor, and he pictured himself smiling and answering their questions as he climbed in. "I just wanted to get a breath of fresh air, so—"

He couldn't possibly wait here till Clare came home. It was the second feature she'd wanted to see, and she'd left in time to see the first. She'd be another three hours or—He glanced at his watch; Clare had been gone eight minutes. It wasn't possible, but only eight minutes ago he had kissed his wife goodbye. She wasn't even at the theater yet!

It would be four hours before she could possibly be home, and he tried to picture himself kneeling out here, fingertips hooked to these narrow strippings, while first one movie, preceded by a slow listing of credits, began, developed, reached its climax and then finally ended. There'd be a newsreel next, maybe, and then an animated cartoon, and then interminable scenes from coming pictures. And then, once more, the beginning of a full-length picture—while all the time he hung out here in the night.

He might possibly get to his feet, but he was afraid to try. Already his legs were cramped, his thigh muscles tired; his knees hurt, his feet felt numb and his hands were stiff. He couldn't possibly stay out here for four hours, or anywhere near it. Long before that his legs and arms would give out; he would be forced to try changing his position often—stiffly, clumsily, his coordination and

Literature in Context

Science Connection

Physics Tom is on the ledge with only a pane of glass between him and safety. Yet he is reluctant to hit the window to break the glass—with good reason. Tom understands Newton's third law of motion: for every action, there is an equal and opposite reaction. For example, the *action* of throwing a ball against a wall has the opposite *reaction* of the ball bouncing away from the wall.

Connect to the Literature

What opposite reaction does Tom fear will result if he hits the glass hard but does not break it?

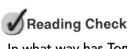

Reading Check

In what way has Tom's situation improved? In what way does it remain the same?

strength gone—and he would fall. Quite realistically, he knew that he would fall; no one could stay out here on this ledge for four hours.

A dozen windows in the apartment building across the street were lighted. Looking over his shoulder, he could see the top of a man's head behind the newspaper he was reading; in another window he saw the blue-gray flicker of a television screen. No more than twenty-odd yards from his back were scores of people, and if just one of them would walk idly to his window and glance out. . . . For some moments he stared over his shoulder at the lighted rectangles, waiting. But no one appeared. The man reading his paper turned a page and then continued his reading. A figure passed another of the windows and was immediately gone.

In the inside pocket of his jacket he found a little sheaf of papers, and he pulled one out and looked at it in the light from the living room. It was an old letter, an advertisement of some sort; his name and address, in purple ink, were on a label pasted to the envelope. Gripping one end of the envelope in his teeth, he twisted it into a tight curl. From his shirt pocket he brought out a book of matches. He didn't dare let go the casing with both hands, but, with the twist of paper in his teeth, he opened the matchbook with his free hand; then he bent one of the matches in two without tearing it from the folder, its red-tipped end now touching the striking surface. With his thumb, he rubbed the red tip across the striking area.

He did it again, then again, and still again, pressing harder each time, and the match suddenly flared, burning his thumb. But he kept it alight, cupping the matchbook in his hand and shielding it with his body. He held the flame to the paper in his mouth till it caught. Then he snuffed out the match flame with his thumb and forefinger, careless of the burn, and replaced the book in his pocket. Taking the paper twist in his hand, he held it flame down, watching the flame crawl up the paper, till it flared bright. Then he held it behind him over the street, moving it from side to side, watching it over his shoulder, the flame flickering and guttering in the wind.

There were three letters in his pocket and he lighted each of them, holding each till the flame touched his hand and then dropping it to the street below. At one point, watching over his shoulder while the last of the letters burned, he saw the man across the street put down his paper and stand—even seeming, to Tom, to glance

▲ **Critical Viewing**
What makes a match such as this one a good choice as a distress signal? What makes it a poor choice? **[Analyze]**

toward his window. But when he moved, it was only to walk across the room and disappear from sight.

There were a dozen coins in Tom Benecke's pocket and he dropped them, three or four at a time. But if they struck anyone, or if anyone noticed their falling, no one connected them with their source, and no one glanced upward.

His arms had begun to tremble from the steady strain of clinging to this narrow perch, and he did not know what to do now and was terribly frightened. Clinging to the window stripping with one hand, he again searched his pockets. But now—he had left his wallet on his dresser when he'd changed clothes—there was nothing left but the yellow sheet. It occurred to him irrelevantly that his death on the sidewalk below would be an eternal mystery; the window closed—why, how, and from where could he have fallen? No one would be able to identify his body for a time, either—the thought was somehow unbearable and increased his fear. All they'd find in his pockets would be the yellow sheet. *Contents of the dead man's pockets,* he thought, *one sheet of paper bearing penciled notations—incomprehensible.*

He understood fully that he might actually be going to die; his arms, maintaining his balance on the ledge, were trembling steadily now. And it occurred to him then with all the force of a revelation that, if he fell, all he was ever going to have out of life he would then, abruptly, have had. Nothing, then, could ever be changed; and nothing more—no least experience or pleasure—could ever be added to his life. He wished, then, that he had not allowed his wife to go off by herself tonight—and on similar nights. He thought of all the evenings he had spent away from her, working; and he regretted them. He thought wonderingly of his fierce ambition and of the direction his life had taken; he thought of the hours he'd spent by himself, filling the yellow sheet that had brought him out here. *Contents of the dead man's pockets,* he thought with sudden fierce anger, *a wasted life.*

He was simply not going to cling here till he slipped and fell; he told himself that now. There was one last thing he could try; he had been aware of it for some moments, refusing to think about it, but now he faced it. Kneeling here on the ledge, the fingertips of one hand pressed to the narrow strip of wood, he could, he knew, draw his other hand back a yard perhaps, fist clenched tight, doing it very slowly till he sensed the outer limit of balance, then, as hard as he was able from the distance, he could drive his fist forward against the glass. If it broke, his fist smashing through, he was safe; he might cut himself badly, and probably would, but with his arm inside the room, he would be secure. But if the glass did not break,

Reading Skill
Analyzing Cause and Effect What effect does Tom hope the burning papers and the falling coins will have?

Reading Skill
Analyzing Cause and Effect What key details explain why Tom grows angry?

✔ **Reading Check**

Why does Tom have only one option left?

the rebound, flinging his arm back, would topple him off the ledge. He was certain of that.

He tested his plan. The fingers of his left hand clawlike on the little stripping, he drew back his other fist until his body began teetering backward. But he had no leverage now—he could feel that there would be no force to his swing—and he moved his fist slowly forward till he rocked forward on his knees again and could sense that his swing would carry its greatest force. Glancing down, however, measuring the distance from his fist to the glass, he saw that it was less than two feet.

It occurred to him that he could raise his arm over his head, to bring it down against the glass. But, experimenting in slow motion, he knew it would be an awkward . . . blow without the force of a driving punch, and not nearly enough to break the glass.

Facing the window, he had to drive a blow from the shoulder, he knew now, at a distance of less than two feet; and he did not know whether it would break through the heavy glass. It might; he could picture it happening, he could feel it in the nerves of his arm. And it might not; he could feel that too—feel his fist striking this glass and being instantaneously flung back by the unbreaking pane, feel the fingers of his other hand breaking loose, nails scraping along the casing as he fell.

He waited, arm drawn back, fist balled, but in no hurry to strike; this pause, he knew, might be an extension of his life. And to live even a few seconds longer, he felt, even out here on this ledge in the night, was infinitely better than to die a moment earlier than he had to. His arm grew tired, and he brought it down and rested it.

Then he knew that it was time to make the attempt. He could not kneel here hesitating indefinitely till he lost all courage to act, waiting till he slipped off the ledge. Again he drew back his arm, knowing this time that he would not bring it down till he struck. His elbow protruding over Lexington Avenue far below, the fingers of his other hand pressed down bloodlessly tight against the narrow stripping, he waited, feeling the sick tenseness and terrible excitement building. It grew and swelled toward the moment of action, his nerves tautening. He thought of Clare—just a wordless, yearning thought—and then drew his arm back just a bit more, fist so tight his fingers pained him, and knowing he was going to do it. Then with full power, with every last scrap of strength he could bring to bear, he shot his arm forward toward the glass, and he said, "*Clare!*"

He heard the sound, felt the blow, felt himself falling forward, and his hand closed on the living-room curtains, the shards and fragments of glass showering onto the floor. And then, kneeling

Literary Analysis
Conflict Why do Tom's imaginings of what might happen build suspense?

there on the ledge, an arm thrust into the room up to the shoulder, he began picking away the protruding slivers and great wedges of glass from the window frame, tossing them in onto the rug. And, as he grasped the edges of the empty window frame and climbed into his home, he was grinning in triumph.

He did not lie down on the floor or run through the apartment, as he had promised himself; even in the first few moments it seemed to him natural and normal that he should be where he was. He simply turned to his desk, pulled the crumpled yellow sheet from his pocket and laid it down where it had been, smoothing it out; then he absently laid a pencil across it to weight it down. He shook his head wonderingly, and turned to walk toward the closet.

There he got out his topcoat and hat and, without waiting to put them on, opened the front door and stepped out, to go find his wife. He turned to pull the door closed and the warm air from the hall rushed through the narrow opening again. As he saw the yellow paper, the pencil flying, scooped off the desk and, unimpeded by the glassless window, sail out into the night and out of his life, Tom Benecke burst into laughter and then closed the door behind him.

Literary Analysis
Conflict Name one conflict that is settled in the story's resolution.

▼ Critical Viewing
After his adventure, how might Tom view the scene in this image? Explain. **[Connect]**

Apply the Skills

Contents of the Dead Man's Pocket

Thinking About the Selection

1. **Respond:** Which of Tom's choices did you think were good? Which did you think were foolish? Explain.
2. **(a) Recall:** What document is Tom working on at the start of the story? **(b) Analyze Cause and Effect:** What long-term goals does he hope to achieve by this work? **(c) Draw Conclusions:** What does his plan tell you about his character?
3. **(a) Recall:** Why does Tom go out on the ledge? **(b) Connect:** Is his decision surprising, given his character? Explain.
4. **(a) Compare and Contrast:** Contrast Tom's attitude toward life at the beginning of the story with his attitude at the end. **(b) Infer:** What causes his attitude to change? **(c) Speculate:** What changes, if any, will Tom make as a result of this experience?
5. **(a) Evaluate:** Do you think that a movie based on Finney's story would be as effective as the story itself? Why or why not? **(b) Discuss:** Share and discuss responses with a partner. Then, discuss whether your partner's response has changed or expanded your own thinking.

Literary Analysis

6. **(a)** What is the main **external conflict** in this story? Explain. **(b)** What is the main **internal conflict** in the story? Explain.
7. **(a)** Identify a moment in the story that had great **suspense**. **(b)** Which conflict helps to create this suspense? Explain.
8. **(a)** How are Tom's conflicts resolved? **(b)** Describe an alternative **resolution** the story might have had.

Reading Skill

9. **(a)** In your opinion, which single **cause** sets the story's cause-and-effect chain in motion? **(b)** Identify two **effects**—one short-term and one long-term—of this event. Use a diagram like this one to record your answer.

| Cause | Cause/Effect | Effect |

10. **(a)** Identify a key detail early in the story that becomes important later on. **(b)** Analyze the causes and effects linked to this detail.

QuickReview

Story at a Glance
An ambitious young businessman takes a big risk to retrieve an important document.

Go **O**nline
——Assessment
For: Self-test
Visit: www.PHSchool.com
Web Code: eqa-6108

Conflict: a struggle between two opposing forces; a conflict may be *external* or *internal*

Resolution: the stage of a plot in which a conflict is settled or resolved

Suspense: a feeling of intense anticipation about the outcome of events

Cause: an event, an action, or a situation that leads to particular events or circumstances

Effect: the result of an event or circumstance

Vocabulary Builder

Practice Answer each question. Explain your responses.

1. Should directions for dealing with an emergency be <u>convoluted</u>?
2. Would you want a surgeon to display <u>deftness</u>?
3. If the temperature fell <u>imperceptibly</u>, would most people notice?

Adding Words to Your Vocabulary An **antonym** is a word that means the opposite of another word. Use a thesaurus to find one antonym for each of the underlined words above. Then, use each antonym correctly in a sentence. (For more on using a thesaurus, see page R7.)

Writing

"Contents of the Dead Man's Pocket" ends with an **irony**—a strong contrast between a character's efforts and what actually happens. Write an **anecdote**, or brief story, with an ironic ending.

- Pick a character, a conflict, an expected end, and a twist.
- As you draft, include details to set up the expected outcome, but include hints that could explain an unexpected one.
- Finally, resolve the conflict with your twist ending.

Ask a classmate to read a draft and tell you how effective your ending is. Consider revising based on your reader's feedback.

For *Grammar, Vocabulary,* and *Assessment,* see **Build Language Skills,** pages 140–141.

Extend Your Learning

Listening and Speaking With other students, form a **problem-solving group** to find solutions to Tom's problem.
- Discuss strategies, supporting your ideas with reasons and examples.
- Respond to one another respectfully, and ask for clarification of any points you do not understand.

Share the results of your discussion with the rest of the class.

Research and Technology Create an **outline for a multimedia report** on the invention of high-rise buildings. Then, present your outline to a small group. Watch for confusion in your audience and clarify points as needed. Afterward, summarize your plan for a report. Ask for questions or comments from the group.

Background

India's Hot Season "Games at Twilight" is set in India during the 1940s—a time and a place in which air conditioning is unknown. From the story's first sentence, you can almost feel the heat of India's hot season rising off the page. The hot season is one of three main south Asian seasons. Falling between the wet season and the cool season, the hot season lasts from early March to mid-June.

Connecting to the Literature

Reading/Writing Connection The heat in this story mirrors the intense feelings of Ravi, its main character. Ravi tries to gain the respect of the older children by winning a game. Describe an older child whom you once looked up to. Use at least three of these words: *appreciate, contrast, differentiate, identify.*

Review

For **Literary Analysis, Reading Skill,** and **Vocabulary Builder,** see page 108.

READ MORE

by Anita Desai
Fire on the Mountain
Baumgartner's Bombay

Meet the Author

Anita **Desai** (b. 1937)

Anita Desai was born in India to a German mother and an Indian father. As a child, she learned German, Hindi, and English. Today, Desai writes in English and is widely regarded as one of India's foremost novelists.

Family and Familiarity Desai's stories are often about the relationships among family members—in the words of one critic, "the tug and pull of Indian family life." Desai has been praised for her ability to create vivid portraits of her characters and for her powerful images.

Fast Facts

▶ Anita Desai published her first story at the age of nine.
▶ In 1993, Desai became the first professor of writing at Massachusetts Institute of Technology (MIT) in more than twenty years.

Go Online
Author Link

For: More on the author
Visit: www.PHSchool.com
Web Code: eqe-9109

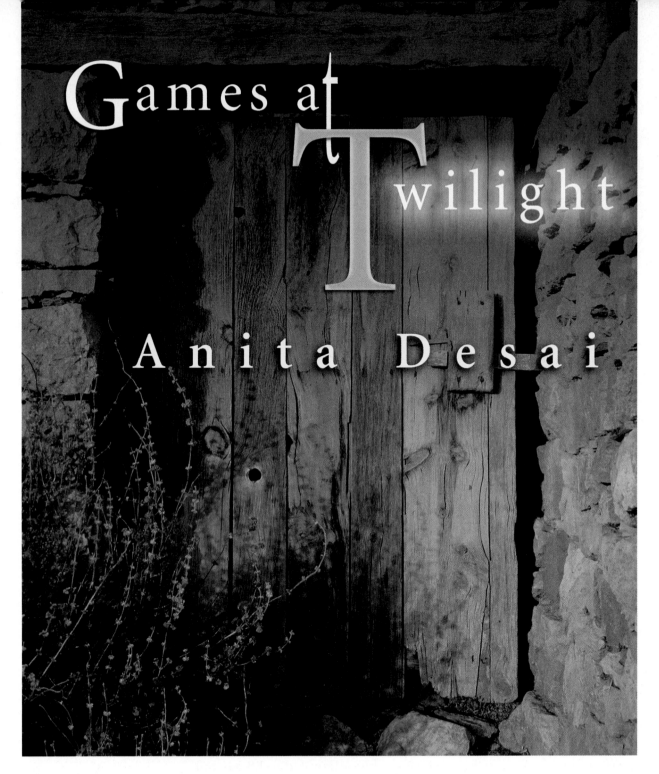

Games at Twilight

Anita Desai

It was still too hot to play outdoors. They had had their tea, they
had been washed and had their hair brushed, and after the long
day of confinement in the house that was not cool but at least a
protection from the sun, the children strained to get out. Their faces
were red and bloated with the effort, but their mother would not
open the door, everything was still curtained and shuttered in a way

that stifled the children, made them feel that their lungs were stuffed with cotton wool and their noses with dust and if they didn't burst out into the light and see the sun and feel the air, they would choke.

"Please, Ma, please," they begged. "We'll play in the veranda and porch—we won't go a step out of the porch."

"You will, I know you will, and then—"

"No—we won't, we won't," they wailed so horrendously that she actually let down the bolt of the front door so that they burst out like seeds from a crackling, over-ripe pod into the veranda, with such wild, maniacal yells that she retreated to her bath and the shower of talcum powder and the fresh sari[1] that were to help her face the summer evening.

They faced the afternoon. It was too hot. Too bright. The white walls of the veranda glared stridently in the sun. The bougainvillea hung about it, purple and magenta, in <u>livid</u> balloons. The garden outside was like a tray made of beaten brass, flattened out on the red gravel and the stony soil in all shades of metal—aluminum, tin, copper and brass. No life stirred at this arid time of day—the birds still drooped, like dead fruit, in the papery tents of the trees; some squirrels lay limp on the wet earth under the garden tap. The outdoor dog lay stretched as if dead on the veranda mat, his paws and ears and tail all reaching out like dying travelers in search of water. He rolled his eyes at the children—two white marbles rolling in the purple sockets, begging for sympathy—and attempted to lift his tail in a wag but could not. It only twitched and lay still.

Then, perhaps roused by the shrieks of the children, a band of parrots suddenly fell out of the eucalyptus tree, tumbled frantically

---

1. sari (sä´ rē) *n.* a long piece of cloth wrapped around the body, forming a skirt and draped over one shoulder; the main garment of Hindu women.

in the still, sizzling air, then sorted themselves out into battle formation and streaked away across the white sky.

The children, too, felt released. They too began tumbling, shoving, pushing against each other, frantic to start. Start what? Start their business. The business of the children's day which is—play.

"Let's play hide-and-seek."

"Who'll be It?"

"You be It."

"Why should I? You be—"

"You're the eldest—"

"That doesn't mean—"

The shoves became harder. Some kicked out. The motherly Mira intervened. She pulled the boys roughly apart. There was a tearing sound of cloth but it was lost in the heavy panting and angry grumbling and no one paid attention to the small sleeve hanging loosely off a shoulder.

"Make a circle, make a circle!" she shouted, firmly pulling and pushing till a kind of vague circle was formed. "Now clap!" she roared and, clapping, they all chanted in melancholy unison: "Dip, dip, dip—my blue ship—" and every now and then one or the other saw he was safe by the way his hands fell at the crucial moment—palm on palm, or back of hand on palm—and dropped out of the circle with a yell and a jump of relief and jubilation.

Raghu was It. He started to protest, to cry "You cheated—Mira cheated—Anu cheated—" but it was too late, the others had all already streaked away. There was no one to hear when he called out, "Only in the veranda—the porch—Ma said—Ma *said* to stay in the porch!" No one had stopped to listen, all he saw were their brown legs flashing through the dusty shrubs, scrambling up brick walls, leaping over compost heaps and hedges, and then the porch stood empty in the purple shade of the bougainvillea and the garden

▲ **Critical Viewing**
Contrast the time of day in this image with the time of day at the beginning of the story. **[Contrast]**

Reading Skill
Analyzing Cause and Effect What key details suggest that the children use this rhyming game to choose who will be "it"?

☑ **Reading Check**

What game do the children decide to play?

was as empty as before; even the limp squirrels had whisked away, leaving everything gleaming, brassy and bare.

Only small Manu suddenly reappeared, as if he had dropped out of an invisible cloud or from a bird's claws, and stood for a moment in the center of the yellow lawn, chewing his finger and near to tears as he heard Raghu shouting, with his head pressed against the veranda wall, "Eighty-three, eighty-five, eighty-nine, ninety . . ." and then made off in a panic, half of him wanting to fly north, the other half counseling south. Raghu turned just in time to see the flash of his white shorts and the uncertain skittering of his red sandals, and charged after him with such a bloodcurdling yell that Manu stumbled over the hosepipe, fell into its rubber coils and lay there weeping, "I won't be It—you have to find them all—all—All!"

"I know I have to, idiot," Raghu said, superciliously[2] kicking him with his toe. "You're dead," he said with satisfaction, licking the beads of perspiration off his upper lip, and then stalked off in search of worthier prey, whistling spiritedly so that the hiders should hear and tremble.

Ravi heard the whistling and picked his nose in a panic, trying to find comfort by burrowing the finger deep—deep into that soft tunnel. He felt himself too exposed, sitting on an upturned flower pot behind the garage. Where could he burrow? He could run around the garage if he heard Raghu come—around and around and around—but he hadn't much faith in his short legs when matched against Raghu's long, hefty, hairy footballer legs. Ravi had a frightening glimpse of them as Raghu combed the hedge of crotons and hibiscus, trampling delicate ferns underfoot as he did so. Ravi looked about him desperately, swallowing a small ball of snot in his fear.

The garage was locked with a great heavy lock to which the driver had the key in his room, hanging from a nail on the wall under his work-shirt. Ravi had peeped in and seen him still sprawling on his string-cot in his vest and striped underpants, the hair on his chest and the hair in his nose shaking with the vibrations of his phlegm-obstructed snores. Ravi had wished he were tall enough, big enough to reach the key on the nail, but it was impossible, beyond his reach for years to come. He had sidled away and sat dejectedly on the flower pot. That at least was cut to his own size.

But next to the garage was another shed with a big green door. Also locked. No one even knew who had the key to the lock. That shed wasn't opened more than once a year when Ma turned out all

▶ **Critical Viewing**
What might Ravi find in a shed like the one shown in the photograph? **[Speculate]**

Literary Analysis
Conflict In what way does this description of Ravi's conflict add suspense?

---

2. superciliously (sōō´ pər sil´ ē əs lē) *adv.* haughtily; in a manner expressing pride in oneself and scorn for the other person.

the old broken bits of furniture and rolls of matting and leaking buckets, and the white ant hills were broken and swept away and Flit sprayed into the spider webs and rat holes so that the whole operation was like the looting of a poor, ruined and conquered city. The green leaves of the door sagged. They were nearly off their rusty hinges. The hinges were large and made a small gap between the door and the walls—only just large enough for rats, dogs, and, possibly, Ravi to slip through.

Ravi had never cared to enter such a dark and depressing mortuary of <u>defunct</u> household goods seething with such unspeakable and alarming animal life but, as Raghu's whistling grew angrier and sharper and his crashing and storming in the hedge wilder, Ravi suddenly slipped off the flower pot and through the crack and was

Vocabulary Builder
defunct (dē funkt´)
adj. no longer in use
or existence; dead

 **Reading Check**

Where does Ravi
decide to hide?

gone. He chuckled aloud with astonishment at his own temerity[3] so that Raghu came out of the hedge, stood silent with his hands on his hips, listening, and finally shouted "I heard you! I'm coming! *Got you*—" and came charging round the garage only to find the upturned flower pot, the yellow dust, the crawling of white ants in a mud-hill against the closed shed door—nothing. Snarling, he bent to pick up a stick and went off, whacking it against the garage and shed walls as if to beat out his prey.

Ravi shook, then shivered with delight, with self-congratulation. Also with fear. It was dark, spooky in the shed. It had a muffled smell, as of graves. Ravi had once got locked into the linen cupboard and sat there weeping for half an hour before he was rescued. But at least that had been a familiar place, and even smelled pleasantly of starch, laundry and, reassuringly, of his mother. But the shed smelled of rats, ant hills, dust and spider webs. Also of less definable, less recognizable horrors. And it was dark. Except for the white-hot cracks along the door, there was no light. The roof was very low. Although Ravi was small, he felt as if he could reach up and touch it with his finger tips. But he didn't stretch. He hunched himself into a ball so as not to bump into anything, touch or feel anything. What might there not be to touch him and feel him as he stood there, trying to see in the dark? Something cold, or slimy— like a snake. Snakes! He leapt up as Raghu whacked the wall with his stick—then quickly realizing what it was, felt almost relieved to hear Raghu, hear his stick. It made him feel protected.

But Raghu soon moved away. There wasn't a sound once his footsteps had gone around the garage and disappeared. Ravi stood frozen inside the shed. Then he shivered all over. Something had tickled the back of his neck. It took him a while to pick up the courage to lift his hand and explore. It was an insect—perhaps a spider—exploring *him*. He squashed it and wondered how many more creatures were watching him, waiting to reach out and touch him, the stranger.

There was nothing now. After standing in that position—his hand still on his neck, feeling the wet splodge of the squashed spider gradually dry—for minutes, hours, his legs began to tremble with the effort, the inaction. By now he could see enough in the dark to make out the large solid shapes of old wardrobes, broken buckets and bedsteads piled on top of each other around him. He recognized an old bathtub—patches of enamel glimmered at him and at last he lowered himself onto its edge.

He contemplated slipping out of the shed and into the fray. He wondered if it would not be better to be captured by Raghu and be

---

3. temerity (tə mer´ ə tē) *n.* recklessness; foolish boldness

returned to the milling crowd as long as he could be in the sun, the light, the free spaces of the garden and the familiarity of his brothers, sisters and cousins. It would be evening soon. Their games would become legitimate. The parents would sit out on the lawn on cane basket chairs and watch them as they tore around the garden or gathered in knots to share a loot of mulberries or black, teeth-splitting *jamun* from the garden trees. The gardener would fix the hosepipe to the water tap and water would fall lavishly through the air to the ground, soaking the dry yellow grass and the red gravel and arousing the sweet, the intoxicating scent of water on dry earth—that loveliest scent in the world. Ravi sniffed for a whiff of it. He half-rose from the bathtub, then heard the despairing scream of one of the girls as Raghu bore down upon her. There was the sound of a crash, and of rolling about in the bushes, the shrubs, then screams and accusing sobs of, "I touched the den—" "You did not—" "I did—" "You liar, you did *not*" and then a fading away and silence again.

Ravi sat back on the harsh edge of the tub, deciding to hold out a bit longer. What fun if they were all found and caught—he alone left unconquered! He had never known that sensation. Nothing more wonderful had ever happened to him than being taken out by an uncle and bought a whole slab of chocolate all to himself, or being flung into the soda-man's pony cart and driven up to the gate by the friendly driver with the red beard and pointed ears. To defeat Raghu—that hirsute,[4] hoarse-voiced football champion—and to be the winner in a circle of older, bigger, luckier children—that would be thrilling beyond imagination. He hugged his knees together and smiled to himself almost shyly at the thought of so much victory, such laurels.[5]

There he sat smiling, knocking his heels against the bathtub, now and then getting up and going to the door to put his ear to the broad crack and listening for sounds of the game, the pursuer and the pursued, and then returning to his seat with the <u>dogged</u> determination of the true winner, a breaker of records, a champion.

It grew darker in the shed as the light at the door grew softer, fuzzier, turned to a kind of crumbling yellow pollen that turned to yellow fur, blue fur, gray fur. Evening. Twilight. The sound of water gushing, falling. The scent of earth receiving water, slaking its thirst in great gulps and releasing that green scent of freshness, coolness. Through the crack Ravi saw the long purple shadows of the shed and the garage lying still across the yard. Beyond that, the white walls of the house. The bougainvillea had lost its lividity, hung in

---

4. hirsute (hʉr′ sōōt′) *adj.* hairy.

5. laurels (lôr′ əlz) *n.* leaves of the laurel tree, worn in a crown as an ancient symbol of victory in a contest.

Vocabulary Builder
dogged (dôg′ id) *adj.* stubborn

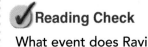Reading Check

What event does Ravi look forward to?

dark bundles that quaked and twittered and seethed with masses of homing sparrows. The lawn was shut off from his view. Could he hear the children's voices? It seemed to him that he could. It seemed to him that he could hear them chanting, singing, laughing. But what about the game? What had happened? Could it be over? How could it when he was still not found?

It then occurred to him that he could have slipped out long ago, dashed across the yard to the veranda and touched the "den." It was necessary to do that to win. He had forgotten. He had only remembered the part of hiding and trying to elude the seeker. He had done that so successfully, his success had occupied him so wholly that he had quite forgotten that success had to be clinched by that final dash to victory and the ringing cry of "Den!"

With a whimper he burst through the crack, fell on his knees, got up and stumbled on stiff, benumbed legs across the shadowy yard, crying heartily by the time he reached the veranda so that when he flung himself at the white pillar and bawled, "Den! Den! Den!" his voice broke with rage and pity at the disgrace of it all and he felt himself flooded with tears and misery.

Out on the lawn, the children stopped chanting. They all turned to stare at him in amazement. Their faces were pale and triangular in the dusk. The trees and bushes around them stood inky and sepulchral,[6] spilling long shadows across them. They stared, wondering at his reappearance, his passion, his wild animal howling. Their mother rose from her basket chair and came toward him, worried, annoyed, saying, "Stop it, stop it, Ravi. Don't be a baby. Have you hurt yourself?" Seeing him attended to, the children went back to clasping their hands and chanting "The grass is green, the rose is red. . . ."

But Ravi would not let them. He tore himself out of his mother's grasp and pounded across the lawn into their midst, charging at them with his head lowered so that they scattered in surprise. "I won, I won, I won," he bawled, shaking his head so that the big tears flew. "Raghu didn't find me. I won, I won—"

It took them a minute to grasp what he was saying, even who he was. They had quite forgotten him. Raghu had found all the others long ago. There had been a fight about who was to be It next. It had

Literary Analysis
Conflict What new internal conflict does Ravi face?

6. **sepulchral** (sə pul´ krəl) *adj.* of the tomb; gloomy.

been so fierce that their mother had emerged from her bath and made them change to another game. Then they had played another and another. Broken mulberries from the tree and eaten them. Helped the driver wash the car when their father returned from work. Helped the gardener water the beds till he roared at them and swore he would complain to their parents. The parents had come out, taken up their positions on the cane chairs. They had begun to play again, sing and chant. All this time no one had remembered Ravi. Having disappeared from the scene, he had disappeared from their minds. Clean.

"Don't be a fool," Raghu said roughly, pushing him aside, and even Mira said, "Stop howling, Ravi. If you want to play, you can stand at the end of the line," and she put him there very firmly.

The game proceeded. Two pairs of arms reached up and met in an arc. The children trooped under it again and again in a lugubrious[7] circle, ducking their heads and intoning

"The grass is green,
The rose is red;
Remember me
When I am dead, dead, dead, dead . . ."

And the arc of thin arms trembled in the twilight, and the heads were bowed so sadly, and their feet tramped to that melancholy refrain so mournfully, so helplessly, that Ravi could not bear it. He would not follow them, he would not be included in this funereal game. He had wanted victory and triumph—not a funeral. But he had been forgotten, left out and he would not join them now. The ignominy[8] of being forgotten—how could he face it? He felt his heart go heavy and ache inside him unbearably. He lay down full length on the damp grass, crushing his face into it, no longer crying, silenced by a terrible sense of his insignificance.

---

7. **lugubrious** (lə gōō′ brē əs) *adj.* very sad, especially in an exaggerated or ridiculous way.
8. **ignominy** (ig′ nə min′ ē) *n.* shame and dishonor.

Reading Skill
Analyzing Cause and Effect What effect had Ravi hoped for in hiding so well? What effect has it actually caused?

Literary Analysis
Conflict Is the resolution of the story what Ravi wanted? Explain.

◀ **Critical Viewing** Contrast the feelings the children express in this image with Ravi's feelings at the end of the selection. **[Contrast]**

Apply the Skills

Games at Twilight

Thinking About the Selection

1. **Respond:** Put yourself in Ravi's place. What would you have done after Raghu left the shed area? Explain your answer.
2. **(a) Recall:** What does Ravi think it would feel like to be "the winner in a circle of older, bigger, luckier children"? **(b) Draw Conclusions:** What do his feelings show about his view of the other children and his view of himself?
3. **(a) Infer:** Why do the other children stop searching for Ravi? **(b) Draw Conclusions:** What do the other children think of Ravi?
4. **(a) Interpret:** What bitter lesson does Ravi learn at the end of the story? **(b) Apply:** Do you think that Ravi's sense of "insignificance" will remain strong? Explain.
5. **(a) Evaluate:** Do you think the story accurately portrays the relations between older and younger children? Explain. **(b) Generalize:** Why might older children treat younger children this way? **(c) Discuss:** Share your response with a partner. Then, discuss whether your partner's response has changed or expanded your own thinking.

Literary Analysis

6. **(a)** What is the main **external conflict** in this story? Explain. **(b)** What is the main **internal conflict** in the story? Explain.
7. **(a)** Identify a moment in the story that had great **suspense**. **(b)** Which conflict helps to create this suspense? Why?
8. **(a)** Are Ravi's conflicts settled by the end of the story? Explain. **(b)** Describe an alternative **resolution** the story might have had.

Reading Skill

9. **(a)** In your opinion, which **cause** sets the story's cause-and-effect chain in motion? **(b)** Identify two **effects** that depend on this event. Use a diagram like this one to record your answer.

10. **(a)** Identify a key detail about the shed that is linked to later events. **(b)** Explain the causes and effects to which this detail is linked.

QuickReview

Story at a Glance
A boy tries to win a game of hide-and-seek by hiding in a dark shed.

Go Online
—Assessment
For: Self-test
Visit: www.PHSchool.com
Web Code: eqa-6109

Conflict: a struggle between two opposing forces; a conflict may be *external* or *internal*

Resolution: the stage of a plot in which a conflict is settled or resolved

Suspense: a feeling of intense anticipation about the outcome of events

Cause: an event, an action, or a situation that leads to a particular event or circumstance

Effect: the result of an event or circumstance

Vocabulary Builder

Practice Answer each question. Explain your responses.

1. To inspire calm, would you paint a room in <u>livid</u> colors?
2. How many calls can you make on a <u>defunct</u> cell phone?
3. Is a lazy person likely to make a <u>dogged</u> effort?

Adding Words to Your Vocabulary An **antonym** of a word is a word that means the opposite. Use a thesaurus to find one antonym for each of the underlined words above. Then, use each antonym correctly in a sentence. (For more on using a thesaurus, see page R7.)

Writing

"Games at Twilight" has an **ironic,** or unexpected, ending: Ravi tries to be invisible during the game but is devastated to learn how invisible he actually is. Write an **anecdote,** or brief story, with an ironic ending.

- Pick a character, a conflict, and a twist ending.
- As you draft, include details that will lead readers to expect an outcome different from the one you have chosen. At the same time, make sure your story leads logically to your surprise ending.
- Finally, resolve the conflict with your twist ending.

Ask a classmate to read a draft and tell you how effective your ending is. Consider revising based on your reader's feedback.

For *Grammar, Vocabulary,* and *Assessment,* see **Build Language Skills,** pp. 140–141.

Extend Your Learning

Listening and Speaking With others, form a **problem-solving group** to find solutions to Ravi's problem.
- Discuss strategies, supporting your ideas with reasons and examples.
- Respond to one another respectfully, and ask for clarification of any points you do not understand.

Share the results of your discussion with the rest of the class.

Research and Technology Create an **outline for a multimedia report** on the history of a children's game such as hide-and-seek. Present your outline to a small group. Watch for confusion in your audience and clarify points as needed. Afterward, summarize your plan for a report. Ask for questions or comments from the group.

Build Language Skills

Contents of the Dead Man's Pocket • Games at Twilight

Vocabulary Skill

Word Origins The word *preliminary* is derived from the Latin word *limen*, meaning "threshold" (the area of floor under a doorway) or "entrance." This word is the origin of *preliminary*, which means "in the beginning stages" or "leading up to something." Other English words that share this origin, such as *eliminate* and *lintel*, also have to do with the idea of a threshold or an entrance.

Practice In a dictionary, look up each of these words: *eliminate, elimination, lintel,* and *preliminary.* Explain the meaning of each. Then, complete the following sentences using each word once.

1. To _____ waste, buy just what you need.
2. Walking through the door, one passes under the _____.
3. The _____ of study halls meant the students took nine classes a day.
4. I have finished a _____ draft of my book.

Grammar Lesson

Personal Pronouns **Pronouns** are words that are used in place of nouns or of words that work together as a noun. The most common pronouns are **personal pronouns**, which refer to the person speaking (first-person pronouns), the person spoken to (second-person pronouns), or the person, place, or thing spoken about (third-person pronouns).

MorePractice

For more practice with personal pronouns, see the Grammar Handbook, p. R39.

Personal Pronouns	Singular	Plural
First Person	I, me, my, mine	we, us, our, ours
Second Person	you, your, yours	you, your, yours
Third Person	he, him, his, she, her, hers, it, its	they, them, their, theirs

Practice Rewrite the sentence, substituting a pronoun for each underlined word or phrase. Then, explain how this substitution changed the information in the sentence.

1. <u>Sarah</u> hopes that <u>the computer</u> will work.
2. <u>The technical documentation</u> is lengthy.
3. <u>Juana</u> adopted <u>Tabby and Fido</u> from the animal shelter.
4. Find out where <u>the actors</u> are rehearsing for the play.
5. Despite the problems, <u>the performance</u> was exceptional.

W̶G̶ Prentice Hall Writing and Grammar Connection: Chapter 16, Section 2

Monitor Your Progress

Test Practice

Standards
Assessed
• 10.1.2
• 10.3.1
• 10.3.3

Reading: Cause and Effect

Directions: *Questions 1–4 are based on the following passage.*

One morning when [the dog] Muggs bit me slightly, more or less in passing, I reached down and grabbed his short stumpy tail and hoisted him into the air. It was a foolhardy thing to do. . . . I carried him to the kitchen and flung him onto the floor and shut the door on him just as he crashed against it. But I forgot about the backstairs. Muggs went up the backstairs and down the frontstairs and had me cornered in the living room. I managed to get up onto the mantel-piece above the fireplace, but it gave way and came down with a tre-mendous crash. . . . Muggs was so alarmed by the racket that when I picked myself up he had disappeared.

—from "The Dog That Bit People" by James Thurber

1. Which of the following is the original cause of the events in the paragraph?
   A The narrator holds Muggs by the tail.
   B The narrator was chasing Muggs.
   C Muggs bites the narrator.
   D Muggs corners the narrator in the living room.

2. Which is not an effect of the narrator's climbing up on the mantelpiece?
   A Muggs disappears.
   B The mantelpiece falls.
   C The narrator falls.
   D Muggs grows even more vicious.

3. What was directly caused by Muggs biting the narrator?
   A The narrator held him in the air.
   B The narrator climbed the mantelpiece.
   C Muggs crashed into the kitchen door.
   D Muggs got hit when a vase crashed.

4. Which item gives a cause and then its effect?
   A Narrator forgets about the backstairs/ Narrator is cornered in living room.
   B Narrator holds dog in air/Narrator gets bitten by dog.
   C Dog attempts to bite narrator/Dog is locked in kitchen.
   D Dog is alarmed by mantel falling/Dog escapes kitchen.

Timed Writing: Exposition [Connections]

Many times the interplay of a character and society form the core of a work. Write an explanation of the cause-effect relationship between a character's culture and the character in either *Contents of the Dead Man's Pocket* or *Games at Twilight*. **(20 minutes)**

 Writing Workshop: *Work in Progress*

Cause-and-Effect Essay

Jot down three questions that interest you. Note one or two sources you think might have information on each topic. Keep this list in your writing portfolio.

Practice these skills with either "Making History With Vitamin C" (p. 144) or "The Marginal World" (p. 155).

Literary Analysis

An **author's purpose** is his or her main reason for writing.

- An author may seek to inform, explain, persuade, describe, or entertain. He or she may also combine these purposes.

- If the primary purpose is to inform or persuade, the author presents a **thesis**—the main point about the subject. To explain and prove the thesis, the author supplies support: evidence, facts, and other details confirming the thesis.

As you read, identify the author's thesis, and look for details that support it.

Reading Skill

A **cause** is an event, an action, or a situation that makes something happen. An **effect** is the event that results. Causes and effects are often linked in a sequence of events. To **analyze cause and effect,** determine which events cause which effects.

- **Reread** passages to determine whether they involve sequences of events. Ask whether the writer indicates causes and effects in these sequences. Look for cause-and-effect terms like *because, as a result, and for that reason,* and so on.
- As you read, use a diagram like this to record causes and effects.

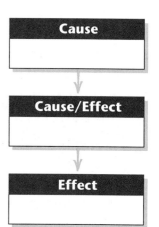

Vocabulary Builder

Making History With Vitamin C

- **deficiency** (dē fish′ ən sē) *n.* lack of something essential (p. 144) *A calcium deficiency can cause weak bones.*

- **replenished** (ri plen′ ish'd) *v.* made complete or full again (p. 145) *She replenished the bowl before it was empty.*

- **incessant** (in ses′ ənt) *adj.* not coming to a stop; constant (p. 145) *His incessant chatter gave me a headache.*

- **obscured** (əb skyoor′d′) *v.* made dark; blocked from view; hid (p. 147) *A tall person obscured my view of the screen.*

The Marginal World

- **mutable** (myoot′ ə bəl) *adj.* changeable (p. 156) *His personality is mutable, and I never know how he will react.*

- **ephemeral** (e fem′ ər əl) *adj.* short-lived (p. 158) *The fog was ephemeral; it passed just after sunrise.*

- **marginal** (mär′ jə nəl) *adj.* at, on, or near the edge (p. 160) *The teacher wrote a few marginal comments on my final draft.*

- **manifestations** (man′ə fes tā′shənz) *n.* appearances; forms (p. 161) *Steam and ice are different manifestations of water.*

Build Understanding • *Making History With Vitamin C*

Background

The Age of Discovery In the 1300s, Europeans began sailing the known world in search of spices and other goods to trade. As navigation improved, they traveled farther. These adventurers risked shipwreck and losing their way. They also risked scurvy, the illness resulting from a lack of vitamin C, as "Making History With Vitamin C" explains.

Connecting to the Literature

Reading/Writing Connection Vitamin C may seem like a small matter, but sailors' access to foods that contained it made a big difference. Describe a small thing crucial to the success of your day or week. Use at least three of these words: *rely, benefit, maximize, reinforce.*

READ MORE

by Le Couteur and Burreson

Napoleon's Buttons

Meet the Author

Penny **Le Couteur** (b. 1943)
Jay **Burreson** (b. 1942)

Born in New Zealand, Penny Le Couteur (lə kōō´ tər) has taught chemistry for more than thirty years. Jay Burreson is also a chemist and runs a high-tech company. The two met in graduate school and have remained friends ever since.

Teaming Up The two friends decided to work together on a book "to tell the stories of the fascinating connections between chemical structures and historical episodes." Each chapter in this book, *Napoleon's Buttons*, examines a different molecule and its role in history.

Napoleon's Buttons takes its title from the chapter on tin. In extreme cold, tin will crumble. When the French leader Napoleon invaded Russia in 1812, his soldiers' tin buttons disintegrated in the freezing air. Many perished of cold in this defeat—some, perhaps, because of their tin buttons.

Go **Online**
Author Link

For: More about the authors
Visit: www.PHSchool.com
Web Code: eqe-9110

Making History With Vitamin C

Penny Le Couteur and Jay Burreson

The Age of Discovery was fueled by molecules of the spice trade, but it was the lack of another, quite different molecule that almost ended it. Over 90 percent of his crew didn't survive Magellan's[1] 1519–1522 circumnavigation of the world—in large part due to scurvy, a devastating disease caused by a <u>deficiency</u> of the ascorbic acid molecule, dietary vitamin C.

Exhaustion and weakness, swelling of the arms and legs, softening of the gums, excessive bruising, hemorrhaging from the nose and mouth, foul breath, diarrhea, muscle pain, loss of teeth, lung and kidney problems—the list of symptoms of scurvy is long and horrible. Death generally results from an acute infection such as pneumonia or some other respiratory ailment or, even in young people, from heart failure. One symptom, depression, occurs at an early stage, but whether it is an effect of the actual disease or a response to the other symptoms is not clear. After all, if you were constantly exhausted and had sores that did not heal, painful and bleeding gums, stinking breath, and diarrhea, and you knew that there was worse to come, would you not be depressed, too?

Scurvy is an ancient disease. Changes in bone structure in Neolithic remains are thought to be compatible with scurvy, and hieroglyphs from ancient Egypt have been interpreted as referring to it. The word *scurvy is* said to be derived from Norse, the language of the seafaring Viking warriors who, starting in the ninth century, raided the Atlantic coast of Europe from their northern homelands

Literary Analysis
Author's Purpose
What does the first paragraph suggest might be the thesis of this selection?

Vocabulary Builder
deficiency (dē fish′ ən sē) *n.* lack of something essential

Reading Skill
Analyzing Cause and Effect Reread the first paragraph after completing the second. What causes scurvy?

---

1. **Magellan's** (mə jel′ ənz) Ferdinand Magellan (*ca.*1480–1521) was a Portuguese explorer in the service of Spain. He commanded the first expedition to sail around the world.

in Scandinavia. A lack of vitamin-rich fresh fruit and vegetables would have been common on board ships and in northern communities during winter. The Vikings supposedly made use of scurvy grass, a form of Arctic cress, on their way to America via Greenland. The first real descriptions of what was probably scurvy date from the Crusades in the thirteenth century.

Scurvy at Sea

In the fourteenth and fifteenth centuries, as longer voyages were made possible by the development of more efficient sets of sails and fully rigged ships, scurvy became commonplace at sea. Oar-propelled galleys, such as those used by the Greeks and Romans, and the small sailing boats of Arab traders had stayed fairly close to the coast. These vessels were not seaworthy enough to withstand the rough waters and huge swells of the open ocean. Consequently, they would seldom venture far from the coast, and supplies could be <u>replenished</u> every few days or weeks. Access to fresh food on a regular basis meant that scurvy was seldom a major problem. But in the fifteenth century, long ocean voyages in large sailing ships heralded not only the Age of Discovery but also reliance on preserved food.

Bigger ships had to carry cargo and arms, a larger crew to handle the more complicated rigging and sails, and food and water for months at sea. An increase in the number of decks and men and the amount of supplies inevitably translated into cramped sleeping and living conditions for the crew, poor ventilation, and a subsequent increase in infectious diseases and respiratory conditions. Consumption (tuberculosis) and the "bloody flux" (a pernicious form of diarrhea) were common as, no doubt, were body and head lice, scabies, and other contagious skin conditions.

The standard sailor's food did nothing to improve his health. Two major factors dictated the seafaring diet. Firstly, aboard wooden ships it was extremely difficult to keep anything, including food, dry and mold free. Water was absorbed through wooden hulls, as the only water-proofing material available was pitch, a dark-colored, sticky resin obtained as a by-product of charcoal manufacture, applied to the outside of the hull. The inside of the hull, particularly where ventilation was poor, would have been extremely humid. Many accounts of sailing journeys describe <u>incessant</u> dampness, as mold and mildew grew on clothing, on leather boots and belts, on bedding, and on books. The standard sailor's fare was salted beef or pork and ship's biscuits known as hardtack, a mixture of flour and water without salt that was baked rock hard and used as a substitute for bread. Hardtack had the

Vocabulary Builder
replenished (ri plen´ ish'd) *v.* made complete or full again

Vocabulary Builder
incessant (in ses´ ənt) *adj.* not coming to a stop; constant

Reading Check

What problems did the lack of vitamin C in sailors' diets cause?

desirable characteristic of being relatively immune to mildew. It was baked to such a degree of hardness that it remained edible for decades, but it was extremely difficult to bite into, especially for those whose gums were inflamed by the onset of scurvy. Typically, ship's biscuits were weevil-infested, a circumstance that was actually welcomed by sailors as the weevil holes increased porosity and made the biscuits easier to break and chew.

The second factor governing diet on wooden ships was the fear of fire. Wooden construction and liberal use of highly combustible pitch meant that constant diligence was necessary to prevent fire at sea. For this reason the only fire permitted on board was in the galley and then only in relatively calm weather. At the first sign of foul weather, galley fires would be extinguished until the storm was over. Cooking was often not possible for days at a time. Salted meat could not be simmered in water for the hours necessary to reduce its saltiness; nor could ship's biscuits be made at least somewhat palatable by dunking them in hot stew or broth.

At the outset of a voyage provisions would be taken on board: butter, cheese, vinegar, bread, dried peas, beer, and rum. The butter was soon rancid, the bread moldy, the dried peas weevil infested, the cheeses hard, and the beer sour. None of these items provided vitamin C, so signs of scurvy were often evident after as little as six weeks out of port. Was it any wonder that the navies of European countries had to resort to the press-gang[2] as a means of manning their ships?

Scurvy's toll on the lives and health of sailors is recorded in the logs of early voyages. By the time the Portuguese explorer Vasco da Gama sailed around the southern tip of Africa in 1497, one hundred of his 160-member crew had died from scurvy. Reports exist of the discovery of ships adrift at sea with entire crews dead from the disease. It is estimated that for centuries scurvy was responsible for more death at sea than all other causes; more than the combined total of naval battles, piracy, shipwrecks, and other illnesses.

Astonishingly, preventives and remedies for scurvy during these years were known—but largely ignored. As early as the fifth century, the Chinese were growing fresh ginger in pots on board their ships. The idea that fresh fruit and vegetables could alleviate symptoms of scurvy was, no doubt, available to other countries in

▲ **Critical Viewing**
Using details from this illustration and the selection, describe the life of a sailor. **[Synthesize]**

Literary Analysis
Author's Purpose
Which details in this paragraph support the idea that vitamin C is important?

---

2. **press-gang** men who round up other men to force them into naval or military service.

Southeast Asia in contact with Chinese trading vessels. It would have been passed on to the Dutch and been reported by them to other Europeans as, by 1601, the first fleet of the English East India Company is known to have collected oranges and lemons at Madagascar[3] on their way to the East. This small squadron of four ships was under the command of Captain James Lancaster, who carried bottled lemon juice with him on his flagship, the *Dragon*. Anyone who showed signs of scurvy was dosed with three teaspoons of lemon juice every morning. On arrival at the Cape of Good Hope, none of the men on board the *Dragon* was suffering from scurvy, but the toll on the other three ships was significant. Despite Lancaster's instructions and example, nearly a quarter of the total crew of this expedition died from scurvy—and not one of these deaths was on his flagship.

Some sixty-five years earlier the crew members on French explorer Jacques Cartier's second expedition to Newfoundland and Quebec were badly affected by a severe outbreak of scurvy, resulting in many deaths. An infusion of needles of the spruce tree, a remedy suggested by the local Indians, was tried with seemingly miraculous results. Almost overnight the symptoms were said to lessen and the disease rapidly disappeared. In 1593 Sir Richard Hawkins, an admiral of the British navy, claimed that within his own experience at least ten thousand men had died at sea from scurvy, but that lemon juice would have been an immediately effective cure.

There were even published accounts of successful treatments of scurvy. In 1617, John Woodall's *The Surgeon's Mate* described lemon juice as being prescribed for both cure and prevention. Eighty years later Dr. William Cockburn's *Sea Diseases, or the Treatise of their Nature, Cause and Cure* recommended fresh fruits and vegetables. Other suggestions such as vinegar, salt water, cinnamon, and whey were quite useless and may have <u>obscured</u> the correct action.

It was not until the middle of the following century that the effectiveness of citrus juice was proven in the first controlled clinical studies of scurvy. Although the numbers involved were very small, the conclusion was obvious. In 1747, James Lind, a Scottish naval surgeon at sea in the *Salisbury*, chose twelve of the crew suffering from scurvy for his experiment. He selected men whose symptoms seemed as similar as possible. He had them all eat the same diet: not the standard salted meat and hardtack, which these patients would have found very difficult to chew, but sweetened gruel, mutton broth, boiled biscuits, barley, sago, rice, raisins, currants, and

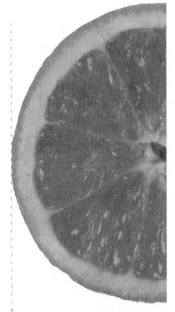

Reading Skill
Analyzing Cause and Effect Which words in this paragraph signal cause-and-effect relationships?

Vocabulary Builder
obscured (əb skyoor'd′) *v.* made dark; blocked from view; hid

**Reading Check**

What factors limited sailors' diets on board a ship?

---

3. Madagascar (mad′ ə gas′ kər) an island in the Indian Ocean off the southeast coast of Africa.

wine. Lind added various supplements to this carbohydrate-based regime. Two of the sailors each received a quart of cider daily. Two others were dosed with vinegar, and another unfortunate pair received diluted elixir of vitriol (or sulfuric acid). Two more were required to drink half a pint of seawater daily, and another two were fed a concoction of nutmeg, garlic, mustard seed, gum myrrh, cream of tartar, and barley water. The lucky remaining pair was issued daily two oranges and one lemon each.

The results were sudden and visible and what we would expect with today's knowledge. Within six days the men who received the citrus fruit were fit for duty. Hopefully, the other ten sailors were then taken off their seawater, nutmeg, or sulfuric acid regimes and also supplied with lemons and oranges. Lind's results were published in *A Treatise of Scurvy*, but it was another forty years before the British navy began the compulsory issue of lemon juice.

If an effective treatment for scurvy was known, why wasn't it acted upon and used routinely? Sadly, the remedy for scurvy, though proven, seems to have not been recognized or believed. A widely held theory blamed scurvy on a diet of either too much salted meat or not enough fresh meat rather than a lack of fresh fruit and vegetables. Also, there was a logistical problem: it was difficult to keep fresh citrus fruit or juice for weeks at a time. Attempts were made to concentrate and preserve lemon juice, but such procedures were time consuming, costly, and perhaps not very effective, as we now know that vitamin C is easily destroyed by heat and light and that long-term storage reduces the amount in fruits and vegetables.

Because of expense and inconvenience, naval officers, physicians, the British admiralty, and shipowners could see no way of growing sufficient greens or citrus fruit on heavily manned vessels. Precious cargo space would have to be used for this purpose. Fresh or preserved citrus fruit was expensive, especially if it was to be allocated daily as a preventive measure. Economy and the profit margin ruled—although, in hindsight, it does seem that this was a false economy. Ships had to be manned above capacity to allow for a 30, 40 or even 50 percent death rate from scurvy. Even without a high death rate, the effectiveness of a crew suffering from scurvy would have been remarkably low. And then there was the humane factor—rarely considered during these centuries.

Another element was the intransigence of the average crew. They were used to eating the standard ship's fare, and although they complained about the monotonous diet of salt meat and ship's biscuit when they were at sea, what they wanted in port was lots of fresh meat, fresh bread, cheese, butter, and good beer. Even if fresh fruit and vegetables were available, the majority of the crew would

Literary Analysis
Author's Purpose
What words suggest that the author's purpose here is to comment on events, not just to give information?

not have been interested in a quick stir-fry of tender crunchy greens. They wanted meat and more meat—boiled, stewed, or roasted. The officers, who generally came from a higher social class, where a wider and more varied diet was common, would have found eating fruit and vegetables in port to be normal and probably highly acceptable. It would not have been unusual for them to be interested in trying exotic new foodstuffs to be found in the locales where they made landfall. Tamarinds, limes, and other fruits high in vitamin C would have been used in the local cuisine that they, unlike the crew, might try. Scurvy was thus usually less of a problem among a ship's officers.

Cook: Hundreds—Scurvy: Nil

James Cook of the British Royal Navy was the first ship's captain to ensure that his crews remained scurvy free. Cook is sometimes associated with the discovery of antiscorbutics, as scurvy-curing foods are called, but his true achievement lay in the fact that he insisted on maintaining high levels of diet and hygiene aboard all his vessels. The result of his meticulous standards was an extraordinarily good level of health and a low mortality rate among his crew. Cook entered the navy at the relatively late age of twenty-seven, but his previous nine years of experience sailing as a merchant seaman mate in the North Sea and the Baltic, his intelligence, and his innate seamanship combined to ensure his rapid promotion within the naval ranks. His first experience with scurvy came aboard the *Pembroke,* in 1758, on his initial voyage across the Atlantic Ocean to Canada to challenge the French hold on the St. Lawrence River. Cook was alarmed by the devastation this common affliction caused and appalled that the deaths of so many crew, the dangerous reduction of working efficiency, and even actual loss of ships were generally accepted as inevitable.

His experience exploring and mapping around Nova Scotia, the Gulf of St. Lawrence, and Newfoundland and his accurate observations of the eclipse of the sun greatly impressed the Royal Society, a body founded in 1645 with the aim of "improving natural knowledge." He was granted command of the ship *Endeavour* and instructed to explore and chart the southern oceans, to investigate new plants and animals, and to make astronomical observations of the transit of planets across the sun.

Less known but nonetheless compelling reasons for this voyage and for Cook's subsequent later voyages were political. Taking possession in the name of Britain of already discovered lands; claiming of new lands still to be discovered, including Terra Australis Incognita, the great southern continent; and the hopes of finding a

Reading Skill
Analyzing Cause and Effect What factors caused Cook to be successful in the Navy?

**Reading Check**

What was James Cook's contribution to maintaining sailors' health?

Northwest Passage were all on the minds of the admiralty. That Cook was able to complete so many of these objectives depended to a large degree on ascorbic acid.

Consider the scenario on June 10, 1770, when the *Endeavour* ran aground on coral of the Great Barrier Reef just south of present-day Cooktown, in northern Queensland, Australia. It was a near catastrophe. The ship had struck at high water; a resulting hole in the hull necessitated drastic measures. In order to lighten the ship, the entire crew heaved overboard everything that could be spared. For twenty-three hours straight they manned the pumps as seawater leaked inexorably into the hold, hauling desperately on cables and anchor in an attempt to plug the hole by fothering, a temporary method of mending a hole by drawing a heavy sail under the hull. Incredible effort, superb seamanship, and good fortune prevailed. The ship eventually slid off the reef and was beached for repairs. It had been a very close call—one that an exhausted, scurvy-inflicted crew could not have summoned the energy to answer.

A healthy, well-functioning crew was essential for Cook to accomplish what he did on his voyages. This fact was recognized by the Royal Society when it awarded him its highest honor, the Copley gold medal, not for his navigational feats but for his demonstration that scurvy was not an inevitable companion on long ocean voyages. Cook's methods were simple. He insisted on maintaining cleanliness throughout the ship, especially in the tight confines of the seamen's quarters. All hands were required to wash their clothes regularly, to air and dry their bedding when the weather permitted, to fumigate between decks, and in general to live up to the meaning of the term *shipshape*. When it was not possible to obtain the fresh fruit and vegetables he thought necessary for a balanced diet, he required that his men eat the sauerkraut he had included in the ship's provisions. Cook touched land at every possible opportunity to replenish stores and gather local grasses (celery grass, scurvy grass) or plants from which he brewed teas.

This diet was not at all popular with the crew, accustomed as they were to the standard seamen's fare and reluctant to try anything new. But Cook was adamant. He and his officers also adhered to this diet, and it was by his example, authority, and determination that his regimen was followed. There is no record that Cook had anyone flogged for refusing to eat sauerkraut or celery grass, but the crew knew the captain would not hesitate to prescribe the lash for opposing his rules. Cook also made use of a more subtle approach. He records that a "Sour Kroutt" prepared from local

▲ **Critical Viewing**
Do the actions of James Cook described in the essay seem to fit with his personality as suggested by this portrait? Explain.
[Connect]

plants was initially made available only to the officers; within a week the lower ranks were clamoring for their share.

Success no doubt helped convince Cook's crew that their captain's strange obsession with what they ate was worthwhile. Cook never lost a single man to scurvy. On his first voyage of almost three years, one-third of his crew died after contracting malaria or dysentery in Batavia (now Jakarta) in the Dutch East Indies (now Indonesia). On his second voyage from 1772 to 1775, he lost one member of his crew to illness—but not to scurvy. Yet on that trip the crew of his companion vessel was badly affected by the problem. The commander, Tobias Furneaux, was severely reprimanded and instructed yet again by Cook on the need for preparation and administration of antiscorbutics. Thanks to vitamin C, the ascorbic acid molecule, Cook was able to compile an impressive list of accomplishments: the discovery of the Hawaiian Islands and the Great Barrier Reef, the first circumnavigation of New Zealand, the first charting of the coast of the Pacific Northwest, and first crossing of the Antarctic Circle.

Literary Analysis
Author's Purpose
How does this paragraph about Captain Cook support the author's thesis about the importance of vitamin C for the Age of Discovery?

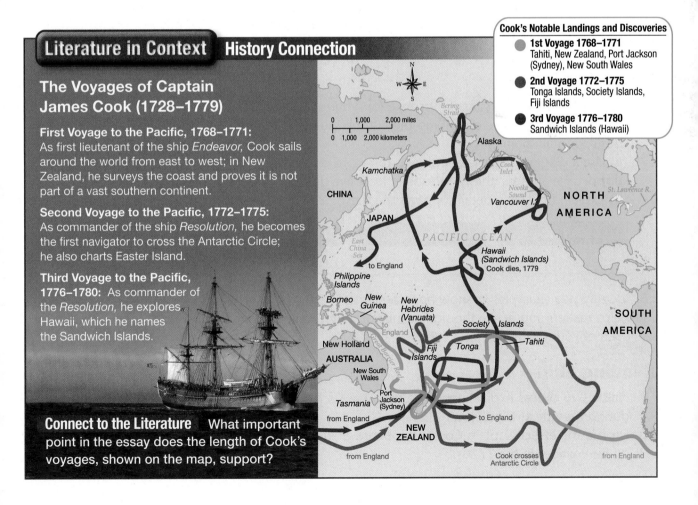

Literature in Context — History Connection

The Voyages of Captain James Cook (1728–1779)

First Voyage to the Pacific, 1768–1771: As first lieutenant of the ship *Endeavor,* Cook sails around the world from east to west; in New Zealand, he surveys the coast and proves it is not part of a vast southern continent.

Second Voyage to the Pacific, 1772–1775: As commander of the ship *Resolution,* he becomes the first navigator to cross the Antarctic Circle; he also charts Easter Island.

Third Voyage to the Pacific, 1776–1780: As commander of the *Resolution,* he explores Hawaii, which he names the Sandwich Islands.

Connect to the Literature What important point in the essay does the length of Cook's voyages, shown on the map, support?

Cook's Notable Landings and Discoveries
- **1st Voyage 1768–1771** Tahiti, New Zealand, Port Jackson (Sydney), New South Wales
- **2nd Voyage 1772–1775** Tonga Islands, Society Islands, Fiji Islands
- **3rd Voyage 1776–1780** Sandwich Islands (Hawaii)

Apply the Skills

Making History With Vitamin C

Thinking About the Selection

1. **Respond:** Which fact in this essay most surprised you? Why?
2. **(a) Recall:** Before the eighteenth century, what was included in a typical sailor's diet? **(b) Analyze Cause and Effect:** Explain why this diet led to widespread illness.
3. **(a) Connect:** In what way did shipowners' concern about saving money add to the problem of scurvy? **(b) Interpret:** What does the delay in correcting the problem reveal about human nature?
4. **Summarize:** What was Captain James Cook's contribution to eliminating scurvy?
5. **(a) Speculate:** What modern inventions related to food preparation or storage do you think would have been most helpful to navigators in the Age of Discovery? Why?
   (b) Discuss: Share your ideas with classmates in a group. Discuss the inventions, and select the three you think are most important. Present them to the class, explaining why the group chose them.

Literary Analysis

6. **(a)** What is the authors' main **purpose** for writing? Explain.
   (b) Write one sentence describing the authors' subject and their **thesis**, or main point.
7. **(a)** Use a diagram like the one shown to record details that **support** the authors' thesis. Include at least five details.
   (b) Explain how each detail supports the thesis.

Detail	Thesis	Detail

8. Identify two examples to show how the writers' choice of words helps readers appreciate the significance of their thesis. Explain each of your examples.

Reading Skill

9. Name two **causes** explaining why scurvy was such a problem during the Age of Discovery.
10. Explain the **effect** Captain Cook's shipboard dietary policies had on his voyages in the 1770s.

QuickReview

Essay at a Glance
During the Age of Discovery, lack of vitamin C on ships caused widespread illness. An English explorer found a solution and persisted in applying it.

Go Online
—Assessment
For: Self-test
Visit: www.PHSchool.com
Web Code: eqa-6110

Author's purpose: an author's reason for writing

Thesis: the main point that an author wants to make

Support: the details that an author provides to explain and prove a thesis

Cause: an event, an action, or a situation that makes something happen

Effect: the event or situation that results from a cause

Vocabulary Builder

Practice Antonyms are words with opposite meanings, such as *day* and *night*. For each numbered word here, choose the best antonym. Then, use each pair of antonyms in a sentence.

1. deficiency: **(a)** shortage, **(b)** obstacle, **(c)** surplus
2. replenished: **(a)** emptied, **(b)** forgave, **(c)** allowed
3. incessant: **(a)** failing, **(b)** brief, **(c)** filthy
4. obscured: **(a)** revealed, **(b)** darkened, **(c)** pierced

Adding Words to Your Vocabulary In the vocabulary list for "Making History With Vitamin C," on page 142, identify the vocabulary word that is related to the word *cease*. Then, using a dictionary, explain the connection between the meanings of the two words. (For more on using a dictionary, see page R6.)

Writing

Write a **proposal for a documentary** on Cook's efforts to solve the problem of scurvy. First, reread the essay for ideas. Then, write an essay on what the documentary should show. Include these elements:

- details about maps, charts, and other objects to display
- summaries of the action to be reenacted
- topics for comment by the actors and narrator

For *Grammar, Vocabulary,* and *Assessment,* see **Build Language Skills,** pages 164–165.

Extend Your Learning

Listening and Speaking In Cook's time, exploration was risky. In a small group, **debate** whether the benefits of manned space expeditions are worth the risks. Brainstorm for ideas. Then, divide into two teams, one arguing for manned missions and the other arguing against them. Next, switch sides and hold a second debate. Afterward, compare the cases each team made.

Research and Technology For a week, keep track of what you eat, using computer software to create a **diet spreadsheet.** Record the foods you eat at each meal, listing ingredients when possible. Review your log and compare your diet to that of the sailors in Cook's day.

Nonfiction

Background

Tides The pull of the moon's gravity is strongest on the part of Earth that is closest to the moon. As the Earth rotates, the area that is closest to the moon changes. The result is tides, the daily changes in the water level at the ocean shore. Each day, the edge of the shore is flooded and then exposed by the tides. Rachel Carson explores the creatures that live in this special zone.

Connecting to the Literature

Reading/Writing Connection For Rachel Carson, tidal action makes the edge of the sea a special place. Describe a place that has meaning to you—a shore you visited once, for example, or a local park. Use at least three of these words: *appeal, appreciate, contrast, display.*

Review

For **Literary Analysis**, **Reading Skill**, and **Vocabulary Builder**, see page 142.

READ MORE

by Rachel Carson

The Edge of the Sea

The Sense of Wonder

Meet the Author

Rachel **Carson** (1907–1964)

A lifelong lover of nature, Rachel Carson trained as a marine biologist at a time when few women pursued the study of the sea. She worked for the United States Fish and Wildlife Service and wrote poetically about nature in books like *The Sea Around Us,* which won the National Book Award.

A Crusade One day a friend wrote to complain that many birds had died on her property after it was sprayed for insects. Carson decided she had to show the world that people were damaging the environment with insecticides. In 1962, she published *Silent Spring,* a pioneering environmental work.

Fast Facts

▶ President John F. Kennedy ordered a committee to investigate Carson's claims in *Silent Spring.*

▶ As a result, the insecticide DDT was eventually banned.

For: More about the author
Visit: www.PHSchool.com
Web Code: eqe-9111

Go Online
Author Link

The Marginal World

Rachel Carson

The edge of the sea is a strange and beautiful place. All through the long history of Earth it has been an area of unrest where waves have broken heavily against the land, where the tides have pressed forward over the continents, receded, and then returned. For no two successive days is the shoreline precisely the same. Not only do the tides advance and retreat in their eternal rhythms, but the level of the sea itself is never at rest. It rises or falls as the glaciers melt or grow, as the floor of the deep ocean basins shifts under its increasing load of sediments, or as the

▲ **Critical Viewing**
Do you find sea life mysterious and beautiful as Carson does? Explain.
[Relate]

earth's crust along the continental margins warps up or down in adjustment to strain and tension. Today a little more land may belong to the sea, tomorrow a little less. Always the edge of the sea remains an elusive and indefinable boundary.

The shore has a dual nature, changing with the swing of the tides, belonging now to the land, now to the sea. On the ebb tide it knows the harsh extremes of the land world, being exposed to heat and cold, to wind, to rain and drying sun. On the flood tide it is a water world, returning briefly to the relative stability of the open sea.

Only the most hardy and adaptable can survive in a region so <u>mutable</u>, yet the area between the tide lines is crowded with plants and animals. In this difficult world of the shore, life displays its enormous toughness and vitality by occupying almost every conceivable niche. Visibly, it carpets the intertidal rocks; or half hidden, it descends into fissures and crevices, or hides under boulders, or lurks in the wet gloom of sea caves. Invisibly, where the casual observer would say there is no life, it lies deep in the sand, in burrows and tubes and passageways. It tunnels into solid rock and bores into peat and clay. It encrusts weeds or drifting spars[1] or the hard, chitinous[2] shell of a lobster. It exists minutely, as the film of

---

1. **spars** (spärs) *n.* pieces of wood or metal, such as masts or booms, for supporting sails on a ship.

2. **chitinous** (kī′ tin əs) *adj.* of the material that forms the tough outer covering of insects, crustaceans, and so on.

bacteria that spreads over a rock surface or a wharf piling; as spheres of protozoa, small as pinpricks, sparkling at the surface of the sea; and as Lilliputian[3] beings swimming through dark pools that lie between the grains of sand.

The shore is an ancient world, for as long as there has been an earth and sea there has been this place of the meeting of land and water. Yet it is a world that keeps alive the sense of continuing creation and of the relentless drive of life. Each time that I enter it, I gain some new awareness of its beauty and its deeper meanings, sensing that intricate fabric of life by which one creature is linked with another, and each with its surroundings.

In my thoughts of the shore, one place stands apart for its revelation of exquisite beauty. It is a pool hidden within a cave that one can visit only rarely and briefly when the lowest of the year's low tides fall below it, and perhaps from that very fact it acquires some of its special beauty. Choosing such a tide, I hoped for a glimpse of the pool. The ebb was to fall early in the morning. I knew that if the wind held from the northwest and no interfering swell ran in from a distant storm the level of the sea should drop below the entrance to the pool. There had been sudden ominous showers in the night, with rain like handfuls of gravel flung on the roof. When I looked out into the early morning the sky was full of a gray dawn light but the sun had not yet risen. Water and air were pallid. Across the bay the moon was a luminous disc in the western sky, suspended above the dim line of distant shore—the full August moon, drawing the tide to the low, low levels of the threshold of the alien sea world. As I watched, a gull flew by, above the spruces. Its breast was rosy with the light of the unrisen sun. The day was, after all, to be fair.

Later, as I stood above the tide near the entrance to the pool, the promise of that rosy light was sustained. From the base of the steep wall of rock on which I stood, a moss-covered ledge jutted seaward into deep water. In the surge at the rim of the ledge the dark fronds of oarweeds swayed, smooth and gleaming as leather. The projecting ledge was the path to the small hidden cave and its pool. Occasionally a swell, stronger than the rest, rolled smoothly over the rim and broke in foam against the cliff. But the intervals between such swells were long enough to admit me to the ledge and long enough for a glimpse of that fairy pool, so seldom and so briefly exposed.

And so I knelt on the wet carpet of sea moss and looked back into the dark cavern that held the pool in a shallow basin. The floor of the cave was only a few inches below the roof, and a mirror had

◄▲ **Critical Viewing**
In what way are these creatures prepared for the life along the shore Carson describes? **[Draw Conclusions]**

Reading Check

Name three places creatures may live along the shore.

---

3. **Lilliputian** (lil′ ə py$\overline{oo}$′ shən) *adj.* tiny (from the name of the tiny people who inhabit Lilliput in *Gulliver's Travels* by Jonathan Swift).

been created in which all that grew on the ceiling was reflected in the still water below.

Under water that was clear as glass the pool was carpeted with green sponge. Gray patches of sea squirts glistened on the ceiling and colonies of soft coral were a pale apricot color. In the moment when I looked into the cave a little elfin starfish hung down, suspended by the merest thread, perhaps by only a single tube foot. It reached down to touch its own reflection, so perfectly delineated that there might have been, not one starfish, but two. The beauty of the reflected images and of the limpid pool itself was the poignant beauty of things that are <u>ephemeral</u>, existing only until the sea should return to fill the little cave.

Whenever I go down into this magical zone of the low water of the spring tides, I look for the most delicately beautiful of all the shore's inhabitants—flowers that are not plant but animal, blooming on the threshold of the deeper sea. In that fairy cave I was not disappointed. Hanging from its roof were the pendent[4] flowers of the hydroid Tubularia, pale pink, fringed and delicate as the wind flower. Here were creatures so exquisitely fashioned that they seemed unreal, their beauty too fragile to exist in a world of crushing force. Yet every detail was functionally useful, every stalk and hydranth[5] and petallike tentacle fashioned for dealing with the realities of existence. I knew that they were merely waiting, in that moment of the tide's ebbing, for the return of the sea. Then in the rush of water, in the surge of surf and the pressure of the incoming tide, the delicate flower heads would stir with life. They would sway on their slender stalks, and their long tentacles would sweep the returning water, finding in it all that they needed for life.

And so in that enchanted place on the threshold of the sea the realities that possessed my mind were far from those of the land world I had left an hour before. In a different way the same sense of remoteness and of a world apart came to me in a twilight hour on a great beach on the coast of Georgia. I had come down after sunset and walked far out over sands that lay wet and gleaming, to the very edge of the retreating sea. Looking back across that immense flat, crossed by winding, waterfilled gullies and here and there holding shallow pools left by the tide, I was filled with awareness that this intertidal area, although abandoned briefly and rhythmically by the sea, is always reclaimed by the rising tide. There at the edge of low

---

4. pendent (pen´ dənt) *adj.* dangling; hanging like a pendant on a necklace or charm.
5. hydranth (hī´ dranth´) *n.* one of the feeding individuals in a hydroid colony; the individuals are all attached at the base to a common tube.

water the beach with its reminders of the land seemed far away. The only sounds were those of the wind and the sea and the birds. There was one sound of wind moving over water, and another of water sliding over the sand and tumbling down the faces of its own wave forms. The flats were astir with birds, and the voice of the willet[6] rang insistently. One of them stood at the edge of the water and gave its loud, urgent cry; an answer came from far up the beach and the two birds flew to join each other.

The flats took on a mysterious quality as dusk approached and the last evening light was reflected from the scattered pools and creeks. Then birds became only dark shadows, with no color discernible. Sanderlings[7] scurried across the beach like little ghosts, and here and there the darker forms of the willets stood out. Often I could come very close to them before they would start up in alarm—the sanderlings running, the willets flying up, crying. Black skimmers[8] flew along the ocean's edge silhouetted against the dull, metallic gleam, or they went flitting above the sand like large, dimly seen moths. Sometimes they "skimmed" the winding creeks of tidal water, where little spreading surface ripples marked the presence of small fish.

The shore at night is a different world, in which the very darkness that hides the distractions of daylight brings into sharper focus the elemental realities. Once, exploring the night beach, I surprised a small ghost crab in the searching beam of my torch. He was lying in a pit he had dug just above the surf, as though watching the sea and waiting. The blackness of the night possessed water, air, and beach. It was the darkness of an older world, before Man. There was no sound but the all-enveloping, primeval sounds of wind blowing over water and sand, and of waves crashing on the beach. There was no other visible life—just one small crab near the sea. I have seen hundreds of ghost crabs in other settings, but suddenly I was filled with the odd sensation that for the first time I

---

6. **willet** (wil′ it) *n.* shorebird, about 16 inches long, with a long bill, found by shallow shores and other waters of North and South America.
7. **sanderlings** (san′ dər liŋz) *n.* small, gray-and-white shorebirds.
8. **skimmers** (skim′ ərz) *n.* shorebirds with bladelike bills, which they use to skim the surface of the water for small fish and crustaceans.

▲ **Critical Viewing**
After reading Carson's thoughts, do you view this scene differently than you would have before reading? Explain. **[Interpret]**

Reading Skill
Analyzing Cause and Effect Reread this paragraph, focusing on the changes Carson describes. What effect does the coming of dusk have on the flats?

 **Reading Check**

What main qualities does Carson associate with life along the seashore?

knew the creature in its own world—that I understood, as never before, the essence of its being. In that moment time was suspended; the world to which I belonged did not exist and I might have been an onlooker from outer space. The little crab alone with the sea became a symbol that stood for life itself—for the delicate, destructible, yet incredibly vital force that somehow holds its place amid the harsh realities of the inorganic world.

The sense of creation comes with memories of a southern coast, where the sea and the mangroves,[9] working together, are building a wilderness of thousands of small islands off the southwestern coast of Florida, separated from each other by a tortuous[10] pattern of bays, lagoons, and narrow waterways. I remember a winter day when the sky was blue and drenched with sunlight; though there was no wind one was conscious of flowing air like cold clear crystal. I had landed on the surf-washed tip of one of those islands, and then worked my way around to the sheltered bay side. There I found the tide far out, exposing the broad mud flat of a cove bordered by the mangroves with their twisted branches, their glossy leaves, and their long prop roots reaching down, grasping and holding the mud, building the land out a little more, then again a little more.

The mud flats were strewn with the shells of that small, exquisitely colored mollusk,[11] the rose tellin, looking like scattered petals of pink roses. There must have been a colony nearby, living buried just under the surface of the mud. At first the only creature visible was a small heron in gray and rusty plumage—a reddish egret that waded across the flat with the stealthy, hesitant movements of its kind. But other land creatures had been there, for a line of fresh tracks wound in and out among the mangrove roots, marking the path of a raccoon feeding on the oysters that gripped the supporting roots with projections from their shells. Soon I found the tracks of a shore bird, probably a sanderling, and followed them a little; then they turned toward the water and were lost, for the tide had erased them and made them as though they had never been.

Looking out over the cove I felt a strong sense of the interchangeability of land and sea in this <u>marginal</u> world of the shore, and of the links between the life of the two. There was also an awareness of the past and of the continuing flow of time, obliterating much that had gone before, as the sea had that morning washed away the tracks of the bird.

Reading Skill
Analyzing Cause and Effect What are two examples of cause-and-effect reasoning here?

Vocabulary Builder
marginal (mär´ jə nəl) *adj.* at, on, or near the edge

---

9. mangroves (maŋ´ grōvz) *n.* tropical trees that grow in swampy ground with spreading branches. The branches send down additional roots, forming a cluster of trunks for each tree.
10. tortuous (tôr´ chōō əs) *adj.* full of twists and turns.
11. mollusk (mäl´ əsk) *n.* one of a large group of soft-bodied animals with shells, including clams and snails.

The sequence and meaning of the drift of time were quietly summarized in the existence of hundreds of small snails—the mangrove periwinkles—browsing on the branches and roots of the trees. Once their ancestors had been sea dwellers, bound to the salt waters by every tie of their life processes. Little by little over the thousands and millions of years the ties had been broken, the snails had adjusted themselves to life out of water, and now today they were living many feet above the tide to which they only occasionally returned. And perhaps, who could say how many ages hence, there would be in their descendants not even this gesture of remembrance for the sea.

The spiral shells of other snails—these quite minute—left winding tracks on the mud as they moved about in search of food. They were horn shells, and when I saw them I had a nostalgic moment when I wished I might see what Audubon[12] saw, a century and more ago. For such little horn shells were the food of the flamingo, once so numerous on this coast, and when I half closed my eyes I could almost imagine a flock of these magnificent flame birds feeding in that cove, filling it with their color. It was a mere yesterday in the life of the earth that they were there; in nature, time and space are relative matters, perhaps most truly perceived subjectively in occasional flashes of insight, sparked by such a magical hour and place.

There is a common thread that links these scenes and memories—the spectacle of life in all its varied <u>manifestations</u> as it has appeared, evolved, and sometimes died out. Underlying the beauty of the spectacle there is meaning and significance. It is the elusiveness of that meaning that haunts us, that sends us again and again into the natural world where the key to the riddle is hidden. It sends us back to the edge of the sea, where the drama of life played its first scene on earth and perhaps even its prelude; where the forces of evolution are at work today, as they have been since the appearance of what we know as life; and where the spectacle of living creatures faced by the cosmic realities of their world is crystal clear.

12. Audubon (ôd´ ə bän´) John James Audubon (1785–1851), an ornithologist, a naturalist, and a painter famous for his paintings of North American birds.

Vocabulary Builder
manifestations (man´ ə fes tā´ shənz) *n.* appearances; forms

Literary Analysis
Author's Purpose
In what way does this final paragraph relate to the thesis identified in the first paragraph?

Apply the Skills

The Marginal World

Thinking About the Selection

1. **Respond:** Which aspects of nature that Carson describes do you find the most intriguing? Why?
2. **(a) Recall:** Which place does Carson first visit? **(b) Infer:** Which details make the place special to her?
3. **(a) Recall:** Name three creatures that Carson describes at length. **(b) Compare and Contrast:** For each, explain how it demonstrates or symbolizes the power of life to endure in a harsh world.
4. **Interpret:** What lesson about life does Carson draw from the "marginal world"? Support your answer with details from the work.
5. **(a) Evaluate:** Carson wrote this essay about fifty years ago. What comment would you add to the essay for today's world? **(b) Discuss:** Share your comment with classmates in a group. Discuss the ideas, and select the three you think are most important. Present them to the class, explaining why the group chose them.

Literary Analysis

6. **(a)** What is Carson's main **purpose** for writing? Explain. **(b)** Write one sentence describing the author's subject and her **thesis,** or main point.
7. **(a)** Use a diagram like the one shown to record details that **support** the author's thesis. Include at least five details. **(b)** Explain how each detail supports the thesis.

8. Identify two examples to show how Carson's descriptions of creatures or places help make her thesis about the "spectacle of life" more convincing to readers. Explain both of your choices.

Reading Skill

9. Identify the **cause** of changes in the water level of the "marginal world."
10. **(a)** Name two **effects** on creatures in the tidal zone caused by the changing water level. **(b)** For each effect, explain how the changing water level brings it about.

QuickReview

Essay at a Glance
Rachel Carson describes the beauty and wonder of life along the ocean shore.

Go  nline
—Assessment
For: Self-test
Visit: www.PHSchool.com
Web Code: eqa-6111

Author's purpose: an author's reason for writing

Thesis: the main point that an author wants to make

Support: the details that an author provides to explain or prove a thesis

Cause: an event, an action, or a situation that makes something happen

Effect: the event or situation that results from a cause

Vocabulary Builder

Practice Antonyms are words with opposite meanings, such as *day* and *night*. For each numbered word here, choose the best antonym. Then, use each pair of antonyms in a sentence.

1. marginal: **(a)** buttery, **(b)** outside, **(c)** central
2. ephemeral: **(a)** enduring, **(b)** weak, **(c)** healthy
3. manifestations: **(a)** upheavals, **(b)** absences, **(c)** questions
4. mutable: **(a)** worried, **(b)** noisy, **(c)** permanent

Adding Words to Your Vocabulary The word *manifestation* comes from the Latin word *manus,* meaning "hand." A *manifestation* makes the presence of a thing so obvious that it is as if one had been "struck by a hand." Using a dictionary, find two other words related to *manus* and explain how the idea of "hand" is related to the meaning of each. (For more on using a dictionary, see page R6.)

Writing

Write a **proposal for a documentary** on the "marginal world." First, reread the essay for ideas. Then, write an essay on what the documentary should show. Include these elements:
- details about the places to be filmed and times to film there
- summaries of the action
- quotations to use from Carson's essay

For *Grammar, Vocabulary,* and *Assessment,* see **Build Language Skills,** pages 164–165.

Extend Your Learning

Listening and Speaking In a small group, **debate** the need to preserve a natural feature in your community. Brainstorm for ideas on the subject. Then, divide into two teams, one arguing for preservation and the other arguing against it. Next, switch sides and hold a second debate. Afterward, compare the cases each team made.

Research and Technology Using computer software, create a **wildlife spreadsheet** on which you record sightings of animals that live in your area. Include dates, times, and your observations. Review your spreadsheet after a week, and record a conclusion about your environment. Compare your conclusion to Carson's.

Build Language Skills

The Marginal World • Making History With Vitamin C

Vocabulary Skill

Word Origins The word *fluent* comes from the Latin word *fluere,* meaning "to flow." *Fluent* means "having a flowing quality." All the forms of *fluent,* and other words that share this origin, also involve the idea of flowing.

The form of a word depends on its function in a sentence. *Fluent* is an adjective that describes the quality of flowing smoothly. *Fluency* is a noun that names the quality.

Practice Tell the part of speech and give an informal definition of each of the following words. Then, compare each of your answers to the information in a dictionary. Use each word correctly in a sentence.

1. fluent
2. fluently
3. fluency
4. influence
5. influential

Grammar Lesson

Relative Pronouns A **relative pronoun** is a pronoun that begins a subordinate clause. The relative pronoun relates the information in the clause to a noun or pronoun in the sentence.

RELATIVE PRONOUNS				
that	which	who	whom	whose

Practice Copy the sentences. Circle the relative pronoun. Underline the noun and the clause that are connected by this relative pronoun.

1. The haircutter who worked on me never stopped talking.
2. The wind, which gusted alarmingly, blew my hat away.
3. The students who won the spelling bee went on to the state finals.
4. The audience members whom the announcer selected became contestants on the show.
5. The suspenders that my sister gave me are missing a button.

MorePractice

For more practice with relative pronouns, see the Grammar Handbook p. R39.

𝒲𝒢 Prentice Hall Writing and Grammar Connection: Chapter 16, Section 2

Reading: Analyzing Cause and Effect

Standards Assessed
• 10.2.4
• 10.4.2
• 10.5.8

Directions: *Read the following selection. Then answer the question.*

I had not been in the state long when I experienced a lightning storm in the mountains. I am normally a fairly careful hiker, but the storm predicted on the radio weather report seemed unlikely on a breezy, sun-filled afternoon. I should have paid attention.

The flash of light was spectacular and spectacularly frightening. When the first crack of thunder roared over the mountains, the sound was so intense, my ears physically hurt. This was a different nature than the benevolent spirit of an hour ago. Squirrels no longer scurried but seemed to fly out of sight. I watched as a tree cracked, and fell—shattering its smaller counterparts. Then I smelled the smoke.

1. Which of the following is an effect of ignoring the storm's warning?
   A delight
   B apathy
   C danger
   D awe

2. What is the first effect of the storm?
   A a radio broadcast
   B a lightning storm
   C loud noise
   D smoke

3. What causes the narrator to ignore the weather report?
   A The narrator was accustomed to storms in the mountains.
   B There were irrelevant warning signs.
   C The narrator was photographing the mountains.
   D There was no sign of an approaching storm.

Timed Writing: Exposition [Connections]

Many times the interplay of a character and society form the core of a work. Write an explanation of the cause-effect relationship between a character's culture and the character in a work from world literature.
(20 minutes)

 ## Writing Workshop: *Work in Progress*

Cause-and-Effect Essay

Questions should lead to other questions as you research cause and effect. While researching, note the progression of causes and effects that produced the final result. Keep these notes in your writing portfolio.

Reading Informational Materials

Technical Articles

In Part 2, you learned to analyze causes and effects in works of literature. If you read "The Marginal World" by Rachel Carson, you know how richly varied the effects a single cycle—the ocean tides—can be. You can learn more about tides in this technical article.

About Technical Articles

A **technical article** is an article that explains a process, provides step-by-step instruction, or presents other specialized information. Technical articles often share these features:

- main heads that divide the article into sections
- subheads that organize the information within a section
- boldfaced words, phrases, or sentences that contain key ideas
- diagrams or charts that illustrate or summarize information
- captions that explain how to apply the diagrams

Reading Skill

A picture is worth a thousand words—and when it comes to a technical article, so is a diagram. Because diagrams can lay out complicated information in a direct way, technical writers often include them in their articles. As you read the following article, **use charts and diagrams** to help you understand and **analyze the causes and effects** it discusses. Follow these steps:

- Read the text. Take note of important circumstances or events.
- Look for notations that tell you where to find a related diagram.
- Study the diagram. Ask yourself whether the visual provides information about a cause, an effect, or about the relation between causes and effects.

Use a chart like this one to help you use the diagrams in "Tides."

Text: Causes and Effects	Related Diagram	What Diagram Shows
moon's gravity tides	Figure 1	

Academic Standards

- Understand specific technical vocabulary. (10.1.1)
- Follow directions to use sophisticated technology. (10.2.3)
- Write technical documents. (10.5.6)

Tides

Joseph D. Exline, Ed.D., Jay M. Pasachoff, Ph.D., et al.

You're standing on a riverbank in the town of Saint John, Canada. In the distance there's a loud roaring sound, like a train approaching. Suddenly a wall of water twice your height thunders past. The surge of water rushes up the river channel so fast that it almost looks as if the river is flowing backward.

This thundering wall of water is an everyday event at Saint John. The town is located where the Saint John River enters the Bay of Fundy, an arm of the Atlantic Ocean. The Bay of Fundy is famous for its dramatic daily tides. When the tide comes in, fishing boats float on the water near the piers, as shown in Figure 1A. But once the tide goes out, so much water flows back to sea that the boats are stranded on the muddy harbor bottom (Figure 1B).

Photographs as well as diagrams and graphics are used to illustrate ideas presented in the text.

Figure 1 The Bay of Fundy in Canada is noted for its great differences in water level at high and low tide. **A.** Near the mouth of the bay, boats float in the Saint John River at high tide. **B.** At low tide, the boats are grounded.

Reading Informational Materials

Headings are used to divide this article into sections. Each heading names the main topic discussed in the section following.

This key idea is boldfaced to help readers find important concepts quickly.

Captions like the one at right are used to identify each photo or diagram and to link it to the text.

What Causes Tides?

The daily rise and fall of Earth's waters on its coastlines are called **tides.** As the tide comes in, the level of the water on the beach rises gradually. When the water reaches its highest point, it is high tide. Then the tide goes out, flowing back toward the sea. When the water reaches its lowest point, it is low tide. **Tides are caused by the interaction of Earth, the moon, and the sun.**

Figure 2 shows the effect of the moon's gravity on the water on Earth's surface. The moon pulls on the water on the side closest to it (point A) more strongly than it pulls on the center of the Earth. This pull creates a bulge of water, called a tidal bulge, on the side of Earth facing the moon. The water at point C is pulled toward the moon less strongly than is Earth as a whole. This water is "left behind," forming a second bulge.

In the places in Figure 2 where there are tidal bulges (points A and C), high tide is occurring along the coastlines. In the places between the bulges (points B and D), low tide is occurring. As Earth rotates, different places on the planet's surface pass through the areas of the tidal bulges and experience the change in water levels.

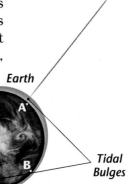

Moon

Earth

Tidal Bulges

Figure 2
The moon's pull on Earth's water causes tidal bulges to form on the side closest to the moon and the side farthest from the moon.

Day	Highest High Tide (m)	Lowest Low Tide (m)
1	1.9	0.2
2	2.1	0.1
3	2.3	0.0
4	2.4	-0.2
5	2.5	-0.2
6	2.6	-0.3
7	1.9	0.3

Figure 3
This table lists the highest high tides and lowest low tides at the mouth of the Savannah River at the Atlantic Ocean in Georgia for one week.

Tables such as this one present numerical data for easy reference.

The Daily Tide Cycle

As Earth turns completely around once each day, people on or near the shore observe the rise and fall of the tides as they reach the area of each tidal bulge. The high tides occur about 12 hours and 25 minutes apart in each location. As Earth rotates, eastern-most points pass through the area of the tidal bulge before points farther to the west. Therefore, high tide occurs later the farther west you go along a coastline.

The Monthly Tide Cycle

Even though the sun is 150 million kilometers from Earth, it is so massive that its gravity also affects the tides. The sun pulls the water on Earth's surface toward it. In Figure 4 (next page), you can follow the positions of the Earth, moon, and sun at different times during a month.

Reading Informational Materials

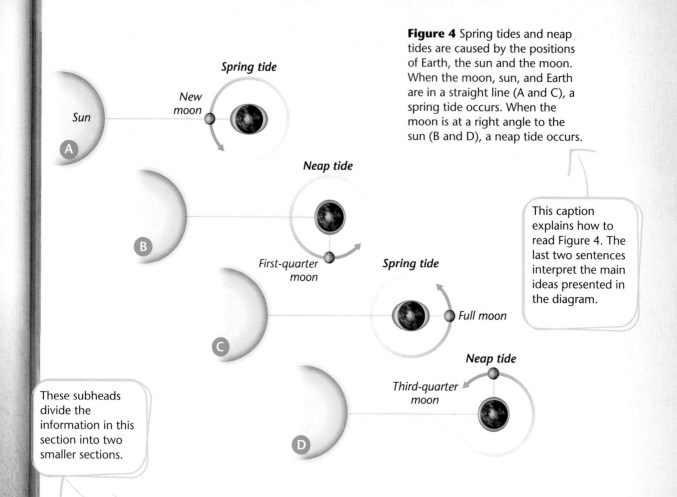

Figure 4 Spring tides and neap tides are caused by the positions of Earth, the sun and the moon. When the moon, sun, and Earth are in a straight line (A and C), a spring tide occurs. When the moon is at a right angle to the sun (B and D), a neap tide occurs.

This caption explains how to read Figure 4. The last two sentences interpret the main ideas presented in the diagram.

These subheads divide the information in this section into two smaller sections.

Spring Tides Twice a month, at the new moon and the full moon, the sun and moon are lined up. Their combined gravitational pull produces the greatest range between high and low tide, called a **spring tide.** These tides get their name not because they occur during the spring season, but from an Old English word, *springen,* which means "to jump."

Neap Tides In between spring tides, at the first and third quarters of the moon, the sun and moon pull at right angles to each other. This line-up produces a **neap tide,** a tide with the least difference between low and high tide. During a neap tide, the sun's gravity pulls some of the water away from the tidal bulge facing the moon. This acts to "even out" the water level over Earth's surface, reducing the difference between high and low tides.

Reading: Using Diagrams to Analyze Causes and Effects

Directions: *Choose the letter of the best answer to each question about the technical article.*

Standards Assessed
- 10.1.1
- 10.2.3
- 10.5.6

1. Which element of Figure 2 represents the cause of "tidal bulges"?
   A Points D and B
   B Moon
   C Points A and C
   D Earth

2. What does Figure 3 show?
   A the number of days it takes for a tide to come in
   B the high points reached by a tide in a month
   C the high and low points of daily tides during a week
   D the movement of a tide over the course of a day

3. Look at Figure 4. When the Moon and Sun are at right angles, what is the effect on the tide?
   A High tide is at its highest.
   B Low tide is at its lowest.
   C There is the greatest difference between high and low tide.
   D There is the least difference between high and low tide.

Reading: Comprehension and Interpretation

Directions: *Write your answers on a separate piece of paper.*

4. Explain two causes and two effects of tides. **[Analysis]**
5. Explain why high tide occurs on the side of Earth opposite the moon, as well as on the side closest to the moon. Use details from the diagrams in your answer. **[Integrating]**

Timed Writing: Exposition [Cognition]

Summarize the main ideas of the article "Tides." Begin with an overview of the subject. Organize your ideas logically. As you draft, define key terms before you begin using them. Make sure that you do not include details that are too specific for a summary. **(20 minutes)**

Tone

The **tone** of a work is the writer's attitude toward his or her subject and audience.

- A writer may treat a subject seriously or playfully, with anger or sadness, or in an objective tone that shows no emotion.
- A writer may address readers formally or casually, may accuse or flatter them, or may confide in them or try to inspire them.

Tone is closely related to **voice,** the personality that a writer shows to readers. Tone may be conveyed by these elements:

- the details the writer chooses to include
- the **diction,** or word choice, that the writer uses
- direct statements of the writer's feelings

<table>
<tr><td>(IN)</td><td>Academic
Standards</td></tr>
</table>

- Examine how the author's perspective influences the structure and tone of the text. (10.2.4)
- Evaluate the use of voice and narrator. (10.3.9)
- Evaluate the aesthetic qualities of style. (10.3.11)

Comparing Tones

In these two essays, "How to Recognize Familiar Faces" and "The Leader in the Mirror," Umberto Eco and Pat Mora look at perceptions and values created by society. However, each writer takes a different tone. Use a chart like the one shown to note elements in each essay that create its distinctive tone.

Element of Tone
Striking Detail:
Diction:
Direct Statements:

Tone
Attitude Toward Subject:
Attitude Toward Reader:

Vocabulary Builder

How to Recognize Familiar Faces

- **context** (kän´ tekst´) *n.* environment or situation in which something is found, especially when it helps explain the thing (p. 174) *I explained my question by establishing its <u>context</u>.*

- **expound** (ek spound´) *v.* explain in detail (p. 175) *He loves to <u>expound</u> on the subject, but we told him to keep it brief.*

- **amiably** (ā´ mē ə blē) *adv.* in a cheerful, friendly way (p. 176) *The restaurant hostess smiled <u>amiably</u> and led us to our table.*

The Leader in the Mirror

- **aspirations** (as´ pə rā´ shənz) *n.* strong ambitions or desires; goals (p. 177) *The actor had <u>aspirations</u> to win an Oscar.*

- **catalyst** (kat´ ə list´) *n.* person or thing that triggers an event or inspires an action (p. 179) *Slipping five times on the walk was the <u>catalyst</u> I needed to start shoveling the snow.*

- **inheritance** (in her´ i təns) *n.* gift handed down to a later generation in a family (p. 179) *The pin was her <u>inheritance</u> from her aunt.*

Build Understanding

Connecting to the Literature

Reading/Writing Connection In their essays, both Mora and Eco pose the question: How does society shape our perceptions of the world? Think of a topic in fashion, sports, or politics that the news media or advertisers present as important. Then, in a few sentences, explain how important you think the topic actually is. Use at least three of these words: *appeal, benefit, maximize, devote.*

Meet the Authors

Umberto **Eco** (b. 1932)

Italian author Umberto Eco has a personal library of more than 30,000 volumes—larger than many school libraries! In fact, he is interested in communication of every kind. At the University of Bologna, he teaches semiotics, the study of communication through signs and symbols. He also follows the information revolution on the Internet with great interest.

An Unlikely Bestseller After publishing many scholarly works, Eco had a surprise world hit with *The Name of the Rose* in 1980. This suspenseful novel tells of a murder in a Benedictine monastery in the Middle Ages.

Pat **Mora** (b. 1942)

Pat Mora was born in El Paso, Texas, just across the border from Juarez, Mexico. A graduate of the University of Texas, she taught school and served as a museum director before becoming a full-time writer.

Celebrating Heritage As a young girl, Mora spoke Spanish at home but did not want her friends at school to know. Now she celebrates her Mexican American background. "I write in part because Hispanic perspectives need to be part of our literary heritage," she explains.

Go Online
Author Link

For: More about the authors
Visit: www.PHSchool.com
Web Code: eqe-9112

HOW TO REACT TO FAMILIAR FACES

UMBERTO ECO

Marilyn Monroe, Andy Warhol. © Andy Warhol Foundation.

Background In this essay, Umberto Eco mentions several celebrities with whom you may not be familiar:

- Anthony Quinn was a film actor who won two Academy Awards.
- Charlton Heston, another film actor, won an Academy Award for his role in the film *Ben-Hur*.
- Johnny Carson was the host of the nighttime talk show *The Tonight Show* for thirty years.
- Oprah Winfrey is a successful talk-show host. She produces her show and also publishes a magazine.

A few months ago, as I was strolling in New York, I saw, at a distance, a man I knew very well heading in my direction. The trouble was that I couldn't remember his name or where I had met him. This is one of those sensations you encounter especially when, in a foreign city, you run into someone you met back home, or vice versa. A face out of <u>context</u> creates confusion. Still, that face was so familiar that, I felt, I should certainly stop, greet him, converse; perhaps he would immediately respond, "My dear Umberto, how are you?" or "Were you able to do that thing you were telling me about?" And I would be at a total loss. It was too late to flee. He was still looking at the opposite side of the street, but now he was beginning to turn his eyes towards me. I might as well make the first move; I would wave and then, from his voice, his first remarks, I would try to guess his identity.

We were now only a few feet from each other, I was just about to break into a broad, radiant smile, when suddenly I recognized him.

▲ **Critical Viewing**
Artist Andy Warhol made these prints repeating movie star Marilyn Monroe's face. Which of Eco's points do the prints help illustrate? **[Connect]**

Vocabulary Builder
context (kän´ tekst´) *n.* environment or situation in which something is found, especially when it helps explain the thing

It was Anthony Quinn. Naturally, I had never met him in my life, nor he me. In a thousandth of a second I was able to check myself, and I walked past him, my eyes staring into space.

Afterwards, reflecting on this incident, I realized how totally normal it was. Once before, in a restaurant, I had glimpsed Charlton Heston and had felt an impulse to say hello. These faces inhabit our memory; watching the screen, we spend so many hours with them that they are as familiar to us as our relatives', even more so. You can be a student of mass communication, debate the effects of reality, or the confusion between the real and the imagined, and <u>expound</u> the way some people fall permanently into this confusion; but still you are not immune to the syndrome.[1] And there is worse.

I have received confidences from people who, appearing fairly frequently on TV, have been subjected to the mass media over a certain period of time. I'm not talking about Johnny Carson or Oprah Winfrey, but public figures, experts who have participated in panel discussions often enough to become recognizable. All of them complain of the same disagreeable experience. Now, as a rule, when we see someone we don't know personally, we don't stare into his or her face at length, we don't point out the person to the friend at our side, we don't speak of this person in a loud voice when he or she can overhear. Such behavior would be rude, even—if carried too far—aggressive. But the same people who would never point to a customer at a counter and remark to a friend that the man is wearing a smart[2] tie behave quite differently with famous faces.

Vocabulary Builder
expound (ek spound´) v. explain in detail

Literary Analysis
Tone What does the writer's choice of the verb *subjected* tell you about his attitude toward mass media?

✓**Reading Check**

How does the writer react at first when he sees Anthony Quinn?

---

1. **syndrome** (sin´ drōm´) n. set of symptoms or characteristics occurring together and defining a disease or condition.
2. **smart** adj. stylish; fashionable.

My guinea pigs[3] insist that, at a newsstand, in the tobacconist's, as they are boarding a train or entering a restaurant toilet, they encounter others who, among themselves, say aloud, "Look there's X." "Are you sure?" "Of course I'm sure. It's X, I tell you." And they continue their conversation <u>amiably</u>, while X hears them, and they don't care if he hears them: it's as if he didn't exist.

Such people are confused by the fact that a protagonist of the mass media's imaginary world should abruptly enter real life, but at the same time they behave in the presence of the real person as if he still belonged to the world of images, as if he were on a screen, or in a weekly picture magazine. As if they were speaking in his absence.

I might as well have grabbed Anthony Quinn by the lapel, dragged him to a phone booth, and called a friend to say, "Talk about coincidence! I've run into Anthony Quinn. And you know something? He seems real!" (After which I would throw Quinn aside and go on about my business.)

The mass media first convinced us that the imaginary was real, and now they are convincing us that the real is imaginary; and the more reality the TV screen shows us, the more cinematic[4] our everyday world becomes.

---

3. **guinea** (gin´ ē) **pigs** subjects of an experiment (so-called because of the use of guinea pigs in laboratory experiments).
4. **cinematic** (sin´ ə mat´ ik) *adj.* of or like movies.

Thinking About the Selection

1. **Respond:** Would you react to a celebrity in the way Eco describes? Explain.

2. **(a) Recall:** Whom does the author see while strolling in New York City? **(b) Summarize:** Why does he plan to wave and then change his mind? **(c) Analyze Cause and Effect:** How does Eco explain his reaction to this familiar face?

3. **(a) Summarize:** According to Eco, how do many people behave when they run into a celebrity? **(b) Infer:** What does Eco suggest is the reason for their behavior?

4. **(a) Analyze:** Explain Eco's understanding of the role that media plays in our attitude toward reality. **(b) Generalize:** According to Eco, what changes in society may the media be causing?

5. **(a) Make a Judgment:** Do you think that the media's treatment of famous people is fair? Why or why not? **(b) Discuss:** Discuss your ideas in a small group. **(c) Evaluate:** Choose the best ideas and share them with the rest of the class.

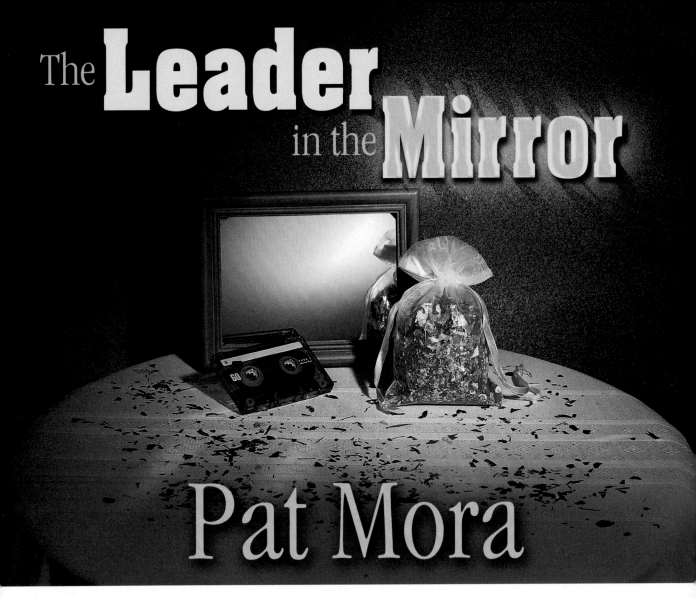

The Leader in the Mirror

Pat Mora

Each year, the newspaper in my hometown of El Paso, Texas, honors the top five academic achievers from the local high schools at an annual banquet. Last year when I addressed the group, the room at the fancy hotel was full of proud students and their relatives. The <u>aspirations</u> of the students were like a dose of powerful vitamins, filling parents, educators and guests with energy.

I began by congratulating the family members and teachers for being steady beacons[1] for those young people. In a society that undervalues families and educators, they had truly lived their commitments.

As I was planning the talk I would give to this group, I wondered how best to create an occasion for reflection. What could I say to the audience about the daily struggle to create a meaningful life?

▲ **Critical Viewing**
What do the objects in this photo suggest about Mora's essay topic? **[Speculate]**

Vocabulary Builder
aspirations (as´ pə rā´ shənz) *n.* strong ambitions or desires; goals

---

1. beacons (bē´ kənz) *n.* guiding lights; shining examples.

I remembered planning parties for my children when they were young: the careful selection of party favors, the mementos for the guests to carry away. Since this banquet was to be a party of sorts, an academic celebration, I asked myself what favors I would choose for each place at the table.

I knew I would be very popular with the students if I could give them keys to a new red car or tickets to an island vacation. But I am a writer, not a millionaire. So I decided to give them imaginary gifts: Each student would receive confetti, a tape recorder, a photograph and a mirror—symbols and metaphors to take with them through life.

I hoped that most of the students were going to enroll in college. The confetti would be for their private celebrations, those solitary moments when they had passed a test that worried them, finished a difficult paper at 2 A.M., found a summer internship.[2] Sometimes, even when no one else is around, it's important to celebrate when we have struggled and succeeded—to sprinkle a little confetti on our own heads.

Why a tape recorder? I read them my poem "Immigrants."

2. internship (in´ tʉrn´ ship´) *n.* temporary job providing training for an inexperienced young person.

Literary Analysis
Tone Which details in this paragraph show that the writer might be amused by students' values?

Immigrants
wrap their babies in the American flag,
feed them mashed hot dogs and apple pie,
name them Bill and Daisy,
buy them blonde dolls that blink blue
eyes or a football and tiny cleats
before the baby can even walk,
speak to them in thick English,
   hallo, babee, hallo,
whisper in Spanish or Polish
when the baby sleeps, whisper
in a dark parent bed, that dark
parent fear, "Will they like
our boy, our girl, our fine american
boy, our fine american girl?"

As a writer, I understand the value and necessity of knowing my past, of keeping that door open. My family stories are my <u>catalyst</u> for creativity. All of us have people in our lives whose voices merit saving if we'll only take the time.

My own father was once a paper boy for the newspaper hosting the banquet. I might not have known that fact, nor his long history of hard work, had I not been listening to him with my tape recorder a few years ago. I did not want the students to wait as long as I had to begin preserving the rich <u>inheritance</u> of their family voices. The strength of their heritage would give them the courage to face the future.

My third gift was a photograph of the El Paso/Juárez border: the Chihuahua Desert, the Rio Grande,[3] a stern mountain, two sprawling border cities. Like our families, our geography is part of who we are.

When I was growing up on the U.S. side of that border, the society around me tried in subtle and not-so-subtle ways to convince me that my Mexican heritage was inferior to that of Anglo-Americans. I hope that today's educators on the border and throughout this nation are now committed to multiculturalism, to motivating the next generation to draw on their heritage as a resource for learning. The U.S. has been described as the first international country: Our varied cultures are our common wealth.

---

3. **El Paso** (el pas´ ō) **/ Juárez** (hwä´ res) **. . . Chihuahua** (chi wä´ wä) **. . . Rio Grande** (rē´ ō grand´) El Paso is a city in Texas on the Rio Grande, the river forming the border between Texas and Mexico. Juárez, in the Mexican state of Chihuahua, is directly across the river.

Borders—and if we're attentive, we realize we all live on borders, whether they are national or not—are sites of tension and sites for learning. Borders invite us to confront differences, inequities and stereotypes. They invite us to work for multicultural cooperation and to celebrate multilingual richness.

The final gift of the evening, a mirror, was for serious gazing. I asked the students if they saw a leader when they looked into their mirrors. My guess is that too many of our young people do not see themselves as leaders because they don't look, dress or sound like the images of leaders presented to us. But leaders come in all colors, shapes and sizes. Some are talkative while others are quiet, but they all share a determination to contribute to the society of the future.

I urged the students to look often in their mirrors and to ask themselves these questions: "Am I satisfied with this world? If not, what will I do to improve it?" For if we are shaped by our surroundings, we in turn shape them. We deceive ourselves if we believe that we can live neutral[4] lives.

One-third of this nation now traces its heritage to regions other than Western Europe. We will continue to squander[5] our talent if our leaders—in politics, science, business, education and the arts—do not reflect our grand variety. I urged the students (and all of us) to ponder the strength of the mountains around us, to rise to the challenges.

Literary Analysis
Tone What tone do the details and diction in this paragraph help to create?

---

4. **neutral** (nōō′ trəl) *adj.* not taking a position; lacking vivid color.
5. **squander** (skwän′ dər) *v.* spend or use wastefully or extravagantly.

Thinking About the Selection

1. **Respond:** How do you think you would have reacted to Mora's speech if you were a student present when she gave it? Why?

2. **(a) Recall:** On what occasion does Mora give her speech?
   (b) Infer: What does the invitation to give this speech show about Mora's own achievements?

3. **(a) Recall:** What "gifts" does Mora give the students?
   (b) Interpret: Explain the meaning or purpose of each.
   (c) Connect: In what way is each gift connected to the idea of respect for one's own heritage?

4. **(a) Make a Judgment:** In your opinion, how important is a person's heritage? Why? **(b) Discuss:** Discuss your ideas in a small group. **(c) Evaluate:** Choose the most thought-provoking ideas and share them with the rest of the class.

Apply the Skills

How to React to Familiar Faces • The Leader in the Mirror

Comparing Tones

1. For each of the following items, describe the author's attitude toward it. Support each answer with two details from the text.
   Eco: (a) the idea of celebrity **(b)** the media that creates celebrity
   Mora: (c) heritage **(d)** consumer goods

2. **(a)** Use a chart like the one shown to record words and phrases that express each writer's **tone**. Analyze the attitude each writer takes in discussing the values or perceptions created by society.
   (b) Based on your chart, write a sentence to compare the mixture of tones in each piece.

	Inspirational	Sarcastic	Analytical	Other
Diction				
Direct Statements				
Other Details				

3. Based on the mix of tones in each piece, describe the voice, or personality "on the page," of each writer.

Writing to Compare Literary Works

In an essay, compare your reactions to the tone in each selection.

- First, discuss the details, diction, and direct statements that help convey the tone in each essay.
- Then, explain how the tone affects your reactions to each essay.
- Finally, explain which tone you found more effective.

Vocabulary Builder

Practice Rewrite each of the following sentences, using a word from the vocabulary list on page 172. Make any changes needed to be sure that the new sentences are grammatical. Then, explain why your chosen word makes sense.

1. The professor likes to give long explanations about his subject.
2. A good trainer encourages athletes' dreams.
3. My singing voice is one of the gifts I got from my father.
4. The politician shook hands in a friendly manner.
5. I did not recognize her out of her usual surroundings.
6. This fertilizer is supposed to be a trigger for plant growth.

QuickReview

Tone: the writer's attitude toward his or her subject and audience, made up in part by *diction* and contributing to the writer's *voice*

Go Online
Assessment

For: Self-test
Visit: www.PHSchool.com
Web Code: eqa-6112

Reading

Directions: *Questions 1–5 are based on the following selection.*

The wind blew. A falling tree bough crashed through the kitchen window. Cleaning solvent, bottled, shattered over the stove. The room was ablaze in an instant!

"Fire!" screamed a voice. The house lights flashed, water pumps shot water from the ceilings. But the solvent spread on the linoleum, licking, eating, under the kitchen door, while the voices took it up in chorus: "Fire, fire, fire!"

The house tried to save itself. Doors sprang tightly shut, but the windows were broken by the heat and the wind blew and sucked upon the fire.

The house gave ground as the fire in ten billion angry sparks moved with flaming ease from room to room and then up the stairs. While scurrying water rats squeaked from the walls, pistoled their water, and ran for more. And the wall sprays let down showers of mechanical rain.

—from "There Will Come Soft Rains" by Ray Bradbury

1. **What are two causes of the fire spreading quickly?**
   A the lights flash and the window breaks
   B the solvent spills and the doors shut
   C rats run for water and the wind blows
   D the windows break and the solvent spills

2. **Which event is not an effect of the fire?**
   A the wall sprays showering the house
   B the solvent spreading across the floor
   C the windows breaking
   D the voices screaming

3. **What is the intended effect of closing all the doors tightly?**
   A to stop the solvent from spreading
   B to trap the water rats inside
   C to cut off air to the fire
   D to block sparks from starting another fire

4. **Which event is both a cause and an effect?**
   A the wind blows
   B the window breaks
   C the voices cry "Fire!"
   D the water rats run for water

5. **The passage enumerates**
   A one action leading to the fire.
   B two actions leading to the fire.
   C three actions leading to the fire.
   D none of the above.

Vocabulary

Directions: *Choose the letter of the sentence in which the word in bold is used correctly.*

Standards Assessed

• 10.1.2
• 10.3.2
• 10.3.6

6. preliminary

A Our preliminary explorations indicate that there is oil there.

B At the preliminary hearing, the judge received the jury's verdict.

C In the recipe, the preliminary step is frosting the cake and serving it.

D He does his preliminary exercises last.

7. priority

A This task is a priority, so I will do it last.

B In the emergency room, a broken leg has priority over a small cut.

C The person who is last in line has priority over anyone else.

D My priority is my job, so I rarely work.

8. fluent

A A fluent runner, she tripped as she rounded the curve.

B His English is fluent, so you will have difficulty understanding him.

C The translator was not fluent, so I could understand him well.

D The dancer's fluent movements charmed the audience.

9. intuitive

A Math is intuitive for him, so he needs to use a calculator.

B She got lost because she has an intuitive sense of direction.

C Winning thirty games, he showed an intuitive grasp of chess.

D It took much careful thought to reach my intuitive conclusion.

10. initial

A My initial words in the conversation were "Good-bye and good luck."

B After his initial hesitation, he grew to enjoy the game.

C In the initial chapters of the book, we finally discover how the story ends.

D In the initial stages of a fire, there is nothing left but ashes.

Directions: *Choose the most likely meaning for each word.*

11. fluency

A quality of acting uncertainly

B quality of flowing smoothly or easily

C quality of ending abruptly

D quality of beginning aggressively

12. influence

A the power of flight

B a flow of ideas from one person to another

C a sudden, abrupt ending

D a large amount of money

13. elimination

A act of depicting a scene

B act of throwing out, as through a door

C act of running away

D act of heating, as when cooking

14. subliminal

A below the acceptable level of order

B stuck between paths

C below the threshold of awareness

D having to do with the deep sea

Spelling Workshop

Easily Confused Words

Certain words are easily confused with each other. The words may sound similar, have related meanings, or have similar spellings.

Choosing the Correct Word The two words in each pair in the word list are easy to confuse. If you use one in place of the other, a spell checker on a word-processing program will not find the error. You need to proofread carefully.

Use a dictionary to determine the difference between the words in each pair. Then, study the word list until you are sure you understand the difference between the words.

Practice *Read each of the following sentences. Then, fill in the letters necessary to complete the correct word from the word pairs.*

1. The criminal was _ _ _secuted for his crime.
2. The weather will _ffect our plans for the picnic.
3. The _ffect of the Internet is improved communications.
4. The flashing lights indicated a power outage was _ _ _inent.
5. We tried to _ _icit a smile from the baby.
6. Have the art experts appr_ _ _ _ the painting.
7. When a group is _ _ _secuted, its members may fear for their lives.
8. _ _ _icit activities are usually criminal activities.
9. He is an _ _inent statesman and won the Nobel Peace Prize last year.
10. Did they appr_ _ e you of the time that the meeting starts?

Word List
affect
effect
eminent
imminent
persecuted
prosecuted
apprise
appraise
illicit
elicit

Monitor Your Progress

Directions: *Write the letter of the sentence in which all words are spelled correctly.*

1. **A** The affact of the new road was to speed up traffic.
   B Did my argument affecte your decision?
   C The bright green wall had a strange effect on the light in the room.
   D The effecte of the treaty isn't known.

2. **A** The district attorney persecuted the case.
   B Certain crimes against the community will always be persacuted.
   C He felt persecuted when they would not stop laughing at him.
   D The protesters were persekuted for obstructing traffic on the highway.

3. **A** Please appraize the value of this antique.
   B Will someone apprase David of the homework assignment?
   C Marla can apraise you of what happened at the meeting.
   D Who can appraise the painting's value?

4. **A** A good moderator will elicit a response from everyone.
   B There is a large elicet market in stolen bicycles.
   C The executive stored his ellicit gains in a foreign bank account.
   D We tried to elisit information from the children.

Directions: *Write the letter of the correct spelling of the word that best completes the sentence.*

1. The time to make up your mind is _____.
   A iminent
   B eminent
   C imminent
   D emminent

2. It will be hard to _____ the case without witnesses.
   A persecute
   B prosecute
   C prosacute
   D presecute

3. The antibiotic had no _____ on her illness.
   A afect
   B efect
   C affect
   D effect

4. No one bothered to _____ our class of the schedule change.
   A appraise
   B appriase
   C apprise
   D apriase

5. The boat smuggled the _____ cargo past the guards.
   A ilicit
   B elicit
   C illicit
   D illisit

6. The _____ judge was respected by everyone.
   A iminent
   B eminent
   C imminent
   D emminent

Writing Workshop

Exposition: Cause-and-Effect Essay

Academic Standards

• Establish a thesis and focus for the piece. (10.4.2)

• Use supporting evidence to develop main ideas within the body of the composition. (10.4.5)

• Write persuasive compositions. (10.5.4)

Whenever something unusual happens, the first question most people ask is, "Why?" A **cause-and-effect essay** can satisfy a reader's curiosity. It might explain why a weird new fashion fad began or what happened as a result of a groundbreaking court decision. Use the steps outlined in this workshop to write a cause-and-effect essay.

Assignment Write a cause-and-effect essay in which you explain a strong cause-and-effect relationship.

What to Include Your cause-and-effect essay should feature these elements:

- a clearly stated topic that identifies the cause-and-effect relationships to be explored

- an effective and logical method of organization

- strong details and examples

- transitions that smoothly and clearly connect your ideas

- error-free grammar, including correct use of pronouns

To preview the criteria on which your cause-and-effect essay may be judged, see the rubric on page 193.

Using the Form
You may use elements of this form in these types of writing:
- news articles
- process explanations
- reflective essays

Writing Workshop: *Work in Progress*

If you have completed the Work-in-Progress assignments, you already have several ideas to use in your cause-and-effect essay. Continue to develop these ideas, or explore a new idea as you complete the Writing Workshop.

To get a feel for cause-and-effect essays, read "Making History With Vitamin C" by Penny Le Couteur and Jay Burreson on page 144.

Prewriting

Choosing Your Topic

To choose a topic that shows a strong cause-and-effect relationship, use one of the following strategies:

- **Scan a newspaper or magazine.** Review print or online articles, looking for ideas that make you ask, "Why?" Keep notes of possible topics and then focus on the subjects that make you most curious. Review your notes and choose a topic to address.

- **Make a list.** With a partner, brainstorm for a list of scientific phenomena, historical events, or popular trends that you find interesting, important, or even confusing. Look over your list to pick a topic you would like to explore.

Narrowing Your Topic

Once you have a topic, make sure that it is a reasonable size for your essay. You may need to focus your essay on a more specific topic. For example, you might not be able to answer "Why did the Great Depression happen?" in a short work. Instead, your essay could focus on why the stock market crashed in October of 1929.

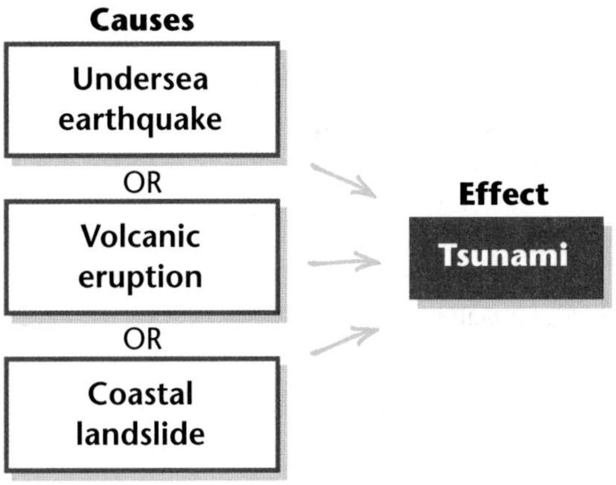

Gathering Details

Make a cause-and-effect chart. Organizing your ideas and details in a cause-and-effect chart can help you form a clear picture of the relationship you will write about. One chart shown here presents three events that can cause one effect. The other chart classifies the possible effects of one cause.

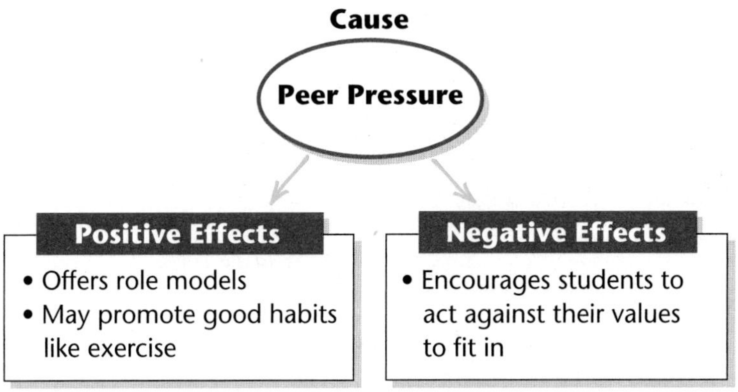

Work in Progress
Review the work you did on pages 141 and 165.

Causes

| Undersea earthquake |
| OR |
| Volcanic eruption |
| OR |
| Coastal landslide |

Effect

Tsunami

Cause

Peer Pressure

Positive Effects
- Offers role models
- May promote good habits like exercise

Negative Effects
- Encourages students to act against their values to fit in

Writing Workshop

Drafting

Shaping Your Writing

Summarize your analysis. Even if you are describing a complicated chain of effects, you will need a clear and direct introduction. Prepare a simplified cause-and-effect chart like the one shown here to summarize your prewriting ideas. The chart can show you which ideas are essential to your topic and which are less critical.

Choose a logical organization. The structure you choose for your essay depends on the information you have.

- **Chronological order** makes sense for many cause-and-effect essays. You can start with the cause and then continue by describing its effects. You could also start with the effect and then go back through its causes one at a time.

- If you are describing multiple causes, consider using an **order of importance organization.** You might begin with your most important cause, or save the most important cause for last.

Cause

Bicycles are built using new, stronger materials.

Effect

New bicycles are faster, more comfortable, and lighter.

Providing Elaboration

Describe details thoroughly. Think about how much your audience of readers already knows about your topic. Be sure to provide full explanations for any unfamiliar words or events.

Use clear transitions. Many words and phrases will help you introduce causes or effects. For example, use *therefore, consequently, as a result,* or *for that reason* to introduce effects. Identify causes with *because, since, as,* or *for the reason that.*

As you write, also look for phrases that help you connect, contrast, or compare ideas. You might use *not only . . . but also* to join two related ideas. Other transitions, such as *however* and *on the other hand,* can introduce contrasting ideas.

To read the complete student model, see page 192.

Student Model: Using Transitions

Some of the water the hurricane carried soaks into the ground, but often there is more water than the land can absorb. As a result, the water quickly runs off to lower areas.

The writer's use of a transitional phrase clarifies the effect being described.

From the Author's Desk

Susan Vreeland

Susan Vreeland
On Showing Causes and Effects

My story "Crayon, 1955" is drawn from a time in my childhood when my great-grandfather, an artist, came to our house to die. What occurred there in that intense time was magical: He introduced me to his world of art. The experience narrated here was the cause of my lifelong interest in art, and resulted, ultimately, in writing *Girl in Hyacinth Blue.*

"Re-visioning . . . is a coaxing process."

——— Susan Vreeland

Professional Model:
from *"Crayon, 1955"*

"Jenny," he said the next day. His voice scraped
^ like a Popsicle stick across the sidewalk. "Let me teach you to paint."

I wasn't sure I wanted him to. The room smelled bad, but not just because of his . . . paints. Once Mom said Gramp's blood ran with turpentine, which I thought was what made his skin waxy and yellow.

Practicing a secret style of shallow breathing, I sat on the edge of the bed and he held my hand inside his spidery one while I held the long brush. He squeezed so tightly, directing where my hand should go, that his long yellow nails jabbed into my palm. I curled up my toes and kept quiet. Like a miracle, In front of me appeared an unrolled white flower with an orange finger inside. "There's nothing so cheerful as a calla lily," he said as we worked. "They grow tall and graceful just like you, and one day, they open themselves to the world."

In my revision, I inserted images that a young girl might think — the simile of a Popsicle stick, and the visual adjective "spidery."

To convey sharply the resulting change in Jenny, in my revision I added, "Like a miracle," an exaggerated simile revealing her astonishment.

In fiction, cause and effect are subtle, sometimes only a suggestion. Jenny's negative reactions to her grandfather change when the painting resulting from his teaching pleases her.

Revising

Revising Your Paragraphs

Color-code to identify related details. Each paragraph in your essay should have a strong, single focus. First, circle the topic sentence of each paragraph. If you cannot find a topic sentence, consider adding one. Then, underline the details that support the topic of the paragraph.

Peer Review: After identifying topic sentences and supporting details, take a close look at the sentences that are neither circled nor underlined. With a partner, discuss whether you should rewrite or delete these sentences. You might also move sentences to another paragraph where they would support the topic more effectively. After revising, explain your decisions to your partner.

To read the complete student model, see page 192.

Student Model: Revising to Strengthen Focus

These storms not only caused trouble for the insurance companies, but also affected the citrus and tourism industries. The citrus growers in Florida lost about half of their grapefruit crop during Hurricane Frances. Hurricanes also bring lightning, which can cause fires in trees or houses. Tourism was also hurt because people do not want to travel into a disaster zone.

> The writer deleted a sentence that offered useful information but did not relate to the topic of the paragraph.

Revising Your Word Choice

Look for careless repetition. Effective writing can use repetition to emphasize key ideas and create a memorable impact, but sloppy repetition weakens your writing. Look for words that appear too often or too close together. Use a thesaurus to find words with related meanings or use a pronoun to replace a noun that appears too frequently.

Too Much Repetition: *Bees buzz* as a result of beating their wings *rapidly*. When an intruder approaches, *bees* beat their wings even more *rapidly*. As a result, *the bees' buzzing rapidly* grows louder.

More Effective: *Bees buzz* as a result of beating their wings *rapidly*. When an intruder approaches, *bees* beat their wings *faster* and their *buzzing* grows louder.

Integrating Grammar Skills

Revising Pronoun-Antecedent Agreement

Antecedents are the nouns for which pronouns stand. A pronoun must agree with its antecedent in number, person, and gender.

Prentice Hall Writing and Grammar Connection: Chapter 24, Section 2

Identifying Incorrect Pronoun-Antecedent Agreement In your writing, check each pronoun to make sure it agrees with its antecedent. Ask three things about the antecedent:

- *Number:* Is it singular or plural?
- *Person:* Is it first person (the one speaking), second person (the one being spoken to), or third person (the one spoken about)?
- *Gender:* Is it masculine, feminine, or neuter?

> ANTECEDENT   PRONOUN
> Marie Curie is known for her work with radium.
>   ANTECEDENT   PRONOUN
> My father and I saw the experiment. We were amazed.

Special Problems With Agreement Use a plural personal pronoun with two or more antecedents joined by *and*.

Lewis and Clark described the expedition in *their* journal.

Use a singular personal pronoun with two or more antecedents joined by *or* or *nor*.

Neither *Lewis* nor *Clark* regretted *his* journey.

Fixing Agreement Errors To fix a pronoun and antecedent that do not agree, choose the pronoun that has the correct number, person, and gender.

1. **Describe the number, person, and gender of the antecedent.**
2. **Choose a pronoun with the same number, person, and gender.** Make sure you choose the correct pronoun case: nominative, objective, or possessive. (*For more on pronoun-antecedent agreement, see pages R45–R46.*)

Apply It to Your Editing

Circle the pronouns in two paragraphs of your draft. Draw an arrow to the antecedent for each pronoun. Evaluate whether or not the pronoun and antecedent agree. Replace any incorrect pronouns.

Writing Workshop

Student Model: Andrew Vanover
Raleigh, NC

Hurricane: Causes and Effects

Everyone dreads the hurricane season. When that time of year comes around, we all lock down and get ready for the harsh winds and power outages. The 2004 season started out with a bang. Large parts of the coast were torn apart as storms rolled in, one after another.

Causes of Hurricanes

Hurricanes form when weather patterns of different temperatures run into each other and start spinning. When a cold front out in the ocean, moving in one direction, comes in contact with a warm front moving in the opposite direction, winds start. These winds start moving in circular motions. As they spin, they pick up speed. These large areas of fast-moving winds generate tornadoes that pull water up into the storm. Hurricanes have high winds with tornadoes, and carry large amounts of water.

When it starts, the storm is classified as a tropical depression. As it becomes stronger, it is called a tropical storm. If the wind speeds get high enough, the tropical storm is categorized as a hurricane.

Effects of Hurricanes: Damage to Property

When the storm hits land, it dumps all its water, and that is when it becomes the most destructive. Some of the water soaks into the ground, but often there is more water than the land can absorb. As a result, the water quickly runs off to lower areas. These run-offs are called flash floods. Flash floods can wash away land and possessions or destroy them by filling them with water. At the same time, hurricane winds can blow over trees and power lines. With the power out, repairs are hard to make quickly. This means power can be out for a week or longer. Hurricanes also bring lightning, which can cause fires in trees or houses.

Effects of Hurricanes: Damage to Business

During the late summer and fall of 2004, the state of Florida was hit by four major hurricanes: Charley, Frances, Ivan, and Jeanne. Each hurricane caused so much damage that it could not be repaired before the next storm hit. The damage was so bad that President Bush asked Congress for 7.1 billion dollars for repairs in Florida. Many people had to board up stores and wait in line for electric generators. In addition, relief workers were sent down to Florida to help deliver meals, water, and ice.

These storms not only caused trouble for the insurance companies, but also affected the citrus and tourism industries. The citrus growers in Florida lost about half of their grapefruit crop during Hurricane Frances. Tourism was also hurt because people do not want to travel into a disaster zone.

Conclusion

The hurricane season of 2004 was more intense than previous years. This is said to be from warm temperatures in the Atlantic Ocean and a decrease in wind shear. We hope that in the future we will better be able to predict and prepare for these hurricanes.

Andrew uses subheads to clearly organize the information. This paragraph explains what causes hurricanes.

Andrew breaks his discussion of the effects of hurricanes into two sections.

In addition, Andrew uses a specific detail to support his broader claims.

Editing and Proofreading

Check your draft for errors in format, grammar, and punctuation.

Focus on Usage Errors: Check your writing for commonly confused words. Remember that *then* refers to time and *than* is used for comparisons. Use *since* to refer to a previous time, not to mean "because." If you are unsure about a word, consult a dictionary or usage guide.

Publishing and Presenting

Consider one of the following ways to share your writing:
Give a class presentation. Use your essay as the basis of a presentation. Use photographs, charts, or diagrams to make the cause-and-effect relationships clear. Practice combining visuals with your writing, deciding when you will show each visual as you share the ideas from your essay.
Use e-mail. Share your writing electronically. Type the essay using word-processing software. Attach the file to an e-mail to a friend or relative. Save printouts of the essay and any responses in your writing portfolio.

Reflecting on Your Writing

Writer's Journal Jot down your thoughts on the experience of writing a cause-and-effect essay. Begin by answering these questions:
- Which prewriting strategy helped shape your final draft the most?
- How did writing change your ideas about your topic?

Rubric for Self-Assessment

To assess your own cause-and-effect essay, use this rubric.

Criteria	Rating Scale *not very* *very*
Focus: How clearly do you identify the cause-and-effect relationship you explore?	1 2 3 4 5
Organization: How effectively do you organize your information?	1 2 3 4 5
Support/Elaboration: How strong are the details and examples you use as support?	1 2 3 4 5
Style: How effectively do you use transitions to connect your ideas?	1 2 3 4 5
Conventions: How correct is your grammar, especially your use of pronouns?	1 2 3 4 5

Communications Workshop

Analyzing Media Presentations

Some television, radio, and Internet sources are truthful, thorough, and objective. Others offer information that is inaccurate, incomplete, or reported in a biased manner. To evaluate media, stay alert and analyze claims critically. Use the following strategies.

Evaluate the Content

To evaluate the information presented in a news program, advertisement, or on a Web site, follow these steps:

Identify evidence. Listen or read for facts, statistics, quotations, and other evidence. If no support is given, consider whether you have any reason to accept the claims in the presentation.

Analyze evidence. Evaluate any evidence provided.

- **Consider relevance.** A fact may be attention-grabbing, but if it has nothing to do with the main idea, it is not evidence.

- **Consider bias.** People quoted in media may present biased, or distorted, evidence. Consider reasons a source might have to favor one version of events over another.

- **Consider inconsistencies or ambiguities.** Ask yourself whether the claims made are contradictory or vague. Consider whether any viewpoints have been left out.

Evaluate the Presentation

Once you know a presentation's content, think about how it delivers this information. Be alert for these media techniques:

- **Charged or Manipulative Language** Saying that "the budget was *finally* approved today," implies criticism of the amount of time it took to approve it.

- **Stereotypes** Watch for stereotypes, or oversimplified ideas about a group of people. Many stereotypes are negative images based on race, gender, age, or role.

- **Cultural Assumptions** Media presentations reflect basic assumptions about what is important or good. Think about whether you agree with such value judgments.

Academic Standards

- Synthesize information from multiple different sources. (10.4.6)
- Compare and contrast the ways in which media genres cover the same event. (10.7.8)
- Identify and evaluate the artistic effects of a media presentation. (10.7.13)

1= poor to 5= excellent

Purpose:
What is the main purpose?_____

Use of Facts
____Relevant support
____Reliable support
____Complete support

Opinions
____Reasonableness
____Breadth

Presentation
____Speaker's clarity
____Graphics
____Speaker's tone
____Music

Does the presentation include charged language?
Does it include charged images?
Does it present stereotypes?

Conclusions
Was the presentation objective?
Was it reliable?

Activity ❯ *Prepare and Deliver a Speech* ❯ Analyze a television newscast or advertisement using the Feedback Form as a guide. Share your conclusions in a class discussion.

Up From Slavery

Booker T. Washington
Signet Classic, 2000

Autobiography Nineteenth-century African American businessman, activist, and educator Booker Taliaferro Washington's *Up from Slavery* is one of the great American autobiographies. Washington's philosophy of self-reliance and his vision of African American success have inspired generations.

Roughing It

Mark Twain
Signet Classic, 1962

Novel A fascinating picture of the American frontier emerges from Twain's fictionalized recollections of his experiences prospecting for gold, speculating in timber, and writing for a series of small Western newspapers during the 1860s. Twain's humor and sarcastic view of life makes the wild west a little more wild.

Jane Eyre

Charlotte Brontë
Signet Classic, 1997

Novel Common sense and a healthy self-respect guide Jane, an orphan, as she journeys through the world. When she takes a job as governess at gloomy Thornfield Hall, owned by the mysterious Mr. Rochester, Jane must confront sinister dangers and her greatest challenge yet—herself.

Lord of the Flies

William Golding
Perigee Book, 1954

Novel A plane crashes on a tropical island in the Pacific, stranding a group of boys. It should be a simple matter for the boys to pull together and wait to be rescued—but conflicts arise. Swept up in a nightmare of fear and bullying, most of the castaways abandon their efforts to stay "civilized." Through this survival story, the author explores the darker side of human nature.

These titles are available in the Penguin/Prentice Hall Literature Library.
Consult your teacher before choosing one.

Think About It The crack of a bat, clouds of dust erupting as the runner slides—the sounds and sights of a baseball game are familiar to most Americans. So too is the anxiety. At critical moments, knowing that everyone is watching, a player has to wonder, "Will I goof up?" As Dave Barry reports, the pressure can make one incredibly, well, butterfingered. If you do happen to make an error, though, laughter is a good way to get back in the game.

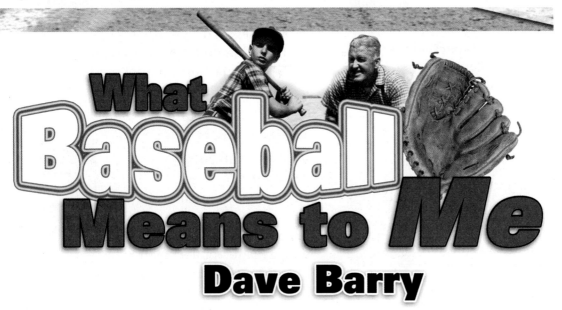

What Baseball Means to Me
Dave Barry

I was on a team called the Indians and had a Herb Score–model glove, named for a player who went on to get hit in the eye by a baseball.

I particularly remember this one game: I was in deep right field, of course, and there were two out in the bottom of the last inning with the tying run on base, and Gerry Sinnott, who already had to shave, was at bat. As I stood there waiting for the pitch, I dreamed a dream that millions of other kids have dreamt: that someday I would grow up and I wouldn't have to be in Little League anymore. In the interim, my feelings could best be summed up by the statement "Oh, please, please, please, God, don't let Gerry Sinnott hit the ball to me."

And of course God, who as you know has a terrific sense of humor, had Gerry Sinnott hit the ball to me. Here is what happened in the next few seconds: Outside of my body, hundreds of spectators, thousands of spectators, arrived at the ball field at that very instant via chartered buses from distant cities to see if I could catch the ball. Inside my body, my brain cells hastily met and came up with a Plan of Action, which they announced to the rest of the body parts. "Listen up, everybody!" they shouted. "We're going to MISS THE BALL! Let's get cracking!"

Instantly my entire body sprang into action, like a complex, sophisticated machine operated by earthworms. The command flashed down from Motor Control to my legs: "GET READY TO RUN!" And soon the excited reply flashed back: "WHICH LEG FIRST?" Before Motor Control could issue a ruling, an urgent message came in from Vision Central, reporting that the ball had already gone by. In fact, it was now a good thirty to forty yards behind my body, rolling into the infield of the adjacent field. Motor Control, reacting quickly to this surprising new input, handled the pressure coolly and decisively, snapping out the command "OKAY! We're going to FALL DOWN!" And my body lunged violently sideways, in the direction opposite the side the ball had passed a full two seconds earlier, flopping onto the ground like some pathetic spawning salmon whose central nervous system had been destroyed by toxic waste, as Gerry Sinnott cruised home.

Meet the Author

In 1988, humor writer **Dave Barry** (b. 1947) was awarded the prestigious Pulitzer Prize. According to his official Web site, "Many people are still trying to figure out how this happened." Self-deprecating humor of this sort is Barry's trademark style. It keeps readers hooked on his syndicated column, which appears in over 500 newspapers.

Readings in Contemporary Humor
Talk About It

Use the following questions to guide a discussion of Barry's essay.

1. Which part of the essay did you find funniest? Why?
2. Reread the first two paragraphs. Look for sentences that end with an unexpected idea. Explain the way that Barry gets readers to expect one idea and then delivers another.
3. With a group, consider the following questions:
   - If you were Barry's friend, what might you have said to him or done with him after the game? Explain your answer.
   - Can hearing about the mistakes that people, such as Barry, have made encourage others to pick themselves up after a defeat? Why?

   Choose a point-person to share your group's ideas with the class.

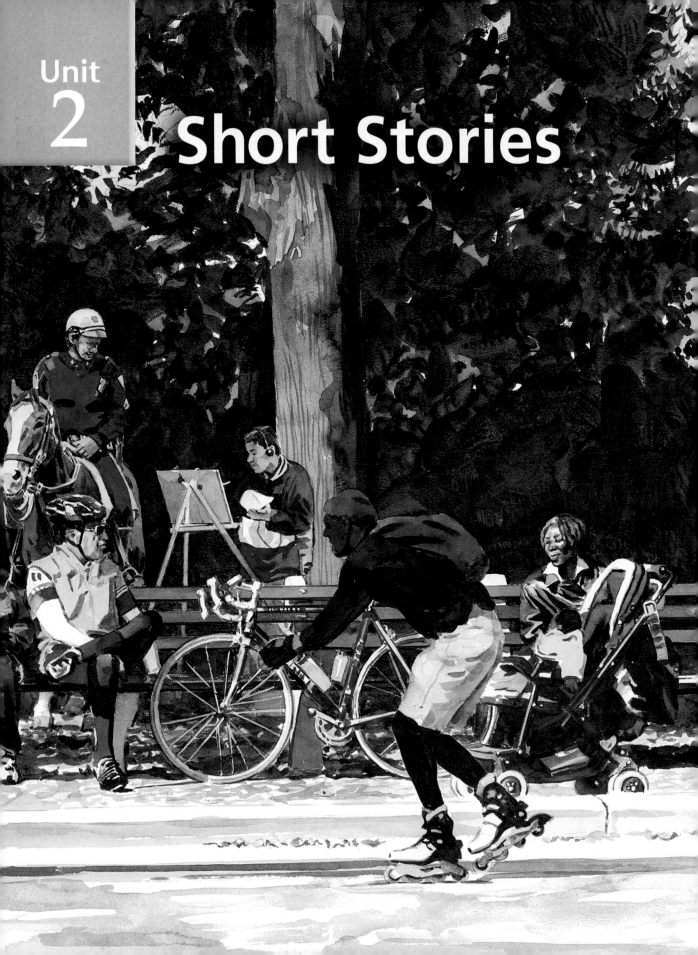

Unit
2

Short Stories

Unit 2 Overview

PART 1: Making Inferences
PART 2: Drawing Conclusions

Academic Standards
In This Unit You Will

- Examine how the author's perspective influences the structure and tone of the text. (10.2.4)
- Analyze many different forms of dramatic literature. (10.3.1)
- Evaluate interactions between characters and how these affect the plot. (10.3.3)
- Evaluate the use of voice and narrator. (10.3.9)
- Use varied and expanded vocabulary. (10.5.7)

Introduction
The Short Story

From the Author's Desk

C. J. Cherryh
Talks About the Form

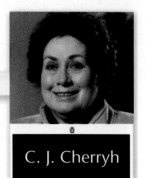

C. J. Cherryh

The **short story** isn't my native medium. I'm a novelist. Novels use very different rules than the short story: novels, unlike stories, have elaborately developed **characters** and an involved **plot** that produces change in the central characters.

▲ **C. J. Cherryh** is an award-winning writer of fantasy and science fiction.

"Compression of Time and Place"

I wanted to try the short story, and knew it was different, but I hadn't been able to produce a good short story idea until I heard Mr. Harlan Ellison, an excellent writer, speak on the basic characteristics of the short story, namely compression of time and place.

Ideally, in Mr. Ellison's words, a short story arranges matters so that the **conflict** comes to a head in one single encounter between individuals who don't know they know as much as they do—and their whole world shakes in that encounter. So a short story, unlike a novel, doesn't have deeply complex characters, doesn't have a complicated **plot,** and doesn't use many **settings.**

◀ **Critical Viewing**
In what ways does this image suggest the "what-if" quality of science fiction that Cherryh discusses? **[Apply]**

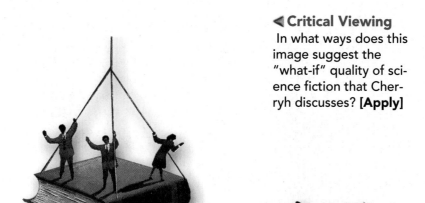

"Follow No Rule Off a Cliff"

Now my own proverb is this: follow no rule off a cliff . . . meaning, don't carry any rule to the point of absurdity. So you will see that, in my story "The Threads of Time," while I have an encounter which creates a shock in two lives, the matter of time is somewhat wider in scope. I took Mr. Ellison's definition for a good guide and applied it at need.

I write **science fiction,** meaning fiction in which science is important. What is science? Knowledge. And what is fiction? Fiction is what-if, in modern Brooklyn or in 1800's London.

Dare we what-if about something as certain as science? Yes—precisely because science should never be too sure of itself, as the quotation shown here indicates.

It is less than five hundred years since an entire half of the world was discovered. . . . The sciences of chemistry and physics go back scarcely one century. The science of aviation goes back forty years. The science of atomics is being born.

And yet we think we know a lot.

from "Mimic"
—*Donald A. Wollheim*

What-if is how science makes progress. What-if breaks us out of the stale daily rut and makes us look at the world in a different way, and scientists read science fiction because it makes them follow trails their knowledge doesn't encourage them to use.

So science fiction is a literature of questions and what-ifs, but it's not a new literature. The first hunters sitting around the fire, telling the first tall tales and what-ifs in the world—that began what we now call science fiction.

More About C. J. Cherryh

C. J. Cherryh (b. 1942) is known for her space opera series— books filled with romantic adventure, vivid details of alien cultures, and interstellar conflict.

She enjoys excitement in her real life on Earth as well. Her adventures include outrunning a dog pack in Thebes, Greece, and falling down a chute in a cave on Crete. Referring to her home in the Pacific Northwest, she says, "I choose to live downwind of five active volcanoes."

Fast Facts

▶ The adventurous Cherryh wants to visit the Amazon and see the Erebus volcano in Antarctica.

▶ She took up figure skating when she was 61 and won a silver medal in a competition six months later.

Exploring Short Stories

Elements of Short Stories

A **short story** is a brief work of fiction intended to be read in one sitting. Due to the brevity of a short story, the writer must limit the number of characters, the range of settings, and the scope of the action.

"I thought it had a pretty good story and interesting characters, but I really didn't like the font."

The following are some of the key elements of a short story:

Plot A short story's **plot** is the progression of events that make up the action. Throughout the course of a story's plot, events unfold, develop to a **climax** (or high point), and are then resolved, or sorted out, during the **resolution.**

Conflict Most plots center around a **conflict,** a problem or struggle. There are two main types of conflict in literature.

- An **external conflict** is a struggle between two characters, between an individual and a group, or between a character and a force, such as nature or fate.

- An **internal conflict** is a struggle within the mind of one character.

In traditional stories, the conflict ends at the resolution. However, in modern stories, characters may experience an **epiphany,** or sudden insight, that changes their feelings about the conflict without necessarily resolving it.

▶ **Critical Viewing** What types of conflict does the painting on p. 203 suggest? **[Interpret]**

Character The **characters** in a story are the individuals who participate in the action. Types of characters include the **protagonist** and **antagonist**—the main character and his or her adversary. The **hero,** a character who exhibits positive traits, is often the protagonist.

Characterization is the writer's process of revealing a character's personality to the reader. Writers can reveal characters both directly and indirectly.

- **Direct:** Writers make direct statements about a character's personality, appearance, habits, goals, values, or beliefs.
- **Indirect:** Writers can report a character's words, thoughts, actions, and interactions with other characters without commenting on them.

The process of showing how a character changes or of revealing different sides of a character's personality is called **character development.**

Setting The **setting** of a story is the time and place of the action. Setting provides a context or backdrop for the action. It can also add complications to the plot or contribute to the mood of the story.

- The setting can be past, present, or future, and it can also include a specific year, season, or hour of day.
- The setting can include the social, economic, or cultural circumstances that affect the characters and their specific geographic location in a country, town, or community.

Theme The **theme** of a short story is its central message or insight about life. A theme is not a summary of "what happens" in a story. Instead, it is a generalization about what the events mean. Themes may be stated or implied.

- A **stated theme** is expressed directly by the author.
- An **implied theme** is suggested indirectly through the experiences of the characters or through the events and the setting of the work.

Check Your Understanding

Choose the letter of the short story element that best represents each item.

1. Martians visit Earth.   **A** theme   **B** plot
2. Two women love one man.   **A** theme   **B** conflict
3. A hero triumphs.   **A** theme   **B** setting
4. A volcano erupts.   **A** setting   **B** character

From the Author's Desk
C. J. Cherryh Introduces "The Threads of Time"

This little story is a good example of why one should never throw creative work away. In the year this was written, I was using a typewriter, which produces paper, and because it was on paper, I filed it. When you use a computer, it's natural simply to highlight and delete something that doesn't fit where it is—or to delete the outtake files when you finish a project.

An Introductory Scene Becomes a Short Story

"The Threads of Time" was the introductory scene for my first published novel, back in 1975. It's set in a very futuristic world, and while one of the characters does appear in the novel that follows, the **setting** of the novel itself is a feudal age. So my editor, Don Wollheim, said the introduction had to go.

I cut it, he published the book—*Gate of Ivrel*—and the little snippet I'd clipped off lay in a manila folder for nearly ten years until someone needed a short-short for a convention program book. I polished the snippet into what you see before you. It's interesting to note that the **central character** in this story became the **antagonist**, not the **hero**, in the novel that followed.

Science Fiction Combines What's Real and What-if

"The Threads of Time" is a time-travel story. It is **science fiction.** But you don't have to believe time-travel exists. In fact, to be a good science fiction reader, you need two things: first, a "sense of wonder," which means being able to look at the real world and say, "But—what if. . .?" And second, you need to engage in "willing suspension of disbelief" as you read. This means you know what part of the story is real, and what part is what-if. Then, you enter into the what-if for the duration of the tale, with your imagination given free rein.

Once you let yourself imagine time travel, for instance, you can think of all the strange effects that might follow. It's so human to wish to relive yesterday, or to leap ahead to a longed-for event. Science fiction allows you to fulfill that wish.

The Threads of Time
C.J. Cherryh

It was possible that the Gates were killing the qhal. They were everywhere, on every world, had been a fact of life for five thousand years, and linked the whole net of qhalur civilization into one present-tense coherency.

They had not, to be sure, invented the Gates. Chance gave them that gift . . . on a dead world of their own sun. One Gate stood—made by unknown hands.

And the qhal made others, imitating what they found. The Gates were instantaneous transfer, not alone from place to place, but, because of the motion of worlds and suns and the traveling galaxies—involving time.

There was an end of time. Ah, qhal *could* venture anything. If one supposed, if one believed, if one were very *sure*, one could step through a Gate to a Gate that would/might exist on some other distant world.

And if one were wrong?
If it did not exist?
If it never had?

▲ Critical Viewing
What do you predict about the setting of this story based on this image? **[Predict]**

C. J. Cherryh
Author's Insight
You aren't expected to know what the word *qhal* means. But an experienced reader will guess that this is another species of intelligent beings.

Time warped in the Gate-passage. One could step across light-years, unaged; so it was possible to outrace light and time. Did one not want to die, bound to a single lifespan? Go forward. See the future. Visit the world/ worlds to come.

But never go back. Never tamper. Never alter the past.

There was an End of Time.

It was the place where qhal gathered, who had been farthest and lost their courage for traveling on. It was the point beyond which no one had courage, where descendants shared the world with living ancestors in greater and greater numbers, the jaded, the restless, who reached this age and felt their will erode away.

It was the place where hope ended. Oh, a few went farther, and the age saw them—no more. They were gone. They did not return.

They went beyond, whispered those who had lost their courage. They went out a Gate and found nothing there.

They died.

Or was it death—to travel without end? And what was death? And was the universe finite at all?

Some went, and vanished, and the age knew nothing more of them.

Those who were left were in agony—of desire to go; of fear to go farther.

Of changes.

This age—did change. It rippled with possibilities. Memories deceived. One remembered, or remembered that one had remembered, and the fact grew strange and dim, contradicting what obviously *was*. People remembered things that never had been true.

And one must never go back to see. Backtiming—had direst possibilities. It made paradox.

But some tried, seeking a time as close to their original exit point as possible. Some came too close, and involved themselves in time-loops, a particularly distressing kind of accident and unfortunate equally for those involved as bystanders.

Among qhal, between the finding of the first Gate and the End of Time, a new kind of specialist evolved: time-menders, who in most extreme cases of disturbance policed the Gates and carefully

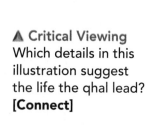

▲ **Critical Viewing**
Which details in this illustration suggest the life the qhal lead? **[Connect]**

researched afflicted areas. They alone were licensed to violate the back-time barrier, passing back and forth under strict non-involvement regulations, exchanging intelligence only with each other, to minutely adjust reality.

Evolved.

Agents recruited other agents at need—but at whose instance? There might be some who knew. It might have come from the far end of time—in that last (or was it last?) age beyond which nothing seemed certain, when the years since the First Gate were more than five thousand, and the Now in which all Gates existed was—very distant. Or it might have come from those who had found the Gate, overseeing their invention. Someone knew, somewhen, somewhere along the course of the stars toward the end of time.

But no one said.

It was hazardous business, this time-mending, in all senses. Precisely *what* was done was something virtually unknowable after it was done, for alterations in the past produced (one believed) changes in future reality. Whole time-fields, whose events could be wiped and redone, with effects which widened the farther down the timeline they proceeded. Detection of time-tampering was almost impossible.

A stranger wanted something to eat, a long time ago. He shot himself his dinner.

A small creature was not where it had been, when it had been.

A predator missed a meal and took another . . . likewise small.

A child lost a pet.

And found another.

And a friend she would not have had. She was happier for it.

She met many people she had never/would never meet.

A man in a different age had breakfast in a house on a hill.

Agent Harrh had acquired a sense about disruptions, a kind of extrasensory queasiness about a just-completed timewarp. He was not alone in this. But the time-menders (Harrh knew three others of his own age) never reported such experiences outside their own

Short Story
Conflict The information here reveals one of the story's conflicts—the hazards of time travel.

C. J. Cherryh
Author's Insight
A thread of causality strings these events together. The little girl might have been the man on the hill's great-grandmother. A chain of events led her to become what she was. Small events could lead us in many possible directions, but the single path we do take defines the future.

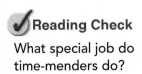Reading Check
What special job do time-menders do?

special group. Such reports would have been meaningless to his own time, involving a past which (as a result of the warp) was neither real nor valid nor perceptible to those in Time Present. Some time-menders would reach the verge of insanity because of this. This was future fact. Harrh knew this.

He had been there.

And he refused to go again to Now, that Now to which time had advanced since the discovery of the Gate—let alone to the End of Time, which was the farthest that anyone imagined. He was one of a few, a very few, licensed to do so, but he refused.

He lived scattered lives in ages to come, and remembered the future with increasing melancholy.

He had visited the End of Time, and left it in the most profound despair. He had seen what was there, and when he had contemplated going beyond, that most natural step out the Gate which stood and beckoned—

He fled. He had never run from anything but that. It remained, a recollection of shame at his fear.

A sense of a limit which he had never had before.

And this in itself was terrible, to a man who had thought time infinite and himself immortal.

In his own present of 1003 since the First Gate, Harrh had breakfast, a quiet meal. The children were off to the beach. His wife shared tea with him and thought it would be a fine morning.

"Yes," he said. "Shall we take the boat out? We can fish a little, take the sun."

"Marvelous," she said. Her gray eyes shone. He loved her—for herself, for her patience. He caught her hand on the crystal table, held slender fingers, not speaking his thoughts, which were far too <u>somber</u> for the morning.

They spent their mornings and their days together. He came back to her, time after shifting time. He might be gone a month; and home a week; and gone two months next time. He never dared cut it too close. They lost a great deal of each other's lives, and so much—so much he could not share with her.

Short Story
Character The details here develop the character of Agent Harrh.

Vocabulary Builder
somber (säm´ bər) *adj.* dark and gloomy

"The island," he said. "Mhreihrrinn, I'd like to see it again."

"I'll pack," she said.

And went away.

He came back to her never aged; and she bore their two sons; and reared them; and managed the accounts: and explained his absences to relatives and the world. *He travels*, she would say, with that right amount of secrecy that protected secrets.

And even to her he could never confide what he knew.

"I trust you," she would say—knowing what he was, but never what he did.

He let her go. She went off to the hall and out the door— He imagined happy faces, holiday, the boys making haste to run the boat out and put on the bright colored sail. She would keep them busy carrying this and that, fetching food and clothes—things happened in

▲ **Critical Viewing**
How is this painting similar to and different from the image of the Gates in your imagination?
[Compare and Contrast]

✓**Reading Check**
From what challenge did Agent Harrh flee?

The Threads of Time ■ 209

shortest order when Mhreihrrinn set her hand to them.

He wanted that, wanted the familiar, the orderly, the homely. He was, if he let his mind dwell on things—afraid. He had the notion never to leave again.

He had been to the Now most recently—5045, and his flesh crawled at the memory. There was recklessness there. There was disquiet. The Now had traveled two decades and more since he had first begun, and he felt it more and more. The whole decade of the 5040's had a queasiness about it, ripples of instability as if the whole fabric of the Now were shifting like a kaleidoscope.

And it headed for the End of Time. It had become more and more like that age, confirming it by its very collapse.

People had illusions in the Now. They perceived what had not been true.

And yet it *was* when he came home.

It had grown to be so—while he was gone.

A university stood in Morurir, which he did not remember.

A hedge of trees grew where a building had been in Morurir.

A man was in the Council who had died.

He would not go back to Now. He had resolved that this morning.

He had children, begotten before his first time-traveling. He had so very much to keep him—this place, this home, this stability—He was very well to do. He had invested well—his own small tampering. He had no lack, no need. He was mad to go on and on. He was done.

But a light distracted him, an opal shimmering beyond his breakfast nook, arrival in that receptor which his fine home afforded, linked to the master gate at Pyvrrhn.

A young man materialized there, opal and light and then solidity, a distraught young man.

"Harrh," the youth said, disregarding the decencies of meeting, and strode forward unasked. "Harrh, is everything all right here?"

Harrh arose from the crystal table even before the shimmer died, beset by that old queasiness of things out of joint. This was Alhir from 390 Since the Gate, an experienced man in the force: he had

▲ **Critical Viewing**
Which figures in this painting might represent the qhal and which might represent the makers of the Gates? Explain.
[Connect]

used a Master Key to come here—had such access, being what he was.

"Alhir," Harrh said, perplexed. "What's wrong?"

"You don't know." Alhir came as far as the door.

"A cup of tea?" Harrh said. Alhir had been here before. They were friends. There were oases along the course of suns, friendly years, places where houses served as rest-stops. In this too Mhreihrrinn was patient. "I've got to tell you— No, don't tell me. I don't want to know. I'm through. I've made up my mind. You can carry that where you're going. —But if you want the breakfast—"

"There's been an accident."

"I don't want to hear."

"He got past us."

"I don't want to know." He walked over to the cupboard, took another cup. "Mhreihrrinn's with the boys down at the beach. You just caught us." He set the cup down and poured the tea, where Mhreihrrinn had sat. "Won't you? You're always welcome here. Mhreihrrinn has no idea what you are. My young friend, she calls you. She doesn't know. Or she suspects. She'd never say.—Sit *down.*"

Alhir had strayed aside, where a display case sat along the wall, a lighted case of <u>mementoes</u> of treasures, of crystal. "Harrh, there was a potsherd here."

"No," Harrh said, less and less comfortable. "Just the glasses. I'm quite sure."

"Harrh, it was very old."

"No," he said. "—I promised Mhreihrrinn and the boys—I mean it. I'm through. I don't want to know."

"It came from Silen. From the digs at the First Gate, Harrh. It was a very valuable piece. You valued it very highly.—You don't remember."

"No," Harrh said, feeling fear thick about him, like a change in atmosphere. "I don't know of such a piece. I never had such a thing. Check your memory, Alhir."

"It was from the ruins by the *First Gate,* don't you understand?" And then Alhir did not exist.

Harrh blinked, remembered pouring a cup of tea. But he was sitting in the chair, his breakfast before him.

He poured the tea and drank.

He was sitting on rock, amid the grasses blowing gently in the wind, on a clifftop by the sea.

He was standing there. "Mhreihrrinn," he said, in the first chill touch of fear.

Short Story
Conflict In this paragraph, the author provides more detail about the conflict between Harrh and the time-menders.

Vocabulary Builder
mementoes (mə men´ tōz) *n.* souvenirs; objects that serve as reminders

C. J. Cherryh
Author's Insight
When Harrh hears this, he is afraid. Why? Look back at the line "a university stood in Morurir" (p. 210).

✓**Reading Check**
What news does Alhir bring Harrh?

◀ **Critical Viewing**
Which details in this painting support the idea that who we are is a direct result of what we remember? **[Support]**

But that memory faded. He had never had a wife, nor children. He forgot the house as well.

Trees grew and faded.

Rocks moved at random.

The time-menders were in most instances the only ones who survived even a little while.

Wrenched loose from time and with lives rooted in many parts of it, they felt it first and lived it longest, and not a few were trapped in backtime and did not die, but survived the horror of it and begot children who further <u>confounded</u> the time-line.

Time, stretched thin in possibilities, adjusted itself.

He was Harrh.

But he was many possibilities and many names.

In time none of them mattered.

He was many names; he lived. He had many bodies; and the souls stained his own.

In the end he remembered nothing at all, except the drive to live.

And the dreams.

And none of the dreams were true.

C. J. Cherryh
Author's Insight After Harrh's initial fear, something has changed. What follows is all his perception, as the orderly progress of time rips loose around him.

Vocabulary Builder
confounded (kən foun´ did) *n.* confused; bewildered

Q. Is time travel possible?

A. Some of the smartest people in the world concern themselves quite seriously with this question. Numerous books have questioned the nature of time, notably the recent work of Stephen Hawking, *A Brief History of Time*, and the work of Albert Einstein, which predicted that time, mass, and the speed of light are all connected. The smallest things in the universe—particles—and the fastest thing in the universe—light—pose intriguing questions about time.

Q. Does this story show "compression of time and place"?

A. It has the encounter I named, certainly, and lives are very much shaken by the information each character brings in. Because this bit began as it did, as the introduction for a novel, it has a few other characteristics. One of these is a reference to a non-appearing character, the wife, who never does make it into the scene. Another characteristic is that time, which is unraveling around Harrh as he sits there, is behaving oddly. In that sense, time is compressed: we are getting a lot of information in an instant. Time is also an eternal expanse, in which he is trapped. So the story hedges the rules, but it uses them, too.

StudentCorner

Q. The mention of "man" and "fingers" hints that the qhal are humanoid, but are they human? Are they our descendants?
—**David Price, Austin, Texas**

A. Yes, their world is connected to ours, and Earth is one of the worlds caught in the time disturbance. What settles out after the disaster is bits and pieces of things that belong on one planet ending up on another, and a handful of people like Harrh being set adrift on a planet other than the one he began on. The disaster happened, relative to our world, about 500 years ago, and left us a few inexplicable relics, but little other damage. Of course, this is all fiction.

 Writing Workshop: *Work in Progress*

Short Story

For a short story you may write, list five positive and five negative traits that you find in other people. Choose one and briefly describe a character who possesses it. Save your Character Description in your writing portfolio.

Apply the Skills

The Short Story

Thinking About the Selection

1. **Respond:** If you could travel in time like Agent Harrh, would you journey to the future or the past? Why?

2. **(a) Recall:** How did the qhal acquire the ability to travel in time? **(b) Infer:** In what ways does this circumstance suggest that the qhal may not have fully understood the consequences of time travel?

3. **(a) Recall:** In his own present of 1003, what changes does Harrh notice? **(b) Recall:** What detail does Alhir notice? **(c) Draw Conclusions:** Why are these changes significant?

4. **(a) Speculate:** What is the "accident" that Alhir reports to Harrh? **(b) Analyze Cause and Effect:** How does this accident affect Harrh?

5. **(a) Define:** Use a chart like the one shown to analyze key terms from the story. **(b) Discuss:** In a group, share and discuss your definitions. Revise them based on the discussion.

Term	What It Means	Why It Is Important
the qhal		
Gate		
time-mender		
the Now		
End of Time		

Short Story Review

6. Which aspect of the story—**plot, setting,** or **character**—does the author emphasize? Support your answer with details.

7. A common **theme** of science fiction is the warning against a misuse of technology. What warning or warnings do you find in this story?

Research the Author

Using the Internet and library sources, investigate one of the several science-fiction worlds that C. J. Cherryh has created. Follow these steps:
- Identify the specific novels in one series.
- Write a brief description of the imagined universe, the beings who populate it, and the conflicts they face.
- Present your findings to the class.

QuickReview

Story at a Glance
A time-traveler's world is threatened.

Go Online
Assessment
For: Self-test
Visit: www.PHSchool.com
Web Code: eqa-6201

Short Story: a brief work of fiction

Plot: a progression of events that make up the action

Setting: time and place of the action

Characters: the personalities who participate in the action of a story

Theme: the central message or insight of a literary work

Unit 2 Part 1

Make Inferences

Skills You Will Learn

Literary Analysis: *Character and Characterization*
Reading Skill: *Relate Your Experiences to Make Inferences About Characters*

Literary Analysis: *Setting*
Reading Skill: *Read On to Confirm Inferences*

Reading Skill: *Evaluate the Credibility of Web Sources*

Literary Analysis: *Points of View*

Literature You Will Read

Reading and Vocabulary Skills Preview

Reading: Make Inferences

Academic Standards

• Understand specific technical vocabulary. (10.1.1)

• Evaluate an author's use of time and sequence. (10.3.6)

• Use varied and expanded vocabulary. (10.5.7)

▶ An **inference** is an insight, based on stated details, about information that is not stated.

Skills and Strategies You Will Learn in Part 1

In Part 1, you will learn

- to **relate your experiences** to **make inferences** about character (p. 218).
- to **read ahead** to **confirm inferences** (p. 244).
- to **make inferences** in order to **evaluate the credibility of Web sources** (p. 270).

Using the Skills and Strategies in Part 1

In Part 1, you will learn to relate your experiences to the details in the story in order to make inferences about the characters. You also will learn how the purpose and structure of nonfiction gives you a basis for inferences and to read ahead to confirm these inferences. Your understanding of a text often depends on information that is not directly stated, so making inferences improves your comprehension of a text.

The example shows how you can apply the skills and strategies in Part 1.

Story Details	Experience
Character's team loses game	Losing isn't fun
Character congratulates winners	

↓

Inference	Confirm
Character is a good sport	Later, character refuses to cheat to win
Character has ethics	

Academic Vocabulary: Words for Understanding Literature

The following words will help you write and talk about your understanding of the literature in this unit.

Word	Definition	Example Sentence
formulate *v.*	express in a fixed or definite way	The expert tried to *formulate* her remarks so they were understandable to amateurs.
perspective *n.*	a specific point of view	I enjoy an essay more if I understand the author's *perspective.*
anticipate *v.*	give advance thought to, expect	An alert reader can sometimes *anticipate* the ending of a story.
indicate *v.*	direct attention to	An essayist will *indicate* the theme.
discern *v.*	recognize clearly	The detective can *discern* clues.

Vocabulary Skill: Word Roots

▶ A **word root** is the part of a word that contains its basic meaning.

In Part 1, you will learn

- the Latin root *-form-* (p. 242)
- the Latin root *-spec-* (p. 268)

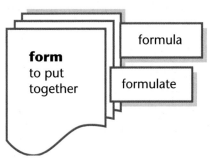

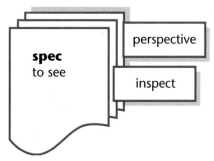

Activity Use a dictionary to identify three ways that the words *perspective* and *formulate* can be used. Then, note which academic disciplines or professions might use that meaning.

Build Skills *A Visit to Grandmother • A Problem*

Practice these skills with either "A Visit to Grandmother" (p. 220) or "A Problem" (p. 233).

IN **Academic Standards**

- Analyze many different forms of dramatic literature. (10.3.1)
- Evaluate interactions between characters and how these affect the plot. (10.3.3)
- Evaluate the use of voice and narrator. (10.3.9)

Literary Analysis

The **characters** are the people, animals, or even objects who perform the actions and experience the events of a story. Writers use two main types of **characterization** to bring characters to life:

- **Direct characterization:** The writer tells readers exactly what a character is like.
- **Indirect characterization:** The writer reveals a character's traits through **dialogue** (the character's words), the character's actions and thoughts, and the effect the character has on others.

To better understand characters and gain insight into the message of a story, notice the **character development**—changes the character undergoes or new aspects of the character the writer reveals.

Reading Skill

An **inference** is an insight you reach based on stated details about information that is not stated. To make inferences, **relate characters and events to your own experience.**

For instance, when reading the story of a space captain on her first voyage, you might compare the captain to leaders whom you have known. Use a chart like the one shown to relate your reading to your experiences.

Story Detail

The new captain's palms are sweating as she addresses the crew.

Your Experience

New camp counselors are nervous about whether campers will obey them.

Inference

The new captain is unsure of herself.

Vocabulary Builder

A Visit to Grandmother

- **indulgence** (in dul′ jəns) *n.* leniency; readiness to tolerate or forgive bad behavior (p. 221) *If you show the child too much indulgence, you may spoil her.*
- **grimacing** (grim′ is iŋ) *v.* making a twisted face showing disgust or pain (p. 222) *Grimacing, I pulled the splinter from my toe.*
- **trace** (trās) *n.* tiny amount; hint (p. 228) *There was not even a trace of cake left.*

A Problem

- **candid** (kan′ did) *adj.* honest; direct (p. 234) *Stop telling tales, and give me a candid answer.*
- **taciturn** (tas′ ə tʉrn′) *adj.* not liking to talk (p. 234) *She was usually taciturn, and at first I did not recognize her voice.*
- **subdued** (səb dood′) *adj.* quiet; lacking energy (p. 238) *The boy was subdued after he was scolded.*

Build Understanding • *A Visit to Grandmother*

Background

Dialect Dialect is the variety of a language spoken in a region or community. Some characters in "A Visit to Grandmother" speak in a southern dialect. In this dialect, *I reckon* means "I believe." *Fixin' to* replaces "about to."

Connecting to the Literature

Reading/Writing Connection In this story, a family misunderstanding lasts for thirty years before finally being aired. Jot down a few notes about the reasons for misunderstandings. Use at least three of these words: *agitate, comprehend, complicate, dissolve.*

READ MORE

by **William Melvin Kelley**
Dancers on the Shore

Meet the Author

William Melvin **Kelley** (b. 1937)

William Melvin Kelley is a man of questions. He says, "I am not a sociologist or a politician or a spokesman. Such people try to give answers. A writer, I think, should ask questions."

Kelley's questions often explore the problems of belonging to a group. His first novel, *A Different Drummer,* reflects his belief in individualism.

A Community Artist At the same time, Kelley's work shows a strong connection to community. He belongs to the Black Arts Movement, the generation of writers, artists, dancers, and musicians that emerged in the 1960s and 1970s. Like others in the movement, he often addresses the moral, cultural, and political questions African Americans face.

Fast Facts

▶ Introducing his class on writing fiction, Kelley notes that "Art may come from the heart, but craft comes from the brain."

▶ Kelley has received a grant to develop a video, *Excavating Harlem,* about the historic African American neighborhood in New York City.

Go **Online**
Author Link

For: More about the author
Visit: www.PHSchool.com
Web Code: eqe-9202

A Visit
to
Grandmother

WILLIAM
MELVIN
KELLEY

Chig knew something was wrong the instant his father kissed her. He had always known his father to be the warmest of men, a man so kind that when people ventured timidly into his office, it took only a few words from him to make them relax, and even laugh. Doctor Charles Dunford cared about people.

But when he had bent to kiss the old lady's black face, something new and almost ugly had come into his eyes: fear, uncertainty, sadness, and perhaps even hatred.

Ten days before in New York, Chig's father had decided suddenly he wanted to go to Nashville to attend his college class reunion, twenty years out. Both Chig's brother and sister, Peter and Connie, were packing for camp and besides were too young for such an affair. But Chig was seventeen, had nothing to do that summer, and his father asked if he would like to go along. His father had given him additional reasons: "All my running buddies got their diplomas and were snapped up by them crafty young gals, and had kids within a year—now all those kids, some of them gals, are your age."

The reunion had lasted a week. As they packed for home, his father, in a far too offhand way, had suggested they visit Chig's grandmother. "We this close. We might as well drop in on her and my brothers."

So, instead of going north, they had gone farther south, had just entered her house. And Chig had a suspicion now that the reunion had been only an excuse to drive south, that his father had been heading to this house all the time.

His father had never talked much about his family, with the exception of his brother, GL, who seemed part con man, part practical joker and part Don Juan;[1] he had spoken of GL with the kind of indulgence he would have shown a cute, but ill-behaved and potentially dangerous, five-year-old.

Chig's father had left home when he was fifteen. When asked why, he would answer: "I wanted to go to school. They didn't have a Negro high school at home, so I went up to Knoxville and lived with a cousin and went to school."

They had been met at the door by Aunt Rose, GL's wife, and ushered into the living room. The old lady had looked up from her seat by the window. Aunt Rose stood between the visitors.

The old lady eyed his father. "Rose, who that? Rose?" She squinted. She looked like a doll, made of black straw, the wrinkles in her face running in one direction like the head of a broom. Her

---

1. **Don Juan** (dän´ wän´) a legendary nobleman, idle and immoral, who fascinates women.

◀ **Critical Viewing**
Predict what the grandmother in the story will be like, judging from this painting. **[Predict]**

Literary Analysis
Characterization
What do you learn about GL through direct characterization?

Vocabulary Builder
indulgence (in dul´ jəns) *n.* leniency; readiness to tolerate or forgive bad behavior

✔**Reading Check**
Whom do Chig and his father go to visit?

hair was white and coarse and grew out straight from her head. Her eyes were brown—the whites, too, seemed light brown—and were hidden behind thick glasses, which remained somehow on a tiny nose. "That Hiram?" That was another of his father's brothers. "No, it ain't Hiram; too big for Hiram." She turned then to Chig. "Now that man, he look like Eleanor, Charles's wife, but Charles wouldn't never send my grandson to see me. I never even hear from Charles." She stopped again.

"It Charles, Mama. That who it is." Aunt Rose, between them, led them closer. "It Charles come all the way from New York to see you, and brung little Charles with him."

The old lady stared up at them. "Charles? Rose, that really Charles?" She turned away, and reached for a handkerchief in the pocket of her clean, ironed, flowered housecoat, and wiped her eyes. "God have mercy, Charles." She spread her arms up to him, and he bent down and kissed her cheek. That was when Chig saw his face, <u>grimacing</u>. She hugged him; Chig watched the muscles in her arms as they tightened around his father's neck. She half rose out of her chair. "How are you, son?"

Chig could not hear his father's answer.

She let him go, and fell back into her chair, grabbing the arms. Her hands were as dark as the wood, and seemed to become part of it. "Now, who that standing there? Who that man?"

"That's one of your grandsons, Mama." His father's voice cracked. "Charles Dunford, junior. You saw him once, when he was a baby, in Chicago. He's grown now."

"I can see that, boy!" She looked at Chig squarely. "Come here, son, and kiss me once." He did. "What they call you? Charles too?"

"No, ma'am, they call me Chig."

She smiled. She had all her teeth, but they were too perfect to be her own. "That's good. Can't have two boys answering to Charles in the same house. Won't nobody at all come. So you that little boy. You don't remember me, do you. I used to take you to church in Chicago, and you'd get up and hop in time to the music. You studying to be a preacher?"

"No, ma'am. I don't think so. I might be a lawyer."

"You'll be an honest one, won't you?"

"I'll try."

"Trying ain't enough! You be honest, you hear? Promise me. You be honest like your daddy."

"All right. I promise."

"Good. Rose, where's GL at? Where's that thief? He gone again?"

"I don't know, Mama." Aunt Rose looked embarrassed. "He say he was going by the store. He'll be back."

Reading Skill
Making Inferences
What feelings does the grandmother have upon seeing her son? Which details support your inference?

Vocabulary Builder
grimacing (grim' is iŋ) v. making a twisted face showing disgust or pain

Literary Analysis
Characterization
Name one trait of the grandmother that is suggested in the dialogue.

"Well, then where's Hiram? You call up those boys, and get them over here—now! You got enough to eat? Let me go see." She started to get up. Chig reached out his hand. She shook him off. "What they tell you about me, Chig? They tell you I'm all laid up? Don't believe it. They don't know nothing about old ladies. When I want help, I'll let you know. Only time I'll need help getting anywheres is when I dies and they lift me into the ground."

She was standing now, her back and shoulders straight. She came only to Chig's chest. She squinted up at him. "You eat much? Your daddy ate like two men."

"Yes, ma'am."

"That's good. That means you ain't nervous. Your mama, she ain't nervous. I remember that. In Chicago, she'd sit down by a window all afternoon and never say nothing, just knit." She smiled. "Let me see what we got to eat."

"I'll do that, Mama." Aunt Rose spoke softly. "You haven't seen Charles in a long time. You sit and talk."

The old lady squinted at her. "You can do the cooking if you promise it ain't because you think I can't."

Aunt Rose chuckled. "I know you can do it, Mama."

"All right. I'll just sit and talk a spell." She sat again and arranged her skirt around her short legs.

Chig did most of the talking, told all about himself before she asked. His father spoke only when he was spoken to, and then, only one word at a time, as if by coming back home, he had become a small boy again, sitting in the parlor while his mother spoke with her guests.

When Uncle Hiram and Mae, his wife, came they sat down to eat. Chig did not have to ask about Uncle GL's absence; Aunt Rose volunteered an explanation: "Can't never tell where the man is at. One Thursday morning he left here and next thing we knew, he was calling from Chicago, saying he went up to see Joe Louis[2] fight. He'll be

▲ **Critical Viewing**
Does the attitude of this young man reflect how Chig reacts during the visit? Explain. **[Connect]**

✓ **Reading Check**
How does the grandmother react to the surprise visit?

---

2. Joe Louis (1914–1981) U.S. boxer and the world heavyweight champion from 1937 to 1949.

here though; he ain't as young and footloose as he used to be."
Chig's father had mentioned driving down that GL was about five
years older than he was, nearly fifty.

Uncle Hiram was somewhat smaller than Chig's father; his short-
cropped kinky hair was half gray, half black. One spot, just off his
forehead, was totally white. Later, Chig found out it had been that
way since he was twenty. Mae (Chig could not bring himself to call
her Aunt) was a good deal younger than Hiram, pretty enough so
that Chig would have looked at her twice on the street. She was a
honey-colored woman, with long eyelashes. She was wearing a
white sheath.

At dinner, Chig and his father sat on one side, opposite Uncle
Hiram and Mae; his grandmother and Aunt Rose sat at the ends.
The food was good; there was a lot and Chig ate a lot. All through
the meal, they talked about the family as it had been thirty years
before, and particularly about the young GL. Mae and Chig asked
questions; the old lady answered; Aunt Rose directed the discussion, steering the old lady onto the best stories; Chig's father
laughed from time to time; Uncle Hiram ate.

▼ **Critical Viewing**
What does this image
suggest about the life
the grandmother and
her family lead?
[Connect]

"Why don't you tell them about the horse, Mama?" Aunt Rose, over Chig's weak protest, was spooning mashed potatoes onto his plate. "There now, Chig."

"I'm trying to think." The old lady was holding her fork halfway to her mouth, looking at them over her glasses. "Oh, you talking about that crazy horse GL brung home that time."

"That's right, Mama." Aunt Rose nodded and slid another slice of white meat on Chig's plate.

Mae started to giggle. "Oh, I've heard this. This is funny, Chig."

The old lady put down her fork and began: Well, GL went out of the house one day with an old, no-good chair I wanted him to take over to the church for a bazaar, and he met up with this man who'd just brung in some horses from out West. Now, I reckon you can expect one swindler[3] to be in every town, but you don't rightly think there'll be two, and God forbid they should ever meet—but they did, GL and his chair, this man and his horses. Well, I wished I'd-a been there; there must-a been some mighty high-powered talking going on. That man with his horses, he told GL them horses was half-Arab, half-Indian, and GL told that man the chair was an antique he'd stole from some rich white folks. So they swapped. Well, I was a-looking out the window and seen GL dragging this animal to the house. It looked pretty gentle and its eyes was most closed and its feet was shuffling.

"GL, where'd you get that thing?" I says.

"I swapped him for that old chair, Mama," he says. "And made myself a bargain. This is even better than Papa's horse."

Well, I'm a-looking at this horse and noticing how he be looking more and more wide awake every minute, sort of warming up like a teakettle until, I swears to you, that horse is blowing steam out its nose.

"Come on, Mama," GL says, "come on and I'll take you for a ride." Now George, my husband, God rest his tired soul, he'd brung home this white folks' buggy which had a busted wheel and fixed it and was to take it back that day and GL says: "Come on, Mama, we'll use this fine buggy and take us a ride."

"GL," I says, "no, we ain't. Them white folks'll burn us alive if we use their buggy. You just take that horse right on back." You see, I was sure that boy'd come by that animal ungainly.

"Mama, I can't take him back," GL says.

"Why not?" I says.

"Because I don't rightly know where that man is at," GL says.

Literary Analysis
Characterization
How does the writer use indirect characterization to reveal GL's character?

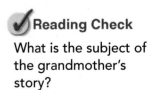

Reading Check

What is the subject of the grandmother's story?

---

3. swindler (swind′ lər) *n.* a cheater; a person who takes the money or property of others using deception.

"Oh," I says. "Well, then I reckon we stuck with it." And I turned around to go back into the house because it was getting late, near dinner time, and I was cooking for ten.

"Mama," GL says to my back. "Mama, ain't you coming for a ride with me?"

"Go on, boy. You ain't getting me inside kicking range of that animal." I was eying that beast and it was boiling hotter all the time. I reckon maybe that man had drugged it. "That horse is wild, GL," I says.

"No, he ain't. He ain't. That man say he is buggy and saddle broke[4] and as sweet as the inside of a apple."

My oldest girl, Essie, had-a come out on the porch and she says: "Go on, Mama. I'll cook. You ain't been out the house in weeks."

"Sure, come on, Mama," GL says. "There ain't nothing to be fidgety about. This horse is gentle as a rose petal." And just then that animal snorts so hard it sets up a little dust storm around its feet.

"Yes, Mama," Essie says, "you can see he gentle." Well, I looked at Essie and then at that horse because I didn't think we could be looking at the same animal. I should-a figured how Essie's eyes ain't never been so good.

"Come on, Mama," GL says.

"All right," I says. So I stood on the porch and watched GL hitching that horse up to the white folks' buggy. For a while there, the animal was pretty quiet, pawing a little, but not much. And I was feeling a little better about riding with GL behind that crazy-looking horse. I could see how GL was happy I was going with him. He was scurrying around that animal buckling buckles and strapping straps, all the time smiling, and that made me feel good.

Then he was finished, and I must say, that horse looked mighty fine hitched to that buggy and I knew anybody what climbed up there would look pretty good too. GL came around and stood at the bottom of the steps, and took off his hat and bowed and said: "Madam," and reached out his hand to me and I was feeling real elegant like a fine lady. He helped me up to the seat and then got up beside me and we moved out down our alley. And I remember how colored folks come out on their porches and shook their heads, saying: "Lord now, will you look at Eva Dunford, the fine lady! Don't she look good sitting up there!" And I pretended not to hear and sat up straight and proud.

We rode on through the center of town, up Market Street, and all the way out where Hiram is living now, which in them days was all woods, there not being even a farm in sight and that's when that

Reading Skill
Making Inferences
Think of a person you know who likes to get attention. How does knowing this person help you understand GL's actions?

---

4. **buggy and saddle broke** trained to carry a mounted rider or to pull a carriage.

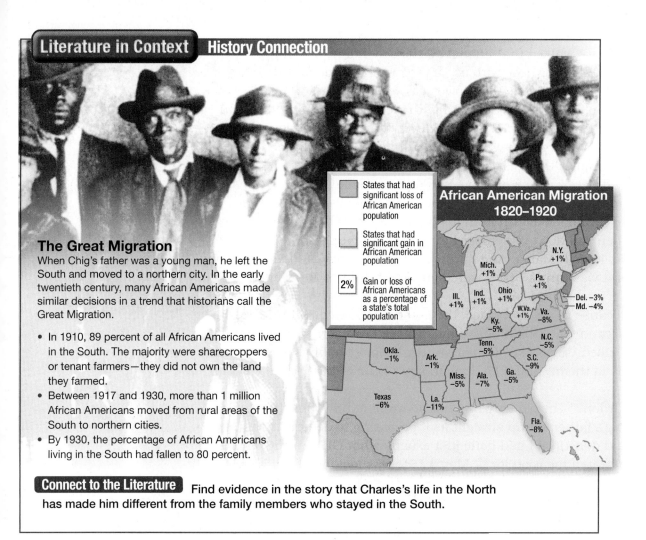

The Great Migration

When Chig's father was a young man, he left the South and moved to a northern city. In the early twentieth century, many African Americans made similar decisions in a trend that historians call the Great Migration.

- In 1910, 89 percent of all African Americans lived in the South. The majority were sharecroppers or tenant farmers—they did not own the land they farmed.
- Between 1917 and 1930, more than 1 million African Americans moved from rural areas of the South to northern cities.
- By 1930, the percentage of African Americans living in the South had fallen to 80 percent.

Connect to the Literature   Find evidence in the story that Charles's life in the North has made him different from the family members who stayed in the South.

horse must-a first realized he weren't at all broke or tame or maybe thought he was back out West again, and started to gallop.

"GL," I says, "now you ain't joking with your mama, is you? Because if you is, I'll strap you purple if I live through this."

Well, GL was pulling on the reins with all his meager strength, and yelling, "Whoa, you. Say now, whoa!" He turned to me just long enough to say, "I ain't fooling with you, Mama. Honest!"

I reckon that animal weren't too satisfied with the road, because it made a sharp right turn just then, down into a gulley and struck out across a hilly meadow. "Mama," GL yells. "Mama, do something!"

I didn't know what to do, but I figured I had to do something so I stood up, hopped down onto the horse's back and pulled it to a stop. Don't ask me how I did that; I reckon it was that I was a mother and my baby asked me to do something, is all.

Reading Check

What happens when GL takes his mother for a buggy ride?

"Well, we walked that animal all the way home; sometimes I had to club it over the nose with my fist to make it come, but we made it, GL and me. You remember how tired we was, Charles?"

"I wasn't here at the time." Chig turned to his father and found his face completely blank, without even a <u>trace</u> of a smile or a laugh.

"Well, of course you was, son. That happened in . . . in . . . it was a hot summer that year and—"

"I left here in June of that year. You wrote me about it."

The old lady stared past Chig at him. They all turned to him; Uncle Hiram looked up from his plate.

"Then you don't remember how we all laughed?"

"No, I don't, Mama. And I probably wouldn't have laughed. I don't think it was funny." They were staring into each other's eyes.

"Why not, Charles?"

"Because in the first place, the horse was gained by fraud. And in the second place, both of you might have been seriously injured or even killed." He broke off their stare and spoke to himself more than to any of them: "And if I'd done it, you would've beaten me good for it."

"Pardon?" The old lady had not heard him; only Chig had heard.

Chig's father sat up straight as if preparing to debate. "I said that if I had done it, if I had done just exactly what GL did, you would have beaten me good for it, Mama." He was looking at her again.

"Why you say that, son?" She was leaning toward him.

"Don't you know? Tell the truth. It can't hurt me now." His voice cracked, but only once. "If GL and I did something wrong, you'd beat me first and then be too tired to beat him. At dinner, he'd always get seconds and I wouldn't. You'd do things with him, like ride in that buggy, but if I wanted you to do something with me, you were always too busy." He paused and considered whether to say what he finally did say: "I cried when I left here. Nobody loved me, Mama. I cried all the way up to Knoxville. That was the last time I ever cried in my life."

"Oh, Charles." She started to get up, to come around the table to him.

He stopped her. "It's too late."

"But you don't understand."

"What don't I understand? I understood then; I understand now."

Tears now traveled down the lines in her face, but when she spoke, her

Vocabulary Builder
trace (trās) *n.* tiny amount; hint

voice was clear. "I thought you knew. I had ten children. I had to give all of them what they needed most." She nodded. "I paid more mind to GL. I had to. GL could-a ended up swinging if I hadn't. But you was smarter. You was more growed up than GL when you was five and he was ten, and I tried to show you that by letting you do what you wanted to do."

"That's not true, Mama. You know it. GL was light-skinned and had good hair and looked almost white and you loved him for that."

"Charles, no. No, son. I didn't love any one of you more than any other."

"That can't be true." His father was standing now, his fists clenched tight. "Admit it, Mama . . . please!" Chig looked at him, shocked; the man was actually crying.

"It may not-a been right what I done, but I ain't no liar." Chig knew she did not really understand what had happened, what he wanted of her. "I'm not lying to you, Charles."

Chig's father had gone pale. He spoke very softly. "You're about thirty years too late, Mama." He bolted from the table. Silverware and dishes rang and jumped. Chig heard him hurrying up to their room.

They sat in silence for a while and then heard a key in the front door. A man with a new, lacquered[5] straw hat came in. He was wearing brown and white two-tone shoes with very pointed toes and a white summer suit. "Say now! Man! I heard my brother was in town. Where he at? Where that rascal?"

He stood in the doorway, smiling broadly, an engaging, open, friendly smile, the innocent smile of a five-year-old.

---

5. lacquered (lak´ərd) *adj.* coated with a hardened protective layer of resinous material, which gives a shine.

◄ **Critical Viewing** What might the grandmother be thinking about in this image, given what you have learned about her? **[Speculate]**

Apply the Skills

A Visit to Grandmother

Thinking About the Selection

1. **Respond:** With which character in the story do you sympathize most strongly? Share your responses in a small group. Record members' thoughts about each character. Review the notes and explain how others' responses affected your viewpoint.
2. **(a) Recall:** What reason does Charles give for leaving home when he was fifteen? **(b) Hypothesize:** What other reasons might he have had? Support your answer with story details.
3. **(a) Recall:** How does Charles react to Mama's story about GL and the horse? **(b) Compare and Contrast:** In what way does his reaction contrast with the way Mama feels about the story?
4. **(a) Connect:** Explain why the story has this effect on Charles. **(b) Speculate:** What might Charles's relationship with his mother be like in the future? Explain.
5. **(a) Summarize:** Describe Mama's approach to raising her children. **(b) Evaluate:** Is her approach sound? Explain.

Literary Analysis

6. Compare and contrast the **characters** of Charles and GL. Use details from the story to support your answer.
7. Identify three examples of **indirect characterization** used to portray Charles. Use a chart like the one shown.

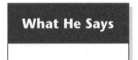  

What He Says	What He Does	What Others Say About Him

8. **(a)** What does Charles say is his reason for visiting Mama? **(b)** In what way is his character **developed** at the end?
9. **(a)** Give two examples of **dialogue** from Mama and two from Charles. **(b)** What do your examples show about how they differ?

Reading Skill

10. **Make an inference** about Charles's feelings toward GL. Explain on which story details your inference is based.
11. Draw an inference about Chig's feelings toward his family. Support your inference with story details and your own experiences.

QuickReview

Who's Who in the Story
Chig: a seventeen-year-old New Yorker
Charles: Chig's father
Mama: Chig's grandmother—Charles's mother
GL: Charles's younger brother

Go Online
—Assessment
For: Self-test
Visit: www.PHSchool.com
Web Code: eqa-6202

Character: a person, an animal, or an object who performs the actions and experiences the events of a story

Characterization: techniques a writer uses to portray characters. Characterization may be *direct* or *indirect*.

Dialogue: characters' own words as spoken in conversation

Inference: an insight, based on stated details, about information that is not stated

Vocabulary Builder

Practice Answer each question, and explain how the meaning of the underlined word influences your answer.

1. What may happen if parents give children too much <u>indulgence</u>?
2. On what occasions might you see someone <u>grimacing</u>?
3. If there is a <u>trace</u> of mud on the rug, is a big cleanup necessary?

Adding Words to Your Vocabulary Use a thesaurus to find one **synonym,** or word with a similar meaning, for each vocabulary list word for "A Visit to Grandmother," on page 218. Then, use each synonym in a sentence. (For more on using a thesaurus, see page R7.)

Writing

Write two brief **retellings** of the events in "A Visit to Grandmother." First, retell the story as Mama would tell it. Then, retell the story from GL's viewpoint.

- Use a story map or plot diagram to list the main events.
- Identify details that will show the difference between the characters' perspectives.
- Use the first-person pronoun *I* to write as the character.

For *Grammar, Vocabulary,* and *Assessment,* see **Build Language Skills,** pages 242–243.

Extend Your Learning

Listening and Speaking Work with a partner to prepare an **overview of speech patterns** of the characters in this story.
- List the major characters in the first column of a chart.
- In the next column, list examples of each character's speech.
- In a third column, identify social and regional factors that affect each character's speech.
Present your analysis to the class, reading examples aloud to help listeners appreciate differences in language.

Research and Technology Write a **report on sources** for a research project about the Great Migration from the rural South to northern cities. Find three to four sources of varied types, including books, the Internet, and CD-ROM references. Evaluate the accuracy and reliability of each. Consider the date of the source, the author's credentials, and whether or not details are verified or contradicted by other sources.

Build Understanding • *A Problem*

Background

Money Lending An IOU, or promissory note, is a promise to pay money or goods. In Russia at the time of this story, a person could "discount" an IOU, selling it to a moneylender for less than full value. Later, the person could "redeem" the note, buying it back by a certain date. In this story, a character commits a crime by forging an IOU and selling it to a moneylender.

Connecting to the Literature

Reading/Writing Connection A young man's actions in the story reflect badly on his family. Think of a person in the news. Write down thoughts about how the person's family might be affected by the media coverage. Use at least three of these words: *cease, define, injure, isolate.*

Review

For **Literary Analysis, Reading Skill,** and **Vocabulary Builder,** see page 218.

READ MORE

by Anton Chekhov
The Seagull
The Cherry Orchard

Meet the Author

Anton **Chekhov** (1860–1904)

Anton Chekhov grew up in the small coastal town of Taganrog in southern Russia. When the family moved to Moscow, he helped support them by writing comic sketches and light short stories. Although he attended medical school and became a doctor, Chekhov devoted himself to writing short stories and dramas.

A Diagnosis Chekhov said that "a writer is not a confectioner, a cosmetic dealer, or an entertainer. He is a man who has signed a contract with his conscience and his sense of duty." Some of Chekhov's works offer a diagnosis of nineteenth-century Russian society, showing how it trapped individuals into hopeless, unproductive lives. Other works humorously reveal universal human weaknesses. Today, he is regarded as one of the greatest modern writers and one of the most important dramatists of all time.

Fast Facts

▶ As a child, Chekhov worked in his father's grocery store.
▶ Chekhov's study of prisoners' lives, *The Island of Sakhalin,* helped reform the Russian prison system.

Go Online
Author Link

For: More about the author
Visit: www.PHSchool.com
Web Code: eqe-9203

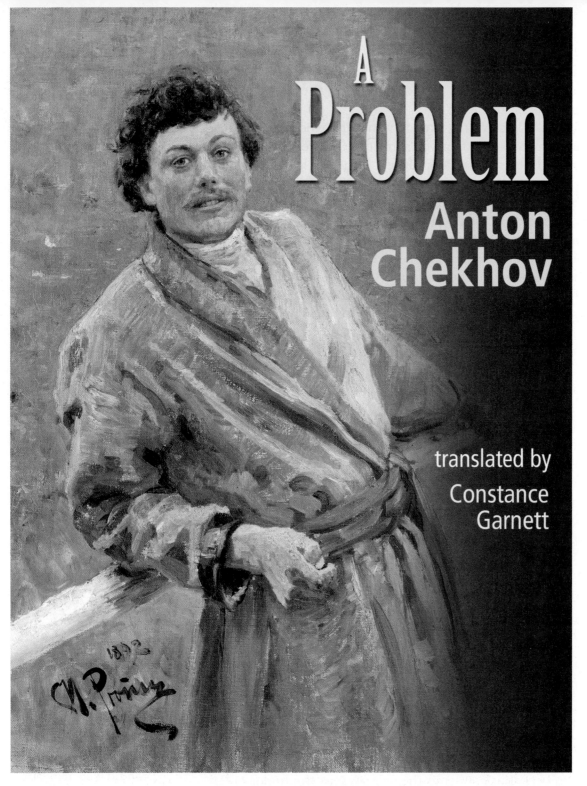

A Problem

Anton Chekhov

translated by
Constance Garnett

The strictest measures were taken that the Uskovs' family secret might not leak out and become generally known. Half of the servants were sent off to the theater or the circus; the other half were sitting in the kitchen and not allowed to leave it. Orders were given that no one was to be admitted. The wife of the Colonel, her sister, and the governess, though they had been initiated into the secret, kept up a pretense of knowing nothing; they sat in the dining room and did not show themselves in the drawing room or the hall.

Sasha Uskov, the young man of twenty-five who was the cause of all the commotion, had arrived some time before, and by the advice of kind-hearted Ivan Markovitch, his uncle, who was taking his part, he sat meekly in the hall by the door leading to the study, and prepared himself to make an open, <u>candid</u> explanation.

The other side of the door, in the study, a family council was being held. The subject under discussion was an exceedingly disagreeable and delicate one. Sasha Uskov had cashed at one of the banks a false promissory note,[1] and it had become due for payment three days before, and now his two paternal uncles and Ivan Markovitch, the brother of his dead mother, were deciding the question whether they should pay the money and save the family honor, or wash their hands of it and leave the case to go to trial.

To outsiders who have no personal interest in the matter such questions seem simple; for those who are so unfortunate as to have to decide them in earnest they are extremely difficult. The uncles had been talking for a long time, but the problem seemed no nearer decision.

"My friends!" said the uncle who was a colonel, and there was a note of exhaustion and bitterness in his voice. "Who says that family honor is a mere convention? I don't say that at all. I am only warning you against a false view; I am pointing out the possibility of an unpardonable mistake. How can you fail to see it? I am not speaking Chinese; I am speaking Russian!"

"My dear fellow, we do understand," Ivan Markovitch protested mildly.

"How can you understand if you say that I don't believe in family honor? I repeat once more; fa-mil-y ho-nor false-ly un-der-stood is a prejudice! Falsely understood! That's what I say: whatever may be the motives for screening a scoundrel, whoever he may be, and helping him to escape punishment, it is contrary to law and unworthy of a gentleman. It's not saving the family honor; it's civic cowardice! Take the army, for instance. . . . The honor of the army is more precious to us than any other honor, yet we don't screen our guilty members, but condemn them. And does the honor of the army suffer in consequence? Quite the opposite!"

The other paternal uncle, an official in the Treasury, a <u>taciturn</u>, dull-witted, and rheumatic man, sat silent, or spoke only of the fact

▲ **Critical Viewing**
Which uncle might this painting portray? Support your answer. **[Connect]**

Vocabulary Builder
candid (kan´ did) *adj.* honest; direct

taciturn (tas´ ə tʉrn´) *adj.* not liking to talk

---

1. promissory note written promise to pay a specified sum on demand; an IOU.

that the Uskovs' name would get into the newspapers if the case went for trial. His opinion was that the case ought to be hushed up from the first and not become public property; but, apart from publicity in the newspapers, he advanced no other argument in support of this opinion.

The maternal uncle, kind-hearted Ivan Markovitch, spoke smoothly, softly, and with a tremor in his voice. He began with saying that youth has its rights and its peculiar temptations. Which of us has not been young, and who has not been led astray? To say nothing of ordinary mortals, even great men have not escaped errors and mistakes in their youth. Take, for instance, the biography of great writers. Did not every one of them gamble, drink, and draw down upon himself the anger of right-thinking people in his young days? If Sasha's error bordered upon crime, they must remember that Sasha had received practically no education; he had been expelled from the high school in the fifth class; he had lost his parents in early childhood, and so had been left at the tenderest age without guidance and good, benevolent influences. He was nervous, excitable, had no firm ground under his feet, and, above all, he had been unlucky. Even if he were guilty, anyway he deserved indulgence² and the sympathy of all compassionate souls. He ought, of course, to be punished, but he was punished as it was by his conscience and the agonies he was enduring now while awaiting the sentence of his relations. The comparison with the army made by the Colonel was delightful, and did credit to his lofty intelligence; his appeal to their feeling of public duty spoke for the chivalry of his soul, but they must not forget that in each individual the citizen is closely linked with the Christian. . . .

"Shall we be false to civic duty," Ivan Markovitch exclaimed passionately, "if instead of punishing an erring boy we hold out to him a helping hand?"

Ivan Markovitch talked further of family honor. He had not the honor to belong to the Uskov family himself, but he knew their distinguished family went back to the thirteenth century; he did not forget for a minute, either, that his precious, beloved sister had been the wife of one of the representatives of that name. In short, the family was dear to him for many reasons, and he refused to admit the idea that, for the sake of a paltry fifteen hundred rubles,³ a blot should be cast on the escutcheon⁴ that was beyond all price. If all the motives he had brought forward were not sufficiently convincing, he, Ivan Markovitch, in conclusion, begged his listeners

Literary Analysis
Characterization
Contrast the Colonel's position with Ivan Markovitch's. What does this contrast indirectly reveal about the two?

Reading Check

Why is Sasha in trouble?

---

2. **indulgence** (in dul´ jəns) *n.* forgiveness; tolerance.
3. **rubles** (roo´ belz) *n.* A ruble is the basic unit of Russian currency.
4. **escutcheon** (e skuch´ ən) *n.* shield displaying a family's coat of arms, symbol of its nobility.

to ask themselves what was meant by crime? Crime is an immoral act founded upon ill-will. But is the will of man free? Philosophy has not yet given a positive answer to that question. Different views were held by the learned. The latest school of Lombroso,[5] for instance, denies the freedom of the will, and considers every crime as the product of the purely anatomical peculiarities of the individual.

"Ivan Markovitch," said the Colonel, in a voice of entreaty, "we are talking seriously about an important matter, and you bring in Lombroso, you clever fellow. Think a little, what are you saying all this for? Can you imagine that all your thunderings and rhetoric will furnish an answer to the question?"

Sasha Uskov sat at the door and listened. He felt neither terror, shame, nor depression, but only weariness and inward emptiness. It seemed to him that it made absolutely no difference to him whether they forgave him or not; he had come here to hear his sentence and to explain himself simply because kind-hearted Ivan Markovitch had begged him to do so. He was not afraid of the future. It made no difference to him where he was: here in the hall, in prison, or in Siberia.

"If Siberia, then let it be Siberia, damn it all!"

He was sick of life and found it insufferably hard. He was inextricably involved in debt; he had not a farthing[6] in his pocket; his family had become detestable to him; he would have to part from his friends and his women sooner or later, as they had begun to be too contemptuous of his sponging on them. The future looked black.

Sasha was indifferent, and was only disturbed by one circumstance; the other side of the door they were calling him a scoundrel and a criminal. Every minute he was on the point of jumping up, bursting into the study and shouting in answer to the detestable metallic voice of the Colonel:

"You are lying!"

"Criminal" is a dreadful word—that is what murderers, thieves, robbers are; in fact, wicked and morally hopeless people. And Sasha was very far from being all that. . . . It was true he owed a great deal and did not pay his debts. But debt is not a crime, and it is unusual for a man not to be in debt. The Colonel and Ivan Markovitch were both in debt. . . .

"What have I done wrong besides?" Sasha wondered.

He had discounted a forged note. But all the young men he knew did the same. Handrikov and Von Burst always forged IOU's from

Reading Skill
Making Inferences
Based on Sasha's thoughts, what can you infer about how mature he is?

---

5. Lombroso Cesare Lombroso (1835–1909), an Italian criminologist who believed that criminals were of a distinct human type and were led to crime by hereditary, inborn characteristics.
6. farthing (fär′ thin) *n.* coin of little value.

their parents or friends when their allowances were not paid at the regular time, and then when they got their money from home they redeemed them before they became due. Sasha had done the same, but had not redeemed the IOU because he had not got the money which Handrikov had promised to lend him. He was not to blame; it was the fault of circumstances. It was true that the use of another person's signature was considered reprehensible; but, still, it was not a crime but a generally accepted dodge, an ugly formality which injured no one and was quite harmless, for in forging the Colonel's signature Sasha had had no intention of causing anybody damage or loss.

"No, it doesn't mean that I am a criminal . . ." thought Sasha. "And it's not in my character to bring myself to commit a crime. I am soft, emotional. . . . When I have the money I help the poor. . . ."

Sasha was musing after this fashion while they went on talking the other side of the door.

"But, my friends, this is endless," the Colonel declared, getting excited. "Suppose we were to forgive him and pay the money. You know he would not give up leading a dissipated life, squandering money, making debts, going to our tailors and ordering suits in our names! Can you guarantee that this will be his last prank? As far as I am concerned, I have no faith whatever in his reforming!"

The official of the Treasury muttered something in reply; after him Ivan Markovitch began talking blandly and suavely again. The Colonel moved his chair impatiently and drowned the other's words with his detestable metallic voice. At last the door opened and Ivan Markovitch came out of the study; there were patches of red on his cleanshaven face.

"Come along," he said, taking Sasha by the hand. "Come and speak frankly from your heart. Without pride, my dear boy, humbly and from your heart."

Sasha went into the study. The official of the Treasury was sitting down; the Colonel was standing before the table with one hand in his pocket and one knee on a chair. It was smoky and stifling in the study. Sasha did not look at the official or the Colonel; he felt suddenly ashamed and uncomfortable. He looked uneasily at Ivan Markovitch and muttered:

"I'll pay it . . . I'll give it back. . . ."

"What did you expect when you discounted the IOU?" he heard a metallic voice.

"I . . . Handrikov promised to lend me the money before now."

Sasha could say no more. He went out of the study and sat down again on the chair near the door. He would have been glad to go away altogether at once, but he was choking with hatred and he awfully wanted to remain, to tear the Colonel to pieces, to say

Literary Analysis
Characterization
How do Sasha's thoughts about himself compare to what you have learned about his character?

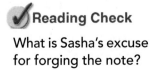Reading Check

What is Sasha's excuse for forging the note?

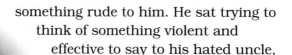

something rude to him. He sat trying to think of something violent and effective to say to his hated uncle, and at that moment a woman's figure, shrouded in the twilight, appeared at the drawing room door. It was the Colonel's wife. She beckoned Sasha to her, and, wringing her hands, said, weeping:

"*Alexandre,* I know you don't like me, but . . . listen to me; listen, I beg you. . . . But, my dear, how can this have happened? Why, it's awful, awful! For goodness' sake, beg them, defend yourself, entreat them."

Sasha looked at her quivering shoulders, at the big tears that were rolling down her cheeks, heard behind his back the hollow, nervous voices of worried and exhausted people, and shrugged his shoulders. He had not in the least expected that his aristocratic relations would raise such a tempest over a paltry fifteen hundred rubles! He could not understand her tears nor the quiver of their voices.

An hour later he heard that the Colonel was getting the best of it; the uncles were finally inclining to let the case go for trial.

"The matter's settled," said the Colonel, sighing. "Enough."

After this decision all the uncles, even the emphatic Colonel, became noticeably depressed. A silence followed.

"Merciful Heavens!" sighed Ivan Markovitch. "My poor sister!"

And he began saying in a <u>subdued</u> voice that most likely his sister, Sasha's mother, was present unseen in the study at that moment. He felt in his soul how the unhappy, saintly woman was weeping, grieving, and begging for her boy. For the sake of her peace beyond the grave, they ought to spare Sasha.

The sound of a muffled sob was heard. Ivan Markovitch was weeping and muttering something which it was impossible to catch through the door. The Colonel got up and paced from corner to corner. The long conversation began over again.

But then the clock in the drawing room struck two. The family council was over. To avoid seeing the person who had moved him to such wrath, the Colonel went from the study, not into the hall, but into the vestibule. . . . Ivan Markovitch came out into the hall. . . .

Literary Analysis
Characterization
How does the writer reveal without directly stating it that Sasha is not sorry?

Vocabulary Builder
subdued (səb do͞od´) *adj.* quiet; lacking energy

▲ ▶ **Critical Viewing**
What do these pictures suggest about the setting of the story? **[Interpret]**

He was agitated and rubbing his hands joyfully. His tear-stained eyes looked good-humored and his mouth was twisted into a smile.

"Capital," he said to Sasha. "Thank God! You can go home, my dear, and sleep tranquilly. We have decided to pay the sum, but on condition that you repent and come with me tomorrow into the country and set to work."

A minute later Ivan Markovitch and Sasha in their greatcoats and caps were going down the stairs. The uncle was muttering something edifying. Sasha did not listen, but felt as though some uneasy weight were gradually slipping off his shoulders. They had forgiven him; he was free! A gust of joy sprang up within him and sent a sweet chill to his heart. He longed to breathe, to move swiftly, to live! Glancing at the street lamps and the black sky, he remembered that Von Burst was celebrating his name day[7] that evening at the "Bear," and again a rush of joy flooded his soul. . . .

"I am going!" he decided.

But then he remembered he had not a farthing, that the companions he was going to would despise him at once for his empty pockets. He must get hold of some money, come what may!

"Uncle, lend me a hundred rubles," he said to Ivan Markovitch.

His uncle, surprised, looked into his face and backed against a lamppost.

"Give it to me," said Sasha, shifting impatiently from one foot to the other and beginning to pant. "Uncle, I entreat you, give me a hundred rubles."

His face worked; he trembled, and seemed on the point of attacking his uncle. . . .

"Won't you?" he kept asking, seeing that his uncle was still amazed and did not understand. "Listen. If you don't, I'll give myself up tomorrow! I won't let you pay the IOU! I'll present another false note tomorrow!"

Petrified, muttering something incoherent in his horror, Ivan Markovitch took a hundred-ruble note out of his pocketbook and gave it to Sasha. The young man took it and walked rapidly away from him. . . .

Taking a sledge, Sasha grew calmer, and felt a rush of joy within him again. The "rights of youth" of which kind-hearted Ivan Markovitch had spoken at the family council woke up and asserted themselves. Sasha pictured the drinking party before him, and, among the bottles, the women, and his friends, the thought flashed through his mind:

"Now I see that I am a criminal; yes, I am a criminal."

7. **name day** feast day of the saint after whom a person is named.

Reading Skill
Making Inferences
Based on this decision and your knowledge of families, make an inference about the uncles' feelings for Sasha's mother.

Literary Analysis
Characterization In what way does Sasha's character develop at the end of the story?

Apply the Skills

A Problem

Thinking About the Selection

1. **Respond:** With which character in the story do you sympathize most strongly? Share your responses in a small group. Record members' thoughts about each character. Review the notes and explain how others' responses affected your viewpoint.
2. **(a) Recall:** Why is Sasha in trouble? **(b) Compare and Contrast:** Compare the position each uncle takes at the beginning of the story toward Sasha's problem.
3. **Infer:** How does Ivan Markovitch change the Colonel's mind?
4. **(a) Evaluate:** Does Ivan Markovitch's attitude help or harm Sasha? Explain. **(b) Take a Position:** What should he have done when Sasha asked him for money after the family meeting?
5. **(a) Evaluate:** Do you think what Sasha did should be punished as a crime? Why or why not? **(b) Relate:** What would you have done if you were one of Sasha's uncles? Explain.

Literary Analysis

6. Compare and contrast the **characters** of Ivan Markovitch and the Colonel. Use details from the story to support your answer.
7. Identify three examples of **indirect characterization** used to portray Sasha. Use a chart like the one shown.

What He Says	What He Does	What Others Say About Him

8. **(a)** What is Sasha's reason for cashing a false note? **(b)** Explain what this reason adds to your understanding of him. **(c)** Explain how his character is **developed** by the end of the story.
9. **(a)** Give two examples of **dialogue** from Sasha and two from one of the uncles. **(b)** What do your examples show about how the two characters differ?

Reading Skill

10. **Make an inference** about how Sasha feels having been caught doing wrong. Support your inference.
11. Draw an inference about Ivan Markovitch's feelings at the end of the story. Support your inference with story details and your own experience.

QuickReview

Story at a Glance
After Sasha cashes a forged IOU, his family must decide whether or not to take care of his debt.

Go **O**nline

—Assessment
For: Self-test
Visit: www.PHSchool.com
Web Code: eqa-6203

Character: a person, an animal, or an object who performs the actions and experiences the events of a story

Characterization: techniques a writer uses to portray characters. Characterization may be *direct* or *indirect*.

Dialogue: characters' own words as spoken in conversation

Inference: an insight, based on stated details, about information that is not stated

Vocabulary Builder

Practice Answer each question, and explain how the meaning of the underlined word influences your answer.

1. Why might you expect a <u>candid</u> answer from a good friend?
2. What might be the best way to speak with a <u>taciturn</u> person?
3. When might it be a good idea to keep your conversation <u>subdued</u>?

Adding Words to Your Vocabulary Use a thesaurus to find one **synonym**, or word with a similar meaning, for each vocabulary list word for "A Problem," on page 218. Then, use each synonym in a sentence. (For more on using a thesaurus, see page R7.)

Writing

Write two brief **retellings** of the events in "A Problem." First, retell the story from the perspective of one of the uncles. Then, tell the story from Sasha's perspective.

- Use a story map or diagram to list the main events.
- Identify details that will show the difference between the characters' perspectives.
- Use the first-person pronoun *I* to write as the character.

For *Grammar, Vocabulary,* and *Assessment,* see **Build Language Skills,** pages 242–243.

Extend Your Learning

Listening and Speaking Work with a partner to prepare an **overview of speech-patterns** of the characters in this story.
- List the major characters in the first column of a chart.
- In the next column, list typical examples of each character's speech.
- In a third column, identify social and regional factors that affect each character's speech. For instance, consider whether older people with established careers tend to speak differently from young people.

Present your analysis to the class, reading examples aloud to help listeners appreciate differences in language.

Research and Technology Write a **report on sources** for a research project about social status in Russia during the nineteenth century. Find three to four sources of varied types, including books, the Internet, and CD-ROM references. Evaluate the accuracy and reliability of each. Consider the date of the source, the author's credentials, and whether or not details are verified or contradicted by other sources.

Build Language Skills

A Visit to Grandmother • *A Problem*

Vocabulary

Word Roots The word *formulate* traces back to the **Latin root *-form-***, meaning "shape" or "form." *Formulate* means "to express in a fixed or definite way"—that is, to give shape or form to a way of expressing things. The meanings of other words containing this root also involve the idea of shape or form.

Practice Using a dictionary, briefly explain what the root contributes to the meaning of each of the following words. Then, use each phrase in a sentence.

1. a *formal* requirement
2. the *information* in an encyclopedia
3. the *formative* years of a child's life
4. a mathematical *formula*

Grammar Lesson

Principal Parts of Regular Verbs A verb has four **principal parts**: the present, the present participle, the past, and the past participle.

The Four Principal Parts of Verbs			
Present	Present Participle	Past	Past Participle
talk	(is) talking	talked	(have) talked
type	(is) typing	typed	(have) typed

MorePractice

For more practice with regular verbs, see the Grammar Handbook, pp. R40 and R44.

Most of the verbs in the English language form the present participle by adding *-ing* to the present. The past and the past participle of most verbs add *-ed* or *-d* to the present.

Practice Identify the principal part of each verb. Then, rewrite each sentence using a different principal part.

1. Jared *is helping* me on a car restoration project.
2. I always *vote* in the election for class president.
3. Several of the figure skaters *tripped* during their routines.
4. I *have discussed* my idea for a term paper topic with my teacher.

W̲G *Prentice Hall Writing and Grammar Connection: Chapter 22, Section 1*

Reading: Make Inferences

Directions: *Read the selection. Then, answer the questions.*

Standards
Assessed
• 10.1.1

The north and the west and the south are good hunting ground, but it is forbidden to go east. It is forbidden to go to any of the Dead Places except to search for metal, and then he who touches the metal must be a priest or the son of a priest. Afterwards, both the man and the metal must be purified!

—from "By the Waters of Babylon" by Stephen Vincent Benét

1. Which of the following is NOT a reasonable inference?

   A The narrator is from a primitive tribe.

   B The narrator is from a hunting people.

   C The narrator is not very smart.

   D The narrator knows the laws of his people.

2. It is reasonable to infer that

   A there is very little metal where the narrator lives.

   B metal is common in the north.

   C metal is found easily in the Dead Places.

   D metal is in the hunting grounds.

3. Use your knowledge and the repetition of "it is forbidden" to choose the best inference.

   A There is a strict monarch.

   B The narrator follows the religious rules of his group.

   C The narrator is part of his government.

   D There are no particular laws—only suggested ways of behaving.

4. The author relies on the reader to have some knowledge of

   A the properties of metals.

   B biology.

   C the ways of primitive tribes.

   D theology.

Timed Writing: Exposition [Connections]

Characters often face a conflict between what others believe are their responsibilities and their personal desires. Choose either "A Problem" or "A Visit to Grandmother." Define the conflict a character faces and discuss the overall effect of this conflict on the character and those around him. **(25 minutes)**

 ## Writing Workshop: *Work in Progress*

Short Story

Write a list of the inventions from the last one hundred years that are part of your daily life. In a small group, review your lists. Then, using the protagonist/antagonist list from your writing portfolio, assign each character an invention that could be important to him or her in a story.

Practice these skills with either "The Street of the Cañon" (p. 246) or "There Will Come Soft Rains" (p. 259).

Literary Analysis

All stories have a **setting**—the time and the place of the story's events. To establish a setting, writers use **description**, or word-pictures appealing to the senses. Settings shape stories in a few ways:

- Setting may determine plot. In a story set in the Arctic wilderness, characters will face challenges not found in a Caribbean resort hotel.

- Setting may shape a character's concerns and values. A character from the days of knights might be concerned with honor. A character from the Stone Age might be concerned only with survival.

As you read, use a chart like the one shown to identify the setting and the details that describe it.

Reading Skill

An **inference** is an insight, based on stated details, about information that is not stated. Drawing inferences helps you make connections between facts or events. For instance, if a writer does not name a setting but describes extreme cold, hunters huddled in igloos, and a night that will last all winter, you can make the inference that the story is set in the Arctic.

After making an inference, **read on** to find additional support. If new details contradict the inference, modify your inference.

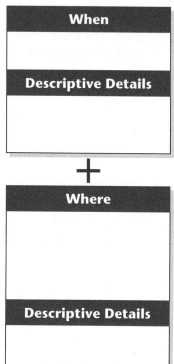

Academic Standards

- Examine how the author's perspective influences the structure and tone of the text. (10.2.4)

- Analyze many different forms of dramatic literature. (10.3.1)

- Evaluate interactions between characters and how these affect the plot. (10.3.3)

When
Descriptive Details

+

Where
Descriptive Details

Vocabulary Builder

The Street of the Cañon

- **nonchalantly** (nän´ shə länt´ lē) *adv.* casually; indifferently (p. 248) *Despite the insult, he shrugged nonchalantly.*

- **imperiously** (im pir´ ē əs lē) *adv.* arrogantly (p. 250) *She gave orders imperiously.*

- **plausibility** (plô´ zə bil´ i tē) *n.* believability; seeming truth (p. 251) *Although his excuse has some plausibility, I just do not believe it.*

There Will Come Soft Rains

- **titanic** (tī tan´ ik) *adj.* powerful; of great size (p. 261) *A single titanic wave sank the ship.*

- **fluttered** (flut´ ər'd) *v.* flapped or vibrated rapidly (p. 262) *The papers fluttered in the wind and then blew away.*

- **tremulous** (trem´ yoo ləs) *adj.* trembling; quivering; timid; fearful (p. 263) *The cup shook in his tremulous hands.*

Build Understanding • *The Street of the Cañon*

Background

Courtship and Marriage in Old Mexico Historically, in some parts of Mexico, a man had to ask a woman's family for permission to marry her. In others, the parents arranged the match. In the town in this story, a man and woman are considered engaged if they walk together in the plaza.

Connecting to the Literature

Reading/Writing Connection The townspeople in this story are quarreling with a neighboring village. In the midst of the conflict, one man plays a daring prank. Write some reasons people use humor during a quarrel. Use at least three of these words: *provoke, accommodate, diminish, mediate.*

READ MORE

by Josephina Niggli
Mexican Village

Meet the Author

Josephina **Niggli** (1910–1983)

Josephina Niggli was born in Monterrey, Mexico, but she grew up on both sides of the border between Mexico and the United States. When Niggli was fifteen, her parents sent her to San Antonio, Texas, to attend school.

Writing for Stage and Screen Niggli published her first book shortly after her high school graduation. Later, she wrote plays. She found theater thrilling, writing, "Once you have experienced the emotion of having a play produced, you are forever lost to the ordinary world."

Later, Niggli worked on movie scripts in Hollywood. In 1945, she published *Mexican Village,* a collection of ten stories that capture the rich local color of Mexico.

Fast Facts

▶ While still in college, Niggli won several prizes for her writing.
▶ Niggli worked as a writer on the film *Sombrero,* which was based on her book *Mexican Village.*

Go Online
Author Link

For: More about the author
Visit: www.PHSchool.com
Web Code: eqe-9204

The Street of the Cañon

of the

Cañon

Josephina Niggli

Dance in Tehuantepec, 1935. Diego Rivera. Los Angeles County Museum of Art.

It was May, the flowering thorn was sweet in the air, and the village of San Juan Iglesias in the Valley of the Three Marys was celebrating. The long dark streets were empty because all of the people, from the lowest-paid cowboy to the mayor, were helping Don Roméo Calderón celebrate his daughter's eighteenth birthday.

On the other side of the town, where the Cañon Road led across the mountains to the Sabinas Valley, a tall slender man, a package clutched tightly against his side, slipped from shadow to shadow. Once a dog barked, and the man's black suit merged into the blackness of a wall. But no voice called out, and after a moment he slid into the narrow, dirt-packed street again.

▲ Critical Viewing
What does this painting suggest about the setting of the story? **[Infer]**

The moonlight touched his shoulder and spilled across his narrow hips. He was young, no more than twenty-five, and his black curly head was bare. He walked swiftly along, heading always for the distant sound of guitar and flute. If he met anyone now, who could say from which direction he had come? He might be a trader from Monterrey, or a buyer of cow's milk from farther north in the Valley of the Three Marys. Who would guess that an Hidalgo man dared to walk alone in the moonlit streets of San Juan Iglesias?

Carefully adjusting his flat package so that it was not too prominent, he squared his shoulders and walked jauntily across the street to the laughter-filled house. Little boys packed in the doorway made way for him, smiling and nodding to him. The long, narrow room with the orchestra at one end was filled with whirling dancers. Rigid-backed chaperones[1] were gossiping together, seated in their straight chairs against the plaster walls. Over the scene was the yellow glow of kerosene lanterns, and the air was hot with the too-sweet perfume of gardenias, tuberoses,[2] and the pungent scent of close-packed humanity.

The man in the doorway, while trying to appear at ease, was carefully examining every smiling face. If just one person recognized him, the room would turn on him like a den of snarling mountain cats, but so far all the laughter-dancing eyes were friendly.

Suddenly a plump, officious little man, his round cheeks glistening with perspiration, pushed his way through the crowd. His voice, many times too large for his small body, boomed at the man in the doorway. "Welcome, stranger, welcome to our house." Thrusting his arm through the stranger's, and almost dislodging the package, he started to lead the way through the maze of dancers. "Come and drink a toast to my daughter—to my beautiful Sarita. She is eighteen this night."

In the square patio the gentle breeze ruffled the pink and white oleander bushes. A long table set up on sawhorses held loaves of flaky crusted French bread, stacks of thin, delicate tortillas, plates of barbecued beef, and long red rolls of spicy sausages. But most of all there were cheeses, for the Three Marys was a cheese-eating valley. There were yellow cheese and white cheese and curded cheese from cow's milk. There was even a flat white cake of goat cheese from distant Linares, a delicacy too expensive for any but feast days.

---

1. chaperones (shap´ ər ōnz´) older or married women who accompany and supervise the behavior of a young person in public.
2. gardenias (gär dēn´ yəz), **tuberoses** (tōōb´ rōz´ əs) two types of plant with especially sweet-smelling flowers.

Reading Skill
Making Inferences
Make an inference about the towns of Hidalgo and San Juan Iglesias. What kinds of details might confirm your inference?

Literary Analysis
Setting To which senses does this description of the setting appeal?

**Reading Check**

What occasion is the village of San Juan Iglesias celebrating?

To set off this feast were bottles of beer floating in ice-filled tin tubs, and another table was covered with bottles of mescal, of tequila, of maguey wine.

Don Roméo Calderón thrust a glass of tequila into the stranger's hand. "Drink, friend, to the prettiest girl in San Juan. As pretty as my fine fighting cocks, she is. On her wedding day she takes to her man, and may she find him soon, the best fighter in my flock. Drink deep, friend. Even the rivers flow with wine."

The Hidalgo man laughed and raised his glass high. "May the earth be always fertile beneath her feet."

Someone called to Don Roméo that more guests were arriving, and with a final delighted pat on the stranger's shoulder, the little man scurried away. As the young fellow smiled after his retreating host, his eyes caught and held another pair of eyes—laughing black eyes set in a young girl's face. The last time he had seen that face it had been white and tense with rage, and the lips clenched tight to prevent an outgushing stream of angry words. That had been in February, and she had worn a white lace shawl over her hair. Now it was May, and a gardenia was a splash of white in the glossy dark braids. The moonlight had mottled his face that February night, and he knew that she did not recognize him. He grinned impudently[3] back at her, and her eyes widened, then slid sideways to one of the chaperones. The fan in her small hand snapped shut. She tapped its parchment tip against her mouth and slipped away to join the dancing couples in the front room. The gestures of a fan translate into a coded language on the frontier. The stranger raised one eyebrow as he interpreted the signal.

But he did not move toward her at once. Instead, he inched slowly back against the table. No one was behind him, and his hands quickly unfastened the package he had been guarding so long. Then he <u>nonchalantly</u> walked into the front room.

The girl was sitting close to a chaperone. As he came up to her he swerved slightly toward the bushy-browed old lady.

"Your servant, señora. I kiss your hands and feet."

The chaperone stared at him in astonishment. Such fine manners were not common to the town of San Juan Iglesias.

"Eh, you're a stranger," she said. "I thought so."

"But a stranger no longer, señora, now that I have met you." He bent over her, so close she could smell the faint fragrance of talcum on his freshly shaven cheek.

"Will you dance the *parada* with me?"

---

3. **impudently** (im′ pyoo dənt lē) *adv.* in a shamelessly bold or provocative way.

Literature in Context

Language Connection

Spanish Vocabulary Set in Mexico the story contains several Spanish words and terms, including

- **cañon** canyon; a narrow valley between high cliffs
- **tío** uncle
- **hola** Spanish exclamation meaning "hi"
- **don** title of respect meaning "sir"; often placed before a man's name
- **parada** literally, "parade"; a dance in which partners stride around together

Connect to the Literature

Why do you think Niggli included these terms in the story? [Hypothesize]

Vocabulary Builder
nonchalantly (nän′ shə länt′ lē) *adv.* casually; indifferently

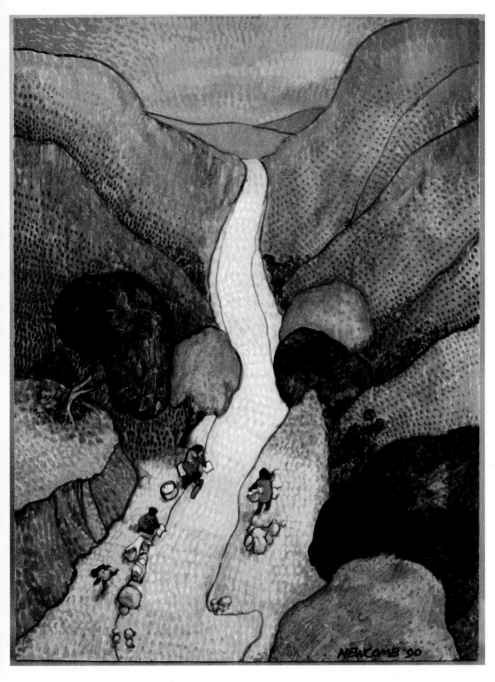

◀ **Critical Viewing**
Identify one way in
which this painting
reflects the setting of
the story. **[Connect]**

This request startled her eyes into popping open beneath the
heavy brows. "So, my young rooster, would you flirt with me, and I
old enough to be your grandmother?"

"Can you show me a prettier woman to flirt with in the Valley of
the Three Marys?" he asked audaciously.

She grinned at him and turned toward the girl at her side. "This
young fool wants to meet you, my child."

The girl blushed to the roots of her hair and shyly lowered her
white lids. The old woman laughed aloud.

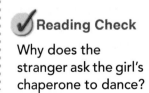

Reading Check

Why does the
stranger ask the girl's
chaperone to dance?

The Street of the Cañon ■ 249

"Go out and dance, the two of you. A man clever enough to pat the sheep has a right to play with the lamb."

The next moment they had joined the circle of dancers and Sarita was trying to control her laughter.

"She is the worst dragon in San Juan. And how easily you won her!"

"What is a dragon," he asked <u>imperiously</u>, "when I longed to dance with you?"

"Ay," she retorted, "you have a quick tongue. I think you are a dangerous man."

In answer he drew her closer to him, and turned her toward the orchestra. As he reached the chief violinist he called out, "Play the *Virgencita*, 'The Shy Young Maiden.'"

The violinist's mouth opened in soundless surprise. The girl in his arms said sharply, "You heard him, the *Borachita*, 'The Little Drunken Girl.'"

With a relieved grin, the violinist tapped his music stand with his bow, and the music swung into the sad farewell of a man to his sweetheart:

> *Farewell, my little drunken one,*
> *I must go to the capital*
> *To serve the master*
> *Who makes me weep for my return.*

The stranger frowned down at her. "Is this a joke, señorita?" he asked coldly.

"No," she whispered, looking about her quickly to see if the incident had been observed. "But the *Virgencita* is the favorite song of Hidalgo, a village on the other side of the mountains in the next valley. The people of Hidalgo and San Juan Iglesias do not speak."

"That is a stupid thing," said the man from Hidalgo as he swung her around in a large turn. "Is not music free as air? Why should one town own the rights to a song?"

The girl shuddered slightly. "Those people from Hidalgo—they are wicked monsters. Can you guess what they did not six months since?"

The man started to point out that the space of time from February to May was three months, but he thought it better not to

appear too wise. "Did these Hidalgo monsters frighten you, señorita? If they did, I personally will kill them all."

She moved closer against him and tilted her face until her mouth was close to his ear. "They attempted to steal the bones of Don Rómolo Balderas."

"Is it possible?" He made his eyes grow round and his lips purse up in disdain. "Surely not that! Why, all the world knows that Don Rómolo Balderas was the greatest historian in the entire Republic. Every school child reads his books. Wise men from Quintana Roo to the Río Bravo bow their heads in admiration to his name. What a wicked thing to do!" He hoped his virtuous tone was not too virtuous for <u>plausibility</u>, but she did not seem to notice.

"It is true! In the night they came. Three devils!"

"Young devils, I hope."

"Young or old, who cares? They were devils. The blacksmith surprised them even as they were opening the grave. He raised such a shout that all of San Juan rushed to his aid, for they were fighting, I can tell you. Especially one of them—their leader."

"And who was he?"

"You have heard of him doubtless. A proper wild one named Pepe Gonzalez."

"And what happened to them?"

"They had horses and got away, but one, I think, was hurt."

The Hidalgo man twisted his mouth remembering how Rubén the candymaker had ridden across the whitewashed line high on the cañon trail that marked the division between the Three Marys' and the Sabinas' sides of the mountains, and then had fallen in a faint from his saddle because his left arm was broken. There was no candy in Hidalgo for six weeks, and the entire Sabinas Valley resented that broken arm as fiercely as did Rubén.

The stranger tightened his arm in reflexed anger about Sarita's waist as she said, "All the world knows that the men of Hidalgo are sons of the mountain witches."

"But even devils are shy of disturbing the honored dead," he said gravely.

"'Don Rómolo was born in our village,' Hidalgo says. 'His bones belong to us.' Well, anyone in the valley can tell you he died in San Juan Iglesias, and here his bones will stay! Is that not proper? Is that not right?"

To keep from answering, he guided her through an intricate dance pattern that led them past the patio door. Over her head he could see two men and a woman staring with amazement at the open package on the table.

Vocabulary Builder
plausibility (plô′ zə bil′ i tē) *n.* believability; seeming truth

Reading Skill
Making Inferences
Make an inference about the stranger's connection to the men who tried to raid the grave.

Reading Check

What did three men from Hidalgo try to do six months earlier?

His eyes on the patio, he asked blandly, "You say the leader was one Pepe Gonzalez? The name seems to have a familiar sound."

"But naturally. He has a talent." She tossed her head and stepped away from him as the music stopped. It was a dance of two *paradas*. He slipped his hand through her arm and guided her into place in the large oval of parading couples. Twice around the room and the orchestra would play again.

"A talent?" he prompted.

"For doing the impossible. When all the world says a thing cannot be done, he does it to prove the world wrong. Why, he climbed to the top of the Prow, and not even the long vanished Joaquín Castillo had ever climbed that mountain before. And this same Pepe caught a mountain lion with nothing to aid him but a rope and his two bare hands."

"He doesn't sound such a bad friend," protested the stranger, slipping his arm around her waist as the music began to play the merry song of the soap bubbles:

> *Pretty bubbles of a thousand colors*
> *That ride on the wind*
> *And break as swiftly*
> *As a lover's heart.*

The events in the patio were claiming his attention. Little by little he edged her closer to the door. The group at the table had considerably enlarged. There was a low murmur of excitement from the crowd.

"What has happened?" asked Sarita, attracted by the noise.

"There seems to be something wrong at the table," he answered, while trying to peer over the heads of the people in front of him. Realizing that this might be the last moment of peace he would have that evening, he bent toward her.

"If I come back on Sunday, will you walk around the plaza with me?"

She was startled into exclaiming, "Ay, no!"

"Please. Just once around."

"And you think I'd walk more than once with you, señor, even if you were no stranger? In San Juan Iglesias, to walk around the plaza with a girl means a wedding."

"Ha, and you think that is common to San Juan alone? Even the devils of Hidalgo respect that law," he added hastily at her puzzled upward glance. "And so they do in all the villages." To cover his lapse[4] he said softly, "I don't even know your name."

Literary Analysis
Setting How does the time and place of the story affect the way Sarita responds to the stranger?

---

4. lapse (laps) *n.* slip; error.

◀ **Critical Viewing**
Compare the mood of
this painting with the
mood of the story.
**[Compare and
Contrast]**

A mischievous grin crinkled the corners of her eyes. "Nor do I
know yours, señor. Strangers do not often walk the streets of San
Juan."

Before he could answer, the chattering in the patio swelled to
louder proportions. Don Roméo's voice lay on top, like thick
cream on milk. "I tell you it is a jewel of a cheese. Such
flavor, such texture, such whiteness. It is a jewel of a cheese."

✔**Reading Check**

What has appeared on
the table on the patio?

The Street of the Cañon ■ 253

"What has happened?" Sarita asked of a woman at her elbow.

"A fine goat's cheese appeared as if by magic on the table. No one knows where it came from."

"Probably an extra one from Linares," snorted a fat bald man on the right.

"Linares never made such a cheese as this," said the woman decisively.

"Silence!" roared Don Roméo. "Old Tío Daniel would speak a word to us."

A great hand of silence closed down over the mouths of the people. The girl was standing on tiptoe trying vainly to see what was happening. She was hardly aware of the stranger's whispering voice although she remembered the words that he said. "Sunday night— once around the plaza."

She did not realize that he had moved away, leaving a gap that was quickly filled by the blacksmith.

▲ Critical Viewing
Which details in this image capture the excitement of the party in the story? [Interpret]

Old Tío Daniel's voice was a shrill squeak, and his thin, stringy neck jutted forth from his body like a turtle's from its shell. "This is no cheese from Linares," he said with authority, his mouth sucking in over his toothless gums between his sentences. "Years ago, when the great Don Rómolo Balderas was still alive, we had such cheese as this—ay, in those days we had it. But after he died and was buried in our own sainted ground, as was right and proper . . ."

"Yes, yes," muttered voices in the crowd. He glared at the interruption. As soon as there was silence again, he continued:

"After he died, we had it no more. Shall I tell you why?"

"Tell us, Tío Daniel," said the voices humbly.

"Because it is made in Hidalgo!"

The sound of a waterfall, the sound of a wind in a narrow cañon, and the sound of an angry crowd are much the same. There were no distinct words, but the sound was enough.

"Are you certain, Tío?" boomed Don Roméo.

"As certain as I am that a donkey has long ears. The people of Hidalgo have been famous for generations for making cheese like this—especially that wicked one, that owner of a cheese factory, Timotéo Gonzalez, father to Pepe, the wild one, whom we have good cause to remember."

"We do, we do," came the sigh of assurance.

"But on the whole northern frontier there are no vats like his to produce so fine a product. Ask the people of Chihuahua, of Sonora. Ask the man on the bridge at Laredo, or the man in his boat at Tampico, '*Hola*, friend, who makes the finest goat cheese?' And the answer will always be the same, 'Don Timotéo of Hidalgo.'"

It was the blacksmith who asked the great question. "Then where did that cheese come from, and we haters of Hidalgo these ten long years?"

No voice said, "The stranger," but with one fluid movement every head in the patio turned toward the girl in the doorway. She also turned, her eyes wide with something that she realized to her own amazement was more apprehension[5] than anger.

But the stranger was not in the room. When the angry, muttering men pushed through to the street, the stranger was not on the plaza. He was not anywhere in sight. A few of the more religious crossed themselves for fear that the Devil had walked in their midst. "Who was he?" one voice asked another. But Sarita, who was meekly listening to a lecture from Don Roméo on the propriety of dancing with strangers, did not have to ask. She had a strong suspicion that she had danced that night within the circling arm of Pepe Gonzalez.

Reading Skill
Making Inferences
Do details here support your inference about the stranger's link with Hidalgo? Explain.

Literary Analysis
Setting What features of the setting make it easy for the stranger to escape?

---

5. **apprehension** (ap´ rē hen´ shən) *n.* anxious feeling; fear.

Apply the Skills

The Street of the Cañon

Thinking About the Selection

1. **Respond:** Would you like to read some of the other stories in Niggli's book *Mexican Village*? Why or why not?

2. **(a) Recall:** What adjectives does the author use to describe the way in which the Hidalgo man walks into the village? **(b) Infer:** What does the man wish to prevent others from learning?

3. **(a) Recall:** Whom does the Hidalgo man first ask to dance? **(b) Infer:** Why does he ask her? **(c) Interpret:** What does Sarita mean when she says, "I think you are a dangerous man"?

4. **(a) Summarize:** Why are the towns quarreling? **(b) Hypothesize:** What might the villagers have done to the stranger if they had known his identity? Support your answer.

5. **(a) Interpret:** Why does the stranger risk danger to dance with Sarita and leave the gift? **(b) Discuss:** In a small group, share your responses. **(c) Evaluate:** As a group, choose the best response to share with the class.

Literary Analysis

6. **(a)** Identify these aspects of the **setting** in "The Street of the Cañon": the country, the town, and the historical period in which the action occurs. **(b)** For each aspect, give an example of a **description** that helps make the setting vivid for readers.

7. Explain why the specific dangers the man from Hidalgo faces might not apply in a story set in a different town or time.

Reading Skill

8. **(a)** Based on the information in the first three paragraphs of the story, what two **inferences** could you make about the stranger's plans? **(b)** For each inference, note at least one detail later in the story that either proves it or disproves it. Record your answers in a chart like the one shown.

Inference	Confirming Details	Disproving Details

9. Make an inference concerning Sarita's feelings about the stranger at the end of the story. Give three details in support.

QuickReview

Who's Who in the Story

Sarita: a beautiful girl of San Juan Iglesias

The stranger: a man from Hidalgo

Don Roméo Calderón: Sarita's father

Don Rómolo Balderas: the dead historian whose burial has caused a feud between the towns

Go Online
Assessment
For: Self-test
Visit: www.PHSchool.com
Web Code: eqa-6204

Setting: the time and place of story events, typically conveyed through *description*

Inference: an insight, based on stated details, about something not stated

Vocabulary Builder

Practice Match each statement with a word from the vocabulary list for "The Street of the Cañon," on page 244. Explain each choice.

1. Some say that a good story should have this quality.
2. A pushy person might act in this way.
3. A nervous person may have difficulty behaving this way.

Adding Words to Your Vocabulary Someone who behaves *imperiously* acts in the manner of an emperor. Using a dictionary, find two words related to *imperiously*. For each word, tell the part of speech and explain how it is related to the idea of an emperor. Then, use it in a sentence. (For more on using a dictionary, see page R6.)

Writing

Write a brief **letter to a friend** summarizing this story. Then, rewrite the summary as part of a **book review** for newspaper readers.

- Change your language as needed for your new audience, replacing informal words with formal ones.
- Add information that a newspaper audience would expect to find in a review, such as information about the writer.

For *Grammar, Vocabulary,* and *Assessment,* see **Build Language Skills,** pages 268–269.

Extend Your Learning

Listening and Speaking Give an **oral reading** of "The Highwayman" by Alfred Noyes.
- Vary your tone of voice to reflect meaning.
- Use gestures as appropriate.
Afterward, lead the class in a comparison of Noyes's poem and "The Street of the Cañon."

Research and Technology With a partner, prepare a **visual art presentation** for the story. Find at least two works of art that reflect the setting and the spirit of the story. To evaluate the art, identify any direct visual references to the setting, such as a canyon. Then, note feelings—humor, mystery—that fit the mood of the story. Present the works you have chosen to the class and explain your choices.

Short Story

Background

The Atomic Age Ray Bradbury published this story in 1950. Five years earlier, the United States had dropped the first atomic bombs on Japan. One year before the story, the Soviet Union had tested its own atomic device. This story reflects the fear at that time that these rival nations might unleash their deadly technology and destroy humanity.

Connecting to the Literature

Reading/Writing Connection The house in this futuristic tale is automated to an astonishing extent. Write a few sentences about the positive or negative aspects of automated machines such as car alarms and ATMs. Use at least three of these words: *maximize, minimize, challenge, display, maintain.*

Review

For **Literary Analysis, Reading Skill,** and **Vocabulary Builder,** see page 244.

READ MORE

by Ray Bradbury

Fahrenheit 451

The Illustrated Man

Meet the Author

Ray **Bradbury** (b. 1920)

Ray Bradbury, one of the world's most celebrated science-fiction and fantasy writers, was born in Waukegan, Illinois, and grew up near Lake Michigan. As a child, he was influenced by the stories of Edgar Allan Poe and developed a fascination with horror movies and futuristic fantasy.

Dreaming the Impossible Bradbury considers most of his work fantasy rather than science fiction, explaining, "Science fiction is the art of the possible. Fantasy is the art of the impossible." One of his dreams remains an impossible fantasy, at least for now—he wants to go to Mars. "But since it's not going to happen," he explains, "I don't worry about it."

Fast Facts

▶ Bradbury worked on developing the Spaceship Earth display at Disney World's Epcot Center.

▶ In 2002, Bradbury was commemorated with a star on the Hollywood Walk of Fame.

Go **Online**
Author Link

For: More about the author
Visit: www.PHSchool.com
Web Code: eqe-9205

There Will Come Soft Rains

Ray Bradbury

The Body of a House, #1 of 8. © Robert Beckmann 1993. Collection: Nevada Museum of Art, Reno.

◀ **Critical Viewing**
What does this painting suggest about the mood of the story? **[Predict]**

In the living room the voice-clock sang, *Tick-tock, seven o'clock, time to get up, time to get up, seven o'clock!* as if it were afraid that nobody would. The morning house lay empty. The clock ticked on, repeating and repeating its sounds into the emptiness. *Seven-nine, breakfast time, seven-nine!*

In the kitchen the breakfast stove gave a hissing sigh and ejected from its warm interior eight pieces of perfectly browned toast, eight eggs sunnyside up, sixteen slices of bacon, two coffees, and two cool glasses of milk.

"Today is August 4, 2026," said a second voice from the kitchen ceiling, "in the city of Allendale, California." It repeated the date three times for memory's sake. "Today is Mr. Featherstone's birthday. Today is the anniversary of Tilita's marriage. Insurance is payable, as are the water, gas, and light bills."

Somewhere in the walls, relays clicked, memory tapes glided under electric eyes.

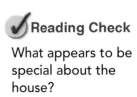

✓ **Reading Check**

What appears to be special about the house?

The Body of a House, #2 of 8. © Robert Beckmann 1993. Collection: Nevada Museum of Art, Reno.

◀ **Critical Viewing**
Compare and contrast
the house in this
painting with the
house at this point in
the story. [**Compare
and Contrast**]

*Eight-one, tick-tock, eight-one o'clock, off to school, off to work,
run, run, eight one*! But no doors slammed, no carpets took the soft
tread of rubber heels. It was raining outside. The weather box on
the front door sang quietly: "Rain, rain, go away; rubbers, raincoats
for today . . ." And the rain tapped on the empty house, echoing.

Outside, the garage chimed and lifted its door to reveal the waiting car. After a long wait the door swung down again.

At eight-thirty the eggs were shriveled and the toast was like
stone. An aluminum wedge scraped them into the sink, where hot
water whirled them down a metal throat which digested and flushed
them away to the distant sea. The dirty dishes were dropped into a
hot washer and emerged twinkling dry.

Nine-fifteen, sang the clock, *time to clean.*

Out of warrens in the wall, tiny robot mice darted. The rooms
were acrawl with the small cleaning animals, all rubber and metal.
They thudded against chairs, whirling their mustached runners,
kneading the rug nap, sucking gently at hidden dust. Then, like
mysterious invaders, they popped into their burrows. Their pink
electric eyes faded. The house was clean.

Ten o'clock. The sun came out from behind the rain. The house
stood alone in a city of rubble and ashes. This was the one house
left standing. At night the ruined city gave off a radioactive glow
which could be seen for miles.

Ten-fifteen. The garden sprinklers whirled up in golden founts,
filling the soft morning air with scatterings of brightness. The water
pelted windowpanes, running down the charred west side where the

Reading Skill
Making Inferences
Make an inference
about the inhabitants
of the house. What
kinds of confirming
details will you look
for as you read on?

house had been burned evenly free of its white paint. The entire west face of the house was black, save for five places. Here the silhouette[1] in paint of a man mowing a lawn. Here, as in a photograph, a woman bent to pick flowers. Still farther over, their images burned on wood in one <u>titanic</u> instant, a small boy, hands flung into the air; higher up, the image of a thrown ball, and opposite him a girl, hands raised to catch a ball which never came down.

The five spots of paint—the man, the woman, the children, the ball—remained. The rest was a thin charcoaled layer.

The gentle-sprinkler rain filled the garden with falling light.

Until this day, how well the house had kept its peace. How carefully it had inquired, "Who goes there? What's the password?" and, getting no answer from lonely foxes and whining cats, it had shut up its windows and drawn shades in an old-maidenly preoccupation with self-protection which bordered on a mechanical paranoia.

It quivered at each sound, the house did. If a sparrow brushed a window, the shade snapped up. The bird, startled, flew off! No, not even a bird must touch the house!

The house was an altar with ten thousand attendants, big, small, servicing, attending, in choirs. But the gods had gone away, and the ritual of the religion continued senselessly, uselessly.

Twelve noon.

A dog whined, shivering, on the front porch.

The front door recognized the dog voice and opened. The dog, once huge and fleshy, but now gone to bone and covered with sores, moved in and through the house, tracking mud. Behind it whirred angry mice, angry at having to pick up mud, angry at inconvenience.

For not a leaf fragment blew under the door but what the wall panels flipped open and the copper scrap rats flashed swiftly out. The offending dust, hair, or paper, seized in miniature steel jaws, was raced back to the burrows. There, down tubes which fed into the cellar, it was dropped into the sighing vent of an incinerator which sat like evil Baal[2] in a dark corner.

The dog ran upstairs, hysterically yelping to each door, at last realizing, as the house realized, that only silence was here.

It sniffed the air and scratched the kitchen door. Behind the door, the stove was making pancakes which filled the house with a rich baked odor and the scent of maple syrup.

The dog frothed at the mouth, lying at the door, sniffing, its eyes turned to fire. It ran wildly in circles, biting at its tail, spun in a frenzy, and died. It lay in the parlor for an hour.

---

1. **silhouette** (sil´ ə wet´) *n.* outline of a figure, filled in with a solid color.
2. **Baal** (bā´ əl) *n.* ancient Near Eastern deity, later associated with evil.

Vocabulary Builder
titanic (tī tan´ ik) *adj.* powerful; of great size

Literary Analysis
Setting What new information have you learned about the setting of the story?

Reading Check

What has happened to the rest of the city?

Two o'clock, sang a voice.

Delicately sensing decay at last, the regiments of mice hummed out as softly as blown gray leaves in an electrical wind.

Two-fifteen.

The dog was gone.

In the cellar, the incinerator glowed suddenly and a whirl of sparks leaped up the chimney.

Two thirty-five.

Bridge tables sprouted from patio walls. Playing cards <u>fluttered</u> onto pads in a shower of pips. Glasses manifested on an oaken bench with egg-salad sandwiches. Music played.

But the tables were silent and the cards untouched.

At four o'clock the tables folded like great butterflies back through the paneled walls.

Four-thirty.

The nursery walls glowed.

Animals took shape: yellow giraffes, blue lions, pink antelopes, lilac panthers cavorting in crystal substance. The walls were glass. They looked out upon color and fantasy. Hidden films clocked through well-oiled sprockets, and the walls lived. The nursery floor was woven to resemble a crisp, cereal meadow. Over this ran aluminum roaches and iron crickets, and in the hot still air butterflies of delicate red tissue wavered among the sharp aroma of animal spoors![3] There was the sound like a great matted yellow hive of bees within a dark bellows, the lazy bumble of a purring lion. And there was the patter of okapi[4] feet and the murmur of a fresh jungle rain, like other hoofs, falling upon the summer-starched grass. Now the walls dissolved into distances of parched weed, mile on mile, and warm endless sky. The animals drew away into thorn brakes and water holes.

It was the children's hour.

Five o'clock. The bath filled with clear hot water.

Six, seven, eight o'clock. The dinner dishes manipulated like magic tricks, and in the study a *click*. In the hearth a fire now blazed up warmly.

Nine o'clock. The beds warmed their hidden circuits, for nights were cool here.

Nine-five. A voice spoke from the study ceiling:

"Mrs. McClellan, which poem would you like this evening?"

The house was silent.

The voice said at last, "Since you express no preference, I shall select a poem at random." Quiet music rose to back the voice. "Sara Teasdale. As I recall, your favorite. . . .

3. spoors (spŏŏrz) *n.* droppings of wild animals.

4. okapi (ō kä′ pē) *n.* African animal related to the giraffe but with a much shorter neck.

Vocabulary Builder
fluttered (flut′ ər'd) *v.* flapped or vibrated rapidly

Literary Analysis
Setting How does this description show that the story is set in a time different from the present?

The Body of a House, #4 of 8. © Robert Beckmann 1993. Collection: Nevada Museum of Art, Reno.

◀ **Critical Viewing**
What does this painting suggest about the future of the house in the story? **[Predict]**

There will come soft rains and the smell of the ground,
And swallows circling with their shimmering sound;

And frogs in the pools singing at night,
And wild plum trees in <u>tremulous</u> white;

Robins will wear their feathery fire,
Whistling their whims on a low fence-wire;

And not one will know of the war, not one
Will care at last when it is done.

Not one would mind, neither bird nor tree,
If mankind perished utterly;

And Spring herself, when she woke at dawn
Would scarcely know that we were gone."

The fire burned on the stone hearth. The empty chairs faced each other between the silent walls, and the music played.

At ten o'clock the house began to die.

The wind blew. A falling tree bough crashed through the kitchen window. Cleaning solvent, bottled, shattered over the stove. The room was ablaze in an instant!

"Fire!" screamed a voice. The house lights flashed, water pumps shot water from the ceilings. But the solvent spread on the linoleum, licking, eating, under the kitchen door, while the voices took it up in chorus: "Fire, fire, fire!"

Vocabulary Builder
tremulous (trem´ yoo ləs) *adj.* trembling; quivering; timid; fearful

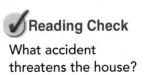Reading Check
What accident threatens the house?

The house tried to save itself. Doors sprang tightly shut, but the windows were broken by the heat and the wind blew and sucked upon the fire.

The house gave ground as the fire in ten billion angry sparks moved with flaming ease from room to room and then up the stairs. While scurrying water rats squeaked from the walls, pistoled their water, and ran for more. And the wall sprays let down showers of mechanical rain.

But too late. Somewhere, sighing, a pump shrugged to a stop. The quenching rain ceased. The reserve water supply which had filled baths and washed dishes for many quiet days was gone.

The fire crackled up the stairs. It fed upon Picassos and Matisses[5] in the upper halls, like delicacies, baking off the oily flesh, tenderly crisping the canvases into black shavings.

Now the fire lay in beds, stood in windows, changed the colors of drapes!

And then, reinforcements.

From attic trapdoors, blind robot faces peered down with faucet mouths gushing green chemical.

The fire backed off, as even an elephant must at the sight of a dead snake. Now there were twenty snakes whipping over the floor, killing the fire with a clear cold venom of green froth.

But the fire was clever. It had sent flame outside the house, up through the attic to the pumps there. An explosion! The attic brain

---

5. **Picassos** (pi kä´ sōz) **and Matisses** (mä tēs´ ez) paintings by the celebrated modern painters Pablo Picasso (1881–1973) and Henri Matisse (1869–1954).

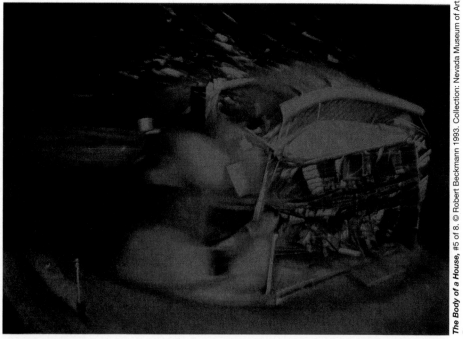

The Body of a House, #5 of 8. © Robert Beckmann 1993. Collection: Nevada Museum of Art, Reno.

◀ **Critical Viewing** Compare and contrast the house in this painting with the house at the end of the story. **[Compare and Contrast]**

which directed the pumps was shattered into bronze shrapnel on the beams.

The fire rushed back into every closet and felt of the clothes hung there.

The house shuddered, oak bone on bone, its bared skeleton cringing from the heat, its wire, its nerves revealed as if a surgeon had torn the skin off to let the red veins and capillaries quiver in the scalded air. Help, help! Fire! Run, run! Heat snapped mirrors like the first brittle winter ice. And the voices wailed Fire, fire, run, run, like a tragic nursery rhyme, a dozen voices, high, low, like children dying in a forest, alone, alone. And the voices fading as the wires popped their sheathings like hot chestnuts. One, two, three, four, five voices died.

In the nursery the jungle burned. Blue lions roared, purple giraffes bounded off. The panthers ran in circles, changing color, and ten million animals, running before the fire, vanished off toward a distant steaming river. . . .

Ten more voices died. In the last instant under the fire avalanche, other choruses, oblivious, could be heard announcing the time, playing music, cutting the lawn by remote-control mower, or setting an umbrella frantically out and in the slamming and opening front door, a thousand things happening, like a clock shop when each clock strikes the hour insanely before or after the other, a scene of maniac confusion, yet unity; singing, screaming, a few last cleaning mice darting bravely out to carry the horrid ashes away! And one voice, with sublime disregard for the situation, read poetry aloud in the fiery study, until all the film spools burned, until all the wires withered and the circuits cracked.

The fire burst the house and let it slam flat down, puffing out skirts of spark and smoke.

In the kitchen, an instant before the rain of fire and timber, the stove could be seen making breakfasts at a psychopathic rate, ten dozen eggs, six loaves of toast, twenty dozen bacon strips, which, eaten by fire, started the stove working again, hysterically hissing!

The crash. The attic smashing into kitchen and parlor. The parlor into cellar, cellar into subcellar. Deep freeze, armchair, film tapes, circuits, beds, and all like skeletons thrown in a cluttered mound deep under.

Smoke and silence. A great quantity of smoke.

Dawn showed faintly in the east. Among the ruins, one wall stood alone. Within the wall, a last voice said, over and over again and again, even as the sun rose to shine upon the heaped rubble and steam:

"Today is August 5, 2026, today is August 5, 2026, today is . . ."

Reading Skill
Making Inferences
Based on the details in this paragraph, what do you infer is happening?

Literary Analysis
Setting In what way has the setting changed by the end of the story?

Apply the Skills

There Will Come Soft Rains

Thinking About the Selection

1. **Respond:** Would you like to read other works by Ray Bradbury? Why or why not?
2. **(a) Recall:** List five automated functions the house performs. **(b) Infer:** What is missing in the routine of activity that the house performs? **(c) Interpret:** What is a likely reason for this absence? Give details in support of your answer.
3. **(a) Infer:** Why does the house continue its activity even when it no longer makes sense? **(b) Analyze:** What does this fact indicate about the human qualities the house does not have?
4. **(a) Make a Judgment:** Do you think Bradbury gives a realistic view of the future of technology? Explain. **(b) Discuss:** Trade answers with a partner. After you have read your partner's response, discuss your answers. **(c) Reflect:** Afterward, write a sentence or two explaining whether your partner's views have influenced your own.

Literary Analysis

5. **(a)** Identify these aspects of the **setting** in "There Will Come Soft Rains": the specific place in which events occur; the historical period. **(b)** For each aspect, give an example of a **description** that helps make this setting vivid for readers.
6. In what ways does the setting change from the beginning to the end of the story?
7. Explain why, in this story, the setting might also be called the main character.

Reading Skill

8. **(a)** Based on information in the first two pages of the story, what two **inferences** could you make about events that occurred before the story opens? **(b)** For each inference, note at least one detail later in the story that either proves it or disproves it. Record your answers in a chart like the one shown.

Inference	Confirming Details	Disproving Details

9. **(a)** What can you infer about the future of the house when the fire starts in the kitchen? **(b)** What information can you learn by reading on to confirm this inference?

QuickReview

Story at a Glance
A fully automated house cheerfully continues taking care of its owners—blind to the fact that they are mysteriously absent.

Go Online
—Assessment
For: Self-test
Visit: www.PHSchool.com
Web Code: eqa-6205

Setting: the time and place in which the events of a story occur, typically conveyed through *description*

Inference: an insight, based on stated details, about information that is not stated

Vocabulary Builder

Practice Match each statement with a word from the vocabulary list for "There Will Come Soft Rains," on page 244. Then, explain each choice.

1. This word might be used to describe a nervous person.
2. The flag did this in the breeze.
3. If you make an effort like this, you are working hard.

Adding Words to Your Vocabulary The word *tremulous* is an adjective. Using a dictionary, find the related adverb and noun. Then, use each of the three words in a sentence. (For more on using a dictionary, see page R6.)

Writing

Write a brief **letter to a friend** summarizing the story. Then, rewrite the summary as part of a **book review** for newspaper readers.

- Change your language as needed for your new audience, replacing informal words with formal ones.
- Add information that a newspaper audience would expect to find in a review, such as information about the writer.

For *Grammar, Vocabulary,* and *Assessment,* see **Build Language Skills,** pages 268–269.

Extend Your Learning

Listening and Speaking Give an **oral reading** of "There Will Come Soft Rains" by Sara Teasdale.
- Vary your tone of voice to reflect meaning.
- Use gestures as appropriate.

Afterward, lead the class in a comparison of Teasdale's poem and the story.

Research and Technology With a partner, prepare a **visual art presentation** for the story. Find at least two works of art that reflect the setting and the spirit of the story. To evaluate the art, identify any direct visual references to the setting, such as a futuristic, high-tech house. Then, note feelings—eeriness, a fake cheeriness—that fit the story's mood. Present the works you have chosen to the class, and explain your choices.

Build Language Skills

Vocabulary Skill

Word Roots The word *perspective* combines the **Latin root-*spec*-** with the prefix *per-*. -*Spec*- traces back to the Latin verb *specere,* meaning "to look." Other words containing the word root -*spec*- also pertain to ways of literally or figuratively looking or seeing.

▶ **Example:** It is important to see things in *perspective*.

Practice Use the following words in a paragraph about trying to solve a crime.

> *inspect, inspection, retrospect, suspect, suspicion, speculate, speculation*

Grammar Lesson

Irregular Verbs A verb has four principal parts: the present, the present participle, the past, and the past participle. A number of very common verbs are irregular. The past and past participle of an **irregular verb** are not formed by adding -*ed* or -*d* to the present form. Some common irregular verbs are shown in the following chart.

The Four Principal Parts of Irregular Verbs			
Present	**Present Participle**	**Past**	**Past Participle**
lend	is lending	lent	[have] lent
fly	is flying	flew	[have] flown
spin	is spinning	spun	[have] spun
begin	is beginning	began	[have] begun

MorePractice

For more practice with verbs, see the Grammar Handbook, p. R44.

Practice Rewrite each sentence using the requested principal parts of the italicized verb.

1. Ashley (become) upset. (present participle)
2. She (see) the coffee stain spreading on her new jeans. (past)
3. She had never (know) such frustration. (past participle)
4. If she hadn't acted fast, the stain would have (become) permanent. (past participle)
5. After some quick scrubbing, she (see) that the stain was all gone. (past)

W͜G Prentice Hall Writing and Grammar Connection: Chapter 22, Section 1

Reading: Make Inferences

Directions: *Read the selection. Then, answer the questions.*

Standards Assessed
• 10.2.4
• 10.3.1
• 10.3.3

We will explore the implications of technological advancement for our students' lives and for the lives of students in the future. The use of computers, the Internet, wireless systems, and hand-held mobile devices have already impacted students' daily routines and parts of their education. Information that once took months to find can be retrieved in milliseconds. We predict that both the dangers of technology and the advantages to the educational community will only increase.

1. Using your prior knowledge, you can infer that the writer is
   A a scientist.
   B a teacher.
   C a salesperson.
   D an inventor.

2. The reader can infer that the remainder of this essay will deal with
   A positive and negative aspects of technology.
   B positive aspects of technology.
   C negative aspects of technology.
   D removing technology from education.

3. Using your own knowledge, you can infer from the second sentence that the author
   A is right about students' technology use.
   B has no knowledge about students.
   C is confused about students' use of technology.
   D is incorrect about students' use of technology.

4. The last sentence leads you to infer that the author
   A advocates increasing technology use.
   B is opposed to increasing technology use.
   C is ignorant about technology.
   D is objective about technology.

Timed Writing: Interpretation [Connections]

"We look forward to a world founded upon four essential freedoms . . . the fourth is freedom from fear."—Franklin D. Roosevelt
Choose either "The Street of the Cañon" or "There Will Come Soft Rains" and discuss how this quotation applies to the characters. Use specific reasons and examples from the text to support your interpretation. **(30 minutes)**

Writing Workshop: *Work in Progress*

Short Story

Using the work in your writing portfolio, make a chart of potential conflicts that the protagonist and antagonist could have. Choose one of these conflicts and add notes about how the invention you assigned the character could help or hinder the resolution of this conflict.

Reading Informational Materials

Web Sites

In Part 1, you learned to make inferences when you read literature. If you read "There Will Come Soft Rains," you made inferences to unlock the secret of the story—that our civilization could fall, as ancient Egypt did.

Inferences are also important in research. When conducting research with print or electronic resources, make logical assumptions and draw conclusions based on the information you find.

Academic Standards

- Use clear research questions and methods to compile evidence from many sources. (10.4.4)
- Synthesize information from multiple different sources. (10.4.6)

About Web Sites as Sources

To find information sources on the Web, many users visit sites known as *search engines*. By entering search terms in the engine, the user can call up a list of sites, or "hits," that feature the search terms or related terms. A Web site may also be called up directly by typing its URL, or address, in a browser window.

Reading Skill

A Web site on Napoleon posted by a sixth-grader may give incorrect dates. One posted by an anti-Napoleon society may minimize his accomplishments. Use what you know about the source of information to **make inferences,** or logical assumptions, about the source's reliability. Before using information from the Web, **evaluate the credibility of Web sources**. Follow this checklist.

Checklist for Evaluating Web Sites

☐ Check the ending of the URL.
- Educational institutions (URL ending ".edu") and government agencies (URL ending ".gov") generally provide reliable information.
- Nonprofit organizations (URL ending ".org") may be unbiased, or they may have an agenda.
- Businesses and individuals (URL ending ".com") may provide information of varying quality.

☐ Consider the credentials of the Web site's sponsor.

☐ Check information against a reliable print source.

☐ Check the "last updated" field on the page.

The URL, or address, of the Web site appears in the browser here.

`http://www.newton.cam.ac.uk/egypt/`

Links in the side margin provide access to information on the topics listed.

Egyptology Resources

Users click on "Museums" to go to the interior Web page shown on page 272.

Popular local items

News & Gossip

Announcements

Bulletin Board

E-mail Addresses

Tomb of Sennefen

Beinlich Wordlist

Wilbour Library Acquisitions

Online Publications

Commercial Items

Server statistics

The first Egyptology site on the Web

This page is set up with the kind assistance of the Newton Institute in the University of Cambridge to provide a World Wide Web resource for Egyptological information. The pages are not a publication of the Newton Institute, and all matters concerning them (e.g., comments, criticisms, and suggestions for items to include) should be sent to Nigel Strudwick.

Click here for guidelines on the format of material.

Click here for site history.

Information on the individual who maintains this Web site is available by clicking his name. Links built into the text are usually shown in blue.

Main pages

Essential Resources

Institutions

Museums

Digs

Publishers, Booksellers

Journals, Magazines

Organizations, Societies

Interesting Egypt Pages

Personal Egypt Pages

Other Resources of Interest

Reading Informational Materials

http://www.newton.cam.ac.uk/egypt/

Museums Online with Egyptian Collections

Many museums, of course, have WWW pages now. I have tried to select some of those which have more specific information on their Egyptian Collections, but I do also include the general Web presences of major museums with relevant material. Some of these links often go directly to the Egypt pages and bypass the home page. A more general set of links will be found in the ABZU indexes.

> Each of these links brings a user to the Web site of a musem that has Egyptian artifacts in its collection.

Egypt
- The Egyptian Museum, Cairo
- The Coptic Museum, Cairo

North America
- Museum of Fine Arts, Boston
- Metropolitan Museum, New York
- Michael C. Carlos Museum, Emory University, Atlanta
- Brooklyn Museum
- Oriental Institute, University of Chicago

Europe
- The British Museum, London COMPASS Project
- The Louvre, Paris
- Musées royaux d'art et d'art historie, Brussels
- Museo Egizio, Torino
- Agyptisches Museum und Papyrussammlung Berlin-Charlottenburg
- Allard Pierson Museum
- Carsten Niebuhr Institute, University of Copenhagen, Papyrus Collection

Back to Egyptology Resources home page

> This link takes the user back to the Egyptology Resources home page.

Reading: Evaluating the Credibility of Web Sources

Directions: *Choose the letter of the best answer to each question about the Web site.*

Standards Assessed

• 10.4.4
• 10.4.6

1. Which statement or phrase from the home page indicates the information on the site is credible?

   A "The first Egyptology site on the web"

   B "Wilbour Library Acquisitions"

   C "This page is set up with the kind assistance of the Newton Institute of the University of Cambridge. . . ."

   D "Click here for guidelines on the format of the material."

2. What is shown by the fact that a university assists the site?

   A The site is carefully monitored by university professors.

   B The site's creator has a good background in his subject.

   C The site is not high-quality enough to make a profit.

   D The site includes interviews with many university professors.

3. Which additional information would help you evaluate the credibility of the site?

   A Facts about Nigel Strudwick's experience

   B The number of visitors to the site

   C Facts about the Wilbour Library

   D The contact information for the site

Reading: Comprehension and Interpretation

Directions: *Write your answers on a separate piece of paper.*

4. Identify the links you would click to learn more about recent developments in the study of ancient Egypt. Explain. **[Applying]**

5. What sort of student or researcher would get the most from this site? Explain your answer. **[Integrating]**

Timed Writing: Persuasion [Critical Stance]

Write a brief letter to the creator of the Egyptology Resources Web site in which you suggest improvements to graphics, layout, or instructions on the site. Support your suggestions using details about the site. As you draft, remember your audience: Phrase criticism constructively and keep a respectful tone. **(20 minutes)**

Comparing Literary Works • *Point of View*

Point of View

Point of view is the perspective from which a story is told. Most stories are told from one of these perspectives:

- **First-person point of view:** The narrator is one of the characters and refers to himself or herself with the pronouns *I* and *me.*
- **Third-person point of view:** The narrator does not participate in the action. Characters are referred to by the third-person pronouns *he, she, him, her, they,* and *them.* A third-person narrator may be **omniscient** (all-knowing), or the narrator's point of view may be **limited** (restricted).

Academic Standards

- Analyze characters' traits through narration and dialogue. (10.3.4)
- Evaluate the use of voice and narrator. (10.3.9)
- Identify and evaluate dialogue, soliloquies, asides, character foils and stage designs in dramatic literature. (10.3.10)

Comparing Points of View

The point of view of a story affects the amount and type of information a reader receives. A writer can control the information the reader receives by using a particular type of narrator:

- An **omniscient third-person narrator** gives readers as much information as the writer desires about every character. Readers may know more about a character than other characters do.
- A **limited third-person narrator** focuses on one character, showing readers what happens through that character's actions and experiences. Readers may only know as much about events as the main character does.
- A **naive first-person narrator** understands less about events in the story that he or she is telling than readers do.

By giving readers more information than the narrator or a character has, writers can create **dramatic irony**—a contrast between what the reader knows and what the narrator or character believes. Compare the use of point of view in these stories by using a chart like this one.

	Story
Pronouns used ➔	
Who tells the story ➔	
Whose thoughts and feelings are shared ➔	

Vocabulary Builder

One Thousand Dollars

- **stipulates** (stip´ yə lāts´) *v.* includes specifically as part of an agreement (p. 276) *In the contract, he stipulates a May deadline.*

- **prudent** (proo͞´ dənt) *adj.* exercising sound judgment; cautious (p. 281) *It is not prudent to go out in the cold without a jacket.*

By the Waters of Babylon

- **purified** (pyoor´ ə fīd´) *v.* rid of impurities or pollution; made pure (p. 282) *Using a filter, he purified the water.*

- **nevertheless** (nev´ ər thə les´) *adv.* in spite of that; however (p. 283) *He expressed regret; nevertheless, the judge ruled harshly.*

Build Understanding

Connecting to the Literature

Reading/Writing Connection In each of these stories, the main character finds himself challenged by unusual circumstances. Make a list of strategies you would recommend for dealing with unexpected situations. Use at least three of the following words: *adapt, alter, respond, simulate, utilize.*

Meet the Authors

O. **Henry** (1862–1910)

A native of North Carolina, O. Henry (the pen name of William Sydney Porter) dropped out of school at age fifteen and by his twenties had made his way to Texas. After working for more than a decade as a bank teller, he was convicted—perhaps unjustly—of embezzling bank funds. In prison, he began to write short stories.

Hundreds of Stories Later Upon his release from jail, O. Henry settled in New York City, where he became a full-time and hugely successful short-story writer. He turned out nearly 300 tales, most of them featuring ironic twists of fate.

Stephen Vincent **Benét** (1898–1943)

Born in Bethlehem, Pennsylvania, Stephen Vincent Benét grew up listening to his father read poetry in the evenings. During World War I, Benét was barred from active army duty because of poor eyesight. Still, he took time off from his studies at Yale University to serve in the State Department during the war.

Touch of the Poet Benét considered himself a poet first and foremost. Much of his work centers on American history and the quest for American ideals. His interest in American history and folklore influenced his epic poem *John Brown's Body,* which won a Pulitzer Prize in 1929.

 **Go Online**
Author Link

For: More about the authors
Visit: www.PHSchool.com
Web Code: eqe-9206

ONE THOUSAND DOLLARS

O. Henry

"**O**ne thousand dollars," repeated Lawyer Tolman, solemnly and severely, "and here is the money."

Young Gillian gave a decidedly amused laugh as he fingered the thin package of new fifty-dollar notes.

"It's such a confoundedly awkward amount," he explained, genially, to the lawyer. "If it had been ten thousand a fellow might wind up with a lot of fireworks and do himself credit. Even fifty dollars would have been less trouble."

"You heard the reading of your uncle's will," continued Lawyer Tolman, professionally dry in his tones. "I do not know if you paid much attention to its details. I must remind you of one. You are required to render to us an account of the manner of expenditure of this $1,000 as soon as you have disposed of it. The will stipulates that. I trust that you will so far comply with the late Mr. Gillian's wishes."

"You may depend upon it," said the young man, politely, "in spite of the extra expense it will entail. I may have to engage a secretary. I was never good at accounts."

Gillian went to his club. There he hunted out one whom he called Old Bryson.

Literary Analysis
Point of View Which words here indicate that the story is told from the third-person point of view?

Vocabulary Builder
stipulates (stip´ yə lāts´) v. includes specifically as part of an agreement

Old Bryson was calm and forty and sequestered. He was in a corner reading a book, and when he saw Gillian approaching he sighed, laid down his book and took off his glasses.

"Old Bryson, wake up," said Gillian. "I've a funny story to tell you."

"I wish you would tell it to someone in the billiard room," said Old Bryson. "You know how I hate your stories."

"This is a better one than usual," said Gillian . . . ; "and I'm glad to tell it to you. It's too sad and funny to go with the rattling of billiard balls. I've just come from my late uncle's firm of legal corsairs. He leaves me an even thousand dollars. Now, what can a man possibly do with a thousand dollars?"

"I thought," said Old Bryson, showing as much interest as a bee shows in a vinegar cruet, "that the late Septimus Gillian was worth something like half a million."

"He was," assented Gillian, joyously, "and that's where the joke comes in. He's left his whole cargo of doubloons[1] to a microbe. That is, part of it goes to the man who invents a new bacillus and the rest to establish a hospital for doing away with it again. There are one or two trifling bequests on the side. The butler and the housekeeper get a seal ring and $10 each. His nephew gets $1,000."

"You've always had plenty of money to spend," observed Old Bryson.

"Tons," said Gillian. "Uncle was the fairy godmother as far as an allowance was concerned."

"Any other heirs?" asked Old Bryson.

"None." Gillian frowned . . . and kicked the upholstered leather of a divan uneasily. "There is a Miss Hayden, a ward of my uncle, who lived in his house. She's a quiet thing—musical—the daughter of somebody who was unlucky enough to be his friend. I forgot to say that she was in on the seal ring and $10 joke, too. I wish I had been. Then I could have had two bottles of brut, tipped the waiter with the ring, and had the whole business off my hands. Don't be superior and insulting, Old Bryson—tell me what a fellow can do with a thousand dollars."

Old Bryson rubbed his glasses and smiled. And when Old Bryson smiled, Gillian knew that he intended to be more offensive than ever.

"A thousand dollars," he said, "means much or little. One man may buy a happy home with it and laugh at Rockefeller.[2] Another could send his wife South with it and save her life. A thousand

---

Literary Analysis
Point of View Whose thoughts are revealed in this short paragraph? Who reveals them?

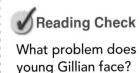

Reading Check

What problem does young Gillian face?

---

1. **doubloons** (də bloonz) *n.* old gold coins of Spanish or Spanish American origin, often associated with pirates.
2. **Rockefeller** John D. Rockefeller (1839–1937), a businessman who became the first American billionaire.

dollars would buy pure milk for one hundred babies during June, July, and August and save fifty of their lives. You could count upon a half hour's diversion with it at faro in one of the fortified art galleries. It would furnish an education to an ambitious boy. I am told that a genuine Corot[3] was secured for that amount in an auction room yesterday. You could move to a New Hampshire town and live respectably two years on it. You could rent Madison Square Garden for one evening with it, and lecture your audience, if you should have one, on the precariousness of the profession of heir presumptive."

"People might like you, Old Bryson," said Gillian, almost unruffled, "if you wouldn't moralize. I asked you to tell me what I could do with a thousand dollars."

"You?" said Bryson, with a gentle laugh. "Why, Bobby Gillian, there's only one logical thing you could do. You can go buy Miss Lotta Lauriere a diamond pendant with the money, and then take yourself off to Idaho and inflict your presence upon a ranch. I advise a sheep ranch, as I have a particular dislike for sheep."

"Thanks," said Gillian, rising. "I thought I could depend upon you, Old Bryson. You've hit on the very scheme. I wanted to chuck the money in a lump, for I've got to turn in an account for it, and I hate itemizing."

Gillian phoned for a cab and said to the driver:

"The stage entrance of the Columbine Theatre."

Miss Lotta Lauriere was assisting nature with a powder puff, almost ready for her call at a crowded matinée, when her dresser mentioned the name of Mr. Gillian.

"Let it in," said Miss Lauriere. "Now, what is it, Bobby? I'm going on in two minutes."

"Rabbit-foot your right ear a little," suggested Gillian, critically. "That's better. It won't take two minutes for me. What do you say to a little thing in the pendant line? I can stand three ciphers[4] with a figure one in front of 'em."

"Oh, just as you say," carolled Miss Lauriere. "My right glove, Adams. Say, Bobby, did you see that necklace Della Stacey had on the other night? Twenty-two hundred dollars it cost at Tiffany's. But, of course—pull my sash a little to the left, Adams."

"Miss Lauriere for the opening chorus!" cried the call boy without.

Literary Analysis
Point of View Which details in the scene with Miss Lotta Lauriere would Gillian know firsthand? Which might he not know?

---

3. Corot (kə rō´) a painting by Jean (zhän) Baptiste (bà tēst´) Camille (kȧ mē´y') Corot (1796–1875), a famous French painter.
4. ciphers (sī´ fərz) *n.* zeroes.

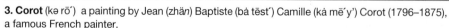

Gillian strolled out to where his cab was waiting.

"What would you do with a thousand dollars if you had it?" he asked the driver.

"Open a s'loon," said the cabby promptly and huskily. "I know a place I could take money in with both hands. It's a four-story brick on a corner. I've got it figured out. Second story— . . . chop suey; third floor—manicures and foreign missions; fourth floor—poolroom. If you was thinking of putting up the cap—"

"Oh, no," said Gillian, "I merely asked from curiosity. I take you by the hour. Drive till I tell you to stop."

Eight blocks down Broadway Gillian poked up the trap[5] with his cane and got out. A blind man sat upon a stool on the sidewalk selling pencils. Gillian went out and stood before him.

"Excuse me," he said, "but would you mind telling me what you would do if you had a thousand dollars?"

"You got out of that cab that just drove up, didn't you?" asked the blind man.

"I did," said Gillian.

"I guess you are all right," said the pencil dealer, "to ride in a cab by daylight. Take a look at that, if you like."

He drew a small book from his coat pocket and held it out. Gillian opened it and saw that it was a bank deposit book. It showed a balance of $1,785 to the blind man's credit.

Gillian returned the book and got into the cab.

"I forgot something," he said. "You may drive to the law offices of Tolman & Sharp, at —— Broadway."

Lawyer Tolman looked at him hostilely and inquiringly through his gold-rimmed glasses.

"I beg your pardon," said Gillian, cheerfully, "but may I ask you a question? It is not an impertinent one, I hope. Was Miss Hayden left anything by my uncle's will besides the ring and the $10?"

"Nothing," said Mr. Tolman.

"I thank you very much, sir," said Gillian, and out he went to his cab. He gave the driver the address of his late uncle's home.

▲ **Critical Viewing** In what ways does the man in this illustration suggest the young Gillian? **[Compare]**

 **Reading Check**

What are three ways other characters suggest Gillian spend the thousand dollars?

---

5. poked up the trap pushed open the roof door of the cab so that the driver would know that he wanted to get out.

Miss Hayden was writing letters in the library. She was small and slender and clothed in black. But you would have noticed her eyes. Gillian drifted in with his air of regarding the world as inconsequent.

"I've just come from old Tolman's," he explained. "They've been going over the papers down there. They found a"—Gillian searched his memory for a legal term—"they found an amendment or a postscript or something to the will. It seemed that the old boy loosened up a little on second thoughts and willed you a thousand dollars. I was driving up this way and Tolman asked me to bring you the money. Here it is. You'd better count it to see if it's right." Gillian laid the money beside her hand on the desk.

Miss Hayden turned white. "Oh!" she said, and again "Oh!"

Gillian half turned and looked out of the window.

"I suppose, of course," he said, in a low voice, "that you know I love you."

"I am sorry," said Miss Hayden, taking up her money.

"There is no use?" asked Gillian, almost light-heartedly.

"I am sorry," she said again.

"May I write a note?" asked Gillian, with a smile. He seated himself at the big library table. She supplied him with paper and pen, and then went back to her secrétaire.

Gillian made out his account of his expenditure of the thousand dollars in these words:

"Paid by the black sheep, Robert Gillian, $1,000 on account of the eternal happiness, owed by Heaven to the best and dearest woman on earth."

Gillian slipped his writing into an envelope, bowed and went his way.

His cab stopped again at the offices of Tolman & Sharp.

"I have expended the thousand dollars," he said, cheerily, to Tolman of the gold glasses, "and I have come to render account of it, as I agreed. There is quite a feeling of summer in the air—do you not think so, Mr. Tolman?" He tossed a white envelope on the lawyer's table. "You will find there a memorandum, sir, of the *modus operandi* of the vanishing of the dollars."

Without touching the envelope, Mr. Tolman went to a door and called his partner, Sharp. Together they explored the caverns of an immense safe. Forth they dragged as trophy of their search a big envelope sealed with wax. This they forcibly invaded, and wagged their venerable heads together over its contents. Then Tolman became spokesman.

"Mr. Gillian," he said, formally, "there was a codicil[6] to your uncle's will. It was intrusted to us privately, with instructions that it

Literary Analysis
Point of View How does the use of a limited third-person narrator help readers see what Gillian is doing in secret?

---

6. **codicil** (käd´ i səl) *n.* an addition to a will changing or explaining the instructions it gives.

be not opened until you had furnished us with a full account of your handling of the $1,000 bequest in the will. As you have fulfilled the conditions, my partner and I have read the codicil. I do not wish to encumber your understanding with its legal phraseology, but I will acquaint you with the spirit of its contents.

"In the event that your disposition of the $1,000 demonstrates that you possess any of the qualifications that deserve reward, much benefit will accrue to you. Mr. Sharp and I are named as the judges, and I assure you that we will do our duty strictly according to justice—with liberality. We are not at all unfavorably disposed toward you, Mr. Gillian. But let us return to the letter of the codicil. If your disposal of the money in question has been <u>prudent</u>, wise, or unselfish, it is in our power to hand you over bonds to the value of $50,000, which have been placed in our hands for that purpose. But if—as our client, the late Mr. Gillian, explicitly provides—you have used this money as you have used money in the past—I quote the late Mr. Gillian—in reprehensible dissipation among disreputable associates—the $50,000 is to be paid to Miriam Hayden, ward of the late Mr. Gillian, without delay. Now, Mr. Gillian, Mr. Sharp and I will examine your account in regard to the $1,000. You submit it in writing, I believe. I hope you will repose confidence in our decision."

Mr. Tolman reached for the envelope. Gillian was a little the quicker in taking it up. He tore the account and its cover leisurely into strips and dropped them into his pocket.

"It's all right," he said, smilingly. "There isn't a bit of need to bother you with this. I don't suppose you'd understand these itemized bets anyway. I lost the thousand dollars on the races. Good day to you, gentlemen."

Tolman & Sharp shook their heads mournfully at each other when Gillian left, for they heard him whistling gayly in the hallway as he started for the elevator.

Vocabulary Builder
prudent (prōō′ dənt) *adj.* exercising sound judgment; cautious

Literary Analysis
Point of View How does the use of a limited third-person narrator help readers know more about what is in the envelope than Mr. Tolman knows?

Thinking About the Selection

1. **Respond:** What would you have done with the thousand dollars if you had been in Bobby Gillian's place?
2. **(a) Recall:** According to his uncle's will, what must Bobby Gillian do after spending the thousand dollars? **(b) Infer:** What are Gillian's feelings about inheriting this amount?
3. **(a) Infer:** Why does Gillian decide to give Miss Hayden the money but not tell the lawyers? **(b) Draw Conclusions:** What do these decisions indicate about his character? **(c) Compare and Contrast:** Compare what these decisions indicate about his character with your first impressions of him.

By the Waters of Babylon
Stephen Vincent Benét

The north and the west and the south are good hunting ground, but it is forbidden to go east. It is forbidden to go to any of the Dead Places except to search for metal, and then he who touches the metal must be a priest or the son of a priest. Afterwards, both the man and the metal must be <u>purified</u>! These are the rules and the laws: they are well made. It is forbidden to cross the great river and look upon the place that was the Place of the Gods—this is most strictly forbidden. We do not even say its name though we know its name. It is there that spirits live, and demons—it is there that there are the ashes of the Great Burning. These things are forbidden—they have been forbidden since the beginning of time.

Vocabulary Builder
purified (pyoor´ ə fid´)
v. rid of impurities or pollution; made pure

My father is a priest; I am the son of a priest. I have been in the Dead Places near us, with my father—at first, I was afraid. When my father went into the house to search for the metal, I stood by the door and my heart felt small and weak. It was a dead man's house, a spirit house. It did not have the smell of man, though there were old bones in a corner. But it is not fitting that a priest's son should show fear. I looked at the bones in the shadow and kept my voice still.

Then my father came out with the metal—a good, strong piece. He looked at me with both eyes but I had not run away. He gave me the metal to hold—I took it and did not die. So he knew that I was truly his son and would be a priest in my time. That was when I was very young—<u>nevertheless</u>, my brothers would not have done it, though they are good hunters. After that, they gave me the good piece of meat and the warm corner by the fire. My father watched over me—he was glad that I should be a priest. But when I boasted or wept without a reason, he punished me more strictly than my brothers. That was right.

After a time, I myself was allowed to go into the dead houses and search for metal. So I learned the ways of those houses—and if I saw bones, I was no longer afraid. The bones are light and old—sometimes they will fall into dust if you touch them. But that is a great sin.

I was taught the chants and the spells—I was taught how to stop the running of blood from a wound and many secrets. A priest must know many secrets—that was what my father said. If the hunters think we do all things by chants and spells, they may believe so—it does not hurt them. I was taught how to read in the old books and how to make the old writings—that was hard and took a long time. My knowledge made me happy—it was like a fire in my heart. Most of all, I liked to hear of the Old Days and the stories of the gods. I asked myself many questions that I could not answer, but it was good to ask them. At night, I would lie awake and listen to the wind—it seemed to me that it was the voice of the gods as they flew through the air.

We are not ignorant like the Forest People—our women spin wool on the wheel, our priests wear a white robe. We do not eat grubs from the tree, we have not forgotten the old writings, although they are hard to understand. Nevertheless, my knowledge and my lack of

◀ **Critical Viewing**
Based on this image, what type of setting do you expect the story to have? **[Connect]**

Literary Analysis
Point of View Which words in the first paragraph on this page tell you that the story is written from the first-person point of view?

Vocabulary Builder
nevertheless (nev´ ər *th*ə les´) *adv.* in spite of that; however

Reading Check

Why are the narrator and his father allowed to bring back metal from the Dead Places?

knowledge burned in me—I wished to know more. When I was a man at last, I came to my father and said, "It is time for me to go on my journey. Give me your leave."

He looked at me for a long time, stroking his beard, then he said at last, "Yes. It is time." That night, in the house of the priesthood, I asked for and received purification. My body hurt but my spirit was a cool stone. It was my father himself who questioned me about my dreams.

He bade me look into the smoke of the fire and see—I saw and told what I saw. It was what I have always seen—a river, and, beyond it, a great Dead Place and in it the gods walking. I have always thought about that. His eyes were stern when I told him—he was no longer my father but a priest. He said, "This is a strong dream."

"It is mine," I said, while the smoke waved and my head felt light. They were singing the Star song in the outer chamber and it was like the buzzing of bees in my head.

He asked me how the gods were dressed and I told him how they were dressed. We know how they were dressed from the book, but I saw them as if they were before me. When I had finished, he threw the sticks three times and studied them as they fell.

"This is a very strong dream," he said. "It may eat you up."

"I am not afraid," I said and looked at him with both eyes. My voice sounded thin in my ears but that was because of the smoke.

He touched me on the breast and the forehead. He gave me the bow and the three arrows.

"Take them," he said. "It is forbidden to travel east. It is forbidden to cross the river. It is forbidden to go to the Place of the Gods. All these things are forbidden."

"All these things are forbidden," I said, but it was my voice that spoke and not my spirit. He looked at me again.

"My son," he said. "Once I had young dreams. If your dreams do not eat you up, you may be a great priest. If they eat you, you are still my son. Now go on your journey."

I went fasting, as is the law. My body hurt but not my heart. When the dawn came, I was out of sight of the village. I prayed and purified myself, waiting for a sign. The sign was an eagle. It flew east.

Sometimes signs are sent by bad spirits. I waited again on the flat rock, fasting, taking no food. I was very still—I could feel the sky above me and the earth beneath. I waited till the sun was beginning to sink. Then three deer passed in the valley, going east—they did not wind me or see me. There was a white fawn with them—a very great sign.

I followed them, at a distance, waiting for what would happen. My heart was troubled about going east, yet I knew that I must go. My head hummed with my fasting—I did not even see the panther spring upon the white fawn. But, before I knew it, the bow was in my hand. I shouted and the panther lifted his head from the fawn. It is not easy to kill a panther with one arrow but the arrow went through his eye and into his brain. He died as he tried to spring—he rolled over, tearing at the ground. Then I knew I was meant to go east—I knew that was my journey. When the night came, I made my fire and roasted meat.

It is eight suns' journey to the east and a man passes by many Dead Places. The Forest People are afraid of them but I am not. Once I made my fire on the edge of a Dead Place at night and, next morning, in the dead house, I found a good knife, little rusted. That was small to what came afterward, but it made my heart feel big. Always when I looked for game, it was in front of my arrow, and twice I passed hunting parties of the Forest People without their knowing. So I knew my magic was strong and my journey clean, in spite of the law.

Toward the setting of the eighth sun, I came to the banks of the great river. It was half-a-day's journey after I had left the god-road— we do not use the god-roads now for they are falling apart into great blocks of stone, and the forest is safer going. A long way off, I had seen the water through trees but the trees were thick. At last, I came out upon an open place at the top of a cliff. There was the great river below, like a giant in the sun. It is very long, very wide. It could eat all the streams we know and still be thirsty. Its name is Ou-dis-sun, the Sacred, the Long. No man of my tribe had seen it, not even my father, the priest. It was magic and I prayed.

Then I raised my eyes and looked south. It was there, the Place of the Gods.

How can I tell what it was like—you do not know. It was there, in the red light, and they were too big to be houses. It was there with the red light upon it, mighty and ruined. I knew that in another moment the gods would see me. I covered my eyes with my hands and crept back into the forest.

Surely, that was enough to do, and live. Surely it was enough to spend the night upon the cliff. The Forest People themselves do not come near. Yet, all through the night, I knew that I should have to cross the river and walk in the places of the gods, although the gods ate me up. My magic did not help me at all and yet there was a fire in my bowels, a fire in my mind. When the sun rose, I thought, "My journey has been clean. Now I will go home from my journey." But, even as I thought so, I knew I could not. If I went to the place of the

Literary Analysis
Point of View What might the reader understand about the "Dead Place" and "the god-roads" that John does not?

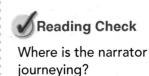

Reading Check

Where is the narrator journeying?

gods, I would surely die, but, if I did not go, I could never be at peace with my spirit again. It is better to lose one's life than one's spirit, if one is a priest and the son of a priest.

Nevertheless, as I made the raft, the tears ran out of my eyes. The Forest People could have killed me without fight, if they had come upon me then, but they did not come. When the raft was made, I said the sayings for the dead and painted myself for death. My heart was cold as a frog and my knees like water, but the burning in my mind would not let me have peace. As I pushed the raft from the shore, I began my death song—I had the right. It was a fine song.

Literary Analysis
Point of View How does the use of a first-person narrator help readers appreciate John's thoughts and actions in this passage?

"I am John, son of John," I sang. "My people are the Hill People.
    They are the men.
I go into the Dead Places but I am not slain.
I take the metal from the Dead Places but I am not blasted.
I travel upon the god-roads and am not afraid. E-yah! I have killed
    the panther, I have killed the fawn!
E-yah! I have come to the great river. No man has come there before.
It is forbidden to go east, but I have gone, forbidden to go on the
    great river, but I am there.
Open your hearts, you spirits, and hear my song.
Now I go to the Place of the Gods, I shall not return.
My body is painted for death and my limbs weak, but my heart is
    big as I go to the Place of the Gods!"

All the same, when I came to the Place of the Gods, I was afraid, afraid. The current of the great river is very strong—it gripped my raft with its hands. That was magic, for the river itself is wide and calm. I could feel evil spirits about me, in the bright morning; I could feel their breath on my neck as I was swept down the stream. Never have I been so much alone—I tried to think of my knowledge, but it was a squirrel's heap of winter nuts. There was no strength in my knowledge any more, and I felt small and naked as a new-hatched bird—alone upon the great river, the servant of the gods.

Yet, after a while, my eyes were opened and I saw. I saw both banks of the river—I saw that once there had been god-roads across it, though now they were broken and fallen like broken vines. Very great they were, and wonderful and broken—broken in the time of the Great Burning when the fire fell out of the sky. And always the current took me nearer to the Place of the Gods, and the huge ruins rose before my eyes.

I do not know the customs of rivers—we are the People of the Hills. I tried to guide my raft with the pole but it spun around. I thought the river meant to take me past the Place of the Gods and

out into the Bitter Water of the legends. I grew angry then—my heart felt strong. I said aloud, "I am a priest and the son of a priest!" The gods heard me—they showed me how to paddle with the pole on one side of the raft. The current changed itself—I drew near to the Place of the Gods.

When I was very near, my raft struck and turned over. I can swim in our lakes—I swam to the shore. There was a great spike of rusted metal sticking out into the river—I hauled myself up upon it and sat there, panting. I had saved my bow and two arrows and the knife I found in the Dead Place but that was all. My raft went whirling downstream toward the Bitter Water. I looked after it, and thought if it had trod me under, at least I would be safely dead. Nevertheless, when I had dried my bow-string and restrung it, I walked forward to the Place of the Gods.

It felt like ground underfoot; it did not burn me. It is not true what some of the tales say, that the ground there burns forever, for I have been there. Here and there were the marks and stains of the

▲ **Critical Viewing**
Does this body of water seem as threatening as the Ou-dis-sun does to the narrator? Explain. **[Compare and Contrast]**

✔ **Reading Check**

How does John feel as he approaches the Place of the Gods?

Great Burning, on the ruins, that is true. But they were old marks and old stains. It is not true either, what some of our priests say, that it is an island covered with fogs and enchantments. It is not. It is a great Dead Place—greater than any Dead Place we know. Everywhere in it there are god-roads, though most are cracked and broken. Everywhere there are the ruins of the high towers of the gods.

How shall I tell what I saw? I went carefully, my strung bow in my hand, my skin ready for danger. There should have been the wailings of spirits and the shrieks of demons, but there were not. It was very silent and sunny where I had landed—the wind and the rain and the birds that drop seeds had done their work—the grass grew in the cracks of the broken stone. It is a fair island—no wonder the gods built there. If I had come there, a god, I also would have built.

How shall I tell what I saw? The towers are not all broken—here and there one still stands, like a great tree in a forest, and the birds nest high. But the towers themselves look blind, for the gods are gone. I saw a fish-hawk, catching fish in the river. I saw a little dance of white butterflies over a great heap of broken stones and columns. I went there and looked about me—there was a carved stone with cut-letters, broken in half. I can read letters but I could not understand these. They said UBTREAS. There was also the shattered image of a man or a god. It had been made of white stone and he wore his hair tied back like a woman's. His name was ASHING, as I read on the cracked half of a stone. I thought it wise to pray to ASHING, though I do not know that god.

How shall I tell what I saw? There was no smell of man left, on stone or metal. Nor were there many trees in that wilderness of stone. There are many pigeons, nesting and dropping in the towers—the gods must have loved them, or, perhaps, they used them for sacrifices. There are wild cats that roam the god-roads, green-eyed, unafraid of man. At night they wail like demons, but they are not demons. The wild dogs are more dangerous, for they hunt in a pack, but them I did not meet till later. Everywhere there are the carved stones carved with magical numbers or words.

I went North—I did not try to hide myself. When a god or a demon saw me, then I would die, but meanwhile I was no longer afraid. My hunger for knowledge burned in me—there was so much that I could not understand. After a while, I knew that my belly was hungry. I could have hunted for my meat, but I did not hunt. It is known that the gods did not hunt as we do—they got their food from enchanted boxes and jars. Sometimes these are still found in the Dead Places—once, when I was a child and foolish, I opened such a jar and tasted it and found the food sweet. But my father found out and punished me for it strictly, for, often, that food is death. Now,

Literary Analysis
Point of View Which details here suggest that John is a naive narrator—that the reader knows more about what John sees than John does?

though, I had long gone past what was forbidden, and I entered the likeliest towers, looking for the food of the gods.

I found it at last in the ruins of a great temple in the mid-city. A mighty temple it must have been, for the roof was painted like the sky at night with its stars—that much I could see, though the colors were faint and dim. It went down into great caves and tunnels—perhaps they kept their slaves there. But when I started to climb down, I heard the squeaking of rats, so I did not go—rats are unclean, and there must have been many tribes of them, from the squeaking. But near there, I found food, in the heart of a ruin, behind a door that still opened. I ate only the fruits from the jars—they had a very sweet taste. There was drink, too, in bottles of glass—the drink of the gods was strong and made my head swim. After I had eaten and drunk, I slept on the top of a stone, my bow at my side.

When I woke, the sun was low. Looking down from where I lay, I saw a dog sitting on his haunches. His tongue was hanging out of his mouth; he looked as if he were laughing. He was a big dog, with a gray-brown coat, as big as a wolf. I sprang up and shouted at him but he did not move—he just sat there as if he were laughing. I did not like that. When I reached for a stone to throw, he moved swiftly out of the way of the stone. He was not afraid of me; he looked at me as if I were meat. No doubt I could have killed him with an arrow, but I did not know if there were others. More-over, night was falling.

I looked about me—not far away there was a great, broken god-road, leading North. The towers were high enough, but not so high, and while many of the dead-houses were wrecked, there were some that stood. I went toward this god-road, keeping to the heights of the ruins, while the dog followed. When I had reached the god-road, I saw that there were others behind him. If I had slept later, they would have come upon me asleep and torn out my throat. As it was, they were sure enough of me; they did not hurry. When I went into the dead-house, they kept watch at the entrance—doubtless they thought they would have a fine hunt. But a dog can-not open a door and I knew, from the books, that the gods did not like to live on the ground but on high.

History Connection

The Babylonian Captivity The title of this story, "By the Waters of Babylon," is an **allusion,** or reference, to Psalm 137 in the Bible. In 586 B.C., King Nebuchadnezzar (neb′ yə kəd nez′ ər) destroyed Jerusalem and exiled the Israelites to Babylon. The Babylonian Captivity, as this period is known, ended in 538 B.C. when King Cyrus of Persia formally freed the Israelites. In Psalm 137, the captive Israelites weep over their lost homeland, Zion, in lines such as this one: "By the rivers of Babylon, there we sat down, yea, we wept, when we remembered Zion."

Connect to the Literature

In what sense are John and his tribe in exile from the home where their ancestors lived?

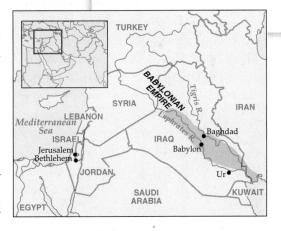

Reading Check

What are two things John sees in the Place of the Gods?

I had just found a door I could open when the dogs decided to rush. Ha! They were surprised when I shut the door in their faces—it was a good door, of strong metal. I could hear their foolish baying beyond it, but I did not stop to answer them. I was in darkness—I found stairs and climbed. There were many stairs, turning around till my head was dizzy. At the top was another door—I found the knob and opened it. I was in a long small chamber—on one side of it was a bronze door that could not be opened, for it had no handle.

▲ **Critical Viewing** Compare this illustration with John's descriptions of the Place of the Gods. **[Compare and Contrast]**

Perhaps there was a magic word to open it, but I did not have the word. I turned to the door in the opposite side of the wall. The lock of it was broken and I opened it and went in.

Within, there was a place of great riches. The god who lived there must have been a powerful god. The first room was a small anteroom—I waited there for some time, telling the spirits of the place that I came in peace and not as a robber. When it seemed to me that they had had time to hear me, I went on. Ah, what riches! Few, even, of the windows had been broken—it was all as it had been. The great windows that looked over the city had not been broken at all though they were dusty and streaked with many years. There were coverings on the floors, the colors not greatly faded, and the chairs were soft and deep. There were pictures upon the walls, very strange, very wonderful—I remember one of a bunch of flowers in a jar—if you came close to it, you could see nothing but bits of color, but if you stood away from it, the flowers might have been picked yesterday. It made my heart feel strange to look at this picture—and to look at the figure of a bird, in some hard clay, on a table and see it so like our birds. Everywhere there were books and writings, many in tongues that I could not read. The god who lived there must have been a wise god and full of knowledge. I felt I had right there, as I sought knowledge also.

Nevertheless, it was strange. There was a washing-place but no water—perhaps the gods washed in air. There was a cooking-place but no wood, and though there was a machine to cook food, there was no place to put fire in it. Nor were there candles or lamps—there were things that looked like lamps but they had neither oil nor wick. All these things were magic, but I touched them and lived—the magic had gone out of them. Let me tell one thing to show. In the washing-place, a thing said "Hot" but it was not hot to the touch—another thing said "Cold" but it was not cold. This must have been a strong magic but the magic was gone. I do not understand—they had ways—I wish that I knew.

It was close and dry and dusty in their house of the gods. I have said the magic was gone but that is not true—it had gone from the magic things but it had not gone from the place. I felt the spirits about me, weighing upon me. Nor had I ever slept in a Dead Place before—and yet, tonight, I must sleep there. When I thought of it, my tongue felt dry in my throat, in spite of my wish for knowledge. Almost I would have gone down again and faced the dogs, but I did not.

I had not gone through all the rooms when the darkness fell. When it fell, I went back to the big room looking over the city and made fire. There was a place to make fire and a box with wood in it,

Literary Analysis
Point of View What might the reader know about the thing that said "Cold" that John does not know?

**Reading Check**

In what way was the life of the gods different from the life John's tribe leads?

though I do not think they cooked there. I wrapped myself in a floor-covering and slept in front of the fire—I was very tired.

Now I tell what is very strong magic. I woke in the midst of the night. When I woke, the fire had gone out and I was cold. It seemed to me that all around me there were whisperings and voices. I closed my eyes to shut them out. Some will say that I slept again, but I do not think that I slept. I could feel the spirits drawing my spirit out of my body as a fish is drawn on a line.

Why should I lie about it? I am a priest and the son of a priest. If there are spirits, as they say, in the small Dead Places near us, what spirits must there not be in that great Place of the Gods? And would not they wish to speak? After such long years? I know that I felt myself drawn as a fish is drawn on a line. I had stepped out of my body—I could see my body asleep in front of the cold fire, but it was not I. I was drawn to look out upon the city of the gods.

It should have been dark, for it was night, but it was not dark. Everywhere there were lights—lines of light—circles and blurs of light—ten thousand torches would not have been the same. The sky itself was alight—you could barely see the stars for the glow in the sky. I thought to myself "This is strong magic" and trembled. There was a roaring in my ears like the rushing of rivers. Then my eyes grew used to the light and my ears to the sound. I knew that I was seeing the city as it had been when the gods were alive.

That was a sight indeed—yes, that was a sight: I could not have seen it in the body—my body would have died. Everywhere went the gods, on foot and in chariots—there were gods beyond number and counting and their chariots blocked the streets. They had turned night to day for their pleasure—they did not sleep with the sun. The noise of their coming and going was the noise of many waters. It was magic what they could do—it was magic what they did.

I looked out of another window—the great vines of their bridges were mended and the god-roads went East and West. Restless, restless, were the gods and always in motion! They burrowed tunnels under rivers—they flew in the air. With unbelievable tools they did giant works—no part of the earth was safe from them, for, if they wished for a thing, they summoned it from the other side of the world. And always, as they labored and rested, as they feasted and made love, there was a drum in their ears—the pulse of the giant city, beating and beating like a man's heart.

Were they happy? What is happiness to the gods? They were great, they were mighty, they were wonderful and terrible. As I looked upon them and their magic, I felt like a child—but a little more, it seemed to me, and they would pull down the moon from the sky. I saw them with wisdom beyond wisdom and knowledge beyond knowledge. And yet not all they did was well done—even I

Literary Analysis
Point of View In what way is John's perception of these scenes different from what yours would be?

could see that—and yet their wisdom could not but grow until all was peace.

Then I saw their fate come upon them and that was terrible past speech. It came upon them as they walked the streets of their city. I have been in the fights with the Forest People—I have seen men die. But this was not like that. When gods war with gods, they use weapons we do not know. It was fire falling out of the sky and a mist that poisoned. It was the time of the Great Burning and the Destruction. They ran about like ants in the streets of their city—poor gods, poor gods! Then the towers began to fall. A few escaped—yes, a few. The legends tell it. But, even after the city had become a Dead Place, for many years the poison was still in the ground. I saw it happen, I saw the last of them die. It was darkness over the broken city, and I wept.

Literary Analysis
Point of View In what way has John's view of the "gods" changed?

All this, I saw. I saw it as I have told it, though not in the body. When I woke in the morning, I was hungry, but I did not think first of my hunger, for my heart was perplexed and confused. I knew the reason for the Dead Places but I did not see why it had happened. It seemed to me it should not have happened, with all the magic they had. I went through the house looking for an answer. There was so much in the house I could not understand—and yet I am a priest and the son of a priest. It was like being on one side of the great river, at night, with no light to show the way.

Then I saw the dead god. He was sitting in his chair, by the window, in a room I had not entered before and, for the first moment, I thought that he was alive. Then I saw the skin on the back of his hand—it was like dry leather. The room was shut, hot and dry—no doubt that had kept him as he was. At first I was afraid to approach him—then the fear left me. He was sitting looking out over the city—he was dressed in the clothes of the gods. His age was neither young nor old—I could not tell his age. But there was wisdom in his face and great sadness. You could see that he would have not run away. He had sat at his window, watching his city die—then he himself had died. But it is better to lose one's life than one's spirit—and you could see from the face that his spirit had not been lost. I knew that, if I touched him, he would fall into dust—and yet, there was something unconquered in the face.

Literary Analysis
Point of View
Does John's new understanding of the "gods" now match the reader's? Explain.

That is all of my story, for then I knew he was a man—I knew then that they had been men, neither gods nor demons. It is a great knowledge, hard to tell and believe. They were men—they went a dark road, but they were men. I had no fear after that—I had no fear going home, though twice I fought off the dogs and once I was hunted for two days by the Forest People. When I saw my father again, I prayed and was purified. He touched my lips and my breast, he said, "You went away a boy. You come back a man and a

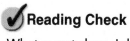 **Reading Check**

What event does John see in his vision?

priest." I said, "Father, they were men! I have been in the Place of the Gods and seen it! Now slay me, if it is the law—but still I know they were men."

He looked at me out of both eyes. He said, "The law is not always the same shape—you have done what you have done. I could not have done it in my time but you come after me. Tell!"

I told and he listened. After that, I wished to tell all the people but he showed me otherwise. He said, "Truth is a hard deer to hunt. If you eat too much truth at once, you may die of the truth. It was not idly that our fathers forbade the Dead Places." He was right—it is better the truth should come little by little. I have learned that, being a priest. Perhaps, in the old days, they ate knowledge too fast.

Nevertheless, we make a beginning. It is not for the metal alone we go to the Dead Places now—there are the books and the writings. They are hard to learn. And the magic tools are broken—but we can look at them and wonder. At least, we make a beginning. And, when I am chief priest we shall go beyond the great river. We shall go to the Place of the Gods—the place newyork—not one man but a company. We shall look for the images of the gods and find the god ASHING and the others—the gods Lincoln and Biltmore[1] and Moses.[2] But they were men who built the city, not gods or demons. They were men. I remember the dead man's face. They were men who were here before us. We must build again.

---

1. Biltmore hotel in New York City.
2. Moses Robert Moses, former New York City municipal official who oversaw many large construction projects.

Thinking About the Selection

1. **(a) Respond:** After returning from the Dead Place, John thinks, "Perhaps, in the old days, they ate knowledge too fast." In your opinion, does our society "eat knowledge too fast"? Explain.
   (b) Discuss: Discuss your response with a partner. Give reasons for your response and listen to your partner's reasons. **(c) Evaluate:** Explain how your response is affected by your discussion.

2. **(a) Infer:** What are the Dead Places and the Place of the Gods?
   (b) Synthesize: How does John's tribe view the Dead Places? Support your answer with details from the story.

3. **(a) Summarize:** After his journey, what key insight does John have about the gods? **(b) Speculate:** Explain why John's father does not want others to know what John has learned about the gods.
   (c) Evaluate: Explain whether you agree or disagree with John's father's advice to John.

Apply the Skills

One Thousand Dollars • By the Waters of Babylon

Comparing Points of View

1. Using a chart like the one shown, compare the way **point of view** is used in "One Thousand Dollars" and in "By the Waters of Babylon" to control the information the reader receives.

Story	Point of View	What Reader Knows	What Character Knows	Effect of Contrast in Knowledge	Impact of Story

2. **(a)** Compare the ways in which the ending of each story surprises the reader. **(b)** For each story, explain how point of view helps prepare for this surprise.

3. **(a)** The reader may find Bobby Gillian's final gesture all the more moving because the reader sees that no one knows what he has done. Explain how point of view makes this effect possible. **(b)** Compare this feeling with the one created by the ending of "By the Waters of Babylon." Why might a modern reader feel humbled by the end of Benét's story?

Writing to Compare Literary Works

Both stories use **dramatic irony**. In an essay, compare and contrast how the irony is achieved in these stories. Consider these elements:

- the point of view from which the story is told
- the character of the narrator
- the nature of the truth that is revealed in the ending

Finally, explain which use of irony you found more effective.

Vocabulary Builder

Practice Answer each of the following sentences *yes* or *no*. Then, explain your response.

1. Is it dangerous to drink water that has been <u>purified</u>?
2. If you are not hungry, might you <u>nevertheless</u> want to eat?
3. If you sell your bicycle, is it fair if the buyer <u>stipulates</u> the price?
4. Would it be <u>prudent</u> to stay up all night before a big test?

Reading and Vocabulary Skills Review

Reading: Inferences

Directions: *Questions 1–5 refer to the following selection.*

The history of the past centuries and millennia has been a history of almost ubiquitous wars, and sometimes desperate battles, leading to mutual destruction. They occurred in the clash of social and political interests and national hostility, be it from ideological or religious incompatibility. All that was the case, and even now many still claim that this past—which has not been overcome—is an immutable pattern. However, parallel with the process of wars, hostility, and alienation of peoples and countries, another process, just as objectively conditioned, was in motion and gaining force; the process of the emergence of a mutually connected and integral world.

"Address to the Forty-Third General Assembly Session"
Mikhail Gorbachev

1. **Using your own experience and the details of the passage, which is the best inference?**
   A Gorbachev's speech will ask for intervention in a world trouble spot.
   B Gorbachev's speech will address mutual space exploration.
   C Gorbachev's speech will call for world peace.
   D Gorbachev's speech will develop the role his country played in the United Nations.

2. **Which additional detail would help the reader make inferences?**
   A Mikhail Gorbachev was the Soviet General Secretary.
   B Mikhail Gorbachev and Ronald Reagan respected each other.
   C Mikhail Gorbachev's policies were controversial in the Soviet Union.
   D Gorbachev's policy of glasnost helped slow the arms race between the US and the USSR.

3. **Which sentence from the passage is a clue to the overall subject of the speech?**
   A the sentence beginning "However"
   B the sentence beginning "They occurred"
   C the sentence beginning "All that"
   D the sentence beginning "The history"

4. **Knowing that this speech was given at the UN would help you infer that the majority of the speech is about**
   A isolationism.
   B cultural integrity.
   C mutual understanding.
   D the structure of the UN.

5. **From your knowledge of history it can be inferred that**
   A Gorbachev didn't mean much of this speech.
   B this was a speech that reflected Gorbachev's proposed actions.
   C Gorbachev never spoke at the UN again.
   D Gorbachev was merely relaying the current Communist philosophy.

Vocabulary

Standards
Assessed

• 10.1.1
• 10.3.6
• 10.5.7

Directions: *Choose the sentence in which the word is used correctly.*

6. *discern*

   A *Discern* the tire to inspect it for flaws.
   B Can you *discern* the spot on the dress?
   C He *discerned* the splinter with tweezers.
   D Either *discern* the plate or replace it.

7. *anticipate*

   A We waited with *anticipate.*
   B *Anticipate* whole into its parts.
   C I *anticipate* what we learned.
   D He can *anticipate* a good result.

8. *formulate*

   A I could not remember that *formulate.*
   B The geese *formulate* a pattern as they fly.
   C I can't *formulate* answers quicky enough to debate her.
   D I find that *formulate* very hard to define.

9. *perspective*

   A Her *perspective* is influenced by her experience.
   B She *perspective* the situation from all angles.
   C The company's *perspective* detailed the losses and profits for investors.
   D They supported their *perspective* opinion with details.

10. *indicate*

   A Did the professor *indicate* which chapters to study?
   B I find that the *indicate* of jobs is very helpful.
   C Isn't there an *indicate* of how the author feels about that subject?
   D The detective can *indicate* clues that others can't figure out.

Directions: *Choose the best definition for each word.*

11. *inform*

   A to shape the mind
   B to bring on or about
   C not suitable to the purpose
   D casual, easy, relaxed

12. *formation*

   A plays in sports
   B the act of giving shape to
   C aerobic exercise
   D the analysis of financial statistics

13. *informal*

   A not seen correctly
   B redundancy
   C not given sufficient information
   D not according to prescribed form

14. *spectator*

   A printer
   B observer
   C gear
   D participant

15. *aspect*

   A the way a person appears or looks
   B the formation of an opinion
   C the process of seeking an answer
   D to logically determine an answer

Writing Workshop

Narration: Short Story

Short stories can take readers to exciting and unusual settings, or they can explore the conflicts and struggles of ordinary life. Follow the steps in this workshop to write a short story that captures the imagination and interest of your readers.

Assignment Write a short story in which you tell about a main character who undergoes a change or learns something.

What to Include Your short story should feature these elements:

- a clear setting—the time and place of the story
- a plot, or series of events, that builds to a dramatic climax
- effective descriptions using sensory details
- a theme that is revealed by the story's end
- error-free grammar, including use of consistent verb tense

To preview the criteria on which your short story may be judged, see the rubric on page 302.

Prewriting

Choosing Your Topic

Sketch and respond. You don't need to be a great artist to get inspiration from drawing. Try sketching a character or setting. Use your imagination to create visual details. Then, review your sketch and jot down the story ideas that it suggests to you.

Gathering Details

Gather details about characters. Before you draft get to know the characters you will develop. Create a character chart describing your characters' unique dreams, fears, habits, and quirks.

Character Chart	
Name	Kei
Appearance	Small frame, dark hair, intense brown eyes
Three Key Adjectives	smart, clumsy, ambitious
Goals	to be a great trumpet player
Habits or Quirks	taps his fingers
Likes	jazz, football, reading
Dislikes	TV, his boss at his after school job

Academic Standards

- Evaluate interactions between characters and how these affect the plot. (10.3.3)
- Analyze characters' traits through narration and dialogue. (10.3.4)
- Review and revise writing. (10.4.10)

Using the Form

You may use elements of this form in these types of writing:

- anecdotes
- scripts
- reflective essays

Work in Progress

Review the work you did on pages 213, 243, and 269.

To get a feel for short stories, read "A Problem" by Anton Chekhov on page 233.

Drafting

Shaping Your Writing

Make a plot diagram. The plot of your story should include exposition to set up the characters, setting, and conflict. Rising action will build to a climax, or point of highest tension. Then, the falling action leads to the resolution. Create a plot diagram like the one here and jot down your major story events to keep your writing on track.

Plot Diagram

Climax — Identify the point of highest interest.

Develop the conflict. — *Rising Action* / *Falling Action* — Reduce the suspense and decrease the tension.

Exposition
Set the scene and introduce the characters.

Resolution
Tie up the loose ends.

Providing Elaboration

Keep pacing in mind. To keep your story moving, introduce the problem early. Then, add details that intensify the problem. You might delay the climax to create more suspense. After the climax, wrap things up quickly to hold your readers' interest.

Revising

Revising Your Overall Structure

Use dialogue to develop characters. Look for points where you can develop characters through dialogue and action. If your characters are from a specific region or background, including their dialect will help readers hear how they sound. Review your draft to identify direct statements that could be replaced with the characters' own words.

Revising Your Sentences

Use active voice. Active voice is livelier and more engaging than the passive voice. In the passive voice, the action is done to the subject. In the active voice, the subject of the sentence performs the action.

> **Passive Voice:** He *had been deserted* by his friends.

> **Active Voice:** His friends *deserted* him.

Reading Writing Connection

To read the complete student model, see page 389.

Student Model: Revising to Use Active Voice

~~Her long skirt was rustled by the cool breeze,~~ and

The cool breeze rustled her long skirt

~~her pace was quickened because she was afraid~~ of the storm.

she began to quicken her pace for fear

Replacing the passive voice with the active voice makes this passage clearer and more forceful.

Integrating Grammar Skills

Revising to Apply Consistent Verb Tense

Correct use of verb tenses indicates clearly when an event occurred. It is often best to stay with a single tense. Mixing tenses can confuse and distract your reader.

Six Basic Verb Tenses	
Present	He *arrives* today.
Past	He *arrived* yesterday.
Future	He *will arrive* tomorrow.
Present Perfect	He *has arrived* already.
Past Perfect	He *had arrived* earlier than expected.
Future Perfect	He *will have arrived* by next week.

Identifying Mixed Tenses To identify mixed tenses, first recognize the verb tenses you use. Compare these examples.

Mixed Tenses: Kei *has knocked* and *was waiting* patiently at the door. Nothing *happens.* Kei *had decided* to leave.

Consistent Tense: Kei *knocked* and *waited* patiently at the door. Nothing *happened.* Kei *decided* to leave.

Mixing tenses is necessary when your work refers to two different times.

> PAST PERFECT   PAST
> Kei <u>*had waited*</u> for ten minutes before the door *opened.*

Fixing Errors To make sure that your verb tenses are consistent, find each verb in your writing.

1. **Identify your overall verb tense as past, present, or future.**
2. **Review the verbs in your writing, circling each one.**
3. **If you find a verb that is not in your basic verb tense, make sure that the tense shift is necessary.** Ask yourself, "Does this action take place in a different time period?"
4. **Revise the verb if the shift is unnecessary.**

Prentice Hall Writing and Grammar Connection: Chapter 22, Section 1

Apply It to Your Editing

Review two paragraphs of your draft. Underline every verb and name its tense. Use the steps you have just learned to fix confusing mixed tenses.

Student Model: Aubrey Weatherford
Broken Arrow, OK

And Then the Rain Came

"Is it wrong for us to have a voice in our lives? We have to fight!" said the woman speaking to the crowd. Scarlett flashed instantly to the night of the fire. She could feel the young man holding her back; she could hear the child screaming in the burning building. She struggled to free herself, tears running down her face. Shaking herself back into reality, Scarlett walked slowly away from the park, the speaker's words fading as she went. There was a dull rumble in the distance, and a flicker of light illuminated the city around her. The cool breeze rustled her long skirt, and she began to quicken her pace for fear of being caught in the storm. Scarlett's mind was spinning, the speaker's words stirring her thoughts. The thought of speaking her opinion and of being able to choose whomever she wanted for public office, though she had never learned exactly what their jobs were—just the thought of having the choice was enough to excite her.

"Little Lady, you had better hurry on home now. There's a gonna be quite a storm a comin'." An old, wrinkled man had approached Scarlett from the shadows, seemingly trying to help. She was looking at him patiently.

"Hey you, crazy man, leave the lady alone. You go on home now, you worthless old fool!" A middle-aged businessman had approached the two.

"Don't talk to him that way! He wasn't bothering me!" Scarlett said.

"You don't need to associate with street people like him. Go on home!"

"You have no right to speak to me in that fashion, good sir. I may associate with whomever I choose."

The businessman turned on his heel and left.

"Thank yer for standing up for me, little lady. Mighty appreciative."

"It was nothing. You remind me so much of, oh, never mind," Scarlett replied.

"I am sure I will walk by here again sometime. I will look for you. Good day, sir." Though Scarlett did not see it, the old man began to come out of the shadows as she made her way down the crowded street, though his appearance had greatly changed. He was no longer a wrinkled, old man but a tall, young man with sandy hair and piercing eyes. Carefully, he watched as Scarlett hurried along the sidewalk. Tiny drops of rain began to fall from the ashen sky as Scarlett disappeared into the crowd. . . .

Aubrey introduces the main character in the first paragraph.

Sensory details describe the setting.

The writer develops the conflict through dialogue.

The writer reveals an interesting twist in the plot.

Go Online
Read More
For: the complete student model
Visit: www.PHSchool.com
Web Code: enm-4201

Editing and Proofreading

Reread your short story carefully to correct errors in grammar, usage, and mechanics.

Focus on Complete Sentences: Check that every sentence in your draft contains a subject and a verb and expresses a complete thought. Review the grammar lesson on page 300 and be sure your verb tenses are accurate.

Publishing and Presenting

Consider one of the following ways to share your writing with classmates:

Give a dramatic reading. Practice reading your story aloud, experimenting with pace, emphasis, and tone. Then, read your story to a group of classmates. After the presentation, discuss which of your story's elements were especially effective when presented dramatically.

Compile an anthology. Join with your classmates to create a class story anthology. Organize the stories by theme and illustrate them with suitable photographs or drawings. Place the collection in your class, school, or community library.

Reflecting on Your Writing

Writer's Journal Jot down your thoughts on the experience of writing a short story. Begin by answering these questions:
- Which ideas from prewriting appear in the final draft of your story?
- Which revision strategies were most effective? Why?
- What advice would you give to another writer who is just beginning to write a short story?

> *Prentice Hall Writing and Grammar Connection: Chapter 5*

Rubric for Self-Assessment

To assess your short story, use the following rubric:

Criteria	Rating Scale
	not very very
Focus: How clear is the story's theme or message?	1 2 3 4 5
Organization: How effectively does the plot build to a climax?	1 2 3 4 5
Support/Elaboration: How effective is your choice of details?	1 2 3 4 5
Style: How well do you describe the characters and setting?	1 2 3 4 5
Conventions: How correct is your grammar, especially your use of verb tense?	1 2 3 4 5

Skills You Will Learn

Literature You Will Read

Reading and Vocabulary Skills Preview

Reading: Draw Conclusions

Academic Standards

- Use knowledge of ancient mythology to understand new words. (10.1.3)
- Analyze many different forms of dramatic literature. (10.3.1)
- Use varied and expanded vocabulary. (10.5.7)

> A **conclusion** is a decision or an opinion that is developed by putting together textual details and your knowledge.

Skills and Strategies You Will Learn in Part 2

In Part 2, you will learn

- to **draw conclusions about a work's theme** by **recognizing** and then **synthesizing key details.** (p. 306)
- to **draw conclusions about the meaning of a symbol** by **identifying patterns in textual details.** (p. 338)
- to **draw conclusions** by **evaluating a critic's judgment.** (p. 366)

Using the Skills and Strategies in Part 2

In Part 2, you will learn to draw conclusions by identifying, evaluating, and synthesizing textual elements. Themes and the meaning of symbols are usually not stated in a literary work. Putting textual details and your own knowledge together will allow you to draw conclusions about the meaning and significance of these elements.

The example shows how you can apply the skills and strategies in Part 2 to a work.

Drawing Conclusions About a Symbol or Theme
Story Detail: Trains stopped in the smallest towns.
Story Detail: All kinds of people relied on train travel.
Story Detail: Strangers chatted together on trains.
Story Detail: Trains provided vital goods and news from distant towns.
Detail: Today, many people choose to travel on planes because they are faster than trains.
Conclusion: Trains represent a time when connections between people were as important as connections between places.

Academic Vocabulary: Words for Understanding Literature

The following words will help you write and talk about your understanding of the literature in this unit.

Word	Definition	Example Sentence
consequently *adv.*	logically following from; as a result of	She broke the laws; *consequently,* she was punished.
predominant *adj.*	superior; most noticeable	The poem's *predominant* mood is sad.
comprehend *v.*	understand; include	The character's behavior is easier to *comprehend* within his culture.
coincide *v.*	occur at the same time	The two plot events *coincide.*
infer *v.*	derive by reasoning; figure out from details	The author never states that he is greedy, but we can *infer* that.

Vocabulary Skill: Etymology

▶ The **etymology** of a word is its origin and development.

In Part 2, you will learn
- the etymology of *consequently.* (p. 336)
- the etymology of *predominant.* (p. 364)

< means "derived from"

MFr stands for the language "Middle French." | **LL** stands for "Late Latin"; **L** stands for "Latin."

sequence (sē' kwəns, kwens) *n.* [MFr < LL, a following < L *sequens:* see SEQUENT]

Activity Look up each word on the chart in a dictionary. In your own words, explain the word's history, including any changes in meaning.

Practice these skills with either "How Much Land Does a Man Need?" (p. 308) or "Civil Peace" (p. 327).

Literary Analysis

The **theme** of a literary work is the central message it communicates. For example, a simple story might have the theme, "Honesty is the best policy." A more complex work might show that "Human suffering cannot be justified or explained." To express a theme, a writer may take one of these approaches:

- Directly state the theme of the work, or have a character directly state it.
- Create patterns of story elements to suggest a larger meaning—for instance, by contrasting a generous man and his selfish brother to say something about generosity.

In many cases, a theme reflects a **philosophical assumption**—the writer's basic beliefs about life. For instance, a writer may make the assumption that being generous leads to happiness. The writer's literary work may reflect this belief.

Reading Skill

When you **draw a conclusion,** you reach a decision or form an opinion based on information in a text. To draw a conclusion identifying the theme of a work, **recognize key details**, combining later details with earlier ones to identify meaningful patterns. Use a chart like the one shown.

 Academic Standards

- Examine how the author's perspective influences the structure and tone of the text. (10.2.4)
- Compare works that express a universal theme. (10.3.5)
- Evaluate the use of voice and narrator. (10.3.9)

Story Detail
Greedy Joe invests in a crooked scheme. He loses his money.

+

Story Detail
Generous John tricks the crooks and saves Joe.

↓

Pattern
Being greedy causes harm. Being generous leads to solutions.

Vocabulary Builder

How Much Land Does a Man Need?

- **piqued** (pēk'd) *adj.* irritated; offended, and so resentful (p. 308) *I am piqued by the fact that you did not tell me that you would be late.*

- **forbore** (fôr bôr') *v.* prevented oneself from doing something; refrained from (p. 311) *The quarterback forbore from responding to the linebackers' taunts.*

- **aggrieved** (ə grēv'd') *adj.* wronged; suffering grief or injury (p. 312) *The tenants were aggrieved by the landlord's delay in fixing the hot-water tank.*

Civil Peace

- **disreputable** (dis rep' yōō tə bəl) *adj.* not respectable; having or deserving a bad reputation (p. 328) *The consumer guide warned against disreputable street vendors.*

- **destitute** (des' tə tōōt') *adj.* lacking the basic necessities of life; poverty-stricken (p. 328) *The city helped families left destitute by the flood.*

- **commiserate** (kə miz' ər āt') *v.* sympathize (with); show sorrow for (p. 333) *We usually commiserate after a tough loss.*

Build Understanding • *How Much Land Does a Man Need?*

Background

Landless in Russia From the sixteenth century to the mid-nineteenth century, Russian peasants were serfs, bound by law to work land they could rent but not own. At the time of the story, peasants were allowed to own property. The memory of earlier times, however, kept peasants, like Pahom in this story, hungry for land.

Connecting to the Literature

Reading/Writing Connection In this story, Pahom dreams of having a little more land and then a little more . . . A modern version of Pahom might wonder, "If only my car were roomier." Jot down a few sentences about which material possessions modern people desire. Use at least three of these words: *accumulate, compile, display, justify.*

READ MORE

by Leo Tolstoy
The Death of Ivan Ilych
"The Kreutzer Sonata"

Meet the Author

Leo **Tolstoy** (1828–1910)

Leo Tolstoy is remembered almost as much for his unusual life as for his work. Born into a rich family, he inherited his family estate at age nineteen. He soon set about trying to improve the lives of the peasants who lived on his land.

Crisis and Renewal After the publication of two major masterpieces, the novels *War and Peace* (1865–1869) and *Anna Karenina* (1875–1877), Tolstoy fell into deep despair, questioning the value of his life and all his previous works. He found salvation and renewal in a mystical spirituality. He gave up small luxuries and worked in the fields. Tolstoy's beliefs about overcoming evil helped to inspire later activists such as Dr. Martin Luther King, Jr.

Fast Facts

▶ Although the young Tolstoy volunteered for the army, he later came to believe that all forms of violence are wrong.

▶ Tolstoy's wife Sonya copied the lengthy novel *War and Peace* by hand seven times to send to various publishers.

Go Online
Author Link
For: more about the author
Visit: www.PHSchool.com
Web Code: eqe-9208

HOW MUCH LAND

1

An elder sister came to visit her younger sister in the country. The elder was married to a shopkeeper in town, the younger to a peasant in the village. As the sisters sat over their tea talking, the elder began to boast of the advantages of town life, saying how comfortably they lived there, how well they dressed, what fine clothes her children wore, what good things they ate and drank, and how she went to the theater, promenades, and entertainments.

The younger sister was <u>piqued</u>, and in turn disparaged the life of a shopkeeper, and stood up for that of a peasant.

"I wouldn't change my way of life for yours," said she. "We may live roughly, but at least we're free from worry. You live in better style than we do, but though you often earn more than you need, you're very likely to lose all you have. You know the proverb, 'Loss and gain are brothers twain.' It often happens that people who're wealthy one day are begging their bread the next. Our way is safer. Though a peasant's life is not a rich one, it's long. We'll never grow rich, but we'll always have enough to eat."

The elder sister said sneeringly:

"Enough? Yes, if you like to share with the pigs and the calves! What do you know of elegance or manners! However much your

Vocabulary Builder
piqued (pēk'd) *adj.*
irritated; offended,
and so resentful

DOES A MAN NEED?

LEO TOLSTOY

translated by Louise and Aylmer Maude

good man may slave, you'll die as you live—in a dung heap—and your children the same."

"Well, what of that?" replied the younger sister. "Of course our work is rough and hard. But on the other hand, it's sure, and we need not bow to anyone. But you, in your towns, are surrounded by temptations; today all may be right, but tomorrow the Evil One may tempt your husband with cards, wine, or women, and all will go to ruin. Don't such things happen often enough?"

Pahom, the master of the house, was lying on the top of the stove and he listened to the women's chatter.

"It is perfectly true," thought he. "Busy as we are from childhood tilling mother earth, we peasants have no time to let any nonsense settle in our heads. Our only trouble is that we haven't land enough. If I had plenty of land, I shouldn't fear the Devil himself!"

The women finished their tea, chatted a while about dress, and then cleared away the tea things and lay down to sleep.

But the Devil had been sitting behind the stove and had heard all that had been said. He was pleased that the peasant's wife had led her husband into boasting and that he had said that if he had plenty of land he would not fear the Devil himself.

"All right," thought the Devil. "We'll have a tussle. I'll give you land enough; and by means of the land I'll get you into my power."

Literary Analysis
Theme What theme does the younger sister state directly in her remarks?

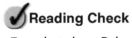
Reading Check

For what does Pahom wish?

2

Close to the village there lived a lady, a small landowner who had an estate of about three hundred acres. She had always lived on good terms with the peasants until she engaged as her manager an old soldier, who took to burdening the people with fines. However careful Pahom tried to be, it happened again and again that now a horse of his got among the lady's oats, now a cow strayed into her garden, now his calves found their way into her meadows—and he always had to pay a fine.

Pahom paid up, but grumbled, and, going home in a temper, was rough with his family. All through that summer Pahom had much trouble because of this manager, and he was actually glad when winter came and the cattle had to be stabled. Though he grudged the fodder when they could no longer graze on the pasture land, at least he was free from anxiety about them.

In the winter the news got about that the lady was going to sell her land and that the keeper of the inn on the high road was bargaining for it. When the peasants heard this they were very much alarmed.

"Well," thought they, "if the innkeeper gets the land, he'll worry us with fines worse than the lady's manager. We all depend on that estate."

So the peasants went on behalf of their village council and asked the lady not to sell the land to the innkeeper, offering her a better price for it themselves. The lady agreed to let them have it. Then the peasants tried to arrange for the village council to buy the whole estate, so that it might be held by them all in common. They met twice to discuss it, but could not settle the matter; the Evil One sowed discord among them and they could not agree. So they decided to buy the land individually, each according to his means; and the lady agreed to this plan as she had to the other.

Presently Pahom heard that a neighbor of his was buying fifty acres, and that the lady had consented to

▼ **Critical Viewing**
Based on details of his appearance, does the peasant in this portrait lead a life similar to Pahom's? Explain.
[Infer]

accept one half in cash and to wait a year for the other half. Pahom felt envious.

"Look at that," thought he, "the land is all being sold, and I'll get none of it." So he spoke to his wife.

"Other people are buying," said he, "and we must also buy twenty acres or so. Life is becoming impossible. That manager is simply crushing us with his fines."

So they put their heads together and considered how they could manage to buy it. They had one hundred rubles[1] laid by. They sold a colt and one half of their bees, hired out one of their sons as a farmhand and took his wages in advance, borrowed the rest from a brother-in-law, and so scraped together half the purchase money.

Having done this, Pahom chose a farm of forty acres, some of it wooded, and went to the lady to bargain for it. They came to an agreement, and he shook hands with her upon it and paid her a deposit in advance. Then they went to town and signed the deeds, he paying half the price down, and undertaking to pay the remainder within two years.

So now Pahom had land of his own. He borrowed seed and sowed it on the land he had bought. The harvest was a good one, and within a year he had managed to pay off his debts both to the lady and to his brother-in-law. So he became a landowner, plowing and sowing his own land, making hay on his own land, cutting his own trees, and feeding his cattle on his own pasture. When he went out to plow his fields, or to look at his growing corn, or at his grass meadows, his heart would fill with joy. The grass that grew and the flowers that bloomed there seemed to him unlike any that grew elsewhere. Formerly, when he had passed by that land, it had appeared the same as any other land, but now it seemed quite different.

3

So Pahom was well contented, and everything would have been right if the neighboring peasants would only not have trespassed on his wheatfields and meadows. He appealed to them most civilly, but they still went on: now the herdsmen would let the village cows stray into his meadows, then horses from the night pasture would get among his corn. Pahom turned them out again and again, and forgave their owners, and for a long time he <u>forbore</u> to prosecute anyone. But at last he lost patience and complained to the District Court. He knew it was the peasants' want of land, and no evil intent on their part, that caused the trouble, but he thought:

---

1. rubles (roo´ bəlz) *n.* A ruble is the basic unit of Russian currency.

Literary Analysis
Theme What do these details about Pahom's motives suggest about his "need" for land?

Vocabulary Builder
forbore (fôr bôr´) *v.* prevented oneself from doing something; refrained from

 **Reading Check**

After acquiring his own land, how does Pahom feel at first?

"I can't go on overlooking it, or they'll destroy all I have. They must be taught a lesson."

So he had them up, gave them one lesson, and then another, and two or three of the peasants were fined. After a time Pahom's neighbors began to bear him a grudge for this, and would now and then let their cattle onto his land on purpose. One peasant even got into Pahom's wood at night and cut down five young lime trees for their bark. Pahom, passing through the wood one day, noticed something white. He came nearer and saw the stripped trunks lying on the ground, and close by stood the stumps where the trees had been. Pahom was furious.

"If he'd only cut one here and there it would have been bad enough," thought Pahom, "but the rascal has actually cut down a whole clump. If I could only find out who did this, I'd get even with him."

He racked his brains as to who it could be. Finally he decided: "It must be Simon—no one else could have done it." So he went to Simon's homestead to have a look around, but he found nothing and only had an angry scene. However, he now felt more certain than ever that Simon had done it, and he lodged a complaint. Simon was summoned. The case was tried, and retried, and at the end of it all Simon was acquitted, there being no evidence against him. Pahom felt still more <u>aggrieved</u>, and let his anger loose upon the Elders and the Judges.

"You let thieves grease your palms," said he. "If you were honest folk yourselves you wouldn't let a thief go free."

So Pahom quarreled with the judges and with his neighbors. Threats to burn his hut began to be uttered. So though Pahom had more land, his place in the community was much worse than before.

About this time a rumor got about that many people were moving to new parts.

"There's no need for me to leave my land," thought Pahom. "But some of the others may leave our village and then there'd be more room for us. I'd take over their land myself and make my estates somewhat bigger. I could then live more at ease. As it is, I'm still too cramped to be comfortable."

One day Pahom was sitting at home when a peasant, passing through the village, happened to drop in. He was allowed to stay the night, and supper was given him. Pahom had a talk with this peasant and asked him where he came from. The stranger answered that he came from beyond the Volga,[2] where he had been working. One word led to another, and the man went on to say that many people were settling in those parts. He told how some people from

---

2. **Volga** (väl′ gə) the major river in western Russia.

Reading Skill
Drawing Conclusions
Which key details in this passage show that the desire for land leads to discord among the peasants?

Vocabulary Builder
aggrieved (ə grēv′d′) *adj.* wronged; suffering grief or injury

Literary Analysis
Theme In what way does this episode reinforce the idea that the desire for land leads to division and unhappiness?

his village had settled there. They had joined the community there and had had twenty-five acres per man granted them. The land was so good, he said, that the rye sown on it grew as high as a horse, and so thick that five cuts of a sickle made a sheaf.[3] One peasant, he said, had brought nothing with him but his bare hands, and now he had six horses and two cows of his own.

Pahom's heart kindled with desire.

"Why should I suffer in this narrow hole, if one can live so well elsewhere?" he thought. "I'll sell my land and my homestead here, and with the money I'll start afresh over there and get everything new. In this crowded place one is always having trouble. But I must first go and find out all about it myself."

Toward summer he got ready and started out. He went down the Volga on a steamer to Samara, then walked another three hundred miles on foot, and at last reached the place. It was just as the stranger had said. The peasants had plenty of land: every man had twenty-five acres of communal land given him for his use, and any-one who had money could buy, besides, at a ruble and a half an acre, as much good freehold land[4] as he wanted.

Having found out all he wished to know, Pahom returned home as autumn came on, and began selling off his belongings. He sold his land at a profit, sold his homestead and all his cattle, and with-drew from membership in the village. He only waited till the spring, and then started with his family for the new settlement.

4

As soon as Pahom and his family reached their new abode, he applied for admission into the council of a large village. He stood treat to the Elders and obtained the necessary documents. Five shares of communal land were given him for his own and his sons' use: that is to say—125 acres (not all together, but in different fields) besides the use of the communal pasture. Pahom put up the buildings he needed and bought cattle. Of the communal land alone he had three times as much as at his former home, and the land was good wheat land. He was ten times better off than he had been. He had plenty of arable[5] land and pasturage, and could keep as many head of cattle as he liked.

At first, in the bustle of building and settling down, Pahom was pleased with it all, but when he got used to it he began to think that even here he hadn't enough land. The first year he sowed wheat on his share of the communal land and had a good crop. He wanted to

---

Reading Skill
Drawing Conclusions
Based on the story so far, draw a conclusion about the amount of land Pahom will need before he is satisfied.

**Reading Check**

After quarreling with his neighbors, what does Pahom decide to do?

---

3. **sheaf** (shēf) *n.* bundle of grain
4. **freehold land** privately owned land that the owner can lease to others for a fee.
5. **arable** (ar´ ə bəl) *adj.* suitable for growing crops.

go on sowing wheat, but had not enough communal land for the purpose, and what he had already used was not available, for in those parts wheat is sown only on virgin soil or on fallow land. It is sown for one or two years, and then the land lies fallow till it is again overgrown with steppe grass. There were many who wanted such land, and there was not enough for all, so that people quarreled about it. Those who were better off wanted it for growing wheat, and those who were poor wanted it to let to dealers, so that they might raise money to pay their taxes. Pahom wanted to sow more wheat, so he rented land from a dealer for a year. He sowed much wheat and had a fine crop, but the land was too far from the village—the wheat had to be carted more than ten miles. After a time Pahom noticed that some peasant dealers were living on separate farms and were growing wealthy, and he thought:

"If I were to buy some freehold land and have a homestead on it, it would be a different thing altogether. Then it would all be fine and close together."

The question of buying freehold land recurred to him again and again.

He went on in the same way for three years, renting land and sowing wheat. The seasons turned out well and the crops were good, so that he began to lay by money. He might have gone on living contentedly, but he grew tired of having to rent other people's land every year and having to scramble for it. Wherever there was good land to be had, the peasants would rush for it and it was taken up at once, so that unless you were sharp about it, you got none. It happened in the third year that he and a dealer together rented a piece of pasture land from some peasants, and they had already plowed it up, when there was some dispute and the peasants went to law about it, and things fell out so that the labor was all lost.

"If it were my own land," thought Pahom, "I should be independent, and there wouldn't be all this unpleasantness."

So Pahom began looking out for land which he could buy, and he came across a peasant who had bought thirteen hundred acres, but having got into difficulties was willing to sell again cheap. Pahom bargained and haggled with him, and at last they settled the price at fifteen hundred rubles, part in cash and part to be paid later. They had all but clinched the matter when a passing dealer happened to stop at Pahom's one day to get feed for his horses. He drank tea with Pahom, and they had a talk. The dealer said that he was just returning from the land of the Bashkirs,[6] far away, where he had bought thirteen thousand acres of land, all for a thousand rubles. Pahom questioned him further, and the dealer said:

Literary Analysis
Theme What common idea comes across in each of the episodes in which Pahom acquires land?

---

6. **Bashkirs** (bash kirz´) *n.* originally nomadic people who live in the plains of southwestern Russia.

▲ **Critical Viewing**
In this painting by
Vincent van Gogh,
what does the radiant
outpouring of the sun
suggest about the
painter's attitude
toward nature and the
land? **[Interpret]**

"All one has to do is to make friends with the chiefs. I gave away about one hundred rubles' worth of silk robes and carpets, besides a case of tea, and I gave wine to those who would drink it; and I got the land for less than three kopecks[7] an acre." And he showed Pahom the title deed, saying:

"The land lies near a river, and the whole steppe[8] is virgin soil."

Pahom plied him with questions, and the dealer said:

"There's more land there than you could cover if you walked a year, and it all belongs to the Bashkirs. They're as simple as sheep, and land can be got almost for nothing."

"There, now," thought Pahom, "with my one thousand rubles, why should I get only thirteen hundred acres, and saddle myself with a debt besides? If I take it out there, I can get more than ten times as much for my money."

5

Pahom inquired how to get to the place, and as soon as the grain dealer had left him, he prepared to go there himself. He left his wife to look after the homestead, and started on his journey, taking his

**Reading Check**

Where does Pahom
decide to go next?

---

7. kopecks (kō′ peks′) *n.* A kopek is a unit of Russian money, equal to one hundredth of a ruble.
8. steppe (step) *n.* high grassland plains stretching from Hungary through Russia into central Asia.

hired man with him. They stopped at a town on their way and bought a case of tea, some wine, and other presents, as the grain dealer had advised.

On and on they went until they had gone more than three hundred miles, and on the seventh day they came to a place where the Bashkirs had pitched their round tents. It was all just as the dealer had said. The people lived on the steppe, by a river, in felt-covered tents. They neither tilled the ground nor ate bread. Their cattle and horses grazed in herds on the steppe. The colts were tethered behind the tents, and the mares were driven to them twice a day. The mares were milked, and from the milk kumiss[9] was made. It was the women who prepared the kumiss, and they also made cheese. As far as the men were concerned, drinking kumiss and tea, eating mutton, and playing on their pipes was all they cared about. They were all stout and merry, and all the summer long they never thought of doing any work. They were quite ignorant, and knew no Russian, but were good-natured enough.

As soon as they saw Pahom, they came out of their tents and gathered around the visitor. An interpreter was found, and Pahom told them he had come about some land. The Bashkirs seemed very glad; they took Pahom and led him into one of the best tents, where they made him sit on some down cushions placed on a carpet, while they sat around him. They gave him some tea and kumiss, and had a sheep killed, and gave him mutton to eat. Pahom took presents out of his cart and distributed them among the Bashkirs, and divided the tea amongst them. The Bashkirs were delighted. They talked a great deal among themselves and then told the interpreter what to say.

"They wish to tell you," said the interpreter, "that they like you and that it's our custom to do all we can to please a guest and to repay him for his gifts. You have given us presents, now tell us which of the things we possess please you best, that we may present them to you."

"What pleases me best here," answered Pahom, "is your land. Our land is crowded and the soil is worn out, but you have plenty of land, and it is good land. I never saw the likes of it."

The interpreter told the Bashkirs what Pahom had said. They talked among themselves for a while. Pahom could not understand what they were saying, but saw that they were much amused and heard them shout and laugh. Then they were silent and looked at Pahom while the interpreter said:

"They wish me to tell you that in return for your presents they will gladly give you as much land as you want. You have only to point it out with your hand and it is yours."

---

9. kumiss (ko͞o′ mis) *n.* fermented mare's or camel's milk that is used as a drink.

The Bashkirs talked again for a while and began to dispute. Pahom asked what they were disputing about, and the interpreter told him that some of them thought they ought to ask their chief about the land and not act in his absence, while others thought there was no need to wait for his return.

6

While the Bashkirs were disputing, a man in a large fox-fur cap appeared on the scene. They all became silent and rose to their feet. The interpreter said: "This is our chief himself."

Pahom immediately fetched the best dressing gown and five pounds of tea, and offered these to the chief. The chief accepted them and seated himself in the place of honor. The Bashkirs at once began telling him something. The chief listened for a while, then made a sign with his head for them to be silent, and addressing himself to Pahom, said in Russian:

"Well, so be it. Choose whatever piece of land you like; we have plenty of it."

"How can I take as much as I like?" thought Pahom. "I must get a deed to make it secure, or else they may say: 'It is yours,' and afterward may take it away again."

"Thank you for your kind words," he said aloud. "You have much land, and I only want a little. But I should like to be sure which portion is mine. Could it not be measured and made over to me? Life and death are in God's hands. You good people give it to me, but your children might wish to take it back again."

"You are quite right," said the chief. "We will make it over to you."

"I heard that a dealer had been here," continued Pahom, "and that you gave him a little land, too, and signed title deeds to that effect. I should like to have it done in the same way."

The chief understood.

"Yes," replied he, "that can be done quite easily. We have a scribe, and we will go to town with you and have the deed properly sealed."

"And what will be the price?" asked Pahom.

"Our price is always the same: one thousand rubles a day."

Pahom did not understand.

"A day? What measure is that? How many acres would that be?"

"We do not know how to reckon it out," said the chief. "We sell it by the day. As much as you can go around on your feet in a day is yours, and the price is one thousand rubles a day."

Pahom was surprised.

"But in a day you can get around a large tract of land," he said.

The chief laughed.

Reading Skill
Drawing Conclusions
Which key details show that the Bashkirs view the land differently from Pahom?

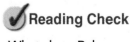

Reading Check

What does Pahom ask of the Bashkirs?

"It will all be yours!" said he. "But there is one condition: If you don't return on the same day to the spot whence you started, your money is lost."

"But how am I to mark the way that I have gone?"

"Why, we shall go to any spot you like and stay there. You must start from that spot and make your round, taking a spade with you. Wherever you think necessary, make a mark. At every turning, dig a hole and pile up the turf; then afterward we will go around with a plow from hole to hole. You may make as large a circuit as you please, but before the sun sets you must return to the place you started from. All the land you cover will be yours."

Pahom was delighted. It was decided to start early next morning. They talked a while, and after drinking some more kumiss and eating some more mutton, they had tea again, and then the night came on. They gave Pahom a featherbed to sleep on, and the Bashkirs dispersed for the night, promising to assemble the next morning at daybreak and ride out before sunrise to the appointed spot.

7

Pahom lay on the featherbed, but could not sleep. He kept thinking about the land.

"What a large tract I'll mark off!" thought he. "I can easily do thirty-five miles in a day. The days are long now, and within a circuit of thirty-five miles what a lot of land there will be! I'll sell the poorer land or let it to peasants, but I'll pick out the best and farm it myself. I'll buy two ox teams and hire two more laborers. About a hundred and fifty acres shall be plowland, and I'll pasture cattle on the rest."

Pahom lay awake all night and dozed off only just before dawn. Hardly were his eyes closed when he had a dream. He thought he was lying in that same tent and heard somebody chuckling outside. He wondered who it could be, and rose and went out, and he saw the Bashkir chief sitting in front of the tent holding his sides and rolling about with laughter. Going nearer to the chief, Pahom asked: "What are you laughing at?" But he saw that it was no longer the chief but the grain dealer who had recently stopped at his house and had told him about the land. Just as Pahom was going to ask: "Have you been here long?" he saw that it was not the dealer, but the peasant who had come up from the Volga long ago, to Pahom's old home. Then he saw that it was not the peasant either, but the Devil himself with hoofs and horns, sitting there and chuckling, and before him lay a man, prostrate on the ground, barefooted, with only trousers and a shirt on. And Pahom dreamed that he looked

Reading Skill
Drawing Conclusions
Which key details in this passage suggest that the Devil is responsible for all of Pahom's land deals?

The Emancipation of the Serfs

Tolstoy published "How Much Land Does a Man Need?" in 1886, a year in which the question in the title was on many Russians' minds.

- In 1861, the ruler of Russia, Tsar Alexander II, freed the serfs.

- The government bought land from the serfs' former masters and sold it to the serfs.

- In some parts of Russia, the price was unrealistically high. In other parts, the parcels were too small.

- To survive, some freed serfs rented land from landowners. Others worked for landowners or went to work in factories. Discontent grew, and many sought further reform.

Russia

1460
The freedom of peasants to leave the land they farmed is limited.

1649
Russian peasants are enserfed.

1773–1774
Peasants rebel.

1861
Alexander II ends serfdom in Russia.

Other Countries

England ends serfdom.
1600s

France ends serfdom.
1789

United States abolishes slavery.
1865

Nineteenth-Century Population of Russia

Nobles, Merchants, and Others
roughly one fifth

Privately Owned Serfs
roughly two fifths

State and Other Peasants
roughly two fifths

Connect to the Literature   Based on Pahom's story, what do you think Tolstoy thought of land reform in Russia? Explain.

---

more attentively to see what sort of man it was lying there, and he saw that the man was dead, and that it was himself. Horror-struck, he awoke.

"What things one dreams about!" thought he.

Looking around he saw through the open door that the dawn was breaking.

"It's time to wake them up," thought he. "We ought to be starting."

He got up, roused his man (who was sleeping in his cart), bade him harness, and went to call the Bashkirs.

"It's time to go to the steppe to measure the land," he said.

The Bashkirs rose and assembled, and the chief came, too. Then they began drinking kumiss again, and offered Pahom some tea, but he would not wait.

"If we are to go, let's go. It's high time," said he.

8

The Bashkirs got ready and they all started; some mounted on horses and some in carts. Pahom drove in his own small cart with

Reading Check

How large a tract of land does Pahom decide he will mark off?

his servant and took a spade with him. When they reached the steppe, the red dawn was beginning to kindle. They ascended a hillock (called by the Bashkirs a *shikhan*) and, dismounting from their carts and their horses, gathered in one spot. The chief came up to Pahom and, stretching out his arm toward the plain:

"See," said he, "all this, as far as your eye can reach, is ours. You may have any part of it you like."

Pahom's eyes glistened: it was all virgin soil, as flat as the palm of your hand, as black as the seed of a poppy, and in the hollows different kinds of grasses grew breast-high.

The chief took off his fox-fur cap, placed it on the ground, and said:

"This will be the mark. Start from here, and return here again. All the land you go around shall be yours."

Pahom took out his money and put it on the cap. Then he took off his outer coat, remaining in his sleeveless undercoat. He unfastened his girdle[10] and tied it tight below his stomach, put a little bag of bread into the breast of his coat, and, tying a flask of water to his girdle, he drew up the tops of his boots, took the spade from his man, and stood ready to start. He considered for some moments which way he had better go—it was tempting everywhere.

"No matter," he concluded, "I'll go toward the rising sun."

He turned his face to the east, stretched himself, and waited for the sun to appear above the rim.

"I must lose no time," he thought, "and it's easier walking while it's still cool."

---

10. girdle (gʉrd´´l) *n.* old term for a belt or sash for the waist.

The sun's rays had hardly flashed above the horizon when Pahom, carrying the spade over his shoulder, went down into the steppe.

Pahom started walking neither slowly nor quickly. After having gone a thousand yards he stopped, dug a hole, and placed pieces of turf one on another to make it more visible. Then he went on; and now that he had walked off his stiffness he quickened his pace. After a while he dug another hole.

Pahom looked back. The hillock could be distinctly seen in the sunlight, with the people on it, and the glittering iron rims of the cartwheels. At a rough guess Pahom concluded that he had walked three miles. It was growing warmer; he took off his undercoat, slung it across his shoulder, and went on again. It had grown quite warm now; he looked at the sun—it was time to think of breakfast.

"The first shift is done, but there are four in a day, and it's too soon yet to turn. But I'll just take off my boots," said he to himself.

He sat down, took off his boots, stuck them into his girdle, and went on. It was easy walking now.

"I'll go on for another three miles," thought he, "and then turn to the left. This spot is so fine that it would be a pity to lose it. The further one goes, the better the land seems."

He went straight on for a while, and when he looked around, the hillock was scarcely visible and the people on it looked like black ants, and he could just see something glistening there in the sun.

"Ah," thought Pahom, "I have gone far enough in this direction; it's time to turn. Besides, I'm in a regular sweat, and very thirsty."

He stopped, dug a large hole, and heaped up pieces of turf. Next he untied his flask, had a drink, and then turned sharply to the left. He went on and on; the grass was high, and it was very hot.

Literary Analysis
Theme How do Pahom's thoughts and actions now reflect his earlier attitude toward acquiring land?

Reading Check

At what sort of pace does Pahom set out?

Pahom began to grow tired: he looked at the sun and saw that it was noon.

"Well," he thought, "I must have a rest."

He sat down, and ate some bread and drank some water; but he did not lie down, thinking that if he did he might fall asleep. After sitting a little while, he went on again. At first he walked easily; the food had strengthened him; but it had become terribly hot and he felt sleepy. Still he went on, thinking: "An hour to suffer, a lifetime to live."

He went a long way in this direction also, and was about to turn to the left again, when he perceived a damp hollow: "It would be a pity to leave that out," he thought. "Flax would do well there." So he went on past the hollow and dug a hole on the other side of it before he made a sharp turn. Pahom looked toward the hillock. The heat made the air hazy: it seemed to be quivering, and through the haze the people on the hillock could scarcely be seen.

"Ah," thought Pahom, "I have made the sides too long; I must make this one shorter." And he went along the third side, stepping faster. He looked at the sun: it was nearly halfway to the horizon, and he had not yet done two miles of the third side of the square. He was still ten miles from the goal.

"No," he thought, "though it will make my land lopsided, I must hurry back in a straight line now. I might go too far, and as it is I have a great deal of land."

So Pahom hurriedly dug a hole and turned straight toward the hillock.

9

Pahom went straight toward the hillock, but he now walked with difficulty. He was exhausted from the heat, his bare feet were cut and bruised, and his legs began to fail. He longed to rest, but it was impossible if he meant to get back before sunset. The sun waits for no man, and it was sinking lower and lower.

"Oh, Lord," he thought, "if only I have not blundered trying for too much! What if I am too late?"

He looked toward the hillock and at the sun. He was still far from his goal, and the sun was already near the rim of the sky.

Pahom walked on and on; it was very hard walking, but he went quicker and quicker. He pressed on, but was still far from the place. He began running, threw away his coat, his boots, his flask, and his cap, and kept only the spade which he used as a support.

"What am I to do?" he thought again. "I've grasped too much and ruined the whole affair. I can't get there before the sun sets."

And this fear made him still more breathless. Pahom kept on running; his soaking shirt and trousers stuck to him, and his

Reading Skill
Drawing Conclusions
Based on details here and earlier, what conclusion can you draw about the chances for Pahom's success?

mouth was parched. His breast was working like a blacksmith's bellows, his heart was beating like a hammer, and his legs were giving way as if they did not belong to him. Pahom was seized with terror lest he should die of the strain.

Though afraid of death, he could not stop.

"After having run all that way they will call me a fool if I stop now," thought he.

And he ran on and on, and drew near and heard the Bashkirs yelling and shouting to him, and their cries inflamed his heart still more. He gathered his last strength and ran on.

The sun was close to the rim of the sky and, cloaked in mist, looked large, and red as blood. Now, yes, now, it was about to set! The sun was quite low, but he was also quite near his goal. Pahom could already see the people on the hillock waving their arms to make him hurry. He could see the fox-fur cap on the ground and the money in it, and the chief sitting on the ground holding his sides. And Pahom remembered his dream.

"There's plenty of land," thought he, "but will God let me live on it? I have lost my life, I have lost my life! Never will I reach that spot!"

Pahom looked at the sun, which had reached the earth: one side of it had already disappeared. With all his remaining strength he rushed on, bending his body forward so that his legs could hardly follow fast enough to keep him from falling. Just as he reached the hillock it suddenly grew dark. He looked up—the sun had already set!

He gave a cry: "All my labor has been in vain," thought he, and was about to stop, but he heard the Bashkirs still shouting and remembered that though to him, from below, the sun seemed to have set, they on the hillock could still see it. He took a long breath and ran up the hillock. It was still light there. He reached the top and saw the cap. Before it sat the chief, laughing and holding his sides. Again Pahom remembered his dream, and he uttered a cry: his legs gave way beneath him, he fell forward and reached the cap with his hands.

"Ah, that's a fine fellow!" exclaimed the chief. "He has gained much land!"

Pahom's servant came running up and tried to raise him, but he saw that blood was flowing from his mouth. Pahom was dead.

The Bashkirs clicked their tongues to show their pity.

His servant picked up the spade and dug a grave long enough for Pahom to lie in, and buried him in it.

Six feet from his head to his toes was all he needed.

Literary Analysis
Theme Rephrase Pahom's question as a statement of a theme in the story.

Apply the Skills

How Much Land Does a Man Need?

Thinking About the Selection

1. **Respond:** Do you sympathize with Pahom? Explain.
2. **(a) Recall:** What event allows Pahom to buy his first parcel of land? **(b) Interpret:** What is his main reason for wanting this land? Support your answer with details from the story.
3. **(a) Summarize:** Explain the events that change Pahom's relations with his neighbors. **(b) Analyze Cause and Effect:** What effect does owning land have on his life?
4. **(a) Hypothesize:** If Pahom had no chances to acquire more land, do you think he could find happiness with what he already has? Explain. **(b) Discuss:** Share and discuss answers with a partner. **(c) Apply:** Based on your discussion, write a sentence explaining the author's attitude toward ambition.
5. **(a) Summarize:** What events take place on the last day of Pahom's life? **(b) Interpret:** Explain the meaning of the last sentence of the story both as a description of Pahom's fate and as an answer to the title of the story.

Literary Analysis

6. **(a)** Using a chart like the one shown, analyze each episode in which Pahom is given the chance to acquire property. **(b)** How are these episodes related? Are they similar or different? Does one lead to another? Explain. **(c)** State the **theme** of the story, explaining how each event helps convey it.

Episode	Character's Response	Reasons for the Response	Result: Peace of Mind/Problems

7. Tolstoy makes the **philosophical assumption** that people should not waste their lives on material things. How might Pahom's life have been different if he had applied this belief?

Reading Skill

8. **(a) Draw a conclusion** about the Bashkirs' values based on their attitude toward land. **(b)** Which details in Tolstoy's depiction of the tribe contribute to his theme? Explain.
9. Draw a conclusion about Pahom's dream, explaining how it helps readers grasp the theme.

QuickReview

Story at a Glance
A peasant discovers that, once he is able to own land, enough is never enough.

Go Online
Assessment
For: Self-test
Visit: www.PHSchool.com
Web Code: eqa-6207

Theme: the central message or insight in a literary work

Philosophical Assumptions: basic beliefs about life that a writer holds to be true

Conclusion: a decision or an opinion one reaches based on details in a text

Vocabulary Builder

Practice **Antonyms** are words with opposite meanings. Rewrite each of the following sentences by replacing the word or phrase in italics with its antonym from the vocabulary list for "How Much Land . . .," on page 306. You may need to change some other words in the sentence. Then, explain which version of the sentence makes the most sense.

1. He *indulged* and ate half the cake.

2. After he took my bicycle, I was *forgiving* and lent him my radio.

3. I was *not hurt* by his insults, and I enjoy his company.

Adding Words to Your Vocabulary Using a thesaurus, find one additional antonym for each of the words in the vocabulary list for "How Much Land . . .," on page 306. Use each antonym correctly in a sentence. (For more on using a thesaurus, see page R7.)

Writing

Write a brief **character analysis** of Pahom. In your analysis, identify his main traits. Give examples of incidents and descriptions in the story that show these traits. Use the following techniques:

- Use phrases such as *for example* to link supporting details to your main idea.
- Use transitional words such as *instead* to connect ideas.

For *Grammar, Vocabulary,* and *Assessment,* see **Build Language Skills,** pages 336–337.

Extend Your Learning

Listening and Speaking Hold a **group discussion** to decide whether Tolstoy's theme applies to modern life. Begin by agreeing on a statement of the story's message. To aid the discussion, follow these tips:

- Express your ideas in understandable and nonoffensive ways.
- Add to others' ideas by giving examples that support them.
- Allow your own ideas to be challenged by others.

Research and Technology In a group, construct and present **visual aids** explaining the landowning system in Tolstoy's Russia. Include a map showing urban and rural populations and a flowchart showing how property was acquired. Present your work to the class.

Build Understanding • *Civil Peace*

Background

The Nigerian Civil War In 1960, the West African nation of Nigeria finally won independence from Britain. The Ibo (ē′ bō′), one people of Nigeria, seceded from the new country, setting up the independent Republic of Biafra. A brutal civil war followed. In 1970, a defeated Biafra rejoined Nigeria. "Civil Peace" unfolds in the aftermath of this war.

Connecting to the Literature

Reading/Writing Connection In "Civil Peace," the main character, Jonathan Iwegbu, shows a survivor's ability to put aside regrets and adapt to life's ups and downs. Write several reasons why a positive outlook can help people manage problems. Use at least three of the following words: *maximize, minimize, isolate, perceive.*

Review

For **Literary Analysis, Reading Skill,** and **Vocabulary Builder,** see page 306.

READ MORE

by Chinua Achebe
Things Fall Apart

Meet the Author

Chinua **Achebe** (b. 1930)

Chinua (chin′ wä′) Achebe (ä chā′ bā) is renowned for novels and stories that explore the conflicts of modern Africans. Achebe was born into the Ibo tribe of Nigeria. He grew up to pursue a varied career as a university teacher and as a director for the Nigerian Broadcasting Corporation. According to one critic, "In the English language, he is the founding father of modern African literature."

Africans Face the West Achebe wrote his first and most celebrated novel, *Things Fall Apart* (1958), in an effort to accurately portray the disruption of Ibo tribal society by Western colonial rule.

Fast Facts

▶ During the civil war in Nigeria, Achebe's house was bombed. He fled, leaving behind a book of his that he had nearly finished printing. When he returned, a single copy of the book remained.

▶ Achebe believes that stories can help people find their way through life's conflicts.

Go Online
Author Link

For: More about the author
Visit: www.PHSchool.com
Web Code: eqe-9209

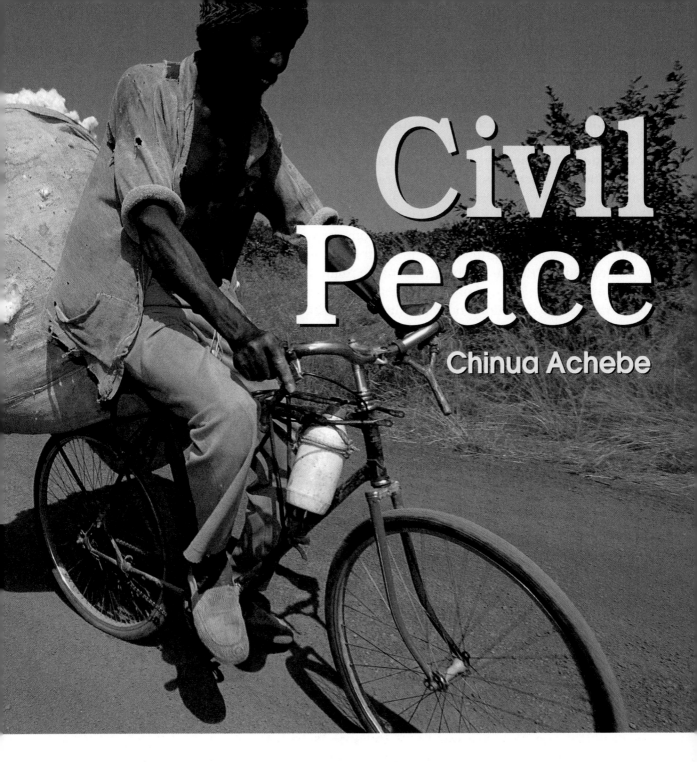

Civil Peace

Chinua Achebe

Jonathan Iwegbu counted himself extraordinarily lucky. "Happy survival!" meant so much more to him than just a current fashion of greeting old friends in the first hazy days of peace. It went deep to his heart. He had come out of the war with five inestimable blessings—his head, his wife Maria's head and the heads of three out of their four children. As a bonus he also had his old bicycle—a miracle too but naturally not to be compared to the safety of five human heads.

The bicycle had a little history of its own. One day at the height of the war it was commandeered "for urgent military action." Hard as its loss would have been to him he would still have let it go without a thought had he not had some doubts about the genuineness of the officer. It wasn't his <u>disreputable</u> rags, nor the toes peeping out of one blue and one brown canvas shoe, nor yet the two stars of his rank done obviously in a hurry in biro,[1] that troubled Jonathan; many good and heroic soldiers looked the same or worse. It was rather a certain lack of grip and firmness in his manner. So Jonathan, suspecting he might be amenable to influence, rummaged in his raffia bag and produced the two pounds with which he had been going to buy firewood which his wife, Maria, retailed to camp officials for extra stock-fish and corn meal, and got his bicycle back. That night he buried it in the little clearing in the bush where the dead of the camp, including his own youngest son, were buried. When he dug it up again a year later after the surrender all it needed was a little palm-oil greasing. "Nothing puzzles God," he said in wonder.

He put it to immediate use as a taxi and accumulated a small pile of Biafran[2] money ferrying camp officials and their families across the four-mile stretch to the nearest tarred road. His standard charge per trip was six pounds and those who had the money were only glad to be rid of some of it in this way. At the end of a fortnight[3] he had made a small fortune of one hundred and fifteen pounds.

Then he made the journey to Enugu and found another miracle waiting for him. It was unbelievable. He rubbed his eyes and looked again and it was still standing there before him. But, needless to say, even that monumental blessing must be accounted also totally inferior to the five heads in the family. This newest miracle was his little house in Ogui Overside. Indeed nothing puzzles God! Only two houses away a huge concrete edifice some wealthy contractor had put up just before the war was a mountain of rubble. And here was Jonathan's little zinc house of no regrets built with mud blocks quite intact! Of course the doors and windows were missing and five sheets off the roof. But what was that? And anyhow he had returned to Enugu early enough to pick up bits of old zinc and wood and soggy sheets of cardboard lying around the neighborhood before thousands more came out of their forest holes looking for the same things. He got a <u>destitute</u> carpenter with one old hammer, a

---

1. biro (bī′ rō) *n.* British expression for "ballpoint pen."
2. Biafran (bē ăf′ rən) *adj.* of the rebellious southeastern region of Nigeria, which declared itself the independent Republic of Biafra in the civil war of 1967.
3. fortnight (fôrt′ nīt′) *n.* British English for "two weeks."

Literary Analysis
Theme What theme is suggested by Jonathan's gratitude for his family's survival?

Vocabulary Builder
disreputable (dis rep′ yōō tə bəl) *adj.* not respectable; having or deserving a bad reputation

Literary Analysis
Theme What do these stories of Jonathan's "blessings" have in common?

Vocabulary Builder
destitute (des′ tə tōōt′) *adj.* lacking the basic necessities of life; poverty-stricken

◀ **Critical Viewing**
Does the expression on this man's face suggest he has a personality similar to Jonathan's? Explain. **[Connect]**

blunt plane and a few bent and rusty nails in his tool bag to turn this assortment of wood, paper and metal into door and window shutters for five Nigerian shillings or fifty Biafran pounds. He paid the pounds, and moved in with his overjoyed family carrying five heads on their shoulders.

His children picked mangoes near the military cemetery and sold them to soldiers' wives for a few pennies—real pennies this time—and his wife started making breakfast akara balls[4] for neighbors in a hurry to start life again. With his family earnings he took his bicycle to the villages around and bought fresh palm-wine which he mixed generously in his rooms with the water which had recently started running again in the public tap down the road, and opened up a bar for soldiers and other lucky people with good money.

✔ Reading Check

How does Jonathan make money after the war?

---

4. **akara** (ə kär′ ə) **balls** *n.* deep-fried balls of ground beans.

At first he went daily, then every other day and finally once a week, to the offices of the Coal Corporation where he used to be a miner, to find out what was what. The only thing he did find out in the end was that that little house of his was even a greater blessing than he had thought. Some of his fellow ex-miners who had nowhere to return at the end of the day's waiting just slept outside the doors of the offices and cooked what meal they could scrounge together in Bournvita tins. As the weeks lengthened and still nobody could say what was what Jonathan discontinued his weekly visits altogether and faced his palm-wine bar.

But nothing puzzles God. Came the day of the windfall when after five days of endless scuffles in queues[5] and counterqueues in the sun outside the Treasury he had twenty pounds counted into his palms as ex-gratia[6] award for the rebel money he had turned in. It was like Christmas for him and for many others like him when the payments began. They called it (since few could manage its proper official name) *egg-rasher.*

As soon as the pound notes were placed in his palm Jonathan simply closed it tight over them and buried fist and money inside his trouser pocket. He had to be extra careful because he had seen a man a couple of days earlier collapse into near-madness in an instant before that oceanic crowd because no sooner had he got his twenty pounds than some heartless ruffian picked it off him. Though it was not right that a man in such an extremity of agony should be blamed yet many in the queues that day were able to remark quietly at the victim's carelessness, especially after he

---

5. **queues** (kyo͞oz) *n.* British English for "lines."
6. **ex-gratia** (eks grāˊ shē ə) as a favor (Latin).

pulled out the innards of his pocket and revealed a hole in it big enough to pass a thief's head. But of course he had insisted that the money had been in the other pocket, pulling it out too to show its comparative wholeness. So one had to be careful.

Jonathan soon transferred the money to his left hand and pocket so as to leave his right free for shaking hands should the need arise, though by fixing his gaze at such an elevation as to miss all approaching human faces he made sure that the need did not arise, until he got home.

He was normally a heavy sleeper but that night he heard all the neighborhood noises die down one after another. Even the night watchman who knocked the hour on some metal somewhere in the distance had fallen silent after knocking one o'clock. That must have been the last thought in Jonathan's mind before he was finally carried away himself. He couldn't have been gone for long, though, when he was violently awakened again.

"Who is knocking?" whispered his wife lying beside him on the floor.

"I don't know," he whispered back breathlessly.

The second time the knocking came it was so loud and imperious that the rickety old door could have fallen down.

"Who is knocking?" he asked them, his voice parched and trembling.

"Na tief-man and him people," came the cool reply. "Make you hopen de door."[7] This was followed by the heaviest knocking of all.

Maria was the first to raise the alarm, then he followed and all their children.

"Police-o! Thieves-o! Neighbors-o! Police-o! We are lost! We are dead! Neighbors, are you asleep? Wake up! Police-o!"

This went on for a long time and then stopped suddenly. Perhaps they had scared the thief away. There was total silence. But only for a short while.

"You done finish?" asked the voice outside. "Make we help you small. Oya, everybody!"

"Police-o! Tief-man-so! Neighbors-o! we done loss-o! Police-o! . . ."

There were at least five other voices besides the leader's.

Literature in Context

Geography Connection

Nigerian Civil War Jonathan is delighted that his home in Enugu still stands—and for good reason. Enugu was at the center of the civil war that broke out in Nigeria in 1967. The war began when the eastern region of Nigeria declared itself the independent Republic of Biafra, with Enugu as its capital. The city was invaded by Nigerian federal troops just five months after independence. The war resulted in horrific famine as well as violence. It ended in 1970 with the defeat of Biafra and the reunification of Nigeria.

Connect to the Literature

Which of Jonathan's experiences can you connect to events of the Nigerian Civil War? Explain.

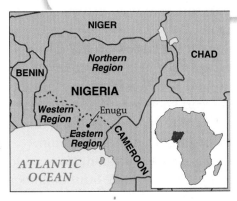

✓ Reading Check

What does Jonathan get in exchange for the rebel money he has saved?

---

7. **"Na tief-man . . hopen de door"** (dialect) "I am a thief with my accomplices. Open the door."

Jonathan and his family were now completely paralyzed by terror. Maria and the children sobbed inaudibly like lost souls. Jonathan groaned continuously.

The silence that followed the thieves' alarm vibrated horribly. Jonathan all but begged their leader to speak again and be done with it.

"My frien," said he at long last, "we don try our best for call dem but I tink say dem all done sleep-o . . . So wetin we go do now? Sometaim you wan call soja? Or you wan make we call dem for you? Soja better pass police. No be so?"

"Na so!" replied his men. Jonathan thought he heard even more voices now than before and groaned heavily. His legs were sagging under him and his throat felt like sandpaper.

"My frien, why you no de talk again. I de ask you say you wan make we call soja?"

"No."

"Awrighto. Now make we talk business. We no be bad tief. We no like for make trouble. Trouble done finish. War done finish and all the katakata wey de for inside. No Civil War again. This time na Civil Peace. No be so?"

"Na so!" answered the horrible chorus.

"What do you want from me? I am a poor man. Everything I had went with this war. Why do you come to me? You know people who have money. We . . ."

"Awright! We know say you no get plenty money. But we sef no get even anini. So derefore make you open dis window and give us one hundred pound and we go commot. Orderwise we de come for inside now to show you guitar-boy like dis . . ."

A volley of automatic fire rang through the sky. Maria and the children began to weep aloud again.

"Ah, missisi de cry again. No need for dat. We done talk say we na good tief. We just take our small money and go nwayorly. No molest. Abi we de molest?"

"At all!" sang the chorus.

"My friends," began Jonathan hoarsely. "I hear what you say and I thank you. If I had one hundred pounds . . ."

"Lookia my frien, no be play we come play for your house. If we make mistake and step for inside you no go like am-o. So derefore . . ."

"To God who made me; if you come inside and find one hundred pounds, take it and shoot me and shoot my wife and children. I swear to God. The only money I have in this life is this twenty-pounds *egg-rasher* they gave me today . . ."

▶ **Critical Viewing**
How does the contrast between this woman's clothing and the landscape reflect the contrast between Jonathan's outlook and his experiences? **[Connect]**

Reading Skill
Drawing Conclusions
Do Jonathan's experiences lead you to agree with the thief that "Trouble done finish" in Nigeria? Explain.

"Ok. Time de go. Make you open dis window and bring the twenty pound. We go manage am like dat."

There were now loud murmurs of dissent among the chorus: "Na lie de man de lie; e get plenty money . . . Make we go inside and search properly well . . . Wetin be twenty pound? . . ."

"Shurrup!" rang the leader's voice like a lone shot in the sky and silenced the murmuring at once. "Are you dere? Bring the money quick!"

"I am coming," said Jonathan fumbling in the darkness with the key of the small wooden box he kept by his side on the mat.

At the first sign of light as neighbors and others assembled to <u>commiserate</u> with him he was already strapping his five-gallon demijohn[8] to his bicycle carrier and his wife, sweating in the open fire, was turning over akara balls in a wide clay bowl of boiling oil. In the corner his eldest son was rinsing out dregs of yesterday's palm-wine from old beer bottles.

"I count it as nothing," he told his sympathizers, his eyes on the rope he was tying. "What is *egg-rasher?* Did I depend on it last week? Or is it greater than other things that went with the war? I say, let *egg-rasher* perish in the flames! Let it go where everything else has gone. Nothing puzzles God."

Vocabulary Builder
commiserate (kə miz′ ər āt′) *v.* sympathize (with); show sorrow for

---

8. demijohn (dem′ i jän′) *n.* large glass or earthenware bottle with a wicker cover.

Apply the Skills

Civil Peace

Thinking About the Selection

1. **Respond:** How did you react to Jonathan's encounter with thieves?
2. **(a) Recall:** What are the "five inestimable blessings" for which Jonathan is grateful? **(b) Infer:** In what sense has the war enhanced Jonathan's appreciation for his life?
3. **(a) Analyze:** Explain how Jonathan reacts to the damage to his house. **(b) Connect:** Considering the other damage the war has done, why might his reaction make sense?
4. **Infer:** By turning over the "egg-rasher" to the thieves, what does Jonathan hope to prevent from happening? Explain.
5. **(a) Infer:** What is Jonathan's reaction to the theft after it has occurred? Explain how you know. **(b) Connect:** In what way is this response consistent with his other responses to loss?
6. **(a) Compare and Contrast:** In what ways is the period the thieves call "Civil Peace" like a civil war? In what ways are they unlike? **(b) Discuss:** Share and discuss your answers with a partner. **(c) Assess:** Based on your discussion, how has your response grown or changed? Explain.

Literary Analysis

7. **(a)** Using a chart like the one shown, analyze the episodes that spark a response in Jonathan. **(b)** How are these episodes related? Are they similar or different? Does one lead to another? Explain. **(c)** State the **theme**, explaining how each event helps convey it.

Episode	Character's Response	Reasons for the Response	Result: Peace of Mind/Problems

8. Achebe makes the **philosophical assumption** that in order to survive, we must be able to let go of what we have lost. Explain what Jonathan might have done about the theft of the "egg-rasher" if he had refused to let go.

Reading Skill

9. **(a) Draw a conclusion** about the thieves' response to the losses of war based on what they say and do. **(b)** What key details support your conclusion? **(c)** Explain how the contrast between their response and Jonathan's adds to Achebe's theme.

Vocabulary Builder

Practice **Antonyms** are words with opposite meanings. Rewrite each sentence by replacing the word in italics with its antonym from the vocabulary list on page 306. You may need to change some other words in the sentence. Then, state which version makes the most sense and explain why.

1. We should not give charity to the most *wealthy.*

2. People go to this bank because it is *respectable.*

3. In times of joy, people may get together to *celebrate.*

Adding Words to Your Vocabulary Using a thesaurus, find one additional antonym for each of the words in the vocabulary list on page 306. Use each antonym correctly in a sentence. (For more on using a thesaurus, see page R7.)

Writing

Write a brief **character analysis** of Jonathan. In your analysis, identify his main traits. Give examples of incidents and descriptions in the story that show these traits. Use the following techniques:

- Use phrases such as *for example* to link supporting details to your main idea.
- Use transitional words such as *instead* to connect ideas.

For *Grammar, Vocabulary,* and *Assessment,* see **Build Language Skills,** pages 336–337.

Extend Your Learning

Listening and Speaking Hold a **group discussion** to decide how Achebe's theme does or does not apply to modern life. Begin by proposing and agreeing on a statement of the author's message. To aid the discussion, follow these tips:

- Express your ideas in understandable and nonoffensive ways.
- Add to others' ideas by giving examples that support them.
- Allow your ideas to be challenged by the contributions of others.

Research and Technology In a group, construct a series of **visual aids** with which you explain the civil war in Nigeria. Include a map showing the distribution of various tribes, as well as a timeline showing events from colonization through independence to the war. Present your final work to the class.

Build Language Skills

How Much Land Does a Man Need? • Civil Peace

Vocabulary Skill

Etymology The word *consequence* came into English from Old French, which had taken it from the Latin word *consequi*, meaning "follow after." A *consequence* is a result that follows a cause. *Consequently* is an adverb that means "following as a result of what came before."

Practice Using a dictionary, look up each of the following words. Compare and contrast the meaning, use, and history of each word to the meaning, use, and history of *consequently*. Then use each word in a sentence.

1. consecutive
2. sequential
3. inconsequential
4. consecutively
5. sequence

Grammar Lesson

Action and Linking Verbs An **action verb** shows physical or mental action. A **linking verb** expresses state of being or tells what the subject is by linking it to one or more words in the predicate.

> **Example:**
> **Action Verb:** Li *worries* about her grades. (shows mental action)
> **Linking Verb:** She *is* a good student. (links *She* to *good student*)

The most common linking verb is *be* in one of its forms—*is, are, was, were,* and so on. Other linking verbs include *feel* when used in a sentence like "I <u>feel</u> ill" and *grew* when used in a sentence like "He <u>grew</u> tall." To tell whether a verb is functioning as a linking verb, replace it with the appropriate form of *be*. If the sentence still makes sense, then the verb is a linking verb.

> **Example:**
> **Action Verb:** I *smelled* a rose. (cannot replace with a form of *be*)
> **Linking Verb:** The rose *smelled* fragrant. (can replace with *was*)

Practice Identify the verb in each sentence and tell whether it is an action verb or a linking verb.

1. Mrs. Lopez grows vegetables and flowers in her garden.
2. The colors of the flowers are lovely.
3. The tomatoes taste delicious.
4. Each year, the garden grows larger.
5. She really enjoys her hobby.

MorePractice

For more practice with action and linking verbs, see Grammar Handbook, p. R40.

*W*G *Prentice Hall Writing and Grammar Connection: Chapter 16, Part 3*

Monitor Your Progress

Test Practice

Standards
Assessed

- 10.2.4
- 10.3.5
- 10.3.9

Reading: Draw Conclusions

Directions: *Read the selection. Then, answer the questions.
At the age of seven, Mari Djata still does not walk. Sassouma
insults Mari Djata's mother, Sogolon, saying that her son cannot
bring her leaves from the baobab tree as other sons do. To prove
Sassouma wrong, Mari Djata has a giant iron rod made for him.*

With a violent jerk he threw his weight on [the iron bar]
and his knees left the ground. . . . In a great effort he straightened up and was on his feet at one go—but the great bar of
iron was twisted and had taken the form of a bow! . . .

Behind Niani there was a young baobab tree and it was there that the
children of the town came to pick leaves for their mothers. With all his
might the son of Sogolon tore up the tree. . . .

—from *Sundiata: An Epic of Old Mali* by D. T. Niane

1. What is the baobab tree a symbol of?
   A nature
   B childhood
   C personal achievement
   D physical beauty

2. What is a likely theme of the selection?
   A Do not judge a person's worth hastily.
   B Pride can lead to destruction.
   C Beauty is in the eye of the beholder.
   D Weak children become weak leaders.

3. The reader can conclude that
   A Mari Djata was lazy.
   B Mari Djata was not well liked.
   C Mari Djata was very strong.
   D Mari Djata was a braggart.

4. Mari Djata is also called
   A son of Sassouma.
   B Niani.
   C son of Sogolon.
   D young baobab.

5. The reader can conclude that baobab leaves
   A are part of a coming-of-age ritual.
   B are important in this culture.
   C give people strength.
   D had healing properties.

Timed Writing: Exposition [Critical Stance]

Discuss how a symbol in either "Civil Peace" or "How Much Land Does
a Man Need?" helps convey the story's theme. State the theme and give
details to show how the symbol supports this theme. **(25 minutes)**

Writing Workshop: *Work in Progress*

Problem-and-Solution Essay

For an essay you may write, define a problem that you see in your
school. Use this problem as the central circle of a web and web all the
possible solutions. Put this work in your writing portfolio.

Practice these skills with either "The Masque of the Red Death" (p. 340) or "The Garden of Stubborn Cats" (p. 351).

IN Academic Standards

- Evaluate the use of literary devices including figurative language, imagery, allegory, and symbolism. (10.3.7)
- Write for different purposes and audiences. (10.5.8)

Literary Analysis

Symbolism is a writer's use of symbols. A **symbol** is a character, a place, a thing, or an event in a literary work that stands for a larger idea. For example, a dog in a story may stand for loyalty. To make something into a symbol, a writer may use these strategies:

- Call on traditional associations—a dog is a symbol of loyalty because dogs are often praised for that virtue.
- Create new associations—if the dog in the story runs away when its owner betrays a friend, a connection is made because both loyalty and the dog "disappear" at the same time.

A story in which all characters, settings, and events are clearly symbolic is called an **allegory.** Use a diagram like this one to identify details that show that an object or a character symbolizes a larger meaning.

Reading Skill

When you **draw a conclusion,** you make a decision or form an opinion based on facts and details in a text. To draw a conclusion about the meaning of a symbol, **identify patterns** that suggest its larger meaning.

- Consider the repeated actions, qualities, and other details that the work associates with the symbol.
- Make a logical guess about the meaning of the symbol—the meaning that best explains its role in the work.

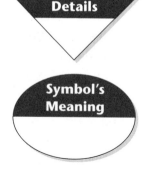

Vocabulary Builder

The Masque of the Red Death

- **august** (ô gust´) *adj.* impressive; majestic (p. 341) *The king was an __august__ figure when he sat on his throne.*
- **impeded** (im pēd´ id) *v.* blocked; obstructed (p. 341) *The pillar __impeded__ my ability to see the screen.*
- **cessation** (se sā´ shən) *n.* halt; stopping (p. 345) *After the sudden __cessation__ of the car alarm, the silence seemed deep.*

The Garden of Stubborn Cats

- **itinerary** (ī tin´ ər er´ ē) *n.* route; travel plan (p. 351) *As part of our __itinerary__, we will be in Cleveland on Sunday.*
- **intrigues** (in´ trēgz) *n.* plots; schemes (p. 352) *The twins whispered together and laughed, cooking up one of their __intrigues__.*
- **indigence** (in´ di jəns) *n.* poverty (p. 359) *Many lost their jobs, and the number of people living in __indigence__ grew.*

Build Understanding • *The Masque of the Red Death*

Background

The Black Death In the 1300s, a plague called the Black Death swept across Europe, killing as many as 25 million people. Most of those who caught the disease died within three to five days after their symptoms appeared. Subsequent outbreaks of plague continued in Europe until recent times. Poe invented the "Red Death" for this story, but his tale plays on an age-old fear.

Connecting to the Literature

Reading/Writing Connection The prince in Poe's story tries to escape the Red Death by locking the doors of his palace—but that may not be enough. Write a few sentences about the risks of hiding from problems. Use at least three of the these words: *guarantee, ignore, resolve, withdraw*.

READ MORE

by Edgar Allan Poe
"The Purloined Letter"
"The Tell-tale Heart"

Meet the Author

Edgar Allan **Poe** (1809–1849)

The son of traveling actors, Edgar Poe lost his mother at an early age. He was then raised by a wealthy Virginia family named Allan, from whom he took his middle name. After winning a writing contest with his story "MS. in a Bottle," Poe became a literary success, winning fame but not fortune. He died in poverty at the age of forty. Today, he is recognized as a master of the short story.

A Single Effect Poe believed that a work of fiction has the most impact if it can be read in one sitting and if all the elements work together to create a "single effect." He is best known for tales in which the single effect is horror. Poe also pioneered detective stories and science fiction.

Fast Facts

▶ The Mystery Writers of America call their annual awards "Edgars" in Poe's honor.
▶ Poe's room at the University of Virginia has been preserved as a mini-museum. The room number is thirteen.

Go Online
Author Link
For: More about the author
Visit: www.PHSchool.com
Web Code: eqe-9210

The Masque[1] of the Red Death

Edgar Allan Poe

The "Red Death" had long devastated the country. No pestilence had ever been so fatal, or so hideous. Blood was its Avatar[2] and its seal—the redness and the horror of blood. There

---

1. **Masque** (mask) *n.* ball at which costumes and masks are worn.
2. **Avatar** (av´ ə tär´) *n.* sign; outward manifestation of an unseen force.

were sharp pains, and sudden dizziness, and then profuse bleeding at the pores, with dissolution. The scarlet stains upon the body and especially upon the face of the victim, were the pest ban which shut him out from the aid and from the sympathy of his fellow men. And the whole seizure, progress and termination of the disease, were the incidents of half an hour.

But the Prince Prospero was happy and dauntless and sagacious. When his dominions were half depopulated, he summoned to his presence a thousand hale and lighthearted friends from among the knights and dames of his court, and with these retired to the deep seclusion of one of his castellated abbeys.[3] This was an extensive and magnificent structure, the creation of the prince's own eccentric yet <u>august</u> taste. A strong and lofty wall girdled it in. This wall had gates of iron. The courtiers, having entered, brought furnaces and massy hammers and welded the bolts. They resolved to leave means neither of ingress or egress[4] to the sudden impulses of despair or frenzy from within. The abbey was amply provisioned. With such precautions the courtiers might bid defiance to contagion. The external world could take care of itself. In the meantime it was folly to grieve, or to think. The prince had provided all the appliances of pleasure. There were buffoons, there were improvisatori, there were ballet dancers, there were musicians, there was Beauty, there was wine. All these and security were within. Without was the "Red Death."

It was toward the close of the fifth or sixth month of his seclusion, and while the pestilence raged most furiously abroad, that the Prince Prospero entertained his thousand friends at a masked ball of the most unusual magnificence.

It was a voluptuous scene, that masquerade. But first let me tell of the rooms in which it was held. There were seven—an imperial suite. In many palaces, however, such suites form a long and straight vista, while the folding doors slide back nearly to the walls on either hand, so that the view of the whole extent is scarcely <u>impeded</u>. Here the case was very different; as might have been expected from the duke's love of the bizarre. The apartments were so irregularly disposed that the vision embraced but little more than one at a time. There was a sharp turn at every twenty or thirty yards, and at each turn a novel effect. To the right and left, in the middle of each wall, a tall and narrow Gothic window looked out upon a closed corridor which pursued the windings of the suite. These windows were of stained glass whose color varied in accordance with the prevailing

---

3. **castellated abbeys** (kas′ tə lāt′ id ab′ ēz) monasteries or convents (religious retreats) with towers like those of a castle.
4. **ingress** (in′ gres′) **or egress** (ē′ gres′) entry or exit.

Vocabulary Builder
august (ô gust′) *adj.* impressive; majestic

Reading Skill
Drawing Conclusions
What details here support the conclusion that the prince thinks he can escape the plague?

Vocabulary Builder
impeded (im pēd′ id) *v.* blocked; obstructed

✓ **Reading Check**
Why has Prince Prospero locked himself and his guests in his castle?

hue of the decorations of the chamber into which it opened. That at the eastern extremity was hung, for example, in blue—and vividly blue were its windows. The second chamber was purple in its ornaments and tapestries, and here the panes were purple. The third was green throughout, and so were the casements. The fourth was furnished and lighted with orange—the fifth with white—the sixth with violet. The seventh apartment was closely shrouded in black velvet tapestries that hung all over the ceiling and down the walls, falling in heavy folds upon a carpet of the same material and hue. But in this chamber only, the color of the windows failed to correspond with the decorations. The panes here were scarlet—a deep blood color.

Now in no one of the seven apartments was there any lamp or candelabrum amid the profusion of golden ornaments that lay scattered to and fro or depended from the roof. There was no light of any kind emanating from lamp or candle within the suite of chambers. But in the corridors that followed the suite, there stood, opposite to each window, a heavy tripod, bearing a brazier[5] of fire that projected its rays through the tinted glass and so glaringly illumined the room. And thus were produced a multitude of gaudy and fantastic appearances. But in the western or black chamber the effect of the firelight that streamed upon the dark hangings through the blood-tinted panes, was ghastly in the extreme, and produced so wild a look upon the countenances of those who entered, that there were few of the company bold enough to set foot within its precincts at all.

It was in this apartment, also, that there stood against the western wall a gigantic clock of ebony.[6] Its pendulum swung to and fro with a dull, heavy, monotonous clang; and when the minute-hand made the circuit of the face, and the hour was to be stricken, there came from the brazen lungs of the clock a sound which was clear and loud and deep and exceedingly musical, but of so peculiar a

Reading Skill
Drawing Conclusions
Judging from the title of the story and the colors of the seventh room, what might the room represent?

---

5. **brazier** (brā′ zhər) *n.* metal pan or bowl used to hold burning coals.
6. **ebony** (eb′ ə nē) *n.* the black or dark wood of certain trees.

note and emphasis that, at each lapse of an hour, the musicians of the orchestra were constrained to pause, momentarily, in their performance, to hearken to the sound; and thus the waltzers perforce ceased their evolutions; and there was a brief disconcert[7] of the whole gay company; and, while the chimes of the clock yet rang, it was observed that the giddiest grew pale, and the more aged and sedate passed their hands over their brows as if in confused reverie or meditation. But when the echoes had fully ceased, a light laughter at once pervaded the assembly; the musicians looked at each other and smiled as if at their own nervousness and folly, and made whispering vows, each to the other, that the next chiming of the clock should produce in them no similar emotion; and then, after the lapse of sixty minutes, (which embrace three thousand and six hundred seconds of the Time that flies), there came yet another chiming of the clock, and then were the same disconcert and tremulousness and meditation as before.

But, in spite of these things, it was a gay and magnificent revel. The tastes of the duke were peculiar. He had a fine eye for colors and effects. He disregarded the decora of mere fashion. His plans

▲ **Critical Viewing**
What details does this scene share with the masque in the story? What differences can you find? **[Compare and Contrast]**

✓ **Reading Check**

How do the partygoers and musicians react when the clock strikes?

---

7. disconcert (dis kän´ surt) *n.* embarrassment; confusion.

The Masque of the Red Death ■ 343

▲ Critical Viewing
Does this painting
capture the mood of
the masque as Poe
describes it? Support
your answer.
[Interpret]

were bold and fiery, and his conceptions glowed with barbaric luster. There are some who would have thought him mad. His followers
felt that he was not. It was necessary to hear and see and touch him
to be *sure* that he was not.

He had directed, in great part, the movable embellishments of
the seven chambers, upon occasion of this great fête; and it was his
own guiding taste which had given character to the masqueraders.
Be sure they were grotesque.[8] There were much glare and glitter
and piquancy and phantasm—much of what has been since seen in
Hernani.[9] There were arabesque figures with unsuited limbs and
appointments. There were delirious fancies such as the madman
fashions. There was much of the beautiful, much of the wanton,
much of the bizarre, something of the terrible, and not a little of

---

8. grotesque (grō tesk´) *adj.* fantastic; distorted; bizarre; marked by strange mismatches of
characteristics.
9. *Hernani* (hʉr nä´ nē) extravagant drama by the French author Victor Hugo.

that which might have excited disgust. To and fro in the seven chambers there stalked, in fact, a multitude of dreams. And these— the dreams—writhed in and about, taking hue from the rooms, and causing the wild music of the orchestra to seem as the echo of their steps. And, anon, there strikes the ebony clock which stands in the hall of the velvet. And then, for a moment, all is still, and all is silent save the voice of the clock. The dreams are stiff-frozen as they stand. But the echoes of the chime die away—they have endured but an instant—and a light, half-subdued laughter floats after them as they depart. And now again the music swells, and the dreams live, and writhe to and fro more merrily than ever, taking hue from the many-tinted windows through which stream the rays from the tripods. But to the chamber which lies most westwardly of the seven, there are now none of the maskers who venture; for the night is waning away; and there flows a ruddier light through the blood-colored panes; and the blackness of the sable[10] drapery appalls; and to him whose foot falls upon the sable carpet, there comes from the near clock of ebony a muffled peal more solemnly emphatic than any which reaches *their* ears who indulge in the more remote gaieties of the other apartments.

But these other apartments were densely crowded, and in them beat feverishly the heart of life. And the revel went whirlingly on, until at length there commenced the sounding of midnight upon the clock. And then the music ceased, as I have told; and the evolutions of the waltzers were quieted; and there was an uneasy cessation of all things as before. But now there were twelve strokes to be sounded by the bell of the clock; and thus it happened, perhaps, that more of thought crept, with more of time, into the meditations of the thoughtful among those who reveled. And thus, too, it happened, perhaps, that before the last echoes of the last chime had utterly sunk into silence, there were many individuals in the crowd who had found leisure to become aware of the presence of a masked figure which had arrested the attention of no single individual before. And the rumor of this new presence having spread itself whisperingly around, there arose at length from the whole company a buzz, or murmur, expressive of disapprobation and surprise— then, finally, of terror, of horror, and of disgust.

In an assembly of phantasms such as I have painted, it may well be supposed that no ordinary appearance could have excited such sensation. In truth the masquerade license of the night was nearly unlimited; but the figure in question had out-Heroded Herod,[11] and

---

10. **sable** (sā´ bəl) *adj.* black; made of the black fur of the marten, an animal in the weasel family.
11. **out-Heroded Herod** (her´ əd) behaved even more excessively than Herod, a Biblical figure noted for his shocking acts.

Reading Skill
Drawing Conclusions
What does the contrast between activities in the first six rooms and the last one suggest about the symbolic meaning of this room?

Vocabulary Builder
cessation (se sā´ shən) *n.* halt; stopping

Reading Check

Who draws the attention of the revelers?

gone beyond the bounds of even the prince's indefinite decorum. There are chords in the hearts of the most reckless which cannot be touched without emotion. Even with the utterly lost, to whom life and death are equally jests, there are matters of which no jest can be made. The whole company, indeed, seemed now deeply to feel that in the costume and bearing of the stranger neither wit nor propriety existed. The figure was tall and gaunt, and shrouded from head to foot in the habiliments[12] of the grave. The mask which concealed the visage was made so nearly to resemble the countenance of a stiffened corpse that the closest scrutiny must have had difficulty in detecting the cheat. And yet all this might have been endured, if not approved, by the mad revelers around. But the mummer[13] had gone so far as to assume the type of the Red Death. His vesture was dabbled in *blood*—and his broad brow, with all the features of the face, was besprinkled with the scarlet horror.

When the eyes of Prince Prospero fell upon this spectral image (which with a slow and solemn movement, as if more fully to sustain its role, stalked to and fro among the waltzers) he was seen to be convulsed, in the first moment with a strong shudder either of terror or distaste; but, in the next, his brow reddened with rage.

"Who dares?" he demanded hoarsely of the courtiers who stood near him—"who dares insult us with this blasphemous mockery? Seize him and unmask him—that we may know whom we have to hang at sunrise, from the battlements!"

It was in the eastern or blue chamber in which stood the Prince Prospero as he uttered these words. They rang throughout the seven rooms loudly and clearly—for the prince was a bold and

---

12. **habiliments** (hə bil´ ə mənts) *n.* clothing.
13. **mummer** (mum´ ər) *n.* masked and costumed person.

▼ Critical Viewing In what way does this image express the fears of the revelers? **[Connect]**

robust man, and the music had become hushed at the waving of his hand.

It was in the blue room where stood the prince, with a group of pale courtiers by his side. At first, as he spoke, there was a slight rushing movement of this group in the direction of the intruder, who at the moment was also near at hand, and now, with deliberate and stately step, made closer approach to the speaker. But from a certain nameless awe with which the mad assumptions of the mummer had inspired the whole party, there were found none who put forth hand to seize him; so that, unimpeded, he passed within a yard of the prince's person; and, while the vast assembly, as if with one impulse, shrank from the centers of the rooms to the walls, he made his way uninterruptedly, but with the same solemn and measured step which had distinguished him from the first, through the blue chamber to the purple—through the purple to the green— through the green to the orange—through this again to the white— and even thence to the violet, ere a decided movement had been made to arrest him. It was then, however, that the Prince Prospero, maddening with rage and the shame of his own momentary coward-ice, rushed hurriedly through the six chambers, while none followed him on account of a deadly terror that had seized upon all. He bore aloft a drawn dagger, and had approached, in rapid impetuosity, to within three or four feet of the retreating figure, when the latter, having attained the extremity of the velvet apartment, turned suddenly and confronted his pursuer. There was a sharp cry—and the dagger dropped gleaming upon the sable carpet, upon which, instantly afterwards, fell prostrate in death the Prince Prospero. Then, summoning the wild courage of despair, a throng of the revel-ers at once threw themselves into the black apartment, and, seizing the mummer, whose tall figure stood erect and motionless within the shadow of the ebony clock, gasped in unutterable horror at find-ing the grave cerements[14] and corpselike mask which they handled with so violent a rudeness, untenanted by any tangible form.

And now was acknowledged the presence of the Red Death. He had come like a thief in the night. And one by one dropped the revelers in the blood-bedewed halls of their revel, and died each in the despairing posture of his fall. And the life of the ebony clock went out with that of the last of the gay. And the flames of the tripods expired. And Darkness and Decay and the Red Death held illimitable dominion over all.

Literary Analysis
Symbolism How does the use of a number of symbols—the black room, the clock, the uninvited guest— show that the story is an allegory?

---

14. cerements (ser´ ə mənts) *n.* burial wrapping for a corpse; shroud.

Apply the Skills

The Masque of the Red Death

Thinking About the Selection

1. **Respond:** Would you like the prince as a friend? Explain.
2. **(a) Recall:** Why does Prince Prospero hide in his palace?
   (b) Contrast: Contrast life outside the palace with life inside it.
3. **(a) Recall:** Briefly describe the rooms in which the masquerade is held. **(b) Infer:** What does the design of the rooms suggest about the prince's tastes and values?
4. **(a) Interpret:** Why does the prince decide to hold the masquerade? **(b) Evaluate:** What does the prince's response to the Red Death suggest about the kind of person he is? Explain.
5. **(a) Analyze:** What message do you think Poe conveys in this story? Support your answer. **(b) Discuss:** Share your answers in a small group. **(c) Evaluate:** As a group, choose the two best-supported ideas. Present them to the class, explaining why you agreed on the two.

Literary Analysis

6. In the story, the uninvited guest might be interpreted as a **symbol** of death. **(a)** Describe two responses of the partygoers to the stranger. **(b)** Explain how these responses are similar to ones associated with death.
7. Identify two other details supporting this interpretation of the stranger.
8. This story can be read as an **allegory.** Explain what the ability of the uninvited guest to enter a fortified palace might symbolize.

Reading Skill

9. **(a)** In a chart like the one shown, identify the pattern of details that shows the importance of the clock. **(b)** Based on your chart, **draw a conclusion** about what the clock symbolizes.
10. Review the description of each of the seven rooms. Based on the patterns you find, what do you think the progression of rooms symbolizes? Explain.

QuickReview

Story at a Glance
A prince tries to shield himself and his friends from the plague that ravages his country.

Go **Online**
——**Assessment**
For: Self-test
Visit: www.PHSchool.com
Web Code: eqa-6209

Symbol: a character, a place, a thing, or an event that stands for a larger idea

Symbolism: a writer's use of symbols in a literary work

Allegory: a story in which all characters, events, and settings are symbolic

Conclusion: a decision or an opinion based on facts and details in a text

Vocabulary Builder

Practice Synonyms are words with similar meanings, such as *happy* and *jolly*. For each set of words below, choose the word that is *not* a synonym for the other two words. Explain your choices.

1. august; dignified; anguished
2. aided; hindered; impeded
3. end; cessation; hesitation

Adding Words to Your Vocabulary Use a dictionary to find another form of these words from the vocabulary list: *impeded* and *cessation*. For example, you might find a noun form for the verb and a verb form for the noun. Use each new word correctly in a sentence. (For more on using a dictionary, see page R6.)

Writing

Poe turns a simple clock into a symbol of doom. Write a brief **narrative** using another object as a symbol. To show what the object stands for, follow these steps:

- Use vivid adjectives to suggest the qualities it symbolizes.
- Provide information about its location and actions.
- Link it to important events.

For *Grammar, Vocabulary*, and *Assessment*, see **Build Language Skills,** pages 364–365.

Extend Your Learning

Listening and Speaking In an *impromptu presentation,* a person speaks without rehearsal or a script. Give an **impromptu speech** to describe one way that modern people, like the guests in the story, can avoid facing their own limitations. For instance, you might describe a fad for plastic surgery or for video games in which players take on powerful roles. When you present your speech, speak slowly and confidently. In addition, project your voice.

Research and Technology Conduct research to learn more about Poe's influence on either mysteries or on detective fiction. Then, present your findings to the class in a **research summary.** Be sure to choose words suited to your audience and to explain literary terms such as *whodunit* and *ratiocination*.

Background

Marcovaldo This story is one of the interrelated short stories in Italo Calvino's *Marcovaldo: or The Seasons in the City.* Set in a grim Italian industrial city in the 1950s and 1960s, the collection presents the adventures of Marcovaldo, an ordinary working man, as he uses his imagination to escape his surroundings.

Connecting to the Literature

Reading/Writing Connection As Marcovaldo discovers, the unexpected can spring up in the most humdrum places. Jot a few notes about a street, path, shop, garden, or another place in your neighborhood that you have only just discovered. Use at least three of these words: *appeal, capture, contradict, emerge.*

Review

For **Literary Analysis, Reading Skill,** and **Vocabulary Builder,** see page 338.

READ MORE

by Italo Calvino
Italian Folktales
Invisible Cities

Meet the Author

Italo **Calvino** (1923–1985)

The son of two Italian botanists, Italo Calvino was born in Cuba. He grew up in San Remo on the Italian Riviera and began his literary career in the Italian city of Turin.

A Writer of Fables According to Calvino, "A classic is a book that has never finished saying what it has to say." In this sense, Calvino's own works are classics. They say much more than appears on the page.

Though his ideas are complex, Calvino conveys them using events and characters as simple as those in a fable or fairy tale. Like a good fable, his stories blend reality and fantasy.

Fast Facts

▶ During World War II, Calvino joined the Italian Resistance to fight the fascist dictatorship that had overrun Italy.

▶ Calvino met his wife, who came from Argentina, when she was working as a translator in Paris.

Go **Online**
—Author Link

For: More about the author
Visit: www.PHSchool.com
Web Code: eqe-9211

The Garden Of Stubborn Cats

Italo Calvino   Translated by William Weaver

The city of cats and the city of men exist one inside the other, but they are not the same city. Few cats recall the time when there was no distinction: the streets and squares of men were also streets and squares of cats, and the lawns, courtyards, balconies, and fountains: you lived in a broad and various space. But for several generations now domestic felines have been prisoners of an uninhabitable city: the streets are uninterruptedly overrun by the mortal traffic of cat-crushing automobiles; in every square foot of terrain where once a garden extended or a vacant lot or the ruins of an old demolition, now condominiums loom up, welfare housing, brand-new skyscrapers; every entrance is crammed with parked cars; the courtyards, one by one, have been roofed by reinforced concrete and transformed into garages or movie houses or storerooms or workshops. And where a rolling plateau of low roofs once extended, copings, terraces, water tanks, balconies, skylights, corrugated-iron sheds, now one general superstructure rises wherever structures can rise; the intermediate differences in height, between the low ground of the street and the supernal[1] heaven of the penthouses, disappear; the cat of a recent litter seeks in vain the <u>itinerary</u> of its fathers, the point from which to make the soft leap from balustrade to cornice to drainpipe, or for the quick climb on the roof-tiles.

Literary Analysis
Symbolism What associations with cats is the author creating?

Vocabulary Builder
itinerary (ī tin´ ər er´ ē)
n. route; travel plan

---

1. supernal (sōō pʉr´ nəl) *adj.* of the heavens; divine.

But in this vertical city, in this compressed city where all voids tend to fill up and every block of cement tends to mingle with other blocks of cement, a kind of counter-city opens, a negative city, that consists of empty slices between wall and wall, of the minimal distances ordained by the building regulations between two constructions, between the rear of one construction and the rear of the next; it is a city of cavities, wells, air conduits, driveways, inner yards, accesses to basements, like a network of dry canals on a planet of stucco and tar, and it is through this network, grazing the walls, that the ancient cat population still scurries.

On occasion, to pass the time, Marcovaldo would follow a cat. It was during the work-break, between noon and three, when all the personnel except Marcovaldo went home to eat, and he—who brought his lunch in his bag—laid his place among the packing-cases in the warehouse, chewed his snack, smoked a half-cigar, and wandered around, alone and idle, waiting for work to resume. In those hours, a cat that peeped in at a window was always welcome company, and a guide for new explorations. He had made friends with a tabby, well fed, a blue ribbon around its neck, surely living with some well-to-do family. This tabby shared with Marcovaldo the habit of an afternoon stroll right after lunch; and naturally a friendship sprang up.

Following his tabby friend, Marcovaldo had started looking at places as if through the round eyes of a cat and even if these places were the usual environs of his firm he saw them in a different light, as settings for cattish stories, with connections practicable only by light, velvety paws. Though from the outside the neighborhood seemed poor in cats, every day on his rounds Marcovaldo made the acquaintance of some new face, and a miau, a hiss, a stiffening of fur on an arched back was enough for him to sense ties and intrigues and rivalries among them. At those moments he thought he had already penetrated the secrecy of the felines' society: and then he felt himself scrutinized by pupils that became slits, under the surveillance of the antennae of taut whiskers, and all the cats around him sat impassive as sphinxes, the pink triangles of their noses convergent on the black triangles of their lips, and the only things that moved were the tips of the ears, with a vibrant jerk like radar. They reached the end of a narrow passage, between squalid blank walls; and, looking around, Marcovaldo saw that the cats that had led him this far had vanished, all of them together, no telling in which direction, even his tabby friend, and they had left him alone. Their realm had territories, ceremonies, customs that it was not yet granted to him to discover.

Reading Skill
Drawing Conclusions
Which details here support the conclusion that cats are not fully at home in the city?

Vocabulary Builder
intrigues (in´ trēgz) *n.* plots; schemes

◄ **Critical Viewing**
In what way does this picture, like the story, express the idea of multiple perspectives on the world? **[Interpret]**

On the other hand, from the cat city there opened unsuspected peepholes onto the city of men: and one day the same tabby led him to discover the great Biarritz Restaurant.

Anyone wishing to see the Biarritz Restaurant had only to assume the posture of a cat, that is, proceed on all fours. Cat and man, in this fashion, walked around a kind of dome, at whose foot some low, rectangular little windows opened. Following the tabby's example, Marcovaldo looked down. They were transoms through which the luxurious hall received air and light. To the sound of gypsy violins, partridges and quails swirled by on silver dishes balanced by the white-gloved fingers of waiters in tailcoats. Or, more precisely, above the partridges and quails the dishes whirled, and above the dishes the white gloves, and poised on the waiters' patent-leather shoes, the gleaming parquet floor, from which hung dwarf potted palms and tablecloths and crystal and buckets like bells with the champagne bottle for their clapper: everything was turned upside-down because Marcovaldo, for fear of being seen, wouldn't stick his head inside the window and confined himself to looking at the reversed reflection of the room in the tilted pane.

 **Reading Check**

To what place does Marcovaldo follow the tabby?

But it was not so much the windows of the dining-room as those of the kitchens that interested the cat: looking through the former you saw, distant and somehow transfigured, what in the kitchens presented itself—quite concrete and within paw's reach—as a plucked bird or a fresh fish. And it was toward the kitchens, in fact, that the tabby wanted to lead Marcovaldo, either through a gesture of altruistic friendship or else because it counted on the man's help for one of its raids. Marcovaldo, however, was reluctant to leave his belvedere over the main room: first as he was fascinated by the luxury of the place, and then because something down there had riveted his attention. To such an extent that, overcoming his fear of being seen, he kept peeking in, with his head in the transom.

In the midst of the room, directly under that pane, there was a little glass fish tank, a kind of aquarium, where some fat trout were swimming. A special customer approached, a man with a shiny bald pate, black suit, black beard. An old waiter in tailcoat followed him, carrying a little net as if he were going to catch butterflies. The gentleman in black looked at the trout with a grave, intent air; then he raised one hand and with a slow, solemn gesture singled out a fish. The waiter dipped the net into the tank, pursued the appointed trout, captured it, headed for the kitchens, holding out in front of him, like a lance, the net in which the fish wriggled. The gentleman in black, solemn as a magistrate[2] who has handed down a capital sentence, went to take his seat and wait for the return of the trout, sautéed "à la meunière."[3]

If I found a way to drop a line from up here and make one of those trout bite, Marcovaldo thought, I couldn't be accused of theft; at worst, of fishing in an unauthorized place. And ignoring the miaus that called him toward the kitchens, he went to collect his fishing tackle.

Nobody in the crowded dining room of the Biarritz saw the long, fine line, armed with hook and bait, as it slowly dropped into the tank. The fish saw the bait, and flung themselves on it. In the fray one trout managed to bite the worm: and immediately it began to rise, rise, emerge from the water, a silvery flash, it darted up high,

---

2. magistrate (maj´ is trāt´) *n.* judge.
3. sautéed "à la meunière" (sô tād´ ä lä mə nyer´) rolled in flour, fried in butter, and sprinkled with lemon juice and chopped parsley.

over the laid tables and the trolleys of hors d'oeuvres, over the blue flames of the crêpes Suzette, until it vanished into the heavens of the transom.

Marcovaldo had yanked the rod with the brisk snap of the expert fisherman, so the fish landed behind his back. The trout had barely touched the ground when the cat sprang. What little life the trout still had was lost between the tabby's teeth. Marcovaldo, who had abandoned his line at that moment to run and grab the fish, saw it snatched from under his nose, hook and all. He was quick to put one foot on the rod, but the snatch had been so strong that the rod was all the man had left, while the tabby ran off with the fish, pulling the line after it. Treacherous kitty! It had vanished.

But this time it wouldn't escape him: there was that long line trailing after him and showing the way he had taken. Though he had lost sight of the cat, Marcovaldo followed the end of the line: there it was, running along a wall; it climbed a parapet, wound through a doorway, was swallowed up by a basement . . . Marcovaldo, venturing into more and more cattish places, climbed roofs, straddled railings, always managed to catch a glimpse—perhaps only a second before it disappeared—of that moving trace that indicated the thief's path.

Now the line played out down a sidewalk, in the midst of the traffic, and Marcovaldo, running after it, almost managed to grab it. He flung himself down on his belly: there, he grabbed it! He managed to seize one end of the line before it slipped between the bars of a gate.

Beyond a half-rusted gate and two bits of wall buried under climbing plants, there was a little rank[4] garden, with a small, abandoned-looking building at the far end of it. A carpet of dry leaves covered the path, and dry leaves lay everywhere under the boughs of the two plane-trees, forming actually some little mounds in the yard. A layer of leaves was yellowing in the green water of a pool. Enormous buildings rose all around, skyscrapers with thousands of windows, like so many eyes trained disapprovingly on that little square patch with two trees, a few tiles, and all those yellow leaves, surviving right in the middle of an area of great traffic.

And in this garden, perched on the capitals and balustrades, lying on the dry leaves of the flowerbeds, climbing on the trunks of the trees or on the drainpipes, motionless on their four paws, their tails making a question-mark, seated to wash their faces, there were tiger cats, black cats, white cats, calico cats, tabbies, angoras, Persians, house cats and stray cats, perfumed cats and mangy cats. Marcovaldo realized he had finally reached the heart of the cats' realm, their secret island. And, in his emotion, he almost forgot his fish.

Literary Analysis
Symbolism Which details reinforce the contrast between a cat's view of the city and a human's view?

Reading Check

Where does the tabby finally lead Marcovaldo?

---

4. rank (raŋk) *adj.* growing vigorously and coarsely.

It had remained, that fish, hanging by the line from the branch of a tree, out of reach of the cats' leaps; it must have dropped from its kidnapper's mouth at some clumsy movement, perhaps as it was defended from the others, or perhaps displayed as an extraordinary prize. The line had got tangled, and Marcovaldo, tug as he would, couldn't manage to yank it loose. A furious battle had meanwhile been joined among the cats, to reach that unreachable fish, or rather, to win the right to try and reach it. Each wanted to prevent the others from leaping: they hurled themselves on one another, they tangled in midair, they rolled around clutching each other, and finally a general war broke out in a whirl of dry, crackling leaves.

After many futile yanks, Marcovaldo now felt the line was free, but he took care not to pull it: the trout would have fallen right in the midst of that infuriated scrimmage of felines.

It was at this moment that, from the top of the walls of the gardens, a strange rain began to fall: fish-bones, heads, tails, even bits of lung and lights.[5] Immediately the cats' attention was distracted from the suspended trout and they flung themselves on the new delicacies. To Marcovaldo, this seemed the right moment to pull the line and regain his fish. But, before he had time to act, from

---

5. lights term for animal organs used for catfood.

▲ **Critical Viewing**
Compare what a cat might find interesting about this scene with what a person might. **[Compare and Contrast]**

a blind of the little villa, two yellow, skinny hands darted out: one was brandishing scissors; the other, a frying pan. The hand with the scissors was raised above the trout, the hand with the frying pan was thrust under it. The scissors cut the line, the trout fell into the pan; hands, scissors and pan withdrew, the blind closed: all in the space of a second. Marcovaldo was totally bewildered.

"Are you also a cat lover?" A voice at his back made him turn round. He was surrounded by little old women, some of them ancient, wearing old-fashioned hats on their heads; others, younger, but with the look of spinsters; and all were carrying in their hands or their bags packages of leftover meat or fish, and some even had little pans of milk. "Will you help me throw this package over the fence, for those poor creatures?"

All the ladies, cat lovers, gathered at this hour around the garden of dry leaves to take the food to their protégés.[6]

"Can you tell me why they are all here, these cats?" Marcovaldo inquired.

"Where else could they go? This garden is all they have left! Cats come here from other neighborhoods, too, from miles and miles around . . ."

"And birds, as well," another lady added. "They're forced to live by the hundreds and hundreds on these few trees . . ."

"And the frogs, they're all in that pool, and at night they never stop croaking . . . You can hear them even on the eighth floor of the buildings around here."

"Who does this villa belong to anyway?" Marcovaldo asked. Now, outside the gate, there weren't just the cat-loving ladies but also other people: the man from the gas pump opposite, the apprentices

Reading Skill
Drawing Conclusions
Based on details of this event, what conclusion can you draw about whether the tabby has brought fish here before?

Reading Check

What happens to Marcovaldo's trout?

---

6. **protégés** (prōt´ ə zhāz´) *n.* those guided and helped by another.

from a mechanic's shop, the postman, the grocer, some passers-by. And none of them, men and women, had to be asked twice: all wanted to have their say, as always when a mysterious and controversial subject comes up.

"It belongs to a Marchesa.[7] She lives there, but you never see her . . ."

"She's been offered millions and millions, by developers, for this little patch of land, but she won't sell . . ."

"What would she do with millions, an old woman all alone in the world? She wants to hold on to her house, even if it's falling to pieces, rather than be forced to move . . ."

"It's the only undeveloped bit of land in the downtown area . . . Its value goes up every year . . . They've made her offers—"

"Offers! That's not all. Threats, intimidation, persecution . . . You don't know the half of it! Those contractors!"

"But she holds out. She's held out for years . . ."

"She's a saint. Without her, where would those poor animals go?"

"A lot she cares about the animals, the old miser! Have you ever seen her give them anything to eat?"

"How can she feed the cats when she doesn't have food for herself? She's the last descendant of a ruined family!"

"She hates cats. I've seen her chasing them and hitting them with an umbrella!"

"Because they were tearing up her flowerbeds!"

"What flowerbeds? I've never seen anything in this garden but a great crop of weeds!"

Marcovaldo realized that with regard to the old Marchesa opinions were sharply divided: some saw her as an angelic being, others as an egoist and a miser.

"It's the same with the birds; she never gives them a crumb!"

▲ **Critical Viewing**
Does this image, like the story, suggest that cats have secrets? Explain. **[Interpret]**

Literary Analysis
Symbolism What relationship with the city do the Marchesa and her property represent?

---

7. Marchesa (mär kā′ zä) *n.* title of an Italian noblewoman.

"She gives them hospitality. Isn't that plenty?"

"Like she gives the mosquitoes, you mean. They all come from here, from that pool. In the summertime the mosquitoes eat us alive, and it's all the fault of that Marchesa!"

"And the mice? This villa is a mine of mice. Under the dead leaves they have their burrows, and at night they come out . . ."

"As far as the mice go, the cats take care of them . . ."

"Oh, you and your cats! If we had to rely on them . . ."

"Why? Have you got something to say against cats?"

Here the discussion degenerated into a general quarrel.

"The authorities should do something: confiscate the villa!" one man cried.

"What gives them the right?" another protested.

"In a modern neighborhood like ours, a mouse-nest like this . . . it should be forbidden . . ."

"Why, I picked my apartment precisely because it overlooked this little bit of green . . ."

"Green, hell! Think of the fine skyscraper they could build here!"

Marcovaldo would have liked to add something of his own, but he couldn't get a word in. Finally, all in one breath, he exclaimed: "The Marchesa stole a trout from me!"

The unexpected news supplied fresh ammunition to the old woman's enemies, but her defenders exploited it as proof of the <u>indigence</u> to which the unfortunate noblewoman was reduced. Both sides agreed that Marcovaldo should go and knock at her door to demand an explanation.

It wasn't clear whether the gate was locked or unlocked; in any case, it opened, after a push, with a mournful creak. Marcovaldo picked his way among the leaves and cats, climbed the steps to the porch, knocked hard at the entrance.

At a window (the very one where the frying pan had appeared), the blind was raised slightly and in one corner a round, pale blue eye was seen, and a clump of hair dyed an undefinable color, and a dry skinny hand. A voice was heard, asking: "Who is it? Who's at the door?", the words accompanied by a cloud smelling of fried oil.

"It's me, Marchesa. The trout man," Marcovaldo explained. "I don't mean to trouble you. I only wanted to tell you, in case you didn't know, that the trout was stolen from me, by that cat, and I'm the one who caught it. In fact the line . . ."

"Those cats! It's always those cats . . ." the Marchesa said, from behind the shutter, with a shrill, somewhat nasal voice. "All my troubles come from the cats! Nobody knows what I go through! Prisoner night and day of those horrid beasts! And with all the refuse people throw over the walls, to spite me!"

Vocabulary Builder
indigence (in´ di jəns)
n. poverty

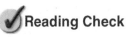

Reading Check

Who owns the garden where the cats gather?

"But my trout . . ."

"Your trout! What am I supposed to know about your trout!"
The Marchesa's voice became almost a scream, as if she wanted to
drown out the sizzle of oil in the pan, which came through the
window along with the aroma of fried fish. "How can I make sense of
anything, with all the stuff that rains into my house?"

"I understand, but did you take the trout or didn't you?"

"When I think of all the damage I suffer because of the cats! Ah,
fine state of affairs! I'm not responsible for anything! I can't tell you
what I've lost! Thanks to those cats, who've occupied house and
garden for years! My life at the mercy of those animals! Go and find
the owners! Make them pay damages! Damages? A whole life
destroyed! A prisoner here, unable to move a step!"

"Excuse me for asking: but who's forcing you to stay?"

From the crack in the blind there appeared sometimes a round,
pale blue eye, sometimes a mouth with two protruding teeth; for a
moment the whole face was visible, and to Marcovaldo it seemed,
bewilderingly, the face of a cat.

▲ **Critical Viewing**
Compare this image
with the garden in the
story, identifying one
similarity and one
difference. **[Compare
and Contrast]**

Reading Skill
Drawing Conclusions
Which details help you
draw the conclusion
that the Marchesa and
the cats stand for
similar ideas?

"They keep me prisoner, they do, those cats! Oh, I'd be glad to leave! What wouldn't I give for a little apartment all my own, in a nice clean modern building! But I can't go out . . . They follow me, they block my path, they trip me up!" The voice became a whisper, as if to confide a secret. "They're afraid I'll sell the lot . . . They won't leave me . . . won't allow me . . . When the builders come to offer me a contract, you should see them, those cats! They get in the way, pull out their claws; they even chased a lawyer off! Once I had the contract right here, I was about to sign it, and they dived in through the window, knocked over the inkwell, tore up all the pages . . ."

All of a sudden Marcovaldo remembered the time, the shipping department, the boss. He tiptoed off over the dried leaves, as the voice continued to come through the slats of the blind, enfolded in that cloud apparently from the oil of a frying pan. "They even scratched me . . . I still have the scar . . . All alone here at the mercy of these demons . . ."

Winter came. A blossoming of white flakes decked the branches and capitals and the cats' tails. Under the snow, the dry leaves dissolved into mush. The cats were rarely seen, the cat lovers even less; the packages of fish-bones were consigned only to cats who came to the door. Nobody, for quite a while, had seen anything of the Marchesa. No smoke came now from the chimneypot of the villa.

One snowy day, the garden was again full of cats, who had returned as if it were spring, and they were miauing as if on a moonlight night. The neighbors realized that something had happened: they went and knocked at the Marchesa's door. She didn't answer: she was dead.

In the spring, instead of the garden, there was a huge building site that a contractor had set up. The steam shovels dug down to great depths to make room for the foundations, cement poured into the iron armatures, a very high crane passed beams to the workmen who were making the scaffoldings. But how could they get on with their work? Cats walked along all the planks, they made bricks fall and upset buckets of mortar, they fought in the midst of the piles of sand. When you started to raise an armature, you found a cat perched on top of it, hissing fiercely. More treacherous pusses climbed onto the masons' backs as if to purr, and there was no getting rid of them. And the birds continued making their nests in all the trestles, the cab of the crane looked like an aviary[8] . . . And you couldn't dip up a bucket of water that wasn't full of frogs, croaking and hopping . . .

---

8. aviary (ā′ vē er′ ē) *n.* building or large cage for housing many birds.

Literary Analysis
Symbolism How do these details confirm the association of the cats with forces resisting the modern city?

Apply the Skills

The Garden of Stubborn Cats

Thinking About the Selection

1. **Respond:** In the story, whom did you find the most sympathetic—Marcovaldo, the Marchesa, or the cats? Why?
2. **(a) Recall:** What is the "negative city"? **(b) Infer:** How have changes in the city altered the way cats live?
3. **(a) Summarize:** How does Marcovaldo find the secret garden of the cats? **(b) Analyze:** List two details from Calvino's descriptions that suggest that such a garden is rare in the city.
4. **(a) Take a Position:** Should the garden of cats remain as it is, or should developers be free to build over it? Support your position. **(b) Discuss:** Share and discuss your opinions with a small group. **(c) Evaluate:** Choose the two best-supported opinions, and share them with the class.

Literary Analysis

5. In the **symbolism** of the story, the cats are a force challenging order—they resist human attempts to define and control the city. Identify three details supporting this interpretation.
6. **(a)** List two other forces in life—natural or human—that resist people's attempts to control space and life in a city. **(b)** Using your answer, explain the meaning of the cats as a **symbol.**
7. This story can be read as an **allegory.** Explain what the final conflict between cats and humans symbolizes.

Reading Skill

8. **(a)** Using a chart like the one shown, list three details showing the pattern in the Marchesa's relationship to the other people in the city. **(b) Draw a conclusion** based on your chart about what she symbolizes.

9. **(a)** What does the Marchesa do for the cats? **(b)** Why do some people believe she is supporting the cats while others think she is not? **(c)** What do your answers indicate about what she symbolizes?

QuickReview

Story at a Glance
Marcovaldo discovers the secret gathering spot of the city's cats—one of the few spots of greenery remaining.

Assessment
For: Self-test
Visit: www.PHSchool.com
Web Code: eqa-6210

Symbol: a character, a place, a thing, or an event that stands for a larger idea

Symbolism: a writer's use of symbols in a literary work

Allegory: a story in which all characters, events, and settings are symbolic

Conclusion: a decision or an opinion based on facts and details in a text

Vocabulary Builder

Practice **Synonyms** are words with similar meanings, such as *happy* and *jolly.* For each set of words below, choose the word that is *not* a synonym for the other two words. Explain your choices.

1. schedule; itinerary; guide

2. poverty; resource; indigence

3. conspiracies; intrigues; circuits

Adding Words to Your Vocabulary Use a dictionary to find another form of the nouns *intrigues* and *indigence.* For example, you might find a related verb or adjective form. Use each new word correctly in a sentence. (For more on using a dictionary, see page R6.)

Writing

Calvino turns cats into a symbol of mischief and mystery. Write a brief **narrative** using another animal as a symbol. To show what the animal stands for, follow these steps:

• Describe it using vivid adjectives that suggest the qualities it symbolizes.

• Provide information about its situation and actions.

• Give it a name that hints at what it represents.

For *Grammar, Vocabulary,* and *Assessment,* see
Build Language Skills, pages 364–365.

Extend Your Learning

Listening and Speaking In an *impromptu presentation,* a person speaks without rehearsal or a script. Give an **impromptu speech** to describe one way that people, like the cats in the story, adapt places to new uses. For instance, you might describe students socializing in a mall or skateboarders skating in a dry park fountain. As you deliver your speech, speak slowly and confidently. In addition, project your voice so that it can be heard in the back of the room.

Research and Technology Find out more about the historic architecture of a European city. Focus on one or two famous structures. Then, present your findings to classmates in a **research summary.** Be sure to choose words suited to your audience and to explain technical terms such as *balustrade* and *gargoyle.*

Build Language Skills

Vocabulary Skill

Etymology The word *predominant* came into the English language from French, which had borrowed the word from Latin. *Predominant* means "ruling before all others" or "superior."

▶ **Example:** A few people have liked the film, but the *predominant* opinion is that it is not worth seeing.

Practice Explain the meaning of the following words based on the meaning of the word root -*dom*-. Then, use each word in a sentence that helps you remember its meaning.

1. dominate
2. dominant

3. predominantly
4. predominance

Grammar Lesson

Active and Passive Voice A verb is in the **active voice** when the subject performs the action. A verb is in the **passive voice** when the action is performed on the subject. Verbs in the passive voice consist of a form of *be* followed by the past participle of the main verb. Usually, active voice is stronger. However, passive voice is used when the writer wants to emphasize the recipient of the action. Passive voice is also used when the subject performing the action is unknown.

Active Voice: The student *answered* the question.

Passive Voice: The question *was answered*.

Practice Change the following sentences from passive voice to active voice. Then, note which is the more effective form:

1. The defendant was found to be guilty by the jury.
2. Horses were brought to America by Europeans.
3. Townspeople were stereotyped by the author.
4. An incorrect conversion factor was used by the chemistry student.
5. Citizens were encouraged by Britain to emigrate to Australia.

W͜G *Prentice Hall Writing and Grammar Connection: Chapter 22, Section 2*

MorePractice

For more practice with the principal parts of verbs, see Grammar Handbook, p. R44.

Reading: Draw Conclusions

Directions: *Read the poem. Then, answer the questions.*

Standards Assessed
• 10.3.7
• 10.5.8

> Black reapers with the sound of steel on stones
> Are sharpening scythes. I see them place the hones
> In their hip-pockets as a thing that's done,
> And start their silent swinging, one by one.
> 5 Black horses drive a mower through the weeds,
> And there, a field rat, startled, squealing bleeds,
> His belly close to the ground. I see the blade,
> Blood-stained, continue cutting weeds and shade.
> —"Reapers" by Jean Toomer

1. What does the rat symbolize?
   A the weak
   B the beauty of nature
   C the strong
   D childhood innocence

2. Black horses are a reference to
   A horses used in battle.
   B horses that are symbolic of power.
   C horses that pulled funeral wagons.
   D the horses of the Crusades.

3. What is the theme of the poem?
   A Nature brings great comfort.
   B Ignorance is bliss.
   C Society is indifferent to suffering.
   D Technology is ruining farming.

4. How do the sounds in the first two lines reinforce the theme?
   A The rhyming words at the end of the lines suggest natural beauty.
   B The repeated *s*-sound suggests the threatening hiss of a blade.
   C The rhythm of the lines suggests the casual speech of the reapers.
   D The repeated long *e*-sound in *reapers* and *steel* suggests brotherhood.

5. Which detail in the last two lines makes the theme clear?
   A A rat, creature of the dark, is finally brought into the light.
   B The rat bravely struggles against fate.
   C Work goes on, regardless of the fate of an individual creature.
   D The blade makes way for civilization.

Timed Writing: Literary Interpretation [Interpretation]

Explain how symbolism contributes to the theme of "The Garden of Stubborn Cats" or "The Masque of the Red Death." Use specific examples from the selection. **(35 minutes)**

 ## Writing Workshop: *Work in Progress*

Problem-and-Solution Essay
Review the problem/solution web from your portfolio and highlight one solution. Write down additional details clarifying the solution.

Reading Informational Materials

Literary Reviews

In Part 2, you learned to draw conclusions when you read literature. Drawing conclusions is also important when reading critical writing, such as reviews. If you read "The Garden of Stubborn Cats," you already have opinions of Italo Calvino's fiction. As you read these reviews of Calvino's work, draw conclusions about each critic's judgments.

About Literary Reviews

In a **literary review,** a type of literary criticism, a writer shares his or her response to a work of literature, whether fiction or nonfiction. Literary reviews typically include the following elements:

- an overview (or a summary) of the work being reviewed
- background information on the writer or on literary trends
- quotations or examples that give the reader a flavor of the work
- an analysis of elements of the work, such as character or style
- the reviewer's evaluation of the work based on his or her analysis

Reading Skill

When reading a review, do not just accept what the critic writes as true. Draw conclusions to **evaluate the critic's judgments.**

- Consider how well the critic supports his or her judgments. For example, if a critic calls a biography "boring," he or she should support that judgment with evidence, such as a quotation of an uninteresting passage.
- Analyze the critic's standards. If the critic calls a novel "great" because it is "action-packed," consider whether the amount of action is the standard by which you would judge a novel.

Use the following checklist to evaluate a review.

Checklist for Evaluating a Review

Does the critic
- ❑ provide sufficient background information?
- ❑ give an adequate overview or summary of the work?
- ❑ suggest the "flavor" of the work through descriptions or quotations?
- ❑ clearly state his or her opinions of the work?
- ❑ support opinions with specific examples or quotations?
- ❑ avoid unmerited praise or unjustified attacks?

Academic Standards

- Analyze many different forms of dramatic literature. (10.3.1)
- Integrate quotations and citations into text. (10.4.7)
- Provide constructive criticism to other writers. (10.4.12)

The New York Times

Calvino's Urban Allegories

The New York Times, January 22, 1984

MARCOVALDO

Or The Seasons in the City. By Italo Calvino. Translated by William Weaver. 121 pp. San Diego: Helen & Kurt Wolff/Harcourt Brace Jovanovich. Cloth, $9.95. Paper, $3.95.

By Franco Ferrucci

A SENTENCE from Italo Calvino's introduction to his "Italian Folktales" reveals the secret behind the magic of the earlier stories in "Marcovaldo": "I believe that fables are true." Conversely, Mr. Calvino believes that reality is fabulous. When he began the stories of "Marcovaldo" in the 1950s and 60s he did not know he was creating a masterwork in the narrative trend labeled the *nouveau roman*[1] by French critics. He simply followed his instincts as a storyteller and achieved a durable balance between the heritage of 20th-century Italian neorealism and a fabulous vision of reality. [. . .]

"Marcovaldo," sensitively translated by William Weaver, is a series of ecological allegories[2] in the form of urban tales. Psychological insights are held back in favor of cartoons in which facts and people succeed one another with the geometrical smoothness of movie animation. Sharp definition and clarity are characteristics of Mr. Calvino's best prose in such books as "The Castle of Crossed Destinies," "The Nonexistent Knight and the Cloven Viscount" and "Cosmicomics." Even early in his career, his rhetorical virtuosity disguised the subtlety and depth of his vision—especially in some of the stories in "Marcovaldo," like "The City Lost in the Snow," "A Saturday of Sun, Sand and Sleep" and "The Wrong Stop." He writes lightly and jauntily; any trace of effort is concealed. But what catches the reader goes beyond the unspotted perfection of the style; it is his uninhibited poetic sense of life.

Each story belongs to a season, and all of them together take their shape from the cycle of the seasons. Marcovaldo lives through the stories as the double of the writer, observing, reflecting and comparing in a perfectly detached way. He is a humble and romantic blue-collar worker lost in the big city, which perverts rhythms and obfuscates cycles. He is trapped in the unreality of this modern city (the setting is vividly evoked in "Marcovaldo at the Supermarket"), a place that even suffocates the life of the animals in the stories [. . .]

What is so much admired by the readers of Mr. Calvino's later "Invisible Cities" was already at work in "Marcovaldo" and with a more cogent narrative drive. "Invisible Cities" seems like a memory, while "Marcovaldo" conveys the sensuous, tangible qualities of life. The opening lines from "The Forest on the Superhighway," a story in "Marcovaldo," might serve as an invitation to readers to meet this tender and humorous Kafka of our days: "Cold has a thousand shapes and a thousand ways of moving in the world: on the sea it gallops like a troop of horses, on the countryside it falls like a swarm of locusts, in the cities like a knife-blade it slashes the streets and penetrates the chinks of unheated houses."

---

1. *nouveau roman* (nōō′ vō rỗ mä̃′) French for "new novel"; term for works of the 1950s and 1960s in which writers rejected realistic representations of life.
2. **allegories** (al′ ə gôr′ ēz) *n.* stories in which characters stand for ideas and so tend to lack individual personalities.

Easy Ironies

The New York Times, November 9, 1983

MARCOVALDO

Or The Seasons in the City. By Italo Calvino.
Translated by William Weaver.

By Anatole Broyard

While Umberto Eco has been on the best-seller list for 20 weeks with "The Name of the Rose," Italo Calvino is the Italian writer who seems to cause the most excitement among American readers. With three books especially—"Cosmicomics," "Invisible Cities" and "If on a winter's night a traveler" — Mr. Calvino has earned comparisons with Jorge Luis Borges and Gabriel García Márquez.[1] After decades of Italian neorealism in the works of authors like Alberto Moravia, Elio Vittorini and Cesare Pavese, Mr. Calvino's fictions appear to be closer to the fantastic Italy of a Fellini film or a painting by Giorgio de Chirico.

He is seen by some critics as an emancipation, as a writer who has brought back humor, lightness and freedom of invention to contemporary Italian fiction. Others find him too light, or all light and no shadow, no substance. He is clever and witty, they concede, but all surface. Italy, it seems, has grown used to taking itself very seriously and is resisting, in fiction at least, the anarchic pleasures of the international modern style.

"Marcovaldo" reads like an attempt to satisfy both schools of thought. The hero for whom the book is named is a Chaplinesque[2] figure posed against the background of a drab and nameless industrial city in the north of Italy. Marcovaldo is Mr. Calvino's Candide,[3] his image of an innocent who survives the 1950s and 60s in a modern metropolis by willfully misreading reality, as Chaplin did, by opposing his optimism to its negative influences.

Since all 20 of these very short stories feature the same character, "Marcovaldo" might just as easily be read as a novel. In fact, some of the stories are so slight that without the support of the others, they seem negligible. Taken together, they have a mild charm. [. . .]

An unskilled laborer with a wife and several children to feed, Marcovaldo is always searching his city for some sign of a relenting. In one story, he finds this relenting in the form of mushrooms springing up under the city's trees. As it turns out, the mushrooms are poisonous. Yet, because there are not enough of them, the poison is not fatal. Marcovaldo and his family enjoy the poisoned, metropolitan pleasure of eating the mushrooms and surviving them. In Mr. Calvino's work, irony too springs up underneath the city's trees. [. . .]

In another story, a herd of cattle passes through the streets in the middle of the night and the whole family wakes up to see it. The story is turned away from this promising epiphany, though, when the eldest boy runs off with the herd and returns, months later, disillusioned with the pastoral life. [. . .]

This may be the trouble with Marcovaldo and with Mr. Calvino's work in general: It leans almost entirely on irony, but of a rather bland or schematic kind. One feels, in reading the book, a sort of fatigue in regard to irony. [. . .]

---

1. **Jorge Luis Borges** (hôr´ he lōō ēs´ bôr´ hes) **and Gabriel García Márquez** (gä´ vrē el´ gär sē´ ä mär´ kes) Borges (1899–1986) and Márquez (b. 1928) are two Latin American writers noted for fantastical stories.
2. **Chaplinesque** (chap´ lin esk´) resembling the characters played by silent movie actor Charlie Chaplin (1889–1977); innocent and optimistic even in the midst of misfortune.
3. **Candide** (kän´ dēd´) hero of French thinker Voltaire's 1759 novel of the same name, whose inexperience helps emphasize the evil he encounters in his travels.

Reading: Evaluating a Critic's Judgments

Directions: *Choose the letter of the best answer to each question about the reviews.*

1. Which topic does each reviewer discuss to provide background information for his review?
   A The paintings of Giorgio de Chirico
   B The distinctive style of the author being reviewed
   C His friendship with the author being reviewed
   D Other novels on the same topic
2. Why might Ferrucci's review give the reader a better sense of Calvino's style than Broyard's review?
   A Ferrucci gives clear reasons for his opinions.
   B Ferrucci summarizes the plot of one of the stories.
   C Ferrucci discusses the views of other critics.
   D Ferrucci quotes a passage from the book being reviewed.
3. Why might Broyard's review seem better balanced than Ferrucci's?
   A Broyard summarizes but does not assess the work.
   B Broyard gives examples from the work.
   C Broyard discusses differing opinions about Calvino.
   D Broyard thinks Calvino's writing has no major faults.

Reading: Comprehension and Interpretation

Directions: *Write your answers on a separate piece of paper.*

4. Identify two descriptions by Ferrucci of Calvino's style. Explain what they indicate about his opinion of the style. [**Generating**]
5. Identify two passages, one from each reviewer, in which the same characteristic of Calvino's writing is discussed. Compare the reviewers' reactions to that characteristic. [**Organizing**]

Timed Writing: Exposition [Critical Stance]

Write a brief essay in which you compare each reviewer's standards. Examine the reasons each reviewer offers for his opinions, and determine what these reasons show about his standards—what he expects from literature. Finally, evaluate each critic's standards, explaining whether you would judge a book using them.
(20 minutes)

Irony and Paradox

 Academic Standards

- Analyze many different forms of dramatic literature. (10.3.1)
- Evaluate the use of literary devices including figurative language, imagery, allegory, and symbolism. (10.3.7)
- Evaluate the impact of contradictions and ironies in the text. (10.3.8)

Irony is the effect created when a writer makes a forceful contrast between words or expectations and reality.

- In **situational irony,** something happens that directly contradicts strong expectations or hopes. *Example:* Someone buys an expensive outfit for a party where the main activity turns out to be playing soccer in the mud.
- **Verbal irony** involves indicating that something is so by saying the opposite. *Example:* Friends call a tall person "Shorty."
- In **dramatic irony,** the reader or audience knows or understands something that a character or speaker does not. *Example:* Fans watch as a confused player spikes the ball and starts a victory dance one foot short of the goal line while opposing linebackers close in.

In addition to irony, writers sometimes use **paradox**—a statement expressing two contradictory ideas yet revealing a truth, or a situation that can be described with such a statement. For example, the following paradox indicates the danger of not telling someone a painful truth: "It is cruel to be kind."

Comparing Uses of Irony and Paradox

In "Like the Sun" and "The Censors," the writers use irony and paradox to explore contradictory ideas of honesty and deceit. Note examples of irony and paradox in the stories using a diagram like the one shown.

Like the Sun		
Sekhar wants to be truthful.	← clashes with →	People dislike the truth.
Example of _irony_		

The Censors		
Juan fears censorship.	← clashes with →	
Example of_____		

Vocabulary Builder

Like the Sun

- **tempering** (tem′ pər iŋ) *n.* changing to make more suitable, usually by mixing with something (p. 372) *I am angry, but I believe in tempering my remarks with politeness.*

- **ingratiating** (in grā′ shē āt′ iŋ) *adj.* acting in a way intended to win someone's favor (p. 374) *Her ingratiating ways charmed us.*

- **scrutinized** (skrōōt′′n īz′d′) *v.* examined carefully (p. 375) *We scrutinized every inch of the yard but never found her ring.*

The Censors

- **irreproachable** (ir′ i prō′ chə bəl) *adj.* above criticism; blameless (p. 377) *His irreproachable record made him the ideal candidate.*

- **ulterior** (ul tir′ ē ər) *adj.* further; beyond what is openly stated or implied (p. 377) *She had an ulterior motive for being extra nice to you.*

- **staidness** (stād′ ness) *n.* state of being settled; calm (p. 378) *His present staidness is a contrast to his wild youth.*

Build Understanding

Connecting to the Literature

Reading/Writing Connection In these stories, characters plan reasonable goals, but the outcomes are far from what they expect. In a few sentences, describe a time when things did not turn out as you planned. Use at least three of these words: *analyze, react, respond, evaluate, predict.*

Meet the Authors

R. K. **Narayan** (1906–2001)

R. K. Narayan spun his tales from the stuff of real life. His hometown of Mysore in southern India probably served as the basis for Malgudi, the setting for much of his fiction. Like the main character in "Like the Sun," Narayan's father was a schoolteacher, and Narayan studied music, a key element of the story, as a youth.

Crossing Languages A native Tamil speaker, Narayan wrote his novels and stories in English, a second language to many Indians. In addition to fiction, he wrote a memoir, *My Days,* and a noted English translation of the ancient Indian epic *Mahabharata.*

Luisa **Valenzuela** (b. 1938)

Born in Buenos Aires, the capital of Argentina, Luisa Valenzuela has lived in places ranging from bustling New York City to Tepoztlán, Mexico, a little village where people still speak the ancient Aztec language. Valenzuela brings the same sense of adventure to her writing by changing spellings, creating new words, and using puns.

Politics and Writing Having lived under a repressive regime, Valenzuela is a strong defender of human rights. In "The Censors," she explores the dilemmas that life in a repressive society poses.

Go Online
Author Link
For: More about the authors
Visit: www.PHSchool.com
Web Code: eqe-9212

LIKE THE SUN

R. K. Narayan

Truth, Sekhar reflected, is like the sun. I suppose no human being can ever look it straight in the face without blinking or being dazed. He realized that, morning till night, the essence of human relationships consisted in <u>tempering</u> truth so that it might not shock. This day he set apart as a unique day—at least one day in the year we must give and take absolute Truth whatever may happen. Otherwise life is not worth living. The day ahead seemed to him full of possibilities. He told no one of his experiment. It was a quiet resolve, a secret pact between him and eternity.

The very first test came while his wife served him his morning meal. He showed hesitation over a tidbit, which she had thought was her culinary masterpiece. She asked, "Why, isn't it good?" At other times he would have said, considering her feelings in the matter, "I feel full-up, that's all." But today he said, "It isn't good. I'm unable to swallow it." He saw her wince and said to himself, Can't be helped. Truth is like the sun.

Vocabulary Builder
tempering (tem´ pər iŋ) *n.* changing to make more suitable, usually by mixing with something

His next trial was in the common room when one of his colleagues came up and said, "Did you hear of the death of so-and-so? Don't you think it a pity?" "No," Sekhar answered. "He was such a fine man—" the other began. But Sekhar cut him short with: "Far from it. He always struck me as a mean and selfish brute."

During the last period when he was teaching geography for Third Form A,[1] Sekhar received a note from the headmaster: "Please see me before you go home." Sekhar said to himself: It must be about these horrible test papers. A hundred papers in the boys' scrawls; he had shirked this work for weeks, feeling all the time as if a sword were hanging over his head.

The bell rang, and the boys burst out of the class.

Sekhar paused for a moment outside the headmaster's room to button up his coat; that was another subject the headmaster always sermonized about.

He stepped in with a very polite "Good evening, sir."

The headmaster looked up at him in a very friendly manner and asked, "Are you free this evening?"

Sekhar replied, "Just some outing which I have promised the children at home—"

"Well, you can take them out another day. Come home with me now."

"Oh . . . yes, sir, certainly . . ." And then he added timidly, "anything special, sir?"

"Yes," replied the headmaster, smiling to himself. . . . "You didn't know my weakness for music?"

"Oh, yes, sir . . ."

"I've been learning and practicing secretly, and now I want you to hear me this evening. I've engaged a drummer and a violinist to accompany me—this is the first time I'm doing it full-dress, and I want your opinion. I know it will be valuable."

Sekhar's taste in music was well known. He was one of the most dreaded music critics in the town. But he never anticipated his musical inclinations would lead him to this trial. . . . "Rather a surprise for you, isn't it?" asked the headmaster. "I've spent a fortune on it behind closed doors. . . ." They started for the headmaster's house. "God hasn't given me a child, but at least let him not deny me the consolation of music," the headmaster said, pathetically, as they walked. He incessantly chattered about music: how he began one day out of sheer boredom; how his teacher at first laughed at him, and then gave him hope; how his ambition in life was to forget himself in music.

---

1. **Third Form A** in British-style schools, an advanced class roughly equivalent to eighth grade in the United States school system.

Literary Analysis
Irony and Paradox
Why is it ironic that today is the day the headmaster will ask for Sekhar's opinion about his musical abilities?

✔ **Reading Check**

What does the headmaster request Sekhar do that evening?

At home the headmaster proved very <u>ingratiating</u>. He sat Sekhar on a red silk carpet, set before him several dishes of delicacies, and fussed over him as if he were a son-in-law of the house. He even said, "Well, you must listen with a free mind. Don't worry about these test papers." He added half humorously, "I will give you a week's time."

"Make it ten days, sir," Sekhar pleaded.

"All right, granted," the headmaster said generously. Sekhar felt really relieved now—he would attack them at the rate of ten a day and get rid of the nuisance.

The headmaster lighted incense sticks. "Just to create the right atmosphere," he explained. A drummer and a violinist, already seated on a Rangoon mat, were waiting for him. The headmaster sat down between them like a professional at a concert, cleared his throat and began an alapana,[2] and paused to ask, "Isn't it good Kalyani?"[3] Sekhar pretended not to have heard the question. The headmaster went on to sing a full song composed by Thyagaraja[4] and followed it with two more. All the time the headmaster was singing, Sekhar went on commenting within himself, He croaks like a dozen frogs. He is bellowing like a buffalo. Now he sounds like loose window shutters in a storm.

The incense sticks burnt low. Sekhar's head throbbed with the medley of sounds that had assailed his eardrums for a couple of hours now. He felt half stupefied. The headmaster had gone nearly hoarse, when he paused to ask, "Shall I go on?" Sekhar replied, "Please don't, sir, I think this will do. . . ." The headmaster looked stunned. His face was beaded with perspiration. Sekhar felt the greatest pity for him. But he felt he could not help it. No judge delivering a sentence felt more pained and helpless. Sekhar noticed that the headmaster's wife peeped in from the kitchen, with eager curiosity. The drummer and the violinist put away their burdens with an air of relief. The headmaster removed his spectacles, mopped his brow, and asked, "Now, come out with your opinion."

"Can't I give it tomorrow, sir?" Sekhar asked tentatively.

"No. I want it immediately—your frank opinion. Was it good?"

"No, sir . . ." Sekhar replied.

"Oh! . . . Is there any use continuing my lessons?"

Vocabulary Builder
ingratiating (in grā´ shē āt´ iŋ) *adj.* acting in a way intended to win someone's favor

▼ **Critical Viewing** What can you conclude about the sitar (si tär´), a traditional Indian instrument, based on this image? Explain. **[Draw Conclusions]**

---

2. **alapana** (äl ä´ pä nä) in classical Indian music, an improvisational exploration of a melody, without a defined beat, and intended to showcase the talent of a singer.
3. **Kalyani** (käl yä´ nē) traditional Indian folk songs.
4. **Thyagaraja** (tē ä´ gä rä´ jä) (1767–1847) revered composer of Indian devotional songs.

"Absolutely none, sir. . . ." Sekhar said with his voice trembling. He felt very unhappy that he could not speak more soothingly. Truth, he reflected, required as much strength to give as to receive.

All the way home he felt worried. He felt that his official life was not going to be smooth sailing hereafter. There were questions of increment and confirmation[5] and so on, all depending upon the headmaster's goodwill. All kinds of worries seemed to be in store for him. . . . Did not Harishchandra[6] lose his throne, wife, child, because he would speak nothing less than the absolute Truth whatever happened?

At home his wife served him with a sullen face. He knew she was still angry with him for his remark of the morning. Two casualties for today, Sekhar said to himself. If I practice it for a week, I don't think I shall have a single friend left.

He received a call from the headmaster in his classroom next day. He went up apprehensively.

"Your suggestion was useful. I have paid off the music master. No one would tell me the truth about my music all these days. Why such antics at my age! Thank you. By the way, what about those test papers?"

"You gave me ten days, sir, for correcting them."

"Oh, I've reconsidered it. I must positively have them here tomorrow. . . ." A hundred papers in a day! That meant all night's sitting up! "Give me a couple of days, sir. . . ."

"No. I must have them tomorrow morning. And remember, every paper must be thoroughly <u>scrutinized</u>."

"Yes, sir," Sekhar said, feeling that sitting up all night with a hundred test papers was a small price to pay for the luxury of practicing Truth.

---

5. **increment and confirmation** salary increase and job security.
6. **Harishchandra** (hə rish chən′ drə) legendary Hindu king who was the subject of many Indian stories. His name has come to symbolize truth and integrity.

Thinking About the Selection

1. **Respond:** Did you sympathize with the headmaster after Sekhar's critique? Explain.

2. **(a) Recall:** What experiment does Sekhar plan at the beginning of the story? **(b) Connect:** What conflict does the experiment create for him?

3. **(a) Draw Conclusions:** Are there any benefits to Sekhar's truth telling? **(b) Support:** Cite story details and logical reasons to support your conclusion.

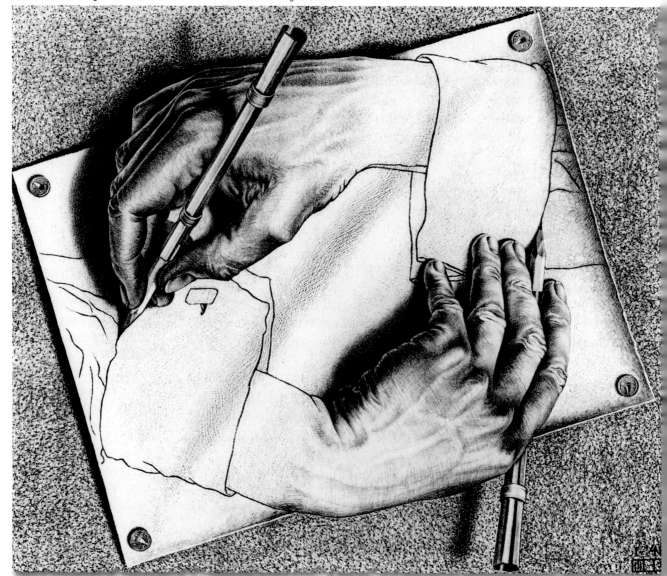

The Censors

Luisa Valenzuela, *translated by* David Unger

Background Like many other Latin American writers, Luisa Valenzuela often addresses political issues in her writing. Her native country, Argentina, now a democracy, has had an unfortunate history of censorship and other human rights violations. In the 1970s, a military regime took power, brutally hunting down suspected political foes and censoring news and mail. In "The Censors," Valenzuela explores the absurd aspects of such oppression.

▲ **Critical Viewing**
What paradox does this work by M. C. Escher present? What might this image suggest about the story? **[Interpret/ Preview]**

Poor Juan! One day they caught him with his guard down before he could even realize that what he had taken as a stroke of luck was really one of fate's dirty tricks. These things happen the minute you're careless, as one often is. Juancito let happiness—a feeling you can't trust—get the better of him when he received from a confidential source Mariana's new address in Paris and knew that she hadn't forgotten him. Without thinking twice, he sat down at his table and wrote her a letter. *The* letter that now keeps his mind off his job during the day and won't let him sleep at night (what had he scrawled, what had he put on that sheet of paper he sent to Mariana?).

Juan knows there won't be a problem with the letter's contents, that it's <u>irreproachable</u>, harmless. But what about the rest? He knows that they examine, sniff, feel, and read between the lines of each and every letter, and check its tiniest comma and most accidental stain. He knows that all letters pass from hand to hand and go through all sorts of tests in the huge censorship offices and that, in the end, very few continue on their way. Usually it takes months, even years, if there aren't any snags; all this time the freedom, maybe even the life, of both sender and receiver is in jeopardy. And that's why Juan's so troubled: thinking that something might happen to Mariana because of his letters. Of all people, Mariana, who must finally feel safe there where she always dreamt she'd live. But he knows that the *Censor's Secret Command* operates all over the world and cashes in on the discount in air fares; there's nothing to stop them from going as far as that hidden Paris neighborhood, kidnapping Mariana, and returning to their cozy homes, certain of having fulfilled their noble mission.

Well, you've got to beat them to the punch, do what everyone tries to do: sabotage the machinery, throw sand in its gears, get to the bottom of the problem so as to stop it.

This was Juan's sound plan when he, like many others, applied for a censor's job—not because he had a calling or needed a job: no, he applied simply to intercept his own letter, a consoling albeit unoriginal idea. He was hired immediately, for each day more and more censors are needed and no one would bother to check on his references.

<u>Ulterior</u> motives couldn't be overlooked by the *Censorship Division*, but they needn't be too strict with those who applied. They knew how hard it would be for the poor guys to find the letter they wanted and even if they did, what's a letter or two when the new

Vocabulary Builder
irreproachable (ir´ i prō´ chə bəl) *adj.* above criticism; blameless

ulterior (ul tir´ ē ər) *adj.* further; beyond what is openly stated or implied

Literary Analysis
Irony and Paradox
What is ironic about the idea of secret police agents taking advantage of cheap airline tickets?

✓ **Reading Check**
What does Juan fear may happen as a result of his letter?

censor would snap up so many others? That's how Juan managed to join the *Post Office's Censorship Division*, with a certain goal in mind.

The building had a festive air on the outside that contrasted with its inner <u>staidness</u>. Little by little, Juan was absorbed by his job, and he felt at peace since he was doing everything he could to get his letter for Mariana. He didn't even worry when, in his first month, he was sent to *Section K* where envelopes are very carefully screened for explosives.

It's true that on the third day, a fellow worker had his right hand blown off by a letter, but the division chief claimed it was sheer negligence on the victim's part. Juan and the other employees were allowed to go back to their work, though feeling less secure. After work, one of them tried to organize a strike to demand higher wages for unhealthy work, but Juan didn't join in; after thinking it over, he reported the man to his superiors and thus got promoted.

You don't form a habit by doing something once, he told himself as he left his boss's office. And when he was transferred to *Section F*, where letters are carefully checked for poison dust, he felt he had climbed a rung in the ladder.

By working hard, he quickly reached *Section E* where the job became more interesting, for he could now read and analyze the letters' contents. Here he could even hope to get hold of his letter, which, judging by the time that had elapsed, had gone through the other sections and was probably floating around in this one.

Soon his work became so absorbing that his noble mission blurred in his mind. Day after day he crossed out whole paragraphs in red ink, pitilessly chucking many letters into the censored basket. These were horrible days when he was shocked by the subtle and conniving ways employed by people to pass on subversive messages; his instincts were so sharp that he found behind a simple "the weather's unsettled" or "prices continue to soar" the wavering hand of someone secretly scheming to overthrow the Government.

His zeal brought him swift promotion. We don't know if this made him happy. Very few letters reached him in *Section B*—only a handful passed the other hurdles—so he read them over and over again, passed them under a magnifying glass, searched for microprint with an electronic microscope, and tuned his sense of smell so that he was beat by the time he made it home. He'd barely manage to warm up his soup, eat some fruit, and fall into bed, satisfied with having done his duty. Only his darling mother worried, but she couldn't get him back on the right track. She'd say, though it wasn't always true: Lola called, she's at the bar with the girls, they miss you,

Vocabulary Builder
staidness (stād′ ness)
n. state of being
settled; calm

Literary Analysis
Irony and Paradox
What is ironic about
Juan's rise to power in
the censorship office?

▶ Critical Viewing
In what way does this
photograph express
Juan's predicament?
[Connect]

they're waiting for you. Or else she'd leave a bottle of red wine on the table. But Juan wouldn't overdo it: any distraction could make him lose his edge, and the perfect censor had to be alert, keen, attentive, and sharp to nab cheats. He had a truly patriotic task, both self-denying and uplifting.

His basket for censored letters became the best fed as well as the most cunning basket in the whole *Censorship Division*. He was about to congratulate himself for having finally discovered his true mission, when his letter to Mariana reached his hands. Naturally, he censored it without regret. And just as naturally, he couldn't stop them from executing him the following morning, another victim of his devotion to his work.

Literary Analysis
Irony and Paradox
What is ironic about Juan's last act of censorship?

Thinking About the Selection

1. **Respond:** Do you think it was a good idea for Juan to become a censor? Why or why not?

2. **(a) Recall:** At the opening of the story, what worries Juan?
   (b) Infer: Judging from this concern, what can you tell about the situation in Juan's country?

3. **(a) Recall:** Why does Juan apply for the job in the censor's office?
   (b) Analyze: What character traits make Juan a good censor?

4. **(a) Summarize:** How does Juan's career as a censor progress?
   (b) Draw Conclusions: Why does Juan's attitude about censorship change?

5. **(a) Generalize:** Explain why a system of censorship might lead anyone to "censor himself or herself," as Juan does. **(b) Draw Conclusions:** What lesson does the story teach about the effects of a repressive government on people?

6. **Evaluate:** Is Valenzuela's use of humor an effective way to convey a serious message? Explain.

7. **Apply:** Think of a situation in which people's ability to express themselves freely is restricted. Explain what someone like Juan might do in that situation.

Apply the Skills

Like the Sun • *The Censors*

Comparing Uses of Irony and Paradox

1. **(a)** Analyze an example of **irony** in "Like the Sun" and in "The Censors." In your analysis, explain why your example shows a contrast, and identify the specific elements in the example that contrast with one another. **(b)** Is the example you identified one of situational, verbal, or dramatic irony? Explain.

2. Explain in what ways each story explores the **paradox** stated:
(a) "Like the Sun": telling the truth is a virtue that leads to punishment.
(b) "The Censors": trying to avoid the censors leads one to censor oneself.

3. Compare the effect of irony and paradox in the two stories. Consider whether these devices simply add humor or whether they emphasize the impossible dilemmas facing a character.

Writing to Compare Literary Works

Both Narayan and Valenzuela use irony or paradox to explore ideas of truth, deception, and honesty. In an essay, compare and contrast the concepts of honesty and deception in the stories. Start by completing a chart like the one shown to analyze how in each story a character's attitude toward truth and honesty changes.

Attitude at Beginning	Later Events	Change in Attitude

In your essay, explain how the use of irony and paradox helps each writer convey his or her ideas.

Vocabulary Builder

Practice For each item, write a sentence in which you use the word pair correctly.

1. irreproachable; award
2. tempering; response
3. scrutinized; report
4. ulterior; deceit
5. staidness; silence
6. ingratiating; interview

QuickReview

Irony: the contrast between words or expectations and reality. There are three types of irony: *verbal, situational,* and *dramatic.*

Paradox: a statement expressing two contradictory ideas yet revealing a truth

Go Online
—Assessment
For: Self-test
Visit: www.PHSchool.com
Web Code: eqa-6211

Reading and Vocabulary Skills Review

Reading: Draw Conclusions

Directions: *Questions 1–5 are based on the following selection.*

"Look there, friend Sancho Panza, where thirty or more monstrous giants rise up, all of whom I mean to engage in battle and slay, and with whose spoils we shall begin to make our fortunes. For this is righteous warfare, and it is God's good service to sweep so evil a breed from off the face of the earth."

"What giants?" said Sancho Panza.

"Those you see there," answered his master, "with the long arms, and some have them nearly two leagues long."

"Look, your worship," said Sancho. "What we see there are not giants but windmills, and what seem to be their arms are the vanes that turned by the wind make the millstone go."

"It is easy to see," replied Don Quixote, "that you are not used to this business of adventures. Those are giants, and if you are afraid, away with you out of here and betake yourself to prayer, while I engage them in fierce and unequal combat."

So saying, he gave the spur to his steed Rocinante, heedless of the cries his squire Sancho sent after him. . . .

—from *Don Quixote* by Miguel de Cervantes

1. **The windmills are**
   A actually giants.
   B objects with a symbolic meaning.
   C objects without symbolic meaning.
   D paradoxical.

2. **Based on the details in this selection, what do you conclude that Don Quixote is probably a symbol of?**
   A practical reality
   B impractical idealism
   C age and wisdom
   D poverty

3. **Based on the details, what do you conclude Sancho Panza is most likely a symbol of?**
   A practical reality
   B impractical idealism
   C poverty
   D the upper class

4. **What could the windmills symbolize?**
   A wealth
   B protection
   C decisions
   D false visions

5. **Based on the details, what do you conclude is a theme of the selection?**
   A Be true to your ideals and others will respect you.
   B Dreamers may seem foolish to others.
   C Those who are practical lead boring, empty lives.
   D Age and experience usually triumph over youthful energy.

Vocabulary

Directions: *Choose the sentence that correctly uses the italicized word.*

Standards Assessed

• 10.1.3
• 10.3.1
• 10.5.7

6. *infer*
   - A The details *infer* that the hero is jealous.
   - B We can *infer* that the hero is jealous.
   - C Parents need to *infer* with teachers.
   - D If you *infer* the table, you will damage it.

7. *coincide*
   - A My birthday and the first day of school *coincide*.
   - B Act I of a play *coincides* with Act II.
   - C The United States Treasury plans to *coincide* the silver dollar.
   - D I prefer outdoor stadiums but sometimes *coincide*.

8. *comprehend*
   - A If you *comprehend* arithmetic, you cannot add 2 and 2.
   - B *Comprehend* your tickets in advance.
   - C Some characters are puzzling, but others are easy to *comprehend*.
   - D I was hungry enough to *comprehend* a whole salad.

9. *predominant*
   - A The simple farmers *predominant*.
   - B The winner of the election was not *predominant*.
   - C The weakest wrestler is always *predominant*.
   - D The poll identified the *predominant* views of the public.

10. *consequently*
   - A She went off her diet and *consequently* gained two pounds.
   - B Arrange the details *consequently*.
   - C They encourage driving *consequently*.
   - D Dressed *consequently*, she drew the eyes of everyone in the room.

Directions: *Choose the most likely meaning for each word in italics.*

11. *sequential*
   - A presented in order
   - B hidden from view or understanding
   - C satisfying to one's hunger or thirst
   - D sparkling

12. *domination*
   - A a weak or failed country
   - B mastery or control over others
   - C an unexpected success
   - D a dark, mysterious way of dressing

13. *predominance*
   - A authority
   - B safety
   - C corruption
   - D followers

14. *inconsequential*
   - A without understanding
   - B without significance
   - C without belief
   - D without argument

Spelling Workshop

SPELLING

Vowel Combinations

Certain words are difficult to spell because they contain unusual letter combinations. Some of these combinations involve vowels.

Did You Use the Right Vowels? Some of the vowel sounds in the words on the list are silent. Silent vowels in combination with vowel sounds you hear make correct spelling difficult. In most cases, two vowels are used to spell a sound that usually takes only one vowel. (Look at porcel<u>ai</u>n, for example, or counterf<u>ei</u>t.)

Read through the list and look at the vowel groupings. If a word gives you problems, make up a mnemonic device, or memory aid, to help you remember to include all the letters. A mnemonic device can be a sentence, a rhyme, or other trick to help you remember.

▶ **Example:** A *u* hides in <u>camouflage</u>

Academic Standards

- Revise writing based on specific criteria. (10.4.11)
- Use varied and expanded vocabulary. (10.5.7)

But it would be unusual for the villain to be friendly

Word List
villain
liaison
guarantee
cantaloupe
counterfeit
porcelain
vacuum
waive
lieutenant
camouflage

Practice Add consonants to the vowels to spell words from the Word List. Focus your attention on the vowel combinations as you reconstruct each word.

1. ieuea
2. aaoue
3. iai
4. aie
5. aouae

6. auu
7. iaio
8. uaaee
9. oeai
10. oueei

Monitor Your Progress

A. Directions: *Write the letter of the sentence in which the underlined word is spelled correctly.*

Standards Assessed
• 10.4.11
• 10.5.7

1. **A** He was the <u>villin</u> of the story.
   B He had been a <u>luetenent</u>.
   C He got into trouble trying to pass <u>counterfeit</u> money.
   D He was caught when he could not <u>garantee</u> that it was genuine.

2. **A** The <u>porceline</u> bowl fell to the floor.
   B In it were several slices of <u>cantaloupe</u>.
   C We tried to <u>camoflage</u> the damage.
   D We cleaned up with a <u>vacume</u>.

3. **A** Derek is the school's <u>laiason</u> with the city.
   B He asked the council to <u>wave</u> late fees.
   C They refused to <u>guarantey</u> cooperation.
   D They feared that the students would <u>camouflage</u> their recent earnings.

4. **A** The museum received a <u>vaccuum</u>-packed article.
   B They were told that it was a priceless <u>porcelain</u> vase.
   C The vase was a <u>counterfit</u>.
   D They never found out what <u>villian</u> had tried to trick them.

B. Directions: *Write the letter of the correct spelling of the word.*

5. Martha finds _____ work interesting.
   A laiason
   B laiaison
   C liaison
   D liaeson

6. They will _____ all fees for children under twelve.
   A waive
   B wave
   C waeve
   D whaive

7. Dave wants to be a _____ commander.
   A lootenent
   B lieutenent
   C lieutenant
   D leiutenant

8. Please eat some of that _____.
   A cantaloupe
   B cantalop
   C cantiloupe
   D cantilope

9. They can ____ the wall with tree branches.
   A camoflage
   B camouflage
   C camoflauge
   D camaflage

10. Ivona will _____ the living room.
    A vacuum
    B vacume
    C vacoume
    D vacuume

Writing Workshop

Exposition: Problem-and-Solution Essay

Individuals, schools, communities, and even entire nations face problems every day. **Problem-and-solution writing** helps to identify the problems and then to offer reasonable remedies. In this workshop, you will write a problem-and-solution essay on a subject of your choice.

Assignment Write a problem-and-solution essay that identifies a problem in your school or community and presents one or more solutions.

What to Include Your problem-and-solution essay should feature the following elements:
- a clear description of a specific, real-life problem
- an analysis of the most important parts of the problem
- proof, such as facts, anecdotes, or examples, that shows the significance of the problem
- a complete explanation of one or more possible solutions
- your personal evaluation of any solutions you discuss
- error-free grammar, including correct subject-verb agreement

To preview the criteria on which your problem-and-solution essay may be assessed, see the rubric on page 393.

 Writing Workshop: *Work in Progress*

If you have completed the Work-in-Progress assignments, you already have a wealth of ideas in your portfolio to use in your problem-and-solution essay. You may continue to develop these ideas, or you might choose to explore a new idea as you complete the Writing Workshop.

IN Academic Standards

- Write persuasive compositions. (10.5.4)
- Produce well-punctuated, legible work. (10.6.3)
- Review and revise writing. (10.4.10)

Using the Form

You may use elements of this form in these types of writing:
- History papers
- Health articles
- Proposals
- Editorials

Reading Writing Connection

To get a feel for problem-and-solution essays, read the Nobel Lecture by Alexander Solzhenitsyn, on page 505.

Prewriting

Choosing Your Topic

To choose a meaningful problem, use one of these strategies:

- **Browse media sources.** Look through newspapers, magazines, and Internet sites for recent stories that discuss a problem. Jot down problems for which you think you can offer solutions.

- **Analyze your audience.** Choose the people you want to reach—community members, students, or others. Consider that group's interests and needs. Conduct brief interviews to identify a problem that troubles your audience.

Narrowing Your Topic

Categorize to narrow your topic. Some problems may be too large for your essay. Focus on manageable, local aspects of an issue.

- Write down these categories: World, Nation, State, Town, and School. Identify one aspect of the problem for each category.

- Focus your essay on the aspect that you wrote under the local categories, such as "Town" or "School." For example, you cannot solve the problem of war in a few pages. However, you can write about the problem of bullies at school.

Gathering Details

Evaluate possible solutions. Before you draft, use a chart to evaluate potential solutions. Look for specific details and consider the advantages and disadvantages of each solution. Offer the best solutions in your essay.

Problem	Solutions	Pros	Cons
overcrowded computer lab	1. teachers split classes into three parts, each with separate deadlines	Students won't need the lab at the same time.	Teachers will have to manage a lot of deadlines.
Details: students have the same deadlines; all need the lab at the same times	2. students sign up for lab time one week in advance	Students will have to plan their work.	Some students may not sign up.

Work in Progress
Review the work you did on pages 337 and 365.

Writing Workshop

Drafting

Shaping Your Writing

Create an Essay Map. For additional support during drafting, write each important idea on an index card. Then, write each supporting detail, such as a fact or an example, on an index card. Using the index cards, arrange the ideas and details in different orders. Once you have determined the best order, number the cards and use them as a map for your writing.

Write an outline. An outline gives you a quick overview of all your points. It also lets you figure out how best to structure, or order, the information and reasoning you want to present. The outlines here show two possible organizations for a problem-and-solution essay.

Providing Elaboration

Address your audience Some audiences, such as your friends or young readers, might respond best to informal language. Other audiences will respect your thinking more if you use formal language.

> **Informal:** Face it—lots of us like to eat junk food for lunch.
>
> **Formal:** When choosing their own meals, many students select foods with little nutritional value.

Stick to the facts. To convince your readers that the problem you have identified is genuine, you must explain it clearly using solid evidence. That means presenting factual information rather than personal opinions. Reserve your opinions for your personal evaluation at the end of the essay.

> **Outline A**
> I. Description of Problem
>   A. One aspect
>   B. Another aspect
> II. Explanation of Solution
>   A. How it solves the first aspect
>   B. How it solves the second aspect
> III. Personal Evaluation

> **Outline B**
> I. Description of Problem
>   A. One aspect
>   B. Another aspect
> II. Explanation of First Solution
>   A. Advantages
>   B. Disadvantages
> III. Explanation of Second Solution
>   A. Advantages
>   B. Disadvantages
> IV. Personal Evaluation

To read the complete student model, see page 392.

Student Model: Drafting with Evidence

There is immense pressure for students to purchase brand name clothes. However, these articles cost more than regular clothes, making it a challenge for many people to afford them.

> This writer strengthened the explanation of the problem by focusing first on evidence, not her own opinion.

From the Author's Desk

C. J. Cherryh

C. J. Cherryh

On Revising to Tighten Sentences

Knowing what to delete is as important as knowing what to write in the first place. The value of that advice is illustrated both by "The Threads of Time" and by the passage below, which I have written especially for this workshop. The last few sentences of "Threads" relate to the novel that the story originally introduced. Now that the story exists on its own, I'd like to strike that final passage. It's too late for that, but in the passage below, I show how the timely deletion of unnecessary words can tighten a narrative.

> *"Perfect sentences are created by good editing."*
> ——C. J. Cherryh

Professional Model:

Original writing by C. J. Cherryh

"Well," I said, ~~taking a moment to look out at the sunset~~ gazing over the porch railing ~~at the gathering dark of the porch which my grandfather had built,~~ "I really ~~think, well,~~ "it was about this time of evening, yes— back ~~sometime~~ in June. ~~when~~ I saw ~~a truly~~ something terrible ~~thing over there~~ in the garden, right ~~over~~ there by the rose bushes."

> I really want the reader to hear the word "June." I set it off with a long dash. Then, I cut out the choppy, chattery little words, and set the rhythms of the sentence to land on "something terrible in the garden." ←

~~The little girl who was standing next to me on the porch looked~~ Eight-year-old Susan glanced up at me, wide-eyed. ~~She had blue eyes. She was my sister's daughter. She was about eight. She looked very scared at first.~~

> "Look" is a neutral word. "Glance" is sharp and fast. Choosing that word for "look" changes the impression in the reader's mind. ←

~~It wasn't fair to scare the girl. She was just like her mother. I used to tell her mother stories, too, when we were both kids in this house.~~ Then those eyes narrowed: "Mama said you~~'re~~ were a liar." ~~," she said.~~

~~Was I surprised? No. I knew my sister.~~ ~~Her mother Louise never believed me, either.~~ Louise hated imagination: ~~and she missed a lot of~~ ever so many true things sat ~~that were~~ right under her nose, but she never believed ~~simply because she wouldn't believe~~ she saw them.

> Do I need to spell out specifically who Louise is? Once the little girl talks about "mama" and I talk about "my sister," I trust my readers to figure it out. ←

Writing Workshop

Revising

Revising Your Overall Structure

Ask questions to assess effectiveness. Review your draft to uncover illogical connections, weakly supported examples, or missing information. Ask yourself the questions listed below. If you have difficulty providing clear answers, adjust your writing.

- Is there a logical flow to my ideas?
- Did I provide enough details to support my ideas?
- Did I provide more details than I really need?
- Does every statement make sense? If not, what did I mean to say?
- Is this statement a fact or an opinion? If it is an opinion, am I sure I want to include it?

Peer Review: Ask a partner to read your draft and then conduct a conference about your work. Your reader can ask about the overall structure as well as specific details. Use your discussion to guide your revisions.

Revising Your Word Choice

Evaluate tone and style. The words you choose establish your **tone**— your attitude toward your subject and audience. You might want to present an optimistic or a pessimistic tone regarding a particular problem or solution.

Optimistic: Our challenge is to discover an effective solution.

Pessimistic: The difficulty will be in finding a workable solution.

Replace dull words. Word choice is also a key part of your writing style. To make your style more interesting, replace dull words and phrases with vivid, expressive writing.

Flat: The board will make the final decision about the program.

Vivid: The fate of the program lies in the hands of the board.

To read the complete student model, see page 392.

Student Model: Revising to Replace Dull Words

beautiful
Diversity is good, yet it is far too often hidden beneath layers

of similarity.

conformity

> The writer replaced dull, lifeless words with more precise and vivid choices.

Integrating Grammar Skills

Revising Subject-Verb Agreement

For a subject and verb to agree, both must be singular or plural.

Identifying Errors Errors in agreement can occur when the subject and verb are separated by other words, phrases, or clauses. In the examples below, subjects are underlined, and verbs are set in italic type.

Prentice Hall Writing and Grammar Connection: Chapter 24, Section 1

Singular Subject and Verb

Incorrect: The decision of the board members *are* final.

Correct: The decision of the board members *is* final.

Plural Subject and Verb

Incorrect: Students who park here seldom *follows* the rules.

Correct: Students who park here seldom *follow* the rules.

Agreement errors also occur with compound subjects and with indefinite pronouns serving as subjects.

Identifying Indefinite Pronouns These are the most common indefinite pronouns categorized by number:

Singular:	anybody, anyone, each, either, every, everybody, neither, nobody, nothing, somebody, something
Plural:	both, few, many, others, several

Singular or Plural: all, any, more, most, none, some

Fixing Errors To correct mismatched subjects and verbs, follow these steps:

1. **Identify the subject and determine whether it is singular or plural.**
2. **Select the verb that matches the subject.**
   - For compound subjects joined by *and,* use the plural form.
   - For singular subjects joined by *or* or *nor,* use the singular form.
   - When the subject is an indefinite pronoun, use the appropriate form of the verb.

Apply It to Your Editing

Circle all the subjects in two paragraphs of your draft. For each subject, draw an arrow to the verb that tells what it does. Make sure that you have used the form of the verb that agrees with the subject.

Writing Workshop

Student Model: Jacquelyn Simone
Endicott, NY

Brand Names

A great majority of youth today have become walking advertisements. A person's worth is not based on the content of their character, but on the contents of their wallets. Labels have become the measure of merit, and the right clothing can lead to success and popularity. Society has forgotten the value of self-expression. Individuality has been dissolved in a world full of expensive brand names and styles. The problem has several main parts:

Expense: Students experience great pressure to purchase brand name clothes. However, these articles cost more than regular clothes, making it a challenge for many people to afford them. Despite these realities, those teens who do not own a popular brand are often shunned or ridiculed.

Sameness: Clothes should be a reflection of who you are, not an imitation of what you wish you were. For many teens, clothes no longer express their individuality. Instead, brand names express someone else's idea of who teens are supposed to be.

Poor Self-Esteem: We have a certain image of the ideal body, which has been fed to us by magazines, television, and movies. Girls are expected to be thin and tall, while boys should be muscular. However, everyone has a different body, and few fit these unrealistic images. The clothes that we are told to buy often suit only that one uncommon body type. The rest of the population is left to try to squeeze into stylish clothes or feel inferior. For many teens, self-esteem drops with every outfit they cannot wear.

The problem is complex, but there are some solutions:

Change the media: Magazines should feature models with more common body types wearing flattering clothing. Fewer television programs should be dedicated to fashion, and more should focus on human character. Department stores should offer a greater selection of sizes, styles, and prices. Clothing manufacturers might be able to make attractive but inexpensive clothes, so that costly brands do not have a fashion monopoly.

Change values: Adults should try to build children's identities so that teens are able to express themselves instead of copying whatever they are told is stylish. Schools could offer seminars on celebrating our personal distinctiveness.

Diversity is beautiful, yet it is far too often hidden beneath layers of conformity. Making more affordable and unique styles could lessen the problem of people being judged based on the brand of their clothes. Clothing can be a wonderful medium of self-expression, but only if we eliminate the pressure of dressing the same as everyone else.

> In her introduction, Jacquelyn clearly explains the problem she will discuss.

> The writer breaks the problem down into its elements.

> Jacquelyn organizes her solutions into two main categories.

> In her conclusion, the writer restates her key points.

Editing and Proofreading

Check your draft for errors in spelling, grammar, and punctuation. **Focus on Clear References:** Make sure you have used *that* and *which* correctly. Use *that* to introduce adjective clauses that are essential to the meaning of the noun and *which* to introduce clauses that are not essential to the meaning of the noun.

Publishing and Presenting

Consider one of the following ways to share your essay with others.

Launch a discussion. Use your essay to launch a class discussion about the problem you have analyzed. Read your essay for your classmates. Then, allow your audience members to ask questions and propose their own solutions.

Submit your essay. If your essay focused on a matter of local interest, send it to your school or community newspaper. If your school or town has its own Web site, consider posting your essay. First, make sure your essay meets the site's criteria for publication, then follow the steps to transfer your work to the new platform.

Reflecting on Your Writing

Writer's Journal Jot down your thoughts about the experience of writing a problem-and-solution essay. Begin by answering these questions:

- Which organizational strategy would you recommend to someone writing a problem-and-solution essay?
- After writing your essay, does the problem seem more or less challenging? Why?

Prentice Hall Writing and Grammar Connection: Chapter 11

Rubric for Self-Assessment

To assess your problem-and-solution essay, use the following rubric:

Criteria	Rating Scale				
	not very				*very*
Focus: How well do you explain a problem?	1	2	3	4	5
Organization: How logically do you present one or more solutions?	1	2	3	4	5
Support/Elaboration: How effectively do you use facts, anecdotes, or examples to support your ideas?	1	2	3	4	5
Style: How confidently do you state your evaluations of the solutions?	1	2	3	4	5
Conventions: How correct is your grammar, especially your use of subject-verb agreement?	1	2	3	4	5

Communications Workshop

Viewing and Evaluating a Speech

Academic Standards

- Summarize a speaker's purpose and point of view. (10.7.1)
- Make judgments about the ideas being discussed. (10.7.7)
- Assess how language and delivery affect mood of the speech. (10.7.10)

Do not believe everything you hear in a speech, regardless of who is presenting it. Listen carefully to analyze the presenter's message and speaking skills.

Evaluate the Content

Identify the purpose. The purpose of a speech may be to pay tribute to someone, inform, entertain, or persuade. The speaker's purpose will help you decide whether or not the speech is effective.

Assess the arguments. A speaker should present and support clear arguments, or ideas. Think about how the details given by the speaker relate to the speaker's argument. A speech should include facts or quotations from trustworthy sources.

Think about logic and accuracy. Review the logic that holds statements in a speech together. Make sure that a supporting detail logically connects to the speaker's argument. Use your own knowledge and experience to test the accuracy of statements and check those that seem unlikely or exaggerated.

Speech Evaluation		
Content	+	−
Purpose	+	−
Argument	+	−
Support	+	−
Language Level	+	−
Word Choice	+	−
Body Language	+	−
Eye Contact	+	−

Evaluate the Speaker's Communication Skills

Think about how well the speaker communicates.

Language Level A good speaker will choose language suited to his or her audience. For example, if most members of the audience are trained scientists, then the speaker may use technical terms freely. When speaking to the general public, the speaker may use common, easy-to-understand terms instead.

Word Choice and Style A speaker may use formal or informal language. Speakers also may use emotionally charged wording. Charged words with powerful connotations, or emotional associations, can make a statement memorable or make opinions appear to be facts. Words with negative connotations can obscure facts. Speakers may also use allusions, references to cultural figures or events, that evoke emotion.

Nonverbal Communication A speaker communicates with far more than words. The speaker's body language, eye contact, gestures, vocal tone, and pacing affect the audience's reaction.

Activity ▶ *Analyze a Media Presentation* ▶ Evaluate a speech presented in class or via media. Use the Speech Evaluation Checklist to help you focus on all the aspects of the speech.

The Fall of the House of Usher and Other Writings

Edgar Allan Poe

Penguin Classic 2003

Short-Story Collection This collection presents an excellent sampling of Poe's short fiction, from the horror tales for which he is best known to the detective mysteries that he pioneered. It also includes works of fantasy and early science fiction.

41 Stories by O. Henry

O. Henry

Signet Classic 1986

Short-Story Collection All of the stories share O. Henry's hallmark: An unexpected twist shakes the reader's preconceived ideas about the conclusion. It is almost impossible to figure out what surprise O. Henry has in store for his reader, although he provides numerous clues. This collection offers the reader the opportunity to pit their detective skills against a master of the unexpected.

The Joy Luck Club

Amy Tan

Putnam 1989

Novel In 1949, four Chinese women begin meeting in San Francisco to play mah jong, invest in stocks, and "say" stories. They call their group the Joy Luck Club. *The Joy Luck Club* intermingles the stories of these women with the stories of their Americanized daughters. The conflicts in generations and cultures form the basis of triumph and tragedy.

Anton Chekhov: Selected Stories

Anton Chekhov

Signet Classic 1982

Short-Story Collection Twenty stories by one of the world's great masters of the short story. Chekhov's stories are vivid moments of real life, told with a power that transcends time and place. This volume includes twelve of his early tales that make their first appearance in English in this paperback edition.

These titles are available in the Penguin/Prentice Hall Literature Library.
Consult your teacher before choosing one.

Think About It Like films or stories, essays can transport you into other worlds by vividly re-creating experiences. In "Flood," Annie Dillard describes her experience of Hurricane Agnes in 1972. Dillard had retreated to Tinker Creek, Virginia, to observe nature and write—and the hurricane put her descriptive powers to the test.

FLOOD
ANNIE DILLARD

It's summer. We had some deep spring sunshine about a month ago, in a drought; the nights were cold. It's been gray sporadically, but not oppressively, and rainy for a week, and I would think: When is the real hot stuff coming, the mind-melting weeding weather? It was rainy again this morning, the same spring rain, and then this afternoon a different rain came: a pounding, three-minute shower. And when it was over, the cloud dissolved to haze. I can't see Tinker Mountain. It's summer now: the heat is on. It's summer now all summer long.

The season changed two hours ago. Will my life change as well? This is a time for resolutions, revolutions. The animals are going wild. I must have seen ten rabbits in as many minutes. Baltimore orioles are here; brown thrashers seem to be nesting down by Tinker Creek across the road. The coot is still around, big as a Thanksgiving turkey, and as careless; it doesn't even glance at a barking dog.

The creek's up. When the rain stopped today I walked across the road to the downed log by the steer crossing. The steers were across the creek, a black clot on a distant hill. High water had touched my log, the log I sit on, and dumped a smooth slope of muck in its lee. The water itself was an opaque pale

green, like pulverized jade, still high and very fast, lightless, like no earthly water. A dog I've never seen before, thin as death, was flushing rabbits.

A knot of yellow, fleshy somethings had grown up by the log. They didn't seem to have either proper stems or proper flowers, but instead only blind, featureless growth, like etiolated potato sprouts in a root cellar. I tried to dig one up from the crumbly soil, but they all apparently grew from a single, well-rooted corm, so I let them go.

Still, the day had an air of menace. A broken whiskey bottle by the log, the brown tip of a snake's tail disappearing between two rocks on the hill at my back, the rabbit the dog nearly caught, the rabies I knew was in the county, the bees who kept unaccountably fumbling at my forehead with their furred feet . . .

I headed over to the new woods by the creek, the motorbike woods. They were strangely empty. The air was so steamy I could barely see. The ravine separating the woods from the field had filled during high water, and a dead tan mud clogged it now. The horny orange roots of one tree on the ravine's jagged bank had been stripped of soil; now the roots hung, an empty net in the air, clutching an incongruous light bulb stranded by receding waters. For the entire time that I walked in the woods, four jays flew around me very slowly, acting generally odd, and screaming on two held notes. There wasn't a breath of wind.

Coming out of the woods, I heard loud shots; they reverberated ominously in the damp air. But when I walked up the road, I saw what it was, and the dread quality of the whole afternoon vanished at once. It was a couple of garbage trucks, huge trash compacters humped like armadillos, and they were making their engines backfire to impress my neighbors' pretty daughters, high school girls who had just been let off the school bus. The long-haired girls strayed into giggling clumps at the corner of the road; the garbage trucks sped away gloriously, as if they had been the Tarleton twins on thoroughbreds cantering away from the gates of Tara.[1] In the distance a white vapor was rising from the waters of Carvin's Cove and catching in trailing tufts in the mountains' sides. I stood on my own porch, exhilarated, unwilling to go indoors.

It was just this time last year that we had the flood. It was Hurricane Agnes, really, but by the time it got here, the weather bureau had demoted it to a tropical storm. I see by a clipping I saved that the date was June twenty-first, the solstice, midsummer's night, the longest daylight of the year; but I didn't notice it at the time. Everything was so exciting, and so very dark.

All it did was rain. It rained, and the creek started to rise. The creek, naturally, rises every time it rains; this didn't seem any different. But it kept raining, and, that morning of the twenty-first, the creek kept rising.

That morning I'm standing at my kitchen window. Tinker Creek is out of its four-foot banks, way out, and it's still coming. The high creek doesn't look like our creek. Our creek splashes transparently over a jumble of rocks; the high creek obliterates everything in flat opacity. It looks like somebody else's creek that has usurped or eaten our creek and is roving frantically to escape, big and ugly, like a blacksnake caught in a kitchen drawer. The color is foul, a rusty cream. Water that has picked up clay soils looks worse than other muddy waters, because the particles of clay are so fine; they spread out and cloud the water so that you can't see light through even an inch of it in a drinking glass.

Everything looks different. Where my eye is used to depth, I see the flat water, near, too near. I see trees I never noticed before, the black verticals of their rain-soaked trunks standing out of the pale water like pilings for a rotted dock. The stillness of grassy banks and stony ledges is gone; I see rushing, a wild sweep and hurry in one direction, as swift and compelling as a waterfall. The Atkins kids are out in their tiny rain gear, staring at the monster creek. It's risen up to their gates; the neighbors are gathering; I go out.

I hear a roar, a high windy sound more like air than like water, like the run-together whaps of a helicopter's propeller after the engine is off, a high million rushings. The air smells damp and acrid, like fuel oil, or insecticide. It's raining.

1. the Tarleton twins . . . the gates of Tara The Tarleton twins are two suitors who try to win the love of the aristocratic Scarlett O'Hara, who lives on the plantation Tara in Margaret Mitchell's novel *Gone With the Wind*, set in the era of the American Civil War.

I'm in no danger; my house is high. I hurry down the road to the bridge. Neighbors who have barely seen each other all winter are there, shaking their heads. Few have ever seen it before: the water is *over* the bridge. Even when I see the bridge now, which I do every day, I still can't believe it: the water was *over* the bridge, a foot or two over the bridge, which at normal times is eleven feet above the surface of the creek.

Now the water is receding slightly; someone has produced empty metal drums, which we roll to the bridge and set up in a square to keep cars from trying to cross. It takes a bit of nerve even to stand on the bridge; the flood has ripped away a wedge of concrete that buttressed the bridge on the bank. Now one corner of the bridge hangs apparently unsupported while water hurls in an arch just inches below.

It's hard to take it all in, it's all so new. I look at the creek at my feet. It smashes under the bridge like a fist, but there is no end to its force; it hurtles down as far as I can see till it lurches round the bend, filling the valley, flattening, mashing, pushed, wider and faster, till it fills my brain.

It's like a dragon. Maybe it's because the bridge we are on is chancy, but I notice that no one can help imagining himself washed overboard, and gauging his chances for survival. You couldn't live. Mark Spitz[2] couldn't live. The water arches where the bridge's supports at the banks prevent its enormous volume from going wide, forcing it to go high; that arch drives down like a diving whale, and would butt you on the bottom. "You'd never know what hit you," one of the men says. But if you survived that part and managed to surface . . . ? How fast can you live? You'd need a windshield. You couldn't keep your head up; the water under the surface is fastest. You'd spin around like a sock in a clothes dryer. You couldn't grab onto a tree trunk without leaving that arm behind. No, you couldn't live. And if they ever found you, your gut would be solid red clay.

It's all I can do to stand. I feel dizzy, drawn, mauled. Below me the flood-water roils to a violent froth that looks like dirty lace, a lace that continuously explodes before my eyes. If I look away, the earth moves backwards, rises and swells, from the fixing of my eyes at one spot against the motion of the flood. All the familiar land looks as though it were not solid and real at all, but painted on a scroll like a backdrop, and that unrolled scroll has been shaken, so the earth sways and the air roars.

Everything imaginable is zipping by, almost too fast to see. If I stand on the bridge and look downstream, I get dizzy; but if I look upstream, I feel as though I am looking up the business end of an avalanche. There are dolls, split wood and kindling, dead fledgling songbirds, bottles, whole bushes and trees, rakes and garden gloves. Wooden, rough-hewn railroad ties charge by faster than any express. Lattice fencing bobs along, and a wooden picket gate. There are so many white plastic gallon milk jugs that when the flood ultimately recedes, they are left on the grassy banks looking from a distance like a flock of white geese.

I expect to see anything at all. In this one way, the creek is more like itself when it floods than at any other time: mediating, bringing things down. I wouldn't be at all surprised to see John Paul Jones[3] coming round the bend, standing on the deck of the *Bon Homme Richard*, or Amelia Earhart[4] waving gaily from the cockpit of her floating Lockheed. Why not a cello, a basket of breadfruit, a casket of antique coins? Here comes the Franklin expedition[5] on snowshoes, and the three magi,[6] plus camels, afloat on a canopied barge!

---

2. Mark Spitz (b. 1950) Olympic swimmer.

3. John Paul Jones (1747–1792) heroic naval officer of the American Revolutionary War.

4. Amelia Earhart (er´ härt´) (1897–1937?) first woman to fly across the Atlantic. She disappeared on a pioneering flight in 1937.

5. the Franklin expedition an ill-fated North American expedition, on which the explorer Sir John Franklin (1786–1847) died.

6. three magi (mā´ jī´) three wise men who present gifts to the baby Jesus in the Bible.

The whole world is in flood, the land as well as the water. Water streams down the trunks of trees, drips from hat-brims, courses across roads. The whole earth seems to slide like sand down a chute; water pouring over the least slope leaves the grass flattened, silver side up, pointing downstream. Everywhere windfall and flotsam twigs and leafy boughs, wood from woodpiles, bottles, and saturated straw spatter the ground or streak it in curving windrows. Tomatoes in flat gardens are literally floating in mud; they look as though they have been dropped whole into a boiling, brown-gravy stew. The level of the water table is at the top of the toe of my shoes. Pale muddy water lies on the flat so that it all but drowns the grass; it looks like a hideous parody of a light snow on the field, with only the dark tips of the grass blades visible.

When I look across the street, I can't believe my eyes. Right behind the road's shoulder are waves, waves whipped in rhythmically peaking scallops, racing downstream. The hill where I watched the praying mantis lay her eggs is a waterfall that splashes into a brown ocean. I can't even remember where the creek usually runs—it is everywhere now. My log is gone for sure, I think—but in fact, I discover later, it holds, rammed between growing trees. Only the cable suspending the steers' fence is visible, and not the fence itself; the steers' pasture is entirely in flood, a brown river. The river leaps its banks and smashes into the woods where the motorbikes go, devastating all but the sturdiest trees. The water is so deep and wide it seems as though you could navigate the *Queen Mary*[7] in it, clear to Tinker Mountain.

What do animals do in these floods? I see a drowned muskrat go by like he's flying, but they all couldn't die; the water rises after every hard rain, and the creek is still full of muskrats. This flood is higher than their raised sleeping platforms in the banks; they must just race for high ground and hold on. Where do the fish go, and what do they do? Presumably their gills can filter oxygen out of this muck, but I don't know how. They must hide from the current behind any barriers they can find, and fast for a few days. They must: otherwise we'd have no fish; they'd all be in the Atlantic Ocean. What about herons and kingfishers, say? They can't see to eat. It usually seems to me that when I see any animal, its business is urgent enough that it couldn't easily be suspended for forty-eight hours. Crayfish, frogs, snails, rotifers? Most things must simply die. They couldn't live. Then I suppose that when the water goes down and clears, the survivors have a field day with no competition. But you'd think the bottom would be knocked out of the food chain—the whole pyramid would have no base plankton, and it would crumble, or crash with a thud. Maybe enough spores and larvae and eggs are constantly being borne down from slower upstream waters to repopulate . . . I don't know.

Some little children have discovered a snapping turtle as big as a tray. It's hard to believe that this creek could support a predator that size: its shell is a foot and a half across, and its head extends a good seven inches beyond the shell. When the children—in the company of a shrunken terrier—approach it

---

7. *Queen Mary* luxury ocean liner, measuring almost 1,000 feet in length.

on the bank, the snapper rears up on its thick front legs and hisses very impressively. I had read earlier that since turtles' shells are rigid, they don't have bellows lungs; they have to gulp for air. And, also since their shells are rigid, there's only room for so much inside, so when they are frightened and planning a retreat, they have to expel air from their lungs to make room for head and feet—hence the malevolent hiss.

The next time I look, I see that the children have somehow maneuvered the snapper into a washtub. They're waving a broom handle at it in hopes that it will snap the wood like a matchstick, but the creature will not deign to oblige. The kids are crushed; all their lives they've heard that this is the one thing you do with a snapping turtle—you shove a broom handle near it, and it "snaps it like a matchstick." It's nature's way; it's sure-fire. But the turtle is having none of it. It avoids the broom handle with an air of patiently repressed rage. They let it go, and it beelines down the bank, dives unhesitatingly into the swirling floodwater, and that's the last we see of it.

A cheer comes up from the crowd on the bridge. The truck is here with a pump for the Bowerys' basement, hooray! We roll away the metal drums, the truck makes it over the bridge, to my amazement—the crowd cheers again. State police cruise by; everything's fine here; downstream people are in trouble. The bridge over by the Bings' on Tinker Creek looks like it's about to go. There's a tree trunk wedged against its railing, and a section of concrete is out. The Bings are away, and a young couple is living there, "taking care of the house." What can they do? The husband drove to work that morning as usual; a few hours later, his wife was evacuated from the front door in a *motorboat*.

I walk to the Bings'. Most of the people who are on our bridge eventually end up over there; it's just down the road. We straggle along in the rain, gathering a crowd. The men who work away from home are here, too; their wives have telephoned them at work this morning to say that the creek is rising fast, and they'd better get home while the gettin's good.

There's a big crowd already there; everybody knows that the Bings' is low. The creek is coming in the recreation-room windows; it's half-way up the garage door. Later that day people will haul out everything salvageable and try to dry it: books, rugs, furniture—the lower level was filled from floor to ceiling. Now on this bridge a road crew is trying to chop away the wedged tree trunk with a long-handled ax. The handle isn't so long that they don't have to stand on the bridge, in Tinker Creek. I walk along a low brick wall that was built to retain the creek away from the house at high water. The wall holds just fine, but now that the creek's receding, it's retaining water around the house. On the wall I can walk right out into the flood and stand in the middle of it. Now on the return trip I meet a young man who's going in the opposite direction. The wall is one brick wide; we can't pass. So we clasp hands and lean out backwards over the turbulent water; our feet interlace like teeth on a zipper, we pull together, stand, and continue on our ways. The kids have spotted a rattlesnake draping itself out of harm's way in a bush; now they all want to walk over the brick wall to the bush, to get bitten by the snake.

The little Atkins kids are here, and they are hopping up and down. I wonder if I hopped up and down, would the bridge go? I could stand at the railing as at the railing of a steamboat, shouting deliriously, "Mark three! Quarter-less-three! Half twain! Quarter twain! . . ." as the current bore the broken bridge out of sight around the bend before she sank. . . .

Everyone else is standing around. Some of the women are carrying curious plastic umbrellas that look like diving bells—umbrellas they don't put up, but on; they don't get under, but in. They can see out dimly, like goldfish in bowls. Their voices from within sound distant, but with an underlying cheerfulness that plainly acknowledges, "Isn't this ridiculous?" Some of the men are wearing their fishing hats. Others duck their heads under folded newspapers held not very high in an effort to compromise between keeping their heads dry and letting rain run up their sleeves. Following some form of courtesy, I guess, they lower these newspapers when they speak with you, and squint politely into the rain.

Women are bringing coffee in mugs to the road crew. They've barely made a dent in the tree trunk, and they're giving up. It's a job for power tools; the water's going down anyway, and the danger is past. Some kid starts doing tricks on a skateboard; I head home.

Meet the Author

During her late twenties, **Annie Dillard (b. 1945)** spent four seasons living near Tinker Creek, Virginia, an area of forests and mountains that brims with wildlife. She was twenty-nine when she wrote *Pilgrim at Tinker Creek,* a profound meditation on nature and religion that won the Pulitzer Prize.

Readings in Contemporary Literature
Talk About It

Use the following items to guide a discussion of "Flood."

1. **(a)** Identify three changes that the flood brings about. **(b)** Why does Dillard say that the creek is "more like itself" during the flood?

2. Dillard compares the flooding creek to a number of things, including a dragon. Choose the three comparisons that were the most vivid for you. Be prepared to explain your choices.

3. With a group, consider the following questions.

   • Do natural disasters bring people together?

   • Do natural disasters make people more or less appreciative of nature?

   Choose a point-person to share your group's ideas with the class.

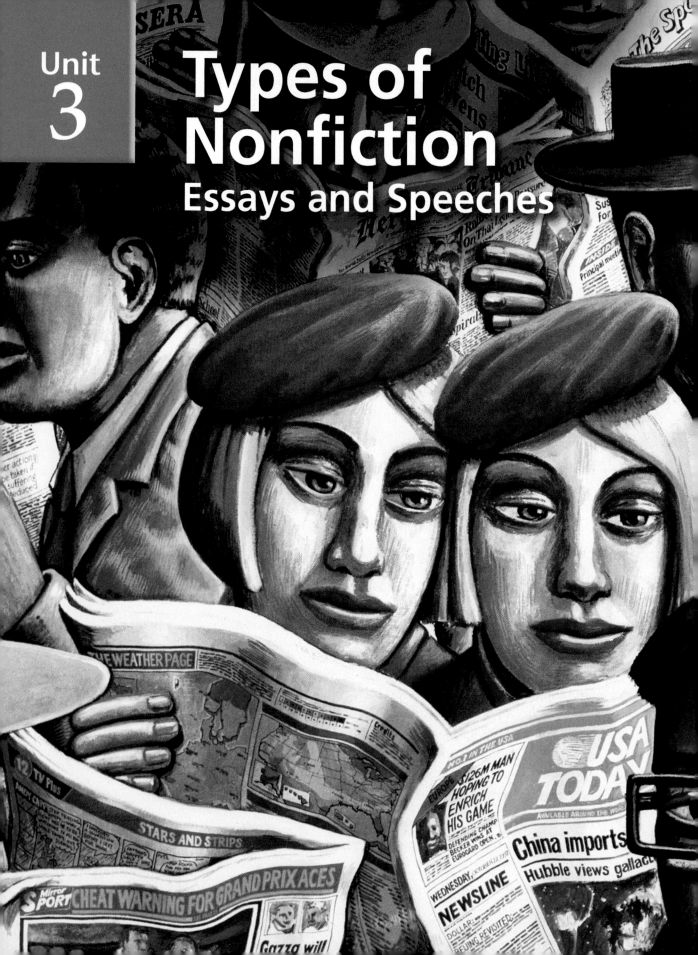

Unit
3

Types of Nonfiction
Essays and Speeches

Unit 3 Overview

PART 1: Analyzing Main Idea and
Supporting Details

PART 2: Evaluating Persuasive Appeals

IN **Academic Standards**

In This Unit You Will

- Examine how the author's perspective influences the structure and tone of the text. (10.2.4)
- Review and revise writing. (10.4.10)
- Revise writing based on specific criteria. (10.4.11)
- Write responses to literature. (10.5.2)
- Write for different purposes and audiences. (10.5.8)

Introduction:
Types of Nonfiction

Erik
Weihenmayer

From the Author's Desk

Erik Weihenmayer

Talks About the Forms

▲ **Erik Weihenmayer**
has achieved the ulti-
mate goal of mountain
climbers by reaching
the tallest peaks on
seven continents.

An **article** is a short nonfiction piece, often found in newspapers, magazines, textbooks, and encyclopedias. It presents facts, explains concepts, or tells about events. A **newspaper article,** for example, explores an event or an issue and fairly presents different points of view.

The Informal Essay

In contrast to an article, an **essay** is usually longer and has more literary value. An **informal essay** gives writers the freedom to bring their own thoughts, feelings, and reflections into the discussion. For example, I have published informal essays on all sorts of topics, from why a blind person would ever enjoy climbing mountains to a comparison of my Everest climb with Sir Edmund Hillary's first ascent of that mountain over fifty years ago.

Although I start with a topic in mind, I never first write the beginning or end of the essay; that's too much pressure. I start with the content I know best or believe in most strongly. Later I mold the begin-ning and end around the middle.

◀ **Critical Viewing** How might reading essays and learning new ideas resem-ble mountain climbing, as this picture suggests? **[Connect]**

Autobiographical Essay to Autobiography

When I write an **autobiographical essay,** it takes self-reflection to chisel out the **themes** that give meaning to my life. A person's life is often rambling, fragmented, and ambiguous, not at all tidy like those of some fictional characters.

As I combined such essays to create my book-length **autobiography,** I faced the same challenge as I did when writing individual essays: how to tell my life as a unified story. I didn't want the book to seem like a series of short, isolated **vignettes,** or brief narratives. How could I find the sinuous strands of my life and weave them together, so that they reoccurred in different ways, constantly building upon each other and strengthening the overall impact?

My editor had great advice. "Think of an autobiography as a tree trunk. Your characters, plots, and themes should flow together and stay connected throughout. Branches or tangents may be extremely interesting, but ultimately lead to dead ends." So, after some coercion, I chopped out two beloved chapters— two autobiographical essays—which I came to realize were branches.

> When she began with that sentence, an aura was cast over her autobiography that bound the disharmonious parts of her life's story together, the way fog shrouds an uneven landscape, the way heat reaches through a rambling house into every room.
>
> **from The World According to Garp**
> —John Irving

I also learned to weave together the threads of my life by reading *The World According to Garp.* In this beautiful yet tragic novel, the "disharmonious parts" of a character's life can form a complete whole.

More About Erik Weihenmayer

Erik Weihenmayer (b. 1968) has not allowed blindness to keep him from para-gliding, biking, long-distance running, skiing, and mountain climbing. He made the cover of *Time* magazine in 2001 after he had reached the summit of Mount Everest. He has said, "I truly believe that we will change what it means to be blind, and we'll do it one mountain at a time." In 2002, he climbed Mount Kosciuszko, thereby completing his quest to climb the highest peak on each of the seven continents.

Fast Facts

▶ Weihenmayer began mountain climbing at age 16. He uses sound and touch to guide him when he climbs.

▶ He and his fiancée climbed Mount Kilimanjaro in Africa and were married near the summit.

Exploring Types of Nonfiction

Characteristics of Essays and Speeches

Essays are short works of nonfiction. Their authors are usually named and are always real people. Speeches are nonfiction literary works that a speaker delivers to an audience.

- An **essay** examines and discusses a topic, often presenting the writer's personal viewpoints. Essays typically explore ideas and opinions.

- A **speech** presents a topic and often marks a specific occasion. There are many types of speeches, ranging from informal talks to formal lectures.

Peanuts, reprinted by permission of United Feature Syndicate, Inc.

Essays or speeches offer more than ideas and facts; they also express a writer's style, tone, perspective, and purpose.

- **Style** is the distinctive way in which an author uses language. Many factors contribute to an author's style, including level of formality, use of figurative language, word choice, sentence patterns, and methods of organization.

- **Tone** is the author's attitude toward both the subject and the audience. When you listen to a speech, you can hear the speaker's tone just as you do when you engage in conversations. Authors of written works convey tone through word choice and details. Tone is often described with a single adjective: *formal, ironic, amused, angry,* and so on.

- **Perspective** is the viewpoint or opinion an author expresses. **Bias** occurs when the presentation of a viewpoint is one-sided and the writer distorts facts or uses emotional language to manipulate the audience.

- **Purpose** is the author's reason for writing or speaking. Common purposes include the following: to inform, to entertain, to persuade, to praise, to celebrate, to warn.

Types of Essays

Essays can be categorized by the mode of composition, or author's purpose.

- A **narrative essay** tells the story of real events or an individual's personal experiences.
- A **descriptive essay** creates an impression about a person, an object, or an experience.
- An **expository essay** provides information, explores ideas, or explains a process.
- A **persuasive essay** attempts to convince readers to take a course of action or adopt the writer's position on an issue.
- A **reflective essay** conveys the writer's thoughts and feelings about a personal experience or an idea.

Types of Speeches

Speeches can be categorized by their levels of formality, which are determined by the speaker, occasion, and purpose.

- An **address** is a formal, prepared speech that is usually delivered by someone of importance.
- A **talk** is an informal speech delivered in a conversational style.
- An **oration** is an eloquent speech given on a formal occasion.
- A **lecture** is a prepared speech that informs or instructs an audience.

▼ **Critical Viewing**
Which type of essay might best suit this photograph? Explain. **[Support]**

Check Your Understanding

Choose the letter of the answer that best matches each numbered item.

1. a writer's unique use of language   **a.** descriptive   **b.** style
2. unfair presentation of facts   **a.** bias   **b.** address
3. a history of World War II   **a.** persuasive   **b.** expository
4. the story of an athletic triumph   **a.** expository   **b.** narrative
5. serious, playful, sarcastic   **a.** tone   **b.** perspective

From the Author's Desk
Erik Weihenmayer Introduces "Everest"

When I first thought about writing an **autobiography,** many people around me said, "It should be an 'inspirational book,' but I had always been uncomfortable with that word. All a blind person has to do is to cross a road independently and people will say, "How inspirational!" Whether a word is used to elevate someone onto a pedestal, or to minimize that person through low expectations, it only serves to separate him from everyone else.

The Fears As Well As the Victories

I started by asking myself, "What books do I like?" They were books like *Dove,* by Robin Lee Graham and Derek Gill: an **autobiography** describing the 16-year-old Graham's sailing trip around the world. The authors envelop you in so much **description** and **reflection** that you feel Graham's disappointments, his yearning, and you celebrate when he ultimately pushes through his human frailties.

So I made a decision to write a book that was honest: not an overly flattering tale of a hero conquering mountains or a stereotyped version of a blind person, but one that revealed moments when I was crushed by sadness, paralyzed by fear, clouded by doubt, and even when I was shallow or just plain mean. If there was inspiration to be found, I wanted it to come from the book's unexpected humor, its intensity of passion, and its gritty, sometimes unpleasant reality.

My Purpose: Connecting With You

By being honest and sharing deeply, I hoped to find those connection points with my **audience,** those archetypal ways which make us human, so my life didn't seem so remote from yours. For me, the greatest compliment would be for a reader to say, "Even though he's blind, in many ways we're the same, and those dreams that I feared were impossible to attain are fully within my reach."

The "Everest" chapter you are about to read is called an "Afterword." I compiled it from my journals soon after I returned from climbing Mt. Everest, and my publisher included it when the paperback edition came out. Although it is a self-contained adventure, it continues the intersecting **themes** of the earlier book: relying on good friends, reaching into the darkness, and pushing past the nay-sayers to breathe in as much joy, fulfillment, and accomplishment as humanly possible.

EVEREST

ERIK WEIHENMAYER

Background The dangers of high-altitude climbing are severe. Many climbers fall sick and even die from illnesses caused by reduced oxygen. Others freeze or plummet to their deaths. Despite these risks, Erik Weihenmayer had successfully reached the summits of five of the world's highest peaks by 1999. In that year, when Pasquale "PV" Scaturro, a geophysicist and expert climber, suggested an expedition to the top of Mount Everest, Weihenmayer readily agreed. He arranged sponsorship from the National Federation of the Blind and, with Scaturro, organized the expedition. The other members of the team included Sherm Bull and his son Brad; Ang Pasang, a Sherpa who had climbed Everest twice; and Weihenmayer's long-time mountaineering buddies Eric "Erie" Alexander, Jeff Evans, Chris Morris, and Mike O'Donnell. On May 25, 2001, Weihenmayer and many of his teammates reached the top of Mount Everest. This excerpt describes the final leg of that adventure.

We left our tents a little before 9:00 P.M. on May 24. Because of our twenty-four-hour delay and the <u>apprehension</u> of other expeditions to share a summit day with me, we moved across the South Col with only one other team behind us. We had no worries of the typical horde clogging the fixed lines but could direct our full focus toward

Vocabulary Builder
apprehension (ap′rē hen′shən) *n.* nervousness; anxiety

the mountain. The wind was blowing so loudly through the col that I couldn't hear the bells jingling from Chris's ice axe. Chris and I expected this, so for the first two hours he clanked his metal axe against rocks he passed. Finally, we worked our way around to the mountain's leeward[1] side, where Everest itself protected us from the wind. Chris had lost his voice, so his verbal directions were <u>sparse</u>. At each anchor, he'd hold the new line with his hand, so I could locate it and clip in. Chris was moving in front of me at his usual rock-solid pace, and I was right on his heels. We were making unbelievable time.

As we got higher up the mountain, four distinct changes had begun to work in my favor. Earlier, in the icefall, each step was very specific, but the terrain above the South Col consisted of steep forty-five-degree snow faces a hundred yards wide, intermingled with ten-to-fifty-foot crumbly rock steps. I could stay in the kicked boot holes of Chris or kick my own steps. Where I stepped had become less important than maintaining internal balance. I could breathe, scan my ice axe, and count on the next step. The slope was often so steep that I could

---

1. **leeward** (lē′ wərd′) *adj.* away from the wind.

Vocabulary Builder
sparse (spärs) *adj.* thinly spread; not plentiful

▼ **Critical Viewing**
How does this photograph of Brad Bull help you appreciate the skills needed to climb Everest? Explain. **[Connect]**

lean forward and feel the rock or snow steps with my gloved hands, and I had trained myself long ago to save energy by landing my feet in the same holds my hands had just left. Finally, when I needed it most, the mountain had given me a pattern.

The thin oxygen of extreme altitude reduced us to a crawl. It was like moving through a bizarre atmosphere of syrup mixed with a narcotic. My team, struggling just to put one foot in front of the other, moved so slowly, it gave me more time to scan my axe across the snow and feel my way forward. The third equalizer was the darkness. With just a trickle of light produced by headlamps, my sighted team could only see a few feet in front of them. Bulky goggles blocked their side vision, and oxygen masks covered much of their visual field. Also, the pure oxygen trickling through their masks would flow up and freeze the lenses of their goggles so that they constantly had to remove them to wipe the lenses clean. Those brief moments when eyes are exposed to the elements, corneas will freeze, and the intense rays of the sun reflecting off the snow cause instant snow blindness. Not once did I ever have to worry about these complications.

In addition, my teammates had chosen smaller masks that rode low and tight across their cheeks and hung mostly below their chins. This allowed climbers to see better and prevented pure oxygen from seeping into their lenses, but also allowed plenty of pure oxygen to escape into the wind. I, on the other hand, had the luxury of choosing the largest mask I could find and wore it high on my face, getting

Narrative Essay
Tone The author matter-of-factly notes the irony that his blindness helped him avoid some problems experienced by the other climbers.

✓ **Reading Check**

What condition reduces the party's progress "to a crawl"?

the most benefit from the oxygen flow and the <u>ambient</u> air around the mask. I'm sure I made a freakish sight with my gigantic mask covering my goggles, like a day long ago in wrestling practice when I had put my sweatshirt on backward, with the hood covering my face, and chased the terrified freshmen around the mat. The consistent terrain, the altitude, the mask, and the darkness were great equalizers. I wouldn't go so far as to claim these gave me an advantage, but it was a matter of perspective. The mountain had gotten desperately harder for everyone else, while it had gotten slightly easier for me.

For two and a half months, all the decisions, the logistics, the backup safety plans had been implemented and executed by PV, and now, somewhere below the Balcony, the exhausting burden of leadership finally took its toll. Suddenly feeling listless and unable to catch his breath even with his oxygen bottle at full flow, PV had <u>arduously</u> turned back. He managed to convince Brad and Sherm, next to him, that he was strong enough to descend alone, in retrospect, a ploy that might have turned deadly, but PV's weary brain had never stopped calculating the big picture. He had refused to divert any energy from the team's summit effort. Through periodic radio checks as PV dropped altitude, I could hear his characteristically hyper voice growing flat, and just below a steep ice bulge, only an hour from Camp Four, PV sat down in the snow. "I'm very tired," he said. "I don't know if I can make it. I might need some assistance." PV's one warning before we left the tent was "If you sit down, you'll stay there." So, beginning to panic, I ripped my radio out of my pocket. "Is anyone near PV who can help him down?" I asked. "Is anyone reading me?" I repeated myself several times to empty static.

A few weeks earlier, Dr. Gipe had received the sad news that a close family friend had been killed in a skiing accident; a three-thousand-foot day in the Death Zone just didn't seem fair to his family, so that night, he had never left his tent. His decision was a tough one to make, but extremely fortunate for PV's sake. "This is Gipe at the South Col," finally came over the radio. "I'm strapping on my crampons right now. I'm going out to get PV." Dr. Gipe met PV about a half an hour from camp, up again and staggering slowly toward the tents.

With the first crisis of the night averted, Chris and I plodded up a steep gully, which led us to the Balcony, a flat snow platform, ten feet wide. Michael Brown arrived first at about 2:00 A.M., with Chris and me right behind. All night, the weather had remained clear, with high clouds to the southeast and distant lightning flashes illuminating the sky, but at the Balcony, our luck suddenly ran out. We walked into a blasting storm. Wind and horizontal snow raked our down suits and covered us with a layer of ice. The lightning strikes were now on

▶ **Critical Viewing**
What two challenges does this photograph suggest mountaineers face in surviving at high altitudes? **[Analyze]**

Vocabulary Builder
ambient (am´bē ənt) *adj.* surrounding; on all sides

Vocabulary Builder
arduously (är´jōō əs lē) *adv.* with great difficulty; laboriously

Narrative Essay
Narration and Exposition The author provides the information readers need to understand the narrative by including some background details about Dr. Gipe.

top of us, exploding like a pyrotechnic show. Chris later said he couldn't see his feet through the blowing snow, which stopped us short, since the southeast ridge above narrowed to fifteen feet wide. Mike O.'s and Didrik's headlamps had simultaneously flickered out, and one of Didrik's crampons had popped off. "Someone come and help us," Mike yelled over the radio. Charley headed back and found them sitting in the snow only twenty feet away.

Chris and I huddled together in the wind, waiting for the others to arrive. "What do you think, Big E?" he asked. "It's lookin' pretty grim." When the others trickled in, Sherm wanted to go on; Charley wanted to turn back, and Erie thought we should wait. For forty-five minutes, we waited, periodic arguments breaking out whether to go on or descend. I was beginning to shiver and forced myself to bounce up and down, and to windmill my arms. We were so close, and I was feeling strong. Turning back was a crushing proposition, but I also wasn't willing to go bullheadedly forward and throw my life away. My mind was starting to settle on the possibility of turning back, when Kevin's voice from Base Camp crackled over my radio. Throughout the expedition, Kevin had been learning to read the satellite weather reports we received every few days over the Internet. From the weather map, it appeared the storm was moving rapidly to the northeast toward Bhutan, and where we stood on the Balcony, we were directly northeast of Base Camp. "Hey you guys, don't quit yet," his voice sounded urgent. "The storm's cleared down here. It just might pass over you."

"Weather is also clearing here," Kami said from Camp Two below.

Chris glanced over at me. Beyond my right hip, shining through the storm clouds, he could see a star. "Let's see if this thing breaks up," he said. Sherm must have felt good tidings, too, because he pushed on. Chris and I followed.

Following the narrow exposed southeast shoulder, I felt the first warmth of the sun about 4:00 A.M.; so high up, no other mountain blocked the sunrise. The weather had thankfully turned spectacular.

Still hours below the South Summit, we were stalled out again. The fixed lines, running up the steepest slope yet, had been frozen over by a hard windswept crust of snow. Jeff and Brad moved ahead, pulling the lines free, an exhausting job at twenty-eight thousand feet. The job was quickly wearing Jeff down, but he said later that with each gasping breath as he heaved the rope free, he envisioned

Erik Weihenmayer
Author's Insight
Kevin's courageous advice represents the idea that leadership isn't only reserved for those who stand on the summit. We're all capable of contributing to something extraordinary.

 **Reading Check**

How does the weather change when the party reaches the Balcony?

the two of us standing on top together. Soon he was beginning to feel faint and dizzy. As he knelt in the snow, Brad, behind him, examined his oxygen equipment and assessed that his regulator, connecting the long tube of his mask to his bottle, had malfunctioned. The internal valves responsible for regulating flow were notoriously prone to freezing shut. "Who's got an extra regulator?" Brad called out over the radio, but tired bodies and brains could not recall who had thrown in the extras in the pre-summit shuffle. "My day's finished if I can't find the extra," Jeff yelled testily.

It may not have been PV's time to summit, but he wasn't through benefiting the team. "Calm down," he advised, lying weakly on his back in his tent. "Everyone take a deep breath. Ang Pasang and Sherm are carrying the extra regulators." Luckily, Ang Pasang was only a hundred feet behind. Together, Brad and Ang Pasang screwed on Jeff's new regulator.

By 8:00 a.m., we had struggled on to the South Summit, 28,700 feet. After a short rest, Chris took off for the summit, cranking it into "Morris gear," and Luis took over in front of me. From the

▲ **Critical Viewing**
What stage of the climb do you think is depicted in this photograph of Weihenmayer and Ang Pasang? Explain.
[Interpret]

South Summit, the true summit is still at least two hours away across the three-hundred-foot-long knife-edge ridge, up the fifty-foot vertical Hillary Step, and finally traversing up a long slightly broader ridge to the summit.

Jeff, exhausted from his two-hour struggle pulling lines, stopped short in front of me. "I'm wasted. I've gotta go down," he said reluctantly. "This'll have to be my summit."

For a moment I wanted to goad him on the way we had done each other on winter training climbs of Colorado fourteeners. "If you wanna turn back, just say the word," we'd jab. "Of course, I'll have to tell everyone you were a whiney little crybaby." But 28,700 feet above sea level wasn't the place to motivate with bravado or ego, so assessing that he was strong enough to get down, I rested a hand on Jeff's shoulder and wished him a safe descent. Jeff had been with me from the beginning, practically introducing me to the mountains. He had shown extraordinary patience as I stumbled along experimenting with brand-new trekking poles. We had even stood together on the summit of Denali[2] and El Capitan,[3] so I knew that reaching the summit of Mt. Everest without him wouldn't feel complete. Suddenly, a wave of heavy exhaustion passed over me, and I felt weary and crumpled. "Maybe I'll go down too," I readied my lips to say, but then Luis was crunching through the snow in front of me, and I forced myself to revive.

Down-climbing the twenty-foot vertical snow face on the backside of the South Summit leading onto the knife-edge ridge went against my survival instinct. The ridge is the width of a picnic table and always heavily corniced[4] with snow. To the left is an eight-thousand-foot drop into Nepal, and on the right, a twelve-thousand-foot drop into Tibet. PV had told me that while crossing the ridge on his 1998 attempt, he had driven his ice axe into the snow and, after withdrawing it, had stared through the small hole into the early morning light of Tibet. In 1995, on Brad's second attempt, a climber in front of him had taken his first step onto the ridge just before the entire right half of it dropped away. The climber jumped back to safety, but a second later he would have ridden the cornice into Tibet. This year, the ridge was drier and more stable. Frozen boot steps traversed along the lefthand side. I'd scan my pole until it dropped

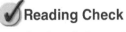
---

2. **Denali** (di nä´ lē) name of the National Park in which Mt. McKinley is located.
3. **El Capitan** (el´ ka´pē tan´) a peak in the Sierra Nevada mountain range in the Yosemite Valley of central California.
4. **corniced** (kôr´ nis´t) *adj.* in architecture, a projecting decorative strip atop a wall or building; here, characterized by overhanging masses of snow or ice.

into a boot mark, then cautiously lower my foot. I knew I couldn't make a mistake here: six hard steady breaths, another solid step, and a relaxed, focused mind like clear water.

Climbing the Hillary Step, I felt I was in my element, feeling the rock under my gloves. I stuck the crampon points of my right foot tenuously into a tiny crack and the left points into a cornice of snow, slid my ascender as high as it would go on the rope, and stood up and quickly reached for the next knob of rock. At the top, I awkwardly belly-flopped onto a flat ledge, slowly pulled myself to my feet, and began traversing the last slope to the summit. For forty minutes I trudged upward. My heavy sluggish muscles felt as if they were pushing through wet cement. With each step closer, the real possibility of standing on top began to trickle through my focused brain. I had speculated success in a conceptual way and as a way to motivate myself when I was down, but it was dangerous to believe it as a fact. A team could be turned back for so many reasons at any time. Just keep moving, I thought. You're not there yet.

Then a body moved down the slope toward me and I felt thin wiry arms beneath a puffy down suit wrapping around me. "Big E!" The voice rasped, so hollow and wispy, I had trouble recognizing it as Chris. His voice tried to say more, but his quaking words dissipated in the wind. Then he leaned in against my ear. "Big E"—his voice gave way to tears, then struggled out in an immense effort—"you're about to stand on top of the world." Then he quickly let go and hurriedly moved down the slope.

Luis and I linked our arms, and in a few steps, the earth flattened and the massive sky closed around me on all sides. "This is Erik, Luis, and Ang Pasang," I said over the radio. "We're on the top. I can't believe it; we're on the top."

"You're the best, Big E!" Kevin yelled from Base Camp. "I love you guys." I could hear the entire Base Camp crew cheering behind him.

"You're the strongest man in the world," PV said.

I turned around, surprised to hear more crampons moving up behind me. "I wasn't gonna let you stand on top and hear about it the rest of my life," Jeff said, with a little pep left in his voice. One of the greatest joys of my summit was that Jeff hadn't turned back at all. From the South Summit, he had watched us down-climb onto the knife-edge ridge and move toward the Hillary Step. Later he told me, "I simply had to follow." Behind Jeff came Erie, Michael B., Didrik, Charley, and Mike O. Sherm had been the first on the team to summit, becoming the oldest man in history to stand on the top of the world, but better than his record was the fact that his son, Brad, had stepped onto the summit right behind him. Nineteen team members made it to the summit: eleven Westerners and eight Sherpas, the most from one team to reach the top in a single day. So it was a crowded summit as we all stood together, hugging and crying on a snow platform the size of a single-car garage.

Another storm was rolling in from the north. "Weather's changing fast," PV called up on the radio. "You guys need to go down immediately." I turned to head down with Erie, when Jeff said, "Wait a second, Big E. You'll only be here once in your life. Look around. Think about where you are and what you've done." So I suspended my nerves for a moment, reached down and touched the snow through my gloved hand, listened to the Sherpa prayer flags flapping in the wind, and heard the infinite sound of space around me, as on my first rock climb. After I had gone blind almost twenty years ago, I would have been proud to find the bathroom, so I said a quick prayer and thanked God for giving me so much. Then it was time to go down.

We descended through heavy snowfall but, thank-

Narrative Essay
Perspective While savoring his historic moment, the author honors achievements of other individuals and of the team.

MODEL SELECTION

Erik Weihenmayer
Author's Insight
Writers describe the world around them in the way they best understand it: I used the senses of touch and hearing.

Erik Weihenmayer
Author's Insight
I wanted to connect the end of my autobiography to the earliest chapters, which describe how I struggled after going blind.

Reading Check

Who surprises Weihenmayer by showing up at Everest's summit?

fully, little wind. Erie took over guiding me, down the Hillary Step, across the knife edge, and contrary to his fears that he wouldn't be strong enough to make the top, he was stronger and more lucid on the way down from Everest's summit than most were on the top of a peak in Colorado. Reaching our tents at about 3:00 P.M., I hugged Erie. "Today," I said, "you were my guardian angel. I'm glad you're here."

That night, Kevin radioed up to report that he had called Ellie on the sat phone with the news. "She screamed loud enough to break the neighbors' windows." He laughed. The next days were exhausting as we fought our way through the screaming wind of the South Col, down the Lhotse Face—where my rubbery legs refused to obey my brain—and finally one last trip through the icefall. At the bottom, in Superman's Palace, of course, the whole team was waiting, and the party lasted long after the sun had sunk below Pumori.

Despite our success, plenty of <u>detractors</u> voiced their opinions on Internet chat rooms and in letters to the editor. I've heard all the ridiculous assumptions.

"Now that a blind guy's climbed it, everyone's going to want to climb it. They're going to think it's easy. People will probably get hurt."

"Why are people thinking this is such a big deal? Anyone can be short-roped to the top by nineteen seeing-eye guides."

My teammates constantly come to my rescue with carefully crafted comebacks like "Before you start spouting a bunch of lies over a public forum, get your facts straight, dude!"

"Don't let 'em get to you," Chris Morris said after I shared with him their comments. "You climbed every inch of that mountain, and then some."

I knew he was right. There were some who would never be convinced, others who still had no idea what to think, but many others for whom the climb forced a higher expectation of their own possibilities. I don't climb mountains to prove to anyone that blind people can do this or that. I climb for the same reason an artist paints a picture: because it brings me great joy. But I'd be lying if I didn't admit my secret satisfaction in facing those cynics and blowing through their doubts, destroying their negative stereotypes, taking their very narrow <u>parameters</u> of what's possible and what's not, and shattering them into a million pieces.

When those parameters are rebuilt, thousands and thousands of people will live with fewer barriers placed before them, and if my climbs can play a small role in opening doors of opportunity and hope for those who will come after us, then I am very proud of what we were able to achieve. . . .

Vocabulary Builder
detractors (dē trak´ tors) *n.* those who discredit someone's accomplishments

Narrative Essay Style The author includes quotations from his critics, which makes the controversy following his climb vivid for the reader.

Vocabulary Builder
parameters (pə ram´ət ərs) *n.* boundaries or limits

Q. **What was the hardest part of writing an autobiography?**

A. Staying honest was a challenge. Writing forces me to examine my perceptions about myself and the world. Many times, after reading a few recently crafted lines, I'd think the passage sounded pretty good, but I'd know it wasn't really what I meant.

Q. **What is your revision process?**

A. At the end of a long day of writing, my wife, Ellie, edits my work. After all that soul searching, what I really want is a pat on the back and for her to say, "Honey, you're brilliant." Instead I get an endless harangue of questions: "What were you thinking at this point?" "Is this really what you mean here?" "How did that affect you?" Inwardly I simmer. She doesn't know what she's talking about, I think. The piece is just perfect. But when I wake up the next morning, the same realization always comes charging through my stubborn brain: Ellie is right and her questions, although painful, have led me to new discoveries.

StudentCorner

Q. **Do you ever think that people's doubts about your abilities made you even stronger and more determined?**
—Jennifer Blaetz, Franklinville, New Jersey

A. Sometimes people's perceptions of our limitations are more damaging than those limitations themselves. In college, I wanted to get a summer job as a dishwasher. I went to most restaurants in town, but each employer had a different reason why I couldn't do the job: "Our kitchen's too small!"—"Our kitchen's too big!"—"The dishes come in too fast!" Previously, I believed that through sheer willpower, I could persuade people to give me a chance, but this experience made me aware that real ceilings exist. Sometimes, however, I feel obligated to bash my head against those ceilings until I break through and feel the sunlight on my face.

 Writing Workshop: *Work in Progress*

Business Letter

For a letter to the editor you may write, think of several issues in the news that spark your interest. Make a list of these issues. Save this Issues List in your writing portfolio.

Apply the Skills

Essays and Speeches

Thinking About the Selection

1. **Respond:** Why does it matter to you—or to people around the world—that a blind man climbed Everest?

2. **(a) Recall:** Identify two challenges that the altitude presents to the climbers. **(b) Connect:** In what ways is Weihenmayer's blindness a benefit as he meets these challenges?
   (c) Generalize: Based on his experience, what statement can you make about turning negatives into positives?

3. **(a) Recall:** How do some critics respond to Weihenmayer's success in reaching the summit of Mount Everest?
   (b) Analyze: Based on the details of Weihenmayer's climb, how would you answer those critics?

4. **(a) Analyze:** Use a chart like the one shown to analyze decisions made by individuals or the team on Mount Everest.
   (b) Discuss: In a small group, discuss your charts. Then, choose one decision to share with the class.

Decision	Results of Decision	Importance to the Team's Success

Essay Review

5. **(a)** Identify three moments when Weihenmayer delays the forward flow of his **narrative essay** to introduce information.
   (b) What information does he share in these moments of **exposition? (c)** In what ways does this information clarify your understanding of the climbers' experience?

6. How does Weihenmayer balance his own **perspective** with the views of others? Explain.

Research the Author

Using the Internet and library resources, write a **report** on Erik Weihenmayer's accomplishments as an athlete. Follow these steps:
   - Research Weihenmayer's successes in scuba diving, distance running, ice climbing, mountain climbing, and skiing.
   - Explain the techniques he developed to compete.
   - Present your report to your class.

QuickReview

Essay at a Glance
The author describes his quest to be the first blind man to climb the world's tallest mountain.

Go Online
Assessment
For: Self-test
Visit: www.PHSchool.com
Web Code: eqa-6301

Narrative Essay: a brief work of nonfiction that tells a true story of actual events or a person's life experiences

Exposition: writing that explains or provides information

Perspective: the viewpoint an author expresses about the subject

Skills You Will Learn

Literary Analysis: *Expository Essay*

Reading Skill: *Summarize to Analyze Main Ideas and Supporting Details*

Reading Skill: *Follow Directions to Perform a Task*

Literary Analysis: *Reflective Essay*

Reading Skill: *Ask Questions to Analyze Main Ideas and Supporting Details*

Literary Analysis: *Humorous Writing*

Literature You Will Read

Reading and Vocabulary Skills Preview

Reading: Analyzing Main Idea and Supporting Details

 Academic Standards

- Revise writing based on specific criteria. (10.4.11)
- Write responses to literature. (10.5.2)

▶ **Analyze a main idea** to identify and evaluate the main point of a work.

Skills and Strategies You Will Learn in Part 1

In Part 1, you will learn
- to **summarize** to **analyze main ideas** (p. 426).
- to **ask questions** as you read to **identify supporting details** (p. 452).
- to **preview** informational materials to help you **follow instructions to perform a task** (p. 448).

Using the Skills and Strategies in Part 1

In Part 1, you will learn to summarize as you read to help you identify main ideas. You will also learn to ask questions to help you identify main ideas and understand their connection to supporting details. You will also use previewing to help you master the main idea and supporting steps in instructions.

▶ **Example:** Minerals are essential to good health. They control the body's water balance and are used by the body to make hormones and enzymes. Eating a variety of foods will help ensure that the body receives enough minerals.

Main Idea	
Minerals are essential to good health.	
Detail	**Detail**
Support body's water balance	Parts of hormones and enzymes

Academic Vocabulary: Words for Interpreting Literature

The following words will help you talk and write about interpretations of literature in this unit.

Word	Definition	Example Sentence
enlighten *v.*	instruct; furnish knowledge to	The lecture was designed to *enlighten* the audience, but it actually just bored them.
emphasis *n.*	expression or action that gives special importance to something	The author gave special *emphasis* to the role of entrepreneurs.
emerge *v.*	become visible or apparent	As you read, the purpose of the essay *emerges*.
speculate *v.*	think seriously; ponder; conjecture	The test requires that the writer *speculate* about a sequence of events in a picture.
confront *v.*	face boldly or defiantly; bring face to face [with]	The author *confronted* the critics in the audience.

Vocabulary Skill: Prefixes

> A **prefix** is a syllable (or group of syllables) joined to the beginning of another word that alters its meaning.

In Part 1, you will learn these prefixes:

   en-/em-   (p. 446)
   con-/com-   (p. 472)

En-/em- are prefixes used to form verbs. *Con-/com-* are prefixes that can also be used as an intensive, a part of a word that adds emphasis to the word root.

Activity With a small group, use a dictionary to make a list of ten words that begin with the prefix *en-*. Explain how the prefix contributes to the meaning of each word.

Practice these skills with either "The Spider and the Wasp" (p. 428) or the excerpt from *Longitude* (p. 437).

Literary Analysis

An **expository essay** is a brief nonfiction work in which an author informs, defines, explains, or discusses. Often, the writer reaches a conclusion through reasoning. The writer's reasoning may be inductive or deductive.

- **Inductive reasoning**—reviewing a number of cases and then making a generalization from them
- **Deductive reasoning**—proving that a conclusion is true by applying a general idea or principle to a specific case

As you read, use a chart to map the writer's reasoning.

Reading Skill

To fully understand an essay, **analyze main ideas and supporting details**—recognize each main point the writer makes and identify its relation to the ideas or facts that explain or illustrate it. To help you organize your thoughts, pause occasionally to summarize. When you **summarize,** you briefly restate only the main ideas and key details.

IN Academic Standards

- Analyze formatting of informal documents. (10.2.1)
- Use supporting evidence to develop main ideas within the body of the composition. (10.4.5)
- Write responses to literature. (10.5.2)

Inductive Reasoning

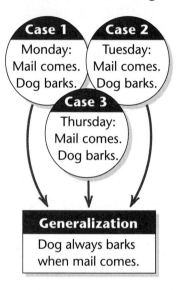

Vocabulary Builder

The Spider and the Wasp

- **instinct** (in´ stiŋkt´) *n.* an inborn pattern of behavior, as opposed to a learned skill (p. 428) *As soon as they hatch, sea turtles use* instinct *to find their way to the sea.*

- **customarily** (kus´ tə mer´ ə lē) *adv.* usually; by habit or tradition (p. 429) *Senior citizens* customarily *receive discounts.*

- **distinct** (di stiŋkt´) *adj.* clearly different; separate (p. 429) *There are two* distinct *sides to the issue.*

- **tactile** (tak´ təl) *adj.* related to the sense of touch (p. 450) *I enjoy the* tactile *sensations of stroking a rabbit's fluffy fur.*

from Longitude

- **haphazardly** (hap´ haz´ ərd lē) *adv.* in an unplanned or a disorganized way (p. 438) *Dirty clothes lay* haphazardly *thrown about the messy room.*

- **configuration** (kən fig´ yə rā´ shən) *n.* arrangement of parts; pattern (p. 438) *We stood in a circular* configuration.

- **derived** (di rīv´d´) *v.* reached by reasoning (p. 439) *We* derived *the answer by solving the equation.*

- **impervious** (im pʉr´ vē əs) *adj.* not affected by (used with *to*) (p. 442) *In my new parka, I am* impervious *to cold.*

Build Understanding • *The Spider and the Wasp*

Background

Instinct vs. Intelligence Petrunkevitch's essay helps readers understand the distinction between instinct and intelligence. An animal's instincts cannot change, even when they lead to harm. Some animals, however, show intelligence: They learn and adjust their behavior to fit their experience.

Connecting to the Literature

Reading/Writing Connection Before writing this essay, Petrunkevitch spent hours watching wasps and spiders. The more you watch animals, the more you learn. When you first see a snake, you might feel fear. If you keep watching, you might feel curiosity. Write a few questions you have about why an animal acts in a certain way. Use at least three of these words: *acquire, compel, equip, function.*

READ MORE

If you enjoy this essay, you might also like *In the Shadow of Man* by Jane Goodall.

Meet the Author

Alexander
Petrunkevitch (1875–1964)

The Russian thinker Alexander Petrunkevitch (pə trσon´ kə vich) was one of the first scientists to explore the secret world of spiders. He classified at least 274 species.

From Politics to Poetry Although Petrunkevitch spent countless hours observing spiders, he did not bury himself away from the world in science. Inspired by his father, who had been jailed for supporting democratic reforms in the Russian government, the younger Petrunkevitch was politically active. He also translated many English poems into Russian.

Fast Facts

▶ Although Petrunkevitch sometimes studied living spiders, much of his work involved analyzing spiders fossilized in amber.
▶ The scientific names for several spider species are based on Petrunkevitch's name.

Go Online
Author Link

For: More about the author
Visit: www.PHSchool.com
Web Code: eqe-9302

THE SPIDER AND THE WASP
Alexander Petrunkevitch

To hold its own in the struggle for existence, every species of animal must have a regular source of food, and if it happens to live on other animals, its survival may be very delicately balanced. The hunter cannot exist without the hunted; if the latter should perish from the earth, the former would, too. When the hunted also prey on some of the hunters, the matter may become complicated.

This is nowhere better illustrated than in the insect world. Think of the complexity of a situation such as the following: There is a certain wasp, *Pimpla inquisitor*, whose larvae feed on the larvae of the tussock moth. *Pimpla* larvae in turn serve as food for the larvae of a second wasp, and the latter in their turn nourish still a third wasp. What subtle balance between fertility and mortality must exist in the case of each of these four species to prevent the extinction of all of them! An excess of mortality over fertility in a single member of the group would ultimately wipe out all four.

This is not a unique case. The two great orders of insects, Hymenoptera and Diptera, are full of such examples of interrelationship. And the spiders (which are not insects but members of a separate order of arthropods) also are killers and victims of insects.

The picture is complicated by the fact that those species which are carnivorous in the larval stage have to be provided with animal

Reading Skill
Analyzing Main Idea and Support Which sentence in this paragraph states the main idea?

food by a vegetarian mother. The survival of the young depends on the mother's correct choice of a food which she does not eat herself.

In the feeding and safeguarding of their progeny[1] the insects and spiders exhibit some interesting analogies to reasoning and some crass examples of blind <u>instinct</u>. The case I propose to describe here is that of the tarantula spiders and their arch-enemy, the digger wasps of the genus Pepsis. It is a classic example of what looks like intelligence pitted against instinct—a strange situation in which the victim, though fully able to defend itself, submits unwittingly to its destruction.

Most tarantulas live in the tropics, but several species occur in the temperate zone and a few are common in the southern U.S. Some varieties are large and have powerful fangs with which they can inflict a deep wound. These formidable-looking spiders do not, however, attack man; you can hold one in your hand, if you are gentle, without being bitten. Their bite is dangerous only to insects and small mammals such as mice; for a man it is no worse than a hornet's sting.

Tarantulas <u>customarily</u> live in deep cylindrical burrows, from which they emerge at dusk and into which they retire at dawn. Mature males wander about after dark in search of females and occasionally stray into houses. After mating, the male dies in a few weeks, but a female lives much longer and can mate several years in succession. In a Paris museum is a tropical specimen which is said to have been living in captivity for 25 years.

A fertilized female tarantula lays from 200 to 400 eggs at a time; thus it is possible for a single tarantula to produce several thousand young. She takes no care of them beyond weaving a cocoon of silk to enclose the eggs. After they hatch, the young walk away, find convenient places in which to dig their burrows and spend the rest of their lives in solitude. Tarantulas feed mostly on insects and millipedes. Once their appetite is appeased, they digest the food for several days before eating again. Their sight is poor, being limited to sensing a change in the intensity of light and to the perception of moving objects. They apparently have little or no sense of hearing, for a hungry tarantula will pay no attention to a loudly chirping cricket placed in its cage unless the insect happens to touch one of its legs.

But all spiders, and especially hairy ones, have an extremely delicate sense of touch. Laboratory experiments prove that tarantulas can distinguish three types of touch: pressure against the body wall, stroking of the body hair, and riffling of certain very

---

1. **progeny** (präj´ ə nē) *n.* offspring; young.

fine hairs on the legs called trichobothria.[2] Pressure against the body, by a finger or the end of a pencil, causes the tarantula to move off slowly for a short distance. The touch excites no defensive response unless the approach is from above where the spider can see the motion, in which case it rises on its hind legs, lifts its front legs, opens its fangs and holds this threatening posture as long as the object continues to move. When the motion stops, the spider drops back to the ground, remains quiet for a few seconds and then moves slowly away.

The entire body of a tarantula, especially its legs, is thickly clothed with hair. Some of it is short and woolly, some long and stiff. Touching this body hair produces one of two <u>distinct</u> reactions. When the spider is hungry, it responds with an immediate and swift attack. At the touch of a cricket's antennae the tarantula seizes the insect so swiftly that a motion picture taken at the rate of 64 frames per second shows only the result and not the process of capture. But when the spider is not hungry, the stimulation of its hairs merely causes it to shake the touched limb. An insect can walk under its hairy belly unharmed.

The trichobothria, very fine hairs growing from disklike membranes on the legs, were once thought to be the spider's hearing organs, but we now know that they have nothing to do with sound. They are sensitive only to air movement. A light breeze makes them vibrate slowly, without disturbing the common hair. When one blows gently on the trichobothria, the tarantula reacts with a quick jerk of its four front legs. If the front and hind legs are stimulated at the same time, the spider makes a sudden jump. This reaction is quite independent of the state of its appetite.

These three <u>tactile</u> responses—to pressure on the body wall, to moving of the common hair, and to flexing of the trichobothria—are so different from one another that there is no possibility of confusing them. They serve the tarantula adequately for most of its needs and enable it to avoid most annoyances and dangers. But they fail the spider completely when it meets its deadly enemy, the digger wasp Pepsis.

These solitary wasps are beautiful and formidable creatures. Most species are either a deep shiny blue all over, or deep blue with

Vocabulary Builder
distinct (di stiŋkt´) *adj.*
clearly different;
separate

Vocabulary Builder
tactile (tak´ təl) *adj.*
related to the sense of
touch

---

2. trichobothria (trik´ ə bäth´ rē ə)

rusty wings. The largest have a wing span of about four inches. They live on nectar. When excited, they give off a pungent odor—a warning that they are ready to attack. The sting is much worse than that of a bee or common wasp, and the pain and swelling last longer. In the adult stage the wasp lives only a few months. The female produces but a few eggs, one at a time at intervals of two or three days. For each egg the mother must provide one adult tarantula, alive but paralyzed. The tarantula must be of the correct species to nourish the larva. The mother wasp attaches the egg to the paralyzed spider's abdomen. Upon hatching from the egg, the larva is many hundreds of times smaller than its living but helpless victim. It eats no other food and drinks no water. By the time it has finished its single gargantuan meal and become ready for wasphood, nothing remains of the tarantula but its indigestible chitinous skeleton.[3]

The mother wasp goes tarantula-hunting when the egg in her ovary is almost ready to be laid. Flying low over the ground late on a sunny afternoon, the wasp looks for its victim or for the mouth of a tarantula burrow, a round hole edged by a bit of silk. The sex of the spider makes no difference, but the mother is highly discriminating as to species. Each species of Pepsis requires a certain species of tarantula, and the wasp will not attack the wrong species. In a cage with a tarantula which is not its normal prey, the wasp avoids the spider, and is usually killed by it in the night.

Yet when a wasp finds the correct species, it is the other way about. To identify the species the wasp apparently must explore the spider with her antennae. The tarantula shows an amazing tolerance to this exploration. The wasp crawls under it and walks over it without evoking any hostile response. The molestation is so great and so persistent that the tarantula often rises on all eight legs, as if it were on stilts. It may stand this way for several minutes. Meanwhile the wasp, having satisfied itself that the victim is of the right species, moves off a few inches to dig the spider's grave. Working vigorously with legs and jaws, it excavates a hole 8 to 10 inches deep with a diameter slightly larger than the spider's girth. Now and again the wasp pops out of the hole to make sure that the spider is still there.

When the grave is finished, the wasp returns to the tarantula to complete her ghastly enterprise. First she feels it all over once more with her antennae. Then her behavior becomes more aggressive.

Literary Analysis
Expository Essay
To support these claims using inductive reasoning, what type of evidence could Petrunkevitch present?

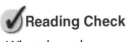**Reading Check**

What does the tarantula allow the wasp to do to it?

---

3. **chitinous** (ki´ tin əs) **skeleton** tough outer covering of an insect's body. The external skeleton gives an insect's body its structure, as an insect has no internal skeleton.

She bends her abdomen, protruding her sting, and searches for the soft membrane at the point where the spider's leg joins its body—the only spot where she can penetrate the horny skeleton. From time to time, as the exasperated spider slowly shifts ground, the wasp turns on her back and slides along with the aid of her wings, trying to get under the tarantula for a shot at the vital spot. During all this maneuvering, which can last for several minutes, the tarantula makes no move to save itself. Finally the wasp corners it against some obstruction and grasps one of its legs in her powerful jaws. Now at last the harassed spider tries a desperate but vain defense. The two contestants roll over and over on the ground. It is a terrifying sight and the outcome is always the same. The wasp finally manages to thrust her sting into the soft spot and holds it there for a few seconds while she pumps in the poison. Almost immediately the tarantula falls paralyzed on its back. Its legs stop twitching; its heart stops beating. Yet it is not dead, as is shown by the fact that if taken from the wasp it can be restored to some sensitivity by being kept in a moist chamber for several months.

After paralyzing the tarantula, the wasp cleans herself by dragging her body along the ground and rubbing her feet, sucks the drop of blood oozing from the wound in the spider's abdomen, then grabs a leg of the flabby, helpless animal in her jaws and drags it down to the bottom of the grave. She stays there for many minutes, sometimes for several hours, and what she does all that time in the dark we do not know. Eventually she lays her egg and attaches it to the side of the spider's abdomen with a sticky secretion. Then she emerges, fills the grave with soil carried bit by bit in her jaws, and finally tramples the ground all around to hide any trace of the grave from prowlers. Then she flies away, leaving her descendant safely started in life.

In all this the behavior of the wasp evidently is qualitatively different from that of the spider. The wasp acts like an intelligent animal. This is not to say that instinct plays no part or that she reasons as man does. But her actions are to the point; they are not

automatic and can be modified to fit the situation. We do not know for certain how she identifies the tarantula—probably it is by some olfactory or chemotactile sense[4]—but she does it purposefully and does not blindly tackle a wrong species.

On the other hand, the tarantula's behavior shows only confusion. Evidently the wasp's pawing gives it no pleasure, for it tries to move away. That the wasp is not simulating sexual stimulation is certain, because male and female tarantulas react in the same way to its advances. That the spider is not anesthetized by some odorless secretion is easily shown by blowing lightly at the tarantula and making it jump suddenly. What, then, makes the tarantula behave as stupidly as it does?

No clear, simple answer is available. Possibly the stimulation by the wasp's antennae is masked by a heavier pressure on the spider's body, so that it reacts as when prodded by a pencil. But the explanation may be much more complex. Initiative in attack is not in the nature of tarantulas; most species fight only when cornered so that escape is impossible. Their inherited patterns of behavior apparently prompt them to avoid problems rather than attack them. For example, spiders always weave their webs in three dimensions, and when a spider finds that there is insufficient space to attach certain threads in the third dimension, it leaves the place and seeks another, instead of finishing the web in a single plane. This urge to escape seems to arise under all circumstances, in all phases of life, and to take the place of reasoning. For a spider to change the pattern of its web is as impossible as for an inexperienced man to build a bridge across a chasm obstructing his way.

In a way the instinctive urge to escape is not only easier but often more efficient than reasoning. The tarantula does exactly what is most efficient in all cases except in an encounter with a ruthless and determined attacker dependent for the existence of her own species on killing as many tarantulas as she can lay eggs. Perhaps in this case the spider follows its usual pattern of trying to escape, instead of seizing and killing the wasp, because it is not aware of its danger. In any case, the survival of the tarantula species as a whole is protected by the fact that the spider is much more fertile than the wasp.

Literary Analysis
Expository Essay
How does the writer link his descriptions of behavior to the concepts identified at the beginning?

Reading Skill
Analyzing Main Idea and Support In what way do the details about web-weaving support the idea that spiders cannot act creatively?

---

4. **olfactory** (äl fak´ tə rē) . . . **chemotactile** (kē´ mō tak´ təl) **sense** An olfactory sense is a sense of smell. A chemotactile sense involves sensitivity by touch to the presence of specific chemicals.

Apply the Skills

The Spider and the Wasp

Thinking About the Selection

1. **Respond:** What fact or idea in the essay surprised you most? Why?

2. **(a) Recall:** What do newly hatched digger wasps feed on? **(b) Compare and Contrast:** Compare the ways in which the wasp and the tarantula each provide for their young.

3. **(a) Classify:** According to Petrunkevitch, is the wasp's behavior closer to reasoning or instinct? **(b) Analyze:** Explain his reasons for the classification. **(c) Make a Judgment:** Do you agree with his point? Explain.

4. **(a) Classify:** In a two-column chart, collect examples of instinctive behavior and intelligent behavior from the essay. **(b) Analyze:** Identify the positive and the negative consequences of each behavior you list. **(c) Generalize:** For an animal in a conflict, does instinct or intelligence provide a greater advantage? Support your answer with details from the essay.

Literary Analysis

5. **(a)** What natural phenomenon does Petrunkevitch explain in this **expository essay?** **(b)** Explain how the essay helps readers understand the difference between instinct and intelligence.

6. **(a)** Explain one way in which Petrunkevitch uses **inductive reasoning** to draw a conclusion about a tarantula's behavior. **(b)** Explain why his conclusion about the role of instinct in the tarantula's failure to defend itself is an example of **deductive reasoning.**

Reading Skill

7. Make a chart like the one shown to identify the **main ideas** and the **supporting details** in the essay. In each box, write the author's main idea about the topic in your own words. Then, find and record supporting details for each main idea.

8. In your own words, **summarize** the essay.

Vocabulary Builder

Practice Write a one-sentence answer to each question. Then, explain how the meaning of the underlined word from the vocabulary list for "The Spider and the Wasp," on page 426, helped you.

1. What is one underline instinct that all dogs have?
2. At what time do you underline customarily wake up?
3. How do scientists decide if two spiders belong to underline distinct species?
4. What fabric do you think has a lot of underline tactile appeal?

Adding Words to Your Vocabulary Use a dictionary to find a word that is similar to each word listed for "The Spider and the Wasp" on page 426. Explain whether the words in each pair share a root.

Writing

Write a **business letter** requesting funds to do more research on tarantulas and wasps. (For the format of a business letter, see page R29.)
- Explain why this topic is of scientific interest and summarize what we currently know, as reported by Petrunkevitch.
- Tell what mysteries could be solved with additional research.
- Use language and logic that will appeal to science professionals.

For *Grammar, Vocabulary,* and *Assessment,*
see **Build Language Skills,** pages 446–447.

Extend Your Learning

Listening and Speaking Deliver a **humorous persuasive speech** encouraging your audience to view wasps and tarantulas as pets.
- Consider what classmates look for in a good pet. Think of humorous examples of how wasps and tarantulas might meet their needs.
- Formulate a clear message—the main idea you want to get across.
- Choose effective language. Slang might seem contemporary, but formal language might command respect.

When you deliver your presentation, speak clearly and with energy.

Research and Technology An *abstract* is a paragraph summing up a research article's main points. Find two additional articles on spiders and write an **abstract** of each. Proofread your work for errors in punctuation or spelling. Check technical vocabulary carefully to make sure it is spelled and used correctly. Use a dictionary or other reference work as necessary.

Essay

Background

Navigation Navigation is the science of finding the position and direction of a craft such as a ship or plane. Since ancient times, mapmakers and sailors have used a system of imaginary lines—longitude and latitude—to identify positions on the Earth's surface.

Connecting to the Literature

Reading/Writing Connection As Sobel explains, before the problem of longitude was solved, sailors ran high risks of getting lost. Think about the last time you were lost. Describe three tools that might have helped you find your location. Use at least three of these words: *perceive, predict, recover, acquire.*

Review

For **Literary Analysis, Reading Skill,** and **Vocabulary Builder,** see page 426.

READ MORE

More by Dava Sobel

Galileo's Daughter

Meet the Author

Dava **Sobel** (b. 1937)

As a child in the Bronx, New York, Dava Sobel enjoyed trips on her family's sailboat, navigated by one of her parents. Years later, she would transform a chapter of navigation history into her first bestseller, *Longitude.*

Curiosity and Inspiration Sobel attended the Bronx High School of Science and went on to become an award-winning science reporter for *The New York Times* and various magazines. In November 1993, she attended a conference about navigation. She became fascinated by the historic contributions of clockmaker John Harrison.

While researching the history of longitude, Sobel stumbled onto the topic of her next book: Italian Renaissance astronomer Galileo and his daughter. She wrote about their relationship in *Galileo's Daughter.*

Fast Facts

▶ *Longitude* was adapted twice for television.
▶ While researching *Longitude*, Sobel traveled to London for research and to stand directly on the prime meridian.

Go **Online**
Author Link

For: More about the author
Visit: www.PHSchool.com
Web Code: eqe-9303

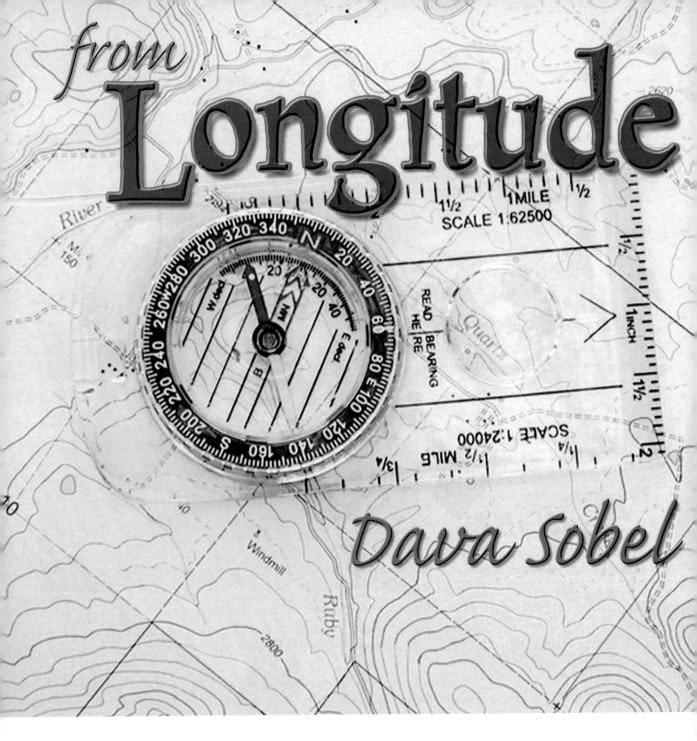

from Longitude

Dava Sobel

When I'm playful I use the meridians of longitude and parallels of latitude for a seine, and drag the Atlantic Ocean for whales.
—Mark Twain, *Life on the Mississippi*

Once on a Wednesday excursion when I was a little girl, my father bought me a beaded wire ball that I loved. At a touch, I could collapse the toy into a flat coil between my palms, or pop it open to make a hollow sphere. Rounded out, it resembled a tiny Earth, because its hinged wires traced the same pattern of intersecting circles that I had seen on the globe in my schoolroom—the thin black lines of latitude and longitude. The few colored beads slid along the wire paths <u>haphazardly</u>, like ships on the high seas.

My father strode up Fifth Avenue to Rockefeller Center with me on his shoulders, and we stopped to stare at the statue of Atlas,[1] carrying Heaven and Earth on his.

The bronze orb that Atlas held aloft, like the wire toy in my hands, was a see-through world, defined by imaginary lines. The Equator. The Ecliptic. The Tropic of Cancer. The Tropic of Capricorn. The Arctic Circle. The prime meridian. Even then I could recognize, in the graph-paper grid imposed on the globe, a powerful symbol of all the real lands and waters on the planet.

Today, the latitude and longitude lines govern with more authority than I could have imagined forty-odd years ago, for they stay fixed as the world changes its <u>configuration</u> underneath them—with continents adrift across a widening sea, and national boundaries repeatedly redrawn by war or peace.

As a child, I learned the trick for remembering the difference between latitude and longitude. The latitude lines, the *parallels*, really do stay parallel to each other as they girdle the globe from the Equator to the poles in a series of shrinking concentric[2] rings. The meridians of longitude go the other way: They loop from the North Pole to the South and back again in great circles of the same size, so they all converge at the ends of the Earth.

---

1. Fifth Avenue . . . Rockefeller Center . . . Atlas landmarks in the borough of Manhattan of New York City. Rockefeller Center features a statue of Atlas, the Greek giant condemned to carry the heavens on his shoulders.

2. concentric (kən sen′ trik) *adj.* having a center in common.

Vocabulary Builder
haphazardly
(hap′ haz′ ərd lē) *adv.*
in an unplanned or a disorganized way
configuration
(kən fig′ yə rā′ shən) *n.*
arrangement of parts; pattern

Lines of latitude and longitude began crisscrossing our world-view in ancient times, at least three centuries before the birth of Christ. By A.D. 150, the cartographer and astronomer Ptolemy had plotted them on the twenty-seven maps of his first world atlas. Also for this landmark volume, Ptolemy listed all the place names in an index, in alphabetical order, with the latitude and longitude of each—as well as he could gauge them from travelers' reports. Ptolemy himself had only an armchair appreciation of the wider world. A common misconception of his day held that anyone living below the Equator would melt into deformity from the horrible heat.

The Equator marked the zero-degree parallel of latitude for Ptolemy. He did not choose it arbitrarily but took it on higher authority from his predecessors, who had <u>derived</u> it from nature while observing the motions of the heavenly bodies. The sun, moon, and planets pass almost directly overhead at the Equator. Likewise the Tropic of Cancer and the Tropic of Capricorn, two other famous parallels, assume their positions at the sun's command. They mark the northern and southern boundaries of the sun's apparent motion over the course of the year.

Ptolemy was free, however, to lay his prime meridian, the zero-degree longitude line, wherever he liked. He chose to run it through the Fortunate Islands (now called the Canary and Madeira Islands) off the northwest coast of Africa. Later mapmakers moved the prime meridian to the Azores and to the Cape Verde Islands,[3] as well as to Rome, Copenhagen, Jerusalem, St. Petersburg, Pisa, Paris, and Philadelphia, among other places, before it settled down at last in London. As the world turns, any line drawn from pole to pole may serve as well as any other for a starting line of reference. The placement of the prime meridian is a purely political decision.

Here lies the real, hard-core difference between latitude and longitude—beyond the superficial difference in line direction that any child can see: The zero-degree parallel of latitude is fixed by the laws of nature, while the zero-degree meridian of longitude shifts like the sands of time. This difference makes finding latitude child's play, and turns the determination of longitude, especially at sea, into an adult dilemma—one that stumped the wisest minds of the world for the better part of human history.

Any sailor worth his salt can gauge his latitude well enough by the length of the day, or by the height of the sun or known guide stars above the horizon. Christopher Columbus followed a straight path across the Atlantic when he "sailed the parallel" on his

---

3. **Azores** (āʹ zôrzʹ) . . . **Cape Verde** (vʉrd) **Islands** two island groups in the Atlantic Ocean; the Azores are off Portugal and the Cape Verde Islands are off the westernmost point of Africa.

◄ **Critical Viewing**
How does this image convey the endurance of the system of longitude and latitude? **[Interpret]**

Vocabulary Builder
derived (di rīvʹdʹ) v.
reached by reasoning

Reading Skill
Analyzing Main Idea and Support What main idea does the writer support using examples like Rome and Copenhagen?

 **Reading Check**

Name an important contribution made to science or navigation by Ptolemy.

1492 journey, and the technique would doubtless have carried him to the Indies had not the Americas intervened.

The measurement of longitude meridians, in comparison, is tempered by time. To learn one's longitude at sea, one needs to know what time it is aboard ship and also the time at the home port or another place of known longitude—at that very same moment. The two clock times enable the navigator[4] to convert the hour difference into a geographical separation. Since the Earth takes twenty-four hours to complete one full revolution of three hundred sixty degrees, one hour marks one twenty-fourth of a spin, or fifteen degrees. And so each hour's time difference between the ship and the starting point marks a progress of fifteen degrees of longitude to the east or west. Every day at sea, when the navigator resets his ship's clock to local noon when the sun reaches its highest point in the sky, and then consults the home-port clock, every hour's discrepancy between them translates into another fifteen degrees of longitude.

Those same fifteen degrees of longitude also correspond to a distance traveled. At the Equator, where the girth of the Earth is greatest, fifteen degrees stretch fully one thousand miles. North or south of that line, however, the mileage value of each degree decreases. One degree of longitude equals four minutes of time the world over, but in terms of distance, one degree shrinks from sixty-eight miles at the Equator to virtually nothing at the poles.

Precise knowledge of the hour in two different places at once—a longitude prerequisite so easily accessible today from any pair of cheap wristwatches—was utterly unattainable up to and including the era of pendulum clocks.[5] On the deck of a rolling ship, such clocks would slow down, or speed up, or stop running altogether. Normal changes in temperature encountered en route from a cold country of origin to a tropical trade zone thinned or thickened a clock's lubricating oil and

---

4. navigator (nav´ ə gāt´ ər) *n.* a person skilled in locating the position and plotting the course of a ship or an aircraft.
5. pendulum (pen´ dyo͞o ləm) **clocks** clocks whose timekeeping movement is regulated by a pendulum, a weight swinging freely from a fixed point.

Literature in Context

Science Connection

Longitude and Latitude The lines of longitude and latitude form an imaginary grid that can be used to name the exact location of any place on Earth.

- The **equator** is the line of latitude on which all points are the same distance from the North and South poles. The sun appears directly overhead at the equator on March 21 and September 21 of each year.
- The **Tropic of Cancer** is 23° 27´ north of the equator. It marks the northernmost latitude at which the sun can appear directly overhead—an event that occurs at noon on June 20 or 21.
- The **Tropic of Capricorn**, at 23° 27´ south, is the southernmost latitude at which the sun can appear directly overhead. The sun reaches its highest position at this tropic at noon on December 20 or 21.
- The **prime meridian** is the line of longitude chosen as the 0° line.

Connect to the Literature

What does this information indicate about how sailors determine latitude by the sun?

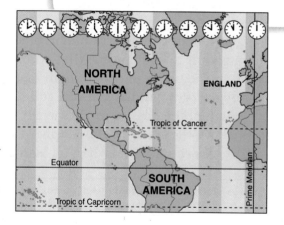

made its metal parts expand or contract with equally disastrous results. A rise or fall in barometric pressure, or the subtle variations in the Earth's gravity from one latitude to another, could also cause a clock to gain or lose time.

For lack of a practical method of determining longitude, every great captain in the Age of Exploration[6] became lost at sea despite the best available charts and compasses. From Vasco da Gama to Vasco Núñez de Balboa, from Ferdinand Magellan to Sir Francis Drake[7]—they all got where they were going willy-nilly, by forces attributed to good luck or the grace of God.

As more and more sailing vessels set out to conquer or explore new territories, to wage war, or to ferry gold and commodities between foreign lands, the wealth of nations floated upon the oceans. And still no ship owned a reliable means for establishing her whereabouts. In consequence, untold numbers of sailors died when their destinations suddenly loomed out of the sea and took them by surprise. In a single such accident, on October 22, 1707, at the Scilly Isles near the southwestern tip of England, four home-bound British warships ran aground and nearly two thousand men lost their lives.

The active quest for a solution to the problem of longitude persisted over four centuries and across the whole continent of Europe. Most crowned heads of state eventually played a part in the longitude story, notably King George III of England and King Louis XIV of France. Seafaring men such as Captain William Bligh of the *Bounty* and the great circumnavigator Captain James Cook, who made three long voyages of exploration and experimentation before his violent death in Hawaii, took the more promising methods to sea to test their accuracy and practicability.

Renowned astronomers approached the longitude challenge by appealing to the clockwork universe: Galileo Galilei, Jean Dominique Cassini, Christiaan Huygens, Sir Isaac Newton, and Edmond Halley,[8] of comet fame, all entreated the moon and stars for help. Palatial observatories were founded at Paris, London, and Berlin for the express purpose of determining longitude by the heavens. Meanwhile, lesser minds devised schemes that depended

Reading Skill
Analyzing Main Idea and Support Which detail in this paragraph supports Sobel's idea that not knowing one's longitude was dangerous?

Literary Analysis
Expository Essay Is the conclusion in the first sentence of this paragraph based on deductive or inductive reasoning?

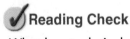Reading Check

What key technical problem prevented sailors from measuring longitude accurately?

---

6. Age of Exploration the period from about 1450 to about 1700, when European navigators sailed to new territories and founded colonies in Africa, the Americas, and Asia.
7. Vasco da Gama (väs´ kô də gä´ mə) . . . **Vasco Núñez de Balboa** (väs´ kô noo͞´ nyeth *the* bal bô´ ə) . . . **Ferdinand Magellan** (mə jel´ ən) . . . **Sir Francis Drake** famous explorers of the fifteenth and sixteenth centuries.
8. Galileo Galilei (gal´ ə lā´ ō gal´ ə lā ē) . . . **Jean-Dominique Cassini** (zhän dō mi nēk´ kä sē´ nē) . . . **Christiaan Huygens** (hī´ gənz) . . . **Sir Isaac Newton** . . . **Edmond Halley** (hal´ ē) pioneering astronomers and scientists of the sixteenth through the eighteenth centuries. Their work redefined people's picture of the universe, replacing traditional views with modern ones.

on the yelps of wounded dogs, or the cannon blasts of signal ships strategically anchored—somehow—on the open ocean.

In the course of their struggle to find longitude, scientists struck upon other discoveries that changed their view of the universe. These include the first accurate determinations of the weight of the Earth, the distance to the stars, and the speed of light.

As time passed and no method proved successful, the search for a solution to the longitude problem assumed legendary proportions, on a par with discovering the Fountain of Youth, the secret of perpetual motion, or the formula for transforming lead into gold.[9] The governments of the great maritime nations—including Spain, the Netherlands, and certain city-states of Italy—periodically roiled the fervor by offering jackpot purses for a workable method. The British Parliament, in its famed Longitude Act of 1714, set the highest bounty of all, naming a prize equal to a king's ransom (several million dollars in today's currency) for a "Practicable and Useful" means of determining longitude.

English clockmaker John Harrison, a mechanical genius who pioneered the science of portable precision timekeeping, devoted his

---

9. Fountain of Youth . . . lead into gold three imaginary goals seriously pursued by inquirers. The Fountain of Youth was supposed to restore youth. Perpetual motion would allow people to generate power endlessly without consuming fuel. A formula to turn the cheap metal lead into the precious metal gold was sought for centuries by alchemists.

▼ **Critical Viewing** Does the appearance of Harrison's marine watch reflect its world-altering importance? Explain. **[Support]**

life to this quest. He accomplished what Newton had feared was impossible: He invented a clock that would carry the true time from the home port, like an eternal flame, to any remote corner of the world.

Harrison, a man of simple birth and high intelligence, crossed swords with the leading lights of his day. He made a special enemy of the Reverend Nevil Maskelyne, the fifth astronomer royal, who contested his claim to the coveted prize money, and whose tactics at certain junctures can only be described as foul play.

With no formal education or apprenticeship to any watchmaker, Harrison nevertheless constructed a series of virtually friction-free clocks that required no lubrication and no cleaning, that were made from materials <u>impervious</u> to rust, and that kept their moving parts perfectly balanced in relation to one another, regardless of how the world pitched or tossed about them. He did away with the pendulum, and he combined different metals inside his works in such a way that when one component expanded or contracted with changes in temperature, the other counteracted the change and kept the clock's rate constant.

His every success, however, was parried by members of the scientific elite, who distrusted Harrison's magic box. The commissioners charged with awarding the longitude prize—Nevil Maskelyne among them—changed the contest rules whenever they saw fit, so as to favor the chances of astronomers over the likes of Harrison and his fellow "mechanics."[10] But the utility and accuracy of Harrison's approach triumphed in the end. His followers shepherded Harrison's intricate, exquisite invention through the design modifications that enabled it to be mass produced and enjoy wide use.

An aged, exhausted Harrison, taken under the wing of King George III, ultimately claimed his rightful monetary reward in 1773—after forty struggling years of political intrigue, international warfare, academic backbiting, scientific revolution, and economic upheaval.

All these threads, and more, entwine in the lines of longitude. To unravel them now—to retrace their story in an age when a network of orbiting satellites can nail down a ship's position within a few feet in just a moment or two—is to see the globe anew.

---

10. **"mechanics"** skilled workers and tradesmen, of a lower class than merchants or aristocrats.

Literary Analysis
Expository Essay
Explain how this paragraph is linked to Sobel's earlier explanations of why it was difficult to keep accurate time at sea.

Vocabulary Builder
impervious
(im pʉr′ vē əs) *adj.* not affected by (used with *to*)

Apply the Skills

from *Longitude*

Thinking About the Selection

1. **Respond:** If you could go back in time, which of the historic figures mentioned in this article would you like to meet? Why?
2. **(a) Recall:** Acccording to Sobel, what two methods can sailors use to estimate their latitude? **(b) Apply:** Using one of these methods, how could you tell whether you were at the equator (the zero-degree latitude)? **(c) Compare and Contrast:** Why is determining latitude easier than determining longitude?
3. **Analyze:** Briefly explain why the invention of an accurate clock was crucial to solving the problem of longitude.
4. **Analyze Cause and Effect:** Why did Harrison have difficulties getting his solution to the problem of longitude recognized?
5. **(a) Speculate:** Identify two ways in which the world would be different without Harrison's clocks. **(b) Discuss:** Share your thoughts with other students, offering improvements as you discuss them. **(c) Evaluate:** Choose the best idea and share it with the class.

Literary Analysis

6. **(a)** What event does Sobel explain in this **expository essay?** **(b)** Briefly explain how she uses facts about astronomy and navigation to help readers understand the significance of this event.
7. Distances in longitude are proportionate to hours: 360 degrees of longitude "equals" twenty-four hours. Using **deductive reasoning,** Sobel applies this principle to the case of two places with a 1-hour time difference. What conclusion does she draw?
8. How does Sobel uses **inductive reasoning** to prove that navigation was perilous without precise longitude measurements?

Reading Skill

9. Using a chart like the one shown, identify the **main ideas** and the **supporting details** in the essay.

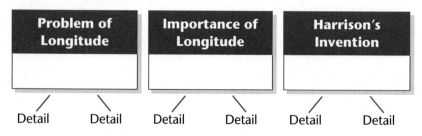

10. In your own words, summarize the essay.

QuickReview

Essay at a Glance
Early navigators struggled with the difficult problem of finding an accurate way to determine longitude at sea.

Go Online
——Assessment
For: Self-test
Visit: www.PHSchool.com
Web Code: eqa-6303

Expository Essay: a brief nonfiction work in which an author informs, defines, explains, or discusses

Inductive Reasoning: drawing a generalization from a number of cases

Deductive Reasoning: proving that a conclusion is true by applying a general principle to a specific case

Main Idea: a writer's main point about the topic of a paragraph or an essay

Supporting Detail: an idea or a fact that explains or illustrates a main idea

Vocabulary Builder

Practice Write a one-sentence answer to each question. Then, explain how the meaning of the underlined word from the vocabulary list for *Longitude,* on page 426, helped you.

1. What might a room look like if it is <u>haphazardly</u> decorated?
2. Has he <u>derived</u> a correct conclusion if he was missing information?
3. What is the <u>configuration</u> of desks in your classroom?
4. Do you think anyone is truly <u>impervious</u> to criticism?

Adding Words to Your Vocabulary Use a dictionary to find a word that begins with the same first syllable as each word listed for *Longitude* on page 426. Explain whether the words in each pair share a common origin. (For more on using a dictionary, see page R6.)

Writing

Imagine that you are John Harrison. Write a **business letter** to King George III explaining your invention. (For the format of a business letter, see page R29.)
- Briefly describe your clock and explain how it determines longitude.
- Mention the resistance you have met from the Royal Society.
- Use language that will appeal to a ruler accustomed to respect.

For *Grammar, Vocabulary,* and *Assessment,* see **Build Language Skills,** pages 446–447.

Extend Your Learning

Listening and Speaking Deliver a **humorous persuasive speech** in which you propose moving the prime meridian to your hometown.
- Come up with humorous ways to meet your audience's interests.
- Formulate a clear message—the main idea you want to get across.
- Choose effective language. Slang might seem contemporary, but formal language might command respect.

When you deliver your presentation, speak clearly and with energy.

Research and Technology An *abstract* is a paragraph summing up a research article's main points. Find two additional articles on navigation and write an **abstract** of each. Proofread your work for errors in punctuation or spelling. Check technical vocabulary carefully. Use a dictionary or other reference work as necessary.

Build Language Skills

The Spider and the Wasp • from *Longitude*

Vocabulary Skill

Prefixes The *prefixes en-* and *em-* mean "in, into, or within." The word *enlighten* is built from the prefix *en-*, which means "in" or "into," and the word "light." Knowing the meaning of the prefix helps you to remember that *enlighten* means "to put [mental] light into" or "to bring someone to understand."

▶ **Example:** The goal of education is to *enlighten* students about a variety of subjects.

Practice Use a dictionary to look up each of the *en-* or *em-* words listed, and fill in the chart. Then, for each word, write a one-sentence explanation of how the prefix contributes to the meaning of the word.

	enmesh	empower	enthrall	empathy	endemic
prefix meaning					
meaning of word					

Grammar Lesson

Direct and Indirect Objects A **direct object** is a noun or pronoun that receives the action of an action verb. To find the direct object of a verb, answer the question "[verb] *whom?*" or "[verb] *what?*"

▶ **Example:** Sam threw Fred the ball.
Threw what? ANSWER/DIRECT OBJECT: the ball

An **indirect object** is used with a direct object and names the person or thing that something is given to or done for. To find the indirect object of a verb, answer the question "[verb] *to or for whom?*" or "[verb] *to or for what?*"

▶ **Example:** Sam threw Fred the ball.
Threw to whom? ANSWER/INDIRECT OBJECT: Fred

Practice Write three sentences in the following pattern: subject, action verb, indirect object, direct object. Then, explain what the direct object and indirect object add to the meaning of the sentences.

W͜G *Prentice Hall Writing and Grammar Connection: Chapter 19, Section 3*

MorePractice

For more practice with verbs that take objects, see the Grammar Handbook, p. R40.

Reading: Main Idea and Supporting Details

Directions: *Read the following selection. Then, answer the questions.*
(1) So one must ask if private luxury has any future at all. (2) I hope and fear: yes. (3) For if it is true that the struggle for difference is a part of the mechanism of evolution, and that the desire to squander has its roots in our natural drives, then luxury can never completely disappear, and the question is only which form it will take in its flight from its own shadow.

—from "The Future of Luxury" by Hans Enzensberger

Standards Assessed
• 10.2.1
• 10.4.5
• 10.5.2

1. Which of the following best captures the main idea of this paragraph?
   A Luxury is disappearing.
   B Luxury has a future.
   C Humans are governed by natural drives.
   D The struggle for difference is part of the mechanism of evolution.

2. Which of the following describes sentence 3?
   A main idea
   B topic sentence
   C supporting detail
   D transition

3. Which of the following would NOT support the main idea of this paragraph?
   A evidence of rising sales of luxury goods
   B discoveries of ancient luxury goods
   C the discovery of a culture without luxuries
   D the invention of a new type of luxury goods

4. The paragraph's main idea is primarily developed by
   A personal reflections.
   B examples.
   C reasons.
   D statistical evidence.

Timed Writing: Explanation [Connections]

"Everything that is unknown is taken to be grand."

—Tacitus

Does knowing the full story about something take all the mystery out of it? Review "The Spider and the Wasp" or the excerpt from *Longitude*. Using details from the selection and from your experience to illustrate your points, explain the meaning of the quotation. **(30 minutes)**

Writing Workshop: *Work in Progress*

Letter to the Editor

Write down two important facts or examples for three of the issues on your Issue List. Use polite, respectful language that would convey the correct tone. Put this work in your writing portfolio.

Technical Directions

In Part 1, you learned about main idea and supporting details when reading literature. These skills are also valuable when you are working with technical directions. The different categories of information are the main ideas. The specific information and steps are the supporting details.

If you read the essay "Longitude," you know that sailors spent centuries trying to get the details right in order to implement a main idea—measuring longitude.

Academic Standards

- Understand specific technical vocabulary. (10.1.1)
- Review and revise writing. (10.4.10)
- Revise writing based on specific criteria. (10.4.11)

About Technical Directions

Technical directions offer step-by-step instruction on how to assemble, operate, or repair a product. Technical directions, along with other informational materials that you **read to perform a task,** often have these features:

- A diagram of the device with the parts listed and labeled
- Numbered steps to follow
- A troubleshooting guide
- Manufacturer's contact information
- Warranty information

Reading Skill

Technical directions are complicated. To ensure that your setup and use of a new device go smoothly, **preview the text.** Look at headings and diagrams to get a sense of the kind of information provided. Identify any unfamiliar terms. Before you begin working, make sure you know the answers to the questions shown.

Questions for Previewing Technical Directions
What does the device do?
What specific functions does it have?
What are the main parts?
What tools or materials are needed?
What are the safety warnings?

Next, **read closely** the steps you must follow to operate the device or to use one of its functions. Look for initial setup instructions—steps that need to be accomplished before any other use can be made of the device. Pay careful attention to the order in which steps must be followed.

How to Use a
Compass

Our compasses have been the accurate and easy-to-use choice of foresters, geologists, surveyors, scientific explorers, sports enthusiasts, military personnel, and many others for 50 years. Most of our compasses include these features:

- Magnetized tungsten steel needle
- Friction-free sapphire bearing
- Permanently clear, antistatic liquid
- Accurate from − 40° to +140°F

Inch Scale —
Direction of Travel Arrow

Orienting Arrow

Magnetic Needle

Base Lines

Index Line

Mile Scale

Rotating Dial, 5°

Orienting Lines

Clear Base Plate

Technical directions usually list the functions the device performs and any special features it has.

This diagram identifies the parts of the compass with labels to help users follow the written instructions.

This section explains the easiest use of the compass. Other sections give instructions for other uses.

Easy as 1-2-3

Point the Base Plate to Your Destination:

Place your compass on the map with the edge along the desired line of travel.

Set the Compass Heading:

Turn the compass Dial until "N" points to the north on your map. Your direction in degrees is read at the Index Line on the Dial.

NOTE: Align the Dial with magnetic north if it is marked on your map. If it is not marked on your map, align the Dial with true north and adjust for declination.

Follow Your Heading:

- Remove the compass from your map and hold it level, so the Magnetic Needle is free to turn.
- Turn your body until the red end of the Needle aligns with the Orienting Arrow and "N" on the Dial.

Find Your Way Without a Map:

Find a heading (field bearing):

1. Select a landmark along the route you want to travel. Hold the compass level and point the Direction of Travel Arrow at the landmark.
2. Find your heading to the landmark by turning the compass dial until the "N" aligns with the red end of the Needle. Read your heading in degrees at the Index Line.
3. Keep the Needle aligned with the "N"; look up; sight on your landmark and walk to it. Repeat this procedure until you reach your destination.

When you know your heading:

1. If you've been given a heading in degrees to travel, turn the Dial so that the heading is set at the Index Line. Hold the compass level in front of you with the Direction of Travel Arrow pointing straight ahead.
2. Turn your body until the red end of the Needle is aligned with the "N" on the dial. You now face your direction of travel.
3. Pick out a landmark in line with your heading and move toward it. Repeat this procedure until you reach your destination.

NOTE: Be aware of nearby iron or steel objects. They may attract the Magnetic Needle if too close to the compass. Even a hidden nail can deflect the needle.

Compass Warranty--------------------

What Is Covered?

We warrant your compass to be free from defects in materials or workmanship, and **we guarantee its accuracy**, for the life of the compass.

What Is Not Covered?

Normal wear, abrasion, melting, misuse, alteration, abuse, or taking apart the compass is not covered by this warranty.

How to Obtain Warranty Service or Repair of Your Compass

Should your compass become defective under the terms of this warranty, call the Customer Satisfaction Department toll free at 1 (800) 123-4567 for return authorization. If, after our inspection, we find that the product was defective in material or workmanship, we shall, at our option, either repair or replace it without charge. If repairs not covered under this warranty are required, we will contact you for approval to proceed. You will be charged for the components repaired or replaced, plus a nominal charge for labor

There are no other express warranties beyond the terms of this limited warranty. In no event shall our company be liable for incidental or consequential damages arising from using our compasses.

Test Practice

Standards
Assessed
• 10.1.1
• 10.4.10
• 10.4.11

Reading: Following Directions to Complete a Task

Directions: *Choose the letter of the best answer to each question about the directions for the compass.*

1. In the "Easy as 1-2-3" version of the directions, which one of these items do you need in order to set your heading?
   A flashlight
   B map
   C mirror
   D guide to local landmarks

2. If you have been given a heading to travel, what is your first step in using the compass?
   A Place the compass on your map with the edge touching a landmark.
   B Turn your body until the Needle is aligned with "N."
   C Hold the compass level in front of you.
   D Turn the Dial to set the heading at the Index Line.

3. In which circumstances will the company NOT repair the compass free of charge?
   A You have already taken the compass apart.
   B The compass broke during shipping.
   C The compass needle is missing.
   D You took the compass with you when hiking.

Reading: Comprehension and Interpretation

Directions: *Write your answers on a separate piece of paper.*

4. Describe the three main parts of the compass. **[Knowledge]**
5. Contrast the function of the Direction of Travel Arrow with the function of the Magnetic Needle. **[Organizing]**

Timed Writing: Persuasion

Write a letter in which you request a repair under warranty for your compass. In your letter, describe a specific damage or defect in the compass. Then, cite details from the warranty to explain the reasons you believe that the problem is covered. **(20 minutes)**

Practice these skills with either "The Sun Parlor" (p. 454) or the selection from "In Commemoration: One Million Volumes" (p. 463).

Academic Standards

- Examine how the author's perspective influences the structure and tone of the text. (10.2.4)
- Write responses to literature. (10.5.2)

Literary Analysis

A **reflective essay** is a brief nonfiction work in which a writer presents the experiences that shaped or inspired his or her thoughts on a topic. In a reflective essay, a writer

- draws on an event, a time period, or an idea from his or her own life and experience.
- weaves a connection between personal experience and a point of general interest, such as a lesson about life.
- reflects on a specific object, scene, occasion, place, or idea.

Look for these characteristics of a reflective essay as you read.

Reading Skill

To fully understand an essay, **analyze main ideas and supporting details**—recognize each main point that the writer makes and identify the ideas or facts that explain or illustrate it. To help you analyze, **ask questions** as you read.

- What is the topic of this passage?
- What is the main point being made?
- Which details support this point?

As you read, use a chart like the one shown to record the main ideas and supporting details.

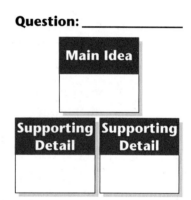

Vocabulary Builder

The Sun Parlor

- **lavished** (lav´ ish′t) *v.* gave with extreme generosity (p. 455) *She lavished candy on us, and we had to borrow a bag to carry it home.*

- **subordinate** (sə bôrd´′n it) *adj.* below another in importance or rank (p. 455) *A private is subordinate to a general.*

- **rejuvenation** (ri jōō´ və nā´ shən) *n.* a making new, youthful, or energetic again (p. 456) *A warm bath is a good method for rejuvenation.*

- **cajoling** (kə jōl´ iŋ) *n.* coaxing with flattery (p. 459) *I resisted her cajoling and did not sign up for the play.*

from One Million Volumes

- **inherent** (in hir´ ənt) *adj.* inborn; natural; characteristic (p. 464) *Her inherent sweetness makes it hard for her to get angry.*

- **dilapidated** (də lap´ ə dāt´ id) *adj.* shabby; broken down (p. 466) *The dilapidated chair broke when I sat on it.*

- **enthralls** (en thrôlz´) *v.* captivates; fascinates (p. 467) *This book enthralls me, and I cannot wait to finish it.*

- **poignant** (poin´ yənt) *adj.* emotionally moving; piercing (p. 469) *The poignant scene with the puppies always makes me cry.*

Build Understanding • *The Sun Parlor*

Background

Parlors and Sun Parlors In past eras, many houses, like the one described in "The Sun Parlor," included a room called the parlor. An early version of the modern living room, the parlor was a place for family members to visit with guests or with each other. A sun parlor, or solarium, enclosed mostly by glass, was intended for enjoying the sun and for reading and talking.

Connecting to the Literature

Reading/Writing Connection The sun parlor in this essay is a room for which the writer has strong protective feelings. Write two or three sentences describing a room that has special significance for you. Use at least three of these words: *derive, embody, evoke, generate.*

READ MORE

by Dorothy West
The Living Is Easy
The Richer, the Poorer

Meet the Author

Dorothy **West** (1907–1998)

Dorothy West enjoyed a comfortable childhood—one made possible by her family's fiery ambition and hard work. Her father, a former slave, came north and built a successful business in Boston.

A Lifetime of Writing By the age of fourteen, West was winning local writing competitions in Boston. A few years later, in 1926, she moved to New York City and contributed to the Harlem Renaissance, an outpouring of African American creativity in the 1920s.

West wrote short stories, novels, and essays. She spent the last half of her life in Oak Bluffs, the village in Martha's Vineyard that is the setting for "The Sun Parlor."

Fast Facts

▶ West's second novel, *The Wedding,* was not published until 1995, though she started it decades earlier.
▶ Oprah Winfrey made the novel into a television movie.

Go **Online**
Author Link

For: More about the author
Visit: www.PHSchool.com
Web Code: eqe-9304

The Sun Parlor
Dorothy West

This is a tale with a moral. I will try not to tax your attention too long. But I have to go way back to begin because it begins with my childhood. It is about houses and children, and which came first.

▲ Critical Viewing
Based on this painting, what feelings do you think will be described in the essay?
[Connect]

There were four of us children, well-schooled in good manners, well-behaved almost all of the time, and obedient to the commands of grown-ups, the power people who could make or break us.

We lived in a beautiful house. The reason I knew that is because all my mother's friends said so, and brought their other friends to see it. On the day appointed for the tour, which included inspection of every room on every floor, my mother would gather us around her and say in her gentlest voice, "I'm sorry, children, but Mrs. So-and-so is coming today and bringing a friend to see our house. You children keep clean and play quietly while they're here. It's not a real visit. They won't stay long. It'll be over before you can say Jack Robinson."

Most often a first-time caller, having <u>lavished</u> praise on everything she saw, including us, proceeded out without any further remarks. But there were others who, when they saw four children good as gold, did not see beyond their size, and asked my mother in outspoken horror, "How can you bear to let children loose in a lovely house like this?"

Every time it happened we were terrified. What would happen to us if my mother decided her house was too good for us and she hated the sight of us? What would we do, where would we go, would we starve?

My mother looked at our stricken faces, and her own face softened and her eyes filled with love. Then she would say to her inquisitor, though she did not say it rudely, "The children don't belong to the house. The house belongs to the children. No room says, *Do not enter.*"

I did not know I could ever forget those sentiments. But once, to my lasting regret, I did. With the passage of years I took my place with grown-ups, and there was another generation, among them the little girl, Sis, who was my mother's treasure. The summer she was eight was the one time I forgot that a child is not <u>subordinate</u> to a house.

We had a cottage in the Highlands of Oak Bluffs of unimpressive size and appearance. My mother loved it for its easy care. It couldn't even stand in the shade of our city house, and there certainly were no special rules for children. No one had ever looked aghast at a child on its premises.

Except me, the summer I painted the sun parlor. I am not a painter, but I am a perfectionist. I threw my whole soul into the project, and worked with such diligence and painstaking care that when the uncounted hours ended I felt that I had painted the Sistine Chapel.[1]

Vocabulary Builder
lavished (lav´ ish'd) *v.* gave with extreme generosity

Vocabulary Builder
subordinate (sə bôrd´'n it) *adj.* below another in importance or rank

✓Reading Check
What does the author say she regrets forgetting?

---

1. the Sistine Chapel (sis´ tēn´ chap´ əl) place of worship in the Vatican, Rome, the Pope's residence. The chapel is famed for scenes painted on its walls and ceiling by Michelangelo.

School vacation began, and Sis arrived for the long holiday, the car pulling up at the edge of the brick walk, and Sis streaking into the house for a round of hugs, then turning to tear upstairs to take off her travel clothes and put on her play clothes, and suddenly her flying feet braking to a stop in front of the sun parlor, its open door inviting inspection.

She who was always in motion, she who never took time for a second look at anything, or cared whether her bed was smooth or crumpled, or noticed what was on her plate as long as it was something to eat—she, in the awakening that came when she was eight, in her first awareness of something outside herself, stood in the doorway of the sun parlor, her face filled with the joy of her discovery, and said in a voice on the edge of tears, "It's the most beautiful room I ever saw in my whole life."

I did not hear her. I did not really hear her. I did not recognize the magnitude of that moment. I let it sink to some low level of my subconscious. All I saw was that her foot was poised to cross the threshold of my chapel.

I let out a little cry of pain. "Sis," I said, "please don't go in the sun parlor. There's nothing in there to interest a child. It's not a place for children to play in. It's a place for grown-ups to sit in. Go and change. Summer is outside waiting for you to come and play wherever you please."

In a little while the sounds of Sis's soaring laughter were mingling with the happy sounds of other vacationing children. They kept any doubt I might have had from surfacing. Sis was surely more herself running free than squirming on a chair in the sun parlor.

All the same I monitored that room, looking for smudges and streaks, scanning the floor for signs of scuffing. The room bore no scars, and Sis showed no trace of frustration.

The summer flowed. My friends admired the room, though they did it without superlatives. To them it was a room I had talked about redoing for a long time. Now I had done it. So much for that.

The summer waned, and Sis went home for school's reopening, as did the other summer children, taking so much life and laughter with them that the ensuing days recovered slowly.

Then my mother's sister, my favorite aunt, arrived from New York for her usual stay at summer's end. She looked ten years younger than her actual years. She seemed to bounce with energy, as if she had gone through some process of <u>rejuvenation</u>. We asked her for the secret.

There was no way for us to know in the brimful days that followed that there really was a secret she was keeping from us. She had had

Reading Skill
Analyzing Main Idea and Support Which details support the idea that Sis's reaction is exceptional?

Literary Analysis
Reflective Essay How is this experience connected to the lesson that the author learned from her mother?

Vocabulary Builder
rejuvenation
(ri jōō′ və nā′ shən) *n.* a making new, youthful, or energetic again

◄ **Critical Viewing**
Do you think this
painting reflects the
author's description of
the summer children?
Why or why not?
[Connect]

a heart attack some months before, and she had been ordered to follow a strict set of rules: plenty of rest during the day, early to bed at night, take her medicine faithfully, carefully watch her diet.

She was my mother's younger sister. My mother had been her babysitter. She didn't want my mother to know that she was back to being a baby again, needing to be watched over, having to be put down for a nap, having to be spoon-fed pap. She kept herself busy around the clock, walking, lifting, sitting up late, eating her favorite foods and forgetting her medicine.

✅ **Reading Check**
What is the matter
with West's aunt?

And then one day standing over the stove involved in the making of a meal that a master chef might envy, she collapsed, and the doctor was called, and the doctor called the ambulance.

She was in the hospital ten days. When she was ready to come home to convalesce, we turned the sun parlor into a sickroom, for the stairs to the upper story were forbidden to her. At night we who, when she slept upstairs, would talk family talk back and forth from our beds far into the night, without her we were now quiet, not wanting our voices to wake her if she was asleep, knowing her recovery depended on rest and quiet.

But at night she slept fitfully. The sleeping house and separation from the flock were unbearable. She was afraid of the sun parlor, seeing it as an abnormal offshoot from the main part of the house, its seven long windows giving access to so many imagined terrors. She did not know if we would hear her if she called. She did not know if she would ever get well.

▲ **Critical Viewing**
In what way does this painting suggest a room apart from the rest of the house, like the sun parlor? **[Connect]**

Reading Skill
Analyzing Main Ideas and Support What main idea do these details about the aunt's stay in the sun parlor suggest?

She did not get well. She went back to the hospital, and for our sakes was brave in her last days, comforting us more than we comforted her.

When it was over, we took the sickbed away and restored the sun parlor to its natural look. But it did not look natural. The sadness resisted the sun's cajoling. It had settled in every corner. The seven long windows streaming light did not help. I closed the door and locked it.

My mother saw the closed door and the key in my hand. She said as a simple statement of fact, "A little girl wanted to love that room, and you wouldn't let her. We learn so many lessons as we go through life."

"I know that now," I said. "I wish I had known it then."

Another summer came, and with it Sis. The sun parlor door was open again, the room full of light with the sadness trying to hide itself whenever she passed. I did not know how to say to her, "You can go in the sun parlor if you want to." I did not know whether she knew it had been a sickroom, and might say, "Take your sun parlor and you-know-what," though in less succinct phrasing. I did not know if she yet knew that nothing can be the same once it has been different.

Other summers passed, older family members died, and mine became the oldest generation. I was living on the Island year-round in the winterized cottage. The sun parlor was just another everyday room, its seven long windows reduced to three of standard size, most of the furniture replaced for sturdier sitting.

Sis was married, a mother, coming to visit when she could— coming, I think, to look for bits and pieces of my mother in me, wanting to see her ways, hear her words through me.

It was a year ago that I asked her the question that had been on my mind, it seems, forever. A dozen times I had bitten it off my tongue because I did not know what she might answer.

"Sis," I said, "do you remember the summer I painted the sun parlor and acted as if I thought more of it than I thought of you? I'm not asking you to forgive me. All I want to know is if sometimes my mother said to you when I went out, 'She's gone.'" My mother always referred to me as "she" when she was annoyed with me. "'She said she'd be gone awhile. You go play in that sun parlor if you want to. There's nothing in there you can hurt. Nothing in that room is worth as much as a child.'"

I saw her lips beginning to part. And I felt my heart trembling.

"I don't want to know the answer. Please don't tell me the answer. I had to ask the question. It's enough for me that you listened."

She smiled.

Vocabulary Builder
cajoling (kə jōl′ iŋ) *n.* coaxing with flattery

Literary Analysis
Reflective Essay
What lesson about life has the author learned?

Apply the Skills

The Sun Parlor

Thinking About the Selection

1. **Respond:** How did you react when West asks Sis not to go into the parlor?
2. **(a) Recall:** What project does West take on to improve the sun parlor? **(b) Infer:** Why does she tell Sis not to go into the room? **(c) Connect:** Does West's response to Sis reflect what her mother taught her about respect for children? Explain.
3. **(a) Compare and Contrast:** Contrast Sis's first reaction to the parlor with her reactions to other things. **(b) Interpret:** What does West mean by calling Sis's reaction part of an "awakening"?
4. **(a) Infer:** Why does the family turn the parlor into a bedroom? **(b) Analyze:** How does this arrangement affect the aunt and the rest of the family? **(c) Interpret:** What point about the room is made by the story of the aunt's stay and her death?
5. **(a) Interpret:** What does West mean when she says to Sis, "It's enough for me that you listened"? **(b) Connect:** Explain how the statement could also indicate the reason West wrote this essay. **(c) Discuss:** In a group, discuss why it is important to West that people "listen." As a group, come up with an explanation and present it to the class.

Literary Analysis

6. Using a chart like the one shown, analyze West's use of the sun parlor as a focus for the elements of her **reflective essay.** For each detail you list, explain its connection to the sun parlor.

7. Explain what point is made by the feelings and events associated with the sun parlor.

Reading Skill

8. **(a)** Reread the first six paragraphs. What is the topic of this section? **(b)** What point is made? **(c)** What details support it?
9. **(a)** What is the next **main idea** you find in the essay? **(b)** Identify three **supporting details** for the idea.

Vocabulary Builder

Practice For each of the following sentences, write a new sentence with the same meaning by using a word from the vocabulary list for "The Sun Parlor," on page 452.

1. I gave in to my brother's wheedling and let him borrow my new video game.
2. The star gets one dressing room, while the lesser-known actors share the other.
3. They showered praise on us for our extremely successful fund drive.
4. The complete recovery of her knee after surgery was a wonder.

Adding Words to Your Vocabulary Using a thesaurus, find an **antonym** (word opposite in meaning) for each of the words in the vocabulary list on page 452. Use each antonym in a sentence in which you make the meaning of the word clear. (For more help using a thesaurus, see page R7.)

Writing

Write a brief **memoir**, or recollection based on personal experience, of a room that has been meaningful to you. Use precise words to paint a vivid picture of the space and to illustrate the power of its memory for you. Make sure that you show, either in your description or your narration of events, why the room has meaning for you.

For *Grammar*, *Vocabulary*, and *Assessment*, see **Build Language Skills**, pages 472–473.

Extend Your Learning

Research and Technology In her essay, West writes that the eight-year-old Sis is at the beginning of an awakening. Gather materials for a brief **multimedia presentation** on the developmental stages children go through between the ages of four and nine. Use the Internet and library sources to conduct research on these stages. Save your materials in a multimedia portfolio.

Listening and Speaking Prepare an **oral recollection** of someone you know who is interesting or important to you. Provide key details that will bring the person to life. Present your recollection to the class.

Build Understanding • from *In Commemoration: One Million Volumes*

Background

Libraries In this essay, Anaya is astounded by the size of the University of New Mexico's library. Libraries perform a variety of functions. For example, a neighborhood library may preserve local history. A university library supports the research of scholars in a variety of subject areas. The Library of Congress guards the historical and cultural record of the United States.

Connecting to the Literature

Reading/Writing Connection In his essay, Anaya talks about a feeling of "exhilaration from reading." List two or three titles of works that have made an impact on you. Briefly explain what you responded to in each. Use at least three of these words: *derive, embody, formulate, evoke.*

Review

For **Literary Analysis, Reading Skill,** and **Vocabulary Builder,** see page 452.

READ MORE

by Rudolfo Anaya

Heart of Aztlán

Meet the Author

Rudolfo **Anaya** (b. 1937)

Rudolfo Anaya was born and raised in the rural village of Pastura in New Mexico. As a child, Anaya's imagination was nourished by *cuentos*—stories that Mexican Americans passed down from one generation to the next.

Teaching and Learning While teaching high school English, Anaya wrote *Bless Me, Ultima,* a highly praised novel about a young boy growing up in New Mexico. The novel was published in 1972. A strong voice of the Mexican American experience, Anaya is considered a founder of Chicano literature.

Anaya went on to teach at the University of New Mexico until his retirement in 1993. In his writing, though, he plays the student as much as the teacher. He explains, "Writing novels seems to be the medium which allows me to bring together all the questions I ask about life."

Fast Facts

▶ In 2002, Anaya was awarded a National Medal of the Arts.
▶ Anaya has also received the Mexican Medal of Friendship.

For: More about the author
Visit: www.PHSchool.com
Author Link Web Code: eqe-9305

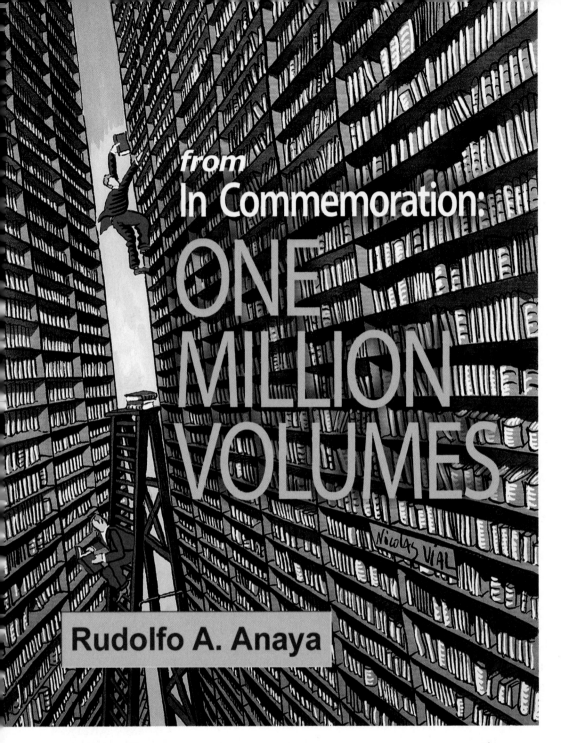

from

In Commemoration:
ONE MILLION VOLUMES

Nicolas VIAL

Rudolfo A. Anaya

A million volumes.

A magic number.

A million books to read, to look at, to hold in one's hand, to learn, to dream. . . .

I have always known there were at least a million stars. In the summer evenings when I was a child, we, all the children of the neighborhood, sat outside under the stars and listened to the stories of the old ones, los viejitos.[1] The stories of the old people taught us to wonder and imagine. Their adivinanzas[2] induced the stirring of our first questioning, our early learning.

I remember my grandfather raising his hand and pointing to the swirl of the Milky Way which swept over us. Then he would whisper his favorite riddle:

> Hay un hombre con tanto dinero
> Que no lo puede contar
> Una mujer con una sábana tan grande
> Que no la puede doblar.

> There is a man with so much money
> He cannot count it
> A woman with a bedspread so large
> She cannot fold it

We knew the million stars were the coins of the Lord, and the heavens were the bedspread of his mother, and in our minds the sky was a million miles wide. A hundred million. Infinite. Stuff for the imagination. And what was more important, the teachings of the old ones made us see that we were bound to the infinity of that cosmic dance of life which swept around us. Their teachings created in us a thirst for knowledge. Can this library with its million volumes bestow that same inspiration?

I was fortunate to have had those old and wise viejitos as guides into the world of nature and knowledge. They taught me with their stories; they taught me the magic of words. Now the words lie captured in ink, but the magic is still there, the power <u>inherent</u> in each volume. Now with book in hand we can participate in the wisdom of mankind.

Each person moves from innocence through rites of passage into the knowledge of the world, and so I entered the world of school in search of the magic in the words. The sounds were no longer the soft sounds of Spanish which my grandfather spoke; the words were in English, and with each new awareness came my first steps toward a million volumes. I, who was used to reading my oraciones en español[3] while I sat in the kitchen and answered the litany to the slap of my mother's tortillas,[4] I now stumbled from sound to word to groups of words, head throbbing, painfully aware that each new

Vocabulary Builder
inherent (in hir´ ənt) *adj.* inborn; natural; characteristic

Literary Analysis
Reflective Essay
Which period in his life is the writer describing?

---

1. **los viejitos** (lôs byā hē´ tôs) *n.* the old ones.
2. **adivinanzas** (a *th*ē vē nan´ sas) *n.* riddles.
3. **oraciones en español** (ô ra syôn´ ās en es pa nyōl´) prayers in Spanish.
4. **tortillas** (tôr tē´ yəs) *n.* thin, flat, round cakes of unleavened cornmeal.

Literature in Context   Culture Connection

Mexican American Pride

Anaya's celebration of his grandfather's *cuentos* shares in the spirit of the Chicano movement of the 1960s.

- Participants in the movement cultivated pride in their Mexican American heritage.
- Leaders included Cesar Chavez (shown in the mural), who unionized grape pickers in California.
- Chicano artists use the symbol of the eagle (seen in the mural) and serpent to reflect their connection with the Aztecs, founders of a great civilization in Mexico.

Connect to the Literature What is one way in which Anaya's essay celebrates his Mexican American heritage? Explain your answer.

Total U.S. Hispanic Population 2002: 37.4 million

- Central and South American 14.3%
- Puerto Rican 8.6%
- Cuban 3.7%
- Other Hispanic 6.5%
- Mexican 66.9%

Source: U.S. Census Bureau, March 2002

---

sound took me deeper into the maze of the new language. Oh, how I clutched the hands of my new guides then!

Learn, my mother encouraged me, learn. Be as wise as your grandfather. He could speak many languages. He could speak to the birds and the animals of the field.

Yes, I remember the cuentos[5] of my grandfather, the stories of the people. Words are a way, he said, they hold joy, and they are a deadly power if misused. I clung to each syllable which lisped from his tobacco-stained lips. That was the winter the snow came, he would say, it piled high and we lost many sheep and cattle, and the trees groaned and broke with its weight. I looked across the llano[6] and saw the raging blizzard, the awful destruction of that winter which was imbedded in our people's mind.

And the following summer, he would say, the grass of the llano grew so high we couldn't see the top of the sheep. And I would look and see what was once clean and pure and green. I could see a million sheep and the pastores[7] caring for them, as I now care for the million words that pasture in my mind.

Reading Skill
Analyzing Main Ideas and Support What main idea do details about his grandfather's stories support?

 **Reading Check**

What does Anaya learn to appreciate from his grandfather and the other *viejitos*?

---

5. **cuentos** (kwen´ tôs) *n.* stories.
6. **llano** (ya´ nō) *n.* plain.
7. **pastores** (pas tô´ rās) *n.* shepherds.

But a million books? How can we see a million books? I don't mean just the books lining the shelves here at the University of New Mexico Library, not just the fine worn covers, the intriguing titles; how can we see the worlds that lie waiting in each book? A million worlds. A million million worlds. And the beauty of it is that each world is related to the next, as was taught to us by the old ones. Perhaps it is easier for a child to see. Perhaps it is easier for a child to ask: How many stars are there in the sky? How many leaves in the trees of the river? How many blades of grass in the llano? How many dreams in a night of dreams?

So I worked my way into the world of books, but here is the paradox, a book at once quenches the thirst of the imagination and ignites new fires. I learned that as I visited the library of my childhood, the Santa Rosa Library. It was only a dusty room in those days, a room sitting atop the town's fire department, which was comprised of one <u>dilapidated</u> fire truck used by the town's volunteers only in the direst emergencies. But in that small room I found my shelter and retreat. If there were a hundred books there we were fortunate, but to me there were a million volumes. I trembled in awe when I first entered that library, because I realized that if the books held as much magic as the words of the old ones, then indeed this was a room full of power.

Miss Pansy, the librarian, became my new guide. She fed me books as any mother would nurture her child. She brought me book after book, and I consumed them all. Saturday afternoons disappeared as the time of day dissolved into the time of distant worlds. In a world that occupied most of my other schoolmates with games, I took the time to read. I was a librarian's dream. My tattered library card was my ticket into the same worlds my grandfather had known, worlds of magic that fed the imagination.

Late in the afternoon, when I was satiated with reading, when I could no longer hold in my soul the characters that crowded there, I heard the call of the llano, the real world of my father's ranchito, the solid, warm world of my mother's kitchen. Then to the surprise and bewilderment of Miss Pansy, I would rush out and race down the streets of our town, books tucked under my shirt, in my pockets, clutched tightly to my breast. Mad with the insanity of books, I would cross the river to get home, shouting my crazy challenge even at la Llorona,[8] and that poor spirit of so many frightening cuentos would wither and withdraw. She was no match for me.

Those of you who have felt the same exhilaration from reading—or from love—will know about what I'm speaking. Alas, the people of the town could only shake their heads and pity my mother. At least

Vocabulary Builder
dilapidated (də lap´ ə dāt´ id) *adj.* shabby; broken down

Literary Analysis
Reflective Essay
What general idea connects this new experience to those Anaya has already narrated?

---

8. la Llorona (la yô rô´ na) spirit of many stories, famous for shouting and crying for her lost love.

one of her sons was a bit touched. Perhaps they were right, for few will trade a snug reality to float on words to other worlds.

And now there are a million volumes for us to read here at the University of New Mexico Library. Books on every imaginable subject, in every field, a history of the thought of the world which we must keep free of censorship, because we treasure our freedoms. It is the word *freedom* which eventually must reflect what this collection, or the collection of any library, is all about. We know that as we preserve and use the literature of all cultures, we preserve and regenerate our own. The old ones knew and taught me this. They eagerly read the few newspapers that were available. They kept their diaries, they wrote décimas[9] and cuentos, and they survived on their oral stories and traditions.

Another time, another library. I entered Albuquerque[10] High School Library prepared to study, because that's where we spent our study time. For better or for worse, I received my first contracts as a writer there. It was a place where budding lovers spent most of their time writing notes to each other, and when my friends who didn't have the gift of words found out I could turn a phrase I quickly had all the business I could do. I wrote poetic love notes for a dime apiece and thus worked my way through high school. And there were fringe benefits, because the young women knew very well who was writing the sweet words, and many a heart I was supposed to capture fell in love with me. And so, a library is also a place where love begins.

A library should be the heart of a city. With its storehouse of knowledge, it liberates, informs, teaches, and <u>enthralls</u>. A library indeed should be the cultural center of any city. Amidst the bustle of work and commerce, the great libraries of the world have provided a sanctuary where scholars and common man alike come to enlarge and clarify knowledge, to read and reflect in quiet solitude.

I knew a place like this. I spent many hours in the old library on Central Avenue and Edith Street. But my world was growing, and quite by accident I wandered up the hill to enroll in the University of New Mexico. And what a surprise lay in store for me. The libraries of my childhood paled in comparison to this new wealth of books housed in Zimmerman Library. Here there were stack after stack of books, and ample space and time to wander aimlessly in this labyrinth of new frontiers.

I had known the communal memory of my people through the newspapers and few books my grandfather read to me and through the rich oral tradition handed down by the old ones; now I discov-

---

Reading Skill
Analyzing Main Ideas and Support Which details illustrate the main idea stated in the last sentence of this paragraph?

Vocabulary Builder
enthralls (en thrôlz´) v. captivates; fascinates

✓ **Reading Check**
During his childhood, where does Anaya spend his free time?

---

9. **décimas** (dā´ sē mas) *n.* ten-line stanzas.
10. **Albuquerque** (al´ bə kʉr´ kē) city in central New Mexico.

ered the collective memory of all mankind at my fingertips. I had only to reach for the books that laid all history bare. Here I could converse with the writers from every culture on earth, old and new, and at the same time I began my personal odyssey, which would add a few books to the collection which in 1981 would come to house a million volumes.

Those were exciting times. Around me swirled the busy world of the university, in many respects an alien world. Like many fellow undergraduates, I sought refuge in the library. My haven during those student university years was the reading room of the west

Literary Analysis
Reflective Essay
What general idea does Anaya use to relate this new period in his life to previous ones?

wing of the old library. There I found peace. The carved vigas[11] decorating the ceiling, the solid wooden tables and chairs and the warm adobe color of the stucco were things with which I was familiar. There I felt comfortable. With books scattered around me, I could read and doze and dream. I took my breaks in the warm sun of the portal, where I ate my tortilla sandwiches, which I carried in my brown paper bag. There, with friends, I sipped coffee as we talked of changing the world and exchanged idealistic dreams.

That is a rich and pleasant time in my memory. No matter how far across the world I find myself in the future, how deep in the creation of worlds with words, I shall keep the simple and <u>poignant</u> memories of those days. The sun set golden on the ocher walls, and the green pine trees and the blue spruce, sacred trees to our people, whispered in the breeze. I remembered my grandfather meeting with the old men of the village in the resolana[12] of one of the men's homes, or against the wall of the church on Sundays, and I remembered the things they said. Later, alone, dreaming against the sun-warmed wall of the library, I continued that discourse in my mind.

Yes, the library is a place where people should gather. It is a place for research, reading, and for the quiet fomentation of ideas, but because it houses the collective memory of our race, it should also be a place where present issues are discussed and debated and researched in order for us to gain the knowledge and insight to create a better future. The library should be a warm place that reflects the needs and aspirations of the people.

◄ **Critical Viewing**
How might Anaya feel about a scene such as this one? How do you know? [**Hypothesize**]

Vocabulary Builder
poignant (pȯin´ yǝnt) *adj.* emotionally moving; piercing

Reading Skill
Analyzing Main Ideas and Support What details support the main idea—that libraries serve a public, as well as private, purpose?

Apply the Skills

from *In Commemoration: One Million Volumes*

Thinking About the Selection

1. **Respond:** Do you share Anaya's feeling that libraries are a place of comfort? Explain.

2. **(a) Recall:** According to Anaya, what did the stories of *los viejitos* teach Anaya and other children? **(b) Compare and Contrast:** Identify a difference and a similarity between the riddles and *cuentos* Anaya learned in childhood and the books he later read.

3. **(a) Interpret:** What does Anaya mean when he writes that "a book at once quenches the thirst of the imagination and ignites new fires"? **(b) Connect:** How is this power of books similar to the power of the riddles and *cuentos* of Anaya's childhood?

4. **(a) Extend:** In today's world, what is the best way to awaken wonder and imagination in people and inspire them to learn? **(b) Discuss:** Share and discuss answers in a small group. **(c) Evaluate:** As a group, choose the best suggestions. Present them to the class.

Literary Analysis

5. Using a chart like the one shown, analyze Anaya's use of libraries as a focus for his **reflective essay.** For each detail you list, explain its connection to libraries.

6. **(a)** Choose three items from your chart, and explain how each is associated with something endless—an uncountable number, for example, or an unquenchable desire. **(b)** For each item you list, explain what general truth about people's imagination it illustrates.

Reading Skill

7. **(a)** Reread up to the paragraph that begins, "But a million books?" What is the topic of this section? **(b)** What point is made? **(c)** What details support it?

8. **(a)** What is the next **main idea** you find in the essay? **(b)** Identify three **supporting details** for the idea.

Vocabulary Builder

Practice For each of the following sentences, write a new sentence with the same meaning by using a word from the vocabulary list for the excerpt from "In Commemoration," on page 452.

1. Getting wet is a risk that is a built-in part of boating.
2. Their reunion was very emotional and touching.
3. My broken-down old bike is dangerous to ride.
4. Today, that comic book is wildly interesting to him, but when he is older, he will not give it a second look.

Adding Words to Your Vocabulary Using a thesaurus, find an **antonym** (word opposite in meaning) for each of the words in the vocabulary list on page 452. Use each antonym in a sentence in which you make the meaning of the word clear. (For more help using a thesaurus, see page R7.)

Writing

Write a brief **memoir,** a recollection based on your personal experience, of a building that has been meaningful to you. Use precise words to paint a vivid picture of the place and to illustrate the power of its memory for you. Make sure that you show, either in your description or your narration of events, why the building has special meaning for you.

For *Grammar, Vocabulary,* and *Assessment,*
see **Build Language Skills,** pages 472–473.

Extend Your Learning

Listening and Speaking Prepare an oral recollection of an organization or institution with which you have been involved, such as a team or community group. Provide key details that will help others understand the spirit of the organization. Present your recollection to the class.

Research and Technology In his essay, Anaya reveals his love of libraries. Gather materials for a multimedia presentation on the history of public libraries in the United States. Using the Internet and library sources, conduct research on those who helped promote public libraries and on their goals and values. Save your materials in a multimedia portfolio.

Build Language Skills

Vocabulary Skill

Prefixes The *prefixes con-* and *com-* come from a Latin word root meaning "with" or "together." Knowing the meaning of these prefixes can help you to understand and remember many English words that begin with them. *Con-* and *com-* can also be used to add emphasis to a word root.

▶ **Example:** When Andrew *confronted* Joel, a person known for his physical prowess, we were *concerned* for Andrew's safety.

Practice Use each of the underlined words in a sentence, according to the meaning given.

1. <u>confluence</u>: the coming together of two rivers
2. <u>complicity</u>: the cooperation of a guilty party in a crime
3. <u>contemporary</u>: at the same time
4. <u>commiserate</u>: offer a shoulder of sympathy to a friend
5. <u>commensurate</u>: proportionate; equal

Grammar Lesson

Subject Complements **Predicate nominatives** and **predicate adjectives** are subject complements. They appear after a linking verb and tell something about the subject of the sentence. A subject and a predicate nominative are two different words for the same person, place, or thing. The linking verb joins them and equates them.

▶ **Example:** Their first choice was <u>you</u>.

A predicate adjective appears with the linking verb and describes the subject of the sentence.

▶ **Example:** Roses are <u>red</u>.

Practice Add a predicate nominative or predicate adjective as indicated to complete the sentence.

1. Jill is (predicate nominative).
2. The nation's capital is (predicate nominative).
3. One danger in the mountains is (predicate nominative).
4. Marine life is (predicate adjective).
5. The delicate shells on the shore looked (predicate adjective).

MorePractice

For more practice with linking verbs, see the Grammar Handbook, p. R40.

W͟G Prentice Hall Writing and Grammar Connection: Chapter 19, Section 4

Reading: Main Idea and Supporting Details

Standards Assessed
- 10.2.4
- 10.5.2

Directions: *Read the selection. Then, answer the questions.*

Now, as a rule, when we see someone we don't know personally, we don't stare into his or her face at length, we don't point out the person to the friend at our side, we don't speak of this person in a loud voice when he or she can overhear. Such behavior would be rude, even—if carried too far—aggressive. But the same people who would never point to a customer at a counter and remark to a friend that the man is wearing a smart tie behave quite differently with famous faces.

—from "How to React to Familiar Faces" by Umberto Eco

1. Which of the following best expresses the main idea of this passage?
   A Public aggressiveness is rude.
   B Some people react differently to celebrities than to ordinary people.
   C Most people worship celebrities because of a lack of fulfillment.
   D People are unfriendly to strangers.

2. If *S* stands for "supporting detail" and *M* stands for "main idea," which characterizes the sequence of sentences in the passage?
   A S-S-M
   B S-M-S
   C M-S-S
   D S-M-M

3. To help readers appreciate what is odd about behavior toward celebrities, the writer
   A gives the opinions of an expert.
   B defends the right to privacy.
   C describes the rules of normal behavior.
   D explains why it is rude to comment on someone's tie.

4. What is the best title for this excerpt?
   A "Different Reactions, Same People"
   B "Aggressive Behavior in Normal People"
   C "Staring at Strangers"
   D "Don't Celebrities Deserve Common Courtesy?"

Timed Writing: Interpretation [Critical Stance]

Review "The Sun Parlor" or "In Commemoration." Interpret the theme of the work. Cite details from the work to support your interpretation.
(30 minutes)

 Writing Workshop: *Work in Progress*

Letter to the Editor
Using the work in your writing portfolio, write an opening sentence for each item in the previous assignment. Each sentence should identify the main point you might want to convey in your letter. Save this work in your writing portfolio.

Humorous Writing

A **humorous essay** or **speech** is a nonfiction composition in which the writer presents people, events, and ideas in unexpected, amusing ways. Often, a humor writer will treat a serious situation lightly or a ridiculous situation seriously. Techniques for creating humor include the following:

- Using **hyperbole**, or exaggeration for effect, a writer describes people, things, or events as if they were much greater than they are—for instance, calling the discovery of a missing sock a "joyous reunion."

- Using **understatement**, a writer speaks for effect of people, things, or events as if they were much less than they are—for instance, saying that "the weather during the party was not ideal" after a tornado carries off two picnic tables.

When a writer uses humor to point out the foolishness of a particular type of human behavior or of a particular institution, the result is called **satire**.

Comparing Humorous Writing

Both Mark Twain in "A Toast to the Oldest Inhabitant . . ." and James Thurber in "The Dog That Bit People" use humor. However, their subjects and their comic techniques are different. Use a chart like the one shown to compare the elements that make these selections humorous.

Academic Standards

- Examine how the author's perspective influences the structure and tone of the text. (10.2.4)
- Revise writing based on specific criteria. (10.4.11)

Hyperbole	Twain:
	Thurber:
Understatement	Twain:
	Thurber:
Satire	Twain:
	Thurber:

Vocabulary Builder

A Toast to the Oldest Inhabitant . . .

- **sumptuous** (sump´ chŏŏ əs) *adj.* lavish; splendid (p. 477) *The committee held a sumptuous dinner for the prize-winners.*

- **blemished** (blem´ ish't) *adj.* damaged; spoiled (p. 477) *The clear sky was not blemished by a single cloud.*

- **commences** (kə mens´ əs) *v.* begins (p. 479) *The teacher commences the class by taking attendance.*

- **vagaries** (vā´ gər ēz) *n.* erratic or unpredictable actions (p. 480) *The kite swooped and soared, following the vagaries of the breeze.*

The Dog That Bit People

- **incredulity** (in´ krə dŏŏ´ lə tē) *n.* unwillingness or inability to believe (p. 481) *Scientists responded to his wild ideas with incredulity.*

- **choleric** (käl´ ər ik) *adj.* having a quick temper; inclined to anger (p. 482) *The choleric boss yelled at the smallest mistakes.*

- **irascible** (i ras´ ə bəl) *adj.* irritable; quick-tempered (p. 483) *A long drive and lack of sleep made her irascible.*

- **indignant** (in dig´ nənt) *adj.* feeling or expressing anger, especially at an injustice (p. 485) *The protesters were indignant about pollution.*

Build Understanding

Connecting to the Literature

Reading/Writing Connection Twain and Thurber are experts at comedy, finding humor in such ordinary parts of life as pets and the weather. Write a sentence or two in which you describe a typical incident or situation in your own life that you find humorous. Use at least three of the following words: *affect, complicate, display, elaborate.*

Meet the Authors

Mark **Twain** (1835–1910)

Mark Twain is the pen name of Samuel Langhorne Clemens, one of America's greatest writers. He is most famous for two classic novels: *The Adventures of Tom Sawyer* (1876) and *The Adventures of Huckleberry Finn* (1884).

A Standup Comic At the height of his fame, Mark Twain was a sought-after, highly paid public speaker. He delivered "A Toast to the Oldest Inhabitant . . ." at the annual dinner of the New England Society on December 22, 1876.

James **Thurber** (1894–1961)

A native of Columbus, Ohio, James Thurber went to work for the U.S. State Department after college. Soon afterward, however, he found his true calling—he became a humorist, writing essays and drawing cartoons for *The New Yorker,* a famous magazine.

Growing Fame, Failing Vision Thurber won fame for his whimsical depictions of human (and animal) silliness. By the 1940s, however, his failing eyesight forced him to reduce the number of cartoon illustrations he produced. By 1952, Thurber was almost totally blind, but he continued to contribute stories and articles to the magazine. His collections, including *The Thurber Carnival* (1945), are considered classics of humor writing.

Go **O**nline
Author Link

For: More about the authors
Visit: www.PHSchool.com
Web Code: eqe-9306

A Toast to the Oldest Inhabitant:

The Weather of New England

Mark Twain

Who can lose it and forget it?
Who can have it and regret it?
Be interposer 'twixt us *Twain*.[1]
— *The Merchant of Venice,* William Shakespeare

Gentlemen: I reverently believe that the Maker who made us all, makes everything in New England[2]—but the weather. I don't know

▲ **Critical Viewing**
Based on this scene, what comments do you think Twain makes about New England weather? **[Preview]**

---

1. *Twain* archaic word for "two" (and a pun on Twain's name).
2. New England the states of the northeastern United States: Maine, Vermont, New Hampshire, Massachusetts, Rhode Island, and Connecticut.

who makes that, but I think it must be raw apprentices in the Weather Clerk's factory, who experiment and learn how in New England, for board and clothes, and then are promoted to make weather for countries that require a good article, and will take their custom elsewhere if they don't get it. There is a <u>sumptuous</u> variety about the New England weather that compels the stranger's admiration—and regret. The weather is always doing something there; always attending strictly to business; always getting up new designs and trying them on the people to see how they will go. But it gets through more business in spring than in any other season. In the spring I have counted one hundred and thirty-six different kinds of weather inside of four and twenty hours. It was I that made the fame and fortune of that man that had that marvelous collection of weather on exhibition at the Centennial[3] that so astounded the foreigners. He was going to travel all over the world and get specimens from all the climes. I said, "Don't you do it; you come to New England on a favorable spring day." I told him what we could do, in the way of style, variety, and quantity. Well, he came, and he made his collection in four days. As to variety—why, he confessed that he got hundreds of kinds of weather that he had never heard of before. And as to quantity—well, after he had picked out and discarded all that was <u>blemished</u> in any way, he

---

3. Centennial international trade fair held in 1876 in Philadelphia to mark the hundredth anniversary of the Declaration of Independence. The fair featured scientific and technological marvels of the day.

not only had weather enough, but weather to spare; weather to hire out; weather to sell; to deposit; weather to invest; weather to give to the poor.

The people of New England are by nature patient and forbearing; but there are some things which they will not stand. Every year they kill a lot of poets for writing about "Beautiful Spring." These are generally casual visitors, who bring their notions of spring from somewhere else, and cannot, of course, know how the natives feel about spring. And so, the first thing they know, the opportunity to inquire how they feel has permanently gone by.

Old Probabilities has a mighty reputation for accurate prophecy, and thoroughly well deserves it. You take up the papers and observe how crisply and confidently he checks off what today's weather is going to be on the Pacific, down South, in the Middle States, in the Wisconsin region; see him sail along in the joy and pride of his power till he gets to New England, and then—see his tail drop. *He* doesn't know what the weather is going to be like in New England.

▲ Critical Viewing
Would a sight like this one make up for living with other types of New England weather? Explain.
[Make a Judgment]

He can't any more tell than he can tell how many Presidents of the United States there's going to be next year.[4] Well, he mulls over it, and by and by he gets out something about like this: Probable nor'-east to sou'-west winds, varying to the southard and westard and eastard and points between; high and low barometer, swapping around from place to place; probable areas of rain, snow, hail, and drought, succeeded or preceded by earthquakes, with thunder and lightning. Then he jots down this postscript from his wandering mind, to cover accidents: "But it is possible that the program may be wholly changed in the meantime."

Yes, one of the brightest gems in the New England weather is the dazzling uncertainty of it. There is only one thing certain about it, you are certain there is going to be plenty of weather—a perfect grand review; but you never can tell which end of the procession is going to move first. You fix up for the drought; you leave your umbrella in the house and sally out with your sprinkling pot, and ten to one you get drowned. You make up your mind that the earthquake is due; you stand from under, and take hold of something to steady yourself, and the first thing you know, you get struck by lightning. These are great disappointments. But they can't be helped. The lightning there is peculiar; it is so convincing! When it strikes a thing, it doesn't leave enough of that thing behind for you to tell whether—well, you'd think it was something valuable, and a Congressman had been there.

And the thunder. When the thunder <u>commences</u> to merely tune up, and scrape, and saw, and key up the instruments for the performance, strangers say, "Why, what awful thunder you have here!" But when the baton is raised and the real concert begins, you'll find that stranger down in the cellar, with his head in the ash barrel.

Now, as to the *size* of the weather in New England—lengthways, I mean. It is utterly disproportioned to the size of that little country. Half the time, when it is packed as full as it can stick, you will see that New England weather sticking out beyond the edges and projecting around hundreds and hundreds of miles over the neighboring states. She can't hold a tenth part of her weather. You can see cracks all about, where she has strained herself trying to do it.

I could speak volumes about the inhuman perversity of the New England weather, but I will give but a single specimen. I like to hear rain on a tin roof, so I covered part of my roof with tin, with an eye to that luxury. Well, sir, do you think it ever rains on the tin? No, sir; skips it every time.

---

4. how many Presidents of the United States there's going to be next year The United States presidential election of 1876 was one of the most disputed, with two declared "winners" when Twain gave this speech. Rutherford B. Hayes was declared the final victor on March 2, 1877.

Literary Analysis
Humorous Essay
What example of understatement can you find in this paragraph?

Literary Analysis
Humorous Essay
What does Twain satirically imply about Congressmen in this paragraph?

Vocabulary Builder
commences (kə mens´ əs) v. begins

Reading Check

According to Twain, how easy is it to predict New England weather?

Mind, in this speech I have been trying merely to do honor to the New England weather—no language could do it justice. But, after all, there are at least one or two things about that weather (or, if you please, effects produced by it) which we residents would not like to part with. If we hadn't our bewitching autumn foliage, we should still have to credit the weather with one feature which compensates for all its bullying <u>vagaries</u>—the ice storm—when a leafless tree is clothed with ice from the bottom to the top—ice that is as bright and clear as crystal; when every bough and twig is strung with ice beads, frozen dewdrops, and the whole tree sparkles, cold and white, like the Shah[5] of Persia's diamond plume. Then the wind waves the branches, and the sun comes out and turns all those myriads of beads and drops to prisms, that glow and burn and flash with all manner of colored fires, which change and change again, with inconceivable rapidity, from blue to red, from red to green, and green to gold—the tree becomes a spraying fountain, a very explosion of dazzling jewels; and it stands there the acme, the climax, the supremest possibility in art or nature, of bewildering, intoxicating, intolerable magnificence! One cannot make the words too strong.

Month after month I lay up my hate and grudge against the New England weather; but when the ice storm comes at last, I say: "There—I forgive you, now—the books are square between us, you don't owe me a cent; go, and sin no more; your little faults and foibles count for nothing—you are the most enchanting weather in the world!"

Vocabulary Builder
vagaries (vā´ gər ēz) *n.* erratic or unpredictable actions

Literary Analysis
Humorous Essay
What makes this paragraph different from the rest of the essay?

---

5. Shah (shä) *n.* formerly, the title of the ruler of Persia (now Iran).

Thinking About the Selection

1. **Respond:** Which part of Twain's essay did you find most clever or amusing? Explain.

2. **(a) Recall:** According to Twain, what quality or feature of New England weather "compels the stranger's admiration"?
   (b) Connect: What point does Twain support with the story of the man who collected and exhibited weather?

3. **(a) Infer:** What is the profession of "Old Probabilities"?
   (b) Interpret: What point is Twain making in the anecdote about this character?

4. **Interpret:** For Twain, does the ice storm make up for the rest of New England weather? Explain.

The Dog That Bit People

Nobody Knew Exactly What Was the Matter with Him, James Thurber.

James Thurber

Probably no one man should have as many dogs in his life as I have had, but there was more pleasure than distress in them for me except in the case of an Airedale named Muggs. He gave me more trouble than all the other fifty-four or -five put together, although my moment of keenest embarrassment was the time a Scotch terrier named Jeannie, who had just had six puppies in the clothes closet of a fourth floor apartment in New York, had the unexpected seventh and last at the corner of Eleventh Street and Fifth Avenue during a walk she had insisted on taking. Then, too, there was the prize winning French poodle, a great big black poodle—none of your little, untroublesome white miniatures—who got sick riding in the rumble seat[1] of a car with me on her way to the Greenwich Dog Show. She had a red rubber bib tucked around her throat and, since a rain storm came up when we were halfway through the Bronx, I had to hold over her a small green umbrella, really more of a parasol. The rain beat down fearfully and suddenly the driver of the car drove into a big garage, filled with mechanics. It happened so quickly that I forgot to put the umbrella down and I will always remember, with sickening distress, the look of <u>incredulity</u> mixed with hatred that came over the face of the particular hardened garage man that came over to see what we wanted,

▲ **Critical Viewing**
Which elements of this drawing by Thurber suggest that Muggs has a difficult personality? **[Analyze]**

Vocabulary Builder
incredulity (in′ krə dōō′ lə tē) *n.* unwillingness or inability to believe

---

1. **rumble seat** in some early automobiles, an open seat in the rear, behind the roofed seat, which could be folded shut when not in use.

when he took a look at me and the poodle. All garage men, and people of that intolerant stripe, hate poodles with their curious hair cut, especially the pom-poms that you got to leave on their hips if you expect the dogs to win a prize.

But the Airedale, as I have said, was the worst of all my dogs. He really wasn't my dog, as a matter of fact: I came home from a vacation one summer to find that my brother Roy had bought him while I was away. A big, burly, choleric dog, he always acted as if he thought I wasn't one of the family. There was a slight advantage in being one of the family, for he didn't bite the family as often as he bit strangers. Still, in the years that we had him he bit everybody but mother, and he made a pass at her once but missed. That was during the month when we suddenly had mice, and Muggs refused to do anything about them. Nobody ever had mice exactly like the mice we had that month. They acted like pet mice, almost like mice somebody had trained. They were so friendly that one night when mother entertained at dinner the Friraliras, a club she and my father had belonged to for twenty years, she put down a lot of little dishes with food in them on the pantry floor so that the mice would be satisfied with that and wouldn't come into the dining room. Muggs stayed out in the pantry with the mice, lying on the floor, growling to himself—not at the mice, but about all the people in the next room that he would have liked to get at. Mother slipped out into the pantry once to see how everything was going. Everything was going fine. It made her so mad to see Muggs lying there, oblivious of the mice—they came running up to her—that she slapped him and he slashed at her, but didn't make it. He was sorry immediately, mother said. He was always sorry, she said, after he bit someone, but we could not understand how she figured this out. He didn't act sorry.

Mother used to send a box of candy every Christmas to the people the Airedale bit. The list finally contained forty or more names. Nobody could understand why we didn't get rid of the dog. I didn't understand it very well myself, but we didn't get rid of him. I think that one or two people tried to poison Muggs—he acted poisoned once in a while—and old Major Moberly fired at him once with his service revolver near the Seneca Hotel in East Broad Street—but Muggs lived to be almost eleven years old and even when he could hardly get around he bit a Congressman who had called to see my father on business. My mother had never liked the Congressman— she said the signs of his horoscope showed he couldn't be trusted (he was Saturn with the moon in Virgo)—but she sent him a box of candy that Christmas. He sent it right back, probably because he suspected it was trick candy. Mother persuaded herself it was all for

Vocabulary Builder
choleric (käl′ ər ik) *adj.* having a quick temper; inclined to anger

Literary Analysis
Humorous Essay
Explain how Thurber uses understatement when comparing Muggs's treatment of family and strangers.

Literary Analysis
Humorous Essay
Which details in this paragraph seem to be hyperboles?

the best that the dog had bitten him, even though father lost an important business association because of it. "I wouldn't be associated with such a man," mother said, "Muggs could read him like a book."

We used to take turns feeding Muggs to be on his good side, but that didn't always work. He was never in a very good humor, even after a meal. Nobody knew exactly what was the matter with him, but whatever it was it made him <u>irascible</u>, especially in the mornings. Roy never felt very well in the morning, either, especially before breakfast, and once when he came downstairs and found that Muggs had moodily chewed up the morning paper he hit him in the face with a grapefruit and then jumped up on the dining room table, scattering dishes and silverware and spilling the coffee. Muggs' first free leap carried him all the way across the table and into a brass fire screen in front of the gas grate but he was back on his feet in a moment and in the end he got Roy and gave him a pretty vicious bite in the leg. Then he was all over it; he never bit anyone more than once at a time. Mother always mentioned that as an argument in his favor; she said he had a quick temper but that he didn't hold a grudge. She was forever defending him. I think she liked him because he wasn't well. "He's not strong," she would say, pityingly, but that was inaccurate; he may not have been well but he was terribly strong.

One time my mother went to the Chittenden Hotel to call on a woman mental healer who was lecturing in Columbus on the subject of "Harmonious Vibrations." She wanted to find out if it was possible to get harmonious vibrations into a dog. "He's a large tan-colored Airedale," mother explained. The woman said that she had never treated a dog but she advised my mother to hold the thought that he did not bite and would not bite. Mother was holding the thought the very next morning when Muggs got the iceman but she blamed that slip-up on the iceman. "If you didn't think he would bite you, he wouldn't," mother told him. He stomped out of the house in a terrible jangle of vibrations.

One morning when Muggs bit me slightly, more or less in passing, I reached down and grabbed his short stumpy tail and hoisted him into the air. It was a foolhardy thing to do and the last time I saw my mother, about six months ago, she said she didn't know what possessed me. I don't either, except that I was pretty mad. As long as I held the dog off the floor by his tail he couldn't get at me, but he twisted and jerked so, snarling all the time, that I realized I couldn't hold him that way very long. I carried him to the kitchen and flung him onto the floor and shut the door on him just as he crashed against it. But I forgot about the backstairs. Muggs went up

Vocabulary Builder
irascible (i ras´ ə bəl)
adj. irritable; quick-tempered

✔**Reading Check**

How does Muggs generally respond to people?

Muggs at His Meals Was an Unusual Sight, James Thurber.

the backstairs and down the frontstairs and had me cornered in the living room. I managed to get up onto the mantelpiece above the fireplace, but it gave way and came down with a tremendous crash throwing a large marble clock, several vases, and myself heavily to the floor. Muggs was so alarmed by the racket that when I picked myself up he had disappeared. We couldn't find him anywhere, although we whistled and shouted, until old Mrs. Detweiler called after dinner that night. Muggs had bitten her once, in the leg, and she came into the living room only after we assured her that Muggs had run away. She had just seated herself when, with a great growling and scratching of claws, Muggs emerged from under a

▲ Critical Viewing How does this drawing of Muggs compare and contrast with the behavior described in the essay? **[Compare and Contrast]**

davenport where he had been quietly hiding all the time, and bit her again. Mother examined the bite and put arnica[2] on it and told Mrs. Detweiler that it was only a bruise. "He just bumped you," she said. But Mrs. Detweiler left the house in a nasty state of mind.

Lots of people reported our Airedale to the police but my father held a municipal office at the time and was on friendly terms with the police. Even so, the cops had been out a couple of times—once when Muggs bit Mrs. Rufus Sturtevant and again when he bit Lieutenant-Governor Malloy—but mother told them that it hadn't been Muggs' fault but the fault of the people who were bitten. "When he starts for them, they scream," she explained, "and that excites him." The cops suggested that it might be a good idea to tie the dog up, but mother said that it mortified him to be tied up and that he wouldn't eat when he was tied up.

Muggs at his meals was an unusual sight. Because of the fact that if you reached toward the floor he would bite you, we usually put his food plate on top of an old kitchen table with a bench along-side the table. Muggs would stand on the bench and eat. I remember that my mother's Uncle Horatio, who boasted that he was the third man up Missionary Ridge,[3] was splutteringly <u>indignant</u> when he found out that we fed the dog on a table because we were afraid to put his plate on the floor. He said he wasn't afraid of any dog that ever lived and that he would put the dog's plate on the floor if we would give it to him. Roy said that if Uncle Horatio had fed Muggs on the ground just before the battle he would have been the first man up Missionary Ridge. Uncle Horatio was furious. "Bring him in! Bring him in now!" he shouted. "I'll feed the — on the floor!" Roy was all for giving him a chance, but my father wouldn't hear of it. He said that Muggs had already been fed. "I'll feed him again!" bawled Uncle Horatio. We had quite a time quieting him.

In his last year Muggs used to spend practically all of his time outdoors. He didn't like to stay in the house for some reason or other—perhaps it held too many unpleasant memories for him. Anyway, it was hard to get him to come in and as a result the garbage man, the iceman, and the laundryman wouldn't come near the house. We had to haul the garbage down to the corner, take the laundry out and bring it back, and meet the iceman a block from home. After this had gone on for some time we hit on an ingenious arrangement for getting the dog in the house so that we could lock him up while the gas meter was read, and so on. Muggs was afraid of only one thing, an electrical storm. Thunder and lightning fright-ened him out of his senses (I think he thought a storm had broken

2. arnica (är´ ni kə) *n.* preparation once used for treating bruises.
3. Missionary Ridge hill near Chattanooga, Tennessee, that was the site of a Civil War battle.

Literary Analysis
Humorous Essay
Which details here suggest that Thurber is satirizing pet-owners?

Vocabulary Builder
indignant (in dig´ nənt) *adj.* feeling or expressing anger, especially at an injustice

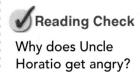

Reading Check

Why does Uncle Horatio get angry?

the day the mantelpiece fell). He would rush into the house and hide under a bed or in a clothes closet. So we fixed up a thunder machine out of a long narrow piece of sheet iron with a wooden handle on one end. Mother would shake this vigorously when she wanted to get Muggs into the house. It made an excellent imitation of thunder, but I suppose it was the most roundabout system for running a household that was ever devised. It took a lot out of mother.

A few months before Muggs died, he got to "seeing things." He would rise slowly from the floor, growling low, and stalk stiff-legged and menacing toward nothing at all. Sometimes the Thing would be just a little to the right or left of a visitor. Once a Fuller Brush salesman[4] got hysterics. Muggs came wandering into the room like Hamlet[5] following his father's ghost. His eyes were fixed on a spot just to the left of the Fuller Brush man, who stood it until Muggs was about three slow, creeping paces from him. Then he shouted. Muggs wavered on past him into the hallway grumbling to himself but the Fuller man went on shouting. I think mother had to throw a pan of cold water on him before he stopped. That was the way she used to stop us boys when we got into fights.

Muggs died quite suddenly one night. Mother wanted to bury him in the family lot under a marble stone with some such inscription as "Flights of angels sing thee to thy rest" but we persuaded her it was against the law. In the end we just put up a smooth board above his grave along a lonely road. On the board I wrote with an indelible pencil "Cave Canem."[6] Mother was quite pleased with the simple classic dignity of the old Latin epitaph.

---

4. **Fuller Brush salesman** salesman for the Fuller Brush Company who went door-to-door demonstrating cleaning equipment, a figure celebrated in comic strips and movies of the 1920s through the 1940s.
5. **Hamlet** the main character of William Shakespeare's play *Hamlet;* in the play, he is visited by the ghost of his murdered father.
6. **"Cave Canem"** (kä′ vā kä′ nem′) Latin for "Beware of the dog."

Literary Analysis
Humorous Essay
Why is this anecdote about the thunder machine an example both of hyperbole and of understatement?

Thinking About the Selection

1. **Respond:** Which of Muggs's escapades did you find the most amusing? Why?

2. **(a) Recall:** Which event does Thurber refer to as his "foolhardy" experience with Muggs? **(b) Analyze:** List reactions you might expect the family to have to this experience, and explain which are missing in the essay.

3. **Hypothesize:** Why do you think the family never does anything to get rid of Muggs?

Apply the Skills

A Toast to the Oldest Inhabitant • The Dog That Bit People

Comparing Humorous Writing

1. **(a)** Find an example of **hyperbole** in each work. **(b)** Find an example of **understatement** in each work. **(c)** Compare Twain's and Thurber's use of these devices, explaining which device each writer uses most.

2. **(a)** Which of the two authors treats a potentially serious subject lightly? **(b)** Which one treats an ordinary subject with exaggerated seriousness? Support your answers with examples.

3. **(a)** Find an example of **satire** in each essay. **(b)** Identify the type of person that is satirized in each example, and explain whether you think satirizing such people is justified.

Writing to Compare Literary Works

In an essay, explain how Twain and Thurber both use **conflict**, or a struggle between opposing forces, to develop the humor of their pieces. Before you write, complete a chart like the one shown. Identify the conflict and the comic details the writer uses to depict it.

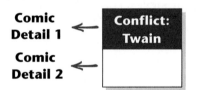
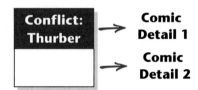

Vocabulary Builder

Practice Complete each of the following sentences in a way that makes sense. Explain your answers.

1. If your personality is *choleric,* you are more likely to _____ .
2. If the décor in a room is *sumptuous,* it is likely to have _____ .
3. When a play *commences,* _____ .
4. An *indignant* citizen is likely to _____ .
5. When given a *blemished* apple, a person might _____ .
6. Sailors who follow the *vagaries* of the wind may end up _____ .
7. When told that all the ice cream in the freezer section has melted, an *irascible* shopkeeper might _____ .
8. The following is a story that people might react to with *incredulity:* _____ .

QuickReview

Humorous Writing: texts meant to amuse. Comic techniques include *hyperbole, understatement,* and *satire.*

Assessment
For: Self-test
Visit: www.PHSchool.com
Web Code: eqa-6306

Main Idea and Supporting Details

Directions: *Questions 1–5 are based on the following selection.*

1 Be-bop (bop for short) was sometimes labeled "New York
2 Jazz," and it is, in fact, the only major school of jazz to which
3 the city can lay proprietary claim. Jazz of the '20s, dominated
4 by Louis Armstrong, originated in New Orleans, migrating to
5 New York only after a formative detour in Chicago. Armstrong
6 inspired '30s swing, the music of the big bands led by Benny
7 Goodman, Artie Shaw, Glenn Miller, Count Basie and Duke
8 Ellington, the "mother bands," as Gillespie called them, whose
9 music the be-boppers both emulated and revolutionized.
10   . . . Bop's wide-ranging allusiveness, its quicksilver expressivity,
11 angular dissonance and shockingly extended palette of pitches and rhythms
12 echoed the international mix, the fluidity and speed of New
13 York life.

—from "Feel the City's Pulse? It's Be-bop, Man!" by Ann Douglas

1. **Which group of lines expresses the main idea of the passage?**
   A   lines 1–3
   B   lines 3–5
   C   lines 6–10
   D   lines 10–13

2. **Which two sentences stand in the relationship of main idea/supporting detail?**
   A   the first and last
   B   the third and second
   C   the second and third
   D   the last and the first

3. **Which is the only major jazz music to which New York can lay claim?**
   A   jazz of the '20s
   B   '30s swing
   C   the music of the big bands
   D   bop

4. **Which of the following words or phrases in lines 10–13 is NOT a supporting detail within the sentence?**
   A   "wide-ranging allusiveness"
   B   "quicksilver expressivity"
   C   "palette of pitches and rhythms"
   D   "New York life"

5. **Which of the following titles best captures the main idea of this passage?**
   A   "Louis Armstrong: Father of Be-bop"
   B   "The Evolution of Be-bop"
   C   "New York: Capital of Be-bop"
   D   "The Big Bands: Forerunners of Be-bop"

Directions: *Choose the sentence in which the numbered word is used correctly.*

Standards
Assessed
• 10.4.4
• 10.5.2

6. **enlighten**
   A Take these to enlighten my load.
   B I should add yellow to enlighten the dark.
   C Enlighten me about the best techniques for solving equations.
   D As soon as the power went out, my first move was to enlighten a match.

7. **emerge**
   A Marroquin finally did emerge from the minor leagues.
   B The president recommended that they emerge with another firm.
   C I had to emerge the reluctant young swimmer to make her first dive.
   D One must emerge anger before speaking.

8. **speculate**
   A This helps to speculate the products.
   B Only a qualified optician can properly speculate a new pair of eyeglasses.
   C We can only speculate about the suspect's motives.
   D People speculate by saving money.

9. **emphasis**
   A The jubilant crowd showed its emphasis for the home team's victory.
   B The jury found the defendant guilty based on the emphasis.
   C Flying takes a great deal of emphasis.
   D The professor placed a strong emphasis on studying Shakespeare.

10. **confront**
    A We needed to confront the hard drive for it to work properly.
    B The coach decided to confront the referee about the bad call.
    C The card never arrived for we forgot to confront the envelope.
    D Playing hockey badly could confront in a serious injury.

Directions: *Choose the word that is closest in meaning to the numbered word.*

11. **conform**
    A be formed in harmony with others
    B decide against
    C challenge against
    D cooperate with

12. **embellish**
    A add in details
    B form a bell curve
    C put sounds together
    D split into groups

13. **commensurate**
    A able to be measured together
    B measured into two equal parts

C measured into two unequal parts
D of separate quality

14. **encapsulate**
    A put together with others
    B put into a summary
    C judge by instinct
    D evaluate by a standard

15. **encamp**
    A to form in a camp
    B to discuss as a group
    C to go with others
    D to divide equally

Writing Workshop

Persuasion: Letter to the Editor

Most newspapers and many magazines include opinion pages that publish **letters to the editor.** These are formal business letters that present the writers' viewpoints about important issues. Follow the steps outlined in this workshop to write your own letter to the editor.

Assignment Write a letter to the editor of a magazine, a newspaper, or an Internet site to share your opinion about a current event.

What to Include Your letter to the editor should feature these elements:
- standard business letter format, including a heading, an inside address, a greeting, a body, a closing, and a signature
- formal, polite language
- a clear statement of opinion supported by relevant facts, examples, or personal experiences
- error-free grammar, including well-combined sentences

To preview the criteria on which your letter may be assessed, see the rubric on page 494.

Prewriting

Choosing Your Topic

Find a hot topic. Watch television, scan newspapers, and listen to neighborhood discussions to identify topics that concern you. List these issues and note differing opinions about each one. Determine which issue, and which opinion, prompts your strongest feelings.

Pro	Hot Topic	Con
Professional athletes have a responsibility to the public.	**Sports heroes as role models**	Excellent athletes are not models for behavior outside the court or off the field.
Restrictions can protect our youngest citizens.	**Laws restricting the Internet**	Freedom of speech is denied by restrictions.

Gathering Details

Collect strong evidence. Select a variety of types of evidence to make your letter both convincing and interesting for readers. Plan to include evidence in these categories:
- facts and statistics
- real-life examples
- personal experiences
- expert opinions

Academic Standards

- Write persuasive compositions. (10.5.4)
- Write for different purposes and audiences. (10.5.8)

Using the Form
You may use elements of this form in these types of writing:
- position papers
- speeches
- proposals

Work in Progress
Review the work you did on pages 421, 447, and 473.

Drafting

Shaping Your Writing

Use the proper format. Your letter to the editor must follow a standard business letter format. These are two commonly accepted conventions:

- **Block format:** each part of the letter begins at the left margin
- **Modified block format:** the heading, closing, and signature are indented to the center of the page

Use a checklist to ensure that you include all six elements of a formal business letter—heading, inside address, salutation, body, closing, and signature. (For more on business letters, see page R29.)

Providing Elaboration

Consider your audience and tone. Your letter will address the general public, so include information that is essential to your case. Be respectful to your audience. Even if you are voicing a complaint, maintain a calm and reasonable tone. Your goal is to persuade, not to insult.

Revising

Revising Your Overall Structure

Evaluate support. As you review your draft, highlight your main ideas to check that they are supported with evidence. If a point is not sufficiently important, omit it. If it is important, add evidence to support it.

To read the complete student model, see page 493.

Student Model: Highlighting to Add Supporting Details

Band programs all over the country have inspired many students

to go into the field of music, but many do not meet the

requirements that students need to compete after high school. ∧

~~I personally know students who have been denied scholarships and have~~

~~had scholarships revoked because they have not been properly trained.~~

> The writer adds support in the form of personal experience.

Revising Your Word Choice

Revise to create appropriate formality. Check that your tone is polite and your style is formal. Replace casual language with formal language.

Casual: The park's a big old mess.

Formal: The park is littered with trash.

Integrating Grammar Skills

Revising to Combine Short Sentences

If you use too many short sentences, your work can seem as if it was written for very young readers rather than a mature audience. To avoid this problem, combine short sentences that express related ideas.

Prentice Hall Writing and Grammar Connection: Chapter 3, Section 1

Methods of Sentence Combining Use **compound verbs** to combine two short sentences:

Choppy: I *cancelled* my cell phone service. I *turned* it in for a refund.

Combined: I *cancelled* my cell phone and *turned* it in for a refund.

You may use **compound objects:**

Choppy: I ate *a sandwich.* I ate *an ice cream cone.*

Combined: I ate *a sandwich* and *an ice cream cone.*

Use **compound predicate nominatives** or **predicate adjectives.**

predicate nominative	predicate adjective
a noun or pronoun that appears with a linking verb and identifies or explains the subject	an adjective that appears with a linking verb and describes the subject
Example: Parakeets are <u>birds</u>.	Example: Parakeets are <u>colorful</u>.

Choppy: My favorite celebrity *is a singer.* She is also *an actress.* She is also *a dancer.*

Combined: My favorite celebrity *is a singer, actress, and dancer.*

Choppy: The bicycle is *very lightweight.* It is *extremely fast.*

Combined: The bicycle is *very lightweight and extremely fast.*

Fixing Choppy Sentences Follow these steps to fix short sentences:

1. **Read your draft aloud,** listening for choppy sentences.
2. **Identify sentences to combine.** Determine which sentences share a common subject or a common predicate.
3. **Try a variety of sentence-combining techniques.** Use the methods above to create a variety of fluid sentences.

Apply It to Your Editing

Reread two paragraphs in your letter. Look for places where a single sentence would express related ideas better than a series of shorter sentences. Combine these sentences using one of the methods above.

Student Model:

Clay Creamans
Independence, KY

Clay Creamans
351 Any Drive
Independence, Kentucky 41051

September 25, 2005

Editor-in-Chief
The Daily Independent
552 Downtown Street
Ashland, Kentucky 41000

Dear Editor-in-Chief:

I am writing in response to the letter you published from Mr. Jones, who complained about our band's playing at the last football game.

The point of high school band programs is to train students to play together, to produce one stirring, harmonious sound. Because of a lack of instruction, education, and familiarity with music and instruments, this is difficult for some students. Band programs all over the country have inspired many students to go into the field of music, but many do not meet the requirements students need to compete after high school. I personally know students who have been denied scholarships and have had scholarships revoked because they have not been properly trained. The Kenton County School District needs to devise a class that will alleviate these problems.

This new music class should have a staff composed of teachers who can play and teach all of the band instruments. Students need one-on-one, as well as group instruction. Of course, hiring a full staff of musicians for every school would cost a lot. Instead, full band directors could be hired for all the schools to share. This would allow students to gain a greater knowledge of music from a larger group of musicians. These teachers would offer more insight into the history and theory of music.

With so many young people interested in fine arts, band directors cannot offer everyone the instruction that is needed. For the band to improve as a whole, everyone has to grow. Many of today's band directors try hard to develop better musicians, yet, because of a lack of time and staffing, they feel disappointed and discouraged.

With adequate time and staffing, students will be able to make music together and demonstrate their talents. With an experienced music staff and better classes, I believe that Mr. Jones will be happier with our band's performance.

Sincerely,

Clay Creamans

Clay Creamans

Clay uses a correct modified block format.

Formal language shows that Clay takes both his opinion and his readers seriously.

Clay supports his argument with personal experiences.

Clay points out an opposing argument and suggests an alternative plan.

The conclusion reinforces Clay's ideas.

Writing Workshop

Editing and Proofreading

Check your draft for errors in format, grammar, and punctuation.

Focus on Accuracy: Make sure that the names of individuals, periodicals, and any quoted experts are spelled correctly. Make sure that any statistics or numerical data are accurately stated, and double-check street addresses.

Publishing and Presenting

Consider one of the following ways to share your writing:

Submit your letter. Send your letter to the editor of the media source you have addressed. When the letter is published, share the newspaper, periodical, or Web site with classmates.

Hold a speaker's corner. Conduct a speaker's corner in which you and your classmates read your letters aloud and discuss the topics presented. To help maintain the flow of the discussion, set time limits for each speaker.

Reflecting on Your Writing

Writer's Journal Jot down your thoughts on the experience of writing a letter to the editor. Begin by answering these questions:
- Which revision strategies improved your final draft the most? Explain.
- Did writing a letter to the editor change the way you feel about your topic? Explain.
- Do you think letters to the editor are an effective way for citizens to voice their concerns and opinions? Why or why not?

Prentice Hall Writing and Grammar Connection: Chapter 15

Rubric for Self-Assessment

To assess your letter to the editor, use the following rubric:

Criteria	Rating Scale				
	not very				*very*
Focus: How clearly do you state your opinion?	1	2	3	4	5
Organization: How accurately do you use standard business letter format?	1	2	3	4	5
Support/Elaboration: How relevant are the facts, examples, or experiences you use to support your opinion?	1	2	3	4	5
Style: How formal and polite is your use of language?	1	2	3	4	5
Conventions: How correct is your grammar, especially your use of well-combined sentences?	1	2	3	4	5

Skills You Will Learn

Literary Analysis: *Persuasive Writing and Rhetorical Devices*
Reading Skill: *Evaluate the Writer's Argument*

Reading Skill: *Analyze the Writer's Assumptions*

Literary Analysis: *Analytic and Interpretive Essays*
Reading Skill: *Distinguish Between Fact and Opinion*

Literary Analysis: *Author's Purposes*

Literature You Will Read

Reading and Vocabulary Skills Preview

Reading: Evaluating Persuasive Appeals

Academic Standards

> **Persuasive appeals** are methods a writer or speaker uses to influence the audience to adopt his or her point of view.

- Examine how the author's perspective influences the structure and tone of the text. (10.2.4)
- Provide constructive criticism to other writers. (10.4.12)

Skills and Strategies You Will Learn in Part 2

In Part 2, you will learn

- to **recognize persuasive techniques** and **evaluate the writer's argument and persuasive techniques.** (p. 498)
- about the **purpose and structure** of informational material to help you **analyze the writer's assumptions.** (p. 514)
- to **distinguish between fact and opinion** as you **evaluate a writer's appeals.** (p. 518)

Using the Skills and Strategies in Part 2

In Part 2, you will learn to distinguish between fact and opinion and evaluate the logic of an argument. You will also practice using the purpose and structure of a work to help you evaluate its contents.

In the following passage, the author's assertions are divided into facts and opinions.

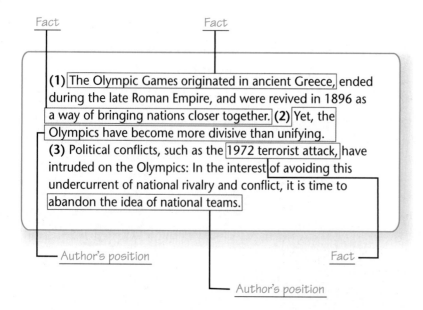

Fact   Fact

(1) The Olympic Games originated in ancient Greece, ended during the late Roman Empire, and were revived in 1896 as a way of bringing nations closer together. (2) Yet, the Olympics have become more divisive than unifying.
(3) Political conflicts, such as the 1972 terrorist attack, have intruded on the Olympics: In the interest of avoiding this undercurrent of national rivalry and conflict, it is time to abandon the idea of national teams.

Author's position

Fact

Author's position

Academic Vocabulary: Words for Interpreting Literature

The following words will help you talk and write about your interpretations of literature in this unit.

Word	Definition	Example Sentence
differentiate v.	distinguish between	The idea is to *differentiate* between them.
disclaim v.	deny or give up a claim	He *disclaimed* authorship of that theory.
inevitable adj.	certain to happen; unavoidable	Ethical dilemmas are an *inevitable* part of life.
insight n.	act or result of understanding the inner nature of things	A good author provides an *insight* into human nature.
motive n.	reason for taking a specific action	The character's *motive* was revealed.

Vocabulary Skill: Prefix

A **prefix** is a syllable or group of syllables joined to the beginning of a word to alter its meaning.

In Part 2, you will learn

- the prefix *in-* or *ir-* (p. 512)
- the prefix *dis-* (p. 532)

Prefixes change the meaning of words. Words that begin with the prefix *in-* or *dis-* often have a meaning that is the opposite of the base word.

Base Word	Meaning	Prefix	New Word	New Meaning
franchise	a set of rights	*dis-*	*disenfranchised*	not having a right or rights
honest	truthful	*dis-*	*dishonest*	not truthful
operative	working	*in-*	*inoperative*	not working

Activity Use a dictionary to define the following words. Then, explain how their meaning changes with the addition of *dis-* or *in-*.

1. associate (dis-)
2. appropriate (in-)
3. regard (dis-)
4. connect (dis-)
5. effective (in-)

Build Skills   Keep Memory Alive • from *Nobel Lecture*

Practice these skills with either "Keep Memory Alive" (p. 500) or the selection from Solzhenitsyn's Nobel Lecture (p. 505).

(IN) **Academic Standards**

- Write for different purposes and audiences. (10.5.8)
- Correctly develop a speech and include quotations. (10.7.2)

Literary Analysis

Persuasive writing, including **speeches,** is intended to convince people to take a particular action or position. Persuasive writers present **arguments,** using reason to support their position. They also use **rhetorical devices,** or verbal techniques that create emphasis and appeal to emotions.

- **Repetition:** the reuse of a key word or idea for emphasis
- **Parallelism:** similar grammatical structures expressing related ideas
- **Slogans and saws:** short, catchy phrases
- **Rhetorical questions:** questions that are intended to have obvious answers, asked for effect

Position	People should oppose the new mall.
Claim	Local businesses will suffer.
Support	Prices at malls are lower.
Technique	Rhetorical question: Do you want your neighbor to lose his business?

Reading Skill

When reading persuasion, **evaluate the writer's argument.** Consider whether the writer supports claims with evidence and reasoning.

   Determine when **persuasive techniques** are effectively used to enhance the impact of the support, and recognize when they are used to cover up a lack of logical support. Use a chart like the one shown to take notes.

Vocabulary Builder

Keep Memory Alive

- **presumptuous** (prē zump′ chōō əs) *adj.* overstepping appropriate bounds; too bold (p. 501) *It would be <u>presumptuous</u> for me to give medical advice, because I'm not a doctor.*

- **bewilderment** (bē wil′ dər mənt) *n.* confusion (p. 501) *Her <u>bewilderment</u> showed on her face.*

- **accomplices** (ə käm′ plis iz) *n.* people who help another person commit a crime (p. 501) *His <u>accomplices</u> kept a lookout while he robbed the bank.*

from Nobel Lecture

- **reciprocity** (res′ ə präs′ ə tē) *n.* relations of exchange; interdependence (p. 506) *<u>Reciprocity</u> between friends means helping each other out of jams.*

- **inexorably** (in eks′ ə rə blē) *adv.* without the possibility of being delayed or stopped (p. 509) *The hurricane moved <u>inexorably</u> up the coast.*

- **oratory** (ôr′ ə tôr′ ē) *n.* act of public speaking; strategies used in such speaking (p. 509) *The speaker's <u>oratory</u> fired up the crowd.*

Build Understanding • *Keep Memory Alive*

Background

The Holocaust The Holocaust was the systematic persecution and murder of Jews and others deemed "unfit" by Germany's Nazi party. The Nazis came to power in Germany in 1933. During World War II (1939–1945), Nazi forces shot Jews throughout German-occupied lands or sent them to concentration camps. There, prisoners like Elie Wiesel were worked to death, starved to death, or killed outright.

Connecting to the Literature

Reading/Writing Connection As Wiesel shows in this speech, testifying to the evils of the past can be an unpleasant but important duty. Explain why it is useful to learn lessons from the past. Use at least three of the following words: *assess, formulate, interpret, comprehend.*

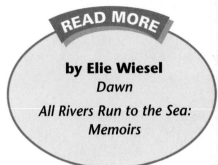

READ MORE

by Elie Wiesel
Dawn

All Rivers Run to the Sea: Memoirs

Meet the Author

Elie **Wiesel** (b. 1928)

The Romanian-born teacher, philosopher, and writer Elie Wiesel was deported to the Nazi death camp at Auschwitz at age fifteen. His parents and sister all perished at the hands of the Nazis.

Survivor and Witness After surviving the war, Wiesel did not write a single word about his wartime experiences for ten years. Finally in 1955, he wrote an account of his experiences, *And the World Kept Silent.* His English adaptation of the work, *Night,* was published in 1960. He says, "I wrote it for the other survivors who found it difficult to speak. And I wanted really to tell them, 'Look, you must speak . . . we must try.'"

Fast Facts

▶ Wiesel was perhaps the first to use the term *Holocaust* to describe the Nazis' brutal program of persecution.
▶ He has been awarded the Congressional Gold Medal of Achievement and the Nobel Peace Prize.

Go Online
—Author Link

For: More about the author
Visit: www.PHSchool.com
Web Code: eqe-9308

Keep Memory Alive

Elie Wiesel

It is with a profound sense of humility that I accept the honor you have chosen to bestow upon me. I know: your choice transcends me. This both frightens and pleases me.

It frightens me because I wonder: do I have the right to represent the multitudes who have perished? Do I have the right to accept this great honor on their behalf? I do not. That would be presumptuous. No one may speak for the dead, no one may interpret their mutilated dreams and visions.

It pleases me because I may say that this honor belongs to all the survivors and their children, and through us, to the Jewish people with whose destiny I have always identified.

I remember: it happened yesterday or eternities ago. A young Jewish boy discovered the kingdom of night. I remember his bewilderment, I remember his anguish. It all happened so fast. The ghetto.[1] The deportation. The sealed cattle car. The fiery altar upon which the history of our people and the future of mankind were meant to be sacrificed.

I remember: he asked his father: "Can this be true? This is the 20th century, not the Middle Ages. Who would allow such crimes to be committed? How could the world remain silent?"

And now the boy is turning to me: "Tell me," he asks. "What have you done with my future? What have you done with your life?"

And I tell him that I have tried. That I have tried to keep memory alive, that I have tried to fight those who would forget. Because if we forget, we are guilty, we are accomplices.

And then I explained to him how naive we were, that the world did know and remain silent. And that is why I swore never to be silent whenever and wherever human beings endure suffering and humiliation. We must always take sides. Neutrality[2] helps the oppressor, never the victim. Silence encourages the tormentor, never the tormented.

---

1. The ghetto (get′ ō) During the Second World War, the Nazis forced Jews in European cities to live in crowded, restricted neighborhoods, or ghettos.
2. Neutrality (nōō tral′ ə tē) *n.* state of not taking sides in a conflict; quality of being unbiased.

◀ Critical Viewing Does this image of children being sent to a Nazi concentration camp add force to Wiesel's point about the necessity of remembering? Explain. **[Support]**

Literary Analysis
Persuasive Writing
Identify two examples of parallelism in the second paragraph.

Vocabulary Builder
presumptuous
(prē zump′ chōō əs)
adj. overstepping appropriate bounds; too bold

bewilderment (bē wil′ dər mənt) *n.* confusion

accomplices (ə käm′ plis iz) *n.* people who help another person commit a crime

Apply the Skills

Keep Memory Alive

Thinking About the Selection

1. **Respond:** Do you share the young Wiesel's shock that the world did not prevent the Holocaust? Why or why not?
2. **(a) Recall:** On whose behalf does Wiesel accept the Nobel Prize? **(b) Draw Conclusions:** Why does he believe the award belongs to those people? **(c) Interpret:** Why does he say that receiving the award both "frightens and pleases" him?
3. **(a) Recall:** What does the boy Wiesel ask the adult Wiesel? **(b) Interpret:** What do his questions imply about Wiesel's adult responsibilities? **(c) Draw Conclusions:** Why does Wiesel believe we have a moral duty to remember?
4. **Extend:** Describe a situation in which silence might do harm.

Literary Analysis

5. Identify the central **argument** in Wiesel's **persuasive speech** and evaluate his reasoning.
6. What **rhetorical devices** does Wiesel use in his speech? Use a chart like the one shown to analyze examples.

	Repetition	Parallelism	Slogans or Saws	Rhetorical Questions
Example				
Effect				

7. **(a)** What assumptions does Wiesel make about a person's obligation to the community? **(b)** Do you agree with these assumptions? **(c)** Share your response with a small group. **(d)** Report your findings to the class.

Reading Skill

8. **(a)** Wiesel says, "If we forget, we are guilty, we are accomplices." Explain his reasons for making the claim. **(b)** Explain whether there are any important facts he has not taken into account. **(c)** Explain whether the claim is logical.
9. **Evaluate** this claim. In your answer, consider the rhetorical power of Wiesel's statement as well as the support he gives.

Vocabulary Builder

Practice **Synonyms** have similar meanings. **Antonyms** have opposite meanings. Explain whether each word pair contains synonyms or antonyms. Write a sentence using both words.

1. presumptuous, modest
2. bewilderment, confusion
3. accomplices, collaborators

Adding Words to Your Vocabulary The word *bewilderment* is related to the idea of confusion. Using a thesaurus, find three additional words that involve this idea. Define each word and use it in a sentence. (For more on using a thesaurus, see page R7.)

Writing

Write a **letter** to Elie Wiesel in which you take a position on his claim that silence makes us accomplices. Use *deductive reasoning*:

- First, identify and state the general definition of an accomplice.
- Next, describe the specific results of silence that Wiesel points out.
- Explain how the general definition of an accomplice applies to those who remain silent.

Use formal language appropriate to your audience, a respected man whom you have not met. Avoid slang or jargon.

For *Grammar, Vocabulary,* and *Assessment,* see **Build Language Skills,** pages 512–513.

Extend Your Learning

Listening and Speaking Hold a group **debate** about this paraphrased claim of Wiesel's: *People who do not speak up against injustice are accomplices to crime.* Choose a note taker and moderator, and divide into teams to argue for and against the statement.

- Listen carefully to the arguments presented.
- Explain how your points relate to what has been said.
- Clarify what others have said by "saying back" their points.

Review the group's notes to identify the best ideas.

Research and Technology Research Wiesel's life, and write a brief **biography** of him. Include details about his life before and after World War II. Look for interesting quotations from the author's memoirs or interviews. Consider typing your notes on a computer, so you can paste quotations from your notes into your biography.

Speech

Background

A Writer in Exile By writing critically about the U.S.S.R. (now Russia and other nations), Alexander Solzhenitsyn faced punishment and censorship. As he explains in his Nobel Lecture, writers and publishers around the world offered their support. When Solzhenitsyn was exiled in 1974, he was first welcomed by fellow author and Nobel Prize winner Heinrich Böll.

Connecting to the Literature

Reading/Writing Connection Free speech is a powerful right. Think about one of your strongest opinions. Now imagine that it is illegal to express that opinion aloud. Write a brief description of your reaction. Use at least three of the following words: *assert, legislate, ignore, interpret.*

Review

For **Literary Analysis, Reading Skill,** and **Vocabulary Builder,** see page 498.

READ MORE

by Alexander Solzhenitsyn
A Day in the Life of Ivan Denisovich
The Gulag Archipelago

Meet the Author

Alexander Solzhenitsyn (b. 1918)

Russian writer Alexander Solzhenitsyn spent years in prison camps because of his political views. Yet he was never intimidated into silence. He experienced the hardship of being a dissident—someone who publicly disagrees with an established system.

A Powerful Voice During the Second World War, Solzhenitsyn was imprisoned for writing letters to a friend that were critical of the Soviet leader, Josef Stalin. In his first novel, *A Day in the Life of Ivan Denisovich*, he described the harsh climate, backbreaking work, and poor diet at the camp in which he was imprisoned. In 1974, after the publication in Paris of parts of *The Gulag Archipelago*, Solzhenitsyn was tried for treason and exiled. In 1994, three years after the fall of the Soviet Union, he returned to his homeland.

Fast Facts

▶ Solzhenitsyn won the Nobel Prize in 1970.
▶ His novel *Cancer Ward* was inspired by his recovery from the disease in the mid-1950s.

For: More about the author
Visit: www.PHSchool.com
Web Code: eqe-9309

from Nobel Lecture

Alexander Solzhenitsyn
Translated by F.D. Reeve

I am, however, encouraged by a keen sense of WORLD LITERATURE as the one great heart that beats for the cares and misfortunes of our world, even though each corner sees and experiences them in a different way.

In past times, also, besides age-old national literatures there existed a concept of world literature as the link between the summits of national literatures and as the aggregate of reciprocal literary influences. But there was a time lag: readers and writers came to know foreign writers only belatedly, sometimes centuries later, so that mutual influences were delayed and the network of national literary high points was visible not to contemporaries but to later generations.

▲ Critical Viewing
Why is it surprising that Solzhenitsyn was sent to a prison camp like this one for writing letters? **[Connect]**

Today, between writers of one country and the readers and writers of another, there is an almost instantaneous <u>reciprocity</u>, as I myself know. My books, unpublished, alas, in my own country, despite hasty and often bad translations have quickly found a responsive world readership. Critical analysis of them has been undertaken by such leading Western writers as Heinrich Böll.[1] During all these recent years, when both my work and my freedom did not collapse, when against the laws of gravity they held on seemingly in thin air, seemingly ON NOTHING, on the invisible, mute surface tension of sympathetic people, with warm gratitude I learned, to my complete surprise, of the support of the world's writing fraternity. On my fiftieth birthday I was astounded to receive greetings from well-known European writers. No pressure put on me now passed unnoticed. During the dangerous weeks when I was being expelled from the Writers' Union,[2] THE PROTECTIVE WALL put forward by prominent writers of the world saved me from worse persecution, and Norwegian writers and artists hospitably prepared shelter for me in the event that I was exiled from my country. Finally, my being nominated for a Nobel Prize was originated not in the land where I live and write but by François Mauriac[3] and his colleagues. Afterward, national writers' organizations expressed unanimous support for me.

As I have understood it and experienced it myself, world literature is no longer an abstraction or a generalized concept invented by literary critics, but a common body and common spirit, a living, heartfelt unity reflecting the growing spiritual unity of mankind. State borders still turn crimson, heated red-hot by electric fences and machine-gun fire; some ministries of internal affairs still suppose that literature is "an internal affair" of the countries under their jurisdiction; and newspaper headlines still herald, "They have no right to interfere in our internal affairs!" Meanwhile, no such thing as INTERNAL AFFAIRS remains on our crowded Earth. Mankind's salvation lies exclusively in everyone's making everything his business, in the people of the East being anything but indifferent to what is thought in the West, and in the people of the West being anything but indifferent to what happens in the East. Literature, one of the most sensitive and responsive tools of human existence, has been the first to pick up, adopt, and assimilate this sense of the growing unity of mankind. I therefore

1. Heinrich (hīn´ riH) **Böll** (böl) (1917–1985) German novelist and winner of the Nobel Prize in Literature.
2. Writers' Union official Soviet writers' organization, which enforced government policies on literature and gave privileges to writers. In addition to being expelled from this union, Solzhenitsyn was forbidden to live in Moscow.
3. François (frän swä´) **Mauriac** (mô´ rē ak´) (1885–1970) French novelist and essayist.

Vocabulary Builder
reciprocity (res´ ə präs´ ə tē) *n.* relations of exchange; interdependence

Literary Analysis
Persuasive Writing
How does repetition of the words *common, unity, West,* and *East* add to the power of this paragraph?

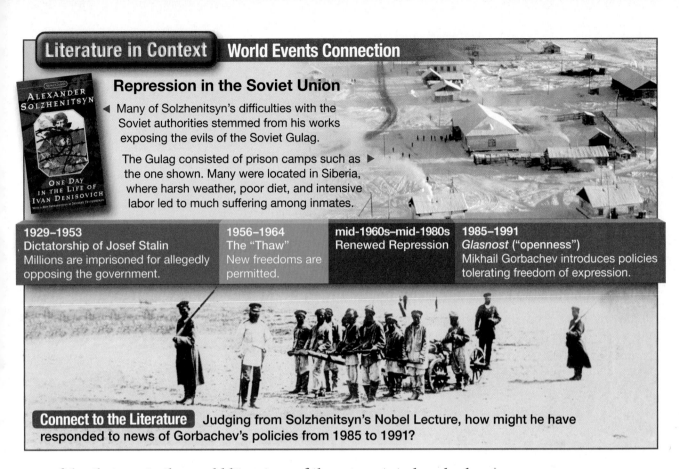

Repression in the Soviet Union

◄ Many of Solzhenitsyn's difficulties with the Soviet authorities stemmed from his works exposing the evils of the Soviet Gulag.

The Gulag consisted of prison camps such as ► the one shown. Many were located in Siberia, where harsh weather, poor diet, and intensive labor led to much suffering among inmates.

1929–1953
Dictatorship of Josef Stalin
Millions are imprisoned for allegedly opposing the government.

1956–1964
The "Thaw"
New freedoms are permitted.

mid-1960s–mid-1980s
Renewed Repression

1985–1991
Glasnost ("openness")
Mikhail Gorbachev introduces policies tolerating freedom of expression.

Connect to the Literature Judging from Solzhenitsyn's Nobel Lecture, how might he have responded to news of Gorbachev's policies from 1985 to 1991?

confidently turn to the world literature of the present, to hundreds of friends whom I have not met face to face and perhaps never will see.

My friends! Let us try to be helpful, if we are worth anything. In our own countries, torn by differences among parties, movements, castes, and groups, who for ages past has been not the dividing but the uniting force? This, essentially, is the position of writers, spokesmen of a national language, of the chief tie binding the nation, the very soil which the people inhabit, and, in fortunate circumstances, the nation's spirit too.

I think that world literature has the power in these frightening times to help mankind see itself accurately despite what is advocated by partisans and by parties. It has the power to transmit the condensed experience of one region to another, so that different scales of values are combined, and so that one people accurately and concisely knows the true history of another with a power of recognition and acute awareness as if it had lived through that history itself—and could thus be spared repeating old mistakes. At the same time, perhaps we ourselves may succeed in developing our own WORLDWIDE VIEW, like any man, with the center of the eye seeing what is nearby but the periphery of vision taking in what is happening in the rest of the world. We will make correlations and maintain worldwide standards.

Reading Check

Name one way in which writers in other countries helped Solzhenitsyn.

from *Nobel Lecture* ■ 507

Who, if not writers, are to condemn their own unsuccessful governments (in some states this is the easiest way to make a living; everyone who is not too lazy does it) as well as society itself, whether for its cowardly humiliation or for its self-satisfied weakness, or the lightheaded escapades of the young, or the youthful pirates brandishing knives?

We will be told: What can literature do against the pitiless onslaught of naked violence? Let us not forget that violence does not and cannot flourish by itself; it is inevitably intertwined with LYING. Between them there is the closest, the most profound and natural bond: nothing screens violence except lies, and the only way lies can hold out is by violence. Whoever has once announced violence as his METHOD must <u>inexorably</u> choose lying as his PRINCIPLE. At birth, violence behaves openly and even proudly. But as soon as it becomes stronger and firmly established, it senses the thinning of the air around it and cannot go on without befogging itself in lies, coating itself with lying's sugary <u>oratory</u>. It does not always or necessarily go straight for the gullet; usually it demands of its victims only allegiance to the lie, only complicity in the lie.

The simple act of an ordinary courageous man is not to take part, not to support lies! Let *that* come into the world and even reign over it, but not through me. Writers and artists can do more: they can VANQUISH LIES! In the struggle against lies, art has always won and always will. Conspicuously, incontestably for everyone. Lies can stand up against much in the world, but not against art.

Once lies have been dispelled, the repulsive nakedness of violence will be exposed—and hollow violence will collapse.

That, my friends, is why I think we can help the world in its red-hot hour: not by the nay-saying of having no armaments,[4] not by abandoning oneself to the carefree life, but by going into battle!

In Russian, proverbs about TRUTH are favorites. They persistently express the considerable, bitter, grim experience of the people, often astonishingly:

ONE WORD OF TRUTH OUTWEIGHS THE WORLD.

On such a seemingly fantastic violation of the law of the conservation of mass and energy are based both my own activities and my appeal to the writers of the whole world.

Vocabulary Builder
inexorably (in eks´ ə rə blē) *adv.* without the possibility of being delayed or stopped

oratory (ôr´ ə tôr´ ē) *n.* act of public speaking; strategies used in such speaking

Reading Skill
Evaluating the Writer's Argument
Does Solzhenitsyn support his claim that "art has always won and always will"? Explain.

◄ **Critical Viewing**
The Berlin Wall once separated East and West Berlin. How does this scene of newspaper readers by the wall support what the author says about truth? **[Connect]**

---

4. **the nay-saying of having no armaments** Solzhenitsyn is referring to the idea that nations should limit the number or kind of weapons that they hold ready for war.

Apply the Skills

from *Nobel Lecture*

Thinking About the Selection

1. **Respond:** Were you stirred by the conclusion? Why or why not?
2. **(a) Recall:** According to Solzhenitsyn, what is a key difference between world literature today and in the past? **(b) Interpret:** Why does he call world literature "one great heart"?
3. **(a) Recall:** According to Solzhenitsyn, what were two ways in which European writers showed support for him? **(b) Connect:** How does this support confirm his view of world literature?
4. **Analyze:** What role does he believe artists have in the struggle against injustice?
5. **Apply:** Identify a situation in which it matters whether people speak up. Explain what Solzhenitsyn might say about it.

Literary Analysis

6. Identify the central **argument** in Solzhenitsyn's **persuasive speech** and evaluate his reasoning.
7. What **rhetorical devices** does Solzhenitsyn use to emphasize his message? Use a chart like the one shown to analyze examples.

	Repetition	Parallelism	Slogans or Saws	Rhetorical Questions
Example				
Effect				

8. **(a)** What assumptions does Solzhenitsyn make about the rights of individuals as opposed to the dictates of the state? **(b)** Do you agree with his assumptions? **(c)** Share your responses with a small group. **(d)** Report your findings to the class.

Reading Skill

9. **(a)** Solzhenitsyn writes, "Once lies have been dispelled . . . hollow violence will collapse." Explain his reasons for making the claim. **(b)** Explain whether there are any important facts he has not taken into account. **(c)** Explain whether the claim is logical.
10. **Evaluate** this claim. In your answer, consider the rhetorical power of the statement as well as the support he gives.

QuickReview

Essay at a Glance
Alexander Solzhenitsyn argues for the power and responsibility of writers.

Go Online
Assessment
For: Self-test
Visit: www.PHSchool.com
Web Code: eqa-6308

Persuasive Writing: nonfiction, including *speeches*, intended to convince readers to take an action or a position on an issue

Argument: the use of reason to support a position

Rhetorical Devices: verbal techniques that create emphasis and appeal to emotion

Vocabulary Builder

Practice **Synonyms** are words with similar meanings. **Antonyms** have opposite meanings. Explain whether each word pair contains synonyms or antonyms. Write a sentence using both words.

1. reciprocity, independence
2. inexorably, avoidably
3. oratory, rhetoric

Adding Words to Your Vocabulary The word *oratory* is related to the art of public speaking. Using a thesaurus, find three additional words that refer to this art. Define each word and use it in a sentence. (For more on using a thesaurus, see page R7.)

Writing

Write a **letter** to Solzhenitsyn in which you evaluate his idea that telling the truth can change the world. Use *deductive reasoning*:

- First, state a general definition of "changing the world."
- Next, describe the effects of truth that Solzhenitsyn identifies.
- Explain whether the examples do or do not illustrate your definition.

Use formal language appropriate to your audience, a respected man you have not met. Avoid slang or jargon.

For *Grammar, Vocabulary,* and *Assessment,* see **Build Language Skills,** pages 512–513.

Extend Your Learning

Listening and Speaking Hold a group **debate** about this paraphrased claim of Solzhenitsyn's: *Telling the truth will bring down an unjust government.* Choose a notetaker and moderator, and divide the group into teams to argue for and against the statement.

- Listen carefully to the arguments presented.
- Explain how your points relate to what has been said.
- Clarify what others have said by "saying back" their points.

Review the group's notes to identify the best ideas.

Research and Technology Research Solzhenitsyn's life and write a brief **biography** of him. Include details about his life in the Soviet Union and in the United States. Look for interesting quotations from his works or interviews. Consider typing your notes on a computer so you can paste quotations into your biography.

Build Language Skills

Vocabulary Skill

Prefixes There are two spelling variations of the **prefix *in-* or *ir-*,** meaning "not." The addition of *in-* or *ir-* usually changes a base word to its antonym. *Inevitable,* which means "not avoidable," is the antonym of *evitable. Irresponsible* is the antonym of *responsible.*

In- can also literally mean "in," as in the word *insight,* which means "seeing and understanding the inner nature of something."

▶ **Example:** An O. Henry story *inevitably* has a surprise ending.

Practice Define the word root, and then write the definition of the word with the prefix added.

1. irrevocable
2. inarticulate
3. irrelevant
4. insurmountable
5. ineligible

Grammar Lesson

Degrees of Adverbs Most adverbs have three different forms called degrees of comparison—the *positive,* the *comparative,* and the *superlative.* Use the comparative to compare two actions or qualities. Use the superlative to compare more than two actions or qualities.

There are different ways to form the comparative and superlative degrees of adverbs. Notice, for example, how the forms of the adverbs in the following chart change to show comparison.

Positive	Comparative	Superlative
soon	sooner	soonest
impressively	more impressively	most impressively
well	better	best

Practice Fill in the following chart.

Positive	Comparative	Superlative
badly		
much	more	
	more elegantly	

MorePractice

For more practice with adverbs and degrees of comparison, see the Grammar Handbook, pp. R41 and R46.

𝒲𝒢 *Writing and Grammar Connection: Chapter 25, Section 1*

Monitor Your Progress

Reading: Evaluate Persuasive Appeals

Directions: *Read the selection. Then, answer the questions.*

Empress Theodora made this speech as rebels threatened to overthrow her and her husband, Justinian I, who ruled the Eastern Roman Empire.

In my opinion, flight is not the right course, even if it should bring us to safety. It is impossible for a person, having been born into this world, not to die, but for one who has reigned it is intolerable to be a fugitive. . . .

If you wish to save yourself, my lord, there is no difficulty. We are rich; over there is the sea, and yonder are the ships. Yet reflect for a moment whether, when you have once escaped to a place of security, you would not gladly exchange such safety for death. As for me, I agree with the adage that the royal purple is the noblest shroud.

—from Speech During the Invasion of Constantinople by Empress Theodora

1. The tone of the passage implies that
   A those who leave are cowards.
   B those who stay are unrealistic.
   C the woman should leave.
   D they should buy freedom.

2. The second paragraph
   A sets up a contradiction that accuses.
   B sets up a logical argument that persuades.
   C sets up a contrast that persuades.
   D sets up a parallel to history that accuses.

3. The use of the word *fugitive* adds strength to the writer's appeal because
   A unusual words are generally persuasive.
   B even royalty has to follow general rules.
   C the word can imply a shameful condition.
   D commoners did not contradict royalty.

4. Therdora's general appeal is that
   A the people should help their rulers.
   B it would be heroic to establish themselves somewhere else.
   C dignity makes life worth living and so is more important than safety.
   D royalty should not abandon the people.

Timed Writing: Persuasion [Critical Stance]

"I think that world literature has the power in these frightening times to help mankind see itself accurately. . . ."—Alexander Solzhenitsyn
Do you think that this statement is correct or incorrect? Support your opinion with specific examples from "Keep Memory Alive" or Solzhenitsyn's Nobel Lecture and from your studies and your experience. **(25 minutes)**

 Writing Workshop: *Work in Progress*

Persuasive Essay

Make a flowchart for the first choice on your topic list. In each supporting box, write a detail that shows why the change is needed or what positive result it would have.

Reading Informational Materials

Newspaper Editorials

In Part 2, you learned about the importance of evaluating persuasive appeals. If you read Solzhenitsyn's Nobel Lecture, you know that persuasive appeals can be quite powerful. As you read these editorials on the ten-year anniversary of a historic event, evaluate the writers' persuasive appeals.

About Newspaper Editorials

Most articles in a newspaper are intended to be objective—the writers report facts and present both sides of an issue. An important exception is a **newspaper editorial,** an essay in which the author presents an opinion about a current event. Typical editorials include a clearly stated opinion about a topic in the news, background information, and arguments in support of the opinion.

Reading Skill

You can better evaluate the arguments in an editorial by **analyzing the writer's assumptions**—the basic ideas that the writer takes for granted. For example, an editorial writer might write "Sports are a vital part of a city's life, and so the mayor should fund the new stadium." In this statement, the writer makes several assumptions:

- Sports are a vital part of city life. (This assumption is stated.)
- The mayor has the power to fund a project such as the stadium. (This assumption is unstated.)
- The mayor has a duty to encourage the city's cultural life, not just provide basic services. (This assumption is unstated.)

The writer's argument is only valid if each assumption is valid. Yet, any one of them might not be true or might not be accepted by all readers. To analyze a writer's assumptions, use a chart like this one.

Academic Standards

- Analyze formatting of informational documents. (10.2.1)
- Evaluate an author's use of time and sequence. (10.3.6)

Writer's Opinion: _____	
Analysis of Assumptions	**My Evaluation of Assumption**
The point is a good one IF one believes . . .	☐ Reasonable
☐ Assumption about what is right or wrong: _____	☐ Reasonable in part
☐ Assumption about human nature: _____	☐ Unreasonable
☐ Assumption about a person's character: _____	
☐ Other assumption: _____	

THE WALL STREET JOURNAL

Editorial, November 9, 1999

On this day in 1989 the world watched as the German people whom the [Berlin] Wall had divided for more than a generation attacked it with hammers, ropes and their bare hands. What the cameras could not capture was that the physical breaching of the Wall would not have been possible without the sustained moral pounding that had softened the foundation upon which it stood. It was a force most literally expressed by Ronald Wilson Reagan two years earlier when he came to Berlin to present his own challenge to the Soviet leader: "Mr. Gorbachev, tear down this wall." At the time, even many of Mr. Reagan's closest sympathizers regarded it as mere boilerplate.

Mr. Reagan knew better. For his was not an optimism grounded in denying unpleasant facts, as his critics like to think. To the contrary, his was an optimism built on a faith in freedom. Freedom, moreover, was not some distant Platonic ideal, but a practical workaday answer. Thus Mr. Reagan could at once acknowledge the threat posed by the Soviet Union while refusing to be intimidated by it. As he went on to say in his now-famous Berlin speech, "In the Communist world, we see failure, technological backwardness, declining standards of health, even want of the most basic kind—too little food."

In other words, for all its strength and brutality, communism was not the invincible monolith it was so often assumed to be by foes and sympathizers alike. [. . .]

Indeed, in looking back to the heady days of the early 1980s perhaps the most striking thing is how persistently Mr. Reagan predicted communism's fall—and how most everyone simply ignored him. Even among his fellow Cold Warriors the Gipper's[1] optimism set him apart. [. . .]

Ronald Reagan did not win the Cold War single-handedly. The contradictions of communism had been building, pushed by brave leaders like Lech Walesa and Vaclav Havel.[2] Clearly too Mikhail Gorbachev played his part, not least in his refusal to use troops to keep the Wall up. Ten years after the Wall came down, Kosovo and Chechnya[3] remind us that we have challenges we could not even have imagined then. But surely the lesson of 1989 is that human beings are born to be free, that a confidence in this proposition is infectious, and that—as Mr. Reagan would no doubt have reminded us—we would do best by our future to look at the pulling down of the Berlin Wall as a beginning, not an end.

---

1. Cold Warriors . . . the Gipper's (gĭ′ pərz) The conflict between the Soviet Union and the United States in the decades after 1945 is known as the Cold War; Ronald Reagan was nicknamed "the Gipper."

2. Lech Walesa (lekh vä wen′ sä) (b. 1943) **. . . Vaclav Havel** (vä′ tslä hä′ vel) (b. 1936) Eastern European leaders of democratic reform, Walesa in Poland and Havel in Czechoslovakia.

3. Kosovo (kô′ sô vô′) **and Chechnya** (chech′ nyə) regions that experienced bloody conflict after the Soviet Union's collapse; Kosovo is in Yugoslavia, and Chechnya was formerly part of the Soviet Union.

The editorial writer identifies the occasion for the editorial and states its topic.

Here the writer states the main opinion in the editorial: The fall of communism was the result of a moral struggle in which Reagan played a decisive role.

The writer strengthens the case by considering other factors in the Cold War besides Reagan's vision.

The New York Times

Editorial, November 10, 1999

> The editorial begins with a statement of the opinion it will support: Gorbachev should be celebrated for his role in the fall of communism.

The Berlin Wall was bound to fall eventually. But that it came down as bloodlessly as it did 10 years ago this week is largely a tribute to one leader. Today Mikhail Gorbachev is a political pariah in Russia and increasingly forgotten in the West. But history will remember him generously for his crucial role in ending the cold war and pulling back the Iron Curtain that Stalin drew across Europe in 1945.[1]

Liquidating the Soviet empire was not what Mr. Gorbachev had in mind when he came to power in 1985. He was shrewd enough to recognize that radical changes were urgently needed to stave off economic and political bankruptcy in Russia and its European satellites. [. . .][2]

> To support the point about Gorbachev's role, the writer reviews his two key reform policies, glasnost and perestroika.

Once Mr. Gorbachev lifted the lid with the openness of *glasnost* and the attempted economic restructuring of *perestroika*,[3] change took on a dynamic of its own. Similar energies were unleashed in the once-captive nations of Eastern Europe as it became clear that he would not send Soviet tanks to bail out the unpopular client regimes that had held sway there since World War II.

As political pressures began to build in the late 1980s, Mr. Gorbachev was left with two options. He could hurtle ahead toward full political and economic freedom. Or he could reverse course and crack down, as so many previous Soviet leaders had done. He chose to do neither. He was too much a creature of his Soviet Communist upbringing to subject his own power to the test of electoral democracy. But he was too enlightened to unleash the kind of thorough repression that might have preserved the Soviet empire for a few more years.

Others stepped in to accelerate the transformations Mr. Gorbachev had begun, and in 1989 fixtures of the Soviet empire began to crumble. [. . .]

Through it all, Mr. Gorbachev and his like-minded foreign minister, Eduard Shevardnadze, stayed their hand, reflecting not only their idealism about reshaping East-West relations but also a pragmatic calculation that the Soviet Union could no longer afford an empire. For permitting its dissolution, Mr. Gorbachev paid a high price. Within two years he had been pushed from power in Moscow. [. . .]

> The writer concludes with a statement, using memorable language, that sums up Gorbachev's role and the historical situation.

History has passed Mr. Gorbachev by. But this week, especially, he deserves to be remembered for what he did and, perhaps more important, what he refused to do. With a wisdom and decency that is sadly rare in international power politics, he chose not to defend a dying system with a final, futile spasm of murderous force.

---

1. **Iron Curtain . . . 1945** At the end of the Second World War, in 1945, Europe was split between western countries, allied with the United States, and eastern countries, dominated by its rival, the Soviet Union, then led by Josef Stalin. West and East were said to be divided by an "iron curtain."
2. **European satellites** Eastern European countries dominated by the Soviet Union.
3. *glasnost* (glaz´ nōst) . . . *perestroika* (per´ ə stroɪ´ kə) policies of Gorbachev's designed to reform the Soviet Union. *Glasnost* involved lifting restrictions on free speech; *perestroika* referred to attempts to reform the government and economy.

Reading: Analyzing the Writer's Assumptions

Standards Assessed

• 10.2.1
• 10.3.6

Directions: *Choose the letter of the best answer to each question.*

1. Which of the following assumptions do the writers of both editorials make?
   A The decisions of individuals do not affect historical events.
   B The fall of the Berlin Wall was a desirable event.
   C Reagan was wise in foreseeing the end of communism.
   D Gorbachev was idealistic in some of his policies.

2. Which of the following assumptions is directly stated in the *New York Times* editorial?
   A The Berlin Wall could not have lasted.
   B Effective change in governments must happen gradually.
   C The existence of the Berlin Wall was shameful.
   D Reagan did not contribute significantly to the fall of the wall.

3. Which of the following assumptions must be made to make the argument in the *Wall Street Journal* editorial valid?
   A Reagan was popular in the Soviet Union.
   B Reagan and Gorbachev had a strong, cooperative relationship.
   C The Soviet Union had no choice but to bring down the Berlin Wall.
   D History is shaped by moral issues, not just power struggles.

Reading: Comprehension and Interpretation

Directions: *Write your answers on a separate piece of paper.*

4. Compare and contrast the writers' interpretations of Gorbachev's role in the fall of the Berlin Wall. Support your answer with quotations from each editorial. **[Organizing]**

5. **(a)** According to the *Wall Street Journal,* how did Reagan contribute to this historic event? **(b)** What response to this opinion might the editorial writer for the *New York Times* give? **[Generating]**

Timed Writing: Persuasion [Critical Stance]

Respond to one of the editorials. Give reasons why readers should or should not accept the argument presented. Cite examples from the text to illustrate your points. **(25–30 minutes)**

Practice these skills with either "What Makes a Degas a Degas?" (p. 520) or "The American Idea" (p. 527).

 Academic Standards

• Examine how the author's perspective influences the structure and tone. (10.2.4)

• Revise writing based on specific criteria. (10.4.11)

• Write responses to literature. (10.5.2)

Literary Analysis

An **analytic essay** is a brief work of nonfiction in which a writer explores a subject by breaking it into parts. In an **interpretive essay,** a writer offers a view of the meaning or significance of an issue of general interest. A single essay may combine features of both types of essay. To bring readers to accept an analysis or interpretation, a writer may use **appeals,** or support, of the following types:

- Using *appeals to authority*, a writer calls on the opinions of experts or other respected people.
- Using *appeals to reason*, a writer calls on logic.
- Using *emotional appeals*, a writer taps a reader's fears, sympathy, or pride.
- Using *appeals to shared values*, a writer calls on beliefs shared by many about what is good, right, or fair.

Reading Skill

To **evaluate a writer's appeals,** decide whether the writer balances logic and facts with emotional appeals. **Distinguish between fact and opinion.**

- A statement of **fact** can be proved true.
- A statement of **opinion** expresses a belief or a viewpoint and should be supported by facts or reason.

Record details on a chart like the one shown to help you decide if the writer has made a strong argument for a position.

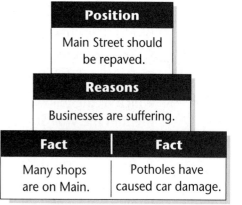

Position
Main Street should be repaved.

Reasons
Businesses are suffering.

Fact	Fact
Many shops are on Main.	Potholes have caused car damage.

Vocabulary Builder

What Makes a Degas a Degas?

- **silhouette** (sil´ ə wet´) *n.* an outline drawing filled in with a solid color (p. 521) *He drew a solid black silhouette of Emily's profile.*

- **simulating** (sim´ yōō lāt´ iŋ) *v.* giving the appearance of (p. 521) *The machine trained pilots by simulating a crash.*

- **spontaneous** (spän tā´ nē əs) *adj.* occurring or seeming to occur without planning (p. 522) *When the judge read the verdict, we burst into spontaneous applause.*

The American Idea

- **emigrants** (em´ i grənts) *n.* people who leave their country or region to settle elsewhere (p. 528) *Many emigrants left Ireland in the 1840s.*

- **relentlessly** (ri lent´ lis lē) *adv.* without pause or easing up; harshly (p. 528) *It rained relentlessly, and we feared a flood.*

- **subversion** (səb vʉr´ zhən) *n.* activity meant to overthrow something established (p. 529) *Disobedience is a subversion of authority.*

Build Understanding • *What Makes a Degas a Degas?*

Background

Degas and Impressionism In the 1860s, a group of French painters known as the Impressionists shocked the art world. Abandoning strict forms, they used short, dabbed brushstrokes to capture fleeting impressions of color and light. Their work had a great impact on Edgar Degas (ed gàŕ_də gä´; 1834–1917). At the same time, as Richard Mühlberger explains in his essay, Degas introduced his own innovative style.

Connecting to the Literature

Reading/Writing Connection In his essay, Mühlberger helps readers look closely at two Degas paintings, revealing details readers might not have noticed. Describe a painting or photograph that you know—or use an artwork in this text as your inspiration. Explain what details in the image others might not notice at first. Use at least three of the following words: *capture, complicate, diminish, identify.*

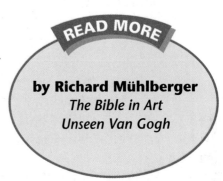

READ MORE

by Richard Mühlberger
The Bible in Art
Unseen Van Gogh

Meet the Author

Richard **Mühlberger** (b. 1938)

Born in New Jersey, Richard Mühlberger has spent over thirty-five years as an art critic and museum administrator. During the 1990s, he was vice-director in charge of education at the Metropolitan Museum of Art in New York City, one of the foremost art museums in the world.

Aiding in Art Appreciation While at the Metropolitan Museum of Art, Mühlberger began producing a series of books that make the works of famous artists accessible to the average viewer. The series includes *What Makes a Degas a Degas?*, from which this selection is taken, and similarly titled books on Van Gogh, Monet, and others.

Fast Facts

▶ Mühlberger also served as director of the Museum of Fine Art in Springfield, Massachusetts.
▶ He has taught art history classes at the Western New England College in Springfield.

Go Online
Author Link
For: More about the author
Visit: www.PHSchool.com
Web Code: eqe-9310

What Makes a Degas a Degas?

Richard Mühlberger

Dancers, Pink and Green, Edgar Degas. The Metropolitan Museum of Art.

Dancers, Pink and Green

Degas's famous ballet paintings witness his enthusiasm for dance and his intimacy with the private backstage areas of the Paris Opéra, the huge complex where the ballet made its home. He was equally familiar with the theater's more public boxes and stalls, where he watched many performances. During his lifetime, he produced about fifteen hundred drawings, prints, pastels, and oil paintings with ballet themes.

In *Dancers, Pink and Green* [left], each ballerina is caught in a characteristic pose as she waits to go on the stage. One stretches and flexes her foot. Another secures her hair, while a third is almost hidden. The fourth dancer, who looks at her shoulder strap as she adjusts it, holds a pose that was a favorite of the artist and one he used in many paintings. An upright beam separates her from the fifth ballerina, who also turns her head but in the opposite direction, full of anticipation. Above her in the distance are the box seats, which Degas simplified into a stack of six red and orange rectangles along the edge of the canvas. The vertical beam the ballerina is touching extends to the top and the bottom of the painting. The multicolored vertical shapes behind the dancers represent a large, painted landscape used as a backdrop for one of the dances. It will provide an immaterial, dreamworld quality to the performance, as it does to the painting.

Subscribers to the Opéra were allowed backstage in the theater, and some took advantage of this access to pester dancers. On the far side of the tall wood column is the partial <u>silhouette</u> of a large man in a top hat. He seems to be trying to keep out of the way, but his protruding profile overlaps a ballerina. None of the dancers pay attention to him. They also ignore one another, for this scene represents the tense moments just before the curtain rises.

Degas discovered that with oil paints he could achieve the same fresh feeling conveyed with pastels. Although this painting took the same amount of time to finish as many of his others and was designed and executed in his studio, Degas wanted to make it look as though it had been executed quickly, backstage. To do this, he imitated the marks of a charcoal pencil with his brush, making narrow black lines that edge the dancers' bodies and costumes. Next, he used his own innovation of <u>simulating</u> the matte[1] finish of pastels by taking the sheen out of oil paint, then filling in the sketchy "charcoal" outlines of his figures with a limited range of colors. The colors he used for the dancers extend to the floor and the background. The technique gives the impression that he applied the

---

1. **matte** (mat) *adj.* dull; not shiny.

Vocabulary Builder
silhouette (sil´ ə wet´) *n.* an outline drawing filled in with a solid color
simulating (sim´ yoo lāt´ iŋ) *v.* giving the appearance of

Literary Analysis
Analytic and Interpretive Essays
What is analytic about this essay?

✓**Reading Check**
What materials did Degas use to execute *Dancers, Pink and Green*?

colors hastily while standing in the wings watching the dancers get ready.

The results of Degas's experiments could have been executed much more quickly had he used pastels instead of oils. What Degas wanted, however, was to make paint look <u>spontaneous</u>. This was part of his lifelong quest: to make viewers feel that they were right there, beside him.

Carriage at the Races

Paul Valpinçon was Degas's best friend in school and remained close to the artist all his life. Degas was a frequent visitor to his country house in Normandy, the northwest region of France, a long journey from Paris. Degas thought that the Normandy countryside was "exactly like England," and the beautiful horse farms there inspired him to paint equestrian subjects. During a visit in 1869, however, Degas found horses secondary to Paul Valpinçon's infant son, Henri. This becomes apparent by looking at the painting *Carriage at the Races* [right].

At first, Degas's composition seems lopsided. In one corner are the largest and darkest objects, a pair of horses and a carriage. Against the lacquered body of the carriage, the creamy white tones of the passengers stand out. They are framed by the dark colors rather than overwhelmed by them.

Degas placed a cream-colored umbrella in the middle of the painting above some of the figures in the carriage. Near it, balanced on the back of the driver's seat, is a black bulldog. Paul Valpinçon himself is the driver. Both Paul and the dog are gazing at the baby, who lies in the shade of the umbrella. With pink, dimpled knees, Henri, not yet a year old, sprawls on the lap of his nurse while his mother looks on.

Ideas From the Exotic, Old, and New

Degas always enjoyed looking at art. One of the thrills of his school years was being allowed to inspect the great paintings in the collection of Paul Valpinçon's father. Throughout his life, the artist drew inspiration from the masterpieces in the Louvre in Paris, one of the greatest museums in the world. He also found ideas in Japanese prints. They were considered cheap, disposable souvenirs in

Vocabulary Builder
spontaneous (spän tā´ nē əs) *adj.* occurring or seeming to occur without planning

Carriage at the Races, 1872, Edgar Degas. Museum of Fine Arts, Boston.

Japan, but were treasured by artists and others in the West as highly original, fascinating works of art. Photographs, then newly invented, also suggested to Degas ways of varying his paintings. He eventually became an enthusiastic photographer himself.

In *Carriage at the Races,* the way in which the horses and carriage are cut off recalls figures in photographs and Japanese prints. For Degas, showing only part of a subject made his paintings more intimate, immediate, and realistic. He wanted viewers to see the scene as if they were actually there.

▲ Critical Viewing
Does the way in which the horses "are cut off" make the picture seem like a photograph, as the essay suggests? **[Assess]**

Apply the Skills

What Makes a Degas a Degas?

Thinking About the Selection

1. **Respond:** Would you like to see more work by Degas? Explain.
2. **(a) Recall:** What effect does Degas seek by outlining the dancers in black lines in *Dancers, Pink and Green*? **(b) Analyze:** What other elements contribute to this effect?
3. **(a) Recall:** What is the dominant image in *Carriage at the Races*? **(b) Analyze:** How does Degas focus attention on this image?
4. **Connect:** What qualities in Degas's paintings suggest that he might have been a good photographer when he took up that hobby? Explain.
5. **(a) Extend:** Identify a way in which television shows or print advertisements create an impression of immediacy and spontaneity, as Degas did. **(b) Discuss:** Share your ideas in a small group. **(c) Evaluate:** Decide on the three most relevant or interesting ideas and present them to the whole class.

Literary Analysis

6. This **interpretive essay** focuses on Degas's achievement. Briefly summarize Mühlberger's view of Degas's "lifelong quest."
7. **(a)** Use a chart like the one shown to organize details of the **analytic** sections of Mühlberger's essay. **(b)** Find two qualities that Mühlberger identifies in these paintings that might make them seem careless or incomplete. **(c)** Explain how Mühlberger uses **persuasive appeals** to reason to strengthen his presentation of the idea that Degas intentionally incorporated these qualities.

Topic:_____

| Dancers: Main Point_____ | → | Supporting Details_____ | → | Conclusions _____ |
| Carriage: Main Point_____ | → | Supporting Details_____ | → | |

Reading Skill

8. **(a)** List two **facts** and two **opinions** that Mühlberger includes about Degas. **(b)** What type of facts does he use to support each opinion? **(c)** Explain whether you agree or disagree with each opinion.

Vocabulary Builder

Practice **Analogies** match relationships between two pairs of words. For each item, choose the word that will make the relationship between the second pair of words most similar to the relationship between the first pair.

1. hatchback : car :: silhouette : **(a)** bracelet, **(b)** portrait, **(c)** carving
2. performing : doing :: simulating : **(a)** pretending, **(b)** believing, **(c)** creating
3. natural : artificial :: spontaneous : **(a)** fresh, **(b)** rehearsed, **(c)** rash

Adding Words to Your Vocabulary Look up *silhouette, boycott,* and *maverick* in a dictionary. Explain what their origins share. Use each in a sentence. (For more on dictionary use, see page R6.)

Writing

Write a **critique,** or critical evaluation, of Mühlberger's essay. Identify one of his central claims, and weigh the evidence he uses to support it. Then, present your evaluation to the class.

- Before you draft, gather examples of the writer's evidence.
- For each piece of evidence, note your ideas about its effectiveness. In one sentence, state whether the writer's evidence is strong.
- Consider discussing each piece of evidence in a separate paragraph.

For *Grammar, Vocabulary,* and *Assessment,* see **Build Language Skills,** pages 532–533.

Extend Your Learning

Listening and Speaking Give a **persuasive speech** in which you explain and defend a new style in music, fashion, or art.
- Prepare your speech in outline form.
- Include logical arguments, examples, and appeals to shared values.
- Address specific concerns that your audience may have, anticipating and answering any objections.

Research and Technology Research an artist associated with French Impressionism, such as Pierre Auguste Renoir or Mary Cassatt. Write the **cover letter** and **résumé** that he or she might have submitted for the job of "French Impressionist." Consult reference works to find a suitable format for cover letters and résumés, and proofread carefully to ensure that you followed the format.

Essay

Background

Coming to America In his essay, Theodore H. White asserts that immigration is key to the idea of America. Since its founding, the United States has welcomed more immigrants than any other nation. From 1820 to 1930, about 60 percent of all immigration worldwide was to the United States. From 1905 to 1914, more than a million people immigrated to the United States each year, seeking opportunity or fleeing oppression.

Connecting to the Literature

Reading/Writing Connection White identifies many reasons that Americans can be proud of their country. The Fourth of July, the Statue of Liberty, veterans on parade—these are some of the reminders of that pride. Explain the significance of something that makes you feel patriotic. Use at least three of the following words: *communicate, display, signify, verify.*

Review

For **Literary Analysis, Reading Skill,** and **Vocabulary Builder,** see page 518.

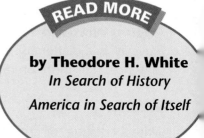

READ MORE

by Theodore H. White
In Search of History
America in Search of Itself

Meet the Author

Theodore H. **White** (1915–1986)

A Boston native, Theodore H. White worked as a newsboy for the *Boston Globe* to help pay for his education at Harvard University. At Harvard, he studied Chinese history and Asian languages. After he graduated, Henry Luce, founder of *Time* magazine, made him *Time*'s correspondent in eastern Asia.

The Making of a Reporter White earned fame writing about the election of John F. Kennedy in *The Making of the President, 1960.* "There is no excitement anywhere in the world, short of war, to match the excitement of the American presidential campaign," White observed. Today, he is viewed as one of the finest political reporters of the twentieth century.

Fast Facts

▶ President Kennedy's widow, Jacqueline Kennedy, chose White to write a magazine essay honoring her husband.
▶ At Harvard's Joan Shorenstein Center, the annual lecture on the press and politics is named in White's honor.

Go **Online**
—Author Link

For: More about the author
Visit: www.PHSchool.com
Web Code: eqe-9311

The American Idea

Theodore H. White

The idea was there at the very beginning, well before Thomas Jefferson put it into words—and the idea rang the call.

Jefferson himself could not have imagined the reach of his call across the world in time to come when he wrote:

"We hold these truths to be self-evident, that all men are created equal, that they are endowed by their Creator with certain unalienable rights, that among these are life, liberty, and the pursuit of happiness."

But over the next two centuries the call would reach the potato patches of Ireland, the ghettoes of Europe, the paddyfields of China, stirring farmers to leave their lands and townsmen their trades and thus unsettling all traditional civilizations.

It is the call from Thomas Jefferson, embodied in the great statue that looks down the Narrows of New York Harbor,[1] and in the immigrants who answered the call, that we now celebrate.

Some of the first European Americans had come to the new continent to worship God in their own way, others to seek their

Literary Analysis
Analytic and Interpretive Essays What emotional appeals does White use in the opening paragraphs of this essay?

---

1. **the great statue that looks down the Narrows of New York Harbor** Statue of Liberty.

fortunes. But, over a century-and-a-half, the new world changed those Europeans, above all the Englishmen who had come to North America. Neither King nor Court nor Church could stretch over the ocean to the wild continent. To survive, the first <u>emigrants</u> had to learn to govern themselves. But the freedom of the wilderness whetted their appetites for more freedoms. By the time Jefferson drafted his call, men were in the field fighting for those new-learned freedoms, killing and being killed by English soldiers, the best-trained troops in the world, supplied by the world's greatest navy. Only something worth dying for could unite American volunteers and keep them in the field—a stated cause, a flag, a nation they could call their own.

When, on the Fourth of July, 1776, the colonial leaders who had been meeting as a Continental Congress in Philadelphia voted to approve Jefferson's Declaration of Independence, it was not puffed-up rhetoric for them to pledge to each other "our lives, our fortunes and our sacred honor." Unless their new "United States of America" won the war, the Congressmen would be judged traitors as <u>relentlessly</u> as would the irregulars-under-arms in the field. . . .

The new Americans were tough men fighting for a very tough idea. How they won their battles is a story for the schoolbooks, studied by scholars, wrapped in myths by historians and poets. But what is most important is the story of the idea that made them into a nation, the idea that had an explosive power undreamed of in 1776.

All other nations had come into being among people whose families had lived for time out of mind on the same land where they were born. Englishmen are English, Frenchmen are French, Chinese are Chinese, while their governments come and go; their national states can be torn apart and remade without losing their nationhood. But Americans are a nation born of an idea; not the place, but the idea, created the United States Government.

The story we celebrate . . . is the story of how this idea worked itself out, how it stretched and changed and how the call for "life, liberty and the pursuit of happiness" does still, as it did in the beginning, mean different things to different people.

The debate began with the drafting of the Declaration of Independence. That task was left to Jefferson of Virginia, who spent two weeks in an upstairs room in a Philadelphia boarding house penning a draft, while John Adams and Benjamin Franklin questioned, edited, hardened his phrases. By the end of that hot and muggy June, the three had reached agreement: the Declaration contained the ringing universal theme Jefferson strove for and, at the same time, voiced American grievances toughly enough to please the feisty Adams and the pragmatic Franklin. After brief debate, Congress passed it.

Vocabulary Builder
emigrants (em´ i grənts) *n.* people who leave their country or region to settle elsewhere
relentlessly (ri lent´ lis lē) *adv.* without pause or easing up; harshly

Reading Skill
Distinguishing Fact From Opinion
Identify one fact and one opinion expressed in the essay so far.

As the years wore on, the great debate expanded between Jefferson and Adams. The young nation flourished and Jefferson chose to think of America's promise as a call to all the world, its promises universal. A few weeks before he died, he wrote, "May it be to the world, what I believe it will be (to some parts sooner, to others later, but finally to all), the signal of arousing men to burst their chains." To Adams, the call meant something else—it was the call for *American* independence, the cornerstone of an *American* state.

Their argument ran through their successive Administrations. Adams, the second President, suspected the French Revolutionaries; Alien and Sedition Acts[2] were passed during his term of office to protect the American state and its liberties against French <u>subversion</u>. But Jefferson, the third President, welcomed the French. The two men, once close friends, became archrivals. Still, as they grew old, their rivalry faded; there was glory enough to share in what they had made; in 1812, they began a correspondence that has since become classic, remembering and taking comfort in the triumphs of their youth.

Adams and Jefferson lived long lives and died on the same day—the Fourth of July, 1826, 50 years to the day from the Continental Congress's approval of the Declaration. Legend has it that Adams breathed on his death bed, "Thomas Jefferson still survives." As couriers set out from Braintree[3] carrying the news of Adams's death, couriers were riding north from Virginia with the news of Jefferson's death. The couriers met in Philadelphia. Horace Greeley,[4] then a youth in Vermont, later remembered: ". . . When we learned . . . that Thomas Jefferson and John Adams, the author and the great champion, respectively, of the Declaration, had both died on that day, and that the messengers bearing South and North, respectively, the tidings of their decease, had met in Philadelphia, under the shadow of that Hall in which our independence was declared, it seemed that a Divine attestation had solemnly hallowed and sanctified the great anniversary by the impressive ministration of Death."

Literature in Context

History Connection

The American Revolution White makes a number of references to the era of the American Revolution.

- **The Declaration of Independence** Written by Thomas Jefferson, the Declaration announced the colonies' decision in 1776 to break away from Great Britain. In the opening paragraph, Jefferson refers to *unalienable* (un āl´ yən ə bəl) *rights*—those rights that cannot be taken or given away.
- **Irregulars-Under-Arms** The colonists who fought the British in the Revolution could be considered irregulars-under-arms. As rebels, they did not belong to a regularly established army.

Connect to the Literature

What contrasting views of the American idea are represented by Jefferson's "unalienable rights" and by Adams's views on immigration?

Vocabulary Builder
subversion (səb vʉr´ zhən) *n.* activity meant to overthrow something established

2. **Alien and Sedition Acts** laws passed by Congress in 1798 restricting immigration and regulating the expression of criticism of the government.
3. **Braintree** town in Massachusetts (now called Quincy) where John Adams lived and died.
4. **Horace Greeley** famous American newspaper publisher.

Apply the Skills

The American Idea

Thinking About the Selection

1. **Respond:** Which idea about America meant the most to you? Why?
2. **(a) Recall:** Identify three groups that White says heard the call of the American idea. **(b) Infer:** How did it affect them?
3. **Compare and Contrast:** What differences does White see between early American settlers and people living elsewhere?
4. **(a) Interpret:** What does White mean when he writes, "Americans are a nation born of an idea"? **(b) Extend:** What might White say defines somebody or something as American?
5. **(a) Take a Position:** Do you agree with White that "life, liberty and the pursuit of happiness" means different things to different people? Why or why not? **(b) Discuss:** Share your ideas in a small group. **(c) Evaluate:** Decide which ideas are the most interesting, and present them to the whole class.

Literary Analysis

6. The author of this **interpretive essay** focuses on the "American idea." **(a)** Briefly summarize White's view. **(b)** Identify two historical details that he uses to support or illustrate his view.
7. Use a chart like this one to organize details of the **analytic** sections of White's essay.

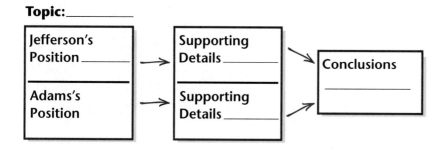

Topic:_____

| Jefferson's Position_____ | → | Supporting Details_____ | → | Conclusions _____ |
| Adams's Position | → | Supporting Details_____ | → | |

8. Explain how White uses the story about Adams and Jefferson and other details and **persuasive appeals** to strengthen his presentation of an "American idea."

Reading Skill

9. List two **facts** that White includes about people or events.
10. **(a)** List two **opinions** that White includes about people or events. **(b)** Which facts does he use to support each opinion?

Vocabulary Builder

Practice **Analogies** match the relationship in one pair of words with that in another. For each item, choose the word that will make the relationships in the first and second pair of words most similar.

1. immigrants : enter :: emigrants : **(a)** leave, **(b)** stay, **(c)** build
2. sadly : sorrowfully :: relentlessly : **(a)** idly, **(b)** loudly, **(c)** continuously
3. entertainment : comedian :: subversion : **(a)** film, **(b)** spy, **(c)** ship

Adding Words to Your Vocabulary The word *subversion* comes from the Latin root *-vers-* or *-vert-,* meaning "to turn." *Subversion* means "an act overturning the established order." Using a dictionary, define *invert* and *convert.* Explain the connection of the meaning of *-vert-* to these definitions. (For more on using a dictionary, see page R6.)

Writing

Write a **critique**, or critical evaluation, of White's essay. Identify one of his central claims, and weigh the evidence he uses to support it.

- Before you draft, gather examples of the writer's evidence.
- Organize your evaluation by discussing the relevance and strength of each piece of evidence in its own paragraph.
- Conclude with a statement that evaluates the overall strength of White's evidence.

For *Grammar, Vocabulary,* and *Assessment,* see **Build Language Skills,** pages 532–533.

Extend Your Learning

Listening and Speaking Give a **persuasive speech** in which you state and defend your own version of the American idea.
- Prepare your speech in outline form.
- Use logical arguments, examples, and appeals to shared values.
- Address specific concerns that your audience may have, anticipating and answering any objections.

Research and Technology Research one of the nation's founders, such as Thomas Jefferson, John Adams, or Benjamin Franklin. Choose one, and write the **cover letter** and **résumé** that he might have submitted for the position of "Founder of the Republic." Consult reference works to find a suitable format for cover letters and résumés, and proofread carefully to ensure that you followed the format.

Build Language Skills

The American Idea • What Makes a Degas a Degas?

Vocabulary Skill

Prefixes The **prefix** *dis-* means "not," "the opposite of," or "apart from." When *dis-* is added to form an adjective, the new word means the opposite of the base word, as in *dishonest* or *disagreeable.* When *dis-* is used to form nouns, it means "the opposite of" or "the lack of," as in *disunion* or *disease. Dis-* in verbs generally means "not," as in *disclaim,* or "not claim."

Practice In a dictionary, look up each of the *dis-* words listed. Explain how the word's definition comes from a meaning opposite to the meaning of the base word. Then, use each word in a sentence.

1. disproportionate   **3.** disgorge   **5.** disapprove

2. disconcerted   **4.** disengage

Grammar Lesson

Degrees of Adjectives Most adjectives have three different forms, called *degrees*—the *positive,* the *comparative,* and the *superlative.* The positive is used to describe one item, group, or person. The comparative is used to describe two items, groups, or people. The superlative is used to describe three or more items, groups, or people.

For most two-syllable adjectives, add *-er* or use *more* or *less* to form the comparative and add *-est* or use *most* or *least* to form the superlative. For adjectives of three or more syllables, use *more, most, less,* and *least.*

Positive	Comparative	Superlative
brave	braver	bravest
alert	more alert	most alert
good	better	best
talented	less talented	least talented

MorePractice

For more practice with adjectives and with degrees of comparison, see the Grammar Handbook, pp. R40–R41 and R46.

Practice Determine if the italicized word is used correctly. Write a brief explanation of why it is, or is not, used correctly.

1. The host's greeting was *warmer.*

2. The weather is the *gloomier* it has been for days.

3. Our team's players were *less talented* than their opponents.

4. She is the *taller* player on our team.

5. Clark was the *more qualified* candidate in the group.

W͞G Prentice Hall Writing and Grammar Connection: Chapter 25, Section 1

Reading: Evaluate Persuasive Appeals

Standards Assessed
- 10.2.4
- 10.4.11
- 10.5.2

Directions: *Read the selection. Then, answer the questions.*

(1) Our constitution does not copy the laws of neighboring states; we are rather a pattern to others than imitators ourselves. (2) Its administration favors the many instead of the few; this is why it is called a democracy. (3) If we look to the laws, they afford equal justice to all in their private differences; if to social standing, advancement in public life falls to reputation for capacity, class considerations not being allowed to interfere with merit; nor again does poverty bar the way, if a man is able to serve the state, he is not hindered by the obscurity of his condition. . . .

—from Pericles' Funeral Oration in Thucydides, *The Peloponnesian War*, trans. Richard Crawley

1. The first sentence seeks to persuade by appealing to which sentiment?
   A shame
   B anger
   C pride
   D compassion

2. Which is the best summary of the author's opinion in the paragraph?
   A Those who fail to advance in a democracy deserve their fate.
   B Democracy is the most just government.
   C Democracy is the form most likely to produce wealth.
   D People should not seek help from the state but should seek to help the state.

3. The clause "If we look to . . . all in their private differences" appeals to a sense of
   A fairness.
   B individualism.
   C greed.
   D economics.

4. The majority of this excerpt is
   A fact.
   B opinion.
   C propaganda.
   D verifiable.

Timed Writing: Persuasion [Critical Stance]

Review the persuasive methods in the selections "The American Idea" and "What Makes a Degas a Degas?" Choose one of these selections and discuss how persuasive techniques are used to convince the reader that the main idea is valid. **(35 minutes)**

Writing Workshop: *Work in Progress*

Persuasive Essay

For a persuasive essay, jot down five local or national practices that you would like to see changed or modified. Prioritize your topic list, numbering the items 1 through 5. Save this work in your writing portfolio.

Author's Purpose

An **author's purpose** is his or her main reason for writing. The following examples illustrate common purposes:

- A journalist might write *to inform* readers about a recent event.
- A short-story writer might write *to entertain* an audience with a humorous or suspenseful tale.
- A speech writer might want *to persuade* readers to take action or share a point of view.
- An essayist might write *to pay tribute to,* or *to commemorate,* a person whom he or she thinks deserves honor.

A writer may have more than a single purpose for writing. Generally, however, one purpose is the most important. For example, a speaker might tell a funny story to make listeners more open to his or her ideas. In this case, the speaker *entertains* in order to fulfill the main purpose—*to persuade.*

> **(IN) Academic Standards**
>
> - Examine how the author's perspective influences the structure and tone of the text. (10.2.4)
> - Revise writing based on specific criteria. (10.4.11)

Comparing Author's Purpose

Both Yoshiko Uchida in *Desert Exile* and N. Scott Momaday in *The Way to Rainy Mountain* write about their personal connections to historic events. Their purposes have something in common—both authors write to inform readers about the past. Writers who write about the past, though, often have another, deeper purpose than informing: They may write to mourn, to heal old wounds, to bear witness to past injustice, or to better understand themselves. As you read, use a chart like the one shown to compare Momaday's and Uchida's ultimate purposes.

	Uchida	Momaday
Details		
Purposes		

Vocabulary Builder

from Desert Exile

- adept (ə dept´) *adj.* expert; highly skilled (p. 538) *The lawyer was <u>adept</u> at arguing a case.*

- unwieldy (un wēl´ dē) *adj.* hard to manage because of shape or weight (p. 539) *The tuba is an <u>unwieldy</u> instrument to carry.*

- assuage (ə swāj´) *v.* lessen (pain or distress); satisfy (thirst, hunger, and so on) (p. 543) *I <u>assuage</u> my loneliness by writing.*

from The Way to Rainy Mountain

- infirm (in furm´) *adj.* weak; feeble (p. 546) *My uncle is <u>infirm</u> and uses a wheelchair.*

- nomadic (nō mad´ ik) *adj.* moving from place to place; without a permanent home (p. 547) *The <u>nomadic</u> shepherds searched for fresh pastures for their flocks.*

- tenuous (ten´ yoo əs) *adj.* slight; flimsy; not substantial or strong (p. 549) *My memory of the tune is <u>tenuous</u>; can you hum it?*

Build Understanding

Connecting to the Literature

Reading/Writing Connection Both Yoshiko Uchida and N. Scott Momaday write to record a vanishing past. Write down a few reasons why it is important for people to mark the past and pass along its lessons. Use at least three of the following words: *cease, dedicate, diminish, maximize, respond.*

Meet the Authors

Yoshiko **Uchida** (1921–1992)

Yoshiko Uchida's childhood was fairly uneventful—until history struck. In 1942, the United States and Japan went to war, and the United States government forced Japanese American families like Uchida's into internment camps. Uchida and her family were sent to Tanforan Racetrack near San Francisco, where they lived in a stable. Later, they were relocated to an internment camp in Utah.

Supporting Awareness After the war, Uchida attended Smith College in Massachusetts. She became a teacher and an award-winning author who wrote more than thirty fiction and nonfiction books. Her ultimate goal, she said, was "to write of meaningful relationships between human beings, to celebrate our common humanity."

N. Scott **Momaday** (b. 1934)

Growing up on the Native American reservations where his parents taught, N. Scott Momaday learned the traditions of his father's Kiowa culture, as well as those of the Navajo, Apache, and Pueblo Indians. At the same time, he received a modern education. "I grew up in two worlds and straddle both those worlds even now," he says. "It has made for confusion and a richness in my life."

A Creative Heritage Momaday has made much of this "richness," celebrating Native American traditions in novels, poetry, and essays. His first novel, *House Made of Dawn,* received a Pulitzer Prize. Momaday earned a doctoral degree from Stanford University, and he now teaches English at the University of Arizona.

Go Online
Author Link
For: More about the authors
Visit: www.PHSchool.com
Web Code: eqe-9312

from Desert Exile

The *Uprooting* of a Japanese-American Family

Yoshiko Uchida

▲ **Critical Viewing** Which details suggest that the family in this photograph is being forced to move to an internment camp?

Background On December 7, 1941, Japan attacked the American naval base at Pearl Harbor, Hawaii. Two months later, under strong political pressure, President Franklin D. Roosevelt ordered more than 100,000 Japanese Americans from their homes and into government-run internment camps. More than thirty years after the war, President Gerald Ford officially apologized to Japanese Americans and signed a proclamation officially ending the old order.

Yoshiko Uchida tells of her own family's experience of wartime internment. In 1942, her father was arrested and taken to Montana by the Federal Bureau of Investigation. A few months later, the rest of the family was ordered to report to the assembly camp at Tanforan.

As the bus pulled up to the grandstand, I could see hundreds of Japanese Americans jammed along the fence that lined the track. These people had arrived a few days earlier and were now watching for the arrival of friends or had come to while away the empty hours that had suddenly been thrust upon them.

As soon as we got off the bus, we were directed to an area beneath the grandstand where we registered and filled out a series of forms. Our baggage was inspected for contraband,[1] a cursory medical check made, and our living quarters assigned. We were to be housed in Barrack 16, Apartment 40. Fortunately, some friends who had arrived earlier found us and offered to help us locate our quarters.

It had rained the day before and the hundreds of people who had trampled on the track had turned it into a miserable mass of slippery mud. We made our way on it carefully, helping my mother who was dressed just as she would have been to go to church. She wore a hat, gloves, her good coat, and her Sunday shoes, because she would not have thought of venturing outside our house dressed in any other way.

Everywhere there were black tar-papered barracks[2] that had been hastily erected to house the 8,000 Japanese Americans of the area who had been uprooted from their homes. Barrack 16, however, was not among them, and we couldn't find it until we had traveled half the length of the track and gone beyond it to the northern rim of the racetrack compound.

Finally one of our friends called out, "There it is, beyond that row of eucalyptus trees." Barrack 16 was not a barrack at all, but a long stable raised a few feet off the ground with a broad ramp the horses had used to reach their stalls. Each stall was now numbered, and

Literary Analysis
Author's Purpose
Which details here show that part of the author's purpose is to pay tribute, or honor?

Reading Check
What kind of building was Barrack 16 before it was turned into housing?

---

1. **contraband** (kän´ trə band´) *n.* prohibited goods.
2. **barracks** (bar´ əks) *n.* large, plain, often temporary housing.

ours was number 40. That the stalls should have been called "apartments" was a euphemism so ludicrous it was comical.

When we reached stall number 40, we pushed open the narrow door and looked uneasily into the vacant darkness. The stall was about ten by twenty feet and empty except for three folded Army cots lying on the floor. Dust, dirt, and wood shavings covered the linoleum that had been laid over manure-covered boards, the smell of horses hung in the air, and the whitened corpses of many insects still clung to the hastily white-washed walls.

High on either side of the entrance were two small windows which were our only source of daylight. The stall was divided into two sections by Dutch doors[3] worn down by teeth marks, and each stall in the stable was separated from the adjoining one only by rough partitions that stopped a foot short of the sloping roof. That space, while perhaps a good source of ventilation for the horses, deprived us of all but visual privacy, and we couldn't even be sure of that because of the crevices and knotholes in the dividing walls.

Because our friends had already spent a day as residents of Tanforan, they had become <u>adept</u> at scrounging for necessities. One found a broom and swept the floor for us. Two of the boys went to the barracks where mattresses were being issued, stuffed the ticking with straw themselves, and came back with three for our cots.

Nothing in the camp was ready. Everything was only half-finished. I wondered how much the nation's security would have been threatened had the Army permitted us to remain in our homes a few more days until the camps were adequately prepared for occupancy by families.

By the time we had cleaned out the stall and set up the cots, it was time for supper. Somehow, in all the confusion, we had not had lunch, so I was eager to get to the main mess hall, which was located beneath the grandstand.

The sun was going down as we started along the muddy track, and a cold, piercing wind swept in from the bay. When we arrived, there were six long weaving lines of people waiting to get into the mess hall. We took our place at the end of one of them, each of us clutching a plate and silverware borrowed from friends who had already received their baggage.

Shivering in the cold, we pressed close together trying to shield Mama from the wind. As we stood in what seemed a breadline for the destitute, I felt degraded, humiliated, and overwhelmed with a longing for home. And I saw the unutterable sadness on my mother's face.

---

3. **Dutch doors** two-part door in which the top half and the bottom half can be opened separately.

Literary Analysis
Author's Purpose
In addition to informing, what purpose might details about dust and dirt serve?

Vocabulary Builder
adept (ə dept′) *adj.*
expert; highly skilled

Literary Analysis
Author's Purpose
What might the author's purpose be in sharing such painful memories?

This was only the first of many lines we were to endure, and we soon discovered that waiting in line was as inevitable a part of Tanforan as the north wind that swept in from the bay stirring up all the dust and litter of the camp.

Once we got inside the gloomy cavernous mess hall, I saw hundreds of people eating at wooden picnic tables, while those who had already eaten were shuffling aimlessly over the wet cement floor. When I reached the serving table and held out my plate, a cook reached into a dishpan full of canned sausages and dropped two onto my plate with his fingers. Another man gave me a boiled potato and a piece of butterless bread.

With 5,000 people to be fed, there were few unoccupied tables, so we separated from our friends and shared a table with an elderly man and a young family with two crying babies. No one at the table spoke to us, and even Mama could seem to find no friendly word to offer as she normally would have done. We tried to eat, but the food wouldn't go down.

"Let's get out of here," my sister suggested.

We decided it would be better to go back to our barrack than to linger in the depressing confusion of the mess hall. It had grown dark by now and since Tanforan had no lights for nighttime occupancy, we had to pick our way carefully down the slippery track.

Once back in our stall, we found it no less depressing, for there was only a single electric light bulb dangling from the ceiling, and a one-inch crevice at the top of the north wall admitted a steady draft of the cold night air. We sat huddled on our cots, bundled in our coats, too cold and miserable even to talk. My sister and I worried about Mama, for she wasn't strong and had recently been troubled with neuralgia,[4] which could easily be aggravated by the cold. She in turn was worrying about us, and of course we all worried and wondered about Papa.

Suddenly we heard the sound of a truck stopping outside.

"Hey, Uchida! Apartment 40!" a boy shouted.

I rushed to the door and found the baggage boys trying to heave our enormous "camp bundle" over the railing that fronted our stall.

"What ya got in here anyway?" they shouted good-naturedly as they struggled with the <u>unwieldy</u> bundle. "It's the biggest thing we got on our truck!"

I grinned, embarrassed, but I could hardly wait to get out our belongings. My sister and I fumbled to undo all the knots we had tied into the rope around our bundle that morning and eagerly pulled out the familiar objects from home.

4. **neuralgia** (nσσ ral´ jə) *n.* severe pain along the path of a nerve.

Vocabulary Builder
unwieldy (un wēl´ dē) *adj.* hard to manage because of shape or weight

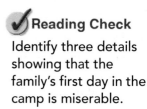**Reading Check**
Identify three details showing that the family's first day in the camp is miserable.

We unpacked our blankets, pillows, sheets, tea kettle, and, most welcome of all, our electric hot plate. I ran to the nearest washroom to fill the kettle with water, while Mama and Kay made up the Army cots with our bedding. Once we hooked up the hot plate and put the kettle on to boil, we felt better. We sat close to its warmth, holding our hands toward it as though it were our fireplace at home.

Before long some friends came by to see us, bringing with them the only gift they had—a box of dried prunes. Even the day before, we wouldn't have given the prunes a second glance, but now they were as welcome as the boxes of Maskey's chocolate my father used to bring home from San Francisco.

Mama managed to make some tea for our friends, and we sat around our steaming kettle, munching gratefully on our prunes. We spent much of the evening talking about food and the lack of it, a concern that grew obsessive over the next few weeks, when we were constantly hungry.

Our stable consisted of twenty-five stalls facing north which were back to back with an equal number facing south, so we were surrounded on three sides. Living in our stable were an assortment of people—mostly small family units—that included an artist, my father's barber and his wife, a dentist and his wife, an elderly retired couple, a group of Kibei [kē′ bā′] bachelors (Japanese born in the United States but educated in Japan), an insurance salesman and his wife, and a widow with two daughters. To say that we all became intimately acquainted would be an understatement. It was, in fact, communal living, with semi-private cubicles provided only for sleeping.

Our neighbors on one side spent much of their time playing cards, and at all hours of the day we could hear the sound of cards being shuffled and money changing hands. Our other neighbors had a teenage son who spent most of the day with his friends, coming home to his stall at night only after his parents were asleep. Family life began to show signs of strain almost immediately, not only in the next stall but throughout the entire camp.

One Sunday our neighbor's son fell asleep in the rear of his stall with the door bolted from inside. When his parents came home from church, no amount of shouting or banging on the door could awaken the boy.

"Our stupid son has locked us out," they explained, coming to us for help.

I climbed up on my cot and considered pouring water on him over the partition, for I knew he slept just on the other side of it. Instead I dangled a broom over the partition and poked and prodded with it,

Literary Analysis
Author's Purpose
Which details suggest that the author relates this incident to amuse readers?

shouting, "Wake up! Wake up!" until the boy finally bestirred himself and let his parents in. We became good friends with our neighbors after that.

About one hundred feet from our stable were two latrines and two washrooms for our section of camp, one each for men and women. The latrines were crude wooden structures containing eight toilets, separated by partitions, but having no doors. The washrooms were divided into two sections. In the front section was a long tin trough spaced with spigots of hot and cold water where we washed our faces and brushed our teeth. To the rear were eight showers, also separated by partitions but lacking doors or curtains. The showers were difficult to adjust and we either got scalded by torrents of hot water or shocked by an icy blast of cold. Most of the Issei[5] were unaccustomed to showers, having known the luxury of soaking in deep pine-scented tubs during their years in Japan, and found the showers virtually impossible to use.

Our card-playing neighbor scoured the camp for a container that might serve as a tub, and eventually found a large wooden barrel. She rolled it to the showers, filled it with warm water, and then climbed in for a pleasant and leisurely soak. The greatest compliment she could offer anyone was the use of her private tub.

The lack of privacy in the latrines and showers was an embarrassing hardship especially for the older women, and many would take newspapers to hold over their faces or squares of cloth to tack up for their own private curtain. The Army, obviously ill-equipped to build living quarters for women and children, had made no attempt to introduce even the most common of life's civilities into these camps for us.

During the first few weeks of camp life everything was erratic and in short supply. Hot water appeared only sporadically, and the minute it was available, everyone ran for the showers or the laundry. We had to be clever and quick just to keep clean, and my sister and I often walked a mile to the other end of the camp where hot water was in better supply, in order to boost our morale with a hot shower.

Even toilet paper was at a premium, for new rolls would disappear as soon as they were placed in the latrines. The shock of the evacuation compounded by the short supply of every necessity brought out the baser instincts of the internees,[6] and there was little inclination for anyone to feel responsible for anyone else. In the early days, at least, it was everyone for himself or herself.

Reading Check

Name two major problems Uchida and other residents of the camp face.

---

5. Issei (ē′ sā′) *n.* Japanese immigrants to North America, especially those who came after 1907 and were ineligible until 1952 to become US citizens.
6. internees (in′ tʉrn′ ēz′) *n.* people detained or confined as prisoners of war or enemy aliens.

One morning I saw some women emptying bed pans into the troughs where we washed our faces. The sight was enough to turn my stomach, and my mother quickly made several large signs in Japanese cautioning people against such unsanitary practices. We posted them in conspicuous spots in the washroom and hoped for the best.

Across from the latrines was a double barrack, one containing laundry tubs and the other equipped with clotheslines and ironing boards. Because there were so many families with young children, the laundry tubs were in constant use. The hot water was often gone by 9:00 a.m., and many women got up at 3:00 and 4:00 in the morning to do their wash, all of which, including sheets, had to be done entirely by hand.

We found it difficult to get to the laundry by 9:00 a.m., and by then every tub was taken and there were long lines of people with bags of dirty laundry waiting behind each one. When we finally got to a tub, there was no more hot water. Then we would leave my mother to hold the tub while my sister and I rushed to the washroom where there was a better supply and carried back bucketfuls of hot water as everyone else learned to do. By the time we had finally hung our laundry on lines outside our stall, we were too exhausted to do much else for the rest of the day.

For four days after our arrival we continued to go to the main mess hall for all our meals. My sister and I usually missed breakfast

▼ Critical Viewing
These photographs show the Manzanar Relocation Center. Compare this camp with Tanforan. **[Compare and Contrast]**

because we were assigned to the early shift and we simply couldn't get there by 7:00 a.m. Dinner was at 4:45 p.m., which was a terrible hour, but not a major problem, as we were always hungry. Meals were uniformly bad and skimpy, with an abundance of starches such as beans and bread. I wrote to my non-Japanese friends in Berkeley shamelessly asking them to send us food, and they obliged with large cartons of cookies, nuts, dried fruit, and jams.

We looked forward with much anticipation to the opening of a half dozen smaller mess halls located throughout the camp. But when ours finally opened, we discovered that the preparation of smaller quantities had absolutely no effect on the quality of the food. We went eagerly to our new mess hall only to be confronted at our first meal with chili con carne, corn, and butterless bread. To <u>assuage</u> our disappointment, a friend and I went to the main mess hall which was still in operation, to see if it had anything better. Much to our amazement and delight, we found small lettuce salads, the first fresh vegetables we had seen in many days. We ate ravenously and exercised enormous self-control not to go back for second and third helpings.

The food improved gradually, and by the time we left Tanforan five months later, we had fried chicken and ice cream for Sunday dinner. By July tubs of soapy water were installed at the mess hall exits so we could wash our plates and utensils on the way out. Being slow eaters, however, we usually found the dishwater tepid and dirty by the time we reached the tubs, and we often rewashed our dishes in the washroom.

Literary Analysis
Author's Purpose
Which details here reveal something about Uchida?

Vocabulary Builder
assuage (ə swāj´) v. lessen (pain or distress); satisfy (thirst, hunger, and so on)

Reading Check
Name two necessities that were in short supply at the camp.

Most internees got into the habit of rushing for everything. They ran to the mess halls to be first in line, they dashed inside for the best tables and then rushed through their meals to get to the wash-tubs before the suds ran out. The three of us, however, seemed to be at the end of every line that formed and somehow never managed to be first for anything.

One of the first things we all did at Tanforan was to make our living quarters as comfortable as possible. A pile of scrap lumber in one corner of camp melted away like snow on a hot day as residents salvaged whatever they could to make shelves and crude pieces of furniture to supplement the Army cots. They also made ingenious containers for carrying their dishes to the mess halls, with handles and lids that grew more and more elaborate in a sort of unspoken competition.

Because of my father's absence, our friends helped us in camp, just as they had in Berkeley, and we relied on them to put up shelves and build a crude table and two benches for us. We put our new camp furniture in the front half of our stall, which was our "living room," and put our three cots in the dark windowless rear section, which we promptly dubbed "the dungeon." We ordered some print fabric by mail and sewed curtains by hand to hang at our windows and to cover our shelves. Each new addition to our stall made it seem a little more like home.

One afternoon about a week after we had arrived at Tanforan, a messenger from the administration building appeared with a telegram for us. It was from my father, telling us he had been released on parole from Montana and would be able to join us soon in camp. Papa was coming home. The wonderful news had come like an unexpected gift, but even as we hugged each other in joy, we didn't quite dare believe it until we actually saw him. . . .

Literary Analysis
Author's Purpose
What do the details here and in the previous paragraph show about how the camp experience has changed the prisoners?

Thinking About the Selection

1. **Respond:** Which part of life in the camps would you have disliked the most? Why?

2. **(a) Recall:** Describe stall number 40. **(b) Analyze:** Why does Uchida feel that calling it an "apartment" was "ludicrous"?

3. **Analyze Cause and Effect:** How do the shortages at the camp affect people's attitudes and behavior? Give details to support your answer.

4. **Draw Conclusions:** What do the conditions at the camp suggest about the government's attitude toward Japanese Americans?

from The Way to Rainy Mountain

N. Scott Momaday

Old Ones Talking, R. Brownell McGrew. Courtesy of the artist.

Background Like other Great Plains tribes, the Kiowa were buffalo hunters. When white settlers came to the Plains, the Kiowa fought them. By the late 1800s, however, United States troops had broken Kiowa resistance and white hunters had all but exterminated the buffalo. Traditional Kiowa life came to an end. In 1868, the Kiowas went to live on a reservation in southwestern Oklahoma.

A single knoll rises out of the plain in Oklahoma, north and west of the Wichita Range.[1] For my people, the Kiowas, it is an old

---

1. Wichita (wich´ ə tô´) **Range** mountain range in southwestern Oklahoma.

landmark, and they gave it the name Rainy Mountain. The hardest weather in the world is there. Winter brings blizzards, hot tornadic winds arise in the spring, and in summer the prairie is an anvil's edge. The grass turns brittle and brown, and it cracks beneath your feet. There are green belts along the rivers and creeks, linear groves of hickory and pecan, willow and witch hazel. At a distance in July or August the steaming foliage seems almost to writhe in fire. Great green and yellow grasshoppers are everywhere in the tall grass, popping up like corn to sting the flesh, and tortoises crawl about on the red earth, going nowhere in the plenty of time. Loneliness is an aspect of the land. All things in the plain are isolate; there is no confusion of objects in the eye, but *one* hill or *one* tree or *one* man. To look upon that landscape in the early morning, with the sun at your back, is to lose the sense of proportion. Your imagination comes to life, and this, you think, is where Creation was begun.

I returned to Rainy Mountain in July. My grandmother had died in the spring, and I wanted to be at her grave. She had lived to be very old and at last <u>infirm</u>. Her only living daughter was with her when she died, and I was told that in death her face was that of a child.

I like to think of her as a child. When she was born, the Kiowas were living the last great moment of their history. For more than a hundred years they had controlled the open range from the Smoky Hill River to the Red, from the headwaters of the Canadian to the fork of the Arkansas and Cimarron.[2] In alliance with the Comanches,[3] they had ruled the whole of the southern Plains. War was their sacred business, and they were among the finest horsemen the world has ever known. But warfare for the Kiowas was pre-eminently a matter of disposition rather than of survival, and they never understood the grim, unrelenting advance of the U.S. Cavalry. When at last, divided and ill-provisioned, they were driven onto the Staked Plains in the cold rains of autumn, they fell into panic. In Palo Duro Canyon they abandoned their crucial stores to pillage and had nothing then but their lives. In order to save themselves, they surrendered to the soldiers at Fort Sill[4] and were imprisoned in the old stone corral that now stands as a military museum. My grandmother was spared the humiliation of those high gray walls by eight or ten years, but she must have known from birth the affliction of defeat, the dark brooding of old warriors.

Critical Viewing
Judging from Momaday's account, what hardships might this Kiowa woman have experienced? **[Speculate]**

Vocabulary Builder
infirm (in furm´) *adj.* weak; feeble

Literary Analysis
Author's Purpose
In this paragraph, which focuses on history, which details reveal something about Momaday?

---

2. Smoky Hill River . . . Cimarron (sim´ ə rän´) the Smoky Hill, Red, Canadian, Arkansas, and Cimarron rivers all run through or near Oklahoma. The area Momaday is defining stretches from central Kansas south through Oklahoma and from the Texas panhandle west to Tulsa, Oklahoma.
3. Comanches (kə man´ chēz) *n.* formerly warlike Native American people of the southern Great Plains, famed for their horsemanship.
4. Fort Sill fort established by the United States government in 1869 to guard against Kiowa and Comanche attacks.

Her name was Aho, and she belonged to the last culture to evolve in North America. Her forebears came down from the high country in western Montana nearly three centuries ago. They were a mountain people, a mysterious tribe of hunters whose language has never been positively classified in any major group. In the late seventeenth century they began a long migration to the south and east. It was a journey toward the dawn, and it led to a golden age. Along the way the Kiowas were befriended by the Crows,[5] who gave them the culture and religion of the Plains. They acquired horses, and their ancient <u>nomadic</u> spirit was suddenly free of the ground. They acquired Tai-me, the sacred Sun Dance doll, from that moment the object and symbol of their worship, and so shared in

Vocabulary Builder
nomadic (nō mad´ ik)
adj. moving from place to place; without a permanent home

✔**Reading Check**
Who gave the Kiowa the culture and religion of the Plains?

---

5. Crows members of a Native American tribe of the northern Plains; like other Plains tribes, they hunted buffalo.

the divinity of the sun. Not least, they acquired the sense of destiny, therefore courage and pride. When they entered upon the southern Plains they had been transformed. No longer were they slaves to the simple necessity of survival; they were a lordly and dangerous society of fighters and thieves, hunters and priests of the sun. According to their origin myth, they entered the world through a hollow log. From one point of view, their migration was the fruit of an old prophecy, for indeed they emerged from a sunless world.

Although my grandmother lived out her long life in the shadow of Rainy Mountain, the immense landscape of the continental interior lay like memory in her blood. She could tell of the Crows, whom she had never seen, and of the Black Hills,[6] where she had never been. I wanted to see in reality what she had seen more perfectly in the mind's eye, and traveled fifteen hundred miles to begin my pilgrimage.

Yellowstone,[7] it seemed to me, was the top of the world, a region of deep lakes and dark timber, canyons and waterfalls. But, beautiful as it is, one might have the sense of confinement there. The skyline in all directions is close at hand, the high wall of the woods and deep cleavages of shade. There is a perfect freedom in the mountains, but it belongs to the eagle and the elk, the badger and the bear. The Kiowas reckoned their stature by the distance they could see, and they were bent and blind in the wilderness.

Descending eastward, the highland meadows are a stairway to the plain. In July the inland slope of the Rockies is luxuriant with flax and buckwheat, stonecrop and larkspur.[8] The earth unfolds and the limit of the land recedes. Clusters of trees, and animals grazing far in the distance, cause the vision to reach away and wonder to build upon the mind. The sun follows a longer course in the day, and the sky is immense beyond all comparison. The great billowing clouds that sail upon it are shadows that move upon the brain like water, dividing light. Farther down, in the land of the Crows and Blackfeet,[9] the plain is yellow. Sweet clover takes hold of the hills and bends upon itself to cover and seal the soil. There the Kiowas paused on their way; they had come to the place where they must change their lives. The sun is at home on the plains. Precisely there does it have the certain character of a god. When the Kiowas came to the land of the Crows, they could see the dark lees of the hills at dawn across the Bighorn River, the profusion of light on the

Literary Analysis
Author's Purpose
What does this paragraph suggest about Momaday's purpose in writing about the Kiowa?

---

6. Black Hills mountain range running from southwestern South Dakota to northeastern Wyoming.
7. Yellowstone Yellowstone National Park, lying mostly in Wyoming but including strips in southern Montana and eastern Idaho.
8. flax and buckwheat, stonecrop and larkspur various types of plants.
9. Blackfeet Native American tribe of the region that includes present-day Montana and parts of Canada.

grain shelves, the oldest deity ranging after the solstices. Not yet would they veer southward to the caldron[10] of the land that lay below; they must wean their blood from the northern winter and hold the mountains a while longer in their view. They bore Tai-me in procession to the east.

A dark mist lay over the Black Hills, and the land was like iron. At the top of a ridge I caught sight of Devil's Tower upthrust against the gray sky as if in the birth of time the core of the earth had broken through its crust and the motion of the world was begun. There are things in nature that engender an awful quiet in the heart of man; Devil's Tower is one of them. Two centuries ago, because they could not do otherwise, the Kiowas made a legend at the base of the rock. My grandmother said:

> *Eight children were there at play, seven sisters and their brother. Suddenly the boy was struck dumb; he trembled and began to run upon his hands and feet. His fingers became claws, and his body was covered with fur. Directly there was a bear where the boy had been. The sisters were terrified; they ran, and the bear after them. They came to the stump of a great tree, and the tree spoke to them. It bade them climb upon it, and as they did so it began to rise in the air. The bear came to kill them, but they were just beyond its reach. It reared against the tree and scored the bark all around with its claws. The seven sisters were borne into the sky, and they became the stars of the Big Dipper.*

From that moment, and so long as the legend lives, the Kiowas have kinsmen in the night sky. Whatever they were in the mountains, they could be no more. However <u>tenuous</u> their well-being, however much they had suffered and would suffer again, they had found a way out of the wilderness.

---

10. caldron (kôl´ drən) *n.* pot for boiling liquids; large kettle.

▲ Critical Viewing
Judging from this photograph of Devil's Tower, why might the landmark inspire Kiowa legends? **[Connect]**

Vocabulary Builder
tenuous (ten´ yo͞o əs) *adj.* slight; flimsy; not substantial or strong

✔**Reading Check**
What change did the Kiowa's beliefs undergo after they left the mountains?

My grandmother had a reverence for the sun, a holy regard that now is all but gone out of mankind. There was a wariness in her, and an ancient awe. She was a Christian in her later years, but she had come a long way about, and she never forgot her birthright. As a child she had been to the Sun Dances; she had taken part in those annual rites, and by them she had learned the restoration of her people in the presence of Tai-me. She was about seven when the last Kiowa Sun Dance was held in 1887 on the Washita River above Rainy Mountain Creek. The buffalo were gone. In order to consummate the ancient sacrifice—to impale the head of a buffalo bull upon the medicine tree—a delegation of old men journeyed into Texas, there to beg and barter for an animal from the Goodnight herd. She was ten when the Kiowas came together for the last time as a living Sun Dance culture. They could find no buffalo; they had to hang an old hide from the sacred tree. Before the dance could begin, a company of soldiers rode out from Fort Sill under orders to disperse the tribe. Forbidden without cause the essential act of their faith, having seen the wild herds slaughtered and left to rot upon the ground, the Kiowas backed away forever from the medicine tree. That was July 20, 1890, at the great bend of the Washita. My grandmother was there. Without bitterness, and for as long as she lived, she bore a vision of deicide.[11]

Now that I can have her only in memory, I see my grandmother in the several postures that were peculiar to her: standing at the wood stove on a winter morning and turning meat in a great iron skillet; sitting at the south window, bent above her beadwork, and afterwards, when her vision failed, looking down for a long time into the fold of her hands; going out upon a cane, very slowly as she did when the weight of age came upon her; praying. I remember her most often at prayer. She made long, rambling prayers out of suffering and hope, having seen many things. I was never sure that I had the right to hear, so exclusive were they of all mere custom and company. The last time I saw her she prayed standing by the side of her bed at night, naked to the waist, the light of a kerosene lamp moving upon her dark skin. Her long, black hair, always drawn and braided in the day, lay upon her shoulders and against her breasts like a shawl. I do not speak Kiowa, and I never understood her prayers, but there was something inherently sad in the sound, some merest hesitation upon the syllables of sorrow. She began in a high and descending pitch, exhausting her breath to silence; then again and again—and always the same

---

11. deicide (dē′ ə sīd′) *n.* killing of a god.

intensity of effort, of something that is, and is not, like urgency in the human voice. Transported so in the dancing light among the shadows of her room, she seemed beyond the reach of time. But that was illusion; I think I knew then that I should not see her again.

Houses are like sentinels in the plain, old keepers of the weather watch. There, in a very little while, wood takes on the appearance of great age. All colors wear soon away in the wind and rain, and then the wood is burned gray and the grain appears and the nails turn red with rust. The windowpanes are black and opaque; you imagine there is nothing within, and indeed there are many ghosts, bones given up to the land. They stand here and there against the sky, and you approach them for a longer time than you expect. They belong in the distance; it is their domain.

Once there was a lot of sound in my grandmother's house, a lot of coming and going, feasting and talk. The summers there were full of excitement and reunion. The Kiowas are a summer people; they abide the cold and keep to themselves, but when the season turns and the land becomes warm and vital they cannot hold still; an old love of going returns upon them. The aged visitors who came to my grandmother's house when I was a child were made of lean and leather, and they bore themselves upright. They wore great black hats and bright ample shirts that shook in the wind. They rubbed fat upon their hair and wound their braids with strips of colored cloth. Some of them painted their faces and carried the scars of old and cherished enmities. They were an old council of warlords, come to remind and be reminded of who they were. Their wives and daughters served them well. The women might indulge themselves; gossip was at once the mark and compensation of their servitude. They made loud and elaborate talk among themselves, full of jest and gesture, fright and false alarm. They went abroad in fringed and flowered shawls, bright beadwork and German silver. They were at home in the kitchen, and they prepared meals that were banquets.

There were frequent prayer meetings, and great nocturnal feasts. When I was a child I played with my cousins outside, where the lamplight fell upon the ground and the singing of the old people rose up around us and carried away into the darkness. There were a lot of good things to eat, a lot of laughter and surprise. And afterwards, when the quiet returned, I lay down with my grandmother and could hear the frogs away by the river and feel the motion of the air.

Now there is a funeral silence in the rooms, the endless wake of some final word. The walls have closed in upon my grandmother's

Literary Analysis
Author's Purpose
Which details here suggest Momaday writes to better understand his memories? Which details pay tribute to his grandmother?

✔ **Reading Check**
Who comes to visit Momaday's grandmother's house in the summer?

house. When I returned to it in mourning, I saw for the first time in my life how small it was. It was late at night, and there was a white moon, nearly full. I sat for a long time on the stone steps by the kitchen door. From there I could see out across the land; I could see the long row of trees by the creek, the low light upon the rolling plains, and the stars of the Big Dipper. Once I looked at the moon and caught sight of a strange thing. A cricket had perched upon the handrail, only a few inches away from me. My line of vision was such that the creature filled the moon like a fossil. It had gone there, I thought, to live and die, for there, of all places, was its small definition made whole and eternal. A warm wind rose up and purled like the longing within me.

The next morning I awoke at dawn and went out on the dirt road to Rainy Mountain. It was already hot, and the grasshoppers began to fill the air. Still, it was early in the morning, and the birds sang out of the shadows. The long yellow grass on the mountain shone in the bright light, and a scissortail hied above the land. There, where it ought to be, at the end of a long and legendary way, was my grandmother's grave. Here and there on the dark stones were ancestral names. Looking back once, I saw the mountain and came away.

Literary Analysis
Author's Purpose
Which details here suggest that Momaday writes to understand himself?

Thinking About the Selection

1. **Respond:** Would you be interested in investigating your own cultural roots in the way Momaday does? Explain.

2. **(a) Recall:** Describe two activities at Momaday's grandmother's house in summer. **(b) Connect:** In what ways are these activities connected to a vanishing way of life?

3. **(a) Support:** In what sense is Momaday's grandmother one of the last representatives of traditional Kiowa culture?
   (b) Draw Conclusions: How does Momaday seem to feel about the disappearance of this way of life? Support your answer with details from the selection.

4. **(a) Interpret:** When Momaday imagines the cricket on the moon, why does he say that "there . . . was its small definition made whole and eternal"? **(b) Draw Conclusions:** In what sense is Momaday's memory of his grandmother like his vision of the cricket?

Apply the Skills

from *Desert Exile: The Uprooting of a Japanese-American Family* • from *The Way to Rainy Mountain*

Comparing Authors' Purposes

1. **(a)** Choose two powerful details from each selection. Using a chart like the one shown, analyze the writer's use of these details.

	Detail	Writer's Reponse to Detail	What Detail Adds to Meaning
Uchida			
Momaday			

   (b) Write a statement in which you identify the writer's purpose in sharing the details you have chosen, and explain your reasoning.

2. **(a)** What general **purpose** for writing do Momaday and Uchida share?
   (b) Identify one major difference in their views of the events and scenes they describe.

Writing to Compare Literary Works

Write an essay to compare the effectiveness of the two selections. Use these questions to get started:

- Which passages best convey the author's purpose?
- In these passages, has the writer included sufficient details to make the writing convincing or moving?
- Which writer generated more sympathy from you? How?

Vocabulary Builder

Given the meaning of each underlined word, explain whether each of the following sentences makes sense.

1. Adept nomadic families avoid collecting unwieldy objects because such possessions cause difficulties when traveling.

2. The infirm man's confidence in the young doctor was tenuous, and the medical degrees posted on the walls did not assuage his fears.

QuickReview

Author's Purpose: the author's main reason for writing. Common purposes are *to inform, to entertain, to persuade, to pay tribute,* and *to commemorate.*

Go Online
—Assessment
For: Self-test
Visit: www.PHSchool.com
Web Code: eqa-6311

Reading

Directions: *Questions 1–5 are based on the following selection.*

1. Four score and seven years ago our fathers brought forth on this continent a new nation, conceived in Liberty, and dedicated to the proposition that all men are created equal.

2. Now we are engaged in a great civil war, testing whether that nation, or any nation so conceived and so dedicated, can long endure. We are met on a great battle-field of that war. We have come to dedicate a portion of that field, as a final resting place for those who here gave their lives that that nation might live. It is altogether fitting and proper that we should do this.

3. But, in a larger sense, we can not dedicate—we can not consecrate—we can not hallow—this ground. The brave men, living and dead, who struggled here, have consecrated it, far above our poor power to add or detract. The world will little note, nor long remember what we say here, but it can never forget what they did here. . . . It is rather for us to be here dedicated to the great task remaining before us—that from these honored dead we take increased devotion to that cause for which they gave the last full measure of devotion. . . .

—from The Gettysburg Address by Abraham Lincoln

1. **Paragraph 1 states**
   A an opinion.
   B a fact.
   C a question.
   D a proposal.

2. **Which sentence in paragraph 2 is an opinion?**
   A "Now we are engaged . . ."
   B "We are met on a great . . ."
   C "We have come to dedicate . . ."
   D "It is altogether fitting . . ."

3. **Which of the following persuasive techniques is most evident in the first sentence of the third paragraph?**
   A logic
   B evidence
   C repetition
   D humor

4. **Lincoln is trying to persuade his listeners of which idea?**
   A A war that is so destructive can never be justified.
   B It is futile to pay tribute to people who are already dead.
   C People should renew their dedication to the war effort.
   D People should cease making war on the United States government.

5. **The repeated use of the words "we" and "us" serve to**
   A remove the sense of brotherhood created in the war.
   B remove the horror of war.
   C add to the audience's sense of partnership with Lincoln.
   D add to the audience's sympathy.

Vocabulary

Directions: *Choose the sentence in which the word given is used correctly.*

6. differentiate
  A The principal said that she could not differentiate such rude behavior.
  B I can hardly differentiate the cars.
  C The recipe instructs us to differentiate the mixture.
  D I need to differentiate my motor.

7. inevitable
  A After winning forty-three matches, his victories began to seem inevitable.
  B My sister is so inevitable that you just cannot reason with her.
  C The cleaner told me the stain was inevitable.
  D They concluded that the mysteries of the universe would remain inevitable.

8. insight
  A Joe's insight let him see distant objects.
  B Chan was able to make money thanks to his insight knowledge.
  C The review gave insight into the film.
  D Agitation could insight a rebellion.

9. motive
  A The motive of the room was Victorian.
  B Detectives motive everyone.
  C The blackmailer's motive was revenge.
  D The motive's gun was displayed.

10. disclaimed
  A He disclaimed knowledge of the plan.
  B Disclaimed taste is a trait of society.
  C Can you please disclaim this for me?
  D It is hard to disclaim between twins.

Directions: *For each word, choose the best definition.*

11. disengage
  A to be interesting
  B to marry
  C to draw apart from
  D to perform a specific military maneuver

12. inappropriate
  A indistinct
  B absence of sense
  C not appropriate
  D able to be switched

13. disregard
  A to set aside or away as unimportant
  B to move along with understanding
  C to see and note as important
  D to see and note for future reference

14. disaffection
  A protest
  B lack of affection
  C excess of love
  D contempt

15. irreparable
  A allowed
  B concerned
  C not able to be repaired
  D able to be put together

Spelling Workshop

Tools for Checking Spelling

Academic Standards

• Use varied and expanded vocabulary. (10.5.7)

• Demonstrate and understanding of sentence construction. (10.6.2)

Computer Spell-checkers Always run spell check on electronic documents. However, remember that spell check does not catch all errors.

- Programs cannot tell if you used the wrong homophone—a word with the same pronunciation as the word you meant, but with a different spelling.
- Programs cannot tell if you have typed another, unrelated word. For example, you might type *gone* when you meant to type *done*.

But Sir, I meant I want to be done in a week. . .
not I want to be gone in a week.
And, I did run the e-mail through spell check. . .

Dictionaries When looking up words in a dictionary, keep in mind that some sounds can be spelled in more than one way. For example, in <u>age</u>, <u>trudge</u>, and <u>just</u>, the "j" sound is spelled three different ways.

Practice Use a dictionary to find the correct spelling of each word. Write the word correctly.

1. misselaneous	4. compasision	7. hipothisise
2. yeild	5. emphasise	8. graffic
3. philosofy	6. competision	9. analize

Rewrite each sentence, spelling all words correctly. Use a dictionary to check the meaning of homophones. Tell whether a spell-check program would catch the errors, and explain why or why not.

1. We visited the state capital building.
2. The zoo had and antelope and a zebra.
3. Use a capitol letter to start a sentence.

Word List

Word List
capital
capitol
emphasize
graphic
hypothesize
analyze
knowledge
composition
yield
miscellaneous

Monitor Your Progress

Directions: *On your paper, write the number of each sentence and the spelling corrections it needs. If a sentence has no errors, write "none." Use a dictionary for help.*

1. The movie that we watched was set in the fuedal era.

2. Until I saw that film, I could not conceive how different life was several hundred years ago.

3. There is a great khasm between that period—the age of shivalry—and now.

4. In the movie, most of the people lived is a tiny village.

5. This pictureskque location was part of the estate of a wealthy lord.

6. This ruler had control over the land, and the people worked for him.

7. When times were good, their storehouses teamed with grain.

8. When there was a bleight, people starved.

9. Health and higene were chronic problems.

10. Across the years, the routine of life changed very little.

11. On pleasant evenings, people sat around the fire and tolled stories.

12. Sometimes, they made up rhymes about great heroes from the past.

13. The landowner also lived quietly.

14. He ate what the peasants grew in the fields, but he received his food on peuter platters.

Directions: *Rewrite each sentence, spelling all words correctly. Use a dictionary for help.*

1. We used a grafic to analize the information.

2. He wrote a composition about the capitol city.

3. You can use capitol letters to emphasize a word.

4. Scientists combine knowlege and experiments to hypothosyze.

5. The research will yeild missellaneous facts.

Persuasion: Persuasive Essay

Persuasion is a part of daily life. You may be persuaded to try an exotic food, audition for a play, or volunteer for a cause. Persuasion is also an important literary mode. A **persuasive essay** is a nonfiction literary work that tries to convince readers to accept a particular point of view or take a specific action. Follow the steps in this workshop to write your own persuasive essay.

Assignment Write a persuasive essay supporting your opinion about an issue that matters to you.

What to Include Your persuasive essay should feature the following elements:

- a clear description of the issue and a clear statement of your opinion
- reliable and varied evidence that supports your opinion
- arguments that acknowledge and refute opposing opinions
- vivid, persuasive language
- a logical organization
- error-free grammar, including correct use of parallel structures

To preview the criteria on which your persuasive essay may be assessed, see the rubric on page 565.

Academic Standards

- Write persuasive compositions. (10.5.4)
- Write for different purposes and audiences. (10.5.8)

Using the Form

You may use elements of this form in these types of writing:

- editorials
- position papers
- letters to the editor
- proposals

Writing Workshop: *Work in Progress*

If you have completed the Work-in-Progress assignments, you already have a wealth of ideas in your portfolio to use in your persuasive essay. You may continue to develop these ideas, or you might choose to explore a new idea as you complete the Writing Workshop.

Reading **Writing** *Connection*

To get a feel for persuasive writing, read the excerpt from Alexander Solzhenitsyn's Nobel Lecture on page 505.

Prewriting

Choosing Your Topic

Use the following strategies to choose a meaningful topic for your essay:

- **Conduct a media review.** Scan newspapers or Internet news sites, listen to radio news, or watch television news shows. Notice any stories that trigger your emotions, whether negative or positive. Your emotional connection to a topic will help you write an effective persuasive essay.

- **List and freewrite.** Think about topics that cause you and others to argue. Make a list of the subjects and issues that have prompted your emotional reactions, and circle the one that most intrigues you. Then, freewrite for three minutes about that topic. Review what you have written and circle any statements of opinion that have emerged. Select the subject with the clearest statement and use it as the starting point for your essay.

Narrowing Your Topic

Conduct research. You may not have enough details about your topic to sufficiently focus your ideas. More information can help you break the topic into meaningful parts. For example, the concept of freedom of speech is far too broad to discuss in a brief essay. However, after you learn more about it, you may choose to write about balanced reporting in television news. Conduct research to identify an aspect of the topic that is manageable in the space of your essay.

Gathering Details

Look at both sides of the issue. An effective persuasive essay anticipates and addresses differing opinions. Use a pro-and-con chart like the one shown to identify counterarguments. In the left column, list arguments that support your opinion. In the right column, list opposing arguments. Then, use the chart to brainstorm for ideas that counter the opposing claims.

Pro-and-Con Chart	
Topic: Honor Students Should Be Rewarded	
Supporting	**Opposing**
• Honor roll students are responsible and dedicated. • They know the material.	• It is unfair to other students. • There would be inequality.

Work in Progress
Review the work you did on pages 513 and 533.

Writing Workshop

Drafting

Shaping Your Writing

Create an effective organization for your essay.

- **Evaluate your arguments.** Write all of your ideas on separate notecards. Then, consider the impact each idea will have on your intended audience. Organize the notecards in order of persuasiveness.

- **Emphasize your strongest argument.** Introduce your topic and state your opinion in a clearly worded thesis statement. In the body of your essay, build your arguments to support your thesis. Consider the organization shown here.

Providing Elaboration

Offer evidence. While your own opinions form the basis for your writing, you need authoritative evidence to convince readers to accept your viewpoint. For each point you make, provide convincing support. Include a variety of types of evidence, including the following:

- **Facts:** information that can be proved true
- **Statistics:** numerical evidence
- **Expert opinion:** information or quotations from experts
- **Case studies:** analysis of an example that illustrates your opinion
- **Anecdotes:** relevant experiences, either your own or those of others

> **Organizing a Persuasive Essay**
>
> - Begin with a statement of your opinion.
> - Explain your second-best argument.
> - Argue against an opposing view.
> - Organize the rest of your arguments in order of persuasiveness.
> - Conclude with your best argument.

Reading Writing Connection

To read the complete student model, see page 564.

Student Model: Supporting Opinion With Evidence

Primarily, honor roll students should be exempt from taking the final exam because they are responsible and dedicated. . .
As one honor student recalled, "One time, I stayed up late, literally, all night so that I could finish a project."

> Convincing anecdotal evidence supports the writer's opinion.

Identify your sources. The inclusion of trustworthy sources strengthens your arguments. Whenever you present a fact or detail gathered from your research, provide the source of the information. If you are quoting someone, use quotation marks. When you quote an expert, tell your readers who the expert is and explain his or her qualifications.

Erik Weihenmayer

On Persuasive Techniques

Erik Weihenmayer

Atop Mt. Kilimanjaro, a sign reads, "You Are Now at the Uhuru Peak. . . ." Sitting on the summit, feeling exhausted, nauseated, and dizzy, I asked my guide, Baltazar, what "Uhuru" meant. He replied, "Freedom." In this passage, I try to persuade you to accept the conclusion about freedom I reached.

"Writing enables me to climb the mountain again."
————Erik Weihenmayer

Professional Model:

from *Touch the Top of the World*

Freedom. It was a word I didn't understand. Freedom from what? Freedom from the limits of my body? From pain? From disappointment? What did it mean? I wanted to believe that by standing atop mountains around the world, I was achieving this kind of freedom, . . . but when standing in these high places, the immense power of the mountains only served to magnify my own fragility, my human need for food, for oxygen, for the help that I received from my team. . . .

First, I ask you a series of difficult questions, which lead you to ponder whether freedom is obtainable.

Then it came to me . . . Perhaps it was the freedom to make of my life what I wanted it to be, or at least the freedom to try, or to fail in the trying. Perhaps freedom itself was unobtainable and the goal was only to reach for it, strive for it, knowing all along that I would fall well short. Perhaps the importance was in the reaching out, and in the impossibility of it all, and in the reaching out through the impossibility, my body planted heavily on the earth but my spirit soaring up and coming impossibly close to its goal.

Second, I try to shatter your traditional definition of freedom by emphasizing the obvious limits of our minds and bodies.

Lastly, I find the answer and suggest, without insisting on, a surprising new understanding of what freedom means.

Writing Workshop

Revising

Revising Your Paragraphs

Test your support. Every paragraph in your essay should play a clear role in supporting your argument. Use these steps to test each paragraph:

- Underline the sentence that states the main idea of the paragraph. If a topic sentence is missing, consider adding one.
- Put a star next to each sentence that supports the main idea. If a sentence is not starred, consider modifying or deleting it.
- If a topic sentence has fewer than two supporting details, add more evidence or reconsider whether the point is worth including.

To read the complete student model, see page 564.

Student Model: Revising to Strengthen a Paragraph

In addition, teachers should not have to give these students the final examination. ★Furthermore, the final exam is an added stress, because students worry and get nervous taking exams. ~~Because they got A's in the first, second, third, and fourth quarters, it is clear that the students know the material very well.~~

> Additional information helps to support the writer's claim.

Revising Your Word Choice

Choose powerful words. Clear, strong language will help make your ideas memorable. Consider these options:

- **Comparatives and Superlatives** Comparative adjectives, such as *sharper* and *bolder,* clarify your ideas. Avoid overuse of predictable or hard to prove superlatives, such as *strongest* or *bravest.*

- **Action Verbs** Strong verbs make your ideas more compelling.
  Linking verb: The policy *is* unfair. (weak)
  Action verb: The policy *cheats* us all. (strong)

- **Connotation** Be aware of **connotations**, the emotions a word sparks. Positive connotations can support your ideas. Negative connotations can emphasize the drawbacks of opposing arguments.
  Neutral: We can look into this problem.
  Positive: We can rise to meet this challenge.
  Negative: We cannot fix this disaster.

Peer Review: Exchange drafts with a partner. Review each other's work, circling ten words in your partner's essay that are weak. Share ideas about possible replacements.

Integrating Grammar Skills

Revising to Create Parallelism

Parallelism is the use of similar grammatical forms or patterns to express similar ideas. Effective use of parallelism can connect your ideas and make them more memorable.

Prentice Hall Writing and Grammar Connection: Chapter 7, Section 4

Identifying Faulty Parallelism Parallel constructions place equal ideas in words, phrases, or clauses of similar types. Ideas are not parallel if the grammatical structure shifts.

	Nonparallel	Parallel
use of verbs	We want <u>to be learning,</u> <u>growing,</u> and <u>to succeed.</u>	We want <u>to learn, to grow,</u> and <u>to succeed.</u>
use of nouns with adjective clauses	Students benefit from <u>limits that are respectful, rea-sonable freedoms,</u> and <u>being inspired by classes.</u>	Students benefit from <u>limits that are respectful,</u> <u>freedoms that are reasonable,</u> and <u>classes that are inspiring.</u>

Fixing Errors Follow these steps to revise nonparallel constructions:

1. **Identify similar or equivalent ideas within a sentence.**
2. **Identify the form in which the ideas are expressed.** Then, read the sentence aloud to hear changes in rhythm or pattern.
3. **Rewrite the sentence so that all the elements match the stronger pattern.** Choose forms that produce the smoothest rhythm or require the fewest words. Look at these examples:
   Nouns: hand, heart, and mind
   Verbs: to seek, to question, and to learn
   Phrases: defending our borders, protecting our resources, securing our futures
   Adverb clauses: wherever we go, whatever we do
   Adjective clauses: she who commits, who practices, who focuses
4. **Punctuate correctly.** Use commas to separate three or more words, phrases, or clauses in a parallel series.

Apply It to Your Editing

Review three paragraphs in your essay, circling sentences that present a series of equivalent ideas. If they have varying grammatical structures, revise them to build parallelism.

Writing Workshop ■ 563

Writing Workshop

Student Model: Esther Herrera
Hialeah, FL

True Reward for Our Achievements

Straight-A students have been rewarded in different ways for their hard work. They have been given the chance to eat breakfast with the principal, they have received gifts and certificates, and they have been publicly acknowledged. Schools hope that these policies will not only serve as a reward to students but also as an inspiration to others to do well in their classes. However, these honor-roll students show little interest in the awards; they want something else. These students should be exempt from taking the final exam because they have demonstrated responsibility and dedication, they know the material, and most importantly, they feel that other students will likely be inspired to achieve the ultimate honor-roll goal.

Primarily, honor-roll students should be exempt from taking the final exam because they are responsible and dedicated. These students have stayed on task throughout the year, going out of their way to turn in a job well done. Sometimes, they sacrificed by staying up late to finish homework assignments. As one honor student recalled, "One time, I stayed up, literally, all night so that I could finish a project. The problem was not finishing it but making sure that it would come out perfect; it did."

In addition, teachers should not have to give these students the final examination. Because they got A's in the first, second, third, and fourth quarters, it is clear that the students know the material very well. Furthermore, the final exam is added stress, because students worry and get nervous taking tests.

On the other hand, eleven out of twenty-five students whom I interviewed believe that such an exemption policy would not be fair to the other students. However, all students were given the same opportunity to get A's. The striking thing about this survey is that many students who were in favor of an exemption policy were not honor students. Instead, they were students who might work harder to earn the privilege of not taking the final exam. What I say to the first eleven students is, Accept the challenge.

In conclusion, honor-roll students should be exempt from taking the final exam because they have already proved themselves. These students deserve a true reward: the knowledge that their efforts have been recognized.

> **Esther clearly states her opinion on the issue.**

> **The writer states the argument and then supports it with valid evidence.**

> **By referring to a survey she conducted, Esther shows that she has done her research and writes with authority.**

> **Here, the writer addresses those who oppose her ideas.**

> **Esther restates her opinion in her conclusion.**

Editing and Proofreading

Check your draft to correct errors in format, grammar, and punctuation.

Focus on Punctuation: Check your draft for punctuation errors. Be especially alert for incorrect use of quotation marks when quoting experts. Put quotation marks around someone else's exact words.

Publishing and Presenting

Consider one of the following ways to share your writing:

Publish for an audience. If your topic relates to a school or community issue, submit your essay to the school or local newspaper. If it appeals to a larger audience, consider submitting it to a national publication.

Deliver a speech. Use your persuasive essay as the basis for an in-class speech followed by a question-and-answer session. Survey your audience before and after your speech to see if you have changed their minds about your topic. Encourage the entire class to join in the question-and-answer period.

Prentice Hall Writing and Grammar Connection: Chapter 7

Reflecting on Your Writing

Writer's Journal Think about the experience of writing a persuasive essay. Begin by answering these questions:

- What did you learn about the process of writing to persuade?
- Did writing this essay change or strengthen your opinion about this topic? Explain.

Rubric for Self-Assessment

To assess your own persuasive essay, use the following rubric:

Criteria	Rating Scale *not very* *very*				
Focus: How clearly do you explain both the issue and your opinion?	1	2	3	4	5
Organization: How well do you organize the elements of your arguments?	1	2	3	4	5
Support/Elaboration: How reliable and varied is your evidence?	1	2	3	4	5
Style: How vivid and persuasive is your language?	1	2	3	4	5
Conventions: How correct is your grammar, especially your use of parallel structures?	1	2	3	4	5

Communications Workshop

Delivering a Persuasive Speech

A convincing **persuasive speech** depends on two key elements: strong writing and a powerful delivery. Your words and presentation style must connect with your audience. Use standard grammar and language to reach the majority of your audience.

Academic Standards

- Recognize and use elements of classical speech forms. (10.7.3)
- Assess how language and delivery affect mood of the speech. (10.7.10)

Plan Your Content

Support your opinion. Your persuasive speech will define and support a position. Gather supporting evidence, such as facts, statistics, expert opinions, and relevant anecdotes. Evaluate your evidence from your audience's point of view.

Use rhetorical devices. Strengthen the argument by using rhetorical devices, such as repetition, questions, or parallel structure. Choose words carefully, paying attention to both their sound and connotations. Try to appeal to your audience's emotions and beliefs.

Focus on your opening and closing. Your introduction needs to grab your audience's attention. Your conclusion should summarize your points in a memorable way.

Prepare Your Delivery

Once you have your words, plan how you will present them.

- **Prepare a reader's script.** Mark a copy of your speech to show words you will emphasize and places you will pause. Slow down to stress key statements; speed up to emphasize emotion or to convey confidence in your evidence. Use a casual tone when telling a personal anecdote. Use a serious tone when quoting an expert.

> START GRADUALLY
> The plans for the new park at Elm Street call for a baseball field,||a
> ENERGETIC
> playground||and a big lawn. It sounds great, but it could be better.
>
> There is one thing missing:||dogs!||We need a dog run. We do not
>
> have a single public dog run in our city. Dr. Sanders, a local
> SLOWER
> veterinarian, estimates that 55 percent of families in our town have a
> EYE CONTACT
> dog. Don't they deserve a place to play? || = PAUSE

- **Establish eye contact.** Keep your audience interested by making eye contact as often as possible. Practice reading your speech so that the words are familiar to you. Use your writing as a guide, but let yourself relax. Audiences connect with speakers who appear natural.

Activity ▶ *Deliver a Persuasive Speech* ▶ Choose a topic that has two sides. Organize a presentation in which you take a stand. Practice your speech in front of a classmate. Revise your presentation and then deliver the speech for your class.

Night
Elie Wiesel
Prentice Hall, 1982

Novel Elie Wiesel was deported to a Nazi death camp at Auschwitz at age fifteen. This work is his story of the horrors he experienced at the hands of the Nazis. It is a fulfill-ment of the author's promise to make sure the world will not forget and will learn from this tragedy. Wiesel is a recipient of the Congres-sional Gold Medal of Achievement and the Nobel Peace Prize.

Immigrant Voices
Edited by Gordon Hutner
Signet, 1999

Anthology This collection recounts the experience of immi-grants arriving in America. Andrew Carnegie details his arrival from Scotland and subsequent journey to fortune, and Marie Zakrzewska, a female physician in the mid-1800s, describes her work among poor immigrants. These autobiographi-cal stories offer insight into the hardships and rewards of forging an American identity while simultaneously maintaining important cultural traditions.

One Day in the Life of Ivan Denisovich
Alexander Solzhenitsyn
Signet, 1993

Novel A Russian soldier, wrongly convicted of treason, is sentenced to spend ten years in a Siberian labor camp, where he faces starvation and deadly cold. The novel documents the daily choices inmates must make between humanity and survival and the dehumanization that is a result. This is the tale of one day in Siberia, a day that most of us cannot even begin to imagine.

Gulliver's Travels
Jonathan Swift
Globe Fearon, 1995

Novel The narrator travels to strange lands—lands with little people and giants and intelligent animals. Yet, from Lilliput to the land of the Houyhnhnms, he finds that the characteristics of these strange creatures are haunting comments on the limitations of humanity. Jonathan Swift's classic satire is riveting, irreverent, and witty.

These titles are available in the Penguin/Prentice Hall Literature Library.
Consult your teacher before choosing one.

Think About It Sometimes, it is the things you have lost that you remember the longest. By writing down your memories, though, you can save the past from being lost forever. A memoir is a work of nonfiction in which the author describes a part of his or her life—a memory. In this selection, the author recalls a poignant memory from his childhood in Ireland. As you read, think about the ways in which the author brings a distant childhood experience to life on the page.

from
Angela's Ashes
Frank McCourt

The other two beds in my room are empty. The nurse says I'm the only typhoid[1] patient and I'm a miracle for getting over the crisis.

The room next to me is empty till one morning a girl's voice says, Yoo hoo, who's there?

I'm not sure if she's talking to me or someone in the room beyond.

Yoo hoo, boy with the typhoid, are you awake?

I am.

Are you better?

I am.

Well, why are you here?

I don't know. I'm still in the bed. They stick needles in me and give me medicine.

What do you look like?

I wonder, What kind of a question is that? I don't know what to tell her.

Yoo hoo, are you there, typhoid boy?

I am.

What's your name?

---

1. typhoid (tī′ foid′) *n.* severe infectious disease causing fever and intestinal disorders.

Frank.

That's a good name. My name is Patricia Madigan. How old are you?

Ten.

Oh. She sounds disappointed.

But I'll be eleven in August, next month.

Well, that's better than ten. I'll be fourteen in September. Do you want to know why I'm in the Fever Hospital?

I do.

I have diphtheria[2] and something else.

What's something else?

They don't know, They think I have a disease from foreign parts because my father used to be in Africa. I nearly died. Are you going to tell me what you look like?

I have black hair.

You and millions.

I have brown eyes with bits of green that's called hazel.

---

2. diphtheria (dif *thir´* ē ə) *n.* severe infectious disease causing high fever and leading to the blockage of breathing passages.

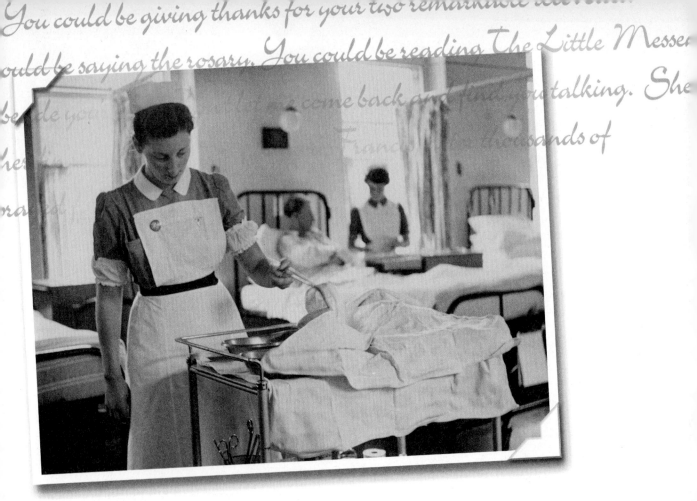

You and thousands.

I have stitches on the back of my right hand and my two feet where they put in the soldier's blood.

Oh, . . . did they?

They did.

You won't be able to stop marching and saluting.

There's a swish of habit[3] and click of beads and then Sister Rita's voice. Now, now, what's this? There's to be no talking between two rooms especially when it's a boy and a girl. Do you hear me, Patricia?

I do, Sister.

Do you hear me, Francis?

I do, Sister.

You could be giving thanks for your two remarkable recoveries. You could be saying the rosary. You could be reading *The Little Messenger of the Sacred Heart* that's beside your beds. Don't let me come back and find you talking.

She comes into my room and wags her finger at me. Especially you, Francis, after thousands of boys prayed for you at the Confraternity. Give thanks, Francis, give thanks.

---

3. habit (hab´ it) *n.* the costume traditionally worn by nuns.

She leaves and there's silence for a while. Then Patricia whispers, Give thanks, Francis, give thanks, and say your rosary, Francis, and I laugh so hard a nurse runs in to see if I'm all right. She's a very stern nurse from the County Kerry[4] and she frightens me. What's this, Francis? Laughing? What is there to laugh about? Are you and that Madigan girl talking? I'll report you to Sister Rita. There's to be no laughing for you could be doing serious damage to your internal apparatus.

She plods out and Patricia whispers again in a heavy Kerry accent, No laughing, Francis, you could be doin' serious damage to your internal apparatus. Say your rosary, Francis, and pray for your internal apparatus.

Mam visits me on Thursdays. I'd like to see my father, too, but I'm out of danger, crisis time is over, and I'm allowed only one visitor. Besides, she says, he's back at work at Rank's Flour Mills and please God this job will last a while with the war on and the English desperate for flour.[5] She brings me a chocolate bar and that proves Dad is working. She could never afford it on the dole.[6] He sends me notes. He tells me my brothers are all praying for me, that I should be a good boy, obey the doctors, the nuns, the nurses, and don't forget to say my prayers. He's sure St. Jude pulled me through the crisis because he's the patron saint of desperate cases and I was indeed a desperate case.

Patricia says she has two books by her bed. One is a poetry book and that's the one she loves. The other is a short history of England and do I want it? She gives it to Seamus, the man who mops the floors every day, and he brings it to me. He says, I'm not supposed to be bringing anything from a dipteria room to a typhoid room with all the germs flying around and hiding between the pages and if you ever catch dipteria on top of the typhoid they'll know and I'll lose my good job and be out on the street singing patriotic songs with a tin cup in my hand, which I could easily do because there isn't a song ever written about Ireland's sufferings I don't know. . . .

Oh, yes, he knows Roddy McCorley. He'll sing it for me right enough but he's barely into the first verse when the Kerry nurse rushes in. What's this, Seamus? Singing? Of all the people in this hospital you should know the rules against singing. I have a good mind to report you to Sister Rita.

Ah, . . . don't do that, nurse.

Very well, Seamus. I'll let it go this one time. You know the singing could lead to a relapse in these patients.

When she leaves he whispers he'll teach me a few songs because singing is good for passing the time when you're by yourself in a typhoid room. He says Patricia is a lovely girl the way she often gives him sweets from the parcel her mother sends every fortnight. He stops mopping the floor and calls to Patricia in the next room, I was telling Frankie you're a lovely girl, Patricia, and she says,

---

4. County Kerry (ker´ ē) southwestern county of Ireland.
5. with the war on and the English desperate for flour the Second World War (1939–1945) caused shortages of food and other basic supplies in England.
6. on the dole unemployed and receiving money from the government in compensation.

You're a lovely man, Seamus. He smiles because he's an old man of forty and he never had children but the ones he can talk to here in the Fever Hospital. He says, Here's the book, Frankie. Isn't is a great pity you have to be reading all about England after all they did to us, that there isn't a history of Ireland to be had in this hospital.

The book tells me all about King Alfred and William the Conqueror and all the kings and queens down to Edward, who had to wait forever for his mother, Victoria, to die before he could be king. The book has the first bit of Shakespeare I ever read.

> I do believe, induced by potent circumstances
> That thou art mine enemy.

The history writer says this is what Catherine, who is a wife of Henry the Eighth, says to Cardinal Wolsey, who is trying to have her head cut off. I don't know what it means and I don't care because it's Shakespeare and it's like having jewels in my mouth when I say the words. If I had a whole book of Shakespeare they could keep me in the hospital for a year.

Patricia says she doesn't know what induced means or potent circumstances and she doesn't care about Shakespeare, she has her poetry book and she reads to me from beyond the wall a poem about an owl and a pussycat that went to sea in a green boat with honey and money and it makes no sense and when I say that Patricia gets huffy and says that's the last poem she'll ever read to me. She says I'm always reciting the lines from Shakespeare and they make no sense either. Seamus stops mopping again and tells us we shouldn't be fighting over poetry because we'll have enough to fight about when we grow up and get married. Patricia says she's sorry and I'm sorry too so she reads me part of another poem[7] which I have to remember so I can say it back to her early in the morning or late at night when there are no nuns or nurses about,

> The wind was a torrent of darkness among the gusty trees,
> The moon was a ghostly galleon tossed upon cloudy seas,
> The road was a ribbon of moonlight over the purple moor,
> And the highwayman came riding
>   Riding riding
> The highwayman came riding, up to the old inn-door.
>
> He'd a French cocked-hat on his forehead, a bunch of lace at his chin,
> A coat of the claret velvet, and breeches of brown doe-skin,
> They fitted with never a wrinkle, his boots were up to the thigh.
> And he rode with jeweled twinkle,
>   His pistol butts a-twinkle,
> His rapier hilt a-twinkle, under the jewelled sky.

---

7. another poem The passage following is from the famous poem "The Highwayman" by Alfred Noyes (1880–1958). A highwayman is a robber in past times who held up travelers.

Every day I can't wait for the doctors and nurses to leave me alone so I can learn a new verse from Patricia and find out what's happening to the highwayman and the landlord's red-lipped daughter. I love the poem because it's exciting and almost as good as my two lines of Shakespeare. The redcoats are after the highwayman because they know he told her, I'll come to thee by moonlight. . . .

I'd love to do that myself, come by moonlight for Patricia in the next room. . . . She's ready to read the last few verses when in comes the nurse from Kerry shouting at her, shouting at me, I told ye there was to be no talking between rooms. Diphtheria is never allowed to talk to typhoid and visa versa. I warned ye. And she calls out, Seamus, take this one. Take the by. Sister Rita said one more word out of him and upstairs with him. We gave ye a warning to stop the blathering but ye wouldn't. Take the by, Seamus, take him.

Ah, now, nurse, sure isn't he harmless. 'Tis only a bit o'poetry.

Take that by, Seamus, take him at once.

He bends over me and whispers, Ah, . . . I'm sorry, Frankie. Here's your English history book. He slips the book under my shirt and lifts me from the bed. He whispers that I'm a feather. I try to see Patricia when we pass through her room but all I can make out is a blur of dark head on a pillow.

Sister Rita stops us in the hall to tell me I'm a great disappointment to her, that she expected me to be a good boy after what God had done for me, after all the prayers said by hundreds of boys at the Confraternity, after all the care

from the nuns and nurses of the Fever Hospital, after the way they let my mother and father in to see me, a thing rarely allowed, and this is how I repaid them lying in the bed reciting silly poetry back and forth with Patricia Madigan knowing very well there was a ban on all talk between typhoid and diphtheria. She says I'll have plenty of time to reflect on my sins in the big ward upstairs and I should beg God's forgiveness for my disobedience reciting a pagan English poem about a thief on a horse and a maiden with red lips who commits a terrible sin when I could have been praying or reading the life of a saint. She made it her business to read that poem so she did and I'd be well advised to tell the priest in confession.

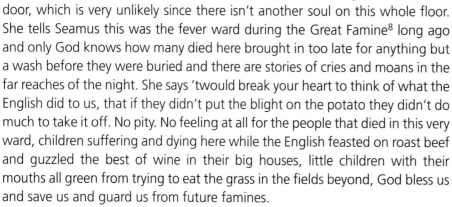

The Kerry nurse follows us upstairs gasping and holding on to the banister. She tells me I better not get the notion she'll be running up to this part of the world every time I have a little pain or a twinge.

There are twenty beds in the ward, all white, all empty. The nurse tells Seamus put me at the far end of the ward against the wall to make sure I don't talk to anyone who might be passing the door, which is very unlikely since there isn't another soul on this whole floor. She tells Seamus this was the fever ward during the Great Famine[8] long ago and only God knows how many died here brought in too late for anything but a wash before they were buried and there are stories of cries and moans in the far reaches of the night. She says 'twould break your heart to think of what the English did to us, that if they didn't put the blight on the potato they didn't do much to take it off. No pity. No feeling at all for the people that died in this very ward, children suffering and dying here while the English feasted on roast beef and guzzled the best of wine in their big houses, little children with their mouths all green from trying to eat the grass in the fields beyond, God bless us and save us and guard us from future famines.

Seamus says 'twas a terrible thing indeed and he wouldn't want to be walking these halls in the dark with all the little green mouths gaping at him. The nurse takes my temperature, 'Tis up a bit, have a good sleep for yourself now that you're away from the chatter with Patricia Madigan below who will never know a gray hair.

She shakes her head at Seamus and he gives her a sad shake back.

Nurses and nuns never think you know what they're talking about. If you're ten going on eleven you're supposed to be simple like my uncle Pat Sheehan who was dropped on his head. You can't ask questions. You can't show you understand what the nurse said about Patricia Madigan, that she's going to die, and you can't show you want to cry over this girl who taught you a lovely poem which the nun says is bad.

The nurse tells Seamus she has to go and he's to sweep the lint from under my bed and mop up a bit around the ward. Seamus tells me . . . that you can't

---

8. Great Famine severe food shortage in Ireland beginning in 1845 caused by the failure of the potato crop. Roughly one million Irish died of starvation in the famine.

catch a disease from a poem. . . . He never heard the likes of it, a little fella shifted upstairs for saying a poem and he has a good mind to go to the *Limerick Leader* and tell them print the whole thing except he has this job and he'd lose it if ever Sister Rita found out. Anyway, Frankie, you'll be outa here one of these fine days and you can read all the poetry you want though I don't know about Patricia below, I don't know about Patricia. . . .

He knows about Patricia in two days because she got out of the bed to go to the lavatory when she was supposed to use a bedpan and collapsed and died in the lavatory. Seamus is mopping the floor and there are tears on his cheeks and he's saying, 'Tis a dirty rotten thing to die in a lavatory when you're lovely in yourself. She told me she was sorry she had you reciting that poem and getting you shifted from the room, Frankie. She said 'twas all her fault.

It wasn't Seamus.

I know and didn't I tell her that.

Meet the Author

Frank McCourt (b. 1930) was born in Brooklyn, New York, but he was raised in Ireland. His father struggled to keep a job, and the family often went hungry. At the age of nineteen, McCourt sailed for America, where he eventually enrolled at New York University and became an English teacher. *Angela's Ashes,* McCourt's Pulitzer Prize-winning memoir, describes the author's youth in Ireland.

Readings in Contemporary Nonfiction
Talk About It

Use these questions to guide a discussion of this excerpt from *Angela's Ashes.*

1. **(a)** Why is Francis in the hospital? **(b)** Do you think the experience is frightening for him? Why or why not?

2. **(a)** Note details that help you understand life in this hospital. Explain your choices. **(b)** Why do the nuns forbid Francis and Patricia to speak to each other?

3. In a group, consider the ways in which strangers facing difficult circumstances, like Francis and Patricia, can help each other.

   • What challenges, both emotional and physical, do Francis and Patricia face while in the hospital?

   • How do Francis and Patricia become friends?

   • What gift does Patricia send to Francis? How does this gift help Francis? How does the giving of the gift help Patricia?

   Choose a point-person to share your group's ideas with the class.

Poetry

Unit 4 Overview

PART 1: Analyzing Main Idea and
Supporting Details
PART 2: Evaluating Persuasive Appeals

Academic Standards
In This Unit You Will

- Examine how the author's perspective influences the structure and tone of text. (10.2.4)
- Analyze many different forms of dramatic literature (10.3.1)
- Evaluate the use of literary devices including figurative language, imagery, allegory, and symbolism. (10.3.7)
- Evaluate the use of voice and narrator. (10.3.9)
- Evaluate the aesthetic qualities of style. (10.3.11)
- Establish a thesis and focus for a piece. (10.4.2)
- Integrate quotations and citations into text. (10.4.7)
- Assess how language and delivery affect mood. (10.7.1)
- Select effective verbal and nonverbal techniques for presentations. (10.7.6)

Introduction:
Poetry

From the Author's Desk

Cornelius Eady
Talks About the Form

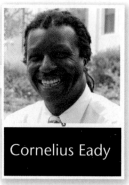

Cornelius Eady

▲ **Cornelius Eady** has explored ways to integrate poetry with music and theater.

When I was in high school, the first poets whose work I encountered were the ones I was assigned to read: Robert Frost, Gwendolyn Brooks, William Carlos Williams, and Langston Hughes.

In the **poetry** I wrote myself, I imitated some of these poets and songs I heard on the radio by using regular rhythms and rhymes.

Jazz Helped Me Understand Poetry

Then, when I was in my late teens or maybe my early twenties, I had a great **epiphany,** or sudden insight, that helped me understand what poetry could express.

I had been lucky enough to get a scholarship to a summer poetry workshop in Rochester, New York, run by the well-known black poet Michael S. Harper. One day, Harper read his poem "Brother John" while also playing a tape of saxophonist John Coltrane's *A Love Supreme.*

Suddenly, I understood what Harper was getting at—that jazz is a language, that when a musician is doing a solo, he is telling you a story. He's telling you where he is from and what he knows. It took me a few more years to work out the implications of that idea for my own poetry. But, eventually, I was able to write poems like jazz riffs, poems that told stories about myself and others, culture and history.

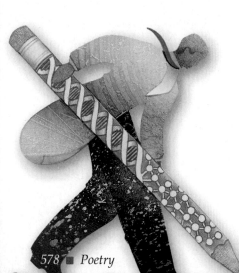

◄ **Critical Viewing** Cornelius Eady compares writing poetry and performing music. Which details in this picture suggest that writing poetry is like a risky performance? **[Interpret]**

Poetry and Music

Poetry and music are alike in so many ways—the term *lyric poetry* reminds us that poetry was once read to the accompaniment of the stringed instrument known as a lyre.

In the quotation shown here, Michael S. Harper compares the progression of a sentence in a poem with the development of a musical solo. And I've always believed that like a saxophone solo or a song, poetry is concerned with breath. A poem is human breath measured out in stanzas and lines.

When I write, I always listen for the music of the lines. There's always a point in the writing process when I start reading passages aloud. And I do that because for my money, a poem should work both on the page and in the air. Hearing the lines is the only way I can test them lyrically, and know for sure that they sing.

A . . . sentence . . . that waits until the end to give you the [meaning] . . . is like a solo that gives you a certain kind of suspense but is also building towards something.

—**Michael S. Harper** in an interview with Graham Lock

More About Cornelius Eady

Cornelius Eady (b. 1954) has received numerous awards for his poetry, and his work is widely anthologized. The traditions of jazz, blues, and gospel music have influenced his poetry. When he listens to jazz, Eady says he hears a story: "I try to find a way to translate or interpret what I hear in music." He has adapted some of his poems as theater pieces. He has also collaborated with jazz musician Diedre Murray on what they call a "jazz opera."

Fast Facts

▶ In Eady's book *You Don't Miss Your Water,* the title of each poem is also the title of a well-known song.

▶ Eady is a co-founder of Cave Canem, a summer workshop and retreat for African American poets. Its title—Latin for "Beware of the Dog"—signifies a safe space in which to dream and work.

Exploring Poetry

Characteristics of Poetry

Poetry is literature in verse form, a controlled arrangement of lines and stanzas. Poems use concise, musical, and emotionally charged language to express multiple layers of meaning.

- **Figurative language** is language that is used imaginatively rather than literally to express ideas or feelings in new ways.
- These **figures of speech** make comparisons between dissimilar things:
  Similes use *like* or *as* to compare two essentially unlike things, as in *"She runs like the wind."*
  Metaphors speak of one thing in terms of another, as in *"All the world's a stage."*
  Personification gives human traits to nonhuman things, as in *"The ocean snarled and pounded against the shore."*
- **Imagery** is descriptive language that creates vivid impressions. These impressions, or **images,** are developed through **sensory language**—details related to sight, sound, taste, touch, smell, and movement.

CALVIN AND HOBBES © 1999 Watterson. Reprinted with permission of UNIVERSAL PRESS.

Poets use a number of **sound devices** to achieve a musical quality.

- **Rhythm** is the pattern created by stressed and unstressed syllables of words in sequence. A pattern of rhythm is called **meter.**
- **Rhyme** is the repetition of identical sounds in the last syllables of words. A pattern of rhyme at the ends of lines is a **rhyme scheme.**
- **Alliteration,** or initial rhyme, is the repetition of the initial consonant sounds of words, as in the words "light" and "lemon." **Assonance,** or vowel rhyme, is the repetition of vowel sounds in nearby words, as in the words "date" and "fade." **Consonance** is the repetition of consonants within nearby words in which the preceding vowels differ, as in the words "milk" and "walk."

Types of Poetry

There are three main types of poetry.

- **Narrative** poetry tells a story and has a plot, characters, and a setting. An **epic** is a long narrative poem about the feats of gods or heroes. A **ballad** is a songlike narrative that has short stanzas and a refrain.

- **Dramatic** poetry tells a story using a character's own thoughts or spoken statements.

- **Lyric** poems express the feelings of a single speaker. Lyrics are the most common type of poem in modern literature.

Poems can also be categorized by form. Poetic forms are defined by specific organizations of line and stanza length, rhythm, and rhyme.

- A **haiku** is a verse form with three unrhymed lines of five, seven, and five syllables. A **tanka** is a verse form with five unrhymed lines of five, seven, five, seven, and seven syllables. Both forms use imagery to convey a single vivid emotion.

- Some poems, described as **free verse,** have neither a set pattern of rhythm nor rhyme.

- A **sonnet** is a fourteen-line lyric poem with formal patterns of rhyme, rhythm, and line structure.

▼**Critical Viewing**
What kind of poetry do you think would best fit this picture? **[Interpret]**

Check Your Understanding

Choose the letter of the answer that best matches each numbered item.

1. fourteen-line lyric poem
   a. haiku   **b.** sonnet

2. comparison of dissimilar things
   a. simile   **b.** lyric

3. vivid descriptive language
   a. epic   **b.** imagery

4. songlike narrative poem
   a. rhyme   **b.** ballad

5. vowel rhyme
   a. assonance   **b.** consonance

From the Author's Desk
Cornelius Eady Introduces His Poems

I grew up in a small, African American neighborhood in the city of Rochester, New York, and some of my strongest memories are of the street where I lived, the tall weeds along the railroad tracks, the bricks on the streets, the way my family and neighbors thought and spoke. Much of this helped to shape the writer I was to become.

Using Images From My Old Neighborhood

At the time I wrote "The Poetic Interpretation of the Twist," I was at work on a group of poems that were all connected by the **theme** of dance and dancing. I was discovering the way a poem sounds and moves was close to what happens when we dance.

All poems have a **rhythm,** a beat to which we write and read. I wanted to find a way to make the elements of my old neighborhood, the **imagery** in my head, "dance" as a poem.

One day I read that "The Twist" was the step that marked the end of couples holding each other on the dance floor! This started me thinking about how we danced that step where I grew up. So I began to write, or "interpret," what I remembered.

A Rhythm That Pulls the Reader Through the Poem

I made the **speaker** in the poem recall the strongest images of that time for me: the way my sister ran, the strange behavior of my father, the smell of the barbershop. That listing begins a rhythm that I hoped would pull the reader across and down the page.

"The Empty Dance Shoes," another poem from this group, is about the *lack* of movement. But even in a poem about not dancing, repeated phrases like "empty pair of dance shoes" help me "dance" around the idea of stillness.

So, as you read these poems, I hope the movement of the lines and the beat of the words will allow you to dance to what you find there.

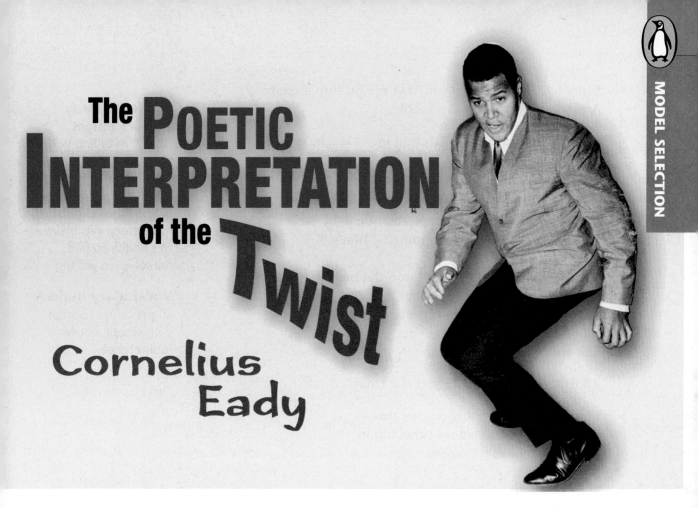

The POETIC INTERPRETATION of the Twist

Cornelius Eady

I know what you're expecting to hear.
You think to yourself: Here's a guy who must understand
   what the twist was all about.
Look at the knuckles of his hands,
Look at his plain, blue shirt hanging out of the back
   of his trousers.
5 The twist must have been the equivalent of
   the high sign
In a secret cult.

I know
I know
I know

10 But listen: I am still confused by the mini-skirt
As well as the deep meaning of vinyl on everything.
The twist was just a children's game to us.
I know you expect there ought to be more to this,
The reason the whole world decided to uncouple,

Poetry
Speaker With this description, the speaker introduces himself and gives the reader a sense of what he is like.

✔ Reading Check

What does the speaker know the reader is expecting to hear?

15 But why should I lie to you? Let me pull up a chair
    And in as few words as possible,
    Re-create my sister,
    Who was renowned for running like a giraffe.
    Let me re-create my neighborhood,
20 A dead-end street next to the railroad tracks.
    Let me re-create
    My father, who would escape the house by bicycle
    And do all the grocery shopping by himself.

    Let's not forget the pool hall and the barbershop,
25 Each with their strange flavors of men,
    And while we're on the subject,
    I must not <u>slight</u> the ragweed,
    The true rose of the street.

    All this will still not give you the twist.

30 Forgive me for running on like this.
    Your question has set an expectation
    That is impossible to meet

    Your question has put on my shoulders
    A troublesome responsibility

35 Because the twist is gone.
    It is the foundation of a bridge
    That has made way for a housing project

    And I am sorry to admit
    You have come to the wrong person.
40 I recall the twist
    The way we recall meeting a distant aunt as a baby
    Or the afternoons spent in homeroom
    Waiting for the last bell.

    My head hurts.
45 I am tired of remembering.
    Perhaps you can refresh my memory
    And tell me
    How we got on this topic?
    As a favor to me,
50 Let's not talk anymore about old dances.

    I have an entire world on the tip of my tongue.

584 ■ Poetry

The EMPTY DANCE SHOES

Cornelius Eady

My friends,
As it has been proven in the laboratory,
An empty pair of dance shoes
Will sit on the floor like a wart
5 Until it is given a reason to move.

Those of us who study inertia[1]
(Those of us covered with wild hair and sleep)
Can state this without fear:
The energy in a pair of shoes at rest
10 Is about the same as that of a clown

Knocked flat by a sandbag.
This you can tell your friends with certainty:
A clown, flat on his back,
Is a lot like an empty pair of
15   dancing shoes.

Cornelius Eady
Author's Insight
Even though the image of the clown shows lack of movement, the short words with a lot of energy reinforce a sense of movement.

---

1. inertia (in ʉr´ shə) *n.* in physics, the tendency of matter at rest to remain at rest or, if moving, to keep doing so in the same direction unless affected by an outside force.

An empty pair of dancing shoes
Is also a lot like a leaf
Pressed in a book.
And now you know a simple truth:
20 A leaf pressed in, say, *The Colossus*
by Sylvia Plath,[2]
Is no different from an empty pair of dance shoes

Even if those shoes are in the middle of the Stardust Ballroom
With all the lights on, and hot music shakes the windows
25   up and down the block.

This is the secret of inertia:
The shoes run on their own sense of the world.
They are in sympathy with the rock the kid skips
over the lake
30 After it settles to the mud.
Not with the ripples,
But with the rock.

A practical and personal <u>application</u> of inertia
Can be found in the question:
35 Whose Turn Is It
To Take Out the Garbage?
An empty pair of dance shoes
Is a lot like the answer to this question,
As well as book-length poems
40 Set in the Midwest.

To sum up:
An empty pair of dance shoes
Is a lot like the sand the 98-pound weakling
brushes from his cheeks
45 As the bully tows away his girlfriend.
Later,

When he spies the coupon at the back of the comic book,
He is about to act upon a different set of scientific principles.
He is ready to dance.

2. *The Colossus* by Sylvia Plath volume of poetry by American poet Sylvia Plath (1932–1963).

Poetry
Repetition Repeating the phrase "An empty pair of dance shoes is like . . ." creates a sense of unity in the poem.

Vocabulary Builder
application (ap´ li kā´ shən) *n.* act of putting something to use

Q. In "The Poetic Interpretation of the Twist," why does the speaker keep "twisting" away from the reader's expectations?

A. The subject seemed easy, but it was hard to find the right words. Sometimes, however, a problem that I have with writing can become an opportunity. So in the first three stanzas, you'll notice a speaker appears and apologizes for not being able to provide what the reader might expect. I hoped this speaker would both disarm and set up a feeling of mystery in the reader.

   I also try to urge the reader to continue by giving instructions: "You think to yourself"; "Look at the knuckles of his hands"; "Look at his plain, blue shirt"; etc. And I hope these instructions will lead the reader on through the different "twists" of the poem.

Q. Was it a challenge to make "The Empty Dance Shoes" lively even though what it describes is not?

A. No, it wasn't a challenge. There came a point in writing these poems when I saw dance and dancers everywhere—in the way someone yawned, or stepped off a bus, for instance. This poem was one way of running with that idea, and having a bit of fun, by making the speaker a know-it-all who tells goofy "facts" about inertia with a straight face.

StudentCorner

Q. What does "inertia" mean in "The Empty Dancing Shoes"?
    —Hayley Arsenault, Mountainville, New York

A. In this poem, "inertia" represents the things that try to stop us, but which we escape by dancing around.

Writing Workshop: *Work in Progress*

Descriptive Essay

For a descriptive essay you might write, fold a piece of paper into three columns: spatial organization, chronological organization, and causal organization. In each, note two things, events, or actions that could be described using that structure. Put this Organization Chart in your portfolio.

Apply the Skills

Poetry

Thinking About the Selections

1. **Respond:** Which poem did you find most intriguing? Explain.
2. **(a) Recall:** In "The Poetic Interpretation of the Twist," what memories does the speaker mention as he tries to remember the dance? **(b) Analyze Cause and Effect:** How is the speaker affected by these memories? **(c) Speculate:** Why do you think the speaker desires to change the subject at the end of the poem?
3. **(a) Recall:** What scientific concept is repeatedly mentioned in "The Empty Dance Shoes"? **(b) Connect:** Note three examples the speaker uses to illustrate this principle. **(c) Compare and Contrast:** How are these examples both similar and different?

Poetry Review

4. Compare the **speakers** in the two poems. In which poem does the speaker's personal life play a more significant role? Explain.
5. **(a)** In the first column of a chart like the one shown, list examples of **figurative language** from "The Empty Dance Shoes" that compare the shoes to other things. In the second column, describe the effect of each example. In the third column, write a one-sentence statement explaining the meaning of the shoes in that example. **(b)** Discuss your chart with a partner, and use the feedback to revise your statements of meaning. Share your revised statements with classmates.

What It Says	Feeling It Creates	What It Means

Research the Author
Create an **annotated poster** that displays the musical or dance imagery in poems by Cornelius Eady. Follow these steps:
- Use the library and Internet to identify six Eady poems that emphasize music or dance. Briefly describe each one.
- Select photographs, drawings, and other images that relate to the music, dance, or performer described in the poems. Use them to illustrate your poster. Display your poster in class.

QuickReview

Selections at a Glance

"The Poetic Interpretation of the Twist" looks back on a bygone dance fad.

"The Empty Dance Shoes" reflects on the idea of inertia and the need to take action.

Go Online
Assessment

For: Self-test
Visit: www.PHSchool.com
Web Code: eqa-6401

Speaker: the voice or identity assumed by the writer of a poem

Figurative Language: language that is used imaginatively rather than literally to express ideas or feelings in new ways

Skills You Will Learn

Literary Analysis: *The Speaker in Narrative and Lyric Poetry*

Reading Skill: *Adjust Your Reading Rate to Read Fluently*

Reading Skill: *Skim, Scan, and Use Text Structure to Read Fluently*

Literary Analysis: *Poetic Forms*

Reading Skill: *Preview to Read Fluently*

Literary Analysis: *Tone and Mood*

Literature You Will Read

Reading and Vocabulary Skills Preview

Reading: Read Fluently

▶**Reading fluently** means reading smoothly and with understanding.

Academic Standards

- Analyze formatting of informational documents. (10.2.1)
- Identify and correctly use clauses, phrases and punctuation. (10.6.1)
- Assess how language and delivery affect mood of the speech. (10.7.1)

Skills and Strategies You Will Learn in Part 1

In Part 1, you will learn

- to **read aloud with fluency** and expression and to **adjust your reading rate** to the difficulty of the text. (p. 592)
- to **read fluently** by **previewing** the work. (p. 627)
- to **preview, skim, scan,** and **use text structure** of informational texts and read them fluently. (p. 622)

Using the Skills and Strategies in Part 1

In Part 1, you will learn strategies for reading fluently both silently and aloud. You will practice reading words and phrases in logical groups. In addition, you will learn how ideas are grouped within the structure of a text to meet a particular purpose.

My heart leaps up when I behold
   A rainbow in the sky:
So was it when my life began;   → group words and phrases
So is it now I am a man;
So be it when I shall grow old,
   Or let me die!   → use punctuation clues
The child is father of the Man;
And I could wish my days to be
Bound each to each by natural piety.

—from "My Heart Leaps Up When I Behold" by William Wordsworth

Academic Vocabulary: Words for Analyzing Literature

The following words will help you talk and write about analyzing literature.

Word	Definition	Example Sentence
visual *adj.*	connected with seeing	The words created a *visual* picture in her mind.
diverse *adj.*	different; varied	Our class has *diverse* tastes in literature.
radical *adj.*	extreme	Beat poetry was a *radical* departure from classic poetic structure.
significance *n.*	meaningful; importance	The *significance* of word sounds in poetry is different from prose.
compensate *v.*	make up for; counterbalance	To *compensate* for the lack of music, the poets used rhyme.

Vocabulary Skill: Suffixes

> A **suffix** is one or more syllables added to the end of a word that alters its meaning and often its part of speech.

In Part 1, you will learn

- the suffixes   *-ance/-ence*   (p. 620)
- the suffix   *-al*   (p. 644)

A suffix generally changes the part of speech of a word. For example, *-ance* or *-ence* changes words to noun form. The suffix *-al* is used to create adjectives and nouns.

Word	Suffix	New Word
signify *v.*	-ance	significance *n.*
correspond *v.*	-ence	correspondence *n.*
music *n.*	-al	musical *adj.*

Activity Add these words to the chart, and complete each column: *reside, analytic, grieve, allow.* Use a dictionary to check each word. Then, use each original word and each new word in a sentence.

You can apply the instruction on this page to these poems.

Poetry Collection 1
The Bridegroom, page 594
The Guitar, page 601
The Fish, page 602
Danny Deever, page 604

Poetry Collection 2
A Tree Telling of Orpheus, page 609
Spring and All, page 614
Mowing, page 616
Making a Fist, page 617

Literary Analysis

In poetry, the **speaker** is the voice that says the words of the poem. The speaker may be the poet, or the speaker may be a character the poet invents to give the poem a particular viewpoint. All poems have a speaker, but some poems have qualities that set them apart as a distinct form.

- In **narrative** poetry, the speaker tells a story in verse.
- In **lyric poetry,** the speaker's thoughts, feelings, and insights create a single, unified impression. Lyric poems include **imagery,** or language that appeals to the senses.

Reading Skill

Read aloud to appreciate and share the musical qualities of poetry. As you read aloud, **read fluently** and **adjust your reading rate**.

- First, read the poem slowly and carefully. Make sure that you understand it and that you can pronounce all the words.
- Use punctuation, and group words for meaning. Do not pause at line-ends unless punctuation indicates that you should.
- Slow down to emphasize an idea or the sounds of words.

To prepare to read aloud, mark a copy of the poem to indicate adjustments to your reading rate. Use a chart like the one shown to help.

Mark the Text	Adjust Reading Rate
Circle punctuation marks.	Pause.
Underline words or sounds to emphasize.	Slow down.
Bracket phrases or groups of words to read together.	Speed up.

Vocabulary Builder

Poetry Collection 1

- **foreboding** (fôr bōd′ iŋ) *n.* a feeling that something bad will happen (p. 595) *Alone in the spooky house, I was filled with <u>foreboding</u>.*

- **monotonously** (mə nät′′n əs lē) *adv.* in a dull, unvarying way (p. 601) *The boring speech continued <u>monotonously</u>.*

- **venerable** (ven′ ər ə bəl) *adj.* worthy of respect because of age or character (p. 602) *He asked for the advice of his <u>venerable</u> elders.*

Poetry Collection 2

- **anguish** (aŋ′ gwish) *n.* extreme suffering, as from grief or pain (p. 612) *Her <u>anguish</u> at the funeral was obvious.*

- **stark** (stärk) *adj.* bare; harsh (p. 615) *The <u>stark</u> room contained only a table and chair.*

- **clenching** (klench′ iŋ) *v.* closing or holding tightly (p. 617) *The child was <u>clenching</u> her fist in anger.*

Build Understanding • *Poetry Collection 1*

Connecting to the Literature

Reading/Writing Connection These poems conjure up feelings of suspense, wonder, or melancholy. Name a story or movie you know that evokes such feelings. In a few sentences, explain your choice. Use at least three of these words: *illustrate, guarantee, plea, predict, react.*

Meet the Author

Alexander **Pushkin** (1799–1837)
"The Bridegroom" (p. 594)
Pushkin is considered the father of modern Russian literature. Though a nobleman, he had great sympathy for poor Russian peasants. In literature, too, he was a rebel, drawing on folklore to express his democratic ideas.

Federico García **Lorca** (1898–1936)
"The Guitar" (p. 601)
Poet and playwright Federico García Lorca is considered one of the greatest Spanish writers. A native of rural Andulasia, García Lorca wrote many of his poems shortly after World War I.

Elizabeth **Bishop** (1911–1979)
"The Fish" (p. 602)
In 1945, Elizabeth Bishop won a poetry contest, leading to the publication of her first poetry collection, *North and South,* which included "The Fish." Her work is noted for its powerful images.

Rudyard **Kipling** (1865–1936)
"Danny Deever" (p. 604)
Rudyard Kipling was born in India to English parents. He worked as a journalist in India, eventually moving to England. In 1907, he was awarded the Nobel Prize in Literature.

Go Online
Author Link
For: More about the authors
Visit: www.PHSchool.com
Web Code: eqe-9402

The Bridegroom

Alexander Pushkin

translated by D. M. Thomas

The Lights of Marriage (detail), Marc Chagall, Kunsthaus, Zurich. © 1998 Artists Rights Society (ARS), New York/ADAGP, Paris.

Background An allusion is a reference to a person, event, place, or artistic work (often, to one that is well known). Pushkin's poem is an extended allusion to a folk tale, "The Robber Bridegroom." From the opening lines, Pushkin's Russian readers would have recognized the story, in which a woman witnesses a horrible crime—and nearly marries the person who committed it.

▲ **Critical Viewing**
Which details in this painting suggest that a marriage touches or is significant to the whole world?
[Interpret]

For three days Natasha,
The merchant's daughter,
Was missing. The third night,
She ran in, distraught.
5 Her father and mother
Plied her with questions.
She did not hear them,
She could hardly breathe.

Stricken with <u>foreboding</u>
10 They pleaded, got angry,
But still she was silent;
At last they gave up.
Natasha's cheeks regained
Their rosy color.
15 And cheerfully again
She sat with her sisters.

Once at the shingle-gate
She sat with her friends
—And a swift troika[1]
20 Flashed by before them;
A handsome young man
Stood driving the horses;
Snow and mud went flying,
Splashing the girls.

25 He gazed as he flew past,
And Natasha gazed.
He flew on. Natasha froze.
Headlong she ran home.
"It was he! It was he!"
30 She cried. "I know it!
I recognized him! Papa,
Mama, save me from him!"

Full of grief and fear,
They shake their heads, sighing.
35 Her father says: "My child,
Tell me everything.
If someone has harmed you,
Tell us . . . even a hint."
She weeps again and
40 Her lips remain sealed.

Vocabulary Builder
foreboding (fôr bōd´ iŋ) *n.* a feeling that something bad will happen

Literary Analysis
Narrative and Lyric Poetry Which details in this stanza does the speaker use to tell a story?

Reading Check

Why do Natasha's mother and father question her?

---

1. troika (troi´ kə) *n.* Russian carriage or sleigh drawn by a team of three horses.

The next morning, the old
Matchmaking woman
Unexpectedly calls and
Sings the girl's praises;
45 Says to the father: "You
Have the goods and I
A buyer for them:
A handsome young man.

"He bows low to no one,
50 He lives like a lord
With no debts nor worries;
He's rich and he's generous,
Says he will give his bride,
On their wedding-day,
55 A fox-fur coat, a pearl,
Gold rings, brocaded² dresses,

"Yesterday, out driving,
He saw your Natasha;
Shall we shake hands
60 And get her to church?"
The woman starts to eat
A pie, and talks in riddles,
While the poor girl
Does not know where to look.

65 "Agreed," says her father;
"Go in happiness
To the altar, Natasha;
It's dull for you here;
A swallow should not spend
70 All its time singing,
It's time for you to build
A nest for your children."

Natasha leaned against
The wall and tried
75 To speak—but found herself
Sobbing; she was shuddering
And laughing. The matchmaker
Poured out a cup of water,
Gave her some to drink,
80 Splashed some in her face.

Reading Skill
Reading Fluently
How many sentences
are there in this stanza
of eight lines?

---

2. brocaded (brō kād′ əd) *adj.* with raised designs woven into the cloth.

Her parents are distressed.
Then Natasha recovered,
And calmly she said:
"Your will be done. Call
85 My bridegroom to the feast,
Bake loaves for the whole world,
Brew sweet mead[3] and call
The law to the feast."

"Of course, Natasha, angel!
90 You know we'd give our lives
To make you happy!"
They bake and they brew;
The worthy guests come,
The bride is led to the feast,
95 Her maids sing and weep;
Then horses and a sledge[4]

With the groom—and all sit.
The glasses ring and clatter,
The toasting-cup is passed
100 From hand to hand in tumult,
The guests are drunk.

BRIDEGROOM
"Friends, why is my fair bride
Sad, why is she not
Feasting and serving?"

105 The bride answers the groom:
"I will tell you why
As best I can. My soul
Knows no rest, day and night
I weep; an evil dream
110 Oppresses me." Her father
Says: "My dear child, tell us
What your dream is."

"I dreamed," she says, "that I
Went into a forest,
115 It was late and dark;
The moon was faintly

3. mead (mēd) *n.* drink made of fermented honey and water.
4. sledge (slej) *n.* sleigh.

Literary Analysis
Narrative and Lyric Poetry How does the omission of details here make the poem seem as if it were being told by a storyteller?

Reading Check

What plans does Natasha's father make for her?

Shining behind a cloud;
I strayed from the path;
Nothing stirred except
120 The tops of the pine-trees.

"And suddenly, as if
I was awake, I saw
A hut. I approach the hut
And knock at the door
125 —Silence. A prayer on my lips
I open the door and enter.
A candle burns. All
Is silver and gold."

BRIDEGROOM
"What is bad about that?
130 It promises wealth."

BRIDE
"Wait, sir, I've not finished.
Silently I gazed
On the silver and gold,
The cloths, the rugs, the silks
135 From Novgorod,[5] and I
Was lost in wonder.

"Then I heard a shout
And a clatter of hoofs . . .
Someone has driven up
140 To the porch. Quickly
I slammed the door and hid
Behind the stove. Now
I hear many voices . . .
Twelve young men come in,

145 "And with them is a girl,
Pure and beautiful.
They've taken no notice
Of the ikons,[6] they sit
To the table without
150 Praying or taking off
Their hats. At the head,

Literary Analysis
Narrative and Lyric
Poetry What details
help the bride's
narrative grow in
excitement?

---

5. Novgorod (näv´ gə räd´) city in northwestern Russia.
6. ikons (ī´ känz´) *n.* sacred religious images.

The eldest brother,
At his right, the youngest;
At his left, the girl.
155　Shouts, laughs, drunken clamor . . . "

BRIDEGROOM
"That betokens merriment."

BRIDE
"Wait, sir, I've not finished.
The drunken din goes on
And grows louder still.
160　Only the girl is sad.

"She sits silent, neither
Eating nor drinking;
But sheds tears in plenty;
The eldest brother
165　Takes his knife and, whistling,
Sharpens it; seizing her by
The hair he kills her
And cuts off her right hand."

"Why," says the groom, "this
170　Is nonsense! Believe me,
My love, your dream is not evil."
She looks him in the eyes.
"And from whose hand
Does this ring come?"
175　The bride said. The whole throng
Rose in the silence.

With a clatter the ring
Falls, and rolls along
The floor. The groom blanches,
180　Trembles. Confusion . . .
"Seize him!" the law commands.
He's bound, judged, put to death.
Natasha is famous!
Our song at an end.

▲ Critical Viewing
What traits does this
young woman seem to
share with Natasha?
Explain which details
in the painting support
your answer.
[Interpret]

The Old Guitarist, 1903, Pablo Picasso. The Art Institute of Chicago. ©2004 Estate of Pablo Picasso/Artists Rights Society (ARS), New York.

▲ **Critical Viewing** Why does the man's pose add to the sad mood of this image? **[Analyze]**

The GUITAR

Federico García Lorca

translated by Elizabeth du Gué Trapier

Now begins the cry
Of the guitar,
Breaking the vaults
Of dawn.
5 Now begins the cry
Of the guitar.
Useless
To still it.
Impossible
10 To still it.
It weeps <u>monotonously</u>
As weeps the water,
As weeps the wind
Over snow.
15 Impossible
To still it.
It weeps
For distant things,
Warm southern sands
20 Desiring white camellias.
It mourns the arrow without a target,
The evening without morning.
And the first bird dead
Upon a branch.
25 O guitar!
A wounded heart,
Wounded by five swords.

Vocabulary Builder
monotonously
(mə nät´ 'n əs lē)
adv. in a dull,
unvarying way

Literary Analysis
**Narrative and Lyric
Poetry** What
feelings do the
images in lines 19–24
convey?

THE FISH

ELIZABETH BISHOP

I caught a tremendous fish
and held him beside the boat
half out of water, with my hook
fast in a corner of his mouth.
5　He didn't fight.
He hadn't fought at all.
He hung a grunting weight,
battered and <u>venerable</u>
and homely. Here and there
10　his brown skin hung in strips
like ancient wallpaper,
and its pattern of darker brown
was like wallpaper:
shapes like full-blown roses
15　stained and lost through age.
He was speckled with barnacles,
fine rosettes of lime,
and infested
with tiny white sea-lice,
20　and underneath two or three
rags of green weed hung down.
While his gills were breathing in
the terrible oxygen
—the frightening gills,
25　fresh and crisp with blood,
that can cut so badly—
I thought of the coarse white flesh
packed in like feathers,
the big bones and the little bones,
30　the dramatic reds and blacks
of his shiny entrails,
and the pink swim-bladder
like a big peony.
I looked into his eyes

35 which were far larger than mine
but shallower, and yellowed,
the irises backed and packed
with tarnished tinfoil
seen through the lenses
40 of old scratched isinglass.[1]
They shifted a little, but not
to return my stare.
—It was more like the tipping
of an object toward the light.
45 I admired his sullen face,
the mechanism of his jaw,
and then I saw
that from his lower lip
—if you could call it a lip—
50 grim, wet, and weaponlike,
hung five old pieces of fish-line,
or four and a wire leader
with the swivel still attached,
with all their five big hooks
55 grown firmly in his mouth.
A green line, frayed at the end
where he broke it, two heavier lines,
and a fine black thread
still crimped from the strain and snap
60 when it broke and he got away.
Like medals with their ribbons
frayed and wavering,
a five-haired beard of wisdom
trailing from his aching jaw.
65 I stared and stared
and victory filled up
the little rented boat,
from the pool of bilge
where oil had spread a rainbow
70 around the rusted engine
to the bailer rusted orange,
the sun-cracked thwarts,[2]
the oarlocks on their strings,
the gunnels[3] —until everything
75 was rainbow, rainbow, rainbow!
And I let the fish go.

▲ Critical Viewing
Does this fish look like the "venerable" old warrior described in the poem? Explain. **[Analyze]**

Literary Analysis
Narrative and Lyric Poetry What details in the conclusion provide a dramatic insight and a surprising action?

---

1. **isinglass** (ī´zin glas´) *n.* transparent material once used in windows.
2. **thwarts** (*th*wôrtz) *n.* seats in a boat for rowers.
3. **gunnels** (gun´ əlz) *n.* upper edges of the sides of a ship or boat.

Danny Deever

Rudyard Kipling

Background In this poem, Kipling writes in **dialect,** a distinct form of a language, spoken by people living in a particular region or belonging to a particular group. The speakers' dialect reflects their working-class British origins.

"What are the bugles blowin' for?" said Files-on-Parade.[1]
"To turn you out, to turn you out," the Color-Sergeant[2] said.
"What makes you look so white, so white?" said Files-on-Parade.
"I'm dreadin' what I've got to watch," the Color-Sergeant said.
5   For they're hangin' Danny Deever, you can hear the Dead
       March play,

---

1. **Files-on-Parade** soldier who directs marching formations.
2. **Color-Sergeant** flag-bearer.

The regiment's in 'ollow square[3] —they're hangin' him today;
They've taken of his buttons off an' cut his stripes away,
An' they're hangin' Danny Deever in the mornin'.

"What makes the rear-rank breathe so 'ard?" said Files-on-
  Parade.
10 "It's bitter cold, it's bitter cold," the Color-Sergeant said.
"What makes that front-rank man fall down?" says Files-on-
  Parade.
"A touch o' sun, a touch o' sun," the Color-Sergeant said.
  They are hangin' Danny Deever, they are marchin' of 'im
    round,
  They 'ave 'alted Danny Deever by 'is coffin on the ground;
15 An' 'e'll swing in 'arf a minute for a sneakin' shootin' hound—
  O they're hangin' Danny Deever in the mornin'!

"'Is cot was right-'and cot to mine," said Files-on-Parade.
"'E's sleepin' out an' far tonight," the Color-Sergeant said.
"I've drunk 'is beer a score o' times," said Files-on-Parade.
20 "'E's drinkin' bitter beer alone," the Color-Sergeant said.
  They are hangin' Danny Deever, you must mark 'im to
    'is place,
  For 'e shot a comrade sleepin'—you must look 'im in the face;
  Nine 'undred of 'is county an' the regiment's disgrace,
  While they're hangin' Danny Deever in the mornin'.

25 "What's that so black agin the sun?" said Files-on-
  Parade.
"It's Danny fightin' 'ard for life," the Color-Sergeant
  said.
"What's that that whimpers over'ead?" said Files-on-
  Parade.
"It's Danny's soul that's passin' now," the Color-Sergeant
  said.
  For they're done with Danny Deever, you can 'ear the
    quick-step play,
30 The regiment's in column, an' they're marchin' us away;
  Ho! the young recruits are shakin', an' they'll want their
    beer to-day,
  After hangin' Danny Deever in the mornin'.

Reading Skill
Reading Fluently
How should the punctuation in lines 13–16 affect your reading rate and pace?

---

3. 'ollow square At a hanging, soldiers standing in ranks form three sides of a square; the gallows occupies the fourth side.

Apply the Skills

Poetry Collection 1

Thinking About the Selections

1. **Respond:** Use a chart like the one shown to identify the images you find most vivid in these poems. Discuss them with a partner. Then, note the choices you share. In the third column, explain how your appreciation of the poems has or has not changed as a result of your discussion.

My Choices	Shared Choices	How My Appreciation Changed

2. **(a) Recall:** In "The Bridegroom," how does Natasha react during the matchmaker's visit? **(b) Connect:** Explain what her "dream" reveals about the reasons for her reaction.
3. **(a) Recall:** List three things in "The Guitar" for which the guitar weeps. **(b) Connect:** Explain how each of these things expresses an unfulfilled desire or something incomplete.
4. **(a) Recall:** What decision does the speaker of "The Fish" make at the end of the poem? **(b) Analyze:** What realization about the fish motivates this decision? Support your answer with details.
5. **(a) Recall:** Who are the two characters who speak in "Danny Deever"? **(b) Contrast:** How are these two characters different?

Literary Analysis

6. **(a)** Identify the best example of **narrative poetry** from among the poems in Poetry Collection 1. Explain your choice.
   (b) Choose the best example of **lyric poetry.** Explain.
7. Identify three examples of visual **imagery**—passages in which a poet creates a picture that appeals to sight.
8. Compare the **speakers** in "The Guitar" and "The Fish." In your response, consider how much or how little you know about the speaker and whether the speaker is the poet or a character.

Reading Skill

9. Choose one of the poems and make notes for reading it aloud. On a copy of the poem, mark where and how you will adjust your reading rate to **read fluently.** Explain your choices.

Quick Review

Poems at a Glance
"The Bridegroom" is a suspenseful narrative about a frightening experience.

"The Guitar" is a poem about the yearning in music.

"The Fish" pays tribute to a fish.

"Danny Deever" presents a discussion between two soldiers about a tragic event.

Go Online
—Assessment
For: Self-test
Visit: www.PHSchool.com
Web Code: eqa-6402

Narrative Poetry: poetry that tells a story

Lyric Poetry: poems that share thoughts or feelings

Speaker: the voice that "says" the words of the poem

Read Fluently: to read smoothly and with understanding

Vocabulary Builder

Practice For each of the following items, write a sentence about the situation described. In each of your sentences, use a word from the vocabulary list for Poetry Collection 1, on page 592.

1. a visit with an elderly, much-admired jazz drummer
2. a doubt about whether you put the ice cream back in the freezer
3. a dripping faucet

Adding Words to Your Vocabulary Using a thesaurus, find two words in addition to *venerable* that can be used to refer to elderly people. Look up each word in a dictionary, and write a brief comparison of the **connotations,** or associated feelings and ideas, of each. (For more on using a thesaurus and a dictionary, see pages R6 and R7.)

Writing

Write your own **lyric poem** in response to one of the poems in Poetry Collection 1.
- Collect ideas for imagery in a chart with columns labeled *sight, hearing, taste, touch,* and *smell.*
- Read your draft aloud to a partner. Ask your partner whether any ideas or images in the poem were unclear. Use your partner's answers to guide you in revising your poem.

For *Grammar, Vocabulary,* and *Assessment,* see **Build Language Skills,** pages 620–621.

Extend Your Learning

Listening and Speaking Present an **oral interpretation** of another Kipling poem that uses dialect. Research any words that are unfamiliar. Then, practice reading the poem aloud. After your presentation, lead a group discussion about whether the dialect helps create a believable speaker.

Research and Technology Working in a group of three, choose one poet from Poetry Collection 1 and find out more about his or her use of language. Create a **report answering research questions.** Consider questions such as these:
- Is the poet's use of language different from that of other poets?
- Does the poet's language reflect a specific region or group?
- Who influenced the poet? Whom has the poet influenced?

Connecting to the Literature

Reading/Writing Connection Each of these poems shows something—an ancient story, a barren road, an afternoon mowing, a clenched fist—from a fresh perspective. Write a few reasons that it is sometimes interesting or helpful to look at a familiar object, place, or situation in a new way. Use at least three of these words: *inspect, perceive, react, stimulate.*

Review

For **Reading Skill, Literary Analysis,** and **Vocabulary Builder,** see page 592.

Meet the Author

Denise **Levertov** (1923–1997)

"A Tree Telling of Orpheus" (p. 609)
When Denise Levertov moved to the United States from England in 1948, she became associated with an experimental community of writers. She said that the freewheeling "open forms" she used allowed her to "explore chaos."

William Carlos **Williams** (1883–1963)

"Spring and All" (p. 614)
William Carlos Williams was both a doctor and a poet. When asked how he managed his double career, he replied that he treated his patients like poems and his poems like patients. Williams also said that a poet should listen "to the language of his locality."

Robert **Frost** (1874–1963)

"Mowing" (p. 616)
Robert Frost worked as a farmer, an editor, and a schoolteacher, absorbing the ebb and flow of New England life. He went on to become one of America's most successful poets, winning many awards, including four Pulitzer Prizes.

Naomi Shihab **Nye** (b. 1952)

"Making a Fist" (p. 617)
Naomi Shihab Nye began publishing poetry in magazines when she was in high school. Her poetry often draws inspiration from the places where she has lived—St. Louis, Missouri, and Jerusalem, in Israel, as well as her current home, San Antonio, Texas.

For: More about the authors
Visit: www.PHSchool.com
Web Code: eqe-9403

A TREE TELLING OF ORPHEUS

Denise Levertov

Background An **allusion** is a reference to a person, event, place, or artistic work. Levertov's poem is an extended allusion to the classic Greek myth of Orpheus. Orpheus' skill on the lyre, an ancient stringed instrument, was so great and his voice so beautiful that trees were said to uproot themselves to follow him. In the end, he was torn limb from limb by his frenzied followers, the Maenads (mē´ nadz´). Flung into a nearby river, his head was said to continue singing as it floated downstream.

> White dawn. Stillness.   When the rippling began
>   I took it for sea-wind, coming to our valley with rumors
>   of salt, of treeless horizons. But the white fog
> didn't stir; the leaves of my brothers remained outstretched,
> 5 unmoving.
>   Yet the rippling drew nearer—and then
> my own outermost branches began to tingle, almost as if
> fire had been lit below them, too close, and their twig-tips
> were drying and curling.
> 10   Yet I was not afraid, only
>   deeply alert.

Literary Analysis
Narrative and Lyric Poetry What clue to the speaker's identity appears in line 4?

I was the first to see him, for I grew
        out on the pasture slope, beyond the forest.
He was a man, it seemed: the two
15 moving stems, the short trunk, the two
arm-branches, flexible, each with five leafless
                      twigs at their ends,
and the head that's crowned by brown or gold grass,
bearing a face not like the beaked face of a bird,
20   more like a flower's.
                  He carried a burden made of
some cut branch bent while it was green,
strands of a vine tight-stretched across it. From this,
when he touched it, and from his voice
25 which unlike the wind's voice had no need of our
leaves and branches to complete its sound,
                            came the ripple,
But it was now no longer a ripple (he had come near and
stopped in my first shadow) it was a wave that bathed me
30   as if rain
              rose from below and around me
          instead of falling.
And what I felt was no longer a dry tingling:

      I seemed to be singing as he sang, I seemed to know
35   what the lark knows; all my sap
          was mounting towards the sun that by now
            had risen, the mist was rising, the grass

Literary Analysis
Narrative and Lyric Poetry What do lines 14–20 tell you about the speaker who is giving the description?

◀ **Critical Viewing** This ancient Greek vessel depicts Orpheus. Which details match the picture of Orpheus you are forming as you read the poem? Which do not? **[Compare and Contrast]**

was drying, yet my roots felt music moisten them
deep under earth.

40   He came still closer, leaned on my trunk:
              the bark thrilled like a leaf still-folded.
Music! There was no twig of me not
                        trembling with joy and fear.

Then as he sang
45 it was no longer sounds only that made the music:
he spoke, and as no tree listens I listened, and language
              came into my roots
                        out of the earth,
                into my bark
50   out of the air,
                into the pores of my greenest shoots
                        gently as dew
and there was no word he sang but I knew its meaning.
He told of journeys,
55   of where sun and moon go while we stand in dark,
        of an earth-journey he dreamed he would take some day
deeper than roots . . .
He told of the dreams of man, wars, passions, griefs,
              and I, a tree, understood words—ah, it seemed
60 my thick bark would split like a sapling's that
                        grew too fast in the spring
when a late frost wounds it.

                        Fire he sang,
that trees fear, and I, a tree, rejoiced in its flames.
65 New buds broke forth from me though it was full summer.
              As though his lyre (now I knew its name)
              were both frost and fire, its chords flamed
up to the crown of me.
                I was seed again.
70   I was fern in the swamp.
                I was coal.

And at the heart of my wood
(so close I was to becoming man or a god)
        there was a kind of silence, a kind of sickness,
75   something akin to what men call boredom,
                        something
(the poem descended a scale, a stream over stones)
                that gives to a candle a coldness

Reading Skill
Reading Fluently
What does the poet's grouping of words in lines 44–52 indicate about the way to read the lines?

Reading Check

What does Orpheus do to cause the tree to respond so powerfully to him?

A Tree Telling of Orpheus ■ 611

              in the midst of its burning, he said.

80   It was then,

          when in the blaze of his power that

                 reached me and changed me

        I thought I should fall my length,

    that the singer began

85   to leave me.   Slowly

        moved from my noon shadow

                to open light,

    words leaping and dancing over his shoulders

    back to me

90   rivery sweep of lyre-tones becoming

    slowly again

        ripple.

    And I

       in terror

95   but not in doubt of

              what I must do

    in anguish, in haste,

          wrenched from the earth root after root,

    the soil heaving and cracking, the moss tearing asunder—

100   and behind me the others: my brothers

    forgotten since dawn. In the forest

    they too had heard,

    and were pulling their roots in pain

    out of a thousand years' layers of dead leaves,

105   rolling the rocks away,

           breaking themselves

                out of

              their depths.

    You would have thought we would lose the sound of the lyre,

110   of the singing

    so dreadful the storm-sounds were, where there was no storm,

        no wind but the rush of our

      branches moving, our trunks breasting the air.

      But the music!

115   The music reached us.

    Clumsily,

       stumbling over our own roots,

           rustling our leaves

             in answer,

120   we moved, we followed.

Literary Analysis
Narrative and Lyric Poetry Why might lines 85–92 be said to have a lyrical quality?

Vocabulary Builder
anguish (aŋ´ gwish) *n.* extreme suffering, as from grief or pain

All day we followed, up hill and down.
                              We learned to dance,
for he would stop, where the ground was flat,
                         and words he said

125   taught us to leap and to wind in and out
around one another in figures the lyre's measure designed.
The singer
              laughed till he wept to see us, he was so glad.
                             At sunset

130   we came to this place I stand in, this knoll[1]
with its ancient grove that was bare grass then.
              In the last light of the day his song became
farewell.
            He stilled our longing.

135   He sang our sun-dried roots back into earth,
watered them: all-night rain of music so quiet
                      we could almost
           not hear it in the
                 moonless dark.

140   By dawn he was gone.
             We have stood here since,
in our new life.
          We have waited.
               He does not return.

145   It is said he made his earth-journey, and lost
what he sought.
         It is said they felled him
and cut up his limbs for firewood.
                And it is said

150   his head still sang and was swept out to sea singing.
Perhaps he will not return.
           But what we have lived
comes back to us.
        We see more.

155   We feel, as our rings increase,
something that lifts our branches, that stretches our furthest
                 leaf-tips
further.
       The wind, the birds,

160   do not sound poorer but clearer,
recalling our agony, and the way we danced.
The music!

---

1. knoll (nōl) *n.* small hill.

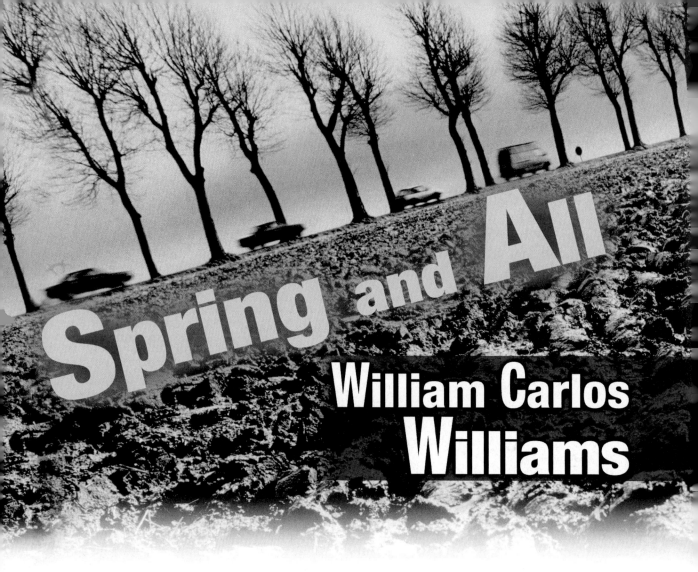

Spring and All

William Carlos Williams

By the road to the contagious hospital
under the surge of the blue
mottled clouds driven from the
northeast—a cold wind. Beyond, the
5 waste of broad, muddy fields
brown with dried weeds, standing and fallen

patches of standing water
the scattering of tall trees

All along the road the reddish
10 purplish, forked, upstanding, twiggy
stuff of bushes and small trees
with dead, brown leaves under them
leafless vines—

Literary Analysis
Narrative and Lyric Poetry To what senses do the images in these stanzas appeal?

Reading Skill
Reading Fluently What punctuation mark indicates a pause at the end of the third stanza?

Lifeless in appearance, sluggish
15 dazed spring approaches—

They enter the new world naked,
cold, uncertain of all
save that they enter. All about them
the cold, familiar wind—

20 Now the grass, tomorrow
the stiff curl of wildcarrot leaf
One by one objects are defined—
It quickens: clarity, outline of leaf

But now the <u>stark</u> dignity of
25 entrance—Still, the profound change
has come upon them: rooted, they
grip down and begin to awaken

▲ **Critical Viewing**
Which details in this
photograph suggest
the hidden power of
spring?

Vocabulary Builder
stark (stärk) *adj.* bare;
harsh

Mowing

ROBERT FROST

Background   A **dialect** is the distinct form of a language spoken by people in a particular region or group. The speaker of this poem uses New England dialect words such as *swale*, referring to a marshland, and *make*, referring to the process of drying out hay. He also uses the outdated word *fay*, meaning "fairy" or "elf." Through these words, Frost creates a speaker who is a man of the land, a traditional New England farmer.

▲ **Critical Viewing** Which word in the poem names one of the tools shown in the painting? Explain how you know. **[Integrate Vocabulary]**

> There was never a sound beside the wood but one,
> And that was my long scythe whispering to the ground.
> What was it it whispered? I knew not well myself;
> Perhaps it was something about the heat of the sun,
> 5   Something, perhaps, about the lack of sound—
> And that was why it whispered and did not speak.
> It was no dream of the gift of idle hours,
> Or easy gold at the hand of fay or elf:
> Anything more than the truth would have seemed too weak
> 10   To the earnest love that laid the swale in rows,
> Not without feeble-pointed spikes of flowers
> (Pale orchises), and scared a bright green snake.
> The fact is the sweetest dream that labor knows.
> My long scythe whispered and left the hay to make.

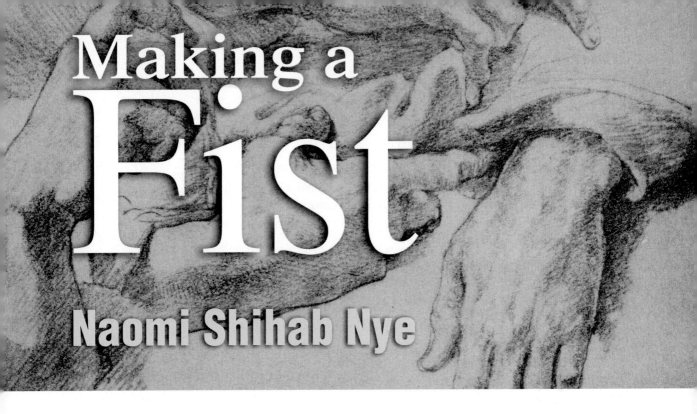

Making a Fist

Naomi Shihab Nye

For the first time, on the road north of Tampico,[1]
I felt the life sliding out of me,
a drum in the desert, harder and harder to hear.
I was seven, I lay in the car
5   watching palm trees swirl a sickening pattern
      past the glass.
My stomach was a melon split wide inside my skin.

"How do you know if you are going to die?"
I begged my mother.
We had been traveling for days.
10   With strange confidence she answered,
"When you can no longer make a fist."

Years later I smile to think of that journey,
the borders we must cross separately,
stamped with our unanswerable woes.
15   I who did not die, who am still living,
still lying in the backseat behind all my questions,
<u>clenching</u> and opening one small hand.

___

1. Tampico (täm pē´ kō) seaport in eastern Mexico.

Literary Analysis
Narrative and Lyric Poetry Identify one detail the poet uses to tell a story and one she uses to present an image or convey a feeling.

Vocabulary Builder
clenching (klench´ in)
v. closing or holding tightly

Apply the Skills

Poetry Collection 2

Thinking About the Selection

1. **Respond:** Use a chart like the one shown to identify the images you find most vivid in these poems. Discuss them with a partner. Then, note the choices you share. In the third column, explain how your appreciation of the poems has or has not changed as a result of your discussion.

My Choices	Shared Choices	How My Appreciation Changed

2. **(a) Recall:** In "A Tree Telling of Orpheus," how do the trees respond when Orpheus begins to leave them? **(b) Analyze:** What is the reason for their reaction?

3. **(a) Recall:** List three details of the landscape in "Spring and All." **(b) Synthesize:** What is the general quality of the landscape?

4. **(a) Infer:** What is the speaker doing in "Mowing"? **(b) Interpret:** What does the speaker imply about accomplishing a task when he says that "The fact is the sweetest dream that labor knows"?

5. **(a) Recall:** What question does the speaker ask in "Making a Fist"? **(b) Take a Position:** Do you think the mother's answer was a good one? Why or why not?

Literary Analysis

6. **(a)** Identify the best example of **narrative poetry** from among the poems in Poetry Collection 2. Explain your choice. **(b)** Choose the best example of **lyric poetry.** Explain.

7. Identify three examples from the poems of visual **imagery**—passages in which a poet creates a picture that appeals to sight.

8. Compare the **speakers** in "Spring and All" and "Making a Fist." In your response, consider how much you know about the speaker and whether the speaker is the poet or a character.

Reading Skill

9. Choose one of the poems and make notes for reading it aloud. On a copy of the poem, mark where and how you will adjust your reading rate to **read fluently.** Explain your choices.

Vocabulary Builder

Practice For each of the following items, write a sentence about the situation described. In each of your sentences, use a word from the vocabulary list for Poetry Collection 2, on page 592.

1. watching the finish of a race while holding something
2. a visit to a dentist
3. a prison cell

Adding Words to Your Vocabulary Using a thesaurus, find two words in addition to *anguish* that can be used to refer to pain or distress. Look up each word in a dictionary, and write a brief comparison of the **connotations,** or associated feelings and ideas, of each. (For more on using a thesaurus and a dictionary, see pages R6 and R7.)

Writing

Write your own **lyric poem** in response to one of these poems.
- Collect ideas for imagery in a chart with columns labeled *sight, hearing, taste, touch,* and *smell.*
- Read your draft aloud to a partner. Ask your partner whether any ideas or images in the poem were unclear. Use your partner's answers to guide you in revising your poem.

For *Grammar, Vocabulary,* and *Assessment,* see **Build Language Skills**, pages 620–621.

Extend Your Learning

Listening and Speaking Present an **oral interpretation** of another Frost poem that uses dialect. Research the meaning of any unfamiliar words. Then, practice reading the poem aloud. After your presentation, lead a group discussion about whether the dialect helps create a believable speaker.

Research and Technology Working in a group of three, find out more about Levertov's, Williams's, or Frost's use of language. Create a **report answering research questions.** Consider questions such as these:
- Is the poet's use of language different from that of other poets?
- Does the poet's language reflect a specific region or group?
- Who influenced the poet? Whom has the poet influenced?

Build Language Skills

Poetry Collection 1 • *Poetry Collection 2*

Vocabulary Skill

Suffixes The **suffix** *-ance* means "the act, process, or quality of" and generally changes words to nouns. If *significance* is broken down into its parts, it means "the act or quality of signifying" or "that which is full of meaning." The **suffix** *-ence* is an alternative spelling of *-ance*.

▶ **Example:** Colors are of great *significance* in that poem.

Practice Predict the meaning of each word based on your knowledge of the suffix and the base word. Check each word's definition in a dictionary. Explain how your prediction compares with the dictionary definition. Then, use each word in a sentence.

1. relevance   **3.** defiance   **5.** conveyance
2. reliance   **4.** deliverance

Grammar Lesson

Prepositions and Prepositional Phrases A **preposition** is a word that relates a noun or pronoun that appears with it to another word in the sentence. The choice of preposition affects the way the other words in a sentence relate to one another. Common prepositions are *on, at, of, across, to, under,* and *with.*

A preposition starts a **prepositional phrase.** A prepositional phrase is a group of words that includes a preposition and a noun or pronoun called the **object of the preposition.**

In each of the following examples, the preposition is underlined and the object of the preposition is in boldface.

MorePractice

For more practice with prepositions, see the Grammar Handbook, p. R41.

Examples:	on the **couch**	under the **couch**	beside the **couch**

Practice Rewrite the sentence, substituting the numbered prepositions for the preposition *to.* Then, write a brief explanation of how the change in preposition changes the sentence.

I am walking <u>to</u> the field.

1. over   **2.** on   **3.** beyond   **4.** in   **5.** around

W︷G Prentice Hall Writing and Grammar Connection: Chapter 18, Section 1

Test Practice

Standards
Assessed

• 10.3.1
• 10.3.9
• 10.7.1

Reading: Read Fluently

Directions: *Questions 1–4 refer to the poem.*

1 O Rose, thou art sick.
The invisible worm
That flies in the night,
In the howling storm,

5 Has found out thy bed
Of crimson joy,
And his dark secret love
Does thy life destroy.

—"The Sick Rose" by William Blake

1. Which word ends a complete thought?
   A sick
   B night
   C storm
   D love

2. What is the connection between lines 3 and 5?
   A Line 5 is about the subject of line 3.
   B Line 3 is about the subject of line 5.
   C Lines 3 and 5 are about the subject of line 2.
   D Lines 3 and 5 are about the subject of line 6.

3. Which group of words shows how a reader would group words when reading?
   A of crimson joy and his dark secret
   B thou art sick the invisible worm
   C his dark secret love does thy
   D the invisible worm that flies in the night

4. The poem consists of
   A 8 sentences.
   B 4 sentences.
   C 2 sentences.
   D 1 sentence.

Timed Writing: Persuasion [Critical Stance]

"Poetry is nearer to vital truth than history." —Plato
Do you think that Plato is correct or incorrect? Write a well-structured argument using specifics from Poetry Collection 1 or Poetry Collection 2 to defend or argue against Plato's assertion. **(40 minutes)**

 ## Writing Workshop: *Work in Progress*

Descriptive Essay

Using the organization chart from your writing portfolio, choose one item to describe. Outline your description using the corresponding organizational structure. Put this outline in your writing portfolio.

Reading Informational Materials

Research Sources

In Part 1, you learned techniques to aid you in reading fluently, including adjusting your reading rate. If you read Federico García Lorca's "The Guitar," you may be interested in reading this research article about the instrument. Practice adjusting your reading rate with the article.

About Research Sources

A **research source** is a text that provides information about a subject. Some research sources are authoritative works intended for the use of researchers, such as encyclopedias, articles, and databases. Such research sources typically feature text aids such as the following:

- "navigational" aids, such as an index, a table of contents, an alphabetical arrangement of entries, or a search engine
- formatting, such as boldface heads or color-coded features

Reading Skill

To locate information in a source efficiently, **preview the text.** First, **skim,** or quickly read through, the table of contents, introduction, and conclusion. Then, **scan** the source, glancing over boldfaced heads and other main elements. As you skim and scan, take note of **text structure,** or patterns of organization, in the source. (Common text structures are shown in the chart.) Identify sections that are likely to contain the information you seek.

Academic Standards

- Analyze formatting of informational documents. (10.2.1)
- Examine how the author's perspective influences the structure and tone of the text. (10.2.4)
- Synthesize information from multiple different sources. (10.4.6)

Common Text Structures

- **sequence,** or **chronological order**—giving information about events in the order of their occurrence

- **spatial order**—giving information about different things according to their location

- **order of importance**—organizing ideas in a logical progression: for example, discussing a whole and then its parts

- **comparison-and-contrast organization**—organizing ideas according to the similarities and differences between subjects

The History of the Guitar
Thomas A. Hill

The writer begins with a discussion of the research sources available on his topic.

Boldface heads help readers locate Hill's discussion of specific topics quickly.

The writer first presents the earliest known facts.

When we attempt to pinpoint the origins of deliberately produced, carefully designed instruments, we run into problems, because the very first instrument makers were not very concerned with posterity. They did not leave written records. One approach we might try, in an effort to find out where the guitar came from, would be an examination of languages.

Ancient Beginnings

The ancient Assyrians,[1] four thousand years ago, had an instrument that they called a *chetarah.* We know little more about it other than that it was a stringed instrument with a sound-box, but the name is intriguing. The ancient Hebrews had their *kinnura,* the Chaldeans[2] their *qitra,* and the Greeks their *cithara* and *citharis*—which Greek writers of the day were careful to emphasize were *not* the same instrument. It is with the Greeks, in fact, that the first clear history of the evolution of an instrument begins; some of this history can again be traced with purely linguistic devices. The cithara and citharis were members of a family of musical instruments called *fides*—a word that is ancient Greek for "strings." From the *fides* family it is easy to draw lines to the medieval French *vielle,* the German *fiedel,* the English *fithele* or *fiddle,* and the *vihuela,* national instrument of medieval Spain. Significantly, much of the music for the vihuela (of which a great deal survives to the present day) can easily be transcribed[3] for the guitar.

In England, the influences of the cithara and citharis led to the evolution of such instruments as the *cither, zither, cittern,* and *gittern,* with which instrument the linguistic parallel we seek is fairly easy to draw. Gitterns dating back to 1330 can be seen in the British Museum. In Spain, there is music for the vihuela that dates back at least that far. What did these instruments look like? Superficially, they bore a substantial resemblance to the guitar as we know it today, although the sides seldom curved in as far as do the sides of the

---

1. **Assyrians** (ə sir´ē ənz) founders of an ancient empire in the Middle East, flourishing in the seventh century B.C.
2. **Chaldeans** (kal dē´ ənz) a people that rose to power in Babylon, an ancient empire of the Middle East, during the sixth century B.C.
3. **transcribed** (tran skrībd´) *v.* adapted a piece of music for an instrument other than the one for which it was originally written.

Here the writer briefly turns to a new pattern of organization—comparison and contrast—to help readers grasp details about instruments of the past.

modern guitar. They were usually strung with *pairs* of strings, or *courses,* much like a modern twelve-string guitar. The two strings of each course were tuned either in unison or an octave[4] apart. For a while, there seemed to be no standard for the number of courses an instrument should have; there are both vihuelas and gitterns with as few as four courses and as many as seven. By the fifteenth century, the vihuela seems to have settled on six as the standard number of courses. . . . In England, the gittern settled down to four courses. . . . Historians of this period do note the existence in Spain of an instrument called the *guitarra.* . . . But no music was being written for this instrument, and nobody seems to have been paying much attention to it.

The African Link

Meanwhile, in Africa, the Arabs had been playing an instrument that they called *al-ud,* or "the wood," for centuries. When the Moors crossed the Straits of Gibraltar[5] in the twelfth century to conquer Spain, they brought this instrument with them. It quickly became popular, and by the time anybody who spoke English was talking about it, al-ud had become *lute.* The lute's main contribution to the evolution of the guitar as we know it today seems to have been the fret, a metal bar on the fingerboard. Until the arrival of the lute, the European forerunners of the guitar had no frets at all. Since the fret made it a little easier to play the same tune the same way more than once, and helped to standardize tunings, it was a resounding success. The first Arabic lutes in Europe had movable frets, tied to the neck, usually about eight in number. Consequently, the first vihuelas to which frets were added also had movable ones.

The lute—or rather the people who brought it to Europe—made another important contribution. The Moorish artistic influence, blowing the cobwebs away from stodgy Spanish art and society, created an artistic climate that encouraged music to flourish. And so the instruments on which the music was played flourished as well, and continued to evolve and improve. This is a contribution that cannot be overestimated.

If any general lines can be drawn, perhaps it can be said that descendants of the original al-ud, crossing the Straits of Gibraltar, collided in Spain with the descendants of the Greek cithara and citharis. Sprinkled with a little bit of gittern influence from England, the result led ultimately to what we know today as the guitar.

The writer concludes with a general summary of the early history of the guitar, carefully qualifying his summary with words such as *perhaps.*

---

4. **unison** (yōōn´ ə sən) . . . **octave** (äk´ tiv) A unison consists of two tones of the same pitch. An octave consists of two tones that are eight notes apart in the scale. The pitches in an octave sound "the same" and are named by the same note.

5. **Moors** (mŏŏrz) . . . **Gibraltar** (ji brôl´ tər) Groups of Moors, an Arab people of North Africa, invaded Spain at various times, beginning in the eighth century A.D. The Straits of Gibraltar are waters dividing Spain from Africa.

Test Practice

Reading: Skimming and Scanning to Identify Text Structures

Standards Assessed
- 10.2.1
- 10.2.4
- 10.4.6

Directions: *Choose the letter of the best answer to each question.*

1. After scanning the boldface heads, what might you reasonably conclude about the organization of the article?
   A It is mainly organized as a comparison.
   B It follows both chronological and spatial organization.
   C Ideas have been organized in the order of importance.
   D Comparison-and-contrast, chronological, and spatial organization have been used.

2. After skimming the first and last paragraphs, which pattern of organization should you conclude the article will probably follow?
   A comparison-and-contrast organization
   B order of importance
   C chronological order
   D spatial order

3. Which pattern is used in the second paragraph?
   A comparison-and-contrast organization
   B order of importance
   C chronological order
   D spatial order

Reading: Comprehension and Interpretation

Directions: *Write your answers on a separate piece of paper.*

4. **(a)** In which part of the world did the earliest instrument described in the essay originate? **(b)** In which country can the early history of the guitar be most clearly traced? **[Knowledge]**

5. What conclusion might you draw from the essay about the power of one culture to influence another? Explain. **[Generating]**

Timed Writing: Research [Connections]

Write a letter to the author commenting on "The History of the Guitar" and requesting information on two related points. As you write, keep your audience in mind—a scholar with whom you are not personally acquainted. Use formal language and a respectful tone. **(20 minutes)**

You can apply the instruction on this page to these poems.

Poetry Collection 1
The clustering clouds . . .,
    page 629
When I went to visit . . ., page 629
My City, page 630
*Do Not Go Gentle into That Good
    Night,* page 633

Poetry Collection 2
One cannot ask loneliness . . .,
    page 637
Was it that I went to sleep . . .,
    page 637
The Waking, page 639
Sonnet 18, page 641

**(IN) Academic
       Standards**

• Analyze many different
  forms of dramatic
  literature. (10.3.1)

• Evaluate the use of literary
  devices including figurative
  language, imagery,
  allegory, and symbolism.
  (10.3.7)

• Identify and correctly use
  clauses, phrases and
  punctuation. (10.6.1)

Literary Analysis

To unify sounds and ideas in a poem, a poet may follow a **poetic form,**
or defined structure. Each poetic form uses a set number of lines and a
distinctive **meter** and pattern of **rhymes.** (For more on these elements,
see pages 580–581.) Traditional poetic forms include the following:

Tanka—a five-line, unrhymed Japanese form

  • The first and third lines contain five syllables. The second,
    fourth, and fifth lines have seven syllables. (The number of
    syllables can vary when a tanka is translated into English.)

  • The briefness of a tanka helps poets focus on a single strong
    image or idea.

Sonnet—a fourteen-line form

  • In a type of sonnet called the **Shakespearean sonnet,** the lines
    are grouped into three **quatrains** (groups of four lines) and a
    couplet, a pair of rhymed lines. The rhyme scheme is *abab,
    cdcd, efef, gg.*

  • Sonnet writers may answer the ideas in one quatrain with ideas
    in another, summing up the poem in the couplet.

  • Sonnets are written in *iambic pentameter.* That is, each line con-
    tains five unaccented and five accented syllables in the pattern
    "da-DUM, da-DUM, da-DUM, da-DUM, da-DUM."

Villanelle—a nineteen-line form

  • The lines are grouped into five three-line stanzas and one four-
    line stanza. The lines rhyme *aba, aba, aba, aba, aba, abaa.*

  • Line 1 is repeated in lines 6, 12, and 18. Line 3 is repeated in
    lines 9, 15, and 19.

  • This repetition can create a chanting effect or suggest intense
    passion.

Use a chart like the one shown to analyze poetic forms as you read.

Analyzing the Form of a Poem	
Number of lines?	
Number of syllables in each line?	
Pattern of accented and unaccented syllables in each line?	
Which lines rhyme?	

Build Skills

Reading Skill

When you **read fluently,** you read smoothly and with understanding, placing emphasis appropriately and pausing where necessary. To increase your fluency when reading a poem, **preview** the work, looking over the text in advance.

- Use footnotes and other text aids to learn unfamiliar words. Practice saying each unfamiliar word by following the pronunciation given, and learn each word's definition.

Punctuation		Type of Pause
.	Period	Full stop
:	Colon	Almost as strong as a period. End with your voice raised just enough so that a listener knows to expect more.
;	Semicolon	Less strong than a colon. Pause briefly, with your voice raised.
,	Comma	A slight pause

- Determine where each sentence in the poem begins and ends. If you notice that a sentence stretches over more than one line, prepare to read it "through" the end of each line, pausing only when the punctuation indicates you should. Refer to the diagram for the type of pause associated with common marks.

- Form a rough idea of the topic and mood of the work. A quick look at the type of words used in the poem may show you whether the mood of the poem is sad or happy, serious or humorous. Read the poem with its mood in mind.

Vocabulary Builder

Poetry Collection 1

- **clustering** (klus´ tər iŋ) *adj.* gathering; forming in a group (p. 629) *I knew from the clustering ants that there had been a spill.*

- **lunar** (lōō´ nər) *adj.* of the moon (p. 629) *Neil Armstrong was the first person to set foot on the lunar surface.*

- **threshold** (thresh´ ōld´) *n.* the bottom of a doorway; entrance or a point of beginning (p. 631) *She opened the door and stepped across the threshold.*

Poetry Collection 2

- **fate** (fāt) *n.* destiny; what happens to a person or thing; final outcome (p. 639) *The judge decided the defendant's fate.*

- **lowly** (lō´ lē) *adj.* humble; of low rank (p. 639) *Starting as a lowly stable boy, he worked hard and became the horse's top trainer.*

- **temperate** (tem´ pər it) *adj.* mild; kept within limits; moderate (p. 641) *This temperate weather is much better than the snow.*

Build Understanding • *Poetry Collection 1*

Connecting to the Literature

Reading/Writing Connection The poems in Poetry Collection 1 include vivid images of a variety of landscapes. Write a brief description of one of your favorite views. Use at least three of the following words: *appreciate, circulate, concentrate, liberate, generate.*

Meet the Authors

Minamoto no Toshiyori (1055?–1129?)
"The clustering clouds . . ." (p. 629)
Japanese poet and critic Minamoto no Toshiyori (mǐ′ nä′ mō′ tō′ nō′ tō′ shē′ yō′ rē′) rebelled against tradition and helped forge a new style. In addition to writing poetry, Toshiyori judged poetry contests.

Ki Tsurayuki (ca. 872–945)
"When I went to visit . . ." (p. 629)
Ki Tsurayuki (kē′ tsoōr′ ĭ′ oō′ kē′) was one of the leading Japanese poets, critics, and diarists of his time. In his preface to a major literary anthology, he said that "The poetry of Japan . . . springs from the heart of man."

James Weldon Johnson (1871–1938)
"My City" (p. 630)
Born in Jacksonville, Florida, James Weldon Johnson became the first African American allowed to practice law in Florida. Johnson also published a newspaper, and was a leader in the civil rights movement.

Dylan Thomas (1914–1953)
"Do Not Go Gentle into That Good Night" (p. 633)
Born in Wales, in Great Britain, Dylan Thomas fell in love with words early in life. Poems poured out of him, and by the age of twenty, he had written most of the poems for which he is famous today.

Go Online
Author Link
For: More about the authors
Visit: www.PHSchool.com
Web Code: eqe-9404

TANKA

The clustering clouds—
Can it be they wipe away
The lunar shadows?
Every time they clear a bit
The moonlight shines the brighter.

— Minamoto no Toshiyori
translated by Donald Keene

When I went to visit
The girl I love so much,
That winter night
The river blew so cold
That the plovers[1] were crying.

— Ki Tsurayuki
translated by Geoffrey Bownas

The Monkey Bridge in Koshu Province, 1841, Hiroshige Hitsu, Christie's, New York.

Vocabulary Builder
clustering (klus´ tər iŋ)
adj. gathering;
forming in a group
lunar (lōō´ nər) *adj.* of
the moon

---

1. plovers (pluv´ ərz) *n.* shorebirds with short tails and long, pointed wings.

MY CITY

James Weldon Johnson

Background   Poets who write Shakespearean sonnets may slightly modify the rhyme scheme. In this sonnet, Johnson uses a modified scheme in the first two quatrains, or groups of four lines. In the rest of the poem, though, he follows classic Shakespearean form.

When I come down to sleep death's endless night,
   The <u>threshold</u> of the unknown dark to cross,
   What to me then will be the keenest loss,
When this bright world blurs on my fading sight?
5 Will it be that no more I shall see the trees
   Or smell the flowers or hear the singing birds
   Or watch the flashing streams or patient herds?
No, I am sure it will be none of these.
But, ah! Manhattan's sights and sounds, her smells,
10 Her crowds, her throbbing force, the thrill that comes
From being of her a part, her subtile spells,
   Her shining towers, her avenues, her slums—
   O God! the stark, unutterable pity,
To be dead, and never again behold my city!

Vocabulary Builder
threshold (thresh′ ōld′)
n. the bottom of a doorway; entrance or a point of beginning

Literary Analysis
Sonnet Which syllables are stressed in the iambic pentameter of line 9?

◄ **Critical Viewing** Which lines in the poem does this photograph best illustrate? Explain. **[Connect]**

Do Not Go Gentle into That Good Night

Dylan Thomas

Do not go gentle into that good night,
Old age should burn and rave at close of day;
Rage, rage against the dying of the light.

Though wise men at their end know dark is right,
5 Because their words had forked no lightning they
Do not go gentle into that good night.

Good men, the last wave by, crying how bright
Their frail deeds might have danced in a green bay,
Rage, rage against the dying of the light.

10 Wild men who caught and sang the sun in flight,
And learn, too late, they grieved it on its way,
Do not go gentle into that good night.

Grave men, near death, who see with blinding sight
Blind eyes could blaze like meteors and be gay,
15 Rage, rage against the dying of the light.

And you, my father, there on the sad height,
Curse, bless, me now with your fierce tears, I pray.
Do not go gentle into that good night.
Rage, rage against the dying of the light.

◄ **Critical Viewing** Which of the four types of men do you think is represented in this painting? Explain. **[Interpret]**

Literary Analysis
Villanelle Where are the first and third lines of the first stanza repeated in this villanelle?

Reading Skill
Reading Fluently Where will you pause when reading lines 16–19? What punctuation indicates each pause?

Apply the Skills

Poetry Collection 1

Thinking About the Selections

1. **Respond:** Which image from the poems in Poetry Collection 1 made the strongest impression on you? Why?
2. **(a) Recall:** What is the weather like when the speaker goes visiting in "When I went to visit . . ."? **(b) Infer:** What does his reaction to such weather indicate about his love? Explain.
3. **(a) Contrast:** Contrast the events actually taking place in "The clustering clouds . . ." with the speaker's interpretation of those events. **(b) Interpret:** What does the poem suggest about the effect of contrasts on our perceptions?
4. **(a) Contrast:** Contrast the landscape the speaker prefers in "My City" with the one he first describes. **(b) Evaluate:** Did the contrast help you appreciate his perspective? Explain.
5. **(a) Interpret:** In "Do Not Go Gentle into That Good Night," what does the speaker mean when he says, "Old age should burn and rave at close of day"? **(b) Analyze:** Explain the disappointment each of the four types of men faces at the end of life.
   (c) Connect: What is the connection among these disappointments and the speaker's advice?

Literary Analysis

6. Which features of **tanka** appear in the translations of "The clustering clouds . . ." and "When I went to visit . . ."?
7. Using a chart like the one shown, analyze the meaning of the three quatrains and the couplet in the **sonnet** "My City."

Message of Quatrain 1	Connection: Quatrains 1 and 2	Connection: Quatrains 2 and 3	Connection: Couplet to Quatrains

8. **(a)** Identify the repeated lines in the **villanelle** "Do Not Go Gentle into That Good Night." **(b)** What feeling does the repetition of these lines help create? **(c)** Discuss answers with a partner. Take notes on how your discussion affected your own thoughts.

Reading Skill

9. **(a)** By previewing the first eight lines of "My City," what information about vocabulary and sentence structure can a reader learn?
   (b) Explain how this information might help a reader **read fluently.**

QuickReview

Poems at a Glance
"When I went to visit . . ." is a tanka about a devoted lover.

"The clustering clouds . . ." is a tanka that takes a humorous look at the moon.

"My City" is a sonnet about the poet's love for his city.

"Do Not Go Gentle into That Good Night" is a cry against death written in villanelle form.

Go Online
Assessment
For: Self-test
Visit: www.PHSchool.com
Web Code: eqa-6404

Poetic Form: a defined structure for a poem. Some of the forms a poem may have are *tanka, sonnet,* or *villanelle.*

Fluent Reading: smooth reading that shows understanding

Vocabulary Builder

Practice For each item, identify the word that does not belong in the group and explain why.

1. clustering, crowding, repairing
2. lunar, rectangular, earthly
3. threshold, doorway, harvest

Adding Words to Your Vocabulary The word *lunar* is related to the words *lunatic, loony,* and *lunette.* Using a dictionary, define each of these three words and explain how its meaning is related to the meaning of *lunar.* Then, use each word in a sentence. (For more on using a dictionary, see page R6.)

Writing

Write your own **tanka**, following the traditional Japanese form.
- Think of a subject for your poem.
- Review the definition of a tanka on page 626.
- As you draft, follow the prescribed syllable pattern for each line.
- Try revising as you draft, jotting down ideas and then rephrasing them to fit the form.

To help follow the form, *invert* normal word order as long as your meaning is clear. For example, you might write, "To the store did he run."

For *Grammar, Vocabulary,* and *Assessment,* see **Build Language Skills,** pages 644–645.

Extend Your Learning

Listening and Speaking In a small group, listen several times to a recording of Dylan Thomas reading "Do Not Go Gentle into That Good Night." Afterward, hold a **poetry reading discussion** in which you explore what the reading added to your appreciation of the poem. Address the speed of the Thomas's reading and the way he emphasizes ideas and brings out rhymes and rhythms in the poem.

Research and Technology Give a **visual presentation** on Japanese art. Locate two or three works of Japanese art that illustrate the general mood or specific descriptions in the tanka in this collection. Research the style of the images. Present the works to the class, explaining your choices and reporting what you learned.

Build Understanding • *Poetry Collection 2*

Connecting to the Literature

Reading/Writing Connection The speakers in these poems each gain insight in moments of solitary reflection. Write a brief paragraph to explain the value of thinking something through on your own. Use at least three of the following words: *restore, revise, evaluate, assess.*

Review

For **Literary Analysis, Reading Skill,** and **Vocabulary Builder,** see pages 626–627.

Meet the Authors

Priest **Jakuren** (1139?–1202)

"One cannot ask loneliness . . ." (p. 637)

Jakuren (jä´ ko͞o´ rən´) was a Buddhist priest whose poems are filled with beautiful yet melancholy imagery. After entering the priesthood at the age of twenty-three, he traveled the Japanese countryside.

Ono **Komachi** (active ca. 833–857)

"Was it that I went to sleep . . ." (p. 637)

A beautiful woman with a strong personality, Ono Komachi (ō´ nō´ kō´ mä´ chē´) was an early Japanese tanka poet. Her poems are marked by passion and energy. The few details known about her life have inspired many legends.

Theodore **Roethke** (1908–1963)

"The Waking" (p. 639)

Born in Michigan, Theodore Roethke developed his great love of nature from observing the plants in his family's commercial greenhouses. This love is often reflected in his poetry. In 1954, Roethke received a Pulitzer Prize for his poetry.

William **Shakespeare** (1564–1616)

Sonnet 18 (p. 641)

Even though he is most famous as a playwright, Shakespeare also wrote brilliant sonnets. Today, the English sonnet, which he perfected, is also known as the Shakespearean sonnet. (For more about Shakespeare and his career, see pages 822–823.)

For: More about the authors
Visit: www.PHSchool.com
Web Code: eqe-9405

TANKA

One cannot ask loneliness
How or where it starts.
On the cypress-mountain,[1]
Autumn evening.

— Priest Jakuren
translated by Geoffrey Bownas

---

1. **cypress-mountain** Cypress trees are
cone-bearing evergreen trees native to
North America, Europe, and Asia.

Triptych of Snow, Moon, and Flower (Center Panel), c.1780s, Shunsho. Museum of Art, Atami, Japan.

Was it that I went to sleep
Thinking of him,
That he came in my dreams?
Had I known it a dream
I should not have wakened.

— Ono Komachi
translated by Geoffrey Bownas

Reading Skill
Read Fluently How
might the mood, or
general feeling, of
each poem affect the
way that you read it?

▲ **Critical Viewing** In what ways does the mood of this image suit each
tanka? Explain. **[Connect]**

The Waking

Theodore Roethke

I wake to sleep, and take my waking slow.
I feel my <u>fate</u> in what I cannot fear.
I learn by going where I have to go.

We think by feeling. What is there to know?
5   I hear my being dance from ear to ear.
I wake to sleep, and take my waking slow.

Of those so close beside me, which are you?
God bless the Ground! I shall walk softly there,
And learn by going where I have to go.

10 Light takes the Tree; but who can tell us how?
The <u>lowly</u> worm climbs up a winding stair;
I wake to sleep, and take my waking slow.

Great Nature has another thing to do
To you and me; so take the lively air,
15 And, lovely, learn by going where to go.

This shaking keeps me steady. I should know.
What falls away is always. And is near.
I wake to sleep, and take my waking slow.
I learn by going where I have to go.

◄ **Critical Viewing** Why might a hiker like this one prefer to "learn by going where to go" rather than following a planned route? **[Apply]**

Vocabulary Builder
fate (fāt) *n.* destiny; what happens to a person or thing; final outcome

Vocabulary Builder
lowly (lō´ lē) *adj.* humble; of low rank

Literary Analysis
Villanelle How has the repetition of lines 1 and 3 changed their significance or associated feelings by the end?

Sonnet 18
William Shakespeare

◄ **Critical Viewing**
Which characteristics of the woman in the sonnet does this woman seem to share? Explain. **[Connect]**

Background   There are two forms of sonnet, the Petrarchan (or Italian) and the Shakespearean. The Petrarchan form is named after the Italian poet Petrarch (pē´ trärk´; 1304–1374). The main difference between the forms is in the rhyme scheme.

Petrarch's sonnets, overflowing with enthusiastic, exaggerated comparisons in praise of his beloved Laura, inspired Shakespeare and other English poets. In Sonnet 18, Shakespeare offers a unique perspective on the comparisons that were popular in the sonnets of the time.

Vocabulary Builder
temperate (tem´ pər it) *adj.* mild; kept within limits; moderate

Literary Analysis
Sonnet In what way does the couplet at the conclusion summarize the main idea of the poem?

> Shall I compare thee to a summer's day?
> Thou art more lovely and more <u>temperate</u>:
> Rough winds do shake the darling buds of May,
> And summer's lease hath all too short a date:
> 5 Sometime too hot the eye of heaven shines,
> And often is his gold complexion dimmed;
> And every fair from fair sometime declines,
> By chance or nature's changing course untrimmed;[1]
> But thy eternal summer shall not fade,
> 10 Nor lose possession of that fair thou owest;[2]
> Nor shall Death brag thou wander'st in his shade,
> When in eternal lines to time thou grow'st:
> > So long as men can breathe, or eyes can see,
> > So long lives this, and this gives life to thee.

---

1. untrimmed *adj.* stripped of ornaments or beautiful features.
2. owest (ō´ ist) *v.* own.

Apply the Skills

Poetry Collection 2

Thinking About the Selections

1. **Respond:** Which poem made the greatest impact on you? Why?
2. **(a) Recall:** What question cannot be asked in "One cannot ask loneliness . . ."? **(b) Connect:** How does the image of the mountain relate to the speaker's thoughts about loneliness?
3. **(a) Recall:** What reason does the speaker in "Was it that I went to sleep . . ." give for dreaming about the man? **(b) Infer:** What do the speaker's comments reveal about her feelings for the man?
4. **(a) Compare and Contrast:** In line 4 of "The Waking," what contrast between thinking and feeling is suggested?
   (b) Interpret: What advice about life is implied in line 19?
5. **(a) Analyze:** Identify three ways in which, according to the speaker in Sonnet 18, a summer day may become less than perfect. **(b) Infer:** What is the main reason the speaker gives for claiming that the woman is superior to a summer's day?

Literary Analysis

6. Which features of **tanka** appear in the translations of "One cannot ask loneliness . . ." and "Was it that I went to sleep . . ."?
7. **(a)** Identify the repeated lines in the **villanelle** "The Waking."
   (b) What feeling does the repetition of these lines help create?
   (c) Discuss answers with a partner. Take notes on how your discussion did or did not change your own thoughts.
8. Using a chart like the one shown, analyze the meaning of the three quatrains and the couplet in the **sonnet** Sonnet 18.

Message of Quatrain 1	Connection: Quatrains 1 and 2	Connection: Quatrains 2 and 3	Connection: Couplet to Quatrains

Reading Skill

9. **(a)** By previewing the first four lines of Sonnet 18, what information about vocabulary and sentence structure can a reader learn? **(b)** Explain how this information might help a reader **read fluently**.

Vocabulary Builder

Practice For each item, identify the word that does not belong in the group and explain why.

1. fate, destiny, loneliness
2. temperate, experienced, extreme
3. lowly, humble, clever

Adding Words to Your Vocabulary The word *temperate* is related to the words *temper, temperance,* and *intemperate.* Using a dictionary, define each of these three words and explain how its meaning is related to the meaning of *temperate.* Then, use each word in a sentence. (For more on using a dictionary, see page R6.)

Writing

Write your own **tanka**, following the traditional Japanese form.
- Think of a subject for your poem.
- Review the definition of a tanka on page 626.
- As you draft, follow the prescribed syllable pattern for each line.
- Try revising as you draft, jotting down ideas and then rephrasing them to fit the form.

To help follow the form, *invert* normal word order as long as your meaning is clear. For example, you might write, "To the store did he run."

For *Grammar, Vocabulary,* and *Assessment,* see **Build Language Skills,** pages 644–645.

Extend Your Learning

Listening and Speaking In a small group, listen several times to a recording of Shakespeare's Sonnet 18. Afterward, hold a **poetry reading discussion** in which you explore what the reading added to your appreciation of the poem. In your discussion, address the speed of the reading and how the reader emphasizes certain ideas as well as rhymes and rhythms.

Research and Technology Give a **visual presentation** on art in Shakespeare's day. Locate two or three works of Elizabethan art that illustrate the mood or specific descriptions in Sonnet 18. Conduct research on the style of the images. Present the works to the class, explaining your choices and reporting what you have learned.

Build Language Skills

Vocabulary Skill

Suffixes The **suffix** *-al* can be used to form adjectives and nouns. When used to change a noun into an adjective, the suffix *-al* means "having the form or character of" or "pertaining to." When *-al* is used to change a verb into a noun, it forms a word that names the result of the action of the verb.

➤ **Example:** vision *n.* + *-al* = visual *adj.*   refuse *v.* + *-al* = refusal *n.*

Practice Copy and complete the chart by supplying the missing words. Then, use each word that ends with the suffix *-al* in a sentence.

deny	season	peruse	part	portray
	seasonal	perusal	partial	
noun	*adjective*	*noun*	*adjective*	*noun*

Grammar Lesson

Direct Objects A **direct object** is a noun or pronoun that receives the action of a transitive verb. It answers the question formed by putting *what* or *whom* after an action verb, as in the following examples. A direct object's function in a sentence is to add specific information.

➤ **Example:**

> **DO**
> Tyrell steers the car. (Tyrell steers *what*?)
> **DO**
> Erin admires her friend. (Erin admires *whom*?)

Verbs such as *am, is, are, was,* and *were* are linking verbs. They do not take direct objects.

Practice The following phrases require a direct object to complete the thought. Copy each phrase and complete it by adding a direct object. Then, rewrite each sentence with a new action verb that makes sense with the direct object you supplied.

1. Damon bought _____.

2. I have no _____.

3. Our basketball team earned

   _____.

4. The judge considered _____.

5. I believe _____.

MorePractice

For more practice with direct objects, see the Grammar Handbook, p. R40.

𝒲𝒢 *Prentice Hall Writing and Grammar Connection: Chapter 19, Section 3*

Monitor Your Progress

Reading Skill: Read Fluently

Directions: *Questions 1–5 are based on the poem.*

1 Five years have past; five summers, with the length
2 Of five long winters! and again I hear
3 These waters, rolling from their mountain springs
4 With a soft inland murmur. Once again
5 Do I behold these steep and lofty cliffs. . . .
        —from "Lines Composed a Few Miles Above
                Tintern Abbey" by William Wordsworth

Standards Assessed

• 10.3.1
• 10.3.7
• 10.6.1

1. Which does line 4 show you must do when reading a poem?
A Pause at the end of a long line.
B Never pause at the end of a line.
C Pause within a line when necessary.
D Never pause within a line.

2. A fluent reader would pause at the end of
A line 1 only.
B line 2 only.
C lines 2 and 3.
D none of the first three lines.

3. Skimming the first few lines suggests the reader read this poem
A quickly and in monotone.
B slowly and carefully.
C at a moderate rate.
D laboriously.

4. In the first two lines, words would best be grouped in
A one group.
B two groups.
C three groups.
D four groups.

5. Before reading this poem aloud, the reader should
A read it several times and mark the poem to show pauses and emphasis.
B read it once.
C mark the poem to show pauses and emphasis.
D read it several times.

Timed Writing: Analysis [Connections]

Review Poetry Collection 1 or Poetry Collection 2. Demonstrate how symbolism conveys theme in one of the poems. **(40 minutes)**

 Writing Workshop: *Work in Progress*

Descriptive Essay

Using the outline from your writing portfolio, add the sensory details that would best convey each item. Cross out items that do not add to your description. Put this work in your writing portfolio.

Tone and Mood

The overall feeling or impression conveyed by a literary work arises from two elements: **tone** and **mood**.

- **Tone** is the author's attitude toward the reader or toward the subject of the work. It can be described with adjectives such as *formal* or *informal, scolding* or *encouraging, humorous* or *serious, matter-of-fact* or *enthusiastic.*
- **Mood**, or atmosphere, is a general, unified feeling conveyed by the various details of a literary work. The mood of a work may be described with adjectives such as *gloomy* or *joyous, menacing* or *cozy.*

Writers create tone and mood through their choice of words, descriptive details, and images. A writer's choice of subject and setting can also help to define a mood. In some works, tone plays a key role. For example, the fun of a humor essay lies in its tone—the writer's absurd approach to his or her subject. In other works, mood is critical. A horror story cannot chill readers unless it creates a creepy mood. Similarly, poets may choose to emphasize tone or mood (or both) in their work.

Comparing Tone and Mood

In the three poems presented here, the poets create unique imaginative worlds. These worlds are defined as much by tone and mood as by the characters and events in the works.

- For example, the mood of "Fear" captures the inner emotional world of a mother.
- By contrast, the mood of "La Belle Dame sans Merci" seeps into every object in the poem, creating an imaginative world in which all things reflect a single feeling.

As you read, compare the imaginative worlds each poet creates. Use a diagram like the one shown.

Vocabulary Builder

La Belle Dam sans Merci

- **haggard** (hag´ ərd) *adj.* having a wild, worn look, as from grief or lack of sleep (p. 651) *He has a haggard look because he studied all night.*

- **sojourn** (sō´ jərn) *v.* stay for a while (p. 652) *Every summer we sojourn for a week at the beach.*

Academic Standards

- Examine how the author's perspective influences the structure and tone of the text. (10.2.4)
- Evaluate the use of voice and narrator. (10.3.9)
- Evaluate the aesthetic qualities of style. (10.3.11)

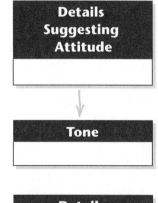

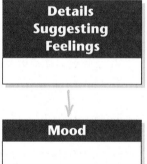

Build Understanding

Connecting to the Literature

The poems of Gabriela Mistral, Gwendolyn Brooks, and John Keats have moods as various as the moods a person might pass through over a day—or a lifetime. Write a brief description of two contrasting moods. Use at least three of the following words: *exhibit, evoke, highlight, reinforce, respond.*

Meet the Authors

Gabriela **Mistral** (1889–1957)

At fifteen, Gabriela Mistral (gā brē ā′ lä mē sträl′) was already a full-time grade-school teacher in her native Chile. Mistral, born Lucila Godoy y Alcayaga [lo͞o sǐ′ lə gō dơ ǐ ē ál kī ä′ gə], published her poetry under a variety of pen names before she settled on Gabriela Mistral. In 1945, she became the first Latin American to receive the Nobel Prize in Literature.

Gwendolyn **Brooks** (1917–2000)

Raised in Chicago, Gwendolyn Brooks began writing poetry at the age of seven. Encouraged by her family, she published her first poem at thirteen. In 1950, Brooks became the first African American writer to win a Pulitzer Prize. She is one of the most highly regarded American poets of the twentieth century.

John **Keats** (1795–1821)

Widely regarded as one of the greatest English poets, John Keats lost both his parents while he was still a boy. He attended school and studied surgery, but his own life was cut tragically short by tuberculosis. Sensing his impending death, Keats wrote the poems many consider his best in about a year, publishing them in 1820. He died in 1821, at the age of twenty-five.

For: More about these authors
Visit: www.PHSchool.com
Web Code: eqe-9406

Fear
Gabriela Mistral

Translated by Doris Dana

I don't want them to turn
my little girl into a swallow.
She would fly far away into the sky
and never fly again to my straw bed,
5   or she would nest in the eaves[1]
where I could not comb her hair.
I don't want them to turn
my little girl into a swallow.

I don't want them to make
10   my little girl a princess.
In tiny golden slippers
how could she play on the meadow?
And when night came, no longer
would she sleep at my side.
15   I don't want them to make
my little girl a princess.

And even less do I want them
one day to make her queen.
They would put her on a throne
20   where I could not go to see her.
And when nighttime came
I could never rock her . . .
I don't want them to make
my little girl a queen!

---

1. eaves (ēvz) *n.* lower edges of a roof.

▲ **Critical Viewing**
Does the mother's expression in this painting express the fears described in the poem? Explain. **[Interpret]**

Literary Analysis
Tone In what tone of voice do you imagine the mother uttering lines 9–12? Why?

THE *Bean Eaters*
Gwendolyn Brooks

They eat beans mostly, this old yellow pair.
Dinner is a casual affair.
Plain chipware on a plain and creaking wood,
Tin flatware.

5 Two who are Mostly Good.
Two who have lived their day,
But keep on putting on their clothes
And putting things away.

And remembering . . .
10 Remembering, with twinklings and twinges,
As they lean over the beans in their rented back room
    that is full of beads and receipts and dolls and cloths,
    tobacco crumbs, vases and fringes.

Literary Analysis
Tone What attitude toward her subject does the speaker show in her use of words like *mostly* and her repetition of *plain*?

Thinking About the Selections

1. **(a) Recall:** Describe the three fears expressed by the speaker of "Fear." **(b) Apply:** What insight does the poem give into the relationship between mothers and their growing daughters?

2. **(a) Recall:** What does the couple in "The Bean Eaters" do as they eat their beans? **(b) Draw Conclusions:** In what way are their lives rich even though they are poor?

3. **Make a Judgment:** Which poem paints a truer picture of an attachment between people? Explain.

La Belle Dame sans Merci[1]

John Keats

O what can ail thee, knight-at-arms,
　　Alone and palely loitering?
The sedge[2] has withered from the lake,
　　And no birds sing.

5　O what can ail thee, knight-at-arms,
　　So <u>haggard</u> and so woe-begone?
The squirrel's granary is full,
　　And the harvest's done.

I see a lily on thy brow,
10　　With anguish moist and fever dew,
And on thy cheeks a fading rose
　　Fast withereth too.

I met a lady in the meads,[3]
　　Full beautiful—a faery's child,
15　Her hair was long, her foot was light,
　　And her eyes were wild.

I made a garland for her head,
　　And bracelets too, and fragrant zone;[4]
She looked at me as she did love,
20　　And made sweet moan.

I set her on my pacing steed,
　　And nothing else saw all day long,
For sidelong would she bend, and sing
　　A faery's song.

Vocabulary Builder
haggard (hag´ ərd)
adj. having a wild,
worn look, as from
grief or lack of sleep

Literary Analysis
Mood What mood do
these signs of poor
health help to create?

Reading Check

Who begins speaking
in the fourth stanza?

---

1. **La Belle Dame** (däm) **sans** (sän) **Merci** (mer sē´) title of a medieval
French poem; literally, "the beautiful lady without mercy."
2. **sedge** (sej) *n.* grassy plant that grows in wet areas or in water.
3. **meads** (mēdz) *n.* old-fashioned or poetic form of *meadows*.
4. **zone** (zōn) *n.* old word for "girdle" or "belt."

25 She found me roots of relish sweet,
     And honey wild, and manna[5] dew,
     And sure in language strange she said—
       'I love thee true.'

     She took me to her elfin grot,[6]
30   And there she wept, and sighed full sore,
     And there I shut her wild wild eyes
       With kisses four.

     And there she lullèd me asleep,
       And there I dreamed—Ah! woe betide!
35   The latest dream I ever dreamed
       On the cold hill's side.

     I saw pale kings and princes too,
       Pale warriors, death-pale were they all;
     They cried—'La Belle Dame sans Merci
40   Hath thee in thrall!'

     I saw their starved lips in the gloam,
       With horrid warning gapèd wide,
     And I awoke and found me here,
       On the cold hill's side.

45   And this is why I sojourn here,
       Alone and palely loitering,
     Though the sedge has withered from the lake,
       And no birds sing.

---

5. **manna** (man´ ə) n. sweet substance obtained from the bark of certain ash trees.
6. **grot** (grät) n. poetic term for "cave."

Thinking About the Selection

1. **(a) Recall:** Identify two details of the setting presented in the first two stanzas. **(b) Infer:** During what season is the poem set? **(c) Connect:** In what way does the setting reinforce the meaning of the poem?

2. **(a) Recall:** Who does the knight meet "in the meads"? **(b) Analyze:** What is his response to this person?

3. **(a) Infer:** At the end of the poem, why is the knight "Alone and palely loitering"? **(b) Draw Conclusions:** What does the poem suggest about the consequences of romantic love?

Apply the Skills

Fear • The Bean Eaters • La Belle Dame sans Merci

Comparing Tone and Mood

1. **(a)** Identify two details in "Fear" and two in "La Belle Dame sans Merci" that give each poem a dreamlike feeling. **(b)** Explain the differences in **mood** between the two poems.

2. **(a)** In "The Bean Eaters," what is the speaker's attitude toward the couple? **(b)** Give two examples of descriptive words and details in the poem that convey this attitude.

3. Explain in what way the use of old-fashioned poetic words and a medieval setting creates a serious, even distant **tone** in "La Belle Dame sans Merci." Support your answer with examples.

4. **(a)** Using a chart like the one shown, compare the tone and mood in each of the three poems. **(b)** Review your chart and compare each speaker's emotional connection with his or her subject, explaining which is most direct and which is most distant.

Tone	Similarities/ Differences	Mood	Similarities/ Differences

QuickReview

Tone: the author's attitude toward the reader or subject

Mood: the general, unified feeling conveyed by the various details of a literary work

Go Online
—**Assessment**
For: Self-test
Visit: www.PHSchool.com
Web Code: eqa-6406

Writing to Compare Literary Works

In an essay, analyze the way the poet generates a mood in each poem. Use these questions to get started:

*   How is the mood of the poem connected with the emotional state of the speaker?
*   How is the mood linked with the feelings of the characters?
*   How is the mood connected to the scenes and objects described?

Conclude your essay by drawing a conclusion about the world of each poem: Is it the inner world of a person, the outer world of everyday experience, or a special world in which outer things reflect an inward state?

Vocabulary Builder

Practice Write a sentence about each of the following people. For each, correctly use a word from the vocabulary list on page 646.

1. a person unable to sleep   **2.** a person on vacation

Reading

Directions: *Questions 1–5 are based on the following excerpt.*

> Oliver has gone up upon a hill,
> sees clearly now: the kingdom of Spain,
> and the Saracens assembled in such numbers:
> helmets blazing, bedecked with gems in gold,
> 5 those shields of theirs, those hauberks sewn with brass,
> and all their spears, the gonfalons affixed;
> cannot begin to count their battle corps,
> there are too many, he cannot take their number.
> —from the *Song of Roland,* translated by Frederick Goldin

1. The excerpt is
A part of a sentence.
B 1 sentence long.
C 3 sentences long.
D 8 sentences long.

2. The phrase "bedecked with gems in gold" refers to
A the narrator.
B Oliver.
C the kingdom of Spain.
D the Saracens.

3. According to the excerpt, what is Oliver unable to do?
A see clearly
B count the Saracen dead
C see the Saracen dead
D determine the number of enemy soldiers

4. When reading aloud, the reader should
A drop his or her voice at the end of each line.
B drop his or her voice after "now."
C drop his or her voice after "gold."
D drop his or her voice after "spears."

5. The reader should plan on reading this excerpt
A faster than a magazine article.
B faster than a quantum physics book.
C slower than a textbook.
D slower than song lyrics.

Test Practice

Vocabulary

Directions: *Choose the best definition of each italicized word.*

Standards Assessed
• 10.2.1
• 10.6.1
• 10.7.1

6. *compensate*
   A to make a circuit
   B to give to charity
   C to make up for
   D to make smaller

7. *significance*
   A the quality of having meaning
   B the quality of being irrelevant
   C the quality of being historical
   D the quality of being traditional

8. *radical*
   A conformity
   B extreme
   C around
   D mathematical

9. *diverse*
   A similar
   B product of a math operation
   C varied
   D comparable

10. *visual*
   A connected with seeing
   B that which appears
   C connected with light
   D able to be calculated

11. *nocturnal*
   A of the night
   B able to be darkened
   C state of being dark
   D the quality of light

12. *external*
   A able to be terminated
   B a person who does not belong to a group
   C of or relating to the outside
   D coming from nature

13. *conventional*
   A forming a large gathering
   B to be capable of following
   C pertaining to the standard
   D dealing with a group idea

14. *remembrance*
   A relating to the past
   B the state of remembering
   C the form of a memory
   D the characterization of the past

15. *compliance*
   A the state of complying
   B the form of a request or wish
   C granting a request or wish
   D related to complying

Writing Workshop

Description: Descriptive Essay

Academic Standards

- Evaluate the aesthetic qualities of style. (10.3.11)
- Revise writing based on specific criteria. (10.4.11)
- Write for different purposes and audiences. (10.5.8)

Descriptive writing portrays people, places, objects, experiences, or ideas in vivid detail so that the reader can create a mental picture of the subject. Use the steps outlined in this workshop to write a descriptive essay.

Assignment Write a descriptive essay about someone or something that is important to you or that you find interesting.

What to Include Your essay should feature these elements:
- precise word choices that create a strong impression
- sensory details of sight, sound, smell, taste, texture, and movement
- figurative language, such as personification, simile, and metaphor
- a logical organization
- error-free grammar, including correct use of prepositional phrases

To preview the criteria on which your descriptive essay may be assessed, see the rubric on page 660.

Prewriting

Choosing Your Topic

Look at pictures. Browse through photographs of people and places that are part of your life. Jot down a list of the ones that stand out in your memory. For each, write a list of details that it brings to mind. Then, review your work and decide which list is most colorful and interesting. Write about that topic.

Gathering Details

Use figurative language. To make your description more vivid, create figurative language by comparing a detail related to your subject with something that is familiar to your readers.

Using the Form
You may use elements of this form in these types of writing:
- short stories
- reflective essays
- character sketches
- scientific observations

Work in Progress
Review the work you did on pages 587, 621, and 645.

Detail	Reminds Me of . . .	Figure of Speech
a star pitcher's fastball	a knife slicing through the air	Metaphor: His fastball is a knife slicing through the air.
	a runaway train	Simile: His fastball is like a runaway train that stops for nothing.
	an emotion, such as anger	Personification: His angry fastball makes batters want to run!

Drafting

Shaping Your Writing

Present a controlling idea. All the details in your essay should build to convey a single main impression. Write one sentence that captures the main idea you want to express. Use the sentence in your introduction. Then, develop that idea in your body paragraphs. In your conclusion, restate your main idea or add a fresh insight.

Providing Elaboration

Fully develop your ideas. In each paragraph, state the main idea, and then extend and elaborate upon it with additional details.

Statement: At track meets, my coach shows few of her reactions.

Extension: She watches quietly from the sidelines.

Elaboration: She offers a smile and an encouraging word before we compete, but she rarely explodes with emotion.

Revising

Revising Your Overall Structure

Frame your description. Review the opening and closing paragraphs of your essay to be sure they frame your work. Circle details in your introduction that vividly establish your topic. Circle details in your conclusion that add insight. If too few details are circled, consider adding some.

To read the complete student model, see page 659.

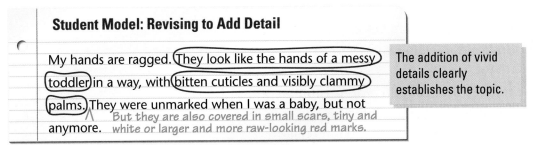

Student Model: Revising to Add Detail

My hands are ragged. They look like the hands of a messy toddler in a way, with bitten cuticles and visibly clammy palms. They were unmarked when I was a baby, but not anymore. But they are also covered in small scars, tiny and white or larger and more raw-looking red marks.

The addition of vivid details clearly establishes the topic.

Revising Your Word Choice

Personalize your voice. To create a genuine voice, choose words that both express your meaning and reflect your personality. Review your essay, circling words or phrases that sound forced. Consider revising your essay with words that are more true to your voice.

Forced: Father always bore a fedora of unobtrusive green.

Genuine: Dad always wore a hat that was a soft, faded green.

Integrating Grammar Skills

Revising to Vary Sentence Patterns

To make your writing more fluid and engaging, vary your style by beginning some sentences with prepositional phrases.

Identifying Prepositional Phrases Prepositions are words that connect a noun or pronoun to another word in the sentence. A preposition and its object—the accompanying noun or pronoun—is called a prepositional phrase. (A prepositional phrase also includes the object's modifiers.)

Prentice Hall Writing and Grammar Connection: Chapter 21, Section 3

Preposition +	Noun/Pronoun		Prepositional Phrase
of	moon	=	of the silvery moon
at	mall		at the local mall

Some prepositional phrases act as adjectives and some act as adverbs. Many prepositions express spatial or time-order relationships, which makes them useful tools when writing description.

Time: after the game; before dinner; at two o'clock; for a day
Space: under the table; near the river; in school; in my hand

Varying Sentences With Prepositional Phrases In these examples, subjects are italicized, verbs are underlined, and prepositional phrases appear in parentheses:

Repeated subject-verb pattern: *She* <u>wakes</u> up early. *She* <u>makes</u> breakfast. *She* <u>makes</u> lunch (after that).
Revision: *She* <u>wakes</u> up early. *She* <u>makes</u> breakfast. (After that), *she* <u>makes</u> lunch.

Follow these steps to vary your sentences in your own writing.

1. **Read your draft aloud.** Listen for overuse of the subject-verb sentence pattern.
2. **Identify sentences that contain a prepositional phrase.**
3. **Rewrite the sentence, starting with the prepositional phrase.** Be sure the phrase is close to the word it modifies.
4. **If the prepositional phrase contains four or more words, set it off from the words that follow with a comma.**

Apply It to Your Editing

Reread the first two paragraphs of your descriptive essay, looking for overuse of the subject-verb sentence pattern. Rewrite some sentences by beginning them with prepositional phrases.

Student Model: Jordan Kurtzman
Brookline, MA

Hands

My hands are ragged. They look like the hands of a messy toddler in a way, with bitten cuticles and visibly clammy palms. But they are also covered in small scars, tiny and white or larger and more raw-looking red marks. They were unmarked when I was a baby, but not anymore. I scar easily.

We had an assignment in drawing class to draw our hands holding an object. The teacher didn't tell us that the object had to be important in our lives until we'd already brought them in, so apparently handcuffs are important to me. The drawing wasn't terrible, but I never spent that much time staring at my hands before. My usual attention span for drawing is, at most, a half an hour, and I usually tend to give up once the shading gets complicated and careful attention must be paid to detail. I'm not a detail person. But in this assignment, I was forced to look at all the craggy grossness of my hands. I tried to stop biting my nails so that I wouldn't have to attempt the stubby, oddly textured things that pass for my fingernails, but it's a habit. I didn't start biting my nails until high school; whenever I have a lot of stress in my life, my nails look like they have been through a shredder.

I often find myself with my hands in my mouth when talking to someone, making for an extremely socially awkward moment. I never know if I should finish the nail-biting process or stop in mid-bite, leaving a partially severed nail.

I can't leave my hands alone. An unpicked cuticle is an incomplete cuticle; a long, unbitten nail is not a true nail. I also have calluses on my fingertips from playing bass, guitar, and violin, and those provide endless fodder for fidgeting. Other people choose to stare off into space; I choose, or am compelled, to endlessly pick at my hands.

My hands are also extremely cold. They are the long-fingered, clammy hands of the Grim Reaper, un-holdable hands. Even my mother has told me that they are cold and clammy. Cold, clammy hands are things that cannot possibly be put in a good light. There is no bright side. I can imagine a palm reader, one who has seen countless hands, recoiling in horror from my hands, pointing at my life line from a distance instead of mapping it out on the skin.

Novels from a certain era always take care to point out the condition of a lady's hands. Long, white, glove-enclosed fingers are lady's hands. Cracked red hands are scullery maid hands. My hands place me squarely in the pot-scrubbing set.

But I'm not sure that I'd want lady's hands. I have a friend who has uncallused, soft and feminine hands. Her fingers are faintly chubby in an extremely cute, cherubic way. They don't look strong or capable, just soft and helpless as those of a baby. My hands, callused, bony, and cold, look strong and capable, not dainty, lily-white, and frail, but tough.

The writer establishes her topic with vivid details.

The author discusses what her topic means, not just what it looks like.

Jordan's genuine voice comes through here. Her sense of humor is evident.

The author draws a clear and interesting message from her description.

Writing Workshop

Editing and Proofreading

Check your draft for errors in spelling, grammar, and punctuation.

Focus on Spelling: Remember to check your spelling even if you use a word processor's spelling software. Spell-checkers cannot tell if you have spelled a word correctly but have used the wrong word. For example, you might have confused *its* and *it's.*

Publishing and Presenting

Consider one of the following ways to share your writing:
Organize a display. Work with classmates to create a display of your essays. Select an appropriate title and organization. For example, you might use one area of the display for essays that describe people. Consider adding artwork or photographs to complement the essays.
Prepare an oral reading. Select music or sound effects to accompany your descriptive essay in an oral reading. Practice until you are confident. Then, deliver your reading for the class. When you are done, gracefully accept applause and express your thanks. If possible, record your reading on audiotape.

Reflecting on Your Writing

Writer's Journal Jot down your thoughts about writing a descriptive essay. Begin by answering these questions:
- What strategies did you find most useful in writing your descriptive essay?
- Did you enjoy using sensory details and figurative language?
- Did writing descriptively sharpen your observation skills?

> *Prentice Hall Writing and Grammar Connection: Chapter 6*

Rubric for Self-Assessment

Evaluate your descriptive essay using the following criteria and rating scale:

Criteria	Rating Scale
	not very ———————— very
Focus: How clear is the impression you create of your subject?	1　2　3　4　5
Organization: How logical is your organization?	1　2　3　4　5
Support/Elaboration: How well do you use sensory details?	1　2　3　4　5
Style: How effective is your use of figurative language?	1　2　3　4　5
Conventions: How correct is your grammar, especially your use of prepositional phrases?	1　2　3　4　5

Paraphrase

Skills You Will Learn	Literature You Will Read

Reading and Vocabulary Skills Preview

Reading: Paraphrase

▶ **Paraphrasing** is restating a text in your own words.

Academic Standards

- Integrate quotations and citations into text. (10.4.7)
- Demonstrate and understanding of sentence construction. (10.6.2)
- Apply appropriate manuscript conventions. (10.6.4)

Skills and Strategies You Will Learn in Part 2

In Part 2, you will learn

- to **form clear pictures** and use them to help you **paraphrase.** (p. 664)
- to **break down long sentences** into parts as a step in **paraphrasing.** (p. 680)
- to **quote, paraphrase, and critique information sources.** (p. 696)

Using the Skills and Strategies in Part 2

In Part 2, you will learn to break complex sentences and ideas into parts and visualize information in order to paraphrase. You will also practice using these skills when reading informational material. Restating information in your own words helps you understand and remember your reading.

The example shows how you can apply the skills and strategies in Part 2.

Example	Paraphrase
Two roads diverged in a wood, and I— *(The first thought creates a word picture.)*	I saw two paths going different ways through the woods.
I took the one less traveled by, *(The second thought tells something the speaker did.)*	I chose the path that most people do not take.
And that has made all the difference. *(The third thought comments on the speaker's choice.)*	Choosing that path made a big difference.

Academic Vocabulary: Words for Analyzing Literature

These words will help you to write and talk about analyzing literature.

Word	Definition	Example Sentence
distort *v.*	twist or change the meaning or intent	When you paraphrase poetry, do not *distort* the meaning.
minimize *v.*	make small; reduce in size, amount, or importance	*Minimize* the reliance on plot to support your thesis.
terminology *n.*	terms or system of terms associated with a specific science, art, and so on	The author uses *terminology* that is unfamiliar to the reader.
recur *v.*	come up or happen again	A question left unanswered is likely to *recur*.
ideology *n.*	doctrines or opinions; study of one basic idea	Each group of critics has its own *ideology*.

Vocabulary Skills You Will Learn in Part 2

> A **suffix** is a syllable or syllables added to the end of a word that alter the meaning of the word and sometimes its function in a sentence.

In Part 2, you will learn

- the suffix *-ize*   (p. 678)
- the suffix *-logy*   (p. 694)

Each of these suffixes indicates a particular part of speech. You can use suffixes as clues to help you determine the meaning and function of a word.

Suffix	Meaning	Examples	Part of Speech
-ize	make, become, or engage in	*humanize, Americanize*	verb
-logy	science or study of	*biology, astrology*	noun

Activity Predict whether each of the following is a noun or verb: *sociology, anthropology, ideology, publicize, summarize, subsidize.* Check your answers in a dictionary. Then, use each word in a sentence.

You can apply the instruction on this page to these poems.

**Academic
Standards**

- Evaluate the use of literary
  devices including figurative
  language, imagery,
  allegory, and symbolism.
  (10.3.7)
- Evaluate the aesthetic
  qualities of style. (10.3.11)
- Apply appropriate
  manuscript conventions.
  (10.6.4)

Literary Analysis

Figurative language is language that is not meant to be taken literally. Poets often use the following **figures of speech,** or specific types of figurative language, to convey their ideas in fresh and innovative ways. Each of these figures of speech is a kind of **analogy,** or comparison of two things that are alike in certain respects but not in others.

- A **simile** is a comparison of unlike things using the word *like* or *as.* A simile is an expressed analogy. *Example:* He runs *like* a cheetah.

- In a **metaphor,** one thing is spoken about as if it were something else. A metaphor is an implied analogy. *Example:* During the holidays, the stores *are* zoos.

- In **personification,** an object, animal, or idea is spoken of as if it were human. *Example:* Our cow was queen of the fair.

Because figurative language is often used to express meaning in concrete pictures, it is an important source of **imagery,** or word-pictures, in poetry.

Reading Skill

To understand a poem, **paraphrase** it, or restate the meaning of lines in your own words. Use a chart like this one to paraphrase as you read.

- Begin by **picturing the imagery,** forming clear pictures of the descriptive details in the poem.
- Then, consider how the lines you will paraphrase are connected with these pictures.

Descriptive Details

"A snapshot in the radiant flood, / Raccoon glares, as any outlaw should. / His craft lies knotted in his paws; / His canny forest ways undo suburban laws."

What I Picture

a raccoon caught in the light when someone opens the back door

My Paraphrase

The raccoon freezes in the light of an open door. He is clever with his paws and can outsmart the person whose yard he is visiting.

Vocabulary Builder

Poetry Collection 1

- countenance (kount´ 'n əns) *n.* face; the look of a face, showing a person's nature (p. 669) *Joe's* <u>countenance</u> *showed the calm he felt.*

- tremulous (trem´ yōō ləs) *adj.* trembling; quivering (p. 669) *I could tell he was nervous by his* <u>tremulous</u> *voice.*

Poetry Collection 2

- flourishes (flʉr´ ish es) *v.* grows vigorously; thrives (p. 674) *This plant* <u>flourishes</u> *in sunlight but has a hard time growing in shade.*

- circuit (sʉr´ kit) *n.* act of going around something (p. 675) *The moon makes a monthly* <u>circuit</u> *of Earth.*

Poetry

Connecting to the Literature

Reading/Writing Connection The poets in Poetry Collection 1 remind us that even ordinary events contain a little bit of the extraordinary. Think of an ordinary daily event. Jot down notes on how this event contributes something special to your day. Use at least three of these words: *create, maximize, enrich, stimulate, display.*

Meet the Author

Yusef **Komunyakaa** (b. 1947)
"Glory" (p. 666)

Poet Yusef Komunyakaa has come a long way in his life. Born in the small rural town of Bogalusa, Louisiana, he is now a creative writing professor at Princeton University in New Jersey. Komunyakaa's collection *Neon Vernacular* earned him a Pulitzer Prize in 1994. He has said that "the writer has to get down to the guts of the thing. . . . "

Eve **Merriam** (1916–1992)
"Metaphor" (p. 668)

Eve Merriam developed a fascination with poetry at an early age. She has written poetry for both children and adults. Merriam has called poetry the most immediate and richest form of communication.

Emily **Dickinson** (1830–1886)
"The Wind—tapped like a tired Man" (p. 669)

Now regarded as one of America's greatest poets, Emily Dickinson was scarcely known during her own time. She never married and spent almost her entire life in the home of her family. As she grew older, she rarely left her house. Although she wrote 1,775 poems, only seven were published during her life—and those were published anonymously.

Go Online
Author Link

For: More about these authors
Visit: www.PHSchool.com
Web Code: eqe-9408

GLORY

Yusef Komunyakaa

Most were married teenagers
Working knockout shifts daybreak
To sunset six days a week—
Already old men playing ball
5   In a field between a row of shotgun houses
& the Magazine Lumber Company.
They were all Jackie Robinson
& Willie Mays, a touch of
Josh Gibson & Satchell Paige[1]
10   In each stance & swing, a promise
Like a hesitation pitch always
At the edge of their lives,
Arms sharp as rifles.
The Sunday afternoon heat
15   Flared like thin flowered skirts
As children & wives cheered.
The men were like cats
Running backwards to snag
Pop-ups & high-flies off
20   Fences, stealing each other's glory.
The old deacons & raconteurs[2]
Who umpired made an *Out* or *Safe*
Into a song & dance routine.
Runners hit the dirt
25   & slid into homeplate,
Cleats catching light,
As they conjured escapes, outfoxing
Double plays. In the few seconds
It took a man to eye a woman
30   Upon the makeshift bleachers,
A stolen base or homerun
Would help another man
Survive the new week.

Literary Analysis
Figurative Language
What does the simile in lines 14–15 tell you about the way in which the heat is rising?

---

1. Jackie Robinson / & Willie Mays . . . / Josh Gibson & Satchell Paige African American baseball stars of the 1920s through the 1970s.
2. deacons & raconteurs (rak´ än tʉrz´) assistant officers of a church and skilled storytellers.

◀ **Critical Viewing**   Which details of the poem are reflected in this photograph? **[Connect]**

Metaphor

Eve Merriam

Morning is
a new sheet of paper
for you to write on.

Whatever you want to say,
5   all day,
until night
folds it up
and files it away.

The bright words and the dark words
10 are gone
until dawn
and a new day
to write on.

Literary Analysis
Figurative Language
What image does the poet use to convey the idea that each morning is a new start?

The Wind— tapped like a tired Man

Emily Dickinson

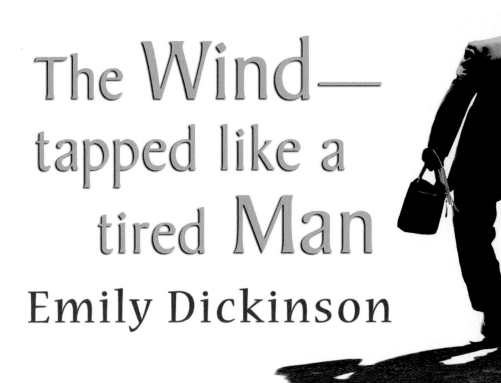

The Wind—tapped like a tired Man—
And like a Host—"Come in"
I boldly answered—entered then
My Residence within

5 A Rapid—footless Guest—
To offer whom a Chair
Were as impossible as hand
A Sofa to the Air—

No Bone had He to bind Him—
10 His Speech was like the Push
Of numerous Humming Birds at once
From a superior Bush—

His <u>Countenance</u>—a Billow—
His Fingers, as He passed
15 Let go a music—as of tunes
Blown <u>tremulous</u> in Glass—

He visited—still flitting—
Then like a timid Man
Again, He tapped—'twas flurriedly—
20 And I became alone—

Apply the Skills

Poetry Collection 1

Thinking About the Selections

1. **Respond:** Which poem spoke to you most directly? Why?
2. **(a) Recall:** What hours do the men in "Glory" work?
   (b) Analyze Cause and Effect: What does the phrase "already old men" suggest about the effect of this work schedule?
   (c) Draw Conclusions: In what way might a "stolen base or home run" help a man "survive the new week"?
3. **(a) Recall:** In "Metaphor," to what does the speaker compare the morning? **(b) Analyze:** To what does she compare a person's actions during the day? **(c) Apply:** What outlook or attitude toward a new day might this poem inspire in readers? Explain.
4. **(a) Recall:** Who is the guest in "The Wind—tapped like a tired Man"? **(b) Analyze:** Identify three ways in which the guest is unlike any other. **(c) Hypothesize:** Do you think the speaker sees the wind as menacing or kind? Explain.

Literary Analysis

5. Among the three poems in Poetry Collection 1, find two examples of a **simile.**
6. Find an example of a **metaphor** in one of the three poems.
7. Identify an example of **personification** in one of the three poems.
8. **(a)** Using a chart like the one shown, explain and evaluate each of the devices you have identified. **(b)** Share and discuss your evaluations with a partner. **(c)** In the last column of the chart, explain whether or not your discussion changed your appreciation of the poems.

Poem	Device	Explanation	First Evaluation	Final Evaluation

Reading Skill

9. **(a)** Describe the image you picture when reading the third stanza of "The Wind—tapped like a tired Man." **(b) Paraphrase** this stanza.
10. **(a)** Paraphrase "Metaphor." **(b)** Compare your paraphrase to the original. What qualities does the poem have that your paraphrase does not?

QuickReview

Poems at a Glance
In **"Glory,"** a baseball game lifts players above their workaday lives.

In **"Metaphor,"** the poet asserts that each day is yours to fill as you wish.

In **"The Wind— tapped like a tired Man,"** the wind is a strange visitor.

Go Online
—Assessment
For: Self-test
Visit: www.PHSchool.com
Web Code: eqa-6407

Figurative Language: language not meant to be interpreted literally, including *simile, metaphor,* and *personification*

Paraphrase: a restatement in your own words of a work or section of a work

Vocabulary Builder

Practice Use the following word pairs correctly in sentences.

1. countenance; mirror   **2.** tremulous; speech

Adding Words to Your Vocabulary Using a thesaurus or a dictionary, find one **synonym,** or word with similar meaning, for each of the words in the vocabulary list for Poetry Collection 1, on page 664. Use each synonym correctly in a sentence. (For more on using a dictionary or thesaurus, see pages R6–R7.)

Writing

Write a **critical essay** to explain which poem you found most effective.
- Decide on the criteria you will use in your evaluation. For example, you might rate the poems based on the strength of the feelings each inspired in you. Alternatively, you might judge each on the basis of how clever the use of language is.
- Review the poems carefully, using your criteria as a guide.
- As you draft, present your evaluation concisely. Then, support each point with relevant quotations from the poems.

For *Vocabulary, Grammar,* and *Assessment,*
see **Build Language Skills,** pages 678–679.

Extend Your Learning

Listening and Speaking With classmates, hold a **group discussion** of Merriam's claim that each new day is like a fresh sheet of paper. Appoint someone to encourage everyone to participate. Express your opinions clearly. Follow these tips:
- If someone else makes a point with which you agree, support his or her point by mentioning further examples or connected ideas.
- If you disagree with someone's point, express your disagreement in a constructive way, offering reasons for your own view.

Research and Technology Write and present a brief **literary history report** explaining how Dickinson's poems were eventually published. Use a variety of research sources, including encyclopedias and the Internet. Check sources against one another, considering the reliability of each.

Build Understanding • *Poetry Collection 2*

Connecting to the Literature

Reading/Writing Connection Being human means being limited—not understanding everything, not always doing the right thing. In each of the poems in Poetry Collection 2, the poets confront life's limitations. Write a sentence about something you once wished you knew or could do. Explain whether or not you were able to overcome this limitation. Use at least three of these words: *compensate, evolve, adapt, rely, achieve.*

Review
For **Literary Analysis, Reading Skill,** and **Vocabulary Builder,** see page 664.

Meet the Authors

Edna St. Vincent **Millay** (1892–1950)
"Conscientious Objector" (p. 673)
Edna St. Vincent Millay was not yet in college when she first won fame as a poet. After graduating from Vassar, in Poughkeepsie, New York, she moved to New York City, where she acted in plays and pursued her writing career. Beautiful and outspoken, she received both praise and scorn for her controversial opinions on issues such as women's rights.

Dahlia **Ravikovitch** (1936–2005)
"Pride" (p. 674)
The Israeli poet Dahlia Ravikovitch was born in a town near Tel Aviv and was raised on a kibbutz, a cooperative settlement. Her father's death in an accident when she was six was a powerful influence on her life and work. Her intensely personal poems are charged with images from nature, history, and religion.

Emily **Dickinson** (1830–1886)
"Tell all the Truth but tell it slant" (p. 675)
Although Emily Dickinson led a reclusive life—she rarely left her home and saw only seven of her poems published in her lifetime—today she shines as one of the brightest stars of American poetry. It was only in 1955 that a scholar, Thomas H. Johnson, was able to assemble her complete works in one book. Dickinson is a truly individual voice in poetry.

For: More about these authors
Visit: www.PHSchool.com
Web Code: eqe-9409

CONSCIENTIOUS OBJECTOR[1]

Edna St. Vincent Millay

I shall die, but that is all that I shall do for Death.

I hear him leading his horse out of the stall; I hear the
    clatter on the barn-floor.
He is in haste; he has business in Cuba, business in the
    Balkans, many calls to make this morning.
But I will not hold the bridle while he cinches the girth.[2]
5 And he may mount by himself: I will not give him a leg up.

Though he flick my shoulders with his whip, I will not tell
    him which way the fox ran.
With his hoof on my breast, I will not tell him where the
    black boy hides in the swamp.
I shall die, but that is all that I shall do for Death; I am not
    on his pay-roll.

I will not tell him the whereabouts of my friends nor of my
    enemies either.
10 Though he promise me much, I will not map him the route to
    any man's door.

Am I a spy in the land of the living, that I should deliver men
    to Death?
Brother, the password and the plans of our city are safe with
    me; never through me
Shall you be overcome.

Literary Analysis
Figurative Language
Identify two details in this stanza that contribute to the personification of Death.

---

1. conscientious (kän´ shē en´ shəs) **objector** one who refuses to participate in warfare for religious or ethical reasons.
2. cinches the girth securely fastens the band that goes around a horse's belly to hold the saddle on.

Pride

Dahlia Ravikovitch
translated by Chana Bloch and Ariel Bloch

I tell you, even rocks crack,
and not because of age.
For years they lie on their backs
in the heat and the cold,
5   so many years,
it almost seems peaceful.
They don't move, so the cracks stay hidden.
A kind of pride.
Years pass over them, waiting.
10 Whoever is going to shatter them
hasn't come yet.
And so the moss <u>flourishes</u>, the seaweed
whips around,
the sea pushes through and rolls back—
15 the rocks seem motionless.
Till a little seal comes to rub against them,
comes and goes away.
And suddenly the rock has an open wound.
I told you, when rocks break, it happens by surprise.
20 And people, too.

Vocabulary Builder
flourishes (flʉr´ ish es)
v. grows vigorously;
thrives

▼ **Critical Viewing**
In what ways does this
photograph show
both the strength and
the fragility identified
in the poem?
[Analyze]

Tell all the Truth but tell it slant
Emily Dickinson

Tell all the Truth but tell it slant—
Success in <u>Circuit</u> lies
Too bright for our infirm Delight
The Truth's superb surprise
5   As Lightning to the Children eased
With explanation kind
The Truth must dazzle gradually
Or every man be blind—

Reading Skill
Paraphrasing Restate the first line in your own words.

Vocabulary Builder
circuit (sʉrˊ kit) *n.* act of going around something

▲ **Critical Viewing**   How does this painting represent the way that, according to the speaker, the truth must be told? **[Interpret]**

Apply the Skills

Poetry Collection 2

Thinking About the Selections

1. **Respond:** Which poems did you agree with most? Why?
2. **(a) Recall:** What are two things the speaker in "Conscientious Objector" will not do? **(b) Apply:** Give your own example of a specific action the speaker would not take. Explain your choice.
3. **(a) Recall:** According to the speaker in "Pride," what may rocks hide from view? **(b) Interpret:** Why might "A kind of pride" lead them to hide this thing? **(c) Extend:** What advice would the speaker in "Pride" give to someone dealing with stress or grief?
4. **(a) Recall:** According to the speaker in "Tell all the Truth but tell it slant," how much of the truth should be told? **(b) Interpret:** What does the speaker mean by the expression "tell it slant"? **(c) Make a Judgment:** Do you agree that truth often takes the form of a "surprise"? Explain.
5. **Extend:** Give an example in which telling the truth is impossible or dangerous, and explain what Dickinson might say about it.

Literary Analysis

6. Among the three poems in Poetry Collection 2, find one example of a **simile**.
7. Find an example of a **metaphor** in one of the three poems.
8. Identify an example of **personification** in one of the three poems.
9. **(a)** Using a chart like the one shown, explain and evaluate each of the devices you have identified. **(b)** Share and discuss your evaluations with a partner. **(c)** In the last column of the chart, explain whether or not your discussion changed your appreciation of the poems.

Poem	Device	Explanation	First Evaluation	Final Evaluation

Reading Skill

10. **(a)** Describe an image you pictured when reading "Tell all the Truth but tell it slant." **(b) Paraphrase** the poem.
11. **(a)** Paraphrase the last two stanzas of "Conscientious Objector." **(b)** Compare your paraphrase to the original. What qualities does the poem have that your paraphrase does not?

QuickReview

Poems at a Glance
In **"Conscientious Objector,"** the speaker views death as the enemy.

In **"Pride,"** the speaker asserts that rocks hide cracks that will one day break them.

"Tell all the Truth but tell it slant" offers a new take on the value of honesty.

Go Online
—Assessment
For: Self-test
Visit: www.PHSchool.com
Web Code: eqa-6408

Figurative Language: language not meant to be interpreted literally, including *simile, metaphor,* and *personification*

Paraphrase: a restatement in your own words of a work or section of a work

Vocabulary Builder

Practice Use the following word pairs correctly in sentences.

1. flourishes; talent   **2.** circuit; speed

Adding Words to Your Vocabulary Using a thesaurus or a dictionary, find one **synonym,** or word with similar meaning, for each of the words in the vocabulary list for Poetry Collection 2, on page 664. Use each synonym correctly in a sentence. (For more on using a dictionary or thesaurus, see pages R6–R7.)

Writing

Write a **critical essay** in which you explain which of the poems in Poetry Collection 2 you found most effective.
- Decide on the criteria you will use in your evaluation. For example, you might rate the poems based on the strength of the feelings each inspired in you. Alternatively, you might judge each on the basis of how clever the use of language is.
- Review the poems carefully, using your criteria as a guide.
- As you draft, present your evaluation concisely. Then, support each point with relevant quotations from the poems.

For *Grammar, Vocabulary,* and *Assessment,*
see **Build Language Skills,** pages 678–679.

Extend Your Learning

Listening and Speaking With classmates, hold a **group discussion** of Dickinson's advice about the best way to tell someone the truth. Appoint someone to encourage everyone to participate. Express your opinions clearly. Follow these tips:
- If someone else makes a point with which you agree, support his or her point by mentioning further examples or connected ideas.
- If you disagree with someone's point, express your disagreement in a constructive way, offering reasons for your own view.

Research and Technology Write and present a brief **literary history report** on Edna St. Vincent Millay's career. Use a variety of research sources, including encyclopedias and the Internet. Check the claims in one source against claims in the others, considering the reliability of each source. Present your report to the class.

Build Language Skills

Poetry Collection 1 • Poetry Collection 2

Vocabulary Skill

Suffixes The **suffix -ize** appears at the ends of verbs. It means "make, become, or engage in." For example, to *minimize* is to "make minimum"—to make as small as possible. In contrast, to *maximize* is to "make maximum"—to make as large as possible.

Practice Write the verb ending in *-ize* that corresponds with the italicized word. Use a dictionary to help you determine the correct spelling of each verb. Then, use each verb you write in a sentence.

1. make into a *drama*
2. engage in *strategy*
3. engage in thinking about *theories*
4. make *legal*
5. become *stable*

Grammar Lesson

Prepositional Phrases A **prepositional phrase** can modify other words by functioning either as an adjective or as an adverb within sentences.

A *prepositional phrase* that serves as an adjective is termed an **adjective phrase.** It modifies a noun or pronoun and tells *what kind* or *which one.*

▶ **Example: Adjective Phrase:** The woman *in the blue dress* is a singer.

A *prepositional phrase* that serves as an adverb is termed an **adverb phrase.** It modifies a verb, an adjective, or an adverb. It tells *where, when, in what way,* or *to what extent.*

▶ **Example: Adverb Phrase:** Her music group sings *at the folk festival.*

Practice Add a prepositional phrase in the blank. The phrase should act as an adverb or adjective phrase and give the reader additional information.

1. The Sanchez family moved _____.
2. Someone _____ told me the news.
3. They relocated _____.
4. They bought a farm _____.
5. The new location will mean a change _____.

MorePractice

For more practice with prepositional phrases, see the Grammar Handbook, p. R40.

WG Prentice Hall Writing and Grammar Connection: Chapter 20, Section 1

Reading: Paraphrasing

Standards Assessed
• 10.3.7
• 10.3.11
• 10.6.4

Directions: *Read this stanza. Then, answer the questions.*

In a shoe box stuffed in an old nylon stocking
Sleeps the baby mouse I found in the meadow,
Where he trembled and shook beneath a stick
Till I caught him up by the tail and brought him in,
5 Cradled in my hand,
A little quaker, the whole body of him trembling, . . .
Wriggling like a minuscule puppy.

—from "The Meadow Mouse" by Theodore Roethke

1. Which best paraphrases the first two lines?
  A In the meadow, I found a shoebox stuffed with an old stocking and a sleeping mouse.
  B I put my pet baby mouse in a shoe box stuffed with an old stocking and buried him in the meadow.
  C I stuffed a mouse in a shoebox with an old stocking and put it in the meadow.
  D I found a baby mouse in the meadow and put him in a shoebox inside an old stocking.

2. Which best paraphrases the last line?
  A squirming like a tiny dog
  B wiggling like a fat dog
  C squeezing through like a large pet going through a small opening
  D teasing a small puppy nobody likes

3. Which choice best paraphrases the stanza as a whole?
  A I found a mouse in a forest and we became fast friends.
  B I was hiking up a mountain with my mouse in a box. The mouse was scared.
  C I found a mouse in a meadow. He was scared of me at first, but now he is sleeping comfortably in a shoebox.
  D My mouse is scared of me, even though he sleeps in a comfortable box with an old nylon stocking.

Timed Writing: Persuasion [Connections]

Choose one poem from Poetry Collection 1 or Poetry Collection 2. Analyze how the visual descriptions in the poem help readers understand its meaning. **(25 minutes)**

Writing Workshop: *Work in Progress*

Analytic Response to Literature

For an analytic response you might write, choose a story or poem that you like. Write five questions about the work's quality. Then, write five questions about how the work achieves its purpose. Put your questions in your writing portfolio.

Build Skills
Poetry Collection 1 • Poetry Collection 2

You can apply the instruction on this page to these poems.

Poetry Collection 1
The Weary Blues, page 682
In Flanders Fields, page 684
Jazz Fantasia, page 685

Poetry Collection 2
The Kraken, page 689
Meeting at Night, page 690
Reapers, page 691

Literary Analysis

To spark the music in words, poets use a variety of **sound devices,** or patterns of word-sounds. These include the following:

- **Alliteration:** repetition of consonant sounds at the beginnings of nearby words, as in "*silent song*"
- **Assonance:** repetition of vowel sounds in nearby stressed syllables, as in "*deep* and *dream´less.*" Unlike rhyming syllables, assonant syllables end in different consonants.
- **Consonance:** repetition of consonant sounds at the ends of nearby stressed syllables with different vowel sounds, as in "*heat* of *light´ning*"
- **Onomatopoeia:** use of words to imitate actual sounds, such as *buzz, tap,* or *splash*

Sound devices can add to the mood of a poem, imitate the sound of events, or reflect or emphasize a poem's meaning. As you read, note how poets use sound devices to create a mood or emphasize their ideas.

Reading Skill

To help you understand poetry, **paraphrase** poems, restating the ideas in your own words. First, **break down long sentences** into parts.
- Identify the main actions and who or what performs them.
- Identify details that show when, where, how, or why each action is performed.

As you read, use a diagram like the one shown to break down sentences.

Breaking Down Long Sentences to Paraphrase

"When fighting for his country, he lost an arm and was suddenly afraid: 'From now on, I shall only be able to do things by halves....'" from "A Man," by Nina Cassian

Who? he
Did what? lost, was suddenly afraid

Paraphrase: He lost his arm fighting in a war and was afraid of what his life would be like.

Vocabulary Builder

Poetry Collection 1

■ **pallor** (pal´ ər) *n.* lack of color; unnatural paleness (p. 683) *By the <u>pallor</u> of his face, I could tell he was frightened.*

■ **ebony** (eb´ ə nē) *adj.* black (p. 683) *The <u>ebony</u> floor contrasts with the white walls.*

Poetry Collection 2

■ **millennial** (mi len´ ē əl) *adj.* of 1,000 years (p. 689) *Built in 1023, the abbey will hold its <u>millennial</u> celebration in 2023.*

■ **slumbering** (slum´ bər iŋ) *adj.* sleeping (p. 689) *Do not wake a <u>slumbering</u> bear.*

Build Understanding • *Poetry Collection 1*

Connecting to the Literature

Reading/Writing Connection Two poems in this grouping are about music. Describe your own favorite type of music. Explain what it is like and what you enjoy about it. Use at least three of these words: *accompany, capture, demonstrate, illuminate, appreciate.*

Meet the Authors

Langston **Hughes** (1902–1967)

"The Weary Blues" (p. 682)

As a young man, Langston Hughes moved from Missouri to Kansas to Illinois to Cleveland, Ohio, where he was voted class poet in high school. Later, he settled in the Harlem section of New York City. He contributed to the Harlem Renaissance, a flowering of African American artistic activity in the 1920s and 1930s. Hughes once defined poetry as "the human soul entire, squeezed like a lemon or lime, drop by drop, into atomic words."

John **McCrae** (1872–1918)

"In Flanders Fields" (p. 684)

Soldier, poet, doctor—John McCrae was a man of many talents. As a teenager in Ontario, Canada, McCrae joined the militia his father commanded. He also began writing poetry, and he published his first poems as a student at the University of Toronto. After earning a degree in medicine, McCrae fought in the Boer War in South Africa (1899–1902) and served as a medical officer in World War I (1914–1918). He died before the war ended.

Carl **Sandburg** (1878–1967)

"Jazz Fantasia" (p. 685)

Carl Sandburg once observed that some poetry was perfect only in form: "All dressed up with nowhere to go." In contrast, his own poetry dresses in blue jeans, going everywhere and speaking in the voices of everyday people. Born in Galesburg, Illinois, Sandburg settled for a time in Chicago. In addition to poetry, Sandburg is famous for his biography of Abraham Lincoln.

For: More about these authors
Visit: www.PHSchool.com
Author Link **Web Code:** eqe-9410

The Weary Blues
Langston Hughes

Droning a drowsy syncopated[1] tune,
Rocking back and forth to a mellow croon,
    I heard a Negro play.
Down on Lenox Avenue[2] the other night
5 By the pale dull <u>pallor</u> of an old gas light
    He did a lazy sway. . . .
    He did a lazy sway. . . .
To the tune o' those Weary Blues.
With his <u>ebony</u> hands on each ivory key
10 He made that poor piano moan with melody.
    O Blues!
Swaying to and fro on his rickety stool
He played that sad raggy tune like a musical fool.
    Sweet Blues!
15 Coming from a black man's soul.
    O Blues!
In a deep song voice with a melancholy tone
I heard that Negro sing, that old piano moan—
    "Ain't got nobody in all this world,
20   Ain't got nobody but ma self.
    I's gwine to quit ma frownin'
    And put ma troubles on the shelf."
Thump, thump, thump, went his foot on the floor.
He played a few chords then he sang some more—
25   "I got the Weary Blues
    And I can't be satisfied.
    Got the Weary Blues
    And can't be satisfied—
    I ain't happy no mo'
30   And I wish that I had died."
And far into the night he crooned that tune.
The stars went out and so did the moon.
The singer stopped playing and went to bed
While the Weary Blues echoed through his head.
35 He slept like a rock or a man that's dead.

Vocabulary Builder
pallor (pal´ ər) *n.* lack of color; unnatural paleness
ebony (eb´ ə nē) *adj.* black

Literary Analysis
Sound Devices Why is "thump, thump, thump" an example of onomatopoeia?

---

1. syncopated (sin´ kə pāt´ id) *adj.* with a catchy or an emphatic rhythm created by accenting beats that are usually unaccented.
2. Lenox Avenue street in Harlem, a historic African American neighborhood in New York City.

◀ Critical Viewing Does this painting express the same mood as Hughes's poem? Explain. **[Interpret]**

IN FLANDERS FIELDS *John McCrae*

Background The devastation of the First World War (1914–1918) brought forth a sad beauty. In the torn-up battlegrounds of Flanders, a region of Belgium, thousands of poppies sprang up, flourishing in the fields cleared by war. McCrae turned these flowers into a symbol that generations have worn to honor the dead.

> In Flanders fields the poppies blow
> Between the crosses, row on row,
>   That mark our place; and in the sky
>   The larks, still bravely singing, fly
> 5 Scarce heard amid the guns below.
>
> We are the Dead. Short days ago
> We lived, felt dawn, saw sunset glow,
>   Loved and were loved, and now we lie
>   In Flanders fields.
>
> 10 Take up our quarrel with the foe:
> To you from failing hands we throw
>   The torch; be yours to hold it high.
>   If ye break faith with us who die
> We shall not sleep, though poppies grow
> 15   In Flanders fields.

◀ **Critical Viewing**
Do you think that this tombstone is a fitting one for McCrae, who died during the war he wrote about? Explain.
[Make a Judgment]

Vocabulary Builder

Practice An **oxymoron** is a phrase combining contradictory or opposing ideas, often used as a figure of speech for poetic effect. Explain whether each phrase below is an oxymoron.

1. ebony pallor   **3.** dark ebony
2. healthy pallor

Adding Words to Your Vocabulary Look up *pallid* in a dictionary. Explain how its meaning is related to the meaning of *pallor.* Then, use both words in sentences. (For more on using a dictionary, see page R6.)

Writing

Using the works in this collection as a model, write a **poem** about your favorite kind of music. Use sound devices to help you create a mood, make your ideas memorable, or capture the sounds that you describe.

- Before you write, jot down the emotions and feelings the type of music inspires in you. Determine the mood you want to convey.
- As you draft, work sound devices such as alliteration and ono-matopoeia into your poem to bring out the energy of your ideas.
- Read your draft aloud and revise to achieve the sounds you want.

For *Grammar, Vocabulary,* and *Assessment,* see **Build Language Skills,** pages 694–695.

Extend Your Learning

Listening and Speaking With a group, consult poetry anthologies to choose three poets whose work you would like to hear read aloud. Find recordings of their works online, in school, or at a library, and hold a **poetry listening.** Then, discuss what hearing the poems adds to your experience of them.

Research and Technology Learn more about the Harlem Renaissance, a movement that Hughes helped define. Choose a visual artist associated with the movement, and prepare a **visual arts presentation** about three of his or her works. In your presentation, compare the artworks to Hughes's poem. Afterward, lead a discussion about the artworks and how they reflect African American experience. Then, collect classmates' questions and report back with answers.

Build Understanding • *Poetry Collection 2*

Connecting to the Literature

Reading/Writing Connection You may be surprised to meet a giant squid and a rat in these poems—such creatures seem the very opposite of poetry! Write two or three sentences in which you describe another "unpoetic" animal. Use at least three of these words: *display, dominate, embody, focus, equate, illustrate.*

Review
For **Literary Analysis, Reading Skill,** and **Vocabulary Builder,** see page 680.

Meet the Authors

Alfred, **Lord Tennyson** (1809–1892)
"The Kraken" (p. 689)
In an age when poets were often celebrities, Alfred, Lord Tennyson was perhaps the most celebrated of all. Named England's poet laureate in 1850, Tennyson cut quite a figure, dressing in a dashing cape and large-brimmed felt hat. When not in London, he lived on the Isle of Wight in a large home that is now an inn. As laureate, he often wrote patriotic verse and poems drawn from history and legend.

Robert **Browning** (1812–1889)
"Meeting at Night" (p. 690)
During his lifetime, Robert Browning was not as famous as his wife, poet Elizabeth Barrett Browning. Today, though, it is Robert who is considered the more innovative poet. He is admired especially for his dramatic monologues, poems in which characters speak directly to readers or other characters. Browning's eerie poem "Childe Roland to the Dark Tower Came" helped inspire Stephen King's *Dark Tower* series.

Jean **Toomer** (1894–1967)
"Reapers" (p. 691)
"My position in America has been a curious one," Jean Toomer once observed. His maternal grandfather was the first African American ever to serve as a state governor (of Louisiana). Reflecting on his diverse ethnic background—French, Dutch, German, and Native American, as well as African American—Toomer called himself the "human race." He won early fame with the 1923 publication of his book *Cane,* an exploration of African American culture.

Go Online
Author Link
For: More about these authors
Visit: www.PHSchool.com
Web Code: eqe-9411

The Kraken
Alfred, Lord Tennyson

◀ Critical Viewing
Which details in the poem does the illustration depict? **[Connect]**

Below the thunders of the upper deep;
Far, far beneath in the abysmal sea,
His ancient, dreamless, uninvaded sleep
The Kraken[1] sleepeth: faintest sunlights flee
5 About his shadowy sides: above him swell
Huge sponges of <u>millennial</u> growth and height;
And far away into the sickly light,
From many a wondrous grot[2] and secret cell
Unnumbered and enormous polypi[3]
10 Winnow[4] with giant arms the <u>slumbering</u> green.
There hath he lain for ages and will lie
Battening[5] upon huge seaworms in his sleep,
Until the latter fire[6] shall heat the deep;
Then once by man and angels to be seen,
15 In roaring he shall rise and on the surface die.

Vocabulary Builder
millennial (mi len´ ē əl) *adj.* of 1,000 years
slumbering (slum´ bər iŋ) *adj.* sleeping

Reading Skill
Paraphrasing What is the main action in lines 7–10, and who or what performs that action?

---

1. Kraken (krä´ kən) *n.* in Scandinavian folklore, a sea monster resembling a giant squid.
2. grot (grät) *n.* grotto; cave.
3. polypi (päl´ i pē) *n.* sea creatures with long, waving tentacles around the mouth, such as the sea anemone or hydra.
4. Winnow (win´ ō) *v.* fan; beat with wings or, here, tentacles.
5. Battening (bat´'n iŋ) *v.* feeding on; growing fat on.
6. the latter fire the apocalypse; the end of the world.

Meeting at Night
ROBERT BROWNING

◄ **Critical Viewing**
Compare the mood of this scene with the mood Browning creates in the poem. **[Compare and Contrast]**

1

The gray sea and the long black land;
And the yellow half-moon large and low;
And the startled little waves that leap
In fiery ringlets from their sleep,
5 As I gain the cove with pushing prow,
And quench its speed i' the slushy sand.

2

Then a mile of warm sea-scented beach;
Three fields to cross till a farm appears;
A tap at the pane, the quick sharp scratch
10 And blue spurt of a lighted match,
And a voice less loud, through its joys and fears,
Than the two hearts beating each to each!

Literary Analysis
Sound Devices Why is "sea-scented beach" an example of both alliteration and of assonance?

Reapers
JEAN TOOMER

Black reapers with the sound of steel on stones
Are sharpening scythes. I see them place the hones[1]
In their hip-pockets as a thing that's done,
And start their silent swinging, one by one.
5 Black horses drive a mower through the weeds,
And there, a field rat, startled, squealing bleeds,
His belly close to ground. I see the blade,
Blood-stained, continue cutting weeds and shade.

---

1. scythes (sīt͟hz) **. . . hones** A scythe is a tool for cutting grain or grass, consisting of a sharp blade attached to a long handle. A hone is a hard stone used to sharpen a metal blade.

▼ **Critical Viewing**
Identify one similarity and one difference between this scene and the scene in the poem. **[Compare and Contrast]**

Apply the Skills

Poetry Collection 2

Thinking About the Selections

1. **Respond:** Which of the three poems left you with the picture you will remember longest? Why?
2. **(a) Recall:** In "The Kraken," what has the Kraken been doing, and how do you know? **(b) Infer:** According to the poem, what is the only thing that could cause a change in the Kraken's activity? **(c) Analyze:** What would be the outcome of such an event?
3. **(a) Interpret:** Describe the journey the speaker makes in "Meeting at Night." **(b) Draw Conclusions:** What is the situation of the two people in the poem? Support your answer.
4. **(a) Analyze:** Identify the series of colors named or suggested in "Meeting at Night." **(b) Connect:** How might this series of colors reflect the speaker's emotional and physical journey?
5. **(a) Infer:** In "Reapers," will the reapers stop their work before it is done? Explain how you know. **(b) Analyze:** What two contrasting ideas are expressed in the final description of the blade? **(c) Draw Conclusions:** What does the poem suggest about life?

Literary Analysis

6. **(a)** Using a chart like the one shown, identify examples of **sound devices** in "The Kraken" and "Reapers."

Alliteration	Consonance	Assonance	Onomatopoeia

   (b) For each device you list, explain what it adds to the poem.
7. Identify two sound devices in "Meeting at Night" that capture the sounds of the events they describe. Explain your answers.
8. **(a)** Compare the effects of sound devices in "Meeting at Night" with the effects of sound devices in one of the other poems. **(b)** Discuss your answer with a partner. **(c)** Together, draw a conclusion about the way that sound devices can be used in poetry. Present your conclusion to the class.

Reading Skill

9. **(a)** Break down the first clause (ending on the colon) of "The Kraken" by identifying the action and who or what is completing the action. **(b) Paraphrase** the clause.
10. **(a)** Paraphrase the second stanza of "Meeting at Night." **(b)** How does this paraphrase help you understand the poem?

QuickReview

Poems at a Glance
In "**The Kraken**," the poet describes a giant creature who sleeps deep below the ocean's surface.

In "**Meeting at Night**," a man travels at night to a romantic appointment.

In "**Reapers**," men are too busy to notice the effects of their work.

Go Online
Assessment
For: Self-test
Visit: www.PHSchool.com
Web Code: eqa-6410

Sound Devices: patterns of sounds in language, including *alliteration, consonance, assonance,* and *onomatopoeia*

Paraphrase: a restatement in your own words of a work or section of a work

Vocabulary Builder

Practice An **oxymoron** is a phrase combining contradictory or opposing ideas, often used as a figure of speech for poetic effect. Explain whether each phrase below is an oxymoron.

1. millennial instant

2. slumbering volcano

3. slumbering children

Adding Words to Your Vocabulary Look up *annual, biennial,* and *centennial* in a dictionary. Explain the meaning of each and its link to *millennial.* (For more on using a dictionary, see page R6.)

Writing

Write a **poem** that, like "The Kraken" or "Reapers," tells about a collision between nature and the world of people. Use sound devices to help you create a mood, make your ideas memorable, or capture the sounds that you describe.

- Before you write, choose a situation that pits nature against people or the developed world. Jot down words that describe the conflict. Based on this list, determine the mood you want to convey.
- As you draft, work sound devices such as alliteration and onomatopoeia into your poem to bring out the energy of your ideas.
- Read your draft aloud and revise to achieve the sounds you want.

For *Grammar, Vocabulary,* and *Assessment,* see **Build Language Skills,** pages 694–695.

Extend Your Learning

Listening and Speaking With a group, consult anthologies to choose three poets whose work you would like to hear. Find recordings of their works online or at a library, and hold a **poetry listening.** Discuss what hearing the poems adds to your experience of them.

Research and Technology Learn more about the Harlem Renaissance, a movement Toomer helped define. Choose a visual artist associated with the movement, and prepare a **visual arts presentation** about three of his or her works. In your presentation, compare the artwork to Toomer's poem. Afterward, lead a discussion about the artworks and how they reflect African American experience. Then, collect classmates' questions and report back with answers.

Build Language Skills

Vocabulary Skill

Suffixes The **suffix** *-logy* means "field of study." It can also refer to the principles, knowledge, or data related to a particular field. Words ending in *-logy* are almost always nouns that name something that is studied or learned.

▶ **Example:** *Biology* is the study of living things.

Practice For each of the following, tell what is studied or learned. Check your answers in a dictionary.

1. criminology
2. technology
3. geology
4. psychology
5. sociology

Grammar Lesson

Infinitives An **infinitive** is a form of the verb that generally appears with the word *to* and acts as a noun, an adjective, or an adverb.

Infinitive (noun)	Last year, my friend Ana learned *to drive.*
Infinitive (adjective)	She was motivated by a desire *to succeed.*
Infinitive (adverb)	Unfortunately, I am still unable *to drive.*

An **infinitive phrase** consists of an infinitive along with any modifiers or complements, all acting together as a single part of speech.

▶ **Example:**
Infinitive phrase: He tried *to answer decisively.*

Practice Identify the infinitive or infinitive phrase in each sentence. Then, use the infinitive or infinitive phrase in a new sentence.

1. Next year, my mom and I plan to visit northern Arizona.
2. In Flagstaff, we should be able to find an inexpensive motel.
3. Mom's dream to see the Grand Canyon will finally come true.
4. To view the orange rocks in Sedona, we will make a short trip from Flagstaff.
5. We also hope to see Monument Valley.

MorePractice

For more practice with infinitives and infinitive phrases, see the Grammar Handbook, p. R43.

W/G Prentice Hall Writing and Grammar Connection: Chapter 20, Section 1

Reading: Paraphrasing

Standards Assessed
- 10.3.11
- 10.7.1
- 10.7.10

Directions: *Read the selection. Then, answer the questions.*

1 Jonson's poetic polish and clarity offered his followers an
2 alternative to John Donne's "rough" lines and complex
3 metaphors. Donne, in turn, influenced other poets, who are
4 often classified as the metaphysical poets.

1. What comparison is made in the first sentence?
   A Jonson's sophisticated manner and Donne's provincial manner
   B Jonson's metaphysics and Donne's metaphors
   C Jonson's style and Donne's style
   D Donne's clarity and Jonson's rough lines

2. What would be a good paraphrase of the first line?
   A Jonson's poetry gave the people who liked his poetry
   B Jonson's clarity gave the people a polish
   C Jonson's clear, revised poetry gave others
   D Jonson's poetry was clear and polished.

3. The phrase "often classified" could be best reworded as
   A "usually grouped together."
   B "commonly celebrated."
   C "normally an active part of."
   D "originally from the same college."

4. The words in the last sentence which should NOT be changed in a paraphrase are
   A "Donne, in turn."
   B "influenced other poets."
   C "are often classified."
   D "metaphysical poets."

Timed Writing: Explanation [Critical Stance]

Review Poetry Collection 1 or Poetry Collection 2. Explain how one poem's imagery contributes to an understanding of the poem's theme.
(40 minutes)

Writing Workshop: *Work in Progress*

Analytic Response to Literature

Use your questions from your writing portfolio. Answer each question with both (1) a statement of your opinion and (2) a textual detail that supports that opinion. Put this work in your writing portfolio.

Reading Informational Materials

Feature Articles

In Part 2, you learned about the importance of paraphrasing as an aid to understanding poetry. Paraphrasing is also an important skill in research writing. If you read Carl Sandburg's "Jazz Fantasia," you may enjoy learning more about jazz in this feature article that incorporates research.

About Feature Articles

A **feature article** in a newspaper or magazine presents a comprehensive view of a person, a place, an event, an activity, or a trend of interest. Feature articles often include these elements:

- a clearly focused topic presented from a particular "angle"—a central theme on which the writer elaborates
- quotations from experts, participants, or observers
- photos, drawings, maps, or other informative graphics

Reading Skill

When taking notes on a feature article or other source, keep in mind the ways in which you will present the information you gather.

- **Quoting** from a source means repeating a section of text word for word within quotation marks (or otherwise set off). (See pages R33–R34 for more on quoting and crediting sources.)
- **Paraphrasing** a source means restating the ideas or information it presents in your own words. Paraphrases of original ideas and of information that is not general knowledge must be credited.
- **Critiquing** a source means evaluating its reliability or credibility.

Review the chart for various notetaking strategies.

	Notetaking Strategy	Example
Quotation	• Copy the statement word for word. • Clearly identify the source.	According to cultural historian Ann Douglas, be-bop music reflected "the international mix, the fluidity and speed of New York life."
Paraphrase	• Note the key facts, double-checking numbers, the spelling of names, and so on. • Clearly identify the source.	According to the most recent count, the 2000 Census, New York City has a population of just over 8 million.

Academic Standards

- Analyze formatting of informational documents. (10.2.1)
- Establish a thesis and focus for the piece. (10.4.2)
- Integrate quotations and citations into text. (10.4.7)

Feel the City's PULSE?
It's Be-bop, Man!

ANN DOUGLAS

The article begins with a quotation, a good way to get the reader's attention.

In 1964, Thelonious Monk, one of the pioneers of be-bop and perhaps jazz's greatest composer, was asked by an interviewer to define jazz. Though Monk disliked questions and usually ignored them, this time he didn't miss a beat: "New York, man. You can feel it. It's around in the air. . . ."

Be-Bop (bop for short) was sometimes labeled "New York Jazz," and it is, in fact, the only major school of jazz to which the city can lay proprietary claim. Jazz of the '20s, dominated by Louis Armstrong, originated in New Orleans, migrating to New York only after a formative detour in Chicago. Armstrong inspired '30s swing, the music of the big bands led by Benny Goodman, Artie Shaw, Glenn Miller, Count Basie and Duke Ellington, the "mother bands," as Gillespie called them, whose music the be-boppers both emulated and revolutionized.

Background information explains swing, a jazz form that influenced be-bop.

. . . Bop's wide-ranging allusiveness, its quicksilver expressivity, angular dissonance and shockingly extended palette of pitches and rhythms echoed the international mix, the fluidity and speed of New York life.

Jamming After Hours

Bop began at roughly the same time as World War II, in 1940 when Monk, then 23, was hired to play with Kenny (Klook) Clarke, the man who transformed jazz drumming, at Minton's Playhouse in Harlem. Gillespie jammed with them after his regular engagement, and Parker joined them a year later. When Minton's closed for the night, they adjourned to Clark Monroe's Uptown House, an after-hours club where an extraordinary teen-age drummer named Max Roach played in the band.

The nation's entrance into the war in late 1941 imposed gas rationing, entertainment taxes and curfews, sharply restricting travel. The swing bands were touring bands, and some of them continued to tour, but now everyone was looking for a long-term base in a big city, easily accessible by public transit.

What hurt swing helped be-bop. The expense and risks of touring (especially down South) had been far greater for black musicians than for white. The cramped quarters of many city clubs suited the young bop musicians, eager to work with the small ensembles that maximized opportunities for experimentation. . . .

The word "be-bop," which both Monk and Gillespie claimed to have coined, described the music's unconventional stop-and-start form, especially Gillespie and Parker's witty eighth-note pair conclusions. The purpose of bop's irregular phrasings, side-sliding harmonies and whirlwind pace, was, in Kenny Clarke's words, to "raise the standards of musicianship," to tell people, "Whatever you go into, go into it intelligently." The be-boppers were the real New York intellectuals, the hippest, smartest men in town.

Having already established that Kenny Clark participated in the creation of be-bop, the writer quotes him as an authority.

The conclusion sums up the writer's "angle": Be-bop has a vital relationship to New York City.

SITES OF BOP'S TRIUMPHS AND TRAGEDIES

Annotations to the map explain the importance of key sites.

1. **Savoy Ballroom** Lenox Avenue and 140th Street, Harlem. Charlie Parker played in this legendary jazz and dance hall with the Jay McShann Orchestra in his early days in New York. . . .

2. **Minton's Playhouse** 210 West 118th Street, Morningside Heights. Charlie Christian, Kenny Clarke, Thelonious Monk, Parker and Gillespie made musical history here in the early 1940s.

3. **St. Peter's Church** 54th Street and Lexington Avenue, Manhattan (also its current site). Monk's funeral took place here on Feb. 22, 1982, with musicians playing for three hours.

4. **52nd Street** between Fifth and Sixth Avenues, known as "The Street." A magical block of jazz clubs . . . including the Onyx, Spotlite, Three Deuces and Kelly's Stable.

5. **Birdland** 1678 Broadway, at 53rd Street, Manhattan. It opened on Dec. 15, 1949, with dozens of (caged) birds on view and Charlie (Bird) Parker presiding.

6. **216 West 19th Street**
Eager to become "a New York musician," Gillespie lived here with his brother, . . . when he first came to town from Philadelphia in 1937, eating for 25 cents a day.

Specific details support and expand the article's description of the New York be-bop scene.

Reading: Quote, Paraphrase, and Critique Sources

Standards Assessed
• 10.2.1
• 10.4.2
• 10.4.7

Directions: *Choose the letter of the best answer to each question.*

1. In which of the following sentences is the final sentence of the article correctly quoted?

   A Ann Douglas says that be-bop musicians were smart.

   B Be-bop musicians were the real New York intellectuals, the hippest, smartest men in town, according to writer Ann Douglas.

   C According to Douglas, be-bop musicians "were the real New York intellectuals, the hippest, smartest men in town."

   D Ann Douglas writes that "be-bop musicians" were the real New York intellectuals.

2. Which of the following statements is the best paraphrase of the first sentence of the second paragraph?

   A Be-bop was always the most popular form of jazz in New York.

   B Be-bop is the only kind of jazz that truly centered in New York.

   C Be-bop (bop for short) was sometimes labeled "New York Jazz."

   D Be-bop and bop are two names for the same kind of music.

3. Which phrase best indicates the credibility of the article as a source?

   A according to Douglas

   B according to Douglas, a historian and *New York Times* writer

   C according to Douglas, who has written on literature

   D according to Douglas, who likes classical music and jazz

Reading: Comprehension and Interpretation

Directions: *Write your answers on a separate piece of paper.*

4. Name two distinctive qualities of be-bop described by Douglas. **[Knowledge]**

5. Explain how the Second World War encouraged be-bop. **[Generating]**

Timed Writing: Persuasion [Connections]

Write a persuasive essay in which you take a position on the following quotation: "Music reflects culture. It is a central means by which a group asserts its relationship to past generations, distinguishes insiders from outsiders, and addresses the future." Support your response with quotations from Douglas's article. **(25–30 minutes)**

Comparing Literary Works · Theme

Theme

A **theme** is the central idea, message, or insight that the author of a literary work conveys. Some authors present a theme by dramatizing the contradictions, conflicts, or complications of life, including the following:

- By having hopes and making plans, people make their lives meaningful—yet if their plans fail, their hopes may seem foolish and their lives empty.
- People strive for what they desire—yet they may long most intensely for what they have lost or can never have.
- People may build their lives around those whom they love— yet if someone betrays their trust, they may feel as if they never knew the person.

By presenting such contradictions or conflicts, writers remind us that life is not just what happens to us. It is also the powerful desires, the joys, and the disappointments that drive us and define us—even in the face of failure.

IN **Academic Standards**

- Examine how the author's perspective influences the structure and tone of the text. (10.2.4)
- Compare works that express a universal theme. (10.3.5)
- Evaluate the impact of ambiguities, contradictions and ironies in the text. (10.3.8)

Comparing Themes

Each of the four poets in this group writes about the meaning of human actions—asking whether our actions add up to something or amount to nothing, whether we should strive for success or strive to find peace in ourselves. Though their general topic is the same, each poet's theme, or insight into that topic, is different. As you read, use a chart like the one shown to note the different insights each poet presents.

Poem:_____

Subject
Human action

↓

Insight About Subject

Vocabulary Builder

All

- lamentation (lam´ ən tā´ shən) *n.* act of crying out in grief; wailing (p. 702) *We heard the widow's mournful lamentation.*

Also All

- wither (with´ ər) *v.* dry up; shrivel from loss of moisture (p. 703) *A tree's leaves will wither without water.*

Success is counted sweetest

- strains (strānz) *n.* musical sounds; melodies (p. 705) *I hear the strains of a distant marching band.*

The Old Stoic

- implore (im plôr´) *v.* plead; ask for earnestly (p. 706) *The characters in the ad implore people to recycle.*

Build Understanding

Connecting to the Literature

Reading/Writing Connection In each of these poems, the poet takes a step back to ask, "Things go wrong so often—how should we respond to this fact of life? What keeps us going?" List three strategies people can use to cope with failure. Use at least three of the following words: *adapt, maximize, minimize, respond.*

Meet the Authors

Bei **Dao** (b. 1949)

In the 1970s, Bei Dao's poems became rallying cries for those Chinese who wanted their country to become more democratic. Since 1989, when government troops gunned down protesters in Tiananmen Square in Beijing, China's capital, Bei Dao has lived abroad.

Shu **Ting** (b. 1952)

As a teenager, Shu Ting (the pen name of Gong Peiyu) was forced by political events in China to leave Beijing, the capital, and live in a small peasant village. She gained fame as a poet while she was still in her twenties, winning China's National Poetry Award in 1981 and 1983.

Emily **Dickinson** (1830–1886)

The daughter of an official of Amherst College in Massachusetts, Emily Dickinson belonged to a generation of writers who redefined American literature. Rather than imitating the works of British poets, Dickinson found her own distinctive voice, at once personal and wise. While thoughtful and expansive in her poetry, Dickinson lived a reclusive life—rarely leaving her home in her later years.

Emily **Brontë** (1818–1848)

The Brontë sisters—Emily, Charlotte, and Anne—spent much of their childhood roaming the bleak, windswept hills of Yorkshire, England, and devising their own imaginary worlds. When Emily was twenty-seven, the three sisters published their poems in a single volume. Emily is most famous for her novel *Wuthering Heights.*

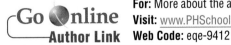

Go **Online**
Author Link

For: More about the authors
Visit: www.PHSchool.com
Web Code: eqe-9412

Bei Dao

translated by Donald Finkel and Xueliang Chen

All is fated,
all cloudy,

all an endless beginning,
all a search for what vanishes,

5   all joys grave,
all griefs tearless,

every speech a repetition,
every meeting a first encounter,

all love buried in the heart,
10   all history prisoned in a dream,

all hope hedged with doubt,
all faith drowned in <u>lamentation</u>.

Every explosion heralds an instant of stillness,
every death reverberates forever.

Literary Analysis
Theme What doubt about people's ability to trust one another is implied in line 8?

Vocabulary Builder
lamentation (lam′ ən tā′ shən) *n.* act of crying out in grief; wailing

Also All

In answer to Bei Dao's "All"

Shu Ting

translated by
Donald Finkel and Jinsheng Yi

Background   Bei Dao and Shu Ting both belonged to a group of Chinese writers known as the Misty Poets. Influenced by Western poets and breaking with Chinese tradition, the Misty Poets used vivid imagery and expressed strong personal emotions. By speaking up for individual feelings, they expressed a quiet opposition to the government of China. In "Also All," Shu Ting answers Bei Dao's poem "All."

> Not all trees are felled by storms.
> Not every seed finds barren soil.
> Not all the wings of dream are broken,
> nor is all affection doomed
> 5 to <u>wither</u> in a desolate heart.
>
> No, not all is as you say.

Vocabulary Builder
wither (with′ər) v. dry up; shrivel from loss of moisture

Not all flames consume themselves,
shedding no light on other lives.
Not all stars announce the night
10   and never dawn. Not every song
will drift past every ear and heart.

No, not all is as you say.

Not every cry for help is silenced,
nor every loss beyond recall.
15   Not every chasm spells disaster.
Not only the weak will be brought to their knees,
nor every soul be trodden under.

It won't all end in tears and blood.
Today is heavy with tomorrow—
20   the future was planted yesterday.
Hope is a burden all of us shoulder
though we might stumble under the load.

Thinking About the Selections

1. **Respond:** Would you rather display "All" or "Also All" on a poster in your classroom? Why?

2. **(a) Recall:** What does the speaker in "All" say about "all joys" and about "all hope"? **(b) Infer:** What do these statements suggest about the speaker's view of life?

3. **(a) Recall:** What does the speaker say all is "a search for"?
   (b) Interpret: To what fact of life might his statement refer?
   (c) Connect: Find another line in the poem that suggests a related idea. Explain your choice.

4. **(a) Recall:** What does the speaker in "Also All" point out about the effect of a storm on trees? **(b) Infer:** Is her viewpoint basically optimistic or pessimistic? Support your answer.
   (c) Interpret: According to the last two lines of "Also All," what responsibility do people have?

5. **(a) Connect:** In what way does "Also All" answer the speaker's points in "All"? **(b) Speculate:** How might the speaker in "All" answer the point in the last two lines of "Also All"?

Success is counted sweetest
Emily Dickinson

Success is counted sweetest
By those who ne'er succeed.
To comprehend a nectar[1]
Requires sorest need.

5   Not one of all the purple Host
Who took the Flag today
Can tell the definition
So clear of Victory

As he defeated—dying—
10   On whose forbidden ear
The distant <u>strains</u> of triumph
Burst agonized and clear!

---

1. nectar (nek´ tər) *n.* in Greek mythology, the drink of the gods; something delicious to drink.

Literary Analysis
Theme What do lines 1–4 suggest about the circumstances in which people care most about success?

Vocabulary Builder
strains (strānz) *n.* musical sounds; melodies

◀ **Critical Viewing** Judging from this athlete's pose, might he agree with Dickinson about success? Explain. **[Connect]**

The Old Stoic[1]

Emily Brontë

Riches I hold in light esteem,
And love I laugh to scorn;
And lust of fame was but a dream
That vanished with the morn:

5   And if I pray, the only prayer
That moves my lips for me
Is, "Leave the heart that now I bear,
And give me liberty!"

Yes, as my swift days near their goal,
10 'Tis all that I <u>implore</u>—
Through life and death a chainless soul,
With courage to endure.

Vocabulary Builder
implore (im plôr´) *v.*
plead; ask for
earnestly

---

1. Stoic (stō´ ik) *n.* follower of an ancient Greek philosophy, stoicism, which teaches that freedom can only be reached through virtue and a detached acceptance of events.

Thinking About the Selections

1. **Respond:** Do you agree with Dickinson's or Brontë's ideas? Why?

2. **(a) Recall:** According to the speaker in "Success is counted sweetest," who appreciates success most? **(b) Interpret:** Why might their appreciation of success be greater than that of others?

3. **(a) Recall:** In "The Old Stoic," what is the speaker's attitude toward riches and love? **(b) Interpret:** To what type of experience does the speaker refer in lines 3–4? **(c) Contrast:** Explain what the speaker values and contrast it with riches, love, and fame.

Apply the Skills

All • Also All • Success is counted sweetest • The Old Stoic

Comparing Themes

1. Summarize the central insights into life expressed in "All" and "Also All."

2. Summarize the central insight in "Success is counted sweetest." Support your answer with quotations from the poem.

3. What reaction might the speaker in "The Old Stoic" have to Dickinson's poem? Support your answer with details from the poems.

4. **(a)** The following diagram lists four possible responses to disappointment and failure. In your own copy of the diagram, list details from the poems that reflect these responses.

(b) Drawing on your analysis, compare the insights into success and failure presented in the poems.

Writing to Compare Literary Works

In an essay, compare the ideas each author presents about people's hopes and the pursuit of success. Use these questions to get started:

- What is the attitude of each poet toward hope and success?
- Which writers might agree? Which might disagree? Why?
- Which details in each poem support its theme most strongly?

Vocabulary Builder

Practice In an **analogy,** the relationship between the second pair of words should be the same as the relationship between the first pair of words. Complete each analogy with a word from the vocabulary list on page 700.

1. puzzles : mysteries :: melodies : _____
2. parade : cheering :: funeral : _____
3. build : destroy :: bloom : _____
4. lawyer : argue :: beggar : _____

QuickReview

Theme: the central idea, message, or insight in a literary work

Assessment
For: Self-test
Visit: www.PHSchool.com
Web Code: eqa-6411

Paraphrasing

Directions: *Questions 1–6 are based on the following poem.*

> The sun that brief December day
> Rose cheerless over hills of gray,
> And, darkly circled, gave at noon
> A sadder light than waning moon.
> 5   Slow tracing down the thickening sky
> Its mute and ominous prophecy,
>
> A portent seeming less than threat,
> It sank from sight before it set.
> A chill no coat, however stout,
> 10   Of homespun stuff could quite shut out,
> A hard, dull bitterness of cold,
> That checked, mid-vein, the circling race
> Of lifeblood in the sharpened face,
> The coming of the snowstorm told.
>
>   —from "Snowbound" by John Greenleaf Whittier

1. What is "cheerless"?
 A the sun
 B December
 C the waning moon
 D the hills

2. Which word could replace "cheerless"?
 A waning
 B sad
 C brief
 D round

3. Which sentence best states the core message of the first four lines?
 A The sun shone brightly.
 B The sun was dim.
 C The day was short.
 D The sky was thick.

4. Based on the context, how would you paraphrase the word "stout" in line 9?
 A fat
 B thick
 C brave
 D thin

5. How many complete sentences are found in the first stanza?
 A one
 B two
 C three
 D six

6. What is the main prophecy or prediction to which line 6 refers?
 A The moon will come out at sunset.
 B It is growing cold.
 C The holiday season is coming.
 D A snowstorm is coming.

Vocabulary

Directions: *Choose the letter of the sentence in which the vocabulary word is used correctly.*

7. *distort*
   A He fired off many questions, but for each, she had a quick distort.
   B A funhouse mirror will usually distort the appearance of what it reflects.
   C A good camera will usually distort the pictures it takes.
   D Distort is very tasty, though I prefer the chocolate layer cake.

8. *minimize*
   A The dentist tried to minimize my discomfort.
   B The head of the business worked hard to minimize profits.
   C It took less than a minimize to finish the quiz.
   D Use a spoon to minimize the ingredients in a big bowl.

9. *ideology*
   A A detective studies ideology.
   B Conflicting ideologies made it difficult for the parties to compromise.
   C He studied birds to be an ideologist.
   D Applying ideology, he bridged the gap.

10. *recur*
    A We expect the child's birth to recur on March 19.
    B If the situation is not remedied, the problem will recur.
    C The dealer will recur the automobile if you do not make your payment.
    D He is a villain and a recur.

11. *terminology*
    A The terminology of the setting made it difficult to comprehend.
    B The article contained difficult terminology.
    C The writer used a lot of words in that terminology.
    D Finally, the terminology took its toll.

Directions: *Choose the best definition for the following words.*

12. *utilize*
    A pretend with
    B make use of
    C reduce the amount
    D employ tools

13. *archaeology*
    A a part of the foot
    B the study of life and cultures of the past
    C someone who studies buildings
    D relating to the science of outer space

14. *personalize*
    A the qualities of a human being
    B relating to a human being
    C to lose one's humanity
    D make specific to one human being

15. *authorize*
    A give authority
    B identify a writer
    C study of authors
    D power to rule

Spelling Workshop

Words With Similar Endings: *-ize, -ise, -yze*

Academic Standards

- Revise writing based on specific criteria. (10.4.11)
- Use varied and expanded vocabulary. (10.5.7)

Endings that sound the same or almost the same can be tricky to spell. How do you choose among the endings *-ize, -ise,* and *-yze*?

Spell the Ending Correctly The endings *-ize, -ise,* and *-yze* can be pronounced "īz." Usually, *-ize* is a suffix added to another word to make a verb, as is the case with *civilize (civil + -ize)* and *characterize (character+ -ize).*

For words with the other two endings, there are no dependable rules, so you have to memorize the spellings. Make a list in your notebook of those words that are troublesome and refer to it or a dictionary if you are unsure of the spelling of a word.

Practice Each set of letters contains the letters of one of the words from the list plus one extra letter. Unscramble each set and eliminate the extra letter to spell a word from the word list.

1. vtaeiesdry
2. zaaienyl
3. leerzisa
4. heriacrzeacty
5. ezsimorpmoc
6. zsipotheheys
7. diyseerchman
8. scuzeblipy
9. immezoers
10. zaboyimles

Word List
characterize
compromise
advertise
merchandise
memorize
analyze
publicize
realize
hypothesize
symbolize

Standards
Assessed

• 10.4.11
• 10.5.7

Directions: *For each item, write the letters of the words that are incorrectly spelled. If all of the underlined words are correct, choose* **No error.**

1. We are working hard to <u>publicize</u> the
                          A
   <u>store's</u> <u>merchandize</u>. <u>No error</u>
   B   C   D

2. The <u>students</u> <u>realize</u> that they must
        A   B
   <u>memorise</u> the rules. <u>No error</u>
        C   D

3. The committee members <u>finally</u>
                          A
   <u>anayzed</u> the problem and reached a
   B
   <u>compromise</u>. <u>No error</u>
   C   D

4. We <u>hypothesised</u> that the author
       A
   <u>symbolized</u> the trial so the work would
   B
   get <u>passed</u> the censors. <u>No error</u>
       C   D

Directions: *Write the letter of the word that is the correct spelling to fill in the blank.*

1. Was it difficult to _____ the chemical
   equations?
   A memorise
   B memoryze
   C memoreyes
   D memorize

2. I did not _____ that we were leaving so
   early.
   A reelize
   B reelise
   C realize
   D realise

3. We will never get a contract unless you
   _____.
   A compromise
   B compramise
   C compromize
   D compromice

4. The skills needed to _____ literature are
   higher-level thinking skills.
   A analize
   B annalyze
   C analyze
   D analyse

5. How would you _____ our new neighbor?
   A caracterize
   B characterise
   C characterice
   D characterize

6. The _____ behind his argument was weak.
   A premese
   B premise
   C premice
   D premize

Writing Workshop

Analytic Response to Literature

Academic Standards

• Establish a thesis and focus for the piece. (10.4.2)

• Write responses to literature. (10.5.2)

• Write for different purposes and audiences. (10.5.8)

If a friend asks about a movie you saw, you might casually respond, "It was OK." However, when you respond to literature in a formal way, you need to dig deeper. An **analytic response to literature** presents a reader's critical response to an entire literary work or focuses on a specific aspect. Follow the steps in this workshop to write an essay analyzing a literary selection of your choice.

Assignment Write an analytic response to a favorite piece of literature. You might analyze a poem, a play, a story, or a screenplay.

What to Include Your analytic response to literature should feature the following elements:

- a thesis statement that presents your personal response to the work being analyzed
- references to specific literary aspects of the work, such as theme or style
- evidence from the literary work or other texts, including accurate quotations, to support your opinions
- effective and logical organization
- error-free grammar, including correct formation of comparisons

To preview the criteria on which your analytic response to literature may be judged, see the rubric on page 719.

Using the Form

You may use elements of this form in these types of writing:

- book reviews
- annotated bibliographies
- articles
- readers' journals

Writing Workshop: *Work in Progress*

If you have completed the Work-in-Progress assignments, you already have a wealth of ideas in your portfolio to use in your analytic response to literature. Continue to develop these ideas, or explore a new idea as you complete the Writing Workshop.

Reading → *Writing Connection*

To get a feel for responses to literature, read two literary reviews of *Marcovaldo* on pages 367–368.

Prewriting

Choosing Your Topic

Use these strategies to find a topic:

- **Book Group Discussion** With a small group, list the literary works that have provoked strong feelings in you. For each item, briefly describe any memorable details about the work or your experience reading it. Review your ideas and choose one work as your topic.

- **Top Five** Choose an awards category, such as bravest character, most dangerous conflict, or best writer. Then, list literary works that fit the category. From the list, choose your topic.

Work in Progress
Review the work you did on pages 679 and 695.

Narrowing Your Topic

Ask your own questions. Decide which aspects of the literary work interested you the most, bothered you the most, or raised questions for you. For example, the actions or personality of one character in particular may have confused you. Jot down two or three questions that you hope to answer by writing your analytical response.

Example questions:
- In *Julius Caesar,* why do Antony and Cassius meet different ends?
- Why does "Contents of the Dead Man's Pocket" end as it does?

Gathering Details

Consider your audience. Identify your audience and assess their knowledge about your topic. If you need to cover subjects that are unfamiliar to your readers, plan to include details that will help them understand. Use a chart like the one shown to plan.

> ### My Topic and Audience
>
> **Topic:** Tennyson's Kraken and the giant squid
>
> **Audience:** classmates
>
> **What they know:** They are familiar with the poem "The Kraken" because we read it in class.
>
> **What they do not know:** They may not be familiar with giant squids, the real sea creatures that might have inspired the legend.

Go back to the source. Find the information you need by skimming the work for details, examples, and passages in the text that relate to your topic. Write each detail or quotation on a separate index card. Then, organize the cards into general categories. For example, you might group all the cards containing details about one character together.

Writing Workshop

Drafting

Shaping Your Writing

Write a thesis statement. Review your notes and consider the main point you want to make about the literary work. Write a statement that expresses that point. Include this thesis in your introduction.

Organize your response. A compelling response to literature can be organized in three parts, as the chart here shows. Each part should relate directly to your thesis.

Providing Elaboration

Use information from the text in various ways. For every major idea in your essay, provide evidence from the literary work or another relevant source. Consider these options:

- Use **exact quotations** to show a character's personality, a poet's use of imagery, or a writer's style. Identify all quotations clearly and use quotation marks.

- Use **paraphrases**—your own restatement of ideas in the text—to clarify a conflict, to present a writer's theme, or to include key concepts. Be sure your paraphrase accurately reflects the original text and that you cite sources for any ideas that are not your own.

- Use **summaries** to provide an overview of a writer's opinion or to explain a series of events. However, do not use summaries to fill up pages with material that is not relevant to your thesis.

Whatever format you use for supporting your ideas, use transitional words and phrases to explain the link between the literature and your thesis.

Use strong, precise language. Choose vivid and exact language. Avoid general or vague statements that will not illuminate your point of view.

Introduction
- State your thesis.
- Give an overview of the work and your response.

Body
- Analyze the key elements that support your thesis.
- Present support, such as quotations and examples.

Conclusion
- Restate your thesis.
- Summarize how the elements contributed to your response.
- Tell readers why the ideas are important.

To read the complete student model, see page 718.

Student Model: Using Precise Language

After the assassination of Caesar in Act III, Antony cleverly manipulates the commoners. His subtle and smooth way of controlling the crowd with a pause in his voice reflects his manipulative ability.

Strong, precise adjectives help the writer convey his ideas clearly.

Cornelius Eady

Cornelius Eady

On Writing Poetry About Music

In my poem "Thelonious Monk" — named for the famous jazz composer and pianist — I was finding a way of duplicating the playfulness in Monk's music. I also wanted to capture another quality — his music is very rhythmic, but also very hard. It's as if you can hear body language — lots of elbows and knees. He forces you to pay attention to melody in a way you wouldn't ordinarily.

There's a link there in terms of the way poetry operates. Poetry makes you look at details or highlights within language that you wouldn't otherwise catch in other circumstances.

> *"Writing a poem about a certain song can yield some really wonderful results."*
>
> —————*Cornelius Eady*

Professional Model:

from "Thelonious Monk"

I know what to do with this math.
Listen to this. It's
Arithmetic, a soundtrack. The motion

Frozen in these lampposts, it
Can be sung. I can lift away
Its logic, make it spin

Like an orbital satellite, find
Gambling's true pitch.
It can be *played*:

Adventure, the trying of
Patience, holding back, holding
Up, laying out, stop-time, . . .

I was trying to get at the quality of Monk's form that's like broken-field running in football. Most of the lines are primarily monosyllabic, and I like to end them with hard percussive words like *It's*.

These lines came out of a story someone told me about Monk. He said he'd seen Monk go up to a lamppost and listen to it, and then Monk went home and tried to play the sound he heard in the lamppost.

I imagined the poem could be Monk saying, "Look, *this* is what I'm up to." I wanted the poem to be representing Monk representing himself.

Writing Workshop

Revising

Revising Your Overall Structure

Cut excess writing. When revising, one of your most important goals is to delete words, phrases, sentences, and even paragraphs that do not add meaning or depth to your essay. As you review your draft, look for these types of unnecessary material:

- **Repeated Ideas:** Extend important ideas with fresh information, but cut repetitions that add nothing new.

- **Unrelated Details:** Be sure that every detail relates directly to your thesis.

- **Inconsistencies:** Make sure that every sentence and every paragraph clearly relates to those that precede and follow.

Peer Review: Exchange drafts with a partner. Highlight passages that include ineffective repetition, unrelated details, or inconsistent statements. Discuss whether to delete the highlighted material. Then, revise your draft, cutting unnecessary language.

To read the complete student model, see page 718.

Student Model: Eliminating Unnecessary Writing

Despite their powers of persuasion, these two show great allegiance to their loved ones. ~~They are loyal to their loved ones.~~ Over Caesar's body, in Act III, Scene i, Antony says he is willing to throw his country into civil war. Later, Cassius kills himself when he thinks that his best friend has been killed, taking loyalty to the extreme. ~~Cassius is also not loyal at all.~~

> The writer deletes a repeated idea and an inconsistent statement to make this paragraph more effective.

Revising Your Word Choice

Use specific terms. The correct use of formal or specialized terms can help you express shades of meaning and add a sense of serious scholarship to your work. Formal terminology may include literary terms, the names of literary movements, references to periods in history, or place names. Review your use of such terms to make sure they are correct.

Nonspecific: the big moment of the play
Specific: the dramatic climax of the play

Nonspecific: the old system of government
Specific: Ancient Roman democracy

Integrating Grammar Skills

Revising Common Usage Problems

Many students misuse certain words when making comparisons.

Identifying Usage Problems With *like, as,* and *as if* When it is not used as a verb (I *like* red), the word *like* is a preposition meaning "similar to" or "such as." Prepositions precede nouns. The word *like* should not be used in place of *as, as if,* or *as though,* which are conjunctions that introduce clauses.

Prentice Hall Writing and Grammar Connection: Chapter 26, Section 2

Incorrect: The sand felt *like* it was a warm slipper. (before a clause)
Correct: The sand felt *like* a warm slipper. (before a noun)
Correct: The sand felt *as if* it were a warm slipper. (before a clause)

Prepositional Phrase vs. Clause

A **prepositional phrase** includes a preposition and a noun or pronoun. It has no subject or verb.

    like a feather   like a snoring elephant

A **clause** has a subject and a verb.

                     S   V
    My friend looked [as if *she* <u>had overslept.</u>]
                      clause

Identifying Usage Problems With *among* and *between* Use *between* to compare two things. Use *among* to compare three or more things.

Incorrect: The cloud hovered *among* the horizon and infinity.
Correct: The cloud hovered *between* the horizon and infinity.

Incorrect: The sunlight danced *between* the many clouds.
Correct: The sunlight danced *among* the many clouds.

Fixing Usage Problems To revise usage problems with *like, as, as if,* or *as though,* follow these steps:

1. **Determine how you are using the word.**
2. **If you have used *like* to introduce a clause, replace it with the conjunction *as, as if,* or *as though.***

To revise usage problems with *among* and *between,* follow these steps:

1. **Identify the number of elements involved in the sentence.**
2. **Use *between* with phrases involving two elements.**
3. **Use *among* with phrases involving three or more elements.**

Apply It to Your Editing

Review two paragraphs of your essay and circle any uses of *like, as, as if, between* or *among.* Revise any incorrect usage.

Writing Workshop

Student Model: Christopher Rich
Omaha, Nebraska

Response to *The Tragedy of Julius Caesar*

In all tales, modern or ancient, characters at odds often differ in obvious ways. One may be likable and honest—a natural leader. The other may be unpleasant and sneaky. However, sometimes enemies are actually very similar. No exception to this rule, Shakespeare's Antony and Cassius of *The Tragedy of Julius Caesar* share many characteristics but come to very different ends.

Marcus Antonius and Caius Cassius, both patricians and warriors, are presented as two of Rome's most noble citizens. Both are seen by plebians as noble and honest, if humanly flawed, men. In truth, they are among the most manipulative characters in the play. Cassius is the first to exploit his power to manipulate, using it to coerce Brutus onto the side of the conspirators. Flattering Brutus, ("I know that virtue to be in you, Brutus, / As well as I do know your outward favor") (I, ii, 90 – 91) and challenging his honor as a Roman, Cassius wins the support of his brother-in-law. Antony, however, shows his ability in a far less conspicuous way. After the assassination of Caesar in Act III, Antony cleverly manipulates the commoners. His subtle and smooth way of controlling the crowd with a pause in his voice reflects his manipulative ability.

Despite their powers of persuasion, these two show great allegiance to their loved ones. Over Caesar's body, in Act III, Scene i, Antony says he is willing to throw his country into civil war. Later, Cassius kills himself when he thinks that his best friend has been killed, taking loyalty to the extreme.

Though people may have many similarities, it is the differences that separate warriors and politicians. Always at the beck and call of the dictator who would be king, Antony is known by the common folk to be a possible successor to the "coronet." Cassius, however, is opposed to Caesar, not only politically but also personally, and is one of Caesar's least favorite people: "Yond Cassius has a lean and hungry look" (I, ii, 194). Cassius himself admits to his own dislike of Caesar by telling a story from their youth, in Act I, Scene ii, lines 97 – 131. It is their differences that determine the eventual fate of each character.

In the end, the obvious similarities of these characters are not as important as their differences. The fate that each meets—Cassius commits suicide and Antony becomes part of the triumvirate that rules Rome—is determined by how each uses his personality traits.

> The writer includes a clear thesis statement in his introduction.

> The writer accurately quotes significant passages from the text.

> Using a point-by-point plan of organization, the writer focuses first on similarities and then moves onto differences.

> In his conclusion, Christopher restates his thesis and provides an insight that takes the analysis further.

Editing and Proofreading

Check your draft for errors in format, grammar, and punctuation.

Focus on Spelling: Double-check the spelling of author and character names to make sure they are correct. If you are unsure about your accuracy, refer back to the literature you are analyzing.

Publishing and Presenting

Consider one of the following ways to share your writing:

Present your response to a book club. Share your response to literature with members of a book club. Invite a group of students, friends, or family to read the work of literature you will address. Set a meeting time and give a brief introduction to the work. Then, read your essay aloud. Follow your reading with a general discussion to share ideas and responses. As you discuss the literature and your analysis, work to be open to the ideas of others rather than simply defending your own.

Publish an online review. Post a literary review on a student or bookstore Web site. Remember to check each site for specific submission requirements. Then, follow correct procedures to retrieve and reproduce your document across platforms.

Reflecting on Your Writing

Writer's Journal Think about the experience of writing an analytic response to literature. Begin by answering these questions:

- Think about your first response to the work. How is your response different now that you have completed a thorough analysis?
- Which strategies would you use again to write a response to literature?

> *Prentice Hall Writing and Grammar Connection: Chapter 13*

Rubric for Self-Assessment

Evaluate your response to literature using the following criteria and rating scale:

Criteria	Rating Scale
	not very very
Focus: How clear is your thesis statement?	1 2 3 4 5
Organization: How logical is your organization?	1 2 3 4 5
Support/Elaboration: How effectively do you include evidence from the literary work to support your opinions?	1 2 3 4 5
Style: How precise and vivid is your use of language?	1 2 3 4 5
Conventions: How correct is your grammar, especially your formation of comparisons?	1 2 3 4 5

Communications Workshop

Delivering an Oral Interpretation of a Literary Work

You can share your ideas about a poem—or anything else you read—by **delivering an oral interpretation** for an audience.

Prepare the Content
Your oral interpretation will combine a careful analysis of the work with your own response.

Advance a judgment about significant ideas. Clearly state the main ideas in the literature. Discuss ways in which the ideas are developed and why they are important.

Support important ideas and viewpoints. Your views will carry more weight if you support them with details from the text. Read passages from the work to share the writer's style and tone with your audience. Choose sections that illustrate key ideas and are pleasing or powerful when read aloud.

Pose questions. Authors do not state all of their ideas directly. Introduce some of the unstated themes of a work by asking a question and then answering it using examples from the works.

Prepare Your Delivery
Preparation is the key to feeling relaxed in front of an audience. These techniques can help you deliver a confident and effective presentation:

- **Organize your ideas.** Write each key idea on a separate notecard. As you rehearse, organize the cards in different orders. Then, number the cards in the best order.
- **Communicate with your voice.** Speak clearly and comfortably without rushing. Use the tone and pitch of your voice to add variety.
- **Use effective body language.** Your gestures and posture send a signal to your audience. Energetic body language shows that you think your subject is important. Maintain eye contact to keep your audience's attention.

Activity **Deliver an Oral Interpretation** ▶ Select a poem, short story, or short piece of nonfiction. Prepare a three-minute interpretation in which you respond to this work. Ask your listeners to use the Feedback Form to evaluate your presentation.

Academic Standards

- Select effective verbal and nonverbal techniques for presentations. (10.7.6)
- Make judgements about the ideas being discussed. (10.7.7)
- Deliver oral responses to literature. (10.7.17)

Feedback Form for an Oral Interpretation

Rating System

1	2	3	4	5
poor		good		excellent

Content
_____ Clear main idea
_____ Effective support
_____ Appropriate quotations from text
_____ Analysis of subtleties in text

Presentation
_____ Logical organization
_____ Clear speaking voice
_____ Varied delivery
_____ Effective gestures and body language

Conclusions
- Is the presentation unified? Does each statement support the main idea?
- Is the speaker's personal response to the literary work clear?

Beowulf

Anonymous
Globe Fearon, 2000

Epic Poem Evil haunts the castle in the form of a monster, and the King and his warriors are powerless to stop the slaughter. Then, the hero from other lands, Beowulf, arrives, and the battle takes on a different twist. This gory tale is not for the faint of heart.

The Song of the Lark

Willa Cather
Signet Classics, 1991

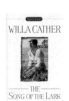

Novel As a child in a small nineteenth-century Colorado town, Thea Kronborg shows a gift for music. She travels to Chicago to fulfill her dream of becoming an opera singer. This novel travels with a young lady who sacrifices a "normal childhood" for her dreams. Thea learns, though, that there is a price to be paid for success. Every teenager who has practiced instead of going out with their friends will understand and empathize with Thea.

Native American Literature

Anthology
Prentice Hall, 2000

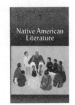

Anthology A range of traditional and contemporary works by Native American writers shows the many sides of the Native American experience. From the ancient Aztecs of Central America to the Penobscot people of New England, the richness and diversity of Native American literature is captured in myths, essays, and contemporary fiction.

Leaves of Grass

Walt Whitman
Signet, 2000

Poetry Whitman prided himself on celebrating common people; his verse sings of ordinary people and ordinary occupations. This poetry has been celebrated and censored, glorified and vilified for both its content and its structure. These poems of America remain as true today as they were in the 1800s.

These titles are available in the Penguin/Prentice Hall Literature Library.
Consult your teacher before choosing one.

Think About It When a series of tiny errors adds up to a massive traffic accident, the result may seem to defy logic and justice. The victims are innocent, yet they have been injured. At the same time, any driver in their circumstances might have caused the damage—and so, in a sense, all drivers are guilty. In this poem, Karl Shapiro investigates the troubling senselessness an accident may reveal.

AUTO WRECK

Karl Shapiro

Its quick soft silver bell beating, beating,
And down the dark one ruby flare
Pulsing out red light like an artery,
The ambulance at top speed floating down
5 Past beacons and illuminated clocks
Wings in a heavy curve, dips down,
And brakes speed, entering the crowd.
The doors leap open, emptying light;
Stretchers are laid out, the mangled lifted
10 And stowed into the little hospital.
Then the bell, breaking the hush, tolls once,
And the ambulance with its terrible cargo
Rocking, slightly rocking, moves away,
As the doors, an afterthought, are closed.

15 We are deranged, walking among the cops
Who sweep glass and are large and composed.
One is still making notes under the light.
One with a bucket douches ponds of blood
Into the street and gutter.
20 One hangs lanterns on the wrecks that cling,
Empty husks of locusts, to iron poles.

Our throats were tight as tourniquets,
Our feet were bound with splints, but now,
Like convalescents intimate and gauche,[1]
25 We speak through sickly smiles and warn
With the stubborn saw of common sense,
The grim joke and the banal resolution.
The traffic moves around with care,
But we remain, touching a wound
30 That opens to our richest horror.
Already old, the question Who shall die?
Becomes unspoken Who is innocent?

For death in war is done by hands;
Suicide has cause and stillbirth, logic;
35 And cancer, simple as a flower, blooms.
But this invites the occult mind,
Cancels our physics with a sneer,
And spatters all we knew of denouement[2]
Across the expedient and wicked stones.

---

1. **gauche** (gōsh) *adj.* awkward.
2. **denouement** (dā′ nōō män′) *n.* resolution; ending that brings a story to completion.

Karl Shapiro (1913–2000) was a teacher, a critic, an editor, and a Pulitzer Prize–winning poet. Shapiro once said that he would like to see the elimination "of the line between poetry and prose." In pursuit of this ideal, he wrote his own poems in everyday American speech, confronting readers with his harsh realism.

Readings in Contemporary Poetry
Talk About It

Use the following questions to guide a discussion of "Auto Wreck."

1. **(a)** In lines 15–19, how do the reactions of the "cops" differ from the reactions of "we"? **(b)** What effect does this contrast have on your understanding of the speaker's state of mind?

2. In a group, review the poem's final stanza, answering the following questions:
   - Why is a fatal accident different from other forms of death?
   - In what ways does the accident challenge reason?

   Choose a point-person to share your group's ideas with the class.

Drama

Unit 5 Overview

PART 1: **Summarizing**
PART 2: **Reading Shakespeare**

Academic Standards
In This Unit You Will

- Analyze formatting of informational documents. (10.2.1)
- Analyze many different forms of dramatic literature. (10.3.1)
- Evaluate interactions between characters and how these affect the plot. (10.3.3)
- Analyze characters' traits through narration and dialogue. (10.3.4)
- Compare works that express a universal theme. (10.3.5)
- Identify and evaluate dialogue, soliloquies, asides, character foils and stage designs in dramatic literature. (10.3.10)

David Henry Hwang
Talks About the Form

David Henry Hwang

For many centuries, **drama** was not considered a literary form. Plays were entertainments performed on stages. Or plays were simply the words actors spoke, regarded much the way we regard scripts for movies and television shows today. William Shakespeare, probably the English language's greatest dramatist, did not even pay much attention to having his plays published during his lifetime.

▲ **David Henry Hwang,** a versatile dramatist, has written stage plays, screenplays, a television miniseries, and the book, or script, for Broadway musicals.

The Journey from Page to Stage: Discovering What "Works"

Though we do think of drama as literature today, plays are really written to be performed, not read from a book. For me, the two most critical moments in the journey from page to stage are the first time I hear my new play read by actors and the first time I see it performed in front of an audience.

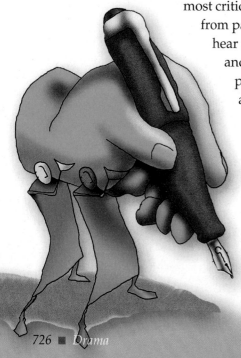

On both occasions, I learn what parts of my drama do and don't "work." When an audience sits silent after a line I thought would be funny, or yawns during a speech I thought would be moving, then I know it's time to rewrite. There's a famous saying that plays are not written, they're rewritten.

◀ **Critical Viewing** David Henry Hwang explains how he enjoys collaborating with other artists to stage his dramas. In what ways does this illustration symbolize such collaboration? **[Connect]**

Dialogue: Writing the Way People Talk

When I first began to explore creative writing, I tried short stories, but didn't really enjoy the form. Plays, however, felt much more enjoyable to me: I was simply writing the way people talk, so my grammar didn't have to be perfect. I didn't even have to use complete sentences! And I loved collaborating with other artists—actors, directors, set designers—to create a show.

As you read a play, become the director yourself and imagine it being staged in your mind. Or gather a group of classmates together and read the lines to one another. Don't worry if your performance isn't perfect. Remember that the work before you was created through a process more chaotic than you might have imagined.

The reality of creating a drama was portrayed in the 1999 Academy Award Winning Best Picture, *Shakespeare In Love,* whose screenplay was co-written by the great British playwright Tom Stoppard. In the passage shown here, Shakespeare ("Will") is rehearsing his new play, "Romeo and Juliet," and gives direction to Viola, who's playing the part of Romeo. This brief scene shows that drama, which may be the liveliest art, is not always the tidiest.

> **Will** *(interfering): No, no, no, no, don't spend it all at once! (He jumps on the stage.)*
> **Viola** *(hesitantly): Yes, sir.*
> **Will** *(to Viola): What will you do in Act Two, when he meets the love of his life?*
> **Viola** *(timidly): Ah, I am very sorry, sir, I have not seen Act Two.*
> **Will** *(stopping short): Of course you have not. I have not written it. Go once more!*
>
> **from *Shakespeare in Love***
> —*Marc Norman and Tom Stoppard*

More About David Henry Hwang

When he was young, David Henry Hwang (b. 1957) considered his Chinese heritage "a minor detail, like having red hair." He became interested in his background, however, when he was in college. His first play was produced while he was still an undergraduate at Stanford. Later, the play *M. Butterfly* established him as a major talent in the world of theater. Hwang has produced texts for Broadway musicals, opera, and even a science-fiction music drama.

Fast Facts
▶ Hwang wrote a screenplay that eventually became the movie *Seven Years in Tibet,* starring Brad Pitt.
▶ He co-authored the book for Elton John and Tim Rice's Broadway show *Aida.*

Exploring Drama

Elements of Drama

Like fiction, drama features **characters** facing a **conflict,** or struggle, that sparks a sequence of events called the **plot.** Sometimes, a drama includes **parallel plots**—two simultaneous sequences. Unlike fiction, however, a drama is a story written to be performed by actors speaking **dialogue,** the characters' words.

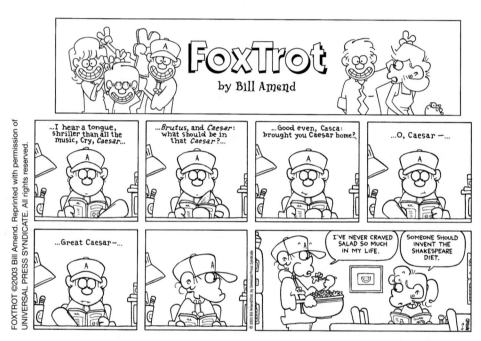

- **Acts** and **scenes** are the basic divisions of drama. A drama may consist of one or more acts, divided into scenes.

- The **script,** or text, of a play contains dialogue and stage directions. **Dialogue** is the words the characters say. **Stage directions** are notes telling how the work is to be performed or staged. Directions are often printed in italics and set off in brackets. Some dramatists use abbreviations such as OS (offstage), DS (downstage, or close to the audience), or US (upstage, or near the rear of the stage).

- **Sets** represent or simulate the place where a scene is set. A set may include such items as painted backdrops and wooden frames.

- **Props** are movable objects, like a spear, that actors use onstage.

In performance, these various elements of drama combine to produce the illusion of reality known as **dramatic effect.** Through this effect, the dramatist explores a **theme,** or central message about life.

Types of Drama and Dramatic Speech

The ancient Greeks developed drama, creating two basic types of plays:

- A **tragedy** shows the downfall or death of the **tragic hero,** or main character. In ancient Greek drama, the hero was an outstanding person brought low by a **tragic flaw,** a mistaken action or defect in character. A **chorus,** or group of performers, sang, danced, and commented on events. The hero's downfall was meant to bring about a **catharsis,** or calming release of tension, in the audience.

  William Shakespeare's tragedies differ from Greek tragedies in several ways. In **Shakespearean tragedy,** the hero has greater free will, or power of choice, and reveals more of an inner life. There is no formal chorus. Patterns of **imagery,** or sensory language, reinforce themes.

- In contrast to tragedy, a **comedy** ends happily after an amusing series of predicaments. If tragedy stresses human greatness in facing inescapable fate, comedy emphasizes human faults and the weaknesses of society itself.

In addition to dialogue involving conversations between two or more characters, dramatists use these types of **dramatic speech:**

- In a **monologue,** a character speaks at length to silent listeners.
- In a **soliloquy,** a character alone on stage reveals private thoughts.
- In an **aside,** a character briefly expresses to the audience private thoughts that other characters on stage cannot hear.

▼ **Critical Viewing**
What type of dramatic speech would you expect to be used in the scene shown here? Explain. **[Interpret]**

Check Your Understanding

Choose the answer that best corresponds to the description in each item.

1. hero reveals more of an inner life

   a. Greek tragedy   **b.** Shakespearean tragedy

2. notes for performance

   a. stage directions

   b. dialogue

3. characters commenting on action

   a. dramatic effect   **b.** chorus

4. text of a play

   a. plot   **b.** script

5. emphasizes amusing human foibles

   a. comedy   **b.** tragedy

From the Author's Desk
David Henry Hwang Introduces *Tibet Through the Red Box*

In 1985, I visited Tibet to research a screenplay I was writing, which would eventually became the movie *Seven Years In Tibet,* starring Brad Pitt. I then traveled to India to meet the Dalai Lama, exiled leader of the Tibetan people, who fled his country when Chinese troops invaded in 1959.

I apologized to him for the fact that my own ancestry was Chinese, like the invaders', yet I was writing a movie about his country. The Dalai Lama draped a prayer-shawl around my neck and said, "Tibet needs more good Chinese." I certainly felt I was in the presence of a profoundly good and spiritual being.

Adaptation: Turning an Existing Story Into a Drama

Almost twenty years later, I was asked to write a play based on a wonderful book by Peter Sís, *Tibet Through the Red Box.* This book told how, when Sís was a boy in Czechoslovakia, his father was sent to Tibet to make a documentary film about the Chinese invasion.

My play would be an **adaptation** of this story, a dramatic version of it. The challenge of adaptation lies in a paradox: In order to preserve the essence of the original story, you must often change a good many of its details.

Parallel Plots and Spectacular Staging

Peter Sís's book focused on his father's adventures in Tibet. In order to keep the **character** of young Peter active, and therefore interesting to the **audience,** I had to find a stronger story for the boy. I constructed **parallel plots:** The action of the play shifts back and forth between the father in Tibet and Peter in Czechoslovakia.

Furthermore, since much of the magic of Sís's book lies in the brilliant and mysterious artwork with which he illustrates his tale, I tried to create a theatrical equivalent through opportunities for spectacular and beautiful **staging:** flying characters, abominable snowmen, martial arts sequences, and many-headed demons.

You can use your imagination to "see" that staging as you read this excerpt from my play.

from Tibet Through the Red Box

David Henry Hwang

CHARACTERS

Peter	A boy	**Vladimir**	Peter's father, a filmmaker
Alenka	Peter's mother	**Yeti**	Abominable Snowman
The Boy Spirit	A guiding spirit who assumes many forms including a cat and the Jingle-Bell Boy	**Ensemble 1 & 2:**	Groups of characters who act as a chorus and serve different functions

Background The play is set in Czechoslovakia and Tibet during the second half of the twentieth century. At that time, the Soviet Union, with Russia as its dominant state, occupied Czechoslovakia. It was also during this period that China, a rival of the Soviet Union, invaded Tibet. In Act I, the Russian government has sent Peter's father, Vladimir, to Tibet to film preparations that the Chinese are making to invade. During his father's absence, Peter was injured while making trouble for the Russian troops. As a result, he is confined to bed. At the same time, an avalanche strands Vladimir in Tibet. Helped by various fantasy characters, including the Boy Spirit, father and son communicate through messages and dreams.

from ACT II

ALENKA (O.S.) Peter, we received another letter — from your Father!

Lights reveal ALENKA *and* PETER, *in bed. She holds the same letter that the* JINGLE-BELL BOY *pinched from* VLADIMIR.

ALENKA All covered with a strange postmark, and these odd little stamps, and characters that can only be Chinese or maybe Japanese or — Peter, he's still alive!
(pause)
I had to run down to the post office to sign for it, and on the way home, of course, I couldn't wait to read it. He is having the most amazing adventures. In a land so strange — lamas, castles, even an abominable snowman! Here — read it.

PETER I read the last one.

ALENKA What is wrong with you?

PETER Everytime we get a letter, it's like we have a big party. If he really cares about us, how come he's not home yet?

ALENKA You are so brave, Peter. The hardest thing of all is not knowing. Where he is, or whether he's even still — whether he's all right. You don't know how strong you are.

PETER Does Father know?

ALENKA Oh, I bet he does. And when he returns you'll be all better, running around like your old self.

PETER How can I get better unless he comes home?
(pause)
How much money does Father make?

ALENKA Why are you —? Enough to survive, like everyone else.

PETER How come, all of a sudden, we can afford paints?

ALENKA I make it a <u>priority</u>, what kind of —?

PETER Is Father a traitor?

ALENKA Who says such a —?

PETER It doesn't matter.

ALENKA Do your friends talk like that? The delinquents?

PETER Mother, they're not —

ALENKA He was sent away by the Russians. But he had no choice!

PETER You said he did.

Drama
Monologue Alenka's short monologue provides the audience with information about the contents of Vladimir's letter.

Drama
Dialogue This conversation reveals Peter's fears about both his father and the attitudes of others in his community.

Vocabulary Builder
priority (prī ôr′ ə tē) *n.* something given more attention than competing alternatives

ALENKA I never said any such —

PETER Before he left.

ALENKA Who are you? The secret police? You tell your friends, your Father loves his country, he's a man of peace. Then send them to me — and I'll cuff them on their pointed heads!

ALENKA *exits, leaving the letter behind.* THE BOY SPIRIT *enters, as the cat.*

THE BOY SPIRIT Meow. Spreading joy and happiness everywhere?

PETER Want me to pull your tail?

THE BOY SPIRIT *(re: the letter)* Oh, you got it.

PETER But I'm not gonna read it. That'll show him.

THE BOY SPIRIT Show him what?

PETER He can't soften me up with, "I miss you, I love you." Not when I know the truth about him.

THE BOY SPIRIT Does that mean you're not even curious about the Abominable Snowman?

The YETI, *an abominable snowman, enters. He is very tall.*

PETER "Abominable snowman."

The YETI *approaches* THE BOY SPIRIT, *who flees, running around the stage.*

PETER Who ever heard of such a stupid —?

The YETI *is tall enough to stand eye to eye with* Peter *in his bed.*

YETI Hello, there!

THE BOY SPIRIT Meow meow meow!

PETER What the —?

YETI Could you help me?

PETER It's the abominable snowman!

YETI Oh my god! Where?

PETER "Where?" You *are* the abominable snowman!

YETI Snowmen are made of snow. This is fur. I am a Yeti. I'm trying to find a city called Prague. In a country called Chicken-slovakia. A boy, about twelve years old, who's stuck in a bed, and can't get himself out. You know anyone like that?

David Henry Hwang
Author's Insight
I wanted to create a benevolent spirit to guide Peter towards greater insights into himself—like the Tibetan Boddhisattvas, who appear in many forms.

Drama
Stage Directions The appearance of the Abominable Snowman onstage intensifies the fantasy and humor of the scene.

Reading Check

Where is Peter's father?

PETER You've got to be kidding.
(off YETI'S confusion)
Boy? Twelve? Bed?

YETI Oh! Oh! Oh! So *you're* Peter. When he sent me on this mission,
I wasn't sure —

PETER "He?"

YETI I mean, to travel all the way to Europe — and, you know, no
one will issue me a passport.

PETER Who sent you?

YETI Your Father, of course. Haven't you read his letter yet?

PETER Why's everyone keep asking
me that?

YETI Not to be boastful or anything,
but . . . a lot of it is about me.
(pause) If you read it, I'll grant
you a magical wish.

PETER Anything?

YETI Anything.

PETER (pulls out the letter)
All right . . . sucker. (reads:) "I
was crossing a mountain pass
when suddenly —"

*Paper cutouts of snowflakes are pro-
jected onto the U.S. wall, moving.*
MUSICIANS *enter with percussion,
simulating the sounds of a snowstorm. U.S.,* VLADIMIR *enters, fighting his way against a blizzard.*

VLADIMIR "A snowstorm took me
by surprise. I was looking for
shelter, but the winds and snow
pushed me to the ground."

U.S., VLADIMIR *is forced to the
ground. He sits in a cross-legged
meditation position for the rest of the
scene.*

▼ **Critical Viewing**
How does the size of
the bed add to the
fantasy of this scene?
[Interpret]

VLADIMIR "I probably lost consciousness, but have some vague memory — like a dream —"

PETER "Of being lifted up —" Hey!

The YETI *mimes lifting* PETER, *as he flies out of his bed.*

VLADIMIR "Lifted up and carried!"

PETER *flies across the stage, with the* YETI *beneath, "carrying" him. Together, they move O.S.*

PETER *(to Yeti:)* What are you doing?

YETI Welcome to the Land of Magic.

YETI *releases* PETER. *He finds he can stand on his own two legs.*

VLADIMIR I awoke in a dark cave, on a bed of leaves. Beside me was a potion of honey and herbs. I drank this potion, and soon my strength began to return.

The projections of snowflakes become silhouettes of YETIS, *moving across the stage.*

VLADIMIR One day, I finally felt well-enough to <u>venture</u> out of my dark cave.

PETER *re-enters (having detached his wires), carried by the* YETI. *Dancers enter in Yeti-like costumes, begin to move through a series of warm-up rituals resembling Tai Chi.*

VLADIMIR After my eyes had adjusted to the light, I could see giant fairy beings moving gently in a kind of slow motion throughout the valley.

YETI *starts to put* PETER *down amidst the* DANCERS.

VLADIMIR They seemed to be working, gathering, tending to young ones, playing in the streams and waterfalls. Was this a lost civilization? I did not know. I crawled back into the cave, but this time I managed not to fall asleep. And I saw . . .

One of the YETIS *places food before* VLADIMIR.

VLADIMIR Slowly, these gentle giants nursed me to recovery.

The DANCERS *begin to assume the almost martial exercises lamas perform when practicing their theological dialectics.*

PETER *(to Yeti:)* What are they doing now?

YETI Practicing for battle.

PETER How tough *are* you guys, anyway?

Drama
Dialogue and Stage Directions Both the dialogue and stage directions dramatize the reading of Vladimir's letter.

Vocabulary Builder
venture (ven´ chər)
v. to do or go at some risk

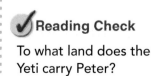

Reading Check
To what land does the Yeti carry Peter?

YETI Look at us — we're big, we're strong, and we love to work out.

PETER And you've got big teeth.

YETI With excellent gums.

PETER OK, I order you to help me fight the Russians. This is gonna be a heck of a lot better than stealing their lunches.

YETI Wait a second.

PETER You promised, remember? Want the whole world to learn Yetis are big liars?

YETI *(to other* YETIS:*)* Guys, we're being called to battle!

ENSEMBLE 1 Battle?

PETER We're gonna get the Russians.

ENSEMBLE 2 The who?

YETI I . . . granted the boy a wish.

ENSEMBLE 2 Oh. Great.

YETI It's a long story, but a wish is a wish!

ENSEMBLE 1 Where are we going?

PETER Prague. Czechoslovakia.

ENSEMBLE 2 Is the food any good?

MUSICIANS *reprise the drumbeat which underscored the attack on the Russians in Act One.*

PETER All right. Let's go back to when everything went wrong. I threw the rock at the Russian soldier, then he followed me into the dead-end alley.

ENSEMBLE 1, ENSEMBLE 2, *and the* YETI *criss-cross the stage, recalling the sequence in Act I.*

PETER This time he's in for a surprise!

THE BOY SPIRIT *enters, dressed as a Russian soldier.*

PETER And here comes the Rooskie!

THE BOY SPIRIT Nyet! Nyet!

PETER I climb up the wall — the exit's blocked!

THE BOY SPIRIT (*bad Russian accent*) Stop, you stupid kid-ski!

PETER He sees me!

Drama
Comedy This interaction stresses the Yeti's humanlike—and funny—sense of pride.

Drama
Stage Directions Music reminds the audience of an event that happened earlier.

Vocabulary Builder
reprise (ri prīz) *n.* repetition of a song, or part of a song, performed earlier

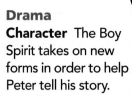

THE BOY SPIRIT I say, stop!

PETER Only this time, I don't even try to escape.

THE BOY SPIRIT Nyet! We have you cornered!

PETER I just stand there, spitting down at them.

THE BOY SPIRIT I never again will lose another lunch to you!

PETER Doing my little victory dance.

THE BOY SPIRIT That's disgusting! Come down — else, I shoot!

PETER Suddenly, out of nowhere —

THE BOY SPIRIT One, two —

PETER The Yeti cavalry appears!

THE BOY SPIRIT What?

YETIS *rush* THE BOY SPIRIT.

YETIS Roar!

THE BOY SPIRIT Oh my god-ski!

PETER He's so scared, he can't even move!

THE BOY SPIRIT The Abominable Snowman?

YETI We're Yeti, why does everyone get that wrong?

PETER Tries to use his gun —

THE BOY SPIRIT N-n-nice snowman . . .

PETER — but his hands are shaking.

YETIS Roar!

THE BOY SPIRIT Bang, bang-ski!

YETI Bullets can't go through our fur.

THE BOY SPIRIT Mama!

ENSEMBLE 2 They only make us angrier!

YETIS Roar, roar!

YETIS *duplicate their martial exercises, which buffet the* "SOLDIER" *without actually touching him.*

PETER They close in, clutching their paws around the soldier's throat —

YETIS *mime the action, as the* "SOLDIER" *falls, clutching his throat.*

Drama

Character The Boy Spirit takes on new forms in order to help Peter tell his story.

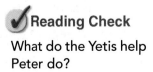

Reading Check

What do the Yetis help Peter do?

THE BOY SPIRIT Aaaargh!

PETER He falls to his knees —

THE BOY SPIRIT *(choking)* Please, please spare me —

PETER I see fear in his eyes —

THE BOY SPIRIT You don't understand — I didn't want to come here —

PETER *(to* YETIS*)* Well hurry up? Aren't you supposed to — you know —?

YETI We're waiting for your command.

PETER Me?

ENSEMBLE 2 After all, this is *your* wish.

ENSEMBLE 1 We're waiting.

THE BOY SPIRIT I have wife and a son . . . just like you.

PETER No you don't. You're nothing like me. You're a monster.

YETI Actually, *we're* the monsters here.

PETER *(to* YETI:*)* Shut up! (to THE BOY SPIRIT:)
I mean you're not a human being.

THE BOY SPIRIT In my back pocket . . .

PETER Not a real one anyway.

THE BOY SPIRIT A letter . . .

PETER You're . . . you're . . .

THE BOY SPIRIT Send it to my son.

YETI Hey, um, Peter, it's hard to hold this position.

ENSEMBLE 2 Yeah, so will you make up your mind?

PETER *screams in frustration.*

PETER All right, let him go.

YETIS *release* THE BOY SPIRIT.

David Henry Hwang
Author's Insight In order for Peter to grow, he must first learn compassion, especially towards those he has long regarded as his enemies.

THE BOY SPIRIT Thank you, thank you for showing mercy.

PETER Get out of here. Before I change my mind.

THE BOY SPIRIT I will remember you always.

▼ **Critical Viewing**
In the production shown here, how do the Yetis convey an illusion of great size and strangeness? **[Interpret]**

MODEL SELECTION

PETER *(to* YETIS:*)* All of you!

YETI But your wish . . .

PETER I don't want any wishes, I'm sick of magic, of Tibet, of this whole stupid business!
(he flies back into his bed)
Everyone just leave me alone.

All exit.

ALENKA *(O.S.)* Peter? I have something to show you.

Alenka *enters, carrying a beautifully lacquered red box.*

ALENKA Isn't it beautiful?

PETER Where'd you get this?

ALENKA I made it — with my own two hands. You think your old mother can only cook and clean and nag?
(pause)
I thought you might like a box — to store your paintings in.

PETER What makes you think I'm painting?

ALENKA Oh, I know you're not. But maybe you will someday. So I am giving you this beautiful red box . . . for all the paintings you have never made.

ALENKA *exits.*

Drama
Props The play's title alerts the audience to the significance of the box Alenka brings.

Q. Was dramatizing Peter's inner life one of your challenges in writing this play?

A. Yes. In the book, we get to know the boy Peter primarily through the memories of the adult Peter, who opens the Red Box for the first time in decades upon Vladimir's death. A play, however, is driven by dramatic events, things that happen, rather than by description. My challenge was to find actions for Peter which would show, rather than describe, his thoughts and feelings.

Q. Vladimir says, "So often, the truth isn't just this or that. One thing or the other." How does a play like this show the different sides of "the truth"?

A. Throughout the play, Peter seeks to know whether his father wanted to leave them, or whether he was forced to go on this journey. He also struggles with whether the Russians are good or evil, and if his friends are right or wrong to respond to the occupation of their country with violence. The play tries to show that "the truth" is not so black-and-white, that there are many sides to every human story.

StudentCorner

Q. What does The Boy Spirit represent?
—Elodie Singer, Boulder, Colorado

A. The Boy Spirit represents the force that guides Peter towards a deeper understanding of the world and himself. In the Tibetan religion, one god can often appear as many different creatures on earth. So Peter's spiritual guide appears in the play as several things, such as his cat, a Russian soldier, and the Dalai Lama himself.

 Writing Workshop: *Work in Progress*

Reflective Essay

For a reflective essay you may write, work in a small group to brainstorm for a list of ten small, everyday events. Then, for five of those events, note specific ways in which they affect people. Include these Event Notes in your writing portfolio.

Drama

Thinking About the Selection

1. **Respond:** What was your favorite line of dialogue in the play? Why?

2. **(a) Recall:** Where is Vladimir, Peter's father? **(b) Infer:** What accusations have some of Peter's peers leveled at Vladimir? Explain how you know.

3. **(a) Recall:** What fantastic or unreal characters appear in this excerpt? **(b) Interpret:** What, if anything, is surprising about the ways in which these characters think and behave?

4. **(a) Analyze:** In what ways do the fantasy characters help Peter connect with his father? **(b) Extend:** How else do they help Peter?

Drama Review

5. **(a)** In a chart like the one shown, list the **conflicts** Peter experiences in this **drama**. **(b)** Then, note **dialogue** and **stage directions** that Hwang uses to dramatize each conflict. In a small group, discuss your findings. **(c)** Working together, select the most effective dramatization of conflict in the excerpt. Choose a point person to share your ideas with the class.

Peter's Conflicts	Stage Direction/ Dialogue	What It Shows

6. In addition to Peter, which **character** is most essential in this excerpt of the play? Explain your choice.

Research the Author

Create a **poster** advertising a speaking appearance at your school by David Hwang. Your poster should highlight information about the author that would be of greatest interest to your classmates.

- Use the Internet and your library to research details of Hwang's life and published works.
- Write a brief note introducing Hwang. Include descriptions of his best-known works and statements by critics. Illustrate your poster with a photograph of Hwang and images from his plays or films.
- Display your poster in class.

QuickReview

Selection at a Glance

The long separation of a boy and his father is filled with stories, dreams, and fantasy.

For: Self-test
Visit: www.PHSchool.com
Web Code: eqa-6501

Drama: a story written to be performed by actors

Conflict: a problem or struggle

Dialogue: speeches or conversation between or among characters

Stage Directions: instructions about how a drama is to be performed

Character: a person or an animal that takes part in a literary work

Summarize

Skills You Will Learn

Literary Analysis: *Protagonist and Antagonist*
Reading Skill: *Retell to Summarize*

Literary Analysis: *Greek Tragedies*
Reading Skill: *Take Notes to Summarize*

Reading Skill: *Evaluate a Critic's Summaries and Responses*

Literary Analysis: *Comparing Universal and Culturally Specific Themes*

Literature You Will Read

Reading and Vocabulary Skills Preview

Reading: Summarize

> **Summarizing** is briefly stating the main events and ideas of a text in your own words.

Academic Standards

- Analyze formatting of informational documents. (10.2.1)
- Examine how the author's perspective influences the structure and tone of the text. (10.2.4)

Skills and Strategies You Will Learn in Part 1

In Part 1, you will learn

- to **summarize** by pausing occasionally to **retell** the most important information. (p. 748)
- to **take notes** to gather details for a **summary.** (p. 770)
- to **evaluate** a critic's **summaries** and responses. (p. 794)

Using the Skills and Strategies in Part 1

In Part 1, you will learn to **retell** the main ideas and events of what you have read. You will also learn strategies for **taking and organizing notes** on the most important information in a text. Finally, you will **evaluate the effectiveness of critics' summaries** in conveying the important elements of a play.

The chart shows how you could use a graphic organizer to take notes on the characters, events, and ideas that would be included in a summary of the first scene of *Antigone.*

Main Characters	Creon	Antigone	Ismene	Chorus
Main Events	Creon says if anyone buries Polyneices that person will be put to death.	Antigone decides to bury her brother Polyneices.	Ismene refuses to help her sister Antigone bury their brother Polyneices.	The Chorus suggests that the gods might have buried Polyneices.
Main Ideas	Creon is proud and harsh.	Antigone is strong-willed and determined.	Ismene is timid.	Maybe Creon is being too harsh.

Academic Vocabulary: Words for Evaluating Literature

The following words will help you talk and write about the literature in this unit.

Word	Definition	Example Sentence
evaluate *v.*	find the value; judge the worth of	Readers must *evaluate* Antigone's actions in the context of the culture.
assess *v.*	judge; measure	To *assess* the relevance of the work, consider whether readers still find it meaningful today.
contradictory *adj.*	in opposition or conflict	The two speakers have *contradictory* opinions.
deficient *adj.*	lacking; incomplete	The plot was *deficient;* events were not connected.
dominant *adj.*	ruling; most important or widespread	The *dominant* themes of the time period are loyalty and duty.

Vocabulary Skill: Word Roots

▶ A **word root** is the most basic part of a word.

In Part 1, you will learn

- the Latin word root *-val-* (p. 792)
- the Latin word root *-dict-* (p. 792)

Knowing these word roots will help you understand the meanings of words that contain them.

Activity Use a dictionary to find the meaning of each word in the chart. Explain what idea is shared by the words with a common root. Then, tell what the word root means. Check your response in a dictionary.

Word Root	Example Words
-val-	value, valor, valid
-dict-	diction, dictate, dictionary

The Birth of Western Theater

From hit Broadway plays to popular television series, contemporary drama owes much to the ancient Greek dramatists. The Greek playwrights gave European culture its first dramatic characters—men and women confronting crisis and the consequences of their own decisions. In their tragedies, the Greeks raised questions of fate, responsibility, and suffering that dramatists explore to this day.

From Ritual to Art

Theater in ancient Greece began as a celebration held in honor of Dionysos (dĭ ə nĭ səs), the god of wine. At his festivals, a chorus would chant songs in honor of the god. According to Greek legend, drama began when Thespis added to the chorus an actor who would take on the role of different characters and hold dialogues with the chorus.

Dramatic Competitions The city of Athens held the first of its annual dramatic festivals in 534 B.C. Competitors each presented three tragedies accompanied by a bawdy, humorous satyr play. In the fifth century B.C., comedies were also produced and judged at the competitions.

Thousands of Athenians attended the annual festival. They viewed the plays in an amphitheater, an outdoor theater like the one shown below. The seats of the amphitheater rose in a semicircle from a level dancing floor, or orchestra area. Painted scenery could be hung at the back. There were no curtains to allow for changes of scenery between acts. The large masks worn by the actors amplified their voices and helped even spectators in back rows identify characters and their emotions.

▼ **Critical Viewing** Judging from this ancient Greek amphitheater, what do you imagine seeing a play here would be like? **[Speculate]**

Dramatic Structure

The playwrights of ancient Greece followed a consistent format. Plays opened with a **prologue,** or exposition, that presented background on the conflict. The entering chorus then sang a **parodos** (par´ əd əs), or opening song. This was followed by the first scene. Additional songs by the chorus, called **odes,** divided scenes, as a curtain falling does in modern theater. At the conclusion of a tragedy, the chorus presented a **paean** (pē´ ən) of thanksgiving to Dionysos. The tragedy concluded with an **exodos** (eks´ ə dəs), or final scene.

The Chorus The chorus was central to the production. During the odes, the leader of the chorus, called the **choragos** (kō rā´ gəs), might exchange thoughts with the group in a dialogue. During the recital, the group would rotate from right to left, singing the **strophe** (strō´ fē), or verse. Then, the chorus would move in the opposite direction during the **antistrophe,** a verse answering the strophe. An **epode,** or stanza that follows the strophe and antistrophe, was included in some odes.

The chorus is probably a survivor from the ritual in which tragedy originated. In the fully developed plays of the fifth century B.C., the chorus plays a number of roles, from a city crowd to a poetic commentator on events. Reacting to the story as it unfolds, the chorus helps direct the audience's responses.

▲ **Critical Viewing**
Which of these photographs shows a modernized production of a Greek tragedy? Which shows a production that re-creates the original staging? Explain how you know. **[Connect]**

Antigone

Antigone is part of a trilogy of plays by Sophocles. Like all Greek tragedies, the plays are based on a myth well known to the original audience. In the myth, Oedipus (ed´ i pəs), raised by adoptive parents, is king of Thebes. A plague strikes his city, and Oedipus discovers that the gods have sent the plague in punishment for his own crimes. A stranger whom he struck down in an argument was, he learns, his real father, Laios (lā´ yəs). His wife, Iocaste, is his mother. Ravaged by this knowledge, Oedipus blinds himself. After his death, his sons, Polyneices (päl´ i nī sēz´) and Eteocles (ē tē´ ə klēz´), battle for the throne, and both die. In *Antigone,* Oedipus' daughter Antigone struggles with the new king, her uncle Creon (krē´ än´), as she strives to do right by her dead brothers.

Build Skills *Antigone,* Prologue through Scene 2

Practice these skills with the first part of *Antigone,* Prologue through Scene 2 (pp. 750–767).

  Academic Standards

- Analyze many different forms of dramatic literature. (10.3.1)
- Evaluate interactions between characters and how these affect the plot. (10.3.3)
- Analyze characters' traits through narration and dialogue. (10.3.4)

Literary Analysis

Greek tragedies, like many other plays and stories, typically focus on a **protagonist,** or main character, and an **antagonist,** the character who is in conflict with the protagonist. The two terms were first applied to Greek tragedies such as *Antigone.*

In a play, the struggle between a protagonist and an antagonist may take the form of a dramatic life-or-death conflict. At the same time, the two characters may stand for larger conflicting ideas or values. The characters' struggle may reflect deep questions of concern to people of all times and places. Here are some of the conflicting ideas in *Antigone*:

- **Protagonist:** Antigone breaks the law in order to stand up for what is right. She believes that the laws of the gods are higher than human laws.

- **Antagonist:** Her antagonist, Creon, insists that everyone must obey the law. He believes that no one is above the law.

Reading Skill

A **summary** is a short statement of the main ideas and events in a work. To summarize, pause occasionally to **retell** what you have read, using only the most important information. Summarizing improves your understanding of a literary work because it leads you to identify its key elements.

As you read *Antigone,* pause to summarize scenes and conversations. Use a chart like the one shown to identify the key elements.

Who is the most important character?

What does the character want?

Who or what gets in the character's way?

What is the outcome?

Vocabulary Builder

Antigone, Prologue through Scene 2

- **sated** (sāt´ id) *adj.* satisfied; provided with more than enough (p. 754) *We were sated after the big lunch.*

- **sententiously** (sen ten´ shəs lē) *adv.* in a way that shows excessive fondness for wise sayings; in lecturing tones (p. 758) *I told him I felt ill, and he answered sententiously, "An apple a day keeps the doctor away."*

- **deflects** (dē flekts´) *v.* turns or makes go to one side (p. 760) *He deflects his opponent's blows by blocking with his forearm.*

- **edict** (ē´ dikt´) *n.* a public order; decree (p. 762) *At the press conference, the mayor gave his edict about stray animals.*

- **brazen** (brā´ zən) *adj.* shameless; bold (p. 763) *There was chocolate all over her mouth, but she told a brazen lie about the cookies.*

- **waver** (wā´ vər) *v.* show indecision; fluctuate (p. 765) *He dipped his toe in the icy water and began to waver about his resolution to dive in.*

Build Understanding

Background

Family Feud Antigone is one of the four children of Oedipus, the former king of Thebes. When Oedipus went into exile for his crimes, Antigone's brothers, Polyneices and Eteocles, fought over who would rule, and Polyneices attacked Thebes. Eventually, the brothers killed each other, and their uncle Creon, who had supported Eteocles, became king. The play opens after the battle in which the two brothers are killed.

READ MORE

More by the Author
Oedipus the King
Oedipus at Colonus
Electra

Connecting to the Literature

Reading/Writing Connection Creon and Antigone refuse to compromise. List situations in which people should compromise, and situations in which they should not. Use three of these words: *display, dominate, abandon, benefit, capture.*

Meet the Author

Sophocles (496?–406 B.C.)

Born in Colonos, near Athens, the Greek dramatist Sophocles (säf´ ə klēz´) wrote 123 plays, of which only 7 still exist. His most famous plays, including *Antigone*, chronicle the lives of Oedipus and his children.

A Much Admired Man Sophocles served as a general in the wars Athens fought with neighboring city-states. Admired for his athleticism, he also excelled at music.

In was in the theater, however, that Sophocles truly shone. He won the prize for tragedy at the Greek dramatic competitions twenty-four times. Earlier plays had featured only two characters on stage at a time. Sophocles was the first to use a third actor in dramatic performance. This innovation changed the genre significantly.

Fast Facts

▶ In drama competitions, Sophocles never placed below second.
▶ Although very successful as a playwright, Sophocles gave up acting early in his career.

Go Online
Author Link

For: More about the author
Visit: www.PHSchool.com
Web Code: eqe-9502

ANTIGONE

SOPHOCLES

translated by
Dudley Fitts and Robert Fitzgerald

PERSONS REPRESENTED

ANTIGONE (an tig´ ə nē´), daughter of Oedipus, former King of Thebes

ISMENE (is mē´ nē), another daughter of Oedipus

EURYDICE (yo͞o rid´ i sē´), wife of Creon

CREON (krē´ än´), King of Thebes, uncle of Antigone and Ismene

HAIMON (hī´ mən), Creon's son, engaged to Antigone

TEIRESIAS (tī rē´ sē əs), a blind prophet

A SENTRY

A MESSENGER

CHORUS

CHORAGOS (kō rā´ gəs), leader of the chorus

A BOY who leads Teiresias

GUARDS

SERVANTS

Prologue—Scene 2

Scene. *Before the palace of* CREON, *King of Thebes. A central double door, and two lateral doors. A platform extends the length of the facade, and from this platform three steps lead down into the "orchestra," or chorus-ground.*

Time. *Dawn of the day after the repulse of the Argive[1] army from the assault on Thebes.*

1. Argive (är′ gïv′) from Argos, the capital of a section of ancient Greece.

Prologue

[ANTIGONE *and* ISMENE *enter from the central door of the Palace.*]

    ANTIGONE. Ismene, dear sister,
        You would think that we had already suffered enough
        For the curse on Oedipus:[2]
        I cannot imagine any grief
5   That you and I have not gone through. And now—
        Have they told you of the new decree of our King Creon?

    ISMENE. I have heard nothing: I know
        That two sisters lost two brothers, a double death
        In a single hour; and I know that the Argive army
10   Fled in the night; but beyond this, nothing.

    ANTIGONE. I thought so. And that is why I wanted you
        To come out here with me. There is something we must do.

    ISMENE. Why do you speak so strangely?

    ANTIGONE. Listen, Ismene:
15   Creon buried our brother Eteocles
        With military honors, gave him a soldier's funeral,
        And it was right that he should; but Polyneices,
        Who fought as bravely and died as miserably,—
        They say that Creon has sworn
20   No one shall bury him, no one mourn for him,
        But his body must lie in the fields, a sweet treasure
        For carrion birds[3] to find as they search for food.
        That is what they say, and our good Creon is coming here
        To announce it publicly; and the penalty—
25   Stoning to death in the public square!
                      There it is,

◀ **Critical Viewing** This Greek temple is dedicated to Poseidon, god of the sea. What does it suggest about the importance of the gods in ancient Greece? Explain. **[Draw Conclusions]**

2. curse on Oedipus reference to the fate of Oedipus, who was doomed by a decree of the gods to kill his father and marry his mother while ignorant of their true identities.

Literary Analysis
Protagonist and Antagonist What conflict between Antigone and Creon does Antigone begin explaining here?

3. carrion (kar′ ē ən) **birds** scavenger birds, such as vultures.

 **Reading Check**

What order will Creon give about Polyneices' body?

And now you can prove what you are:
A true sister, or a traitor to your family.

ISMENE. Antigone, you are mad! What could I possibly do?

30 **ANTIGONE.** You must decide whether you will help me or not.

ISMENE. I do not understand you. Help you in what?

ANTIGONE. Ismene, I am going to bury him. Will you come?

ISMENE. Bury him! You have just said the new law forbids it.

ANTIGONE. He is my brother. And he is your brother, too.

35 **ISMENE.** But think of the danger! Think what Creon will do!

ANTIGONE. Creon is not strong enough to stand in my way.

ISMENE. Ah sister!
Oedipus died, everyone hating him
For what his own search brought to light, his eyes
40 Ripped out by his own hand; and Iocaste died,
His mother and wife at once: she twisted the cords
That strangled her life; and our two brothers died,
Each killed by the other's sword. And we are left:
But oh, Antigone,
45 Think how much more terrible than these
Our own death would be if we should go against
    Creon
And do what he has forbidden! We are only women,
We cannot fight with men, Antigone!
The law is strong, we must give in to the law
50 In this thing, and in worse. I beg the Dead
To forgive me, but I am helpless: I must yield
To those in authority. And I think it is dangerous
    business
To be always meddling.

    ANTIGONE.   If that is what you think,
55 I should not want you, even if you asked to come.
You have made your choice, you can be what you want to be.
But I will bury him; and if I must die,
I say that this crime is holy: I shall lie down
With him in death, and I shall be as dear
60 To him as he to me.
           It is the dead,
Not the living, who make the longest demands;
We die for ever . . .
           You may do as you like,

Reading Skill
Summarizing Review Ismene's speech and then retell the tragic history of Antigone's family.

Literary Analysis
Protagonist and Antagonist What details in Antigone's speech give the reader reason to sympathize with Antigone?

65 Since apparently the laws of the gods mean
        nothing to you.

    ISMENE. They mean a great deal to me; but I
        have no strength
    To break laws that were made for the
        public good.

    ANTIGONE. That must be your excuse, I
        suppose. But as for me,
    I will bury the brother I love.

70 **ISMENE.**   Antigone,
    I am so afraid for you!

    ANTIGONE.   You need not be:
    You have yourself to consider, after
        all.

    ISMENE. But no one must hear of this,
        you must tell no one!
75 I will keep it a secret, I promise!

    ANTIGONE.   Oh tell it! Tell
        everyone!
    Think how they'll hate you when it
        all comes out
    If they learn that you knew about
        it all the time!

    ISMENE. So fiery! You should be
        cold with fear.

80 **ANTIGONE.** Perhaps. But I am doing only what I must.

    ISMENE. But can you do it? I say that you cannot.

    ANTIGONE. Very well: when my strength gives out, I shall do no
        more.

    ISMENE. Impossible things should not be tried at all.

    ANTIGONE. Go away, Ismene:
85 I shall be hating you soon, and the dead will too,
    For your words are hateful. Leave me my foolish plan:
    I am not afraid of the danger; if it means death,
    It will not be the worst of deaths—death without honor.

    ISMENE. Go then, if you feel that you must.
90 You are unwise,
    But a loyal friend indeed to those who love you.

[*Exit into the Palace.* ANTIGONE *goes off, left. Enter the* CHORUS.]

▲ **Critical Viewing**
Which details of this
image convey the
intense emotions of
Antigone and Ismene's
conversation?
[Analyze]

✔ **Reading Check**

What does Antigone
ask Ismene to decide?

Antigone, Prologue ■ *753*

Parodos

CHORUS. [STROPHE 1]

Now the long blade of the sun, lying
Level east to west, touches with glory
Thebes of the Seven Gates.[4] Open, unlidded
Eye of golden day! O marching light

5 Across the eddy and rush of Dirce's stream,[5]
Striking the white shields of the enemy
Thrown headlong backward from the blaze of morning!

CHORAGOS. Polyneices their commander
Roused them with windy phrases,

10 He the wild eagle screaming
Insults above our land,
His wings their shields of snow,
His crest their marshalled helms.

CHORUS. [ANTISTROPHE 1]

Against our seven gates in a yawning ring

15 The famished spears came onward in the night;
But before his jaws were <u>sated</u> with our blood,
Or pinefire took the garland of our towers,
He was thrown back; and as he turned, great Thebes—
No tender victim for his noisy power—

20 Rose like a dragon behind him, shouting war.

CHORAGOS. For God hates utterly
The bray of bragging tongues;
And when he beheld their smiling,
Their swagger of golden helms,

25 The frown of his thunder blasted
Their first man from our walls.

CHORUS. [STROPHE 2]

We heard his shout of triumph high in the air
Turn to a scream; far out in a flaming arc
He fell with his windy torch, and the earth struck him.

30 And others storming in fury no less than his
Found shock of death in the dusty joy of battle.

CHORAGOS. Seven captains at seven gates
Yielded their clanging arms to the god
That bends the battle-line and breaks it.

35 These two only, brothers in blood,
Face to face in matchless rage,
Mirroring each the other's death,
Clashed in long combat.

4. Seven Gates The city of Thebes was defended by walls containing seven entrances.

5. Dirce's (dur´ sēz) **stream** small river near Thebes into which the body of Dirce, one of the city's early queens, was thrown after her murder.

Vocabulary Builder
sated (sāt´ id) *adj.*
satisfied; provided with more than enough

**Reading Skill
Summarizing**
Reread the Parodos, and summarize Polyneices' attack on Thebes.

CHORUS.   [ANTISTROPHE 2]

But now in the beautiful morning of victory
40   Let Thebes of the many chariots sing for joy!
With hearts for dancing we'll take leave of war:
Our temples shall be sweet with hymns of praise,
And the long night shall echo with our chorus.

Scene 1

CHORAGOS. But now at last our new King is coming:
Creon of Thebes, Menoikeus'[6] son.
In this auspicious dawn of his reign
What are the new complexities
5   That shifting Fate has woven for him?
What is his counsel? Why has he summoned
The old men to hear him?

[*Enter* CREON *from the Palace, center. He addresses the* CHORUS *from the top step.*]

CREON. Gentlemen: I have the honor to inform you that our
Ship of State, which recent storms have threatened to
10   destroy, has come safely to harbor at last, guided by the merciful wisdom of Heaven. I have summoned you here this
morning because I know that I can depend upon you: your
devotion to King Laïos was absolute; you never hesitated in
your duty to our late ruler Oedipus; and when Oedipus died,
15   your loyalty was transferred to his children. Unfortunately,
as you know, his two sons, the princes Eteocles and
Polyneices, have killed each other in battle; and I, as
the next in blood, have suceeded to the full power of
the throne.
20   I am aware, of course, that no Ruler can expect complete
loyalty from his subjects until he has been tested in
office. Nevertheless, I say to you at the very outset
that I have nothing but contempt for the kind of
Governor who is afraid, for whatever reason, to follow
25   the course that he knows is best for the State; and as for
the man who sets private friendship above the public
welfare,—I have no use for him, either. I call God to
witness that if I saw my country headed for ruin, I
should not be afraid to speak out plainly; and I need
30   hardly remind you that I would never have any dealings

6. Menoikeus' (me noī′ kē əs)

✓ Reading Check

What does Creon indicate that he puts above private friendship?

▶ **Critical Viewing** What elements of this actor's appearance reflect Creon's status as king? **[Interpret]**

with an enemy of the people. No one values friendship more
highly than I; but we must remember that friends made at
the risk of wrecking our Ship are not real friends at all.
These are my principles, at any rate, and that is why I

35   have made the following decision concerning the sons of
Oedipus: Eteocles, who died as a man should die,
fighting for his country, is to be buried with full military
honors, with all the ceremony that is usual when the greatest heroes die; but his brother Polyneices, who broke his

40   exile to come back with fire and sword against his native
city and the shrines of his fathers' gods, whose one idea
was to spill the blood of his blood and sell his own people
into slavery—Polyneices, I say, is to have no burial: no man
is to touch him or say the least prayer for him; he shall lie

45   on the plain, unburied; and the birds and the scavenging
dogs can do with him whatever they like.
    This is my command, and you can see the wisdom behind
    it. As long as I am King, no traitor is going to be honored
    with the loyal man. But whoever shows by word and

50   deed that he is on the side of the State,—he shall have
    my respect while he is living, and my reverence when he
    is dead.

CHORAGOS. If that is your will, Creon son of Menoikeus,
    You have the right to enforce it: we are yours.

55 CREON. That is my will. Take care that you do your part.

CHORAGOS. We are old men: let the younger ones carry it out.

CREON. I do not mean that: the sentries have been appointed.

CHORAGOS. Then what is it that you would have us do?

CREON. You will give no support to whoever breaks this law.

60 CHORAGOS. Only a crazy man is in love with death!

CREON. And death it is; yet money talks, and the wisest
    Have sometimes been known to count a few coins too many.

[Enter SENTRY from left.]

SENTRY. I'll not say that I'm out of breath from running, King,
    because every time I stopped to think about what I have to

65   tell you, I felt like going back. And all the time a voice kept
    saying, "You fool, don't you know you're walking straight into
    trouble?"; and then another voice: "Yes, but if you let somebody
    else get the news to Creon first, it will be even worse than
    that for you!" But good sense won out, at least I hope it was

Literary Analysis
Protagonist and Antagonist How do Creon's words in lines 42–49 show that he is Antigone's antagonist?

Reading Skill Summarizing Summarize the main points in Creon's speech.

70 good sense, and here I am with a story that makes no sense
at all; but I'll tell it anyhow, because, as they say, what's
going to happen's going to happen, and—

CREON. Come to the point. What have you to say?

SENTRY. I did not do it. I did not see who did it. You must not
75 punish me for what someone else has done.

CREON. A comprehensive defense! More effective, perhaps,
If I knew its purpose. Come: what is it?

SENTRY. A dreadful thing . . . I don't know how to put it—

CREON. Out with it!

80 **SENTRY.**   Well, then;
The dead man—
            Polyneices—

[*Pause. The* SENTRY *is overcome, fumbles for words.* CREON *waits
impassively.*]

                                        out there—
                                someone,—
85   New dust on the slimy flesh!

[*Pause. No sign from* CREON.]

        Someone has given it burial that way, and
        Gone . . .

[*Long pause.* CREON *finally speaks with deadly control.*]

CREON. And the man who dared do this?

SENTRY.   I swear I
90   Do not know! You must believe me!
                            Listen:
        The ground was dry, not a sign of digging, no,
        Not a wheeltrack in the dust, no trace of anyone.
        It was when they relieved us this morning: and one of them,
95   The corporal, pointed to it.
                        There it was,
        The strangest—
                Look:
        The body, just mounded over with light dust: you see?
100   Not buried really, but as if they'd covered it
        Just enough for the ghost's peace. And no sign
        Of dogs or any wild animal that had been there.

        And then what a scene there was! Every man of us
        Accusing the other: we all proved the other man did it,

Reading Skill
Summarizing Summa-
rize the sentry's report
through line 102.

✔ Reading Check

What has happened to
Polyneices' body?

105   We all had proof that we could not have done it.
    We were ready to take hot iron in our hands,
    Walk through fire, swear by all the gods,
    It was not I!
    I do not know who it was, but it was not I!

[CREON'S *rage has been mounting steadily, but the* SENTRY *is too intent upon his story to notice it.*]

110   And then, when this came to nothing, someone said
    A thing that silenced us and made us stare
    Down at the ground: you had to be told the news,
    And one of us had to do it! We threw the dice,
    And the bad luck fell to me. So here I am,
115   No happier to be here than you are to have me:
    Nobody likes the man who brings bad news.

    CHORAGOS. I have been wondering, King: can it be that the
        gods have done this?

    CREON. [*Furiously*] Stop!
    Must you doddering wrecks
120   Go out of your heads entirely? "The gods!"
    Intolerable!
    The gods favor this corpse? Why? How had he served them?
    Tried to loot their temples, burn their images,
    Yes, and the whole State, and its laws with it!
125   Is it your senile opinion that the gods love to honor bad men?
    A pious thought!—
                No, from the very beginning
    There have been those who have whispered together,
    Stiff-necked anarchists, putting their heads together,
130   Scheming against me in alleys. These are the men,
    And they have bribed my own guard to do this thing.

    Money!   [*Sententiously*]
    There's nothing in the world so demoralizing as money.
    Down go your cities,
135   Homes gone, men gone, honest hearts corrupted,
    Crookedness of all kinds, and all for money!
    [*To* SENTRY]   But you—!
    I swear by God and by the throne of God,
    The man who has done this thing shall pay for it!
140   Find that man, bring him here to me, or your death
    Will be the least of your problems: I'll string you up
    Alive, and there will be certain ways to make you
    Discover your employer before you die;

Literary Analysis
Protagonist and Antagonist What does Creon's fear of people scheming against him show about his conflict with Antigone?

Vocabulary Builder
sententiously (sen ten′ shəs lē) *adv.* in a way that shows excessive fondness for wise sayings; in lecturing tones

And the process may teach you a lesson you seem
   to have missed:
145 The dearest profit is sometimes all too dear:
That depends on the source. Do you understand
   me?
A fortune won is often misfortune.

SENTRY. King, may I speak?

CREON.   Your very voice distresses me.

150 **SENTRY.** Are you sure that it is my voice, and not your
   conscience?

CREON. By God, he wants to analyze me now!

SENTRY. It is not what I say, but what has been done,
   that hurts you.

CREON. You talk too much.

SENTRY.   Maybe; but I've done nothing.

155 **CREON.** Sold your soul for some silver: that's all you've done.

SENTRY. How dreadful it is when the right judge judges wrong!

CREON. Your figures of speech
May entertain you now; but unless you bring me the man,
You will get little profit from them in the end.

[*Exit* CREON *into the Palace.*]

160 **SENTRY.** "Bring me the man"—!
I'd like nothing better than bringing him the man!
But bring him or not, you have seen the last of me here.
At any rate, I am safe!

[*Exit* SENTRY.]

Ode I

CHORUS.   [STROPHE 1]
Numberless are the world's wonders, but none
More wonderful than man; the stormgray sea
Yields to his prows, the huge crests bear him high;
Earth, holy and inexhaustible, is graven
5 With shining furrows where his plows have gone
Year after year, the timeless labor of stallions.
                              [ANTISTROPHE 1]
The lightboned birds and beasts that cling to cover,
The lithe fish lighting their reaches of dim water,
All are taken, tamed in the net of his mind;
10 The lion on the hill, the wild horse windy-maned,

▲ **Critical Viewing**
What does this ancient
Greek helmet indicate
about the type of
weapons against
which the sentry was
prepared to defend
himself? **[Infer]**

Reading Check

What does Creon
order the sentry to
do?

Resign to him; and his blunt yoke has broken
The sultry shoulders of the mountain bull.

[STROPHE 2]

Words also, and thought as rapid as air,
He fashions to his good use; statecraft is his,
15 And his the skill that <u>deflects</u> the arrows of snow,
The spears of winter rain: from every wind
He has made himself secure—from all but one:
In the late wind of death he cannot stand.

[ANTISTROPHE 2]

O clear intelligence, force beyond all measure!
20 O fate of man, working both good and evil!
When the laws are kept, how proudly his city stands!
When the laws are broken, what of his city then?
Never may the anarchic man find rest at my hearth,
Never be it said that my thoughts are his thoughts.

Scene 2

[*Re-enter* SENTRY *leading* ANTIGONE.]

CHORAGOS. What does this mean? Surely this captive woman
Is the Princess, Antigone. Why should she be taken?

SENTRY. Here is the one who did it! We caught her
In the very act of burying him.—Where is Creon?

5 **CHORAGOS.** Just coming from the house.

[*Enter* CREON, *center.*]

CREON.   What has happened?
Why have you come back so soon?

SENTRY. [*Expansively*]   O King,
A man should never be too sure of anything:
10 I would have sworn
That you'd not see me here again: your anger
Frightened me so, and the things you threatened me with;
But how could I tell then
That I'd be able to solve the case so soon?

15 No dice-throwing this time: I was only too glad to come!

Here is this woman. She is the guilty one:
We found her trying to bury him.
Take her, then; question her; judge her as you will.
I am through with the whole thing now, and glad of it.

20 **CREON.** But this is Antigone! Why have you brought her here?

SENTRY. She was burying him, I tell you!

CREON. [*Severely*]   Is this the truth?

SENTRY. I saw her with my own eyes. Can I say more?

CREON. The details: come, tell me quickly!

25 **SENTRY.**   It was like this:
After those terrible threats of yours, King,
We went back and brushed the dust away from the body.
The flesh was soft by now, and stinking,
So we sat on a hill to windward and kept guard.
30 No napping this time! We kept each other awake.
But nothing happened until the white round sun
Whirled in the center of the round sky over us:
Then, suddenly,
A storm of dust roared up from the earth, and the sky
35 Went out, the plain vanished with all its trees
In the stinging dark. We closed our eyes and endured it.
The whirlwind lasted a long time, but it passed;
And then we looked, and there was Antigone!
I have seen
40 A mother bird come back to a stripped nest, heard
Her crying bitterly a broken note or two
For the young ones stolen. Just so, when this girl
Found the bare corpse, and all her love's work wasted,
She wept, and cried on heaven to damn the hands
45 That had done this thing.
                    And then she brought more dust
And sprinkled wine three times for her brother's ghost.

We ran and took her at once. She was not afraid,
Not even when we charged her with what she had done.
50 She denied nothing.
              And this was a comfort to me,
And some uneasiness: for it is a good thing
To escape from death, but it is no great pleasure
To bring death to a friend.
55   Yet I always say
There is nothing so comfortable as your own safe skin!

CREON. [*Slowly, dangerously*] And you, Antigone,

Literary Analysis
Protagonist and Antagonist Has Creon realized that he is Antigone's antagonist before this point? Explain.

Reading Check

What has the sentry seen Antigone doing?

You with your head hanging,—do you confess this thing?

ANTIGONE. I do. I deny nothing.

60 **CREON.** [*To* SENTRY]   You may go.

                                            [*Exit* SENTRY.]

[*To* ANTIGONE] Tell me, tell me briefly:
Had you heard my proclamation touching this matter?

ANTIGONE. It was public. Could I help hearing it?

CREON. And yet you dared defy the law.

65 **ANTIGONE.**   I dared.
It was not God's proclamation. That final Justice
That rules the world below makes no such laws.

Your <u>edict</u>, King, was strong,
But all your strength is weakness itself against
70 The immortal unrecorded laws of God.
They are not merely now: they were, and shall be,
Operative forever, beyond man utterly.

I knew I must die, even without your decree:
I am only mortal. And if I must die
75 Now, before it is my time to die,
Surely this is no hardship: can anyone
Living, as I live, with evil all about me,
Think Death less than a friend? This death of mine
Is of no importance; but if I had left my brother
80 Lying in death unburied, I should have suffered.
Now I do not.
              You smile at me. Ah Creon,
Think me a fool, if you like; but it may well be
That a fool convicts me of folly.

85 **CHORAGOS.** Like father, like daughter: both headstrong, deaf to
     reason!
She has never learned to yield.

CREON.   She has much to learn.
The inflexible heart breaks first, the toughest iron
Cracks first, and the wildest horses bend their necks
90 At the pull of the smallest curb.
                   Pride? In a slave?
This girl is guilty of a double insolence,
Breaking the given laws and boasting of it.
Who is the man here,
95 She or I, if this crime goes unpunished?
Sister's child, or more than sister's child,

Or closer yet in blood—she and her sister
Win bitter death for this!
[*To* SERVANTS]   Go, some of you,
100 Arrest Ismene. I accuse her equally.
Bring her: you will find her sniffling in the house there.

Her mind's a traitor: crimes kept in the dark
Cry for light, and the guardian brain shudders;
But how much worse than this
105 Is <u>brazen</u> boasting of barefaced anarchy!

ANTIGONE. Creon, what more do you want than my death?

CREON.   Nothing.
That gives me everything.

ANTIGONE.   Then I beg you: kill me.
110 This talking is a great weariness: your words
Are distasteful to me, and I am sure that mine
Seem so to you. And yet they should not seem so:
I should have praise and honor for what I have done.
All these men here would praise me
115 Were their lips not frozen shut with fear of you.

                                        [*Bitterly*]

Ah the good fortune of kings,
Licensed to say and do whatever they please!

CREON. You are alone here in that opinion.

ANTIGONE. No, they are with me. But they keep their tongues in
        leash.

120 **CREON.** Maybe. But you are guilty, and they are not.

ANTIGONE. There is no guilt in reverence for the dead.

CREON. But Eteocles—was he not your brother too?

ANTIGONE. My brother too.

CREON.   And you insult his memory?

125 **ANTIGONE.** [*Softly*] The dead man would not say that I insult it.

CREON. He would: for you honor a traitor as much as him.

ANTIGONE. His own brother, traitor or not, and equal in blood.

CREON. He made war on his country. Eteocles defended it.

ANTIGONE. Nevertheless, there are honors due all the dead.

130 **CREON.** But not the same for the wicked as for the just.

ANTIGONE. Ah Creon, Creon,

Vocabulary Builder
brazen (brā′ zən)
adj. shameless; bold

Reading Skill
Summarizing Summarize the argument in lines 120–130.

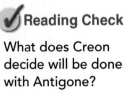Reading Check

What does Creon decide will be done with Antigone?

Which of us can say what the gods hold wicked?

CREON. An enemy is an enemy, even dead.

ANTIGONE. It is my nature to join in love, not hate.

135 **CREON.** [*Finally losing patience*] Go join them, then; if you
        must have your love,
Find it in hell!

CHORAGOS. But see, Ismene comes:

[*Enter* ISMENE, *guarded.*]

    Those tears are sisterly, the cloud
    That shadows her eyes rains down gentle sorrow.

140 **CREON.** You too, Ismene,
    Snake in my ordered house, sucking my blood
    Stealthily—and all the time I never knew

▼ Critical Viewing
What details of this
image suggest that
the chorus is pleading
with one of the
characters? Explain.
[**Analyze**]

That these two sisters were aiming at my throne!

Ismene,

145 Do you confess your share in this crime, or deny it?
Answer me.

ISMENE. Yes, if she will let me say so. I am guilty.

ANTIGONE. [*Coldly*] No, Ismene. You have no right to say so.
You would not help me, and I will not have you help me.

150 **ISMENE.** But now I know what you meant; and I am here
To join you, to take my share of punishment.

ANTIGONE. The dead man and the gods who rule the dead
Know whose act this was. Words are not friends.

ISMENE. Do you refuse me, Antigone? I want to die with you:
155 I too have a duty that I must discharge to the dead.

ANTIGONE. You shall not lessen my death by sharing it.

ISMENE. What do I care for life when you are dead?

ANTIGONE. Ask Creon. You're always hanging on his opinions.

ISMENE. You are laughing at me. Why, Antigone?

160 **ANTIGONE.** It's a joyless laughter, Ismene.

ISMENE.   But can I do nothing?

ANTIGONE. Yes. Save yourself. I shall not envy you.
There are those who will praise you; I shall have honor, too.

ISMENE. But we are equally guilty!

165 **ANTIGONE.**   No more, Ismene.
You are alive, but I belong to Death.

CREON. [*To the* CHORUS] Gentlemen, I beg you to observe these
girls:
One has just now lost her mind; the other,
It seems, has never had a mind at all.

170 **ISMENE.** Grief teaches the steadiest minds to <u>waver</u>, King.

CREON. Yours certainly did, when you assumed guilt with the
guilty!

ISMENE. But how could I go on living without her?

CREON.   You are.
She is already dead.

175 **ISMENE.**   But your own son's bride!

Literary Analysis
Protagonist and Antagonist How does the contrast between the sisters emphasize Antigone's role as the protagonist?

Vocabulary Builder
waver (wā′ vər) v. show indecision; fluctuate

**Reading Check**

What does Ismene say she wants to do?

CREON. There are places enough for him to push his plow.
   I want no wicked women for my sons!

ISMENE. O dearest Haimon, how your father wrongs you!

CREON. I've had enough of your childish talk of marriage!

180 **CHORAGOS.** Do you really intend to steal this girl from your
      son?

CREON. No; Death will do that for me.

CHORAGOS.   Then she must die?

CREON. [*Ironically*] You dazzle me.

                              —But enough of this talk!

185   [*To* GUARDS] You, there, take them away and guard them
      well:
      For they are but women, and even brave men run
      When they see Death coming.
                        [*Exit* ISMENE, ANTIGONE, *and* GUARDS.]

Literary Analysis
Protagonist and Antagonist What fact may force Haimon to become involved in the conflict between Creon and Antigone?

Literature in Context   Humanities Connection

Greek Chorus

In ancient Greek theater, the chorus was central to both the production and the meaning of a tragedy. Through dance and song, the chorus helped to tell the story, commented on the action, and divided the scenes with *odes* (songs). The chorus's commentary often expressed the audience's feelings. For Sophocles, a member of the chorus was an Everyman, an average Athenian citizen. A Greek chorus consisted of 12 or 15 young men, called *choreuts*, who were about to do their required military service.

Objects like this vase reveal the importance of music and dance to Greek culture.

◀ In a modern-day production, this chorus reacts to events taking place on stage.

Connect to the Literature   Identify a speech by the chorus in Scene 2 that probably mirrored the thoughts and feelings of the audience. Explain your choice.

Ode II

CHORUS. [STROPHE 1]

Fortunate is the man who has never tasted God's vengeance!
Where once the anger of heaven has struck, that house is
    shaken
For ever: damnation rises behind each child
Like a wave cresting out of the black northeast,
5   When the long darkness under sea roars up
And bursts drumming death upon the windwhipped sand.

[ANTISTROPHE 1]

I have seen this gathering sorrow from time long past
Loom upon Oedipus' children: generation from generation
Takes the compulsive rage of the enemy god.
10   So lately this last flower of Oedipus' line
Drank the sunlight! but now a passionate word
And a handful of dust have closed up all its beauty.

[STROPHE 2]

    What mortal arrogance
    Transcends the wrath of Zeus?[7]
15   Sleep cannot lull him, nor the effortless long months
Of the timeless gods: but he is young for ever,
And his house is the shining day of high Olympos.[8]
    All that is and shall be,
    And all the past, is his.
20   No pride on earth is free of the curse of heaven.

[ANTISTROPHE 2]

    The straying dreams of men
    May bring them ghosts of joy:
But as they drowse, the waking embers burn them;
Or they walk with fixed eyes, as blind men walk.
25   But the ancient wisdom speaks for our own time:
    Fate works most for woe
    With Folly's fairest show.
Man's little pleasure is the spring of sorrow.

7. Zeus (zo͞os) King of all Greek gods, he was believed to throw lightning bolts when angry.

8. Olympos (ō lim′ pəs) mountain in Greece where the gods were believed to live in ease and splendor (also spelled "Olympus").

Reading Skill
Summarizing
Summarize the main ideas in the concluding ode.

Apply the Skills

Antigone, Prologue through Scene 2

Thinking About the Selection

1. **Respond:** Do you sympathize with Antigone? Explain.
2. **(a) Recall:** At the opening of the play, what does Antigone tell Ismene she plans to do? **(b) Analyze:** What reasons does Ismene give as she urges Antigone not to disobey Creon? **(c) Infer:** What does their argument reveal about the personality of each character? Support your answer with details.
3. **(a) Recall:** Identify two of the accusations Creon makes against Polyneices in his speech about "the Ship of State." **(b) Analyze:** What is the key belief or principle that he states in this speech?
4. **(a) Interpret:** What does Antigone mean when she says, "Your edict, King, was strong, / But all your strength is weakness itself against / The immortal unrecorded laws of God"? **(b) Compare and Contrast:** Compare Antigone's position with Creon's.
5. **(a) Apply:** Antigone refuses to change her mind about her actions. Do you think she is showing strength of will or stubbornness? Explain. **(b) Discuss:** In a small group, share and discuss your responses. **(c) Evaluate:** Then, choose three responses to share with the class.

Literary Analysis

6. **(a)** Using a chart like the one shown, identify actions and language that present Antigone, the **protagonist,** in a sympathetic light. **(b)** Identify passages that show that Creon, the **antagonist,** is hostile to her.

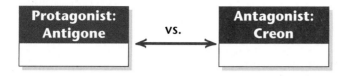

7. **(a)** In Ode I, what powers does the Chorus say humanity possesses? **(b)** Against what force is humanity powerless? **(c)** Does the Chorus favor Creon or Antigone in this ode? Explain.

Reading Skill

8. **(a) Summarize** the following conversations:
   • between Antigone and Ismene at the end of Scene 2
   • between Ismene and Creon at the end of Scene 2
   (b) How does summarizing aid your understanding of the work?

QuickReview

Play at a Glance
Defying the order of her uncle, King Creon of Thebes, Antigone buries her brother. When Creon finds out, he sentences her to death.

For: Self-test
Visit: www.PHSchool.com
Web Code: eqa-6502

Protagonist: the main character in a play or story
Antagonist: the character who is in conflict with the protagonist

Summarizing: restating in your own words the main events and ideas in a story or play

Vocabulary Builder

Practice In each item, find the two words that make the most logical pair, and identify the word that does not belong. Explain your choices.

1. sated, full, standing
2. sententiously, pompously, randomly
3. deflects, reverses, admires
4. edict, law, forecast
5. brazen, shy, cooked
6. waver, decide, smooth

Adding Words to Your Vocabulary Like the vocabulary word *sated,* the words *satiated* and *insatiable* are both forms of the word *sate.* Using a dictionary, find out what each of these last three words means and use each word correctly in a sentence. (For more on using a dictionary, see page R6.)

Writing

In *Antigone,* Sophocles explores the universal theme of conflict between the individual and society. In an **essay,** identify the message that the author is communicating about this conflict in Scenes 1 and 2 of *Antigone.* Explain what that message means to people today and why the message is still important centuries after the play was written.

For **Grammar, Vocabulary,** and **Assessment,** see **Build Language Skills,** pages 792–793.

Extend Your Learning

Research and Technology Create an **advertising poster** for a historically accurate performance of *Antigone.* Include an illustration and appropriate text that capture the essence of the performance. Conduct research to find information about the following:
- the design of the ancient Greek theater
- the costumes
- the actors' use of masks

Listening and Speaking The myths behind Antigone continue to influence culture today. Present an **oral report** on the influence of Greek mythology on contemporary literature and language. Include at least three examples of English words, such as *titanic* or *narcissist,* that are related to figures of Greek myth. Invite classmates to share their own examples.

Practice these skills with *Antigone,* Scenes 3 through 5 (pp. 771–789).

IN **Academic Standards**

- Use knowledge of ancient mythology to understand new words. (10.1.3)
- Analyze many different forms of dramatic literature. (10.3.1)
- Compare works that express a universal theme. (10.3.5)

Literary Analysis

Greek tragedies are serious dramas that were written for festivals beginning in the sixth century B.C. in Greece. They all share certain characteristics:

- They are based on myths that were familiar to the original audience of the time.
- They tell of a reversal of fortune, from good to bad, experienced by a man or woman of noble birth.
- This downfall results from the character's own actions.
- *Fate* is the force ensuring that these actions will bring doom.
- The main character may have a *tragic flaw,* a characteristic that leads to his or her downfall.

The **theme,** or central message, of a Greek tragedy is often a warning against excess, such as pride or passion. Tragedies demonstrate the limitations of human knowledge, sympathy, and foresight. They remind us that every decision involves choosing—and living with the unforeseen consequences.

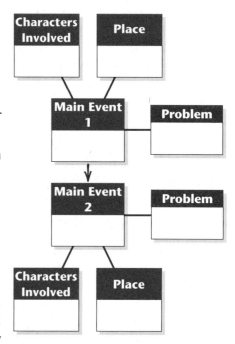

Reading Skill

To **summarize** a play, briefly state the most important actions and ideas in your own words. To gather details for a summary, **take notes.** Write down the most important elements of what you read: the characters, the places, the problems, and the key events. Use a chart like the one shown to take notes that will help you summarize *Antigone.*

Vocabulary Builder

Antigone, Scenes 3 through 5

- **deference** (def´ ər əns) *n.* a yielding to the ideas, wishes, and so on of another (p. 771) *Out of deference to him, she gave up her seat.*

- **contempt** (kən tempt´) *n.* scorn; the attitude of someone who looks down on something or someone else (p. 772) *He expressed his contempt by ignoring his opponent.*

- **vile** (vīl) *adj.* evil; low; extremely disgusting (p. 775) *The week-old food tasted vile.*

- **piety** (pī´ ə tē) *n.* loyalty and devotion to family, the divine, or some other object of respect (p. 776) *Her elders were pleased by her piety.*

- **lamentation** (lam´ ən tā´ shən) *n.* expression of grief; weeping (p. 778) *The crowd broke into loud lamentation when the sad news of the death was announced.*

- **rash** (rash) *adj.* too hasty in speech or action; reckless (p. 789) *It was rash to wander from the trail just to chase a butterfly.*

Scenes 3–5

Review and Anticipate In Scenes 1 and 2, Antigone defies the order of her uncle, King Creon of Thebes, and symbolically buries her brother Polyneices. When Creon discovers her guilt, he sentences Antigone to death, refusing to pardon her just because she is his niece. As Scene 2 ends, the chorus sings, *"Fate works most for woe / With Folly's fairest show."* The remaining scenes show the truth of these words.

Scene 3

    CHORAGOS. But here is Haimon, King, the last of all your sons.
        Is it grief for Antigone that brings him here,
        And bitterness at being robbed of his bride?
[*Enter* HAIMON.]

    CREON. We shall soon see, and no need of diviners.[1]
5   —Son,
        You have heard my final judgment on that girl:
            Have you come here hating me, or have you come
            With deference and with love, whatever I do?

        HAIMON. I am your son, father. You are my guide.

1. **diviners** (də vīn′ ərz) *n.* those who claim to forecast the future.

Vocabulary Builder
deference (def′ ər əns) *n.* a yielding to the ideas, wishes, and so on of another

◀ **Critical Viewing**
What do the ruins of this temple suggest about the endurance of Greek works of art? **[Interpret]**

10   You make things clear for me, and I obey you.
     No marriage means more to me than your continuing
          wisdom.

     CREON. Good. That is the way to behave: subordinate
     Everything else, my son, to your father's will.
     This is what a man prays for, that he may get
15   Sons attentive and dutiful in his house,
     Each one hating his father's enemies,
     Honoring his father's friends. But if his sons
     Fail him, if they turn out unprofitably,
     What has he fathered but trouble for himself
20   And amusement for the malicious?
                                   So you are right
     Not to lose your head over this woman.
     Your pleasure with her would soon grow cold, Haimon,
     And then you'd have a hellcat in bed and elsewhere.
25   Let her find her husband in Hell!
     Of all the people in this city, only she
     Has had <u>contempt</u> for my law and broken it.

     Do you want me to show myself weak before the people?
     Or to break my sworn word? No, and I will not.
30   The woman dies.
     I suppose she'll plead "family ties." Well, let her.
     If I permit my own family to rebel,
     How shall I earn the world's obedience?
     Show me the man who keeps his house in hand,
35   He's fit for public authority.
                              I'll have no dealings
     With law-breakers, critics of the government:
     Whoever is chosen to govern should be obeyed—
     Must be obeyed, in all things, great and small,
40   Just and unjust! O Haimon,
     The man who knows how to obey, and that man only,
     Knows how to give commands when the time comes.
     You can depend on him, no matter how fast
     The spears come: he's a good soldier, he'll stick it out.

45   Anarchy, anarchy! Show me a greater evil!
     This is why cities tumble and the great houses rain down,
     This is what scatters armies!

     No, no: good lives are made so by discipline.
     We keep the laws then, and the lawmakers,
50   And no woman shall seduce us. If we must lose,
     Let's lose to a man, at least! Is a woman stronger than we?

CHORAGOS. Unless time has rusted my wits,
What you say, King, is said with point and dignity.

HAIMON. [*Boyishly earnest*] Father:
55 Reason is God's crowning gift to man, and you are right
To warn me against losing mine. I cannot say—
I hope that I shall never want to say!—that you
Have reasoned badly. Yet there are other men
Who can reason, too; and their opinions might be helpful.
60 You are not in a position to know everything
That people say or do, or what they feel:
Your temper terrifies them—everyone
Will tell you only what you like to hear.
But I, at any rate, can listen; and I have heard them
65 Muttering and whispering in the dark about this girl.
They say no woman has ever, so unreasonably,
Died so shameful a death for a generous act:
"She covered her brother's body. Is this indecent?
She kept him from dogs and vultures. Is this a crime?
70 Death?—She should have all the honor that we can give her!"

This is the way they talk out there in the city.

You must believe me:
Nothing is closer to me than your happiness.
What could be closer? Must not any son
75 Value his father's fortune as his father does his?
I beg you, do not be unchangeable:
Do not believe that you alone can be right.
The man who thinks that,
The man who maintains that only he has the power
80 To reason correctly, the gift to speak, the soul—
A man like that, when you know him, turns out empty.

It is not reason never to yield to reason!

In flood time you can see how some trees bend,
And because they bend, even their twigs are safe,
85 While stubborn trees are torn up, roots and all.
And the same thing happens in sailing:
Make your sheet fast, never slacken,—and over you go,
Head over heels and under: and there's your voyage.
Forget you are angry! Let yourself be moved!
90 I know I am young; but please let me say this:
The ideal condition
Would be, I admit, that men should be right by instinct;
But since we are all too likely to go astray,

Literary Analysis
Greek Tragedies
What basic limitation
of human beings does
Haimon describe?

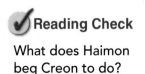

Reading Check

What does Haimon
beg Creon to do?

The reasonable thing is to learn from those who can teach.

95 **CHORAGOS.** You will do well to listen to him, King,
If what he says is sensible. And you, Haimon,
Must listen to your father.—Both speak well.

CREON. You consider it right for a man of my years and
    experience
To go to school to a boy?

100 **HAIMON.**   It is not right
If I am wrong. But if I am young, and right,
What does my age matter?

CREON. You think it right to stand up for an
    anarchist?

HAIMON. Not at all. I pay no respect to criminals.

105 **CREON.** Then she is not a criminal?

HAIMON. The City would deny it, to a man.

CREON. And the City proposes to teach me
    how to rule?

HAIMON. Ah. Who is it that's talking like a
    boy now?

CREON. My voice is the one voice giving orders
    in this City!

110 **HAIMON.** It is no City if it takes orders from one
    voice.

CREON. The State is the King!

HAIMON.   Yes, if the State is
    a desert.

                      [*Pause*]

CREON. This boy, it seems, has sold out to
    a woman.

HAIMON. If you are a woman: my concern is only
    for you.

115 **CREON.** So? Your "concern"! In a public brawl
    with your father!

HAIMON. How about you, in a public brawl with
    justice?

CREON. With justice, when all that I do is
    within my rights?

▼ **Critical Viewing**
Which details of this image from a production of *Antigone* show that Creon and Haimon are father and son? **[Analyze]**

HAIMON. You have no right to trample on God's right.

CREON. [*Completely out of control*] Fool, adolescent fool! Taken
in by a woman!

120 **HAIMON.** You'll never see me taken in by anything <u>vile</u>.

CREON. Every word you say is for her!

HAIMON. [*Quietly, darkly*]   And for you.
And for me. And for the gods under the earth.

CREON. You'll never marry her while she lives.

125 **HAIMON.** Then she must die.—But her death will cause another.

CREON. Another?
Have you lost your senses? Is this an open threat?

HAIMON. There is no threat in speaking to emptiness.

CREON. I swear you'll regret this superior tone of yours!
130   You are the empty one!

HAIMON.   If you were not my father,
I'd say you were perverse.

CREON. You girlstruck fool, don't play at words with me!

HAIMON. I am sorry. You prefer silence.

135 **CREON.**   Now, by God—!
I swear, by all the gods in heaven above us,
You'll watch it, I swear you shall!
[*To the* SERVANTS]   Bring her out!
Bring the woman out! Let her die before his eyes!
140   Here, this instant, with her bridegroom beside her!

HAIMON. Not here, no; she will not die here, King.
And you will never see my face again.
Go on raving as long as you've a friend to endure you.

[*Exit* HAIMON.]

CHORAGOS. Gone, gone.
145   Creon, a young man in a rage is dangerous!

CREON. Let him do, or dream to do, more than a man can.
He shall not save these girls from death.

CHORAGOS.   These girls?
You have sentenced them both?

150 **CREON.**   No, you are right.
I will not kill the one whose hands are clean.

Vocabulary Builder
vile (vīl) *adj.* evil; low;
extremely disgusting

Literary Analysis
Greek Tragedies
How do Haimon's
words in line 125
warn of the fateful
consequences of
Creon's decision?

Reading Check

How does Creon
respond to Haimon's
arguments?

CHORAGOS. But Antigone?

CREON. [*Somberly*]   I will carry her far away
Out there in the wilderness, and lock her
155   Living in a vault of stone. She shall have food,
As the custom is, to absolve the State of her death.
And there let her pray to the gods of hell:
They are her only gods:
Perhaps they will show her an escape from death,
160   Or she may learn,
             though late,
That <u>piety</u> shown the dead is pity in vain.

[*Exit* CREON.]

Ode III

CHORUS. Love, unconquerable   [STROPHE]
Waster of rich men, keeper
Of warm lights and all-night vigil
In the soft face of a girl:
5   Sea-wanderer, forest-visitor!
Even the pure Immortals cannot escape you,
And mortal man, in his one day's dusk,
Trembles before your glory.

Surely you swerve upon ruin   [ANTISTROPHE]
10   The just man's consenting heart,
As here you have made bright anger
Strike between father and son—
And none has conquered but Love!
A girl's glance working the will of heaven:
15   Pleasure to her alone who mocks us,
Merciless Aphrodite.[2]

Scene 4

CHORAGOS. [*As* ANTIGONE *enters guarded*] But I can no longer
    stand in awe of this,
Nor, seeing what I see, keep back my tears.
Here is Antigone, passing to that chamber
Where all find sleep at last.

5   **ANTIGONE** Look upon me, friends, and pity me   [STROPHE 1]
Turning back at the night's edge to say
Good-by to the sun that shines for me no longer;
Now sleepy Death
Summons me down to Acheron,[3] that cold shore:
10   There is no bridesong there, nor any music.

Literature in Context

Culture Connection

Ancient Greek Funeral Rites
In ancient Greek funeral ritual, the body was washed and laid out. Mourners sang ritual songs of grief. A funeral procession followed. The body was in many cases burned, and its ashes were buried in a grave or tomb. Without rites such as these, the Greeks believed, the soul would remain trapped between the underworld and the world of the living.

Connect to the Literature

How do Creon's decisions about Polyneices and Antigone blur the boundaries between the dead and the living?

Vocabulary Builder
piety (pī´ ə tē) *n.* loyalty and devotion to family, the divine, or some other object of respect

2. Aphrodite (af´ rə dīt´ ē) goddess of beauty and love who is sometimes vengeful in her retaliation for offenses.

3. Acheron (ak´ ər än´) In Greek mythology, river in the underworld over which the dead are ferried.

CHORUS. Yet not unpraised, not without a kind of honor,
  You walk at last into the underworld;
  Untouched by sickness, broken by no sword.
  What woman has ever found your way to death?

ANTIGONE.   [ANTISTROPHE 1]
15 How often I have heard the story of Niobe,[4]
  Tantalos'[5] wretched daughter, how the stone
  Clung fast about her, ivy-close: and they say
  The rain falls endlessly
  And sifting soft snow; her tears are never done.
20 I feel the loneliness of her death in mine.

CHORUS. But she was born of heaven, and you
  Are woman, woman-born. If her death is yours,
  A mortal woman's, is this not for you
  Glory in our world and in the world beyond?

ANTIGONE.   [STROPHE 2]
25 You laugh at me. Ah, friends, friends,
  Can you not wait until I am dead? O Thebes,
  O men many-charioted, in love with Fortune,
  Dear springs of Dirce, sacred Theban grove,
  Be witnesses for me, denied all pity,
30 Unjustly judged! and think a word of love
  For her whose path turns
  Under dark earth, where there are no more tears.

CHORUS. You have passed beyond human daring and come
      at last
  Into a place of stone where Justice sits.
35 I cannot tell
  What shape of your father's guilt appears in this.

ANTIGONE.   [ANTISTROPHE 2]
  You have touched it at last: that bridal bed
  Unspeakable, horror of son and mother mingling:
  Their crime, infection of all our family!
40 O Oedipus, father and brother!
  Your marriage strikes from the grave to murder mine.
  I have been a stranger here in my own land:
  All my life
  The blasphemy of my birth has followed me.

45 **CHORUS.** Reverence is a virtue, but strength
  Lives in established law: that must prevail.
  You have made your choice,
  Your death is the doing of your conscious hand.

4. Niobe (nī´ ō bē´) a queen of Thebes who was turned to stone while weeping for her slain children. Her seven sons and seven daughters were killed by Artemis and Apollo, the divine twins of Leto, after Leto complained that Niobe insulted her by bragging of maternal superiority. It was Zeus who turned the bereaved Niobe to stone, but her lament continued and her tears created a stream.

Reading Skill
Summarizing
Summarize the conversation between Antigone and the chorus in lines 1–20.

5. Tantalos' (tan´ tə ləs) Niobe's father, who was condemned to eternal frustration in the underworld because he revealed the secrets of the gods.

Literary Analysis
Greek Tragedies In lines 45–48, which does the chorus say is responsible for Antigone's doom—fate or her own choices?

Reading Check

What punishment for Antigone does Creon announce?

ANTIGONE. [EPODE]

Then let me go, since all your words are bitter,
50 And the very light of the sun is cold to me.
Lead me to my vigil, where I must have
Neither love nor <u>lamentation</u>; no song, but silence.

                            [CREON *interrupts impatiently.*]

CREON. If dirges and planned lamentations could put off death,
Men would be singing forever.
55 [*To the* SERVANTS]   Take her, go!
You know your orders: take her to the vault
And leave her alone there. And if she lives or dies,
That's her affair, not ours: our hands are clean.

ANTIGONE. O tomb, vaulted bride-bed in eternal rock,
60 Soon I shall be with my own again
Where Persephone[6] welcomes the thin ghosts underground:
And I shall see my father again, and you, mother,
And dearest Polyneices—
                dearest indeed
65 To me, since it was my hand
That washed him clean and poured the ritual wine:
And my reward is death before my time!

And yet, as men's hearts know, I have done no wrong,
I have not sinned before God. Or if I have,
70 I shall know the truth in death. But if the guilt
Lies upon Creon who judged me, then, I pray,
May his punishment equal my own.

CHORAGOS.   O passionate heart,
Unyielding, tormented still by the same winds!

75 **CREON.** Her guards shall have good
    cause to regret their delaying.

ANTIGONE. Ah! That voice is like
    the voice of death!

CREON. I can give you no reason to
    think you are mistaken.

ANTIGONE. Thebes, and you my
    fathers' gods,
And rulers of Thebes, you see
    me now, the last
80 Unhappy daughter of a line of
    kings,

Vocabulary Builder
lamentation (lam´ ən
tā´ shən) *n.* expression
of grief; weeping

6. **Persephone** (pər sef´ ə nē)
queen of the underworld.

▼ **Critical Viewing**
What does the
actress's pose in this
image suggest about
Antigone's attitude
toward Creon?
Explain. **[Interpret]**

Your kings, led away to death. You will remember
What things I suffer, and at what men's hands,
Because I would not transgress the laws of heaven.

> [*To the* GUARDS, *simply*]

Come: let us wait no longer.

> [*Exit* ANTIGONE, *left, guarded.*]

Ode IV

CHORUS.   [STROPHE 1]

> All Danae's beauty[7] was locked away
> In a brazen cell where the sunlight could not come:
> A small room, still as any grave, enclosed her.
> Yet she was a princess too,
>
> 5   And Zeus in a rain of gold poured love upon her.
> O child, child,
> No power in wealth or war
> Or tough sea-blackened ships
> Can prevail against untiring Destiny!

[ANTISTROPHE 1]

> 10   And Dryas' son[8] also, that furious king,
> Bore the god's prisoning anger for his pride:
> Sealed up by Dionysos[9] in deaf stone,
> His madness died among echoes.
> So at the last he learned what dreadful power
> 15   His tongue had mocked:
> For he had profaned the revels,
> And fired the wrath of the nine
> Implacable Sisters[10] that love the sound of the flute.

[STROPHE 2]

> And old men tell a half-remembered tale
> 20   Of horror done where a dark ledge splits the sea
> And a double surf beats on the gray shores:
> How a king's new woman, sick
> With hatred for the queen he had imprisoned,
> Ripped out his two sons' eyes with her bloody hands
> 25   While grinning Ares[11] watched the shuttle plunge
> Four times: four blind wounds crying for revenge,

[ANTISTROPHE 2]

> Crying, tears and blood mingled.—Piteously born,
> Those sons whose mother was of heavenly birth!
> Her father was the god of the North Wind
> 30   And she was cradled by gales,
> She raced with young colts on the glittering hills
> And walked untrammeled in the open light:

7. Danae's (dan´ ā ēz´) **beauty** Danae was imprisoned when it was foretold that she would mother a son who would kill her father, King Acrisios. Her beauty attracted Zeus, who visited her in the form of a shower of gold. Perseus was born of the union, and Danae was exiled with the child. Years later, as prophesied, the boy did kill Acrisios, whom he failed to recognize as his grandfather.

8. Dryas' (drī´ əs) **son** Lycorgos (lī kʉr´ gəs), whose opposition to the worship of Dionysos was severely punished by the gods. He drove the followers of Dionysos from Thrace and was driven insane. Lycorgos recovered from his madness while imprisoned in a cave, but he was later blinded by Zeus as additional punishment.

9. Dionysos (dī´ ə nī´ səs) god of wine, in whose honor the Greek plays were performed.

10. nine / Implacable Sisters nine Muses, or goddesses, of science and literature. *Implacable* (im plak´ ə bəl) means "unforgiving."

11. Ares (er´ ēz´) god of war.

Reading Check

Why does Antigone believe that she is not guilty of a crime?

But in her marriage deathless Fate found means
To build a tomb like yours for all her joy.

Scene 5

[*Enter blind* TEIRESIAS, *led by a boy. The opening speeches of*
TEIRESIAS *should be in singsong contrast to the realistic lines of*
CREON.]

TEIRESIAS. This is the way the blind man comes, Princes, Princes,
Lock-step, two heads lit by the eyes of one.

CREON. What new thing have you to tell us, old Teiresias?

TEIRESIAS. I have much to tell you: listen to the prophet, Creon.

5 **CREON.** I am not aware that I have ever failed to listen.

TEIRESIAS. Then you have done wisely, King, and ruled well.

CREON. I admit my debt to you.[12] But what have you to say?

TEIRESIAS. This, Creon: you stand once more on the edge of fate.

CREON. What do you mean? Your words are a kind of dread.

10 **TEIRESIAS.** Listen, Creon:
I was sitting in my chair of augury,[13] at the place
Where the birds gather about me. They were all a-chatter,
As is their habit, when suddenly I heard
A strange note in their jangling, a scream, a
15 Whirring fury; I knew that they were fighting,
Tearing each other, dying
In a whirlwind of wings clashing. And I was afraid.
I began the rites of burnt-offering at the altar,
But Hephaistos[14] failed me: instead of bright flame,
20 There was only the sputtering slime of the fat thigh-flesh
Melting: the entrails dissolved in gray smoke,
The bare bone burst from the welter. And no blaze!

This was a sign from heaven. My boy described it,
Seeing for me as I see for others.

25 I tell you, Creon, you yourself have brought
This new calamity upon us. Our hearths and altars
Are stained with the corruption of dogs and carrion birds
That glut themselves on the corpse of Oedipus' son.
The gods are deaf when we pray to them, their fire
30 Recoils from our offering, their birds of omen
Have no cry of comfort, for they are gorged
With the thick blood of the dead.

12. my debt to you Creon is admitting that he would not have acquired the throne if Teiresias had not moved the former king, Oedipus, to undertake an investigation that led eventually to his own downfall.

13. chair of augury the seat near the temple from which Teiresias would deliver his predictions about the future. Augury is the practice of reading the future from omens, such as the flight of birds.

14. Hephaistos (hē fes′ təs) god of fire and the forge, who would be invoked, as he was by Teiresias, for aid in the starting of ceremonial fires.

Reading Skill
Summarizing Take brief notes on lines 10–32. Then, identify two details that you would not include in a brief summary of the speech.

O my son,

These are no trifles! Think: all men make mistakes,

35 But a good man yields when he knows his course is wrong,
And repairs the evil. The only crime is pride.

Give in to the dead man, then: do not fight with a corpse—
What glory is it to kill a man who is dead?
Think, I beg you:

40 It is for your own good that I speak as I do.
You should be able to yield for your own good.

CREON. It seems that prophets have made me their
especial province.
All my life long
I have been a kind of butt for the dull arrows

45 Of doddering fortunetellers!

No, Teiresias:

If your birds—if the great eagles of God
himself
Should carry him stinking bit by bit to
heaven,
I would not yield. I am not afraid of
pollution:

50 No man can defile the gods.

Do what you will,

Go into business, make money,
speculate
In India gold or that synthetic gold from
Sardis,[15]
Get rich otherwise than by my consent to
bury him.

55 Teiresias, it is a sorry thing when a wise
man
Sells his wisdom, lets out his words for
hire!

TEIRESIAS. Ah Creon! Is there no man left in the
world—

CREON. To do what?—Come, let's have the aphorism![16]

TEIRESIAS. No man who knows that wisdom outweighs any
wealth?

60 **CREON.** As surely as bribes are baser than any baseness.

15. Sardis (sär´ dis) capital of ancient Lydia, which produced the first coins made from an alloy of gold and silver.

16. aphorism (af´ ə riz´ əm) *n.* brief saying. Creon is taunting the prophet and suggesting that the old man relies on profound-sounding expressions to make an impression.

✔**Reading Check**

What does Teiresias come to tell Creon?

▶ **Critical Viewing** Judging from this image, what type of relationship do Creon and Teiresias have? Explain. **[Infer]**

TEIRESIAS. You are sick, Creon! You are deathly sick!

CREON. As you say: it is not my place to challenge a prophet.

TEIRESIAS. Yet you have said my prophecy is for sale.

CREON. The generation of prophets has always loved gold.

65 **TEIRESIAS.** The generation of kings has always loved brass.

CREON. You forget yourself! You are speaking to your King.

TEIRESIAS. I know it. You are a king because of me.

CREON. You have a certain skill; but you have sold out.

TEIRESIAS. King, you will drive me to words that—

70 **CREON.** Say them, say them!
Only remember: I will not pay you for them.

TEIRESIAS. No, you will find them too costly.

CREON. No doubt. Speak:
Whatever you say, you will not change my will.

75 **TEIRESIAS.** Then take this, and take it to heart!
The time is not far off when you shall pay back
Corpse for corpse, flesh of your own flesh.
You have thrust the child of this world into living night,
You have kept from the gods below the child that is theirs:
80 The one in a grave before her death, the other,
Dead, denied the grave. This is your crime:
And the Furies[17] and the dark gods of Hell
Are swift with terrible punishment for you.

Do you want to buy me now, Creon?

85 Not many days,
And your house will be full of men and women weeping,
And curses will be hurled at you from far
Cities grieving for sons unburied, left to rot
Before the walls of Thebes.

90 These are my arrows, Creon: they are all for you.

[*To* BOY] But come, child: lead me home.
Let him waste his fine anger upon younger men.
Maybe he will learn at last
To control a wiser tongue in a better head.

[*Exit* TEIRESIAS.]

95 **CHORAGOS.** The old man has gone, King, but his words
Remain to plague us. I am old, too,
But I cannot remember that he was ever false.

17. Furies (fyๅๅr′ ēz) goddesses of vengeance who punished those who committed crimes against their own families.

CREON. That is true. . . . It troubles me.
   Oh it is hard to give in! but it is worse
100 To risk everything for stubborn pride.

CHORAGOS. Creon: take my advice.

CREON.   What shall I do?

CHORAGOS. Go quickly: free Antigone from her vault
   And build a tomb for the body of Polyneices.

105 **CREON.** You would have me do this?

CHORAGOS.   Creon, yes!
   And it must be done at once: God moves
   Swiftly to cancel the folly of stubborn men.

CREON. It is hard to deny the heart! But I
110 Will do it: I will not fight with destiny.

CHORAGOS. You must go yourself, you cannot leave it to others.

CREON. I will go.
                —Bring axes, servants:
   Come with me to the tomb. I buried her, I
115 Will set her free.
                Oh quickly!
   My mind misgives—
   The laws of the gods are mighty, and a man must serve them
   To the last day of his life!

                                        [*Exit* CREON.]

Pæan

CHORAGOS.
   God of many names   [STROPHE 1]

CHORUS.   O Iacchos[18]
                        son
   of Kadmeian Semele[19]
5   O born of the Thunder!
   Guardian of the West
                Regent
   of Eleusis' plain[20]
                O Prince of maenad Thebes[21]
10 and the Dragon Field by rippling Ismenos:[22]

CHORAGOS.   [ANTISTROPHE 1]
   God of many names

CHORUS.
                the flame of torches

18. Iacchos (ē′ ə kəs) one of several alternate names for Dionysos.

19. Kadmeian Semele (sem′ ə lē′) Semele was a mortal and the mother of Dionysos. She was the daughter of Thebes' founder, Kadmos.

20. Eleusis' (e loo′ sis) **plain** Located north of Athens, this plain was a site of worship for Dionysos and Demeter.

21. maenad (mē′ nad′) **Thebes** The city is here compared to a maenad, one of Dionysos' female worshipers. Such a follower would be thought of as uncontrolled or disturbed.

22. Dragon Field . . . Ismenos (is mē′ nas) The Dragon Field was located by the banks of Ismenos, a river near Thebes. Kadmos created warriors by sowing in the Dragon Field the teeth of the dragon he killed there.

Reading Check

What does Teiresias say is Creon's two-part crime?

flares on our hills
                the nymphs of Iacchos
15   dance at the spring of Castalia:[23]

from the vine-close mountain
                  come ah come in ivy:
Evohe evohe![24] sings through the streets of Thebes

CHORAGOS.   [STROPHE 2]
    God of many names

20 **CHORUS.**   Iacchos of Thebes
    heavenly Child
            of Semele bride of the Thunderer!
    The shadow of plague is upon us:
                      come
25   with clement[25] feet
              oh come from Parnasos[26]
    down the long slopes
               across the lamenting water

CHORAGOS.   [ANTISTROPHE 2]
    Io[27] Fire! Chorister of the throbbing stars!
30   O purest among the voices of the night!
    Thou son of God, blaze for us!

CHORUS. Come with choric rapture of circling Maenads
    Who cry *Io Iacche!*[28]
            God of many names!

Exodus

[*Enter* MESSENGER, *left.*]

MESSENGER. Men of the line of Kadmos,[29] you who live
    Near Amphion's citadel:[30]
                 I cannot say
    Of any condition of human life "This is fixed,
5   This is clearly good, or bad." Fate raises up,
    And Fate casts down the happy and unhappy alike:
    No man can foretell his Fate.
                 Take the case of Creon:
    Creon was happy once, as I count happiness:
10   Victorious in battle, sole governor of the land,
    Fortunate father of children nobly born.
    And now it has all gone from him! Who can say
    That a man is still alive when his life's joy fails?
    He is a walking dead man. Grant him rich,

23. **Castalia** (kas tā´ lē ə) location of a site sacred to Apollo.
24. **Evohe** (ē vō´ ē) triumphant shout of affirmation.
25. **clement** kind; favorable
26. **Parnasos** (pär nas´ əs) mountain that was sacred to both Dionysos and Apollo, located in central Greece.
27. **Io** (ē´ ō´) Greek word for "behold" or "hail."
28. **Io Iacche** (ē´ ō´ ē´ ə ke) cry of celebration used by Dionysian worshipers.

29. **Kadmos** (kad´ məs) founder of the city of Thebes, whose daughter, Semele, gave birth to Dionysos.
30. **Amphion's** (am fi´ ənz) **citadel** Amphion was a king of Thebes credited with erecting the walls of the fortress, or citadel, by using a magic lyre.

15   Let him live like a king in his great house:
     If his pleasure is gone, I would not give
     So much as the shadow of smoke for all he owns.

CHORAGOS. Your words hint at sorrow: what is your news for us?

MESSENGER. They are dead. The living are guilty of their death.

20 **CHORAGOS.** Who is guilty? Who is dead? Speak!

MESSENGER.   Haimon.
     Haimon is dead; and the hand that killed him
     Is his own hand.

CHORAGOS.   His father's? or his own?

25 **MESSENGER.** His own, driven mad by the murder his father had
     done.

CHORAGOS. Teiresias, Teiresias, how clearly you saw it all!

MESSENGER. This is my news: you must draw what conclusions
     you can from it.

CHORAGOS. But look: Eurydice, our Queen:
     Has she overheard us?
                    [*Enter* EURYDICE *from the Palace, center.*]

30 **EURYDICE.** I have heard something, friends:
     As I was unlocking the gate of Pallas'[31] shrine,
     For I needed her help today, I heard a voice
     Telling of some new sorrow. And I fainted
     There at the temple with all my maidens about me.
35   But speak again: whatever it is, I can bear it:
     Grief and I are no strangers.

MESSENGER.   Dearest Lady,
     I will tell you plainly all that I have seen.
     I shall not try to comfort you: what is the use,
40   Since comfort could lie only in what is not true?
     The truth is always best.
                              I went with Creon
     To the outer plain where Polyneices was lying,
     No friend to pity him, his body shredded by dogs.
45   We made our prayers in that place to Hecate[32]
     And Pluto,[33] that they would be merciful. And we bathed
     The corpse with holy water, and we brought
     Fresh-broken branches to burn what was left of it,
     And upon the urn we heaped up a towering barrow
50   Of the earth of his own land.
                              When we were done, we ran

◀ **Critical Viewing** In what way do both the play and this vessel show the importance of conflict in Greek art? **[Synthesize]**

31. Pallas' (pal′ əs) of Pallas Athena, the goddess of wisdom.

Reading Skill
Summarizing Identify three details in lines 37–50 that you would not include in summarizing the speech.

32. Hecate (hek′ ə tē) A goddess of the underworld, the resting place of dead souls in Greek mythology.

33. Pluto (plo͞ot′ ō) Chief god of the underworld, who ruled the souls of the dead in Greek mythology.

✔ **Reading Check**

In the Pæan, from whom does the chorus ask help?

Antigone, Exodus ■ 785

To the vault where Antigone lay on her couch of stone.
One of the servants had gone ahead,
And while he was yet far off he heard a voice
55 Grieving within the chamber, and he came back
And told Creon. And as the King went closer,
The air was full of wailing, the words lost,
And he begged us to make all haste. "Am I a prophet?"
He said, weeping, "And must I walk this road,
60 The saddest of all that I have gone before?
My son's voice calls me on. Oh quickly, quickly!
Look through the crevice there, and tell me
If it is Haimon, or some deception of the gods!"

We obeyed; and in the cavern's farthest corner
65 We saw her lying:
She had made a noose of her fine linen veil
And hanged herself. Haimon lay beside her,
His arms about her waist, lamenting her,
His love lost underground, crying out
70 That his father had stolen her away from him.

When Creon saw him the tears rushed to his eyes
And he called to him: "What have you done, child? Speak
    to me.
What are you thinking that makes your eyes so strange?
O my son, my son, I come to you on my knees!"
75 But Haimon spat in his face. He said not a word,
Staring—
                And suddenly drew his sword
And lunged. Creon shrank back, the blade missed; and the
    boy,
Desperate against himself, drove it half its length
80 Into his own side, and fell. And as he died
He gathered Antigone close in his arms again,
Choking, his blood bright red on her white cheek.
And now he lies dead with the dead, and she is his
At last, his bride in the houses of the dead.

[*Exit* EURYDICE *into the Palace.*]

85 **CHORAGOS.** She has left us without a word. What can this mean?

MESSENGER. It troubles me, too; yet she knows what is best,
Her grief is too great for public lamentation,
And doubtless she has gone to her chamber to weep

▶ Critical Viewing
Do you think the
actress portraying
Eurydice effectively
conveys tragic grief?
Explain. **[Evaluate]**

For her dead son, leading her maidens in his dirge.

90 **CHORAGOS.** It may be so: but I fear this deep silence.

[*Pause*]

MESSENGER. I will see what she is doing. I will go in.

[*Exit* MESSENGER *into the Palace.*]

[*Enter* CREON *with attendants, bearing* HAIMON'S *body.*]

CHORAGOS. But here is the King himself: oh look at him,
Bearing his own damnation in his arms.

CREON. Nothing you say can touch me any more.
95　My own blind heart has brought me
From darkness to final darkness. Here you see
The father murdering, the murdered son—
And all my civic wisdom!

Haimon my son, so young, so young to die,
100　I was the fool, not you; and you died for me.

CHORAGOS. That is the truth; but you were late in learning it.

CREON. This truth is hard to bear. Surely a god
Has crushed me beneath the hugest weight of heaven,
And driven me headlong a barbaric way
105　To trample out the thing I held most dear.

The pains that men will take to come to pain!

Literary Analysis
Greek Tragedies
In what sense might
Creon's loss of his son
be fitting punishment
for his misjudgment?

✓ **Reading Check**

What has happened to
Antigone and
Haimon?

[*Enter* MESSENGER *from the Palace.*]

MESSENGER. The burden you carry in your hands is heavy,
    But it is not all: you will find more in your house.

CREON. What burden worse than this shall I find there?

110 **MESSENGER.** The Queen is dead.

CREON. O port of death, deaf world,
    Is there no pity for me? And you, Angel of evil,
    I was dead, and your words are death again.
    Is it true, boy? Can it be true?
115   Is my wife dead? Has death bred death?

MESSENGER. You can see for yourself.
[*The doors are opened, and the body of* EURYDICE *is disclosed within.*]

CREON. Oh pity!
    All true, all true, and more than I can bear!
    O my wife, my son!

120 **MESSENGER.** She stood before the altar, and her heart
    Welcomed the knife her own hand guided,
    And a great cry burst from her lips for Megareus[34] dead,
    And for Haimon dead, her sons; and her last breath
    Was a curse for their father, the murderer of her sons.
125   And she fell, and the dark flowed in through her closing eyes.

CREON. O God, I am sick with fear.
    Are there no swords here? Has no one a blow for me?

MESSENGER. Her curse is upon you for the deaths of both.

CREON. It is right that it should be. I alone am guilty.
130   I know it, and I say it. Lead me in,
    Quickly, friends.
    I have neither life nor substance. Lead me in.

CHORAGOS. You are right, if there can be right in so much
      wrong.
    The briefest way is best in a world of sorrow.

135 **CREON.** Let it come,
    Let death come quickly, and be kind to me.
    I would not ever see the sun again.

CHORAGOS. All that will come when it will; but we, meanwhile,
    Have much to do. Leave the future to itself.

140 **CREON.** All my heart was in that prayer!

CHORAGOS. Then do not pray any more: the sky is deaf.

34. Megareus (mə gaʹ rē əs) oldest son of Creon and Eurydice, who was killed in the civil war by Argive forces invading Thebes.

CREON. Lead me away. I have been <u>rash</u> and foolish.
    I have killed my son and my wife.
    I look for comfort; my comfort lies here dead.
145   Whatever my hands have touched has come to nothing.
    Fate has brought all my pride to a thought of dust.

[*As* CREON *is being led into the house, the* CHORAGOS *advances and speaks directly to the audience.*]

CHORAGOS. There is no happiness where there is no wisdom;
    No wisdom but in submission to the gods.
    Big words are always punished,
150   And proud men in old age learn to be wise.

Vocabulary Builder
rash (rash) *adj.* too hasty in speech or action; reckless

Literary Analysis
Greek Tragedies
In what way have events forced Creon to confront his own limitations?

Apply the Skills

Antigone, Scenes 3 through 5

Thinking About the Selection

1. **Respond:** Do you think Creon should have changed his decision regarding Antigone? Why or why not?
2. **(a) Recall:** In Scene 3, lines 55–94, what advice does Haimon give his father? **(b) Analyze:** Describe Creon's response to the advice. **(c) Contrast:** Contrast Haimon's main concerns with Creon's.
3. **(a) Recall:** What does Creon have done to Antigone? **(b) Make a Judgment:** Is upholding the law Creon's only motive, or is he also guided by a desire to appear strong? Support your answer with details from the play.
4. **(a) Recall:** What prophecy does Teiresias make about Creon? **(b) Analyze Cause and Effect:** What action does Creon take because of the prophecy?
5. **(a) Summarize:** What does Creon find at the stone chamber? **(b) Connect:** In what way is the prophecy of Teiresias fulfilled?
6. **(a) Interpret:** Why does Creon say in the Exodus, "I have neither life nor substance"? **(b) Make a Judgment:** Does Creon deserve his fate? Explain.

Literary Analysis

7. Identify three characteristics of a **Greek tragedy** that *Antigone* displays. Support your answer.
8. **(a)** What is Antigone's **tragic flaw?** Explain. **(b)** To what extent does this flaw lead to her downfall? To what extent is her downfall due to **fate?** Explain.
9. **(a)** Use a chart like this one to explore the play's **theme.** **(b)** Share and discuss answers with a partner. **(c)** Explain whether your discussion has changed your thoughts on the theme of the play.

Lines From Exodus	What Does It Say?	What Does It Mean?	Why Is It Important?
94–106			
142–150			

Reading Skill

10. **Summarize** Scenes 3 through 5 scene by scene.

Vocabulary Builder

Practice Replace each underlined word with its synonym from the vocabulary list on page 770. Then, use the phrase correctly in a sentence.

1. a great <u>wailing</u>
2. a <u>thoughtless</u> action
3. a <u>nasty</u> remark
4. show <u>meekness</u> before
5. given out of <u>reverence</u>
6. his <u>disdain</u> for

Adding Words to Your Vocabulary Using a dictionary, find the verb forms of the nouns *deference* and *lamentation.* For each pair, explain the common idea that both the meaning of the verb and the noun express. (For more on using a dictionary, see page R6.)

Writing

In *Antigone,* Creon puts the state above family loyalty—and loses his family. Write a brief **reflective essay** on Creon's fate. As you write, consider these questions:

- Is Creon's fate just punishment for his decisions?
- Was there a single right course of action for him to take?
- What does his fate suggest about human action in general?

Use quotations from the play to support your main points.

For *Grammar, Vocabulary, and Assessment,* see **Build Language Skills,** pages 792–793.

Extend Your Learning

Listening and Speaking Hold a **mock trial** in which both sides in the dispute between Antigone and Creon are argued before the class. Select students to play various roles: judge, several defense attorneys, several prosecuting attorneys, and witnesses. Have attorneys for both sides provide witnesses. The class should act as a jury to decide which argument is more convincing.

Research and Technology Research and compose a one-paragraph **playbill note** on the history of Thebes to be included in a program for a production of *Antigone.* Include illustrations for your note. Remember that your audience consists of theatergoers with a casual interest in your subject, not scholars. Choose details that your audience will find interesting and informative.

Build Language Skills

Antigone

Vocabulary Skill

Word Roots The **word root -*dict*-** means "speak" or "say." For example, the word *contradictory* describes things that *say* the opposite of each other.

The Latin **word root -*val-*,** meaning courage or strength, is also the basis for several English words. For example, something that is *valid* has a *strong* foundation in logic.

Practice In a dictionary, look up each of the following words. For each word, explain how the root's meaning contributes to the meaning of the word.

1. predict **2.** validate **3.** diction **4.** benediction **5.** evaluation

Grammar Lesson

Participles and Gerunds A **participle** is a verb form used as an adjective to modify a noun or pronoun.

Examples: *a <u>creaking</u> floor* (present participle)
      a <u>fried</u> egg (past participle)

A **participial phrase** consists of a participle and its complements and modifiers. Participial phrases can add details to descriptions.

Example: *a dress <u>designed by her aunt</u>*

A **gerund** is a verb form ending in *-ing* that acts as a noun. A **gerund phrase** includes a gerund with its modifiers and complements.

Example: *<u>Dancing</u> is my favorite pastime.*

Practice Combine each pair of sentences by using a participial or gerund phrase.

1. The sprinter strained to reach the finish line. The sprinter leaned forward.

2. Ramon studied all week. He did well on the final exam.

3. The city council recognized the need to conserve resources. They passed a recycling law.

4. She played the guitar. It was beautiful.

*W*_G *Prentice Hall Writing and Grammar Connection: Chapter 20, Section 1*

MorePractice

For more practice with participles and participial phrases, see the Grammar Handbook, pp. R43 and R44.

Reading Skill: Summarize

Standards Assessed
- 10.3.1
- 10.3.3
- 10.3.4

Directions: *Read the selection. Then, answer the questions.*

In Sophocles' Oedipus at Colonus, *translated by Dudley Fitts and Robert Fitzgerald, Creon is holding Oedipus' daughters, Antigone and Ismene, against their will in order to capture Oedipus himself. Theseus, King of Athens, intervenes on behalf of Oedipus. Creon responds to Theseus as follows.*

CREON: It was not that I thought this state unmanly, son of Aegeus; nor ill-governed, either; rather I did this thing in the opinion that no one here would love my citizens so tenderly as to keep them against my will. And surely, I thought, no one would give welcome to [Oedipus], an unholy man, a parricide,[1] a man with whom his mother had been found! . . . You will do as you wish in this affair, for even though my case is right and just, I am weak, without support. Nevertheless, old as I am, I'll try to hold you answerable.

1. **parricide** person who murders his or her father.

1. Who is speaking in this excerpt?
   A Oedipus
   B Creon
   C Theseus
   D Antigone

2. What is a main idea in the speech?
   A Oedipus should be forgiven.
   B The laws are unjust.
   C You should not welcome a man like Oedipus.
   D I hope to reconcile with Oedipus.

3. What is Creon's most significant action?
   A He kidnaps Antigone and Ismene.
   B He answers Theseus.
   C He talks about Oedipus.
   D He kills Oedipus.

4. Which of the following details would be least important to include in a summary?
   A Creon is looking for Oedipus.
   B Creon is old and weak.
   C Creon has Antigone and Ismene.
   D Creon is speaking to Theseus.

Timed Writing: Persuasion [Connections]

Write a persuasive essay in which you condemn or condone Antigone's actions in *Antigone*. **(30 minutes)**

 ## Writing Workshop: *Work in Progress*

Reflective Essay

Use the Event Notes from your writing portfolio. For each of the five events you chose, write a brief answer to this question: What might be different if this event had not taken place? Put the answers in your writing portfolio.

Reading Informational Materials

Drama Reviews

In Part 1, you learned how to summarize when reading literature. Summarizing is also important when reading informational materials such as articles, editorials, and reviews. Writing and reading summaries helps you identify the most important ideas in a text, evaluate the ideas, and form your own opinions. If you read *Antigone,* you will probably be interested in these reviews of a work based on the play.

Academic Standards

- Evaluate the aesthetic qualities of style. (10.3.11)
- Write responses to literature. (10.5.2)
- Select effective verbal and nonverbal techniques for presentations. (10.7.6)

About Drama Reviews

Drama reviews are essays that convey a writer's opinion about a performance he or she has seen. The writer, known as a critic, examines each aspect of the play in order to help readers decide whether they want to see the performance. Drama reviews include these features:

- a useful summary of the story line
- a critique of the direction and acting, explaining whether the play's message was effectively expressed
- examples, quotations, facts, or other support for opinions
- judgments about the staging, which includes lighting, costumes, makeup, sound, and set design

Reading Skill

The author of a drama review should provide a summary of the play as well as the critic's considered judgments about the quality of both the play and the production. Readers have less reason to trust a review if the critic leaves out crucial information, demonstrates lack of knowledge, or does not support judgments with valid reasons. Use the following chart to **evaluate a critic's summaries and responses.**

	Criticisms	Specific Reason Given	Was This Aspect of the Production Omitted From the Review?
Acting			
Directing			
Sound and Lighting			
Costuming			
Scenery			

OFF BROADWAY...

Santa Claus Meets Sophocles

A Review of *Antigone: As Played and Danced by the Three Fates on Their Way to Becoming the Three Graces*

MATTHEW MURRAY

The critic takes a friendly tone, addressing the reader directly in the first paragraph to engage the reader's interest.

If you're familiar with Sophocles's classic Greek tragedy and have a solid working knowledge of Greek mythology, you might well appreciate the opportunity to see Big Dance Theater's production of Wellman's interpretation of the story, which is playing at Classic Stage Company through May 23. If you don't know Sophocles' original, or you have only a casual familiarity with it, chances are you'll be utterly baffled by what you see onstage.

The full title of Wellman's play is *Antigone: As Played and Danced by the Three Fates on Their Way to Becoming the Three Graces*. That should give you an idea of what you're in for: a highly deconstructed[1] take on Sophocles' story.

As the Fates (one who spins the thread of life, one who weaves it into actions, and one who determines when it must be snipped) existed eons before Sophocles, this story bears only a perfunctory similarity to his. The story the Fates enact features a handful of characters from the play, and is overseen by a narrator (and disc jockey) named E Shriek, whom Wellman describes as "an unknown god of unknown origin."

The critic provides a concise summary of the play.

As the play progresses, the Fates become the Three Graces, and pass along the story of the young Antigone and the steadfast uncle she defied to Sophocles himself. (Well, as represented by a hand puppet.) The story is told and retold until it reaches the version we currently know, at which point the play stops: what *is* is of no interest to Wellman. He's more concerned with what was and what might have been.

That idea, and the stagecraft used to present it, are the most engaging parts of this *Antigone*. Director Paul Lazar and choreographer[2] Annie-B Parson have done an excellent job of making the play visually appealing, providing almost constant movement onstage, and no shortage of surprises in the way the Fates' journeys are conveyed. (They employ microphones, dust busters, yellow slippers and toy pianos.)

Cynthia Hopkins has provided a few attractive songs for the production; Joanne Howard's set design is spartan,[3] but handsome and occasionally surprising; Claudia Stephens's costumes provide nice definition for the characters; Jay Ryan's lights are colorful and inventive; and Jane Shaw's sound design is never overdone. Leroy Logan, as E Shriek, is a fine combination of paternal and frightening, Santa Claus by way of Socrates (and Sophocles).

In this paragraph, the critic briefly evaluates other key aspects of the production: music, set design, lighting, sound, and acting.

It's the lack of immediacy and freshness that hurts this *Antigone* more than anything else: the production never feels as crisp and well-defined as it needs to be. The theatrical concept on which Wellman and Lazar have collaborated is daring and intelligent, but it's currently missing the piquant[4] energy needed to really put it across.

1. **deconstructed** (dē kən strukt´ id) *adj.* (said of a text) having been broken into its elements in order to question its meaning.
2. **choreographer** (kôr´ ē äg´ rə fər) *n.* a person who creates and directs dances.
3. **spartan** (spärt´'n) *adj.* very plain; lacking ornament.
4. **piquant** (pē´ kənt) *adj.* exciting agreeable interest or curiosity.

Curtain Up

A "Prequel" to *Antigone*

A Review of *Antigone: As Played and Danced by the Three Fates on Their Way to Becoming the Three Graces*

Elyse Sommers

> The critic gives readers background information to help them "place" the work in the contemporary theater scene.

The 55-minute dance theater piece currently at the Classic Stage Theater is a collaboration made in avant-garde[1] heaven: a text by the wizard of word play Mac Wellman, direction and musical staging by the Big Dance Theater's director Paul Lazar and choreographer Annie-B Parson.

The prolific and always surprising Wellman's first journey into Greek myth is more musical tone poem than play. His deconstruction or prequel to Sophocles' *Antigone* is brilliantly acted out and danced by the production's four performers.

> The critic comments on the performance of each actor.

Wellman has kept all the traditional parts: Creon, Antigone's sister Ismene, Creon's son Haemon, Creon's wife Eurydice (who in Wellman's version is also Teiresias) and the chorus of Theban citizens. But in this highly stylized collaboration, all these parts are played by the chameleonic,[2] maskless Three Fates (Deirdre O'Connell, Molly Hickock and Rebecca Wisocky), who are also Three Facts, on their way to becoming the Three Graces. O'Connell is a moving Antigone. Wisocky, an actor-dancer

Author: Mac Wellman
Director: Paul Lazar
Choreography & Musical Staging: Annie-B Parson
Cast: Nancy Ellis, Molly Hickock, Leroy Logan, Deirdre O'Connell & Rebecca Wisocky
Songs: Cynthia Hopkins
Running time: 60 minutes without intermission

Classic Stage
136 East 13th Street
(212/677-4210)
www.classicstage.org
4/27/04 through 5/23/04;
opening 5/02/04
Tuesday through Friday
8:00pm / Saturday 2:00pm &
8:00pm / Sunday 3:00pm

whose enormous range I've long admired, is a mesmerizing and quite humorous Creon whose kingly edicts are delivered into a microphone. Hickock takes on the roles of Teiresias and Eurydice, as well as sharing the Chorus scenes with a fourth Fate, Nancy Ellis.

> A review includes the contact information readers will need if they plan to attend the show.

If all this sounds more than a little confusing and inaccessible, anyone not well schooled in the Greek tale is indeed likely to be swept with a sense of "this is all Greek to me." Still, if you just sit back and watch the four women dance and deliver the bursts of babbling dialogue, you'll gradually get the general sense if not all of it.

> Here, the critic advises readers that they will need prior knowledge of *Antigone* to understand this version.

To add to the fun (yes, much of this IS fun with quite a few laugh-out-loud moments), there's a nondancing narrator with the intriguing name of Shriek Operator. This character is zestfully portrayed by Leroy Logan. The staging overall is appropriately spare with just a few simple but apt and often amusing props.

---

1. avant-garde (ə vänt´ gärd´) *adj.* any new or unconventional movements, especially in the arts.
2. chameleonic (kə mē´ lē än´ ik) *adj.* capable of assuming a variety of appearances.

Reading: Evaluating a Critic's Summaries and Responses

Standards Assessed
- 10.3.11
- 10.5.2
- 10.7.6

Directions: *Choose the letter of the best answer to each question.*

1. How do both critics use their opening paragraphs to prepare their readers for what they can expect in this production?
   A Both critics provide an outline of the story of *Antigone*.
   B Both critics agree that this production uses dance effectively.
   C Both critics state that this interpretation differs from the classic play.
   D Both critics note that adding a narrator helps this production.

2. In what way does Murray demonstrate that he has been open-minded in his assessment?
   A Murray disregards the original story of *Antigone*.
   B Murray praises the show for its originality.
   C Murray describes the characters and their roles in the story.
   D Murray includes both positive and negative judgments, and he explains his reasoning.

3. Which detail supports Sommers's view that the play is confusing?
   A Mac Wellman wrote the play.
   B Props are few and simple.
   C Four actresses play all of the parts.
   D There is dancing in the play.

Reading: Comprehension and Interpretation

Directions: *Write your answers on a separate piece of paper.*

4. Identify a passage from each review that discusses the same aspect of the production. Compare the critics' opinions. **[Organizing]**

5. Explain how each review would influence your decision to see this production. **[Applying]**

Timed Writing: Exposition [Critical Stance]

Write a brief essay in which you summarize and evaluate each reviewer's overall response to the play. Use specific examples from the reviews to support your opinion. **(30 minutes)**

Universal and Culturally Specific Themes

The **theme** of a literary work is its message. The theme may have aspects that are **culturally specific**, reflecting the circumstances and beliefs of the writer's culture. In contrast, the theme may also have aspects that are **universal,** or that are meaningful to people of all times and places.

For instance, an ancient poem might tell of an arrogant warrior who does not obey his people's traditions and who is finally punished by the gods.

- The poem's theme is culturally specific because it reflects the beliefs of the culture: "The gods punish those who do not obey our traditions."
- The poem also expresses a universal theme, one that people of all times and places can appreciate: "No one is above the law."

Comparing Themes

In the ancient Greek play *Antigone,* Antigone courageously defies a king. In the nineteenth-century European drama *An Enemy of the People,* a doctor courageously defies his boss, the mayor.

The "local" or culturally specific elements of each play are different—kings are not the same as mayors or bosses, and Antigone speaks of her duty to the gods while Dr. Stockmann thinks about his own conscience. Yet both plays express an important universal theme: "People may be torn between duty to authority and some higher value." As you read, use a diagram like the one shown to compare the universal and the culturally specific aspects of the two plays.

Academic Standards

- Compare works that express a universal theme. (10.3.5)
- Analyze how literature is related to the themes and issues of its historical period. (10.3.12)

Character: Dr. Stockmann

Situation

He must decide whether to lie to protect his town.

Culturally Specific Elements

- duty as doctor versus duty as townsman
-

Universal Elements

- higher duty versus duty to community
-

Vocabulary Builder

from An Enemy of the People

- **exorbitant** (eg zôr′ bi tənt) *adj.* going beyond what is reasonable; excessive (p. 801) *The price of the dress is* exorbitant—*it costs a full week's salary!*

- **impending** (im pend′ iŋ) *adj.* about to happen (p. 803) *Residents evacuated when they heard alerts of an* impending *storm.*

- **impetuosity** (im pech′ o͞o äs′ i tē) *n.* quality of acting suddenly, with great force and little thought (p. 805) *Impetuosity led him to buy a car without even a test drive.*

- **adamant** (ad′ ə mənt) *adj.* not giving in; unyielding; firm (p. 805) *I am willing to compromise, but he remains* adamant.

Build Understanding

Connecting to the Literature

Reading/Writing Connection In both *Antigone* and *An Enemy of the People,* a character makes an unpopular decision and then must deal with the consequences. In a few sentences, give advice to a person in such a situation. In giving your advice, use at least three of the following words: *assess, emphasize, maintain, accomplish.*

Meet the Author

Henrik **Ibsen** (1828–1906)

Born in Skien, Norway, Henrik Ibsen was a pioneer of modern realistic drama. The popular drama of his day specialized in idealized heroes, ridiculous buffoons, and happy endings. Breaking with convention, Ibsen showed ordinary people facing grimly realistic problems. Instead of developing perfect heroes and utter villains, he presented psychologically complex characters with a mix of good and bad motives.

Creating Controversy Ibsen also offered a brutally honest look at cutting-edge issues of his day. For instance, his play *A Doll House* concerns women's rights, a subject that was highly controversial in the nineteenth century. Outraged by such inflammatory subject matter, critics condemned him. In the end, though, Ibsen triumphed. Today, his plays are considered classics, and his realistic approach to character, plot, dialogue, and staging continues to influence drama.

For a biography of Sophocles (496? B.C.– 406 B.C.), the author of *Antigone*, see page 749.

For: More about the author
Visit: www.PHSchool.com
Web Code: eqe-9503

from An Enemy of the People

Henrik Ibsen

Background At the opening of the play, the future looks good for Dr. Thomas Stockmann's hometown. The town has finally opened a health resort for visitors, who come to drink and bathe in the local water, which is said to have healthful effects. Just when the town is beginning to benefit from the new business, however, Dr. Stockmann makes an alarming discovery. Sewage from a nearby industrial town is polluting the water. As Dr. Stockmann explains to his wife, his oldest child, Petra, and a few friends, the town will have to relocate the pipes that feed the baths in order to prevent the spread of disease. He has sent a report on the problem to his brother Peter, mayor of the town. The next morning, Peter pays him a visit.

MAYOR STOCKMANN (*entering from the hall*). Good morning.

DR. STOCKMANN. Good to see you, Peter!

MRS. STOCKMANN. Morning, Peter. How's everything with you?

MAYOR STOCKMANN. Just so-so, thank you. (*To the* DOCTOR.) Yesterday, after office hours, I received a report from you, discussing the condition of the water at the baths.

DR. STOCKMANN. Yes. Have you read it?

MAYOR STOCKMANN. I have.

DR. STOCKMANN. What have you got to say about it?

MAYOR STOCKMANN. (*glancing at the others*). Hm—

MRS. STOCKMANN. Come along, Petra.

(*She and* PETRA *go into the room on the left.*)

MAYOR STOCKMANN. (*after a moment*). Was it necessary to press all these investigations behind my back?

DR. STOCKMANN. Well, as long as I didn't have absolute proof, then—

MAYOR STOCKMANN. And now you think you do?

DR. STOCKMANN. You must be convinced of that yourself.

MAYOR STOCKMANN. Is it your object to put this document before the board of directors by way of an official recommendation?

DR. STOCKMANN. Of course. Something has to be done about this. And fast.

MAYOR STOCKMANN. As usual, in your report you let your language get out of hand. You say, among other things, that what we're offering our summer visitors is guaranteed poison.

DR. STOCKMANN. But, Peter, how else can you describe it? You've got to realize—this water *is* poison for internal *or* external use! And it's foisted on poor, suffering creatures who turn to us in good faith and pay us <u>exorbitant</u> fees to gain their health back again!

MAYOR STOCKMANN. And then you arrive at the conclusion, by your line of reasoning, that we have to build a sewer to drain off these so-called impurities from Mølledal,[1] and that all the water mains have to be relaid.

DR. STOCKMANN. Well, do you see any other way out? I don't.

MAYOR STOCKMANN. I invented a little business this morning down at the town engineer's office. And in a half-joking way, I brought up these proposals as something we perhaps ought to take under advisement[2] at some time in the future.

DR. STOCKMANN. Some time in the future!

MAYOR STOCKMANN. He smiled at my whimsical extravagance—naturally. Have you gone to the trouble of estimating just what these proposed changes would cost? From the information I received, the expenditure would probably run up into several hundred thousand crowns.[3]

---

1. **Mølledal** (möl′ ə däl′) fictional Norwegian town.
2. **to take under advisement** to think over carefully.
3. **crowns** *n.* A crown is the Norwegian unit of currency; *krone* (krō′ nə) in Norwegian.

◀ **Critical Viewing**
Judging from Dr. Stockmann's expression in this film still, how might others respond to his discovery? **[Predict]**

Vocabulary Builder
exorbitant (eg zôr′ bi tənt) *adj.* going beyond what is reasonable; excessive

Literary Analysis
Themes What details of the issue raised by Dr. Stockmann are characteristic of life in modern, industrial times?

✔ **Reading Check**
What problem does Dr. Stockmann's town face?

DR. STOCKMANN. As high as that?

MAYOR STOCKMANN. Yes. But that's not the worst. The work would extend over at least two years.

DR. STOCKMANN. Two years? Two full years?

MAYOR STOCKMANN. At the least. And meanwhile what do we do with the baths? Shut them down? Yes, we'll have to. Do you really think anyone would make the effort to come all the distance here if the rumor got out that the water was contaminated?

DR. STOCKMANN. Yes, but Peter, that's what it is.

MAYOR STOCKMANN. And then all this happens now—just now, when the baths were being recognized. Other towns in this area have the same resources for development as health resorts. Don't you think they'll leap at the chance to attract the whole flow of tourists to them? No question of it. And there we are, left stranded. We'll most likely have to abandon the whole costly enterprise; and then you'll have ruined the town you were born in.

DR. STOCKMANN. I—ruined—!

MAYOR STOCKMANN. It's through the baths alone that this town has any future to speak of. You can see that just as plain as I can.

DR. STOCKMANN. But then what do you think ought to be done?

MAYOR STOCKMANN. From your report I'm unable to persuade myself that the condition of the baths is as critical as you claim.

DR. STOCKMANN. Look, if anything, it's worse! Or it'll be that by summer, when the warm weather comes.

MAYOR STOCKMANN. Once again. I think you're exaggerating considerably. A capable doctor must know the right steps to take—he should be able to control toxic[4] elements, and to treat them if they make their presence too obvious.

DR. STOCKMANN. And then—? What else—?

MAYOR STOCKMANN. The water system for the baths as it now stands is simply a fact and clearly has to be accepted as such. But in time the directors will more than likely agree to take under consideration to what extent—depending on the funds available—they can institute certain improvements.

DR. STOCKMANN. And you can think I'd play along with that kind of trickery!

MAYOR STOCKMANN. Trickery?

Literary Analysis
Themes What ideas in the mayor's speech might provoke feelings of guilt in most people?

---

4. **toxic** (täk´ sik) *adj.* poisonous.

DR. STOCKMANN. Yes, it's a trick—a deception, a lie, an out-and-out crime against the public and society at large!

MAYOR STOCKMANN. As I've already observed, I've not yet persuaded myself that there's any real <u>impending</u> danger here.

DR. STOCKMANN. Yes, you have! There's no alternative. My report is perfectly accurate, I know that! And you're very much aware of it, Peter, but you won't admit it. You're the one who got the baths and the water system laid out where they are today; and it's *this*—it's this hellish miscalculation that you won't concede. Pah! You don't think I can see right through you?

MAYOR STOCKMANN. And even if it were true? Even if I seem a bit overanxious about my reputation, it's all for the good of the town. Without moral authority I could hardly guide and direct affairs in the way I believe serves the general welfare. For this reason—among many others—it strikes me as imperative[5] that your report not be submitted to the board of directors. It has to be withheld for the common good. Then, later, I'll bring the matter up for discussion, and we'll do the very best we can, as quietly as possible. But nothing—not the slightest word of this catastrophe must leak out to the public.

DR. STOCKMANN. My dear Peter, there's no stopping it now.

MAYOR STOCKMANN. It must and it will be stopped.

DR. STOCKMANN. I'm telling you, it's no use. Too many people know already.

MAYOR STOCKMANN. Know already! Who? Not those fellows from the *Courier*—?

DR. STOCKMANN. Why, of course they know. The independent liberal press is going to see that you do your duty.

MAYOR STOCKMANN (*after a short pause*). You're an exceptionally thoughtless man, Thomas. Haven't you considered the consequences that can follow for you?

DR. STOCKMANN. Consequences? For me?

MAYOR STOCKMANN. For you and your family as well.

DR. STOCKMANN. What the devil does *that* mean?

MAYOR STOCKMANN. I think, over the years, I've proved a helpful and accommodating brother to you.

DR. STOCKMANN. Yes, you have, and I'm thankful to you for that.

---

5. **imperative** (im per′ ə tiv) *adj.* absolutely necessary; urgent.

Vocabulary Builder
impending (im pend′ iŋ) *adj.* about to happen

Literary Analysis
Themes What situations in modern life does Peter's suggestion call to mind?

Literary Analysis
Themes Which details of this scene emphasize the universal theme of "brother against brother"?

 **Reading Check**

What does the mayor wish to do about Dr. Stockmann's discovery?

MAYOR STOCKMANN. I'm not after thanks. Because, in part, I was forced into it—for my own sake. I always hoped I could keep you in check somewhat if I helped better your economic status.

DR. STOCKMANN. What? Just for your own sake—!

MAYOR STOCKMANN. In part, I said. It's embarrassing for a public servant when his closest relative goes and compromises himself again and again.

DR. STOCKMANN. And that's what you think I do?

MAYOR STOCKMANN. Yes, unfortunately you do, without your knowing it. You have a restless, unruly, combative nature. And then this unhappy knack[6] of bursting into print on all kinds of likely and unlikely subjects. You're no sooner struck by an idea than right away you have to scribble a newspaper article on it, or a whole pamphlet even.

DR. STOCKMANN. Well, but isn't it a citizen's duty to inform the public if he comes on a new idea?

MAYOR STOCKMANN. Oh, the public doesn't need new ideas. The public is served best by the good, old, time-tested ideas it's always had.

DR. STOCKMANN. That's putting it plainly!

MAYOR STOCKMANN. I have to talk to you plainly for once. Up till now I've always tried to avoid that because I know how irritable you are; but now I'm telling you the truth, Thomas. You have no conception

---

6. **knack** (nak) *n.* trick; particular skill.

▼ **Critical Viewing**
How might concern for his children, one of whom is shown here, affect Dr. Stockmann's handling of his conflict with the town? Why? **[Speculate]**

how much you injure yourself with your <u>impetuosity</u>. You complain about the authorities and, yes, the government; you rail against them—and insist you're being passed over and persecuted. But what can you expect—someone as troublesome as you.

DR. STOCKMANN. Ah—so I'm troublesome, too?

MAYOR STOCKMANN. Yes, Thomas, you're a very troublesome man to work with. I know from experience. You show no consideration at all. You seem to forget completely that I'm the one you can thank for your post here as staff physician at the baths—

DR. STOCKMANN. I was the inevitable[7] choice—I and nobody else! I was the first to see that this town could become a flourishing spa;[8] and I was the *only* one who could see it then. I stood alone fighting for that idea for years; and I wrote and wrote—

MAYOR STOCKMANN. Unquestionably. But the right moment hadn't arrived yet. Of course you couldn't judge that from up there in the wilds. But when the opportune time came, and I—and a few others—took the matter in hand—

DR. STOCKMANN. Yes, and bungled the whole magnificent plan. Oh yes, it's really coming out now what a brilliant crew you've been!

MAYOR STOCKMANN. All that's coming out, to my mind, is your usual hunger for a good fight. You want to attack your superiors—it's your old pattern. You can't stand any authority over you; you resent anyone in a higher position and regard him as a personal enemy—and then one weapon's as good as another to use. But now I've acquainted you with the vital interests at stake here for this whole town—and, naturally, for me as well. And so I'm warning you, Thomas, I'll be <u>adamant</u> about the demand I am going to make of you.

DR. STOCKMANN. What demand?

MAYOR STOCKMANN. Since you've been so indiscreet as to discuss this delicate issue with outsiders, even though it should have been kept secret among the directors, it of course can't be hushed up now. All kinds of rumors will go flying around, and the maliciously inclined will dress them up with trimmings of their own. It'll therefore be necessary that you publicly deny these rumors.

DR. STOCKMANN. I! How? I don't understand.

MAYOR STOCKMANN. We can expect that, after further investigation, you'll arrive at the conclusion that things are far from being as critical or dangerous as you'd first imagined.

7. inevitable (in ev´ i tə bəl) *adj.* certain to happen; that which cannot be avoided or evaded.
8. spa (spä) *n.* health resort where people drink and bathe in mineral waters.

Vocabulary Builder
impetuosity (im pech´ ōō äs´ i tē) *n.* quality of acting suddenly, with great force and little thought

Vocabulary Builder
adamant (ad´ ə mənt) *adj.* not giving in; unyielding; firm

Literary Analysis
Themes What ideas about rumors lead to Dr. Stockmann's new predicament?

**Reading Check**

What does the mayor tell Dr. Stockmann he must do?

DR. STOCKMANN. Ah—you expect that!

MAYOR STOCKMANN. Moreover, we expect that you'll support and publicly affirm your confidence in the present directors to take thorough and conscientious measures, as necessary, to remedy any possible defects.

DR. STOCKMANN. But that's utterly out of the question for me, as long as they try to get by with patchwork. I'm telling you that, Peter; and it's my unqualified opinion—!

MAYOR STOCKMANN. As a member of the staff, you're not entitled to any personal opinions.

DR. STOCKMANN (*stunned*). Not entitled—?

MAYOR STOCKMANN. As a staff member, I said. As a private person—why, that's another matter. But as a subordinate official at the baths, you're not entitled to express any opinions that contradict your superiors.

DR. STOCKMANN. That's going too far! I, as a doctor, a man of science, aren't entitled to—!

MAYOR STOCKMANN. What's involved here isn't a purely scientific problem. It's a mixture of both technical and economic considerations.

DR. STOCKMANN. I don't care what . . . it is! I want the freedom to express myself on any problem under the sun!

MAYOR STOCKMANN. Anything you like—except for the baths. We forbid you that.

DR. STOCKMANN (*shouting*). You forbid—! You! A crowd of—!

MAYOR STOCKMANN. *I* forbid it—I, your supervisor. And when I forbid you, then you obey.

Literary Analysis
Themes Why might the idea of obedience to authority be universal?

Thinking About the Selection

1. **Respond:** Do you sympathize at all with Mayor Stockmann? Explain.

2. **(a) Recall:** What problem does Dr. Stockmann report to his brother? **(b) Connect:** What solution does he propose?

3. **(a) Recall:** What information does the mayor acquire from an engineer about the proposed solution? **(b) Infer:** What effect does this information have on his reaction?

4. **(a) Draw Conclusions:** What is the mayor's main goal with regard to the problem? Explain. **(b) Connect:** What is the mayor willing to sacrifice to achieve this goal? **(c) Make a Judgment:** Is he being realistic or immoral? Explain.

5. **Compare and Contrast:** Compare and contrast the two brothers.

Apply the Skills

from *An Enemy of the People* • *Antigone*

Comparing Universal and Culturally Specific Themes

1. **(a)** Use a chart like the one shown to analyze both universal and culturally specific elements of Dr. Stockmann's situation in *An Enemy of the People.* **(b)** Complete another chart like the one shown, using details from Antigone's speech in *Antigone,* Scene 2, lines 65–84. **(c)** Referring to your chart, draw a conclusion about the universal **themes** in each play.

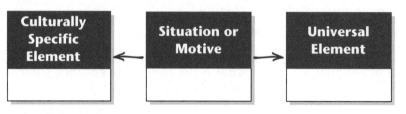

2. Compare Antigone's situation and motives to Dr. Stockmann's. Quote from both plays to support your ideas.

3. **(a)** Review Creon's speech in *Antigone,* Scene 1, lines 8–53, and describe his situation and attitude. **(b)** Compare Creon's reasoning with Mayor Stockmann's, quoting from both plays in support of your answer.

4. To what extent do you think Antigone and Dr. Stockmann act out of pride in their own virtue? Explain.

Writing to Compare Themes

In an essay, discuss whether or not *Antigone* and *An Enemy of the People* express the same universal theme. Use these questions to get started:

- What are the culturally specific elements in each work?

- What universal ideas does each play suggest?

- What is your position about the general problem in each play?

- Which side are you on?

Vocabulary Builder

Practice For each item, write a sentence in which you use the word pair correctly.

1. impending; worry

2. adamant; argue

3. exorbitant; budget

4. impetuosity; regret

Reading: Summarize

Directions: *Questions 1–4 refer to the following selection.*

All tragedies have a tragic hero, or protagonist. This character is usually of high or noble birth. The protagonist finds himself in a difficult situation for one of two reasons: Either he creates the situation because of a flaw in his character or the situation is fated. Sometimes, the situation involves a combination of the two. For example, Oedipus is doomed by fate but makes his situation worse. The tragic hero ultimately experiences disaster.

Tragedies are timeless: the protagonist is a character with whom any audience will sympathize. Audiences can identify with the hero's feelings of helplessness as he tries to fix his mistakes.

1. **What is the best paraphrase of the first sentence in paragraph 2?**
   A Audiences today like the main character.
   B Audiences can understand the main character's feelings.
   C Audiences want to see the main character fail.
   D Audiences want to learn more about the hero.

2. **Which of the following details could be left out of a summary?**
   A The protagonist is a character for whom audiences feel sympathy.
   B Audiences can identify with the main character's feelings of helplessness.
   C Oedipus makes his situation worse.
   D The tragic hero ultimately experiences disaster.

3. **Which detail should be entered in the empty oval in the chart (right)?**
   A identifies with hero
   B marked by fate
   C understands how situation could happen
   D feels sympathy

4. **What is the best one-sentence summary of the first paragraph?**
   A For a tragic hero, fate interferes and the main character experiences disaster.
   B The main character in a tragedy is a character of high status who experiences a downfall because of fate or some problem in his character.
   C A tragedy is a play about a character who cannot avoid his fate no matter what he does.
   D Oedipus is a tragic hero because no matter what he does, he cannot avoid the tragic fate that is waiting for him.

Vocabulary

Directions: *Choose the letter of the sentence that uses the vocabulary word correctly.*

5. evaluate

  A The emergency instructions called for the audience to *evaluate* the premises.

  B Part of a job of a baseball manager is to *evaluate* the talent of the players.

  C The speaker urged the audience to *evaluate* their wealth by investing.

  D I will not change my mind no matter how many times you *evaluate* your opinion.

6. assess

  A After the wound became infected, the patient developed an *assess* on his arm.

  B Only the most trusted advisers had regular *assess* to the president.

  C A jeweler is called on to *assess* gems.

  D To *assess* those in need of help, give to charity.

7. contradictory

  A The themes seemed *contradictory,* but we later realized they were consistent.

  B The main highway was *contradictory* by a huge rock slide.

  C The whole village made an effort to *contradictory* the homes that had been damaged by the storm.

  D In football, a defensive lineman's main task is *contradictory.*

8. deficient

  A To arrive on time, we took the most *deficient* route.

  B The waiter offered us another round of desserts, but we said one was *deficient.*

  C If workers are *deficient* in performing their duties, they can be reprimanded.

  D The audience applauded at the pianist's *deficient* performance.

9. dominant

  A The purpose of a political convention is to *dominant* a candidate for office.

  B Her voice was so *dominant,* we could hardly hear it above the others.

  C The character feels a mix of emotions, but the *dominant* one is anger.

  D The group with the most members will *dominant* the meeting.

Directions: *Choose the answer that is closest in meaning to the given word.*

10. valedictorian

  A a soldier awarded a medal for bravery

  B a student who speaks at graduation

  C a person who receives a degree

  D a teacher of proper speech

11. malediction

  A curse

  B portfolio

  C mistake

  D strength

12. valuable

  A worth a lot

  B sale price

  C willing to help

  D blessing

13. indication

  A a sign that tells what is happening

  B a belt that connects moving parts

  C a gang of criminals

  D smuggled goods

Writing Workshop

Narration: Reflective Essay

Unlike a reflection in a mirror, reflective writing does not simply describe something, or show what it looks like. Reflective writing examines what something means. A **reflective essay** describes a personal experience, memory, object, or idea and explains why and how it is significant. Use the steps outlined in this workshop to write your own reflective essay.

Assignment Write a reflective essay that describes a personal experience and explains its special meaning for you.

What to Include Your reflective essay should feature these elements:
- an insight or observation about life based on your personal experience
- a thorough explanation of the events that inspire this insight
- a logical organization that balances past events and your present understanding
- use of sensory details and images to describe scenes and incidents
- error-free grammar, especially the use of verbal phrases to vary sentence lengths

To preview the criteria on which your reflective essay may be judged, see the rubric on page 814.

Prewriting

Choosing Your Topic

Brainstorm for a list. Make a list of memorable events you have witnessed or experienced. You might review a yearbook, scrapbook, journal, or photo album to recall moments from your life. Choose an experience that holds special meaning for you.

Gathering Details

Gather sensory details. Create a list of words and phrases that both describe your experience and appeal to the senses of sight, hearing, touch, taste, and smell. Include words that spark clear, vivid pictures of the setting, people, and events. As you work, try to identify a strong image that captures a key part of your central insight. Look at these examples:

  Sight: snowy trails through dark trees
  Hearing: lonesome sound of birds in woods
  Smell: scent of pines

 Academic Standards

- Evaluate the use of literary devices including figurative language, imagery, allegory, and symbolism. (10.3.7)
- Review and revise writing. (10.4.10)
- Write biographical or autobiographical narratives. (10.5.1)

Using the Form
You may use elements of this form in these types of writing:
- journals
- responses to literature
- autobiographical narratives
- travel reports

To get a feel for reflective essays, read "The Sun Parlor" by Dorothy West on page 454.

Work in Progress
Review the work you did on pages 741 and 793.

Drafting

Shaping Your Writing

Choose a logical organization. Balance your description of events from the past with your present thoughts. Consider using *chronological order* to describe the events in sequence. Alternatively, consider using *order of importance organization* to interweave descriptions of the most memorable parts of the event.

Chronological Order	Order of Importance
Introduction	**Introduction**
Setting and first event: what happened	Setting: why it is meaningful
Next events: what happened	Each event: why each one is meaningful
Conclusion: Explanation of overall insight gained through this experience	Most important moment: why it is critical
	Conclusion: Explanation of overall insight gained

Providing Elaboration

Use effective imagery. Use sensory images to create word pictures.

- A **simile** compares two unlike things using the words *like* or *as*. (My eyes were <u>as wide as saucers</u>.)

- A **metaphor** compares two unlike things by stating that one thing is the other. (Suddenly, a <u>herd of children stampeded</u> through the room.)

- **Personification** applies human qualities or behavior to something nonhuman. (<u>Disappointment grabbed me</u> and would not let go.)

Revising

Revising Your Overall Structure

Revise for unity. Reread your draft and highlight any sentences that do not support your overall meaning. Cut or rewrite those sentences.

> **Reading** **Writing** *Connection*
>
> To read the complete student model, see page 813.

Student Model: Revising for Unity

The magical miniature world was enclosed in a glass case.

My father brought it up to my bedroom and warned me

never to touch the glass for fear I would destroy its per-

fection. ~~I also had a number of other toys there in the room.~~

> Deleting a detail unrelated to the main idea strengthens the essay's focus.

Revising Your Word Choice

Revise to replace vague words. Review your essay, circling vague words. Consider more precise replacements.

Vague: It was one of the *best things* I had ever seen.

Precise: It was one of the *most colorful packages* I had ever seen.

Integrating Grammar Skills

Revising to Combine Sentences with Verbal Phrases

The repetition of too many sentences with the same structure can create choppy, uninteresting writing. Use verbal phrases to combine a series of short choppy sentences into longer, more flowing ones.

Prentice Hall Writing and Grammar Connection: Chapter 20, Section 1

Identifying Verbal Phrases

Verbal phrases use verbs and act as nouns, adjectives, or adverbs.

The Three Types of Verbal Phrases

Participial Phrase	Gerund Phrase	Infinitive Phrase
a participle—a form of a verb that can act as an adjective—and its modifiers	a gerund—a verb ending in *-ing* that functions as a noun—and its modifiers	an infinitive—a form of verb that appears with the word *to* and acts as a noun, adjective, or adverb—and its modifiers
Walking by herself, Sara felt peaceful. *(modifies Sara)*	*Speaking in public* is scary. *(acts as subject)*	Her advice was *to start small. (acts as predicate nominative)*

A verbal phrase should be close to the word it modifies.

Misplaced: *Eating fish,* the scientists saw a baby seal.

Correct: The scientists saw a baby seal *eating fish.*

Combining Sentences Using Verbal Phrases Use verbal phrases to combine choppy sentences. Follow these steps:

1. **Express the ideas from a short sentence as a verbal phrase.**
2. **Insert the phrase into a new sentence, locating it near the word or words being modified.**
3. **Punctuate the new sentence correctly.** Look at this example:

Choppy sentences: The cheetah moves silently. It stalks its prey.

Combined sentence: Stalking its prey, the cheetah moves silently.

Apply It to Your Editing

Review the last four paragraphs of your essay. Look for short sentences that might be combined using participial, gerund, or infinitive phrases. Avoid misplaced modifiers by locating phrases in your combined sentences as close as possible to the words they modify.

Student Model: Samantha Duffy
Santa Clarita, CA

The Dollhouse

I was sitting on my couch eating chocolate chip ice cream when the front door was flung open. Suddenly, a huge colorfully wrapped box with a giant red bow appeared. The only other thing I could see was the strong hands of a man gripping the box tightly. He placed it carefully on the table in front of me.

My father, glowing with pleasure, emerged from behind the box and said, "My daughter deserves the best present that money can buy for her birthday, and here it is. Go on, open it. What are you waiting for?"

I stood up and ripped the shiny paper from the box, but I could not help but stare when I saw what the paper had been hiding.

"Thank you, Daddy, it's truly beautiful," I said, hoping my eyes did not reveal the confusion I felt as I looked at the item.

In front of me was a delicately handcrafted dollhouse, and inside was a family of tiny porcelain dolls. The furniture in the dollhouse looked real, except that it had no flaws. There were pretty paintings on the wall and little glass chandeliers. It was amazing how peaceful and perfect the family inside appeared.

It would have been a terrific birthday present except for one thing: The magical miniature world was enclosed in a glass case. My father brought it up to my bedroom and warned me never to touch the glass for fear I would destroy its perfection. The dollhouse was there for me to admire but never to touch or play with.

The dollhouse sat in the same place for many years. I obeyed my father and never touched it. At first, I was intrigued by this beautiful world and did as I was supposed to: I admired it. Time passed, though, and I started to find it boring and useless. I began to look at the dollhouse in a new light. Those pretty porcelain dolls had no expression. They would never experience life or feel the way real people do because in that perfect world there was no emotion.

On my eighth birthday, I received a gift that taught me a lot about what I want out of life: Many times I had imagined myself in that house, never being able to interact with the outside world. I do not think I could stand to be so closed off. I would much rather be a part of the world and feel and see everything possible. The dollhouse made me realize that as long as I opened myself up to the world, I would never be lonely. But if I shut the world out of my life, like one of those porcelain perfections, then I would be completely by myself.

The essay focuses on the author's personal experience.

Samantha orders events sequentially.

She clearly sets events in a specific place and time of her life.

The writer shares the insight she gained through reflection.

Samantha includes a truth about life that she learned through personal experience.

Writing Workshop

Editing and Proofreading

Correct errors in spelling, grammar, and punctuation.

Focus on Punctuation: Check that you have used commas correctly throughout your essay. Read the essay aloud and notice where you pause naturally. Consider whether or not these pauses need to be punctuated with commas.

Publishing and Presenting

Consider one of the following ways to share your writing with classmates:

Publish electronically. Share your essay by uploading it onto a classroom computer or Web site. Ask readers to share their reactions by posting them online. Share your favorite responses with the class.

Give a reading. Practice reading your essay aloud. Emphasize specific emotions or ideas by varying the speed and volume of your reading. Mark your draft to indicate these changes. Then, read your essay aloud to your class.

Reflecting on Your Writing

Writer's Journal Jot down your thoughts on your experience of writing a reflective essay. Begin by answering these questions:

- In what ways was writing a reflective essay different from telling the same story to friends in a conversation?
- Which revision strategy improved your essay the most? Why?

> *Prentice Hall Writing and Grammar Connection: Chapter 4*

Rubric for Self-Assessment

To assess your own reflective essay, use the following rubric:

Criteria	Rating Scale not very very				
Focus: How clearly do you connect the events with your insight?	1	2	3	4	5
Organization: How easy is it for readers to follow your interweaving of past events with your present understanding?	1	2	3	4	5
Support/Elaboration: How thorough is your description of events and ideas?	1	2	3	4	5
Style: How effectively do you use details to describe scenes and incidents?	1	2	3	4	5
Conventions: How correct is your grammar, especially your use of verbals to vary sentence length?	1	2	3	4	5

Skills You Will Learn

Literature You Will Read

Reading and Vocabulary Skills Preview

Reading: Reading Shakespearean Drama

 Academic Standards

> **Shakespearean drama** refers to the plays of William Shakespeare, which have a formal structure and are developed according to specific conventions.

- Analyze characters' traits through narration and dialogue. (10.3.4)
- Compare works that express a universal theme. (10.3.5)
- Apply appropriate manuscript conventions. (10.6.4)

Shakespeare's plays use language that may be unfamiliar to modern readers. For this reason, **reading Shakespeare** requires paying special attention to punctuation and rhyme scheme and using strategies for understanding the meaning of the text. Once you unlock the meaning, you will discover that Shakespeare's plays communicate universal themes, messages, and ideas that are relevant to people across time.

Skills and Strategies You Will Learn in Part 2

In Part 2, you will learn

- to **use text aids** to understand text. (p. 820)
- to **paraphrase** to enhance understanding. (p. 846)
- to **analyze imagery.** (p. 868)
- to **read between the lines** to find the deeper meaning of what characters say. (p. 892)
- to **compare and contrast characters** to add to understanding. (p. 910)
- to understand the use of **text format** in informational materials to help you **use signs.** (p. 928)

Using the Skills and Strategies in Part 2

In Part 2, you will learn strategies to help you understand Shakepearean drama. For example, you will practice paraphrasing, analyzing imagery, and reading between the lines to clarify the meaning of difficult passages. You will also practice using text aids, as in this example:

Original Line: Accout'red as I was, I plungèd in. . . .

Word Eplained in Side Notes: *Accout'red* means "dressed in armor."

Paraphrase: Dressed in armor, I jumped in.

Academic Vocabulary: Words for Evaluating Literature

You can use the following words to talk and write about your opinions about the selections in this unit.

Word	Definition	Example Sentence
credible *adj.*	believable; reliable	Some believe it is not *credible* that Shakespeare wrote these plays.
integrity *n.*	honesty; sincerity	Many Shakespearean experts bring scholarly *integrity* to the argument.
legitimate *adj.*	lawful; reasonable; justifiable	Many believe that Shakespeare was the *legitimate* author of these plays.
superficial *adj.*	of or being on the surface; shallow; concerned only with the obvious or apparent	This is a question that can be settled only through careful research, not *superficial* guesses.
document *v.*	provide with factual support	It is difficult to *document* authorship of the plays.

Vocabulary Skill: Word Roots

▶ A **word root** is the part of the word that contains its basic meaning.

In Part 2 you will learn

- the Latin word root *-cred-*
- the Latin word root *-doc-*

Knowing roots can help you determine what unfamiliar words mean.

Activity Look up these words in a dictionary. Use the information in each entry to identify the root of the word. Then, explain how knowing the root helps you to understand and remember the word's meaning.

-cred-	-doc-
credit, credible, incredulous	documentary, doctrine, doctor

The Birth of Modern Theater

In Shakespeare's day, London was already a bustling city. Ships swept up and down the Thames River to dock in London and fuel the city with trade. Nearly 200,000 people crowded into London, making it the largest city in Europe. Reeking of garbage, ringing with street vendors' cries, Shakespeare's London was packed with danger and opportunity. In this stew of excitement, the first modern theaters were born.

The Globe Before the 1570s, Londoners had turned to traveling acting companies for entertainment. City officials, afraid of public unruliness, riots, and moral corruption, frequently cracked down on public performances. In 1576, an actor named James Burbage built the first public theater north of the city. Other theaters followed. In 1599, Shakespeare's company built the Globe theater in Southwark, a neighorhood south of London.

Most of Shakespeare's plays were performed at the Globe, which was built around a roofless courtyard. The sun provided the only lighting; performances were given only during the day. Surrounding the courtyard were three levels of galleries with benches where wealthier

Reconstructing the Globe

playgoers sat. For only a penny, though, a person could stand in the courtyard, called the pit, and watch the performance.

Popcorn and Pickpockets Audiences were boisterous, cheering and booing loudly. Hazelnuts were Elizabethan "popcorn"; people munched on them all during a performance. Pickpockets were a constant danger, and fistfights occasionally broke out. Built to hold between 2,500 and 3,000 people, the theater drew the largest crowds on holidays.

The Stage The stage was a platform that extended into the pit. Actors entered and left the stage from doors located behind the platform. The galleries behind and above the stage were used as dressing and storage rooms. The second-level gallery right above the stage, however, was used as an upper stage.

By modern standards, Elizabethan theater was hardly "realistic." No scenery was used: Settings were indicated in the dialogue. The actors wore Elizabethan clothing, not costumes. Women were not allowed on stage: Young boys played the female roles. Shakespeare did not depend on realistic staging. Instead, he brought his world to life on stage at the Globe through imagination and words.

◀ ▼ **Critical Viewing** Judging from these reconstructions, what features did the Globe share with modern theaters? **[Compare and Contrast]**

In 1987, years of fund-raising and effort resulted in a remarkable birthday present for the playwright. Work began on a faithful reconstruction of the Globe.

The design of the reconstruction is based on archaeological evidence and a drawing by Wenceslaus Hollar, an artist of the time. A contract drawn up in 1600 for the Fortune playhouse, a theater built by the same carpenter who built the Globe, provides additional details. In 1989, the foundation of the original Globe was uncovered, providing even more information about the theater.

The new Globe, like the original, is made of wood. Traditional sixteenth-century carpentry techniques were used for much of the theater's construction. A thatched roof protects the stage and galleries, and lime plaster covers the walls. After long years of fund-raising and construction, the theater opened to its first full season on June 8, 1997, with a production of *Henry V.*

Practice these skills as you read *The Tragedy of Julius Caesar*, Act I.

Literary Analysis

Like other tragedies, **Shakespeare's tragedies** are plays that tell of a reversal of fortune, from good to bad, experienced by a man or woman, usually of noble birth. Shakespeare's tragedies also have these distinctive features:

- They are sometimes based on **historical characters.**
- The **hero** often displays a **tragic flaw,** a characteristic that brings about his downfall.
- Shakespeare emphasizes the hero's **internal conflict.**
- Commoners often play key **supporting roles** and provide **comic relief,** humorous scenes that serve as a break from the intense emotions of the play.

Shakespeare's plays are structured in five acts. In his tragedies, the **crisis**—the turning point that determines how the play will end—occurs in Act III. The **climax,** or point of greatest emotional intensity, often occurs in Act V, when the **catastrophe,** or disaster, befalls the hero.

Act III

The Crisis

Act II

Rising Action

Act IV

Falling Action

Act I

Exposition

Act V

The Catastrophe—often, the Climax

Reading Skill

Shakespeare's plays contain unfamiliar language and references. When **reading Shakespearean drama, use text aids**:

- Review the list of *dramatis personae* (the cast of characters).
- Read the background information provided (p. 821).
- As you read the play, consult the notes, called **glosses,** beside the text. These notes define words and explain references.

Vocabulary Builder

- **replication** (rep´ li kā´ shən) *n.* duplicate; reproduction (p. 826) *His house is an exact replication of mine.*

- **servile** (sʉr´ vəl) *adj.* slavelike; humbly submissive to authority (p. 828) *The butler bowed in a servile manner.*

- **spare** (sper) *adj.* lean; thin (p. 835) *She has a spare frame and is underweight.*

- **infirmity** (in fʉr´ mə tē) *n.* weakness; physical defect (p. 837) *A doctor cured his infirmity.*

- **portentous** (pôr ten´ təs) *adj.* ominous; giving signs of evil to come (p. 839) *The portentous clouds promised snow.*

- **prodigious** (prō dij´ əs) *adj.* of great size or power (p. 840) *The runner made a prodigious effort just before the finish line.*

Build Understanding • *The Tragedy of Julius Caesar*

Background

Ancient Rome A republic since 509 B.C., Rome was ruled for decades by two public officials called *consuls* along with the senate, made up of high-born *patricians,* or aristocrats, and assemblies of *plebeians,* or lower-class citizens.

By the era of Julius Caesar (100–44 B.C.), Rome ruled an empire won by military expansion. Powerful generals arose, and the balance of power grew unstable. Civil war was common. When a general named Pompey tried to make himself sole consul, another popular general, Julius Caesar, defeated him. As Shakespeare's play opens, all of Rome wonders whether Caesar will become emperor, ending the Republic.

Connecting to the Literature

Reading/Writing Connection In *The Tragedy of Julius Caesar,* many feel threatened by Caesar's new power. Write a few sentences about the different ways people may react to another person's success. Use at least three of these words: *confront, manipulate, speculate, stimulate,* and *tolerate.*

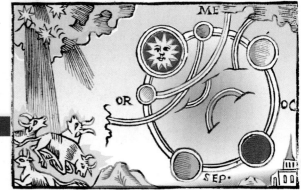

from *Shakespeare Alive!*

Joseph Papp and Elizabeth Kirkland

Joseph Papp, the founder of the New York Shakespeare festival, devoted his life to making Shakespeare accessible to all. In *Shakespeare Alive!* he re-creates England in Shakespeare's day. As he explains, Shakespeare and his audience viewed nature and society as a unified whole.

In the heavenly kingdom . . . several levels of archangels and angels spread downwards from God's throne, and each level knew its place. . . . The universe was a hierarchy too, and each planet and star was assigned to a specific position. . . . The animal world was another very stratified society in which each species had its king: the eagle was the king of birds; the whale the king of fish; and the lion, of course, king of beasts.

The Great Chain of Being, stretching from the lowliest creature in the natural world all the way up to God, connected these worlds to each other, and the hierarchy of one was mirrored in the others. . . .

Since all living things were linked by the Great Chain of Being, violations of order in society were thought to set off violent disturbances in the heavens or the world of nature. . . . In *Julius Caesar* [Act I, Scene iii], strange and terrible goings-on are reported in Rome as the conspirators hatch an assassination plot against the emperor. . . .

Play

William **Shakespeare** (1564–1616)

His characters are known by name around the world. The phrases he coined still slip into people's conversations. Filmmakers, painters, and composers reuse his plots. Writers continue to sift through his thirty-seven plays and his poems, borrowing titles, stories, and insights into the human soul. Nearly 400 years after his death, William Shakespeare's plays are still read and produced internationally. He is regarded as the greatest writer in the English language.

What's Past Is Prologue Shakespeare was born in Stratford-on-Avon, northwest of London. Based on a baptism record for April 26, 1564, scholars estimate that his birth date was April 23 of the same year. Shakespeare's father, John, a successful glove maker and businessman, was a respected leader in the community. His mother, born Mary Arden, was the daughter of John's landlord.

No written evidence of Shakespeare's boyhood exists. Based on his father's status, though, scholars speculate that young Will attended the Stratford Grammar School. In addition to studying Latin grammar, Shakespeare and his classmates would have read the Roman playwrights Plautus and Terence and the Roman poets Ovid, Horace, and Virgil. They would also have studied logic, history, natural history, and some Greek. When Shakespeare left school, he would have had a solid foundation in classical literature.

Scholars pick up the written trail of Shakespeare's life in 1582. Records show that he married Anne Hathaway in late November or early December of that year. Anne was twenty-six; William was eighteen. They had a daughter, Susanna, in 1583, and twins, Judith and Hamnet, two years later.

All the World's a Stage For a brief time, Shakespeare may have worked as a country schoolmaster. In the 1580s, however, he found his true calling—the theater. Some speculate that traveling performers, stopping off in Stratford on their way to London, introduced him to the magic of the stage. At the age of eighteen or nineteen, Shakespeare was probably already acting in plays in London. Friends in the city helped him financially and professionally, and he advanced quickly.

By 1594, Shakespeare was part owner of the Lord Chamberlain's Men, one of the most successful theater companies in London. More

Author Link

For: More information about William Shakespeare
Visit: www.PHSchool.com
Web Code: eqe-9504

importantly, in view of his contributions to English literature, he was the company's chief playwright. Many of Shakespeare's enduring plays first took form as scripts he wrote for performances by the Lord Chamberlain's Men. In 1599, the company built the Globe theater, and it was at the Globe that audiences first saw the plays of Shakespeare.

In 1603, following the death of Elizabeth I, James I became king and took control of the Lord Chamberlain's Men. He renamed the company the King's Men. Shakespeare, a major stockholder in the company, continued to write for and act with the group.

Parting Is Such Sweet Sorrow Around 1610, Shakespeare, now a prosperous middle-class man enriched by his theatrical career, retired to Stratford. He lived in the second-largest house in the town, invested in grain and farmland, and continued to write plays.

Shakespeare wrote his will on March 25, 1616. He left the bulk of his property to his oldest daughter, Susanna, and a smaller sum to his other daughter, Judith. (Hamnet had died in 1596.) By law, his widow automatically received a lifetime income from the estate. On April 23, 1616 (his birthday, if scholars are correct), Shakespeare died.

Familiar Expressions Taken from Shakespeare

You have probably quoted Shakespeare without even realizing it! Look for familiar expressions and phrases in the following list. You may be surprised at how many lines by Shakespeare you already know!

"Eaten out of house and home," *Henry IV,* Part 2, Act II, Scene i

"Cruel to be kind," *Hamlet,* Act III, Scene iv

"Knock, knock! Who's there . . .?" *Macbeth,* Act II, Scene iii

"Too much of a good thing," *As You Like It,* Act IV, Scene i

"Neither a borrower nor a lender be," *Hamlet,* Act I, Scene iii

"Something wicked this way comes," *Macbeth,* Act IV, Scene i

"To thine own self be true," *Hamlet,* Act I, Scene iii

"A tower of strength," *Richard III,* Act V, Scene iii

The Tragedy of
Julius Caesar

William Shakespeare

Julius Caesar

Octavius Caesar ⎤
Marcus Antonius ⎥— Triumvirs* After the Death of Julius Caesar
M. Aemilius Lepidus ⎦

Cicero ⎤
Publius ⎥— Senators
Popilius Lena ⎦

Marcus Brutus ⎤
Cassius ⎥
Casca ⎥
Trebonius ⎥
Ligarius ⎥— Conspirators Against Julius Caesar
Decius Brutus ⎥
Metellus Cimber ⎥
Cinna ⎦

Flavius ⎤
Marullus ⎦— Tribunes

Artemidorus of Cnidos — Teacher of Rhetoric

Cinna ⎤
Another Poet ⎦— Poets

Lucilius ⎤
Titinius ⎥
Messala ⎥— Friends to Brutus and Cassius
Young Cato ⎥
Volumnius ⎦

Varro ⎤
Clitus ⎥
Claudius ⎥
Strato ⎥— Servants to Brutus
Lucius ⎥
Dardanius ⎦

Pindarus ——— Servant to Cassius

Calpurnia ——— Wife to Caesar

Portia ——— Wife to Brutus

Soothsayer

Senators, Citizens, Guards, Attendants, and so on

Scene: During most of the play, at Rome; afterward near Sardis, and near Philippi.

* **Triumvirs** (tri um´ virz) *n.* in ancient Rome, a group of three leaders who shared power equally.

→»»»»»» ACT I «««««««←

Scene i. Rome. A street.

[*Enter* FLAVIUS, MARULLUS, *and certain* COMMONERS[1] *over the stage.*]

    FLAVIUS. Hence! Home, you idle creatures, get you home!
      Is this a holiday? What, know you not,
      Being mechanical,[2] you ought not walk
      Upon a laboring day without the sign
5   Of your profession?[3] Speak, what trade art thou?

    CARPENTER. Why, sir, a carpenter.

    MARULLUS. Where is thy leather apron and thy rule?
      What dost thou with thy best apparel on?
      You, sir, what trade are you?

10 **COBBLER.** Truly, sir, in respect of a fine workman,[4] I am but, as
      you would say, a cobbler.[5]

    MARULLUS. But what trade art thou? Answer me directly.

    COBBLER. A trade, sir, that, I hope, I may use with a safe con-
      science, which is indeed, sir, a mender of bad soles.

1. COMMONERS (kam´ ən ərz) *n.* people not of the nobility or upper classes.

2. mechanical *n.* of the working class.

3. sign / Of your profession work clothes and tools.

4. in respect of a fine workman in relation to a skilled worker.

5. cobbler (a pun) "mender of shoes" or "a clumsy, bungling worker."

✔Reading Check

What fact about the commoners attracts Flavius' attention?

15 FLAVIUS. What trade, thou knave?[6] Thou naughty knave what trade?

COBBLER. Nay, I beseech you, sir, be not out with me: yet, if you be out,[7] sir, I can mend you.[8]

MARULLUS. What mean'st thou by that? Mend me, thou saucy
20 fellow?

COBBLER. Why, sir, cobble you.

FLAVIUS. Thou art a cobbler, art thou?

COBBLER. Truly, sir, all that I live by is with the awl:[9] I meddle with no tradesman's matters, nor women's matters;
25 but withal,[10] I am indeed, sir, a surgeon to old shoes: when they are in great danger, I recover them. As proper men as ever trod upon neat's leather[11] have gone upon my handiwork.

FLAVIUS. But wherefore art not in thy shop today?
30 Why dost thou lead these men about the streets?

COBBLER. Truly, sir, to wear out their shoes, to get myself into more work. But indeed, sir, we make holiday to see Caesar and to rejoice in his triumph.[12]

MARULLUS. Wherefore rejoice? What conquest brings he home?
35 What tributaries[13] follow him to Rome,
To grace in captive bonds his chariot wheels?
You blocks, you stones, you worse than senseless things!
O you hard hearts, you cruel men of Rome,
Knew you not Pompey?[14] Many a time and oft
40 Have you climbed up to walls and battlements,
To tow'rs and windows, yea, to chimney tops,
Your infants in your arms, and there have sat
The livelong day, with patient expectation,
To see great Pompey pass the streets of Rome.
45 And when you saw his chariot but appear,
Have you not made an universal shout,
That Tiber[15] trembled underneath her banks
To hear the replication of your sounds
Made in her concave shores?[16]
50 And do you now put on your best attire?
And do you now cull out[17] a holiday?
And do you now strew flowers in his way
That comes in triumph over Pompey's blood?[18]
Be gone!

Reading Skill
Using Text Aids
Explain how glosses, or sidenotes, 7 and 8 help you to understand Marullus' reaction in lines 19–20.

9. awl (ôl) *n.* small, pointed tool for making holes in leather.
10. withal (with ôl') *adv.* nevertheless (also a pun on "with awl").
11. neat's leather leather made from the hides of cattle.
12. triumph (trī' əmf) *n.* procession celebrating the return of a victorious general.
13. tributaries (trib' yoo ter' ēz) *n.* captives.
14. Pompey (päm' pē) A Roman general and triumvir defeated by Caesar in 48 B.C. and later murdered.
15. Tiber (tī' bər) river that flows through Rome.
16. concave shores hollowed-out banks; over-hanging banks.
17. cull out pick out; select.
18. Pompey's blood Pompey's sons, whom Caesar has just defeated.

Vocabulary Builder
replication (rep' li kā' shən) *n.* duplicate; reproduction

▶ **Critical Viewing**
Judging from this Roman painting, how might the characters be dressed? Explain.
[Connect]

55 Run to your houses, fall upon your knees,
Pray to the gods to intermit the plague[19]
That needs must light on this ingratitude.

FLAVIUS. Go, go, good countrymen, and, for this fault,
Assemble all the poor men of your sort;
60 Draw them to Tiber banks and weep your tears
Into the channel, till the lowest stream
Do kiss the most exalted shores of all.[20]

[*All the commoners exit.*]

19. intermit the plague
(plāg) stop the calamity or
trouble.

**20. the most exalted shores
of all** the highest banks.

Reading Check

What does Marullus
think about the
people celebrating in
the streets?

See, whe'r their basest mettle[21] be not moved,
They vanish tongue-tied in their guiltiness.

65 Go you down that way toward the Capitol;
This way will I. Disrobe the images,
If you do find them decked with ceremonies.[22]

MARULLUS. May we do so?
You know it is the feast of Lupercal.[23]

70 **FLAVIUS.** It is no matter; let no images
Be hung with Caesar's trophies. I'll about
And drive away the vulgar[24] from the streets;
So do you too, where you perceive them thick.
These growing feathers plucked from Caesar's wing

75 Will make him fly an ordinary pitch,[25]
Who else would soar above the view of men
And keep us all in <u>servile</u> fearfulness.   [Exit]

21. **whe'r their basest mettle** whether the most inferior material of which they are made.

22. **Disrobe the images . . . decked with ceremonies** strip the statues . . . covered with decorations.

23. **feast of Lupercal** (loo′ pər kal) ancient Roman festival celebrated on February 15.

24. **vulgar** (vul′ gər) *n.* common people.

25. **pitch** upward flight of a hawk.

Vocabulary Builder
servile (sʉr′ vəl) *adj.*
slavelike; humbly
submissive to authority

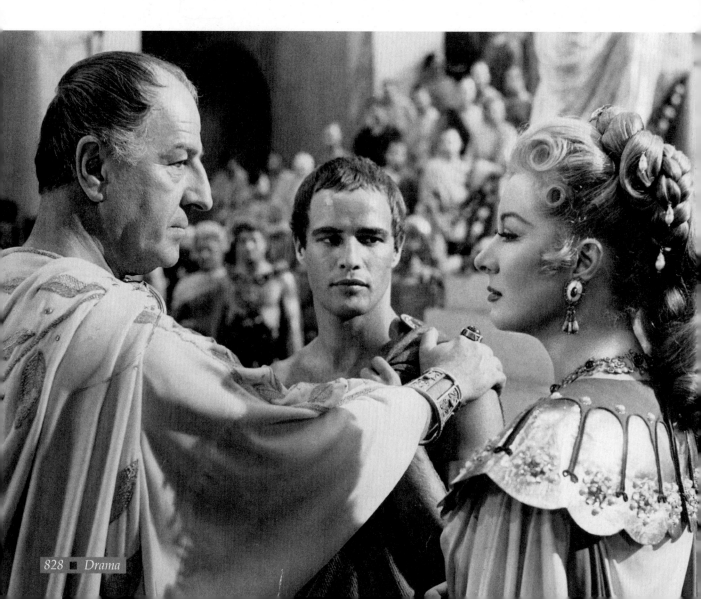

Scene ii. A public place.

[*Enter* CAESAR, ANTONY (*for the course*),[1] CALPURNIA, PORTIA, DECIUS, CICERO, BRUTUS, CASSIUS, CASCA, *a* SOOTHSAYER; *after them,* MARULLUS *and* FLAVIUS.]

CAESAR. Calpurnia!

CASCA. Peace, ho! Caesar speaks.

CAESAR. Calpurnia!

CALPURNIA. Here, my lord.

CAESAR. Stand you directly in Antonius' way
When he doth run his course. Antonius!

5 **ANTONY.** Caesar, my lord?

CAESAR. Forget not in your speed, Antonius,
To touch Calpurnia; for our elders say
The barren, touchèd in this holy chase,
Shake off their sterile curse.[2]

ANTONY. I shall remember:
10 When Caesar says "Do this," it is performed.

CAESAR. Set on, and leave no ceremony out.

SOOTHSAYER. Caesar!

CAESAR. Ha! Who calls?

CASCA. Bid every noise be still; peace yet again!

15 **CAESAR.** Who is it in the press[3] that calls on me?
I hear a tongue, shriller than all the music,
Cry "Caesar." Speak; Caesar is turned to hear.

SOOTHSAYER. Beware the ides of March.[4]

CAESAR. What man is that?

BRUTUS. A soothsayer bids you beware the ides of March.

20 **CAESAR.** Set him before me; let me see his face.

CASSIUS. Fellow, come from the throng; look upon Caesar.

CAESAR. What say'st thou to me now? Speak once again.

SOOTHSAYER. Beware the ides of March.

CAESAR. He is a dreamer, let us leave him. Pass.

[*A trumpet sounds. Exit all but* BRUTUS *and* CASSIUS.]

◀ **Critical Viewing** What do the actors' poses in this movie still imply about the relation between Caesar (left) and Antony (middle)? **[Infer]**

1. *for the course* ready for the foot race that was part of the Lupercal festivities.

Reading Skill
Using Text Aids
What information about the relationship between Caesar and Calpurnia do you find in the "Characters" list, on page 825?

Literary Analysis
Shakespeare's Tragedies What is Caesar's rank?

2. **barren . . . sterile curse** It was believed that women who were unable to bear children (such as Calpurnia), if touched by a runner during this race, would then be able to bear children.

3. **press** *n.* crowd.

4. **ides of March** in the ancient Roman calendar, March 15.

✓ **Reading Check**

How does Caesar respond to the soothsayer's warning?

25 **CASSIUS.** Will you go see the order of the course?[5]

BRUTUS. Not I.

CASSIUS. I pray you do.

BRUTUS. I am not gamesome:[6] I do lack some part
Of that quick spirit[7] that is in Antony.
30 Let me not hinder, Cassius, your desires;
I'll leave you.

CASSIUS. Brutus, I do observe you now of late;
I have not from your eyes that gentleness
And show of love as I was wont[8] to have;
35 You bear too stubborn and too strange a hand[9]
Over your friend that loves you.

BRUTUS.   Cassius,
Be not deceived: if I have veiled my look,
I turn the trouble of my countenance
Merely upon myself.[10] Vexèd I am
40 Of late with passions[11] of some difference,[12]
Conceptions only proper to myself,[13]
Which give some soil,[14] perhaps, to my behaviors;
But let not therefore my good friends be grieved
(Among which number, Cassius, be you one)
45 Nor construe any further my neglect
Than that poor Brutus, with himself at war,
Forgets the shows of love to other men.

CASSIUS. Then, Brutus, I have much mistook your passion;
By means whereof this breast of mine hath buried[15]
50 Thoughts of great value, worthy cogitations.[16]
Tell me, good Brutus, can you see your face?

BRUTUS. No, Cassius; for the eye sees not itself
But by reflection, by some other things.

CASSIUS. 'Tis just.[17]
55 And it is very much lamented,[18] Brutus,
That you have no such mirrors as will turn
Your hidden worthiness into your eye,
That you might see your shadow.[19] I have heard
Where many of the best respect[20] in Rome
60 (Except immortal Caesar), speaking of Brutus,
And groaning underneath this age's yoke,[21]
Have wished that noble Brutus had his eyes.

BRUTUS. Into what dangers would you lead me, Cassius,
That you would have me seek into myself
65 For that which is not in me?

---

5. **order of the course** the race.

6. **gamesome** (gām′ səm) *adj.* having a liking for sports.
7. **quick spirit** lively disposition.

8. **wont** (wōnt) *adj.* accustomed.

9. **bear . . . hand** treat too harshly and too like a stranger.

10. **if I . . . upon myself** if I have been less open, it is because I am troubled with myself.
11. **passions** *n.* feelings; emotions.
12. **of some difference** in conflict.
13. **Conceptions . . . myself** thoughts that concern only me.
14. **soil** *n.* blemish.

15. **By means . . . buried** because of which I have kept to myself.
16. **cogitations** (käj ə tā′ shənz) *n.* thoughts.

17. **'Tis just** it is true.
18. **lamented** (lə men′ təd) *v.* regretted.

19. **turn . . . shadow** reflect your hidden noble qualities so you could see their image.
20. **the best respect** the best reputation.
21. **this age's yoke** the tyranny of Caesar.

CASSIUS. Therefore, good Brutus, be prepared to hear;
  And since you know you cannot see yourself
  So well as by reflection, I, your glass
  Will modestly discover to yourself
70 That of yourself which you yet know not of.[22]
  And be not jealous on[23] me, gentle Brutus:
  Were I a common laughter,[24] or did use
  To stale with ordinary oaths my love
  To every new protester;[25] if you know
75 That I do fawn on men and hug them hard,
  And after scandal[26] them; or if you know
  That I profess myself in banqueting
  To all the rout,[27] then hold me dangerous.

[*Flourish of trumpets and shout*]

22. your glass . . . know not of your mirror will make known to you without exaggeration the qualities you have of which you are unaware.

23. be not jealous on do not be suspicious of.

24. common laughter object of ridicule.

25. To stale . . . new protester to cheapen my friendship by avowing it to anyone who promises to be my friend.

26. scandal *v.* slander; gossip about.

27. profess myself . . . rout declare my friendship to the common crowd.

◀ **Critical Viewing**
What does the expression of this actor in the role of Cassius convey about Cassius' intelligence? Explain. **[Infer]**

✔ **Reading Check**
According to Cassius, what does Brutus not realize about himself?

BRUTUS. What means this shouting? I do fear the people
    Choose Caesar for their king.

80 **CASSIUS.**   Ay, do you fear it?
    Then must I think you would not have it so.

    BRUTUS. I would not, Cassius, yet I love him well.
    But wherefore do you hold me here so long?
    What is it that you would impart to me?
85   If it be aught toward the general good,[28]
    Set honor in one eye and death i' th' other,
    And I will look on both indifferently;[29]
    For let the gods so speed[30] me, as I love
    The name of honor more than I fear death.

90 **CASSIUS.** I know that virtue to be in you, Brutus,
    As well as I do know your outward favor.[31]
    Well, honor is the subject of my story.
    I cannot tell what you and other men
    Think of this life, but for my single self,
95   I had as lief not be,[32] as live to be
    In awe of such a thing as I myself.[33]
    I was born free as Caesar; so were you:
    We both have fed as well, and we can both
    Endure the winter's cold as well as he:
100   For once, upon a raw and gusty day,
    The troubled Tiber chafing with[34] her shores,

Literary Analysis

Shakespeare's Tragedies What internal conflict in Brutus do lines 79–82 reveal?

28. aught . . . good anything to do with the public welfare.

29. indifferently (in dif′ ər ənt lē) *adv.* without preference; impartially.

30. speed *v.* give good fortune to.

31. favor *n.* face; appearance.

32. as lief not be just as soon not exist.

33. such a thing as I myself another human being (Caesar).

34. chafing with raging against.

Literature in Context

History Connection

Roman Society Brutus and Cassius fear that the common people will support Caesar in his bid to become emperor. Their fear reflects tensions in Roman society of the time.

- Poor *plebeians* (commoners), including farmers who could no longer compete with wealthy landowners, flooded Rome.
- They created a restless mass of unemployed poor.
- Some leaders took their side and won power with their support.
- Other leaders took the side of the *patricians* (aristocrats) and the wealthy plebeians.
- The conflict between rich and poor led to civil unrest, including riots and assassinations.

Connect to the Literature

Which scenes in Act I best reflect the division in Roman society? Explain.

Caesar said to me "Darest thou, Cassius, now
Leap in with me into this angry flood,
And swim to yonder point?" Upon the word,

105 Accout'red[35] as I was, I plungèd in
And bade him follow: so indeed he did.
The torrent roared, and we did buffet[36] it
With lusty sinews,[37] throwing it aside
And stemming it with hearts of controversy.[38]

110 But ere we could arrive the point proposed,
Caesar cried "Help me, Cassius, or I sink!"
I, as Aeneas,[39] our great ancestor,
Did from the flames of Troy upon his shoulder
The old Anchises bear, so from the waves of Tiber

115 Did I the tired Caesar. And this man
Is now become a god, and Cassius is
A wretched creature, and must bend his body
If Caesar carelessly but nod on him.
He had a fever when he was in Spain,

120 And when the fit was on him, I did mark
How he did shake: 'tis true, this god did shake.
His coward lips did from their color fly,[40]
And that same eye whose bend[41] doth awe the world
did lose his[42] luster: I did hear him groan;

125 Ay, and that tongue of his, that bade the Romans
Mark him and write his speeches in their books,
Alas, it cried, "Give me some drink, Titinius,"
As a sick girl. Ye gods! It doth amaze me,
A man of such a feeble temper[43] should

130 So get the start of[44] the majestic world,
And bear the palm[45] alone.   [*Shout. Flourish of trumpets*]

BRUTUS. Another general shout?
    I do believe that these applauses are
    For some new honors that are heaped on Caesar.

135 **CASSIUS.** Why, man, he doth bestride the narrow world
    Like a Colossus,[46] and we petty men
    Walk under his huge legs and peep about
    To find ourselves dishonorable[47] graves.
    Men at some time are masters of their fates:

140 The fault, dear Brutus, is not in our stars,[48]
    But in ourselves, that we are underlings.[49]
    Brutus and Caesar: what should be in that "Caesar"?
    Why should that name be sounded[50] more than yours?
    Write them together, yours is as fair a name;

35. Accout'red (ə kōō′ trəd) *adj.* dressed in armor.
36. buffet (buf′ it) *v.* struggle against.
37. lusty sinews (sin′ yōōz) strong muscles.
38. stemming it . . . controversy making progress against it with our intense rivalry.
39. Aeneas (i nē′ əs) Trojan hero of the poet Virgil's epic poem *Aeneid,* who carried his old father, Anchises, from the burning city of Troy and later founded Rome.

40. His coward lips . . . fly color fled from his lips, which were like cowardly soldiers fleeing from a battle.
41. bend *n.* glance.
42. his *pron.* its.
43. feeble temper weak physical constitution.
44. get the start of outdistance.
45. palm *n.* leaf of a palm tree carried or worn as a symbol of victory; victor's prize.
46. Colossus (kə läs′ əs) *n.* gigantic ancient statue of Apollo, a Greek and Roman god, that was set at the entrance to the harbor of Rhodes; ships would sail under its legs.
47. dishonorable (dis än′ ər ə bəl) *adj.* shameful (because they will not be of free men).
48. stars *n.* destinies. The stars were thought to control people's lives.
49. underlings *n.* inferior people.
50. sounded *v.* spoken or announced by trumpets.

Reading Check

What has Cassius done to help Caesar in the past?

145 Sound them, it doth become the mouth as well;
Weigh them, it is as heavy; conjure[51] with 'em,
"Brutus" will start[52] a spirit as soon as "Caesar."
Now, in the names of all the gods at once,
Upon what meat doth this our Caesar feed,
150 That he is grown so great? Age, thou art shamed!
Rome, thou hast lost the breed of noble bloods!
When went there by an age, since the great flood,[53]
But it was famed with[54] more than with one man?
When could they say (till now) that talked of Rome,
155 That her wide walks encompassed but one man?
Now is it Rome indeed, and room enough,
When there is in it but one only man.
O, you and I have heard our fathers say,
There was a Brutus[55] once that would have brooked[56]
160 Th' eternal devil to keep his state in Rome
As easily as a king.

    BRUTUS. That you do love me, I am nothing jealous;[57]
What you would work me to,[58] I have some aim;[59]
How I have thought of this, and of these times,
165 I shall recount hereafter. For this present,
I would not so (with love I might entreat you)
Be any further moved. What you have said
I will consider; what you have to say
I will with patience hear, and find a time
170 Both meet[60] to hear and answer such high things.
Till then, my noble friend, chew upon[61] this:
Brutus had rather be a villager
Than to repute himself a son of Rome
Under these hard conditions as this time
Is like to lay upon us.

175 **CASSIUS.**   I am glad
That my weak words have struck but thus much show
Of fire from Brutus.

[*Enter* CAESAR *and his* TRAIN.[62]]

    BRUTUS. The games are done, and Caesar is returning.

    CASSIUS. As they pass by, pluck Casca by the sleeve,
180 And he will (after his sour fashion) tell you
What hath proceeded worthy note today.

    BRUTUS. I will do so. But look you, Cassius,
The angry spot doth glow on Caesar's brow,
And all the rest look like a chidden train:[63]

---

51. conjure (kän´ jər) *v.* summon a spirit by a magic spell.

52. start *v.* raise.

53. great flood in Greek mythology, a flood that drowned everyone except Deucalion and his wife Pyrrha, who were saved by the god Zeus because of their virtue.

54. But it was famed with without the age being made famous by.

55. Brutus Lucius Junius Brutus had helped expel the last king of Rome and had helped found the Republic in 509 B.C.

56. brooked *v.* put up with.

Reading Skill
Using Text Aids How does the Background on page 821 along with note 55 help you understand Cassius' appeal to Brutus?

57. nothing jealous not at all doubting.

58. work me to persuade me of.

59. aim *n.* idea.

60. meet *adj.* fit; suitable

61. chew upon think about.

Literary Analysis
Shakespeare's Tragedies What tragic flaw in Brutus' character might lines 172–175 reveal?

62. train *n.* attendants.

63. a chidden train scolded attendants.

185   Calpurnia's cheek is pale, and Cicero
    Looks with such ferret[64] and such fiery eyes
    As we have seen him in the Capitol,
    Being crossed in conference[65] by some senators.

CASSIUS. Casca will tell us what the matter is.

190 **CAESAR.** Antonius.

ANTONY. Caesar?

CAESAR. Let me have men about me that are fat,
    Sleek-headed men, and such as sleep a-nights.
    Yond Cassius has a lean and hungry look;
195   He thinks too much: such men are dangerous.

ANTONY. Fear him not, Caesar, he's not dangerous;
    He is a noble Roman, and well given.[66]

CAESAR. Would he were fatter! But I fear him not.
    Yet if my name were liable to fear,
200   I do not know the man I should avoid
    So soon as that <u>spare</u> Cassius. He reads much,
    He is a great observer, and he looks
    quite through the deeds of men.[67] He loves no plays,
    As thou dost, Antony; he hears no music;
205   Seldom he smiles, and smiles in such a sort[68]
    As if he mocked himself, and scorned his spirit
    That could be moved to smile at anything.
    Such men as he be never at heart's ease
    Whiles they behold a greater than themselves,
210   And therefore are they very dangerous.
    I rather tell thee what is to be feared
    Than what I fear; for always I am Caesar.
    Come on my right hand, for this ear is deaf,
    And tell me truly what thou think'st of him.

[A trumpet sounds. CAESAR *and his* TRAIN *exit.]*

215 **CASCA.** You pulled me by the cloak; would you speak with me?

BRUTUS. Ay, Casca; tell us what hath chanced[69] today,
    That Caesar looks so sad.

CASCA. Why, you were with him, were you not?

BRUTUS. I should not then ask Casca what had chanced.

220 **CASCA.** Why, there was a crown offered him; and being
    offered him, he put it by[70] with the back of his hand, thus;
    and then the people fell a-shouting.

64. ferret (fer′ it) *n.* small animal, like a weasel, with reddish eyes.
65. crossed in conference opposed in debate.
66. well given well disposed.
67. looks . . . deeds of men sees through people's actions to their motives.

Vocabulary Builder
spare (sper) *adj.* lean; thin

68. sort way.

69. hath chanced has happened.
70. put it by pushed it away.

**Reading Check**

Why does Cassius compare Brutus and Caesar?

BRUTUS. What was the second noise for?

CASCA. Why, for that too.

225 **CASSIUS.** They shouted thrice; what was the last cry for?

CASCA. Why, for that too.

BRUTUS. Was the crown offered him thrice?

CASCA. Ay, marry,[71] was't, and he put it by thrice, every time
   gentler than other; and at every putting-by mine honest
230 neighbors shouted.

CASSIUS. Who offered him the crown?

CASCA. Why, Antony.

BRUTUS. Tell us the manner of it, gentle Casca.

CASCA. I can as well be hanged as tell the manner of it:
235   it was mere foolery; I did not mark it. I saw Mark Antony
    offer him a crown—yet 'twas not a crown neither, 'twas
    one of these coronets[72]—and, as I told you, he put it by
    once; but for all that, to my thinking, he would fain[73]
    have had it. Then he offered it to him again; then he
240   put it by again; but to my thinking, he was very
    loath to lay his fingers off it. And then he offered it
    the third time. He put it the third time by; and still[74]
    as he refused it, the rabblement[75] hooted, and
    clapped their chopt[76] hands, and threw up their sweaty
245   nightcaps,[77] and uttered such a deal of stinking
    breath because Caesar refused the crown, that it had,
    almost, choked Caesar; for he swounded[78] and
    fell down at it. And for mine own part, I durst
    not laugh, for fear of opening my lips
250   and receiving the bad air.

CASSIUS. But, soft,[79] I pray you; what, did Caesar swound?

CASCA. He fell down in the market place, and foamed at mouth,
    and was speechless.

BRUTUS. 'Tis very like he hath the falling-sickness.[80]

255 **CASSIUS.** No, Caesar hath it not; but you, and I,
    And honest Casca, we have the falling-sickness.[81]

CASCA. I know not what you mean by that, but I am sure
    Caesar fell down. If the tag-rag people[82] did not clap him
    and hiss him, according as he pleased and displeased
260   them, as they use[83] to do the players in the theater,
    I am no true man.

Reading Skill
Using Text Aids
According to the
Literature in Context
feature on page 832,
why might the
common people
support Caesar?

71. marry *interjection* truly.

72. coronets (kôr´ ə nets´) *n.*
ornamental bands used as
crowns.

73. fain (fān) *adv.* gladly.

74. still *adv.* every time.

75. rabblement (rab´ əl mənt)
n. mob.

76. chopt (chäpt) *adj.* chapped.

77. nightcaps *n.* workers'
caps.

78. swounded *v.* swooned;
fainted.

79. soft *adv.* slowly.

80. falling-sickness *n.* epilepsy.

**81. we have the falling-
sickness** We are losing power
and falling in status under
Caesar's rule.

82. tag-rag people the rab-
ble; lower-class people.

83. use *v.* are accustomed.

BRUTUS. What said he when he came unto himself?

CASCA. Marry, before he fell down, when he perceived the common herd was glad he refused the crown, he plucked me ope his doublet[84] and offered them his throat to cut. An I had been a man of any occupation,[85] if I would not have taken him at a word, I would I might go to hell among the rogues. And so he fell. When he came to himself again, he said, if he had done or said anything amiss, he desired their worships to think it was his <u>infirmity</u>.[86] Three or four wenches,[87] where I stood, cried "Alas, good soul!" and forgave him with all their hearts; but there's no heed to be taken of them; if Caesar had stabbed their mothers, they would have done no less.

BRUTUS. And after that, he came thus sad away?

CASCA. Ay.

CASSIUS. Did Cicero say anything?

CASCA. Ay, he spoke Greek.

CASSIUS. To what effect?

CASCA. Nay, an I tell you that, I'll ne'er look you i' th' face again. But those that understood him smiled at one another and shook their heads; but for mine own part, it was Greek to me. I could tell you more news too: Marullus and Flavius, for pulling scarfs off Caesar's images, are put to silence.[88] Fare you well. There was more foolery yet, if I could remember it.

CASSIUS. Will you sup with me tonight, Casca?

CASCA. No, I am promised forth.[89]

CASSIUS. Will you dine with me tomorrow?

CASCA. Ay, if I be alive, and your mind hold,[90] and your dinner worth the eating.

CASSIUS. Good; I will expect you.

CASCA. Do so. Farewell, both.   [*Exit*]

BRUTUS. What a blunt[91] fellow is this grown to be! He was quick mettle[92] when he went to school.

CASSIUS. So is he now in execution[93] Of any bold or noble enterprise, However he puts on this tardy form.[94]

265, 270, 275, 280, 285, 290, 295

(line numbers in left margin: 265, 270, 275, 280, 285, 290, 295)

84. doublet (dub′ lit) *n.* close-fitting jacket.

85. An I . . . occupation if I had been a workingman (or a man of action).

86. infirmity *n.* Caesar's illness is epilepsy.

87. wenches (wench′ əz) *n.* young women.

Vocabulary Builder
infirmity (in fur′ mə tē) *n.* weakness; physical defect

88. for pulling . . . silence For taking decorations off statues of Caesar, they have been silenced (by being forbidden to take part in public affairs, exiled, or perhaps even executed).

89. am promised forth have a previous engagement.

90. hold *v.* does not change.

91. blunt *adj.* dull; not sharp.

92. quick mettle of a lively disposition.

93. execution *n.* carrying out, doing.

94. tardy form sluggish appearance.

✓ **Reading Check**

How does Caesar respond when he is offered the crown?

The Tragedy of Julius Caesar, Act I, Scene ii ■ 837

300

This rudeness is a sauce to his good wit,[95]
Which gives men stomach to disgest[96] his words
With better appetite.

BRUTUS. And so it is. For this time I will leave you.
Tomorrow, if you please to speak with me,

305

I will come home to you; or if you will,
Come home to me, and I will wait for you.

CASSIUS. I will do so. Till then, think of the world.[97]

[*Exit* BRUTUS.]

Well, Brutus, thou art noble; yet I see
Thy honorable mettle may be wrought

310

From that it is disposed;[98] therefore it is meet
That noble minds keep ever with their likes;
For who so firm that cannot be seduced?
Caesar doth bear me hard,[99] but he loves Brutus.
If I were Brutus now, and he were Cassius,

315

He should not humor me.[100] I will this night,
In several hands,[101] in at his windows throw,
As if they came from several citizens,
Writings, all tending to the great opinion[102]
That Rome holds of his name; wherein obscurely

320

Caesar's ambition shall be glancèd at.[103]
And after this, let Caesar seat him sure;[104]
For we will shake him, or worse days endure. [*Exit*]

Scene iii. A street.

[*Thunder and lightning. Enter from opposite sides,* CASCA *and* CICERO.]

CICERO. Good even, Casca; brought you Caesar home?
Why are you breathless? And why stare you so?

CASCA. Are not you moved, when all the sway of earth[1]
Shakes like a thing unfirm? O Cicero,

5

I have seen tempests, when the scolding winds
Have rived[2] the knotty oaks, and I have seen
Th' ambitious ocean swell and rage and foam,
To be exalted with[3] the threat'ning clouds;
But never till tonight, never till now,

10

Did I go through a tempest dropping fire.
Either there is a civil strife in heaven,
Or else the world, too saucy[4] with the gods,
Incenses[5] them to send destruction.

CICERO. Why, saw you anything more wonderful?

---

95. wit *n.* intelligence.
96. disgest *v.* digest.

97. the world present state of affairs.

98. wrought . . . is disposed shaped (like iron) in a way different from its usual form.
99. bear me hard dislike me.

100. humor me win me over.
101. several hands different handwritings.
102. tending to the great opinion pointing out the great respect.
103. glancèd at hinted at.
104. seat him sure establish himself securely.

1. all the sway of earth the stable order of Earth.

2. Have rived have split.

3. exalted with lifted up to.

4. saucy *adj.* rude; impudent.
5. Incenses *v.* enrages.

15 **CASCA.** A common slave—you know him well by sight—
Held up his left hand, which did flame and burn
Like twenty torches joined, and yet his hand,
Not sensible of[6] fire, remained unscorched.
Besides—I ha' not since put up my sword—
20 Against[7] the Capitol I met a lion,
Who glazed[8] upon me and went surly by
Without annoying me. And there were drawn
Upon a heap[9] a hundred ghastly[10] women,
Transformèd with their fear, who swore they saw
25 Men, all in fire, walk up and down the streets.
And yesterday the bird of night[11] did sit
Even at noonday upon the market place,
Hooting and shrieking. When these prodigies[12]
Do so conjointly meet,[13] let not men say,
30 "These are their reasons, they are natural,"
For I believe they are <u>portentous</u> things
Unto the climate that they point upon.[14]

CICERO. Indeed, it is a strange-disposèd[15] time:
But men may construe things after their fashion,[16]
35 Clean from the purpose[17] of the things themselves.
Comes Caesar to the Capitol tomorrow?

CASCA. He doth; for he did bid Antonius
Send word to you he would be there tomorrow.

CICERO. Good night then, Casca; this disturbèd sky
Is not to walk in.

40 **CASCA.**   Farewell, Cicero.   [*Exit* CICERO.]

[*Enter* CASSIUS.]

CASSIUS. Who's there?

CASCA.   A Roman.

CASSIUS.   Casca, by your voice.

CASCA. Your ear is good. Cassius, what night is this?

CASSIUS. A very pleasing night to honest men.

CASCA. Who ever knew the heavens menace so?

45 **CASSIUS.** Those that have known the earth so full of faults.
For my part, I have walked about the streets,
Submitting me unto the perilous night,
And thus unbracèd,[18] Casca, as you see,
Have bared my bosom to the thunder-stone;[19]
50 And when the cross[20] blue lightning seemed to open

Reading Skill
Using Text Aids
According to the information on page 821, why would Shakespeare's audience have connected these unnatural events with the political situation in the play?

6. **sensible of** sensitive to.
7. **Against** *prep.* opposite or near.
8. **glazed** *v.* stared.
9. **were drawn . . . heap** huddled together.
10. **ghastly** (gast´ lē) *adj.* ghostlike; pale.
11. **bird of night** owl.
12. **prodigies** (präd´ ə jēz) *n.* extraordinary happenings.
13. **conjointly meet** occur at the same time and place.
14. **portentous** (pôr ten´ təs) **. . . upon** bad omens for the country they point to.

Vocabulary Builder
portentous (pôr ten´ təs) *adj.* ominous; giving signs of evil to come

15. **strange-disposèd** abnormal.
16. **construe . . . fashion** explain in their own way.
17. **Clean from the purpose** different from the real meaning.
18. **unbracèd** *adj.* with jacket open.
19. **thunder-stone** *n.* thunderbolt.
20. **cross** *adj.* zigzag.

Reading Check

After his conversation with Brutus, what does Cassius say he will do?

The breast of heaven, I did present myself
Even in the aim and very flash of it.

CASCA. But wherefore did you so much tempt the heavens?
It is the part[21] of men to fear and tremble
55   When the most mighty gods by tokens send
Such dreadful heralds to astonish[22] us.

CASSIUS. You are dull, Casca, and those sparks of life
That should be in a Roman you do want,[23]
Or else you use not. You look pale, and gaze,
60   And put on fear, and cast yourself in wonder,[24]
To see the strange impatience of the heavens;
But if you would consider the true cause
Why all these fires, why all these gliding ghosts,
Why birds and beasts from quality and kind,[25]
65   Why old men, fools, and children calculate,[26]
Why all these things change from their ordinance,[27]
Their natures and preformèd faculties,
To monstrous quality,[28] why, you shall find
That heaven hath infused them with these spirits[29]
70   To make them instruments of fear and warning
Unto some monstrous state.[30]
Now could I, Casca, name to thee a man
Most like this dreadful night,
That thunders, lightens, opens graves, and roars
75   As doth the lion in the Capitol;
A man no mightier than thyself, or me,
In personal action, yet <u>prodigious</u> grown
And fearful,[31] as these strange eruptions are.

CASCA. 'Tis Caesar that you mean, is it not, Cassius?

80 CASSIUS. Let it be who it is; for Romans now
Have thews[32] and limbs like to their ancestors;
But, woe the while![33] Our fathers' minds are dead,
And we are governed with our mothers' spirits;
Our yoke and sufferance[34] show us womanish.

85 CASCA. Indeed, they say the senators tomorrow
Mean to establish Caesar as a king;
And he shall wear his crown by sea and land,
In every place save here in Italy.

CASSIUS. I know where I will wear this dagger then;
90   Cassius from bondage will deliver[35] Cassius.
Therein,[36] ye gods, you make the weak most strong;

---

21. part *n.* role.

22. by tokens . . . to astonish by portentous signs send such awful announcements to frighten and stun.

23. want *v.* lack.

24. put on . . . in wonder show fear and are amazed.

25. from quality and kind acting contrary to their nature.

26. calculate *v.* make predictions.

27. ordinance (ôrd´ 'n əns) *n.* regular behavior.

28. preformèd . . . quality established function to unnatural behavior.

29. infused . . . spirits filled them with supernatural powers.

30. monstrous state abnormal condition of government.

31. fearful *adj.* causing fear.

Vocabulary Builder
prodigious (prō dij´ əs) *adj.* of great size or power

32. thews (*th*yo͞oz) *n.* muscles or sinews; strength.

33. woe the while alas for the times.

34. yoke and sufferance slavery and meek acceptance of it.

35. will deliver will set free.

36. Therein (*th*er in´) *adv.* in that way (that is, by giving the weak the power to end their own lives).

Therein, ye gods, you tyrants do defeat.
Nor stony tower, nor walls of beaten brass,
Nor airless dungeon, nor strong links of iron,
95 Can be retentive to[37] the strength of spirit;
But life, being weary of these worldly bars,
Never lacks power to dismiss itself.
If I know this, know all the world besides,
That part of tyranny that I do bear
I can shake off at pleasure.   [*Thunder still*]

100 **CASCA.**   So can I;
So every bondman in his own hand bears
The power to cancel his captivity.

CASSIUS. And why should Caesar be a tyrant then?
Poor man, I know he would not be a wolf
105 But that he sees the Romans are but sheep;
He were no lion, were not Romans hinds.[38]
Those that with haste will make a mighty fire
Begin it with weak straws. What trash is Rome,
What rubbish and what offal,[39] when it serves
110 For the base matter[40] to illuminate
So vile a thing as Caesar! But, O grief,
Where hast thou led me? I, perhaps, speak this
Before a willing bondman; then I know
My answer must be made.[41] But I am armed,
115 And dangers are to me indifferent.

CASCA. You speak to Casca, and to such a man
That is no fleering tell-tale.[42] Hold, my hand.
Be factious[43] for redress of all these griefs,[44]
And I will set this foot of mine as far
As who goes farthest.   [*They clasp hands.*]

120 **CASSIUS.**   There's a bargain made.
Now know you, Casca, I have moved already
Some certain of the noblest-minded Romans
To undergo[45] with me an enterprise
Of honorable dangerous consequence;[46]
125 And I do know, by this[47] they stay for me
In Pompey's porch;[48] for now, this fearful night,
There is no stir or walking in the streets,
And the complexion of the element[49]
In favor's like[50] the work we have in hand,
130 Most bloody, fiery, and most terrible.

[*Enter* CINNA.]

37. **be retentive to** confine.

Literary Analysis
Shakespeare's Tragedies What main conflict has Shakespeare established in Act I?

38. **hinds** (hīndz) *n.* female deer; peasants; servants.
39. **offal** (ôf´ əl) *n.* refuse; waste.
40. **base matter** inferior or low material; foundation materials.
41. **speak this . . . answer must be made** say this before a willing servant of Caesar's; then I know I will have to answer for my words.
42. **fleering tell-tale** sneering tattletale.
43. **factious** (fak´ shəs) *adj.* active in forming a faction or a political party.
44. **redress** (ri dres´) **of all these griefs** setting right all these grievances.
45. **undergo** (un´ dər gō´) *v.* undertake.
46. **consequence** (kän´ sə kwens´) *n.* importance.
47. **by this** by this time.
48. **Pompey's porch** portico of Pompey's Theater.
49. **complexion of the element** condition of the sky; weather.
50. **In favor's like** in appearance is like.

Reading Check

What connection does Cassius make between the night's strange events and Caesar's rise to power?

CASCA. Stand close[51] awhile, for here comes one in haste.

CASSIUS. 'Tis Cinna; I do know him by his gait;[52]
    He is a friend. Cinna, where haste you so?

CINNA. To find out you. Who's that? Metellus Cimber?

135 **CASSIUS.** No, it is Casca, one incorporate
    To our attempts.[53] Am I not stayed for,[54] Cinna?

CINNA. I am glad on't.[55] What a fearful night is this!
    There's two or three of us have seen strange sights.

CASSIUS. Am I not stayed for? Tell me.

CINNA.   Yes, you are.
140   O Cassius, if you could
    But win the noble Brutus to our party—

CASSIUS. Be you content. Good Cinna, take this paper,
    And look you lay it in the praetor's chair,[56]
    Where Brutus may but find it;[57] and throw this
145   In at his window: set this up with wax
    Upon old Brutus'[58] statue. All this done,
    Repair[59] to Pompey's porch, where you shall find us.
    Is Decius Brutus and Trebonius there?

CINNA. All but Metellus Cimber, and he's gone
150   To seek you at your house. Well, I will hie,[60]
    And so bestow these papers as you bade me.

CASSIUS. That done, repair to Pompey's Theater.   [*Exit* CINNA.]
    Come, Casca, you and I will yet ere day
    See Brutus at his house; three parts of him
155   Is ours already, and the man entire
    Upon the next encounter yields him ours.

CASCA. O, he sits high in all the people's hearts;
    And that which would appear offense[61] in us,
    His countenance,[62] like richest alchemy,[63]
160   Will change to virtue and to worthiness.

CASSIUS. Him, and his worth, and our great need of him,
    You have right well conceited.[64] Let us go,
    For it is after midnight, and ere day
    We will awake him and be sure of him.   [*Exit*]

---

51. close *adj.* hidden.

52. gait (gāt) *n.* style of walking.

53. incorporate (in kôr´ pə rit) /
To our attempts part of our efforts.
54. stayed for waited for.
55. on't (ônt) *contraction* of it.

Reading Skill
Using Text Aids Why might you need to consult glosses 56 and 57 to understand Cassius' plan?

56. praetor's (prē´ tərz)
chair Roman magistrate's (or judge's) chair.
57. Where . . . find it where only Brutus (as the chief magistrate) will find it.
58. old Brutus' Lucius (loo´ shəs) Junius Brutus, the founder of the Roman Republic.
59. Repair *v.* go.
60. hie (hī) *v.* hurry.

61. offense (ə fens´) *n.* crime.
62. countenance (koun´ tə nəns) *n.* support.
63. alchemy (al´ kə mē) *n.* an early form of chemistry in which the goal was to change metals of little value into gold.
64. conceited (kən sēt´ id) *v.* understood.

▲ **Critical Viewing** Which details in this relief sculpture indicate the respect and awe with which Romans regarded their leaders? **[Interpret]**

Apply the Skills

The Tragedy of Julius Caesar, Act I

Thinking About the Selection

1. **Respond:** Which character interests you most so far? Why?
2. **(a) Recall:** At the opening of the play, how do common Romans such as the Cobbler react to Caesar's return? **(b) Interpret:** What do noble Romans such as Flavius and Cassius fear or resent about Caesar's success? Support your answer with quotations.
3. **(a) Recall:** What warning does the soothsayer give Caesar? **(b) Infer:** What does Caesar's reaction show about him?
4. **(a) Analyze:** Using a chart like the one shown, analyze Brutus' values as expressed in the speech noted. **(b) Analyze:** Using the same chart, analyze Cassius' speech appealing to those values.

Speech		What Does It Say?	What Does It Mean?	Why Is It Important?
Brutus	Scene ii, lines 82–89			
Cassius	Scene ii, lines 135–161			

5. **(a) Draw Conclusions:** What is Cassius planning to do with the help of Cinna, Casca, and other noble Romans? Support your answer with details from the text. **(b) Hypothesize:** Why is it important to them to win Brutus' support?
6. **Generalize:** Identify the quality that stands out most in each of the following characters: Brutus, Cassius, and Caesar.

Literary Analysis

7. Summarize what you learn in Act I of this **Shakespearean tragedy.**
8. Given what you have read so far, explain what **tragic flaw** in Brutus' character might lead him to disaster.

Reading Skill

9. The **text aids** before the play include a background section on ancient Rome (p. 821). Identify two passages in Act I that are clarified by this background information. Explain your choices.
10. In Scene ii, how do glosses 73 and 74 help readers understand what happened in the marketplace?

QuickReview

Act I at a Glance
Returning from war, Caesar is greeted with enthusiasm by the crowds. Cassius and other nobles, who worry about Caesar's ambition to rule as emperor, seek Brutus' help.

Go Online
Assessment
For: Self-test
Visit: www.PHSchool.com
Web Code: eqa-6505

Tragedy: a form of drama that shows a reversal of fortune experienced by a character usually of noble birth. The *hero's* downfall is the result of a *tragic flaw.*

Text Aids: special features that help readers understand a literary work

Vocabulary Builder

Practice Replace the underlined word with an antonym, a word that is opposite in meaning. Explain your answers.

1. The fine art collector bought a <u>replication</u>.
2. His <u>servile</u> behavior makes me uncomfortable.
3. This suit was not tailored for someone with a <u>spare</u> build.
4. His <u>infirmity</u> is due to chance, not to the way he lives.
5. I found the unlocked door <u>portentous</u>.
6. She has a <u>prodigious</u> appetite.

Adding Words to Your Vocabulary Use a dictionary to find the noun and verb forms of *portentous.* Then, use all three words in sentences. (For more on using a dictionary, see page R6.)

Writing

List four key characters in Act I, and write **character descriptions** to help actors prepare to play the roles. Include the following:

- age and physical description
- personality
- background on the characters' experiences, social standing, and feelings about other characters.

For *Grammar, Vocabulary,* and *Assessment,* see **Build Language Skills,** pages 926–927.

Extend Your Learning

Listening and Speaking With a partner, give a **dramatic reading** of Cassius' discussion with Brutus in lines 132–177 of Scene ii. Review Act I for hints about the personality of each man. Let your knowledge of the character guide your tone of voice and attitude. Practice your parts, and present your reading to the class. Lead the class in a discussion comparing and contrasting the experience of reading the scene silently to oneself with the experience of hearing it performed with different voices for the different roles.

Research and Technology Using library or Internet sources, learn more about the transition from republic to empire in ancient Rome, focusing on Julius Caesar's role in this shift. Make a **timeline** showing important events and actions.

Practice these skills with *The Tragedy of Julius Caesar,* Act II.

Literary Analysis

The Tragedy of Julius Caesar is written in blank verse. **Blank verse** is a poetic form characterized by unrhymed lines written in iambic pentameter.

- An **iamb** is a *foot* (unit of rhythm) in which an unstressed syllable is followed by a stressed syllable: da-DUH.
- **Pentameter** refers to a rhythmic pattern in which each line has five feet.
- In **iambic pentameter,** the typical line has five iambs, or five stressed syllables each preceded by an unstressed syllable:

Shakespeare's "upperclass" characters speak in iambic pentameter. Lower-born characters speak in prose. Sometimes, Shakespeare breaks the rhythmic pattern in a line to add contrast or emphasis.

Reading Skill

Paraphrasing a line or passage from a work means restating its meaning in your own words. To paraphrase when **reading Shakespearean drama,** follow these steps:

- Look for punctuation showing where sentences end.
- For each sentence, identify the subject and verb and put them into the usual order. You may also need to add helping verbs and use modern verb and pronoun forms.

As you read, paraphrase using a diagram like the one shown.

Academic Standards

- Analyze characters' traits through narration and dialogue. (10.3.4)
- Evaluate the use of voice and narrator. (10.3.9)

Original Lines

Verb   Subj.
"O conspiracy, / Sham'st thou to show thy dang'rous brow by night, / When evils are most free?"
-Scene i, lines 77–79

↓

Paraphrase

O conspiracy, are you ashamed to show your dangerous face even at night, when it is easiest to be evil?

Vocabulary Builder

- **augmented** (ôg ment´ id) *adj.* made greater; enhanced (p. 848) *Her augmented library has hundreds more books.*

- **entreated** (en trēt´ id) *v.* begged; pleaded with (p. 849) *He entreated her for mercy.*

- **insurrection** (in´ sə rek´ shən) *n.* rebellion (p. 849) *The insurrection against the government started in the town square.*

- **resolution** (rez´ ə lōō´ shən) *n.* strong determination; a plan or decision (p. 851) *Lou stuck to his plans with firm resolution.*

- **wrathfully** (rath´ fəl lē) *adv.* with intense anger (p. 853) *She shook her fist wrathfully.*

- **imminent** (im´ ə nənt) *adj.* about to happen (p. 861) *The lightning flash meant thunder was imminent.*

Review and Anticipate In Act I, as Caesar returns victorious from war, the common people are calling for him to be crowned emperor. Fearful of Caesar's ambitions and unwilling to surrender their own power, Cassius and others conspire against Caesar. Cassius attempts to win the support of Brutus, a highly respected Roman. Although Brutus is a friend of Caesar's, he worries about Caesar's ambition. In the meantime, Caesar receives a warning to "beware the ides of March." Act II opens on the evening before that fateful day. As you read, note how Caesar's own pride leads him to ignore danger. Note also the contrasts that emerge between Brutus and the conspirators.

➤➤➤➤➤➤➤ ACT II ⫷⫷⫷⫷⫷⫷⫷

Scene i. Rome.

[*Enter* BRUTUS *in his orchard.*]

BRUTUS. What, Lucius, ho!
I cannot, by the progress of the stars,
Give guess how near to day. Lucius, I say!
I would it were my fault to sleep so soundly.
5   When, Lucius, when? Awake, I say! What, Lucius!

[*Enter* LUCIUS.]

LUCIUS. Called you, my lord?

BRUTUS. Get me a taper in my study, Lucius.
When it is lighted, come and call me here.

LUCIUS. I will, my lord.   [*Exit*]

10   **BRUTUS.** It must be by his death; and for my part,
I know no personal cause to spurn at[1] him,
But for the general.[2] He would be crowned.
How that might change his nature, there's the question.
It is the bright day that brings forth the adder,[3]
15   And that craves[4] wary walking. Crown him that,
And then I grant we put a sting in him
That at his will he may do danger with.
Th' abuse of greatness is when it disjoins
Remorse from power;[5] and, to speak truth of Caesar,
20   I have not known when his affections swayed[6]
More than his reason. But 'tis a common proof[7]
That lowliness[8] is young ambition's ladder,

Literary Analysis
Blank Verse Explain which character, Brutus or Lucius, speaks in blank verse and why.

1. spurn at kick against; rebel against.
2. the general the public good.
3. adder (ad´ ər) *n.* poisonous snake.
4. craves *v.* requires.
5. disjoins . . . power separates mercy from power.
6. affections swayed emotions ruled.
7. proof *n.* experience.
8. lowliness (lō´ lē nəs) *n.* humility.

**Reading Check**

What does Brutus fear may happen if Caesar is crowned?

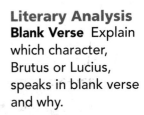

Whereto the climber upward turns his face;
But when he once attains the upmost round,
25   He then unto the ladder turns his back,
Looks in the clouds, scorning the base degrees[9]
By which he did ascend. So Caesar may;
Then lest he may, prevent.[10] And, since the quarrel
Will bear no color for the thing he is,[11]
30   Fashion it[12] thus: that what he is, <u>augmented</u>
Would run to these and these extremities;[13]
And therefore think him as a serpent's egg
Which hatched, would as his kind grow mischievous,
And kill him in the shell.

[*Enter* LUCIUS.]

35 **LUCIUS.** The taper burneth in your closet,[14] sir.
Searching the window for a flint,[15] I found
This paper thus sealed up, and I am sure
It did not lie there when I went to bed. [*Gives him the letter*]

    BRUTUS. Get you to bed again; it is not day.
40   Is not tomorrow, boy, the ides of March?

    LUCIUS. I know not, sir.

    BRUTUS. Look in the calendar and bring me word.

9. base degrees low steps or people in lower positions.
10. lest . . . prevent in case he may, we must stop him.
11. the quarrel . . . the thing he is our complaint cannot be justified in terms of what he now is.
12. Fashion it state the case.
13. extremities (ek strem′ ə tēz) *n.* extremes (of tyranny).

Vocabulary Builder
augmented (ôg ment′ id) *adj.* made greater; enhanced

14. closet *n.* study; small, private room for reading, meditation, and so on.
15. flint *n.* hard stone which, when struck with steel, makes sparks.

Literature in Context

Language Connection

Archaic Word Forms Shakespeare uses some word forms that are now archaic, or out of date. For modern readers, these words give his work a tone that is both more formal and more poetic than contemporary English. These archaic forms include the following:

thou *pron.* subjective case of a pronoun meaning "you" (the form used with family, friends, or the young)

thee *pron.* you (objective case of *thou*)

thy *pron.* your (possessive case of *thou*)

burneth *v.* third-person singular present tense of *burn*

'tis *contraction* it is

doth *v.* third-person singular present tense of *do*

dost *v.* second-person singular present tense of *do* (used with *thou*)

sham'st *v.* second-person singular present tense of *shame* (used with *thou*)

Connect to the Literature

What does this archaic language add to your experience of the play? What challenges does it pose?

LUCIUS. I will, sir.   [*Exit*]

BRUTUS. The exhalations[16] whizzing in the air
45   Give so much light that I may read by them.
                                    [*Opens the letter and reads*]

          "Brutus, thou sleep'st; awake, and see thyself.
          Shall Rome, &c.[17] Speak, strike, redress.
          Brutus, thou sleep'st; awake."

      Such instigations[18] have been often dropped
50   Where I have took them up.
      "Shall Rome, &c." Thus must I piece it out:[19]
      Shall Rome stand under one man's awe?[20] What, Rome?
      My ancestors did from the streets of Rome
      The Tarquin[21] drive, when he was called a king.
55   "Speak, strike, redress." Am I <u>entreated</u>
      To speak and strike? O Rome, I make thee promise,
      If the redress will follow, thou receivest
      Thy full petition at the hand of[22] Brutus!

[*Enter* LUCIUS.]

LUCIUS. Sir, March is wasted fifteen days.   [*Knock within*]

60 **BRUTUS.** 'Tis good. Go to the gate; somebody knocks.

                                              [*Exit* LUCIUS.]

      Since Cassius first did whet[23] me against Caesar,
      I have not slept.
      Between the acting of a dreadful thing
      And the first motion,[24] all the interim is
65   Like a phantasma,[25] or a hideous dream.
      The genius and the mortal instruments[26]
      Are then in council, and the state of a man,
      Like to a little kingdom, suffers then
      The nature of an <u>insurrection</u>.

[*Enter* LUCIUS.]

70 **LUCIUS.** Sir, 'tis your brother[27] Cassius at the door,
      Who doth desire to see you.

    BRUTUS.   Is he alone?

    LUCIUS. No, sir, there are moe[28] with him.

    BRUTUS.   Do you know them?

    LUCIUS. No, sir; their hats are plucked about their ears,
      And half their faces buried in their cloaks,
75   That by no means I may discover them

---

16. exhalations (eks´ hə lā´ shənz) *n.* meteors.

17. &c. et cetera (et set´ ər ə); Latin for "and so forth."

18. instigations (in´ stə gā´ shənz) *n.* urgings, incitements, or spurs to act.

19. piece it out figure out the meaning.

20. under one man's awe in fearful reverence of one man.

21. Tarquin (tär´ kwin) king of Rome driven out by Lucius Junius Brutus, Brutus' ancestor.

Vocabulary Builder
entreated (en trēt´ id)
v. begged; pleaded

22. Thy full . . . hand of all you ask from.

23. whet (hwet) *v.* sharpen; incite.

24. motion *n.* idea; suggestion.

25. all the interim . . . a phantasma (fan taz´ mə) all the time between seems like a hallucination.

26. mortal instruments bodily powers.

Vocabulary Builder
insurrection (in´ sə rek´ shən) *n.* rebellion

27. brother *n.* brother-in-law. (Cassius was married to Brutus' sister.)

28. moe *n.* more.

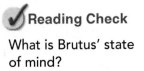
Reading Check

What is Brutus' state of mind?

By any mark of favor.[29]

BRUTUS. Let 'em enter. [*Exit* LUCIUS.]
They are the faction. O conspiracy,
Sham'st thou to show thy dang'rous brow by night,
When evils are most free? O, then by day
80   Where wilt thou find a cavern dark enough
To mask thy monstrous visage? Seek none, conspiracy;
Hide it in smiles and affability:
For if thou path, thy native semblance on,[30]
Not Erebus[31] itself were dim enough
85   To hide thee from prevention.[32]

[*Enter the conspirators,* CASSIUS, CASCA, DECIUS, CINNA, METELLUS
CIMBER, *and* TREBONIUS.]

CASSIUS. I think we are too bold upon[33] your rest.
Good morrow, Brutus; do we trouble you?

BRUTUS. I have been up this hour, awake all night.
Know I these men that come along with you?

90   **CASSIUS.** Yes, every man of them; and no man here
But honors you; and every one doth wish
You had but that opinion of yourself
Which every noble Roman bears of you.
This is Trebonius.

BRUTUS. He is welcome hither.

CASSIUS. This, Decius Brutus.

95   **BRUTUS.** He is welcome too.

CASSIUS. This, Casca; this, Cinna; and this, Metellus Cimber.

BRUTUS. They are all welcome.
What watchful cares do interpose themselves
Betwixt your eyes and night?[34]

100   **CASSIUS.** Shall I entreat a word?[35] [*They whisper.*]

DECIUS. Here lies the east; doth not the day break here?

CASCA. No.

CINNA. O, pardon, sir, it doth; and yon gray lines
That fret[36] the clouds are messengers of day.

105   **CASCA.** You shall confess that you are both deceived.
Here, as I point my sword, the sun arises,
Which is a great way growing on[37] the south,
Weighing[38] the youthful season of the year.

Literary Analysis
Blank Verse Which
interjection does
Shakespeare use to
maintain iambic
pentameter in lines 77
and 79?

Reading Skill
Paraphrasing Para-
phrase Cassius' words
in lines 90–93.

Some two months hence, up higher toward the north
110 He first presents his fire; and the high[39] east
Stands as the Capitol, directly here.

BRUTUS. Give me your hands all over, one by one.

CASSIUS. And let us swear our <u>resolution</u>.

BRUTUS. No, not an oath. If not the face of men,
115 The sufferance of our souls, the time's abuse[40]—
If these be motives weak, break off betimes,[41]
And every man hence to his idle bed.
So let high-sighted[42] tyranny range on
Till each man drop by lottery.[43] But if these
120 (As I am sure they do) bear fire enough
To kindle cowards and to steel with valor
The melting spirits of women, then, countrymen,
What need we any spur but our own cause
To prick us to redress?[44] What other bond
125 Than secret Romans, that have spoke the word,
And will not palter?[45] And what other oath
Than honesty to honesty[46] engaged
That this shall be, or we will fall for it?
Swear priests and cowards and men cautelous,[47]
130 Old feeble carrions[48] and such suffering souls
That welcome wrongs; unto bad causes swear
Such creatures as men doubt; but do not stain
The even[49] virtue of our enterprise,
Nor th' insuppressive mettle[50] of our spirits,
135 To think that or our cause or[51] our performance
Did need an oath; when every drop of blood
That every Roman bears, and nobly bears,
Is guilty of a several bastardy[52]
If he do break the smallest particle
140 Of any promise that hath passed from him.

CASSIUS. But what of Cicero? Shall we sound him?[53]
I think he will stand very strong with us.

CASCA. Let us not leave him out.

CINNA.   No, by no means.

METELLUS. O, let us have him, for his silver hairs
145 Will purchase us a good opinion,
And buy men's voices to commend our deeds.
It shall be said his judgment ruled our hands;
Our youths and wildness shall no whit[54] appear,
But all be buried in his gravity.

39. high *adj.* due.

Vocabulary Builder
resolution (rez′ ə lo͞o′
shən) *n.* strong
determination; a plan
or decision

**40. the face . . . time's
abuse** the sadness on men's
faces, the patient endurance
of our souls, the present abuses (that is, Caesar's abuses of
power).

41. betimes (bē tīmz′)
adv. quickly.

42. high-sighted *adj.*
arrogant (a reference to a
hawk about to swoop down
on prey).

43. by lottery by chance or in
his turn.

44. prick us to redress goad
or spur us on to correct these
evils.

45. palter (pôl′ tər) *v.* talk
insincerely.

46. honesty personal honor.

47. cautelous (kôt′ ə ləs) *adj.*
deceitful.

48. carrions (kar′ ē ənz) *n.*
men who are nearly corpses.

49. even *adj.* constant.

50. insuppressive mettle
uncrushable courage.

51. or . . . or either our
cause or.

52. guilty . . . bastardy is no
true Roman.

53. sound him find out his
opinion.

54. no whit (hwit) not the
least bit.

Reading Check

Why does Brutus think
the conspirators
should not swear an
oath?

150 **BRUTUS.** O, name him not! Let us not break with him;[55]
    For he will never follow anything
    That other men begin.

    CASSIUS.   Then leave him out.

    CASCA. Indeed, he is not fit.

    DECIUS. Shall no man else be touched but only Caesar?

155 **CASSIUS.** Decius, well urged. I think it is not meet
    Mark Antony, so well beloved of Caesar,
    Should outlive Caesar; we shall find of[56] him
    A shrewd contriver;[57] and you know, his means,
    If he improve[58] them, may well stretch so far
160   As to annoy[59] us all; which to prevent,
    Let Antony and Caesar fall together.

    BRUTUS. Our course will seem too bloody, Caius Cassius,
    To cut the head off and then hack the limbs,
    Like wrath in death and envy afterwards;[60]
165   For Antony is but a limb of Caesar.
    Let's be sacrificers, but not butchers, Caius.

55. break with him confide in him.

56. of *prep.* in.
57. contriver (kən triv′ ər) *n.* schemer.
58. improve *v.* increase.
59. annoy *n.* harm.
60. Like . . . envy afterwards as if we were killing in anger with hatred afterward.

▼ **Critical Viewing**
What details of this image emphasize the differences between Brutus, on the left, and the other conspirators? **[Analyze]**

We all stand up against the spirit of Caesar,
And in the spirit of men there is no blood.
O, that we then could come by Caesar's spirit,[61]
170 And not dismember Caesar! But, alas,
Caesar must bleed for it. And, gentle[62] friends,
Let's kill him boldly, but not <u>wrathfully</u>;
Let's carve him as a dish fit for the gods,
Not hew him as a carcass fit for hounds.
175 And let our hearts, as subtle masters do,
Stir up their servants[63] to an act of rage,
And after seem to chide 'em.[64] This shall make
Our purpose necessary, and not envious;
Which so appearing to the common eyes,
180 We shall be called purgers,[65] not murderers.
And for Mark Antony, think not of him;
For he can do no more than Caesar's arm
When Caesar's head is off.

CASSIUS.   Yet I fear him;
For in the ingrafted[66] love he bears to Caesar—

185 **BRUTUS.** Alas, good Cassius, do not think of him.
If he love Caesar, all that he can do
Is to himself—take thought[67] and die for Caesar.
And that were much he should,[68] for he is given
To sports, to wildness, and much company.

190 **TREBONIUS.** There is no fear in him; let him not die,
For he will live and laugh at this hereafter.

[*Clock strikes.*]

BRUTUS. Peace! Count the clock.

CASSIUS.   The clock hath stricken three.

TREBONIUS. 'Tis time to part.

CASSIUS.   But it is doubtful yet
Whether Caesar will come forth today or no;
195 For he is superstitious grown of late,
Quite from the main[69] opinion he held once
Of fantasy, of dreams, and ceremonies.[70]
It may be these apparent prodigies,[71]
The unaccustomed terror of this night,
200 And the persuasion of his augurers[72]
May hold him from the Capitol today.

DECIUS. Never fear that. If he be so resolved,
I can o'ersway him;[73] for he loves to hear

---

61. **come by Caesar's spirit** get hold of the principles of tyranny for which Caesar stands.

62. **gentle** *adj.* honorable; noble.

Vocabulary Builder
wrathfully (ra th′ fəl lē)
adv. with intense anger

63. **their servants** that is, the hands or the passions.

64. **chide 'em** scold them.

65. **purgers** (pʉrj ərz) *n.* healers.

66. **ingrafted** (in graft′ id) *adj.* deeply rooted.

67. **take thought** become melancholy.

68. **that were much he should** It is unlikely he would do that.

69. **Quite from the main** quite changed from the strong.

70. **ceremonies** *n.* omens.

71. **apparent prodigies** obvious omens of disaster.

72. **augurers** (ô′ gər ərz) *n.* augurs; officials who interpreted omens to decide if they were favorable or unfavorable for an undertaking.

73. **I can o'ersway him** I can change his mind.

Reading Check

According to Brutus, why should Antony not be killed?

205 That unicorns may be betrayed with trees,[74]
And bears with glasses,[75] elephants with holes,[76]
Lions with toils,[77] and men with flatterers;
But when I tell him he hates flatterers
He says he does, being then most flatterèd.
Let me work;
210 For I can give his humor the true bent,[78]
And I will bring him to the Capitol.

CASSIUS. Nay, we will all of us be there to fetch him.

BRUTUS. By the eighth hour; is that the uttermost?[79]

CINNA. Be that the uttermost, and fail not then.

215 METELLUS. Caius Ligarius doth bear Caesar hard,[80]
Who rated[81] him for speaking well of Pompey.
I wonder none of you have thought of him.

BRUTUS. Now, good Metellus, go along by him.
He loves me well, and I have given him reasons;
220 Send him but hither, and I'll fashion[82] him.

CASSIUS. The morning comes upon 's; we'll leave you, Brutus.
And, friends, disperse yourselves; but all remember
What you have said, and show yourselves true Romans.

BRUTUS. Good gentlemen, look fresh and merrily.
225 Let not our looks put on[83] our purposes,
But bear it[84] as our Roman actors do,
With untired spirits and formal constancy.[85]
And so good morrow to you every one.   [*Exit all but* BRUTUS.]
Boy! Lucius! Fast asleep? It is no matter;
230 Enjoy the honey-heavy dew of slumber.
Thou hast no figures nor no fantasies
Which busy care draws in the brains of men;
Therefore thou sleep'st so sound.

[*Enter* PORTIA.]

PORTIA.   Brutus, my lord.

BRUTUS. Portia, what mean you? Wherefore rise you now?
235 It is not for your health thus to commit
Your weak condition to the raw cold morning.

PORTIA. Nor for yours neither. Y'have ungently, Brutus,
Stole from my bed; and yesternight at supper
You suddenly arose and walked about,
240 Musing and sighing, with your arms across;
And when I asked you what the matter was,

---

74. unicorns . . . trees reference to the belief that standing in front of a tree as a unicorn charges and then stepping aside at the last moment causes the unicorn to bury its horn in the tree and so allows it to be caught.

75. glasses *n.* mirrors.

76. holes *n.* pitfalls.

77. toils *n.* nets; snares.

78. give his humor the true bent bend his feelings in the right direction.

79. uttermost *adj.* latest.

80. doth bear Caesar hard has a grudge against Caesar.

81. rated *v.* berated; scolded forcefully.

82. fashion *v.* mold.

83. put on show.
84. bear it carry it off.
85. formal constancy consistent dignity.

Reading Skill
Paraphrasing Paraphrase Brutus' speech in lines 229–233 and explain which punctuation mark helps you identify the conclusion he draws.

Literary Analysis
Blank Verse How does shifting the accent to the first and fourth syllables in line 240 add dramatic energy to this speech?

You stared upon me with ungentle looks.
I urged you further; then you scratched your head,
And too impatiently stamped with your foot.
245 Yet I insisted, yet you answered not,
But with an angry wafter[86] of your hand
Gave sign for me to leave you. So I did,
Fearing to strengthen that impatience
Which seemed too much enkindled, and withal
250 Hoping it was but an effect of humor,
Which sometime hath his[87] hour with every man.
It will not let you eat, nor talk, nor sleep,
And could it work so much upon your shape
As it hath much prevailed on your condition,[88]
255 I should not know you[89] Brutus. Dear my lord,
Make me acquainted with your cause of grief.

BRUTUS. I am not well in health, and that is all.

PORTIA. Brutus is wise and, were he not in health,
He would embrace the means to come by it.

260 **BRUTUS.** Why, so I do. Good Portia, go to bed.

PORTIA. Is Brutus sick, and is it physical[90]
To walk unbracèd and suck up the humors[91]
Of the dank morning? What, is Brutus sick,
And will he steal out of his wholesome bed,
265 To dare the vile contagion of the night,
And tempt the rheumy and unpurgèd air[92]
To add unto his sickness? No, my Brutus:
You have some sick offense[93] within your mind,
Which by the right and virtue of my place
270 I ought to know of; and upon my knees
I charm[94] you, by my once commended[95] beauty,
By all your vows of love, and that great vow[96]
Which did incorporate and make us one,
That you unfold to me, your self, your half,
275 Why you are heavy,[97] and what men tonight
Have had resort to you; for here have been
Some six or seven, who did hide their faces
Even from darkness.

BRUTUS.   Kneel not, gentle Portia.

PORTIA. I should not need, if you were gentle Brutus.
280 Within the bond of marriage, tell me, Brutus,
Is it excepted[98] I should know no secrets
That appertain[99] to you? Am I your self

---

86. **wafter** (wäf′ tər) *n.* wave.

87. **his** *pron.* its.

88. **condition** *n.* disposition; mood.
89. **I should not know you** I would not recognize you as.

90. **physical** *adj.* healthy.
91. **walk unbracèd . . . humors** walk with jacket unfastened and take in the dampness.

92. **tempt . . . air** risk exposing yourself to the night air, which is likely to cause rheumatism and has not been purified by the sun.
93. **sick offense** harmful sickness.
94. **charm** *v.* beg.
95. **commended** *adj.* praised.
96. **great vow** marriage vow.
97. **heavy** *adj.* sorrowful.
98. **excepted** *v.* made an exception that.
99. **appertain** (ap′ ər tān′) *v.* belong.

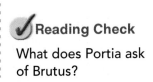

Reading Check

What does Portia ask of Brutus?

But, as it were, in sort or limitation,[100]
To keep with you at meals, comfort your bed,
285 And talk to you sometimes? Dwell I but in the suburbs[101]
Of your good pleasure? If it be no more,
Portia is Brutus' harlot, not his wife.

BRUTUS. You are my true and honorable wife,
As dear to me as are the ruddy drops[102]
290 That visit my sad heart.

PORTIA. If this were true, then should I know this secret.
I grant I am a woman; but withal[103]
A woman that Lord Brutus took to wife.
I grant I am a woman; but withal
295 A woman well reputed, Cato's daughter.[104]
Think you I am no stronger than my sex,
Being so fathered and so husbanded?
Tell me your counsels,[105] I will not disclose 'em.
I have made strong proof of my constancy,
300 Giving myself a voluntary wound

▲ **Critical Viewing**
What do the pose and
expressions of Brutus
and Portia in this film
still reveal about their
feelings? **[Interpret]**

100. in sort or limitation in a
limited way (legal terms).
101. suburbs *n.* outskirts.
102. ruddy drops blood.
103. withal (wi*th* ôl´) *adv.*
nevertheless.

104. Cato's daughter Marcus
Porcius (pôr´ shəs) Cato (Cato
the Younger; 95–46 B.C.) supported Pompey in his quarrel
with Caesar and killed himself
rather than allow himself to be
captured by Caesar.
105. counsels *n.* secrets.

856 ■ *Drama*

Here in the thigh; can I bear that with patience,
And not my husband's secrets?

BRUTUS.   O ye gods,
Render[106] me worthy of this noble wife!   [*Knock*]
Hark, hark! One knocks. Portia, go in a while,
305   And by and by thy bosom shall partake
The secrets of my heart.
All my engagements[107] I will construe to thee,
All the charactery of my sad brows.[108]
Leave me with haste.   [*Exit* PORTIA.]

[*Enter* LUCIUS *and* CAIUS LIGARIUS.]

Lucius, who's that knocks?

310 **LUCIUS.** Here is a sick man that would speak with you.

BRUTUS. Caius Ligarius, that Metellus spake of.
Boy, stand aside. Caius Ligarius! How?

CAIUS. Vouchsafe good morrow from a feeble tongue.

BRUTUS. O, what a time have you chose out,[109] brave Caius,
315   To wear a kerchief![110] Would you were not sick!

CAIUS. I am not sick, if Brutus have in hand
Any exploit worthy the name of honor.

BRUTUS. Such an exploit have I in hand, Ligarius,
Had you a healthful ear to hear of it.

320 **CAIUS.** By all the gods that Romans bow before,
I here discard my sickness! Soul of Rome,
Brave son, derived from honorable loins,[111]
Thou, like an exorcist,[112] hast conjured up
My mortifièd spirit.[113] Now bid me run,
325   And I will strive with things impossible.
Yea, get the better of them. What's to do?

BRUTUS. A piece of work that will make sick men whole.

CAIUS. But are not some whole that we must make sick?

BRUTUS. That must we also. What it is, my Caius,
330   I shall unfold[114] to thee, as we are going
To whom it must be done.

CAIUS.   Set on[115] your foot,
And with a heart new-fired I follow you,
To do I know not what; but it sufficeth[116]
That Brutus leads me on.   [*Thunder*]

BRUTUS.   Follow me, then.   [*Exit*]

---

106. **Render** (ren´ dər) *v.* make.

Literary Analysis
Blank Verse By breaking the pattern of iambic pentameter, which words are emphasized in lines 307 and 308?

107. **engagements** *n.* commitments.

108. **All the charactery of my sad brows** all that is written on my sad face.

109. **chose out** picked out.

110. **To wear a kerchief** Caius wears a scarf to protect himself from drafts because he is sick.

111. **derived from honorable loins** descended from Lucius (loo´ shəs) Junius Brutus, founder of the Roman Republic.

112. **exorcist** (ek´ sôr sist) *n.* one who calls up spirits.

113. **mortifièd** (môrt´ ə fī ed) *adj.* deadened.

114. **unfold** *v.* disclose.

115. **Set on** advance.

116. **sufficeth** (sə fis´ eth) *v.* is enough.

Reading Check

Why does Portia feel that Brutus should confide in her?

Scene ii. *Caesar's house.*

[*Thunder and lightning. Enter* JULIUS CAESAR *in his nightgown.*]

    CAESAR. Nor heaven nor earth have been at peace tonight:
        Thrice hath Calpurnia in her sleep cried out,
        "Help, ho! They murder Caesar!" Who's within?

[*Enter a* SERVANT.]

    SERVANT. My lord?

5 **CAESAR.** Go bid the priests do present[1] sacrifice,
        And bring me their opinions of success.

    SERVANT. I will, my lord.   [*Exit*]

[*Enter* CALPURNIA.]

    CALPURNIA. What mean you, Caesar? Think you to walk forth?
        You shall not stir out of your house today.

10 **CAESAR.** Caesar shall forth. The things that threatened me
        Ne'er looked but on my back; when they shall see
        The face of Caesar, they are vanishèd.

Reading Skill
Paraphrasing Paraphrase Caesar's remarks in lines 1–3, rearranging the subject and verb in line 2.

1. **present** *adj.* immediate.

Literature in Context | Culture Connection

Roman Augurs

In the play, Caesar orders his "priests," or augurs (ô´ gərz), to make a sacrifice to determine whether he should go to the Senate.

▲ Another class of priest, the *haruspices* (hə rus´ pə sēs´), examined the patterns in the innards of a sacrificed animal.

- In ancient Rome, augurs were officials who examined signs to determine whether the gods would grant success to a particular venture or plan.
- After receiving a negative judgment from the augurs, a Roman leader might postpone an attack or cancel a meeting.
- By the first century A.D., there were sixteen official augurs.

Augurs watched for signs ▶ such as thunder and lightning and the flights of birds. They also observed the pecking of sacred chickens. Omens related to birds were called *auspices*.

Connect to the Literature What does Caesar's own interpretation of his augurs' omen show about the straightforwardness of augury?

CALPURNIA. Caesar, I never stood on ceremonies,[2]
    Yet now they fright me. There is one within,
15   Besides the things that we have heard and seen,
    Recounts most horrid sights seen by the watch.[3]
    A lioness hath whelpèd[4] in the streets,
    And graves have yawned, and yielded up their dead;
    Fierce fiery warriors fought upon the clouds
20   In ranks and squadrons and right form of war,[5]
    Which drizzled blood upon the Capitol;
    The noise of battle hurtled[6] in the air,
    Horses did neigh and dying men did groan,
    And ghosts did shriek and squeal about the street.
25   O Caesar, these things are beyond all use,[7]
    And I do fear them.

CAESAR.   What can be avoided
    Whose end is purposed[8] by the mighty gods?
    Yet Caesar shall go forth; for these predictions
    Are to the world in general as to Caesar.[9]

30 **CALPURNIA.** When beggars die, there are no comets seen;
    The heavens themselves blaze forth[10] the death of princes.

CAESAR. Cowards die many times before their deaths;
    The valiant never taste of death but once.
    Of all the wonders that I yet have heard,
35   It seems to me most strange that men should fear,
    Seeing that death, a necessary end,
    Will come when it will come.

[*Enter a* SERVANT.]

                What say the augurers?

SERVANT. They would not have you to stir forth today.
    Plucking the entrails of an offering forth,[11]
40   They could not find a heart within the beast.

CAESAR. The gods do this in shame of[12] cowardice:
    Caesar should be a beast without a heart
    If he should stay at home today for fear.
    No, Caesar shall not; Danger knows full well
45   That Caesar is more dangerous than he.
    We are two lions littered[13] in one day,
    And I the elder and more terrible,
    And Caesar shall go forth.

CALPURNIA.   Alas, my lord,
    Your wisdom is consumed in confidence.[14]

---

2. stood on ceremonies paid attention to omens.

3. Recounts . . . watch tells about the awful sights seen by the watchman.

4. whelpèd *v.* given birth.

5. right form of war proper military formation of war.

6. hurtled (hʉrt′ əld) *v.* clashed.

7. beyond all use contrary to all experience.

8. is purposed is intended.

9. for these . . . as to Caesar because these predictions apply to the rest of the world as much as they apply to Caesar.

10. blaze forth proclaim with meteors and comets.

Reading Skill
Paraphrasing Paraphrase the ideas in lines 32–33.

11. Plucking . . . forth pulling out the insides of a sacrificed animal (which were then "read" by augurs).

12. in shame of in order to shame.

13. littered *v.* born.

14. confidence *n.* overconfidence.

✓ Reading Check

Why does Calpurnia urge Caesar to stay home?

---

50 Do not go forth today. Call it my fear
That keeps you in the house and not your own.
We'll send Mark Antony to the Senate House,
And he shall say you are not well today.
Let me, upon my knee, prevail in this.

55 **CAESAR.** Mark Antony shall say I am not well,
And for thy humor,[15] I will stay at home.

[*Enter* DECIUS.]

Here's Decius Brutus, he shall tell them so.

DECIUS. Caesar, all hail! Good morrow, worthy Caesar;
I come to fetch you to the Senate House.

60 **CAESAR.** And you are come in very happy time[16]
To bear my greeting to the senators,
And tell them that I will not come today.
Cannot, is false; and that I dare not, falser:
I will not come today. Tell them so, Decius.

CALPURNIA. Say he is sick.

15. humor *n.* whim.

16. in very happy time at just the right moment.

Literature in Context

History Connection

The Roman Senate Caesar is preparing to meet the Senate, the oldest Roman political institution. By this time, the Senate had evolved into the most powerful part of the Roman government:

* Before Caesar's rise to power, the Senate was made up of 500 to 600 members.
* The Senate met in the Curia in the Roman Forum (see page 870).
* Senators were appointed for life. Originally, all were from the *patrician*, or aristocratic, class.
* The Senate shaped policy through advice it issued to various officials, its powers to appoint officials, and its power to negotiate with foreign countries.
* After Caesar won his victory over Pompey, he eliminated his enemies in the Senate and packed it with supporters, including men of lower rank and people from outlying provinces.

Connect to the Literature

How does this information help explain the motives of the conspirators, many of whom are senators?

65 **CAESAR.**   Shall Caesar send a lie?
Have I in conquest stretched mine arm so far
To be afeard to tell graybeards[17] the truth?
Decius, go tell them Caesar will not come.

DECIUS. Most mighty Caesar, let me know some cause,
70 Lest I be laughed at when I tell them so.

CAESAR. The cause is in my will: I will not come.
That is enough to satisfy the Senate.
But for your private satisfaction,
Because I love you, I will let you know.
75 Calpurnia here, my wife, stays me at home.
She dreamt tonight she saw my statue,
Which, like a fountain with an hundred spouts,
Did run pure blood, and many lusty Romans
Came smiling and did bathe their hands in it.
80 And these does she apply for[18] warnings and portents
And evils <u>imminent</u>, and on her knee
Hath begged that I will stay at home today.

DECIUS. This dream is all amiss interpreted;
It was a vision fair and fortunate:
85 Your statue spouting blood in many pipes,
In which so many smiling Romans bathed,
Signifies that from you great Rome shall suck
Reviving blood, and that great men shall press
For tinctures, stains, relics, and cognizance.[19]
90 This by Calpurnia's dream is signified.

CAESAR. And this way have you well expounded[20] it.

DECIUS. I have, when you have heard what I can say;
And know it now, the Senate have concluded
To give this day a crown to mighty Caesar.
95 If you shall send them word you will not come,
Their minds may change. Besides, it were a mock
Apt to be rendered,[21] for someone to say
"Break up the Senate till another time,
When Caesar's wife shall meet with better dreams."
100 If Caesar hide himself, shall they not whisper
"Lo, Caesar is afraid"?
Pardon me, Caesar, for my dear dear love
To your proceeding[22] bids me tell you this,
And reason to my love is liable.[23]

17. afeard to tell graybeards afraid to tell old men (the senators).
18. apply for consider to be.

Vocabulary Builder
imminent (im´ ə nənt) *adj.* about to happen

19. shall press . . . cognizance Decius interprets Calpurnia's dream with a double meaning. To Caesar he suggests that people will beg for badges to show they are Caesar's servants; to the audience, that people will seek remembrances of his death.

20. expounded (eks pound´ id) *v.* interpreted; explained.
21. mock . . . rendered jeering comment likely to be made.
22. proceeding *n.* advancing in your career.
23. reason . . . liable my judgment about what I should or should not say is not as strong as my affection for you is.

Reading Check

What does Decius say about the dream?

105 **CAESAR.** How foolish do your fears seem now, Calpurnia!
I am ashamèd I did yield to them.
Give me my robe,²⁴ for I will go.

[*Enter* BRUTUS, LIGARIUS, METELLUS CIMBER, CASCA, TREBONIUS,
CINNA, *and* PUBLIUS.]

And look where Publius is come to fetch me.

PUBLIUS. Good morrow, Caesar.

CAESAR.   Welcome, Publius.
110 What, Brutus, are you stirred so early too?
Good morrow, Casca. Caius Ligarius.
Caesar was ne'er so much your enemy²⁵
As that same ague²⁶ which hath made you lean.
What is't o'clock?

BRUTUS.   Caesar, 'tis strucken eight.

115 **CAESAR.** I thank you for your pains and courtesy.

[*Enter* ANTONY.]

See! Antony, that revels²⁷ long a-nights,
Is notwithstanding up. Good morrow, Antony.

ANTONY. So to most noble Caesar.

CAESAR.   Bid them prepare²⁸ within.
I am to blame to be thus waited for.
120 Now, Cinna; now, Metellus; what Trebonius,
I have an hour's talk in store for you;
Remember that you call on me today;
Be near me, that I may remember you.

TREBONIUS. Caesar, I will [*aside*] and so near will I be,
125 That your best friends shall wish I had been further.

CAESAR. Good friends, go in and taste some wine with me,
And we (like friends) will straightway go together.

BRUTUS. [*Aside*] That every like is not the same,²⁹ O Caesar,
The heart of Brutus earns³⁰ to think upon.   [*Exit*]

Scene iii. *A street near the Capitol, close to Brutus' house.*

[*Enter* ARTEMIDORUS, *reading a paper.*]

ARTEMIDORUS. "Caesar, beware of Brutus; take heed off Cassius;
come not near Casca; have an eye to Cinna; trust not
Trebonius; mark well Metellus Cimber; Decius Brutus loves
thee not; thou hast wronged Caius Ligarius. There is but

24. robe *n.* toga.

**25. Caius Ligarius . . . your
enemy** Caesar had recently
pardoned Ligarius for supporting Pompey during the civil
war.
26. ague (ā´ gyōō) *n.* fever.

27. revels (rev´ əlz) *v.* makes
merry.

28. prepare *v.* set out
refreshments.

**Reading Skill
Paraphrasing** Para-
phrase lines 124–125.

**29. That every like . . . the
same** that is, that everyone
who seems *like* a friend may
actually be an enemy.
30. earns *v.* sorrows.

5   one mind in all these men, and it is bent against Caesar. If
thou beest not immortal, look about you: security gives way
to conspiracy.[1] The mighty gods defend thee!
                                        Thy lover,[2] ARTEMIDORUS."

     Here will I stand till Caesar pass along,
10   And as a suitor[3] will I give him this.
     My heart laments that virtue cannot live
     Out of the teeth of emulation.[4]
     If thou read this, O Caesar, thou mayest live;
     If not, the Fates with traitors do contrive.[5]   [*Exit*]

Scene iv. *Another part of the street.*

[*Enter* PORTIA *and* LUCIUS.]

     PORTIA. I prithee,[1] boy, run to the Senate House;
     Stay not to answer me, but get thee gone.
     Why dost thou stay?

     LUCIUS.   To know my errand, madam.

     PORTIA. I would have had thee there and here again
5   Ere I can tell thee what thou shouldst do there.

1. security . . . conspiracy
overconfident carelessness
allows the conspiracy to proceed.
2. lover *n.* devoted friend.
3. suitor (sōōt´ ər) *n.* person
who requests, petitions, or
entreats.
**4. Out of the teeth of
emulation** beyond the reach
of envy.
5. contrive *v.* conspire.

1. prithee (prith´ ē) "pray
thee"; ask you please.

◀ **Critical Viewing**
When might Caesar
have participated in an
event like the one
depicted on this cup?
Explain. **[Speculate]**

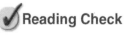**Reading Check**

What does
Artemidorus plan to
do?

O constancy,[2] be strong upon my side;
Set a huge mountain 'tween my heart and tongue!
I have a man's mind, but a woman's might.[3]
How hard it is for women to keep counsel![4]
Art thou here yet?

10 **LUCIUS.**   Madam, what should I do?
Run to the Capitol, and nothing else?
And so return to you, and nothing else?

PORTIA. Yes, bring me word, boy, if thy lord look well,
For he went sickly forth; and take good note
15 What Caesar doth, what suitors press to him.
Hark, boy, what noise is that?

LUCIUS. I hear none, madam.

PORTIA.   Prithee, listen well.
I heard a bustling rumor like a fray,[5]
And the wind brings it from the Capitol.

20 **LUCIUS.** Sooth,[6] madam, I hear nothing.

[*Enter the* SOOTHSAYER.]

PORTIA. Come hither, fellow. Which way hast thou been?

SOOTHSAYER. At mine own house, good lady.

PORTIA. What is't o'clock?

SOOTHSAYER.   About the ninth hour, lady.

PORTIA. Is Caesar yet gone to the Capitol?

25 **SOOTHSAYER.** Madam, not yet; I go to take my stand,
To see him pass on the Capitol.

PORTIA. Thou hast some suit[7] to Caesar, hast thou not?

SOOTHSAYER. That I have, lady; if it will please Caesar
To be so good to Caesar as to hear me,
30 I shall beseech him to befriend himself.

PORTIA. Why, know'st thou any harm's intended towards him?

SOOTHSAYER. None that I know will be, much that I fear may
      chance.
Good morrow to you. Here the street is narrow;
The throng that follows Caesar at the heels,
35 Of senators, of praetors,[8] common suitors,

> **Critical Viewing** Judging from its ruins, how might the Forum in Rome have compared to a modern city center?

2. **constancy** (kän´ stən sē) *n.* firmness of mind or purpose; resoluteness.
3. **might** *n.* strength.
4. **keep counsel** keep secrets.

Literary Analysis
Blank Verse Why might Shakespeare present Lucius' lines in blank verse in this scene?

5. **fray** (frā) *n.* fight; brawl.
6. **Sooth** (sŌŌth) *interjection* truly.
7. **suit** (sŌŌt) *n.* petition.
8. **praetors** (prē´ tərz) *n.* Roman officials of the rank below consul.

Will crowd a feeble man almost to death.
I'll get me to a place more void,[9] and there
Speak to great Caesar as he comes along.

[*Exit*]

PORTIA. I must go in. Ay me, how weak a thing
40   The heart of woman is! O Brutus,
The heavens speed[10] thee in thine enterprise![11]
Sure, the boy heard me—Brutus hath a suit
That Caesar will not grant—O, I grow faint.
Run, Lucius, and commend me[12] to my lord;
45   Say I am merry; come to me again,
And bring me word what he doth say to thee.

[*Exit separately*]

9. void (void) *adj.* empty.

10. speed *v.* make successful.
11. enterprise (en´ tər prīz´) *n.* undertaking; project.

12. commend me give my kind regards.

Apply the Skills

The Tragedy of Julius Caesar, Act II

Thinking About the Selection

1. **Respond:** If you had been a Roman citizen, would you have sided with the conspirators? Why or why not?
2. **(a) Recall:** In Act II, Scene i, what coming event disturbs Brutus? **(b) Interpret:** In Scene i, lines 32–34, what point does Brutus make in comparing Caesar to a serpent's egg? **(c) Evaluate:** Are Brutus' reasons for joining the conspiracy convincing or flawed? Explain.
3. **(a) Compare and Contrast:** In a chart like the one shown, write Caesar's reactions to the events listed. **(b) Draw Conclusions:** In the third column, explain what each reaction reveals about Caesar's character and values. **(c) Discuss:** Explain your responses to other students in a small group and listen to other students' ideas. Then, in the last column, explain why your thinking has or has not changed.

Event	Caesar's Reaction	What It Reveals	After Discussion
augur's sacrifice			
Decius' flattery			

Literary Analysis

4. **(a)** Copy lines 42–43 of Scene ii and mark them to indicate the stressed (´) and unstressed (~) syllables. **(b)** Which line of **blank verse** illustrates perfect iambic pentameter? **(c)** Explain how the rhythm of the other line reinforces the importance of certain words.
5. Examine the dialogue of the following characters from Acts I and II: Flavius, the Cobbler, Brutus, and Portia. **(a)** Indicate whether each typically speaks in blank verse or prose. **(b)** Identify each as an aristocrat or a commoner based on your findings.

Reading Skill

6. **Paraphrase** Brutus' two questions in line 234 of Scene i. Make your new sentences sound like modern English.
7. **(a)** List four words in Portia's final speech in Scene iv that are no longer used or no longer used in the same sense. For each, give a modern word that means the same thing. **(b) Paraphrase** the speech.

QuickReview

Act II at a Glance
Worried about Caesar's ambitions, Brutus joins the conspirators. Meanwhile, Caesar goes to the Capitol, believing the Senate will crown him.

Go Online
—Assessment

For: Self-test
Visit: www.PHSchool.com
Web Code: eqa-6506

Blank Verse:
unrhymed lines of poetry written in iambic pentameter

Iambic Pentameter:
the rhythmic pattern of a line of poetry in which five unstressed syllables are each followed by a stressed syllable

Paraphrasing:
restating in your own words the meaning of a line or passage from a literary work

Vocabulary Builder

Practice A **synonym** of a word is a word that has a similar meaning: for example, *start* is a synonym of *begin.* For each of the following items, explain whether or not the words are synonyms.

1. augmented, angered
2. entreated, appealed
3. insurrection, revolt
4. resolution, glory
5. wrathfully, furiously
6. imminent, enduring

Adding Words to Your Vocabulary Use a dictionary to find a word that is another part of speech for *augmented, entreated, resolution, wrathfully,* and *imminent.* (For more on using a dictionary, see page R6.)

Writing

Write a brief **character analysis** of Brutus, explaining his motivations, strengths, and weaknesses.

- Jot down notes on his key decisions and speeches in Act II.
- Using a two-column chart, list strengths and weaknesses.
- As you draft, support each point you make with examples or quotations from the play.

For *Grammar, Vocabulary,* and *Assessment,* see **Build Language Skills,** pages 926–927.

Extend Your Learning

Listening and Speaking Hold a **debate** on the following question: *Are the conspirators justified in plotting against Caesar?* Each side in the debate should organize arguments, following this form:

- Introduce your position.
- Provide evidence for your position.
- Conclude with a summary.

Research and Technology Using books, reference articles, and reliable Internet sources, find out more about the life that married aristocratic women like Calpurnia and Portia led in ancient Rome. Then, write a **women's history report** comparing these two characters with the typical upper-class woman of the time. Consider the role of each in political affairs and in relation to her husband.

Build Skills   *The Tragedy of Julius Caesar,* Act III

Practice these skills with *The Tragedy of Julius Caesar,* Act III.

Academic Standards

- Analyze characters' traits through narration and dialogue. (10.3.4)
- Evaluate the use of literary devices including figurative language, imagery, allegory, and symbolism. (10.3.7)
- Identify and evaluate dialogue, soliloquies, asides, character foils and stage designs in dramatic literature. (10.3.10)

Literary Analysis

In plays, most of the information is expressed through characters' words and actions. Plays feature the following types of **dramatic speeches**:

- **Dialogue:** the conversations between characters
- **Soliloquy:** a long speech in which a character, usually alone on stage, speaks as if to himself or herself, unheard by any other character
- **Aside:** a remark a character makes, usually to the audience, that is not heard by other characters on stage
- **Monologue:** a long speech by one character usually heard by the other characters

As you read, notice what characters reveal in soliloquies and asides.

Reading Skill

Writers sometimes use **imagery,** language that appeals to the senses, to make abstract ideas vivid and concrete. In Act III, Shakespeare uses many images that focus on words and the body:

- wounds that speak
- burying Caesar's body rather than speaking praise of him
- "plucking" a poet's name out of his heart

In each case, a reference to words—speech, praise, names—is coupled with an image of a person's physical body—a corpse, blood, the heart. In this way, Shakespeare links physical violence in Rome with disrespect for laws—the words that bind society. Use a chart like the one shown to record such images.

Reference to Words
And waving our red weapons o'er our heads, Let's all cry **"Peace, freedom, and liberty!"**

Imagery of the Body
Swords covered in **blood** from Caesar's body

Connection
The words name the ideals the conspirators use to justify killing Caesar.

Vocabulary Builder

- **confounded** (kən foun´ did) *adj.* made to feel confused (p. 873) *Confounded, he gave up.*

- **spectacle** (spek´ tə kəl) *n.* strange or remarkable sight (p. 877) *I was fascinated by the spectacle of ten acrobats performing.*

- **prophesy** (präf´ ə sī) *v.* predict what will happen (p. 878) *Who can truly prophesy the future?*

- **strife** (strīf) *n.* struggle; conflict (p. 878) *Afraid of causing strife, I did not take sides.*

- **discourse** (dis´ kôrs´) *v.* speak (on a topic) formally and at length (p. 879) *He wanted to discourse on seashells.*

- **interred** (in tʉr'd´) *v.* buried (said of a dead body) (p. 882) *They interred the body at the cemetery.*

Review and Anticipate Having ignored the warnings of the soothsayer in Act I and those of his wife, Calpurnia, in Act II, Caesar proceeds to the Capitol on the ides of March. Decius has told him that the Senate is ready to confer a crown upon him. Caesar is accompanied by the conspirators, led by Cassius and Brutus, as well as by his friend Mark Antony. Meanwhile, Artemidorus plans to reveal the conspiracy to Caesar. As Act III unfolds, Caesar approaches the Capitol, and events take a fateful, irreversible turn.

⇒»»»»»» ACT III «««««««←

Scene i. Rome. Before the Capitol.

[*Flourish of trumpets. Enter* CAESAR, BRUTUS, CASSIUS, CASCA, DECIUS, METELLUS CIMBER, TREBONIUS, CINNA, ANTONY, LEPIDUS, ARTEMIDORUS, PUBLIUS, POPILIUS, *and the* SOOTHSAYER.]

CAESAR. The ides of March are come.

SOOTHSAYER. Ay, Caesar, but not gone.

ARTEMIDORUS. Hail, Caesar! Read this schedule.[1]

DECIUS. Trebonius doth desire you to o'er-read,
5   At your best leisure, this his humble suit.[2]

ARTEMIDORUS. O Caesar, read mine first; for mine's a suit
     That touches[3] Caesar nearer. Read it, great Caesar.

CAESAR. What touches us ourself shall be last served.

ARTEMIDORUS. Delay not, Caesar; read it instantly.

CAESAR. What, is the fellow mad?

10 **PUBLIUS.**   Sirrah, give place.[4]

CASSIUS. What, urge you your petitions in the street?
     Come to the Capitol.

[CAESAR *goes to the Capitol, the rest following.*]

POPILIUS. I wish your enterprise today may thrive.

CASSIUS. What enterprise, Popilius?

POPILIUS.   Fare you well.

                                   [*Advances to* CAESAR]

15 **BRUTUS.** What said Popilius Lena?

CASSIUS. He wished today our enterprise might thrive.
     I fear our purpose is discoverèd.

1. schedule (skeˊ jōol) *n.* paper.
2. suit *n.* petition; plea.

3. touches *v.* concerns.

Literary Analysis
Dramatic Speeches
How does the dialogue between Artemidorus and Caesar create suspense?

4. give place get out of the way.

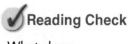

Reading Check

What does Artemidorus want Caesar to do?

BRUTUS. Look how he makes to[5] Caesar; mark him.

CASSIUS. Casca, be sudden,[6] for we fear prevention.

20   Brutus, what shall be done? If this be known,
       Cassius or Caesar never shall turn back,[7]
       For I will slay myself.

BRUTUS.   Cassius, be constant.[8]
       Popilius Lena speaks not of our purposes;
       For look, he smiles, and Caesar doth not change.[9]

25 **CASSIUS.** Trebonius knows his time; for look you, Brutus,
       He draws Mark Antony out of the way.

                    [*Exit* ANTONY *and* TREBONIUS.]

DECIUS. Where is Metellus Cimber? Let him go
       And presently prefer his suit[10] to Caesar.

BRUTUS. He is addressed.[11] Press near and second[12] him.

30 **CINNA.** Casca, you are the first that rears your hand.

CAESAR. Are we all ready? What is now amiss
       That Caesar and his Senate must redress?[13]

METELLUS. Most high, most mighty, and most puissant[14] Caesar,

---

5. **makes to** approaches.

6. **be sudden** be quick.

7. **Cassius . . . back** either Cassius or Caesar will not return alive.

8. **constant** *adj.* firm; calm.

9. **change** *v.* that is, change the expression on his face.

10. **presently prefer his suit** immediately present his petition.

11. **addressed** *adj.* ready.

12. **second** *v.* support.

13. **amiss . . . redress** wrong that Caesar and his Senate must correct.

14. **puissant** (pyo͞o′ i sənt) *adj.* powerful.

Literature in Context   History Connection

The Roman Forum

Caesar receives petitioners at the Senate House in the Roman Forum. Consisting of a plaza, or open space lined with buildings, the Forum (shown here) was the center of government and commercial activity in ancient Rome.

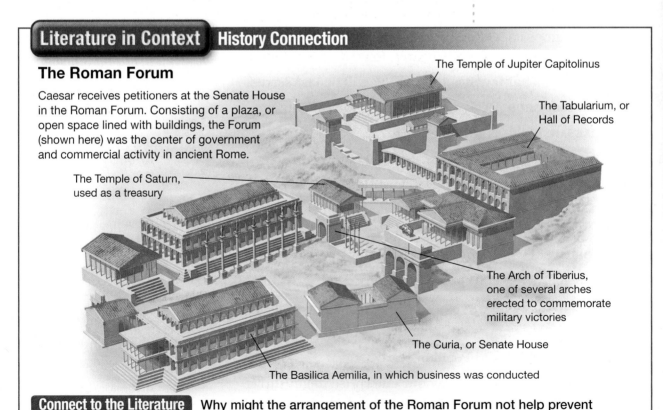

The Temple of Jupiter Capitolinus

The Tabularium, or Hall of Records

The Temple of Saturn, used as a treasury

The Arch of Tiberius, one of several arches erected to commemorate military victories

The Curia, or Senate House

The Basilica Aemilia, in which business was conducted

Connect to the Literature   Why might the arrangement of the Roman Forum not help prevent public attacks such as the one the conspirators have planned?

Metellus Cimber throws before thy seat
An humble heart.   [*Kneeling*]

35 **CAESAR.**   I must prevent thee, Cimber.
These couchings and these lowly courtesies[15]
Might fire the blood of ordinary men,
And turn preordinance and first decree
Into the law of children.[16] Be not fond[17]

40 To think that Caesar bears such rebel blood
That will be thawed from the true quality[18]
With that which melteth fools—I mean sweet words,
Low-crookèd curtsies, and base spaniel fawning.[19]
Thy brother by decree is banishèd.

45 If thou dost bend and pray and fawn for him,
I spurn[20] thee like a cur out of my way.
Know, Caesar doth not wrong, nor without cause
Will he be satisfied.

METELLUS. Is there no voice more worthy than my own,

50 To sound more sweetly in great Caesar's ear
For the repealing[21] of my banished brother?

15. couchings . . . courtesies
low bowings and humble
gestures of reverence.
**16. And turn . . . law of
children** and change what
has already been decided as
children might change their
minds.
17. fond *adj.* foolish (enough).
18. rebel . . . quality unstable
disposition that will lose its
firmness.
**19. base spaniel
fawning** low doglike cringing.
20. spurn *v.* kick disdainfully.
21. repealing *n.* recalling;
ending the banishment.

✔**Reading Check**

What worries Cassius?

▼ **Critical Viewing** Judging from these ruins of the Roman
Forum, how large might the crowds around the Senate have
been on the ides of March? Explain. **[Hypothesize]**

BRUTUS. I kiss thy hand, but not in flattery, Caesar,
Desiring thee that Publius Cimber may
Have an immediate freedom of repeal.[22]

CAESAR. What, Brutus?

55 **CASSIUS.**   Pardon, Caesar; Caesar, pardon!
As low as to thy foot doth Cassius fall
To beg enfranchisement[23] for Publius Cimber.

CAESAR. I could be well moved, if I were as you;
If I could pray to move,[24] prayers would move me;
60 But I am constant as the Northern Star,
Of whose true-fixed and resting[25] quality
There is no fellow[26] in the firmament.[27]
The skies are painted with unnumb'red sparks,
They are all fire and every one doth shine;
65 But there's but one in all doth hold his[28] place.
So in the world; 'tis furnished well with men,

▼ **Critical Viewing**
Which details in this
picture suggest
Caesar's ignorance?
Which suggest the
conspirators'
cunning? **[Analyze]**

And men are flesh and blood, and apprehensive;[29]
Yet in the number I do know but one
That unassailable holds on his rank,[30]
70   Unshaked of motion;[31] and that I am he,
Let me a little show it, even in this—
That I was constant[32] Cimber should be banished,
And constant do remain to keep him so.

CINNA. O Caesar—

CAESAR.   Hence! Wilt thou lift up Olympus?[33]

DECIUS. Great Caesar—

75 **CAESAR.**   Doth not Brutus bootless[34] kneel?

CASCA. Speak hands for me!   *[They stab* CAESAR.]

CAESAR. *Et tu, Brutè?*[35] Then fall, Caesar.   [*Dies*]

CINNA. Liberty! Freedom! Tyranny is dead!
  Run hence, proclaim, cry it about the streets.

80 **CASSIUS.** Some to the common pulpits,[36] and cry out
  "Liberty, freedom, and enfranchisement!"

BRUTUS. People, and senators, be not affrighted.
  Fly not; stand still; ambition's debt is paid.[37]

CASCA. Go to the pulpit, Brutus.

DECIUS.   And Cassius too.

85 **BRUTUS.** Where's Publius?[38]

CINNA. Here, quite <u>confounded</u> with this mutiny.[39]

METELLUS. Stand fast together, lest some friend of Caesar's
  Should chance—

BRUTUS. Talk not of standing. Publius, good cheer;
90   There is no harm intended to your person,
Nor to no Roman else. So tell them, Publius.

CASSIUS. And leave us, Publius, lest that the people
  Rushing on us should do your age some mischief.

BRUTUS. Do so; and let no man abide[40] this deed
95   But we the doers.

[*Enter* TREBONIUS.]

CASSIUS. Where is Antony?

TREBONIUS.   Fled to his house amazed.[41]
  Men, wives, and children stare, cry out and run,
As[42] it were doomsday.

---

29. **apprehensive** (ap´ rə hen´ siv) *adj.* able to understand.
30. **one / That unassailable . . . rank** one who, unattackable, maintains his position.
31. **Unshaked of motion** unmoved by his own or others' impulses.
32. **constant** *adj.* determined.

33. **Olympus** (ō lim´ pəs) *n.* mountain in Greece on which the Greek gods were said to live.
34. **bootless** (boot´ lis) *adv.* uselessly.

Reading Skill
Analyzing Imagery
In what way does line 76 combine ideas of words with images of violence?

35. *Et tu, Brutè?* Latin for "And you, too, Brutus?"
36. **pulpits** (pul´ pits) *n.* speakers' platforms.
37. **ambition's . . . paid** ambition received what it deserved.
38. **Publius** (poob´ lē əs) an elderly senator.

Vocabulary Builder
confounded (kən foun´ did) *adj.* made to feel confused

39. **mutiny** (myoot´ 'n ē) *n.* revolt against authority, such as a rebellion of soldiers against their officers.

40. **let no man abide** let no man take responsibility for.
41. **amazed** *adj.* astounded.
42. **As** *conj.* as if.

Reading Check

What do the conspirators do to Caesar?

BRUTUS.   Fates, we will know your pleasures.
That we shall die, we know; 'tis but the time,

100   And drawing days out, that men stand upon.[43]

CASCA. Why, he that cuts off twenty years of life
Cuts off so many years of fearing death.

BRUTUS. Grant that, and then is death a benefit.
So are we Caesar's friends, that have abridged

105   His time of fearing death. Stoop, Romans, stoop,
And let us bathe our hands in Caesar's blood
Up to the elbows, and besmear our swords.
Then walk we forth, even to the market place,[44]
And waving our red weapons o'er our heads,

110   Let's all cry "Peace, freedom, and liberty!"

CASSIUS. Stoop then, and wash. How many ages hence
Shall this our lofty scene be acted over
In states unborn and accents yet unknown!

BRUTUS. How many times shall Caesar bleed in sport,[45]

115   That now on Pompey's basis lies along[46]
No worthier than the dust!

CASSIUS.   So oft as that shall be,
So often shall the knot[47] of us be called
The men that gave their country liberty.

DECIUS. What, shall we forth?

CASSIUS.   Ay, every man away.

120   Brutus shall lead, and we will grace his heels[48]
With the most boldest and best hearts of Rome.

[*Enter a* SERVANT.]

BRUTUS. Soft,[49] who comes here? A friend of Antony's.

SERVANT. Thus, Brutus, did my master bid me kneel;
Thus did Mark Antony bid me fall down;

125   And, being prostrate, thus he bade me say:
Brutus is noble, wise, valiant, and honest;
Caesar was mighty, bold, royal,[50] and loving.
Say I love Brutus and I honor him;
Say I feared Caesar, honored him, and loved him.

130   If Brutus will vouchsafe that Antony
May safely come to him and be resolved[51]
How Caesar hath deserved to lie in death,
Mark Antony shall not love Caesar dead
So well as Brutus living; but will follow

---

43. 'tis but the time . . . upon It is only the time of death and the length of life that people care about.

Reading Skill
Analyzing Imagery
Find an example of an image linking blood and words in lines 103—110.

44. market place the open area of the Roman Forum, the center of government, business, and public life in ancient Rome.

45. in sport for amusement; the deed will be acted out in plays.
46. on Pompey's basis lies along by the pedestal of Pompey's statue lies stretched out.
47. knot *n.* group.

48. grace his heels do honor to his heels; follow him.

49. Soft *interjection* wait.

50. royal *adj.* showing noble generosity.

51. be resolved have it explained.

135　　The fortunes and affairs of noble Brutus
　　　　Thorough the hazards of this untrod state⁵²
　　　　With all true faith. So says my master Antony.

　　BRUTUS. Thy master is a wise and valiant Roman;
　　　　I never thought him worse.
140　　Tell him, so⁵³ please him come unto this place,
　　　　He shall be satisfied and, by my honor,
　　　　Depart untouched.

　　SERVANT.　　　　　I'll fetch him presently.⁵⁴

　　　　　　　　　　　　　　　　　[Exit SERVANT]

　　BRUTUS. I know that we shall have him well to friend.⁵⁵

　　CASSIUS. I wish we may. But yet have I a mind
145　　That fears him much; and my misgiving still
　　　　Falls shrewdly to the purpose.⁵⁶

[Enter ANTONY.]

　　BRUTUS. But here comes Antony. Welcome, Mark Antony.

　　ANTONY. O mighty Caesar! Dost thou lie so low?
　　　　Are all thy conquests, glories, triumphs, spoils,
150　　Shrunk to this little measure? Fare thee well.
　　　　I know not, gentlemen, what you intend,
　　　　Who else must be let blood,⁵⁷ who else is rank.⁵⁸
　　　　If I myself, there is no hour so fit
　　　　As Caesar's death's hour, nor no instrument
155　　Of half that worth as those your swords, made rich
　　　　With the most noble blood of all this world.
　　　　I do beseech ye, if you bear me hard,⁵⁹
　　　　Now, whilst your purpled hands⁶⁰ do reek and smoke,
　　　　Fulfill your pleasure. Live⁶¹ a thousand years,
160　　I shall not find myself so apt⁶² to die;
　　　　No place will please me so, no mean of death,⁶³
　　　　As here by Caesar, and by you cut off,
　　　　The choice and master spirits of this age.

　　BRUTUS. O Antony, beg not your death of us!
165　　Though now we must appear bloody and cruel,
　　　　As by our hands and this our present act
　　　　You see we do, yet see you but our hands
　　　　And this the bleeding business they have done.
　　　　Our hearts you see not; they are pitiful;⁶⁴
170　　And pity to the general wrong of Rome—
　　　　As fire drives out fire, so pity pity⁶⁵—
　　　　Hath done this deed on Caesar. For your part,

---

52. Thorough . . . state
through the dangers of this
new state of affairs.

53. so *conj.* if it should.

54. presently *adv.*
immediately.

55. to friend as a friend.

**56. my misgiving . . . to the
purpose** my doubts always
turn out to be justified.

Literary Analysis
Dramatic Speeches
What is Antony's
purpose in delivering
this monologue?

57. be let blood (a pun) "be
bled for medical purposes" or
"be killed."
58. rank (a pun) "too powerful"
or "swollen with disease and
therefore in need of bloodlet-
ting."
59. bear me hard have a
grudge against me.
60. purpled hands bloody
hands.
61. Live if I live.
62. apt *adj.* ready.
63. mean of death way of
dying.

64. pitiful *adj.* full of pity or
compassion.
65. pity pity pity for Rome
drove out pity for Caesar.

　**Reading Check**

What does Antony ask
of the conspirators?

To you our swords have leaden[66] points, Mark Antony:
Our arms in strength of malice, and our hearts
175 Of brothers' temper,[67] do receive you in
With all kind love, good thoughts, and reverence.

CASSIUS. Your voice[68] shall be as strong as any man's
In the disposing of new dignities.[69]

BRUTUS. Only be patient till we have appeased
180 The multitude, beside themselves with fear,
And then we will deliver[70] you the cause
Why I, that did love Caesar when I struck him,
Have thus proceeded.

ANTONY.   I doubt not of your wisdom.
Let each man render me his bloody hand.
185 First, Marcus Brutus, will I shake with you;
Next, Caius Cassius, do I take your hand;
Now, Decius Brutus, yours; now yours, Metellus;
Yours, Cinna; and, my valiant Casca, yours;
Though last, not least in love, yours, good Trebonius.
190 Gentlemen all—alas, what shall I say?
My credit[71] now stands on such slippery ground
That one of two bad ways you must conceit[72] me,
Either a coward or a flatterer.
That I did love thee, Caesar, O, 'tis true!
195 If then thy spirit look upon us now,
Shall it not grieve thee dearer[73] than thy death
To see thy Antony making his peace,
Shaking the bloody fingers of thy foes,
Most noble, in the presence of thy corse?[74]
200 Had I as many eyes as thou hast wounds,
Weeping as fast as they stream forth thy blood,
It would become me better than to close[75]
In terms of friendship with thine enemies.
Pardon me, Julius! Here wast thou bayed,[76] brave hart;[77]
205 Here didst thou fall, and here thy hunters stand,
Signed in thy spoil[78] and crimsoned in thy Lethe.[79]
O world, thou wast the forest to this hart;
And this indeed, O world, the heart of thee.
How like a deer, stroken[80] by many princes.
210 Dost thou here lie!

CASSIUS. Mark Antony—

ANTONY.   Pardon me, Caius Cassius.
The enemies of Caesar shall say this;
Then, in a friend, it is cold modesty.[81]

66. **leaden** *adj.* dull; blunt.
67. **Our arms . . . / Of brothers' temper** our arms strengthened with the desire to do harm and our hearts filled with brotherly feelings.
68. **voice** *n.* vote.
69. **dignities** *n.* offices.

70. **deliver** *v.* tell to.

Literary Analysis
Dramatic Speeches
In this monologue, what image of his state of mind does Antony create for the conspirators?

71. **credit** *n.* reputation.
72. **conceit** (kən sēt´) *v.* think of.
73. **dearer** *adv.* more deeply.
74. **corse** *n.* corpse.
75. **close** (clōz) *v.* reach an agreement.
76. **bayed** *v.* cornered.
77. **hart** (härt) *n.* deer.

Reading Skill
Analyzing Imagery
What images of the body does Antony use to contrast his real grief with his words of friendship?

78. **Signed in thy spoil** marked by signs of your slaughter.
79. **Lethe** (lē´ thē) river in Hades, the mythological Greek underworld inhabited by the dead; here, a river of blood.
80. **stroken** *v.* struck down.

81. **cold modesty** calm, moderate speech.

CASSIUS. I blame you not for praising Caesar so;

215 But what compact[82] mean you to have with us?
Will you be pricked[83] in number of our friends,
Or shall we on,[84] and not depend on you?

ANTONY. Therefore I took your hands, but was indeed
Swayed from the point by looking down on Caesar.
220 Friends am I with you all, and love you all,
Upon this hope, that you shall give me reasons
Why, and wherein, Caesar was dangerous.

BRUTUS. Or else were this a savage spectacle.
Our reasons are so full of good regard[85]
225 That were you, Antony, the son of Caesar,
You should be satisfied.

ANTONY.   That's all I seek;
And am moreover suitor that I may
Produce[86] his body to the market place,
And in the pulpit, as becomes a friend,
230 Speak in the order[87] of his funeral.

BRUTUS. You shall, Mark Antony.

CASSIUS.   Brutus, a word with you.
[*Aside to* BRUTUS] You know not what you do; do not consent
That Antony speak in his funeral.
Know you how much the people may be moved
By that which he will utter?

235 **BRUTUS.**   By your pardon:
I will myself into the pulpit first,
And show the reason of our Caesar's death.
What Antony shall speak, I will protest[88]
He speaks by leave and by permission,
240 And that we are contented Caesar shall
Have all true rites and lawful ceremonies.
It shall advantage more than do us wrong.[89]

CASSIUS. I know not what may fall;[90] I like it not.

BRUTUS. Mark Antony, here, take you Caesar's body.
245 You shall not in your funeral speech blame us,
But speak all good you can devise of Caesar,
And say you do't by our permission;
Else shall you not have any hand at all
About his funeral. And you shall speak
250 In the same pulpit whereto I am going,
After my speech is ended.

82. compact (käm´ pakt) *n.* agreement.
83. pricked *v.* marked down; included.
84. on proceed.

Vocabulary Builder
spectacle (spek´ tə kəl) *n.* strange or remarkable sight

85. so full of good regard so carefully considered.

86. Produce *v.* bring forth.
87. order *n.* course of the ceremonies.

Literary Analysis
Dramatic Speeches
Why does Cassius wish to prevent others from hearing what he says in this aside to Brutus?

88. protest *v.* declare.

89. advantage . . . wrong benefit us more than hurt us.
90. what may fall what may happen.

✓**Reading Check**

What rules must Antony follow in delivering his funeral speech for Caesar?

ANTONY.   Be it so;
    I do desire no more.

BRUTUS. Prepare the body then, and follow us.

[*Exit all but* ANTONY.]

ANTONY. O pardon me, thou bleeding piece of earth,
255   That I am meek and gentle with these butchers!
    Thou art the ruins of the noblest man
    That ever livèd in the tide of times.[91]
    Woe to the hand that shed this costly blood!
    Over thy wounds now do I <u>prophesy</u>
260   (Which like dumb mouths do ope their ruby lips
    To beg the voice and utterance of my tongue),
    A curse shall light upon the limbs of men;
    Domestic fury and fierce civil <u>strife</u>
    Shall cumber[92] all the parts of Italy;
265   Blood and destruction shall be so in use,[93]
    And dreadful objects so familiar,
    That mothers shall but smile when they behold
    Their infants quartered with the hands of war,
    All pity choked with custom of fell deeds;[94]
270   And Caesar's spirit, ranging[95] for revenge,
    With Atè[96] by his side come hot from hell,
    Shall in these confines[97] with a monarch's voice
    Cry "Havoc,"[98] and let slip[99] the dogs of war,
    That this foul deed shall smell above the earth
275   With carrion[100] men, groaning for burial.

[*Enter* OCTAVIUS' SERVANT.]

    You serve Octavius Caesar, do you not?

SERVANT. I do, Mark Antony.

ANTONY. Caesar did write for him to come to Rome.

SERVANT. He did receive his letters and is coming,
280   And bid me say to you by word of mouth—
    O Caesar!   [*Seeing the body*]

ANTONY. Thy heart is big;[101] get thee apart and weep.
    Passion, I see, is catching, for mine eyes,
    Seeing those beads of sorrow stand in thine,
285   Began to water. Is thy master coming?

SERVANT. He lies tonight within seven leagues[102] of Rome.

ANTONY. Post[103] back with speed, and tell him what hath
    chanced.[104]
    Here is a mourning Rome, a dangerous Rome,
    No Rome of safety for Octavius yet.
290   Hie hence and tell him so. Yet stay awhile;
    Thou shalt not back till I have borne this corse
    Into the market place; there shall I try[105]
    In my oration[106] how the people take
    The cruel issue[107] of these bloody men;
295   According to the which, thou shalt <u>discourse</u>
    To young Octavius of the state of things.
    Lend me your hand.   [*Exit*]

Scene ii. The Forum

[*Enter* BRUTUS *and goes into the pulpit, and* CASSIUS, *with the*
PLEBEIANS.[1]]

    PLEBEIANS. We will be satisfied![2] Let us be satisfied!

▲ **Critical Viewing** Which scene in the play might this image depict?
Explain. **[Connect]**

103. Post *v.* hasten.
104. hath chanced has
happened.
105. try *v.* test.
106. oration (ō rā´ shən) *n.*
formal public speech.
107. cruel issue outcome of
the cruelty.

Vocabulary Builder
discourse (dis´ kôrs´)
v. speak (on a topic)
formally and at length

1. Plebeians (ple bē´ ənz) *n.*
commoners; members of the
lower class.
2. be satisfied get an
explanation.

Reading Check

What is Antony's real
response to Caesar's
death?

BRUTUS. Then follow me, and give me audience, friends.
Cassius, go you into the other street
And part the numbers.[3]

5   Those that will hear me speak, let 'em stay here;
Those that will follow Cassius, go with him;
And public reasons shall be renderèd
Of Caesar's death.

FIRST PLEBEIAN.   I will hear Brutus speak.

SECOND PLEBEIAN. I will hear Cassius, and compare their reasons,

10   When severally[4] we hear them renderèd.

[*Exit* CASSIUS, *with some of the* PLEBEIANS.]

THIRD PLEBEIAN. The noble Brutus is ascended. Silence!

BRUTUS. Be patient till the last.
Romans, countrymen, and lovers,[5] hear me for my
cause, and be silent, that you may hear. Believe me

15   for mine honor, and have respect to mine honor, that
you may believe. Censure[6] me in your wisdom, and
awake your senses,[7] that you may the better judge. If
there be any in this assembly, any dear friend of
Caesar's, to him I say that Brutus' love to Caesar was

20   no less than his. If then that friend demand why
Brutus rose against Caesar, this is my answer: Not
that I loved Caesar less, but that I loved Rome more.
Had you rather Caesar were living, and die all slaves,
than that Caesar were dead, to live all free men? As

25   Caesar loved me, I weep for him; as he was fortunate,
I rejoice at it; as he was valiant, I honor him; but, as
he was ambitious, I slew him. There is tears, for his
love; joy, for his fortune; honor, for his valor; and
death, for his ambition. Who is here so base,[8] that

30   would be a bondman?[9] If any, speak; for him have I
offended. Who is here so rude,[10] that would not be a
Roman? If any, speak; for him have I offended. Who is
here so vile,[11] that will not love his country? If any,
speak; for him have I offended. I pause for a reply.

35 **ALL.** None, Brutus, none!

BRUTUS. Then none have I offended. I have done no
more to Caesar than you shall do to Brutus. The
question of his death is enrolled in the Capitol;[12] his
glory not extenuated,[13] wherein he was worthy, nor

40   his offenses enforced,[14] for which he suffered death.

---

3. part the numbers divide the crowd.

4. severally (sev´ ər əl ē) *adv.* separately.

5. lovers *n.* dear friends.

6. Censure (sen´ shər) *v.* judge.
7. senses *n.* powers of reason.

Literary Analysis
Dramatic Speeches
What is Brutus' purpose in delivering this monologue?

8. base *adj.* low.

9. bondman *n.* slave.

10. rude *adj.* uncivilized.

11. vile (vīl) *adj.* mean; low-born; of low character.

12. The question . . . in the Capitol The issues that led to his death are on record in the Capitol.

13. extenuated (ek sten´ yōō āt´ id) *adj.* undervalued; made less of.

14. enforced (en fôrs´d´) *adj.* exaggerated.

[*Enter* MARK ANTONY, *with* CAESAR'S *body.*]

Here comes his body, mourned by Mark Antony,
who, though he had no hand in his death, shall receive
the benefit of his dying, a place in the commonwealth,
as which of you shall not? With this I depart, that, as
45 I slew my best lover for the good of Rome, I have the
same dagger for myself, when it shall please my
country to need my death.

ALL. Live, Brutus! Live, live!

FIRST PLEBEIAN. Bring him with triumph home unto his house.

50 **SECOND PLEBEIAN.** Give him a statue with his ancestors.

THIRD PLEBEIAN. Let him be Caesar.

FOURTH PLEBEIAN.   Caesar's better parts[15]
Shall be crowned in Brutus.

FIRST PLEBEIAN. We'll bring him to his house with shouts and
clamors.

BRUTUS. My countrymen—

SECOND PLEBEIAN.   Peace! Silence! Brutus speaks.

55 **FIRST PLEBEIAN.** Peace, ho!

BRUTUS. Good countrymen, let me depart alone,
And, for my sake, stay here with Antony.
Do grace to Caesar's corpse, and grace his speech
Tending to Caesar's glories,[16] which Mark Antony
60 By our permission, is allowed to make.
I do entreat you, not a man depart,
Save I alone, till Antony have spoke.   [*Exit*]

FIRST PLEBEIAN. Stay, ho! And let us hear Mark Antony.

THIRD PLEBEIAN. Let him go up into the public chair;
65 We'll hear him. Noble Antony, go up.

ANTONY. For Brutus' sake, I am beholding[17] to you.

FOURTH PLEBEIAN. What does he say of Brutus?

THIRD PLEBEIAN.   He says, for Brutus' sake,
He finds himself beholding to us all.

FOURTH PLEBEIAN. 'Twere best he speak no harm of Brutus
here!

FIRST PLEBEIAN. This Caesar was a tyrant.

70 **THIRD PLEBEIAN.**   Nay, that's certain.
We are blest that Rome is rid of him.

Literary Analysis
Dramatic Speeches
In this monologue, how does Brutus emphasize his sincerity?

15. **parts** *n.* qualities.

16. **Do grace . . . glories**
Show respect for Caesar's body and for the speech telling of Caesar's achievements.

17. **beholding** *adj.* indebted.

Reading Check

What reason for killing Caesar does Brutus offer to the plebeians?

SECOND PLEBEIAN. Peace! Let us hear what Antony can say.

ANTONY. You gentle Romans—

ALL.   Peace, ho! Let us hear him.

ANTONY. Friends, Romans, countrymen, lend me your ears;

75 I come to bury Caesar, not to praise him.
The evil that men do lives after them,
The good is oft <u>interrèd</u> with their bones;
So let it be with Caesar. The noble Brutus
Hath told you Caesar was ambitious.

80 If it were so, it was a grievous fault,
And grievously hath Caesar answered[18] it.
Here, under leave of Brutus and the rest
(For Brutus is an honorable man,
So are they all, all honorable men),

85 Come I to speak in Caesar's funeral.
He was my friend, faithful and just to me;
But Brutus says he was ambitious,
And Brutus is an honorable man.
He hath brought many captives home to Rome,

90 Whose ransoms did the general coffers[19] fill;
Did this in Caesar seem ambitious?

Literary Analysis
Dramatic Speeches
How is Antony's monologue both similar to and different from Brutus' in lines 12–34?

Vocabulary Builder
interred (in tʉr'd´) v. buried (said of a dead body)

18. **answered** v. paid the penalty for.
19. **general coffers** public treasury.

▼ **Critical Viewing**
What does this film still of Antony addressing the plebeians suggest about the power of his words? Explain. **[Interpret]**

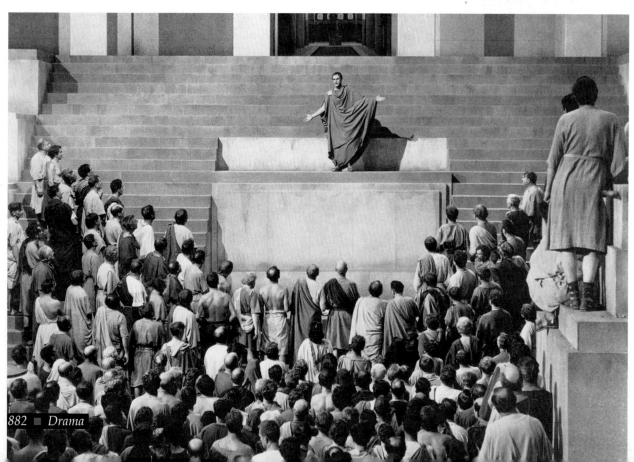

When that the poor have cried, Caesar hath wept;
Ambition should be made of sterner stuff.
Yet Brutus says he was ambitious;
95 And Brutus is an honorable man.
You all did see that on the Lupercal
I thrice presented him a kingly crown,
Which he did thrice refuse. Was this ambition?
Yet Brutus says he was ambitious;
100 And sure he is an honorable man.
I speak not to disprove what Brutus spoke,
But here I am to speak what I do know.
You all did love him once, not without cause;
What cause withholds you then to mourn for him?
105 O judgment, thou art fled to brutish beasts,
And men have lost their reason! Bear with me;
My heart is in the coffin there with Caesar,
And I must pause till it come back to me.

FIRST PLEBEIAN. Methinks there is much reason in his sayings.

110 **SECOND PLEBEIAN.** If thou consider rightly of the matter,
Caesar has had great wrong.

THIRD PLEBEIAN.   Has he, masters?
I fear there will a worse come in his place.

FOURTH PLEBEIAN. Marked ye his words? He would not take
the crown,
Therefore 'tis certain he was not ambitious.

115 **FIRST PLEBEIAN.** If it be found so, some will dear abide it.[20]

SECOND PLEBEIAN. Poor soul, his eyes are red as fire with
weeping.

THIRD PLEBEIAN. There's not a nobler man in Rome than
Antony.

FOURTH PLEBEIAN. Now mark him, he begins again to speak.

ANTONY. But yesterday the word of Caesar might
120 Have stood against the world; now lies he there,
And none so poor to[21] do him reverence.
O masters! If I were disposed to stir
Your hearts and minds to mutiny and rage,
I should do Brutus wrong and Cassius wrong,
125 Who, you all know, are honorable men.
I will not do them wrong; I rather choose
To wrong the dead, to wrong myself and you,
Than I will wrong such honorable men.

Literary Analysis
Dramatic Speeches
Contrast Antony's stated purpose in this monologue with the probable effect of lines 92–100 on his audience.

Reading Skill
Analyzing Imagery In lines 106–108, which images link Antony's heart and inability to continue speaking?

20. **dear abide it** pay dearly for it.

21. **so poor to** low enough in rank to.

Reading Check

What effect does Antony's speech have on the crowd?

But here's a parchment with the seal of Caesar;
130 I found it in his closet; 'tis his will.
Let but the commons²² hear this testament,
Which, pardon me, I do not mean to read,
And they would go and kiss dead Caesar's wounds,
And dip their napkins²³ in his sacred blood;
135 Yea, beg a hair of him for memory,
And dying, mention it within their wills,
Bequeathing it as a rich legacy
Unto their issue.²⁴

FOURTH PLEBEIAN. We'll hear the will; read it, Mark Antony.

140 **ALL.** The will, the will! We will hear Caesar's will!

ANTONY. Have patience, gentle friends, I must not read it.
It is not meet²⁵ you know how Caesar loved you.
You are not wood, you are not stones, but men;
And being men, hearing the will of Caesar,
145 It will inflame you, it will make you mad.
'Tis good you know not that you are his heirs;
For if you should, O, what would come of it?

FOURTH PLEBEIAN. Read the will! We'll hear it, Antony!
You shall read us the will, Caesar's will!

150 **ANTONY.** Will you be patient? Will you stay awhile?
I have o'ershot myself²⁶ to tell you of it.
I fear I wrong the honorable men
Whose daggers have stabbed Caesar; I do fear it.

FOURTH PLEBEIAN. They were traitors. Honorable men!

155 **ALL.** The will! The testament!

SECOND PLEBEIAN. They were villains, murderers! The will!
Read the will!

ANTONY. You will compel me then to read the will?
Then make a ring about the corpse of Caesar,
160 And let me show you him that made the will.
Shall I descend? And will you give me leave?

ALL. Come down.

SECOND PLEBEIAN. Descend.   [ANTONY *comes down*.]

THIRD PLEBEIAN. You shall have leave.

165 **FOURTH PLEBEIAN.** A ring! Stand round.

FIRST PLEBEIAN. Stand from the hearse,²⁷ stand from the body!

SECOND PLEBEIAN. Room for Antony, most noble Antony!

22. commons *n.* plebeians; commoners.

23. napkins *n.* handkerchiefs.

24. issue *n.* children; offspring.

25. meet *adj.* fitting; suitable.

26. o'ershot myself gone further than I meant to.

Reading Skill
Analyzing Imagery
In what way does the action on stage connect Caesar's body and the words in his will?

27. hearse (hŭrs) *n.* coffin.

ANTONY. Nay, press not so upon me; stand far²⁸ off.

ALL. Stand back! Room! Bear back.

170 **ANTONY.** If you have tears, prepare to shed them now.
　　You all do know this mantle;²⁹ I remember
　　The first time ever Caesar put it on:
　　'Twas on a summer's evening, in his tent,
　　That day he overcame the Nervii.³⁰
175　Look, in this place ran Cassius' dagger through;
　　See what a rent³¹ the envious³² Casca made;
　　Through this the well-belovèd Brutus stabbed,
　　And as he plucked his cursèd steel away,
　　Mark how the blood of Caesar followed it,
180　As³³ rushing out of doors, to be resolved³⁴
　　If Brutus so unkindly³⁵ knocked, or no;
　　For Brutus, as you know, was Caesar's angel.
　　Judge, O you gods, how dearly Caesar loved him!
　　This was the most unkindest cut of all;
185　For when the noble Caesar saw him stab,
　　Ingratitude, more strong than traitors' arms,
　　Quite vanquished him. Then burst his mighty heart;
　　And, in his mantle muffling up his face,
　　Even at the base of Pompey's statue

28. far *adv.* farther.

29. mantle (man´ təl) *n.* cloak; toga.

30. Nervii (nʉr´ vē ī) *n.* warlike European tribe conquered by Caesar in 57 B.C.
31. rent *n.* hole; tear; rip.
32. envious (en´ vē əs) *adj.* spiteful.

33. As *conj.* as if.
34. to be resolved to learn for certain.
35. unkindly *adj.* cruelly; also, unnaturally.

✓ Reading Check

To what spot does Antony move to read the will?

▲ **Critical Viewing** Compare this image with the one on page 882. Which details here suggest Antony's growing bond with his audience? **[Contrast]**

190　(Which all the while ran blood) great Caesar fell.
　　　O, what a fall was there, my countrymen!
　　　Then I, and you, and all of us fell down,
　　　Whilst bloody treason flourished[36] over us.
　　　O, now you weep, and I perceive you feel
195　The dint[37] of pity; these are gracious drops.
　　　Kind souls, what[38] weep you when you but behold
　　　Our Caesar's vesture[39] wounded? Look you here,
　　　Here is himself, marred as you see with[40] traitors.

FIRST PLEBEIAN. O piteous spectacle!

200　**SECOND PLEBEIAN.** O noble Caesar!

THIRD PLEBEIAN. O woeful day!

FOURTH PLEBEIAN. O traitors, villains!

FIRST PLEBEIAN. O most bloody sight!

SECOND PLEBEIAN. We will be revenged.

205　**ALL.** Revenge! About![41] Seek! Burn! Fire! Kill! Slay!
　　　Let not a traitor live!

ANTONY. Stay, countrymen.

FIRST PLEBEIAN. Peace there! Hear the noble Antony.

SECOND PLEBEIAN. We'll hear him, we'll follow him, we'll die
210　with him!

ANTONY. Good friends, sweet friends, let me not stir you up
　　　To such a sudden flood of mutiny.
　　　They that have done this deed are honorable.
　　　What private griefs[42] they have, alas, I know not,
215　That made them do it. They are wise and honorable,
　　　And will, no doubt, with reasons answer you.
　　　I come not, friends, to steal away your hearts;
　　　I am no orator, as Brutus is;
　　　But (as you know me all) a plain blunt man
220　That love my friend, and that they know full well
　　　That gave me public leave to speak[43] of him.
　　　For I have neither writ, nor words, nor worth,
　　　Action, or utterance,[44] nor the power of speech
　　　To stir men's blood; I only speak right on.[45]
225　I tell you that which you yourselves do know,
　　　Show you sweet Caesar's wounds, poor poor dumb mouths,
　　　And bid them speak for me. But were I Brutus,
　　　And Brutus Antony, there were an Antony
　　　Would ruffle up your spirits, and put a tongue

36. flourished (flʉr´ ish'd)
v. swaggered; waved a sword in triumph.
37. dint n. stroke; blow.
38. what adv. why.
39. vesture (ves´ chər)
n. clothing.
40. with prep. by.

41. About let's go.

42. private griefs personal grievances.
43. public leave to speak permission to speak in public.
44. neither writ . . . utterance (ut´ ər əns) neither a written speech, nor fluency, nor reputation, nor gestures, nor style of speaking
45. right on directly.

Reading Skill
Analyzing Imagery
Which images in Antony's speech combine ideas of words, the body, and violence?

230 In every wound of Caesar's that should move
The stones of Rome to rise and mutiny.

ALL. We'll mutiny.

FIRST PLEBEIAN. We'll burn the house of Brutus.

THIRD PLEBEIAN. Away, then! Come, seek the conspirators.

ANTONY. Yet hear me, countrymen. Yet hear me speak.

235 **ALL.** Peace, ho! Hear Antony, most noble Antony!

ANTONY. Why, friends, you go to do you know not what:
Wherein hath Caesar thus deserved your loves?
Alas, you know not; I must tell you then:
You have forgot the will I told you of.

240 **ALL.** Most true, the will! Let's stay and hear the will.

ANTONY. Here is the will, and under Caesar's seal.
To every Roman citizen he gives,
To every several[46] man, seventy-five drachmas.

SECOND PLEBEIAN. Most noble Caesar! We'll revenge his death!

245 **THIRD PLEBEIAN.** O royal[47] Caesar!

ANTONY. Hear me with patience.

ALL. Peace, ho!

ANTONY. Moreover, he hath left you all his walks,
His private arbors, and new-planted orchards,[48]
250 On this side Tiber; he hath left them you,
And to your heirs forever: common pleasures,[49]
To walk abroad and recreate yourselves.
Here was a Caesar! When comes such another?

FIRST PLEBEIAN. Never, never! Come, away, away!
255 We'll burn his body in the holy place,
And with the brands[50] fire the traitors' houses.
Take up the body.

SECOND PLEBEIAN. Go fetch fire.

THIRD PLEBEIAN. Pluck down benches.

260 **FOURTH PLEBEIAN.** Pluck down forms, windows,[51] anything!

[*Exit* PLEBEIANS *with the body.*]

ANTONY. Now let it work:[52] Mischief, thou art afoot,
Take thou what course thou wilt.

[*Enter* SERVANT.]

How now, fellow?

---

46. several *adj.* individual.

47. royal *adj.* showing noble generosity.
48. walks . . . orchards parks, his private stands of trees, and newly planted gardens.
49. common pleasures public places of recreation.

Reading Skill
Analyzing Imagery
Moved by news of Caesar's words, what action does the crowd take involving Caesar's body?

50. brands *n.* torches.
51. forms, windows benches and shutters.
52. work *v.* spread and expand, as yeast does; follow through to a conclusion.

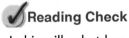
Reading Check

In his will, what has Caesar left the citizens of Rome?

SERVANT. Sir, Octavius is already come to Rome.

ANTONY. Where is he?

265 **SERVANT.** He and Lepidus are at Caesar's house.

ANTONY. And thither[53] will I straight to visit him;
He comes upon a wish.[54] Fortune is merry,
And in this mood will give us anything.

SERVANT. I heard him say, Brutus and Cassius
270 Are rid[55] like madmen through the gates of Rome.

ANTONY. Belike[56] they had some notice of the people,[57]
How I had moved them. Bring me to Octavius. [*Exit*]

Scene iii. *A street.*

[*Enter* CINNA THE POET, *and after him the* PLEBEIANS.]

CINNA. I dreamt tonight[1] that I did feast with Caesar,
And things unluckily charge my fantasy.[2]
I have no will to wander forth of doors,[3]
Yet something leads me forth.

5 **FIRST PLEBEIAN.** What is your name?

SECOND PLEBEIAN. Whither are you going?

THIRD PLEBEIAN. Where do you dwell?

FOURTH PLEBEIAN. Are you a married man or a bachelor?

SECOND PLEBEIAN. Answer every man directly.[4]

10 **FIRST PLEBEIAN.** Ay, and briefly.

FOURTH PLEBEIAN. Ay, and wisely.

THIRD PLEBEIAN. Ay, and truly, you were best.

CINNA. What is my name? Whither am I going? Where do I
dwell? Am I a married man or a bachelor? Then, to answer
15 every man directly and briefly, wisely and truly: wisely I say,
I am a bachelor.

SECOND PLEBEIAN. That's as much as to say, they are fools that
marry; you'll bear me a bang[5] for that, I fear. Proceed
directly.

20 **CINNA.** Directly, I am going to Caesar's funeral.

FIRST PLEBEIAN. As a friend or an enemy?

CINNA. As a friend.

SECOND PLEBEIAN. That matter is answered directly.

---

53. thither *adv.* there.
54. upon a wish as I wished.

55. Are rid have ridden.
56. Belike *adv.* probably.
57. notice of the people word about the mood of the people.

Literary Analysis
Dramatic Speeches
To whom is Cinna's speech addressed?

1. tonight *adv.* last night.
2. things . . . fantasy the events that have happened give an unlucky meaning to my dream.
3. forth of doors outdoors.
4. directly *adv.* in a straight-forward manner.

5. bear me a bang get a blow from me.

FOURTH PLEBEIAN. For your dwelling, briefly.

25 **CINNA.** Briefly, I dwell by the Capitol.

THIRD PLEBEIAN. Your name, sir, truly.

CINNA. Truly, my name is Cinna.

FIRST PLEBEIAN. Tear him to pieces! He's a conspirator.

CINNA. I am Cinna the poet! I am Cinna the poet!

30 **FOURTH PLEBEIAN.** Tear him for his bad verses! Tear him for his bad verses!

CINNA. I am not Cinna the conspirator.

FOURTH PLEBEIAN. It is no matter, his name's Cinna; pluck but his name out of his heart, and turn him going.[6]

35 **THIRD PLEBEIAN.** Tear him, tear him! [*They attack him.*]
Come, brands, ho! Firebrands![7] To Brutus', to Cassius'!
Burn all! Some to Decius' house, and some to
Casca's; some to Ligarius'! Away, go!

[*Exit all the* PLEBEIANS *with* CINNA.]

Reading Skill
Analyzing Imagery
How does a confusion about Cinna's name place his body in danger?

6. turn him going send him on his way.

7. Firebrands *n.* burning pieces of wood; also, people who stir up others to revolt.

▼ **Critical Viewing**
This ancient relief depicts a consultation with priests about an important matter. How might such artworks have inspired Romans' confidence in their government?

Extispicium relief (inspection of entrails) from the Forum of Trajan, Rome. Louvre, Paris, France.

Apply the Skills

The Tragedy of Julius Caesar, Act III

Thinking About the Selection

1. **Respond:** As a Roman, would you have applauded Antony's speech? Explain.
2. **(a) Recall:** What does Caesar say when he sees Brutus among the assassins? **(b) Infer:** What feelings do these words convey?
3. **(a) Summarize:** Explain how Brutus justifies the assassination in his speech to the crowd. **(b) Analyze:** Explain how Antony turns the crowd against the conspirators. Support your answer.
4. **Make a Judgment:** Is Caesar responsible for his death? Explain.

Literary Analysis

5. On a chart like the one shown, identify each speech as an **aside**, a **soliloquy**, or a **monologue.** Then, paraphrase the speech and identify who hears it.

Lines	Type of Speech	Paraphrase	Who Hears It?
Scene i, lines 148–163			
Scene i, lines 254–275			
Scene ii, lines 261–262			

6. Contrast the thoughts and feelings Antony expresses in his **dialogue** with other characters in Scene i, lines 218–222 with the thoughts and feelings he shares in his speech in Scene i, lines 254–275.
7. How does Antony's monologue in Scene ii, lines 74–253 help move the plot along?
8. **(a)** Contrast the style and purpose of Antony's and Brutus' funeral speeches. **(b)** Share your ideas with a partner. **(c)** Explain whether learning another person's responses changed your own and why.

Reading Skill

9. **(a)** Give three examples of **imagery** in Act III related to the human body and to words. **(b) Analyze the imagery** by explaining how words and bodies are linked in each example.

QuickReview

Act III at a Glance
Caesar is assassinated by the conspirators. Brutus persuades the people that the assassination was justified, but Antony stirs up the crowd's desire for revenge.

Go Online
—Assessment

For: Self-test
Visit: www.PHSchool.com
Web Code: eqa-6507

Aside: remark a character makes that is not heard by others on stage

Soliloquy: a long speech in which a character, usually alone on stage, speaks as if to him- or herself, unheard by others

Monologue: a long speech by a character

Imagery: language that appeals to the senses

Vocabulary Builder

Practice Analogies match the relationships between pairs of words. In each item, match the relationship between the first two words by choosing the correct word to complete the second pair. Explain your answers.

1. vague : definite :: confounded : **(a)** certain, **(b)** lost, **(c)** unclear
2. insult : offended :: spectacle: **(a)** educated, **(b)** fascinated, **(c)** drowsy
3. remember : past :: prophesy : **(a)** sky, **(b)** present, **(c)** future
4. tuxedo : T-shirt :: discourse : **(a)** jeans, **(b)** lecture, **(c)** chat
5. stored : attic :: interred : **(a)** museum, **(b)** cemetery, **(c)** exit
6. merriment : laughter :: strife : **(a)** shouting, **(b)** singing, **(c)** blushing

Adding Words to Your Vocabulary Use a dictionary to find the vocabulary word on page 868 that is the same in both noun and verb form. Use each form in a sentence. (For more on dictionaries, see page R6.)

Writing

Imagine that you are one of the tribunes in the play. Write a **letter to the editor** of the *Roman Times* expressing your feelings about the changing loyalties of the common people. Be sure to
- describe the changes in loyalty.
- state your opinion of the changes.
- support your ideas with evidence from the play.

For *Grammar, Vocabulary,* and *Assessment,*
see **Build Language Skills,** pages 926–927.

Extend Your Learning

Listening and Speaking Give a **dramatic reading** of one of the soliloquies or monologues in Act III. Mark up a copy of the speech, underlining the main points. Mark repetition or parallelism (similar sentence structures). Determine how your voice should change with each repetition—growing louder or softer. Perform the speech for the class.

Research and Technology Prepare a **map** showing the locations of important sites in ancient Rome, including those in which scenes in Act III are set. Annotate your map, identifying each site and explaining its importance.

Practice these skills with *The Tragedy of Julius Caesar*, Act IV.

Literary Analysis

Conflict, a struggle between opposing forces, creates drama:

- In an **external conflict**, a character struggles with an outside force, such as another character, a group of characters, or a force such as the weather.

- In an **internal conflict**, the character struggles with his or her own opposing beliefs, desires, or values.

The Tragedy of Julius Caesar involves a number of different conflicts. Internal and external conflicts are in many cases directly related. For instance, earlier in the play, the external conflict between Brutus and Caesar creates an internal conflict for Brutus—he wishes to check Caesar's ambition, but he also considers Caesar a friend.

Reading Skill

When **reading Shakespearean drama**, you need to **read between the lines** to find the deeper meaning of a character's words or actions.

- Keep the larger situation in mind as you read. For instance, early in Act IV, Antony describes Lepidus as "Meet to be sent on errands." Note that Antony has been deciding which of his political rivals will die and which will share power. Between the lines, he is saying, "Fit to run errands—and nothing else."

- Follow indirect references. For example, when Lucilius reports on Cassius, Brutus says, "Thou has described / A hot friend cooling." "A hot friend" refers to Cassius, whom Brutus worries is no longer his ally.

Use a chart like the one shown to read between the lines.

Academic Standards

- Analyze many different forms of dramatic literature. (10.3.1)
- Identify and evaluate dialogue, soliloquies, asides, character foils and stage designs in dramatic literature. (10.3.10)

What Does It Say?

"Meet to be sent on errands"

↓

What Does It Mean?

Lepidus is fit to run errands— and nothing else.

↓

Why Is It Important?

Antony is deciding who will die and who will gain power.

Vocabulary Builder

- **legacies** (leg′ ə sēz) *n.* money, property, or position left in a will to someone (p. 893) *The legacies in his will included a gift to charity.*

- **chastisement** (chas′ tiz mənt) *n.* severe criticism; punishment (p. 897) *As chastisement, the child was sent to bed early.*

- **rash** (rash) *adj.* given to acting without thinking; impulsive (p. 898) *Do not be so rash; think before you act.*

- **mirth** (murth) *n.* joyfulness; merriment (p. 898) *The children were full of mirth and laughed joyfully.*

Review and Anticipate In Act III, after the conspirators assassinate Caesar, Brutus and Antony both speak at his funeral. Brutus explains that Caesar's death was necessary to keep Romans free. Antony, however, convinces the crowd that Caesar was a great man while Brutus is a traitor. The crowd rushes off to find and destroy the conspirators.

As Act IV opens, Antony and his allies Octavius and Lepidus are deciding which of their political rivals are to be killed. Meanwhile, conflict is brewing between their enemies, Cassius and Brutus.

⋙⋙⋙ ACT IV ⋘⋘⋘

Scene i. A house in Rome.

[*Enter* ANTONY, OCTAVIUS, *and* LEPIDUS.]

ANTONY. These many then shall die; their names are pricked.[1]

OCTAVIUS. Your brother too must die; consent you, Lepidus?

LEPIDUS. I do consent—

OCTAVIUS.   Prick him down, Antony.

LEPIDUS. Upon condition Publius shall not live,
5   Who is your sister's son, Mark Antony.

ANTONY. He shall not live; look, with a spot I damn him.[2]
But, Lepidus, go you to Caesar's house;
Fetch the will hither, and we shall determine
How to cut off some charge in <u>legacies</u>.[3]

10 **LEPIDUS.** What, shall I find you here?

OCTAVIUS. Or[4] here or at the Capitol.   [*Exit* LEPIDUS.]

ANTONY. This is a slight unmeritable[5] man,
Meet[6] to be sent on errands; is it fit,
The threefold world[7] divided, he should stand
One of the three to share it?

15 **OCTAVIUS.**   So you thought him,
And took his voice[8] who should be pricked to die
In our black sentence and proscription.[9]

ANTONY. Octavius, I have seen more days[10] than you;

---

1. **pricked** *v.* checked off.

2. **with a spot . . . him** with a mark on the tablet, I condemn him.

3. **cut off some charge in legacies** save costs by changing the amount of gifts left in the will.

Vocabulary Builder
legacies (leg´ ə sēz) *n.* money, property, or position left in a will to someone

4. **Or** *conj.* either.

5. **slight unmeritable** insignificant and without merit.

6. **Meet** *adj.* suitable.

7. **threefold world** three areas of the Roman Empire—Europe, Asia, and Africa.

8. **voice** *n.* vote; opinion.

9. **black . . . proscription** list of those sentenced to death or exile.

10. **have seen more days** am older.

And though we lay these honors on this man,

20 To ease ourselves of divers sland'rous loads,[11]
He shall but bear them as the ass bears gold,
To groan and sweat under the business,
Either led or driven, as we point the way;
And having brought our treasure where we will,

25 Then take we down his load, and turn him off,
(Like to the empty ass) to shake his ears
And graze in commons.[12]

OCTAVIUS. You may do your will;
But he's a tried and valiant soldier.

ANTONY. So is my horse, Octavius, and for that

30 I do appoint him store of provender.[13]
It is a creature that I teach to fight,
To wind,[14] to stop, to run directly on,
His corporal motion governed by my spirit.[15]
And, in some taste,[16] is Lepidus but so.

35 He must be taught, and trained, and bid go forth.
A barren-spirited[17] fellow; one that feeds
On objects, arts, and imitations,[18]
Which, out of use and staled[19] by other men,
Begin his fashion.[20] Do not talk of him

40 But as a property.[21] And now, Octavius,
Listen great things. Brutus and Cassius
Are levying powers;[22] we must straight make head.[23]
Therefore let our alliance be combined,
Our best friends made,[24] our means stretched;[25]

45 And let us presently[26] go sit in council
How covert matters may be best disclosed,
And open perils surest answerèd.[27]

OCTAVIUS. Let us do so; for we are at the stake,
And bayed about with many enemies;[28]

50 And some that smile have in their hearts, I fear,
Millions of mischiefs.[29] [*Exit*]

Scene ii. Camp near Sardis.

[*Drum. Enter* BRUTUS, LUCILIUS, LUCIUS, *and the* ARMY. TITINIUS *and*
PINDARUS *meet them.*]

BRUTUS. Stand ho!

LUCILIUS. Give the word, ho! and stand.

BRUTUS. What now, Lucilius, is Cassius near?

---

11. divers sland'rous loads various burdens of blame.

12. in commons on public pasture.

Literary Analysis
Conflict What is the conflict between Antony and Octavius?

13. appoint . . . provender give him a supply of food.

14. wind (wīnd) *v.* turn.

15. His . . . spirit his bodily movements governed by my mind.

16. taste *n.* degree; measure.

17. barren-spirited without ideas of his own.

18. feeds / On objects, arts, and imitations enjoys curiosities, clever ways, and fashions.

19. staled *v.* cheapened.

20. Begin his fashion he begins to use. (He is hopelessly behind the times.)

21. property *n.* tool; object.

22. levying powers enlisting troops.

23. straight make head quickly gather soldiers.

24. best friends made closest allies chosen.

25. stretched *adj.* used to full advantage.

26. presently *adv.* immediately.

27. How . . . answerèd how hidden dangers may be discovered and known dangers met.

28. at the stake . . . enemies surrounded by enemies like a bear tied to a stake and set upon by many dogs. (Bear-baiting was a popular amusement in Elizabethan England.)

29. mischiefs *n.* plans to injure us.

LUCILIUS. He is at hand, and Pindarus is come

5   To do you salutation[1] from his master.

BRUTUS. He greets me well. Your master, Pindarus,
     In his own change, or by ill officers,
     Hath given me some worthy cause to wish
     Things done undone;[2] but if he be at hand,
     I shall be satisfied.[3]

10 **PINDARUS.**   I do not doubt
     But that my noble master will appear
     Such as he is, full of regard[4] and honor.

BRUTUS. He is not doubted. A word, Lucilius,
     How he received you; let me be resolved.[5]

15 **LUCILIUS.** With courtesy and with respect enough,
     But not with such familiar instances,[6]
     Nor with such free and friendly conference[7]
     As he hath used of old.

1. To do you salutation to bring you greetings.

2. In his own . . . done undone Whether his actions are due to a change in his feelings toward me or to bad advice from subordinates, he has made me wish we did not do what we did.

3. be satisfied obtain an explanation.

4. full of regard worthy of respect.

5. resolved *adj.* fully informed.

6. familiar instances marks of friendship.

7. conference *n.* conversation.

**Reading Check**

What is Brutus' present attitude toward Cassius?

▲ Critical Viewing Which details in this film still reflect the fact that Antony dominates over both Lepidus and Octavius? **[Interpret]**

BRUTUS.   Thou hast described
A hot friend cooling. Ever note, Lucilius,
20   When love begins to sicken and decay
It useth an enforcèd ceremony.[8]
There are no tricks in plain and simple faith;
But hollow[9] men, like horses hot at hand,[10]
Make gallant show and promise of their mettle;[11]

[*Low march within*]

25   But when they should endure the bloody spur,
They fall their crests, and like deceitful jades
Sink in the trial.[12] Comes his army on?

LUCILIUS. They mean this night in Sardis to be quartered;[13]
The greater part, the horse in general,[14]
Are come with Cassius.

[*Enter* CASSIUS *and his Powers.*[15]]

30   **BRUTUS.**   Hark! He is arrived.
March gently[16] on to meet him.

CASSIUS. Stand, ho!

BRUTUS. Stand, ho! Speak the word along.

FIRST SOLDIER. Stand!

35   **SECOND SOLDIER.** Stand!

THIRD SOLDIER. Stand!

CASSIUS. Most noble brother, you have done me wrong.

BRUTUS. Judge me, you gods! Wrong I mine enemies?
And if not so, how should I wrong a brother?

40   **CASSIUS.** Brutus, this sober form[17] of yours hides wrongs;
And when you do them—

BRUTUS.   Cassius, be content.[18]
Speak your griefs softly; I do know you well.
Before the eyes of both our armies here
(Which should perceive nothing but love from us)
45   Let us not wrangle. Bid them move away;
Then in my tent, Cassius, enlarge[19] your griefs,
And I will give you audience.

CASSIUS.   Pindarus,
Bid our commanders lead their charges[20] off
A little from this ground.

---

8. **enforcèd ceremony** forced formality.

9. **hollow** *adj.* insincere.

10. **hot at hand** full of spirit when reined in.

11. **mettle** *n.* spirit; high character; courage.

12. **They fall . . . the trial** They drop their necks, and like worn-out, worthless horses, fail the test.

13. **quartered** *v.* provided with places to stay.

14. **horse in general** cavalry.

15. ***Powers*** *n.* forces; troops.

16. **gently** *adv.* slowly.

17. **sober form** serious manner.

18. **be content** be patient.

Reading Skill
Reading Between the Lines Brutus and Cassius are standing near their troops. Why does Brutus suggest meeting in his tent?

19. **enlarge** *v.* freely express.

20. **charges** *n.* troops.

50 **BRUTUS.** Lucilius, do you the like, and let no man
Come to our tent till we have done our conference.
Let Lucius and Titinius guard our door.

[*Exit all but* BRUTUS *and* CASSIUS]

Scene iii. *Brutus' tent.*

CASSIUS. That you have wronged me doth appear in this:
You have condemned and noted[1] Lucius Pella
For taking bribes here of the Sardians;
Wherein my letters, praying on his side,[2]
5   Because I knew the man, was slighted off.[3]

BRUTUS. You wronged yourself to write in such a case.

CASSIUS. In such a time as this it is not meet
That every nice offense should bear his comment.[4]

BRUTUS. Let me tell you, Cassius, you yourself
10   Are much condemned to have an itching palm,[5]
To sell and mart[6] your offices for gold
To undeservers.

CASSIUS.   I an itching palm?
You know that you are Brutus that speaks this,
Or, by the gods, this speech were else your last.

15 **BRUTUS.** The name of Cassius honors[7] this corruption,
And <u>chastisement</u> doth therefore hide his head.

CASSIUS. Chastisement!

BRUTUS. Remember March, the ides of March remember.
Did not great Julius bleed for justice' sake?
20   What villain touched his body, that did stab,
And not[8] for justice? What, shall one of us,
That struck the foremost man of all this world
But for supporting robbers,[9] shall we now
Contaminate our fingers with base bribes,
25   And sell the mighty space of our large honors[10]
For so much trash[11] as may be graspèd thus?
I had rather be a dog, and bay[12] the moon,
Than such a Roman.

CASSIUS.   Brutus, bait[13] not me;
I'll not endure it. You forget yourself
30   To hedge me in.[14] I am a soldier, I,
Older in practice, abler than yourself
To make conditions.[15]

1. **noted** *v.* publicly denounced.

2. **praying on his side** pleading on his behalf.

3. **slighted off** disregarded.

4. **every . . . comment** every petty fault should receive its criticism.

5. **condemned . . . palm** accused of having a hand eager to accept bribes.

6. **mart** *v.* trade.

7. **honors** *v.* gives respectability to.

Vocabulary Builder
chastisement (chas´ tiz mənt) *n.* severe criticism; punishment

Reading Skill
Reading Between the Lines When Brutus asks who stabbed Caesar "not for justice," what is he suggesting about Cassius?

8. **And not** except.

9. **But . . . robbers** Here Brutus says, for the first time, that Caesar's officials were also involved in taking bribes and that this was a motive in his assassination.

10. **honors** *n.* reputations.

11. **trash** *n.* that is, money.

12. **bay** *v.* howl at.

13. **bait** harass (as a bear tied to a stake is harassed by dogs).

14. **hedge me in** restrict my actions.

15. **make conditions** manage affairs.

 **Reading Check**

Of what does Brutus accuse Cassius?

BRUTUS. Go to! You are not, Cassius.

CASSIUS. I am.

BRUTUS. I say you are not.

35 **CASSIUS.** Urge[16] me no more, I shall forget myself;
Have mind upon your health;[17] tempt me no farther.

BRUTUS. Away, slight[18] man!

CASSIUS. Is't possible?

BRUTUS. Hear me, for I will speak.
Must I give way and room to your <u>rash</u> choler?[19]
40 Shall I be frighted when a madman stares?

CASSIUS. O ye gods, ye gods! Must I endure all this?

BRUTUS. All this? Ay, more: fret till your proud heart break.
Go show your slaves how choleric[20] you are,
And make your bondmen[21] tremble. Must I budge?[22]
45 Must I observe you?[23] Must I stand and crouch[24]
Under your testy humor?[25] By the gods,
You shall digest the venom of your spleen,[26]
Though it do split you; for, from this day forth,
I'll use you for my <u>mirth</u>, yea, for my laughter,
When you are waspish.[27]

50 **CASSIUS.** Is it come to this?

BRUTUS. You say you are a better soldier:
Let it appear so; make your vaunting[28] true,
And it shall please me well. For mine own part,
I shall be glad to learn of[29] noble men.

55 **CASSIUS.** You wrong me every way; you wrong me, Brutus;
I said, an elder soldier, not a better.
Did I say, better?

BRUTUS. If you did, I care not.

CASSIUS. When Caesar lived, he durst[30] not thus have
moved[31] me.

BRUTUS. Peace, peace, you durst not so have tempted him.

60 **CASSIUS.** I durst not?

BRUTUS. No.

CASSIUS. What? Durst not tempt him?

BRUTUS. For your life you durst not.

▶ **Critical Viewing**
What does this ancient Roman sculpture suggest about the Roman attitude toward war? **[Interpret]**

16. Urge *v.* drive onward.
17. health *n.* safety.
18. slight *adj.* insignificant.

Vocabulary Builder
rash (rash) *adj.* given to acting without thinking; impulsive

19. choler (käl´ ər) *n.* anger.
20. choleric (käl´ ər ik) *adj.* quick-tempered.
21. bondmen *n.* slaves.
22. budge *v.* flinch away from you.
23. observe you show reverence toward you.
24. crouch *v.* bow.
25. testy humor irritability.

Vocabulary Builder
mirth (mʉrth) *n.* joyfulness; merriment

26. digest . . . spleen eat the poison of your spleen. (The spleen was thought to be the source of anger.)
27. waspish *adj.* bad-tempered.
28. vaunting (vônt´ iŋ) *n.* boasting.
29. learn of hear about; learn from.
30. durst *v.* dared.
31. moved *v.* angered.

CASSIUS. Do not presume too much upon my love;
I may do that I shall be sorry for.

65 **BRUTUS.** You have done that you should be sorry for.
There is no terror, Cassius, in your threats;
For I am armed so strong in honesty
That they pass by me as the idle wind,
Which I respect not. I did send to you

70 For certain sums of gold, which you denied me;
For I can raise no money by vile means.
By heaven, I had rather coin my heart
And drop my blood for drachmas[32] than to wring
From the hard hands of peasants their vile trash

75 By any indirection.[33] I did send
To you for gold to pay my legions,[34]
Which you denied me. Was that done like Cassius?
Should I have answered Caius Cassius so?
When Marcus Brutus grows so covetous[35]

80 To lock such rascal counters[36] from his friends,
Be ready, gods, with all your thunderbolts,
Dash him to pieces!

CASSIUS.   I denied you not.

BRUTUS. You did.

CASSIUS.   I did not. He was but a fool
That brought my answer back. Brutus hath rived[37] my heart.

85 A friend should bear his friend's infirmities;
But Brutus makes mine greater than they are.

BRUTUS. I do not, till you practice them on me.

CASSIUS. You love me not.

BRUTUS.   I do not like your faults.

CASSIUS. A friendly eye could never see such faults.

90 **BRUTUS.** A flatterer's would not, though they do appear
As huge as high Olympus.

CASSIUS. Come, Antony, and young Octavius, come,
Revenge yourselves alone[38] on Cassius,
For Cassius is aweary of the world:

95 Hated by one he loves; braved[39] by his brother;
Checked like a bondman;[40] all his faults observed,
Set in a notebook, learned and conned by rote[41]
To cast into my teeth. O, I could weep
My spirit from mine eyes! There is my dagger,

100 And here my naked breast; within, a heart

32. **drachmas** (drak′ məz) *n.* silver coins of ancient Greece.
33. **indirection** *n.* irregular methods.
34. **legions** *n.* Roman military divisions of several thousand soldiers.
35. **covetous** (kuv′ ət əs) *adj.* greedy.
36. **rascal counters** worthless coins.
37. **rived** (rivd) *v.* broken.

38. **alone** *adv.* only.
39. **braved** *adj.* defied; challenged.
40. **Checked like a bondman** scolded like a slave.
41. **conned by rote** memorized.

 **Reading Check**

What is the second accusation Brutus makes against Cassius?

Dearer than Pluto's mine,[42] richer than gold;
If that thou be'st a Roman, take it forth.
I, that denied thee gold, will give my heart.
Strike as thou didst at Caesar; for I know,
105 When thou didst hate him worst, thou lovedst him better
Than ever thou lovedst Cassius.

BRUTUS.   Sheathe your dagger.
Be angry when you will, it shall have scope.[43]
Do what you will, dishonor shall be humor.[44]
O Cassius, you are yokèd[45] with a lamb
110 That carries anger as the flint[46] bears fire,
Who, much enforcèd,[47] shows a hasty spark,
And straight[48] is cold again.

CASSIUS.   Hath Cassius lived
To be but mirth and laughter to his Brutus
When grief and blood ill-tempered vexeth him?

▼ **Critical Viewing** In this film still, do Brutus and Cassius look as if
they will be able to settle their conflict? Explain. **[Hypothesize]**

42. **Pluto's mine** all the riches in the Earth.
43. **scope** *n.* free play.
44. **dishonor . . . humor** I will consider any insults to be just the effect of your irritable disposition.
45. **yokèd** *adj.* in partnership.
46. **flint** *n.* hard mineral that, when struck by steel, makes sparks.
47. **enforcèd** *adj.* provoked.
48. **straight** *adv.* immediately.

Reading Skill
Reading Between the Lines In this situation, what does Cassius' use of the phrase "his Brutus" suggest?

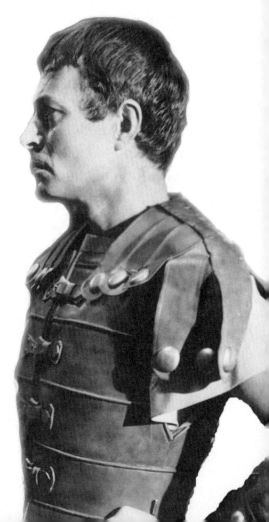

BRUTUS. When I spoke that, I was ill-tempered too.

CASSIUS. Do you confess so much? Give me your hand.

BRUTUS. And my heart too.

CASSIUS.   O Brutus!

BRUTUS.   What's the matter?

CASSIUS. Have not you love enough to bear with me
When that rash humor⁴⁹ which my mother gave me
Makes me forgetful?

49. **humor** *n.* temperament.

BRUTUS.   Yes, Cassius, and from henceforth,
When you are overearnest with your Brutus,
He'll think your mother chides, and leave you so.⁵⁰

50. **your mother . . . so** it is just your inherited disposition and let it go at that.

[*Enter a* POET, *followed by* LUCILIUS, TITINIUS, *and* LUCIUS.]

POET. Let me go in to see the generals;
There is some grudge between 'em; 'tis not meet
They be alone.

LUCILIUS. You shall not come to them.

POET. Nothing but death shall stay me.

CASSIUS. How now? What's the matter?

POET. For shame, you generals! What do you mean?
Love, and be friends, as two such men should be;
For I have seen more years, I'm sure, than ye.

CASSIUS. Ha, ha! How vilely doth this cynic⁵¹ rhyme!

BRUTUS. Get you hence, sirrah! Saucy⁵² fellow, hence!

CASSIUS. Bear with him, Brutus, 'tis his fashion.

BRUTUS. I'll know his humor when he knows his time.⁵³
What should the wars do with these jigging⁵⁴ fools?
Companion,⁵⁵ hence!

51. **cynic** *n.* rude fellow.
52. **Saucy** *adj.* rude; insolent.
53. **I'll know . . . time** I'll accept his eccentricity when he chooses a proper time to exhibit it.
54. **jigging** *adj.* rhyming.
55. **Companion** *n.* fellow (used to show contempt).

CASSIUS.   Away, away, be gone!   [*Exit* POET.]

BRUTUS. Lucilius and Titinius, bid the commanders
Prepare to lodge their companies tonight.

CASSIUS. And come yourselves, and bring Messala with you
Immediately to us.   [*Exit* LUCILIUS *and* TITINIUS.]

BRUTUS.   Lucius, a bowl of wine.   [*Exit* LUCIUS.]

CASSIUS. I did not think you could have been so angry.

BRUTUS. O Cassius, I am sick of many griefs.

Literary Analysis
Conflict How does the arrival of the poet help end the conflict between Cassius and Brutus?

Reading Check

What happens in the quarrel between Cassius and Brutus?

CASSIUS. Of your philosophy you make no use,
145   If you give place to accidental evils.[56]

BRUTUS. No man bears sorrow better. Portia is dead.

CASSIUS. Ha? Portia?

BRUTUS. She is dead.

CASSIUS. How scaped I killing when I crossed you so?[57]
150   O insupportable and touching[58] loss!
        Upon[59] what sickness?

BRUTUS.   Impatient of my absence,
        And grief that young Octavius with Mark Antony
        Have made themselves so strong—for with her death
        That tidings[60] came—with this she fell distract,[61]
155   And (her attendants absent) swallowed fire.

CASSIUS. And died so?

BRUTUS.   Even so.

CASSIUS.   O ye immortal gods!

[*Enter* LUCIUS, *with wine and tapers.*]

BRUTUS. Speak no more of her. Give me a bowl of wine.
        In this I bury all unkindness, Cassius.   [*Drinks*]

CASSIUS. My heart is thirsty for that noble pledge.

56. Of your philosophy . . . evils As a Stoic, Brutus believed that chance misfortunes should not disturb his peace of mind.

57. How scaped . . . you so? How did I escape being killed when I opposed you so?

58. touching *adj.* deeply wounding.

59. Upon *prep.* as a result of.

Literary Analysis

Conflict With what internal conflict has Brutus been struggling?

60. with . . . tidings came That is, Brutus received two messages at the same time: news of Portia's death and news of Octavius and Antony's success.

61. fell distract became distraught.

Literature in Context

Humanities Connection

Stoicism Brutus follows a philosophy called Stoicism (stō´ i siz´ əm), a school of thought established by the ancient Greek thinker Zeno sometime after 312 B.C. Stoicism stresses the following ideas:

- The universe is ruled by unchanging natural laws.
- A wise person lives a virtuous life, using reason to understand natural laws and to act accordingly.
- A wise person is not ruled by his or her emotions.
- Using reason, a wise person distinguishes between what is truly in his or her power and what is not.
- A wise person does not allow events that he or she does not control—even the loss of a loved one—to affect him or her.

Connect to the Literature

How do Brutus' Stoic beliefs affect his actions in Act IV?

The Greek philosopher Epictetus (A.D. 50?–135?), a famous teacher of Stoic ideas

<table>
<tr><td>160</td><td>Fill, Lucius, till the wine o'erswell the cup;
I cannot drink too much of Brutus' love.</td></tr>
</table>

[*Drinks. Exit* LUCIUS.]

[*Enter* TITINIUS *and* MESSALA.]

BRUTUS. Come in, Titinius! Welcome, good Messala.
Now sit we close about this taper here,
And call in question[62] our necessities.

62. call in question examine.

CASSIUS. Portia, art thou gone?

165 **BRUTUS.**   No more, I pray you.
Messala, I have here receivèd letters
That young Octavius and Mark Antony
Come down upon us with a mighty power,[63]
Bending their expedition toward Philippi.[64]

63. power *n.* army.
64. Bending . . . Philippi (fi lip´ ī) directing their rapid march toward Philippi, a city in Macedonia.
65. selfsame tenure same message.
66. proscription . . . outlawry proclamation of death sentences and lists of those condemned.

170 **MESSALA.** Myself have letters of the selfsame tenure.[65]

BRUTUS. With what addition?

MESSALA. That by proscription and bills of outlawry[66]
Octavius, Antony, and Lepidus
Have put to death an hundred senators.

175 **BRUTUS.** Therein our letters do not well agree.
Mine speak of seventy senators that died
By their proscriptions, Cicero being one.

CASSIUS. Cicero one?

MESSALA.   Cicero is dead,
And by that order of proscription.
180 Had you your letters from your wife, my lord?

BRUTUS. No, Messala.

MESSALA. Nor nothing in your letters writ of her?

BRUTUS. Nothing, Messala.

MESSALA.   That methinks is strange.

BRUTUS. Why ask you? Hear you aught[67] of her in yours?

67. aught (ôt) *pron.* anything at all.

185 **MESSALA.** No, my lord.

BRUTUS. Now as you are a Roman, tell me true.

MESSALA. Then like a Roman bear the truth I tell,
For certain she is dead, and by strange manner.

BRUTUS. Why, farewell, Portia. We must die, Messala.
190 With meditating that she must die once,
I have the patience to endure it now.

Reading Skill
Reading Between the Lines In this situation, why might Messala ask Brutus about news of Portia?

Reading Check

What has happened to Brutus' wife, Portia?

MESSALA. Even so great men great losses should endure.

CASSIUS. I have as much of this in art[68] as you,
But yet my nature could not bear it so.

195 **BRUTUS.** Well, to our work alive.[69] What do you think
Of marching to Philippi presently?[70]

CASSIUS. I do not think it good.

BRUTUS.   Your reason?

CASSIUS.   This it is:
'Tis better that the enemy seek us;
So shall he waste his means, weary his soldiers,
200 Doing himself offense,[71] whilst we, lying still,
Are full of rest, defense, and nimbleness.

BRUTUS. Good reasons must of force[72] give place to better.
The people 'twixt Philippi and this ground
Do stand but in a forced affection;[73]
205 For they have grudged us contribution.[74]
The enemy, marching along by them,
By them shall make a fuller number up,[75]
Come on refreshed, new-added[76] and encouraged;
From which advantage shall we cut him off
210 If at Philippi we do face him there,
These people at our back.

CASSIUS.   Hear me, good brother.

BRUTUS. Under your pardon.[77] You must note beside
That we have tried the utmost of our friends,
Our legions are brimful, our cause is ripe.
215 The enemy increaseth every day;
We, at the height, are ready to decline.
There is a tide in the affairs of men
Which, taken at the flood, leads on to fortune;
Omitted,[78] all the voyage of their life
220 Is bound[79] in shallows and in miseries.
On such a full sea are we now afloat,
And we must take the current when it serves,
Or lose our ventures.[80]

CASSIUS.   Then, with your will,[81] go on;
We'll along ourselves and meet them at Philippi.

225 **BRUTUS.** The deep of night is crept upon our talk,
And nature must obey necessity,
Which we will niggard with a little rest.[82]
There is no more to say?

---

68. have . . . art have as much Stoicism in theory.

69. to our work alive Let us go about the work we have to do as living men.

70. presently *adv.* immediately.

71. offense *n.* harm.

72. of force of necessity.

73. Do stand . . . affection support us only out of fear of force.

74. grudged us contribution given us aid and supplies grudgingly.

75. shall make . . . up will add more to their numbers.

76. new-added reinforced.

77. Under your pardon excuse me.

Reading Skill
Reading Between the Lines What does Brutus' speech indicate about the chances that he and Cassius will lose the war?

78. Omitted *adj.* neglected.
79. bound *adj.* confined.
80. ventures *n.* things put at risk in hope of profit—as a merchant risks goods in sending them by sea.
81. with your will as you wish.
82. niggard . . . rest satisfy stingily with a short sleep.

CASSIUS. No more. Good night.
Early tomorrow will we rise and hence.[83]

[*Enter* LUCIUS.]

BRUTUS. Lucius, my gown.[84] [*Exit* LUCIUS.]
230   Farewell, good Messala.
Good night, Titinius. Noble, noble Cassius,
Good night, and good repose.

CASSIUS.   O my dear brother,
This was an ill beginning of the night.
Never come[85] such division 'tween our souls!
Let it not, Brutus.

[*Enter* LUCIUS, *with the gown.*]

235 **BRUTUS.**   Everything is well.

CASSIUS. Good night, my lord.

BRUTUS.   Good night, good brother.

TITINIUS, MESSALA. Good night, Lord Brutus.

BRUTUS.   Farewell, every one.

                                     [*Exit*]

Give me the gown. Where is thy instrument?[86]

LUCIUS. Here in the tent.

BRUTUS.   What, thou speak'st drowsily?
240 Poor knave,[87] I blame thee not; thou art o'erwatched.[88]
Call Claudius and some other of my men;
I'll have them sleep on cushions in my tent.

LUCIUS. Varro and Claudius!

[*Enter* VARRO *and* CLAUDIUS.]

VARRO. Calls my lord?

245 **BRUTUS.** I pray you, sirs, lie in my tent and sleep.
It may be I shall raise[89] you by and by
On business to my brother Cassius.

VARRO. So please you, we will stand and watch your pleasure.[90]

BRUTUS. I will not have it so; lie down, good sirs;
250 It may be I shall otherwise bethink me.[91]
                  [VARRO *and* CLAUDIUS *lie down.*]
Look. Lucius, here's the book I sought for so;
I put it in the pocket of my gown.

LUCIUS. I was sure your lordship did not give it me.

---

83. **hence** leave.

84. **gown** *n.* dressing gown; robe.

85. **Never come** may there never again come.

86. **instrument** *n.* lute (probably), a small stringed instrument related to the guitar.

87. **knave** (nāv) *n.* servant.
88. **o'erwatched** *adj.* weary with too much watchfulness.

89. **raise** *v.* wake.
90. **watch your pleasure** stay alert for your command.
91. **otherwise bethink me** change my mind.

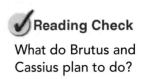

Reading Check

What do Brutus and Cassius plan to do?

BRUTUS. Bear with me, good boy, I am much forgetful.

255 Canst thou hold up thy heavy eyes awhile,
And touch thy instrument a strain or two?[92]

LUCIUS. Ay, my lord, an't[93] please you.

BRUTUS. It does, my boy.
I trouble thee too much, but thou art willing.

LUCIUS. It is my duty, sir.

260 **BRUTUS.** I should not urge thy duty past thy might;
I know young bloods[94] look for a time of rest.

LUCIUS. I have slept, my lord, already.

BRUTUS. It was well done, and thou shalt sleep again;
I will not hold thee long. If I do live,
265 I will be good to thee.

[*Music, and a song*]

This is a sleepy tune. O murd'rous[95] slumber!
Layest thou thy leaden mace[96] upon my boy,
That plays thee music? Gentle knave, good night;
I will not do thee so much wrong to wake thee.
270 If thou dost nod, thou break'st thy instrument;
I'll take it from thee; and, good boy, good night.
Let me see, let me see; is not the leaf[97] turned down
Where I left reading? Here it is, I think.

[*Enter the ghost of* CAESAR.]

How ill this taper burns. Ha! Who comes here?
275 I think it is the weakness of mine eyes
That shapes this monstrous apparition.[98]
It comes upon[99] me. Art thou anything?
Art thou some god, some angel, or some devil,
That mak'st my blood cold, and my hair to stare?[100]
280 Speak to me what thou art.

GHOST. Thy evil spirit, Brutus.

BRUTUS. Why com'st thou?

GHOST. To tell thee thou shalt see me at Philippi.

BRUTUS. Well; then I shall see thee again?

GHOST. Ay, at Philippi.

285 **BRUTUS.** Why, I will see thee at Philippi then.

[*Exit* GHOST.]

---

92. touch . . . a strain or two? play a melody or two on your instrument.
93. an't if it.

94. young bloods young bodies.

95. murd'rous *adj.* deathlike.
96. mace (mās) *n.* staff of office (an allusion to the practice of tapping a person on the shoulder with a mace when arresting him).

97. leaf *n.* page.
98. monstrous apparition ominous ghost.
99. upon *prep.* toward.
100. stare *n.* stand on end.

Reading Skill
Reading Between the Lines Brutus is planning to march to battle at Philippi. In this situation, what might the ghost's warning mean?

Now I have taken heart thou vanishest.
Ill spirit, I would hold more talk with thee.
Boy! Lucius! Varro! Claudius! Sirs, awake!
Claudius!

290 **LUCIUS.** The strings, my lord, are false.[101]

BRUTUS. He thinks he still is at his instrument.
Lucius, awake!

LUCIUS. My lord?

BRUTUS. Didst thou dream, Lucius, that thou so criedst out?

295 **LUCIUS.** My lord, I do not know that I did cry.

BRUTUS. Yes, that thou didst. Didst thou see anything?

LUCIUS. Nothing, my lord.

BRUTUS. Sleep again, Lucius. Sirrah Claudius!
[*To* VARRO] Fellow thou, awake!

300 **VARRO.** My lord?

CLAUDIUS. My lord?

BRUTUS. Why did you so cry out, sirs, in your sleep?

BOTH. Did we, my lord?

BRUTUS.   Ay. Saw you anything?

VARRO. No, my lord, I saw nothing.

CLAUDIUS.   Nor I, my lord.

305 **BRUTUS.** Go and commend me[102] to my brother
      Cassius;
      Bid him set on his pow'rs betimes before,[103]
      And we will follow.

BOTH.   It shall be done, my lord.   [*Exit*]

101. **false** *adj.* out of tune.

Literary Analysis
Conflict What
internal conflict might
the ghost's warning
create for Brutus?

▼ **Critical Viewing**
What does this
ancient Roman coin
suggest about how
war was fought at the
time? **[Interpret]**

102. **commend me** carry my
greetings.
103. **set on . . . before**
advance his troops early,
before me.

Apply the Skills

The Tragedy of Julius Caesar, Act IV

Thinking About the Selection

1. **Respond:** Do you sympathize with anyone in Act IV? Why?
2. **(a) Recall:** In Scene i, what opinion of Lepidus does Antony express? **(b) Infer:** Why is Octavius surprised to hear this opinion? **(c) Connect:** In what way is Antony's behavior toward Lepidus similar to his manipulation of the crowd at Caesar's funeral?
3. **(a) Recall:** What are two accusations Brutus makes against Cassius in Scene iii? **(b) Compare and Contrast:** What difference in their characters does their argument emphasize?
4. **(a) Make a Judgment:** Which character in Act IV do you think would make the best leader for Rome? Explain. **(b) Discuss:** Share your ideas and the reasons for them in a small group discussion. **(c) Evaluate:** As a group, choose the two best candidates and present the reasons for your choices to the class.

Literary Analysis

5. **(a)** Using a diagram like the one shown, identify three **external conflicts** shown or referred to in Act IV. **(b)** Describe two of the **internal conflicts** Brutus experiences in Act IV.

Force 1	Conflict: External / Internal	Force 2
→		←
→		←
→		←

6. **(a)** Explain the connection Brutus makes in Scene iii, lines 18–28 between his reasons for joining the conspirators and his conflict with Cassius. **(b)** Do you think Brutus will feel an internal conflict over his decision to join the conspirators? Explain.

Reading Skill

7. **(a)** To whom is Brutus referring as "a brother" in Scene ii, lines 38–39? **(b)** What is the meaning of what he says?
8. **(a)** What does Cassius say in Scene iii, lines 92–98? **(b)** What is the situation? **(c) Read between the lines** to explain the unspoken significance of his words.

QuickReview

Act IV at a Glance
Antony and Octavius discuss who they must kill. Brutus, whose wife Portia has died, quarrels with Cassius. Later, Caesar's ghost visits Brutus and hints at dangers to come.

Go Online
Assessment
For: Self-test
Visit: www.PHSchool.com
Web Code: eqa-6508

Conflict: the struggle between opposing forces in a literary work. The conflict in a work may be *external* or *internal*.

Reading Between the Lines: finding the deeper meaning of a character's words or actions by relating them to the larger situation

Vocabulary Builder

Practice For each word from the vocabulary list on page 892, write a definition in your own words. Then, write a brief paragraph in which you use the word correctly to describe a profession or career.

1. legacies
2. chastisement
3. mirth
4. rash

Adding Words to Your Vocabulary Using a dictionary, give three different meanings of the word *rash.* Explain which of the meanings are historically connected to the same root word and how. (For more on using a dictionary, see page R6.)

Writing

Imagine that you are a journalist at the time of Caesar's murder. Write an **editorial** to express your opinion on Rome's future.

- Jot down notes on the major events and issues in the play.
- List consequences Rome faces because of the battle between the conspirators and Antony's allies.
- Mark each consequence as desirable or undesirable and add a note explaining why.
- As you draft your editorial, explain the consequences you foresee. Give reasons for each opinion you express.

For *Grammar, Vocabulary,* and *Assessment,* see **Build Language Skills,** pages 926–927.

Extend Your Learning

Listening and Speaking Working in a group, create a **profile** of Brutus for a magazine-style TV news show. Include interviews with Brutus' friends and colleagues and with members of his family, each played by a different member of the group. Incorporate quotations and other details from the play.

Research and Technology Using computer software, produce a **slide-show presentation** on the philosophy of Stoicism. Conduct research to identify the main beliefs of the movement. In your presentation, explain ways in which Brutus' behavior and attitudes reflect or do not reflect the ideas of Stoicism.

Practice these skills with *The Tragedy of Julius Caesar,* Act V.

Literary Analysis

Traditionally, a **tragic hero** is a person, usually of noble birth, who suffers a catastrophe. The hero's choices leading to the catastrophe may reflect a personal shortcoming, such as pride, called a **tragic flaw.** While **Shakespeare's tragic heroes** incorporate these traditional elements, he develops them in new ways:

- He adds complexity to his heroes, who may have opposing desires and who may suffer hesitation and doubt before acting.

- He presents a character's inner turmoil directly, through devices like the *soliloquy,* a speech in which a character thinks aloud.

- He focuses on the choices characters make rather than on fate.

- His characters' problems often concern the difference between the reasons for an action and its outcome. For example, Brutus acts for reasons of honor—the right reasons—but in a world of men who are less than honorable, the results are disastrous.

Academic Standards

- Evaluate interactions between characters and how these affect the plot. (10.3.3)
- Identify and evaluate dialogue, soliloquies, asides, character foils and stage designs in dramatic literature. (10.3.10)

Reading Skill

Shakespeare may emphasize the important qualities of one character by presenting another character with contrasting qualities. When **reading Shakespearean drama,** you can often gain understanding by **comparing and contrasting characters.** Look for similarities and differences in the characters' personalities, situations, behavior, and attitudes.

Brutus	Cassius
nobleman	nobleman
idealistic	practical

Vocabulary Builder

- **fawned** (fônd) *v.* flattered; acted with excessive concern for the wishes and moods of another, as a servant might (p. 912) *She fawned on her new boss as if he were a king.*

- **presage** (prē sāj´) *v.* give a warning sign about a future event (p. 913) *His frown seemed to presage a stern lecture.*

- **demeanor** (di mēn´ ər) *n.* way of conducting oneself; behavior (p. 915) *The child's cooperative demeanor earned him a gold star.*

- **disconsolate** (dis kän´ sə lit) *adj.* so unhappy that nothing brings comfort (p. 918) *Disconsolate, he would not stop weeping for his loss.*

- **misconstrued** (mis´ kən strōōd´) *v.* misinterpreted (p. 918) *I misconstrued the directions and wound up lost.*

- **meditates** (med´ ə tāts´) *v.* thinks deeply (p. 921) *The philosopher quietly meditates on a new idea.*

Review and Anticipate By the end of Act IV, Cassius and Brutus have patched up their quarrel. Brutus persuades Cassius to agree to his strategy—taking the battle to the enemy. He reasons that they should march to the city of Philippi and attack before Octavius and Antony swell their forces with new recruits. The act ends ominously as Brutus is visited by Caesar's ghost. Before disappearing, the ghost tells Brutus that they will meet again at Philippi. As Act V opens, the two armies are poised for battle on the plains of Philippi. Nothing less than the future of Rome is at stake.

→»»»»»» ACT V «««««««

Scene i. *The plains of Philippi.*

[*Enter* OCTAVIUS, ANTONY, *and their Army.*]

    OCTAVIUS. Now, Antony, our hopes are answerèd;
        You said the enemy would not come down,
        But keep the hills and upper regions.
        It proves not so; their battles[1] are at hand;
5   They mean to warn[2] us at Philippi here,
        Answering before we do demand of them.[3]

    ANTONY. Tut, I am in their bosoms,[4] and I know
        Wherefore[5] they do it. They could be content
        To visit other places, and come down
10   With fearful bravery,[6] thinking by this face[7]
        To fasten in our thoughts[8] that they have courage;
        But 'tis not so.

[*Enter a* MESSENGER.]

    MESSENGER.   Prepare you, generals,
        The enemy comes on in gallant show;
        Their bloody sign[9] of battle is hung out,
15   And something to be done immediately.

    ANTONY. Octavius, lead your battle softly[10] on
        Upon the left hand of the even[11] field.

    OCTAVIUS. Upon the right hand I; keep thou the left.

    ANTONY. Why do you cross me in this exigent?[12]

20 **OCTAVIUS.** I do not cross you; but I will do so.   [*March*]

[*Drum. Enter* BRUTUS, CASSIUS, *and their Army;* LUCILIUS, TITINIUS, MESSALA, *and others.*]

---

1. battles *n.* armies.
2. warn *v.* challenge.
3. Answering . . . of them appearing in opposition to us before we challenge them.
4. am in their bosoms know what they are thinking.
5. Wherefore *conj.* why.
6. fearful bravery show of magnificence and pretend courage concealing fear.
7. face *n.* appearance.
8. fasten in our thoughts convince us.

Reading Skill
Comparing and Contrasting What contrast between Octavius and Antony is suggested by their opening speeches?

9. bloody sign red flag.
10. softly *adv.* slowly.
11. even *adj.* level.
12. exigent *n.* critical situation.

✔**Reading Check**

What news does the messenger bring Octavius and Antony?

The Tragedy of Julius Caesar, Act V, Scene i ■ 911

BRUTUS. They stand, and would have parley.[13]

CASSIUS. Stand fast, Titinius, we must out and talk.

OCTAVIUS. Mark Antony, shall we give sign of battle?

ANTONY. No, Caesar, we will answer on their charge.[14]
25   Make forth;[15] the generals would have some words.

OCTAVIUS. Stir not until the signal.

BRUTUS. Words before blows; is it so, countrymen?

OCTAVIUS. Not that we love words better, as you do.

BRUTUS. Good words are better than bad strokes, Octavius.

30 **ANTONY.** In your bad strokes, Brutus, you give good words;
     Witness the hole you made in Caesar's heart,
     Crying "Long live! Hail, Caesar!"

CASSIUS.   Antony,
     The posture[16] of your blows are yet unknown;
     But for your words, they rob the Hybla bees,[17]
     And leave them honeyless.

35 **ANTONY.**   Not stingless too.

BRUTUS. O, yes, and soundless too;
     For you have stol'n their buzzing, Antony,
     And very wisely threat before you sting.

ANTONY. Villains! You did not so, when your vile daggers
40   Hacked one another in the sides of Caesar.
     You showed your teeth[18] like apes, and <u>fawned</u> like hounds,
     And bowed like bondmen,[19] kissing Caesar's feet;
     Whilst damnèd Casca, like a cur,[20] behind
     Struck Caesar on the neck. O you flatterers!

45 **CASSIUS.** Flatterers! Now, Brutus, thank yourself;
     This tongue had not offended so today,
     If Cassius might have ruled.[21]

OCTAVIUS. Come, come, the cause.[22] If arguing make us sweat,
     The proof[23] of it will turn to redder drops.
50   Look,
     I draw a sword against conspirators.
     When think you that the sword goes up[24] again?
     Never, till Caesar's three and thirty wounds
     Be well avenged; or till another Caesar
55   Have added slaughter to the sword of traitors.[25]

BRUTUS. Caesar, thou canst not die by traitors' hands,
     Unless thou bring'st them with thee.

---

13. parley *n.* conference between enemies.

14. answer on their charge meet them when they attack.
15. Make forth go forward.

16. posture *n.* quality.
17. Hybla bees bees from the town of Hybla in Sicily, noted for their sweet honey.
18. showed your teeth grinned.

Vocabulary Builder
fawned (fônd) *v.* flattered; acted with excessive concern for the wishes and moods of another, as a servant might

19. bondmen *n.* slaves.
20. cur *n.* dog.
21. If Cassius might have ruled if Cassius had had his way when he urged that Antony be killed.

Literary Analysis
Shakespeare's Tragic Heroes Which of Brutus' earlier decisions would Cassius call tragic?

22. cause *n.* business at hand.
23. proof *n.* test.
24. goes up goes into its scabbard.
25. till another Caesar... traitors until I, another Caesar, have also been killed by you.

OCTAVIUS.   So I hope.
    I was not born to die on Brutus' sword.

BRUTUS. O, if thou wert the noblest of thy strain,²⁶
60   Young man, thou couldst not die more honorable.

CASSIUS. A peevish²⁷ schoolboy, worthless²⁸ of such honor,
    Joined with a masker and a reveler.²⁹

ANTONY. Old Cassius still!

OCTAVIUS.   Come, Antony; away!
    Defiance, traitors, hurl we in your teeth.
65   If you dare fight today, come to the field;
    If not, when you have stomachs.³⁰

                    [*Exit* OCTAVIUS, ANTONY, *and Army.*]

CASSIUS. Why, now blow wind, swell billow, and swim bark!³¹
    The storm is up, and all is on the hazard.³²

BRUTUS. Ho, Lucilius, hark, a word with you.

                    [LUCILIUS *and* MESSALA *stand forth.*]

LUCILIUS.   My lord?

                    [BRUTUS *and* LUCILIUS *converse apart.*]

CASSIUS. Messala.

MESSALA.   What says my general?

70 **CASSIUS.**   Messala,
    This is my birthday; as this very day
    Was Cassius born. Give me thy hand, Messala:
    Be thou my witness that against my will
    (As Pompey was)³³ am I compelled to set³⁴
75   Upon one battle all our liberties.
    You know that I held Epicurus strong,³⁵
    And his opinion; now I change my mind.
    And partly credit things that do <u>presage</u>.
    Coming from Sardis, on our former ensign³⁶
80   Two mighty eagles fell,³⁷ and there they perched,
    Gorging and feeding from our soldiers' hands,
    Who to Philippi here consorted³⁸ us.
    This morning are they fled away and gone,
    And in their steads do ravens, crows, and kites³⁹
85   Fly o'er our heads and downward look on us
    As we were sickly prey; their shadows seem
    A canopy most fatal,⁴⁰ under which
    Our army lies, ready to give up the ghost.

26. **noblest of thy strain** best of your family.
27. **peevish** silly.
28. **worthless** *adj.* unworthy.
29. **a masker and a reveler** one who attends masquerades and parties; Antony.

30. **stomachs** appetites for battle.

31. **bark** ship.
32. **on the hazard** at stake.
33. **As Pompey was** Against his own judgment, Pompey was urged to do battle against Caesar. The battle resulted in Pompey's defeat and murder.
34. **set** stake.
35. **held Epicurus strong** believed in Epicurus' philosophy that the gods do not interest themselves in human affairs and that omens are merely superstitions.

Vocabulary Builder
presage (prē sāj´)v.
give a warning sign about a future event

36. **former ensign** (en´ sīn´) standard-bearer (soldier carrying a flag) farthest in front.
37. **fell** swooped down.
38. **consorted** *v.* accompanied.
39. **ravens, crows, and kites** scavenger birds, said to gather before a battle.
40. **A canopy most fatal** a rooflike covering foretelling death.

✓ Reading Check

What is Cassius' complaint about the battle they are about to fight?

MESSALA. Believe not so.

CASSIUS.   I but believe it partly,
90   For I am fresh of spirit and resolved
      To meet all perils very constantly.⁴¹

BRUTUS. Even so, Lucilius.

CASSIUS.   Now, most noble Brutus,
      The gods today stand friendly, that we may,
      Lovers⁴² in peace, lead on our days to age!
95   But since the affairs of men rests still incertain,⁴³
      Let's reason with the worst that may befall.⁴⁴
      If we do lose this battle, then is this
      The very last time we shall speak together.
      What are you then determinèd to do?

100 **BRUTUS.** Even by the rule of that philosophy⁴⁵
      By which I did blame Cato⁴⁶ for the death
      Which he did give himself; I know not how,
      But I do find it cowardly and vile,
      For fear of what might fall, so to prevent
105   The time of life,⁴⁷ arming myself with patience
      To stay the providence⁴⁸ of some high powers
      That govern us below.

CASSIUS.   Then, if we lose this battle,
      You are contented to be led in triumph⁴⁹
      Thorough⁵⁰ the streets of Rome?

41. very constantly most resolutely.
42. Lovers *n.* true friends.
43. rests still incertain always remain uncertain.
44. reason . . . befall reason about the worst that may happen.
45. that philosophy here, Stoicism.
46. Cato Marcus Porcius Cato (Cato the Younger) supported Pompey in his quarrel with Caesar and killed himself after Pompey's defeat.
47. so to prevent . . . life thus to anticipate the natural end of life.
48. stay the providence await the ordained fate.

Reading Skill
Comparing and Contrasting Contrast the outlook Brutus expresses here with Cassius' misgivings in lines 70–88.

49. in triumph as a captive in the victor's procession.
50. Thorough *prep.* through.

Literature in Context

History Connection

Roman Triumphs Brutus and Cassius reflect on the humiliation they will experience if they are defeated and brought in triumph to Rome. A *triumph,* held to celebrate a general's victory, included these events:

- Temples were decorated and sacrifices were held.
- The victorious general and his troops marched through the city to the Capitol, preceded by the Roman Senators and trumpeters.
- The triumphant general, dressed in a royal purple toga and holding a laurel branch, rode in a golden chariot drawn by four white horses.
- On display were the spoils of war, including carts full of treasure, and exotic animals.
- Captive enemy leaders—and even their children—were marched in front of the general.
- The people of Rome gathered to view and cheer the spectacle.

Connect to the Literature
Why would Cassius and Brutus wish to escape at any cost being led as prisoners in a triumph?

BRUTUS. No, Cassius, no; think not, thou noble Roman,
110
That ever Brutus will go bound to Rome;
He bears too great a mind. But this same day
Must end that work the ides of March begun;
And whether we shall meet again I know not.
115
Therefore our everlasting farewell take.
Forever, and forever, farewell, Cassius!
If we do meet again, why, we shall smile;
If not, why then this parting was well made.

CASSIUS. Forever, and forever, farewell, Brutus!
120
If we do meet again, we'll smile indeed;
If not, 'tis true this parting was well made.

BRUTUS. Why then, lead on. O, that a man might know
The end of this day's business ere it come!
But it sufficeth that the day will end,
125
And then the end is known. Come, ho! Away!   [*Exit*]

Scene ii. *The field of battle.*

[*Call to arms sounds. Enter* BRUTUS *and* MESSALA.]

BRUTUS. Ride, ride, Messala, ride, and give these bills[1]
Unto the legions on the other side.[2]

[*Loud call to arms*]

Let them set on at once; for I perceive
But cold <u>demeanor</u>[3] in Octavius' wing,
5
And sudden push gives them the overthrow,[4]
Ride, ride, Messala! Let them all come down.[5]   [*Exit*]

Scene iii. *The field of battle.*

[*Calls to arms sound. Enter* CASSIUS *and* TITINIUS.]

CASSIUS. O, look, Titinius, look, the villains[1] fly!
Myself have to mine own turned enemy.[2]
This ensign here of mine was turning back;
I slew the coward, and did take it[3] from him.

5
TITINIUS. O Cassius, Brutus gave the word too early,
Who, having some advantage on Octavius,
Took it too eagerly; his soldiers fell to spoil,[4]
Whilst we by Antony are all enclosed.

[*Enter* PINDARUS.]

PINDARUS. Fly further off, my lord, fly further off!
10
Mark Antony is in your tents, my lord.

Literary Analysis
Shakespeare's Tragic Heroes What details of Brutus' preoccupation with honor, expressed here, reflect his decision to join the conspirators?

1. **bills** written orders.
2. **other side** wing of the army commanded by Cassius.
3. **cold demeanor** (di mēn′ ər) lack of spirit in their conduct.
4. **sudden push . . . overthrow** sudden attack will defeat them.
5. **Let . . . down** attack all at once.

Vocabulary Builder
demeanor (di mēn′ ər) *n.* way of conducting oneself; behavior

1. **villains** here, cowards among his own men.
2. **Myself . . . enemy** I have become an enemy to my own soldiers.
3. **it** here, the ensign's banner.
4. **fell to spoil** began to loot.

 **Reading Check**

How well is the battle going for Cassius and his forces?

Fly, therefore, noble Cassius, fly far off!

CASSIUS. This hill is far enough. Look, look, Titinius!
Are those my tents where I perceive the fire?

TITINIUS. They are, my lord.

CASSIUS. Titinius, if thou lovest me,
15 Mount thou my horse and hide[5] thy spurs in him
Till he have brought thee up to yonder troops
And here again, that I may rest assured
Whether yond troops are friend or enemy.

TITINIUS. I will be here again even with a thought.[6] [*Exit*]

20 **CASSIUS.** Go, Pindarus, get higher on that hill;
My sight was ever thick.[7] Regard[8] Titinius,
And tell me what thou not'st about the field.

[*Exit* PINDARUS.]

This day I breathèd first. Time is come round,
And where I did begin, there shall I end.
25 My life is run his compass.[9] Sirrah, what news?

PINDARUS. [*Above*] O my lord!

CASSIUS. What news?

PINDARUS. [*Above*] Titinius is enclosèd round about
With horsemen that make to him on the spur;[10]
30 Yet he spurs on. Now they are almost on him.
Now, Titinius! Now some light.[11] O, he lights too!
He's ta'en![12] [*Shout*] And, hark! They shout for joy.

CASSIUS. Come down; behold no more.
O, coward that I am, to live so long,
35 To see my best friend ta'en before my face!

[*Enter* PINDARUS.]

Come hither, sirrah.
In Parthia did I take thee prisoner;
And then I swore thee, saving of thy life,[13]
That whatsoever I did bid thee do,
40 Thou shouldst attempt it. Come now, keep thine oath.
Now be a freeman, and with this good sword,
That ran through Caesar's bowels, search[14] this bosom.
Stand not[15] to answer. Here, take thou the hilts,
And when my face is covered, as 'tis now,
45 Guide thou the sword—Caesar, thou art revenged,
Even with the sword that killed thee. [*Dies*]

5. hide sink.

6. even with a thought as quick as a thought.
7. thick dim.
8. Regard observe.

9. his compass its full course.

10. make . . . spur ride toward him at top speed.
11. light dismount from their horses.
12. ta'en taken; captured.

13. swore thee . . . thy life made you promise when I spared your life.
14. search penetrate.
15. Stand not do not wait.

Literary Analysis
Shakespeare's Tragic Heroes What heroic qualities does Cassius show?

▲ **Critical Viewing** Can you tell whether the horseman in this picture is the friend or enemy of the foot soldiers? Explain what your answer shows about the conclusions Cassius draws in battle. **[Connect]**

PINDARUS. So, I am free; yet would not so have been,
Durst[16] I have done my will. O Cassius!
Far from this country Pindarus shall run,
50 Where never Roman shall take note of him.

[*Exit*]

[*Enter* TITINIUS *and* MESSALA.]

MESSALA. It is but change,[17] Titinius; for Octavius
Is overthrown by noble Brutus' power,
As Cassius' legions are by Antony.

TITINIUS. These tidings[18] will well comfort Cassius.

MESSALA. Where did you leave him?

16. **Durst** if I had dared.

17. **change** an exchange.
18. **these tidings** *n.* this news.

Reading Check

What does Cassius think has happened to Titinius?

The Tragedy of Julius Caesar, Act V, Scene iii ■ 917

TITINIUS.   All <u>disconsolate</u>,
55 With Pindarus his bondman, on this hill.

MESSALA. Is not that he that lies upon the ground?

TITINIUS. He lies not like the living. O my heart!

MESSALA. Is not that he?

TITINIUS.   No, this was he, Messala,
60 But Cassius is no more. O setting sun,
    As in thy red rays thou dost sink to night,
    So in his red blood Cassius' day is set.
    The sun of Rome is set. Our day is gone;
    Clouds, dews,[19] and dangers come; our deeds are done!
65 Mistrust of my success[20] hath done this deed.

MESSALA. Mistrust of good success hath done this deed.
    O hateful Error, Melancholy's child,[21]
    Why dost thou show to the apt thoughts of men
    The things that are not?[22] O Error, soon conceived,[23]
70 Thou never com'st unto a happy birth,
    But kill'st the mother that engend'red thee![24]

TITINIUS. What, Pindarus! Where art thou, Pindarus?

MESSALA. Seek him, Titinius, whilst I go to meet
    The noble Brutus, thrusting this report
75 Into his ears. I may say "thrusting" it;
    For piercing steel and darts envenomèd[25]
    Shall be as welcome to the ears of Brutus
    As tidings of this sight.

TITINIUS.   Hie[26] you, Messala,
    And I will seek for Pindarus the while.   [*Exit* MESSALA.]
80 Why didst thou send me forth, brave[27] Cassius?
    Did I not meet thy friends, and did not they
    Put on my brows this wreath of victory,
    And bid me give it thee? Didst thou not hear their shouts?
    Alas, thou hast <u>misconstrued</u> everything!
85 But hold thee,[28] take this garland on thy brow;
    Thy Brutus bid me give it thee, and I
    Will do his bidding. Brutus, come apace,[29]
    And see how I regarded[30] Caius Cassius.
    By your leave,[31] gods. This is a Roman's part:[32]
90 Come, Cassius' sword, and find Titinius' heart.   [*Dies*]

[*Call to arms sounds. Enter* BRUTUS, MESSALA, YOUNG CATO, STRATO,
VOLUMNIUS, *and* LUCILIUS.]

Vocabulary Builder
disconsolate (dis kän´ sə lit) *adj.* so unhappy that nothing brings comfort

19. dews *n.* in Shakespeare's day, dew was considered harmful to the health
20. Mistrust . . . success fear that I would not succeed.

Literary Analysis
Shakespeare's Tragic Heroes According to Messala, what flaw doomed Cassius?

21. hateful Error, Melancholy's child That is, those who are of a gloomy temperament are likely to deceive themselves because they expect the worst.
22. Why dost . . . are not? Why do you fill the receptive imagination of men with false ideas?
23. conceived *v.* formed; born.
24. mother . . . thee Cassius (in this case), who conceived the error.

25. envenomèd (en ven´ əm ed) *adj.* poisoned.

26. Hie *v.* hurry.

27. brave *adj.* noble.

Vocabulary Builder
misconstrued (mis´ kən strood´) *v.* misinterpreted

28. hold thee wait a moment.
29. apace *adv.* quickly.
30. regarded *v.* honored.
31. By your leave with your permission.
32. part *n.* role; duty.

BRUTUS. Where, where, Messala, doth his body lie?

MESSALA. Lo, yonder, and Titinius mourning it.

BRUTUS. Titinius' face is upward.

CATO.   He is slain.

BRUTUS. O Julius Caesar, thou art mighty yet!
95   Thy spirit walks abroad, and turns our swords
         In our own proper entrails.³³   [*Low calls to arms*]

CATO.   Brave Titinius!
         Look, whe'r³⁴ he have not crowned dead Cassius.

BRUTUS. Are yet two Romans living such as these?
         The last of all the Romans, fare thee well!
100   It is impossible that ever Rome
         Should breed thy fellow.³⁵ Friends, I owe moe³⁶ tears
         To this dead man than you shall see me pay.
         I shall find time, Cassius; I shall find time.
         Come, therefore, and to Thasos³⁷ send his body;
105   His funerals shall not be in our camp,
         Lest it discomfort us.³⁸ Lucilius, come,
         And come, young Cato; let us to the field.
         Labeo and Flavius set our battles³⁹ on.
         'Tis three o'clock; and, Romans, yet ere night
110   We shall try fortune in a second fight.   [*Exit*]

Scene iv. *The field of battle.*

[*Call to arms sounds. Enter* BRUTUS, MESSALA, YOUNG CATO, LUCILIUS,
and FLAVIUS.]

BRUTUS. Yet, countrymen, O, yet hold up your heads!

[*Exit, with followers*]

CATO. What bastard¹ doth not? Who will go with me?
         I will proclaim my name about the field.
         I am the son of Marcus Cato,² ho!
5   A foe to tyrants, and my country's friend.
         I am the son of Marcus Cato, ho!

[*Enter* SOLDIERS *and fight.*]

LUCILIUS. And I am Brutus, Marcus Brutus, I;
         Brutus, my country's friend; know me for Brutus!³

[YOUNG CATO *falls.*]

         O young and noble Cato, art thou down?
10   Why, now thou diest as bravely as Titinius,

Literary Analysis
Shakespeare's Tragic Heroes What noble or heroic qualities does Brutus display in his reactions to Cassius' death?

33. **own proper entrails** very own inner organs.

34. **whe'r** whether.

35. **fellow** equal.
36. **moe** *n.* more.
37. **Thasos** an island not far from Philippi.
38. **discomfort us** discourage our soldiers.

39. **battles** armies.

1. **bastard** person who is not a true Roman.
2. **Marcus Cato** Brutus' wife's father.
3. **And I am Brutus** Lucilius impersonates Brutus in order to protect him and confuse the enemy.

Reading Check

What error has led to Cassius' and Titinius' deaths?

And mayst be honored, being Cato's son.

FIRST SOLDIER. Yield, or thou diest.

LUCILIUS.   Only I yield to die.[4]
There is so much that thou wilt kill me straight;[5]
Kill Brutus, and be honored in his death.

15 **FIRST SOLDIER.** We must not. A noble prisoner!

[*Enter* ANTONY.]

SECOND SOLDIER. Room, ho! Tell Antony, Brutus is ta'en.

FIRST SOLDIER. I'll tell thee news. Here comes the general.
Brutus is ta'en, Brutus is ta'en, my lord.

ANTONY. Where is he?

20 **LUCILIUS.** Safe, Antony; Brutus is safe enough.
I dare assure thee that no enemy
Shall ever take alive the noble Brutus.
The gods defend him from so great a shame!
When you do find him, or alive or dead,
25 He will be found like Brutus, like himself.[6]

ANTONY. This is not Brutus, friend, but, I assure you,
A prize no less in worth. Keep this man safe;
Give him all kindness. I had rather have
Such men my friends than enemies. Go on,
30 And see whe'r Brutus be alive or dead,
And bring us word unto[7] Octavius' tent
How everything is chanced.[8]   [*Exit*]

Scene v. *The field of battle.*

[*Enter* BRUTUS, DARDANIUS, CLITUS, STRATO, *and* VOLUMNIUS.]

BRUTUS. Come, poor remains[1] of friends, rest on this rock.

CLITUS. Statilius showed the torchlight,[2] but, my lord,
He came not back; he is or ta'en or slain.

BRUTUS. Sit thee down, Clitus. Slaying is the word;
5   It is a deed in fashion. Hark thee, Clitus. [*Whispers*]

CLITUS. What, I, my lord? No, not for all the world!

BRUTUS. Peace then, no words.

CLITUS.   I'll rather kill myself.

BRUTUS. Hark thee, Dardanius. [*Whispers*]

DARDANIUS.   Shall I do such a deed?

---

4. Only . . . die I will surrender only to die.
5. much . . . straight much honor in it that you will kill me immediately.

6. like himself behaving in a noble way.

7. unto in.
8. How everything is chanced how everything has turned out; what has happened.

1. poor remains pitiful survivors.
2. showed the torchlight signaled with a torch.

CLITUS. O Dardanius!

10 **DARDANIUS.** O Clitus!

CLITUS. What ill request did Brutus make to thee?

DARDANIUS. To kill him, Clitus. Look, he <u>meditates</u>.

CLITUS. Now is that noble vessel[3] full of grief,
    That it runs over even at his eyes.

15 **BRUTUS.** Come hither, good Volumnius; list[4] a word.

VOLUMNIUS. What says my lord?

BRUTUS.   Why, this, Volumnius:
    The ghost of Caesar hath appeared to me
    Two several[5] times by night; at Sardis once,
    And this last night here in Philippi fields.
    I know my hour is come.

20 **VOLUMNIUS.**   Not so, my lord.

BRUTUS. Nay, I am sure it is, Volumnius.
    Thou seest the world, Volumnius, how it goes;
    Our enemies have beat us to the pit.[6]

                         [*Low calls to arms*]

    It is more worthy to leap in ourselves
25   Than tarry till they push us.[7] Good Volumnius,
    Thou know'st that we two went to school together;
    Even for that our love of old, I prithee[8]
    Hold thou my sword-hilts whilst I run on it.

VOLUMNIUS. That's not an office[9] for a friend, my lord.

                         [*Call to arms still*[10]]

30 **CLITUS.** Fly, fly, my lord, there is no tarrying here.

BRUTUS. Farewell to you; and you; and you, Volumnius.
    Strato, thou hast been all this while asleep;
    Farewell to thee too, Strato. Countrymen,
    My heart doth joy that yet in all my life
35   I found no man but he was true to me.
    I shall have glory by this losing day
    More than Octavius and Mark Antony
    By this vile conquest shall attain unto.[11]
    So fare you well at once, for Brutus' tongue
40   Hath almost ended his life's history.
    Night hangs upon mine eyes; my bones would rest,
    That have but labored to attain this hour.[12]

Vocabulary Builder
meditates (med´ ə
tāts´) *v.* thinks deeply

3. **vessel** container of liquid;
here, a metaphor for Brutus.
4. **list** hear.

5. **several** separate.

Literary Analysis
**Shakespeare's Tragic
Heroes** Why does this
scene of Brutus
weeping add
complexity or depth
to his character?

6. **pit** trap or grave.
7. **tarry . . . us** wait until they
kill us.
8. **prithee** (prith´ ē)
interjection ask you, please;
"pray thee."
9. **office** task.
10. **still** continuing.

Literary Analysis
**Shakespeare's Tragic
Heroes** What tragic
flaw in Brutus is
revealed in lines
33–35?

11. **By this . . . unto** by this
evil victory shall gain. (Brutus
sees the victory of Octavius
and Antony as causing the
downfall of Roman freedom.)
12. **this hour** time of death.

**Reading Check**

What does Brutus ask
of his servants?

[*Call to arms sounds. Cry within, "Fly, fly, fly!"*]

CLITUS. Fly, my lord, fly!

BRUTUS.   Hence! I will follow.

[*Exit* CLITUS, DARDANIUS, *and* VOLUMNIUS.]

I prithee, Strato, stay thou by thy lord,
45   Thou art a fellow of a good respect.[13]
Thy life hath had some smatch[14] of honor in it;
Hold then my sword, and turn away thy face,
While I do run upon it. Wilt thou, Strato?

STRATO. Give me your hand first. Fare you well, my lord.

50 **BRUTUS.** Farewell, good Strato—Caesar, now be still;
I killed not thee with half so good a will.
[*Dies*]

[*Call to arms sounds. Retreat sounds. Enter* ANTONY, OCTAVIUS, MESSALA, LUCILIUS, *and the Army.*]

OCTAVIUS. What man is that?

MESSALA. My master's man.[15] Strato, where is thy master?

STRATO. Free from the bondage you are in, Messala;
55   The conquerors can but make a fire of him
For Brutus only overcame himself,[16]
And no man else hath honor[17] by his death.

LUCILIUS. So Brutus should be found. I thank thee, Brutus,
That thou hast proved Lucilius' saying[18] true.

60 **OCTAVIUS.** All that served Brutus, I will entertain them.[19]
Fellow, wilt thou bestow[20] thy time with me?

STRATO. Ay, if Messala will prefer[21] me to you.

OCTAVIUS. Do so, good Messala.

MESSALA. How died my master, Strato?

65 **STRATO.** I held the sword, and he did run on it.

MESSALA. Octavius, then take him to follow thee,
That did the latest service to my master.

ANTONY. This was the noblest Roman of them all.
All the conspirators save[22] only he
70   Did that[23] they did in envy of great Caesar;
He, only in a general honest thought[24]
And common good to all, made one of them.[25]
His life was gentle,[26] and the elements
So mixed[27] in him that Nature might stand up

13. **respect** reputation.
14. **smatch** smack or taste.

Reading Skill
Comparing and
Contrasting What do
the differences in the
way in which Brutus
and Cassius meet
death show about
their characters?

15. **man** servant.
16. **Brutus only overcame himself** only Brutus, no one else, defeated Brutus.
17. **no man else hath honor** no other man gains honor.
18. **Lucilius' saying** See Act V, Scene iv, lines 21–22.
19. **entertain them** take them into my service.
20. **bestow** spend.
21. **prefer** recommend.

22. **save** except.
23. **that** what.
24. **only in a general honest thought** with only public-minded motives.
25. **made one of them** became one of the conspirators.
26. **gentle** noble.
27. **So mixed** well balanced.

75   And say to all the world, "This was a man!"

   OCTAVIUS. According to his virtue,[28] let us use[29] him
      With all respect and rites of burial.
      Within my tent his bones tonight shall lie,
      Most like a soldier ordered honorably.[30]
80   So call the field[31] to rest, and let's away
      To part[32] the glories of this happy day.   [*Exit all.*]

▲ **Critical Viewing**
Which details in this
film still suggest the
respect that Octavius
and Antony have for
Brutus, even in
defeat? **[Analyze]**

28. virtue excellence.
29. use treat.
30. ordered honorably
treated with honor.
31. field army.
32. part share.

Apply the Skills

***The Tragedy of Julius Caesar*, Act V**

Thinking About the Selection

1. **Respond:** How did you respond to Brutus' death?
2. **(a) Recall:** What do Cassius and Brutus each plan to do if they lose the battle? **(b) Analyze Cause and Effect:** In making these plans, what do they hope to avoid? Support your answer. **(c) Draw Conclusions:** What do their plans show about their values?
3. **(a) Recall:** What does Cassius believe has happened to Titinius when Titinius rides to his tents? **(b) Analyze Cause and Effect:** What does his interpretation of events lead him to do?
   (c) Connect: In what way is this reaction like his reaction in Act I to signs that Caesar would become king?
4. **(a) Interpret:** What does Brutus mean when he says, "My heart doth joy that yet in all my life / I found no man but he was true to me"? **(b) Make a Judgment:** Do these lines express a positive attitude or a blindness toward others? Explain. **(c) Discuss:** Discuss your interpretation with a partner. Then, explain whether or not the discussion changed your mind and why.

Literary Analysis

5. **(a)** Using a chart like the one shown, give examples showing that Brutus and Caesar have the qualities of traditional **tragic heroes.**

Noble Birth	Suffers Catastrophe	Tragic Flaw

   (b) Which character has more characteristics of **Shakespeare's tragic heroes?** Support your answer with details from the text.
6. **(a)** Give two examples of situations in which Brutus expects others to act honorably and they fail to do so. **(b)** What is the outcome of each situation? **(c)** What do these situations suggest about Brutus' view of himself and the world?

Reading Skill

7. **(a) Compare and contrast** Cassius and Brutus. Give specific examples in support of your points. **(b)** What do the differences between the two help to emphasize about Brutus' character?

Act V at a Glance
The armies of Brutus and Cassius meet the forces of Antony and Octavius. Learning of Cassius' death and recognizing his own defeat, Brutus kills himself. Antony ends the play with a tribute to Brutus.

Go Online
Assessment
For: Self-test
Visit: www.PHSchool.com
Web Code: eqa-6509

Tragic Hero: the main character of a play, usually of noble birth, who suffers a catastrophe
Tragic Flaw: the personal shortcoming that leads a tragic hero to make disastrous errors

Comparing and Contrasting Characters: finding similarities and differences in the characters' personalities, situations, behavior, and attitudes

Vocabulary Builder

Practice Use a vocabulary word from the list on page 910 to write a complete sentence about each numbered item. Explain your choices.

1. being too eager to please
2. watching the sun set
3. learning a new language
4. losing a friend
5. hearing distant thunder
6. making a good impression

Adding Words to Your Vocabulary The vocabulary word *misconstrued* begins with the prefix *mis-*. Using a dictionary, find the word formed by adding *mis-* to another word from the vocabulary list. Explain how adding *mis-* changes the meaning of the vocabulary word. (For more on using a dictionary, see page R6.)

Writing

An **obituary** is a notice that someone has died. Write an obituary for a character who dies in *Julius Caesar.*

- Review the play for details about the character's life and personality.
- Choose an effective organization. For example, open with the circumstances of death and a brief introduction of the character's life.
- Use details to construct a unified picture of the character's life.

For *Grammar, Vocabulary,* and *Assessment,* see **Build Language Skills,** pages 926–927.

Extend Your Learning

Listening and Speaking With a small group of students, hold a **group screening** of a filmed production of *Julius Caesar.* Afterward, discuss the production, starting with these questions:

- How effective was each actor in a major role?
- How effective was the staging of the action?
- In what ways did the production surprise you, given your reading of the play?

Have two members of the group serve as notetakers. Afterward, review the discussion notes, and analyze the differences in members' responses. Make a chart showing the reactions to the film.

Research and Technology Prepare a **research note** to the play in which you explain what happened in Rome after the events depicted in *Julius Caesar.* Conduct research on Marc Antony, Octavius, and general Roman history. Share your research note with classmates.

Build Language Skills

The Tragedy of Julius Caesar

Vocabulary Skill

Word Roots The **word root** *-cred-* means "believe." Words that contain this word root have meanings related to *believing* or *truth*. For example, a *credible* witness is one who can be believed.

The **word root** *-doc-* comes from a Latin word meaning "teach." Words containing this word root have meanings related to the passing on of information. For example, a *document* provides information.

Practice In a dictionary, look up each of the words listed. For each, explain how the root's meaning contributes to the word's meaning.

1. docudrama   3. doctrinaire   5. credential

2. credited   4. docent

Grammar Lesson

Clauses A **clause** is a group of words that has both a subject and a verb. An **independent clause** can stand by itself as a sentence.

> **Independent Clause:** *We visited the plains.*

A **subordinate clause**, however, cannot stand by itself. There are three types of subordinate clauses: **adjective clauses, adverb clauses,** and **noun clauses.**

> **Adjective Clause:** Shelly forgot to return the calculator *that he borrowed from Tito.* (modifies *calculator*)

> **Adverb Clause:** *Although it was cold out,* we jumped in the pool. (modifies *jumped*)

> **Noun Clause:** *Whatever you decide* is fine with me. (functions as the subject of the sentence)

Practice Complete each sentence by adding the type of clause asked for in parentheses.

1. (Independent clause) when he was small.

2. She placed her hand on the page (adverb clause).

3. (Noun clause) came alive.

4. While his mother read, (independent clause).

5. He loved literature (adjective clause).

MorePractice

For more practice with clauses, see the Grammar Handbook, pp. R43–R44.

𝒲𝒢 Prentice Hall Writing and Grammar Connection: Chapter 20, Section 2

Reading: Reading Shakespeare

Standards
Assessed

• 10.2.1
• 10.2.4

Directions: *Read the selection. Then, answer the questions.*

CALIBAN.   I must eat my dinner.
This island's mine by Sycorax my mother,
Which thou tak'st from me. When thou camest first,
Thou strok'st me and made much of me; wouldst give me
Water with berries in't; and teach me how
To name the bigger light, and how the less,[1]
That burn by day and night. And then I lov'd thee
And show'd thee all the qualities o' th' isle, . . .
          —from *The Tempest*, Act I, Scene ii, by William Shakespeare

1. bigger . . . less see the Bible, Gen. 1:16: "And God made two great lights; the greater light to rule the day, and the lesser light to rule the night."

1. Which of the following is the best para-phrase of Caliban's speech?

A I abused you and treated you like a slave, but you forgave me.

B I have always served you loyally.

C You were kind to me and I returned your kindness, but you betrayed me.

D I was trapped by this rock, and you freed me, but then you betrayed me.

2. What does the annotation help the reader do?

A understand the allusions

B understand the vocabulary

C find the rhythm of the speech

D understand the setting

Timed Writing: Explanation [Critical Stance]

Choose one honorable character in *The Tragedy of Julius Caesar* and explain why this character behaved honorably. Begin by formulating your own definition of honorable behavior. Consider both the obligations that people have to their own consciences, as well as to each other. As you write, use specifics from the text for support.
(40 minutes)

Writing Workshop: *Work in Progress*

Research Report

For a research report you might write, fold a piece of paper in three and label the three sections as follows; "to persuade," "to recommend," and "to inform." Under each label, write one or two topics on which you might write a report with the purpose described. Put these notes in your portfolio.

Reading Informational Materials

Signs

In Part 2, you learned skills to help you in **reading Shakespeare**. Reading signs and reading Shakespeare both require you to construct a larger picture from a few details. Paying attention to basic details is an important part of understanding something as simple as a sign or as complex as a historical drama.

Academic Standards

- Analyze formatting of informational documents. (10.2.1)
- Write for different purposes and audiences. (10.5.8)

About Signs

Signs are publicly displayed posters, placards, or other markers that communicate information. The information is presented so that it is available at any time to anyone. For example, when you approach a store, you may see a sign that reads "open" or "closed." Without asking a question or opening a book, you have taken in important information—you know whether or not you can enter. Signs can provide the following types of information:

- Rules
- Warnings
- Hours of operation
- Identifying information, as for an animal in the zoo
- Background information, as for museum exhibits

The signs you will read here are from the Folger Shakespeare Library in Washington, D.C. The first one appears at the visitors' entrance; the second one informs visitors about Queen Elizabeth I, who ruled England at the time Shakespeare's plays were written and first performed.

Reading Skill

When you read a sign, you usually have a specific purpose—you need particular information. In a museum, you may want to use **signs as research aids.** Once you have identified your purpose, you can use the physical presentation, or appearance of the text, to easily locate the information you need. **Use text format**—the size, color, and arrangement of different parts of the text—to help you locate information quickly.

Practice connecting your purpose to your reading of signs by using a K-W-L chart as you read the signs in this lesson. Your purpose is reflected in the questions you ask in the "What I Want to Know" column.

What I **Know**	What I **W**ant to Know	What I **Learned**
This is a museum.		

FOLGER
SHAKESPEARE LIBRARY

VISITOR ENTRANCE

ELIZABETHAN THEATRE
BOX OFFICE OPENS
ONE HOUR BEFORE EVENTS

EXHIBITIONS

◄ELIZABETHAN GARDEN

MONDAY–SATURDAY
10:00 A.M. – 4:00 P.M.

RESEARCH ENTRANCE ►
READING ROOM • MUSEUM SHOP
ADMINISTRATIVE OFFICES

CLOSED ALL FEDERAL HOLIDAYS

For clarity and ease of reading, each piece of information starts on a separate line.

The more important information is printed in a larger type size.

Elizabeth I

"TO BE A KING AND WEAR A CROWN is a thing more glorious to them that see it than it is pleasant to them that bear it." These words, spoken by Elizabeth I to her Parliament in 1601, might just as well be echoed by any head of state today. All the perks of office—the fine clothes, jewels, servants, and now, private planes and media attention—are there to be enjoyed, but they come with the high price of responsibility to the people and the nation. Elizabeth was not elected, she inherited this responsibility from her father, Henry VIII, but she took it seriously and was educated to be a prince. In 1558 after the death of her Catholic sister Mary, Elizabeth came to the throne and reigned for forty-four years. Though she restored the Protestant church to England, she resisted extremes in religion as well as policy. She also resisted pressure by her male council and Parliament to marry, turning the many offers for her hand into a game of political chess. She was a true "career woman" long before the term was coined; her job was her life.

Now, four hundred years after Elizabeth's death in March of 1603, the Folger Library honors her memory and her reign. Because Emily and Henry Folger focused their collecting on the age of Shakespeare, when Elizabeth was queen, the Folger Library has the largest collection of artifacts relating to Elizabeth in America. She has never really gone out of style. Every generation has re-read her through their own ideas of womanhood, and today perhaps we can appreciate her political skills more than did any other era. In her "Golden Speech" quoted above, she also said: "though you have had and may have many princes more mighty and wise sitting in this seat, yet you never had or shall have any that will be more careful and loving."

Major support for this exhibition comes from the Winton and Carolyn Blount Exhibition Fund of the Folger Shakespeare Library.

Monitor Your Progress

Test Practice

Standards Assessed
• 10.2.1
• 10.5.8

Reading: Using Signs as Research Aids

Directions: *Choose the letter of the best answer to each question about the two signs.*

1. Judging from the arrangement and size of text, which piece of information did the designers of the visitor-entrance sign consider most important?
   A hours of operation
   B the location of the reading room
   C the location of the museum shop
   D the name of the museum

2. On which of the following research topics does the sign introducing "Elizabeth I" give information?
   A English-speaking theater past and present
   B the ascension of Elizabeth I to the throne of England
   C the monarchy following the death of Elizabeth I
   D Shakespeare's connection to Elizabeth I

Reading: Comprehension and Interpretation

Directions: *Write your answers on a separate piece of paper.*

3. Given the notice "Closed All Federal Holidays," name three holidays on which you expect the Folger Shakespeare Library to be closed. **[Generating]**

4. Of the three facilities listed under the heading "Research Entrance," which would be the most important for someone engaged in a research project? Explain. **[Evaluating]**

5. Which idea expressed in the sign introducing the exhibit "Elizabeth I" is most important for a present-day museum-goer? Why? **[Evaluating]**

Timed Writing: Description [Connections]

In an essay, make a detailed proposal for a research project that might be aided by a visit to the Folger Shakespeare Library. Explain the ways in which signs used in the exhibits would add to the efficiency and accuracy of the researcher's task. **(35 minutes)**

Character Motivation

A **character's motivation** consists of the passions, convictions, and even illusions that guide his or her actions and shape his or her words. To develop your own understanding of a character's motivation, answer the following questions as you read:

Academic Standards

- Evaluate interactions between characters and how these affect the plot. (10.3.3)
- Analyze characters' traits through narration and dialogue. (10.3.4)

- What does the character say is important to him or her?
- What goals does the character pursue?
- How does the character feel and behave toward other characters?
- What is the character's family and social background?
- Are there any striking similarities or differences between this character and others? If so, what are they?

Comparing Characters' Motivations

Both William Shakespeare's *The Tragedy of Julius Caesar* and Lorraine Hansberry's *A Raisin in the Sun* feature characters motivated by a concern for dignity. As you read, compare the ideas of dignity that motivate Walter and Mama in *A Raisin in the Sun* with those motivating Cassius, Brutus, and Caesar in *Julius Caesar*. You can narrow your comparison by focusing on these passages from Shakespeare's play:

Character: _____

Challenge to Character's Dignity	
Character's Response	
What Character Finds Essential	

- Act I, Scene ii, lines 90–161 (pp. 832–834)—Cassius explains why he opposes Caesar's rise to power.
- Act II, Scene i, lines 114–140 (p. 851)—Brutus explains why the conspirators should not swear an oath and what their true motives should be.
- Act III, Scene i, lines 58–73 (pp. 872–873)—Caesar explains why he will not pardon a man he has exiled.

Use a diagram like the one shown to help track your comparison.

Vocabulary Builder

- **looming** (lо̄о̄m′ iŋ) *adj.* appearing unclearly but in a threatening form; threatening to occur (p. 935) *I could not make out the name on the ship looming in the fog.*

- **dignity** (dig′ nə tē) *n.* quality of deserving respect and honor; self-respect (p. 936) *Though the others lost our respect, she remained a figure of great dignity.*

Build Understanding

Connecting to the Literature

Reading/Writing Connection Cold, hunger, illness, and poverty—people can endure a great deal. The characters in *A Raisin in the Sun* and in *Julius Caesar,* however, wonder whether life without dignity is worth living. Write a few thoughts on what people need to maintain their self-respect. Use at least three of the following words: *respond, focus, perceive, equate.*

Meet the Author

Lorraine **Hansberry** (1930–1965)

An important voice of the civil rights era, Lorraine Hansberry grew up in Chicago. "Both of my parents were strong-minded, civic-minded, exceptionally race-minded people who made enormous sacrifices on behalf of the struggle for civil rights throughout their lifetimes," she once recalled.

Biographical Inspiration When Hansberry was about eight years old, her parents tried to move to a white neighborhood. Property owners in the neighborhood blocked African American families from purchasing homes there. Hansberry's father fought the restrictions all the way to the U.S. Supreme Court, where he eventually won his case. Years later, Hansberry used that experience as the basis of her award-winning play *A Raisin in the Sun,* which opened on Broadway in 1959.

For a biography of William Shakespeare (1564–1616), the author of *The Tragedy of Julius Caesar,* see page 822.

For: More about the author
Visit: www.PHSchool.com
Web Code: eqe-9505

from A Raisin in the Sun
from Act I, Scene II

Lorraine Hansberry

Background The Youngers are an African American family living in Chicago some time after World War II. During this period, African Americans faced a shortage of economic opportunities and were deprived of many civil rights. Walter Younger, his wife Ruth, and their son Travis live with Walter's mother and his younger sister Beneatha. Walter's father has passed away. When the family learns that Walter's mother is to receive a check from the father's insurance, Walter pleads with his mother to give him money to invest in a store he wants to open with friends. She wants instead to purchase a new home and to pay for Beneatha's education.

WALTER: (*Picks up the check*) Do you know what this money means to me? Do you know what this money can do for us? (*Puts it back*) Mama—Mama—I want so many things . . .

MAMA: Yes, son—

WALTER: I want so many things that they are driving me kind of crazy . . . Mama—look at me.

MAMA: I'm looking at you. You a good-looking boy. You got a job, a nice wife, a fine boy and—

WALTER: A job. (*Looks at her*) Mama, a job? I open and close car doors all day long. I drive a man around in his limousine and I say, "Yes, sir; no, sir; very good, sir; shall I take the Drive, sir?" Mama, that ain't no kind of job . . . that ain't nothing at all. (*Very quietly*) Mama, I don't know if I can make you understand.

MAMA: Understand what, baby?

WALTER: (*Quietly*) Sometimes it's like I can see the future stretched out in front of me—just plain as day. The future, Mama. Hanging over there at the edge of my days. Just waiting for me—a big, <u>looming</u> blank space—full of nothing. Just waiting for me. But it

Literary Analysis
Character Motivation Explain what type of life Walter seems to desire.

Vocabulary Builder
looming (lo͞om′ iŋ) *adj.* appearing unclearly but in a threatening form; threatening to occur

◀ **Critical Viewing** This photograph is from the 2004 Broadway production of *A Raisin in the Sun*. Which details of the image suggest Mama's key role in running the family? **[Interpret]**

from *A Raisin in the Sun* ■ 935

don't have to be. (*Pause. Kneeling beside her chair*) Mama—sometimes when I'm downtown and I pass them cool, quiet-looking restaurants where them white boys are sitting back and talking 'bout things . . . sitting there turning deals worth millions of dollars . . . sometimes I see guys don't look much older than me—

MAMA: Son—how come you talk so much 'bout money?

WALTER: (*With immense passion*) Because it is life, Mama!

MAMA: (*Quietly*) Oh—(*Very quietly*) So now it's life. Money is life. Once upon a time freedom used to be life—now it's money. I guess the world really do change . . .

WALTER: No—it was always money, Mama. We just didn't know about it.

MAMA: No . . . something has changed. (*She looks at him*) You something new, boy. In my time we was worried about not being lynched and getting to the North if we could and how to stay alive and still have a pinch of <u>dignity</u> too . . . Now here come you and Beneatha—talking 'bout things we ain't never even thought about hardly, me and your daddy. You ain't satisfied or proud of nothing we done. I mean that you had a home; that we kept you out of trouble till you was grown; that you don't have to ride to work on the back of nobody's streetcar—You my children—but how different we done become.

WALTER: (*A long beat. He pats her hand and gets up*) You just don't understand, Mama, you just don't understand.

Thinking About the Selection

1. **Respond:** Do you sympathize more with Walter or his mother? Explain.

2. **(a) Recall:** What does Walter do for a living? **(b) Infer:** How does this job make him feel about the future? Support your answer with a quotation from the selection.

3. **(a) Interpret:** Why does Walter think that money "is life"? **(b) Make a Judgment:** Do you agree with him? Explain why or why not.

4. **(a) Summarize:** What is Mama's reaction to Walter's complaint? **(b) Compare and Contrast:** Compare Mama's goals in life with Walter's.

5. **Make a Judgment:** In your opinion, should Mama give Walter the money, or should she use it for a new home? Explain.

Apply the Skills

The Tragedy of Julius Caesar • from *A Raisin in the Sun*

Comparing Characters' Motivations

1. **(a)** Using a chart like the one shown, analyze Walter's **motivation** in the scene from *A Raisin in the Sun.*
   (b) Compare Walter's feelings to those that Cassius expresses in *The Tragedy of Julius Caesar,* Act I, Scene ii, lines 90–161.

Social Background	Personality	Feelings	Values	Goals

2. **(a)** What ideals motivate Brutus' speech in Act II, Scene i, lines 114–140? **(b)** Compare these ideals to those described by Walter's mother. **(c)** What is one difference between Brutus' goal in joining the conspiracy and Walter's dream of having a business?

3. **(a)** Summarize Caesar's ideas about his own dignity, as expressed in *Julius Caesar,* Act III, Scene i, lines 58–73. **(b)** Is his notion of dignity more like that of Walter or of Walter's mother, or is it different from both? Explain.

Writing to Compare Literary Works

Write a brief essay in which you compare the ideas of dignity that motivate characters in *The Tragedy of Julius Caesar* with those that motivate Walter and Walter's mother in *A Raisin in the Sun.* Use these questions to get started:

- What are each character's beliefs, goals, feelings, personality, and background?
- What are the merits and drawbacks of each character's ideals?
- Which character best represents your own ideals?

Vocabulary Builder

Practice **Analogies** match the relationship in one pair of words with the relationship in another pair. For each item, choose the word that best completes the analogy.

1. looming : fading :: bored : **(a)** excited
   (b) disinterested
   (c) sad

2. dignity : insult :: property : **(a)** investment
   (b) vandalism
   (c) purchase

QuickReview

Character Motivation: the passions, convictions, and illusions that guide a character's actions and shape his or her words

Go **O**nline
Author Link
For: Self-test
Visit: www.PHSchool.com
Web Code: eqa-6510

Reading

Directions: *Questions 1–5 are based on the following selection.*

    SEYTON. The queen, my lord, is dead.
    MACBETH. She should[1] have died hereafter;
    There would have been time for such a word.[2]
    Tomorrow, and tomorrow, and tomorrow,
5   Creeps in this petty pace from day to day,
    To the last syllable of recorded time;
    And all our yesterdays have lighted fools
    The way to dusty death. Out, out, brief candle!
    Life's but a walking shadow, a poor player
10   That struts and frets his hour upon the stage
    And then is heard no more. It is a tale
    Told by an idiot, full of sound and fury
    Signifying nothing.
—from *The Tragedy of Macbeth*, Act V, Scene v, by William Shakespeare

1. should would.
2. word i.e., the announcement of her death.

1. **By reading between the lines, what mood do you find is expressed in the passage?**
   A enthusiasm
   B anger
   C despair
   D optimism

2. **Which of the following is the best paraphrase of the last five lines?**
   A Life is meaningless.
   B Life is full of rich experiences.
   C Life is full of dramatic possibilities.
   D Make the most of the present because the future is uncertain.

3. **Which concern is conveyed by the image "Out, out, brief candle"?**
   A longing for death
   B wish for his personal safety
   C the strange workings of the mind
   D the cruelty of nature

4. **Which of the following is an image of life?**
   A last syllable
   B dusty death
   C lighted fools
   D poor player

5. **Which of the following is the best paraphrase of the phrase "sound and fury" in line 12?**
   A delight and disappointment
   B pain and natural disasters
   C sensation and emotion
   D music and excitement

Directions: *Choose the sentence that uses the given word correctly.*

Standards
Assessed

• 10.3.4
• 10.3.5
• 10.6.4

6. credible
  A   Because the witness obviously lied, the jury found his testimony *credible.*
  B   His alibi was confirmed by witnesses and was deemed *credible.*
  C   Hercules was able to perform many *credible* feats of strength that were far beyond the capacity of normal men.
  D   The broken, darkened window made for a *credible* holiday display.

7. integrity
  A   Eggs spoiled the omelette's *integrity.*
  B   Focusing a camera results in photographs of low *integrity.*
  C   The *integrity* of the rock music coming from next door was overwhelming.
  D   A bank must maintain a spotless record of *integrity* before customers will trust it.

8. superficial
  A   Even a *superficial* reading of the article revealed numerous errors.
  B   An appreciation of a literary work requires a *superficial* reading of the text.
  C   Greek gods had *superficial* powers.
  D   The judge's *superficial* attitude intimidated most of the lawyers.

9. legitimate
  A   My e-mail malfunctioned, which was a *legitimate* for a paper being late.
  B   Counterfeit currency is usually *legitimate.*
  C   The judge will *legitimate* the jury without a lawyer's intervention.
  D   We found *legitimate* difficulties that needed to be addressed.

10. document
  A   If you *document* two slices, there will be only one left for Harry.
  B   To *document* the meeting, he took notes.
  C   A *document* was needed to finish the electronic connection.
  D   They *document* each game, so we have no idea who won.

Directions: *Choose the answer that is closest in meaning to the given word.*

11. credence
  A   fraudulent   C   belief
  B   fact   D   frivolous

12. incredulous
  A   doubting   C   frightened
  B   gullible   D   dutiful

13. docile
  A   round   C   warm
  B   cold   D   obedient

14. indoctrinate
  A   instruct   C   destroy
  B   erode   D   astonish

15. credo
  A   explanations   C   convictions
  B   strategies   D   pathways

Spelling Workshop

Words With Double Letters

Words with one or more sets of **double letters** are common in English. Some of these words can cause spelling problems even for good spellers.

Seeing Double Words with double letters can cause all sorts of spelling problems. If a word has one set of double letters, like *dilemma,* it is often hard to remember which letter to double. And when a word has two or more sets of double letters, like *embarrass,* people tend to forget to double one of them. Look carefully at the words in the list and make up clues to help yourself remember any that you tend to spell wrong.

Word List
commitment
embarrass
accommodations
questionnaire
appalling
connoisseur
harass
millennium
bookkeeper
dilemma

Practice Read the clues that tell how many times the given letters appear in each word. Write the word from the Word List that matches each clue. Use each word only once.

1. l-2, n-2
2. p-2, l-2
3. r-2, s-2
4. k-2, p-1
5. r-1, s-2
6. c-2, m-2
7. l-1, m-2
8. m-2, t-1, m-1, t-1
9. t-1, n-2, r-1
10. n-2, s-2

A. Directions: *Write the letter of the sentence in which the underlined word is spelled correctly.*

1. A Each member received a <u>questionairre</u>.
    B Did the officers mean to <u>embarass</u> us with some of the things they asked?
    C For example, they asked about our <u>committment</u> to education.
    D Wouldn't it be <u>appalling</u> if no one responded?

2. A A few years ago, office workers faced a <u>dillema</u>.
    B Not only a new century, but a new <u>milennium</u>, began.
    C Every <u>bookkeeper</u> needed to change dates from 19__ to 20__.
    D Was it fair to <u>harrass</u> employees who forgot to fix their own records?

3. A The <u>conoisseur</u> liked to travel in style.
    B The <u>accomodations</u> he chose were always the finest.
    C He also had a <u>commitment</u> to dining at the best restaurants.
    D Clearly, spending huge amounts of money did not <u>embarras</u> him.

4. A Tour guides must sometimes deal with a <u>dillemma</u>.
    B They know that unruly travelers sometimes <u>harass</u> others on the trips.
    C Should they request separate <u>acomodations</u> for these tourists?
    D After all, it would be <u>apalling</u> if another tourist's trip were ruined by one lout's rudeness.

B. Directions: *Write the letter of the correct spelling of the word that completes the sentence.*

1. Only a few generations are able to witness a new _____.
    A milennium   C millenium
    B millennium   D milenium

2. She is a _____ of classical music.
    A connoisseur   C connoiseur
    B conoiseur   D conoisseur

3. A long _____ came in the mail.
    A questionair   C questionnaire
    B questionnair   D questionaire

4. It was a _____ because both events were on the same day.
    A dillemma   C dillema
    B dilema   D dilemma

5. I am _____ by their rude behavior.
    A embarased   C embarassed
    B embarrazed   D embarrassed

6. We can't find _____; all the lodging is booked.
    A acomodations   C accommodations
    B accomodations   D acommodations

Research Writing: Research Report

Research writing presents, interprets, and analyzes information gathered through comprehensive study of a subject. Writing a research report is a good way to learn about a topic that is outside your own experience. As you gather information from outside sources, you gain a deeper understanding of the subject, and you can then share this knowledge with readers. Use the steps outlined in this workshop to write a research report.

Assignment Write a research report on a topic that interests you and is substantial enough to merit an in-depth study.

What to Include Your research report should feature these elements:
- a specific, narrow topic that is summarized in a thesis statement
- relevant information from primary and secondary sources
- a logical organization of details and ideas
- correct documentation of sources, following an accepted format
- error-free grammar, including correct use of adverb clauses

To preview the criteria on which your research report may be assessed, see the rubric on page 953.

Writing Workshop: *Work in Progress*

If you have completed the Work-in-Progress assignment, you have several ideas in your portfolio that you might wish to pursue in your research report. You may continue to develop these ideas, or you might choose to explore a new idea as you complete this Writing Workshop.

 Academic Standards

- Use clear research questions and methods to compile evidence from many sources. (10.4.4)
- Synthesize information from multiple different sources. (10.4.6)
- Write expository compositions. (10.5.3)

Using the Form
You may use elements of research writing in these types of texts:
- biographies
- opinion papers
- lab reports
- annotated bibliographies

Reading / Writing Connection

To get a feel for research writing, read "Making History With Vitamin C" by Penny Le Couteur and Jay Burreson on page 144.

Prewriting

Choosing Your Topic

Scan your notebooks. Follow your instincts and interests when looking for a topic. Review the notes you have taken in any subject—from history to math to drama. Use a marker or self-sticking notes to highlight ideas that fascinate you. Then, choose one that you want to investigate further.

Review periodicals. Flip through newspaper and magazine articles for topics that you find intriguing. For example, you might consider researching the history behind a story that is currently in the news. Determine what you already know about the topic and what you would like to learn. Use a chart like the one shown to organize your thoughts.

What I Know	What I Want to Know

Work in Progress
Review the work you did on page 927.

Narrowing Your Topic

Develop a research plan. Plan your research by starting with a *working thesis statement*—a sentence that summarizes the idea you intend to address in your report.

Working Thesis Statement: Dreams are important in a variety of ways.

Based on this statement, determine the types of sources you will need to consult. For example, you may decide that you need to gain a broad overview of a subject before investigating specific categories.

My Plan	Possible Sources
Step 1: Get a solid overview about dreams and dream theory.	• Books on dream theory • Web sites (credible ones)
Step 2: Gather specific details and current information.	• Psychology journals (online and print) • Biographies of historical figures • Interviews with working psychologists

As you gather information and refine your ideas, revise your thesis statement so that it is more precise. Plan to include the final version of your thesis statement in the introduction of your report.

Writing Workshop

Gathering Details

Make a list of open-ended research questions. Create a list of questions you would like to answer through research. As you conduct your research, refer to your list to maintain your focus. The information you find may also inspire other ideas. Include new questions, but be sure that you continue to focus or narrow your topic rather than expand it.

Use a variety of primary and secondary sources. Consult *primary sources*—firsthand or original accounts of events. Primary sources include interview transcripts, journals, letters, eyewitness accounts, and speeches. They may also include newspaper accounts from the past.

Also consult *secondary sources* that report or comment on facts and events, such as books, encyclopedia entries, and magazine articles. Consider using specialized types of secondary sources as well, such as those listed in this chart.

Resource	Information
Almanacs	Social, political, and economic statistics
Atlases	Tables, charts, maps, and illustrations
Government publications	Information on laws, government programs, and topics such as agriculture and economics
Microfiche	Back issues of periodicals
Databases	Indexes to online and print sources

Document sources and organize your notes. As you gather information, carefully record each key detail and its source.

- **Source Cards:** Write the identifying information—title, author, publisher, and date of publication—of every resource you consult. Use a separate notecard for each source. Label each card with a letter (*A, B, C,* and so on) or with a code word, such as the author's last name.

- **Notecards:** Record each relevant fact or idea you discover on its own notecard. *Paraphrase,* or restate in your own words, the ideas of other authors. If you quote passages directly, use quotation marks and make sure your quotations are accurate. Include the letter or code word you have chosen to identify the source of the information.

Evaluate the validity of information and the bias of sources. As you gather information, evaluate its *validity,* or trustworthiness. Make sure the authors have the education, training, or personal experience to speak with authority. Notice any evidence of *bias,* or a tendency to make unfair judgments about certain topics. Evidence of bias includes the use of stereotypes, unsupported statements, or overly dramatic claims. Make sure opinions are grounded in evidence that is convincing and factual. Note your evaluations on your source notecards as you work. Later, you can decide whether to use the information and how to present it.

Source Card:

[A]
Kreisler, Kristin V. "Why We Dream What We Dream." <u>Reader's Digest,</u> Feb. 1995: 28, 30, 34-36, 38.

Notecard:

a dream helped Jack Nicklaus fix his golf swing

Source Card: A

Drafting

Shaping Your Writing

Refine your thesis statement. Your working thesis statement should have evolved into a focused declaration as you gathered information. Now, make sure it can be proved using the facts and ideas you have compiled through research.

> **Final Thesis Statement:**
> Dreams make a difference in people's lives—not only to the individuals who dream them, but to society.

Organize your information. Choose an organizational strategy that matches the content and purpose of your writing. Consider using one of the strategies described in this chart.

Organizational Strategy	Uses
Chronological Order offers information in the sequence in which it happened	historical topics; science experiments
Part-to-Whole Order examines how categories affect a larger subject	science experiments; historical topics
Order of Importance presents information in order of increasing or decreasing importance	persuasive arguments; supporting a bold or challenging thesis
Comparison-and-Contrast presents similarities and differences	addressing two or more subjects

Use an outline. Construct an outline to order your ideas and supporting information before writing. Write a draft of your introduction and conclusion. Then, write the topic sentence for each body paragraph. Under each topic sentence, note the evidence you will use to support it.

Synthesize ideas. Effective research writing does not merely present facts and details, but synthesizes—gathers, orders, and interprets—those elements. As you draft, synthesize information into a unified whole.

Providing Elaboration

Use and credit sources. You may choose any of the following methods to present the ideas, facts, and examples you discover in your research. In all cases, you must credit your source.

- **Direct Quotation** Use the author's exact words when they are interesting or persuasive. Indicate any omissions with ellipsis points. Enclose direct quotations in quotation marks.
- **Paraphrase** Restate an author's ideas in your own words.
- **Summary** Compress a complex idea into a briefer version.

If a fact is available only in one source, include documentation.

Incorporate graphic aids and visuals. Consider using illustrations, photographs, graphs, or charts to clarify facts, highlight trends, or add dramatic impact. You may include visuals you discover in your research materials. If so, provide full credit for them.

David Henry
Hwang

David Henry Hwang

On Using Research

As someone born and raised in California, I disliked New York very much. However, I have grown to love the city and now call it my home. The one aspect of New York I did enjoy was discovering Broadway. When I later wrote an article about Broadway, I relied on research as well as my own observations.

Professional Model:

from "Place of a Lifetime..."

Shows premiered here that helped a young nation define its identity: plays like *A Streetcar Named Desire* (at the Ethel Barrymore Theatre, on West 47th Street), musicals like *Guys and Dolls* (at the 46th Street Theatre, now renamed the Richard Rodgers).

Along with most theatre artists, I believe each of these theatres is home to at least one ghost; before leaving each evening, a stagehand will turn on the "ghost light," a single bulb that burns all night, to scare away bad spirits and attract good ones. Very little else about New York captured my imagination on that first visit; I only lasted four days before fleeing back to the West Coast, vowing never to return.

Now, more than 20 years later, I am a devoted New Yorker who has been privileged to see five of my shows performed on Broadway. I sometimes feel that my first hit, *M. Butterfly*, afflicted me with a Broadway virus: an unshakable affection for those aging theatres—roughly 40 in total—and the life that inhabits and surrounds them. . . .

"My first Broadway producer . . . once told me that a success here is 'a shot fired round the world.'"

—**David Henry Hwang**

I just don't know in my head which great plays were produced in which theatres; I had to look this information up.

As with most legends, there are several different explanations for the origin of the "ghost light." Among the explanations I found in different books, this one seemed most common.

Here, I jump forward in time to demonstrate how my views of New York have completely changed.

Revising

Revising Your Paragraphs

Revise to strengthen coherence. Make sure that all of the elements in your draft follow your organizational strategy and appear in logical, or coherent, order.

- On a separate piece of paper, write the main idea of each paragraph.
- Review this list—an abbreviated version of your report—to see whether your ideas flow logically from paragraph to paragraph.
- Rearrange paragraphs or sections that do not build in a logical way. Consider eliminating any that stray from your thesis statement.

To read the complete student model, see page 950.

> ### Student Model: Revising to Strengthen Coherence
>
> *Reorder*
> 1. Introduction
> 2. Creative People and Problem Solving
> 3. Foretelling the Future
> 4. History of Dream Interpretation—Aristotle, Freud
> 5. Symbols in Dreams
> 6. Dreaming at Different Life Stages

> The author reordered her paragraphs to present the ideas of Aristotle and Freud before she turns to her contemporary research.

Peer Review: Share your draft and list of main ideas with a partner. Ask your partner to consider how well each main idea builds on the last in a logical flow. Consider moving paragraphs or sections to improve your report's coherence. Explain to your partner your reasons for specific revision choices.

Revise to avoid plagiarism. To avoid plagiarism—the unethical presentation of someone else's ideas as if they were your own—you must cite sources for direct quotations, paraphrased information, or facts that are specific to a single source. Reread your draft, circling any words or ideas that are not your own. Follow the instructions on page 948 and pages R33–R34 to correctly cite those passages.

Revising Your Word Choice

Revise for conciseness. Your research report will be more effective if you avoid unnecessary complexity or wordiness. Reread your draft, circling any words that add clutter without meaning. Consider omitting those words or replacing them with better choices.

Wordy: Thus, in conclusion, one can see from careful observation that political conflict often leads to economic change.

Concise: In conclusion, political conflict often leads to economic change.

Documenting Sources

Citing Sources

When citing sources in your report, follow a specific format. Modern Language Association (MLA) style calls for parenthetical citations or references. For print works, the citation usually gives the author's or editor's name followed by a page number. If the work does not have an author, use a keyword or phrase from the title. For Web sources, use the author's name if it is available, the title of the article, if any, or the title of the site itself. Include a screen number if screens on the site are numbered.

Citing a Print Work: . . . men have more action-oriented dreams, while women imagine more emotional one-on-one struggles with loved ones (Van de Castle 45).

Citing a Web Source: Unsolvedmysteries.com shows how dreams can bring luck with the report of a lottery winner from Maine ("Winning the Lottery," screen 1).

Creating a Works-Cited List or Bibliography

Publication information for each source you cite must appear at the end of your report. MLA style calls for a Works-Cited list, in which you list alphabetically the works you cite.

- For books, the Works-Cited entry usually takes the form of the author's name, last name first, followed by the title of the work. The entry gives full publication information, including the city of publication, the name of the publisher, and the year of publication.

- For articles in periodicals, the entry usually takes the form of the author's name, last name first, followed by the title of the article, then the name of the magazine. Publication information includes the date of the issue, the volume and issue number if any, and the pages on which the article appears. If the article is continued on a later, nonconsecutive page, give the number of the first page, followed by a plus sign.

- For general Web sites, give any of the following information that is available, in the order indicated: author's name, the title of the page, the title of the site, the date of last update, and the name of the sponsoring organization. Give screen numbers, if any. Give the date that you consulted the site, and conclude with the full URL, or address, for the material.

For more information on MLA style, see pages R33–R34.

Integrating Grammar Skills

Revising to Combine Sentences Using Adverb Clauses

Avoid too many choppy, short sentences by combining some sentences using adverb clauses.

Two sentences: She had sent the letter. The mail was delayed.

Combined: Although the mail was delayed, she had sent the letter.

Prentice Hall Writing and Grammar Connection: Chapter 3, Section 1

Identifying Adverb Clauses A clause is a group of words with a subject and a verb. An *independent clause* can stand alone as a complete sentence, but a *subordinate clause* cannot stand alone. An adverb clause is a subordinate clause that begins with a subordinating conjunction and tells *where, when, in what way, to what extent, under what condition,* or *why.*

When: *Before I got on the plane,* I was afraid of flying.

Condition: Dave will carry the box *if you will open the door.*

Why: I gave her my number *so she could call me later.*

In what way: The child swam *as if she had been born in the water.*

Combining Sentences When using adverb clauses to combine two shorter sentences, follow these steps.

1. **Identify the relationship between the ideas in the two sentences.**

2. **Select a subordinating conjunction that clarifies that relationship.** Add the conjunction to the appropriate sentence to create an adverb clause. Then, add this new clause to the other sentence.

3. **When a subordinate clause begins a sentence, use a comma to separate it from the rest of the sentence.**

Subordinating Conjunctions			
after	although	as	as if
as long as	because	before	even though
if	since	so that	than
though	unless	until	when
whenever	where	wherever	while

Apply It to Your Editing

Review the introduction and conclusion of your report and highlight any short sentences that appear in series. Combine sentences to clarify connections, using an appropriate subordinating conjunction.

Writing Workshop

Student Model:
Lisa Maiden
Phoenix, AZ

In Your Dreams

Ever since humans have existed, dreams have made a difference in people's lives. Julius Caesar's wife, Calpurnia, once dreamed that Caesar's statue spurted blood like a fountain while the Romans smiled and bathed in it. This nightmarish picture foreshadowed reality when Caesar was later assassinated. In 1793, Marie Antoinette had a dream of a red sun and pillar. After the sun rose, it suddenly set; this immediately preceded her beheading. Then, there is Robert Louis Stevenson, who believed his best stories came from dreams, including the infamous "Dr. Jekyll and Mr. Hyde." Neils Bohr dreamed of sitting on the sun with planets whizzing around him on small cords; he then developed the model of an atom. Even Genghis Khan claimed to receive his battle plans from his sleepy nights.

Who were the early interpreters of such dreams? Aristotle and Freud, of course, were among the scholars who labored over dream interpretation. Aristotle suggested that dreams were formed by disturbances in the body. Freud, however, believed that dreams were powerful tools for uncovering unconscious wishes. He said, "The purpose of dreams is to allow us to satisfy in fantasies the instinctual urges that society judges unacceptable" (Dreams: History, 2000).

Even today, creative people use their dreams in solving problems. A 1995 *Reader's Digest* article entitled "Why We Dream What We Dream" provides many examples. One such dreamer was the scientist Dmitri Ivanovich Mendeleev. He "saw" the periodic table of the elements in a dream and wrote it down the following day. Later, only one correction was needed. Screenwriter James Cameron dreamed of a robot with a red eye staring back at him. He woke up and wrote the script for *The Terminator.* Steve Allen's hit song "This Could Be the Start of Something Big" also began from a dream, as did the new way of swinging the club that allowed Jack Nicklaus to overcome his golfing problem (Kreisler, 28–38).

Besides being helpful in the creative aspect, dreams have, in many cases, foretold the future. In the weeks prior to his murder, Abraham Lincoln dreamed the White House was in mourning for an assassinated president. The video *The Secret World of Dreams* tells of a man whose dreams indicated a chronic illness even before it was diagnosed, as well as a man whose recurring nightmares of an explosion prepared him for the real thing and enabled him to save the life of a coworker. Unsolved mysteries.com shows

> The writer begins by introducing the topic in a concise sentence.

> Lisa correctly quotes and cites one of her sources.

> The writer incorporates the source of her information into the flow of her discussion.

> The writer demonstrates the wide variety of sources she consulted in her research.

how dreams can bring luck with the report of a lottery winner from Maine whose dreams revealed a winning ticket (Unsolved Mysteries Home Page, screen 1). Given such cases as these, it is no mystery that modern psychology still believes in the prophetic power of dreams.

However, to understand one's dreams, one must uncover the meaning of dream symbols. Psychoanalyst Sigmund Freud said that the secret to the symbols in dreams lies within the dreamer (Bentley, p. 4). In other words, individuals can interpret dream symbols from their own lives and the imagery around them—not just by using a dream dictionary. Sleeps.com gives just a few examples of these symbols. For instance, to most dreamers, clothing symbolizes mood, attitude, or state of mind. One who wears a uniform in a dream may be influenced too much by society, while having clothes that are too short may suggest a longing for the pleasures of youth now gone. Death is also a recurring symbol. Whether the dreamer attends a funeral or is in a coffin, these pictures signify a change in one's attitude toward life or one's emotional balance. Finally, other people occur in dreams as reflections of the dreamer's own personality traits. For instance, if a dreamer is faced by the stares of others, that person may be worried about making a bad impression on other people (Dream Analysis and Interpretation, screens 6, 7).

While dreams can be interpreted according to symbols, the most common types of dreams vary throughout the human life cycle. People at different places in their lives tend to dream differently. Children's dreams reflect new impressions that they encounter each day. Bold geometric shapes are not just building blocks with which they play—they represent a fixation with family relationships. For example, a triangle would signify the relationship among the father, mother, and child. Dreams of giants indicate a child's impression of his or her own size and sense of self-worth. Naturally, everything is bigger to a child, but a child with giant proportions compared to the world around him may have an increasing self-awareness (Bentley, p. 25). Much like a scene from *The Nutcracker,* toys come to life as the child lives out fantasies, showing developments of the young person's persona. As children become teens, they dream more about romance. Among adults, men and women dream differently. "It's biology and social conditioning," says Milton Kramer, director of the Bethesda Oak Hospital's Sleep Center in Cincinnati. Research has shown that men dream twice as often of other men as they do of women, while women tend to have an equal number of dreams of both sexes (*New Scientist,* p. 2). A study by Robert Van de Castle, author of

Each paragraph includes a topic sentence, which is then supported in the paragraph with details.

Our Dreaming Mind, analyzed 1,000 dreams and found that men have more action-oriented dreams, while women imagine more emotional one-on-one struggles with loved ones (Van de Castle 45).

Studies are also beginning to show that a person's attitude can influence his or her dreams. University of Pennsylvania professor Aaron Beck found that angry people are the ones throwing the punches in their dreams, while depressed people often find themselves the victims of rejection. However, people who have a hard time standing up for themselves are the ones likely to suffer from restless nightmares (Kreisler 36).

Through the fascinating history of dreams, the interpretation of some dream symbols, and the secret dreams of different sleepers, it is evident that dreams are important. They provide valuable insights, help solve problems, spark new thoughts and creations, and may even foretell the future. Maybe people should pay more attention to their dreams. The hours one spends sleeping could be the key to a better life.

Works Cited

Bentley, Peter. *Book of Dream Symbols.* San Francisco: Chronicle Books, 1995.

"Dream Analysis and Interpretation, Doing It!" *Dream Central.* 9 March 2000: 6, 7.
    <http://www.sleeps.com/analysis.html>

"Dreams: History." ThinkQuest. 22 Mar. 2000.
    <http://library.thinkquest.org/11130/data/history/history.html>

Kreisler, Kristin V. "Why We Dream What We Dream." *Reader's Digest*
    Feb. 1995: 28+.

Kramer, Milton. Personal Interview. 10 March 2000.

Mestel, Rosie. "Get Real, Siggi." *New Scientist* 26 April 1997: 2,5. 21 March 2000.
    <http://www.newscientist.com/ns/970426/siggi.html>

Randall, Dr. Alexander, V. "Great Dreams in History." *Dr. -Dream's Resources
    for People Who Dream.* 10 June 1996. 7 March 2000: 1–3.
    <http://www.dr-dream.com/hist.htm>

The Secret World of Dreams. Videotape. Questar Video, 1997. 80 Min.

Van de Castle, Robert L. *Our Dreaming Mind.* New York: Ballantine, 1995.

"Winning the Lottery in Your Dreams." *Unsolved Mysteries.* 11 March 2000: 1.
    <http://unsolvedmysteries.com/usm397.html>

> Using a standard format, Lisa lists the sources from which her information was drawn.

Editing and Proofreading

Check your draft to correct errors in format, grammar, and punctuation. **Focus on Accuracy in Citations:** Carefully check the spelling, punctuation, and format of titles, including the use of quotation marks, underlining, and italics. Check the spelling of authors' names, and make sure that you have capitalized titles correctly.

Publishing and Presenting

Consider one of the following ways to share your writing:
Publish on the Internet. Post your research report on a Web site that publishes student writing, or send it to the Web site editors as an e-mail.
Share a multimedia presentation. Use your research report as the basis for a multimedia presentation, and include graphics, music, and other elements to engage your audience. If possible, rehearse your presentation with a live audience to coordinate the smooth combination of elements. Incorporate audience feedback to improve your report or presentation. Make sure you allow time for your audience to ask questions.

Reflecting on Your Writing

Writer's Journal Jot down your thoughts on the experience of writing a research report. Begin by answering these questions:

- Which reference source was most useful? How did you locate that source?
- What was the most important thing you learned about your topic?

Rubric for Self-Assessment

To assess your own research report, use the following rubric:

Criteria	Rating Scale
	not very very
Focus: How specific is your thesis statement?	1 2 3 4 5
Organization: How logical and effective is your organization?	1 2 3 4 5
Support/Elaboration: How varied and reliable is your evidence?	1 2 3 4 5
Style: How concise is your phrasing of ideas?	1 2 3 4 5
Conventions: How accurately and thoroughly have you cited sources for ideas that are not your own?	1 2 3 4 5

Delivering a Multimedia Presentation of a Research Report

Academic Standards

• Use visual aids to enhance presentations. (10.7.4)

• Identify and evaluate the artistic effects of a media presentation. (10.7.13)

• Deliver expository presentations. (10.7.15)

Transform your research report into a **multimedia presentation** by adding sounds and visuals that create drama and interest for an audience. A successful multimedia presentation offers clear ideas and information about a topic, using a variety of supporting media. When preparing your presentation, consider using an overhead or a slide projector, a video or an audio player, a computer, or other electronic audiovisual device.

Prepare the Content

Consider your topic, audience, and available equipment when choosing which media to use.

• Using an outline of your report, decide which parts can be presented effectively using visuals or sounds. Plan in such a way that media will appear at points throughout your presentation.

• Choose media that suits your topic. For example, if your topic is American life during World War II, you might play popular music of that time as a soundtrack.

• Make sure that all visual images can be seen by the entire audience. Photocopy and enlarge small images to show them effectively.

Prepare Your Delivery

To smoothly integrate words, sounds, and images in your presentation, you must practice it.

• Rehearse your presentation with the multimedia equipment. Practice making adjustments to the equipment.

• Before the presentation, double-check your equipment to make sure that everything is in working condition and properly connected.

• Have a backup plan in case your equipment fails. You might prepare copies of illustrations or graphic organizers to hand out.

• Do not read your research report word for word. Instead, talk to your audience, articulating your ideas with energy. To make sure you stay on track, refer to your notes each time you shift to a new idea.

Feedback Form for a Multimedia Presentation

Rating System

1	2	3	4	5
poor		good		excellent

Content
___ Clearly expressed ideas
___ Media that illustrates ideas
___ Use of varied media
___ Effective pacing of media use

Presentation
___ Equipment functioning
___ Smooth delivery
___ Media visible and audible
___ Media supports topic without overwhelming it

Activity *Share a Multimedia Presentation* Prepare a media presentation to share research that you have done. Practice your presentation, making sure that your media choices do not detract from your topic. Ask your listeners to use the Feedback Form to evaluate your presentation.

Romeo and Juliet: An Adapted Classic

William Shakespeare
Globe Fearon, 1996

Play This play tells the story of two teenagers from families who have hated each other for decades. Against the odds, Romeo and Juliet fall in love and plan to leave the city and their families behind. The play encompasses love, humor, and tragedy—and sword fights!

A Raisin in the Sun

Lorraine Hansberry
Vintage Books, 1994

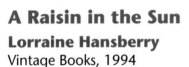

Play If a large amount of money were coming your way, how would you use it? That question drives the action in *A Raisin in the Sun,* the first play by an African American woman to be produced on Broadway. An African American family living in Chicago in the 1950s, the Younger family debate their options in a society that wants to restrict their freedom. Not until the tense climax of this gripping drama do we learn whether they will find the strength to unite and claim a better future.

Short Dramas and Teleplays

Prentice Hall, 2000
Plays and Teleplays

The authors represented in this volume encompass a variety of periods and styles. Although all of the selections are short dramas or teleplays (plays written for television), many of them were adapted from novels, such as *The Prince and the Pauper* and *The Adventures of Tom Sawyer* by Mark Twain. Others have been adapted from short stories, such as "The Purloined Letter" by Edgar Allan Poe.

Ibsen: Four Major Plays

Henrik Ibsen
Signet, 1992

Play These four plays are among the greatest and best known of Ibsen's works and exemplify his contributions to theater—his frank probing of social problems, realistic dialogue, and the depiction of his characters' inner lives and actions. Included in this collection is *A Doll House,* a play that prompted an outcry and a debate about the role of women in European society in the late 1800s.

These titles are available in the Penguin/Prentice Hall Literature Library.
Consult your teacher before choosing one.

Think About It When a student graduates from high school or college, he or she takes a big step forward. To help students grasp the significance of this step—and to let them know that others have taken it and survived!—speakers at a graduation ceremony share their experiences and vision of the world. As you read the commencement speech given by rock star Billy Joel, think about what his experiences show about what it means to become an adult.

Hold Fast Your Dreams—and Trust Your Mistakes

Billy Joel

Commencement Speech at Fairfield University
Fairfield, Connecticut
May 19, 1991

When I was first asked to speak to the graduating class of Fairfield University, my initial reaction was not too dissimilar to a certain philosophy professor who is a member of the faculty here. I had to ask myself, What makes me qualified to do this? What relevance do I have to the future lives of these young people? After all, I did not even go to college, and I did write a song called "Only the Good Die Young." So, why me?

After meeting with a group of Fairfield students, I realized what I might be able to share with you from my perspective. I have lived what many would consider to be an unorthodox life, but it has always been an interesting one.

It is true that I did not graduate from high school; but like you, I did spend years majoring in my own area of study. I am a graduate of the University of Rock and Roll, Class of 1970. My diploma was a check—a week's worth of wages earned from playing long nights in smoky, crowded clubs in the New York area. Through the years, I have been given platinum albums, Grammys, keys to cities, and many other awards which are considered prestigious in my profession. But the greatest award I have ever received was that check—my diploma—made out to Billy Joel in 1970. This particular check was enough to cover my rent and my expenses. It was also enough to convince me that I no longer needed to work in a factory or be a short-order cook or pump gas or paint houses or do any of the other day jobs I had done in order to make ends meet. That check meant that I was now able to make a living solely by doing the thing that I loved most—making music. It meant that I had become self-reliant as a musician. I will never forget that day. I consider it to be one of the most important days in my life.

I also remember the twenty-one-year-old Billy Joel and I often wonder what it would be like if we could, somehow, meet each other. Here I am, forty-two, exactly twice his age. What would I think of him? Would I find him to be naive, arrogant, simplistic, crude, noble, hopelessly idealistic? Perhaps all of these things. But more important, what would he think of me? Have I fulfilled his dream? Have I created the kind of music he would have wanted to have written? Have I compromised any of his ideals? Have I broken any of the promises I made to him? Have I lost the desire to be the best he could be? Would he be disappointed in me? Would he even like me?

That twenty-one-year-old has been the biggest pain in the neck I have had to endure in my life. Yet he has had more influence on the work I have done than anyone else for the last twenty-one years. He has been my greatest teacher, my deepest conscience, my toughest editor, and my harshest critic. He has significantly shaped my life. I can say to you today that what you are at this moment in your lives you will always be in your hearts.

When I met with your fellow students, they asked me what is the most powerful lesson I have learned. After eleven years of classical training, I learned to play the piano, but I realized that I was not destined to be another Van Cliburn. I learned to write songs, although what I really wanted to write were symphonies like Beethoven. I have learned to perform, but somehow I knew I would never be able to move like Michael Jackson or sing like Ray Charles.

Out of respect for things that I was never destined to do, I have learned that my strengths are a result of my weaknesses, my success is due to my failures, and my style is directly related to my limitations. You see, the only original things I have ever done have been accidents, mistakes, flubs, foul-ups, and their attendant solutions. I have an inherent talent for stumbling onto something. I am an expert at making bad choices and illogical decisions. I have discovered that after all those years of musical instruction, after all that practice to be perfect, after all that hard work trying to compose the right notes, I am gifted with the knack of hitting exactly the wrong notes at precisely the right time.

This is the secret of originality. Think about it. You may have learned all there is to know about reproducing the art of someone else, but only you can commit a colossal blunder in your own exquisite style. This is what makes you unique. But then you are faced with solving the problem. This is what makes you inventive. Commit enough blunders and you become an artist. Solve all the

problems you have created and they will call you a genius.

I have learned that no matter how successful or proficient or accomplished I might think I am, I am always going to make mistakes. I will always have to face some difficulties. I am always going to have to deal with the possibility of failure, and I will always be able to utilize these things in my work. So I am no longer afraid of becoming lost, because the journey back always reveals to me something new about my life and about my own humanity, and that is, ultimately, good for the artist.

Meet the Author

Billy Joel (b. 1949) grew up on Long Island, in the suburbs of New York City. He studied classical music as a child, but it was a performance by the Beatles that convinced him to become a professional musician. One of the most successful popular artists of his generation, Joel has sold more than 100 million records worldwide. He was inducted into the Rock and Roll Hall of Fame in 1999.

Readings in Contemporary Speeches
Talk About It

Use these questions to guide a discussion of the speech.

1. **(a)** What did Billy Joel receive that he felt was his "college diploma"? **(b)** How did getting it change his life? Explain.

2. **(a)** In what ways did making mistakes help Billy Joel? **(b)** Has making a mistake ever helped you? Explain.

3. In a group, discuss how the young Billy influenced Joel's career.

   - Why do you think Joel says that his younger self has been "the biggest pain in [his] neck"?
   - Which values do you think the young Joel may have held that his older self may have struggled to fulfill?
   - Do you think that the person you are today is important to the person you will become? Why or why not?

   Choose a point-person to share your group's ideas with the class.

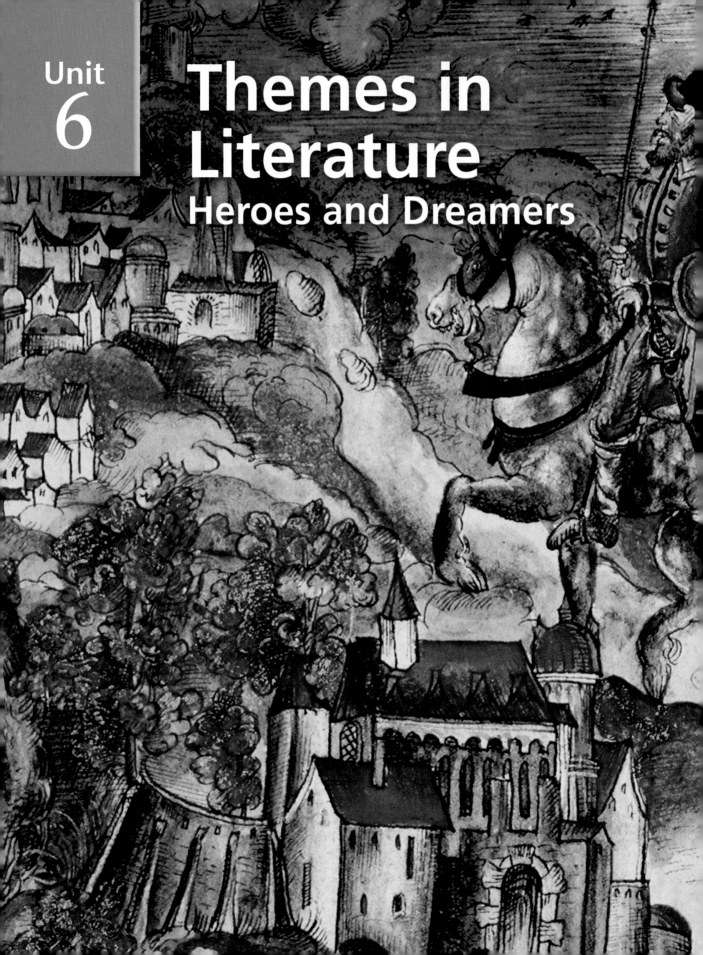

Unit 6

Themes in Literature
Heroes and Dreamers

Unit 6 Overview

PART 1: Analyzing the Influence of Cultural and Historical Context

PART 2: Comparing and Contrasting

(IN) **Academic Standards**
In This Unit You Will

- Examine how the author's perspective influences the structure and tone of the text. (10.2.4)

- Analyze many different forms of dramatic literature. (10.3.1)

- Evaluate interactions between characters and how these affect the plot. (10.3.3)

Unit 6

Introduction

Themes in Literature: Heroes and Dreamers

John Phillip Santos

From the Author's Desk

John Phillip Santos

Talks About Themes in the Oral Tradition

When you write about your **personal mythology**—blending stories of your own with **oral traditions** handed down by word of mouth in your family—you're writing autobiography, yes, but you're also writing about some of the oldest themes and mysteries known to humans: Who are we? Where did we come from? Where are we going? Where do I fit into the story?

Since humans could first use language, we have been seeking answers to these questions and recording them in **myths, epics, and legends** told around campfires. We have also recorded our answers in written form, **poetry** and **prose,** to share with others, now and into the future.

Stories of Ancestors

I began looking for answers to these questions in stories of the people and the lands where my family came from—South Texas, Mexico, and Spain.

How much of who we are was handed down from those ancestors? What happened to their old gods? When did we embrace new ones?

I found clues to these mysteries in unexpected places, in food, in seemingly insignificant objects, documents, and photographs left behind by my ancestors, and in the tales that many of my elders told me.

▲ **John Phillip Santos** reveals in his memoir how the past is still alive in the values and attitudes of modern generations of Mexican Americans.

◀ **Critical Viewing** Which details in this picture relate to Santos's ideas about telling one's life story and linking it to the past? **[Connect]**

962 Themes in Literature

Every Life Contains a Story

I began reading authors from all over the world—Cervantes and Edmund Spenser, Jorge Luis Borges, and the Ugandan poet Okot p'Bitek. As diverse as their voices and tales might be, one common theme was emerging. All of them offered us their personal stories so we would delve more deeply into the mystery of what it is to be human.

This is not about telling stories of important people. It doesn't matter who you are. As Laura (Riding) Jackson suggests, every life contains a story waiting to be told. You can tell your own story in conversations with friends and family, in poems, fiction, or in non-fiction, but we're all waiting to hear your story, which is unlike any other, ever.

> "There is something to be told about us for the telling of which we all wait. . . . We know we are explainable, and not explained. . . . Until the missing story of ourselves is told, nothing besides told can suffice us: we shall go on quietly craving it."
> **from The Telling**
> —Laura (Riding) Jackson

We tell these stories to come to know ourselves, but don't expect answers. In the great human mystery, there are plenty of clues but few solutions. In many ways, the deeper you go, the greater the mystery will become. That's the fun part.

More About John Phillip Santos

John Phillip Santos (b. 1957) is well-known as a filmmaker, producer, and journalist. He began his memoir, *Places Left Unfinished at the Time of Creation,* in order to solve the mystery of his grandfather's death in 1939.

In his book, Santos explores his Mexican American roots by moving back through time to the land his ancestors knew to find the "hidden light left behind in the past." His memoir combines personal memories with ancient history and literary sources, suggesting the great and mysterious influence of the past.

Fast Facts

▶ Santos has written over forty film scripts for television documentaries.
▶ He was the first Mexican American to win a Rhodes scholarship to Oxford University in England.

Themes in Literature

Themes in the Oral Tradition

Long before it was written down, literature was part of the **oral tradition,** the passing on of narratives and sayings by word of mouth. Stories lightened work and sweetened leisure, and people exchanged tales while doing chores or sitting around campfires. Storytellers, expressing what fascinated or moved them, explored **universal themes,** ideas about life shared by many cultures: for example, the value of friendship and the need for courage.

In telling their tales, people naturally used **archetypes,** the characters, situations, images, and symbols that appear in the narratives of many different cultures. Here are common **archetypical characters and ideas:**

- the **wise and virtuous king,** whose reign brings in a **golden age,** or time of peace and prosperity

- the **dreamer,** a character who imagines new possibilities and defies danger to bring an important gift to society

- the **hero,** who is an unpromising youth but who blossoms into a wise, strong, and courageous leader

- the struggle between the **protagonist,** the main character, and the **antagonist,** a person or force that opposes the protagonist

The presentation of these archetypes might vary depending on the **historical context,** the social and cultural background of the storyteller and the audience. Yet, the presence of archetypes in different times and places suggests that they arise from our common humanity. Some scholars even believe that archetypal patterns express truths about the human mind and unconscious.

WILEY@WILEYTOONS.COM DIST. BY THE WASHINGTON POST WRITERS GROUP   WWW.

Forms That Express Archetypes

Anonymous storytellers developed recognizable forms as they built narratives from archetypal patterns. At first, these narrative forms lived only in the memory and therefore might be recited in many different versions. Later, as stories were written, their content was fixed and the idea of an individual author emerged. These are the types of stories in which archetypes are often found.

- **Myths** explain the actions of gods and the humans who interact with them. They may also explain the causes of natural phenomena.
- **Legends** are traditional stories about the past that are usually based on historical fact.
- **Epics** are long narrative poems about a larger-than-life **epic hero.** The epic hero's career is important to the history of a group.
- **Folk tales** focus on human or animal heroes, not gods.
- **Fairy tales** are a kind of folk tale recounting the adventures of spirits who appear as very small humans.

Each of these forms expresses the **values,** or model behaviors, cherished by a society. Some ideas are **shared values,** which are held by many societies. Others are **culturally distinct values,** which are specific to a group. Similarly, **cultural details** in a narrative relate to the beliefs and customs that give a particular group its **identity,** or sense of self.

Modern fiction, though written by an individual rather than fashioned by a group, can express universal themes. It can also express a **parody,** or humorous mockery, of an archetypal pattern.

▼ Critical Viewing
Which type of archetypal story might take place in a setting like this?

Check Your Understanding

Complete each item with the most appropriate term from the list.

　　universal theme　　epic　　dreamer　　myth　　archetype

1. One archetypal character is the _____, who brings a gift to society.
2. A(n) _____ explains the actions of gods and humans.
3. The need for courage in life is a(n) _____.
4. A(n) _____ is a character or situation that appears in many stories.
5. A(n) _____ tells about the deeds of a culturally important hero.

From the Author's Desk
John Phillip Santos Introduces His Work

My book, *Places Left Unfinished at the Time of Creation*, began in a curiosity about a family secret from the distant past: My grandfather Juan Jose's mysterious death in the San Antonio River on a cold January morning in 1939.

Even though I grew up in a very close family with two formidable grandmothers and lots of uncles, aunts, and cousins, I was already sixteen when I first learned of the strange circumstances of my abuelo's (ä bwə′ lōz)—grandfather's—death. Maybe I never asked.

Cultural Context: A Door Into the Past

But that mystery prompted me to learn more about the link between my family and the mythologies of the past. It set me on a quest for abuelo Juan Jose's story, and that story opened up another chain of stories, about the Mexicans of my hometown, old San Antonio, the landscapes of Texas and Mexico, the Conquest of Mexico by the Spanish that began the whole story, and tales of the indigenous civilizations that had preceded the arrival of the Spaniards. I discovered that my family story was a portal into an infinite past; my grandfather's story was part of a larger undiscovered myth of our ancestry.

The passages from my book that you will read, which begin on the next page, describe some of the ways I sought to recover that mythic story.

Family Stories and Powerful Objects

There are memories of time spent with the oldest members of my family, stories told to me by relatives like my Uncle Lico, who sought out genealogies and other knowledge of the family's remote past. Certain powerful objects remembered from childhood unlock troves of memories. And in the absence of written records of the family's history, journeys into the lands of our origins, north and south of the border, become an important part of my search.

I wanted to explore the **theme of my own identity** by telling my family's story and ended up finding a hidden mythology that connected us to the great human tale, the one that is incalculably old, but still being written.

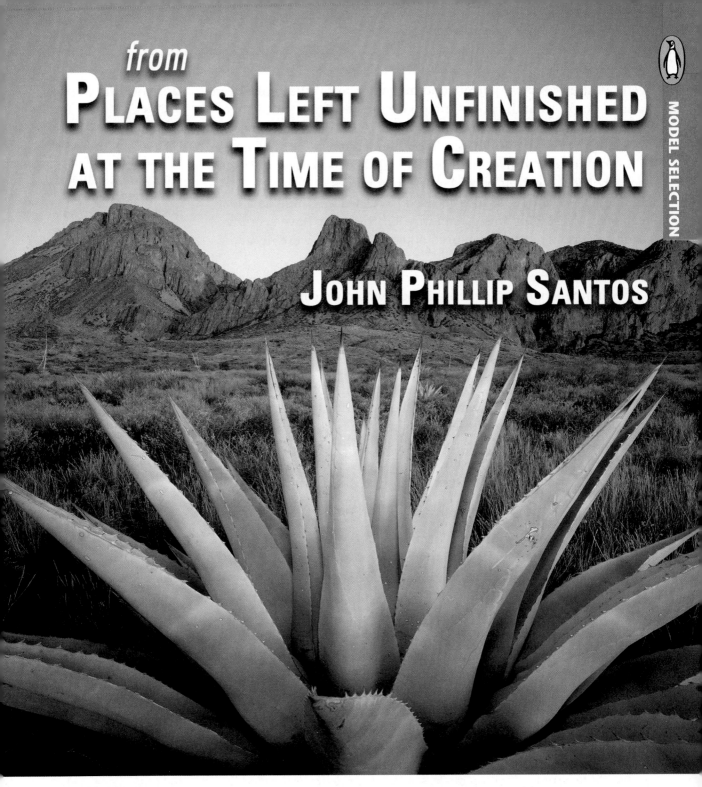

from PLACES LEFT UNFINISHED AT THE TIME OF CREATION

JOHN PHILLIP SANTOS

. . . The past can be difficult to conjure again when so little has been left behind. A few photographs, a golden medal, a pair of eyeglasses as delicate as eggshells, an old Bible, a letter or two. Some families in Mexico have troves of their ancestors' belongings, from pottery of the ancients and exquisite paintings of Mexico City in the eighteenth century to helmets and shields of the Spaniards, and even hundred-year-old parrots and maguey plants[1] that have been handed down, from the great-grandparents who first tended them.

By comparison, the Santos are traveling light through time. In my family, virtually nothing has been handed down, not because there was nothing to give, but after leaving Mexico to come to Texas—so many loved ones left behind, cherished places and things abandoned—the antepasados[2] ceased to regard anything as a keepsake. Everything was given away. Or they may have secretly clung so closely to their treasured objects that they were never passed on.

Then they were lost.

My mother's mother, Leandra Lopez, whom we called simply "Grandmother," sat in her cluttered dark house on West Russell Street like an aged Tejana[3] sphinx during the last ten years of her life. Through the year, she filed away embossed death notices and patron saint prayer cards of departed family and friends in the black leather address book I consulted to write out her Christmas cards every year. In early December, I would sit down with her and first cross out the entries for all those who had "passed onward," as she used to say. By each name in the book, she had already scratched a cross with thick black pencil lines.

Memo Montalvo from Hebbronville, Texas. According to Grandmother, a good man. He had married a not-very-pretty cousin from Laredo.

Efraín Vela from Mier, Tamaulipas. Son of a cousin on her father's side whom she never spoke to. Supposedly, he was the keeper of the family coat of arms, awarded to the family by the Viceroy of Nueva España himself. What would happen to it now?

Socorro Mendiola, from Alice, Texas. She and Grandmother had taught school together in a one-room schoolhouse in Cotulla in 1910. Then Socorro became a Franciscan nun, breaking the heart of Grandmother's cousin, Emeterio Vela, whom, she noted with a sigh, had died just last year.

And every year, by the degrees of each ended life, as the world grew older, our addressing marathons grew shorter—though Grandmother would change the subject if I pointed out this mortal ratio.

Inside her rolltop writing desk, she kept a mysterious wooden polygonal[4] star that had a different swatch of old Mexican fabrics

John Phillip Santos
Author's Insight The idea there was nothing left behind was a part of our family myth. There were actually many keepsakes; it just didn't seem so at first. But looking for the stories of my ancestors set me on the path to write.

John Phillip Santos
Author's Insight
As your family's chief mythologist, you will always want to be useful to your elders when they need the services of a scribe.

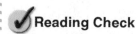
Reading Check

How did the author help his grandmother every year?

---

1. maguey (mag´wā´) **plants** *n.* fleshy-leaved plants common to Mexico, Central America and the southwestern U.S.; used for making rope and tequila.

2. antepasados (än tā pä sä´ dōs) *n.* forebears, ancestors.

3. Tejana (tā jä´ nä) *adj.* Texan.

4. polygonal (pə lig´ə nəl) *adj.* many-sided.

▲ Critical Viewing Why might an old photograph like this one be important to the author? [Connect]

glued on each <u>facet</u>. The multicolored curiosity smelled like Mexico, all cumin, wild honey, and smoky rose, and when you shook it, a small solitary object rattled inside. A stone? A marble? A gem? To me, it seemed like some magician's puzzle, and locked inside were all of the secrets of old Mexico.

During one of our annual Christmas-card sessions, I asked her if I could have that star, instead of the customary reward of a box of animal crackers and five dollars in change, which she laboriously fished out of her zippered, yellowing plastic coin purse. Grandmother was almost completely blind by then, so I put her hand to the last of the Hallmark Christmas cards in the place for her to sign her name. She slowly scratched out Leandra Vela Lopez, and told me no, I could not have the star.

I never saw it again.

My uncle, Lico Lopez, her son, ferreted out the past as a passionate genealogist who used research, fantasy, and spells of breathless diabetic madness to craft his ancestral charts of the Lopez and Vela families. Some are elaborate discs, in which each outward concentric ring represents a new generation. In these, as you delve closer to the center, you also go deeper into the past. In others, quickly dashed off as notes to himself, ragged trees and jagged lines are drawn between names like Evaristo, Viviano, Blas, and Hermenegilda. In one, going back to 1763, the capstone slot contains the cryptic entry,

"King of Spain,"

from whom, presumably, he believed we were descended. Subtle faculties and proclivities[5] were passed, speechlessly, through the flesh of successive generations. The ghosts of Spanish royalty mingled with Indios, Negros, and people from every part of the world—in Uncle Lico's secret genealogy of Mexico. Yet, despite the uninterest and ridicule of many, he managed to recover numerous family names and stories.

Lico knew I had some of the same magnetic attraction to the past that fueled his manic genealogies, as if the molecules of our bodies were <u>polarized</u> in a way that drew us both back in time, back, <u>inexorably</u>, toward the ancestors. Before he died, suddenly, in San Antonio, of a heart attack, he sent me all of the notes and charts accumulated in his forty years of digging in the family root cellars. He also gave me a receipt, dated May 25, 1928, laminated and mounted on wood, from my grandfather's grocery store, Leonides Lopez Groceries, in Cotulla, Texas. In my grandfather's filigreed

---

5. **proclivities** (prō kliv´ə tēs) *n.* natural or habitual inclinations.

wrought iron pencil script, it details a sale on that day of *harina* (flour), *azúcar* (sugar), *fideos* (vermicelli), *manteca* (lard), *papas* (potatoes), and other assorted dry goods, for a total of $5.05.

A relic like this is the exception, though. A trunkful of the Santos family photographs disappeared when Madrina moved out of the old house on Cincinnati Street. She swears she remembers seeing it fall off the truck near the corner of Zarzamora Street, where La Poblanita bakery was located. It was a pine box the size of a shipping trunk, stuffed with heirloom photographs. She can't remember why she said nothing at the time. It fell off a truck onto the dusty streets of old San Antonio de Bejar one day and was left behind, abandoned, lost.

In one photo that survived it is 1960, and the whole Santos tribe is standing on the porch of my grandmother's house, in early evening shadows. It must have been Easter because my many cousins and I are in church clothes, standing in the yard around the trunk of a great sycamore tree. My aunts and uncles are there, partly old Mexican, partly new American, looking handsome, hopeful, proud of the brood standing in front of them. In the very middle of the scene, *las Ancianas*, Grandmother Santos, whom we called "Uela," short for *abuela*, and Madrina, her sister, are standing regally in a perfect moment, radiating the indelible light of Mexico. On the porch, Mother and an aunt have my newborn twin brothers, George and Charles, wrapped in blankets in their arms. My father looks serious, with a distant gaze, in a dark suit and silky tie. To one side, standing apart from us, is one of my eldest cousins, René, who would be killed in Vietnam just seven years later.

These are the memento mori[6] of the Santos. There are a few photographs, rosary chains of half-remembered stories, carried out of another time by the old Mexicans I grew up with. In dreams, the ancestors who have passed on visit with me, in this world, and in a world that lies perhaps within, amidst, and still beyond this world— a mystical limbo dimension that the descendants of the Aztecs call *el Inframundo*. In the *Inframundo*, all that has been forgotten still lives. Nothing is lost. All remembrance is redeemed from oblivion.

These ancestors, living and dead, have asked me the questions they were once asked: Where did our forebears come from and what have we amounted to in this world? Where have we come to in the span of all time, and where are we headed, like an arrow shot long ago into infinite empty space? What messages and markings of the ancient past do we carry in these handed-down bodies we live in today?

---

6. **memento mori** (mə men′tō mōr′ē) *n.* reminder of death.

John Phillip Santos
Author's Insight
Old family photographs and other newer media are treasure troves heaping with evidence from the past. Some of my earliest drafts are composed of collages of this "tribal media."

✓ Reading Check

What happened to the box of the author's heirloom family photographs?

With these questions swirling inside me, I have rediscovered some stories of the family past in the landscapes of Texas and Mexico, in the timeless language of stone, river, wind, and trees. Tío Abrín, twin brother to my great-grandfather Jacobo, was a master of making charcoal. He lived in the hill country, where the cedars needed to make charcoal were planted a century ago to supply the industry. Today, long after he worked there, walking in that central Texas landscape crowded with deep green cedar, I feel old Abrán's presence, like the whisper of a tale still waiting to be told, wondering whether my intuition and the family's history are implicitly intertwined. Even if everything else had been lost— photographs, stories, rumors, and suspicions—if nothing at all from the past remained for us, the land remains, as the original book of the family.

It was always meant to be handed down. . . .

◀ Critical Viewing
How might Santos have used his grandmother's address book, shown here, to reconstruct family history?
[Hypothesize]

Once they arrived in Texas during the revolution, maybe the Santos and Garcia families simply wanted to forget their past in Mexico—the dusty streets, broken-down houses, and hunger. They wanted to burn away the memory of when the families came north across the Rio Grande. Northern Mexico became one of the most violent and chaotic battlefields of *la Revolución* of 1910, a revolution that was to last eleven years. But for the first years, the revolution was only distant thunder, more of a concern to Mexicans well to the south of Coahuila in states such as Guerrero, Puebla, and Mexico City. The family's flight from Coahuila was in 1914, the year Pancho Villa, along with a myriad of other revolutionary bands, rose up to occupy the bare constellation of towns across the parched high Norteño desert where they had made their homes. San Antonio provided them a convenient escape from the fighting, and—despite other intentions—a shelter for memory, instead of its negation.

For my cousins, as for my brothers and me, the homes of *las Viejitas*[7] were sanctuaries where Coahuila was still alive, and places where the inhibitions and proprieties of the Gringo world of San Antonio, Texas, outside did not apply. Those were days when the taco and the tamal[8] were stigmatized in public, and Spanish was seldom heard on downtown streets. The old tíos[9] had to speak English, often haltingly, to get along in the working world. Most of *las Viejitas*, staying in their homes, spoke only Spanish, or at least pretended not to speak English. When Uela spoke Spanish, her sentences moved in one steady arc, like a bow across a violin, and her words were delicately pronounced, so that you could hear every tinkle of an old chandelier, every gust of a Coahuila wind falling to a hush, and the grain of a rustling squash blossom.

The migrations continued through the century. In the 1960s, my parents moved us from one of the old neighborhoods of the city to a new suburb at the city's northwestern edge, in order to get us into the better public schools in San Antonio. We were the first Mexicans in the neighborhood, in a two-floor house with a two-car garage, a built-in dishwasher, central air-conditioning, and intercom consoles in every room. We spoke English to each other, and Spanish to the old ones in the family. When the mariachis played in our backyard, the rapid plucking of the bajo sexto[10] and the shimmering trumpet lines echoed off the neighbors' houses and drew them out to listen. Out there in that virgin neighborhood, it always felt as if we were closer to the iridescent Texas sky, stripped of the protective canopy of sycamore, wisteria, china berry, and live oak that arched over so many of the streets of our old, secret Mexican city, San Antonio de Bejar.

That old San Antonio was part of the hoary earth of the ancestors. Out there in the suburb at the edge of the city, following the early Gemini and Apollo space missions, I read books about space and prepared for the day in the future, which would undoubtedly come, when I would leave this planet in a rocket of my own.

---

7. *las Viejitas* (läs bē′ ā hē′ täs) *n.* literally, "little old ladies." Santos is using this as a term of endearment for his elderly women relatives.
8. tamal (tä′ mäl) *n.* tamale, a steamed corn husk filled with meat and cornmeal.
9. tíos (ti′ ōs) *n.* uncles.
10. bajo sexto (bä′ hō seks′ tō) *n.* six-string bass.

John Phillip Santos
Author's Insight
It's important to understand that family history happens inside of world history. The 1910 Revolución in Mexico caused my family, among many others, to flee Mexico for Texas.

Themes in Literature
Cultural Context Details about the difficulties many Mexicans faced in Texas in the early 1900s help make the author's experiences more meaningful.

**Reading Check**

Why did Santos's forbears flee Mexico in 1914?

Today, in New York City, I live in a world *las Viejitas* never visited, very far from the land they knew well. I have been to places they never imagined, like England, Europe, Turkey, Peru, and the Sudan. Yet, wherever I go, there is a ribbon of primordial Mexican night, the color of obsidian,[11] snaking in a dream through the skies high over my head. Sometimes it is easily visible to me, like a burning galaxy, sometimes it is not. Sometimes it drizzles a fine rain of voices, images, and stories. And *las Viejitas* are here now, too, as they have always been, invisible yet abiding. They are keeping a vigil over the stories they told to me as if they are a *compromiso,* a promise that has been handed on. I have always felt connected, oriented, and imparted to by them, but unsure how I fit into a story that was never meant to be told.

---

11. **obsidian** (əb sid′ ē ən) *n.* dark or black volcanic glass.

▼ Critical Viewing In what ways does this photograph suggest a journey from the past into the future? **[Interpret]**

Q. **Where does the book's title come from?**

A. When I was a kid, my great aunt told me a story about a mysterious place in northern Mexico that hid a deep secret about the creation of the world. The story appears in an early chapter, and its strange understanding of the world helped me to understand what I was really writing about. If the world is unfinished, then surely we are too. The original title was *Immaterial America*. But I like long titles. *Places* told a part of my father's family's story. My new book, which deals with my mother's family, will be titled *The Farthest Home Is in an Empire of Fire*. I've imagined one more volume in this series of autobiographical books, and it will probably have a long title, too.

Q. **In what traditions do you see your work?**

A. As a writer from Texas who grew up speaking English and studied American literature, I see the book coming partly out of that tradition. But I also grew up speaking Spanish and reading great Mexican and Latin American literature.

Student Corner

Q. **Why do you feel that stories and heirlooms like photographs need to be passed down through generations?**
—Robin Posey, St. Paul, Minnesota

A. Every life has its story, but the lives of a family together inevitably tell a larger story about humanity that one life alone cannot fathom. Whatever is passed down through generations will shape the memory of the past that tells us where we came from and how we got here. As writers, we want to reclaim that story, and tell it to others, so that they will tell their tales, and on and on.

 Writing Workshop: *Work in Progress*

Writing for Assessment

To practice timed writing, list two common themes or insights you have encountered in literature. Choose one and write for fifteen minutes on the topic. Save this timed essay in your writing portfolio.

Apply the Skills

Exploring Themes in Literature

Thinking About the Selection

1. **Respond:** How important do you think it is for a family to actively preserve its history and traditions? Explain your answer.

2. **(a) Recall:** Why does the Santos family move to San Antonio? **(b) Analyze Cause and Effect:** Why might these circumstances have affected their desire to remember the past?

3. **(a) Interpret:** What does Santos mean when he says his family is "traveling light through time"? **(b) Generalize:** Do you think this tendency to "travel light" is unusual or common among modern-day families? Explain.

4. **(a) Compare and Contrast:** In what specific ways is Santos's life different from those of his Mexican ancestors? **(b) Analyze:** How does Santos maintain a connection to his family's past?

Reviewing Themes in Literature

5. **(a)** Using a chart like the one shown, identify passages containing **cultural details** that help the Santos family maintain its **identity** over time. **(b)** Compare your findings with those of a classmate. Eliminate duplications and rewrite the complete list in order of importance. **(c)** Discuss the values each item on your list represents to the Santos family. Share your ideas with the class.

Passage	Cultural Detail	Why It Is Important

6. What role does the **oral tradition** play in helping Santos understand his family's past?

Research the Author

Create an **annotated map** of the places where Santos and his family settled in Mexico and Texas. Follow these steps:
- Reread the selection and make a list of the places.
- Use library and Internet sources to study each place.
- Draw or adapt a poster-sized map showing these locations.
- For each location, write a brief note about the significant events that occurred while the family or Santos himself lived there.
- Display the map in class.

QuickReview

Selection at a Glance
The author traces the journey of his family from Mexico to Texas and beyond.

Go **O**nline
— **Assessment**
For: Self-test
Visit: www.PHSchool.com
Web Code: eqa-6601

Cultural details: beliefs, values, traditions, and customs of a group, society, or civilization

Identity: a sense of one's self as both an individual and as a member of an ethnic, religious, or racial group

Oral Tradition: the passing of songs, stories, and poems from generation to generation by word-of-mouth

Unit 6
Part 1
Cultural Context

Skills You Will Learn

Literary Analysis: *Myths*
Reading Skill: *Generate Questions to Analyze Cultural Context*

Literary Analysis: *Epics and Epic Heroes*
Reading Skill: *Acquire Background Knowledge to Analyze Cultural Context*

Reading Skill: *Make Generalizations to Build Historical Context*

Literary Analysis: *Comparing Uses of Archetypal Narrative Patterns*

Literature You Will Read

Reading: Cultural Context

**Academic
Standards**

• Examine how the author's
perspective influences the
structure and tone of the
text. (10.2.4)

• Evaluate the aesthetic
qualities of style. (10.3.11)

> **Analyzing cultural context** means determining how a
> work reflects the customs and concerns of the culture that
> produced it.

Skills and Strategies You Will Learn in Part 1

In Part 1, you will learn

• to **generate questions** in order to **analyze cultural context.**
  (p. 980)

• to **use text aids and selection details to acquire
  background knowledge** about **cultural context.** (p. 1004)

• to use **research** to **make generalizations** that build **cultural
  context.** (p. 1030)

Using the Skills and Strategies in Part 1

In Part 1, you will learn to **generate questions to analyze the
cultural context** of a work. You will also learn to **acquire background
knowledge about cultural context** by referring to the **textual aids
and details** in a selection. Then, you will practice using research to
make generalizations about the culture that produced the text.

This example shows some questions that have been generated to
analyze the cultural context of this text.

I will proclaim to the world the deeds of
Gilgamesh. This was the man to whom all
things were known; this was the king who
knew the countries of the world. . . .
  In Uruk he built walls, a great rampart, and
the temple of blessed Eanna, for the god of
the firmament Anu, and for Ishtar the
goddess of love. Look at it still today; the
outer wall where the cornice runs, it shines
with the brilliance of copper. . . .

Cultural Questions
What kind of government
did the culture have?

What did the culture value?

Which details indicate how
advanced the culture is?

What were the culture's
religious beliefs?

Academic Vocabulary: Words for Developing Concepts in Literature

The following words will help you write and talk about the cultural context of the selections in this part.

Word	Definition	Example Sentence
incorporate *v.*	make part of something	*Incorporate* specific quotations from the text into your essay.
initiate *v.*	bring into practice or use; start	The beat poets *initiated* a new type of poetry.
unify *v.*	join together; unite	To *unify* the essay, we should add transitions.
manipulate *v.*	manage or control skillfully, often in an underhanded way	A good author lets events speak for themselves and does not *manipulate* the reader's response.
visual *adj.*	related to seeing	The play's *visual* effects were wonderful!

Vocabulary Skill: Context Clues

▶ **Context clues** are in the information surrounding a word and can be used to determine the word's meaning.

In Part 1, you will learn to use context clues
- in combination with word roots.
- to choose between multiple meanings.

Knowing the meaning of a word's root can give you a clue to the word's meaning. For more clues, look at the context, or surroundings, of the word.

Activity Write three sentences in which the context illustrates the meaning of each of these words: *incorporate, manipulate,* and *visual.* Include at least one context clue in each sentence, and explain how the clue or clues point to the meaning of the word.

> CONTEXT CLUE   CONTEXT CLUE
> Instead of just recording the music, we filmed the concert on videotape that we could watch when we got back.
> WORD ROOT   CONTEXT CLUE
> MEANING "SEE"
> Conclusion: A *videotape* is a tape on which pictures and sounds can be recorded.

Practice these skills with "Prometheus and the First People" (p. 982) or "The Orphan Boy and the Elk Dog" (p. 991).

Literary Analysis

Myths are stories that are part of an oral tradition: Before being written, they were told and retold from one generation to the next. Myths reflect the culture of the people who originated and shared them.

- Some myths explain a natural phenomenon or a specific custom by telling of its **origins**—how it came to be. These myths reveal the beliefs of ancient cultures.

- Myths include characters with exceptional characteristics. These characteristics emphasize qualities that the culture admired or feared.

- Some myths tell of a **quest**, or search, for knowledge or some important object. These myths reveal what was important to the culture.

- Other myths tell of a **transgression**, or the violation of a rule. These myths teach the values of the culture.

Academic Standards

- Examine how the author's perspective influences the structure and tone of the text. (10.2.4)
- Analyze many different forms of dramatic literature. (10.3.1)

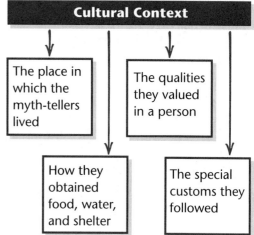

Cultural Context

The place in which the myth-tellers lived → How they obtained food, water, and shelter

The qualities they valued in a person → The special customs they followed

Reading Skill

To understand a myth, **analyze cultural context,** or determine ways in which the myth reflects the lives and concerns of those who told it. Before you read, **generate questions** about cultural context. Ask yourself one question about each element shown in the chart. Then, note details in the myth that help you answer your questions.

Vocabulary Builder

Prometheus and the First People

- **toil** (toil) *n.* hard, tiring work (p. 982) *After much toil, I finally finished building the wall.*

- **heedless** (hēd´ lis) *adj.* careless; thoughtless (p. 982) *His heedless remark was hurtful.*

- **counsel** (koun´ səl) *n.* advice; discussion (p. 985) *He sought his brother's counsel whenever he had to make a hard decision.*

- **disembarked** (dis´ im bärk´´t) *v.* left a ship to go ashore (p. 987) *They disembarked at the dock and waved goodbye to the ship's crew.*

The Orphan Boy and the Elk Dog

- **surpassed** (sər pas´´d) *v.* went beyond; excelled (p. 993) *Her score was so high, it surpassed her expectations.*

- **emanating** (em´ ə nāt´ iŋ) *v.* coming forth, as from a source (p. 996) *We were curious about the light emanating from the woods.*

- **relish** (rel´ ish) *n.* enjoyment (p. 996) *Her vivid gestures show that she talks with relish.*

- **stifle** (stī´ fəl) *v.* smother; hold back (p. 998) *She grew bored and could not stifle a yawn.*

Background

The Greek Gods Many of the characters in "Prometheus and the First People" are Olympians, the family of gods and goddesses ruled by Zeus and his wife Hera. Each god and goddess governs an aspect of nature or human life. For example, Ares (er´ ēz´) is the god of war.

Connecting to the Literature

Reading/Writing Connection In the myth of Prometheus, the ancient Greeks explain how human beings learned to cope in the world. Make a list of several inventions humans use for comfort and protection. Use at least three of the following words: *anticipate, assemble, speculate, study.*

READ MORE

by Olivia E. Coolidge

The Trojan War

Meet the Author

The Ancient Greeks and Olivia E. Coolidge (b. 1908)

Thousands of years ago in Greece, the Mycenaeans (mī´ sə nē´ ənz) told stories of a great sea god. Their civilization collapsed around 1200 B.C., but settlers from the north, the Dorians, blended the old myths with their own stories. Classical Greek mythology was born.

The ancient Greeks represented the Olympic gods as having human qualities. Just as the typical Greek household was dominated by the father, so Zeus dominates the Olympic gods.

Retelling the Tale Olivia E. Coolidge, who retells the myth of Prometheus, was born in London, England, where she studied Latin, Greek, and philosophy.

Fast Facts

▶ Many traditions of Western civilization, including democracy, science, and philosophy, began with the ancient Greeks.

▶ For centuries, Greek myth has been an inspiration for writers and artists.

Go Online
Author Link

For: more about the authors
Visit: www.PHSchool.com
Web Code: eqe-9602

PROMETHEUS AND THE FIRST PEOPLE

OLIVIA E. COOLIDGE

Humanity's Beginnings

The Greeks have several stories about how man came to be. One declares that he was created in the age of Kronos,[1] or Saturn, who ruled before Zeus [zōōs]. At that time, the legend says, there was no sorrow, toil, sickness, or age. Men lived their lives in plenty and died as though they went to sleep. They tilled[2] no ground, built no cities, killed no living thing, and among them war was unknown. The earth brought forth strawberries, cherries, and ears of wheat for them. Even on the bramble bushes grew berries good to eat. Milk and sweet nectar flowed in rivers for men to drink, and honey dripped from hollow trees. Men lived in caves and thickets, needing little shelter, for the season was always spring.

Another legend declares that Zeus conceived of animals first and he entrusted their creation to Prometheus [prō mē′ thē əs] and Epimetheus [ep ə mē′ thē əs], his brother. First, Epimetheus undertook to order all things, but he was a heedless person and soon got into trouble. Finally he was forced to appeal to Prometheus.

"What have you done?" asked Prometheus.

"Down on the earth," answered his brother, "there is a green, grassy clearing, ringed by tall oak trees and shaded by steep slopes from all but the midday sun. There I sat and the animals came to me, while I gave to each the gifts which should be his from this time

Vocabulary Builder
toil (toil) *n.* hard, tiring work

heedless (hēd′ lis) *adj.* careless; thoughtless

Literary Analysis
Myths Which details show you that this myth will explain the origins of something?

▶ **Critical Viewing** Which details in this painting of Prometheus suggest that he fears the gods' anger? **[Analyze]**

---

1. **Kronos** (krō′ nəs) son of the sky and the earth; father of Zeus.
2. **tilled** *v.* cultivated; plowed or hoed.

forward. Air I gave to the birds, seas to the fishes, land to four-footed creatures and the creeping insects, and to some, like the moles, I gave burrows beneath the earth."

"That was well done," answered Prometheus. "What else did you do?"

"Strength," said Epimetheus, "I gave to lions and tigers, and the fierce animals of the woods. Size I gave to others like the great whales of the sea. The deer I made swift and timid, and the insects I made tiny that they might escape from sight. I gave warm fur to the great bears and the little squirrels, keen eyes and sharp talons[3] to the birds of prey, tusks to the elephant, hide to the wild boar, sweet songs and bright feathers to the birds. To each I gave some special excellence, that whether large or small, kind or terrible, each might live in his own place, find food, escape enemies, and enjoy the wide world which is his to inhabit."

"All this is very good," said his brother, Prometheus. "You have done well. Wherein lies your trouble?"

"Because I did not think it out beforehand," said the heedless brother sadly, "I did not count how many animals there were to be before I started giving. Now when I have given all, there comes one last animal for whom I have neither skill nor shape, nor any place to dwell in. Everything has been given already."

"What is this animal," said Prometheus, "who has been forgotten?"

"His name," said Epimetheus, "is Man."

Thus it was that the future of man was left to Prometheus, who was forced to make man different from all other creatures. Therefore he gave him the shape of the gods themselves and the privilege of walking upright as they do. He gave him no special home, but made him ruler over the whole earth, and over the sea and air. Finally, he gave him no special strength or swiftness, but stole a spark from heaven and lighted a heavenly fire within his mind which should teach him to understand, to count, to speak, to remember. Man learned from it how to build cities, tame animals, raise crops, build boats, and do all the things that animals cannot. Prometheus also kindled fire on earth that man might smelt[4] metals and make tools. In fact, from this heavenly fire of Prometheus all man's greatness comes.

Before this time fire was a divine thing and belonged only to the gods. It was one of their greatest treasures, and Zeus would never have given Prometheus permission to use it in the creation of man. Therefore when Prometheus stole it, Zeus was furious indeed. He chained Prometheus to a great,

3. talons (tal´ ənz) *n.* claws (of birds of prey).
4. smelt *v.* purify metal by melting it.

Reading Skill
Analyzing Cultural Context What question does this paragraph suggest to you about the region where the Greeks lived?

▼ **Critical Viewing** What does this ancient Greek statue show about how the Greeks viewed the human form? Explain. **[Interpret]**

lofty rock, where the sun scorched him by day and the cruel frost tortured him by night. Not content with that, he sent an eagle to tear him, so that, though he could not die, he lived in agony. For many centuries Prometheus hung in torment, but he was wiser than Zeus, and by reason of a secret he had, he forced Zeus in later ages to set him free. By then, also, Zeus had learned that there is more in ruling than power and cruelty. Thus, the two at last were friends.

The Coming of Evil

After the punishment of Prometheus, Zeus planned to take his revenge on man. He could not recall the gift of fire, since it had been given by one of the immortals,[5] but he was not content that man should possess this treasure in peace and become perhaps as great as were the gods themselves. He therefore took <u>counsel</u> with the other gods, and together they made for man a woman. All the gods gave gifts to this new creation. Aphrodite [af´ rə dīt´ ē] gave her fresh beauty like the spring itself. The goddess Athene [ə thē´ nē] dressed her and put on her a garland of flowers and green leaves. She had also a golden diadem[6] beautifully decorated with figures of animals. In her heart Hermes [hʉr´ mēz´] put cunning, deceit, and curiosity. She was named Pandora [pan dôr´ ə], which means All-Gifted, since each of the gods had given her something. The last gift was a chest in which there was supposed to be great treasure, but which Pandora was instructed never to open. Then Hermes, the Messenger, took the girl and brought her to Epimetheus.

Epimetheus had been warned by his brother to receive no gifts from Zeus, but he was a heedless person, as ever, and Pandora was very lovely. He accepted her, therefore, and for a while they lived together in happiness, for Pandora besides her beauty had been given both wit and charm. Eventually, however, her curiosity got the better of her, and she determined to see for herself what treasure it was that the gods had given her. One day when she was alone, she went over to the corner where her chest lay and cautiously lifted the lid for a peep. The lid flew up out of her hands and knocked her aside, while before her frightened eyes dreadful, shadowy shapes flew out of the box in an endless stream. There were hunger, disease, war, greed, anger, jealousy, toil, and all the griefs and hardships to which man from that day has been subject. Each was terrible in appearance, and as it passed, Pandora saw something of

Literary Analysis
Myths Why is Prometheus' gift of fire a transgression?

Vocabulary Builder
counsel (kōun´ səl) *n.* advice; discussion

✔ Reading Check

Why does Zeus punish Prometheus?

---

5. immortals (i môrt´ ′lz) *n.* those who do not die.
6. diadem (dī´ ə dem´) *n.* crown.

the misery that her thoughtless action had brought on her descendants. At last the stream slackened,[7] and Pandora, who had been paralyzed with fear and horror, found strength to shut her box. The only thing left in it now, however, was the one good gift the gods had put in among so many evil ones. This was hope, and since that time the hope that is in man's heart is the only thing which has made him able to bear the sorrows that Pandora brought upon him.

The Great Flood

When evil first came among mankind, people became very wicked. War, robbery, treachery, and murder prevailed throughout the world. Even the worship of the gods, the laws of truth and honor, reverence[8] for parents and brotherly love were neglected.

Finally, Zeus determined to destroy the race of men altogether, and the other gods agreed. All the winds were therefore shut up in a cave except the South Wind, the wet one. He raced over the earth with water streaming from his beard and long, white hair. Clouds gathered around his head, and dew dripped from his wings and the ends of his garments. With him went Iris, the rainbow goddess, while below Poseidon [pō sī´ dən] smote the earth with his trident until it shook and gaped open, so that the waters of the sea rushed up over the land.

Fields and farmhouses were buried. Fish swam in the tops of the trees. Sea beasts were quietly feeding where flocks and herds had grazed before. On the surface of the water, boars, stags, lions, and tigers struggled desperately to keep afloat. Wolves swam in the midst of flocks of sheep, but the sheep were not frightened by them, and the wolves never thought of their natural prey. Each fought for his own life and forgot the others. Over them wheeled countless birds, winging far and wide in the hope of finding something to rest upon. Eventually they too fell into the water and were drowned.

Literature in Context

Culture Connection

The Twelve Olympian Gods
The ancient Greeks worshiped a family of gods said to have their home on Mount Olympus:

Zeus (zo͞os) ruler of the gods

Hera (hir´ ə) queen of the gods; goddess of marriage

Aphrodite (af´ rə dīt´ ē) goddess of love and beauty

Apollo (ə päl´ ō) god of music, poetry, and light

Ares (er´ ēz´) god of war

Artemis (är´ tə mis) goddess of the moon, wild animals, and hunting

Athene (ə thē´ nē) goddess of wisdom

Demeter (di mēt´ ər) goddess of grain and agriculture

Hephaestus (hē fes´ təs) god of fire; blacksmith of the gods

Hermes (hur´ mēz´) messenger of the gods; god of business, science, and speech

Hestia (hes´ tē ə) goddess of the hearth

Poseidon (pō sī´ dən) god of earthquakes, the sea, and horses

Connect to the Literature

According to this myth, what is the relationship between the gods and humans like?

---

7. slackened (slak´ ənd) *v.* diminished; became less active.
8. reverence (rev´ ə rəns) *n.* feeling or display of great respect.

All over the water were men in small boats or makeshift rafts. Some even had oars which they tried to use, but the waters were fierce and stormy, and there was nowhere to go. In time all were drowned, until at last there was no one left but an old man and his wife, Deucalion [dōō kāl´ ē ən] and Pyrrha [pir´ ə]. These two people had lived in truth and justice, unlike the rest of mankind. They had been warned of the coming of the flood and had built a boat and stocked it. For nine days and nights they floated until Zeus took pity on them and they came to the top of Mount Parnassus, the sacred home of the Muses.[9] There they found land and <u>disembarked</u> to wait while the gods recalled the water they had unloosed.

When the waters fell, Deucalion and Pyrrha looked over the land, despairing. Mud and sea slime covered the earth; all living things had been swept away. Slowly and sadly they made their way down the mountain until they came to a temple where there had been an oracle.[10] Black seaweed dripped from the pillars now, and the mud was over all. Nevertheless the two knelt down and kissed the temple steps while Deucalion prayed to the goddess to tell them what they should do. All men were dead but themselves, and they were old. It was impossible that they should have children to people the earth again. Out of the temple a great voice was heard speaking strange words.

"Depart," it said, "with veiled heads and loosened robes, and throw behind you as you go the bones of your mother."

Pyrrha was in despair when she heard this saying. "The bones of our mother!" she cried. "How can we tell now where they lie? Even if we knew, we could never do such a dreadful thing as to disturb their resting place and scatter them over the earth like an armful of stones."

"Stones!" said Deucalion quickly. "That must be what the goddess means. After all Earth is our mother, and the other thing is too horrible for us to suppose that a goddess would ever command it."

Accordingly both picked up armfuls of stones, and as they went away from the temple with faces veiled, they cast the stones behind them. From each of those Deucalion cast sprang up a man, and from Pyrrha's stones sprang women. Thus the earth was repeopled, and in the course of time it brought forth again animals from itself, and all was as before. Only from that time men have been less sensitive and have found it easier to endure toil, and sorrow, and pain, since now they are descended from stones.

Vocabulary Builder
disembarked (dis´ im bärk´ 't) v. left a ship to go ashore

Literary Analysis
Myth What fact of life does the myth of Deucalion and Pyrrha explain?

---

9. **Muses** (myōōz´ iz) *n.* nine goddesses who rule over literature and the arts and sciences.
10. **oracle** (ôr´ ə kəl) *n.* person who, when consulted on a matter, is said to reveal the will of the gods.

Apply the Skills

Prometheus and the First People

Thinking About the Selection

1. **Respond:** What questions would you like to ask Zeus? Explain.
2. **(a) Recall:** What problem does Epimetheus face when it is humanity's turn to receive a gift? **(b) Contrast:** Contrast the gifts Prometheus gives humanity with the gifts Epimetheus gives the animals. **(c) Evaluate:** Which gift is most valuable? Why?
3. **(a) Recall:** Which of Prometheus' actions angers Zeus? **(b) Infer:** Why does it anger him? **(c) Draw Conclusions:** How did the Greeks view Zeus? Support your answer with details from the text.
4. **(a) Analyze Cause and Effect:** What changes does Pandora bring to the world by opening the box? **(b) Connect:** How does her mistake solve the problem Prometheus caused for the gods?
5. **(a) Evaluate:** What ideas about human limitations do these myths express? Explain. **(b) Discuss:** Share and discuss responses with a partner. Work together to formulate a response that represents both of your opinions. Share your idea with the class.

Literary Analysis

6. Using a chart like the one shown, identify which characteristics of **myths** are found in "Prometheus and the First People." Support your choices by supplying examples from the text.

What the Story Explains	Exceptional or Fantastic Characters	Quest	Transgression

7. **(a)** What do the myths suggest about the value the ancient Greeks placed on the human power to reason? Explain. **(b)** In what way does the story of Pandora show that the gift of intelligence is also a curse? **(c)** Working from your previous answer, draw a conclusion about the ancient Greek view of humanity.
8. **(a)** Why does Zeus save Deucalion and Pyrrha? **(b)** Draw a conclusion about ancient Greek values from their story.

Reading Skill

9. **(a)** Give two examples of questions you might ask to **analyze the cultural context** of the myth. **(b)** Explain what answers the myth suggests, and support your answer with details from the text.

QuickReview

Myths at a Glance
Three myths explain the introduction of unhappiness in the world.

Go Online
Assessment
For: Self-test
Visit: www.PHSchool.com
Web Code: eqa-6602

Myth: a story that is part of a culture's oral tradition; myths often explain the *origins* of some thing or custom.

Analyzing Cultural Context: determining the ways in which a myth reflects the lives and concerns of those who told it

Vocabulary Builder

Practice Copy each of the following word pairs. If the words have similar meanings, write *S* for **synonyms.** If the words have opposite meanings, write *A* for **antonyms.** Explain each of your choices.

1. toil, work

2. heedless, cautious

3. counsel, recommendation

4. disembarked, boarded

Adding Words to Your Vocabulary Using a dictionary, find three meanings for *counsel,* including its meanings as a noun and as a verb. For each meaning, write a sentence using the word correctly. (For more on using a dictionary, see page R6.)

Writing

In a small group, write a **myth** about the origin of some aspect of human life, such as how gossip or forgiveness entered the world. Follow these steps:

- Agree on a topic that group members find interesting.
- Have one member write an opening sentence.
- Each group member should take a turn writing a sentence that follows from the one before until the myth is complete.
- As a group, review the story as it progresses, and make any revisions agreed upon by the group members.

Present your myth to the class.

For *Grammar, Vocabulary,* and *Assessment,*
see **Build Language Skills,** pages 1002–1003.

Extend Your Learning

Listening and Speaking Locate another Greek myth about the gods and humans. Present a **retelling** of the story to your class. Afterward, have classmates summarize the myth you have retold. Then, lead a discussion in which you compare and contrast the myth to "Prometheus and the First People."

Research and Technology Myths were oral literature before they were written down. Conduct research on the Greek written alphabet. Write a brief **language report** in which you draw a conclusion about the importance of the Greek alphabet for later systems of writing.

Myth

Background

Horses in America "The Orphan Boy and the Elk Dog" explains the origin of an important part of the North American Blackfeet culture—horses. Horses did not always exist in North America. Spanish explorer Hernando Cortés brought the first horses to Mexico in 1519, and they quickly spread northward. By the 1600s, many Native American tribes had captured and tamed wild horses.

Connecting to the Literature

Reading/Writing Connection This myth tells how the Blackfeet acquired a crucial kind of transportation—the horse. List the reasons you depend on modes of transportation other than walking. Use at least three of these words: *rely, depend, enable, transport*.

Review

For **Literary Analysis**, **Reading Skill**, and **Vocabulary Builder**, see page 980.

READ MORE

by the Authors

Blackfeet Tales of Glacier Park

Meet the Authors

The **Blackfeet**

The Blackfeet are one of the many Native American nations that have lived on the Great Plains of North America. At one time, most Plains Indians were farmers who lived in one place, grew their own food, and sometimes hunted buffalo on foot. Then, in the 1600s, many tribes captured and tamed wild horses.

New Way of Life In time, the Blackfeet became skillful riders, and horses transformed their way of life. A mounted hunter could search for game more efficiently. Hunting replaced farming, and the tribes followed the buffalo herds.

Today, the Blackfeet live on reservations in Montana and in Canada. Myths like "The Orphan Boy and the Elk Dog" reflect the importance of the horse in early Blackfeet culture.

Fast Facts

▶ The name "Blackfeet" is a reference to the dark moccasins worn by early Blackfeet people.

▶ About the time the Blackfeet discovered horses, they also began hunting with guns acquired from European settlers.

Go Online
Author Link

For: More about the authors
Visit: www.PHSchool.com
Web Code: eqe-9603

THE ORPHAN BOY AND THE ELK DOG

NATIVE AMERICAN (BLACKFEET)

The Color of Sun, Howard Terpnin. Licensed by The Greenwich Workshop, Inc.

◀ **Critical Viewing**
Use the selection title and this painting to predict what this story is about. **[Predict]**

I n the days when people had only dogs to carry their bundles, two orphan children, a boy and his sister, were having a hard time. The boy was deaf, and because he could not understand what people said, they thought him foolish and dull-witted. Even his relatives wanted nothing to do with him. The name he had been given at birth, while his parents still lived, was Long Arrow. Now he was like a beaten, mangy dog, the kind who hungrily roams outside a camp, circling it from afar, smelling the good meat boiling in the kettles but never coming close for fear of being kicked. Only his sister, who was bright and beautiful, loved him.

Then the sister was adopted by a family from another camp, people who were attracted by her good looks and pleasing ways. Though they wanted her for a daughter, they certainly did not want the awkward, stupid boy. And so they took away the only person who cared about him, and the orphan boy was left to fend for

Reading Skill
Analyzing Cultural Context What questions about Blackfeet culture does the first paragraph suggest?

Reading Check

What difficulties does Long Arrow face?

himself. He lived on scraps thrown to the dogs and things he found on the refuse heaps. He dressed in remnants of skins and frayed robes discarded by the poorest people. At night he bedded down in a grass-lined dugout, like an animal in its den.

Eventually the game was hunted out near the camp that the boy regarded as his, and the people decided to move. The lodges were taken down, belongings were packed into rawhide bags and put on dog travois,[1] and the village departed. "Stay here," they told the boy. "We don't want your kind coming with us."

For two or three days the boy fed on scraps the people had left behind, but he knew he would starve if he stayed. He had to join his people, whether they liked it or not. He followed their tracks, frantic that he would lose them, and crying at the same time. Soon the sweat was running down his skinny body. As he was stumbling, running, panting, something suddenly snapped in his left ear with a sound like a small crack, and a wormlike substance came out of that ear. All at once on his left side he could hear birdsongs for the first time. He took this wormlike thing in his left hand and hurried on. Then there was a snap in his right ear and a wormlike thing came out of it, and on his right side he could hear the rushing waters of a stream. His hearing was restored! And it was razor-sharp—he could make out the rustling of a tiny mouse in dry leaves a good distance away. The orphan boy laughed and was happy for the first time in his life. With renewed courage he followed the trail his people had made.

In the meantime the village had settled into its new place. Men were already out hunting. Thus the boy came upon Good Running, a kindly old chief, butchering a fat buffalo cow he had just killed. When the chief saw the boy, he said to himself, "Here comes that poor good-for-nothing boy. It was wrong to abandon him." To the boy Good Running said "Rest here, grandson, you're sweaty and covered with dust. Here, have some tripe."[2]

The boy wolfed down the meat. He was not used to hearing and talking yet, but his eyes were alert and Good Running also noticed a change in his manner. "This boy," the chief said to himself, "is neither stupid nor crazy." He gave the orphan a piece of the hump meat, then a piece of liver, then a

Reading Skill
Analyzing Cultural Context In this paragraph, what do you learn about Blackfeet life?

▼ **Critical Viewing**
From this picture, what can you tell about the life of the Blackfeet? Explain. **[Analyze]**

---

1. travois (trə voi´) *n.* sled with two poles and a net or platform in between, pulled along the ground by a person or an animal.
2. tripe (trīp) *n.* walls of the stomach of a buffalo or other grazing animal, used as food.

piece of raw kidney, and at last the very best kind of meat—a slice of tongue. The more the old man looked at the boy, the more he liked him. On the spur of the moment he said, "Grandson, I'm going to adopt you; there's a place for you in my tipi. And I'm going to make you into a good hunter and warrior." The boy wept, this time for joy. Good Running said, "They called you a stupid, crazy boy, but now that I think of it, the name you were given at birth is Long Arrow. I'll see that people call you by your right name. Now come along."

The chief's wife was not pleased. "Why do you put this burden on me," she said, "bringing into our lodge this good-for-nothing, this slow-witted crazy boy? Maybe you're a little slow-witted and crazy yourself!"

"Woman, keep talking like that and I'll beat you! This boy isn't slow or crazy; he's a good boy, and I have taken him for my grandson. Look—he's barefooted. Hurry up, and make a pair of moccasins for him, and if you don't do it well I'll take a stick to you."

Good Running's wife grumbled but did as she was told. Her husband was a kind man, but when aroused, his anger was great.

So a new life began for Long Arrow. He had to learn to speak and to understand well, and to catch up on all the things a boy should know. He was a fast learner and soon <u>surpassed</u> other boys his age in knowledge and skills. At last even Good Running's wife accepted him.

He grew up into a fine young hunter, tall and good-looking in the quilled buckskin outfit the chief's wife made for him. He helped his grandfather in everything and became a staff for Good Running to lean on. But he was lonely, for most people in the camp could not forget that Long Arrow had once been an outcast. "Grandfather," he said one day, "I want to do something to make you proud and show people that you were wise to adopt me. What can I do?"

Good Running answered, "Someday you will be a chief and do great things."

"But what's a great thing I could do now, Grandfather?"

The chief thought for a long time. "Maybe I shouldn't tell you this," he said. "I love you and don't want to lose you. But on winter nights, men talk of powerful spirit people living at the bottom of a faraway lake. Down in that lake the spirit people keep mystery animals who do their work for them. These animals are larger than a great elk, but they carry the burdens of the spirit people like dogs. So they're called Pono-Kamita—Elk Dogs. They are said to be swift, strong, gentle, and beautiful beyond imagination. Every fourth generation, one of our young warriors has gone to find these spirit folk and bring back an Elk Dog for us. But none of our brave young men has ever returned."

Vocabulary Builder
surpassed (sər pas´´d)
v. went beyond; excelled

Literary Analysis
Myth What mythical qualities do the Elk Dogs have?

**Reading Check**

Identify two ways Long Arrow's life has improved.

"Grandfather, I'm not afraid. I'll go and find the Elk Dog."

"Grandson, first learn to be a man. Learn the right prayers and ceremonies. Be brave. Be generous and open-handed. Pity the old and the fatherless, and let the holy men of the tribe find a medicine for you which will protect you on your dangerous journey. We will begin by purifying you in the sweat bath."

So Long Arrow was purified with the white steam of the sweat lodge. He was taught how to use the pipe, and how to pray to the Great Mystery Power. The tribe's holy men gave him a medicine[3] and made for him a shield with designs on it to ward off danger.

Then one morning, without telling anybody, Good Running loaded his best travois dog with all the things Long Arrow would need for traveling. The chief gave him his medicine, his shield, and his own fine bow and, just as the sun came up, went with his grandson to the edge of the camp to purify him with sweet-smelling cedar smoke. Long Arrow left unheard and unseen by anyone else. After a while some people noticed that he was gone, but no one except his grandfather knew where and for what purpose.

Following Good Running's advice, Long Arrow wandered south-ward. On the fourth day of his journey he came to a small pond, where a strange man was standing as if waiting for him. "Why have you come here?" the stranger asked.

"I have come to find the mysterious Elk Dog."

"Ah, there I cannot help you," said the man, who was the spirit of the pond. "But if you travel further south, four-times-four days, you might chance upon a bigger lake and there meet one of my uncles. Possibly he might talk to you; then again, he might not. That's all I can tell you."

---

3. medicine in Native American culture, an object, a ceremony, a song, and so on with religious or magical power.

Literary Analysis
Myth What quest does Long Arrow undertake?

▼ Critical Viewing
Judging from this photograph, what qualities of horses might impress someone who had never seen one before?

Long Arrow thanked the man, who went down to the bottom of the pond, where he lived.

Long Arrow wandered on, walking for long hours and taking little time for rest. Through deep canyons and over high mountains he went, wearing out his moccasins and enduring cold and heat, hunger and thirst.

Finally Long Arrow approached a big lake surrounded by steep pine-covered hills. There he came face to face with a tall man, fierce and scowling and twice the height of most humans. This stranger carried a long lance with a heavy spearpoint made of shining flint. "Young one," he growled, "why did you come here?"

"I came to find the mysterious Elk Dog."

The stranger, who was the spirit of the lake, stuck his face right into Long Arrow's and shook his mighty lance. "Little one, aren't you afraid of me?" he snarled.

"No, I am not," answered Long Arrow, smiling.

The tall spirit man gave a hideous grin, which was his way of being friendly. "I like small humans who aren't afraid," he said, "but I can't help you. Perhaps our grandfather will take the trouble to listen to you. More likely he won't. Walk south for four-times-four days, and maybe you'll find him. But probably you won't." With that the tall spirit turned his back on Long Arrow and went to the bottom of the lake, where he lived.

Long Arrow walked on for another four-times-four days, sleeping and resting little. By now he staggered and stumbled in his weakness, and his dog was not much better off. At last he came to the biggest lake he had ever seen, surrounded by towering snow-capped peaks and waterfalls of ice. This time there was nobody to receive him. As a matter of fact, there seemed to be no living thing around. "This must be the Great Mystery Lake," thought Long Arrow. Exhausted, he fell down upon the shortgrass meadow by the lake, fell down among the wild flowers, and went to sleep with his tired dog curled up at his feet.

When Long Arrow awoke, the sun was already high. He opened his eyes and saw a beautiful child standing before him, a boy in a dazzling white buckskin robe decorated with porcupine quills of many colors. The boy said, "We have been expecting you for a long time. My grandfather invites you to his lodge. Follow me."

Telling his dog to wait, Long Arrow took his medicine shield and his grandfather's bow and went with the wonderful child. They came to the edge of the lake. The spirit boy pointed to the water and

Literary Analysis
Myth What mythical qualities does the stranger have?

**Reading Check**

Who has directed Long Arrow to the Great Mystery Lake?

said, "My grandfather's lodge is down there. Come." The child turned himself into a kingfisher[4] and dove straight to the bottom.

Afraid, Long Arrow thought, "How can I follow him and not be drowned?" But then he said to himself, "I knew all the time that this would not be easy. In setting out to find the Elk Dog, I already threw my life away." And he boldly jumped into the water. To his surprise, he found it did not make him wet, that it parted before him, that he could breathe and see. He touched the lake's sandy bottom. It sloped down, down toward a center point.

Long Arrow descended this slope until he came to a small flat valley. In the middle of it stood a large tipi of tanned buffalo hide. The images of two strange animals were drawn on it in sacred vermilion[5] paint. A kingfisher perched high on the top of the tipi flew down and turned again into the beautiful boy, who said, "Welcome. Enter my grandfather's lodge."

Long Arrow followed the spirit boy inside. In the back at the seat of honor sat a black-robed old man with flowing white hair and such power <u>emanating</u> from him that Long Arrow felt himself in the presence of a truly Great One. The holy man welcomed Long Arrow and offered him food. The man's wife came in bringing dishes of buffalo hump, liver, tongues, delicious chunks of deer meat, the roasted flesh of strange, tasty water birds, and meat pounded together with berries, chokecherries, and kidney fat. Famished after his long journey, Long Arrow ate with <u>relish</u>. Yet he still looked around to admire the furnishings of the tipi, the painted inner curtain, the many medicine shields, wonderfully wrought weapons, shirts and robes decorated with porcupine quills in rainbow colors, beautifully painted rawhide containers filled with wonderful things, and much else that dazzled him.

After Long Arrow had stilled his hunger, the old spirit chief filled the pipe and passed it to his guest. They smoked, praying silently. After a while the old man said, "Some came before you from time to time, but they were always afraid of the deep water, and so they went away with empty hands. But you, grandson, were brave enough to plunge in, and therefore you are chosen to receive a wonderful gift to carry back to your people. Now, go outside with my grandson."

The beautiful boy took Long Arrow to a meadow on which some strange animals, unlike any the young man had ever seen, were galloping and gamboling, neighing and nickering. They were truly won-

---

4. **kingfisher** n. type of water bird that dives for its food.
5. **vermilion** (vər mil′ yən) n. bright red.

derful to look at, with their glossy coats fine as a maiden's hair, their long manes and tails streaming in the wind. Now rearing, now nuzzling, they looked at Long Arrow with gentle eyes which belied their fiery appearance.

"At last," thought Long Arrow, "here they are before my own eyes, the Pono-Kamita, the Elk Dogs!"

"Watch me," said the mystery boy, "so that you learn to do what I am doing." Gracefully and without effort, the boy swung himself onto the back of a jet-black Elk Dog with a high, arched neck. Larger than any elk Long Arrow had ever come across, the animal carried the boy all over the meadow swiftly as the wind. Then the boy returned, jumped off his mount, and said, "Now you try it." A little timidly Long Arrow climbed up on the beautiful Elk Dog's back. Seemingly regarding him as feather-light, it took off like a flying arrow. The young man felt himself soaring through the air as a bird does, and experienced a happiness greater even than the joy he had felt when Good Running had adopted him as a grandson.

When they had finished riding the Elk Dogs, the spirit boy said to Long Arrow, "Young hunter from the land above the waters, I want you to have what you have come for. Listen to me. You may have noticed that my grandfather wears a black medicine robe as long as a woman's dress, and that he is always trying to hide his feet. Try to get a glimpse of them, for if you do, he can refuse you nothing. He will then tell you to ask him for a gift, and you must ask for these three things: his rainbow-colored quilled belt, his black medicine robe, and a herd of these animals which you seem to like."

Long Arrow thanked him and vowed to follow his advice. For four days the young man stayed in the spirit chief's lodge, where he ate well and often went out riding on the Elk Dogs. But try as he would, he could never get a look at the old man's feet. The spirit chief always kept them carefully covered. Then on the morning of the fourth day, the old one

Literature in Context

Culture Connection

Traditional Great Plains Culture
Before the westward push of white settlers ended their traditional way of life, the Blackfeet and other Native American tribes of the Great Plains shared a common culture.

- The life of the Plains peoples revolved around the buffalo—they ate buffalo meat, slept in tipis made from buffalo hides, sewed with thread made from buffalo sinews, and carried water in buffalo stomachs.

- Plains tribes prized the virtues of a warrior—bravery, the ability to endure pain, skill with a bow, and masterful horsemanship.

- Young men sought spiritual assistance by fasting and going on vision quests.

Connect to the Literature

Which details in the story illustrate these elements of Plains culture?

Reading Check

What creatures does Long Arrow find in the spirit chief's lake?

was walking out of the tipi when his medicine robe caught in the entrance flap. As the robe opened, Long Arrow caught a glimpse of a leg and one foot. He was awed to see that it was not a human limb at all, but the glossy leg and firm hoof of an Elk Dog! He could not <u>stifle</u> a cry of surprise, and the old man looked over his shoulder and saw that his leg and hoof were exposed. The chief seemed a little embarrassed, but shrugged and said, "I tried to hide this, but you must have been fated to see it. Look, both of my feet are those of an Elk Dog. You may as well ask me for a gift. Don't be timid; tell me what you want."

Long Arrow spoke boldly: "I want three things: your belt of rainbow colors, your black medicine robe, and your herd of Elk Dogs."

"Well, so you're really not timid at all!" said the old man. "You ask for a lot, and I'll give it to you, except that you cannot have all my Elk Dogs; I'll give you half of them. Now I must tell you that my black medicine robe and my many-colored belt have Elk Dog magic in them. Always wear the robe when you try to catch Elk Dogs; then they can't get away from you. On quiet nights, if you listen closely to the belt, you will hear the Elk Dog dance song and Elk Dog prayers. You must learn them. And I will give you one more magic gift: this long rope woven from the hair of a white buffalo bull. With it you will never fail to catch whichever Elk Dog you want."

The spirit chief presented him with the gifts and said, "Now you must leave. At first the Elk Dogs will not follow you. Keep the medicine robe and the magic belt on at all times, and walk for four days toward the north. Never look back—always look to the north. On the fourth day the Elk Dogs will come up beside you on the left. Still don't look back. But after they have overtaken you, catch one with the rope of white buffalo hair and ride him home. Don't lose the black robe, or you will lose the Elk Dogs and never catch them again."

Long Arrow listened carefully so that he would remember. Then the old spirit chief had his wife make up a big pack of food, almost too heavy for Long Arrow to carry, and the young man took leave of his generous spirit host. The mysterious boy once again turned himself into a kingfisher and led Long Arrow to the surface of the lake, where his faithful dog greeted him joyfully. Long Arrow fed the dog, put his pack of food on the travois, and started walking north.

On the fourth day the Elk Dogs came up on his left side, as the spirit chief had foretold. Long Arrow snared the black one with the arched neck to ride, and he caught another to carry the pack of food. They galloped swiftly on, the dog barking at the big Elk Dogs' heels.

Vocabulary Builder
stifle (stī′ fəl) *v.*
smother; hold back

Reading Skill
Analyzing Cultural Context Given the details in this paragraph, what questions might you ask about Blackfeet ceremonies and songs?

When Long Arrow arrived at last in his village, the people were afraid and hid. They did not recognize him astride his beautiful Elk Dog but took him for a monster, half man and half animal. Long Arrow kept calling, "Grandfather Good Running, it's your grandson. I've come back bringing Elk Dogs!"

Recognizing the voice, Good Running came out of hiding and wept for joy, because he had given Long Arrow up for lost. Then all the others emerged from their hiding places to admire the wonderful new animals.

Long Arrow said, "My grandfather and grandmother who adopted me, I can never repay you for your kindness. Accept these wonderful Elk Dogs as my gift. Now we no longer need to be humble footsloggers, because these animals will carry us swiftly everywhere we want to go. Now buffalo hunting will be easy. Now our tipis will be larger, our possessions will be greater, because an Elk Dog travois can carry a load ten times bigger than that of a dog. Take them, my grandparents. I shall keep for myself only this black male and this black female, which will grow into a fine herd."

"You have indeed done something great, grandson," said Good Running, and he spoke true. The people became the bold riders of the Plains and soon could hardly imagine how they had existed without these wonderful animals.

After some time Good Running, rich and honored by all, said to Long Arrow, "Grandson, lead us to the Great Mystery Lake so we can camp by its shores. Let's visit the spirit chief and the wondrous boy; maybe they will give us more of their power and magic gifts."

Long Arrow led the people southward and again found the Great Mystery Lake. But the waters would no longer part for him, nor would any of the kingfishers they saw turn into a boy. Nor, gazing down into the crystal-clear water, could they discover people, Elk Dogs, or a tipi. There was nothing in the lake but a few fish.

**Reading Skill
Analyzing Cultural Context** What question about Blackfeet culture might the details here help answer?

**Literary Analysis
Myth** What does this myth explain?

The Orphan Boy and the Elk Dog ■ 999

Apply the Skills

The Orphan Boy and the Elk Dog

Thinking About the Selection

1. **Respond:** Would you like to travel with Long Arrow? Explain.
2. **(a) Recall:** Why do the villagers shun Long Arrow at the beginning of the story? **(b) Analyze:** What does this behavior suggest about the villagers?
3. **(a) Recall:** What reason does Long Arrow give for asking Good Running for a "great" thing to do? **(b) Infer:** What does his reason show about Long Arrow's feelings for Good Running?
4. **(a) Summarize:** List three obstacles Long Arrow faces on his journey. **(b) Analyze:** Explain how he overcomes each one.
5. **(a) Infer:** What type of animal is an "Elk Dog"? **(b) Analyze Cause and Effect:** Explain why the "Elk Dogs" will lead to changes in the tribe's life.
6. **(a) Interpret:** What lessons does the myth teach about helping others? **(b) Discuss:** Share and discuss responses with a partner. Work together to formulate a response that represents both of your opinions. Share that response with the class.

Literary Analysis

7. Using a chart like the one shown, identify which characteristics of **myths** are found in "The Orphan Boy and the Elk Dog." Support your choices by supplying examples from the text.

What the Story Explains	Exceptional or Fantastic Characters	Quest	Transgression

8. **(a)** What qualities help Long Arrow overcome the obstacles he faces on his quest? Support your answer with details from the text. **(b)** Working from your answer, draw a conclusion about the qualities the Blackfeet valued in a person.
9. **(a)** What advice does Good Running give Long Arrow before his journey? **(b)** Draw a conclusion about the customs and beliefs of the Blackfeet based on this advice.

Reading Skill

10. **(a)** Give two examples of questions you might ask to **analyze the cultural context** of the myth. **(b)** Explain the answers that the myth suggests, and provide details from the text.

Vocabulary Builder

Practice Copy each of the following word pairs. If the words have similar meanings, write *S* for **synonyms**. If the words have opposite meanings, write *A* for **antonyms**. Explain each of your choices.

1. surpassed, failed
2. emanating, absorbing
3. relish, pleasure
4. stifle, conceal

Adding Words to Your Vocabulary Using a dictionary, find three meanings for *relish,* including its meanings as a noun and as a verb. For each meaning, write a sentence using the word correctly.

Writing

In a small group, write a **myth** about the origin of some feature of your everyday world, such as television, computers, or automobiles. Follow these steps:

- Agree on a topic that group members find interesting.
- Have one member write an opening sentence.
- Each group member should take a turn writing a sentence that follows from the one before until the myth is complete.
- As a group, review the story as it progresses, and make any revisions agreed upon by the group members.

Present your myth to the class.

For *Grammar, Vocabulary,* and *Assessment,* see **Build Language Skills,** pages 1002–1003.

Extend Your Learning

Listening and Speaking Locate another Native American myth in which the origin of an animal is explained. Present your own **retelling** of the myth to your class. Afterward, have classmates summarize the myth you have retold. Then, lead a discussion in which you compare and contrast the myth to "The Orphan Boy and the Elk Dog."

Research and Technology Myths were oral literature before they were written down. Conduct research on the evolution of written languages among Native Americans. Write a brief **language report** in which you draw a conclusion about the reasons that writing evolved in these cultures.

Build Language Skills

Vocabulary Skill

Context Clues and Word Roots A **context clue** is information surrounding a word that can be used to determine its meaning. A word's root also provides clues to its meaning. For example, in the sentence *We will incorporate a short new dance into the larger show,* the word *incorporate* contains the **word root -corp-,** which means "body." Knowing the meaning of the word root and examining the context in which the word appears can help you figure out that *incorporate* means "to combine into a larger body" or "to make part of something."

Practice Use the context clues and your knowledge of -corp- to help you figure out the meaning of the word in italics. Write the definition and explain how you determined it.

1. My mom bought stock in a *corporation* that produces health food.
2. Members of the diplomatic *corps* report to the Secretary of State.
3. Each red *corpuscle* of blood contains hemoglobin to carry oxygen.
4. The *corpulent* man could barely fit through the door.

Grammar Lesson

Simple and Compound Sentences A **clause** is a group of words with a subject and a verb. An **independent clause** is a clause that can stand on its own as a sentence. A **simple sentence** consists of a single independent clause. A **compound sentence** contains two or more independent clauses linked by a semicolon or a coordinating conjunction (such as *and, but, or, for, nor, so,* and *yet*). In the following examples, subjects are underlined once and verbs are underlined twice.

    Simple: The <u>myth</u> of Prometheus <u>explains</u> the origin of fire.
    Compound: <u>Myths</u> <u>explain</u> the world; <u>legends</u> <u>record</u> great deeds.

Practice Identify each of the following sentences as *simple* or *compound*. Rewrite each compound sentence as two simple sentences.

1. Gilgamesh was a real king, but his feats are magnified in the epic.
2. Roland was a hero and model character of early French literature.
3. The *Mahabharata* and the *Ramayana* are two great epics of India.
4. Sundiata led the African kingdom of Mali; his nickname was "the Lion King."
5. Beowulf came from Sweden but won fame as a hero in Denmark.

MorePractice

For more practice with independent clauses, see Grammar Handbook, p. R43.

Reading: Cultural Context

Standards
Assessed
• 10.2.4
• 10.3.1

Directions: *Read the selection. Then, answer the questions.*

One day [the cat, Lady Myōbu], wandered onto the veranda, and Lady Uma, the nurse in charge of her, called out, "Oh, you naughty thing! Please come inside at once." But the cat paid no attention and went on basking sleepily in the sun. Intending to give her a scare, the nurse called for the dog, Okinamaro.

"Okinamaro, where are you?" she cried. "Come here and bite Lady Myōbu!" The foolish Okinamaro, believing that the nurse was in earnest, rushed at the cat, who, startled and terrified, ran behind the blind in the Imperial Dining Room, where the Emperor happened to be sitting. Greatly surprised, His Majesty picked up the cat and held her in his arms. He summoned his gentlemen-in-waiting. When Tadataka, the Chamberlain, appeared, His Majesty ordered that Okinamaro be chastised and banished to Dog Island. The attendants all started to chase the dog amid great confusion.

—from *The Pillow Book* by Sei Shōnagon, translated by Ivan Morris

1. From the selection, you can infer that
   A the nurse will be in trouble.
   B the nurse will be rewarded.
   C the nurse hates dogs but loves cats.
   D the nurse will be praised for her prank.

2. The passage portrays the Emperor's court as
   A very formal, with elaborate protocol.
   B primitive by Western standards.
   C a place with many people around.
   D being isolated from everyone.

3. Which statement best describes the court life portrayed in the selection?
   A Court was held in a one-room hut.
   B Women were banned from court.
   C Gentlemen-in-waiting served the ruler.
   D There was no nobility, or upper class.

4. From the selection, one can conclude that
   A this culture could support luxury.
   B this culture worshiped animals.
   C this culture was divided politically.
   D this culture indulged in frivolous games.

Timed Writing: Analysis [Connections]

Review "The Orphan Boy and the Elk Dog" or "Prometheus and the First People." Write an analysis of how the selection reflects the values of the culture that produced it. Use specific examples. **(45 minutes)**

Writing Workshop: *Work in Progress*

Writing for Assessment

Use the timed essay from your writing portfolio. Skim the paper for any obvious errors in logic. Put a check mark beside logical problems, but do not stop reading. Return the edited piece to your portfolio.

Practice these skills with either the selection from *Sundiata* (p. 1006) or the selection from the *Ramayana* (p. 1019).

(IN) Academic Standards

- Examine how the author's perspective influences the structure and tone of the text. (10.2.4)
- Analyze many different forms of dramatic literature. (10.3.1)
- Evaluate the aesthetic qualities of style. (10.3.11)

Literary Analysis

An **epic** is an extended narrative poem about the deeds of heroes. The typical **epic hero** is a warrior, and his character may be based on a historic or a legendary figure. In a number of epics, the hero strives to win immortality or undying fame through great deeds, especially in combat. The typical hero has the following characteristics:

- He has a high position in society and the virtues of a warrior, such as strength, courage, and perseverance.
- He defends his family's honor, and he acts ethically, fighting evil and striving for justice.
- He may be marked by the gods or by fate and so may benefit from special blessings or suffer from special burdens.

Background	Support
At age twelve, boys in this culture are initiated.	Footnote 2
Men in this culture are free to express their emotions.	The two friends cry when they part.

Reading Skill

To understand an epic, **analyze cultural context,** or determine ways in which the epic reflects the culture in which it was composed. You can **acquire background knowledge** about the culture in these ways:

- Read introductory sections, footnotes, and other text aids.
- Draw conclusions from the details in the selection.

Take notes on cultural context using a chart like the one shown.

Vocabulary Builder

from **Sundiata**

- **fathom** (fa*th*′ əm) *v.* understand thoroughly (p. 1007) *I cannot <u>fathom</u> his strange act.*

- **innuendo** (in′ yo͞o en′ dō) *n.* indirect insult or accusation; insinuation (p. 1008) *She will not accuse him directly, but her <u>innuendo</u> let him know she suspects him.*

- **estranged** (ə strānj′d) *adj.* kept apart; in the condition of having had affection turn into indifference or hostility (p. 1008) *The two friends were <u>estranged</u> after an especially bitter quarrel.*

- **affront** (ə frunt′) *n.* open insult (p. 1012) *Their snickers were an <u>affront</u> to her pride.*

from the **Ramayana**

- **decrepitude** (dē krep′ ə to͞od′) *n.* feebleness; condition of being worn out by age or illness (p. 1020) *His love for the ratty old chair blinded him to its extreme <u>decrepitude</u>.*

- **august** (ô gust′) *adj.* inspiring awe; worthy of respect (p. 1020) *The musicians grew silent when the <u>august</u> conductor entered.*

- **secular** (sek′ yə lər) *adj.* of worldly, as opposed to religious, matters (p. 1021) *The singer sang both religious and <u>secular</u> songs.*

- **esoteric** (es′ ə ter′ ik) *adj.* beyond the understanding or knowledge of most people (p. 1025) *Quantum mechanics is <u>esoteric</u>.*

Epic

Background

A Great Leader *Sundiata* tells the tale of Mari (or Sogolon) Djata, also known as Sundiata. Nearly 1,000 years ago, a warrior named Sumanguru took control of the area around Mali in West Africa and oppressed its Malinke people. A hero arose to unite the people, defeat Sumanguru, and usher in a period of peace. That hero was Sundiata.

Connecting to the Literature

Reading/Writing Connection The epic hero in *Sundiata* spends his early life being insulted for his physical weakness. Write a few sentences about why his culture might have valued physical strength. Use at least three of these words: *acquire, attain, derive, dominate.*

Meet the Author

D. T. **Niane** (b.1932), Mamadou **Kouyaté,** and the **Malinke**

Sundiata's people, the Malinke, are one of the Mande peoples of West Africa. Mande society is divided into different classes of people, from nobles to commoners. In his day, Sundiata's people traded in gold. After his victory over Sumanguru, Sundiata conquered neighboring lands and built an extensive kingdom known as the Mali empire.

The Griot Tradition Sundiata's achievements were celebrated over the centuries by West African oral historians known as griots (grē´ ōz). The twentieth-century griot Mamadou Kouyaté (mä´ mä dōō kōō ya´ te) continued this tradition. "I derive my knowledge from my father Djeli Kedian, who also got it from his father," Kouyaté explained. "History holds no mystery for us." The scholar D. T. Niane (nĭ´ yan) wrote an account of Sundiata based on Kouyaté's retellings.

Fast Facts

▶ Kouyaté belongs to the same clan as the kings of Old Mali.
▶ The English translation of *Sundiata* first appeared in 1965.

For: more about the authors
Visit: www.PHSchool.com
Web Code: eqe-9604

from
SUNDIATA:
AN EPIC OF OLD MALI

D.T. NIANE

Characters in *Sundiata*

Balla Fasséké (bä´ lä fä sä´ kä): Griot and counselor of Sundiata

Boukari (bōō kä´ rē): Son of the king and Namandjé, one of his wives; also called Manding (män´ diŋ) Boukari

Dankaran Touman (dän´ kä rän tōō´ män): Son of the king and his first wife, Sassouma, who is also called Sassouma Bérété

Djamarou (jä mä´ rōō): Daughter of Sogolon and the king; sister of Sundiata and Kolonkan

Farakourou (fä rä kōō´ rōō): Master of the forges

Gnankouman Doua (nän kōō´ män dōō´ ə): The king's griot; also called, simply, Doua

Kolonkan (kō lōn´ kən): Sundiata's eldest sister

Namandjé (nä män´ jē): One of the king's wives

Naré Maghan (nä´ rä mäg´ hän): Sundiata's father; the king of Mali before Sundiata

Nounfaïri (nōōn´ fä ē´ rē): Soothsayer and smith; father of Farakourou

Sassouma Bérété (sä sōō´ mä be´ re te): The king's first wife

Sogolon (sô gô lōn´): Sundiata's mother; also called Sogolon Kedjou (kä´ jōō)

Sundiata (sōōn dyä´ tä): Legendary king of Mali; referred to as Djata (dyä´ tä) and Sogolon Djata ("son of Sogolon"), and Mari (mä´ rē) Djata.

CHILDHOOD

God has his mysteries which none can <u>fathom</u>. You, perhaps, will be a king. You can do nothing about it. You, on the other hand, will be unlucky, but you can do nothing about that either. Each man finds his way already marked out for him and he can change nothing of it.

Sogolon's son had a slow and difficult childhood. At the age of three he still crawled along on all-fours while children of the same age were already walking. He had nothing of the great beauty of his father Naré Maghan. He had a head so big that he seemed unable to support it; he also had large eyes which would open wide whenever anyone entered his mother's house. He was taciturn[1] and used to spend the whole day just sitting in the middle of the house. Whenever his mother went out he would crawl on all-fours to rummage about in the calabashes[2] in search of food, for he was very greedy.

Malicious tongues began to blab. What three-year-old has not yet taken his first steps? What three-year-old is not the despair of his parents through his whims and shifts of mood? What

---

1. **taciturn** (tas´ ə tʉrn´) *adj.* almost always silent; not liking to talk.
2. **calabashes** (kal´ ə bash´ iz) *n.* dried, hollow shells of gourds (squashlike fruits), used as bowls, cups, and so on.

◀ **Critical Viewing** Contrast this depiction of Mari (or Sogolon) Djata with the child described in the opening paragraphs. **[Contrast]**

three-year-old is not the joy of his circle through his backwardness in talking? Sogolon Djata (for it was thus that they called him, prefixing his mother's name to his), Sogolon Djata, then, was very different from others of his own age. He spoke little and his severe face never relaxed into a smile. You would have thought that he was already thinking, and what amused children of his age bored him. Often Sogolon would make some of them come to him to keep him company. These children were already walking and she hoped that Djata, seeing his companions walking, would be tempted to do likewise. But nothing came of it. Besides, Sogolon Djata would brain the poor little things with his already strong arms and none of them would come near him any more.

The king's first wife was the first to rejoice at Sogolon Djata's infirmity. Her own son, Dankaran Touman, was already eleven. He was a fine and lively boy, who spent the day running about the village with those of his own age. He had even begun his initiation in the bush.[3] The king had had a bow made for him and he used to go behind the town to practice archery with his companions. Sassouma was quite happy and snapped her fingers at Sogolon, whose child was still crawling on the ground. Whenever the latter happened to pass by her house, she would say, "Come, my son, walk, jump, leap about. The jinn didn't promise you anything out of the ordinary,[4] but I prefer a son who walks on his two legs to a lion that crawls on the ground." She spoke thus whenever Sogolon went by her door. The <u>innuendo</u> would go straight home and then she would burst into laughter, that diabolical laughter which a jealous woman knows how to use so well.

Her son's infirmity weighed heavily upon Sogolon Kedjou; she had resorted to all her talent as a sorceress to give strength to her son's legs, but the rarest herbs had been useless. The king himself lost hope.

How impatient man is! Naré Maghan became imperceptibly <u>estranged</u> but Gnankouman Doua never ceased reminding him of the hunter's words. Sogolon became pregnant again. The king hoped for a son, but it was a daughter called Kolonkan. She resembled her mother and had nothing of her father's beauty. The disheartened king debarred Sogolon from his house and she lived in semi-disgrace for a while. Naré Maghan married the daughter of one of his allies, the king of the Kamaras. She was called Namandjé and

Literary Analysis
Epics In what two ways is Mari (or Sogolon) Djata set apart from other children?

Vocabulary Builder
innuendo (in´ yoo en´ dō) *n.* indirect insult or accusation; insinuation

estranged (e strānj´d) *adj.* kept apart; in the condition of having had affection turn into indifference or hostility

---

3. **initiation in the bush** education in tribal lore given to twelve-year-old West African boys so they can become full members of the tribe.
4. **The jinn . . . ordinary** Jinn are supernatural beings said to influence human affairs. They promised that the son of Sogolon would make Mali a great empire.

her beauty was legendary. A year later she brought a boy into the world. When the king consulted soothsayers[5] on the destiny of this son he received the reply that Namandjé's child would be the right hand of some mighty king. The king gave the newly-born the name of Boukari. He was to be called Manding Boukari or Manding Bory later on.

Naré Maghan was very perplexed. Could it be that the stiff-jointed son of Sogolon was the one the hunter soothsayer had foretold?

"The Almighty has his mysteries," Gnankouman Doua would say and, taking up the hunter's words, added, "The silk-cotton tree emerges from a tiny seed."

One day Naré Maghan came along to the house of Nounfaïri, the blacksmith seer of Niani. He was an old, blind man. He received the king in the anteroom which served as his workshop. To the king's question he replied, "When the seed germinates growth is not always easy; great trees grow slowly but they plunge their roots deep into the ground."

"But has the seed really germinated?" said the king.

"Of course," replied the blind seer. "Only the growth is not as quick as you would like it; how impatient man is."

This interview and Doua's confidence gave the king some assurance. To the great displeasure of Sassouma Bérété the king restored Sogolon to favor and soon another daughter was born to her. She was given the name of Djamarou.

However, all Niani talked of nothing else but the stiff-legged son of Sogolon. He was now seven and he still crawled to get about. In spite of all the king's affection, Sogolon was in despair. Naré Maghan aged and he felt his time coming to an end. Dankaran Touman, the son of Sassouma Bérété, was now a fine youth.

One day Naré Maghan made Mari Djata come to him and he spoke to the child as one speaks to an adult. "Mari Djata, I am growing old and soon I shall be no more among you, but before death takes me off I am going to give you the present each king gives his successor. In Mali every prince has his own griot. Doua's father was my father's griot, Doua is mine and the son of Doua, Balla Fasséké here, will be your griot. Be inseparable friends from this day forward. From his mouth you will hear the history of your ancestors, you will learn the art of governing Mali according to the principles which our ancestors have bequeathed to us. I have served my term and done my duty too. I have done everything which a king of Mali ought to do. I am handing an enlarged

---

5. **soothsayers** (sōōth′ sā′ ərz) *n.* people who profess to foretell the future.

kingdom over to you and I leave you sure allies. May your destiny be accomplished, but never forget that Niani is your capital and Mali the cradle of your ancestors."

The child, as if he had understood the whole meaning of the king's words, beckoned Balla Fasséké to approach. He made room for him on the hide he was sitting on and then said, "Balla, you will be my griot."

"Yes, son of Sogolon, if it pleases God," replied Balla Fasséké.

The king and Doua exchanged glances that radiated confidence.

THE LION'S AWAKENING

A short while after this interview between Naré Maghan and his son the king died. Sogolon's son was no more than seven years old. The council of elders met in the king's palace. It was no use Doua's defending the king's will which reserved the throne for Mari Djata, for the council took no account of Naré Maghan's wish. With the help of Sassouma Bérété's intrigues, Dankaran Touman was

▼ **Critical Viewing** Why might Mari Djata have difficulty gathering leaves from a baobab tree like this one? **[Analyze]**

proclaimed king and a regency council[6] was formed in which the queen mother was all-powerful. A short time after, Doua died.

As men have short memories, Sogolon's son was spoken of with nothing but irony and scorn. People had seen one-eyed kings, one-armed kings, and lame kings, but a stiff-legged king had never been heard tell of. No matter how great the destiny promised for Mari Djata might be, the throne could not be given to someone who had no power in his legs; if the jinn loved him, let them begin by giving him the use of his legs. Such were the remarks that Sogolon heard every day. The queen mother, Sassouma Bérété, was the source of all this gossip.

Having become all-powerful, Sassouma Bérété persecuted Sogolon because the late Naré Maghan had preferred her. She banished Sogolon and her son to a back yard of the palace. Mari Djata's mother now occupied an old hut which had served as a lumber-room of Sassouma's.

The wicked queen mother allowed free passage to all those inquisitive people who wanted to see the child that still crawled at the age of seven. Nearly all the inhabitants of Niani filed into the palace and the poor Sogolon wept to see herself thus given over to public ridicule. Mari Djata took on a ferocious look in front of the crowd of sightseers. Sogolon found a little consolation only in the love of her eldest daughter, Kolonkan. She was four and she could walk. She seemed to understand all her mother's miseries and already she helped her with the housework. Sometimes, when Sogolon was attending to the chores, it was she who stayed beside her sister Djamarou, quite small as yet.

Sogolon Kedjou and her children lived on the queen mother's leftovers, but she kept a little garden in the open ground behind the village. It was there that she passed her brightest moments looking after her onions and gnougous.[7] One day she happened to be short of condiments and went to the queen mother to beg a little baobab leaf.[8]

---

6. **regency** (rē´ jən sē) **council** group that rules instead of the king or queen when the king or queen is still a child or is otherwise incapable of ruling.
7. **gnougous** (no͞o´ go͞oz´) *n.* root vegetables.
8. **baobab** (bā´ ō bab´) **leaf** The baobab is a thick-trunked tree; its leaves are used to flavor foods.

Reading Skill
Analyzing Cultural Context What do the details here indicate about the way in which West African society was ruled?

Literary Analysis
Epics In what way is the honor of Mari Djata's family threatened?

✓ **Reading Check**

After the king's death, who takes power in the kingdom?

"Look you," said the malicious Sassouma, "I have a calabash full. Help yourself, you poor woman. As for me, my son knew how to walk at seven and it was he who went and picked these baobab leaves. Take them then, since your son is unequal to mine." Then she laughed derisively with that fierce laughter which cuts through your flesh and penetrates right to the bone.

Sogolon Kedjou was dumbfounded. She had never imagined that hate could be so strong in a human being. With a lump in her throat she left Sassouma's. Outside her hut Mari Djata, sitting on his useless legs, was blandly eating out of a calabash. Unable to contain herself any longer, Sogolon burst into sobs and seizing a piece of wood, hit her son.

"Oh son of misfortune, will you never walk? Through your fault I have just suffered the greatest <u>affront</u> of my life! What have I done, God, for you to punish me in this way?"

Mari Djata seized the piece of wood and, looking at his mother, said, "Mother, what's the matter?"

"Shut up, nothing can ever wash me clean of this insult."

"But what then?"

"Sassouma has just humiliated me over a matter of a baobab leaf. At your age her own son could walk and used to bring his mother baobab leaves."

"Cheer up, Mother, cheer up."

"No. It's too much. I can't."

"Very well then, I am going to walk today," said Mari Djata. "Go and tell my father's smiths to make me the heaviest possible iron rod. Mother, do you want just the leaves of the baobab or would you rather I brought you the whole tree?"

"Ah, my son, to wipe out this insult I want the tree and its roots at my feet outside my hut."

▲ **Critical Viewing**
What relationship in the epic might this picture illustrate? Explain. **[Connect]**

Vocabulary Builder
affront (ə frunt´) *n.* open insult

Literary Analysis
Epics Why is Mari Djata's response here suitable for an epic hero?

Balla Fasséké, who was present, ran to the master smith, Farakourou, to order an iron rod.

Sogolon had sat down in front of her hut. She was weeping softly and holding her head between her two hands. Mari Djata went calmly back to his calabash of rice and began eating again as if nothing had happened. From time to time he looked up discreetly at his mother who was murmuring in a low voice, "I want the whole tree, in front of my hut, the whole tree."

All of a sudden a voice burst into laughter behind the hut. It was the wicked Sassouma telling one of her serving women about the scene of humiliation and she was laughing loudly so that Sogolon could hear. Sogolon fled into the hut and hid her face under the blankets so as not to have before her eyes this heedless boy, who was more preoccupied with eating than with anything else. With her head buried in the bedclothes Sogolon wept and her body shook violently. Her daughter, Sogolon Djamarou, had come and sat down beside her and she said, "Mother, Mother, don't cry. Why are you crying?"

Mari Djata had finished eating and, dragging himself along on his legs, he came and sat under the wall of the hut for the sun was scorching. What was he thinking about? He alone knew.

The royal forges were situated outside the walls and over a hundred smiths worked there. The bows, spears, arrows and shields of Niani's warriors came from there. When Balla Fasséké came to order the iron rod, Farakourou said to him, "The great day has arrived then?"

"Yes. Today is a day like any other, but it will see what no other day has seen."

The master of the forges, Farakourou, was the son of the old Nounfaïri, and he was a soothsayer like his father. In his workshops there was an enormous iron bar wrought by his father, Nounfaïri. Everybody wondered what this bar was destined to be used for. Farakourou called six of his apprentices and told them to carry the iron bar to Sogolon's house.

When the smiths put the gigantic iron bar down in front of the hut the noise was so frightening that Sogolon, who was lying down, jumped up with a start. Then Balla Fasséké, son of Gnankouman Doua, spoke.

"Here is the great day, Mari Djata. I am speaking to you, Maghan, son of Sogolon. The waters of the Niger can efface the stain from the body, but they cannot wipe out an insult. Arise, young lion, roar, and may the bush know that from henceforth it has a master."

Reading Skill
Analyzing Cultural Context What do these details suggest about the role of blacksmiths and warriors in West African culture?

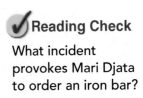

Reading Check

What incident provokes Mari Djata to order an iron bar?

The apprentice smiths were still there, Sogolon had come out and everyone was watching Mari Djata. He crept on all-fours and came to the iron bar. Supporting himself on his knees and one hand, with the other hand he picked up the iron bar without any effort and stood it up vertically. Now he was resting on nothing but his knees and held the bar with both his hands. A deathly silence had gripped all those present. Sogolon Djata closed his eyes, held tight, the muscles in his arms tensed. With a violent jerk he threw his weight on to it and his knees left the ground. Sogolon Kedjou was all eyes and watched her son's legs which were trembling as though from an electric shock. Djata was sweating and the sweat ran from his brow. In a great effort he straightened up and was on his feet at one go—but the great bar of iron was twisted and had taken the form of a bow!

Then Balla Fasséké sang out the "Hymn to the Bow," striking up with his powerful voice:

> "Take your bow, Simbon,
> Take your bow and let us go.
> Take your bow, Sogolon Djata."

Literary Analysis
Epics What qualities of an epic hero does Mari Djata display here?

Literature in Context   Culture Connection

Griot: The Mind of the People

In West Africa, the griot (pronounced "gree-oh") is the storyteller and historian of a village. The griot memorizes the births, deaths, marriages, hunts, and wars of the people and its ancestors. Sometimes speaking or singing for days, the griot recites these events as stories, often to musical accompaniment. To the Mandinka, the griot is the "mind" of the people, an oral library of history and culture.

► Children gather closely around a griot to hear a story.

▲ Many griots use talking drums, like this one, as they tell their stories.

Connect to the Literature   Given this information, explain why Naré Maghan's decision to appoint a griot for Mari Djata shows his confidence in his son.

When Sogolon saw her son standing she stood dumb for a moment, then suddenly she sang these words of thanks to God, who had given her son the use of his legs:

"Oh day, what a beautiful day,
Oh day, day of joy;
Allah[9] Almighty, you never created a finer day.
So my son is going to walk!"

Standing in the position of a soldier at ease, Sogolon Djata, supported by his enormous rod, was sweating great beads of sweat. Balla Fasséké's song had alerted the whole palace and people came running from all over to see what had happened, and each stood bewildered before Sogolon's son. The queen mother had rushed there and when she saw Mari Djata standing up she trembled from head to foot. After recovering his breath Sogolon's son dropped the bar and the crowd stood to one side. His first steps were those of a giant. Balla Fasséké fell into step and pointing his finger at Djata, he cried:

"Room, room, make room!
The lion has walked;
Hide antelopes,
Get out of his way."

Behind Niani there was a young baobab tree and it was there that the children of the town came to pick leaves for their mothers. With all his might the son of Sogolon tore up the tree and put it on his shoulders and went back to his mother. He threw the tree in front of the hut and said, "Mother, here are some baobab leaves for you. From henceforth it will be outside your hut that the women of Niani will come to stock up."

Reading Skill
Analyzing Cultural Context What do the images in the griot's song indicate about the region in which the Malinke live?

---

9. Allah (al′ ə) Muslim name for God.

Apply the Skills

from *Sundiata: An Epic of Old Mali*

Thinking About the Selection

1. **Respond:** Did you enjoy Mari Djata's triumph? Explain.
2. **(a) Recall:** What is Mari Djata's main difficulty? **(b) Infer:** How does this problem affect the way people treat his mother?
3. **(a) Recall:** What does the king specify as his wish for Mari Djata? **(b) Analyze Cause and Effect:** How do the soothsayers' predictions help prompt the king's wishes?
4. **(a) Recall:** After the king's death, where does Sassouma Bérété force Sogolon and Mari Djata to live? **(b) Infer:** Why does Sassouma Bérété treat Mari Djata and Sogolon as she does?
5. **(a) Analyze Cause and Effect:** Explain how an insult from Sassouma leads Mari Djata to overcome his own problem. **(b) Predict:** Do you think that Mari Djata has taught Sassouma Bérété a lesson once and for all? Explain.
6. **(a) Generalize:** What main lesson do you think is intended in retelling Mari Djata's experiences? Support your answer with details from the text. **(b) Discuss:** Working in a small group, share your ideas. **(c) Evaluate:** As a group, choose the best three ideas and share them with the class.

Literary Analysis

7. Some heroes battle dragons or warriors. Explain two ways in which the challenges Mari Djata faces differ from other **epic** struggles.
8. Using a chart like the one shown, give specific examples showing which qualities of an **epic hero** Mari Djata possesses.

Noble Birth	Warrior Virtues	Acts Honorably	Chosen by the Gods or Fate

Reading Skill

9. **(a)** List three things that you learned about West African **cultural context** from the features that appear before the selection. **(b)** List two things you learned about West African culture from the selection or from the footnotes. **(c)** For each item of context you list, briefly explain how knowing that item helps you to understand *Sundiata*. Give specific examples.

QuickReview

Epic at a Glance
As a child, Mali's future king Mari Djata overcomes a crippling condition to defend his mother's honor.

Go Online
Assessment
For: Self-test
Visit: www.PHSchool.com
Web Code: eqa-6604

Epic: a long narrative or narrative poem about the deeds of heroes

Epic Hero: a warrior, often based on a historic or legendary figure, who strives to win immortality through great deeds

Analyzing Cultural Context: determining ways in which a literary work reflects the culture in which it was composed

Vocabulary Builder

Practice Write a sentence about each situation described below, using a word from the vocabulary list for *Sundiata,* on page 1004.

1. ceasing to socialize with a group of friends
2. the purchase of a large python and a kitten to keep as pets
3. an exchange of snide remarks
4. an effort to harm someone's reputation

Adding Words to Your Vocabulary Referring to a dictionary, explain the relationship between the meanings of the word *fathom* as a noun and as a verb. Use both meanings in sentences. (For more on using a dictionary, see page R6.)

Writing

Write a **newspaper report** of events at the end of the selection. First, take notes in which you identify main characters and outline story events. As you draft, include the following elements:
- a catchy headline
- information telling *who, what, where, when, how,* and *why*
- believable quotations from participants and onlookers
- comments on the significance of the events

For *Grammar, Vocabulary,* and *Assessment,* see **Build Language Skills,** pages 1028–1029.

Extend Your Learning

Listening and Speaking With two classmates, present an **improvised dialogue** between a queen of Mali, her son, a rival queen, and a sage regarding an insult the rival has delivered to the queen. Apply what you have learned about West African culture, and be sure that characters speak in a way suited to their position. Take 10 minutes to prepare and no more than 10 minutes for the presentation.

Research and Technology Locate audiovisual resources about culture and history in Old Mali. As you review the material, jot down the thoughts, opinions, and questions that occur to you. Then, write a **summary of research notes** explaining what you learned, what thoughts you had about the material, and what questions you still have. Note any connections you found to the material in *Sundiata.*

Epic

Background

Hinduism The *Ramayana,* the great Hindu epic telling of Prince Rama, is one of the sacred books of Hinduism, the major religion of India. Hinduism involves a belief in many gods, each representing an aspect of life and nature. The most important gods are Brahma, the creator; Vishnu, the preserver; and Siva, the destroyer.

Connecting to the Literature

Reading/Writing Connection Ancient heroes like Rama have much in common with superheroes today. Briefly describe a few qualities of today's superheroes. Use at least three of the following words: *embody, evoke, intervene, prevail.*

Review

For **Literary Analysis, Reading Skill,** and **Vocabulary Builder,** see page 1004.

Meet the Authors

Hindu Tradition and R.K. Narayan (1906–2001)

The foundations of Hindu culture were laid around 1500 B.C., when a warrior people, the Aryans, invaded northern India. The Aryans enforced the caste system, in which society is rigidly divided into castes, or groups, each with its own occupation and duties. The caste system supports Hindu emphasis on righteous behavior and spiritual self-improvement.

From Poet-Sage to Modern Novelist The earliest surviving version of Rama's story, credited to the poet-sage Valmiki, dates to perhaps 300 B.C. Among the story's most recent retellers is Indian novelist R.K. Narayan. According to Narayan, "All imaginative writing in India has had its origin in . . . the 10,000-year-old epics of India."

Fast Facts

▶ To this day, Hindus take Rama as their model for conduct.
▶ According to legend, Valmiki earned his name, which means "a white ant hill," when he meditated without moving for so long that ants built a nest over his body.

Go Online
Author Link

For: More about Hinduism and the author
Visit: www.PHSchool.com
Web Code: eqe-9605

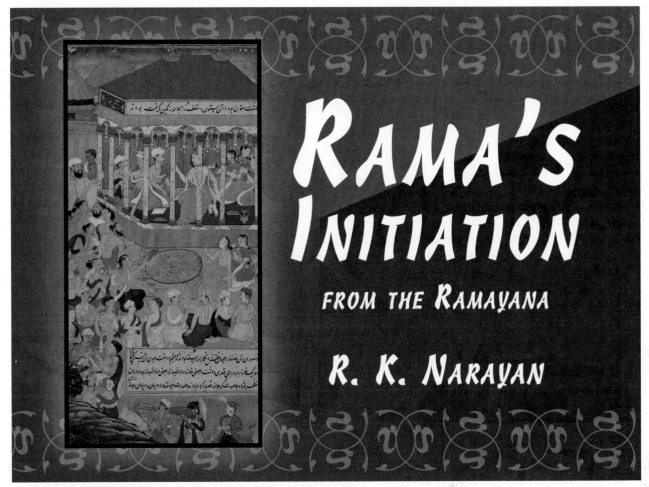

RAMA'S INITIATION

FROM THE RAMAYANA

R. K. NARAYAN

Persian translation of the *Ramayana* of Valmiki (detail). Indian manuscript, late 16th century, Mughal, school of Akbar. Courtesy of the Freer Gallery of Art, Smithsonian Institution, Washington, D.C.

Steeped in the Hindu religion of India, the Ramayana *is the story of Prince Rama (rä´ mə), son of King Dasaratha (dä sä rä´ tä). With the guidance of several Hindu sages, or wise men, Rama confronts and overcomes many obstacles, including a test of strength to win his wife Sita. Just as he is about to inherit his throne, he is banished and spends fourteen years in exile before returning to his kingdom. Through the challenges he meets, he reaches a spiritual and moral state so perfect that many associate him with Krishna, the incarnation, or embodiment, of the Hindu god Vishnu (vēsh´ n̄ō).*

This excerpt tells of adventures from Rama's childhood that occur before his fourteen-year banishment. Even as boys, he and his brother Lakshmana (läks mä´ nä) show extraordinary strength and skill.

The new assembly hall, Dasaratha's latest pride, was crowded all day with visiting dignitaries, royal emissaries, and citizens coming in with representations or appeals for justice. The King was always accessible, and fulfilled his duties as the ruler of Kosala without grudging the hours spent in public service.

On a certain afternoon, messengers at the gate came running in to announce, "Sage Viswamithra" [vish wä′ mē trä]. When the message was relayed to the King, he got up and hurried forward to receive the visitor. Viswamithra, once a king, a conqueror, and a dreaded name until he renounced his kingly role and chose to become a sage (which he accomplished through severe austerities[1]), combined in himself the sage's eminence and the king's authority and was quick tempered and positive. Dasaratha led him to a proper seat and said, "This is a day of glory for us; your gracious presence is most welcome. You must have come from afar. Would you first rest?"

"No need," the sage replied simply. He had complete mastery over his bodily needs through inner discipline and austerities, and was above the effects of heat, cold, hunger, fatigue, and even decrepitude. The King later asked politely, "Is there anything I can do?" Viswamithra looked steadily at the King and answered, "Yes. I am here to ask of you a favor. I wish to perform, before the next full moon, a *yagna*[2] at Sidhasrama [sēd häs rä′ mä]. Doubtless you know where it is?"

"I have passed that sacred ground beyond the Ganges many times."

The sage interrupted. "But there are creatures hovering about waiting to disturb every holy undertaking there, who must be overcome in the same manner as one has to conquer the five-fold evils[3] within before one can realize holiness. Those evil creatures are endowed with immeasurable powers of destruction. But it is our duty to pursue our aims undeterred. The *yagna* I propose to perform will strengthen the beneficial forces of this world, and please the gods above."

"It is my duty to protect your sublime[4] effort. Tell me when, and I will be there."

The sage said, "No need to disturb your august self. Send your son Rama with me, and he will help me. He can."

"Rama!" cried the King, surprised, "When I am here to serve you."

Viswamithra's temper was already stirring. "I know your greatness," he said, cutting the King short. "But I want Rama to go with me. If you are not willing, you may say so."

The air became suddenly tense. The assembly, the ministers and officials, watched in solemn silence. The King looked miserable. "Rama is still a child, still learning the arts and practicing the use of

**Reading Skill
Analyzing Cultural Context** What background information on page 1018 helps explain the king's treatment of the sage?

**Vocabulary Builder
decrepitude** (dē krep′ ə to͞od′) *n.* feebleness; condition of being worn out by age or illness

**Literary Analysis
Epics** What typical epic conflict does the sage describe here?

**Vocabulary Builder
august** (ô gust′) *adj.* inspiring awe; worthy of respect

---

1. **austerities** (ô ster′ ə tēz) *n.* acts or habits of self-denial.
2. *yagna* (yäg nä′) *n.* Sanskrit term for sacrifice.
3. **five-fold evils** In Hindu belief, the five evils are lust, anger, miserliness, egoism, and envy.
4. **sublime** (sə blīm′) *adj.* noble; grand.

arms." His sentences never seemed to conclude, but trailed away as he tried to explain. "He is a boy, a child, he is too young and tender to contend with demons."

"But I know Rama," was all that Viswamithra said in reply.

"I can send you an army, or myself lead an army to guard your performance. What can a stripling[5] like Rama do against those terrible forces . . . ? I will help you just as I helped Indra[6] once when he was harassed and deprived of his kingdom."

Viswamithra ignored his speech and rose to leave. "If you cannot send Rama, I need none else." He started to move down the passage.

The King was too stricken to move. When Viswamithra had gone half way, he realized that the visitor was leaving unceremoniously and was not even shown the courtesy of being escorted to the door. Vasishtha [vä sē′ shtä], the King's priest and guide, whispered to Dasaratha, "Follow him and call him back," and hurried forward even before the King could grasp what he was saying. He almost ran as Viswamithra had reached the end of the hall and, blocking his way, said, "The King is coming; please don't go. He did not mean . . ."

A wry smile played on Viswamithra's face as he said without any trace of bitterness, "Why are you or anyone agitated? I came here for a purpose; it has failed: no reason to prolong my stay."

"Oh, eminent one, you were yourself a king once."

"What has that to do with us now?" asked Viswamithra, rather irked, since he hated all reference to his <u>secular</u> past and wanted always to be known as a Brahma Rishi.[7]

Vasishtha answered mildly, "Only to remind you of an ordinary man's feelings, especially a man like Dasaratha who had been childless and had to pray hard for an issue . . ."

"Well, it may be so, great one; I still say that I came on a mission and wish to leave, since it has failed."

"It has not failed," said Vasishtha, and just then the King came up to join them in the passage; the assembly was on its feet.

Dasaratha made a deep obeisance and said, "Come back to your seat, Your Holiness."

"For what purpose, Your Majesty?" Viswamithra asked.

"Easier to talk seated . . ."

"I don't believe in any talk," said Viswamithra; but Vasishtha pleaded with him until he returned to his seat.

When they were all seated again, Vasishtha addressed the King: "There must be a divine purpose working through this seer, who

---

5. stripling (strip′ lin) *n.* young boy passing into manhood.
6. Indra (in′ drə) Hindu god associated with rain and thunderbolts.
7. Brahma Rishi (brä′ mä rí′ shē) enlightened wise person.

Literary Analysis
Epics In what way is Rama singled out as an epic hero?

Vocabulary Builder
secular (sek′ yə lər) *adj.* of worldly, as opposed to religious, matters

Reading Check

What does Viswamithra ask of the king?

Rama and Sita, 1740. Victoria and Albert Museum, London.

may know but will not explain. It is a privilege that Rama's help should be sought. Do not bar his way. Let him go with the sage."

"When, oh when?" the King asked anxiously.

"Now," said Viswamithra. The King looked woebegone and desperate, and the sage relented enough to utter a word of comfort. "You cannot count on the physical proximity of someone you love, all the time. A seed that sprouts at the foot of its parent tree remains stunted until it is transplanted. Rama will be in my care, and he will be quite well. But ultimately, he will leave me too. Every human being, when the time comes, has to depart and seek his fulfillment in his own way."

"Sidhasrama is far away . . .?" began the King.

"I'll ease his path for him, no need for a chariot to take us there," said Viswamithra, reading his mind.

▲ **Critical Viewing**
Which details in this painting indicate that Rama is an epic hero? **[Analyze]**

"Rama has never been separated from his brother Lakshmana. May he also go with him?" pleaded the King, and he looked relieved when he heard Viswamithra say, "Yes, I will look after both, though their mission will be to look after me. Let them get ready to follow me; let them select their favorite weapons and prepare to leave."

Dasaratha, with the look of one delivering hostages into the hand of an enemy, turned to his minister and said, "Fetch my sons."

Following the footsteps of their master like his shadows, Rama and Lakshmana went past the limits of the city and reached the Sarayu River, which bounded the capital on the north. When night fell, they rested at a wooded grove and at dawn crossed the river. When the sun came over the mountain peak, they reached a pleasant grove over which hung, like a canopy, fragrant smoke from numerous sacrificial fires. Viswamithra explained to Rama, "This is where God Shiva[8] meditated once upon a time and reduced to ashes the god of love when he attempted to spoil his meditation. From time immemorial saints praying to Shiva come here to perform their sacrifices, and the pall of smoke you notice is from their sacrificial fires."

A group of hermits emerged from their seclusion, received Viswamithra, and invited him and his two disciples to stay with them for the night. Viswamithra resumed his journey at dawn and reached a desert region at midday. The mere expression "desert" hardly conveys the absolute aridity of this land. Under a relentless sun, all vegetation had dried and turned to dust, stone and rock crumbled into powdery sand, which lay in vast dunes, stretching away to the horizon. Here every inch was scorched and dry and hot beyond imagination. The ground was cracked and split, exposing enormous fissures everywhere. The distinction between dawn, noon, and evening did not exist here, as the sun seemed to stay overhead and burn the earth without moving. Bleached bones lay where animals had perished, including those of monstrous serpents with jaws open in deadly thirst; into these enormous jaws had rushed (says the poet) elephants desperately seeking shade, all dead and fossilized, the serpent and the elephant alike. Heat haze rose and singed the very heavens. While traversing this ground, Viswamithra noticed the bewilderment and distress on the faces of the young men, and transmitted to them mentally two mantras[9] (called "Bala" and "Adi-Bala"). When they meditated on and recited these incantations, the arid atmosphere was transformed for the

**Reading Skill
Analyzing Cultural
Context** What
background
information helps
explain details in this
paragraph?

**Literary Analysis
Epics** What do these
descriptive details
show about the power
of the evil forces Rama
will battle?

Reading Check

Whom does the king
send to accompany
Rama and
Viswamithra?

---

8. Shiva (shē´ və) Hindu god of destruction and reproduction; along with Vishnu and Brahma, one of the three most important gods in Hinduism.
9. mantras (man´ trəz) *n.* sacred syllables or hymns chanted in prayer.

rest of their passage and they felt as if they were wading through a cool stream with a southern summer breeze blowing in their faces. Rama, ever curious to know the country he was passing through, asked, "Why is this land so terrible? Why does it seem accursed?"

"You will learn the answer if you listen to this story—of a woman fierce, ruthless, eating and digesting all living creatures, possessing the strength of a thousand mad elephants."

Thataka's Story

The woman I speak of was the daughter of Suketha [sōō kā′ tä] a *yaksha*,[10] a demigod of great valor, might, and purity. She was beautiful and full of wild energy. When she grew up she was married to a chieftain named Sunda. Two sons were born to them— Mareecha [mä′ rē chä] and Subahu [sä bä′ hōō]—who were endowed with enormous supernatural powers in addition to physical strength; and in their conceit and exuberance they laid waste their surroundings. Their father, delighted at their pranks and infected by their mood, joined in their activities. He pulled out ancient trees by their roots and flung them about, and he slaughtered all creatures that came his way. This depredation came to the notice of the great savant[11] Agasthya [ä gus tē yä′] (the diminutive[12] saint who once, when certain demoniac beings hid themselves at the bottom of the sea and Indra appealed for his help to track them, had sipped off the waters of the ocean). Agasthya had his hermitage in this forest, and when he noticed the destruction around, he cursed the perpetrator of this deed and Sunda fell dead. When his wife learned of his death, she and her sons stormed in, roaring revenge on the saint. He met their challenge by cursing them. "Since you are destroyers of life, may you become *asuras*[13] and dwell in the nether worlds." (Till now they had been demigods. Now they were degraded to demonhood.) The three at once underwent a transformation; their features and stature became forbidding, and their natures changed to match. The sons left to seek the company of superdemons. The mother was left alone and lives on here, breathing fire and wishing everything ill. Nothing flourishes here; only heat and sand remain. She is a scorcher. She carries a trident with spikes; a cobra entwined on her arm is her armlet. The name of this fearsome creature is Thataka [tä tä′ kä]. Just as the presence of a little *loba* (meanness) dries up and disfigures a whole human

Literary Analysis
Epics Why is Thataka a suitable opponent for an epic hero?

---

10. *yaksha* Sanskrit term for a good nature spirit.
11. savant (sə vänt′) *n.* learned person.
12. diminutive (də min′ yōō tiv) *adj.* much smaller than ordinary or average.
13. *asuras* (ä sōō′ räz) in Hindu belief, group of demons at war with gods and human beings.

personality, so does the presence of this monster turn into desert a region which was once fertile. In her restlessness she constantly harasses the hermits at their prayers; she gobbles up anything that moves and sends it down her entrails.

Touching the bow slung on his shoulder, Rama asked, "Where is she to be found?"

Before Viswamithra could answer, she arrived, the ground rocking under her feet and a storm preceding her. She loomed over them with her eyes spitting fire, her fangs bared, her lips parted revealing a cavernous mouth; and her brows twitching in rage. She raised her trident and roared, "In this my kingdom, I have crushed out the minutest womb of life and you have been sent down so that I may not remain hungry."

Rama hesitated; for all her evil, she was still a woman. How could he kill her? Reading his thoughts, Viswamithra said, "You shall not consider her a woman at all. Such a monster must receive no consideration. Her strength, ruthlessness, appearance, rule her out of that category. Formerly God Vishnu himself killed Kyathi [kyä′ tē], the wife of Brigu [brë′ go͞o], who harbored the *asuras* fleeing his wrath, when she refused to yield them. Mandorai, [mänd rä′ ē] a woman bent upon destroying all the worlds, was vanquished by Indra and he earned the gratitude of humanity. These are but two instances. A woman of demoniac tendencies loses all consideration to be treated as a woman. This Thataka is more dreadful than Yama, the god of death, who takes a life only when the time is ripe. But this monster, at the very scent of a living creature, craves to kill and eat. Do not picture her as a woman at all. You must rid this world of her. It is your duty."

Rama said, "I will carry out your wish."

Thataka threw her three-pronged spear at Rama. As it came flaming, Rama strung his bow and sent an arrow which broke it into fragments. Next she raised a hail of stones under which to crush her adversaries. Rama sent up his arrows, which shielded them from the attack. Finally Rama's arrow pierced her throat and ended her career; thereby also inaugurating Rama's life's mission of destroying evil and demonry in this world. The gods assembled in the sky and expressed their joy and relief and enjoined Viswamithra, "Oh, adept and master of weapons, impart without any reserve all your knowledge and powers to this lad. He is a savior." Viswamithra obeyed this injunction and taught Rama all the <u>esoteric</u> techniques in weaponry. Thereafter the presiding deities of various weapons, *asthras* [äs′ träz], appeared before Rama submissively and declared, "Now we are yours: command us night or day."

Reading Skill
Analyzing Cultural Context What do the details in this paragraph suggest about the place of women in Hindu culture?

Literary Analysis
Epics What does Rama's victory show about his destiny as an epic hero?

Vocabulary Builder
esoteric (es′ ə ter′ ik) *adj.* beyond the understanding or knowledge of most people

Apply the Skills

Rama's Initiation **from the** *Ramayana*

Thinking About the Selection

1. **Respond:** What was your reaction to the killing of Thataka? Why?
2. **(a) Recall:** What favor does Viswamithra ask of King Dasaratha? **(b) Hypothesize:** Why does he want Rama, rather than the king, to perform the favor?
3. **(a) Recall:** List three details describing the region through which Rama, Lakshmana, and Viswamithra pass. **(b) Analyze:** How does the land seem different to Rama and Lakshmana when they use Viswamithra's mantras? **(c) Draw Conclusions:** What does this episode suggest about the sage's power?
4. **(a) Recall:** Summarize the outcome of Rama's first battle. **(b) Interpret:** This part of the epic is called "Rama's Initiation." Into what activity or way of life is he initiated?
5. **(a) Make a Judgment:** Do you find Viswamithra a worthy teacher for Rama? List examples of Viswamithra's qualities and behavior that support your answer. **(b) Discuss:** Share your ideas in a small group discussion. **(c) Evaluate:** As a group, choose the best ideas and present them to the class.

Literary Analysis

6. **(a)** What is the goal of the sage's **epic** journey? **(b)** What is Rama's goal in accompanying the sage? **(c)** Compare and contrast these goals with the goals of epic heroes who fight for honor or glory.

Noble Birth	Warrior Virtues	Acts Honorably	Chosen by the Gods or Fate

7. Using a chart like the one shown, give specific examples showing which qualities of an **epic hero** Rama possesses.
8. **(a)** Why does Rama hesitate before fighting Thataka? **(b)** Does his hesitation suit the character of an epic hero? Explain.

Reading Skill

9. **(a)** List three things that you learned about Hindu **cultural context** from the features that appear before the selection. **(b)** List two things you learned about Hindu culture from the selection or from the footnotes. **(c)** For each item of context you list, briefly explain how knowing that item helps you to understand the *Ramayana.* Give specific examples.

QuickReview

Epic at a Glance
Prince Rama, a son of King Dasaratha, accepts his own destiny by agreeing to accompany the sage Viswamithra on a perilous journey.

Go Online
Assessment
For: Self-test
Visit: www.PHSchool.com
Web Code: eqa-6605

Epic: a long narrative or narrative poem about the deeds of heroes

Epic Hero: a warrior, often based on a historic or legendary figure, who strives to win immortality through great deeds

Analyzing Cultural Context: determining ways in which a literary work reflects the culture in which it was composed

Vocabulary Builder

Practice Write a sentence about each of the following situations by using a word from the vocabulary list for the *Ramayana* on page 1004.

1. a building with peeling paint, a sagging door, and a broken fence
2. a judge seated at the head of a courtroom
3. a successful lawyer who is also very spiritual
4. a scientist's most difficult theory

Adding Words to Your Vocabulary Using a thesaurus, find two **synonyms**, or words with equivalent meanings, for *august* and two for *esoteric.* Then, explain the similarities and differences in the meanings of the words. (For more on using a thesaurus, see page R7.)

Writing

Write a **newspaper report** of events at the end of the selection. First, take notes in which you identify main characters and outline story events. As you draft, include the following elements:

- a catchy headline
- information on *who, what, where, when, how,* and *why*
- believable quotations from participants and onlookers
- comments on the significance of the events

For *Grammar, Vocabulary,* and *Assessment,* see **Build Language Skills,** pages 1028–1029.

Extend Your Learning

Listening and Speaking With two classmates, present an **improvised dialogue** between an Indian king, his son, and a sage about venturing forth against the demons of the world. Apply what you have learned about Hindu culture, and be sure that characters speak in a way suited to their position. Take 10 minutes to prepare, and use no more than 10 minutes for the presentation.

Research and Technology Locate audiovisual resources about the culture and history of classical India. As you review the material, jot down the thoughts, opinions, and questions that occur to you. Then, write a **summary of research notes** explaining what you learned, what thoughts you had about the material, and what questions you still have. Note connections you found to the *Ramayana.*

Build Language Skills

from *Sundiata: An Epic of Old Mali* • from the *Ramayana*

Vocabulary Skill

Context Clues and Multiple Meanings Many words have more than one meaning. The **context** of a word, or the surroundings in which it is used, can help you determine the meaning that applies in a particular case. For example, the word root -*man*-, meaning "hand," is the root of *manifest*. *Manifest* is an adjective meaning "able to be touched by the hand" or "evident." *Manifest* is also a noun meaning "an itemized list"—a list that makes evident the contents of a ship or a box.

Adjective: His sweaty palms made his nervousness manifest.

Noun: I checked the manifest for the box to see if an item was missing.

Practice Use a dictionary to find two meanings for each word. Write a sentence that illustrates each meaning.

1. manual   **2.** manage   **3.** maneuver

Grammar Lesson

Complex and Compound-Complex Sentences An **independent clause** contains a subject and verb and can stand alone as a complete sentence. A **subordinate clause** has a subject and verb but cannot stand alone as a complete sentence.

- A **complex sentence** contains one independent clause and one or more subordinate clauses.
- A **compound-complex sentence** contains at least one subordinate clause and at least two independent clauses.

In these examples, the independent clauses are underlined once and the subordinate clauses are underlined twice.

Complex: After reading about knights, Don Quixote became a knight.
Complex: Sancho Panza, who accompanied Don Quixote, was a simple peasant, although Don Quixote called Panza his squire.
Compound-complex: When Cervantes wrote about Don Quixote, the age of knighthood was over, and Spain had become a power.

Practice Identify each sentence as complex or compound-complex, and indicate which clauses are independent and which are subordinate.

1. King Arthur was probably a real historical figure, but he was not really a king as we understand the term today.

2. The real Arthur led the Celts of Britain when Germanic tribes invaded the island in the sixth century.

3. After they fled central Britain, the Celts flourished in Wales and Cornwall in the west; they also settled in Brittany, which is on the western coast of France.

Reading: Analyzing Cultural Context

Standards
Assessed
• 10.2.4
• 10.3.1
• 10.3.11

Directions: *Read this ancient Egyptian poem, and then answer the questions.*

> I think I'll go home and lie very still,
>   feigning terminal illness.
> Then the neighbors will all troop over to stare,
>   my love, perhaps, among them.
> How she'll smile while the specialists
>   snarl in their teeth!—
>
> she perfectly well knows what ails me.

—"I Think I'll Go Home and Lie Very Still," translated by John L. Foster

1. Judging from the context of the poem, what is the best definition of *feigning*?
   A with
   B pretending
   C extremely serious
   D known

2. The fact that the poem is from ancient Egypt helps the reader
   A understand the specialists of the time.
   B understand the universal nature of human behavior.
   C understand the culture of ancient Egypt.
   D understand the nature of the speaker.

3. The line "the neighbors will all troop over to stare" demonstrates
   A the particular customs of ancient Egypt.
   B a ritual that was part of that region.
   C a universal human curiosity.
   D the military background of the speaker.

4. What does the poem show about interpersonal relations in ancient Egypt?
   A The concept of love was foreign to ancient Egyptians.
   B Love was considered a serious illness.
   C People lived isolated lives.
   D People felt the pain of disappointed love just as they do today.

Timed Writing: Explanation [Connections]

Select a character from either *Sundiata* or the *Ramayana*. In an essay, explain how the character's role is determined by his or her culture. Use details from the text to support your points. **(50 minutes)**

Writing Workshop: *Work in Progress*

Writing for Assessment

Use the timed essay from your writing portfolio to practice quick revision. Look at the places where you have placed a check mark and revise as little as possible to correct the logic. Attempt to revise phrases or clauses rather than entire sentences. Save this work in your writing portfolio.

Reading Informational Materials

Research Sources

In Part 1, you learned how to analyze the cultural context of a literary work. Research sources, such as encyclopedias, atlases, and almanacs, can add to your understanding of cultural context by providing valuable historical, economic, geographic, and cultural information. If you read *Sundiata,* you may be interested in this atlas entry about Mali.

About Research Sources

Research sources are publications, such as encyclopedias, certain Web sites, and atlases, that present information. The following are features found in many research sources:

- heads and subheads that help you quickly locate information
- statements of fact rather than opinion
- statistics, or numerical data
- visuals, such as maps, graphs, diagrams, charts, icons, and symbols

Reading Skill

You can use research sources to understand the cultural context of a literary work—the life of the people who created it. To build a picture of this life, **make generalizations**—formulate statements that explain, connect, or sum up a number of the facts that you find in sources.

- Ask a general question about your topic. Then, identify the facts that help answer your question. Finally, state the answer to your question in a sentence. Your answer will be a generalization.

Question	Facts	Generalization
What is the standard of living in Mali?	Poverty is a main political issue.	The standard of life is probably not high.

- Look for connections between facts or patterns joining them. Then, brainstorm for general nouns, such as *influence,* or adjectives, such as *warlike,* that sum up these connections. Use your chosen words to formulate a generalization.

Fact	Pattern	General Words	Generalization
Language: French Currency: franc	French things in Malinese life	*influence* *relationship*	Mali has been influenced by the French.

Academic Standards

- Analyze formatting of informational documents. (10.2.1)
- Compare first-hand and second-hand accounts of an event. (10.2.2)

Adapted from *Dorling Kindersley*
World Reference Atlas

Central and Western Africa

MALI

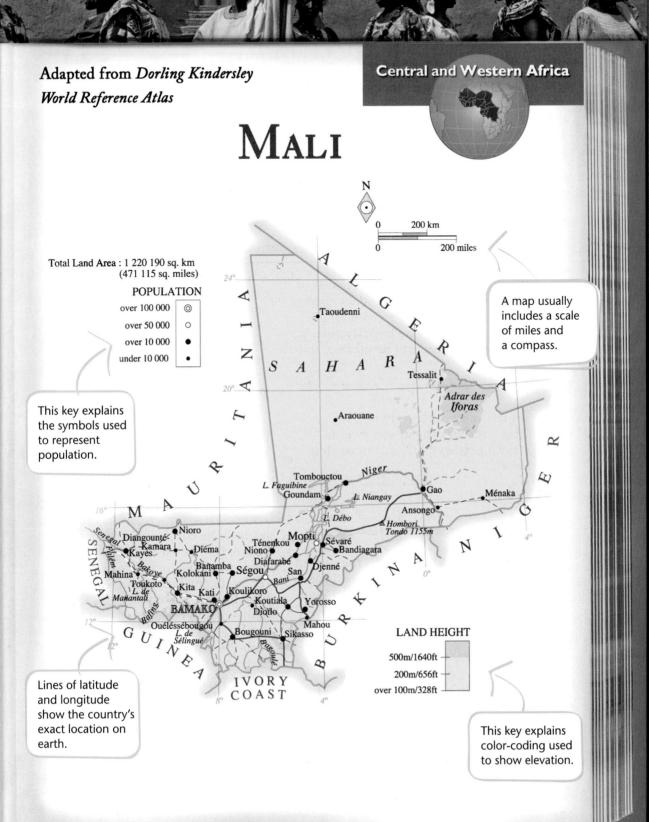

Total Land Area : 1 220 190 sq. km
(471 115 sq. miles)

POPULATION

over 100 000	◎
over 50 000	○
over 10 000	●
under 10 000	•

LAND HEIGHT

500m/1640ft	
200m/656ft	
over 100m/328ft	

This key explains the symbols used to represent population.

A map usually includes a scale of miles and a compass.

Lines of latitude and longitude show the country's exact location on earth.

This key explains color-coding used to show elevation.

Mali

Official Name: Republic of Mali
Capital: Bamako
Population: 10.8 million
Currency: CFA franc
Official Language: French

Key facts are summari ed here.

Mali is landlocked in the heart of West Africa. Its mostly flat terrain comprises virtually uninhabited Saharan plains in the north and more fertile savanna land in the south, where most of the population live. The River Niger irrigates the central and southwestern regions of the country. Following independence in 1960, Mali experienced a long period of largely single-party rule. It became a multiparty democracy in 1992.

Heads are set off to make locating information easy.

CLIMATE

In the south, intensely hot, dry weather precedes the westerly rains. Mali's northern half is almost rainless.

TRANSPORTATION

 Has no fleet   Bamako-Senou

Mali is linked by rail with the port of Dakar in Senegal, and by good roads to the port of Abidjan in Ivory Coast.

Icons are used to call out basic information.

TOURISM

 16,000 visitors   Down 33% in 1994

Tourism is largely safari-oriented, although the historic cities of Djénné, Gao and Mopti, lying on the banks of the River Niger, also attract visitors. A national domestic airline began operating in 1990.

PEOPLE

 Bambara, Fulani, Senufo, Soninke, French   24 people per sq. mile

Mali's most significant ethnic group, the Bambara, is also politically dominant. The Bambara speak the lingua franca of the River Niger, which is shared with other groups including the Malinke. The relationship between the Bambara–Malinke majority and the Tuareg nomads of the Saharan north is often tense and sometimes violent. As with elsewhere in Africa, the extended family, often based around the village, is a vital social security system and a link between the urban and rural poor. There are a few powerful women in Mali but, in general, women have little status.

POLITICS

The successful transition to multiparty politics in 1992 followed the overthrow in the previous year of Moussa Traoré, Mali's dictator for 23 years. The army's role was crucial in leading the coup, while Colonel Touré, who acted as interim president, was responsible for the swift return to civilian rule in less than a year. The change marks Mali's first experience of multipartyism. Maintaining good relations with the Tuaregs, after a peace agreement in 1991, is a key issue. However, the main challenge facing President Alpha Oumar Konaré's government is to alleviate poverty while placating the opposition, which feels that the luxury of multipartyism is something that Mali cannot afford.

Text provides more in-depth information.

Reading: Making Generalizations

Directions: *Choose the letter of the best answer to each question about the atlas entry for Mali.*

1. Which of the following generalizations can be supported by the information presented on the map?
   A Life in Mali centers around deep-sea fishing.
   B Most of the population lives in the southwestern region of Mali.
   C The peoples of the desert dominate the country politically.
   D Mali is a land of craggy mountains and deep valleys.

2. Which of the following facts does not support this generalization: "The people of Mali have adopted many European ways"?
   A Mali has a multiparty, democratic political system.
   B The currency of Mali is modeled on the French franc.
   C Mali has a national airline.
   D Malinese depend on extended tribal and family connections.

Reading: Comprehension and Interpretation

Directions: *Write your answers on a separate piece of paper.*

3. **(a)** Which part of Mali almost always goes without rain?
   (b) Does the city of Taoudenni receive much rain? Explain.
   [Integrating]

4. What important change occurred to the political system of Mali in the 1990s? **[Organizing]**

5. A review of a new novel set in Mali states that the story presents a realistic picture of the country's violent conflicts. From what backgrounds might the characters in conflict come? Explain.
   [Integrating]

Timed Writing: Research [Connections]

Write a **research plan** based on an interesting fact or detail in this Mali atlas entry. Explain the topic you would like to investigate further. Then, make a list of questions and explain how specific research sources could be used to answer each question. **(45 minutes)**

Archetypal Narrative Patterns

Archetypal narrative patterns are basic storytelling patterns found in the stories of cultures around the world. These patterns often appear in stories originally passed along orally, such as fairy tales and myths. Patterns make the stories easier to remember and retell, and help to create drama and a storytelling rhythm.

Common archetypal narrative patterns include the following:

- a series of tests that a character must pass
- a quest or task a character must perform
- characters, events, or objects that come in threes
- a greedy, cruel, or jealous relative who behaves unfairly
- a hero who triumphs over stronger forces through cleverness or virtue
- a mysterious or supernatural guide who points the way
- a just end that rewards good or punishes evil

Comparing Archetypal Narrative Patterns

Many readers are interested in the drama of a work or the insights it conveys. Certain methods of studying literature, however, require critics to focus on narrative patterns and other structures of a work. By analyzing and comparing patterns in stories, critics attempt to study literature in an objective way. Their results may also reveal something about the way human beings organize and understand information—the inner "machinery" of the human mind. As you read "Cupid and Psyche" and "Ashputtle," analyze the narrative patterns in each story, using a chart like the one shown.

(IN) Academic Standards

- Analyze many different forms of dramatic literature. (10.3.1)
- Evaluate the use of literary devices including figurative language, imagery, allegory, and symbolism. (10.3.7)

Story Detail	Archetypal Pattern
three sisters	characters that come in threes
help from the birds	

Vocabulary Builder

Cupid and Psyche

- **adulation** (a´ jōō lā´ shən) *n.* high or excessive praise; intense admiration (p. 1036) *Rock stars may grow used to the <u>adulation</u> of fans.*

- **diligence** (dil´ ə jəns) *n.* constant, careful effort (p. 1038) *He worked with <u>diligence</u> and finished his report early.*

- **allay** (a lā´) *v.* relieve; lessen; calm (p. 1040) *One look at the dog's sweet face will <u>allay</u> your fear of him.*

Ashputtle

- **plague** (plāg) *v.* pester; harass; torment (p. 1045) *She is studying for a test, so do not <u>plague</u> her with questions.*

- **jeered** (jir'd) *v.* made fun of; mocked; taunted (p. 1045) *The fans <u>jeered</u> when the opposing outfielder dropped the ball.*

- **nimbly** (nim´ blē) *adv.* in a quick, easy, light way; with agility (p. 1048) *The acrobat ran <u>nimbly</u> across the highwire.*

Build Understanding

Connecting to the Literature

Reading/Writing Connection As "Cupid and Psyche" and "Ashputtle" show, life is full of tests—tests of strength, of trust, or of truth. Write a few sentences to describe such a test as it is depicted in literature or the movies. Use at least three of these words: *emphasize, equate, complicate, react.*

Meet the Author

Lucius **Apuleius** (ca. A.D. 124–170)
Sally **Benson** (1900–1972)

Although the tale of Cupid and Psyche goes back to Greek mythology, the best-known version is in the *Metamorphoses* by the ancient Roman writer Lucius Apuleius (loo′ shəs ap′ yoo lē′ əs). This work is often considered the world's first novel.

A Modern Reteller Sally Benson won fame with her short stories. Her collection *Meet Me in St. Louis,* based on her own Missouri childhood, was adapted as a movie musical.

Jakob **Grimm** (1785–1863)
Wilhelm **Grimm** (1786–1859)

Born in the German state of Hesse, Jakob and Wilhelm Grimm grew up in poverty after their father died. Although both studied law, they were most interested in language and literature. Eventually both brothers found work as librarians.

A National Literature The brothers began collecting tales that people told in Hesse and neighboring places. They also wrote books on literature, and Jakob made contributions to linguistics. Today, they are most remembered for the folktales they preserved, including "Rumpelstiltskin" and "Snow White."

Go Online
Author Link
For: More about the authors
Visit: www.PHSchool.com
Web Code: eqe-9606

Cupid and Psyche

retold by SALLY BENSON

There once lived a king and queen who had three daughters. The two elder daughters were beautiful, but the youngest daughter, Psyche,[1] was the loveliest maiden in the whole world. The fame of her beauty was so great that strangers from neighboring countries came in crowds to admire her, paying her the homage which is only due Venus[2] herself. In fact, Venus found her altars deserted, as men turned their devotion to the exquisite young girl. People sang her praises as she walked the streets, and strewed chaplets and flowers before her.

This <u>adulation</u> infuriated Venus. Shaking her silken locks in indignation, she exclaimed, "Am I then to be eclipsed by a mortal girl? In vain did that royal shepherd whose judgment was approved by Jupiter himself give me the palm of beauty over my illustrious rivals, Minerva and Juno.[3] I will give this Psyche cause to repent of so unlawful a beauty."

She complained to her son, Cupid, and led him to the land where Psyche lived, so that he could see for himself the insults the girl unconsciously heaped upon his mother. "My dear son," said Venus, "punish that beauty. Give thy mother a revenge as sweet as her injuries are great. Infuse into the bosom of that haughty girl a passion for some low, mean, unworthy being, so that she may reap a shame as great as her present joy and triumph."

Vocabulary Builder
adulation (a´ jōō lā´ shən) *n.* high or excessive praise; intense admiration

---

1. **Psyche** (sī´ kē)
2. **Venus** (vē´ nəs) the Roman goddess of love and beauty.
3. **royal shepherd. . . Minerva** (mi nur´ və) **and Juno** (jōō´ nō) In Greek and Roman mythology, Paris, a prince who lived as a shepherd, was called to judge who was most beautiful of three goddesses: Juno, queen of the gods; Minerva, goddess of wisdom; or Venus, goddess of love.

Now, there were two fountains in Venus's garden, one of sweet waters, the other of bitter. Cupid filled two amber vases, one from each fountain and, suspending them from the top of his quiver, hastened to Psyche's chamber, where she lay asleep. He shed a few drops from the bitter fountain over her lips, though she looked so beautiful in her sleep that he was filled with pity. Then he touched her side with the point of his arrow. At the touch, she awoke and opened her eyes on Cupid, who was so startled by their blue enchantment that he wounded himself with his own arrow. He hovered over her, invisible, and to repair the damage he had done, he poured the water from the sweet fountain over her silken ringlets.

Psyche, thus frowned upon by Venus, derived no benefit from all her charms. All eyes were still cast eagerly upon her and every mouth spoke her praise, but neither king, royal youth, or common man presented himself to demand her hand in marriage. Her two elder sisters were married to royal princes, but Psyche, in her lonely apartment, wept over her beauty, sick of the flattery it aroused, while love was denied her.

Her parents, afraid that they had unwittingly incurred the anger of the gods, consulted the oracle of Apollo,[4] and received this answer: "The girl is destined for the bride of no mortal lover. Her future husband awaits her on the top of the mountain. He is a monster whom neither the gods nor men can resist."

This dreadful decree of the oracle filled all the people with dismay, and her parents abandoned themselves to grief. But Psyche said, "Why, my dear parents, do you now lament me? You should rather have grieved when the people showered undeserved honors upon me and with one voice called me 'Venus.' I now perceive I am a victim to that name. I submit. Lead me to that rock to which my unhappy fate has destined me."

She dressed herself in gorgeous robes, and her beauty was so dazzling that people turned away as it was more than they could bear. Then, followed by wailing and lamenting crowds, she and her parents ascended the mountain. On the summit, her father and mother left her alone, and returned home in tears.

While Psyche stood on the ridge of the mountain, panting with fear and sobbing aloud, the gentle Zephyrus[5] raised her from the earth and bore her with an easy motion into a flowery dale. There she lay down on a grassy bank and fell asleep. She awoke refreshed, and saw near by a pleasant grove of tall and stately trees. She

Literary Analysis
Archetypal Narrative Patterns Which archetypal pattern does the fact that there are three sisters illustrate?

Reading Check
Why is Venus angry with Psyche?

---

4. **oracle** (ôr´ ə kəl) **of Apollo** (ə päl´ ō) Apollo was the Greek and Roman god of light, music, and medicine. An oracle was a person who revealed the will of the gods in answer to people's questions.
5. **Zephyrus** (zef´ ə rəs) in Greek mythology, god of the west wind.

entered it, and discovered a fountain sending forth clear and crystal waters, and near it stood a magnificent palace that was too stupendous to have been the work of mortal hands. Drawn by admiration and wonder, she walked through the huge doors. Inside, golden pillars supported the vaulted roof, and the walls were hung with delightful paintings. She wandered through the empty rooms marveling at what she saw, when suddenly a voice addressed her. "Sovereign lady," it said, "all that you see is yours. We whose voices you hear are your servants and shall obey all your commands with the utmost care and <u>diligence</u>. Retire, therefore, to your chamber and repose on your bed of down, and when you see fit, repair to the bath. Supper awaits you in the adjoining alcove when it pleases you to take your seat there."

Psyche listened with amazement, and, going to her room, she lay down and rested. Then, after a refreshing bath, she went to the alcove, where a table wheeled itself into the room without any visible aid. It was covered with the finest delicacies and the most wonderful wines. There even was music from invisible performers.

She had not yet seen her destined husband. He came only in the hours of darkness and fled before dawn, but his accents were full of love and inspired a like passion in her. She often begged him to stay and let her behold him, but he would not consent. On the contrary, he charged her to make no attempt to see him, for it was his pleasure, for the best of reasons, to remain concealed. "Why should you wish to behold me?" he asked. "Have you any doubt of my love? If you saw me, perhaps you would fear me, perhaps adore me. But all I ask of you is to love me. I would rather have you love me as an equal than adore me as a god."

This reasoning satisfied Psyche for a time and she lived quite happily alone in the huge palace. But at length she thought of her parents who were in ignorance of her fate, and of her sisters with whom she wished to share the delights of her new home. These thoughts preyed on her mind and made her think of her splendid mansion as a prison. When her husband came one night, she told

▲ **Critical Viewing**
Which details of this painting suggest Cupid's love for Psyche? **[Analyze]**

Vocabulary Builder
diligence (dil′ ə jəns) *n.* constant, careful effort

him of her distress, and at last drew from him an unwilling consent that her sisters should be brought to see her.

So, calling Zephyrus, she told him of her husband's command, and he soon brought them across the mountain down to their sister's valley. They embraced her, and Psyche's eyes filled with tears of joy. "Come," she said, "enter my house and refresh yourselves." Taking them by their hands, she led them into her golden palace and committed them to the care of her numerous train[6] of attendant voices, to refresh themselves in her baths and at her table, and to show them all her treasures. The sight of all these splendid things filled her sisters with envy, and they resented the thought that she possessed such splendor which far exceeded anything they owned.

They asked her numberless questions, and begged her to tell them what sort of person her husband was. Psyche replied that he was a beautiful youth who generally spent the daytime in hunting upon the mountains. The sisters, not satisfied with this reply, soon made her confess that she had never seen him. They then proceeded to fill her bosom with dire suspicions. "Call to mind," they said, "the Pythian oracle[7] that declared that you were destined to marry a direful and tremendous monster. The inhabitants of this valley say that your husband is a terrible and monstrous serpent, who nourishes you for a while with dainties that he may by and by devour you. Take our advice. Provide yourself with a lamp and a sharp knife. Put them in concealment so that your husband may not discover them, and when he is sound asleep, slip out of bed, bring forth your lamp and see for yourself whether what they say is true or not. If it is, hesitate not to cut off the monster's head, and thereby recover your liberty."

Psyche resisted these persuasions as well as she could, but they did not fail to have their effect on her mind, and when her sisters were gone, their words and her own curiosity were too strong for her to resist. She prepared her lamp and a sharp knife, and hid them out of sight of her husband. When he had fallen into his first sleep, she silently arose, and uncovering her lamp beheld him. He lay there, the most beautiful and charming of the gods, with his golden ringlets wandering over his snowy neck and crimson cheek. On his shoulders were two dewy wings, whiter than snow, with shining feathers.

As she leaned over with the lamp to have a closer view of his face, a drop of burning oil fell on his shoulder, and made him wince with

6. train (trān) *n.* group of followers, such as servants.
7. Pythian (pith'ē ən) **oracle** oracle of Apollo, called Pythian after Python, the monstrous snake that Apollo killed.

Literary Analysis
Archetypal Narrative Patterns What test does Cupid set for Psyche?

Reading Check

What do Psyche's sisters persuade her to do?

Cupid and Psyche ■ 1039

pain. He opened his eyes and fixed them full upon her. Then, without saying a word, he spread his white wings and flew out of the window. Psyche cried out and tried to follow him, falling from the window to the ground. Cupid, beholding her as she lay in the dust, stopped his flight for an instant and said, "O foolish Psyche! Is it thus you repay my love? After having disobeyed my mother's commands and made you my wife, will you think me a monster and cut off my head? But go. Return to your sisters whose advice you seem to think better than mine. I inflict no other punishment on you than to leave you forever. Love cannot dwell with suspicion."

He soared into the air, leaving poor Psyche prostrate on the ground.

When she recovered some degree of composure, she looked around her. The palace and gardens had vanished, and she found herself in an open field not far from the city where her sisters dwelt. She went to them and told them the whole story of her misfortune, at which, pretending to grieve, they inwardly rejoiced. "For now," they said, "he will perhaps choose one of us." With this idea, without saying a word of her intentions, each of them rose early the next morning and ascended the mountain and, having reached the top, called upon Zephyrus to receive her and bear her to his lord. Then, leaping into space, and not being sustained by Zephyrus, they fell down the precipice and were dashed to pieces.

Psyche, meanwhile, wandered day and night, without food or rest, in search of her husband. One day, seeing a lofty mountain in the distance, she sighed and said to herself, "Perhaps my love, my lord, inhabits there."

On the mountain top was a temple and she no sooner entered it than she saw heaps of corn, some in loose ears and some in sheaves,[8] with mingled ears of barley. Scattered about lay sickles and rakes, and all the instruments of harvest, without order, as if thrown carelessly out of the weary reapers' hands in the sultry hours of the day.

Psyche put an end to this unseemly confusion by separating and sorting everything to its proper place and kind, believing that she ought to neglect none of the gods, but endeavor by her piety to engage them all in her behalf. The holy Ceres,[9] whose temple it was, finding her so religiously employed, spoke to her, "O Psyche, truly worthy of our pity, though I cannot shield you from the frowns of Venus, yet I can teach you how to best <u>allay</u> her displeasure. Go then, and voluntarily surrender yourself to her, and try by modesty and submission to win her forgiveness, and perhaps her favor will restore you to the husband you have lost."

▶ **Critical Viewing**
For some artists, Psyche is a symbol of the human soul striving after wisdom. Which details in this painting support this interpretation? **[Interpret]**

Literary Analysis
Archetypal Narrative Patterns In what other stories have you encountered a mysterious building like the palace?

Vocabulary Builder
allay (a lā´) v. relieve; lessen; calm

---

8. sheaves (shēvz) n. bundles of stalks of grain.
9. Ceres (sir´ ēz´) Roman goddess of farming.

Psyche obeyed the commands of Ceres and journeyed to the temple of Venus. Venus received her in a fury of anger. "Most undutiful and faithless of servants," she said, "do you at last remember that you really have a mistress? Or have you come to see your sick husband, yet laid up with the wound given him by his loving wife? You are so ill-favored and disagreeable that the only way you can merit your lover must be by dint of industry and diligence. I will make trial of your housewifery."

She ordered Psyche to be led to the storehouse of her temple, where a great quantity of wheat, barley, millet, beans and lentils, which was used as food for her pigeons, lay scattered about the floors. Then Venus said, "Take and separate all these grains into their proper parcels, and see that you get it done before evening."

Psyche, in consternation over the enormous task, sat stupid and silent. While she sat despairing, Cupid stirred up the little ant, a native of the fields, to take compassion on her. The leader of the ant-hill, followed by whole hosts of his six-legged subjects, went to work and sorted each grain to its parcel. And when all was done, the ants vanished out of sight.

At twilight, Venus returned from the banquet of the gods, crowned with roses. Seeing the task done, she exclaimed, "This is no work of yours, wicked one, but his, whom to your own and his misfortune you have enticed." So saying, she threw her a piece of black bread for her supper and went away.

Next morning Venus ordered Psyche to be called and said to her, "Behold yonder grove which stretches along the margin of the water. There you will find sheep feeding without a shepherd, with gold-shining fleeces on their backs. Go, fetch me a sample of that precious wool from every one of their fleeces."

Psyche obediently went to the river side, prepared to do her best to execute the command. But the river god inspired the reeds with harmonious murmurs, which seemed to say, "O maiden, severely tried, tempt not the dangerous flood, nor venture among formidable rams on the other side, for as long as they are under the influence of the rising sun they burn with a cruel rage to destroy mortals with their sharp horns or rude teeth. But when the noontide sun has driven the cattle to the shade, and the serene spirit of the flood has lulled them to rest, you may then cross in safety, and you will find the woolly gold sticking to the bushes and the trunks of the trees."

✓ Reading Check

What does Cupid do after Psyche exposes his identity?

She followed the compassionate river god's instructions and soon returned to Venus with her arms full of the golden fleece. Venus, in a rage, cried, "I know very well it is by none of your own doings that you have succeeded in this task. And I am not satisfied yet that you have any capacity to make yourself useful. But I have another task for you. Here, take this box, and go your way to the infernal shade and give this box to Proserpina[10] and say, 'My mistress, Venus, desires you to send her a little of your beauty, for in tending her sick son, she has lost some of her own.' Be not too long on your errand, for I must paint myself with it to appear at the circle of gods and goddesses this evening."

Psyche was now sure that her destruction was at hand, being obliged to go with her own feet down to the deathly regions of Erebus.[11] So as not to delay, she went to the highest tower prepared to hurl herself headlong from it down to the shades below. But a voice from the tower said to her, "Why, poor unlucky girl, dost thou design to put an end to thy days in so dreadful a manner? And what cowardice makes thee sink under this last danger who hast been so miraculously supported in all thy former perils?"

Then the voice told her how she might reach the realms of Pluto[12] by way of a certain cave, and how to avoid the perils of the road, how to pass by Cerberus,[13] the three-headed dog, and prevail on Charon,[14] the ferryman, to take her across the black river and bring her back again. And the voice added, "When Proserpina has given you the box filled with her beauty, of all things this is chiefly to be observed by you, that you never once open or look into the box, nor allow your curiosity to pry into the treasure of the beauty of the goddesses."

Psyche, encouraged by this advice, obeyed in all things, and traveled to the kingdom of Pluto. She was admitted to the palace of Proserpina, and without accepting the delicate seat or delicious banquet that was offered her, but content with coarse bread for her food, she delivered her message from Venus. Presently the box was returned to her, shut, and filled with the precious commodity. She returned the way she came, happy to see the light of day once more.

Having got so far successfully through her dangerous task, a desire seized her to examine the contents of the box. "What," she

---

10. **infernal shade . . . Proserpina** (prō sʉr′ pi nə) In Greek and Roman mythology, the dead inhabit an "infernal shade," or dark region under the earth. Proserpina, daughter of Ceres, is the wife of Pluto, the god who rules this region.
11. **Erebus** (er′ ə bəs) in Greek mythology, the place under the earth through which the dead pass before entering the underworld.
12. **Pluto** (plo͞ot′ ō) Roman god of the underworld.
13. **Cerberus** (sʉr′ bər əs) in Greek and Roman mythology, the three-headed dog guarding the entrance to the underworld.
14. **Charon** (ker′ ən) in Greek mythology, the ferryman who carried the dead over the river Styx into the underworld.

Literary Analysis
Archetypal Narrative Patterns Identify an archetypal pattern developed here.

said to herself, "shall I, the carrier of this divine beauty, not take the least bit to put on my cheeks to appear to more advantage in the eyes of my beloved husband!" She carefully opened the box, and found nothing there of any beauty at all, but an infernal and truly Stygian[15] sleep, which, being set free from its prison, took possession of her. She fell down in the road, unconscious, without sense or motion.

Cupid had recovered from his wound and was no longer able to bear the absence of his beloved Psyche. He slipped through the smallest crack in the window of his chamber and flew to the spot where Psyche lay. He gathered up the sleep from her body and closed it again in the box. Then he waked Psyche with a light touch from one of his arrows.

"Again," he said, "hast thou almost perished by the same curiosity. But now perform exactly the task imposed on you by my mother, and I will take care of the rest."

Swift as lightning, he left the earth and penetrated the heights of heaven. Here he presented himself before Jupiter with his supplication. The god lent a favoring ear, and pleaded the cause of the lovers so earnestly with Venus that he won her consent. Then he sent Mercury to bring Psyche up to the heavenly assemblage, and when she arrived, he handed her a cup of ambrosia[16] and said, "Drink this, Psyche, and be immortal. Nor shall Cupid ever break away from the knot in which he is tied, but these nuptials[17] shall be perpetual."

Psyche became at last united to Cupid forever.

---

15. **Stygian** (stij′ ē ən) *adj.* of the river Styx, a mythological river crossed by the dead on their way to the underworld.
16. **ambrosia** (am brō′ zhə) *n.* food of the gods.
17. **nuptials** (nup′ shəlz) *n.* wedding.

Thinking About the Selection

1. **Respond:** Do you think Psyche was wrong to disobey Cupid by uncovering his identity? Explain.

2. **(a) Recall:** What reason does Venus give for sending Cupid to Psyche? **(b) Compare and Contrast:** Compare her plan with its actual outcome.

3. **(a) Summarize:** What tasks does Venus require Psyche to perform? **(b) Connect:** In the third task, in what way does Psyche repeat her earlier mistake with Cupid?

4. **(a) Interpret:** What does Cupid mean when he says, "Love cannot dwell with suspicion"? **(b) Draw Conclusions:** What lesson does the story suggest about love? Explain.

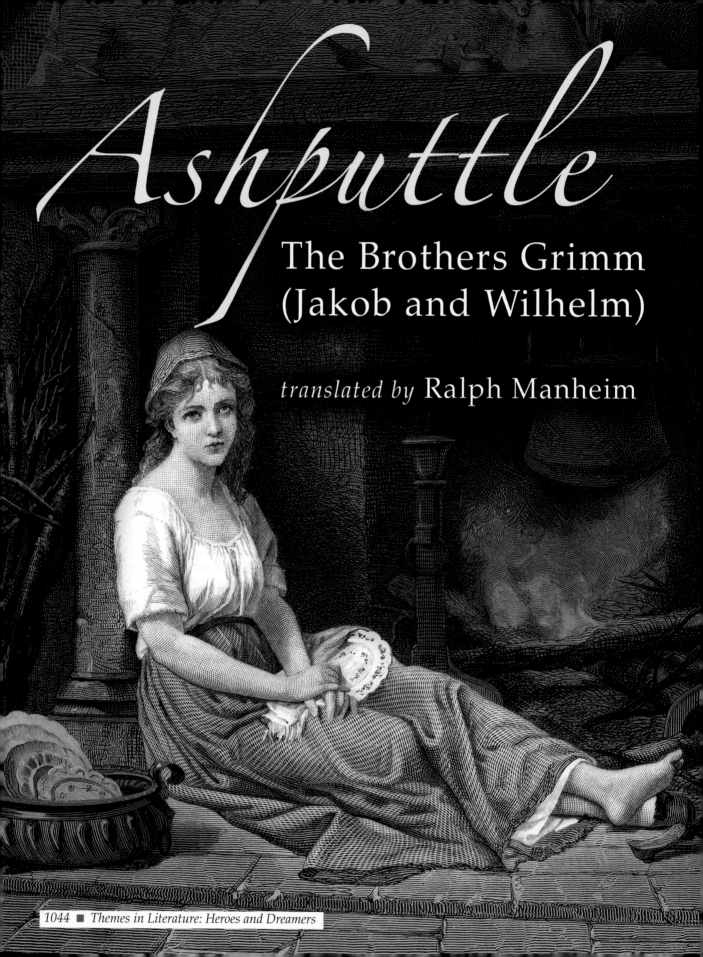

Ashputtle

The Brothers Grimm
(Jakob and Wilhelm)

translated by Ralph Manheim

A rich man's wife fell sick and, feeling that her end was near, she called her only daughter to her bedside and said: "Dear child, be good and say your prayers; God will help you, and I shall look down on you from heaven and always be with you." With that she closed her eyes and died. Every day the little girl went out to her mother's grave and wept, and she went on being good and saying her prayers. When winter came, the snow spread a white cloth over the grave, and when spring took it off, the man remarried.

His new wife brought two daughters into the house. Their faces were beautiful and lily-white, but their hearts were ugly and black. That was the beginning of a bad time for the poor stepchild. "Why should this silly goose sit in the parlor[1] with us?" they said. "People who want to eat bread must earn it. Get into the kitchen where you belong!" They took away her fine clothes and gave her an old gray dress and wooden shoes to wear. "Look at the haughty princess in her finery!" they cried and, laughing, led her to the kitchen. From then on she had to do all the work, getting up before daybreak, carrying water, lighting fires, cooking and washing. In addition the sisters did everything they could to <u>plague</u> her. They <u>jeered</u> at her and poured peas and lentils[2] into the ashes, so that she had to sit there picking them out. At night, when she was tired out with work, she had no bed to sleep in but had to lie in the ashes by the hearth. And they took to calling her Ashputtle because she always looked dusty and dirty.

One day when her father was going to the fair, he asked his two stepdaughters what he should bring them. "Beautiful dresses," said one. "Diamonds and pearls," said the other. "And you, Ashputtle. What would you like?" "Father," she said, "break off the first branch that brushes against your hat on your way home, and bring it to me." So he bought beautiful dresses, diamonds and pearls for his two stepdaughters, and on the way home, as he was riding through a copse,[3] a hazel branch brushed against him and knocked off his hat. So he broke off the branch and took it home with him. When he got home, he gave the stepdaughters what they had asked for, and gave Ashputtle the branch. After thanking him, she went to her mother's grave and planted the hazel sprig over it and cried so hard that her tears fell on the sprig and watered it. It grew and became a beautiful tree. Three times a day Ashputtle went and sat under it and wept and prayed. Each time a little white bird came and perched on the tree, and when Ashputtle made a wish the little bird threw down what she had wished for.

---

1. **parlor** (pär´lər) *n.* room set aside for entertaining guests; living room.
2. **lentils** (lent´'ls) *n.* pea-like, edible seeds of the lentil, a plant in the pea family.
3. **copse** (käps) *n.* group of small trees growing thickly together.

Vocabulary Builder
plague (pläg) *v.* pester; harass; torment

jeered (jir'd) *v.* made fun of; mocked; taunted

Literary Analysis
Archetypal Narrative Patterns What other stories do you know that feature a heroine faced with cruel relatives?

Reading Check

Describe the way that Ashputtle's stepsisters treat her.

Now it so happened that the king arranged for a celebration. It was to go on for three days and all the beautiful girls in the kingdom were invited, in order that his son might choose a bride. When the two stepsisters heard they had been asked, they were delighted. They called Ashputtle and said: "Comb our hair, brush our shoes, and fasten our buckles. We're going to the wedding at the king's palace." Ashputtle obeyed, but she wept, for she too would have liked to go dancing, and she begged her stepmother to let her go. "You little sloven!"[4] said the stepmother. "How can you go to a wedding when you're all dusty and dirty? How can you go dancing when you have neither dress nor shoes?" But when Ashputtle begged and begged, the stepmother finally said: "Here, I've dumped a bowlful of lentils in the ashes. If you can pick them out in two hours, you may go." The girl went out the back door to the garden and cried out: "O tame little doves, O turtledoves, and all the birds under heaven, come and help me put

> the good ones in the pot,
> the bad ones in your crop."[5]

Two little white doves came flying through the kitchen window, and then came the turtledoves, and finally all the birds under heaven came flapping and fluttering and settled down by the ashes. The doves nodded their little heads and started in, peck peck peck peck, and all the others started in, peck peck peck peck, and they sorted out all the good lentils and put them in the bowl. Hardly an hour had passed before they finished and flew away. Then the girl brought the bowl to her stepmother, and she was happy, for she thought she'd be allowed to go to the wedding. But the stepmother said: "No, Ashputtle. You have nothing to wear and you don't know how to dance; the people would only laugh at you." When Ashputtle began to cry, the stepmother said: "If you can pick two bowlfuls of lentils out of the ashes in an hour, you may come." And she thought: "She'll never be able to do it." When she had dumped the two bowlfuls of lentils in the ashes, Ashputtle went out the back door to the garden and cried out: "O tame little doves, O turtledoves, and all the birds under heaven, come and help me put

> the good ones in the pot,
> the bad ones in your crop."

Then two little white doves came flying through the kitchen window, and then came the turtledoves, and finally all the birds under heaven came flapping and fluttering and settled down by the ashes. The doves nodded their little heads and started in, peck peck peck peck, and all the

Literary Analysis
Archetypal Narrative Patterns What task does Ashputtle's stepmother set for her?

Literary Analysis
Archetypal Narrative Patterns What does the fact that the birds help her suggest about Ashputtle's character?

---

4. **sloven** (sluv´ ən) *n.* dirty or untidy person.
5. **crop** (kräp) *n.* part of a bird's throat in which it stores food.

others started in, peck peck peck peck, and they sorted out all the good lentils and put them in the bowls. Before half an hour had passed, they had finished and they all flew away. Then the girl brought the bowls to her stepmother, and she was happy, for she thought she'd be allowed to go to the wedding. But her stepmother said: "It's no use. You can't come, because you have nothing to wear and you don't know how to dance. We'd only be ashamed of you." Then she turned her back and hurried away with her two proud daughters.

When they had all gone out, Ashputtle went to her mother's grave. She stood under the hazel tree and cried:

> *"Shake your branches, little tree,*
> *Throw gold and silver down on me."*

Whereupon the bird tossed down a gold and silver dress and slippers embroidered with silk and silver. Ashputtle slipped into the dress as fast as she could and went to the wedding. Her sisters and stepmother didn't recognize her. She was so beautiful in her golden dress that they thought she must be the daughter of some foreign king. They never dreamed it could be Ashputtle, for they thought she was sitting at home in her filthy rags, picking lentils out of the ashes. The king's son came up to her, took her by the hand and danced with her. He wouldn't dance with anyone else and he never let go her hand. When someone else asked for a dance, he said: "She is my partner."

She danced until evening, and then she wanted to go home. The king's son said: "I'll go with you, I'll see you home," for he wanted to find out whom the beautiful girl belonged to. But she got away from him and slipped into the dovecote.[6] The king's son waited until her father arrived, and told him the strange girl had slipped into the dovecote. The old man thought: "Could it be Ashputtle?" and he sent for an ax and a pick and broke into the dovecote, but there was no one inside. When they went indoors, Ashputtle was lying in the ashes in her filthy clothes and a dim oil lamp was burning on the chimney piece, for Ashputtle had slipped out the back end of the dovecote and run to the hazel tree. There she had taken off her fine clothes and put them on the grave, and the bird had taken

▲ Critical Viewing Name another fairy tale that this picture might illustrate. Explain. **[Connect]**

✓ Reading Check

How does it come about that Ashputtle is able to attend the wedding?

---

6. dovecote (duv´ kōt´) *n.* small house with compartments for nesting birds.

them away. Then she had put her gray dress on again, crept into the kitchen and lain down in the ashes.

Next day when the festivities started in again and her parents and stepsisters had gone, Ashputtle went to the hazel tree and said:

> "*Shake your branches, little tree,*
> *Throw gold and silver down on me.*"

Whereupon the bird threw down a dress that was even more dazzling than the first one. And when she appeared at the wedding, everyone marveled at her beauty. The king's son was waiting for her. He took her by the hand and danced with no one but her. When others came and asked her for a dance, he said: "She is my partner." When evening came, she said she was going home. The king's son followed her, wishing to see which house she went into, but she ran away and disappeared into the garden behind the house, where there was a big beautiful tree with the most wonderful pears growing on it. She climbed among the branches as <u>nimbly</u> as a squirrel and the king's son didn't know what had become of

⋀ Critical Viewing
What is the test represented in this illustration? **[Connect]**

Vocabulary Builder
nimbly (nim´ blē) *adv.*
in a quick, easy, light way; with agility

her. He waited until her father arrived and said to him: "The strange girl has got away from me and I think she has climbed up in the pear tree." Her father thought: "Could it be Ashputtle?" He sent for an ax and chopped the tree down, but there was no one in it. When they went into the kitchen, Ashputtle was lying there in the ashes as usual, for she had jumped down on the other side of the tree, brought her fine clothes back to the bird in the hazel tree, and put on her filthy gray dress.

On the third day, after her parents and sisters had gone, Ashputtle went back to her mother's grave and said to the tree:

> "*Shake your branches, little tree,*
> *Throw gold and silver down on me.*"

Whereupon the bird threw down a dress that was more radiant than either of the others, and the slippers were all gold. When she appeared at the wedding, the people were too amazed to speak. The king's son danced with no one but her, and when someone else asked her for a dance, he said: "She is my partner."

When evening came, Ashputtle wanted to go home, and the king's son said he'd go with her, but she slipped away so quickly that he couldn't follow. But he had thought up a trick. He had arranged to have the whole staircase brushed with pitch,[7] and as she was running down it the pitch pulled her left slipper off. The king's son picked it up, and it was tiny and delicate and all gold. Next morning he went to the father and said: "No girl shall be my wife but the one this golden shoe fits." The sisters were overjoyed, for they had beautiful feet. The eldest took the shoe to her room to try it on and her mother went with her. But the shoe was too small and she couldn't get her big toe in. So her mother handed her a knife and said: "Cut your toe off. Once you're queen you won't have to walk any more." The girl cut her toe off, forced her foot into the shoe, gritted her teeth against the pain, and went out to the king's son. He accepted her as his bride-to-be, lifted her up on his horse, and rode away with her. But they had to pass the grave. The two doves were sitting in the hazel tree and they cried out:

> "Roocoo, roocoo,
> There's blood in the shoe.
> The foot's too long, the foot's too wide,
> That's not the proper bride."

He looked down at her foot and saw the blood spurting. At that he turned his horse around and took the false bride home again. "No," he said, "this isn't the right girl; let her sister try the shoe on." The sister went to her room and managed to get her toes into the shoe, but her heel was too big. So her mother handed her a knife and said: "Cut off a chunk of your heel. Once you're queen you won't have to walk any more." The girl cut off a chunk of her heel, forced her foot into the shoe, gritted her teeth against the pain, and went out to the king's son. He accepted her as his bride-to-be, lifted her up on his horse, and rode away with her. As they passed the hazel tree, the two doves were sitting there, and they cried out:

> "Roocoo, roocoo,
> There's blood in the shoe.
> The foot's too long, the foot's too wide,
> That's not the proper bride."

He looked down at her foot and saw that blood was spurting from her shoe and staining her white stocking all red. He turned his horse around and took the false bride home again. "This isn't the right girl, either," he said. "Haven't you got another daughter?" "No," said the man, "there's only a puny little kitchen drudge[8] that my dead wife left me. She couldn't possibly be the bride." "Send her

---

7. **pitch** (pich) *n.* sticky substance used for waterproofing.
8. **drudge** (druj) *n.* person whose job consists of hard, unpleasant work.

Literary Analysis
Archetypal Narrative Patterns How does the number of dances Ashputtle attends reflect an archetypal narrative element?

✓ Reading Check

How does the prince propose to find the woman he wishes to marry?

Ashputtle ■ 1049

up," said the king's son, but the mother said: "Oh no, she's much too dirty to be seen." But he insisted and they had to call her. First she washed her face and hands, and when they were clean, she went upstairs and curtseyed to the king's son. He handed her the golden slipper and sat down on a footstool, took her foot out of her heavy wooden shoe, and put it into the slipper. It fitted perfectly. And when she stood up and the king's son looked into her face, he recognized the beautiful girl he had danced with and cried out: "This is my true bride!" The stepmother and the two sisters went pale with fear and rage. But he lifted Ashputtle up on his horse and rode away with her. As they passed the hazel tree, the two white doves called out:

> "Roocoo, roocoo,
> No blood in the shoe.
> Her foot is neither long nor wide,
> This one is the proper bride."

Then they flew down and alighted on Ashputtle's shoulders, one on the right and one on the left, and there they sat.

On the day of Ashputtle's wedding, the two stepsisters came and tried to ingratiate themselves and share in her happiness. On the way to church the elder was on the right side of the bridal couple and the younger on the left. The doves came along and pecked out one of the elder sister's eyes and one of the younger sister's eyes. Afterward, on the way out, the elder was on the left side and the younger on the right, and the doves pecked out both the remaining eyes. So both sisters were punished with blindness to the end of their days for being so wicked and false.

**Literary Analysis
Archetypal Narrative Patterns** Which events show that evil is punished in the story?

Thinking About the Selection

1. **Respond:** Do you sympathize with Ashputtle, or do you think she should have stood up for herself more? Explain.
2. **(a) Recall:** What does Ashputtle do with her father's gift? **(b) Infer:** What do her actions suggest about her character? **(c) Contrast:** Contrast Ashputtle with her stepmother and stepsisters.
3. **(a) Recall:** What type of help does Ashputtle receive? **(b) Connect:** What lesson about life is suggested by the fact that a person like Ashputtle receives this help?
4. **(a) Support:** In what way do the schemes of the stepmother and stepsisters lead to their punishment? **(b) Connect:** In what way do these events support the lesson of "Ashputtle"?

Apply the Skills

Cupid and Psyche • *Ashputtle*

Comparing Archetypal Narrative Patterns

1. Using a chart like this one, identify the **archetypal narrative patterns** in "Cupid and Psyche" and "Ashputtle."

Heroine	Powerful Older Woman	Ideal Lover	Rivals for Love	Supernatural Assistance

2. Compare the special tasks that Psyche must perform with the special tasks that Ashputtle must perform. Consider each of these structural elements: **(a)** the number of tasks; **(b)** who assigns the task and why; **(c)** the difficulty of the task; and **(d)** by what means the character completes the task.

3. Explain how your comparison of the tasks shows that the stories follow archetypal narrative patterns.

Writing to Compare Literary Works

Write an essay to compare archetypal narrative patterns in the two stories. Use these questions to get started:

- What was similar and what was different in the archetypal patterns in each story?
- What lesson does each story convey using archetypal patterns?
- What effect did the use of archetypal characters and narrative patterns have on your appreciation of each story?

Vocabulary Builder

Practice Given the meaning of the italicized words, explain whether each of the following sentences is likely to be true.

1. His complete failure won him much *adulation.*
2. Work with *diligence,* and you will accomplish much.
3. To *allay* his fear of snakes, I told him the story of how Uncle Bob was eaten by a python.
4. We *jeered* at the team to show our support.
5. You have already called him five times; do not *plague* him.
6. Carrying several bags of groceries and supported by crutches, I moved *nimbly* across the parking lot.

QuickReview

Archetypal Narrative Patterns: basic storytelling patterns found in the stories of cultures around the world

Assessment
For: Self-test
Visit: www.PHSchool.com
Web Code: eqa-6606

Reading

Directions: *Questions 1–5 are based on the following selection.*

[The poor fisherman] lifted his eyes to heaven and cried: "Allah[1] knows that I cast my net only four times a day. I have already cast it for the third time and caught no fish at all. Surely He will not fail me again!"

With this the fisherman hurled his net far out into the sea and waited for it to sink to the bottom. When at length he brought it to land he found in it a bottle made of yellow copper. The mouth was stopped with lead and bore the seal of our master Solomon, son of David.[2] The fisherman rejoiced and said: "I will sell this in the market of the coppersmiths. It must be worth ten pieces of gold." He shook the bottle and . . . there burst from it a great column of smoke which spread along the shore and rose so high that it almost touched the heavens. Taking shape, the smoke resolved itself into a jinnee.[3]

—from *The Thousand and One Nights,* translated by N. J. Dawood

1. Allah Arabic word for God.
2. Solomon, son of David David and Solomon were great Jewish leaders who are considered prophets by Muslims.
3. jinnee supernatural creature of Arabian legend.

1. **From the passage, what can you conclude about economic or social ranks in Arabic or Persian society of the time?**
   A Most people were reasonably well off.
   B Poor people had to struggle to support their families.
   C Fishermen were in the upper class of society.
   D The poor always lived near the sea.

2. **What can you conclude about the commercial activity of the society?**
   A Almost everyone earned their living on the sea.
   B Goods were sold or traded at marketplaces.
   C Copper was more valuable than gold.
   D Cans and bottles of soda pop littered the beaches.

3. **What does the passage show about the use of metals?**
   A Copper was more valuable than gold.
   B Lead was more valuable than copper.
   C Copper and gold were the only metals in use.
   D Metal objects were fashioned and sold.

4. **What does the second footnote reveal about the Muslim faith?**
   A It reveres some of the same religious figures as the Jewish faith.
   B It is very critical of kings.
   C Its scripture is written in the Hebrew language.
   D It stresses the need for compassion.

5. **What does the appearance of a jinnee show about the cultural context?**
   A People who committed crimes were imprisoned in bottles.
   B Magic was a crime.
   C There were no servants and masters.
   D People believed in the supernatural.

Vocabulary

Directions: *Choose the letter of the sentence that uses the italicized vocabulary word correctly.*

6. A My boss will *incorporate* my idea in her plan.
   B The negative campaign ads were able to *incorporate* driving a wedge.
   C The business leaders met *incorporate* headquarters.
   D She coughed, trying to *incorporate* the poison she had swallowed.

7. A The new store was *initiate* profitable but has begun losing money lately.
   B Runners *initiate* the race at the end.
   C She stuck her finger in the cement to *initiate* the letters of her name.
   D The diplomat wanted to *initiate* a new round of peace talks.

8. A The chorus chanted the lyrics in *unify*.
   B A good politician will *unify* the party.
   C When the club members *unify*, they will break apart into separate groups.
   D Adding milk will help *unify* the coffee and make it weaker.

9. A The skilled puppeteer was able to *manipulate* three puppets at once.
   B The loser must *manipulate* by turning in the money to the other players.
   C You can *manipulate* others if you do not interact with them.
   D The *manipulate* government is in charge of the city beaches and parks.

10. A A person with *visual* talents is usually colorblind.
    B Yellow is a *visual* signal for drivers.
    C The Bill of Rights protects *visual* liberties such as freedom of religion.
    D Turn up the volume on the *visual* as you watch the audio.

Directions: *Study each sentence for context clues about the meaning of the word in italics. Then, choose the applicable meaning of the word.*

11. **The writer sent in her *manuscript.***
    A a booklet giving directions on how to operate equipment
    B the copy of an author's work that is submitted to a publisher
    C written by hand
    D block-lettered text

12. **Science examines the *corporeal,* not the spiritual, world.**
    A related to the body or to physical reality
    B related to the supernatural
    C having a large body
    D the military rank below sergeant

13. **Try to *envision* the future by studying recent advances in science.**
    A picture in the mind; imagine
    B listen carefully; hear every word
    C watch over protectively; take care of
    D point out the flaws in; criticize

14. **He had a nasty sneer on his *visage.***
    A the part of the head that is covered
    B face, the aspect of a person recognized by sight
    C cruel and unusual punishment
    D a face-to-face meeting

Writing for Assessment: Timed Essay

Timed essays are tools teachers use to assess students' mastery of a subject. Most timed writing assignments require you to respond to a question or prompt within a brief time limit. Use the steps in this workshop to practice writing for assessment.

Assignment Write an essay in response to either of the following prompts or to another that your teacher provides.
- Traditional heroic figures were usually male, physically strong, and clever. In an essay, compare such a traditional hero to a modern hero.
- Select an issue that affects students in your school. Write an essay describing the issue and recommending solutions.

What to Include Your timed essay should feature these elements:
- answers or responses that match the questions asked
- a clear thesis or main idea supported with evidence
- a logical and effective organizational plan
- on-time completion
- error-free grammar, including correct sentence formation
- correct spelling and punctuation

To preview the criteria on which your timed writing may be assessed, see the rubric on page 1058.

Prewriting

Spend a quarter of your time on prewriting.

Choosing Your Topic

Read the questions. In many cases, you will be asked to choose from a selection of essay topics. Read all the questions and eliminate those that do not immediately spark a response. To test yourself, quickly think of three details that you could use to answer a prompt. If you have to think for too long, try another question.

Gathering Details

Use keywords. Reread the question and circle keywords that indicate the form your response should take.
- *Discuss:* support a generalization with facts and examples
- *Explain:* clarify by probing reasons, causes, and effects
- *Analyze:* examine how various factors contribute to a whole

Then, write a thesis statement that introduces your answer and focuses your topic. Using this statement to guide you, jot down the details you will discuss.

Using the Form
You will use writing-for-assessment strategies in these situations:
- end-of-year tests
- standardized tests
- college entrance exams, such as SAT and ACT

Work-in-Progress
Review the work you did on pages 975, 1003, and 1029.

Drafting

Spend about half your time drafting.

Shaping Your Writing

Organize your composition. Choose a structure that suits the type of essay you are asked to write. Using a standard structure saves time and allows you to focus on content:

- **Compare-and-contrast organization:** Use this method to show how subjects are alike or different. You might discuss your topic point by point or subject by subject.
- **Chronological organization:** Present events in the order in which they occurred. Use dates and transitions to clarify the order.
- **Nestorian organization:** Use the plan shown in the chart if you are writing to persuade or to evaluate.

Nestorian Organization

Introduction
Second-most persuasive point
↓
Third-most persuasive point
↓
Remaining points, decreasing in importance
↓
Most persuasive point
Conclusion

Providing Elaboration

Include facts and examples. Review the details you collected during prewriting. Number your best ideas in the order in which you will use them. This can help you remember to include your most effective facts, examples, and observations.

Revising

Spend about a quarter of your time revising and editing.

Revising Your Paragraphs

Revise to refine paragraph unity. Ideas within each paragraph should support a clear topic sentence. Try this strategy:

- Mark the topic sentence in each paragraph. If you do not find one, either add one or consider deleting the paragraph.
- Review each paragraph to make sure you have effectively supported the topic sentence.
- Delete irrelevant details. Add supporting details as necessary. Insert revisions neatly and cross out any deletions with a single line.

Revising Your Word Choice

Delete unnecessary words. Strengthen your draft quickly by deleting hedging words, or unnecessary qualifiers, such as the following:

what I mean is	*to the extent that*	*the thing is*
needless to say	*it seems*	*quite*

Integrating Grammar Skills

Revising to Correct Fragments and Run-on Sentences

Fragments and run-on sentences can make your writing confusing and may lower your score on the assignment.

Identifying and Correcting Fragments and Run-ons A complete sentence has a subject and a verb and expresses a complete thought.

Prentice Hall Writing and Grammar Connection: Chapter 21, Section 4

Fragment: A *fragment* is a group of words that does not express a complete thought but is punctuated as if it were a sentence. To correct fragments, combine them with nearby sentences or add words to complete the thought.

> **Fragment:** She felt relieved. *After passing the test.*
> **Combined:** *After passing the test,* she felt relieved.
>
> **Fragment:** *The results of the election.*
> **Expanded:** The results of the election were discussed far and wide.

Run-on: A *run-on* is two or more complete sentences that are not properly joined or separated.

> **Fused:** They hiked quickly they stopped to eat lunch.
> **Comma splice:** They hiked quickly, they stopped to eat lunch.

Fixing Errors Use these steps to correct fragments and run-ons.

1. **Decide if a problematic sentence is a fragment or a run-on.**

2. **If it is a fragment, add information to make a complete thought or combine the fragment with another sentence.**

3. **If it is a run-on, split it into two sentences.** You might also add a comma or a conjunction to make it a correct single sentence.

Correcting a Run-on Sentence	
Run-on: They wandered through the store they bought a novel.	
Use a period to separate a run-on into two sentences. Begin each with a capital letter.	They wandered through the store. They bought a novel.
Use a comma and a coordinating conjunction, such as *and, but, or, for,* or *nor,* to combine two related independent clauses.	They wandered through the store, and they bought a novel.

Apply It to Your Editing

Review the sentences in your draft to find fragments and run-ons. Neatly correct any problems using the strategies that have been presented.

Student Model: Aleksandra Wojtalewicz
Long Beach, CA

In an essay, discuss the U.S. Constitution. (a) Explain how it came to be.
(b) Analyze how a document written so long ago can still be of use today.

In May 1787, in Philadelphia, the Constitutional Convention discussed what was happening to the government. Through debates and compromises, a draft defining the new government was finally completed. Each man signed the Constitution, which would mold and shape the government of the United States.

It took many skilled statesmen to contribute to this document. Without their knowledge, the Constitution would probably lack the power limits of the judicial, executive, and legislative branches and certain rights of the people. Without the Constitution, the country would not function smoothly because it would not have a plan to follow. The Constitution impacts the everyday problems that occur in the government. Who would have thought that this document would have such a great impact 211 years later?

In the presidential election of 2000, people waited impatiently until midnight to find out who would be the next president. The time came and went and the United States did not have a president-elect. The United States did not have a future president for about 38 days. During that time, candidates postured for the camera but also followed the rules set by the Constitution to try and reach a resolution. The case went from court to court, finally reaching the U.S. Supreme Court. In the end, the Supreme Court decided to stop recounting, and a president-elect was finally named.

Was the presidential election dilemma of 2000 the fault of the Constitution? The Constitution does not provide an obvious solution to problems such as an incorrect count of votes. There was a lot of talk in the media during the election of 2000 about changing the electoral-college system to allow the candidates to be elected by popular vote. This system was put into place with the signing of the Constitution. Under the original system, a board of electors represented the will of each state. Each cast two ballots.

How could a 211-year-old piece of paper have an influence on the wealthiest country in the world? If the Constitutional Convention had never met, then the United States would probably never have had this document. Even at the most difficult times, the Constitution provides a way for justice to be served.

The first two paragraphs provide an answer to part (a) of the question.

Here, the writer explains the key information in the Constitution.

A transitional sentence indicates that the essay will move to address the second question.

A conclusion presents the writer's insights into the issue.

Editing and Proofreading

Check your draft to correct errors in spelling, grammar, and punctuation.

Focus on Clarity: Review your draft and make sure that your handwriting is legible, that any deletions are clearly indicated with clean strikethroughs, and that any revisions or additions are clearly shown.

Publishing and Presenting

Consider one of the following ways to share your writing:

Hold a test-taking forum. Read your essay aloud to classmates and then listen to their essays responding to the same question. Discuss the strengths and weaknesses in each response and create a list of tips to remember when writing for assessment. If the class agrees, organize the tips into a document to share with other students. Post this list to your school or other academic Web site.

Publish your composition electronically. Post your composition on a Web site, or upload it onto a classroom computer. You might also e-mail it to family members who want to monitor your progress at school.

Reflecting on Your Writing

Writer's Journal Jot down your thoughts about writing a timed essay. Begin by answering these questions.

- Did you have enough time? If you were going to write this essay again, what would you do differently?
- What advice would you give to a friend before he or she takes a timed writing exam?

> *Prentice Hall Writing and Grammar Connection: Chapter 14*

Rubric for Self-Assessment

To assess your timed essay, use the following rubric:

Criteria	Rating Scale
	not very very
Focus: How completely do you answer the question prompt?	1 2 3 4 5
Organization: How logical and effective is the organization?	1 2 3 4 5
Support/Elaboration: How fully do you support the thesis statement and topic sentences with evidence?	1 2 3 4 5
Style: How well do you avoid fragments and run-ons?	1 2 3 4 5
Conventions: How correct is your spelling and punctuation?	1 2 3 4 5

Skills You Will Learn

Literary Analysis: *Legends and Legendary Heroes*
Reading Skill: *Drawing Conclusions to Compare and Contrast Worldviews*

Literary Analysis: *Parody*
Reading Skill: *Analyze Illusion and Reality to Compare and Contrast Worldviews*

Reading Skill: *Compare and Contrast Writers' Purposes*

Literary Analysis: *Comparing Themes and Worldviews*

Literature You Will Read

Reading and Vocabulary Skills Preview

Reading: Compare and Contrast Worldviews

 Academic Standards

> **Comparing and contrasting worldviews** means finding similarities and differences in the basic beliefs and values expressed by authors or characters.

- Examine how the author's perspective influences the structure and tone of the text. (10.2.4)
- Analyze many different forms of dramatic literature. (10.3.1)

Skills and Strategies You Will Learn in Part 2

In Part 2, you will learn

- to **identify contrasts in worldviews** by **drawing conclusions** from characters' attitudes and reactions. (p. 1062)
- to **analyze contrasts between illusion and reality.** (p. 1096)
- to **compare and contrast writers' purposes.** (p. 1126)

Using the Skills and Strategies in Part 2

In Part 2, you will learn to compare and contrast worldviews by drawing conclusions from characters' attitudes and reactions. You will also learn to identify different views of appearance and reality. You will practice comparing and contrasting writers' purposes.

Pius gave an uncertain laugh. "As a matter of fact, one of the reasons I came up here was to invite you to the wedding—it's next month."

Salongo carefully laid down the spear he was rubbing upon a piece of clean barkcloth and stared at his friend as if he had suddenly grown another head. "What a fool you are! . . . At your age you ought to have more sense."

For a moment Pius was full of misgivings. Was he, after all, behaving like a fool? Then he thought of Sarah, and the wonders she had worked with his house and his shamba in the short time they had been together. He felt reassured.

—from "The Winner" by Barbara Kimenye

Example

Salongo's Worldview	Pius's Worldview
suspicious, traditional, dislikes change, certain	hopeful, traditional, welcomes change, hesitant

Academic Vocabulary: Words for Developing Concepts in Literature

The following words will help you write and talk about differing world-views in the literature in this part.

Word	Definition	Example Sentence
coordinate *v.*	place in the same order or system; adjust	We need to *coordinate* the lights and music in our presentation.
evolve *v.*	develop slowly over time	These details help the characters' relationship *evolve* into a deep friendship.
lucid *adj.*	well reasoned; clearly expressed	Although she was annoyed about the new plan, she wrote a *lucid* editorial.
intense *adj.*	strong and focused	The *intense* imagery evokes a strong response from the reader.
synthesize *v.*	put together elements to form a whole	The director *synthesized* the elements of Miller's drama.

▶ The **context** is the situation in which a word is used.

In Part 2, you will use context clues
- in combination with word roots (p. 1094)
- to clarify meaning (p. 1124)

Activity Use reference tools to find three products or companies that have used the word roots *-luc-/-lum-* or *-volv-/-volt-* as part of their name. Explain how these roots and the context of the company's function help you understand the meaning of the word.

I used a large flashlight to *illuminate* the dark corners of the closet.

context clue   word root meaning "light"   context clue

Conclusion: To *illuminate* is probably to light up.

Practice these skills with "Morte d'Arthur" (p. 1064) or "Arthur Becomes King of Britain" (p. 1077).

Literary Analysis

Legends are popular stories about the past that have been handed down for generations. Most legends have some basis in historical fact. Legends share the following characteristics:

- A focus on the life and adventures of **legendary heroes,** or characters who are human yet "larger than life"
- A deep concern with right and wrong.
- Support for feelings of national pride

Legends help shape a people's cultural identity and reflect the values of a community or nation.

Reading Skill

A **worldview** consists of values and beliefs held by a culture. When a writer retells a legend, the retelling may reflect two worldviews—that of the writer and that of the original tale. To understand a retelling, **compare and contrast** worldviews.

- **Identify details** that indicate characters' beliefs and their reasons for acting or feeling as they do. In addition, identify details suggesting the writer's attitudes.
- **Draw a conclusion** from these details about the values and basic beliefs of the different characters and of the writer.

IN **Academic Standards**

- Examine how the author's perspective influences the structure and tone of the text. (10.2.4)
- Analyze many different forms of dramatic literature. (10.3.1)
- Evaluate the aesthetic qualities of style. (10.3.11)

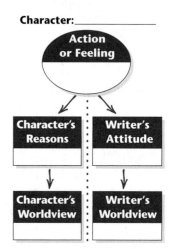

Character:_____

Action or Feeling

Character's Reasons → Character's Worldview

Writer's Attitude → Writer's Worldview

Vocabulary Builder

Morte d'Arthur

- **disparagement** (di spar′ ij mənt) *n.* comments expressing a low opinion of or lack of respect for (p. 1066) *The critic's <u>disparagement</u> of her painting upset her.*
- **brandished** (bran′ dish'd) *v.* showed, waved, or shook in a threatening, or triumphant manner (p. 1069) *As he ran home, he <u>brandished</u> his excellent report card.*
- **languid** (lan′ gwid) *adj.* without energy; drooping, as from exhaustion (p. 1070) *His <u>languid</u> arms dangled by his side.*

Arthur Becomes King of Britain

- **stickler** (stik′ lər) *n.* person who insists on strict obedience to rules or standards (p. 1078) *She is a <u>stickler</u> for perfect grammar.*
- **petulantly** (pech′ ə lənt lē) *adv.* in a manner that expresses impatience or irritation, especially over a minor matter (p. 1079) *The child <u>petulantly</u> refuses to let anyone tie her shoes.*
- **surmise** (sər mīz′) *n.* guess; idea based on evidence that is not conclusive (p. 1082) *His <u>surmise</u> about how I felt was wrong.*

Build Understanding • *Morte d'Arthur*

Background

Legends of King Arthur The figure of King Arthur, the legendary ruler of England, may be based on a historical Welsh ruler who resisted Germanic invaders of Britain in the 500s. The first English prose version of the legends, *Le Morte d'Arthur,* was written around 1470 by Sir Thomas Malory. In "Morte d'Arthur," Alfred, Lord Tennyson adapts the tale of Arthur's passing.

Connecting to the Literature

Reading/Writing Connection In "Morte d'Arthur," Tennyson contrasts the ideals of the past with the confusing, unheroic life of the present. Make a list of reasons the past may often seem better than the present. Use at least three of the following words: *appeal, cite, differentiate, diminish, repress.*

READ MORE

by Alfred, Lord Tennyson
"The Charge of the Light Brigade"

Meet the Author

Alfred, **Lord Tennyson** (1809–1892)

Alfred, Lord Tennyson was born in eastern Lincolnshire in England. His work was immensely popular during his lifetime and won him the friendship of Queen Victoria. In 1850, Tennyson was appointed poet laureate of England.

A Life's Work
It took Tennyson more than forty years to complete *The Idylls of the King,* his epic retelling of the King Arthur legends. By conjuring up a golden Arthurian age—and the problems that doomed it—Tennyson expressed the questions people of his own time had about life.

Fast Facts
▶ Tennyson was known as "the poet of the people."
▶ A large man, Tennyson impressed others with his broad-brimmed hat, his cloak, and his booming voice.

Go **Online**
Author Link
For: More about the author
Visit: www.PHSchool.com
Web Code: eqe-9608

Morte d'Arthur

Alfred, Lord Tennyson

How Sir Bedivere Cast the Sword Excalibur Into the Water, Aubrey Beardsley. Houghton Library, Harvard University.

The Epic

At Francis Allen's on the Christmas eve—
The game of forfeits[1] done—the girls all kissed
Beneath the sacred bush and passed away—
The parson Holmes, the poet Everard Hall,

5   The host, and I sat round the wassail bowl,[2]
Then halfway ebbed; and there we held a talk,
How all the old honor had from Christmas gone,
Or gone or dwindled down to some odd games
In some odd nooks like this; till I, tired out

10 With cutting eights[3] that day upon the pond,
Where, three times slipping from the outer edge,
I bumped the ice into three several stars,
Fell in a doze; and half-awake I heard
The parson taking wide and wider sweeps,

15 Now harping on the church commissioners,
Now hawking at geology and schism;[4]
Until I woke, and found him settled down
Upon the general decay of faith
Right through the world: "at home was little left,

20 And none abroad; there was no anchor, none,
To hold by." Francis, laughing, clapped his hand
On Everard's shoulder, with "I hold by him."
"And I," quoth Everard, "by the wassail-bowl."
"Why yes," I said, "we knew your gift that way

25 At college; but another which you had—
I mean of verse (for so we held it then)—
What came of that?" "You know," said Frank, "he burnt
His epic, his King Arthur, some twelve books"—
And then to me demanding why: "O, sir,

30 He thought that nothing new was said, or else
Something so said 'twas nothing—that a truth
Looks freshest in the fashion of the day;
God knows; he has a mint of reasons; ask.
It pleased *me* well enough." "Nay, nay," said Hall,

35 "Why take the style of those heroic times?
For nature brings not back the mastodon,
Nor we those times; and why should any man
Remodel models? these twelve books of mine

---

1. forfeits (fôr´ fits) *n.* game in which something is taken away as a penalty for making a mistake.
2. wassail (wäs´ əl) **bowl** *n.* punch bowl.
3. cutting eights ice-skating in such a way that the skates cut figure eights in the ice.
4. schism (siz´ əm) *n.* division within an organization, especially a church, because of a difference of opinion.

◄ **Critical Viewing**
Which elements of this illustration seem magical and which realistic? Explain. **[Analyze]**

Reading Skill
Comparing Worldviews What do lines 13–21 show about people's worldview in the poet's time?

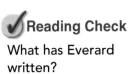

Reading Check

What has Everard written?

Were faint Homeric echoes,[5] nothing-worth,
40 Mere chaff and draff, much better burnt." "But I,"
Said Francis, "picked the eleventh from this hearth,
And have it; keep a thing, its use will come.
I hoard it as a sugarplum for Holmes."
He laughed, and I, though sleepy, like a horse
45 That hears the corn-bin open, pricked my ears;
For I remembered Everard's college fame
When we were freshmen. Then at my request
He brought it; and the poet, little urged,
But with some prelude of <u>disparagement</u>,
50 Read, mouthing out his hollow o's and a's,
Deep-chested music, and to this result.

Morte d'Arthur

So all day long the noise of battle rolled
Among the mountains by the winter sea,
Until King Arthur's table, man by man,
55 Had fallen in Lyonnesse[6] about their lord,
King Arthur; then, because his wound was deep,
The bold Sir Bedivere uplifted him,
Sir Bedivere, the last of all his knights,
And bore him to a chapel nigh the field,
60 A broken chancel[7] with a broken cross,
That stood on a dark strait of barren land.
On one side lay the ocean, and on one
Lay a great water, and the moon was full.
    Then spake King Arthur to Sir Bedivere:
65 "The sequel of today unsolders[8] all
The goodliest fellowship of famous knights
Whereof this world holds record. Such a sleep
They sleep—the men I loved. I think that we
Shall never more, at any future time,
70 Delight our souls with talk of knightly deeds,
Walking about the gardens and the halls
Of Camelot, as in the days that were.
I perish by this people which I made—
Though Merlin[9] sware that I should come again
75 To rule once more—but let what will be be,

Vocabulary Builder
disparagement
(di spar´ ij mənt) *n.*
comments expressing a low opinion of or lack of respect for

---

5. **Homeric** (hō mer´ ik) **echoes** imitations of the Greek poet Homer (of the eighth century B.C.).
6. **Lyonnesse** (lī´ ə nes´) *n.* legendary country off the southwestern coast of England, supposed to have sunk beneath the sea.
7. **chancel** (chan´ səl) *n.* part of a church around the altar.
8. **unsolders** (un säd´ ərz) *v.* separates.
9. **Merlin** sorcerer who advised King Arthur.

I am so deeply smitten through the helm
That without help I cannot last till morn.
Thou therefore take my brand Excalibur,
Which was my pride; for thou rememberest how
80   In those old days, one summer noon, an arm
Rose up from out the bosom of the lake,
Clothed in white samite,[10] mystic, wonderful,
Holding the sword—and how I rowed across
And took it, and have worn it, like a king;
85   And, wheresoever I am sung or told
In aftertime, this also shall be known.
But now delay not; take Excalibur,
And fling him far into the middle mere;[11]
Watch what thou seest, and lightly[12] bring me word."
90   To him replied the bold Sir Bedivere:
"It is not meet,[13] Sir King, to leave thee thus,
Aidless, alone, and smitten through the helm.
A little thing may harm a wounded man.
Yet I thy hest will all perform at full,[14]
95   Watch what I see, and lightly bring thee word."
        So saying, from the ruined shrine he stepped
And in the moon athwart the place of tombs,
Where lay the mighty bones of ancient men,
Old knights, and over them the sea wind sang
100 Shrill, chill, with flakes of foam. He, stepping down
By zigzag paths and juts of pointed rock,
Came on the shining levels of the lake.
        There drew he forth the brand Excalibur,
And o'er him, drawing it, the winter moon,
105 Brightening the skirts of a long cloud, ran forth
And sparkled keen with frost against the hilt;
For all the haft twinkled with diamond sparks,
Myriads of topaz-lights, and jacinth-work[15]
Of subtlest jewelry. He gazed so long
110 That both his eyes were dazzled, as he stood,
This way and that dividing the swift mind,
In act to throw; but at the last it seemed
Better to leave Excalibur concealed
There in the many-knotted water flags,[16]

Literary Analysis
Legends How does the story of Excalibur show Arthur to be a legendary hero?

Reading Skill
Comparing Worldviews What does Sir Bedivere's response show about the importance of obedience in Arthurian times?

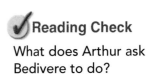

Reading Check

What does Arthur ask Bedivere to do?

---

10. samite (sam´ it) *n.* heavy silk fabric worn in the Middle Ages.
11. mere (mir) *n.* old or poetic word for "lake."
12. lightly *adv.* old or poetic word for "quickly."
13. meet *adj.* old or poetic word for "proper."
14. I thy hest will all perform at full I will carry out your order completely.
15. topaz-lights, and jacinth-work yellow and reddish-orange jewels.
16. water flags marsh plants.

115 That whistled stiff and dry about the marge.[17]
So strode he back slow to the wounded king.
     Then spake King Arthur to Sir Bedivere:
"Hast thou performed my mission which I gave?
What is it thou hast seen, or what hast heard?"
120   And answer made the bold Sir Bedivere:
"I heard the ripple washing in the reeds,
And the wild water lapping on the crag."
     To whom replied King Arthur, faint and pale:
"Thou hast betrayed thy nature and thy name,
125 Not rendering[18] true answer, as beseemed
Thy fealty,[19] nor like a noble knight;
For surer sign had followed, either hand,
Or voice, or else a motion of the mere.
This is a shameful thing for men to lie.
130 Yet now, I charge thee, quickly go again
As thou art lief and dear, and do the thing
I bade thee, watch, and lightly bring me word."
     Then went Sir Bedivere the second time
Across the ridge, and paced beside the mere,
135 Counting the dewy pebbles, fixed in thought;
But when he saw the wonder of the hilt,
How curiously and strangely chased,[20] he smote
His palms together, and he cried aloud:
     "And if indeed I cast the brand away;
140 Surely a precious thing, one worthy note,
Should thus be lost forever from the earth,
Which might have pleased the eyes of many men.
What good should follow this, if this were done?
What harm, undone? deep harm to disobey,
145 Seeing obedience is the bond of rule.
Were it well to obey then, if a king demand
An act unprofitable, against himself?
The king is sick, and knows not what he does.
What record, or what relic of my lord
150 Should be to aftertime, but empty breath
And rumors of a doubt? But were this kept,
Stored in some treasure-house of mighty kings,
Some one might show it at a joust of arms,
Saying, 'King Arthur's sword, Excalibur,
155 Wrought by the lonely maiden of the lake;

> **Critical Viewing**
Judging from this manuscript page, were the Arthur stories told only in England? Explain. **[Draw Conclusions]**

**Reading Skill
Comparing
Worldviews** To what values does Arthur appeal in lines 124–126?

**Literary Analysis
Legends** How does Bedivere's debate with himself emphasize a concern with right and wrong?

---

17. marge (märj) *n.* margin; edge.
18. rendering (ren´ dər iŋ) *v.* giving.
19. beseemed (bē sēm´ əd) / **Thy fealty** (fē´ əl tē) was suitable to the loyalty you owe your lord.
20. chased *adj.* decorated by engraving or embossing.

Nine years she wrought it, sitting in the deeps
Upon the hidden bases of the hills.'
So might some old man speak in the aftertime
To all the people, winning reverence;
160 But now much honor and much fame were lost."
    So spake he, clouded with his own conceit,
And hid Excalibur the second time,
And so strode back slow to the wounded king.
    Then spoke King Arthur, breathing heavily:
165 "What is it thou hast seen, or what hast heard?"
    And answer made the bold Sir Bedivere:
"I heard the water lapping on the crag,
And the long ripple washing in the reeds."
    To whom replied King Arthur, much in wrath:
170 "Ah, miserable and unkind, untrue,
Unknightly, traitor-hearted! Woe is me!
Authority forgets a dying king,
Laid widowed of the power in his eye
That bowed the will. I see thee what thou art,
175 For thou, the latest-left of all my knights,
In whom should meet the offices[21] of all,
Thou wouldst betray me for the precious hilt;
Either from lust of gold, or like a girl
Valuing the giddy pleasure of the eyes.
180 Yet, for a man may fail in duty twice,
And the third time may prosper, get thee hence;
But, if thou spare to fling Excalibur,
I will arise and slay thee with my hands."
    Then quickly rose Sir Bedivere, and ran,
185 And, leaping down the ridges lightly, plunged
Among the bulrush beds,[22] and clutched the sword,
And strongly wheeled and threw it. The great brand
Made lightnings in the splendor of the moon,
And flashing round and round, and whirled in an arch,
190 Shot like a streamer of the northern morn,[23]
Seen where the moving isles of winter shock[24]
By night, with noises of the northern sea.
So flashed and fell the brand Excalibur;
But ere he dipped the surface, rose an arm
195 Clothed in white samite, mystic, wonderful,
And caught him by the hilt, and <u>brandished</u> him

---

21. **offices** *n.* duties.
22. **bulrush** (bŏŏl′ rush′) **beds** growth of marsh plants.
23. **a streamer of the northern morn** northern lights; the aurora borealis.
24. **the moving isles of winter shock** icebergs crash.

Vocabulary Builder
brandished (bran′ dish'd) *v.* showed, waved, or shook in a threatening or triumphant manner

Reading Check

What does Sir Bedivere do on his third visit to the shore?

Three times, and drew him under in the mere.
And lightly went the other to the king.

    Then spoke King Arthur, drawing thicker breath:
200 "Now see I by thine eyes that this is done.
Speak out; what is it thou hast heard, or seen?"

    And answer made the bold Sir Bedivere:
"Sir King, I closed mine eyelids, lest the gems
Should blind my purpose, for I never saw,
205 Nor shall see, here or elsewhere, till I die,
Not though I live three lives of mortal men,
So great a miracle as yonder hilt.
Then with both hands I flung him, wheeling him;
But when I looked again, behold an arm,
210 Clothed in white samite, mystic, wonderful,
That caught him by the hilt, and brandished him
Three times, and drew him under in the mere."

    And answer made King Arthur, breathing hard:
"My end draws nigh; 'tis time that I were gone.
215 Make broad thy shoulders to receive my weight,
And bear me to the margin; yet I fear
My wound hath taken cold, and I shall die."

    So saying, from the pavement he half rose,
Slowly, with pain, reclining on his arm,
220 And looking wistfully with wide blue eyes
As in a picture. Him Sir Bedivere
Remorsefully regarded through his tears,
And would have spoken, but he found not words,
Then took with care, and kneeling on one knee,
225 O'er both his shoulders drew the <u>languid</u> hands,
And rising bore him through the place of tombs.

    But, as he walked, King Arthur panted hard,
Like one that feels a nightmare on his bed
When all the house is mute. So sighed the king,
230 Muttering and murmuring at his ear, "Quick, quick!
I fear it is too late, and I shall die."
But the other swiftly strode from ridge to ridge,
Clothed with his breath, and looking, as he walked,
Larger than human on the frozen hills.
235 He heard the deep behind him, and a cry
Before. His own thought drove him like a goad.[25]
Dry clashed his harness[26] in the icy caves

The Dream of Arthur in Avalon (detail), Sir Edward Burne-Jones. The
Museo de Arte de Ponce. The Luis A. Ferrè Foundation Inc. Ponce,
Puerto Rico.

▲ **Critical Viewing**
Which details in this
painting contrast
Arthur's warrior life
with the civilized life
he fought to protect?
[Contrast]

Vocabulary Builder
languid (laŋ´ gwid) *adj.*
without energy;
drooping, as from
exhaustion

---

25. goad (gōd) *n.* sharp-pointed stick used to drive oxen.
26. harness (här´ nis) *n.* armor.

And barren chasms, and all to left and right
The bare black cliff clanged round him, as he based
240 His feet on juts of slippery crag that rang
Sharp-smitten with the dint of armèd heels—
And on a sudden, lo! the level lake,
And the long glories of the winter moon.
      Then saw they how there hove a dusky barge,
245 Dark as a funeral scarf from stem to stern,
Beneath them; and descending they were ware
That all the decks were dense with stately forms
Black-stoled, black-hooded, like a dream—by these
Three queens with crowns of gold—and from them rose
250 A cry that shivered to the tingling stars,
And, as it were one voice, an agony
Of lamentation, like a wind that shrills
All night in a waste land, where no one comes,
Or hath come, since the making of the world.
255   Then murmured Arthur, "Place me in the barge,"
And to the barge they came. There those three queens
Put forth their hands, and took the king, and wept.
But she that rose the tallest of them all
And fairest laid his head upon her lap,
260 And loosed the shattered casque, and chafed his hands,
And called him by his name, complaining loud,
And dropping bitter tears against his brow
Striped with dark blood; for all his face was white
And colorless, and like the withered moon
265 Smote by the fresh beam of the springing east;
And all his greaves and cuisses dashed with drops
Of onset; and the light and lustrous curls—
That made his forehead like a rising sun
High from the dais-throne—were parched with dust;
270 Or, clotted into points and hanging loose,
Mixed with the knightly growth that fringed his lips.
So like a shattered column lay the king;
Not like that Arthur who, with lance in rest,
From spur to plume a star of tournament,
275 Shot through the lists at Camelot, and charged
Before the eyes of ladies and of kings.
      Then loudly cried the bold Sir Bedivere:
"Ah! my Lord Arthur, whither shall I go?
Where shall I hide my forehead and my eyes?
280 For now I see the true old times are dead,
When every morning brought a noble chance,

Literary Analysis
Legends Why is the arrival of the mysterious barge appropriate to the death of a legendary hero?

Reading Skill
Comparing Worldviews How does the arrival of the three queens reflect a belief in supernatural forces or mystical events?

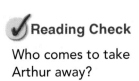Reading Check

Who comes to take Arthur away?

And every chance brought out a noble knight.
Such times have been not since the light that led
The holy Elders with the gift of myrrh.[27]
285 But now the whole ROUND TABLE is dissolved
Which was an image of the mighty world;
And I, the last, go forth companionless,
And the days darken round me, and the years,
Among new men, strange faces, other minds."
290   And slowly answered Arthur from the barge:
"The old order changeth, yielding place to new,
And God fulfills himself in many ways,
Lest one good custom should corrupt the world.
Comfort thyself: what comfort is in me?
295 I have lived my life, and that which I have done
May He within himself make pure! but thou,
If thou shouldst never see my face again,
Pray for my soul. More things are wrought by prayer
Than this world dreams of. Wherefore, let thy voice
300 Rise like a fountain for me night and day.
For what are men better than sheep or goats
That nourish a blind life within the brain,
If, knowing God, they lift not hands of prayer
Both for themselves and those who call them friend?
305 For so the whole round earth is every way
Bound by gold chains about the feet of God.
But now farewell. I am going a long way
With these thou seest—if indeed I go—
For all my mind is clouded with a doubt—
310 To the island-valley of Avilion;[28]
Where falls not hail, or rain, or any snow,
Nor ever wind blows loudly, but it lies
Deep-meadowed, happy, fair with orchard lawns
And bowery[29] hollows crowned with summer sea,
315 Where I will heal me of my grievous wound."
      So said he, and the barge with oar and sail
Moved from the brink, like some full-breasted swan
that, fluting a wild carol ere her death,
Ruffles her pure cold plume, takes the flood

Literary Analysis
Legends Which ideas in Bedivere's speech encourage English national pride?

Reading Skill
Comparing Worldviews What is the main difference between Bedivere's and Arthur's view of the world?

---

27. **the light . . . of myrrh** (mŭr) star that guided the three kings ("the holy Elders") with their gifts of myrrh (a gum from plants, used to make incense and perfume), to Bethlehem at the birth of Jesus.
28. **island-valley of Avilion** According to ancient British myth, heroes were taken after death to the island paradise of Avalon, called "Avilion" here.
29. **bowery** (bou´ ər ē) *adj.* enclosed by overhanging boughs of trees or by vines.

320 With swarthy webs. Long stood Sir Bedivere
Revolving many memories, till the hull
Looked one black dot against the verge of dawn,
And on the mere the wailing died away.

      Here ended Hall, and our last light, that long
325 Had winked and threatened darkness, flared and fell;
At which the parson, sent to sleep with sound,
And waked with silence, grunted "Good!" but we
Sat rapt: it was the tone with which he read—
Perhaps some modern touches here and there
330 Redeemed it from the charge of nothingness—
Or else we loved the man, and prized his work;
I know not; but we sitting, as I said,
The cock crew loud, as at that time of year
The lusty bird takes every hour for dawn.
335 Then Francis, muttering, like a man ill-used,
"There now—that's nothing!" drew a little back,
And drove his heel into the smoldered log,
That sent a blast of sparkles up the flue.
And so to bed, where yet in sleep I seemed
340 To sail with Arthur under looming shores,
Point after point; till on to dawn, when dreams
Begin to feel the truth and stir of day,
To me, methought, who waited with the crowd,
There came a bark that, blowing forward, bore
345 King Arthur; like a modern gentleman
Of stateliest port;[30] and all the people cried,
"Arthur is come again: he cannot die."
Then those that stood upon the hills behind
Repeated—"Come again, and thrice as fair";
350 And, further inland, voices echoed—"Come
With all good things, and war shall be no more."
At this a hundred bells began to peal,
That with the sound I woke, and heard indeed
The clear church bells ring in the Christmas morn.

Literary Analysis
Legends In what way do lines 344–351 suggest that faith and the opportunity for noble action might return in modern times, as strong as in the Arthur legend?

---

30. Of stateliest port who carried himself in a most majestic or dignified manner.

Apply the Skills

Morte d'Arthur

Thinking About the Selection

1. **Respond:** If you had been in Sir Bedivere's position, would you have obeyed Arthur's request? Explain.
2. **(a) Recall:** What occasion is celebrated at the opening of the poem? **(b) Interpret:** What complaint does the parson make on this occasion?
3. **(a) Recall:** In Everard's poem, what has happened to Arthur and his knights? **(b) Interpret:** When Bedivere says that "'the true old times are dead,'" what does he imply will vanish from the world?
4. **(a) Recall:** What does Arthur specifically request of Bedivere? **(b) Interpret:** Why does Bedivere fear that if he obeys Arthur's request, "much honor and much fame were lost"? **(c) Connect:** What attitude toward the past do Bedivere and the parson share?
5. **(a) Support:** Find passages in the poem in which the poet suggests that hope remains even though Arthur is gone. **(b) Discuss:** Share examples and interpretations with a partner. **(c) Evaluate:** Choose two of the best examples, and present them to the class.

Life Story of Legendary Hero	Concern with Right and Wrong	Reflections of National Pride

Literary Analysis

6. Which features of **legends** are present in this poem? Use a chart like the one shown to gather examples from the selection.
7. In what way does the end of the poem suggest that King Arthur still unites the people of England, past and present?

Reading Skill

8. Arthur says, "The old order changeth, yielding place to new." **(a)** Describe the "old order" of Arthur's reign, using details from the poem. **(b)** What do the parson's complaints show about the "new order" of modern times? **(c) Compare and contrast** the parson's **worldview** with the worldview of the old order.
9. In the narrator's dream, the people cry, "'Arthur is come again: he cannot die.'" Based on this dream, explain what basic values or beliefs Tennyson might hold.

Vocabulary Builder

Practice Answer each of the following questions. Explain your responses.

1. Are football players noted for their <u>languid</u> movements?
2. If you want to make friends with someone you have just met, should you start with a <u>disparagement</u> of his or her clothes?
3. Why scold a child who <u>brandished</u> a pair of scissors while running?

Adding Words to Your Vocabulary Using a dictionary, determine the meaning of *languish*. Explain the relationship between *languish* and *languid*. (For more on using a dictionary, see page R6.)

Writing

The death of King Arthur is big news. Write a brief **script for a television news report** in which you present the story to the nation. Follow these tips:

- First, take notes on *who* is involved, *what* happened, and *where, when, why,* and *how* it happened.
- Outline the various perspectives you will offer. You might open with a news anchor, cut next to footage of the barge, and conclude with a discussion among commentators.
- As you draft, clearly identify each speaker and describe the visuals.

For *Grammar, Vocabulary,* and *Assessment,* see **Build Language Skills,** pages 1094–1095.

Extend Your Learning

Listening and Speaking Watch a movie based on the legends of King Arthur. As you watch, fill out a two-column **"influences" chart.** In one column, note aspects of the film that the director probably took directly from the legends. In the other column, note aspects that probably represent modern influences. Present your findings to the class.

Research and Technology Conduct research about a type of technology that would have been common in the days of Arthur. Technologies might include metal-making, shipbuilding, or navigation. Write a brief **technical report** in which you explain, in step-by-step form, one of the processes used by people of the era.

Build Understanding • *Arthur Becomes King of Britain*

Background

Legends of King Arthur Tales of King Arthur, legendary ruler of Britain, and of the knights of his Round Table have been retold for centuries. Sir Thomas Malory wrote the first English prose version of the legends, *Le Morte d'Arthur,* in 1470. In "Arthur Becomes King of Britain," an excerpt from his series *The Once and Future King,* T. H. White modernizes Malory's version of the legends.

Connecting to the Literature

Reading/Writing Connection In this excerpt, T. H. White presents the young hero-to-be Arthur. Make a list of examples of heroism. Then, explain whether you think people can learn to become heroic. Use at least three of the following words: *adapt, rely, respond, focus.*

Review

For **Literary Analysis, Reading Skill,** and **Vocabulary Builder,** see page 1062.

READ MORE

by T.H. White
The Sword in the Stone

The Book of Merlyn

Meet the Author

T. H. **White** (1906–1964)

Terence Hanbury White is widely known for his tales of Britain's national hero, King Arthur, but he was born in India when it was still a British colony. White was educated at Cambridge University in England, where he received first-class honors in English.

Finding a Passion After school, White went to work as a teacher. When his autobiographical work *England Have My Bones* met with success, the thirty-year-old White became a full-time writer. The four-part novel *The Once and Future King,* a comic retelling of the King Arthur legends, is White's most famous work.

Fast Facts

▶ White's interests included flying and deep-sea diving.
▶ White's version of the Arthur legends has inspired movies as well as the musical *Camelot* (1960).

Go **Online**
Author Link

For: More about the author
Visit: www.PHSchool.com
Web Code: eqe-9609

Arthur Becomes King of Britain

from THE ONCE AND FUTURE KING

T. H. WHITE

The Crowning of Arthur, Royal MS. By permission of the British Library.

K ing Pellinore arrived for the important weekend in a high
state of flurry.

"I say," he exclaimed, "do you know? Have you heard? Is
it a secret, what?"

"Is what a secret, what?" they asked him.

"Why, the King," cried his majesty. "You know, about the King?"

"What's the matter with the King?" inquired Sir Ector. "You don't
say he's comin' down to hunt with those darned hounds of his or
anythin' like that?"

▲ **Critical Viewing**
Which details in this
illustration indicate
the importance and
which the humor of
Arthur's becoming
king? **[Analyze]**

"He's dead," cried King Pellinore tragically. "He's dead, poor fellah, and can't hunt any more."

Sir Grummore stood up respectfully and took off his cap of maintenance.

"The King is dead," he said. "Long live the King."

Everybody else felt they ought to stand up too, and the boys' nurse burst into tears.

"There, there," she sobbed. "His loyal highness dead and gone, and him such a respectful gentleman. Many's the illuminated picture I've cut out of him, from the Illustrated Missals,[1] aye, and stuck up over the mantel. From the time when he was in swaddling bands,[2] right through them world towers till he was a-visiting the dispersed areas as the world's Prince Charming, there wasn't a picture of 'im but I had it out, aye, and give 'im a last thought o' nights."

"Compose yourself, Nannie," said Sir Ector.

"It is solemn, isn't it?" said King Pellinore, "what? Uther the Conqueror, 1066 to 1216."

"A solemn moment," said Sir Grummore. "The King is dead. Long live the King."

"We ought to pull down the curtains," said Kay, who was always a <u>stickler</u> for good form, "or half-mast[3] the banners."

"That's right," said Sir Ector. "Somebody go and tell the sergeant-at-arms."

It was obviously the Wart's duty to execute this command, for he was now the junior nobleman present, so he ran out cheerfully to find the sergeant. Soon those who were left in the solar[4] could hear a voice crying out, "Nah then, one-two, special mourning fer 'is lite majesty, lower awai on the command Two!" and then the flapping of all the standards, banners, pennons, pennoncells, banderolls, guidons, streamers and cognizances[5] which made gay the snowy turrets of the Forest Sauvage.

"How did you hear?" asked Sir Ector.

"I was pricking through the purlieus[6] of the forest after that Beast, you know, when I met with a solemn friar of orders gray, and he told me. It's the very latest news."

"Poor old Pendragon," said Sir Ector.

"The King is dead," said Sir Grummore solemnly. "Long live the King."

Reading Skill
Comparing Worldviews Which details in the nurse's speech reflect a modern outlook? Which details reflect medieval life?

Vocabulary Builder
stickler (stik´ lər) *n.* person who insists on strict obedience to rules or standards

▼ **Critical Viewing**
What does the ornamented hilt of this sword indicate about a knight's attitude toward his weapons? **[Infer]**

---

1. Missals (mis´ əlz) *n.* books produced by the Roman Catholic Church for solemn religious purposes.
2. swaddling (swäd´´lin) **bands** in former times, long, narrow bands of cloth wrapped around a newborn baby.
3. half-mast *v.* lower a flag halfway down a pole as a sign of mourning.
4. solar (sō´ lər) *n.* sun room.
5. standards . . . cognizances (käg´ nə zən´ səz) banners or flags.
6. purlieus (pɜrl´ yōōz´) *n.* outlying part of a forest, in which forest laws were not enforced.

"It is all very well for you to keep on mentioning that, my dear Grummore," exclaimed King Pellinore <u>petulantly</u>, "but who is this King, what, that is to live so long, what, accordin' to you?"

"Well, his heir," said Sir Grummore, rather taken aback.

"Our blessed monarch," said the Nurse tearfully, "never had no hair. Anybody that studied the loyal family knowed that."

"Good gracious!" exclaimed Sir Ector. "But he must have had a next-of-kin?"

"That's just it," cried King Pellinore in high excitement. "That's the excitin' part of it, what? No hair and no next of skin, and who's to succeed to the throne? That's what my friar was so excited about, what, and why he was asking who could succeed to what, what? What?"

"Do you mean to tell me," exclaimed Sir Grummore indignantly, "that there ain't no King of Gramarye?"

"Not a scrap of one," cried King Pellinore, feeling important. "And there have been signs and wonders of no mean might."

"I think it's a scandal," said Sir Grummore. "God knows what the dear old country is comin' to. Due to these lollards and communists, no doubt."

"What sort of signs and wonders?" asked Sir Ector.

"Well, there has appeared a sort of sword in a stone, what, in a sort of a church. Not in the church, if you see what I mean, and not in the stone, but that sort of thing, what, like you might say."

"I don't know what the Church is coming to," said Sir Grummore.

"It's in an anvil,"[7] explained the King.

"The Church?"

"No, the sword."

"But I thought you said the sword was in the stone?"

"No," said King Pellinore. "The stone is outside the church."

"Look here, Pellinore," said Sir Ector. "You have a bit of a rest, old boy, and start again. Here, drink up this horn of mead[8] and take it easy."

"The sword," said King Pellinore, "is stuck through an anvil which stands on a stone. It goes right through the anvil and into the stone. The anvil is stuck to the stone. The stone stands outside a church. Give me some more mead."

"I don't think that's much of a wonder," remarked Sir Grummore. "What I wonder at is that they should allow such things to happen. But you can't tell nowadays, what with all these Saxon agitators."[9]

Vocabulary Builder
petulantly (pech´ ə lənt lē) *adv.* in a manner that expresses impatience or irritation, especially over a minor matter

Literary Analysis
Legends Why is humor like this surprising in a retelling of a legend?

Reading Check

What news does King Pellinore bring?

---

7. anvil (an´ vəl) *n.* iron or steel block on which a blacksmith rests metal to hammer it into shape.
8. mead (mēd) *n.* drink made of fermented honey and water.
9. Saxon (sak´ sən) **agitators** (aj´ i tāt´ ərz) The Saxons were a Germanic people who conquered parts of England in ancient times. Agitators are those who stir up people for a cause.

"My dear fellah," cried Pellinore, getting excited again, "it's not where the stone is, what, that I'm trying to tell you, but what is written on it, what, where it is."

"What?"

"Why, on its pommel."[10]

"Come on, Pellinore," said Sir Ector. "You just sit quite still with your face to the wall for a minute, and then tell us what you are talkin' about. Take it easy, old boy. No need for hurryin'. You sit still and look at the wall, there's a good chap, and talk as slow as you can."

"There are words written on this sword in this stone outside this church," cried King Pellinore piteously, "and these words are as follows. Oh, do try to listen to me, you two, instead of interruptin' all the time about nothin', for it makes a man's head go ever so."

"What are these words?" asked Kay.

"These words say this," said King Pellinore, "so far as I can understand from that old friar of orders gray."

"Go on, do," said Kay, for the King had come to a halt.

"Go on," said Sir Ector, "what do these words on this sword in this anvil in this stone outside this church, say?"

"Some red propaganda, no doubt," remarked Sir Grummore.

King Pellinore closed his eyes tight, extended his arms in both directions, and announced in capital letters, "Whoso Pulleth Out This Sword of this Stone and Anvil, is Rightwise King Born of All England."

"Who said that?" asked Sir Grummore.

"But the sword said it, like I tell you."

"Talkative weapon," remarked Sir Grummore skeptically.

"It was written on it," cried the King angrily. "Written on it in letters of gold."

"Why didn't you pull it out then?" asked Sir Grummore.

"But I tell you that I wasn't there. All this that I am telling you was told to me by that friar I was telling you of, like I tell you."

"Has this sword with this inscription been pulled out?" inquired Sir Ector.

"No," whispered King Pellinore dramatically. "That's where the whole excitement comes in. They can't pull this sword out at all, although they have all been tryin' like fun, and so they have had to proclaim a tournament all over England, for New Year's Day, so that the man who comes to the tournament and pulls out the sword can be King of all England forever, what, I say?"

Literary Analysis
Legends Why is the formal sound of the words on the stone suitable to a legend?

Reading Skill
Comparing Worldviews How do these details about the choosing of the next king suggest a belief in mysterious powers guiding human affairs?

---

10. **pommel** (päm´ əl) *n.* knob at the end of the hilt of some swords.

▲ **Critical Viewing** Which details in this illustration suggest the importance of Arthur's sword as a symbol of England? **[Interpret]**

"Oh, father," cried Kay. "The man who pulls the sword out of the stone will be the King of England. Can't we go to the tournament, father, and have a shot?"

"Couldn't think of it," said Sir Ector.

"Long way to London," said Sir Grummore, shaking his head.

"My father went there once," said King Pellinore.

Kay said, "Oh, surely we could go? When I am knighted I shall have to go to a tournament somewhere, and this one happens at just the right date. All the best people will be there, and we should see the famous knights and great kings. It does not matter about the sword, of course, but think of the tournament, probably the greatest there has ever been in Gramarye, and all the things we should see and do. Dear father, let me go to this tourney, if you love me, so that I may bear away the prize of all, in my maiden fight."

"But, Kay," said Sir Ector, "I have never been to London."

"All the more reason to go. I believe that anybody who does not go for a tournament like this will be proving that he has no noble blood in his veins. Think what people will say about us, if we do not go and have a shot at that sword. They will say that Sir Ector's family was too vulgar and knew it had no chance."

"We all know the family has no chance," said Sir Ector, "that is, for the sword."

"Lot of people in London," remarked Sir Grummore, with a wild surmise. "So they say."

He took a deep breath and goggled at his host with eyes like marbles.

"And shops," added King Pellinore suddenly, also beginning to breathe heavily.

"Dang it!" cried Sir Ector, bumping his horn mug on the table so that it spilled. "Let's all go to London, then, and see the new King!"

They rose up as one man.

"Why shouldn't I be as good a man as my father?" exclaimed King Pellinore.

"Dash it all," cried Sir Grummore. "After all, it is the capital!"

"Hurray!" shouted Kay.

"Lord have mercy," said the nurse.

At this moment the Wart came in with Merlyn, and everybody was too excited to notice that, if he had not been grown up now, he would have been on the verge of tears.

"Oh, Wart," cried Kay, forgetting for the moment that he was only addressing his squire, and slipping back into the familiarity of their boyhood. "What do you think? We are all going to London for a great tournament on New Year's Day!"

"Are we?"

"Yes, and you will carry my shield and spears for the jousts,[11] and I shall win the palm of everybody and be a great knight!"

"Well, I am glad we are going," said the Wart, "for Merlyn is leaving us too."

"Oh, we shan't need Merlyn."

"He is leaving us," repeated the Wart.

"Leavin' us?" asked Sir Ector. "I thought it was we that were leavin'?"

"He is going away from the Forest Sauvage."

Sir Ector said, "Come now, Merlyn, what's all this about? I don't understand all this a bit."

"I have come to say Goodbye, Sir Ector," said the old magician. "Tomorrow my pupil Kay will be knighted, and the next week my other pupil will go away as his squire. I have outlived my usefulness here, and it is time to go."

"Now, now, don't say that," said Sir Ector. "I think you're a jolly useful chap whatever happens. You just stay and teach me, or be the librarian or something. Don't you leave an old man alone, after the children have flown."

"We shall all meet again," said Merlyn. "There is no cause to be sad."

"Don't go," said Kay.

"I must go," replied their tutor. "We have had a good time while we were young, but it is in the nature of Time to fly. There are many things in other parts of the kingdom which I ought to be attending to just now, and it is a specially busy time for me. Come, Archimedes,[12] say Goodbye to the company."

"Goodbye," said Archimedes tenderly to the Wart.

"Goodbye," said the Wart without looking up at all.

"But you can't go," cried Sir Ector, "not without a month's notice."

"Can't I?" replied Merlyn, taking up the position always used by philosophers who propose to dematerialize. He stood on his toes, while Archimedes held tight to his shoulder—began to spin on them slowly like a top—spun faster and faster till he was only a blur of grayish light—and in a few seconds there was no one there at all.

"Goodbye, Wart," cried two faint voices outside the solar window.

"Goodbye," said the Wart for the last time—and the poor fellow went quickly out of the room.

Literature in Context

History Connection

Tournaments The first tournaments were held in France in the 1100s. Groups of knights would split into two sides and fight each other. Death and injury often resulted. In the 1200s, the real battles were replaced with mock ones called *jousts*. In a joust, two horsemen would charge at each other with blunt weapons. Each would try to knock the other from his horse. Jousting tournaments were social gatherings attended by ladies and common people as well as by knights.

Connect to the Literature

In light of these facts, should Kay be nervous about his first jousting tournament? Explain.

Reading Check

Why is Merlyn leaving Sir Ector's household?

---

11. **win the palm** be the winner. A palm leaf is a symbol of victory.
12. **Archimedes** (är′ kə mē′ dēz′) Merlin's owl, who is able to talk.

▲ **Critical Viewing** Contrast the idea of knighthood conveyed by this illustration with the concerns of Pellinore and Kay. **[Contrast]**

The knighting took place in a whirl of preparations. Kay's sumptuous bath had to be set up in the box room, between two towel-horses and an old box of selected games which contained a worn-out straw dart-board—it was called fléchette in those days—because all the other rooms were full of packing. The nurse spent the whole time constructing new warm pants for everybody, on the principle that the climate of any place outside the Forest Sauvage must be treacherous to the extreme, and, as for the sergeant, he polished all the armor till it was quite brittle and sharpened the swords till they were almost worn away.

At last it was time to set out.

Perhaps, if you happen not to have lived in the Old England of the twelfth century, or whenever it was, and in a remote castle on the borders of the Marches at that, you will find it difficult to imagine the wonders of their journey.

The road, or track, ran most of the time along the high ridges of the hills or downs, and they could look down on either side of them upon the desolate marshes where the snowy reeds sighed, and the ice crackled, and the duck in the red sunsets quacked loud on the winter air. The whole country was like that. Perhaps there would be a moory marsh on one side of the ridge, and a forest of a hundred thousand acres on the other, with all the great branches weighted in white. They could sometimes see a wisp of smoke among the trees, or a huddle of buildings far out among the impassable reeds, and twice they came to quite respectable towns which had several inns to boast of, but on the whole it was an England without civilization. The better roads were cleared of cover for a bow-shot on either side of them, lest the traveler should be slain by hidden thieves.

They slept where they could, sometimes in the hut of some cottager who was prepared to welcome them, sometimes in the castle of a brother knight who invited them to refresh themselves, sometimes in the firelight and fleas of a dirty little hovel with a bush tied to a pole outside it—this was the signboard used at that time by inns—and once or twice on the open ground, all huddled together for warmth between their grazing chargers. Wherever they went and wherever they slept, the east wind whistled in the reeds, and the geese went over high in the starlight, honking at the stars.

London was full to the brim. If Sir Ector had not been lucky enough to own a little land in Pie Street, on which there stood a respectable inn, they would have been hard put to it to find a lodging. But he did own it, and as a matter of fact drew most of his dividends from that source, so they were able to get three beds between the five of them. They thought themselves fortunate.

Reading Skill Comparing Worldviews How does this section connect past and present views of the world?

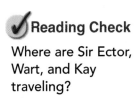

Reading Check

Where are Sir Ector, Wart, and Kay traveling?

On the first day of the tournament, Sir Kay managed to get them on the way to the lists at least an hour before the jousts could possibly begin. He had lain awake all night, imagining how he was going to beat the best barons in England, and he had not been able to eat his breakfast. Now he rode at the front of the cavalcade, with pale cheeks, and Wart wished there was something he could do to calm him down.

For country people, who only knew the dismantled tilting ground[13] of Sir Ector's castle, the scene which met their eyes was ravishing. It was a huge green pit in the earth, about as big as the arena at a football match. It lay ten feet lower than the surrounding country, with sloping banks, and the snow had been swept off it. It had been kept warm with straw, which had been cleared off that morning, and now the close-worn grass sparkled green in the white landscape. Round the arena there was a world of color so dazzling and moving and twinkling as to make one blink one's eyes. The wooden grandstands were painted in scarlet and white. The silk pavilions of famous people, pitched on every side, were azure and green and saffron and checkered. The pennons and pennoncells which floated everywhere in the sharp wind were flapping with every color of the rainbow, as they strained and slapped at their flagpoles, and the barrier down the middle of the arena itself was done in chessboard squares of black and white. Most of the combatants and their friends had not yet arrived, but one could see from those few who had come how the very people would turn the scene into a bank of flowers, and how the armor would flash, and the scalloped sleeves of the heralds jig in the wind, as they raised their brazen trumpets to their lips to shake the fleecy clouds of winter with joyances[14] and fanfares.

"Good heavens!" cried Sir Kay. "I have left my sword at home."

"Can't joust without a sword," said Sir Grummore. "Quite irregular."

"Better go and fetch it," said Sir Ector. "You have time."

"My squire will do," said Sir Kay. "What an awful mistake to make! Here, squire, ride hard back to the inn and fetch my sword. You shall have a shilling[15] if you fetch it in time."

The Wart went as pale as Sir Kay was, and looked as if he were going to strike him. Then he said, "It shall be done, master," and

▲ **Critical Viewing**
Which features of this sculpture convey the dignity of a king? **[Interpret]**

---

13. **tilting ground** ground on which a joust takes place.
14. **joyances** (joi´ əns iz) *n.* old word meaning "rejoicing."
15. **shilling** (shil´ iŋ) *n.* British silver coin.

turned his ambling palfrey[16] against the stream of newcomers. He began to push his way toward their hostelry[17] as best he might.

"To offer me money!" cried the Wart to himself. "To look down at this beastly little donkey-affair off his great charger and to call me Squire! Oh, Merlyn, give me patience with the brute, and stop me from throwing his filthy shilling in his face."

When he got to the inn it was closed. Everybody had thronged to see the famous tournament, and the entire household had followed after the mob. Those were lawless days and it was not safe to leave your house—or even to go to sleep in it—unless you were certain that it was impregnable.[18] The wooden shutters bolted over the downstairs windows were two inches thick, and the doors were double-barred.

"Now what do I do," asked the Wart, "to earn my shilling?"

He looked ruefully at the blind little inn, and began to laugh.

"Poor Kay," he said. "All that shilling stuff was only because he was scared and miserable, and now he has good cause to be. Well, he shall have a sword of some sort if I have to break into the Tower of London.

"How does one get hold of a sword?" he continued. "Where can I steal one? Could I waylay some knight, even if I am mounted on an ambling pad, and take his weapons by force? There must be some swordsmith or armorer in a great town like this, whose shop would be still open."

He turned his mount and cantered off along the street. There was a quiet churchyard at the end of it, with a kind of square in front of the church door. In the middle of the square there was a heavy stone with an anvil on it, and a fine new sword was stuck through the anvil.

"Well," said the Wart, "I suppose it is some sort of war memorial, but it will have to do. I am sure nobody would grudge Kay a war memorial, if they knew his desperate straits."

He tied his reins round a post of the lych gate,[19] strode up the gravel path, and took hold of the sword.

"Come, sword," he said. "I must cry your mercy and take you for a better cause.

"This is extraordinary," said the Wart. "I feel strange when I have hold of this sword, and I notice everything much more clearly. Look at the beautiful gargoyles[20] of the church, and of the monastery

Literary Analysis
Legends What does Wart's reaction have in common with the reaction a legendary hero would have in these circumstances?

Reading Skill
Comparing Worldviews Which details here reflect modern attitudes and which reflect the world of legend?

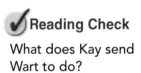
Reading Check
What does Kay send Wart to do?

---

16. **palfrey** (pôl´ frē) *n.* old term for a saddle horse, especially one for women.
17. **hostelry** (häs´ təl rē) *n.* inn.
18. **impregnable** (im preg´ nə bəl) *adj.* not capable of being captured or entered by force.
19. **lych** (lich) **gate** roofed gate at the entrance to a churchyard.
20. **gargoyles** (gär´ goilz´) *n.* grotesque sculptures of animals or fantastic creatures decorating a building.

◄ **Critical Viewing**
What does this
illustration suggest
about Merlin's
character and
abilities? Explain.
[Interpret]

which it belongs to. See how splendidly all the famous banners in the aisle are waving. How nobly that yew[21] holds up the red flakes of its timbers to worship God. How clean the snow is. I can smell something like fetherfew and sweet briar—and is it music that I hear?"

It was music, whether of pan-pipes or of recorders, and the light in the churchyard was so clear, without being dazzling, that one could have picked a pin out twenty yards away.

"There is something in this place," said the Wart. "There are people. Oh, people, what do you want?"

Nobody answered him, but the music was loud and the light beautiful.

"People," cried the Wart, "I must take this sword. It is not for me, but for Kay. I will bring it back."

---

21. yew (yo͞o) *n.* type of evergreen tree with red cones.

There was still no answer, and Wart turned back to the anvil. He saw the golden letters, which he did not read, and the jewels on the pommel, flashing in the lovely light.

"Come, sword," said the Wart.

He took hold of the handles with both hands, and strained against the stone. There was a melodious consort[22] on the recorders, but nothing moved.

The Wart let go of the handles, when they were beginning to bite into the palms of his hands, and stepped back, seeing stars.

"It is well fixed," he said.

He took hold of it again and pulled with all his might. The music played more strongly, and the light all about the churchyard glowed like amethysts; but the sword still stuck.

"Oh, Merlyn," cried the Wart, "help me to get this weapon."

There was a kind of rushing noise, and a long chord played along with it. All round the churchyard there were hundreds of old friends. They rose over the church wall all together, like the Punch-and-Judy[23] ghosts of remembered days, and there were badgers and nightingales and vulgar crows and hares and wild geese and falcons and fishes and dogs and dainty unicorns and solitary wasps and corkindrills and hedgehogs and griffins and the thousand other animals he had met. They loomed round the church wall, the lovers and helpers of the Wart, and they all spoke solemnly in turn. Some of them had come from the banners in the church, where they were painted in heraldry, some from the waters and the sky and the fields about—but all, down to the smallest shrew mouse, had come to help on account of love. Wart felt his power grow.

"Put your back into it," said a luce (or pike) off one of the heraldic banners, "as you once did when I was going to snap you up. Remember that power springs from the nape of the neck."

"What about those forearms," asked a badger gravely, "that are held together by a chest? Come along, my dear embryo,[24] and find your tool."

A merlin sitting at the top of the yew tree cried out, "Now then, Captain Wart, what is the first law of the foot? I thought I once heard something about never letting go."

"Don't work like a stalling woodpecker," urged a tawny owl affectionately. "Keep up a steady effort, my duck, and you will have it yet."

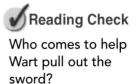
---

22. **consort** (kän′ sôrt′) *n.* piece of music composed for a small group.
23. **Punch-and-Judy** puppets of the quarrelsome Punch and his wife, Judy, who fight constantly in a comical way.
24. **embryo** (em′ brē ō′) *n.* anything in an early stage of development.

A white-front said. "Now, Wart, if you were once able to fly the great North Sea, surely you can coordinate a few little wing-muscles here and there? Fold your powers together, with the spirit of your mind, and it will come out like butter. Come along, Homo sapiens,[25] for all we humble friends of yours are waiting here to cheer."

The Wart walked up to the great sword for the third time. He put out his right hand softly and drew it out as gently as from a scabbard.

There was a lot of cheering, a noise like a hurdy-gurdy[26] which went on and on. In the middle of this noise, after a long time, he saw Kay and gave him the sword. The people at the tournament were making a frightful row.

"But this is not my sword," said Sir Kay.

"It was the only one I could get," said the Wart. "The inn was locked."

"It is a nice-looking sword. Where did you get it?"

"I found it stuck in a stone, outside a church."

Sir Kay had been watching the tilting nervously, waiting for his turn. He had not paid much attention to his squire.

"That is a funny place to find one," he said.

"Yes, it was stuck through an anvil."

"What?" cried Sir Kay, suddenly rounding upon him. "Did you just say this sword was stuck in a stone?"

"It was," said the Wart. "It was a sort of war memorial."

Sir Kay stared at him for several seconds in amazement, opened his mouth, shut it again, licked his lips, then turned his back and plunged through the crowd. He was looking for Sir Ector, and the Wart followed after him.

"Father," cried Sir Kay, "come here a moment."

"Yes, my boy," said Sir Ector. "Splendid falls these professional chaps do manage. Why, what's the matter, Kay? You look as white as a sheet."

"Do you remember that sword which the King of England would pull out?"

"Yes."

"Well, here it is. I have it. It is in my hand. I pulled it out."

Sir Ector did not say anything silly. He looked at Kay and he looked at the Wart. Then he stared at Kay again, long and lovingly, and said, "We will go back to the church."

"Now then, Kay," he said, when they were at the church door. He looked at his firstborn kindly, but straight between the eyes. "Here

Literary Analysis

Legends How does this event mark Wart as a legendary hero?

Literary Analysis

Legends Contrast Wart's everyday language with the significance of the event he describes.

---

25. **Homo sapiens** (hō′ mō sā′ pē enz′) scientific name for human beings.
26. **hurdy-gurdy** (hur′ dē gur′ dē) *n.* musical instrument played by turning a crank.

is the stone, and you have the sword. It will make you the King of England. You are my son that I am proud of, and always will be, whatever you do. Will you promise me that you took it out by your own might?"

Kay looked at his father. He also looked at the Wart and at the sword.

Then he handed the sword to the Wart quite quietly.

He said, "I am a liar. Wart pulled it out."

As far as the Wart was concerned, there was a time after this in which Sir Ector kept telling him to put the sword back into the stone—which he did—and in which Sir Ector and Kay then vainly tried to take it out. The Wart took it out for them, and stuck it back again once or twice. After this, there was another time which was more painful.

He saw that his dear guardian was looking quite old and powerless, and that he was kneeling down with difficulty on a gouty[27] knee.

"Sir," said Sir Ector, without looking up, although he was speaking to his own boy.

"Please do not do this, father," said the Wart, kneeling down also. "Let me help you up, Sir Ector, because you are making me unhappy."

"Nay, nay, my lord," said Sir Ector, with some very feeble old tears. "I was never your father nor of your blood, but I wote[28] well ye are of an higher blood than I wend[29] ye were."

"Plenty of people have told me you are not my father," said the Wart, "but it does not matter a bit."

"Sir," said Sir Ector humbly, "will ye be my good and gracious lord when ye are King?"

"Don't!" said the Wart.

"Sir," said Sir Ector, "I will ask no more of you but that you will make my son, your foster-brother, Sir Kay, seneschal[30] of all your lands?"

Kay was kneeling down too, and it was more than the Wart could bear.

"Oh, do stop," he cried. "Of course he can be seneschal, if I have got to be this King, and, oh, father, don't kneel down like that, because it breaks my heart. Please get up, Sir Ector, and don't make everything so horrible. Oh, dear, oh, dear, I wish I had never seen that filthy sword at all."

And the Wart also burst into tears.

Reading Skill
Comparing Worldviews What details of the conversation between Sir Ector and Kay reflect both modern and medieval values?

Literary Analysis
Legends How does the change in the kind of words Sir Ector uses emphasize the legendary importance of the event?

---

27. gouty (gout´ ē) *adj.* having gout, a disease causing swelling and severe pain in the joints.
28. wote (wōt) *v.* old world meaning "know."
29. wend (wend) *v.* thought (past tense of *ween*, an old word meaning "think.")
30. seneschal (sen´ ə shəl) *n.* steward, or manager, in the house of a medieval noble.

Apply the Skills

Arthur Becomes King of Britain

Thinking About the Selection

1. **Respond:** Who is your favorite character in this retelling of the Arthur legend? Why?
2. **(a) Recall:** How is the new king of England to be chosen? **(b) Draw Conclusions:** What does this method suggest about the reason men become kings in the world of the story?
3. **(a) Recall:** What does Kay ask Wart to do when Kay discovers he is missing his sword? **(b) Analyze:** Describe the two reactions Wart has to Kay's request. **(c) Contrast:** Based on this incident, contrast the characters of Wart and Kay.
4. **(a) Recall:** Who or what offers advice to Wart as he attempts to pull the sword from the stone? **(b) Interpret:** How does this episode add to the sense of the importance of Wart's action?
5. **(a) Draw a Conclusion:** At the end of the tale, what lesson about duty is suggested by Sir Ector's new behavior toward Wart? **(b) Discuss:** Discuss responses with a partner. Then, explain whether your discussion changed your thoughts about the story.

Literary Analysis

6. Which features of **legends** are present in this excerpt? Use a chart like the one shown to gather examples from the text.
7. What point about heroes might the author be making by mixing ordinary and legendary characteristics in Wart? Explain.

Life Story of Legendary Hero	Concern with Right and Wrong	Reflections of National Pride

Reading Skill

8. **(a)** Based on King Pellinore's tales of "'signs and wonders,'" draw a conclusion about his basic beliefs. **(b)** Describe Sir Grummore's reaction to the report. **(c) Compare and contrast** Pellinore's and Grummore's **worldviews**.
9. **(a)** Find three examples in which characters speak casually or in slang about legendary events. **(b)** What might these examples suggest about the difference between the author's worldview and the worldview of those who originally told the legend of Arthur?

QuickReview

Legend at a Glance
In this part of the legend, Sir Ector, his son Kay, and his foster son Wart (Arthur) travel to London and make a surprising discovery.

Go Online
—Assessment
For: Self-test
Visit: www.PHSchool.com
Web Code: eqa-6608

Legends: stories about the past that have been handed down for generations

Worldview: the values and basic beliefs of a culture or group of people

Vocabulary Builder

Practice Answer each of the following questions. Explain your responses.

1. Will a <u>stickler</u> for cleanliness complain when you spill milk?
2. If you want to impress someone, should you behave <u>petulantly</u>?
3. Is it fair to jail a person based on a neighbor's <u>surmise</u>?

Adding Words to Your Vocabulary Using a thesaurus, find two **synonyms**, or words with similar meanings, for *surmise*. Explain any differences in the meanings of the three words. (For more on using a thesaurus, see page R7.)

Writing

The discovery that Wart will be king of England is big news. Write a brief **script for a television news report** to present the story to the nation. Follow these tips:
- First, take notes on *who* is involved, *what* happened, and *where, when, why,* and *how* it happened.
- Outline the various perspectives you will offer. You might open with a news anchor, and cut next to footage of the sword.
- As you draft, identify each speaker and describe each visual.

For *Grammar, Vocabulary,* and *Assessment,* see **Build Language Skills,** pages 1094–1095.

Extend Your Learning

Listening and Speaking Watch a movie based on the legends of King Arthur. As you watch, fill out a two-column **"influences" chart.** In one column, note aspects of the film that the director probably took directly from the legends. In the other column, note aspects that probably represent modern influences. Present your findings to the class.

Research and Technology Conduct research about a type of technology that would have been common in the days of Arthur. Technologies might include metal-making, shipbuilding, or navigation. Write a brief **technical report** in which you explain, in step-by-step form, one of the processes used by people of the era.

Build Language Skills

Morte d'Arthur • Arthur Becomes King of Britain

Vocabulary Skill

Words in Context Like a word's root, a word's **context** provides clues to its meaning. For example, the word *lucid* contains the word root *-luc-*, which means "light." In the context of the sentence *He made a lucid argument that anyone could follow,* you can figure out that *lucid* means "readily apparent, as if well lit" or "clear."

Practice Using context clues and the meaning of the word root, define each italicized word. Then, check your definition in a dictionary.

1. The *translucent* glass gave everything a smoky look.

2. Fireflies light up, but their *luminescence* is not related to body heat.

3. She is such a *luminary* that her birthday is a national holiday.

Grammar Lesson

Using Commas Correctly Commas are used to separate or join similar sentence elements and to show the relationship between ideas.

- Use commas to separate three or more words, phrases, or clauses in a series.

  SERIES: I read Ralph Waldo Emerson's **speeches, poems,** and **essays.**

- Use a comma and a coordinating conjunction (*and, but, or, nor, for, so,* and *yet*) to link two independent clauses in a compound sentence.

  COMPOUND SENTENCE: I liked the essays, **but** I disliked the poems.

- Use commas to set off introductory, parenthetical, and nonessential words, phrases, and clauses.

  INTRODUCTORY: **Actually,** we also read Henry David Thoreau.
  PARENTHETICAL: Thoreau, **who was against the Mexican War,** preached civil disobedience.
  APPOSITIVE: Gandhi, **the father of India's independence,** drew on Thoreau's ideas.

MorePractice

For more practice with commas, use the Grammar Handbook, p. R47.

Practice Rewrite the following sentences, correcting any errors with commas. If no corrections are necessary, write *correct.*

1. Emerson who lived in the nineteenth century is associated with romanticism an idealistic philosophical movement of the time.

2. The author, Nathaniel Hawthorne, is also considered a romantic.

3. Hawthorne's vision however is much less hopeful than Emerson's for he was less optimistic about people's ability to change.

Reading: Compare and Contrast Worldviews

Standards Assessed
- 10.2.4
- 10.3.1
- 10.3.11

Directions: *Read the selection. Then, answer the questions.*

"Black. Black Wordsworth. White Wordsworth was my brother. We share one heart. I can watch a small flower like the morning glory and cry."

. . . He pulled out a printed sheet from his hip-pocket and said, "On this paper is the greatest poem about mothers and I'm going to sell it to you at a bargain price. For four cents."

I went inside and I said, "Ma, you want buy a poetry for four cents?"

My mother said, "Tell that blasted man I haul his tail away from my yard, you hear."

I said to B. Wordsworth, "My mother say she ain't have four cents."

B. Wordsworth said, "It is the poet's tragedy."

—from "B. Wordsworth" by V. S. Naipal

1. What does the dialogue convey about the characters' background?
   A They are well-educated.
   B The characters know each other.
   C The characters live in a large city.
   D The characters are not poets.

2. Which statement best describes B. Wordsworth's worldview?
   A He hopes to be a famous poet.
   B He likes to wander around writing poetry.
   C He tries to cheat everyone.
   D He is a person who learns about nature.

3. Which statement best describes the mother's worldview?
   A She values logic.
   B She has a low opinion of wandering poets.
   C She fears contact with people unlike herself.
   D She wants to improve the world.

4. What is the narrator's attitude toward the exchange?
   A The narrator is fascinated by it.
   B The narrator is an observer.
   C The narrator pretends indifference.
   D The narrator is horrified by it.

Timed Writing: Analysis [Connections]

Review "Arthur Becomes King of Britain" or "Morte d'Arthur." Analyze the conflict that one of the characters faces between responsibility and personal desires. Use specific examples to support your analysis.
(25 minutes)

Writing Workshop: *Work in Progress*

Comparison-and-Contrast Essay

For a comparison-and-contrast essay you may write, choose two literary works. Freewrite about each piece separately for two to four minutes. Then, circle the ideas that are similar in your freewrites and underline the ideas that are different. Save these freewrites in your writing portfolio.

Practice these skills with either the selection from *A Connecticut Yankee in King Arthur's Court* (p. 1098) or the selection from *Don Quixote* (p. 1113).

Literary Analysis

A **parody** is a humorous work in which the author imitates the style or ideas of other works in an exaggerated or a ridiculous way. For example, the following passage parodies the style, conflict, characters, and themes typical of sports stories:

> John was tense as he flipped the final peanut into the air. Then, he exploded into action. In one flawless move, he snapped his head back, and the peanut dropped neatly into his mouth.

The drama of the passage is ridiculously exaggerated because of the silliness of the topic. As you read, consider which works the author of the parody imitates.

Reading Skill

A serious work of literature reflects the writer's **worldview,** or basic beliefs and values. In a parody of the work, another writer may portray this worldview as an illusion.

As you read, **compare and contrast** illusion and reality in the narrative as shown in the different characters' beliefs and actions. Use a chart like the one shown.

Academic Standards

- Examine how the author's perspective influences the structure and tone of the text. (10.2.4)
- Select effective verbal and nonverbal techniques for presentations. (10.7.6)
- Assess how language and delivery affect mood of the speech. (10.7.10)

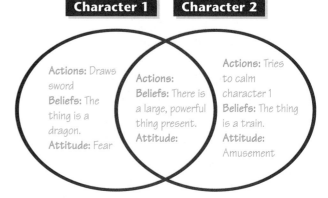

Character 1 **Character 2**

Actions: Draws sword
Beliefs: The thing is a dragon.
Attitude: Fear

Actions:
Beliefs: There is a large, powerful thing present.
Attitude:

Actions: Tries to calm character 1
Beliefs: The thing is a train.
Attitude: Amusement

Vocabulary Builder

from *A Connecticut Yankee . . .*

- **rudiments** (rōō′ də mənts) *n.* basics; slight beginning (p. 1102) *First graders learn only the rudiments of arithmetic.*
- **calamity** (kə lam′ ə tē) *n.* terrible misfortune; disaster (p. 1102) *The hurricane was a great calamity.*
- **multitudes** (mul′ tə tōōdz) *n.* crowds; large number of people or things (p. 1105) *Outside the stadium, multitudes swarmed.*

from *Don Quixote*

- **lucidity** (lōō sid′ ə tē) *n.* clarity; quality of being readily understood (p. 1114) *The students did well because of the lucidity of the teacher's explanations.*
- **sonorous** (sə nôr′ əs) *adj.* having a rich or impressive sound (p. 1117) *His sonorous voice echoed across the room.*
- **extolled** (ek stōl′d′) *adj.* praised (p. 1118) *The joys of country living are much extolled.*

Background

Yankees and Knights In literature, the days of the legendary King Arthur are typically depicted as a time of great deeds and noble characters. Mark Twain paints a different picture of Arthur's world. Hank Morgan, the hero of Twain's *A Connecticut Yankee in King Arthur's Court,* is a nineteenth-century "Yankee," or New Englander. Hank has all the shrewdness and can-do attitude often associated with New Englanders. His ingenuity is tested, though, in King Arthur's court.

Connecting to the Literature

Reading/Writing Connection Hank Morgan runs into trouble when he travels through time—unintentionally. List two reasons someone might want to travel in time and two difficulties the person might encounter. Use at least three of these words: *accommodate, withdraw, violate, react, perceive.*

READ MORE

by Mark Twain

The Adventures of Tom Sawyer

Meet the Author

Mark **Twain** (1835–1910)

Samuel Clemens, who later won fame as Mark Twain, grew up in the small Mississippi River port of Hannibal, Missouri. He left school early to learn the printing trade and later found work as a steamboat pilot. After the Civil War, he headed west, hunting for silver in Nevada and gold in California while writing accounts of his travels.

A Connecticut Writer In 1870, Twain married Olivia Langdon and began to raise a family. Settling in Hartford, Connecticut, he penned his popular boyhood tale *The Adventures of Tom Sawyer* and a string of other bestsellers.

Fast Facts

▶ In the year Twain was born, Halley's Comet appeared in Earth's skies; he died in the year of its next appearance.

▶ He took his pen name from a riverboat cry, "Mark twain!", meaning the water was deep enough for safe passage.

Go Online
Author Link

For: More about the author
Visit: www.PHSchool.com
Web Code: eqe-9610

from
A Connecticut Yankee in King Arthur's Court

Mark Twain

The practical Hank Morgan is manager of an arms factory in Connecticut in 1879. One day, in a fight with an employee named Hercules, he is knocked unconscious. Awakening in a strange place, he finds himself the prisoner of a knight in armor, Sir Kay. On their way to King Arthur's court, Hank meets Clarence, a friendly young page. Hank is unsure of where he is, and he is astonished when Clarence tells him that it is June 19 in the year 528. Hank knows that a solar eclipse occurred at noon on June 21 in the year 528 but that no eclipse is predicted for his own year. If an eclipse occurs, he reasons, it will confirm that he has traveled in time. In the meantime, he is taken to a dungeon to await execution.

CHAPTER V—An Inspiration

I was so tired that even my fears were not able to keep me awake long.

When I next came to myself, I seemed to have been asleep a very long time. My first thought was, "Well, what an astonishing dream I've had! I reckon I've waked only just in time to keep from being hanged or drowned or burned or something. . . . I'll nap again till the whistle blows, and then I'll go down to the arms factory and have it out with Hercules."

But just then I heard the harsh music of rusty chains and bolts, a light flashed in my eyes, and that butterfly,[1] Clarence, stood before me! I gasped with surprise; my breath almost got away from me.

"What!" I said, "you here yet? Go along with the rest of the dream! scatter!"

But he only laughed, in his light-hearted way, and fell to making fun of my sorry plight.

"All right," I said resignedly, "let the dream go on; I'm in no hurry."

"Prithee[2] what dream?"

"What dream? Why, the dream that I am in Arthur's court—a person who never existed; and that I am talking to you, who are nothing but a work of the imagination."

"Oh, la, indeed! and is it a dream that you're to be burned to-morrow? Ho-Ho—answer me that!"

The shock that went through me was distressing. I now began to reason that my situation was in the last degree serious, dream or no

**Reading Skill
Comparing
Worldviews** What illusion does Hank think he has? What illusion does Clarence think Hank has?

✓**Reading Check**

What danger is Hank facing?

---

1. butterfly *n.* sociable, lighthearted person.
2. Prithee (pri*th′* ē) *interjection* old term for "please."

◀ **Critical Viewing** Based on this illustration, predict whether this selection will be serious or humorous. Explain your reasoning. **[Predict]**

dream; for I knew by past experience of the lifelike intensity of dreams, that to be burned to death, even in a dream, would be very far from being a jest, and was a thing to be avoided, by any means, fair or foul, that I could contrive. So I said beseechingly:

"Ah, Clarence, good boy, only friend I've got—for you *are* my friend, aren't you?—don't fail me; help me to devise some way of escaping from this place!"

"Now do but hear thyself! Escape? Why, man, the corridors are in guard and keep of men-at-arms."

"No doubt, no doubt. But how many, Clarence? Not many, I hope?"

"Full a score.[3] One may not hope to escape." After a pause—hesitatingly: "and there be other reasons—and weightier."

"Other ones? What are they?"

"Well, they say—oh, but I daren't, indeed and indeed, I daren't!"

"Why, poor lad, what is the matter? Why do you blench? Why do you tremble so?"

"Oh, in sooth, there is need! I do want to tell you, but—"

"Come, come, be brave, be a man—speak out, there's a good lad!"

He hesitated, pulled one way by desire, the other way by fear; then he stole to the door and peeped out, listening; and finally crept close to me and put his mouth to my ear and told me his fearful

_____

3. **a score** twenty.

▼ **Critical Viewing**
What contrasting worldviews does this film still suggest? Explain. **[Interpret]**

news in a whisper, and with all the cowering apprehension of one who was venturing upon awful ground and speaking of things whose very mention might be freighted with death.

"Merlin, in his malice, has woven a spell about this dungeon, and there bides not the man in these kingdoms that would be desperate enough to essay to cross its lines with you! Now God pity me, I have told it! Ah, be kind to me, be merciful to a poor boy who means thee well; for an thou betray me I am lost!"

I laughed the only really refreshing laugh I had had for some time; and shouted:

"Merlin has wrought a spell! *Merlin*, forsooth! That cheap old humbug,[4] that maundering old ass? Bosh, pure bosh, the silliest bosh in the world! Why, it does seem to me that of all the childish, idiotic, chuckleheaded, chicken-livered superstitions that ev—oh, [curse] Merlin!"

But Clarence had slumped to his knees before I had half finished, and he was like to go out of his mind with fright.

"Oh, beware! These are awful words! Any moment these walls may crumble upon us if you say such things. Oh, call them back before it is too late!"

Now this strange exhibition gave me a good idea and set me to thinking. If everybody about here was so honestly and sincerely afraid of Merlin's pretended magic as Clarence was, certainly a superior man like me ought to be shrewd enough to contrive some way to take advantage of such a state of things. I went on thinking, and worked out a plan. Then I said:

"Get up. Pull yourself together; look me in the eye. Do you know why I laughed?"

"No—but for our blessed Lady's sake, do it no more."

"Well, I'll tell you why I laughed. Because I'm a magician myself."

"Thou!" The boy recoiled a step, and caught his breath, for the thing hit him rather sudden; but the aspect which he took on was very, very respectful. I took quick note of that; it indicated that a humbug didn't need to have a reputation in this asylum; people stood ready to take him at his word, without that. I resumed.

"I've known Merlin seven hundred years, and he—"

"Seven hun—"

"Don't interrupt me. He has died and come alive again thirteen times, and traveled under a new name every time: Smith, Jones, Robinson, Jackson, Peters, Haskins, Merlin—a new alias every time he turns up. I knew him in Egypt three hundred years ago; I knew him in India five hundred years ago—he is always blethering

4. **humbug** *n.* con artist; impostor; one who misrepresents himself or herself in order to take advantage of others.

Literary Analysis
Parody Which phrases in Clarence's speech imitate the style of tales of knights?

Reading Skill
Comparing Worldviews What does Hank reveal about his values here?

Reading Skill
Comparing Worldviews How does Hank take advantage of Clarence's beliefs about the world?

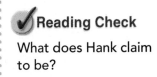**Reading Check**

What does Hank claim to be?

around in my way, everywhere I go; he makes me tired. He don't amount to shucks, as a magician; knows some of the old common tricks, but has never got beyond the <u>rudiments</u>, and never will. He is well enough for the provinces[5]—one-night stands and that sort of thing, you know—but dear me, *he* oughtn't to set up for an expert—anyway not where there's a real artist. Now look here, Clarence, I am going to stand your friend, right along, and in return you must be mine. I want you to do me a favor. I want you to get word to the king that I am a magician myself—and the Supreme Grand High-yu-Muckamuck and head of the tribe, at that; and I want him to be made to understand that I am just quietly arranging a little <u>calamity</u> here that will make the fur fly in these realms if Sir Kay's project is carried out and any harm comes to me. Will you get that to the king for me?"

The poor boy was in such a state that he could hardly answer me. It was pitiful to see a creature so terrified, so unnerved, so demoralized. But he promised everything; and on my side he made me promise over and over again that I would remain his friend, and never turn against him or cast any enchantments upon him. Then he worked his way out, staying himself with his hand along the wall, like a sick person.

Presently this thought occurred to me: how heedless I have been! When the boy gets calm, he will wonder why a great magician like me should have begged a boy like him to help me get out of this place; he will put this and that together, and will see that I am a humbug.

I worried over that heedless blunder for an hour, and called myself a great many hard names, meantime. But finally it occurred to me all of a sudden that these animals didn't reason; that *they* never put this and that together; that all their talk showed that they didn't know a discrepancy when they saw it. I was at rest, then.

But as soon as one is at rest, in this world, off he goes on something else to worry about. It occured to me that I had made another blunder: I had sent the boy off to alarm his betters with a threat—I intending to invent a calamity at my leisure; now the people who are the readiest and eagerest and willingest to swallow miracles are the very ones who are hungriest to see you perform them; suppose I should be called on for a sample? Suppose I should be asked to name my calamity? Yes, I had made a blunder; I ought to have invented my calamity first. "What shall I do? what can I say, to gain a little time?" I was in trouble again; in the deepest kind of trouble: . . . "There's a footstep!—they're coming. If I had only just a moment to think. . . . Good, I've got it. I'm all right."

Vocabulary Builder
rudiments (roō′ də ments) *n.* basics; slight beginning

calamity (kə lam′ ə tē) *n.* terrible misfortune; disaster

Literary Analysis
Parody Which phrases in Hank's speech are humorously out of step with traditional ideas of a mighty sorcerer?

Reading Skill
Comparing Worldviews What do Hank's thoughts here show about his worldview? What do they suggest about the worldview of Clarence and others of his time?

---

5. for the provinces (präv′ ins iz) for unsophisticated audiences in places far from a big city.

You see, it was the eclipse. It came into my mind, in the nick of time, how Columbus, or Cortez, or one of those people, played an eclipse as a saving trump once, on some savages, and I saw my chance. I could play it myself, now; and it wouldn't be any plagiarism, either, because I should get it in nearly a thousand years ahead of those parties.

Clarence came in, subdued, distressed, and said:

"I hasted the message to our liege the king, and straightway he had me to his presence. He was frighted even to the marrow, and was minded to give order for your instant enlargement,[6] and that you be clothed in fine raiment and lodged as befitted one so great; but then came Merlin and spoiled all; for he persuaded the king that you are mad, and know not whereof you speak; and said your threat is but foolishness and idle vaporing. They disputed long, but in the end, Merlin, scoffing, said, 'Wherefore hath he not *named* his brave calamity? Verily it is because he cannot.' This thrust did in a most sudden sort close the king's mouth, and he could offer naught to turn the argument; and so, reluctant, and full loth to do you the discourtesy, he yet prayeth you to consider his perplexed case, as noting how the matter stands, and name the calamity—if so be you have determined the nature of it and the time of its coming. Oh, prithee delay not; to delay at such a time were to double and treble the perils that already compass thee about. Oh, be thou wise—name the calamity!"

I allowed silence to accumulate while I got my impressiveness together, and then said:

"How long have I been shut up in this hole?"

"Ye were shut up when yesterday was well spent. It is nine of the morning now."

"No! Then I have slept well, sure enough. Nine in the morning now! And yet it is the very complexion of midnight, to a shade. This is the 20th, then?"

"The 20th—yes."

"And I am to be burned alive to-morrow." The boy shuddered.

"At what hour?"

"At high noon."

"Now then, I will tell you what to say." I paused, and stood over that cowering lad a whole minute in awful silence; then, in a voice deep, measured, charged with doom, I began, and rose by dramatically graded stages to my colossal climax, which I delivered in as sublime and noble a way as ever I did such a thing in my life: "Go back and tell the king that at that hour I will smother the whole world in the dead blackness of midnight; I will blot out the sun, and

Literary Analysis
Parody Given the nature of the argument Clarence describes, why does the formality of his language seem exaggerated?

Reading Check

How do the King and Merlin respond to Hank's threat of a "calamity"?

---

6. **enlargement** *n.* old term for "release."

he shall never shine again; the fruits of the earth shall rot for lack of light and warmth, and the peoples of the earth shall famish and die, to the last man!"

I had to carry the boy out myself, he sunk into such a collapse. I handed him over to the soldiers, and went back.

Literary Analysis
Parody What circumstances in the story make Hank's imitation of a magician's speech comical?

CHAPTER VI—The Eclipse

In the stillness and the darkness, realization soon began to supplement knowledge. The mere knowledge of a fact is pale; but when you come to *realize* your fact, it takes on color. It is all the difference between hearing of a man being stabbed to the heart, and seeing it done. In the stillness and the darkness, the knowledge that I was in deadly danger took to itself deeper and deeper meaning all the time; a something which was realization crept inch by inch through my veins and turned me cold.

But it is a blessed provision of nature that at times like these, as soon as a man's mercury[7] has got down to a certain point there comes a revulsion, and he rallies. Hope springs up, and cheerfulness along with it, and then he is in good shape to do something for himself, if anything can be done. When my rally came, it came with a bound. I said to myself that my eclipse would be sure to save me, and make me the greatest man in the kingdom besides; and straightway my mercury went up to the top of the tube, and my solicitudes all vanished. I was as happy a man as there was in the world. I was even impatient for tomorrow to come, I so wanted to gather in that great triumph and be the center of all of the nation's wonder and reverence. Besides, in a business way it would be the making of me; I knew that.

Reading Skill
Comparing Worldviews What does Hank indicate about his values in the last sentence of this paragraph?

Meantime there was one thing which had got pushed into the background of my mind. That was the half-conviction that when the nature of my proposed calamity should be reported to those superstitious people, it would have such an effect that they would want to compromise. So, by and by when I heard footsteps coming, that thought was recalled to me, and I said to myself, "As sure as anything, it's the compromise. Well, if it is good, all right, I will accept; but if it isn't, I mean to stand my ground and play my hand for all it is worth."

The door opened, and some men-at-arms appeared. The leader said:

"The stake is ready. Come!"

---

7. mercury referring to the liquid metal used in a thermometer; the mercury rises and falls in the thermometer with the temperature.

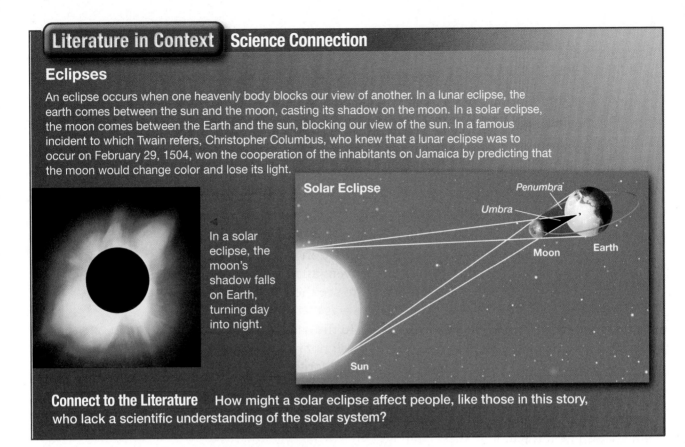

An eclipse occurs when one heavenly body blocks our view of another. In a lunar eclipse, the earth comes between the sun and the moon, casting its shadow on the moon. In a solar eclipse, the moon comes between the Earth and the sun, blocking our view of the sun. In a famous incident to which Twain refers, Christopher Columbus, who knew that a lunar eclipse was to occur on February 29, 1504, won the cooperation of the inhabitants on Jamaica by predicting that the moon would change color and lose its light.

Solar Eclipse

Penumbra

Umbra

Moon

Earth

Sun

In a solar eclipse, the moon's shadow falls on Earth, turning day into night.

Connect to the Literature   How might a solar eclipse affect people, like those in this story, who lack a scientific understanding of the solar system?

The stake! The strength went out of me, and I almost fell down. It is hard to get one's breath at such a time, such lumps come into one's throat, and such gaspings; but as soon as I could speak, I said:

"But this is a mistake—the execution is tomorrow."

"Order changed; been set forward a day. Haste thee!"

I was lost. There was no help for me. I was dazed, stupefied; I had no command over myself; I only wandered purposelessly about, like one out of his mind; so the soldiers took hold of me, and pulled me along with them, out of the cell and along the maze of underground corridors, and finally into the fierce glare of daylight and the upper world. As we stepped into the vast inclosed court of the castle I got a shock; for the first thing I saw was the stake, standing in the center, and near it the piled fagots[8] and a monk. On all four sides of the court the seated <u>multitudes</u> rose rank above rank, forming sloping terraces that were rich with color. The king and the queen sat in their thrones, the most conspicuous figures there, of course.

To note all this, occupied but a second. The next second Clarence had slipped from some place of concealment and was

Reading Skill
Comparing Worldviews What reasoning does Hank follow to determine that he will not succeed in creating his illusion?

Vocabulary Builder
multitudes (mul´ tə tōōdz´) *n.* crowds; large number of people or things

✔**Reading Check**
What new problem upsets Hank's plans?

---

8. fagots (fag´ əts) *n.* bundles of sticks used as fuel.

pouring news into my ear, his eyes beaming with triumph and gladness. He said:

"'Tis through *me* the change was wrought! And main hard have I worked to do it, too. But when I revealed to them the calamity in store, and saw how mighty was the terror it did engender, then saw I also that this was the time to strike! Wherefore I diligently pretended, unto this and that and the other one, that your power against the sun could not reach its full until the morrow; and so if any would save the sun and the world, you must be slain today, while your enchantments are but in the weaving and lack potency. Odsbodikins, it was but a dull lie, a most indifferent invention, but you should have seen them seize it and swallow it, in the frenzy of their fright, as it were salvation sent from heaven; and all the while was I laughing in my sleeve the one moment, to see them so cheaply deceived, and glorifying God the next, that He was content to let the meanest[9] of His creatures be His instrument to the saving of thy life. Ah, how happy has the matter sped! You will not need to do the sun a *real* hurt—ah, forget not that, on your soul forget it not! Only make a little darkness—only the littlest little darkness, mind, and cease with that. It will be sufficient. They will see that I spoke

Literary Analysis
Parody In what way is Clarence's scheming a parody of Hank's?

▼ **Critical Viewing**
How might Hank escape the predicament shown? **[Speculate]**

falsely—being ignorant, as they will fancy—and with the falling of the first shadow of that darkness you shall see them go mad with fear; and they will set you free and make you great! Go to thy triumph, now! But remember—ah, good friend, I implore thee remember my supplication, and do the blessed sun no hurt. For *my* sake, thy true friend."

I choked out some words through my grief and misery; as much as to say I would spare the sun; for which the lad's eyes paid me back with such deep and loving gratitude that I had not the heart to tell him his good-hearted foolishness had ruined me and sent me to my death.

As the soldiers assisted me across the court the stillness was so profound that if I had been blindfold I should have supposed I was in a solitude instead of walled in by four

---

9. meanest *adj.* lowest; least significant.

thousand people. There was not a movement perceptible in those masses of humanity; they were as rigid as stone images, and as pale; and dread sat upon every countenance. This hush continued while I was being chained to the stake; it still continued while the fagots were carefully and tediously piled about my ankles, my knees, my thighs, my body. Then there was a pause, and a deeper hush, if possible, and a man knelt down at my feet with a blazing torch; the multitude strained forward, gazing, and parting slightly from their seats without knowing it; the monk raised his hands above my head, and his eyes toward the blue sky, and began some words in Latin; in this attitude he droned on and on, a little while, and then stopped. I waited two or three moments; then looked up; he was standing there petrified. With a common impulse the multitude rose slowly up and stared into the sky. I followed their eyes; as sure as guns, there was my eclipse beginning! The life went boiling through my veins; I was a new man! The rim of black spread slowly into the sun's disk, my heart beat higher and higher, and still the assemblage and the priest stared into the sky, motionless. I knew that this gaze would be turned upon me, next. When it was, I was ready. I was in one of the most grand attitudes I ever struck, with my arm stretched up pointing to the sun. It was a noble effect. You could *see* the shudder sweep the mass like a wave. Two shouts rang out, one close upon the heels of the other:

"Apply the torch!"

"I forbid it!"

The one was from Merlin, the other from the king. Merlin started from his place—to apply the torch himself, I judged. I said:

"Stay where you are. If any man moves—even the king—before I give him leave, I will blast him with thunder, I will consume him with lightnings!"

The multitude sank meekly into their seats, and I was just expecting they would. Merlin hesitated a moment or two, and I was on pins and needles that little while. Then he sat down, and I took a good breath; for I knew I was master of the situation now. The king said:

"Be merciful, fair sir, and essay no further in this perilous matter, lest disaster follow. It was reported to us that your powers could not attain unto their full strength until the morrow; but—"

"Your Majesty thinks the report may have been a lie? It *was* a lie."

That made an immense effect; up went appealing hands everywhere, and the king was assailed with a storm of supplications that I might be bought off at any price, and the calamity stayed.

The king was eager to comply. He said:

Reading Skill
Comparing Worldviews What are the differing ways in which Hank and the crowd interpret the eclipse?

Reading Check

What surprising event occurs just before Hank is about to be executed?

from *A Connecticut Yankee in King Arthur's Court* ■ 1107

"Name any terms, reverend sir, even to the halving of my kingdom; but banish this calamity, spare the sun!"

My fortune was made, I would have taken him up in a minute, but I couldn't stop an eclipse; the thing was out of the question. So I asked time to consider. The king said:

"How long—ah, how long, good sir? Be merciful; look, it groweth darker, moment by moment. Prithee how long?"

"Not long. Half an hour—maybe an hour."

▲ **Critical Viewing**
What qualities of Hank Morgan are conveyed by this actor's expression and pose? **[Analyze]**

There were a thousand pathetic protests, but I couldn't shorten up any, for I couldn't remember how long a total eclipse lasts. I was in a puzzled condition, anyway, and wanted to think. Something was wrong about that eclipse, and the fact was very unsettling. If this wasn't the one I was after, how was I to tell whether this was the sixth century, or nothing but a dream? Dear me, if I could only prove it was the latter! Here was a glad new hope. If the boy was right about the date, and this was surely the 20th, it *wasn't* the sixth century. I reached for the monk's sleeve, in considerable excitement, and asked him what day of the month it was.

Hang him, he said it was the *twenty-first*! It made me turn cold to hear him. I begged him not to make any mistake about it; but he was sure; he knew it was the 21st. So, that feather-headed boy had botched things again! The time of the day was right for the eclipse; I had seen that for myself, in the beginning, by the dial[10] that was near by. Yes, I *was* in King Arthur's court, and I might as well make the most of it I could.

The darkness was steadily growing, the people becoming more and more distressed. I now said:

"I have reflected, Sir King. For a lesson, I will let this darkness proceed, and spread night in the world; but whether I blot out the sun for good, or restore it shall rest with you. These are the terms, to wit: You shall remain king over all your dominions, and receive all the glories and honors that belong to the kingship; but you shall appoint me your perpetual minister and executive, and give me for my services one per cent. of such actual increase of revenue[11] over

Reading Skill
Comparing Worldviews How does Hank resolve the question of whether he is suffering from an illusion of his own?

Literary Analysis
Parody What two types of language does Hank mix together in this speech? Explain.

---

10. dial *n.* sundial, or device used to measure time by the position of the sun in the sky.

11. revenue (rev´ ə nōō´) *n.* money taken in by a government in the form of taxes, fees, and penalties.

and above its present amount as I may succeed in creating for the state. If I can't live on that, I sha'n't ask anybody to give me a lift. Is it satisfactory?"

There was a prodigious roar of applause, and out of the midst of it the king's voice rose, saying:

"Away with his bonds, and set him free! and do him homage, high and low, rich and poor, for he is become the king's right hand, is clothed with power and authority, and his seat is upon the highest step of the throne! Now sweep away this creeping night, and bring the light and cheer again, that all the world may bless thee."

But I said:

"That a common man should be shamed before the world, is nothing; but it were dishonor to the *king* if any that saw his minister naked should not also see him delivered from his shame. If I might ask that my clothes be brought again—"

"They are not meet," the king broke in. "Fetch raiment of another sort; clothe him like a prince!"

My idea worked. I wanted to keep things as they were till the eclipse was total, otherwise they would be trying again to get me to dismiss the darkness, and of course I couldn't do it. Sending for the clothes gained some delay, but not enough. So I had to make another excuse. I said it would be but natural if the king should change his mind and repent to some extent of what he had done under excitement; therefore I would let the darkness grow awhile, and if at the end of a reasonable time the king had kept his mind the same, the darkness should be dismissed. Neither the king nor anybody else was satisfied with that arrangement, but I had to stick to my point.

It grew darker and darker and blacker and blacker, while I struggled with those awkward sixth-century clothes. It got to be pitch-dark, at last, and the multitude groaned with horror to feel the cold uncanny night breezes fan through the place and see the stars come out and twinkle in the sky. At last the eclipse was total, and I was very glad of it, but everybody else was in misery; which was quite natural. I said:

"The king, by his silence, still stands to the terms." Then I lifted up my hand—stood just so a moment—then I said, with the most awful solemnity: "Let the enchantment dissolve and pass harmless away!"

There was no response, for a moment, in that deep darkness and that graveyard hush. But when the silver rim of the sun pushed itself out, a moment or two later, the assemblage broke loose with a vast shout and came pouring down like a deluge to smother me with blessings and gratitude.

And Clarence was not the last of the wash, to be sure.

Literary Analysis
Parody Which elements of the situation make the king's solemn words into a parody?

Reading Skill
Comparing Worldviews How do two different ideas of events lead both Hank and the crowd to feel relieved?

Apply the Skills

from *A Connecticut Yankee in King Arthur's Court*

Thinking About the Selection

1. **Respond:** Do you sympathize with Clarence? Why or why not?
2. **(a) Recall:** What threat does Hank face? **(b) Infer:** Why does he think he may be dreaming?
3. **(a) Recall:** What does Clarence say Merlin has woven? **(b) Analyze:** What story about himself does this information prompt Hank to tell?
4. **(a) Interpret:** What does the deal Hank strikes with King Arthur show about his character? **(b) Make a Judgment:** Is Hank's manipulation of Clarence and the king justified? Why or why not?
5. **(a) Speculate:** List two triumphs and two problems Hank might experience as a minister at Arthur's court. **(b) Discuss:** Discuss your ideas with a partner. **(c) Evaluate:** Together, choose your two best ideas and present them to the class.

Literary Analysis

6. **(a)** Identify the main personality traits of Clarence, Merlin, and King Arthur. **(b)** Of these traits, which would the characters in the original King Arthur legends probably not display? Explain. **(c)** In what way is Twain's tale a **parody** of the Arthur legends?
7. **(a)** Using a chart like the one shown, give examples that show specific ways in which Hank is a **parody** of a heroic figure.

Arthurian Hero	Hank Morgan
1. wins with great strength or supernatural power	1.
2. desires glory	2.
3. serves his king out of loyalty	3.
4. other	4.

(b) In what ways does Hank show the genuinely heroic nature of American common sense? Explain.

Reading Skill

8. **(a) Compare and contrast** two of Hank's and Clarence's reactions to danger. **(b)** What does the contrast suggest about common illusions in Arthur's day?

QuickReview

Story at a Glance
Nineteenth-century Yankee Hank Morgan travels in time to the days of the legendary King Arthur.

Go Online
Assessment
For: Self-test
Visit: www.PHSchool.com
Web Code: eqa-6609

Parody: a humorous work in which the author imitates another work or literary form in an exaggerated or a ridiculous way

Comparing and Contrasting: examining two or more things to determine their similarities and differences

Vocabulary Builder

Practice Replace the underlined word in each sentence with its **antonym,** or word of opposite meaning, from the vocabulary list for *A Connecticut Yankee in King Arthur's Court,* on page 1096. Then, explain which version of the sentence makes better sense.

1. To master the <u>subtleties</u> of the saxophone, take advanced lessons.
2. The entire nation mourned his <u>success</u>.
3. The band was successful, so <u>handfuls</u> of people lined up for the show.

Adding Words to Your Vocabulary Using a dictionary, explain the connection between the words *rude* and *rudiments*. Then, use each word correctly in a sentence. (For more on using a dictionary, see page R6.)

Writing

Write a **parody** in which a twenty-first century time traveler lands in King Arthur's world.
- Outline the events of your story.
- As you draft, clearly depict both the reality of what is happening and the illusions in characters' minds.

For *Grammar, Vocabulary,* and *Assessment,* see **Build Language Skills,** pages 1124–1125.

Extend Your Learning

Listening and Speaking Working with a partner, defend one of the following ideas. Have your partner defend the other:
- *The present is better than the past because we know more now.*
- *The past was better because people then had stronger values.*

Each of you should give a five-minute **oral presentation** to the class on your position, using examples from Twain's work. Have your classmates summarize the opinions you offer and provide constructive comments comparing the effectiveness of your presentations.

Research and Technology Working with a group, conduct research for a **biographical brochure** on Mark Twain. Devise several research questions to guide your work. Then, use biographical dictionaries, the Internet, and other sources to find answers.

Build Understanding • from *Don Quixote*

Background

The Age of Chivalry The days of knights were long gone when Miguel de Cervantes wrote *Don Quixote,* his parody of medieval romance—tales of knightly adventure. In these stories, knights live by the code of chivalry, rules for conduct that stress courage and courtesy.

Connecting to the Literature

Reading/Writing Connection The title character in *Don Quixote* thinks he is a character in a tale of knightly adventure. Write a brief description of a fictional character whose life you might like to lead. Use at least three of these words: *achieve, appreciate, commit, dedicate, enhance.*

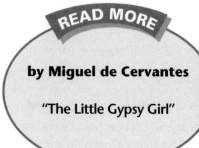

READ MORE

by Miguel de Cervantes

"The Little Gypsy Girl"

Meet the Author

Miguel de Cervantes (1547–1616)

Born near Madrid, Spain, Miguel de Cervantes (mē gel´ də sər vän´ tēz) joined the army as a young man. Returning to Spain from a war, he was captured by pirates, who enslaved him for five years. Even after returning home, Cervantes's troubles were not over: Financial problems eventually led to fines and imprisonment.

A Change of Fortune Cervantes's luck changed when he published his novel *Don Quixote* (dän´ kē hōt´ ē). Although the book did not make him rich, it did ease his debts and win him fame. Cervantes is widely regarded as Spain's greatest writer.

Fast Facts

▶ Published in two parts in 1605 and 1615, *Don Quixote* helped establish the novel as a respected literary form.
▶ Tradition has it that Cervantes wrote at least part of *Don Quixote* while he was in prison.

Go Online
Author Link

For: More information about the author
Visit: www.PHSchool.com
Web Code: eqe-9611

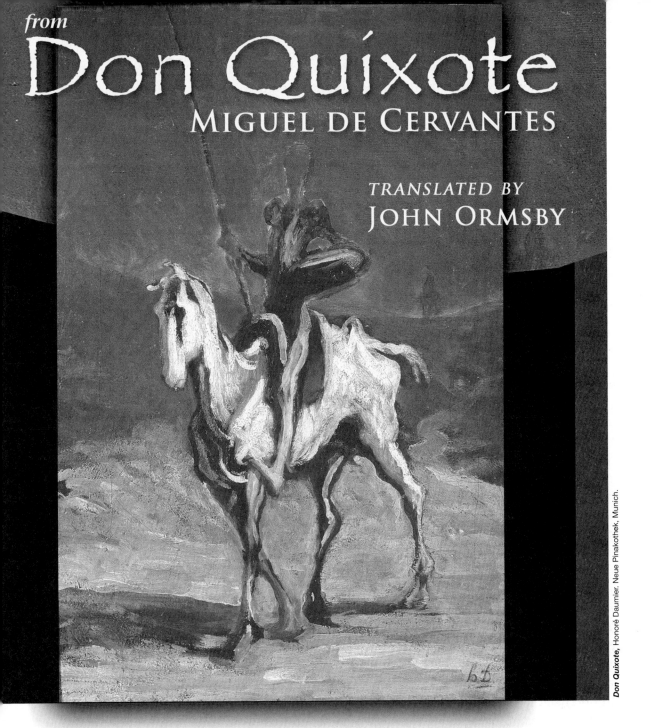

from

Don Quixote
MIGUEL DE CERVANTES

TRANSLATED BY
JOHN ORMSBY

Don Quixote, Honoré Daumier. Neue Pinakothek, Munich.

CHAPTER I
Which Treats of the Character and Pursuits of the Famous Gentleman Don Quixote[1] of La Mancha[2]

In a village of La Mancha, which I prefer to leave unnamed, there lived not long ago one of those gentlemen that keep a lance in the

---

1. **Don Quixote** (dän´ kē hōt´ ē).
2. **La Mancha** province (region) in south-central Spain.

lance-rack, an old shield, a lean hack, and a greyhound for hunting. A stew of rather more beef than mutton, hash on most nights, bacon and eggs on Saturdays, lentils on Fridays, and a pigeon or so extra on Sundays consumed three quarters of his income. The rest went for a coat of fine cloth and velvet breeches and shoes to match for holidays, while on weekdays he cut a fine figure in his best homespun. He had in his house a housekeeper past forty, a niece under twenty, and a lad for the field and marketplace, who saddled the hack as well as handled the pruning knife. The age of this gentleman of ours was bordering on fifty. He was of a hardy constitution, spare, gaunt-featured, a very early riser, and fond of hunting. Some say that his surname was Quixada or Quesada (for there is no unanimity among those who write on the subject), although reasonable conjectures tend to show that he was called Quexana. But this scarcely affects our story; it will be enough not to stray a hair's breadth from the truth in telling it.

You must know that the above-named gentleman devoted his leisure (which was mostly all the year round) to reading books of chivalry—and with such ardor and avidity that he almost entirely abandoned the chase and even the management of his property. To such a pitch did his eagerness and infatuation go that he sold many an acre of tillage land to buy books of chivalry to read, bringing home all he could find.

But there were none he liked so well as those written by the famous Feliciano de Silva, for their <u>lucidity</u> of style and complicated conceits[3] were as pearls in his sight, particularly when in his reading he came upon outpourings of adulation[4] and courtly challenges. There he often found passages like *"the reason of the unreason with which my reason is afflicted so weakens my reason that with reason I complain of your beauty"*; or again, *"the high heavens, that of your divinity divinely fortify you with the stars, render you deserving of the desert your greatness deserves."*

Over this sort of folderol[5] the poor gentleman lost his wits, and he used to lie awake striving to understand it and worm out its meaning; though Aristotle[6] himself could have made out or extracted nothing, had he come back to life for that special purpose. He was rather uneasy about the wounds which Don Belianís gave and received, because it seemed to him that, however skilled the

---

3. conceits (kən sēts´) *n.* elaborate comparisons or metaphors.
4. adulation (a´ joo lā´ shən) *n.* intense or excessive praise or admiration.
5. folderol (fäl´ də räl´) *n.* mere nonsense.
6. Aristotle (ar´ is tät´´l) ancient Greek thinker and scientist.

Literary Analysis
Parody Which details in this paragraph make the formal-sounding chapter title on page 1113 seem ridiculous?

Vocabulary Builder
lucidity (loo sid´ ə tē) *n.* clarity; quality of being readily understood

Literary Analysis
Parody What qualities of the language of heroic tales are mocked in the quotations in this paragraph?

surgeons who had cured him, he must have had his face and body covered all over with seams and scars. He commended, however, the author's way of ending his book, with a promise to go on with that interminable adventure, and many a time he felt the urge to take up his pen and finish it just as its author had promised. He would no doubt have done so, and succeeded with it too, had he not been occupied with greater and more absorbing thoughts.

Many an argument did he have with the priest of his village (a learned man, and a graduate of Sigüenza[7]) as to which had been the better knight, Palmerín of England or Amadís of Gaul. Master Nicolás, the village barber, however, used to say that neither of them came up to the Knight of Phœbus, and that if there was any that could compare with *him* it was Don Galaor, the brother of Amadís of Gaul, because he had a spirit equal to every occasion, and was no wishy-washy knight or a crybaby like his brother, while in valor he was not a whit behind him.

In short, he became so absorbed in his books that he spent his nights from sunset to sunrise, and his days from dawn to dark, poring over them; and what with little sleep and much reading his brain shriveled up and he lost his wits. His imagination was stuffed with all he read in his books about enchantments, quarrels, battles, challenges, wounds, wooings, loves, agonies, and all sorts of impossible nonsense. It became so firmly planted in his mind that the whole fabric of invention and fancy he read about was true, that to him no history in the world was better substantiated. He used to say the Cid Ruy Díaz[8] was a very good knight but that he was not to be compared with the Knight of the Burning Sword who with one backstroke cut in half two fierce and monstrous giants. He thought more of Bernardo del Carpio because at Roncesvalles he slew Roland in spite of enchantments, availing himself of Hercules' trick when he strangled Antæus the son of Terra in his arms. He approved highly of the giant Morgante, because, although of the giant breed which is always arrogant and ill-mannered, he alone was affable and well-bred. But above all he admired Reinaldos of Montalbán, especially when he saw him sallying forth from his castle and robbing everyone he met, and when beyond the seas he stole that image of Mohammed which, as his history says, was

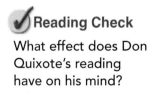

▲ Critical Viewing
What feelings or ideas might Don Quixote associate with images such as the ones on these pages? Explain. **[Connect]**

Reading Skill
Comparing Worldviews Why might Don Quixote's illusion be so appealing to him?

✓ Reading Check
What effect does Don Quixote's reading have on his mind?

---

7. **Sigüenza** (sē gwän´ sä) one of a group of "minor universities" granting degrees that were often laughed at by Spanish humorists.
8. **Cid Ruy Díaz** (sēd roo´ ē dē´ äs) famous Spanish soldier Ruy Díaz de Vivar; called "the Cid," a derivation of the Arabic word for "lord."

entirely of gold. To have a bout of kicking at that traitor of a Ganelon he would have given his housekeeper, and his niece into the bargain.

In a word, his wits being quite gone, he hit upon the strangest notion that ever madman in this world hit upon. He fancied it was right and requisite, no less for his own greater renown than in the service of his country, that he should make a knight-errant of himself, roaming the world over in full armor and on horseback in quest of adventures. He would put into practice all that he had read of as being the usual practices of knights-errant: righting every kind of wrong, and exposing himself to peril and danger from which he would emerge to reap eternal fame and glory. Already the poor man saw himself crowned by the might of his arm Emperor of Trebizond[9] at least. And so, carried away by the intense enjoyment he found in these pleasant fancies, he began at once to put his scheme into execution.

The first thing he did was to clean up some armor that had belonged to his ancestors and had for ages been lying forgotten in a corner, covered with rust and mildew. He scoured and polished it as best he could, but the one great defect he saw in it was that it had no closed helmet, nothing but a simple morion.[10] This deficiency, however, his ingenuity made good, for he contrived a kind of half-helmet of pasteboard which, fitted on to the morion, looked like a whole one. It is true that, in order to see if it was strong and fit to

▲ **Critical Viewing**
In this illustration, which elements convey Don Quixote's condition? **[Analyze]**

---

9. Trebizond (treb´ i zänd´) in medieval times, a Greek empire off the southeast coast of the Black Sea.

10. morion (mōr´ ē än´) *n.* old-fashioned soldier's helmet with a brim, covering the top part of the head.

withstand a cut, he drew his sword and gave it a couple of slashes, the first of which undid in an instant what had taken him a week to do. The ease with which he had knocked it to pieces disconcerted him somewhat, and to guard against the danger he set to work again, fixing bars of iron on the inside until he was satisfied with its strength. Then, not caring to try any more experiments with it, he accepted and commissioned it as a helmet of the most perfect construction.

He next proceeded to inspect his nag, which, with its cracked hoofs and more blemishes than the steed of Gonela, that "*tantum pellis et ossa fuit*,"[11] surpassed in his eyes the Bucephalus of Alexander or the Babieca of the Cid.[12] Four days were spent in thinking what name to give him, because (as he said to himself) it was not right that a horse belonging to a knight so famous, and one with such merits of its own, should be without some distinctive name. He strove to find something that would indicate what it had been before belonging to a knight-errant, and what it had now become. It was only reasonable that it should be given a new name to match the new career adopted by its master, and that the name should be a distinguished and full-sounding one, befitting the new order and calling it was about to follow. And so, after having composed, struck out, rejected, added to, unmade, and remade a multitude of names out of his memory and fancy, he decided upon calling it Rocinante. To his thinking this was a lofty, <u>sonorous</u> name that nevertheless indicated what the hack's[13] status had been before it became what now it was, the first and foremost of all the hacks in the world.

Having got a name for his horse so much to his taste, he was anxious to get one for himself, and he spent eight days more pondering over this point. At last he made up his mind to call himself Don Quixote—which, as stated above, led the authors of this veracious history to infer that his name quite assuredly must have been Quixada, and not Quesada as others would have it. It occurred to him, however, that the valiant Amadís was not content to call himself Amadís and nothing more but added the name of his kingdom and country to make it famous and called himself Amadís of Gaul. So he, like a good knight, resolved to add on the name of his own region and style himself Don Quixote of La Mancha. He believed that this accurately described his origin and country, and that he did it honor by taking its name for his own.

Reading Skill
Comparing Worldviews How does the writer's view of the helmet differ from Don Quixote's?

Literary Analysis
Parody How does the contrast between the "lofty, sonorous name" and the horse's actual qualities add to the parody?
Vocabulary Builder
sonorous (sə nôr´ əs) *adj.* having a rich or impressive sound

Reading Check

What three steps has Don Quixote taken to transform himself into a knight?

---

11. "***tantum pellis et ossa fuit***" (tän´ tum pel´ is et äs´ ə fōō´ it) "creature made of skin and bones" (Latin).
12. **Bucephalus** (byōō sef´ ə ləs) **of Alexander or the Babieca** (bäb ē ā´ kä) **of the Cid** Bucephalus was Alexander the Great's war horse; Babieca was the Cid's war horse.
13. **hack's** A hack is an old, worn-out horse.

from *Don Quixote* ■ 1117

So then, his armor being furbished, his morion turned into a helmet, his hack christened, and he himself confirmed, he came to the conclusion that nothing more was needed now but to look for a lady to be in love with, for a knight-errant without love was like a tree without leaves or fruit, or a body without a soul.

"If, for my sins, or by my good fortune," he said to himself, "I come across some giant hereabouts, a common occurrence with knights-errant, and knock him to the ground in one onslaught, or cleave him asunder at the waist, or, in short, vanquish and subdue him, will it not be well to have someone I may send him to as a present, that he may come in and fall on his knees before my sweet lady, and in a humble, submissive voice say, 'I am the giant Caraculiambro, lord of the island of Malindrania, vanquished in single combat by the never sufficiently <u>extolled</u> knight Don Quixote of La Mancha, who has commanded me to present myself before your grace, that your highness may dispose of me at your pleasure'?"

Oh, how our good gentleman enjoyed the delivery of this speech, especially when he had thought of someone to call his lady! There was, so the story goes, in a village near his own a very good-looking farm-girl with whom he had been at one time in love, though, so far as is known, she never knew it nor gave a thought to the matter. Her name was Aldonza Lorenzo, and upon her he thought fit to confer the title of Lady of his Thoughts. Searching for a name not too remote from her own, yet which would aim at and bring to mind that of a princess and great lady, he decided upon calling her Dulcinea del Toboso, since she was a native of El Toboso. To his way of thinking, the name was musical, uncommon, and significant, like all those he had bestowed upon himself and his belongings.

CHAPTER VIII

Of the Good Fortune Which the Valiant Don Quixote Had in the Terrible and Undreamed-of Adventure of the Windmills, With Other Occurrences Worthy to Be Fitly Recorded

At this point they came in sight of thirty or forty windmills that are on that plain.

"Fortune," said Don Quixote to his squire, as soon as he had seen them, "is arranging matters for us better than we could have hoped. Look there, friend Sancho Panza,[14] where thirty or more monstrous giants rise up, all of whom I mean to engage in battle

---

14. Sancho Panza a simple countryman whom Don Quixote takes as his squire. In contrast to Don Quixote, Panza is practical and has common sense.

Vocabulary Builder
extolled (ek stōld´)
adj. praised

Literary Analysis
Parody Which phrases in Don Quixote's speech contribute to the parody of tales of knights?

and slay, and with whose spoils we shall begin to make our fortunes. For this is righteous warfare, and it is God's good service to sweep so evil a breed from off the face of the earth."

"What giants?" said Sancho Panza.

"Those you see there," answered his master, "with the long arms, and some have them nearly two leagues[15] long."

"Look, your worship," said Sancho. "What we see there are not giants but windmills, and what seem to be their arms are the vanes that turned by the wind make the millstone go."

"It is easy to see," replied Don Quixote, "that you are not used to this business of adventures. Those are giants, and if you are afraid, away with you out of here and betake yourself to prayer, while I engage them in fierce and unequal combat."

So saying, he gave the spur to his steed Rocinante, heedless of the cries his squire Sancho sent after him, warning him that most certainly they were windmills and not giants he was going to attack. He, however, was so positive they were giants that he neither heard the cries of Sancho, nor perceived, near as he was, what they were.

"Fly not, cowards and vile beings," he shouted, "for a single knight attacks you."

A slight breeze at this moment sprang up, and the great vanes began to move.

"Though ye flourish more arms than the giant Briareus, ye have to reckon with me!" exclaimed Don Quixote, when he saw this.

So saying, he commended himself with all his heart to his lady Dulcinea, imploring her to support him in such a peril. With lance braced and covered by his shield, he charged at Rocinante's fullest gallop and attacked the first mill that stood in front of him. But as he drove his lance-point into the sail, the wind whirled it around with such force that it shivered the lance to pieces. It swept away

Don Quixote, **Pablo Picasso**, Bridgeman Art Library, London/New York. © 2004 Estate of Pablo Picasso/Artists Rights Society (ARS), New York.

▲ **Critical Viewing**
In this picture, how does the physical contrast between Sancho Panza and Don Quixote reflect their different views of the world? **[Connect]**

✓ **Reading Check**
Which "enemy" does Don Quixote decide to battle?

---

15. leagues (lēgz) *n.* A league is a distance of about three miles.

with it horse and rider, and they were sent rolling over the plain, in sad condition indeed.

Sancho hastened to his assistance as fast as the animal could go. When he came up he found Don Quixote unable to move, with such an impact had Rocinante fallen with him.

"God bless me!" said Sancho. "Did I not tell your worship to watch what you were doing, because they were only windmills? No one could have made any mistake about it unless he had something of the same kind in his head."

"Silence, friend Sancho," replied Don Quixote. "The fortunes of war more than any other are liable to frequent fluctuations. Moreover I think, and it is the truth, that that same sage Frestón who carried off my study and books, has turned these giants into mills in order to rob me of the glory of vanquishing them, such is the enmity he bears me. But in the end his wicked arts will avail but little against my good sword."

"God's will be done," said Sancho Panza, and helping him to rise got him up again on Rocinante, whose shoulder was half dislocated.

▼ **Critical Viewing**
Which details in this painting capture the humor of Don Quixote's "battle" with the windmills? **[Analyze]**

Then, discussing the adventure, they followed the road to Puerto Lápice, for there, said Don Quixote, they could not fail to find adventures in abundance and variety, as it was a well-traveled thoroughfare. For all that, he was much grieved at the loss of his lance, and said so to his squire.

"I remember having read," he added, "how a Spanish knight, Diego Pérez de Vargas by name, having broken his sword in battle, tore from an oak a ponderous bough or branch. With it he did such things that day, and pounded so many Moors, that he got the surname of Machuca, and he and his descendants from that day forth were called Vargas y Machuca. I mention this because from the first oak I see I mean to tear such a branch, large and stout. I am determined and resolved to do such deeds with it that you may deem yourself very fortunate in being found worthy to see them and be an eyewitness of things that will scarcely be believed."

"Be that as God wills," said Sancho, "I believe it all as your worship says it. But straighten yourself a little, for you seem to be leaning to one side, maybe from the shaking you got when you fell."

"That is the truth," said Don Quixote, "and if I make no complaint of the pain it is because knights-errant are not permitted to complain of any wound, even though their bowels be coming out through it."

"If so," said Sancho, "I have nothing to say. But God knows I would rather your worship complained when anything ailed you. For my part, I confess I must complain however small the ache may be, unless this rule about not complaining applies to the squires of knights-errant also."

Don Quixote could not help laughing at his squire's simplicity, and assured him he might complain whenever and however he chose, just as he liked. So far he had never read of anything to the contrary in the order of knighthood.

Sancho reminded him it was dinner time, to which his master answered that he wanted nothing himself just then, but that Sancho might eat when he had a mind. With this permission Sancho settled himself as comfortably as he could on his beast, and taking out of the saddlebags what he had stowed away in them, he jogged along behind his master munching slowly. From time to time he took a pull at the wineskin with all the enjoyment that the thirstiest tavernkeeper in Málaga might have envied. And while he went on in this way, between gulps, he never gave a thought to any of the promises his master had made him, nor did he rate it as hardship but rather as recreation going in quest of adventures, however dangerous they might be.

Literary Analysis
Parody How does the contrast between Don Quixote's ridiculous defeat and his brave words add to the parody?

Reading Skill
Comparing Worldviews What contrasting views of bodily comfort do Don Quixote and Sancho Panza have?

Apply the Skills

from *Don Quixote*

Thinking About the Selection

1. **Respond:** Which of Don Quixote's ideas or actions did you find funniest? Why?
2. **(a) Recall:** What does Don Quixote spend most of his time doing before he decides to become a knight? **(b) Analyze Cause and Effect:** In what way does this activity bring about his decision?
3. **(a) Recall:** Why does Don Quixote attack the windmills? **(b) Connect:** How does he explain his failure to conquer them? **(c) Hypothesize:** What would happen to his dreams of knightly adventure if he admitted the truth about the windmills?
4. **Speculate:** Why do you think Sancho agrees to go adventuring with Don Quixote?
5. **(a) Draw Conclusions:** Does Cervantes team Don Quixote with Sancho Panza for humorous effect, to teach a lesson about life, or both? Explain. **(b) Discuss:** Discuss your ideas with a small group. **(c) Evaluate:** Share two of the best ideas with the class.

Literary Analysis

6. In what way is Don Quixote's adventure with the windmills a **parody** of an episode in a romance or legend?
7. **(a)** Using a chart like the one shown, give examples showing specific ways in which Don Quixote is a parody of a heroic knight.

Legendary Knight	Don Quixote
1. wears shining armour	1.
2. rides a great steed	2.
3. pledges love to a lady	3.
4. conquers giants	4.
5. other _____	5.

   (b) Do you think Don Quixote is a genuine hero as well as a parody of one? Explain.

Reading Skill

8. **(a)** Compare and contrast Don Quixote's responses with Sancho Panza's in two situations. **(b)** In what way do these contrasts emphasize the fact that Don Quixote's beliefs are illusions?
9. **(a)** Compare Don Quixote's situation at the opening of the selection with his situation at the end. **(b)** What needs might his illusions satisfy that his earlier life did not?

QuickReview

Selection at a Glance
Centuries too late, Don Quixote decides that he is a knight and goes in search of adventure.

Go Online
—Assessment
For: Self-test
Visit: www.PHSchool.com
Web Code: eqa-6610

Parody: a humorous work in which the author imitates another work or literary form in an exaggerated or a ridiculous way

Comparing and Contrasting: examining two or more things to determine their similarities and differences

Vocabulary Builder

Practice Replace the underlined word in each sentence with its **antonym,** or word of opposite meaning, from the vocabulary list for *Don Quixote,* on page 1096. Then, explain which version of the sentence makes better sense.

1. The <u>vagueness</u> of his idea convinced other scientists to accept it.
2. The speaker's <u>squeaky</u> voice soothed his listeners.
3. I knew we had similar tastes when she <u>criticized</u> my favorite poet.

Adding Words to Your Vocabulary Using a dictionary, determine the meaning of the words *sonnet* and *sonata.* Explain how each is related to *sonorous.* Then, use each word correctly in a sentence. (For more on using a dictionary, see page R6.)

Writing

Following Cervantes's lead, write a **parody** in which Don Quixote takes on a twenty-first century challenge. Follow these tips:
- Choose a situation that Don Quixote might misunderstand.
- Jot notes on how Don Quixote will interpret each event.
- As you draft, clearly depict both the reality of what is happening and the illusion in Don Quixote's mind.

For *Grammar, Vocabulary,* and *Assessment,* see
Build Language Skills, pages 1124–1125.

Extend Your Learning

Listening and Speaking Working with a partner, defend one of the following ideas and have your partner defend the other:
- *It is nobler to dream like Don Quixote than to be limited by reality.*
- *It is best to face reality directly, like Sancho Panza.*

Each of you should give a five-minute **oral presentation** to the class on your position. Have your classmates summarize the opinions you offer and provide constructive comments comparing the effectiveness of your presentations.

Research and Technology With a group, create a **biographical brochure** on Cervantes. Devise several research questions. Then, use biographical dictionaries, the Internet and other sources to find answers. Present your work in an attractive format.

Build Language Skills

Vocabulary Skill

Words in Context Many words have more than one meaning. For example, *coordinate* is usually a verb meaning "to place in the same order or system" or "to adjust," but it can also be an adjective meaning "in the same order" or "of equal rank" or a noun referring to one of an equal or matched pair.

Verb: We must *coordinate* our plans so that one of us is always here.
Adjective: Put a comma between *coordinate* adjectives.
Noun: Each point on the graph has an x *coordinate* and a y *coordinate*.

Practice Use context to determine which meaning given most clearly applies in each sentence. Then, write a new sentence using one of the word's other meanings.

1. During the *revolution,* many leaders were exiled. **(a)** a complete turn around; **(b)** a radical change that overthrows a government

2. No one could follow the politician's *convoluted* explanation. **(a)** rolled into coils; **(b)** extremely complicated

3. The publisher issued the first *volume* three months ago. **(a)** paper bound together in book **(b)** the amount of space something occupies **(c)** the loudness of a sound

4. The peasants began *revolting* when the government tried to prevent them from gathering rainwater. **(a)** overthrowing something established; **(b)** disgusting

Grammar Lesson

Using Semicolons Use a semicolon to join independent clauses not already joined by a coordinating conjunction (*and, but, or, nor, for, so,* and *yet*).

▶ **Example:** The poet came to our school; she critiqued our work.

Use semicolons to separate items in a series when one or more of the items includes a comma.

▶ **Example:** I sent notes to Mrs. Jones, our science teacher; Mrs. Jensen, my history teacher; and Mrs. Seltz, my coach.

Practice Use a semicolon to combine these sentences.

1. The coach called practice for Monday. Monday is usually our day off.

2. Lacrosse is a growing sport. Lacrosse is a Native American sport.

3. For a long time, lacrosse was an East Coast sport. Recently lacrosse has grown in popularity around the country.

MorePractice

For more practice with semicolons, use the Grammar Handbook, pp. R47–R48.

Reading: Compare and Contrast Worldviews

Standards Assessed
- 10.2.4
- 10.7.6
- 10.7.10

Directions: *Read this passage. Then, answer the questions.*

The city of cats and the city of men exist one inside the other, but they are not the same city. Few cats recall the time when there was no distinction: the streets and squares of men were also streets and squares of cats, and the lawns, courtyards, balconies, and fountains: you lived in a broad and various space. But for several generations now domestic felines have been prisoners of an uninhabitable city: the streets are uninterruptedly overrun by the mortal traffic of cat-crushing automobiles; in every square foot of terrain where once a garden extended or a vacant lot or the ruins of an old demolition, now condominiums loom up, welfare housing, brand-new skyscrapers; every entrance is crammed with parked cars. . . .

from "The Garden of Stubborn Cats" by Italo Calvino,
translated by William Weaver

1. Which contrast most clearly reflects the contrasting worldviews in the passage?
   A cat lovers vs. cat haters
   B traditional vs. modern
   C liberty vs. tyranny
   D wealth vs. poverty

2. Which statement best reflects the narrator's view of the changes he describes?
   A He welcomes the changes.
   B He sees them as harsh but necessary.
   C He finds the changes unpleasant.
   D He has no opinion about them.

3. The narrator's tone can best be described as
   A exasperated.
   B approving.
   C nostalgic.
   D annoyed.

4. The structure of the passage reinforces the concept of
   A chaos and destruction.
   B strict order.
   C out-of-control growth.
   D structured planning.

Timed Writing: Analysis [Critical Stance]

Review either the selection from *Don Quixote* or from *A Connecticut Yankee in King Arthur's Court.* Write an analysis of how appearance and reality are portrayed in the selection. Use specifics from the text to support your points. **(50 minutes)**

Writing Workshop: *Work in Progress*

Comparison-and-Contrast Essay

Use the freewriting from your writing portfolio to develop a Venn diagram of similarities and differences. Save the Venn diagram in your writing portfolio.

Reading Informational Materials

Position Statements

In Part 2, you learned about the importance of comparing worldviews when interpreting literature. Analyzing and comparing viewpoints is equally important when evaluating information sources. If you read the excerpt from *Don Quixote,* you know how different the same object can look from different perspectives. When Don Quixote saw giants and adventures, Sancho Panza saw only windmills—and trouble. As you read the following position statements on an art project in New York City, compare and contrast the different views they represent.

About Position Statements

A **position statement** is a written presentation of a person's or an organization's considered opinion on a given topic. For example, a public interest group might issue a position statement about a proposed law on the environment. Most position statements include these elements:

- background information about the issue
- a clear statement of the person's or organization's point of view
- facts and details that logically support the opinion
- a call for action

Reading Skill

You can better evaluate position statements and other sources by **comparing and contrasting the writers' purposes.** Most position statements are primarily written to persuade but may have additional purposes, such as informing an audience, paying tribute to a person, or even entertaining readers. For instance, a persuasive writer may include an entertaining story to win reader's interest. To compare position statements, fill out a chart like the one shown for each.

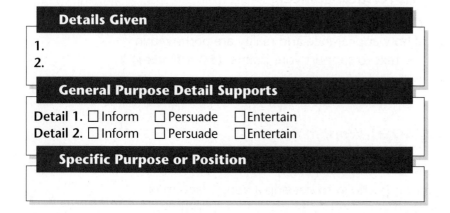

Academic Standards

- Examine how the author's perspective influences the structure and tone of the text. (10.2.4)
- Review and revise writing. (10.4.10)
- Provide constructive criticism to other writers. (10.4.12)

SPECIAL EXHIBITIONS

● Home
● Special Exhibitions

Christo and Jeanne-Claude: *The Gates*, Central Park, New York

More about this Exhibition

The evolution of the widely anticipated outdoor work of art for New York City initiated in 1979 by the husband-and-wife collaborators Christo and Jeane-Claude is the subject of the exhibition "Christo and Jeanne-Claude: *The Gates*, Central Park, New York," on view at The Metropolitan Museum of Art through July 25, 2004. Fifty-one preparatory drawings and collages by Christo, sixty-four photographs, and eleven maps and technical diagrams document the soon-to-be-realized work of art, which when completed will consist of 7,500 saffron-colored gates placed at twelve-foot intervals throughout twenty-three miles of pedestrian walkways lacing Central Park from 59th Street to 110th Street and from Central Park West to Fifth Avenue.

"*The Gates*, Central Park, New York City, 1979–2005" will be on view in Central Park for sixteen days in February 2005. This outdoor project—in which 193 gates will surround the Metropolitan Museum in the park, all the way to the glass wall of The American Wing—will be entirely financed by Christo and Jeanne-Claude.

The exhibition is made possible by an anonymous donor.

Philippe de Montebello, director, The Metropolitan Museum of Art, commented: "We are delighted to present the blueprints, if you will, of this far-reaching project, which the public will be able to preview here at the Museum. At long last Christo and Jeanne-Claude's project will see fruition, and our exhibition will trace the full course of its evolution. This work of massive scope, when realized, will surely constitute a tribute to the grandeur of Central Park and New York City, and reaffirm the continuity of culture and the centrality of art to the life of our city and all cities."

> This page gives details about *The Gates* and about an exhibition of sketches for the project.

> A quotation from the director of the museum presents a clearly favorable position on the value of the project.

● Current Exhibitions ● Upcoming Exhibitions ● Past Exhibitions ● Traveling Exhibitions ● Printing Instructions

http://www.christojeanneclaude.net

Welcome Page | Artworks in Progress | Exhibitions/Collections | Bibliography | About the Artists | Contact

Christo and Jeanne-Claude

The Gates
Project for Central Park, New York City

© 2005 Christo and Jeanne-Claude

Photo: Wolfgang Volz/laif/Redux

As Christo and Jeanne-Claude have always done for their projects, *The Gates* will be entirely financed by the artists with the sale of preparatory studies, drawings, collages, and scale models, earlier works of the fifties and sixties, and original lithographs on other subjects.

The artists do not accept sponsorship or donations. All materials used in the project will be recycled.

The final installation of the 7,503 gates will be done, in five days, simultaneously by hundreds of workers. The unfurling of the fabric panels will bloom in one day.

A written contract has been drafted between the City of New York and the Department of Parks and Recreation and the artists.

The contract requires the artists to provide, among other terms and conditions:

- Personal and property liability insurance holding harmless the City, the Department of Parks and Recreation and the Central Park Conservancy.
- Restoration Bond providing funds for complete removal.
- Clearance for the usual activities in the park and access of Rangers, maintenance, clean-up, police and emergency vehicles.
- The artists shall pay all costs of the Park's supervision directly related to the project.

> The artists responsible for *The Gates* use both facts and colorful descriptive language such as *bloom* to give readers a sense of their project.

> Details about the artists' contract with the city may reassure critical readers about the cost and consequences of the project.

- Neither vegetation nor rock formations shall be disturbed.
- *The Gates* will be clear of rocks, tree roots and low branches.
- The people of New York will continue to use Central Park as usual.
- After the removal, the site shall be inspected by the Department of Parks and Recreation, which will be holding the security until satisfaction.

For those who will walk through *The Gates*, following the walkways, and staying away from the grass, *The Gates* will be a golden ceiling creating warm shadows. When seen from the buildings surrounding Central Park, *The Gates* will seem like a golden river appearing and disappearing through the bare branches of the trees and will highlight the shape of the footpaths.

The 16-day-duration work of art, free to all, will be a long-to-be-remembered joyous experience for every New Yorker, as a democratic expression that Olmsted[1] invoked when he conceived a "central" park. The luminous moving fabric will underline the organic design of the park, while the rectangular poles will be a reminder of the geometric grid pattern of the city blocks around the park. *The Gates* will harmonize with the beauty of Central Park.

> Here the artists use descriptive details and historical facts to express their position: The work of art will give spectators pleasure while affirming the beauty of the park.

> A preliminary sketch for the project, incorporating a map of the park, helps bring the project to life for readers.

Christo: *The Gates, Project for Central Park, New York City.* Collage, 2002. In two parts. 12" x 30 1/2" and 26 1/4" x 30 1/2".

©2002 Christo   **Photo:** Wolfgang Volz/laif/Redux

---

1. Olmsted (1822–1903) Frederick Law Olmsted, landscape architect and social thinker who helped to design Central Park, New York City, the nation's first large urban park. Olmsted intended his designs to make beauty available to everyone.

Send comments

Who's in charge
of this site

What's on this site

Forgotten Delights

Christo's _Gates_: Art in Individual Minds and Public Places
Copyright © Dianne L. Durante 2004.

A great work of art [. . .] transforms the artist's message into an unforgettable image. Such a work is not merely pretty décor: it gives you a guide to living your life.

At its best, art can literally help you keep your goals in sight. A work of visual art condenses a whole view of the world. You can hold it in your mind as a single, concrete image of what sort of person you'd like to become: a person with the pride of Michelangelo's _David_, or the elegance of _Madame Récamier_.[1] You can use it to recall the sort of world you want to live in: the peace of a Constable landscape, the bustle and energy of Canaletto's Venice, the drama of a Delacroix. . . .[2]

The writer builds her argument. First, she defines the role of art. Next, she evaluates the Central Park project by applying her own definition of art.

What message will _The Gates_ convey? None at all. If you examine every fiber of the million square feet of fabric, you won't be a nanometer closer to knowing what sort of person you'd like to be, what you should focus on, what sort of world you'd like to live in. Prominent art historians and critics at the Whitney, the Museum of Modern Art and _The New York Times_ haven't even tried to proclaim any meaning in _The Gates_. They merely assert that it will draw attention to Central Park. . . .

The writer concludes by recommending specific actions.

If you want to enjoy art in Central Park, do your best to avoid Christo's giant slalom poles. Instead, seek out the dozens of figurative sculptures scattered through the Park, from _Duke Ellington_ to the Delacorte Clock, from the Maine Monument to _Samuel Morse_, from _Still Hunt_ to the Untermeyer Fountain. Like genuine works of art ever since the caveman's time, these have the potential to speak to you.

---

1. **Michelangelo's** (mī′ kəl an′ jə loz′) _David . . . Madame Récamier_ (rā kà myā′) Sculptor and painter Michelangelo (1475–1564) chiseled a famous sculpture depicting the biblical hero David, who killed Goliath. The beautiful, witty, socially successful Frenchwoman Madame Récamier (1777 –1849) was the subject of a number of paintings by nineteeth-century artists.

2. **Constable . . . Delacroix** (də là krwà′) Englishman John Constable (1776–1837) is famous for his paintings of the English countryside. Italian Antonio Canaletto (1697–1768) is noted for his paintings of Venice, Italy. Frenchman Eugène Delacroix (1798–1863) painted dramatic depictions of battles and of life in other cultures.

Reading: Comparing and Contrasting Writers' Purposes

Standards Assessed
• 10.2.4
• 10.4.10
• 10.4.12

Directions: *Choose the letter of the best answer to each question about the position statements.*

1. Of the following details from these Web sites, which is included mainly to persuade readers?
   A *Metropolitan Museum*: the contents of the exhibition
   B *Christo and Jeanne-Claude*: the comparison of *The Gates* to "a golden river"
   C *Forgotten Delights*: the list of sculptures in Central Park
   D *Metropolitan Museum*: the number of gates in the project

2. Which detail is included mainly to inform readers?
   A *Metropolitan Museum*: the quotation from the museum director
   B *Christo and Jeanne-Claude*: the time the work will remain up
   C *Forgotten Delights*: the discussion of the purposes of art
   D *Forgotten Delights*: the claim that critics "haven't even tried to proclaim any meaning in *The Gates*"

3. Which is the most accurate comparison of the sites?
   A All three are written to persuade readers to support *The Gates.*
   B The main purpose of the museum statement is to inform; the information on the other sites is used to persuade.
   C All three articles are written primarily to inform readers.
   D The Christo and Jeanne-Claude statement is intended to persuade; the main purpose of the other sites is to inform.

Reading: Comprehension and Interpretation

Directions: *Write your answers on a separate piece of paper.*

4. Explain why the Forgotten Delights Web site opposes *The Gates.* In your answer, show the connection between this opposition and specific ideas about the purpose of art. **[Integrating]**

5. What response might Christo and Jeanne-Claude make to the *Forgotten Delights* article?

Timed Writing: Persuasion [Critical Stance]

Write a **position statement** in which you explain your support for or opposition to *The Gates.* First, summarize reasons to oppose or to support the project. Then, explain your own viewpoint. Use details or quotations from at least one of the position statements to support your comments. **(45 minutes)**

Comparing Literary Works • Theme and Worldview

Theme and Worldview

The **theme** of a literary work is the central message or insight that it conveys. Many themes are **universal**, or found in the literature of different times and places. For example, the struggle of good and evil is a universal theme. At the same time, a particular writer's expression of a theme will reflect a specific **worldview**—the basic beliefs and values that shape the writer's experience and outlook.

- In past times, many writers portrayed a well-ordered world in which every event happens for a reason, a world defended by true heroes. Such writers might show good people being rewarded while bad people are punished.
- In modern times, many writers depict a chaotic or an indifferent world filled with ordinary, limited people. Such writers might show good people as having greater peace of mind than bad people. At the same time, they might show bad people succeeding while good people suffer great losses.

Comparing Themes and Worldviews

Both "Damon and Pythias," an ancient legend, and "Two Friends," a modern short story, center on the theme of friendship and honor. Yet, in each work, the theme is filtered through a different worldview and so takes on a different meaning.

As you read, identify the central message or insight in each story. Then, using a chart like the one shown, compare the different worldviews represented in each.

Note that an important clue to the theme and worldview of a story is the way in which it ends. Ask yourself, for example, whether good characters are rewarded and bad ones punished.

 Academic Standards

- Examine how the author's perspective influences the structure and tone of the text. (10.2.4)
- Analyze many different forms of dramatic literature. (10.3.1)
- Evaluate the aesthetic qualities of style. (10.3.11)

Theme

expressed through . . .
↓

Type of Characters
❑ "larger-than-life" ❑ ordinary

Language They Speak
❑ eloquent; formal ❑ everyday

Challenge They Face
❑ unique to them ❑ part of a larger conflict

Ending
❑ Justice is done. ❑ Justice is not done.

Vocabulary Builder

Damon and Pythias

- **dire** (dīr) *adj.* urgent; terrible; calling for quick action (p. 1135) *The dire problem must be solved at once.*

- **impediments** (im ped´ ə mənts) *n.* things that slow something or someone down or that get in the way (p. 1135) *Work boots are impediments to running.*

- **serenity** (sə ren´ ə tē) *n.* state of calm or peace (p. 1136) *The stream created a mood of serenity.*

Two Friends

- **ardent** (är´ dənt) *adj.* intensely enthusiastic or devoted (p. 1138) *She is an ardent soccer fan and goes to every game.*

- **jauntiness** (jôn´ tē nəs) *n.* carefree, easy attitude (p. 1140) *With a casual jauntiness, he tossed the crumpled-up paper into the trash.*

- **relent** (ri lent´) *v.* become less strong, severe, or intense (p. 1143) *Will the downpour relent soon?*

Build Understanding

Connecting to the Literature

Reading/Writing Connection In both "Damon and Pythias" and "Two Friends," the loyalty between two men is put to an extreme test. Write a few sentences about the qualities a person must have in order to be a true friend. Use at least three of the following words: *appreciate, rely, display, conduct,* and *benefit.*

Meet the Authors

Ancient Greek Legends and Their Retellers

Like other legends, "Damon and Pythias" exaggerates the characteristics of people to provide examples of the best—and the worst—conduct. In this way, a legend serves as a cultural how-to manual, showing people which virtues they should honor and cultivate.

Retelling the Tales Over the centuries, the legend of Damon and Pythias has been retold and adapted in many forms, including plays. William F. Russell, a recent reteller of this and many other myths and legends, is also the author of *Family Learning* and *Classic Myths to Read Aloud.*

Guy de **Maupassant** (1850–1893)

In his short stories, Guy de Maupassant often focuses on the environment in which his characters live. The outcome of events in his work is determined by forces beyond a character's control, such as family history, social circumstances, and the character's basic disposition. His stories provide a fascinating record of nineteenth-century life.

A Productive Life Maupassant seemed destined for success. A gifted writer born into an aristocratic family, he won the attention of famous authors while he was still a young man. He soon became famous in his own right. Unfortunately, his career was cut short by illness. He died while still in his early forties. Yet, he left a fortune to every future reader: 300 short stories.

For: More about the authors
Visit: www.PHSchool.com
Web Code: eqe-9612

DAMON
AND
PYTHIAS

Retold by WILLIAM F. RUSSELL, ED.D

D amon [dā′ mən] and Pythias [pi*th*′ ē əs] were two noble young men who lived on the island of Sicily in a city called Syracuse. They were such close companions and were so devoted to each other that all the people of the city admired them as the highest examples of true friendship. Each trusted the other so completely that nobody could ever have persuaded one that the other had been unfaithful or dishonest, even if that had been the case.

Now it happened that Syracuse was, at that time, ruled by a famous tyrant named Dionysius [dī′ ə nis′ ē əs],[1] who had gained the throne for himself through treachery, and who from then on flaunted his power by behaving cruelly to his own subjects and to all strangers and enemies who were so unfortunate as to fall into his clutches. This tyrant, Dionysius, was so unjustly cruel that once, when he awoke from a restless sleep during which he dreamt that a certain man in the town had attempted to kill him, he immediately had that man put to death.

It happened that Pythias had, quite unjustly, been accused by Dionysius of trying to overthrow him, and for this supposed crime of treason Pythias was sentenced by the king to die. Try as he might, Pythias could not prove his innocence to the king's satisfaction, and so, all hope now lost, the noble youth asked only for a few days' freedom so that he could settle his business affairs and see to it that his relatives would be cared for after he was executed. Dionysius, the hardhearted tyrant, however, would not believe Pythias' promise to return and would not allow him to leave unless he left behind him a hostage, someone who would be put to death in his place if he should fail to return within the stated time.

Literary Analysis
Theme and Worldview What subject or theme is suggested at the story's opening?

---

1. Dionysius Dionysius the Elder (ca. 430 B.C.–367 B.C.), ruler of ancient Syracuse.

Pythias immediately thought of his friend Damon, and he unhesitatingly sent for him in this hour of <u>dire</u> necessity, never thinking for a moment that his trusty companion would refuse his request. Nor did he, for Damon hastened straightaway to the palace—much to the amazement of King Dionysius—and gladly offered to be held hostage for his friend, in spite of the dangerous condition that had been attached to this favor. Therefore, Pythias was permitted to settle his earthly affairs before departing to the Land of the Shades,[2] while Damon remained behind in the dungeon, the captive of the tyrant Dionysius.

After Pythias had been released, Dionysius asked Damon if he did not feel afraid, for Pythias might very well take advantage of the opportunity he had been given and simply not return at all, and then he, Damon, would be executed in his place. But Damon replied at once with a willing smile: "There is no need for me to feel afraid, O King, since I have perfect faith in the word of my true friend, and I know that he will certainly return before the appointed time—unless, of course, he dies or is held captive by some evil force. Even so, even should the noble Pythias be captured and held against his will, it would be an honor for me to die in his place."

Such devotion and perfect faith as this was unheard of to the friendless tyrant; still, though he could not help admiring the true nobility of his captive, he nevertheless determined that Damon should certainly be put to death should Pythias not return by the appointed time.

And, as the Fates would have it, by a strange turn of events, Pythias *was* detained far longer in his task than he had imagined. Though he never for a single minute intended to evade the sentence of death to which he had been so unjustly committed, Pythias met with several accidents and unavoidable delays. Now his time was running out and he had yet to overcome the many <u>impediments</u> that had been placed in his path. At last he succeeded in clearing away all the hindrances, and he sped back the many miles to the palace of the king, his heart almost bursting with grief and fear that he might arrive too late.

Meanwhile, when the last day of the allotted time arrived, Dionysius commanded that the place of execution should be readied at once, since he was still ruthlessly determined that if one of his victims escaped him, the other should not. And so, entering the chamber in which Damon was confined, he began to utter words of sarcastic pity for the "foolish faith," as he termed it, that the young man of Syracuse had in his friend.

---

2. **Land of the Shades** in Greek mythology, place where people go when they die.

Vocabulary Builder
dire (dīr) *adj.* urgent; terrible; calling for quick action

▲ Critical Viewing
As he appears on this coin, does Dionysius seem to have the characteristics of the man in the legend? Explain. **[Interpret]**

Vocabulary Builder
impediments (im pedʹ ə mənts) *n.* things that slow something or someone down or that get in the way

✔ Reading Check

What does Damon agree to do for his friend Pythias?

In reply, however, Damon merely smiled, since, in spite of the fact that the eleventh hour had already arrived, he still believed that his lifelong companion would not fail him. Even when, a short time later, he was actually led out to the site of his execution, his <u>serenity</u> remained the same.

Great excitement stirred the crowd that had gathered to witness the execution, for all the people had heard of the bargain that had been struck between the two friends. There was much sobbing and cries of sympathy were heard all around as the captive was brought out, though he himself somehow retained complete composure even at this moment of darkest danger.

Presently the excitement grew more intense still as a swift runner could be seen approaching the palace courtyard at an astonishing speed, and wild shrieks of relief and joy went up as Pythias, breathless and exhausted, rushed headlong through the crowd and flung himself into the arms of his beloved friend, sobbing with relief that he had, by the grace of the gods, arrived in time to save Damon's life.

This final exhibition of devoted love and faithfulness was more than even the stony heart of Dionysius, the tyrant, could resist. As the throng of spectators melted into tears at the companions' embrace, the king approached the pair and declared that Pythias was hereby pardoned and his death sentence canceled. In addition, he begged the pair to allow him to become their friend, to try to be as much a friend to them both as they had shown each other to be.

Thus did the two friends of Syracuse, by the faithful love they bore to each other, conquer the hard heart of a tyrant king, and in the annals of true friendship there are no more honored names than those of Damon and Pythias—for no person can do more than be willing to lay down his life for the sake of his friend.

Vocabulary Builder
serenity (sə ren′ ə tē) *n.* state of calm or peace

Literary Analysis
Theme and Worldview What details here show that good people are rewarded?

Thinking About the Selection

1. **Respond:** When were you most anxious about the legend's outcome? Explain.

2. **(a) Recall:** What does Damon risk for Pythias? **(b) Interpret:** What does his decision show you about their friendship?

3. **(a) Infer:** Why is Damon patient and not fearful as he waits for Pythias? **(b) Take a Position:** Could a friendship like the one between Damon and Pythias exist in our own times? Why or why not?

Two Friends
Guy de Maupassant
translated by Gordon R. Silber

The following story is set during the Franco-Prussian War, a conflict between France and Germany that began on July 19, 1870. The Germans won a series of victories, one of which ended in the capture of the French leader, Napoleon III. On September 19, 1870, the German army established a blockade around Paris. Movement in and out of the city was severely restricted. Led by a provisional government and plagued by famine and hopelessness, Paris managed to hold out until January 28, 1871, when the city surrendered. As Maupassant's story begins, the city is on the verge of surrender.

⋀ Critical Viewing
What insight into friendship does this painting convey?
[Interpret]

Paris was blockaded, starved, in its death agony. Sparrows were becoming scarcer and scarcer on the rooftops and the sewers were being depopulated. One ate whatever one could get.

As he was strolling sadly along the outer boulevard one bright January morning, his hands in his trousers pockets and his stomach empty, M.[1] Morissot [mô rē sō´], watchmaker by trade but local militiaman for the time being, stopped short before a fellow militiaman whom he recognized as a friend. It was M. Sauvage [sō väzh´], a riverside acquaintance.

Every Sunday, before the war, Morissot left at dawn, a bamboo pole in his hand, a tin box on his back. He would take the Argenteuil [àr zhän të´y´] railroad, get off at Colombes, and walk to Marante Island. As soon as he arrived at this ideal spot he would start to fish; he fished until nightfall.

Every Sunday he would meet a stout, jovial little man, M. Sauvage, a haberdasher[2] in Rue Notre-Dame-de-Lorette, another <u>ardent</u> fisherman. Often they spent half a day side by side, line in hand and feet dangling above the current. Inevitably they had struck up a friendship.

Some days they did not speak. Sometimes they did; but they understood one another admirably without saying anything because they had similar tastes and responded to their surroundings in exactly the same way.

On a spring morning, toward ten o'clock, when the young sun was drawing up from the tranquil stream wisps of haze which floated off in the direction of the current and was pouring down its vernal warmth on the backs of the two fanatical anglers,[3] Morissot would sometimes say to his neighbor, "Nice, isn't it?" and M. Sauvage would answer, "There's nothing like it." And that was enough for them to understand and appreciate each other.

On an autumn afternoon, when the sky, reddened by the setting sun, cast reflections of its scarlet clouds on the water, made the whole river crimson, lighted up the horizon, made the two friends look as ruddy as fire, and gilded the trees which were already brown and beginning to tremble with a wintery shiver, M. Sauvage would look at Morissot with a smile and say, "Fine sight!" And Morissot, awed, would answer, "It's better than the city, isn't it?" without taking his eyes from his float.

As soon as they recognized one another they shook hands energetically, touched at meeting under such changed circumstances.

Vocabulary Builder
ardent (är´ dənt) *adj.* intensely enthusiastic or devoted

Literary Analysis
Theme and Worldview What idea about friendship does this paragraph suggest?

---

1. **M.** abbreviation for *Monsieur* (mə syʉr´), "Mister" or "Sir" in French.
2. **haberdasher** (hab´ ər dash´ ər) *n.* person in the business of selling men's clothing.
3. **anglers** (aŋ´ glərz) *n.* people who fish with hook and line.

Les Maisons Cabassud à la Ville D'Avray, Camille Corot

M. Sauvage, with a sigh, grumbled, "What goings-on!" Morissot groaned dismally, "And what weather! This is the first fine day of the year."

The sky was, in fact, blue and brilliant.

They started to walk side by side, absent-minded and sad. Morissot went on, "And fishing! Ah! Nothing but a pleasant memory."

"When'll we get back to it?" asked M. Sauvage.

They went into a little café and had an absinthe,[4] then resumed their stroll along the sidewalks.

Morissot stopped suddenly, "How about another, eh?" M. Sauvage agreed, "If you want." And they entered another wine shop.

On leaving they felt giddy, muddled, as one does after drinking on an empty stomach. It was mild. A caressing breeze touched their faces.

The warm air completed what the absinthe had begun. M. Sauvage stopped. "Suppose we went?"

"Went where?"

"Fishing, of course."

"But where?"

"Why, on our island. The French outposts are near Colombes. I know Colonel Dumoulin; they'll let us pass without any trouble."

 **Critical Viewing**
What does this painting suggest about the pace of life in the French countryside? Explain. **[Interpret]**

Reading Check
What pleasure do M. Morissot and M. Sauvage share?

---

4. absinthe (ab´ sin*th*´) *n.* type of liqueur.

Morissot trembled with eagerness: "Done! I'm with you." And they went off to get their tackle.

An hour later they were walking side by side on the highway. They reached the villa which the Colonel occupied. He smiled at their request and gave his consent to their whim. They started off again, armed with a pass.

Soon they passed the outposts, went through the abandoned village of Colombes, and reached the edge of the little vineyards which slope toward the Seine. It was about eleven.

Opposite, the village of Argenteuil seemed dead. The heights of Orgemont and Sannois dominated the whole countryside. The broad plain which stretches as far as Nanterre was empty, absolutely empty, with its bare cherry trees and its colorless fields.

Pointing up to the heights, M. Sauvage murmured, "The Prussians are up there!" And a feeling of uneasiness paralyzed the two friends as they faced this deserted region.

"The Prussians!" They had never seen any, but for months they had felt their presence—around Paris, ruining France, pillaging, massacring, starving the country, invisible and all-powerful. And a kind of superstitious terror was superimposed on the hatred which they felt for this unknown and victorious people.

Morissot stammered, "Say, suppose we met some of them?"

His Parisian <u>jauntiness</u> coming to the surface in spite of everything, M. Sauvage answered, "We'll offer them some fish."

But they hesitated to venture into the country, frightened by the silence all about them.

Finally M. Sauvage pulled himself together: "Come on! On our way! But let's go carefully." And they climbed over into a vineyard, bent double, crawling, taking advantage of the vines to conceal themselves, watching, listening.

A stretch of bare ground had to be crossed to reach the edge of the river. They began to run, and when they reached the bank they plunged down among the dry reeds.

Morissot glued his ear to the ground and listened for sounds of anyone walking in the vicinity. He heard nothing. They were indeed alone, all alone.

Reassured, they started to fish.

Opposite them Marante Island, deserted, hid them from the other bank. The little building which had housed a restaurant was shut up and looked as if it had been abandoned for years.

M. Sauvage caught the first gudgeon.[5] Morissot got the second, and from then on they pulled in their lines every minute or two with

Vocabulary Builder
jauntiness (jônt′ ē nəs)
n. carefree, easy
attitude

Literary Analysis
Theme and Worldview Which details here show that the men are not exceptional heroes?

---

5. gudgeon (guj′ ən) *n.* small European freshwater fish.

a silvery little fish squirming on the end, a truly miraculous draught.

Skillfully they slipped the fish into a sack made of fine net which they had hung in the water at their feet. And happiness pervaded their whole being, the happiness which seizes upon you when you regain a cherished pleasure of which you have long been deprived.

The good sun was pouring down its warmth on their backs. They heard nothing more; they no longer thought about anything at all; they forgot about the rest of the world—they were fishing!

But suddenly a dull sound which seemed to come from underground made the earth tremble. The cannon were beginning.

Morissot turned and saw, over the bank to the left, the great silhouette of Mount Valérien wearing a white plume on its brow, powdersmoke which it had just spit out.

And almost at once a second puff of smoke rolled from the summit, and a few seconds after the roar still another explosion was heard.

Then more followed, and time after time the mountain belched forth death-dealing breath, breathed out milky-white vapor which rose slowly in the calm sky and formed a cloud above the summit.

M. Sauvage shrugged his shoulders. "There they go again," he said.

As he sat anxiously watching his float bob up and down, Morissot was suddenly seized by the wrath which a peace-loving man will feel toward madmen who fight, and grumbled, "Folks sure are stupid to kill one another like that."

M. Sauvage answered, "They're worse than animals."

And Morissot, who had just pulled in a bleak,[6] went on, "And to think that it will always be like this as long as there are governments."

M. Sauvage stopped him: "The Republic[7] wouldn't have declared war—"

Morissot interrupted: "Under kings you have war abroad; under the Republic you have war at home."

And they started a leisurely discussion, unraveling great political problems with the sane reasonableness of easygoing, limited individuals, and found themselves in agreement on the point that men would never be free. And Mount Valérien thundered unceasingly, demolishing French homes with its cannon, crushing out lives, putting an end to the dreams which many had dreamt, the joys which many had been waiting for, the happiness which

Literary Analysis
Theme and Worldview What goals or ideals do the men seem to have?

✔ **Reading Check**

What risk do the men decide to take?

---

6. bleak *n.* small European freshwater fish with silvery scales.
7. The Republic the temporary republican government that assumed control of France when Napoleon III was captured by the Prussians.

many had hoped for, planting in wives' hearts, in maidens' hearts, in mothers' hearts, over there, in other lands, sufferings which would never end.

"That's life for you," opined M. Sauvage.

"You'd better say 'That's death for you,'" laughed Morissot.

But they shuddered in terror when they realized that someone had just come up behind them, and looking around they saw four men standing almost at their elbows, four tall men, armed and bearded, dressed like liveried[8] servants, with flat caps on their heads, pointing rifles at them.

The two fish lines dropped from their hands and floated off down stream.

In a few seconds they were seized, trussed up,[9] carried off, thrown into a rowboat and taken over to the island.

And behind the building which they had thought deserted they saw a score of German soldiers.

A kind of hairy giant who was seated astride a chair smoking a porcelain pipe asked them in excellent French: "Well, gentlemen, have you had good fishing?"

Then a soldier put down at the officer's feet the sack full of fish which he had carefully brought along. The Prussian smiled: "Aha! I see that it didn't go badly. But we have to talk about another little matter. Listen to me and don't get excited.

"As far as I am concerned, you are two spies sent to keep an eye on me. I catch you and I shoot you. You were pretending to fish in order to conceal your business. You have fallen into my hands, so much the worse for you. War is like that.

"But—since you came out past the outposts you have, of course, the password to return. Tell me that password and I will pardon you."

The two friends, side by side, pale, kept silent. A slight nervous trembling shook their hands.

The officer went on: "No one will ever know. You will go back placidly. The secret will disappear with you. If you refuse, it is immediate death. Choose."

▲ **Critical Viewing**
What does this officer's posture suggest about his attitude and training? Explain. **[Interpret]**

---

8. liveried (liv´ ər ēd) *adj.* uniformed
9. trussed up tied up.

They stood motionless, mouths shut.

The Prussian quietly went on, stretching out his hand toward the stream: "Remember that within five minutes you will be at the bottom of that river. Within five minutes! You have relatives, of course?"

Mount Valérien kept thundering.

The two fishermen stood silent. The German gave orders in his own language. Then he moved his chair so as not to be near the prisoners and twelve men took their places, twenty paces distant, rifles grounded.

The officer went on: "I give you one minute, not two seconds more."

Then he rose suddenly, approached the two Frenchmen, took Morissot by the arm, dragged him aside, whispered to him, "Quick, the password? Your friend won't know. I'll pretend to <u>relent</u>."

Morissot answered not a word.

The Prussian drew M. Sauvage aside and put the same question.

M. Sauvage did not answer.

They stood side by side again.

And the officer began to give commands. The soldiers raised their rifles.

Then Morissot's glance happened to fall on the sack full of gudgeons which was lying on the grass a few steps away.

A ray of sunshine made the little heap of still squirming fish gleam. And he almost weakened. In spite of his efforts his eyes filled with tears.

He stammered, "Farewell, Monsieur Sauvage."

M. Sauvage answered, "Farewell, Monsieur Morissot."

They shook hands, trembling from head to foot with a shudder which they could not control.

The officer shouted, "Fire!"

The twelve shots rang out together.

M. Sauvage fell straight forward, like a log. Morissot, who was taller, tottered, half turned, and fell crosswise on top of his comrade, face up, as the blood spurted from his torn shirt.

The German gave more orders.

His men scattered, then returned with rope and stones which they tied to the dead men's feet. They carried them to the bank.

Mount Valérien continued to roar, its summit hidden now in a mountainous cloud of smoke.

Two soldiers took Morissot by the head and the feet, two others seized M. Sauvage. They swung the bodies for a moment then let go. They described an arc and plunged into the river feet first, for the weights made them seem to be standing upright.

Vocabulary Builder
relent (ri lent´) *v.* to become less strong, severe, or intense

Literary Analysis
Theme and Worldview Which actions show the heroism of M. Morissot and M. Sauvage?

Reading Check

What does the German officer order the men to do?

There was a splash, the water trembled, then grew calm, while tiny wavelets spread to both shores.

A little blood remained on the surface.

The officer, still calm, said in a low voice: "Now the fish will have their turn."

And he went back to the house.

And all at once he caught sight of the sack of gudgeons in the grass. He picked it up, looked at it, smiled, shouted, "Wilhelm!"

A soldier in a white apron ran out. And the Prussian threw him the catch of the two and said: "Fry these little animals right away while they are still alive. They will be delicious."

Then he lighted his pipe again.

Literary Analysis
Theme and Worldview What details of this ending emphasize the injustice of the heroes' fate?

Thinking About the Selection

1. **Respond:** Were you shocked by the ending of the story? Explain.

2. **(a) Recall:** Before the siege, what did Morissot and Sauvage do together on Sundays? **(b) Analyze Cause and Effect:** Why does the situation in Paris force them to change their habits?

3. **(a) Analyze Cause and Effect:** What circumstances lead the two friends to risk going outside town? **(b) Support:** Identify two details from the selection showing the pleasure the two experience when fishing. **(c) Interpret:** What aspects of life does fishing represent for them?

4. **(a) Analyze:** Use details from the story to describe the friendship of the two men. **(b) Draw Conclusions:** What role does friendship play in the decision each man makes in the ending?

5. **(a) Synthesize:** What message does Maupassant convey by contrasting the cruelty of war with the pleasures of fishing? **(b) Interpret:** How do the last two paragraphs add to the story's message?

Apply the Skills

Damon and Pythias • Two Friends

Comparing Theme and Worldview

1. **(a)** For each story, fill in a chart like the one shown.

Friends	Powerful Person	Test of Loyalty	Result of Test?

   (b) Draw a conclusion based on your chart about the theme of each story. **(c)** Explain what the themes of the two stories have in common.

2. What is the relationship between loyalty and power in the worldview of each story?

3. **(a)** Describe the way in which Damon and Pythias each face probable death. **(b)** Compare the way in which they face death with Morrisot and Sauvage's final goodbye.

4. **(a)** What is the difference between heroism in Maupassant's worldview and heroism in the worldview of the legend? **(b)** Which view makes heroism seem most "heroic"? Explain.

Writing to Compare Literary Works

Write an essay to evaluate the themes and worldviews reflected in "Damon and Pythias" and "Two Friends." Use these questions to get started:

- In which story is friendship presented more realistically?
- Which story does a better job teaching a clear lesson?
- Which story shows the forces opposing friendship?
- Which worldview is closer to your own perspective? Why?

Vocabulary Builder

Give an example of the items described. Explain your answers.

1. a *dire* emergency
2. *impediments* faced on a shopping trip
3. music that inspires a mood of *serenity*
4. the actions of an *ardent* fan
5. clothing or accessories that give a look of *jauntiness*
6. reasons a person arguing with another might *relent*

QuickReview

Theme: the central message or insight conveyed in a literary work. Many themes are *universal.*

Worldview: the basic beliefs and values that shape a writer's experience.

Go Online
Assessment

For: Self-test
Visit: www.PHSchool.com
Web Code: eqa-6611

Reading

Directions: *Questions 1–5 are based on the following selection.*

Three days later the village priest of Ani called on the headmaster. . . . "I have heard," he said after the usual exchange of cordialities, "that our ancestral footpath has recently been closed. . . ."

"Yes," replied Mr. Obi. "We cannot allow people to make a highway of our school compound."

"Look here, my son," said the priest bringing down his walking-stick, "this path was here before you were born and before your father was born. The whole life of the village depends on it. Our dead relatives depart by it and our ancestors visit us by it. But most important, it is the path of children coming in to be born. . . ."

Mr. Obi listened with a satisfied smile on his face.

"The whole purpose of our school," he said finally, "is to eradicate just such beliefs as that. Dead men do not require footpaths. The whole idea is just fantastic. Our duty is to teach your children to laugh at such ideas."

"What you say may be true," replied the priest, "but we follow the practices of our fathers. If you reopen the path we shall having nothing to quarrel about. What I always say is: let the hawk perch and let the eagle perch." He rose to go.

from "Dead Men's Path" by Chinua Achebe

1. **Which phrase best describes the priest's worldview?**
   A old-fashioned and stubborn
   B traditional but accommodating
   C modern and scientific
   D deeply concerned with bettering the lot of humanity

2. **Which phrase best describes the headmaster's worldview?**
   A cynical and pessimistic
   B generous and optimistic
   C narrowminded and superstititious
   D modern and opinionated

3. **Why does the priest think the path is important?**
   A It provides a route to the fields where food for the community is harvested.
   B It is vital to the community's traditional beliefs about birth and death.
   C It allows older community members to visit the school and learn new ways.
   D The tolls charged for using it provide a source of revenue for the church.

4. **What does the priest mean when he tells the headmaster, "Let the hawk perch and let the eagle perch"?**
   A My way is better than your way.
   B Let us be tolerant of each other's views.
   C Let us be less materialistic.
   D Modern ideas like yours must be pounced on and destroyed.

Vocabulary

Directions: *Choose the letter of the sentence that uses the vocabulary word correctly.*

5. coordinate
  A If we *coordinate* our efforts, we will get the job done more efficiently.
  B When you *coordinate* information, you refuse to share it with anyone else.
  C On Sunday, the church will *coordinate* several new ministers.
  D Someone ought to *coordinate* her ego and make her less conceited.

6. lucid
  A The plot was too *lucid* to follow.
  B We used *lucid* to paint the walls yellow.
  C Her *lucid* arguments convinced me.
  D The *lucid* fabric is opaque.

7. evolve
  A Parades *evolve* many people.
  B Old-fashioned vinyl records used to *evolve* around a spindle.
  C The worst jobs *evolve* to new workers.
  D Will the change be drastic, or will it *evolve* more slowly?

8. intense
  A An *intense* person is usually easygoing and somewhat vague.
  B An *intense* person is usually highly emotional or focused.
  C The verb is in the past *intense*.
  D To all *intense* and purposes, the decision was made by us.

9. synthesize
  A The *synthesize* fabric was invented and produced at a factory.
  B *Synthesizing* data is one of the most difficult thinking skills.
  C A *synthesized* action causes trouble.
  D *Synthesize* your swimming with mine.

Directions: *Study each sentence for context clues about the meaning of the word in italics. Then, choose the correct meaning of the word as it is used in the sentence.*

10. The Internet was a *revolutionary* force in modern communications.
  A showing drastic change; radical
  B conforming to the status quo
  C person who rebels against authority
  D happening slowly over time

11. The clock has a *luminous* dial that you can see in the dark.
  A very unclear
  B glowing
  C related to the spoken word
  D frightening; threatening

12. She wore a *voluminous* sweater that stretched down below her knees.
  A consisting of many books
  B dark colored
  C too small to be noticed
  D having a great size or bulk

13. I was confused and asked for *illumination*.
  A the act of turning on a light
  B lights used as decoration
  C clarification; explanation
  D the act of darkening

Spelling Workshop

Spelling on College Entrance Exams

You will find a few spelling items in the English sections of most college entrance exams. To do well on them, look for small, easy errors; recall some basic rules; and know your own spelling problems.

Testing Tips Though spelling is not the most important part of college entrance exams, spelling items do occur in writing or English usage sections of most tests. The following recommendations will help you prepare for items of this type.

- Look for homophone errors, easily confused words, or simple words spelled incorrectly. Remember, for example, that *who's*, not *whose*, is the spelling for "who is."
- Review word formation rules that people sometimes forget.
  - When adding endings to multisyllable words whose final letters are a vowel followed by a consonant, double the final consonant if the accent is on the final syllable.
  - When adding prefixes to words, do not drop any letters.
  - When adding suffixes to words ending consonant +*y*, remember that the final *y* usually changes to *i*. In words ending consonant +*e*, the final *e* is usually dropped when the suffix begins with a vowel—but not when the base word ends in *ce* or *ge*.
- Know the words that give you trouble and work out memory tricks to help with them. If you cannot remember where the *y* comes in *rhythm*, try making up a saying with the letters r-h-y, or just remember the letter group.

Word List

emigrate

immigrate

transmittal

reevaluate

liveliness

irreplaceable

machinations

specious

concede

dissemble

Okay, I'm looking for *their, there, they're, emigrate, immigrate, irreplaceable, supercede*............

Monitor Your Progress

Test Practice

Standards Assessed
• 10.4.11
• 10.4.12

A. Directions: *Write the letter of the item that contains a spelling, punctuation, capitalization, or usage error. Write E if there are no errors in the sentence.*

1. Although I knew that <u>Professor Chin</u> was
   A
   <u>infuriated,</u> she <u>manages</u> to <u>dissemble</u> her
   B   **C**   **D**
   true feelings with a smile. No <u>error</u>
   E

2. The <u>women's</u> choir sang traditional
   A
   <u>American</u> songs with a <u>livliness</u> that had the
   B   **C**
   audience clapping <u>their</u> hands and singing
   D
   along. No error
   E

3. The judge thought that <u>Lewis Davis, Jr.,</u> a
   A
   known <u>criminal,</u> would offer a <u>specious</u>
   B   **C**
   story about his <u>whereabouts; however, he</u>
   D
   said nothing. No error
   E

4. Voters were fed up with the <u>mackinations</u>
   A
   of the ruling <u>party,</u> an arrogant group
   B
   <u>whose</u> members were only interested in
   C
   staying in office and <u>filling</u> their own
   D
   pockets. No error
   E

B. Directions: *Write the letter of the version of the underlined section that makes the item correct and appropriate. If you think the original version is best, choose "NO CHANGE."*

Boris knew that the papers of <u>transmittal were irreplaceable, since</u> they allowed <u>his family to immigrate.</u> However, he could not find them anywhere. After much frantic <u>searching, he had to conceed</u> that they were lost. With a heavy heart, <u>he begins to reevaluate</u> his plans for leaving Lutonia.

1. **A** NO CHANGE
   B transmittal was irreplaceable, since
   C transmital were irreplaceable, since
   D transmittal were irreplaceable, though

2. **A** NO CHANGE
   B their family to immigrate
   C his family to emigrate
   D their family to emigrate

3. **A** NO CHANGE
   B searching he had to conceed
   C searching, they had to conceed
   D searching, he had to concede

4. **A** NO CHANGE
   B he began to reevaluate
   C he begins to revaluate
   D he began to revaluate

Writing Workshop

Exposition: Comparison-and-Contrast Essay

Comparing and contrasting are ways of thinking that you apply every day perhaps without realizing you are doing so. By noticing similarities and differences, you clarify your understanding of things. A **comparison-and-contrast** essay explores the similarities and differences between or among two or more topics, thus bringing both into clearer focus. Use the steps outlined in this workshop to write a comparison-and-contrast essay.

Assignment Write a comparison-and-contrast essay about two literary characters, two concepts, or two events.

What to Include Your essay should include these elements:
- a purpose for comparing and contrasting
- a clear thesis statement
- supporting evidence, including facts and examples that show similarities and differences between two or more subjects
- transitions that show clear relationships between ideas
- an effective organizational plan suited to your topic and purpose
- error-free grammar and varied sentence structure and length

To preview the criteria on which your comparison-and-contrast essay may be assessed, see the rubric on page 1157.

 Writing Workshop: *Work in Progress*

If you have completed the Work-in-Progress assignments, you have several ideas in your portfolio that you might pursue in your essay. Continue to develop these ideas, or explore a new idea as you complete this Writing Workshop.

 Academic Standards
- Provide constructive criticism to other writers. (10.4.12)
- Write for different purposes and audiences. (10.5.8)
- Produce well-punctuated, legible work. (10.6.3)

Using the Form
You will use comparison and contrast in these types of writing:
- profiles of historical figures
- reviews of literature or performances
- descriptive essays

Reading Writing Connection

To get a feel for comparison-and-contrast writing, read the excerpt from "The Marginal World" by Rachel Carson on page 155.

Prewriting

Choosing Your Topic

Your comparison-and-contrast essay should explore subjects that share traits but are significantly different. Use these strategies to choose a topic:

- **List related topics.** Think of a broad subject area, such as music, sports, or fictional characters. Then, list specific items. For example, you might list favorite athletes or unusual places. Look for similarities—and differences—between two or more items on your list. Choose one set as your subject.

- **Fill in a sentence frame.** Find at least three ways to complete a sentence frame. Then, choose your best idea to explore in your essay.
  Sample Sentence Frame: I often confuse _____ and _____ because they are both _____. However, they are also different because of _____ and _____.

Narrowing Your Topic

Consider your purpose. The comparisons and contrasts you explore should fulfill a larger purpose or idea such as one of the following:

- **To persuade**—You believe one of your subjects is better than the other and you want to convince your readers to share your opinion.
- **To reflect**—Both subjects are meaningful to you, but in different ways, and you want to explore why this is the case.
- **To describe**—The similarities and differences in your subjects are very striking and you want to portray them.

Formulate a thesis statement. Write a sentence describing your subject that incorporates a sense of your larger purpose. You will include this thesis statement in your introduction.

Gathering Details

Evaluate your topic. Be sure your topics offer enough interesting similarities and differences. To evaluate your topic choices, use a Venn diagram.

Conduct research. Consider conducting research to further explore your analysis. For example, after creating a Venn diagram like the one shown, a writer might read movie industry journals to find the average time between a movie's release into theaters and its release onto DVD.

Work-in-Progress
Review the work you did on pages 1095 and 1125.

Going to a Movie Theater   **Watching a DVD**

- big screen
- live audience (comedies are funnier)
- see the movie sooner

- same movie
- same running time

- home comfort
- extra features
- no audience noise
- see the movie later

Writing Workshop

Drafting

Shaping Your Writing

Choose an organization. Most comparison-and-contrast essays are organized in one of two ways. In *subject-by-subject organization,* you analyze all of the features of one subject and then all the features of the second subject. In *point-by-point organization,* you discuss one point about both subjects and then move on to a second point. Select an organizational structure that best suits your subjects.

Types of Organization	
Subject-by-Subject	**Point-by-Point**
Subject A • Point 1 • Point 2 Subject B • Point 1 • Point 2	Point A • Subject 1 • Subject 2 Point B • Subject 1 • Subject 2

Use your thesis statement and purpose. Include your thesis in your introduction. Check that the ideas you include in each body paragraph connect directly to your thesis statement and purpose. Restate or reevaluate your thesis statement in your conclusion.

Providing Elaboration

Support opinions. Using a wide variety of evidence can make your ideas more convincing and add interest to your essay.

- **Examples:** Illustrations clarify similarities and differences.
- **Facts:** Hard evidence helps readers understand each subject.
- **Quotations:** The exact words of experts add authority.

Use transitions. Help readers follow the logic of your comparisons and contrasts by using effective transitions to show the relationships between ideas. These transitional words and phrases are especially useful:

similarly	*on the other hand*	*conversely*
however	*although*	*nevertheless*
in contrast	*whereas*	*by comparison*

For the complete student model, see page 1156.

Student Model: Using Transitions to Clarify Connections

Letter writers, phone callers, and e-mailers are generally not limited by time either. They can create and share their communications round the clock.

Despite their similarities, letters, phone calls, and e-mail communicate differently.

> The writer uses a transitional phrase to signal a shift from comparison to contrast.

From the Author's Desk

John Phillip Santos
On Making Comparisons

John Phillip
Santos

In the following passage from my book, I wanted to find a way to illuminate the history of Mexican Americans by comparing and contrasting my family's name—Santos—with its literal meaning in Spanish and earlier versions of the name that had been used in the past.

"You're part of a long tradition of writers."
—John Phillip Santos

Professional Model:

from *Places Left Unfinished at the Time of Creation*

It is ~~It's~~ a common name my family carries, ~~through a skyful of generations~~ out of our Mexican past. It is a name that invokes the saints and embroiders daily prayers of Latinos in North and South America. The old ones in the family say the name was once *de Los Santos.* "From the saints." But no one remembers when or why it was shortened. There were Santos in San Antonio two hundred years ago. In the records for the year 1793 at the Mission San Antonio de Valero, which later became the Alamo, you find the names of Manuel and Jorge de Los Santos, referred to as "Indios," but it's not clear whether they are our ancestors.

It sometimes seems as if Mexicans are to forgetting what the Jews are to remembering. We have made selective forgetting a sacramental obligation. Leave it all in the past, all that you were, and all that you could not be. There is pain enough in the present to go around. Some memories cannot not be abandoned. Let the past reclaim all the rest forever, and let stories come to their fitting end.

In this early section of the book, by asking readers to move between English and Spanish, I am slowly preparing them for the mix of the two languages that I use in telling the story to come.

By adding this passage, I was able to establish the broader historical background of our Mexican families from San Antonio. This allowed me to compare our experience to the storied legacy of Jewish people.

After comparing traditions of remembering and forgetting to a sacramental obligation, I wanted the rest of the paragraph to have a chant-like quality. The final sentences are short, written with short words, making the passage seem solemn and ceremonial.

Writing Workshop

Revising

Revising Your Paragraphs

Revise to balance your organization. An effective comparison-and-contrast essay provides a thorough analysis of each subject being compared. Follow these steps to check the balance of your coverage:

- First, use one color to highlight places where you discuss one subject. Use another color to highlight places where you discuss another subject. Use other colors for any additional subjects.

- Next, review your highlighted draft to determine whether you have addressed each subject equally. Add details to support under-developed subjects.

Peer Review: Ask a partner to read your essay and identify which subject you have explored most effectively. Discuss whether or not the other subject or subjects need additional support. Consider developing an idea further or adding details to provide more thorough comparisons and contrasts.

For the complete student model, see page 1156.

Student Model: Revising to Create Balance

Letters convey a personal touch and make recipients especially happy when received. They can be saved, to be reread (often over and over) at a later time. Unlike a letter, e-mail is usually more spontaneous and less likely to be reread. Phone call messages quickly fade. Of all three modes, letters take the longest time between the sender and the receiver.

> The writer adds information about her third topic to create a better balance.

Revising Your Word Choice

Revise for precision. When you compare and contrast, you discuss topics that share many traits. To clearly distinguish one from the other, use words that are specific and precise.

Vague: The effects used in the *Star Wars* movies were *good,* but today's computerized images *are also good.*

Specific: The effects used in the first *Star Wars* movies were *convincing,* but today's computerized images *are totally lifelike.*

Integrating Grammar Skills

Revising to Vary Sentence Structure and Length

A sequence of too many sentences of the same length and structure can be monotonous, causing readers to lose interest. Vary sentence lengths, sentence beginnings, and subject-verb order to create an engaging flow in your writing.

Prentice Hall Writing and Grammar Connection: Chapter 21, Section 3

Vary sentence length. The constant use of short sentences can make your writing seem undeveloped and choppy. Work to identify whether you have too many short sentences in sequence and combine some to create a better flow. Reserve a short, punchy sentence for an idea you want to emphasize.

Choppy: I like lakes more than the ocean. It is easier to swim. You can fish. You can water ski. Lakes are nice at all times of day. They are pretty in all weather. I feel at home on a lake.

Flowing: I like lakes more than the ocean because it is easier to swim, fish, and water ski. Lakes are beautiful at all times of day and in all weather. I feel at home on a lake.

Vary sentence beginnings. Avoid using the same parts of speech to start a series of sentences. Vary your sentence beginnings by using different parts of speech, phrases, and clauses.

Adjective: *Blue* skies always remind her of home.

Prepositional phrase: *Until then,* she was not sure she would make friends at her new school.

Adverb clause: *Wherever she went,* she still thought about the people she had left.

Complement: *Spending lunchtime alone* was most distressing to her. (complement of verb *was*)

Vary subject-verb order. You can also create variety in your sentences by reversing the usual subject-verb order.

Original: The statue stood outside the theater.

Inverted: Outside the theater stood the statue.

Apply It to Your Editing

Review three body paragraphs of your draft, highlighting sequences of sentences of similar length and structure. Add variety to your sentences by changing sentence lengths, altering sentence beginnings, or inverting subject-verb order.

Writing Workshop

Student Model: Amanda Goodman
Glen Rock, NJ

You've Got Mail

Personal communications have gone through a major evolution in modern times. The letter gave way to the telephone call, and now they have both been overwhelmed in popularity by e-mail. While the three modes of communication have a lot in common, there are differences that let each stand out on its own.

Letters, phone calls, and e-mail are similar because they all involve personal communication. They allow people to share ideas and feelings with other people. Communicators do not have to be face to face; they can be across the world and get the same points across. Letter writers, phone callers, and e-mailers are generally not limited by time either. They can create and share their communications round the clock.

Despite their similarities, letters, phone calls, and e-mail communicate differently. Letters convey a personal touch and make recipients especially happy when received. They can be saved, to be reread (often over and over) at a later time. Unlike a letter, e-mail is usually more spontaneous and less likely to be reread. Phone call messages quickly fade. Of all three modes, letters take the longest time between the sender and the receiver. If time is important, letters are probably the worst format to use.

E-mail is seldom personal. It is more convenient than "snail mail," though. You never have to move away from your computer. Plus, you can edit without cross-outs. Once you send an e-mail, it is delivered instantly. This speed has its disadvantages. Because people create e-mails with such haste, they often do not stop to think carefully about what they want to say—or correct grammar or spelling mistakes—before they click an e-mail on its way.

A phone call is extremely personal, and it shows that you have set aside time for the other person. You are able to hear the tone of voice and expression of the other person. Phone calls may be expensive, temporary, and time-sensitive—unlike a letter or an e-mail, which a recipient can read when he or she has the time. Another problem with the phone is that once you say something, you cannot take it back, in contrast to the way you can edit writing.

There is a time and a place for all three types of communication. People are often so busy that they have time only for e-mail, but maybe people should set aside some time to write a letter or call a friend.

In her introduction, Amanda identifies the subjects she will compare.

In this paragraph, the writer discusses the similarities that the three formats share.

In the third, fourth, and fifth paragraphs, the writer addresses the unique qualities of each form.

Transitions help clarify the contrasts between subjects.

Editing and Proofreading

Check your draft to correct errors in spelling, grammar, and punctuation.

Focus on Transitional Words: Double-check the meanings of the transitional words you have used, and make sure they are punctuated correctly. If you start a sentence with a coordinating conjunction, such as *however* or *nevertheless,* follow it with a comma.

Publishing and Presenting

Consider one of the following ways to share your writing:

Present a shared reading. With a partner, deliver an oral presentation of your essay. First, present to a small group. Read the paragraphs that discuss one subject while having your partner read the paragraphs that discuss the other subject. Ask for listeners' comments to improve your presentation before sharing it with another group.

Create a class book. Compile a collection of comparison-and-contrast essays. Devise a title that reflects the content of the collection and place the finished book in your classroom or school library.

Reflecting on Your Writing

Writer's Journal Jot down your thoughts on writing a comparison-and-contrast essay. Begin by answering these questions.

- Which prewriting strategies helped you the most?
- In what ways did writing about these subjects help you understand their relationship in a new way?

Rubric for Self-Assessment

To assess your comparison-and-contrast essay, use the following rubric:

Criteria	Rating Scale
	not very very
Focus: How clear is your purpose and thesis?	1 2 3 4 5
Organization: How effectively does your organization show comparisons and contrasts?	1 2 3 4 5
Support/Elaboration: How varied and convincing is your evidence?	1 2 3 4 5
Style: How well do you use transitions to connect ideas?	1 2 3 4 5
Conventions: How correct is your grammar? How consistently and well do you vary sentence lengths and structures?	1 2 3 4 5

Comparing Media Coverage

The same event can be described in varying ways, resulting in different messages being delivered to an audience. The following techniques will help you assess the objectivity and effectiveness of different media presentations and compare the delivery of information.

Evaluate Coverage

Choose two different reports of the same event. Evaluate each report separately to start the comparison.

Background Does the reporter have a cultural or political agenda—a particular viewpoint or opinion to support? Knowing the background of the person or group structuring the information allows you to actively listen for potential *bias,* or a tendency to favor unfairly one side of an issue.

Facts and Opinions Are the items presented as facts verifiable? Are facts accompanied by music or images that add an emotional dimension? Does the reporter add comments that are not facts of the story?

Actively Listen and Watch Is the language factual, emotional and objective, or emotional and subjective? Is the pacing of speech designed to elicit an emotional response from the audience?

Compare Coverage

After you evaluate the reports, compare them.

Emphasis Note the facts that each report highlights. Which points are omitted from one, but not the other? Which report contains more opinions? Compare the items that each reporter chose to emphasize.

Techniques Compare the techniques each presentation uses to convey information. Note the use of music, pictures, and colors that might evoke responses from the audience. Compare how each report uses language and pacing to convey a specific tone or attitude.

Evaluate

After you have compared the two reports, write a statement explaining which one is more factual and objective.

> **Activity** > Compare Media Coverage > Choose two different media sources and evaluate the same story as presented by each group. Use the checklist to analyze the basic elements of the stories.

 Academic Standards

- Evaluate the aesthetic qualities of style. (10.3.11)
- Write persuasive compositions. (10.5.4)
- Deliver persuasive arguments. (10.7.18)

Comparing Media Coverage

For each report, note the following:

Purpose _____

Background _____
_____

The majority of information is factual _____
_____

The majority of information is opinion _____
_____

There is a balance of fact and opinion _____
_____

Visuals are neutral
Visuals are dramatic

Language is factual
Language is emotional

Facial expressions reinforce language

The Prince and the Pauper: A Pacemaker Classic

Mark Twain
Globe Fearon, 1993

Novel This story is set in England in the 1500s and is inspired by historical facts. Two boys happen to look exactly alike. However, one is a prince, heir to the kingdom of England, and the other is from the poverty-stricken streets. Follow what happens to both boys as they switch places and each tries to live in a world very different from his own. What begins as a frivolous adventure turns dark and dangerous.

Myths and Legends from Ancient Greece and Around the World

Prentice Hall Anthology
Prentice Hall, 2000

Anthology These are the legends and myths that have been told and retold throughout generations. The Greek gods, sitting on Mt. Olympus and dabbling in the lives of mortals, form the core of this collection. King Arthur, Norse myths, and Trickster gods are also included. These explanations of how things came to be and why people behave as they do are fascinating reading.

Early Irish Myths and Sagas

Betty Radice
Penguin Group, 1981

Collection These early Irish stories represent the oral tradition at the dawn of Western civilization. Written in beautiful, elusive language, the stories weave reality and fantasy to create a world where men mingle freely with the gods.

The Once and Future King

T. H. White
Ace Books, 1987

Novel This is an epic of King Arthur and his Camelot. Merlyn, Guinevere, Lancelot, and the knights of the Round Table are characters in this book, which follows Arthur as he grows up and consolidates his power. Magicians and kings build a kingdom but sacrifice their own personal desires. This retelling is based largely on Sir Thomas Malory's *Le Morte d'Arthur*.

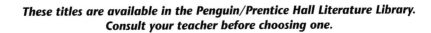

These titles are available in the Penguin/Prentice Hall Literature Library.
Consult your teacher before choosing one.

Think About It The right word can make a gloomy day cheerful—the wrong word can take all the joy out of sunshine. In this story, a young girl tests her power to change the look of things by telling tales. As you read, decide whether you sympathize with her—or with her victims!

THE OPEN WINDOW
SAKI
(H.H. MUNRO)

"My aunt will be down presently, Mr. Nuttel," said a very self-possessed young lady of fifteen; "in the meantime you must try and put up with me."

Framton Nuttel endeavored to say the correct something that should duly flatter the niece of the moment without unduly discounting the aunt that was to come. Privately he doubted more than ever whether these formal visits on a succession of total strangers would do much towards helping the nerve cure which he was supposed to be undergoing.

"I know how it will be," his sister had said when he was preparing to migrate to this rural retreat; "you will bury yourself down there and not speak to a living soul, and your nerves will be worse than ever from moping. I shall just give you letters of introduction[1] to all the people I know there. Some of them, as far as I can remember, were quite nice."

Framton wondered whether Mrs. Sappleton, the lady to whom he was presenting one of the letters of introduction, came into the nice division.

"Do you know many of the people round here?" asked the niece, when she judged that they had had sufficient silent communion.

"Hardly a soul," said Framton. "My sister was staying here, at the rectory, you know, some four years ago, and she gave me letters of introduction to some of the people here."

He made the last statement in a tone of distinct regret.

"Then you know practically nothing about my aunt?" pursued the self-possessed young lady.

"Only her name and address," admitted the caller. He was wondering whether Mrs. Sappleton was in the married or widowed state. An undefinable something about the room seemed to suggest masculine habitation.

"Her great tragedy happened just three years ago," said the child; "that would be since your sister's time."

"Her tragedy?" asked Framton; somehow in this restful country spot tragedies seemed out of place.

"You may wonder why we keep that window wide open on an October afternoon," said the niece, indicating a large French window that opened on to a lawn.

"It is quite warm for the time of the year," said Framton; "but has that window got anything to do with the tragedy?"

"Out through that window, three years ago to a day, her husband and her two young brothers went off for their day's shooting. They never came back. In crossing the moor to their favorite snipe-shooting ground[2] they were all three engulfed in a treacherous piece of bog.[3] It had been that dreadful wet summer, you know, and places that were safe in other years gave way suddenly without warning. Their bodies were never recovered. That was the dreadful part of it." Here the child's voice lost its self-possessed note and became falteringly human. "Poor aunt always thinks that they will come back some day, they and the little brown spaniel that was lost with them, and walk in at that window just as they used to do. That is why the window is kept open every evening till it is quite dusk. Poor dear aunt, she has often told me how they went out, her husband with his white waterproof coat over his arm, and Ronnie, her youngest brother, singing, 'Bertie, why do you bound?' as he always did to tease her, because she said it got on her nerves. Do you know, sometimes on

---

1. letters of introduction letters introducing two strangers, written by someone who knows them both. The person to whom such a letter is written is obliged to provide hospitality to the person carrying the letter.
2. snipe-shooting ground area for hunting snipe—wading birds that live chiefly in marshy places and have long, flexible bills.
3. bog small swamp; wet, spongy ground.

still, quiet evenings like this, I almost get a creepy feeling that they will walk in through that window—"

She broke off with a little shudder. It was a relief to Framton when the aunt bustled into the room with a whirl of apologies for being late in making her appearance.

"I hope Vera has been amusing you?" she said.

"She has been very interesting," said Framton.

"I hope you don't mind the open window," said Mrs. Sappleton briskly; "my husband and brothers will be home directly from shooting, and they always come in this way. They've been out for snipe in the marshes today, so they'll make a fine mess over my poor carpets. So like you menfolk, isn't it?"

She rattled on cheerfully about the shooting and the scarcity of birds, and the prospects for duck in the winter. To Framton, it was all purely horrible. He made a desperate but only partially successful effort to turn the talk on to a less ghastly topic; he was conscious that his hostess was giving him only a fragment of her attention, and her eyes were constantly straying past him to the open window and the lawn beyond. It was certainly an unfortunate coincidence that he should have paid his visit on this tragic anniversary.

"The doctors agree in ordering me complete rest, an absence of mental excitement, and avoidance of anything in the nature of violent physical exercise," announced Framton, who labored under the tolerably widespread delusion that total strangers and chance acquaintances are hungry for the least detail of one's ailments and infirmities, their cause and cure. "On the matter of diet they are not so much in agreement," he continued.

"No?" said Mrs. Sappleton, in a voice which only replaced a yawn at the last moment. Then she suddenly brightened into alert attention—but not to what Framton was saying.

"Here they are at last!" she cried. "Just in time for tea, and don't they look as if they were muddy up to the eyes!"

Framton shivered slightly and turned towards the niece with a look intended to convey sympathetic comprehension. The child was staring out through the open window with dazed horror in her eyes. In a chill shock of nameless fear Framton swung round in his seat and looked in the same direction.

In the deepening twilight three figures were walking across the lawn towards the window; they all carried guns under their arms, and one of them was additionally burdened with a white coat hung over his shoulders. A tired brown spaniel kept close at their heels. Noiselessly they neared the house, and then a hoarse young voice chanted out of the dusk: "I said, Bertie, why do you bound?"

Framton grabbed wildly at his stick and hat; the hall door, the gravel drive, and the front gate were dimly noted stages in his headlong retreat. A cyclist coming along the road had to run into the hedge to avoid imminent collision.

"Here we are, my dear," said the bearer of the white mackintosh,[4] coming in through the window; "fairly muddy, but most of it's dry. Who was that who bolted out as we came up?"

"A most extraordinary man, a Mr. Nuttel," said Mrs. Sappleton; "could only talk about his illnesses, and dashed off without a word of goodbye or apology when you arrived. One would think he had seen a ghost."

"I expect it was the spaniel," said the niece calmly; "he told me he had a horror of dogs. He was once hunted into a cemetery somewhere on the banks of the Ganges[5] by a pack of pariah dogs, and had to spend the night in a newly dug grave with the creatures snarling and grinning and foaming just above him. Enough to make anyone lose their nerve."

Romance at short notice was her specialty.

---

4. **mackintosh** (mak′ in täsh′) *n.* waterproof raincoat.
5. **Ganges** (gan′ jēz) river in northern India and Bangladesh.

Meet the Author
Saki (1870–1916) is the pen name of Hector Hugh Munro. Born to British parents in Burma (now Myanmar), Saki lived in England for most of his life. He began by writing political satires for newspapers and then turned to fiction. Today, Saki is best known for his witty, sometimes cruel short stories, many of which feature humorous surprise endings.

Readings in Classic Fiction
Talk About It
Use these questions to guide a discussion of "The Open Window."

1. **(a)** Why is Framton visiting the country? **(b)** Why is this detail critical to the story?

2. **(a)** When Mrs. Sappleton announces that she sees the hunters returning, what did you think was actually happening? **(b)** Did you enjoy the surprise of the story? Why?

3. In a group, consider how social conventions—the unwritten rules and expectations for people's behavior—affect people's lives.
   • What role does the convention of "small-talk" play in the story?
   • What social conventions guide your behavior?
   • What is the purpose of these rules?
   • What are the positive and negative aspects of social conventions?

   Choose a point-person to share your group's ideas with the class.

RESOURCES

GLOSSARY

High utility and academic vocabulary words appear in green.

A

abruptly (ə brupt´ lē) *adv.* unexpectedly; happening in a way that seems too sudden

accomplices (ə käm´ plis iz) *n.* people who help others commit a crime

adamant (ad´ ə mənt) *adj.* not giving in; unyielding; firm

adept (ə dept´) *adj.* expert; highly skilled

adulation (a´ joō lā´ shən) *n.* high or excessive praise; intense admiration

affront (ə frunt´) *n.* open insult

aggrieved (ə grēv´d´) *v.* caused grief or injury; wronged

allay (a lā´) *v.* relieve; lessen; calm

ambient (am´ bē ənt) *adj.* surrounding; part of the atmosphere or environment

amenable (ə mē´ nə bəl) *adj.* responsive; open (to influence)

amiably (ā´ mē ə blē) *adv.* in a cheerful, friendly way

anticipate (an tis´ ə pāt´) *v.* give advance thought to; expect

apathy (ap´ ə *th*ē) *n.* without emotion

application (ap´ li kā´ shən) *n.* act of putting something to use

arabesques (ar´ ə besks´) *n.* elaborate decorative designs of intertwined lines

ardent (är´ dənt) *adj.* intensely enthusiastic or devoted

arduously (är´joō əs lē) *adv.* with great difficulty; laboriously

aspirations (as´ pə rā´ shənz) *n.* strong ambitions or desires; goals

assess (ə ses´) *v.* judge, measure

assimilate (ə sim´ ə lāt´) *v.* absorb or incorporate

assuage (ə swāj´) *v.* lessen (pain or distress); satisfy (thirst, hunger, and so on)

augmented (ôg ment´ id) *adj.* made greater; enhanced

august (ô gust´) *adj.* impressive; majestic

B

bewilderment (bē wil´ dər mənt) *n.* confusion

blemished (blem´ ish´t) *adj.* damaged; spoiled

bloated (blōt´ ed) *adj.* swollen

brandished (bran´ dish´d) *v.* showed, waved, or shook in a threatening or triumphant manner

brazen (brā´ zən) *adj.* shameless; bold

buffer (buf´ ər) *v.* lessen a shock; cushion

C

cajoling (kə jōl´ iŋ) *n.* coaxing with flattery

calamity (kə lam´ ə tē) *n.* terrible misfortune; disaster

candid (kan´ did) *adj.* honest; direct

canopied (kan´ ə pēd) *adj.* covered by a cloth suspended from poles or a framework

catalyst (kat´ ə list´) *n.* person or thing that triggers an event or inspires an action

cessation (se sā´ shən) *n.* halt; stopping

chastisement (chas´ tiz mənt) *n.* severe criticism; punishment

choleric (käl´ ər ik) *adj.* having a quick temper; inclined to anger

circuit (sʉr´ kit) *n.* act of going around something

coincide (kō´ in sīd´) *v.* occur at the same time

commences (kə mens´ əs) *v.* begins

commiserate (kə miz´ ər āt´) *v.* sympathize (with); show sorrow for

compensate (käm´ pən sāt´) *v.* make up for; counterbalance

comprehend (käm´ prē hend´) *v.* understand; include

configuration (kən fig´ yə rā´ shən) *n.* arrangement of parts; pattern

confounded (kən foun´ did) *n.* confused; bewildered

conniving (kə nīv´ iŋ) *adj.* conspiring; cooperating secretly (with someone)

consequently (kän´ si kwent´ lē) *adv.* logically following from; as a result of

contempt (kən tempt´) *n.* scorn; the attitude of someone who looks down on something or someone else

context (kän´ tekst´) *n.* environment, situation, or surroundings in which something is found, especially when these help explain the thing

contradictory (kän´ trə dik´ tə rē) *adj.* in opposition or conflict

convoluted (kän´ və lōōt´ id) *adj.* intricate; twisted

coordinate (kō ôrd´´nāt´) *v.* place in the same order, rank, or system; adjust

counsel (koun´ səl) *n.* advice; discussion

countenance (kount´´n əns) *n.* face; the look of a person's face showing his or her nature or feelings

credible (kred´ ə bəl) *adj.* believable; reliable

customarily (kus´ tə mer´ ə lē) *adv.* usually; by habit; by tradition

D

debut (dā byoo´) *n.* first public appearance

decrepitude (dē krep´ ə tood´) *n.* feebleness; condition of being worn out by age or illness

deference (def´ ər əns) *n.* a yielding to the ideas, wishes, and so on of another

defiance (dē fī´ əns) *n.* the act of defying; open resistance to authority

deficiency (dē fish´ ən sē) *n.* lack of something essential

deficient (dē fish´ ənt) *adj.* lacking in some essential quality; incomplete; inadequate in amount

deflects (dē flekts´) *v.* turns or makes go to one side

deftness (deft´ nes) *n.* skillfulness

defunct (dē funkt´) *adj.* no longer in use or existence; dead

demeanor (di mēn´ ər) *n.* way of conducting oneself; behavior

derived (di rīv´d´) *v.* reached by reasoning

destitute (des´ tə toot´) *adj.* lacking the basic necessities of life; poverty-stricken

differentiate (dif´ər en´ shē āt´) *v.* distinguish between; discriminate

dignity (dig´ nə tē) *n.* quality of deserving respect and honor; self-respect

dilapidated (də lap´ ə dāt´ id) *adj.* shabby; broken down

diligence (dil´ ə jəns) *n.* constant, careful effort

dimpled (dim´ pəld) *adj.* marked with small hollows or indentations

dingy (din´ jē) *adj.* dirty-looking; shabby

dire (dīr) *adj.* urgent; terrible; calling for quick action

disapprobation (dis´ ap´ rə bā´ shən) *n.* disapproval

discern (di surn´) *v.* perceive or recognize clearly

disclaim (dis klām´) *v.* deny or give up a claim

disconsolate (dis kän´ sə lit) *adj.* so unhappy that nothing brings comfort

discourse (dis´ kôrs´) *v.* to speak formally and at length

disembarked (dis´ im bärk´d´) *v.* left a ship to go ashore

disparaged (di spar´ ij´d) *v.* spoke slightingly of; belittled

disparagement (di spar´ ij mənt) *n.* comments expressing a low opinion of or lack of respect for

disreputable (dis rep´ yoo tə bəl) *adj.* not respectable; having or deserving a bad reputation

distinct (di stiŋkt´) *adj.* clearly different; separate

distort (di stôrt) *v.* twist or change the meaning or intent

diverse (də vurs´) *adj.* different, varied

document (däk´ yoo mənt) *v.* provide with factual support for a statement or hypothesis

dogged (dôg´ id) *adj.* stubborn

dominant (dä´ mə nənt) *adj.* ruling; main

E

ebony (eb´ ə nē) *adj.* black

edict (ē´ dikt´) *n.* public order; decree

eloquent (el´ə kwənt) *adj.* expressing meaning clearly, forcefully, and memorably

emanating (em´ ə nāt´ iŋ) *v.* coming forth, as from a source

emigrants (em´ i grənts) *n.* people who leave their country or region to settle elsewhere

encroaching (en krōch´ iŋ) *adj.* intruding on, especially in a gradual manner

enthralls (en thrôlz´) *v.* captivates; fascinates

entreated (en trēt´ id) *v.* begged; pleaded

ephemeral (e fem´ ər əl) *adj.* short-lived

equestrian (ē kwes´ trē ən) *adj.* of a ride on horseback; related to horseback riding

equilibrium (ē´ kwi lib´ rē əm) *n.* a state of balance

esoteric (es´ ə ter´ ik) *adj.* beyond the understanding or knowledge of most people

estranged (e strānj´d´) *adj.* kept apart; in the condition of having had affection turn into indifference or hostility

evaluate (ē val´yoo āt´) *v.* find the value or the amount of; judge the worth of

evolve (ē välv´) *v.* develop by gradual changes; unfold

exorbitant (eg zôr´ bi tənt) *adj.* going beyond what is reasonable; excessive

expound (ek spound´) *v.* explain in detail

extolled (ek stōl´d´) *adj.* praised

extricating (eks´ tri kāt´ iŋ) *v.* setting free; removing from a difficult situation

F

facet (fas´ it) *n.* any of a number of sides or aspects

fathom (fa*th*´ əm) *v.* understand thoroughly

fawned (fônd) *v.* flattered; acted timidly with, as a servant might

flourishes (flur´ ish es) *v.* grows vigorously; thrives

fluttered (flut´ ər´d) *v.* flapped or vibrated rapidly

forbore (fôr bôr´) *v.* prevented oneself from doing something; refrained from

formulate (fôr´ myoo lāt´) *v.* express in a fixed or definite way

furtively (fur´ tiv lē) *adv.* secretively; sneakily; stealthily

G

grimacing (grim´ is iŋ) *v.* making a twisted face showing disgust or pain

H

haggard (hag´ ərd) *adj.* having a wild, worn look, as from grief or lack of sleep

haphazardly (hap´ haz´ ərd lē) *adv.* in an unplanned or a disorganized way

heedless (hēd´ lis) *adj.* careless; thoughtless

I

ideology (ī´ dē äl´ə jē) *n.* doctrines; system of beliefs;

imminent (im´ ə nənt) *adj.* about to happen

impeded (im pēd´ id) *v.* blocked; obstructed

impediments (im ped´ ə mənts) *n.* things that slow something or someone down or that get in the way

impending (im pend´ iŋ) *adj.* about to happen

imperceptibly (im´ pər sep´ tə blē) *adv.* so slowly or slightly as to be barely noticeable

imperiously (im pir´ ē əs lē) *adv.* arrogantly

impervious (im pɥr´ vē əs) *adj.* not affected by (with *to*)

impetuosity (im pech´ ōō äs´ i tē) *n.* quality of acting suddenly, with great force and little thought

implore (im plôr´) *v.* plead; ask for earnestly

incessant (in ses´ ənt) *adj.* not coming to a stop; constant

incorporate (in kôr´pə rāt´) *v.* to make part of something

incredulity (in´ krə dōō´ lə tē) *n.* unwillingness or inability to believe

indicate (in´di kāt´) *v.* direct attention to; point out

indigence (in´ di jəns) *n.* poverty

indignant (in dig´ nənt) *adj.* feeling or expressing anger, especially at an injustice

indulgence (in dul´ jəns) *n.* leniency; readiness to tolerate or forgive bad behavior

inevitable (in ev´i tə bəl) *adj.* certain to happen; unavoidable

inexorably (in eks´ə rə blē) *adv.* without the possibility of being delayed or stopped

infer (in fɥr´) *v.* derive by reasoning; to figure out from details

infirm (in fɥrm´) *adj.* weak; feeble

infirmity (in fɥr´ mə tē) *n.* illness; weakness; physical defect

ingratiating (in grā´ shē āt´ iŋ) *adj.* acting in a way intended to win someone's favor

inherent (in hir´ ənt) *adj.* inborn; natural; characteristic

inheritance (in her´ i təns) *n.* gift handed down to a later generation in a family

initiate (i nish´ē āt´) *v.* bring into practice or use; start

innovation (in´ ə vā´ shən) *n.* invention; a new thing or way of doing something

innuendo (in´ yōō en´ dō) *n.* indirect insult or accusation; insinuation

insight (in´ sīt´) *n.* the act or result of understanding the inner nature of things

instinct (in´ stiŋkt´) *n.* inborn pattern of behavior, as opposed to a learned skill

insurrection (in´ sə rek´ shən) *n.* rebellion

integrity (in teg´ rə tē) *n.* honesty; sincerity

intense (in tens´) *adj.* strong and focused; showing strong emotion; extreme

interminable (in tɥr´ mi nə bəl) *adj.* seemingly endless

interred (in tɥr´d´) *v.* buried (said of a dead body)

intrigues (in´ trēgz) *n.* plots; schemes

irascible (i ras´ ə bəl) *adj.* irritable; quick-tempered

irreproachable (ir´ i prō´ chə bəl) *adj.* above criticism; blameless

irretrievable (ir´ i trev´ ə bəl) *adj.* impossible to regain or recover

itinerary (ī tin´ ər er´ ē) *n.* route; travel plan

J

jauntiness (jôn´ tē nəs) *n.* carefree, easy attitude

jeered (jir´d) *v.* made fun of; mocked; taunted

L

lamentation (lam´ ən tā´ shən) *n.* act of crying out in grief; wailing

languid (laŋ´ gwid) *adj.* without energy; drooping, as from exhaustion

lavished (lav´ ish´d) *v.* gave with extreme generosity

legacies (leg´ ə sēz) *n.* money, property, or position left in a will to someone

legitimate (lə ji´ tə mit´) *adj.* lawful; reasonable; justifiable

livid (liv´ id) *adj.* discolored, as by a bruise; red with anger

looming (lōōm´ iŋ) *adj.* appearing unclearly but in a threatening form; threatening to occur

lucid (lōō´ sid) *adj.* readily apparent; clear

lucidity (lōō sid´ ə tē) *n.* clarity; quality of being readily understood

lucrative (lōō´ krə tiv) *adj.* producing wealth; profitable

M

maligned (mə līnd´) *adj.* spoken ill of

manifestations (man´ ə fes tā´ shənz) *n.* appearing or showings (of) ; forms (of)

manipulate (mə nip´ yōō lāt´) v. manage or control through clever moves; handle

marginal (mär´ jə nəl) adj. at, on, or near the edge

meditates (med´ ə tāts´) v. thinks deeply

melancholy (mel´ ən käl´ ē) adj. sad; gloomy

mementoes (mə men´ tōz) n. souvenirs; objects that serve as reminders

millennial (mi len´ ē əl) adj. of 1,000 years

minimize (min´ i mīz´) v. make small; reduce in size, amount, or importance

mirth (murth) n. joyfulness or merriment

misconstrued (mis´ kən strōōd´) v. misinterpreted

motive (mō´tiv) n. a person's reason for taking a specific action

multitudes (mul´ tə tōōdz) n. crowds; large number of people or things

mutable (myōōt´ ə bəl) adj. changeable

N

neutrality (nōō tral´ ə tē) n. state of not taking sides in a conflict; quality of being unbiased

nevertheless (nev´ ər thə les´) adv. in spite of that; however

nimbly (nim´ blē) adv. in a quick, easy, light way; with agility

nomadic (nō mad´ ik) adj. moving from place to place; without a permanent home

nonchalantly (nän´ shə länt´ lē) adv. casually; indifferently

O

obscured (əb skyōōr'd´) v. made dark; blocked from view; hid

oratory (ôr´ ə tôr´ ē) n. act of public speaking; strategies characteristic of such speaking

P

pallor (pal´ ər) n. lack of color; paleness

perceive (pər sēv´) v. see; understand

perspective (pər spek´ tiv) n. a specific point of view

petulantly (pech´ ə lənt lē) adv. in a manner that expresses impatience or irritation, especially over a minor matter

piety (pī´ ə tē) n. loyalty and devotion to the family, the divine, or some other object of respect

piqued (pēk'd) adj. offended, and so resentful

plague (plāg) v. pester; harass; torment

plausibility (plô´ zə bil´ i tē) n. believability; seeming truth

poignant (poin´ yənt) adj. emotionally moving; piercing

polarized (pō´ lə rīzd´) adj. divided into two opposing groups

portentous (pôr ten´ təs) adj. ominous; giving signs of evil to come

pragmatic (prag mat´ ik) adj. practical; concerned more with actual practice than with questions of principles

predominant (prē däm´ə nənt) adj. coming before other things; superior; most noticeable

presage (prē sāj´) v. give a warning sign about a future event

presumptuous (prē zump´ chōō əs) adj. overstepping appropriate bounds; too bold

priority (prī ôr´ ə tē) n. something given or meriting more attention than competing alternatives

prodigious (prō dij´ əs) adj. of great size or power

prolonged (prō lôn´´d) adj. extended; lengthy

prophesy (präf´ ə sī´) v. predict what will happen

prow (prou) n. the front of a boat or ship

prudent (prōō´ dənt) adj. exercising sound judgment; cautious

purified (pyōōr´ ə fīd´) v. rid of impurities or pollution; made pure

R

radical (rad´ i kəl) adj. extreme in opinions or effects

rash (rash) adj. acting without thinking; impulsive

reciprocity (res´ ə präs´ ə tē) n. relations of exchange; interdependence

recur (ri kur´) v. come up or happen again

rejuvenation (ri jōō və nā´ shən) n. a making new, youthful, or energetic again

relent (ri lent´) v. become less strong, severe, or intense

relentlessly (ri lent´ lis lē) adv. without pause or easing up; harshly

relish (rel´ ish) n. enjoyment

repertoire (rep´ ər twär´) n. a stock of works, such as songs, that a performer is prepared to present

replenished (ri plen´ ish'd) v. made complete or full again

replication (rep´ li kā´ shən) n. duplicate; reproduction

reprise (rə prēz´) n. repetition of a song, or part of a song, performed earlier

resolution (rez´ ə lōō´ shən) n. strong determination; a plan made with such determination

rudiments (rōō´ də mənts) n. basics; slight beginning

S

sated (sāt´ id) v. satisfied; provided with more than enough

scrutinized (skrōōt´'nīz'd´) v. examined carefully

secular (sek´ yə lər) adj. of worldly, as opposed to religious, matters

self-sufficiency (self´ sə fish´ ən sē) n. independence

sententiously (sen ten´ shəs lē) *adv.* in a way that shows excessive fondness for wise sayings; in lecturing tones

serenity (sə ren´ ə tē) *n.* state of calm or peace

significance (sig nif´ə kəns) *n.* meaning; importance

silhouette (sil´ ə wet´) *n.* depiction of a person in outline, filled in with a solid color

simulating (sim´ yōō lāt´ iŋ) *v.* giving the false appearance of

slight (slīt) *v.* treat with disrespect or indifference

slumbering (slum´ bər iŋ) *adj.* sleeping

sojourn (sō´ jʉrn) *v.* stay for a while

solemn (säl´ əm) *adj.* deeply serious; formal

somber (säm´ bər) *adj.* dark and gloomy

sonorous (sə nôr´ əs) *adj.* having a rich or impressive sound

spare (sper) *adj.* lean; thin

sparse (spärs) *adj.* thinly spread; not plentiful

spectacle (spek´ tə kəl) *n.* strange or remarkable sight

spontaneous (spän tā´nē əs) *adj.* seeming to occur without study or planning; impulsive

staidness (stād´ ness) *n.* state of being settled; calm

staunch (stônch) *adj.* steadfast; strong; loyal

stickler (stik´ lər) *n.* person who insists on strict obedience to rules or standards

stifle (stī´ fəl) *v.* smother; hold back

stipulates (stip´ yə lāts´) *v.* includes specifically as part of an agreement

strains (strānz) *n.* musical sounds; melodies

strife (strīf) *n.* struggle; conflict

stupefied (stōō´ pə fīd´) *adj.* dazed; stunned

subdued (səb dōōd´) *adj.* quiet; lacking energy

subjective (səb jek´ tiv) *adj.* of a person's thoughts and feelings

subordinate (sə bôrd´'n it) *adj.* below another in importance or rank

subtle (sut´'l) *adj.* not obvious or direct

subversion (səb vʉr´ zhən) *n.* activity aimed at ruining or overthrowing something established

sumptuous (sump´ chōō əs) *adj.* lavish; splendid

supercilious (sōō´ pər sil´ ē əs) *adj.* expressing an attitude of superiority; contemptuous

superficial (sōō´pər fish´ əl) *adj.* of or being on the surface; shallow; concerned only with the obvious or apparent

surmise (sər mīz´) *n.* guess; idea based on evidence that is not conclusive

surpassed (sər pas´'d) *v.* went beyond; excelled

synthesize (sin´ thə sīz´) *v.* put together elements to form a whole

T

taciturn (tas´ ə tʉrn´) *adj.* not liking to talk

tactile (tak´ təl) *adj.* related to the sense of touch

tempering (tem´ pər iŋ) *n.* changing to make more suitable, usually by mixing with something

tentative (ten´ tə tiv) *adj.* hesitant; not confident

tenuous (ten´ yōō əs) *adj.* slight; flimsy; not substantial or strong

terminology (tʉr´ mə näl´ ə jē) *n.* the terms or system of terms associated with a specific science, art profession, and so on

thrall (thrôl) *n.* complete power over another; complete absorption by

titanic (tī tan´ik) *adj.* powerful or of great size

toil (toil) *n.* hard, tiring work

trace (trās) *n.* a tiny amount

tremulous (trem´ yōō ləs) *adj.* trembling; quivering; timid; fearful

U

ulterior (ul tir´ ē ər) *adj.* further; beyond what is openly stated or implied

unify (yōō´ nə fī´) *v.* join together; unite

unwieldy (un wēl´ dē) *adj.* hard to manage because of shape or weight

V

vagaries (vā´ gər ēz) *n.* erratic or unpredictable actions

venture (ven´ chər) *v.* do or go at some risk

vile (vīl) *adj.* evil; low; disgusting

visual (vizh´ yōō əl) *adj.* related to sight or seeing

W

waver (wā´ vər) *v.* show indecision; fluctuate

wither (with´ r) *v.* dry up; shrivel from loss of moisture

wrathfully (rath´ fəl lē) *adv.* with intense anger

USING A DICTIONARY

A **dictionary** is a reference book containing an alphabetical list of words along with their pronunciations, their definitions, and other information about them. Dictionaries are helpful when you need to find the meaning, the pronunciation, or the part of speech of a word. Dictionaries provide the *denotation* of each word, or its objective meaning. You may also consult a dictionary to trace a word's *etymology*, or its origins. Etymology explains how words change, how they are borrowed from other languages, and how new words are invented, or "coined."

A Sample Dictionary Entry

Here is an entry from a dictionary. Notice what it tells about the word *anthology*.

> **anthology** (an thäl′ə jē) *n.*, *pl.* **–gies** [Gr. *anthologia*, a garland, collection of short poems < *anthologos*, gathering flowers < *anthos*, flower + *legein*, to gather] a collection of poems, stories, songs, excerpts, and so on, chosen by the compiler

The etymology of *anthology* is given in brackets, using the symbol <, which means "comes from" or "is derived from." In this case, the Greek words for "flower" and "gather" combined to form a Greek word that meant "a garland," and then that word became an English word that means "a collection of literary flowers"—a collection of literature like the one you are reading now.

Idiomatic Expressions

Dictionaries also provide information about idiomatic expressions. An *idiomatic expression* is a phrase that means something different from the combined meanings of its individual words. For example, *lay eyes on* is an idiomatic expression meaning "to see." Another common idiomatic expression is *drop everything*, which means, "stop what you are doing." In a dictionary, idiomatic expressions are usually included in the entry for a key word in the expression.

Activity

Look up the word *gauntlet* in a dictionary. **(a)** What is its etymology? **(b)** Explain what its etymology reveals about the development of Middle English. **(c)** What idiomatic expressions are associated with the word *gauntlet*?

USING A THESAURUS

A **thesaurus** is a book of synonyms, or words that have similar meanings. Words in a thesaurus are often arranged by concept, such as "wisdom," or "wealth." Use a thesaurus to increase your vocabulary or to find alternative words to express your meaning.

- Do not choose a word just because it sounds interesting or smart. Choose the word that expresses exactly the meaning you intend.
- When choosing a word, note both its *denotative* and *connotative* meanings. A word's connotations are the emotional associations that it calls to mind. The connotation may not reflect your intentions even if the denotation does.
- To avoid errors, look up the word in a dictionary to check its precise meaning and to make sure you are using it properly.

A Sample Thesaurus Entry

Here is an entry from a thesaurus. Notice what it tells about the word *book*.

> **book** *noun*
>
> A printed and bound work: tome, volume. *See* WORDS.
>
> **book** *verb* 1. To register in or as if in a book: catalog, enroll, inscribe, list, set down, write down. *See* REMEMBER. 2. To cause to be set aside, as for one's use, in advance: bespeak, engage, reserve. *See* GET.

If the word can be used as different parts of speech, as *book* can, the thesaurus entry provides synonyms for the word as each part of speech. A thesaurus entry also gives specific synonyms for each connotation of the word.

Activity

Look up the word *deception* in a thesaurus. **(a)** What are three synonyms for this word? **(b)** Explain how the connotations of the synonyms differ.

THE HISTORY OF ENGLISH

A Merging of Cultures

Old English English began about the year 500 when Germanic tribes from the middle of Europe traveled west and settled in Britain. These peoples—the Angles, Saxons, and Jutes—spoke a Germanic language that combined with the Danish and Norse spoken by Vikings who invaded Britain. Some Latin elements entered the language when Christian missionaries arrived. The result was Old English, which looked like this:

> Hwaet! We Gar-Dena in gear-dagum,
> peod-cyninga, prym gefrunon,
> hu da aepelingas ellen fremedon!

These words are the opening lines of the Old English epic poem *Beowulf*, probably composed in the eighth century. In modern English, they mean: "Listen! We know the ancient glory of the Spear-Danes, and the heroic deeds of those noble kings!"

Middle English The biggest change in English took place after the Norman Conquest of Britain in 1066. The Normans spoke a dialect of Old French, and Old English changed dramatically when the Normans became the new aristocracy. From about 1100 to 1500, the people of Britain spoke what we now call Middle English.

> A Knyght ther was, and that a worthy man,
> That fro the tyme that he first bigan
> To riden out, he loved chivalrie,
> Trouthe and honour, fredom and curtesie.

These lines from the opening section of Geoffrey Chaucer's *Canterbury Tales* (c. 1400) are much easier for us to understand than the lines from *Beowulf*. They mean: "There was a knight, a worthy man who, from the time he began to ride, loved chivalry, truth, honor, freedom, and courtesy."

Modern English During the Renaissance, with its emphasis on reviving classical culture, Greek and Latin languages exerted a strong influence on the English language. In addition, Shakespeare added about two thousand words to the language. Grammar, spelling, and pronunciation continued to change. Modern English was born.

> But soft! What light through yonder window breaks?
> It is the East, and Juliet is the sun!

These lines from Shakespeare's *Romeo and Juliet* (c. 1600) need no translation, although it is helpful to know that *soft* meant "speak softly" in Shakespeare's time. Since Shakespeare's day, conventions of usage and grammar have continued to change. For example, the *th* at the end of some verb forms has become *s*. In Shakespeare's time, it was correct to say "Romeo *hath* fallen in love." In our time, it is correct to say "he *has* fallen in love." However, the changes of the past five hundred years are not nearly as drastic as the changes from Old English to Middle English, or from Middle English to Modern English. We still speak Modern English.

Old Words, New Words

Modern English has a larger vocabulary than any other language in the world. The *Oxford English Dictionary* contains about a half million words, and it is estimated that another half million scientific and technical terms do not appear in the dictionary. Here are the main ways that new words enter the language:

- **War**—Conquerors introduce new ideas—and new vocabulary, such as *anger*, from Old Norse.
- **Immigration**—When large groups of people move from one country to another, they bring their languages with them, such as *boycott*, from Ireland.
- **Travel and Trade**—Those who travel to foreign lands and those who do business in faraway places bring new words back with them, such as *shampoo,* from Hindi, a language of India.
- **Science and Technology**—In our time, the amazing growth of science and technology adds multitudes of new words to English, such as *Internet*.

English is also filled with **borrowings**, words taken directly from other languages. Sometimes, borrowed words maintain the same meanings they have in their original languages: *pajamas* (Hindi), *sauna* (Finnish), *camouflage* (French), *plaza* (Spanish). Sometimes borrowed words take on new meanings. *Sleuth*, for example, an Old Norse word for *trail*, now means the person who follows a trail—a detective.

Mythology contributed to our language too. Some of the days of the week are named after Norse gods—Wednesday was Woden's Day, Thursday was Thor's Day. Greek and Roman myths have given us many words, such as *jovial* (from the god Jove, or Jupiter), *martial* (from the god Mars), *mercurial* (from the god Mercury), and *herculean* (from the hero Hercules).

Americanisms are words, phrases, or usages that originated in American English or that are unique to the way Americans speak. They are expressions of our national character in all its variety: *easy as pie, prairie dog, bamboozle, panhandle, halftime, fringe benefit, bookmobile, jackhammer, southpaw, lickety split.*

Activity

Look up the following words in a dictionary. Describe the most probable ways in which these words entered American English.

    kindle   batik   façade   halcyon   download

The Influence of English

There are about three hundred million native English speakers, and about the same number who speak English as a second language. Although more people speak Mandarin Chinese, English is the dominant language of trade, tourism, international diplomacy, science, and technology.

Language is a vehicle of both communication and culture, and the cultural influence of English in the twenty-first century is unprecedented in the history of the world's languages. Beyond business and science, English spreads through sports, pop music, Hollywood movies, television, and journalism. A book that is translated into English reaches many more people than it would in its native language alone. Perhaps most significantly, English dominates the Internet. The next time you log on, notice how many Web sites from around the world also have an English version. The global use of English is the closest the world has ever come to speaking an international language.

Activity

Choose one area of culture—such as sports, fashion, the arts, or technology—and identify three new words that English has recently added to the world's vocabulary. **(a)** In what ways does a shared language benefit the world? **(b)** In what ways might a global language be a detriment to the world?

LITERARY TERMS

ACT *See* Drama.

ALLEGORY An *allegory* is a story or tale with two or more levels of meaning—a literal level and one or more symbolic levels. The events, setting, and characters in an allegory are symbols for ideas and qualities.

ALLITERATION *Alliteration* is the repetition of initial consonant sounds. Writers use alliteration to give emphasis to words, to imitate sounds, and to create musical effects. In the following line from Theodore Roethke's "The Waking" (p. 639), there is alliteration of the *f* sound:

I *f*eel my *f*ate in what I cannot *f*ear.

ALLUSION An *allusion* is a reference to a well-known person, place, event, literary work, or work of art. The title of the story "By the Waters of Babylon" (p. 282) is an allusion to the Bible's Psalm 137, in which the Hebrew people lament their exile in Babylon. It begins, "By the rivers of Babylon, there we sat down, yea, we wept. . . ."

ANALOGY An *analogy* makes a comparison between two or more things that are similar in some ways but otherwise unalike.

ANECDOTE An *anecdote* is a brief story about an interesting, amusing, or strange event told to entertain or to make a point. In the excerpt from "The Way to Rainy Mountain" (p. 545), N. Scott Momaday tells anecdotes about his grandmother to reveal her character and provide a glimpse into a vanishing way of life.

See also Narrative.

ANTAGONIST An *antagonist* is a character or force in conflict with a main character, or protagonist.

ANTICLIMAX Some stories end in an anticlimax. Like a climax, an *anticlimax* is the turning point in a story. However, an anticlimax is always a letdown. It is the point at which you learn that the story will not turn out in a way that truly resolves the problem or satisfies the reader. The conclusion of Keats's "La Belle Dame sans Merci" (p. 650) is an anticlimax.

ARCHETYPE An *archetype* is a type of character, detail, image, or situation that appears in literature from around the world and throughout history. Some critics believe that archetypes reveal deep truths about human experience.

ASIDE An *aside* is a short speech delivered by a character in a play in order to express his or her thoughts and feelings. Traditionally, the aside is directed to the audience and is presumed not to be heard by the other characters.

ASSONANCE *Assonance* is the repetition of vowel sounds followed by different consonants in two or more stressed syllables. Assonance is found in this phrase from Elizabeth Bishop's "The Fish" (p. 602): "frayed and wavering."

ATMOSPHERE *See* Mood.

AUTOBIOGRAPHICAL ESSAY *See* Essay.

AUTOBIOGRAPHY An *autobiography* is a form of non-fiction in which a writer tells his or her own life story. An autobiography may tell about the person's whole life or only a part of it. An example of an autobiography is Erik Weihenmayer's *Touch the Top of the World* (p. 411).

See also Biography *and* Nonfiction.

BALLAD A *ballad* is a songlike poem that tells a story, often one dealing with adventure and romance. Most ballads are written in four- to six-line stanzas and have regular rhythms and rhyme schemes. A ballad often features a *refrain*—a regularly repeated line or group of lines.

See also Oral Tradition.

BIOGRAPHY A *biography* is a form of nonfiction in which a writer tells the life story of another person. Biographies have been written about many famous people, historical and contemporary, but they can also be written about "ordinary" people.

See also Autobiography *and* Nonfiction.

BLANK VERSE *Blank verse* is poetry written in unrhymed iambic pentameter lines. This verse form was widely used by William Shakespeare.

See also Meter.

CHARACTER A *character* is a person or an animal who takes part in the action of a literary work. The main character, or protagonist, is the most important character in a story. In Chinua Achebe's story "Civil Peace" (p. 327), Jonathan Iwegbu is the protagonist. This character often changes in some important way as a result of the story's events.

Characters are sometimes classified as round or flat, dynamic or static. A *round character* shows many different traits—faults as well as virtues. A *flat character* shows only one trait. A *dynamic character* develops and grows during the course of the story; a *static character* does not change.

See also Characterization *and* Motivation.

CHARACTERIZATION *Characterization* is the act of creating and developing a character. In *direct characterization*, the author directly states a character's traits. For example, in "The Masque of the Red Death" (p. 340), Poe directly characterizes Prince Prospero: "But the Prince Prospero was happy and dauntless and sagacious."

In *indirect characterization*, an author gives clues about a character by describing what a character looks like, does, and says, as well as how other characters react to him or her. It is up to the reader to draw conclusions about the character based on this indirect information.

The most effective indirect characterizations usually result from showing characters acting or speaking.

See also Character.

CLIMAX The *climax* of a story, novel, or play is the high point of interest or suspense. The events that make up the rising action lead up to the climax. The events that make up the falling action follow the climax.

See also Conflict; Plot; *and* Anticlimax.

COMEDY A *comedy* is a literary work, especially a play, that has a happy ending. Comedies often show ordinary characters in conflict with society. These conflicts are introduced through misunderstandings, deceptions, and concealed identities. When the conflict is resolved, the result is the correction of moral faults or social wrongs. Types of comedy include *romantic comedy*, which involves problems among lovers, and the *comedy of manners*, which satirically challenges the social customs of a sophisticated society. Comedy is often contrasted with tragedy, in which the protagonist meets an unfortunate end.

COMIC RELIEF *Comic relief* is a technique that is used to interrupt a serious part of a literary work by introducing a humorous character or situation.

CONFLICT A *conflict* is a struggle between opposing forces. Characters in conflict form the basis of stories, novels, and plays.

There are two kinds of conflict: external and internal. In an *external conflict,* the main character struggles against an outside force. This force may be another character, as in "Civil Peace" (p. 327), in which Jonathan Iwegbu struggles with the leader of the thieves. The outside force could also be the standards or expectations of a group, such as the oppression and censorship that Juan struggles against in "The Censors" (p. 376). The outside force may be nature itself, as when Erik

Weihenmayer struggles to climb Mt. Everest in *Touch the Top of the World* (p. 411).

An *internal conflict* involves a character in conflict with himself or herself. In *Julius Caesar* (p. 824), Brutus experiences an internal conflict when trying to decide whether to assassinate Caesar.

See also Plot.

CONNOTATION The *connotation* of a word is the set of ideas associated with it in addition to its explicit meaning.

See also Denotation.

CONSONANCE *Consonance* is the repetition of final consonant sounds in stressed syllables with different vowel sounds, as in *hat* and *sit.*

CONTEMPORARY INTERPRETATION A *contemporary interpretation* is a literary work of today that responds to and sheds new light on a well-known, earlier work of literature. Such an interpretation may refer to any aspect of the older work, including plot, characters, settings, imagery, language, and theme. T.H. White's *The Once and Future King* (p. 1077) provides a modern version of the legend of King Arthur.

COUPLET A *couplet* is a pair of rhyming lines, usually of the same length and meter. In the following couplet from Sonnet 29 by William Shakespeare, the speaker comforts himself with the thought of his love:

> For thy sweet love remember'd such wealth brings
> That then I scorn to change my state with kings.

See also Stanza.

DENOTATION The *denotation* of a word is its dictionary meaning, independent of other associations that the word may have. The denotation of the word *lake,* for example, is "an inland body of water." "Vacation spot" and "place where the fishing is good" are connotations of the word *lake.*

See also Connotation.

DENOUEMENT *See* Plot.

DESCRIPTION A *description* is a portrait in words of a person, place, or object. Descriptive writing uses sensory details, those that appeal to the senses: sight, hearing, taste, smell, and touch. Description can be found in all types of writing. Anita Desai's "Games at Twilight" (p. 129) has vivid descriptive passages.

DESCRIPTIVE ESSAY *See* Essay.

DEVELOPMENT *See* Plot.

DIALECT *Dialect* is a special form of a language, spoken by people in a particular region or group. It may involve changes to the pronunciation, vocabulary, and sentence structure of the standard form of the language. Rudyard Kipling's "Danny Deever" (p. 604) is a poem written in the Cockney dialect of English, used by working-class Londoners.

DIALOGUE A *dialogue* is a conversation between characters that may reveal their traits and advance the action of a narrative. In fiction or nonfiction, quotation marks indicate a speaker's exact words, and a new paragraph usually indicates a change of speaker. Following is an exchange between two characters in "The Monkey's Paw" (p. 32):

> "*What's that?*" cried the old woman, starting up.
> "A rat," said the old man in shaking tones—"a rat. It passed me on the stairs."

Quotation marks are not used in *script*, the printed copy of a play. Instead, the dialogue follows the name of the speaker, as in this example from *Julius Caesar* (p. 824):

> **PORTIA.** Is Caesar yet gone to the Capitol?

DICTION *Diction* refers to an author's choice of words, especially with regard to range of vocabulary, use of slang and colloquial language, and level of formality. This sentence from "The Masque of the Red Death" (p. 340) is an example of formal diction containing many words derived from Latin: "This was an extensive and magnificent structure, the creation of the prince's own eccentric yet august taste."

See also Connotation *and* Denotation.

DIRECT CHARACTERIZATION *See* Characterization.

DRAMA A *drama* is a story written to be performed by actors. The script of a drama is made up of *dialogue*—the words the actors say—and *stage directions*, which are descriptions of how and where action happens.

The drama's *setting* is the time and place in which the action occurs. It is indicated by one or more *sets*, including furniture and backdrops, that suggest interior or exterior scenes. *Props* are objects, such as a sword or a cup of tea, that are used onstage.

At the beginning of most plays, a brief *exposition* gives the audience some background information about the characters and the situation. Just as in a story or novel, the plot of a drama is built around characters in conflict.

Dramas are divided into large units called *acts,* which are divided into smaller units called *scenes*. A long play may include many sets that change with the scenes, or it may indicate a change of scene with lighting. *Julius Caesar* (p. 824) is a play in five acts.

See also Dialogue; Genre; Stage Directions; *and* Tragedy.

DRAMATIC IRONY *See* Irony.

DRAMATIC MONOLOGUE A *dramatic monologue* is a poem in which a character reveals himself or herself by speaking to a silent listener or thinking aloud.

DRAMATIC POETRY *Dramatic poetry* is poetry that utilizes the techniques of drama. The dialogue between the bride and the bridegroom at the end of "The Bridegroom" (p. 594) is an example.

END RHYME *See* Rhyme.

EPIC An *epic* is a long narrative poem about the deeds of gods or heroes. *Sundiata: An Epic of Old Mali* (p. 1006) and the *Ramayana* (p. 1019) are examples of the genre.

An epic is elevated in style and usually follows certain patterns. In Greek epics and in the epics modeled after them, the poet begins by announcing the subject and asking a Muse—one of the nine goddesses of the arts, literature, and sciences—to help.

An *epic hero* is the larger-than-life central character in an epic. Through behavior and deeds, the epic hero displays qualities that are valued by the society in which the epic originated.

See also Epic Simile *and* Narrative Poem.

EPIC SIMILE An *epic simile*, also called *Homeric simile*, is an elaborate comparison of unlike subjects. In this example from the *Odyssey,* Homer compares the bodies of men killed by Odysseus to a fisherman's catch heaped up on the shore:

> Think of a catch that fishermen haul in to a
>   half-moon bay
> in a fine-meshed net from the whitecaps of the sea:
> how all are poured out on the sand, in throes
>   for the salt sea,
> twitching their cold lives away in Helios' fiery air:
> so lay the suitors heaped on one another.

See also Figurative Language *and* Simile.

EPIPHANY An *epiphany* is a character's sudden flash of insight into a conflict or situation. At the end of the poem "The Fish" (p. 602), the speaker has an epiphany that causes her to release the fish.

ESSAY An *essay* is a short nonfiction work about a particular subject. While classification is difficult, five types of essays are sometimes identified.

A *descriptive essay* seeks to convey an impression about a person, place, or object. In "Flood" (p. 396), Annie Dillard describes scenes from a flood.

An *expository essay* gives information, discusses ideas, or explains a process. In "The Spider and the Wasp"(p. 428), Alexander Petrunkevitch compares and contrasts the two creatures mentioned in the title.

A *narrative essay* tells a true story. In "The Dog That Bit People" (p. 481), James Thurber tells the story of a troublesome pet. An *autobiographical essay* is a narrative essay in which the writer tells a story from his or her own life.

A *persuasive essay* tries to convince readers to do something or to accept the writer's point of view. In "Keep Memory Alive" (p. 500), Elie Wiesel argues the importance of speaking out against evil.

A *visual essay* is an exploration of a topic that conveys its ideas through visual elements as well as language. Like a standard essay, a visual essay presents an author's views of a single topic. Unlike other essays, however, much of the meaning in a visual essay is conveyed through illustrations or photographs. "What Makes a Degas a Degas?" (p. 520) is an example of such an essay.

See also Description; Exposition; Genre; Narration; Nonfiction; *and* Persuasion.

EXPOSITION *Exposition* is writing or speech that explains a process or presents information. In the plot of a story or drama, the exposition is the part of the work that introduces the characters, the setting, and the basic situation.

See also Plot.

EXPOSITORY ESSAY *See* Essay.

EXTENDED METAPHOR In an *extended metaphor*, as in regular metaphor, a writer speaks or writes of a subject as though it were something else. An extended metaphor sustains the comparison for several lines or for an entire poem. In *Julius Caesar* (p. 824), Brutus uses an extended metaphor in Act II, Scene i, lines 21–27, when he speaks of "ambition's ladder."

See also Figurative Language *and* Metaphor.

FALLING ACTION *See* Plot.

FANTASY A *fantasy* is a work of highly imaginative writing that contains elements not found in real life. Examples of fantasy include stories that involve supernatural elements, such as fairy tales, and stories that deal with imaginary places and creatures.

See also Science Fiction.

FICTION *Fiction* is prose writing that tells about imaginary characters and events. The term is usually used for novels and short stories, but it also applies to dramas and narrative poetry. Some writers rely on their imaginations alone to create their works of fiction. Others base their fiction on actual events and people, to which they add invented characters, dialogue, and plot situations.

See also Genre; Narrative; *and* Nonfiction.

FIGURATIVE LANGUAGE *Figurative language* is writing or speech not meant to be interpreted literally. It is often used to create vivid impressions by setting up comparisons between dissimilar things.

Some frequently used figures of speech are *metaphors, similes*, and *personifications*.

See also Literal Language.

FLASHBACK A *flashback* is a means by which authors present material that occurred earlier than the present time of the narrative. Authors may include this material in the form of a characters' memories, dreams, or accounts of past events, or they may simply shift their narrative back to the earlier time.

FOIL A *foil* is a character who provides a contrast to another character. In *Julius Caesar* (p. 824), the impetuous and resentful Cassius is a foil for the cooler and more rational Brutus.

FOOT *See* Meter.

FORESHADOWING *Foreshadowing* is the use in a literary work of clues that suggest events that have yet to occur. This technique helps to create suspense, keeping readers wondering about what will happen next.

See also Suspense.

FREE VERSE *Free verse* is poetry not written in a regular pattern of meter or rhyme. Cornelius Eady's "The Poetic Interpretation of the Twist" (p. 583) is an example.

GENRE A *genre* is a category or form of literature. Literature is commonly divided into three major types of writing: poetry, prose, and drama. For each type, there are several distinct genres, as follows:

1. Poetry: Lyric Poetry, Dramatic Poetry, Narrative Poetry, including Epic Poetry

2. Prose: Novels and Short Stories (fiction) and Biographies, Autobiographies, Letters, Essays, and Reports (nonfiction)

3. Drama: Serious Drama and Tragedy, Comic Drama, Melodrama, and Farce

See also Drama; Poetry; *and* Prose.

HAIKU The *haiku* is a three-line verse form. The first and third lines of a haiku each have five syllables. The second line has seven syllables. A haiku seeks to convey a single vivid emotion by means of images from nature.

HOMERIC SIMILE *See* Epic Simile.

HYPERBOLE A *hyperbole* is a deliberate exaggeration or overstatement. In Mark Twain's "The Notorious Jumping Frog of Calaveras County," the claim that Jim Smiley would follow a bug as far as Mexico to win a bet is a hyperbole. As this example shows, hyperboles are often used for comic effect.

IAMB *See* Meter.

IDIOM An *idiom* or *idiomatic expression* is an expression that is characteristic of a language, region, community or class of people. Idiomatic expressions mean something more than or different from the meaning of the words making them up. Following is an example of an idiom from T. H. White's *The Once and Future King* (p. 1077): "Think what people will say about us, if we do not go and *have a shot* at that sword."

See *also* Dialect.

IMAGE An *image* is a word or phrase that appeals to one or more of the five senses—sight, hearing, touch, taste, or smell. Writers use images to re-create sensory experiences in words.

See also Description.

IMAGERY *Imagery* is the descriptive or figurative language used in literature to create word pictures for the reader. These pictures, or images, are created by details of sight, sound, taste, touch, smell, or movement.

INDIRECT CHARACTERIZATION *See* Characterization.

INTERNAL RHYME *See* Rhyme.

IRONY *Irony* is the general term for literary techniques that portray differences between appearance and reality, or expectation and result. In *verbal irony*, words are used to suggest the opposite of what is meant. In *dramatic irony*, there is a contradiction between what a character thinks and what the reader or audience knows to be true. In *irony of situation*, an event occurs that directly contradicts the expectations of the characters, the reader, or the audience.

LITERAL LANGUAGE *Literal language* uses words in their ordinary senses. It is the opposite of *figurative language*. If you tell someone standing on a diving board to jump in, you speak literally. If you tell someone on the street to "go jump in a lake," you are speaking figuratively.

See also Figurative Language.

LYRIC POEM A *lyric poem* is a poem written in highly musical language that expresses the thoughts, observations, and feelings of a single speaker.

MAIN CHARACTER *See* Character.

METAPHOR A *metaphor* is a figure of speech in which one thing is spoken of as though it were something else. Unlike a simile, which compares two things using *like* or *as*, a metaphor implies a comparison between them. In "A Tree Telling of Orpheus" (p. 609), the speaker is a tree and describes music as if it were water: "my roots felt music moisten them."

See also Extended Metaphor *and* Figurative Language.

METER The *meter* of a poem is its rhythmical pattern. This pattern is determined by the number and arrangements of stressed syllables, or beats, in each line. To describe the meter of a poem, you must scan its lines. Scanning involves marking the stressed and unstressed syllables, as shown with the following two lines from *Julius Caesar* (p. 824):

> Wĕ bóth hăve féd ăs wéll, ănd wé căn bóth
> Ĕndúre thĕ wínter's cóld ăs wéll ăs hé . . .

As you can see, each stressed syllable is marked with a slanted line (´) and each unstressed syllable with a horseshoe symbol (˘). The stressed and unstressed syllables are then divided by vertical lines (|) into groups called *feet*. The following types of feet are common in English poetry:

1. *Iamb:* a foot with one unstressed syllable followed by a stressed syllable, as in the word *again*

2. *Trochee:* a foot with one stressed syllable followed by an unstressed syllable, as in the word *wonder*

3. *Anapest:* a foot with two unstressed syllables followed by one strong stress, as in the phrase *on the beach*

4. *Dactyl:* a foot with one strong stress followed by two unstressed syllables, as in the word *wonderful*

5. *Spondee:* a foot with two strong stresses, as in the word *spacewalk*

Depending on the type of foot that is most common in them, lines of poetry are described as *iambic, trochaic, anapestic,* and so forth.

Lines are also described in terms of the number of feet that occur in them, as follows:

1. *Monometer:* verse written in one-foot lines
   All things
   Must pass
   Away.

2. *Dimeter:* verse written in two-foot lines

Thomas | Jefferson
What do | you say
Under the | gravestone
Hidden | away?
—Rosemary and Stephen Vincent Benét,
"Thomas Jefferson, 1743–1826"

3. *Trimeter:* verse written in three-foot lines

I know | not whom | I meet
I know | not where | I go.

4. *Tetrameter:* verse written in four-foot lines

5. *Pentameter:* verse written in five-foot lines

6. *Hexameter:* verse written in six-foot lines

7. *Heptameter:* verse written in seven-foot lines

    Blank verse, used by Shakespeare in *Julius Caesar* (p. 824), is poetry written in unrhymed iambic pentameter.

    Free verse, used by Cornelius Eady in "The Poetic Interpretation of the Twist" (p. 583), is poetry that does not follow a regular pattern of meter and rhyme.

MONOLOGUE A *monologue* in a play is a long speech by one character that, unlike a *soliloquy*, is addressed to another character or characters. An example from Shakespeare's *Julius Caesar* (p. 824) is the famous speech by Antony to the Roman people in Act III, Scene ii. It begins, "Friends, Romans, countrymen, lend me your ears. . . ." (line 74).

See also Soliloquy.

MONOMETER *See* Meter.

MOOD *Mood*, or *atmosphere*, is the feeling created in the reader by a literary work or passage. The mood is often suggested by descriptive details. Often the mood can be described in a single word, such as lighthearted, frightening, or despairing. Notice how this passage from Edgar Allan Poe's "The Masque of the Red Death" (p. 340) contributes to an eerie, fearful mood:

> And now was acknowledged the presence of the Red Death. He had come like a thief in the night. And one by one dropped the revelers in the blood-bedewed halls of their revel, and died each in the despairing posture of his fall.

See also Tone.

MORAL A *moral* is a lesson taught by a literary work, especially a fable—many fables, for example, have a stated moral at the end. It is customary, however, to discuss contemporary works in terms of the themes they explore, rather than a moral that they teach.

MOTIVATION *Motivation* is a reason that explains or partially explains why a character thinks, feels, acts, or behaves in a certain way. Motivation results from a combination of the character's personality and the situation he or she must deal with. In *Antigone* (p. 750), the protagonist is motivated by loyalty to her dead brother and reverence for the laws of the gods.

See also Character *and* Characterization.

MYTH A myth is a *fictional* tale that describes the actions of gods and heroes or explains the causes of natural phenomena. Unlike legends, myths emphasize supernatural rather than historical elements. Many cultures have collections of myths, and the most familiar in the Western world are those of the ancient Greeks and Romans. "Prometheus and the First People"(p. 982) is a retelling of a famous ancient Greek myth.

See also Oral Tradition.

NARRATION *Narration* is writing that tells a story. The act of telling a story in speech is also called narration. Novels and short stories are fictional narratives. Nonfiction works—such as news stories, biographies, and autobiographies—are also narratives. A narrative poem tells a story in verse.

See also Anecdote, Essay, Narrative Poem, Nonfiction, Novel, *and* Short Story.

NARRATIVE A *narrative* is a story told in fiction, nonfiction, poetry, or drama.

See also Narration.

NARRATIVE ESSAY *See* Essay.

NARRATIVE POEM A *narrative poem* is one that tells a story. Alexander Pushkin's "The Bridegroom" (p. 594) is a narrative poem that tells how Natasha, a merchant's daughter, outwits a thief and murderer.

See also Dramatic Poetry; Epic; *and* Narration.

NARRATOR A *narrator* is a speaker or character who tells a story. The writer's choice of narrator determines the story's *point of view*, or the perspective from which the story is told. By using a consistent point of view, a writer controls the amount and type of information revealed to the reader.

    When a character in the story tells the story, that character is a *first-person narrator*. This narrator may be a major character, a minor character, or just a witness. Readers see only what this character sees, hear only what he or she hears, and so on. Stephen Vincent Benét's "By the Waters of Babylon" (p. 282) is told by a first-person narrator. Viewing unfolding events from this character's perspective, the reader shares in his discoveries and feels more suspense than another point of view would provide.

When a voice outside the story narrates, the story has a *third-person narrator*. An *omniscient,* or all-knowing, third-person narrator can tell readers what any character thinks and feels. For example, in "The Monkey's Paw" (p. 32), we know the thoughts of the father, the wife, and the son. A *limited third-person narrator* sees the world through one character's eyes and reveals only that character's thoughts. In Jack Finney's "Contents of the Dead Man's Pocket" (p. 110), the narrator reveals only Tom's thoughts and feelings.

See also Speaker.

NONFICTION *Nonfiction* is prose writing that presents and explains ideas or that tells about real people, places, ideas, or events. To be classified as nonfiction, a work must be true. Dorothy West's "The Sun Room" (p. 454) is a true account of events related to a particular room in a house.

See also Autobiography; Biography; *and* Essay.

NOVEL A *novel* is a long work of fiction. It has a plot that explores characters in conflict. A novel may also have one or more subplots, or minor stories, and several themes.

OCTAVE *See* Stanza.

ONOMATOPOEIA *Onomatopoeia* is the use of words that imitate sounds. *Whirr, thud, sizzle*, and *hiss* are typical examples. Writers can deliberately choose words that contribute to a desired sound effect.

ORAL TRADITION The *oral tradition* is the retelling of songs, stories, and poems passed orally, or by spoken word, from generation to generation. Many folk songs, ballads, fairy tales, legends, and myths originated in the oral tradition.

See also Myth.

OXYMORON An *oxymoron* is a combination of words that contradict each other. Examples are "deafening silence," "honest thief," "wise fool," and "bittersweet." This device is effective when the apparent contradiction reveals a deeper truth.

PARADOX A *paradox* is a statement that seems contradictory but that actually may express a deeper truth. Because a paradox is surprising, it catches the reader's attention.

PARALLELISM *See* Rhetorical Devices.

PENTAMETER *See* Meter.

PERSONIFICATION *Personification* is a type of figurative language in which a nonhuman subject is given human characteristics. Denise Levertov personifies a tree in her poem "A Tree Telling of Orpheus" (p. 609). In fact, the tree is the speaker in this poem: "I listened, and language came into my roots . . ."

See also Figurative Language.

PERSUASION *Persuasion* is writing or speech that attempts to convince the reader to adopt a particular opinion or course of action.

PERSUASIVE ESSAY *See* Essay.

PLOT *Plot* is the sequence of events in a literary work. In most novels, dramas, short stories, and narrative poems, the plot involves both characters and a central conflict. The plot usually begins with an *exposition* that introduces the setting, the characters, and the basic situation. This is followed by the *inciting incident*, which introduces the central conflict. The conflict then increases during the *development* until it reaches a high point of interest or suspense, the *climax*. All the events leading up to the climax make up the *rising action*. The climax is followed by the *falling action*, which leads to the *denouement,* or *resolution,* in which the conflict is resolved and in which a general insight may be conveyed.

POETRY *Poetry* is one of the three major types of literature, the others being prose and drama. Most poems make use of highly concise, musical, and emotionally charged language. Many also make use of imagery, figurative language, and special devices of sound such as rhyme. Poems are often divided into lines and stanzas and often employ regular rhythmical patterns, or meters. Poetry that does not follow a regular metrical pattern is called *free verse*.

See also Genre.

POINT OF VIEW *See* Narrator.

PROSE *Prose* is the ordinary form of written language. Most writing that is not poetry, drama, or song is considered prose. Prose is one of the major categories of literature and occurs in two forms: fiction and nonfiction.

See also Fiction; Genre; *and* Nonfiction.

PROTAGONIST The *protagonist* is the main character in a literary work.

See also Antagonist *and* Character.

PUN A *pun* is a play on words involving a word with two or more different meanings or two words that sound alike but have different meanings. In *Julius Caesar* (p. 824), there is a pun on the phrase *mend you* (Act I, Scene i, lines 17-18): "yet if you be out [angry], sir, I can mend you." The speaker is a cobbler and by *mend you* he means both "mend your shoes" and "improve your disposition."

QUATRAIN A *quatrain* is a stanza, or section, of a poem made up of four lines, usually with a definite rhythm and rhyme scheme.

REPETITION *Repetition* is the use of any element of language—a sound, a word, a phrase, a clause, or a sentence—more than once.

Poets use many kinds of repetition. *Alliteration, assonance, consonance, rhyme,* and *rhythm* are repetitions of certain sounds and sound patterns. A *refrain* is a repeated line or group of lines. In both prose and poetry, repetition is used for musical effects and for emphasis.

See also Alliteration; Assonance; Consonance; Rhyme; *and* Rhythm.

RESOLUTION *See* Plot.

RHETORICAL DEVICES *Rhetorical devices* are special patterns of words and ideas that create emphasis and stir emotion, especially in speeches or other oral presentations. *Parallelism,* for example, is the repetition of a grammatical structure in order to create a rhythm and make words more memorable. In "Keep Memory Alive" (p. 500), Elie Wiesel uses parallelism: "Neutrality helps the oppressor, never the victim. Silence encourages the tormentor, never the tormented."

Other common rhetorical devices include *restatement,* expressing the same idea in different words, and *rhetorical questions,* questions with obvious answers.

RHYME *Rhyme* is the repetition of sounds at the ends of words. *End rhyme* occurs when the rhyming words come at the ends of lines, as in "The Desired Swan Song" by Samuel Taylor Coleridge:

> Swans sing before they die—'twere no bad *thing*
> Should certain persons die before they *sing.*

Internal rhyme occurs when one of the rhyming words appears within a line, as in these lines from "The Waking" (p. 639):

> God bless the Ground! I shall walk softly *there,*
> And learn by going *where* I have to go.

Exact rhyme involves the repetition of the same final vowel and consonant sounds in words like *ball* and *hall.* *Slant rhyme* involves the repetition of words that sound alike but do not rhyme exactly, like *grove* and *love.*

See also Repetition *and* Rhyme Scheme.

RHYME SCHEME A *rhyme scheme* is a regular pattern of rhyming words in a poem. The rhyme scheme of a poem is indicated by using different letters of the alphabet for each new rhyme. In an *aabb* stanza, for example, line 1 rhymes with line 2 and line 3 rhymes with line 4. "Meeting at Night" (p. 690) uses an *abccba* rhyme scheme in each of its two stanzas:

The gray sea and the long black land;	a
And the yellow half-moon large and low;	b
And the startled little waves that leap	c
In fiery ringlets from their sleep,	c
As I gain the cove with pushing prow,	b
And quench its speed i' the slushy sand.	a

Many poems use the same pattern of rhymes, though not the same rhymes, in each stanza.

See also Rhyme.

RHYTHM *Rhythm* is the pattern of *beats,* or *stresses,* in spoken or written language. Some poems follow a very specific pattern, or meter, whereas prose and free verse may use the natural rhythms of everyday speech.

See also Meter.

RISING ACTION *See* Plot.

ROUND CHARACTER *See* Character.

SATIRE A *satire* is a literary work that ridicules the foolishness and faults of individuals, an institution, society, or even humanity in general.

SCENE *See* Drama.

SCIENCE FICTION *Science fiction* is writing that tells about imaginary events involving science or technology. Many science-fiction stories are set in the future. C. J. Cherryh's science-fiction story "The Threads of Time" (p. 205) plays with the dimension of time.

See also Fantasy.

SENSORY LANGUAGE *Sensory language* is writing or speech that appeals to one or more of the senses.

See also Image.

SESTET *See* Stanza.

SET *See* Drama.

SETTING The *setting* of a literary work is the time and place of the action. Time can include not only the historical period—past, present, or future—but also a specific year, season, or time of day. Place may involve not only the geographical place—a region, country, state, or town—but also the social, economic, or cultural environment.

In some stories, setting serves merely as a backdrop for action, a context in which the characters move and speak. In others, however, setting is a crucial element.

See also Mood.

SHORT STORY A *short story* is a brief work of fiction. In most short stories, one main character faces a conflict that is resolved in the plot of the story. Great craftsmanship must go into the writing of a good story, for it has to accomplish its purpose in relatively few words.

See also Fiction *and* Genre.

SIMILE A *simile* is a figure of speech in which the words *like* or *as* are used to compare two apparently dissimilar items. The comparison, however, surprises the reader into a fresh perception by finding an unexpected likeness. In "The Guitar" (p. 601), for example, García Lorca says that the guitar "weeps monotonously / As weeps the water, / As weeps the wind / Over snow."

SOLILOQUY A *soliloquy* is a long speech expressing the thoughts of a character alone on stage. In William Shakespeare's *Julius Caesar* (p. 824), Brutus delivers a soliloquy in which he confirms and justifies his participation in the plot to assassinate Caesar (Act II, Scene i, lines 10–34): "It must be by his death . . ."

See also Monologue.

SONNET A *sonnet* is a fourteen-line lyric poem, usually written in rhymed iambic pentameter. The *English*, or *Shakespearean*, sonnet consists of three quatrains (four-line stanzas) and a couplet (two lines), usually rhyming *abab cdcd efef gg*. The couplet usually comments on the ideas contained in the preceding twelve lines. The sonnet is usually not printed with the stanzas divided, but a reader can see distinct ideas in each. (See the English sonnet by William Shakespeare on page 640.)

The *Italian*, or *Petrarchan*, sonnet consists of an octave (eight-line stanza) and a sestet (six-line stanza). Often, the octave rhymes *abbaabba* and the sestet rhymes *cdecde*. The octave states a theme or asks a question. The sestet comments on the theme or answers the question.

See also Lyric Poem; Meter; *and* Stanza.

SPEAKER The *speaker* is the imaginary voice assumed by the writer of a poem. In many poems, the speaker is not identified by name. When reading a poem, remember that the speaker within the poem may be a person, an animal, a thing, or an abstraction. The speaker in the following stanza by Emily Dickinson is a person who has died:

Because I could not stop for Death—
He kindly stopped for me—

The Carriage held but just Ourselves—
And Immortality.

STAGE DIRECTIONS *Stage directions* are notes included in a drama to describe how the work is to be performed or staged. These instructions are printed in italics and are not spoken aloud. They are used to describe sets, lighting, sound effects, and the appearance, personalities, and movements of characters.

See also Drama.

STANZA A *stanza* is a repeated grouping of two or more lines in a poem that often share a pattern of rhythm and rhyme. Stanzas are sometimes named according to the number of lines they have—for example, a *couplet*, two lines; a *quatrain*, four lines; a *sestet*, six lines; and an *octave*, eight lines.

See also Sonnet.

STATIC CHARACTER *See* Character.

STYLE *Style* refers to an author's unique way of writing. Elements determining style include diction; tone; characteristic use of figurative language, dialect, or rhythmic devices; and typical grammatical structures and patterns.

See also Diction *and* Tone.

SURPRISE ENDING A *surprise ending* is a conclusion that violates the expectations of the reader but in a way that is both logical and believable.

O. Henry's "One Thousand Dollars" (p. 276) and Saki's "The Open Window" (p. 1160) have surprise endings. Both authors were masters of this form.

SUSPENSE *Suspense* is a feeling of uncertainty about the outcome of events in a literary work. Writers create suspense by raising questions in the minds of their readers.

SYMBOL A *symbol* is a character, place, thing or event that stands for something else, often an abstract idea. For example, a flag is a piece of cloth, but it also represents the idea of a country. Writers sometimes use conventional symbols like flags. Frequently, however, they create symbols of their own through emphasis or repetition. In "The Garden of Stubborn Cats" (p. 351), for example, the cats come to symbolize nature's stubborn resistance to human development.

TETRAMETER *See* Meter.

THEME A *theme* is a central message or insight into life revealed through a literary work.

The theme of a literary work may be stated directly or implied. When the theme of a work is implied, readers think about what the work suggests about people or life.

Archetypal themes are those that occur in folklore and literature across the world and throughout history. The hero who makes civilization possible, the theme of "Prometheus and the First People" (p. 982), is an example of an archetypal theme.

TONE The *tone* of a literary work is the writer's attitude toward his or her audience and subject. The tone can often be described by a single adjective, such as *formal* or *informal*, *serious* or *playful*, *bitter* or *ironic*. When Valenzuela discusses the fate of Juan in "The Censors" (p. 376), she uses an ironic tone: ". . . another victim of his devotion to his work."

See also Mood.

TRAGEDY A *tragedy* is a work of literature, especially a play, that tells of a catastrophe, a disaster or great misfortune, for the main character. In ancient Greek drama, the main character was always a significant person—a king or a hero—and the cause of the tragedy was often a tragic flaw, or weakness, in his or her character. In modern drama, the main character can be an ordinary person, and the cause of the tragedy can be some evil in society itself. Tragedy not only arouses fear and pity in the audience, but also, in some cases, conveys a sense of the grandeur and nobility of the human spirit.

Shakespeare's *Julius Caesar* (p. 824) is a tragedy. Brutus suffers from the tragic flaw of blindness to reality and people's motives. His noble-mindedness is almost a form of arrogance. This flaw ultimately leads to his death.

See also Drama.

TRIMETER *See* Meter.

UNDERSTATEMENT An *understatement* is a figure of speech in which the stated meaning is purposely less than (or "under") what is really meant. It is the opposite of *hyperbole*, which is a deliberate exaggeration.

UNIVERSAL THEME A *universal theme* is a message about life that can be understood by most cultures. Many folk tales and examples of classic literature address universal themes such as the importance of courage, the effects of honesty, or the danger of greed.

VERBAL IRONY *See* Irony.

VILLANELLE A *villanelle* is a nineteen-line lyric poem written in five three-line stanzas and ending in a four-line stanza. It uses two rhymes and repeats two refrain lines that appear initially in the first and third lines of the first stanza. These lines then appear alternately as the third line of subsequent three-line stanzas and, finally, as the last two lines of the poem. Theodore Roethke's "The Waking" (p. 639) is a villanelle.

VISUAL ESSAY A *visual essay* is an exploration of a topic that conveys its ideas through visual elements as well as language. Like a standard essay, a visual essay presents an author's views of a single topic. Unlike other essays, however, much of the meaning in a visual essay is conveyed through illustrations or photographs.

VOICE *Voice* is a writer's distinctive "sound" or way of "speaking" on the page. It is related to such elements as word choice, sentence structure, and tone. It is similar to an individual's speech style and can be described in the same way—fast, slow, blunt, meandering, breathless, and so on.

Voice resembles *style*, an author's typical way of writing, but style usually refers to a quality that can be found throughout an author's body of work, while an author's voice may sometimes vary from work to work.

See also Style.

TIPS FOR DISCUSSING LITERATURE

As you read and study literature, discussion with other readers can help you understand, enjoy, and develop interpretations of what you read. Use the following tips to practice good speaking and listening skills while participating in group discussions of literature.

Understand the Purpose of Your Discussion

When you discuss literature, your purpose is to broaden your understanding and appreciation of a work by testing your own ideas and hearing the ideas of others. Stay focused on the literature you are discussing and keep your comments relevant to that literature. Starting with one focus question will help to keep your discussion on track.

Communicate Effectively

Effective communication requires thinking before speaking. Plan the points that you want to make and decide how you will express them. Organize these points in logical order and cite details from the work to support your ideas. Jot down informal notes to help keep your ideas focused.

Remember to speak clearly, pronouncing words slowly and carefully so that others can understand your points. Also, keep in mind that some literature touches readers deeply—be aware of the possibility of counterproductive emotional responses and work to control them. Negative emotional responses can also be conveyed through body language, so work to demonstrate respect in your demeanor as well as in your words.

Encourage Everyone to Participate

While some people are comfortable participating in discussions, others are less eager to speak up in groups. However, everyone should work to contribute thoughts and ideas. To encourage the entire group's participation, try the following strategies:

- If you enjoy speaking, avoid monopolizing the conversation. After sharing your ideas, encourage others to share theirs.
- Try different roles. For example, have everyone take turns being the facilitator or host of the discussion.
- Use a prop, such as a book or gavel. Pass the prop around the group, allowing whomever is holding the prop to have the floor.

Make Relevant Contributions

Especially when responding to a short story, a poem, or a novel, avoid simply summarizing the plot. Instead, consider *what* you think might happen next, *why* events take place as they do, or *how* a writer provokes a response in you. Let your ideas inspire deeper thought or discussion about the literature.

Consider Other Ideas and Interpretations

A work of literature can generate a wide variety of responses in different readers—and that can make your discussions exciting. Be open to the idea that many interpretations can be valid. To support your own ideas, point to the events, descriptions, characters, or other literary elements in the work that produced your interpretation. To consider someone else's ideas, decide whether details in the work support the interpretation he or she presents. Be sure to convey your criticism of the ideas of others in a respectful and supportive manner.

Ask Questions and Extend the Contributions of Others

Get in the habit of asking questions to help you clarify your understanding of another reader's ideas. You can also use questions to call attention to possible areas of confusion, to points that are open to debate, or to errors.

In addition, offer elaboration of the points that others make by providing examples and illustrations. To move a discussion forward, pause occasionally to summarize and evaluate tentative conclusions reached by the group members. Then, continue the discussion with a fresh understanding of the material and ideas you have already covered.

Manage Differing Opinions and Views

Each participant brings his or her own personality, experiences, ideas, cultural background, likes and dislikes to the experience of reading, making disagreement almost inevitable. As differences arise, be sensitive to each individual's point of view. Do not personalize disagreements, but keep them focused on the literature or ideas under discussion.

When you meet with a group to discuss literature, use a chart like the one shown to analyze the discussion.

Work Being Discussed:	
Focus Question:	
Your Response:	Another Student's Response:
Supporting Evidence:	Supporting Evidence:
One New Idea That You Considered About the Work During the Discussion:	

LITERARY CRITICISM

Criticism is writing that explores the meaning and techniques of literary works, usually in order to evaluate them. Writing criticism can help you think through your experience of a work of literature and can also help others to deepen their own understanding. All literary criticism shares similar goals:

- **Making connections** within or between works, or between a work of literature and its context
- **Making distinctions** or showing differences between elements of a single work or aspects of two or more works
- **Achieving insights** that were not apparent from a superficial reading
- **Making a judgment** about the quality or value of a literary work

Critics use various **theories of literary criticism** to understand, appreciate, and evaluate literature. Some theories focus on the context of the work while others focus on the work itself. Sometimes critics combine one or more theories. These charts show a few examples of the many theories of criticism:

Focus on Contexts		Focus on the Work Itself
HUMAN EXPERIENCE	**Mythic Criticism** Explores universal situations, characters, and symbols called archetypes as they appear in a literary work	**Formal Criticism** Shows how the work reflects characteristics of the genre, or literary type, to which it belongs
CULTURE AND HISTORY	**Historic Criticism** Analyzes how circumstances or ideas of an era influence a work	
AUTHOR'S LIFE	**Biographical Criticism** Explains how the author's life sheds light on the work	

Examples of Literary Theories in Action

- **Mythic Criticism:** discussing how the Greek myth "Prometheus and the First People," p. 982, reveals Prometheus as an archetypal character
- **Historical Criticism:** showing how William Shakespeare was influenced by Elizabethan concepts of nature and politics in *Julius Caesar*, p. 824
- **Biographical Criticism:** showing that Emily Dickinson's family relationships influenced the theme of "Success is counted sweetest," p. 705
- **Formal Criticism:** analyzing how "Contents of the Dead Man's Pocket," p. 110, combines short-story elements like plot, suspense, setting, character, and theme

Apply It To Your Reading

Choose one selection from this textbook and explore it using two different theories of literary criticism. Write an essay explaining how the unique focus of each theory helped you appreciate different aspects of the selection.

LITERARY MOVEMENTS

Our literary heritage has been shaped by a number of **literary movements**, directions in literature characterized by shared assumptions, beliefs, and practices. This chart shows, in chronological order, some important literary movements. While these movements developed at particular historical moments, all of them may still influence individual writers working today.

Movement	Beliefs and Practices	Examples
Classicism Europe during the Renaissance (c. 1300–1625)	• Looks to classical literature of ancient Greece and Rome as models • Values logic, clarity, balance, and restraint • Prefers "ordered" nature of parks and gardens	the clarity and restraint of Robert Frost's verse ("Mowing," p. 616)
Romanticism Europe during the late 1700s and the early 1800s	• Rebels against Classicism • Values imagination and emotion • Prefers "wild" nature of forests	the visionary encounters in Keats's poetry ("La Belle Dame sans Merci," p. 650)
Realism Europe and America from the mid-1800s to the 1890s	• Rebels against Romanticism's search for the ideal • Focuses on everyday life and social problems	the realistic rendering of Russian life in Anton Chekhov's fiction ("A Problem," p. 233)
Naturalism Europe and America during the late 1800s and early 1900s	• Assumes people cannot choose their fate but are shaped by psychological and social forces • Views society as a competitive jungle	the portrayal of characters as victims of social forces in Guy de Maupassant's fiction ("Two Friends," p. 1137)
Modernism World-wide between 1890 and 1945	• In response to the First World War, questions human reason • Focuses on studies of the unconscious and the art of primitive peoples • Experiments with language and form	the experiments with free verse and sound effects in Carl Sandburg's poetry ("Jazz Fantasia," p. 685)
Post-Modernism World-wide after 1945; still prevalent today	• Believes works of art comment on themselves • Finds inspiration in information technology	the self-consciousness about tradition in John Phillip Santos's nonfiction (from *Places Left Unfinished at the Time of Creation*, p. 967)

TIPS FOR IMPROVING READING FLUENCY

When you were younger, you learned to read. Then, you read to expand your experiences or for pure enjoyment. Now, you are expected to read to learn. As you progress in school, you are given more and more material to read. The tips on these pages will help you improve your reading fluency, or your ability to read easily, smoothly, and expressively.

Keeping Your Concentration

One common problem that readers face is the loss of concentration. When you are reading an assignment, you might find yourself rereading the same sentence several times without really understanding it. The first step in changing this behavior is to notice that you do it. Becoming an active, aware reader will help you get the most from your assignments. Practice using these strategies:

- Cover what you have already read with a note card as you go along. Then, you will not be able to reread without noticing that you are doing it.

- Set a purpose for reading beyond just completing the assignment. Then, read actively by pausing to ask yourself questions about the material as you read.

- Use the Reading Strategy instruction and notes that appear with each selection in this textbook.

- Stop reading after a specified period of time (for example, 5 minutes) and summarize what you have read. To help you with this strategy, use the Reading Check questions that appear with each selection in this textbook. Reread to find any answers you do not know.

Reading Check

What common problem do many readers face?

Reading Phrases

Fluent readers read phrases rather than individual words. Reading this way will speed up your reading and improve your comprehension. Here are some useful ideas:

- Experts recommend rereading as a strategy to increase fluency. Choose a passage of text that is neither too hard nor too easy. Read the same passage aloud several times until you can read it smoothly. When you can read the passage fluently, pick another passage and keep practicing.

- Read aloud into a tape recorder. Then, listen to the recording, noting your accuracy, pacing, and expression. You can also read aloud and share feedback with a partner.

- Use the *Prentice Hall Listening to Literature* audiotapes or CDs to hear the selections read aloud. Read along silently in your textbook, noticing how the reader uses his or her voice and emphasizes certain words and phrases.

Reading Check

In what ways will reading phrases rather than individual words affect your reading?

Understanding Key Vocabulary

If you do not understand some of the words in an assignment, you may miss out on important concepts. Therefore, it is helpful to keep a dictionary nearby when you are reading. Follow these steps:

- Before you begin reading, scan the text for unfamiliar words or terms. Find out what those words mean before you begin reading.
- Use context—the surrounding words, phrases, and sentences—to help you determine the meanings of unfamiliar words.
- If you are unable to understand the meaning through context, refer to the dictionary.

Reading Check

Why should you look up words you do not know when reading an assignment?

Paying Attention to Punctuation

When you read, pay attention to punctuation. Commas, periods, exclamation points, semicolons, and colons tell you when to pause or stop. They also indicate relationships between groups of words. When you recognize these relationships, you will read with greater understanding and expression. Look at the chart below.

Punctuation Mark	Meaning
comma	brief pause
period	pause at the end of a thought
exclamation point	pause that indicates emphasis
semicolon	pause between related but distinct thoughts
colon	pause before giving explanation or examples

Using the Reading Fluency Checklist

Use the checklist below each time you read a selection in this textbook. In your Language Arts journal or notebook, note which skills you need to work on and chart your progress each week.

Reading Fluency Checklist

- ☐ Preview the text to check for difficult or unfamiliar words.
- ☐ Practice reading aloud.
- ☐ Read according to punctuation.
- ☐ Break down long sentences, starting with the main subject and main verb.
- ☐ Read groups of words for meaning rather than reading single words.
- ☐ Read with expression (change your tone of voice to add meaning to the word).

Reading is a skill that can be improved with practice. The key to improving your fluency is to read. The more you read, the better your reading will become.

TYPES OF WRITING

Writing is a process that begins with the exploration of ideas and ends with the presentation of a final draft. Often, the types of writing are grouped into modes according to form and purpose.

Narration

Whenever writers tell any type of story, they are using **narration.** Most narratives share certain elements, such as characters, a setting, a sequence of events, and, often, a theme. Following are some types of narration:

Autobiographical Writing Autobiographical writing tells a true story about an important period, experience, or relationship in the writer's life. Effective autobiographical writing includes

- A series of events that involve the writer as the main character
- Details, thoughts, feelings, and insights from the writer's perspective
- A conflict or an event that affects the writer
- A logical organization that tells the story clearly
- Insights that the writer gained from the experience

Types of autobiographical writing include personal narratives, autobiographical sketches, reflective essays, eyewitness accounts, and memoirs.

Short Story A short story is a brief, creative narrative. Most short stories include

- Details that establish the setting in time and place
- A main character who undergoes a change or learns something during the course of the story
- A conflict or a problem to be introduced, developed, and resolved
- A plot, the series of events that make up the action of the story
- A theme or message about life

Types of short stories include realistic stories, fantasies, historical narratives, mysteries, thrillers, science-fiction stories, and adventure stories.

Description

Descriptive writing is writing that creates a vivid picture of a person, place, thing, or event. Most descriptive writing includes

- Sensory details—sights, sounds, smells, tastes, and physical sensations
- Vivid, precise language
- Figurative language or comparisons
- Adjectives and adverbs that paint a word picture
- An organization suited to the subject

Types of descriptive writing include description of ideas, observations, travel brochures, physical descriptions, functional descriptions, remembrances, and character sketches.

Persuasion

Persuasion is writing or speaking that attempts to convince people to accept a position or take a desired action. Following are some types of persuasion:

Persuasive Essay A persuasive essay presents a position on an issue, urges readers to accept that position, and may encourage a specific action. An effective persuasive essay

- Explores an issue of importance to the writer
- Addresses an issue that is arguable
- Uses facts, examples, statistics, or personal experiences to support a position
- Tries to influence the audience through appeals to the readers' knowledge, experiences, or emotions
- Uses clear organization to present a logical argument

Forms of persuasion include editorials, position papers, persuasive speeches, grant proposals, advertisements, and debates.

Advertisements An advertisement is a planned communication meant to be seen, heard, or read. It attempts to persuade an audience to buy a product or service, accept an idea, or support a cause. Advertisements may appear in printed or broadcast form. An effective advertisement includes

- A memorable slogan to grab the audience's attention
- A call to action
- Persuasive and/or informative text
- Striking visual or aural images
- Information about price, location, date, and time

Several common types of advertisements are public-service announcements, billboards, merchandise ads, service ads, and political campaign literature.

Exposition

Exposition is writing that relies on facts to inform or explain. Effective expository writing reflects a well-thought-out organization—one that includes a clear introduction, body, and conclusion. Here are some types of exposition:

Comparison-and-Contrast Essay A comparison-and-contrast essay analyzes the similarities and differences between or among two or more things. An effective comparison-and-contrast essay

- Identifies a purpose for comparison and contrast
- Identifies similarities and differences between or among two or more things, people, places, or ideas
- Gives factual details about the subjects
- Uses an organizational plan suited to the topic and purpose

Cause-and-Effect Essay A cause-and-effect essay examines the relationship between events, explaining how one event or situation causes another. A successful cause-and-effect essay includes

- A discussion of a cause, event, or condition that produces a specific result
- An explanation of an effect, outcome, or result
- Evidence and examples to support the explanation
- A logical organization that makes the explanation clear

Problem-and-Solution Essay A problem-and-solution essay describes a problem and offers one or more solutions to it. It describes a clear set of steps to achieve a result. An effective problem-and-solution essay includes

- A clear statement of the problem, with its causes and effects summarized for the reader
- The most important aspects of the problem
- A proposal of at least one realistic solution
- Facts, statistics, data, or expert testimony to support the solution
- A clear organization that makes the relationship between problem and solution obvious

Research Writing

Research writing is based on information gathered from outside sources. A research paper—a focused study of a topic—helps writers explore and connect ideas, make discoveries, and share their findings with an audience. An effective research paper

- Focuses on a specific, narrow topic, which is usually summarized in a thesis statement
- Presents relevant information from a wide variety of sources
- Uses a clear organization that includes an introduction, body, and conclusion
- Includes a bibliography or works-cited list that identifies the sources from which the information was drawn

Other types of writing that depend on accurate and insightful research include multimedia presentations, statistical reports, annotated bibliographies, and experiment journals.

Response to Literature

When you write a **response-to-literature essay,** you give yourself the opportunity to discover *what, how,* and *why* a piece of writing affected you. An effective response

- Contains a reaction to a poem, story, essay, or other work of literature
- Analyzes the content of a literary work, its related ideas, or the work's effect on the reader
- Presents a thesis statement to identify the nature of the response
- Focuses on a single aspect of the work or gives a general overview
- Supports opinion with evidence from the work addressed

The following are just a few of the ways you might respond in writing to a literary work: reader's response journals, literary letters, and literary analyses.

Writing for Assessment

One of the most common types of school **assessment** is the written test. When a test includes an essay, you are expected to write a response that includes

- A clearly stated and well-supported thesis
- Specific information about the topic derived from your reading or from class discussion
- A clear organization

In your school career, you will probably encounter questions that ask you to address each of the following types of writing: explaining a process; defending a position; comparing, contrasting, or categorizing; and showing cause and effect.

Workplace Writing

Workplace writing is probably the format you will use most after you finish school. In general, workplace writing is fact-based and meant to communicate specific information in a structured format. Effective workplace writing

- Communicates information concisely
- Includes details that provide necessary information and anticipate potential questions
- Is error-free and neatly presented

Common types of workplace writing include business letters, memorandums, résumés, forms, and applications.

WRITING FRIENDLY LETTERS

A friendly letter is an informal letter to a friend, a family member, or anyone with whom the writer wants to communicate in a personal way. Most friendly letters are made up of five parts:

- the heading
- the salutation, or greeting
- the body
- the closing
- the signature

The purpose of a friendly letter is often one of the following:

- to share personal news and feelings
- to send or to answer an invitation
- to express thanks

Model Friendly Letter

In this friendly letter, Betsy thanks her grandparents for a birthday present and gives them some news about her life.

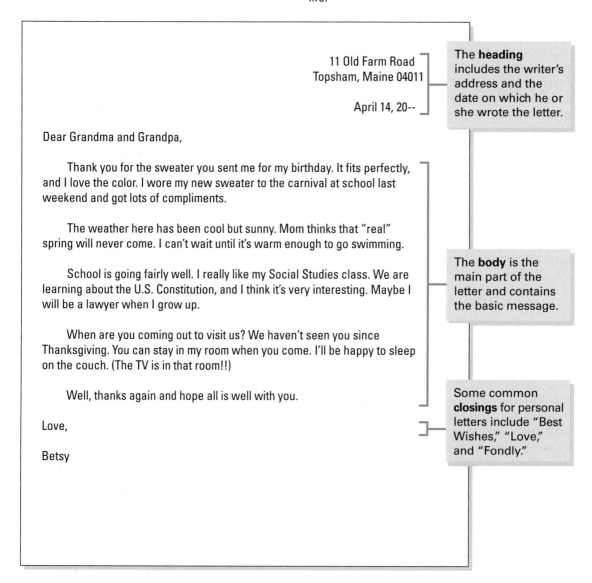

11 Old Farm Road
Topsham, Maine 04011

April 14, 20--

The **heading** includes the writer's address and the date on which he or she wrote the letter.

Dear Grandma and Grandpa,

Thank you for the sweater you sent me for my birthday. It fits perfectly, and I love the color. I wore my new sweater to the carnival at school last weekend and got lots of compliments.

The weather here has been cool but sunny. Mom thinks that "real" spring will never come. I can't wait until it's warm enough to go swimming.

School is going fairly well. I really like my Social Studies class. We are learning about the U.S. Constitution, and I think it's very interesting. Maybe I will be a lawyer when I grow up.

When are you coming out to visit us? We haven't seen you since Thanksgiving. You can stay in my room when you come. I'll be happy to sleep on the couch. (The TV is in that room!!)

Well, thanks again and hope all is well with you.

Love,

Betsy

The **body** is the main part of the letter and contains the basic message.

Some common **closings** for personal letters include "Best Wishes," "Love," and "Fondly."

WRITING BUSINESS LETTERS

Business letters follow one of several acceptable formats. In **block format,** each part of the letter begins at the left margin. A double space is used between paragraphs. In **modified block format,** some parts of the letter are indented to the center of the page. No matter which format is used, all letters in business format have a heading, an inside address, a salutation, or greeting, a body, a closing, and a signature. These parts are shown and annotated on the model business letter below, formatted in modified block style.

Model Business Letter
In this letter, Yolanda Dodson uses modified block format to request information.

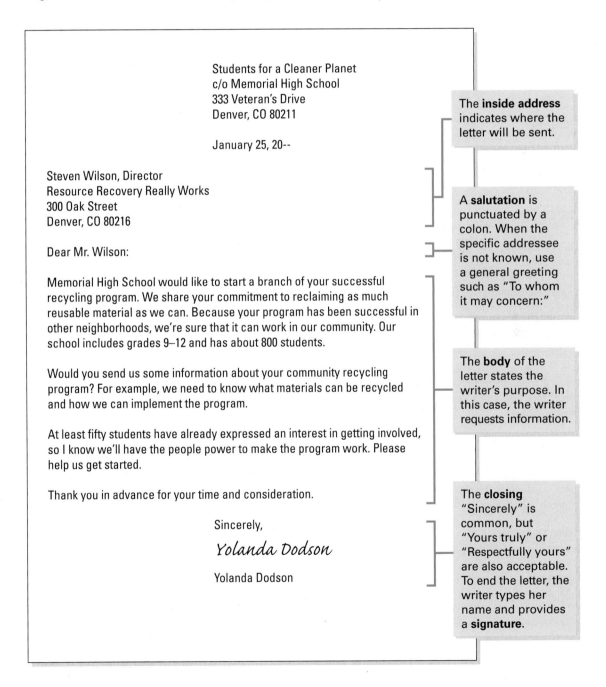

Students for a Cleaner Planet
c/o Memorial High School
333 Veteran's Drive
Denver, CO 80211

January 25, 20--

Steven Wilson, Director
Resource Recovery Really Works
300 Oak Street
Denver, CO 80216

Dear Mr. Wilson:

Memorial High School would like to start a branch of your successful recycling program. We share your commitment to reclaiming as much reusable material as we can. Because your program has been successful in other neighborhoods, we're sure that it can work in our community. Our school includes grades 9–12 and has about 800 students.

Would you send us some information about your community recycling program? For example, we need to know what materials can be recycled and how we can implement the program.

At least fifty students have already expressed an interest in getting involved, so I know we'll have the people power to make the program work. Please help us get started.

Thank you in advance for your time and consideration.

Sincerely,

Yolanda Dodson

Yolanda Dodson

The **inside address** indicates where the letter will be sent.

A **salutation** is punctuated by a colon. When the specific addressee is not known, use a general greeting such as "To whom it may concern:"

The **body** of the letter states the writer's purpose. In this case, the writer requests information.

The **closing** "Sincerely" is common, but "Yours truly" or "Respectfully yours" are also acceptable. To end the letter, the writer types her name and provides a **signature.**

WRITING A RÉSUMÉ

A résumé summarizes your educational background, work experiences, relevant skills, and other employment qualifications. It also tells potential employers how to contact you. An effective résumé presents the applicant's name, address, and phone number. It follows an accepted résumé organization, using labels and headings to guide readers. A résumé should outline the applicant's educational background, life experiences, and related qualifications using precise and active language.

Model Résumé

With this résumé, James, a college student, hopes to find a full-time job.

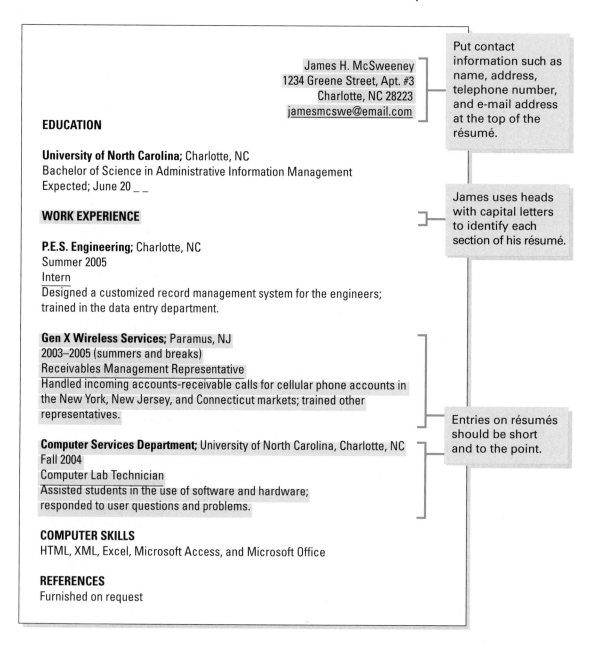

James H. McSweeney
1234 Greene Street, Apt. #3
Charlotte, NC 28223
jamesmcswe@email.com

Put contact information such as name, address, telephone number, and e-mail address at the top of the résumé.

EDUCATION

University of North Carolina; Charlotte, NC
Bachelor of Science in Administrative Information Management
Expected; June 20 _ _

WORK EXPERIENCE

James uses heads with capital letters to identify each section of his résumé.

P.E.S. Engineering; Charlotte, NC
Summer 2005
Intern
Designed a customized record management system for the engineers; trained in the data entry department.

Gen X Wireless Services; Paramus, NJ
2003–2005 (summers and breaks)
Receivables Management Representative
Handled incoming accounts-receivable calls for cellular phone accounts in the New York, New Jersey, and Connecticut markets; trained other representatives.

Entries on résumés should be short and to the point.

Computer Services Department; University of North Carolina, Charlotte, NC
Fall 2004
Computer Lab Technician
Assisted students in the use of software and hardware; responded to user questions and problems.

COMPUTER SKILLS
HTML, XML, Excel, Microsoft Access, and Microsoft Office

REFERENCES
Furnished on request

USING THE INTERNET

Introduction to the Internet

The Internet is a series of networks that are interconnected all over the world. The Internet allows users to have almost unlimited access to information stored on the networks. Dr. Berners-Lee, a physicist, created the Internet in the 1980s by writing a small computer program that allowed pages to be linked together using key words. The Internet was mostly text-based until 1992, when a computer program called the NCSA Mosaic (National Center for Supercomputing Applications) was created at the University of Illinois. This program was the first Web browser. The development of Web browsers greatly eased the ability of the user to navigate through all the pages stored on the Web. Very soon, the appearance of the Web was altered as well. More appealing visuals were added, and sound, too, was implemented. This change made the Web more user-friendly and more appealing to the general public.

Using the Internet for Research

Key Word Search

Before you begin a search, you should identify your specific topic. To make searching easier, narrow your subject to a key word or a group of key words. These are your search terms, and they should be as specific as possible. For example, if you are looking for the latest concert dates for your favorite musical group, you might use the band's name as a key word. However, if you were to enter the name of the group in the query box of the search engine, you might be presented with thousands of links to information about the group that is unrelated to what you want to know. You might locate such information as band member biographies, the group's history, fan reviews of concerts, and hundreds of sites with related names containing information that is irrelevant to your search. Because you used such a broad key word, you might need to navigate through all that information before you could find a link or subheading for concert dates. In contrast, if you were to type in "Duplex Arena and [band name]," you would have a better chance of locating pages that contain this information.

How to Narrow Your Search

If you have a large group of key words and still do not know which ones to use, write out a list of all the words you are considering. Once you have completed the list, scrutinize it. Then, delete the words that are least important to your search, and highlight those that are most important.

These **key search connectors** can help you fine-tune your search:

AND: Narrows a search by retrieving documents that include both terms. For example: *baseball* AND *playoffs*

OR: Broadens a search by retrieving documents including any of the terms. For example: *play-offs* OR *championships*

NOT: Narrows a search by excluding documents containing certain words. For example: *baseball* NOT *history of*

Tips for an Effective Search

1. Remember that search engines can be case-sensitive. If your first attempt at searching fails, check your search terms for misspellings and try again.

2. If you are entering a group of key words, present them in order from the most important to the least important key word.

3. Avoid opening the link to every single page in your results list. Search engines present pages in descending order of relevancy. The most useful pages will be located at the top of the list. However, read the description of each link before you open the page.

4. Some search engines provide helpful tips for specializing your search. Take the opportunity to learn more about effective searching.

Other Ways to Search

Using Online Reference Sites How you search should be tailored to what you are hoping to find. If you are looking for data and facts, use reference sites before you jump onto a simple search engine. For example, you can find reference sites to provide definitions of words, statistics about almost any subject, biographies, maps, and concise information on many topics. Here are some useful online reference sites:

Online libraries

Online periodicals

Almanacs

Encyclopedias

You can find these sources using subject searches.

Conducting Subject Searches As you prepare to go online, consider your subject and the best way to find information to suit your needs. If you are looking for general information on a topic and you want your search results to be extensive, consider the subject search indexes on most search engines. These indexes, in the form of category and subject lists, often appear on the first page of a search engine. When you click on a specific highlighted word, you will be presented with a new screen containing subcategories of the topic you chose.

Evaluating the Reliability of Internet Resources

Just as you would evaluate the quality, bias, and validity of any other research material you locate, check the source of information you find online. Compare these two sites containing information about the poet and writer Langston Hughes:

Site A is a personal Web site constructed by a college student. It contains no bibliographic information or links to sites that he used. Included on the site are several poems by Langston Hughes and a student essay about the poet's use of symbolism. It has not been updated in more than six months.

Site B is a Web site constructed and maintained by the English Department of a major university. Information on Hughes is presented in a scholarly format, with a bibliography and credits for the writer. The site includes links to other sites and indicates new features that are added weekly.

For your own research, consider the information you find on Site B to be more reliable and accurate than that on Site A. Because it is maintained by experts in their field who are held accountable for their work, the university site will be a better research tool than the student-generated one.

Tips for Evaluating Internet Sources

1. Consider who constructed and who now maintains the Web page. Determine whether this author is a reputable source. Often, the URL endings indicate a source.
   - Sites ending in *.edu* are maintained by educational institutions.
   - Sites ending in *.gov* are maintained by government agencies (federal, state, or local).
   - Sites ending in *.org* are normally maintained by nonprofit organizations and agencies.
   - Sites ending in *.com* are commercially or personally maintained.

2. Skim the official and trademarked Web pages first. It is safe to assume that the information you draw from Web pages of reputable institutions, online encyclopedias, online versions of major daily newspapers, or government-owned sites produce information as reliable as the material you would find in print. In contrast, unbranded sites or those generated by individuals tend to borrow information from other sources without providing documentation. As information travels from one source to another, it could have been muddled, misinterpreted, edited, or revised.

3. You can still find valuable information in the less "official" sites. Check for the writer's credentials, and then consider these factors:
   - Do not be misled by official-looking graphics or presentations.
   - Make sure that the information is updated enough to suit your needs. Many Web pages will indicate how recently they have been updated.
   - If the information is borrowed, notice whether you can trace it back to its original source.

Respecting Copyrighted Material

Because the Internet is a relatively new and quickly growing medium, issues of copyright and ownership arise almost daily. As laws begin to govern the use and reuse of material posted online, they may change the way that people can access or reprint material.

Text, photographs, music, and fine art printed online may not be reproduced without acknowledged permission of the copyright owner.

CITING SOURCES AND PREPARING MANUSCRIPT

In research writing, cite your sources. In the body of your paper, provide a footnote, an end-note, or a parenthetical citation, identifying the sources of facts, opinions, or quotations. At the end of your paper, provide a bibliography or a works-cited list, a list of all the sources you cite. Follow an established format, such as Modern Language Association (MLA) Style.

Works-Cited List (MLA Style)

A works-cited list must contain accurate information sufficient to enable a reader to locate each source you cite. The basic components of an entry are as follows:

- Name of the author, editor, translator, or group responsible for the work
- Title of the work
- Place and date of publication
- Publisher

For print materials, the information required for a cita-tion generally appears on the copyright and title pages of a work. For the format of works-cited list entries, consult the examples at right and in the chart on page R34.

Parenthetical Citations (MLA Style)

A parenthetical citation briefly identifies the source from which you have taken a specific quotation, fac-tual claim, or opinion. It refers the reader to one of the entries on your works-cited list. A parenthetical cita-tion has the following features:

- It appears in parentheses.
- It identifies the source by the last name of the author, editor, or translator.
- It gives a page reference, identifying the page of the source on which the information cited can be found.

Punctuation A parenthetical citation generally falls out-side a closing quotation mark but within the final punc-tuation of a clause or sentence. For a long quotation set off from the rest of your text, place the citation at the end of the excerpt without any punctuation following.

Special Cases

- If the author is an organization, use the organiza-tion's name, in a shortened version if necessary.
- If you cite more than one work by the same author, add the title or a shortened version of the title.

Sample Works-Cited Lists

Carwardine, Mark, Erich Hoyt, R. Ewan Fordyce, and Peter Gill. *The Nature Company Guides: Whales, Dolphins, and Porpoises.* New York: Time-Life Books, 1998.

"Discovering Whales." *Whales on the Net.* Whales in Danger. 31 March 2006. <http://www.omplace.com/omsites/discover>

Neruda, Pablo. "Ode to Spring." *Odes to Opposites.* Trans. Ken Krabbenhoft. Ed. and illus. Ferris Cook. Boston: Little, Brown and Company, 1995.

The Saga of the Volsungs. Trans. Jesse L. Byock. London: Penguin Books, 1990.

List an anonymous work by title

List both the title of the work and the title of the collection in which it is found.

Sample Parenthetical Citations

It makes sense that baleen whales such as the blue whale, the bowhead whale, the humpback whale, and the sei whale (to name just a few) grow to immense sizes (Carwardine, Hoyt, and Fordyce 19–21). The blue whale has grooves running from under its chin to partway along the length of its underbelly. As in some other whales, these grooves expand and allow even more food and water to be taken in (Ellis 18–21).

Authors' last names

Page numbers where information can be found

MLA Style for Listing Sources

Book with one author	Pyles, Thomas. *The Origins and Development of the English Language.* 2nd ed. New York: Harcourt Brace Jovanovich, Inc., 1971.
Book with two or three authors	McCrum, Robert, William Cran, and Robert MacNeil. *The Story of English.* New York: Penguin Books, 1987.
Book with an editor	Truth, Sojourner. *Narrative of Sojourner Truth.* Ed. Margaret Washington. New York: Vintage Books, 1993.
Book with more than three authors or editors	Donald, Robert B., et al. *Writing Clear Essays.* Upper Saddle River, NJ: Prentice Hall, Inc., 1996.
Single work from an anthology	Hawthorne, Nathaniel. "Young Goodman Brown." *Literature: An Introduction to Reading and Writing.* Ed. Edgar V. Roberts and Henry E. Jacobs. Upper Saddle River, NJ: Prentice Hall, Inc., 1998. 376–385. [Indicate pages for the entire selection.]
Introduction in a published edition	Washington, Margaret. Introduction. *Narrative of Sojourner Truth.* By Sojourner Truth. New York: Vintage Books, 1993. v–xi.
Signed article in a weekly magazine	Wallace, Charles. "A Vodacious Deal." *Time* 14 Feb. 2000: 63.
Signed article in a monthly magazine	Gustaitis, Joseph. "The Sticky History of Chewing Gum." *American History* Oct. 1998: 30–38.
Unsigned editorial or story	"Selective Silence." Editorial. *Wall Street Journal* 11 Feb. 2000: A14. [If the editorial or story is signed, begin with the author's name.]
Signed pamphlet or brochure	[Treat the pamphlet as though it were a book.]
Pamphlet with no author, publisher, or date	*Are You at Risk of Heart Attack?* n.p. n.d. ["n.p. n.d." indicates that there is no known publisher or date.]
Filmstrips, slide programs, videocassettes, DVDs, and other audiovisual media	*The Diary of Anne Frank.* Dir. George Stevens. Perf. Millie Perkins, Shelley Winters, Joseph Schildkraut, Lou Jacobi, and Richard Beymer. 1959. Twentieth Century Fox, 2004.
Radio or television program transcript	"Nobel for Literature." Narr. Rick Karr. *All Things Considered.* National Public Radio. WNYC, New York. 10 Oct. 2002. Transcript.
Internet	"Fun Facts About Gum." *NACGM.* National Association of Chewing Gum Manufacturers. 19 Dec. 1999 <http://www.nacgm.org/consumer/funfacts.html> [Indicate the date you accessed the information. Content and addresses at Web sites change frequently.]
Newspaper	Thurow, Roger. "South Africans Who Fought for Sanctions Now Scrap for Investors." *Wall Street Journal* 11 Feb. 2000: A1+ [For a multipage article that does not run on consecutive pages, write only the first page number on which it appears, followed by a plus sign.]
Personal interview	Smith, Jane. Personal interview. 10 Feb. 2000.
CD (with multiple publishers)	Simms, James, ed. *Romeo and Juliet.* By William Shakespeare. CD-ROM. Oxford: Attica Cybernetics Ltd.; London: BBC Education; London: HarperCollins Publishers, 1995.
Signed article from an encyclopedia	Askeland, Donald R. "Welding." *World Book Encyclopedia.* 1991 ed.

GUIDE TO RUBRICS

What is a rubric?

A rubric is a tool, often in the form of a chart or a grid, that helps you assess your work. Rubrics are particularly helpful for writing and speaking assignments.

To help you or others assess, or evaluate, your work, a rubric offers several specific criteria to be applied to your work. Then, the rubric helps you or an evaluator indicate your range of success or failure according to those specific criteria. Rubrics are often used to evaluate writing for standardized tests.

Using a rubric will save you time, focus your learning, and improve the work you do. When you know what the rubric will be before you begin writing a persuasive essay, for example, you will be aware as you write of specific criteria that are important in that kind of an essay. As you evaluate the essay before giving it to your teacher, you will focus on the specific areas that your teacher wants you to master—or on areas that you know present challenges for you. Instead of searching through your work randomly for any way to improve it or correct its errors, you will have a clear and helpful focus on specific criteria.

How are rubrics constructed?

Rubrics can be constructed in several different ways.

- Your teacher may assign a rubric for a specific assignment.
- Your teacher may direct you to a rubric in your textbook.
- Your teacher and your class may construct a rubric for a particular assignment together.
- You and your classmates may construct a rubric together.
- You may create your own rubric with criteria you want to evaluate in your work.

How will a rubric help me?

A rubric will help you assess your work on a scale. Scales vary from rubric to rubric but usually range from 6 to 1, 5 to 1, or 4 to 1, with 6, 5, or 4 being the highest score and 1 being the lowest. If someone else is using the rubric to assess your work, the rubric will give your evaluator a clear range within which to place your work. If you are using the rubric yourself, it will help you make improvements to your work.

What are the types of rubrics?

- A **holistic rubric** has general criteria that can apply to a variety of assignments. See p. R-37 for an example of a holistic rubric.
- An **analytic rubric** is specific to a particular assignment. The criteria for evaluation address the specific issues important in that assignment. See p. R-36 for examples of analytic rubrics.

Sample Analytic Rubrics

Rubric With a 4-point Scale

The following analytic rubric is an example of a rubric to assess a persuasive essay. It will help you evaluate focus, organization, support, elaboration, and style conventions.

	Focus	Organization	Support/Elaboration	Style Conventions
4	Demonstrates highly effective word choice; clearly focused on task.	Uses clear, consistent organizational strategy.	Provides convincing, well-elaborated reasons to support the position.	Incorporates transitions; includes very few mechanical errors.
3	Demonstrates good word choice; stays focused on persuasive task.	Uses clear organizational strategy with occasional inconsistencies.	Provides two or more moderately elaborated reasons to support the position.	Incorporates some transitions; includes few mechanical errors.
2	Shows some good word choices; minimally stays focused on persuasive task.	Uses inconsistent organizational strategy; presentation is not logical.	Provides several reasons, but few are elaborated; only one elaborated reason.	Incorporates few transitions; includes many mechanical errors.
1	Shows lack of attention to persuasive task.	Demonstrates lack of organizational strategy.	Provides no specific reasons or does not elaborate.	Does not connect ideas; includes many mechanical errors.

Rubric With a 6-point Scale

The following analytic rubric is an example of a rubric to assess a persuasive essay. It will help you evaluate presentation, position, evidence, and arguments.

	Presentation	Position	Evidence	Arguments
6	Essay clearly and effectively addresses an issue with more than one side.	Essay clearly states a supportable position on the issue.	All evidence is logically organized, well presented, and supports the position.	All reader concerns and counterarguments are effectively addressed.
5	Most of essay addresses an issue that has more than one side.	Essay clearly states a position on the issue.	Most evidence is logically organized, well presented, and supports the position.	Most reader concerns and counterarguments are effectively addressed.
4	Essay adequately addresses issue that has more than one side.	Essay adequately states a position on the issue.	Many parts of evidence support the position; some evidence is out of order.	Many reader concerns and counterarguments are adequately addressed.
3	Essay addresses issue with two sides but does not present second side clearly.	Essay states a position on the issue, but the position is difficult to support.	Some evidence supports the position, but some evidence is out of order.	Some reader concerns and counterarguments are addressed.
2	Essay addresses issue with two sides but does not present second side.	Essay states a position on the issue, but the position is not supportable.	Not much evidence supports the position, and what is included is out of order.	A few reader concerns and counterarguments are addressed.
1	Essay does not address issue with more than one side.	Essay does not state a position on the issue.	No evidence supports the position.	No reader concerns or counterarguments are addressed.

Sample Holistic Rubric

Holistic rubrics such as this one are sometimes used to assess writing assignments on standardized tests. Notice that the criteria for evaluation are focus, organization, support, and use of conventions.

Points	Criteria
6 Points	• The writing is strongly focused and shows fresh insight into the writing task. • The writing is marked by a sense of completeness and coherence and is organized with a logical progression of ideas. • A main idea is fully developed, and support is specific and substantial. • A mature command of the language is evident, and the writing may employ characteristic creative writing strategies. • Sentence structure is varied, and writing is free of all but purposefully used fragments. • Virtually no errors in writing conventions appear.
5 Points	• The writing is clearly focused on the task. • The writing is well organized and has a logical progression of ideas, though there may be occasional lapses. • A main idea is well developed and supported with relevant detail. • Sentence structure is varied, and the writing is free of fragments, except when used purposefully. • Writing conventions are followed correctly.
4 Points	• The writing is clearly focused on the task, but extraneous material may intrude at times. • Clear organizational pattern is present, though lapses may occur. • A main idea is adequately supported, but development may be uneven. • Sentence structure is generally fragment free but shows little variation. • Writing conventions are generally followed correctly.
3 Points	• Writing is generally focused on the task, but extraneous material may intrude at times. • An organizational pattern is evident, but writing may lack a logical progression of ideas. • Support for the main idea is generally present but is sometimes illogical. • Sentence structure is generally free of fragments, but there is almost no variation. • The work generally demonstrates a knowledge of writing conventions, with occasional misspellings.
2 Points	• The writing is related to the task but generally lacks focus. • There is little evidence of organizational pattern, and there is little sense of cohesion. • Support for the main idea is generally inadequate, illogical, or absent. • Sentence structure is unvaried, and serious errors may occur. • Errors in writing conventions and spellings are frequent.
1 Point	• The writing may have little connection to the task and is generally unfocused. • There has been little attempt at organization or development. • The paper seems fragmented, with no clear main idea. • Sentence structure is unvaried, and serious errors appear. • Poor word choice and poor command of the language obscure meaning. • Errors in writing conventions and spelling are frequent.
Unscorable	The paper is considered unscorable if: • The response is unrelated to the task or is simply a rewording of the prompt. • The response has been copied from a published work. • The student did not write a response. • The response is illegible. • The words in the response are arranged with no meaning. • There is an insufficient amount of writing to score.

Student Model

Persuasive Writing

This persuasive letter, which would receive a top score according to a persuasive rubric, is a response to the following writing prompt, or assignment:

With the increased use of technology in the workplace, the skills that high-school graduates must possess have changed. Write a letter to your principal advocating new technology courses that could give high-school graduates a competitive edge.

Dear Principal:

I am writing to alert you to an urgent need in our school's curriculum. We need computer graphics courses!

> The letter begins with an engaging introduction that clearly states the persuasive focus.

Although you would have to find funds to buy the equipment, I've concluded that setting up this course would be well worth it. By adding this course, you would be adding many high-paying career options for students. Computer graphics is a type of art, and businesses all around us involve art in some form. You see computer graphics in commercials, movies, news broadcasts, weather broadcasts, architectural design, and business presentations. Workers with computer graphics skills are well paid because they are in such high demand.

You may argue that the school already has computer science classes. Good point! I'm in a computer science class, and it is mainly programming. Once we did have an assignment to design a graphic of a pumpkin. You wouldn't believe how much coding it takes to get a simple, animated drawing. In order to get a really creative image with definite lines, shading, lifelike colors, and texture, you need to use computer graphics software designed especially for that purpose. With software, you can make images that move and talk smoothly and environments with realistic colors and lighting. This is the same graphics software that businesses use for commercials, movies, and brochures. Students should be learning how to use this software.

> The author effectively counters an opposing argument to increase the persuasive power of her own argument.

Most important, computer graphics is a subject area that allows students to express their creativity. Adding a computer graphics course would have a positive effect on students. Course participants would enjoy doing their assignments, so they would earn good grades and turn in creative work. The energy and enthusiasm they would bring to their projects would catch the attention of the community at large. As a result, they would make the school and the principal look good.

> A positive argument that is well supported enhances the letter's persuasive appeal.

As you can see, adding a computer graphics course could be a very profitable idea for you, the students, and the community. You would be ensuring the success of the students who desire an art or computer career. You would be opening hundreds of different career pathways. Wouldn't it be great to know you were the reason for these students' success? Thanks for your time and consideration.

Sincerely,
Dawn Witherspoon

GRAMMAR, USAGE, AND MECHANICS

Parts of Speech

Nouns

A **noun** is the name of a person, place, or thing. A **common noun** names any one of a class of people, places, or things. A **proper noun** names a specific person, place, or thing.

Common Noun	Proper Noun
city	Washington, D.C.

Exercise A **Distinguishing Between Common and Proper Nouns.** Identify each noun as *common* or *proper*. Supply a proper noun of the same category for each common noun. Supply a common noun of the same category for each proper noun.

1. town
2. war
3. continent
4. Wilhelm
5. League of Nations
6. England
7. country
8. general
9. battle
10. June

Pronouns

A **pronoun** is a word that stands for a noun or for a word that takes the place of a noun.

A **personal pronoun** refers to (1) the person speaking, (2) the person spoken to, or (3) the person, place, or thing spoken about.

	Singular	Plural
First Person	I, me, my, mine	we, us, our, ours
Second Person	you, your, yours	you, your, yours
Third Person	he, him, his, she, her, hers, it, its	they, them, their, theirs

Antecedents are nouns (or words that take the place of nouns) for which pronouns stand. In the following sentence, the pronoun *it* stands for the noun *Florida*.

Florida is popular because it has a warm climate.

Exercise B **Identifying Pronouns and Antecedents.** Identify the pronoun and antecedent in each sentence. If a pronoun has no antecedent, write *none*.

1. I enjoy Ithaca, located on Cayuga Lake.
2. It was settled in 1789.
3. De Witt Clinton, the American statesman, made his home in Ithaca.
4. Residents of Ithaca enjoy its great natural beauty.
5. There are many cliffs and deep ravines, and their beauty is overwhelming.

A **reflexive pronoun** ends in *-self* or *-selves* and adds information to a sentence by pointing back to a noun or a pronoun earlier in the sentence.

"If you were honest folk *yourselves* you wouldn't let a thief go free." — Leo Tolstoy, p. 308

An **intensive pronoun** ends in *-self* or *-selves* and simply adds emphasis to a noun or a pronoun in the same sentence.

After a time, I *myself* was allowed to go into the dead houses and search for metal.
— Stephen Vincent Benét, p. 282

Exercise C **Identifying Personal, Reflexive, and Intensive Pronouns.** Identify each pronoun and label it *personal, reflexive,* or *intensive.*

1. Taos, New Mexico, sits in the hills near its neighbor, Santa Fe.
2. The city itself has long been attractive to visitors from other states and countries.
3. They enjoy the beauty of the land and the spirit of the residents there.
4. At the Kit Carson Home and Museum, you can look at objects owned by Carson himself.
5. Literary buffs can occupy themselves at the D. H. Lawrence Ranch and Shrine.

A **demonstrative pronoun** directs attention to a specific person, place, or thing.

this	these	that	those

These are the juiciest pears I have ever tasted.

A **relative pronoun** begins a subordinate clause and connects it to another idea in the sentence.

The poet *who* wrote "Fear" is Gabriela Mistral.

An **interrogative pronoun** is used to begin a question. The five interrogative pronouns are *what, which, who, whom,* and *whose.*

Exercise D **Recognizing Demonstrative, Relative, and Interrogative Pronouns.** Identify the pronoun in each of the following sentences. Then, label each *demonstrative, relative,* or *interrogative.*

1. Visitors who come to Houston find a thriving city in southeast Texas.

2. These are often people interested in the history and culture of the area.

3. Which would you like to see: the ballet or the opera?

4. The Houston Grand Opera, whose home is the Civic Center Complex, performs at the Gus Worthman Theater Center.

5. That is the theater of the Houston Ballet.

An **indefinite pronoun** refers to a person, place, or thing, often without specifying which one.

all anyone each everyone few one someone

> And then, for a moment, *all* is still, . . .
>
> — Edgar Allan Poe, p. 340

Exercise E **Supplying Indefinite Pronouns.** Complete each sentence by adding an indefinite pronoun.

1. Has __?__ here visited Cleveland, Ohio?

2. __?__ of the attractions in Cleveland's park system include a zoo and an aquarium.

3. The Metropolitan Park System gives __?__ a chance to enjoy nature.

4. A __?__ of Cleveland's roads lead to Lake Erie.

5. Not __?__ can name __?__ of the Great Lakes.

Verbs

A **verb** is a word that expresses time while showing an action, a condition, or the fact that something exists.

An **action verb** indicates the action of someone or something.

An action verb is **transitive** if it directs action toward someone or something named in the same sentence.

> He *dusted* his hands, muttering.
>
> — Jack Finney, p. 110

An action verb is **intransitive** if it does not direct action toward something or someone named in the same sentence.

> I *smiled* and looked up at the crew . . .
>
> — Lynne Cox, p. 58

Exercise F **Identifying Transitive and Intransitive Action Verbs.** Identify the action verb in each sentence, and label it *transitive* or *intransitive*.

1. People often imagine New Mexico as a faraway, quiet place.

2. In fact, New Mexico has developed into a vital, vibrant, and diverse state.

3. Many interesting and unusual events have occurred in New Mexico.

4. For instance, the federal government selected Los Alamos as a site for nuclear research in 1942.

5. Some people wonder about supposed extraterrestrial landings in Roswell.

A **linking verb** is a verb that connects the subject of a sentence with a noun or a pronoun that renames or describes the subject. The noun, pronoun, or phrase acting as a noun that renames the subject is called a **predicate nominative.**

> Romance at short notice *was* her specialty.
>
> — Saki, p. 1160

Exercise G **Recognizing Linking Verbs.** Write each sentence, underlining the linking verb. Draw an arrow showing which words are linked by the verb.

1. Santa Fe is the second-oldest city in the United States.

2. The Palace of the Governors is now the home of major museums.

3. This building had been the seat of government during the Spanish and Mexican occupations.

4. Native American and Hispanic cultures remain influential in New Mexico.

5. Native Americans seem eager to contribute to the social and economic affairs of the state.

A **helping verb** is a verb that can be added to another verb to make a verb phrase.

> Nor *did* I <u>suspect</u> that these experiences could be part of a novel's meaning.

Exercise H **Supplying Helping Verbs.** Add a helping verb to complete each sentence.

1. Alcatraz Island __?__ become home to numerous colonies of birds.

2. The island's natural and manmade features __?__ preserved by the National Park Service.

3. The name of the island __?__ attributed to a Spanish explorer.

4. He might __?__ called it *Isla de los Alcatraces* (Island of the Pelicans) because the birds were plentiful there.

5. *Alcatraz* __?__ become the anglicized form of the original name.

Adjectives

An **adjective** describes a noun or a pronoun or gives a noun or a pronoun a more specific meaning. Adjectives answer these questions:

> *What* kind? *blue* lamp, *large* tree
> *Which* one? *this* table, *those* books

How many?   *five* stars, *several* buses

How much?   *less* money, *enough* votes

The articles *the, a,* and *an* are adjectives. *An* is used before a word beginning with a vowel sound.

A noun may sometimes be used as an adjective.

   diamond necklace   *summer* vacation

Exercise I Recognizing Adjectives. Write the adjectives, including articles, in each sentence below.

1. Parrots are found in the warm tropical areas of the planet.
2. A small number of species inhabit the cooler temperate regions.
3. The colorful birds have red, green, blue, and yellow plumage.
4. Parrots eat a wide variety of hearty seeds and nutritious fruits.
5. Parrots are monogamous, often remaining with a single mate for life.

Adverbs

An **adverb** modifies a verb, an adjective, or another adverb. Adverbs answer the questions *where, when, in what way,* or *to what extent.*

   He could stand *there.* (modifies verb *stand*)

   He was *blissfully* happy. (modifies adjective *happy*)

   It ended *too* soon. (modifies adverb *soon*)

Exercise J Recognizing Adverbs. Identify the adverbs in each sentence below. Then, tell which word each adverb modifies.

1. Cowries are a very common variety of sea snails that are generally found in warm tropical waters.
2. They are mostly nocturnal animals, and they usually feed on algae.
3. A few species crawl slowly among corals and feed hungrily upon them.
4. These small creatures often have brilliantly colored shells.
5. For many years, cowry shells were used quite frequently by people in Africa, Asia, and Melanesia as a form of currency.

Prepositions

A **preposition** relates a noun or a pronoun that appears with it to another word in the sentence.

   before the end   *near* me   *inside* our fence

Exercise K Identifying Prepositions. Write the prepositions in the following sentences.

1. The headlines announced a truce between the nations.
2. Cut two pounds of apples into quarter-inch slices.
3. A window with a northern exposure is perfect for the plant.
4. The passengers in the back of the boat got wet from the spray.
5. Ted found the map underneath the woodpile behind the barn.

Conjunctions

A **conjunction** connects words or groups of words.

A **coordinating conjunction** connects similar kinds or groups of words.

   mother *and* father   simple *yet* stylish

Correlative conjunctions are used in pairs to connect similar words or groups of words.

   both Sue *and* Meg   *neither* he *nor* I

A **subordinating conjunction** connects two complete ideas by placing one idea below the other in rank or importance.

   You would know him *if* you saw him.

Exercise L Identifying Conjunctions. Write the conjunctions in the following sentences. Then, label each *coordinating, correlative,* or *subordinating.*

1. Are you familiar with the Navajo art of sandpainting or drypainting?
2. Even though it has its roots in Navajo ceremonies, sandpainting is also a commercial art form.
3. Most scholars agree that the Navajos borrowed the idea of sandpainting and changed it to fit their own ideas.
4. Because early sandpaintings were not permanent, there is little evidence to prove how this process occurred.
5. This sandpainting is both permanent and colorful.

Sentences, Phrases, and Clauses

Sentences

A **sentence** is a group of words with a subject and a predicate. Together, these parts express a complete thought.

A **fragment** is a group of words that does not express a complete thought.

Exercise A Recognizing Sentence Fragments. Write *F* for each item that is a fragment and *S* for complete sentences.

1. Consists of woodwind, brass, and percussion instruments.

2. Originally a section in ancient Greek theaters.

3. Dancers and instrumentalists used this area.

4. The part reserved for musicians called the orchestra pit.

5. The term *orchestra* now designates an area of seating in an auditorium.

The Four Structures of Sentences

There are two kinds of clauses: independent and subordinate. An independent clause can stand by itself as a sentence; a subordinate clause cannot. These can be used to form four basic sentence structures: *simple, compound, complex,* and *compound-complex.*

A **simple sentence** consists of a single independent clause.

A **compound sentence** consists of two or more independent clauses.

The clauses in a compound sentence can be joined by a comma and a coordinating conjunction *(and, but, for, nor, or, so, yet)* or by a semicolon (;).

A **complex sentence** consists of one independent clause and one or more subordinate clauses.

The independent clause in a complex sentence is often called the *main clause* to distinguish it from the subordinate clause or clauses.

A **compound-complex sentence** consists of two or more independent clauses and one or more subordinate clauses.

Phrases

A **phrase** is a group of words, without a subject and a verb, that functions in a sentence as one part of speech.

A **prepositional phrase** is a group of words that includes a preposition and a noun or a pronoun that is the object of the preposition.

    outside my window   **below the counter**

Exercise B Identifying Prepositional Phrases. In each sentence, identify the prepositional phrase or phrases. Write each on a piece of paper, underline the preposition, and circle its object.

1. In 1868, San Francisco selected the roughly 1,000 acres of the Golden Gate Park.

2. Few were pleased by this selection because of its windy landscape.

3. When John McLaren became superintendent in 1890, the site was suffering from neglect and overuse.

4. Under his supervision, an international exposition was held during 1894; nothing was preserved from it except the Japanese Tea Garden and a museum.

5. It has been a popular setting for a variety of gatherings.

An **adjective phrase** is a prepositional phrase that modifies a noun or a pronoun by telling *what kind* or *which one.*

    The wooden gates *of that lane* stood open.

An **adverb phrase** is a prepositional phrase that modifies a verb, an adjective, or an adverb by pointing out *where, when, in what way,* or *to what extent.*

    On a sudden impulse, he got to his feet. . . .
                 — Jack Finney, p. 110

Exercise C Identifying Adjective and Adverb Phrases. Write the sentences, underlining each prepositional phrase. Identify each as either an *adjective phrase* or an *adverb phrase.*

1. Charlemagne was an influential figure in French history.

2. During the Middle Ages, he became the first true ruler of France.

3. In 771, Charlemagne inherited the territory of his father and brother.

4. He soon initiated a long series of wars against rival factions throughout western Europe.

5. Around this time, he also provided military aid to the pope in Rome.

An **appositive phrase** is a noun or a pronoun with modifiers, placed next to a noun or a pronoun to identify it or add information and details.

    M. Morissot, watchmaker by trade but local militiaman for the time being, stopped short. . . .
            — Guy de Maupassant, p. 1137

Exercise D Using Appositives and Appositive Phrases Write each pair of sentences as a single sentence with an appositive or appositive phrase.

1. The ostrich is a native of Africa and parts of Asia. The ostrich is the largest of all birds.

2. Mrs. Gordon had a piano in her parlor. Her parlor was a room for special guests.

3. The restaurant serves lobster in a delicious Newburg sauce. Newburg sauce is a creamy sauce with butter and wine.

4. Marjorie is one of the most interesting people I know. She is a gourmet, an expert ventriloquist, and a very good poet.

5. Donny's father is a neurologist. He is a specialist on the nervous system.

A **participial phrase** is a participle with its modifiers or complements. The entire phrase acts as an adjective.

> *Choosing such a tide,* I hoped for a glimpse of the pool.   — Rachel Carson, p. 155

Exercise E Recognizing Participial Phrases. Write the participial phrase in each sentence. Then, write the word the participial phrase modifies.

1. Pioneering in different fields, the French have been leaders in the scientific world.

2. The French government, having supported scientific research for more than 350 years, has made many advances possible.

3. In 1635, the Royal Garden became one of the first scientific research centers sponsored by a government.

4. King Louis XIV, known as the Sun King, founded the Royal Academy of Science.

5. Revered as the father of modern chemistry, Antoine Lavoisier gave much to science.

A **gerund** is a form of a verb that is used as a noun. It ends in -*ing*. A **gerund phrase** is a gerund with modifiers or a complement, all acting together as a noun.

> . . . *moving along the ledge* was quite as easy as he had thought it would be. — Jack Finney, p. 110

Exercise F Identifying Gerunds and Gerund Phrases. Write the gerund or gerund phrase in each sentence. Identify the function of each as *subject, direct object, indirect object, predicate nominative, object of a preposition,* or *appositive.*

1. In 1642, the French king Louis XIV began the difficult task of ruling.

2. As he was only four years old, the running of France was left to his mother and her counselor until Louis was older.

3. After the death of his mother's counselor, Louis instituted a new policy: governing without a prime minister.

4. One of Louis's obsessions was expanding the power and influence of France.

5. Louis made conquering the Netherlands and defeating the English his priorities.

An **infinitive** is the form of a verb using *to*. It acts as a noun, adjective, or adverb. An **infinitive phrase** is an infinitive with modifiers, complements, or a subject, all acting together as a single part of speech.

> *To be dead,* and never again behold my city!
> —Dreams, p. 630

Exercise G Identifying Infinitives and Infinitive Phrases. Write the infinitive or infinitive phrase in each of the following sentences. Label each *subject, direct object, predicate nominative, object of a preposition, adjective,* or *adverb.*

1. Charles de Gaulle was to lead France through World War II and the difficult post-war years.

2. In the 1930's, De Gaulle thought the French army was unprepared for the war it was about to fight.

3. After the French government surrendered in 1940, De Gaulle felt he had but one choice, to escape.

4. He resolved to form a new French government in England.

5. He continued to command the resistance groups and the Free French army.

Clauses

A **clause** is a group of words with a subject and a verb.

An **independent clause** has a subject and a verb and can stand by itself as a complete sentence.

A **subordinate clause** has a subject and a verb but cannot stand by itself as a complete sentence; it can only be part of a sentence.

Exercise H Recognizing Independent and Subordinate Clauses. Write and label the independent and subordinate clauses in these sentences.

1. The luxury of baths, which we have come to associate with Rome, was imported from the East.

2. The earliest Roman literature, which contained translations from Greek classics, was based on Greek models.

3. Roman boys, who received better training than the girls did, were taught the Greek classics.

4. The Greeks were conquered by Rome, but culturally the Greeks were the conquerors.

5. Romans were proud of their civilization, although much of it was Greek in origin.

An **adjective clause** is a subordinate clause that modifies a noun or a pronoun by telling *what kind* or *which one.*

> The people *who read the book* loved it.

An **adverb clause** modifies a verb, an adjective, an adverb, or a verbal by telling *where, when, in what way, to what extent, under what condition,* or *why.*

They read it *as soon as it was published.*

A **noun clause** is a subordinate clause that acts as a noun.

Whoever reads it is overcome with joy.

Parallelism

Parallelism is the placement of equal ideas in words, phrases, or clauses of similar type.

Parallel Words: The camp has excellent facilities for *riding, hiking,* and *swimming.*
Parallel Phrases: Jennings had gone to the country *to rest, to think,* and *to catch a few fish.*
Parallel Clauses: A news story should tell *what happened, when it happened,* and *who was involved.*

Exercise I **Correcting Faulty Parallelism.** Rewrite each sentence, correcting the faulty parallelism.

1. Joel likes imitating people and to tell jokes.
2. My desires were to visit the museum and seeing everything in the displays.
3. These plants need water and looking after.
4. The guidance counselor recommended studying harder and to turn off the television set at homework time.
5. A successful ballerina needs skill, stamina, and to have good coordination.

Verb Usage

The Four Principal Parts of Verbs

A verb has four **principal parts:** the *present,* the *present participle,* the *past,* and the *past participle.*

Regular verbs form the past and past participle by adding *-ed* to the present form.

Present: walk
Present Participle: (am) walking
Past: walked
Past Participle: (have) walked

The past and past participle of an **irregular verb** are not formed by adding *-ed* or *-d* to the present form. Irregular verbs form the past and past participle by changing form. Whenever you are in doubt about the principal parts of an irregular verb, use a dictionary to check them.

Present: go
Present Participle: (am) going
Past: went
Past Participle: (have) gone

Exercise A **Using the Principal Parts of Verbs.** Choose the principal part that is correct in each of the following sentences.

1. Many books have been (wrote, written) on the value of money worldwide.
2. Writers have (gave, given) much thought to this topic.
3. Economists have long (knew, known) that the value of money fluctuates.
4. They have (threw, thrown) new light on that which gives money value.
5. For example, a dollar (buyed, bought) more in the 1920s than it does today.

Pronoun Usage

Pronoun Case

The **case** of a pronoun is the form it takes to show its use in a sentence. There are three pronoun cases: *nominative, objective,* and *possessive.*

The **nominative case** is used to rename the subject of the sentence. The nominative case pronouns are *I, you, he, she, it, we, you, they.*

As the subject: *She* is brave
Renaming the subject: The leader is *she.*

The **objective case** is used as the direct object, indirect object, or object of the preposition. The objective case pronouns are *me, you, him, her, it, us, you, them.*

As a direct object: Tom called *me.*
As an indirect object: My friend gave *me* advice.
As an object of preposition: The coach gave pointers to *me.*

The **possessive case** is used to show ownership. The possessive pronouns are *my, your, his, her, its, our, their, mine, yours, his, hers, its, ours, theirs.*

Exercise A **Using All Three Cases.** Choose the correct word in each of the parentheses to complete the sentences below.

1. The doctor told both William and (she, her) his reasons for prescribing the medicine.
2. (He, Him) and (she, her) make a fine team.

3. (Their, They're) contributions cannot be overestimated.

4. These sketches are definitely (her's, hers).

5. Mozart and the young Beethoven were similar in (their, they're) musical styles.

6. Why can't we reach David and (they, them)?

7. Unquestionably, the outstanding speaker was (she, her).

8. Between (we, us), nobody expected such a victory.

9. Those skates surely are (their's, theirs).

10. The team waited for (him, he) until (he, him) arrived.

Agreement

Subject and Verb Agreement

To make a subject and verb agree, make sure that both are singular or both are plural.

Many *storms are* the cause of beach erosion.

In the case of a plural and a singular subject joined by *or* or *nor,* choose the form of the verb that agrees with the closer of the two.

Either the *cats* or the *dog is* hungry.

Neither *Angie* nor *her sisters were* present.

Exercise A **Making Subjects Agree With Their Verbs.** Choose the verb in parentheses that agrees with the subject of each sentence.

1. The old books in the attic (was, were) thrown away.

2. Neither the coach nor the players (holds, hold) much hope of winning.

3. The director and stage manager (has, have) a meeting tomorrow.

4. Phil or Mary usually (opens, open) the office each day.

5. Flights from this airport (leaves, leave) infrequently.

Pronoun-Antecedent Agreement

Pronouns must agree with their antecedents in number and gender. Use singular pronouns with singular antecedents and plural pronouns with plural antecedents. Many errors in pronoun-antecedent agreement occur when a plural pronoun is used to refer to a singular antecedent for which the gender is not specified.

Incorrect: Everyone did their best.

Correct: Everyone did his or her best.

The following indefinite pronouns are singular: *anybody, anyone, each, either, everybody, everyone, neither, nobody, no one, one, somebody, someone.*

The following indefinite pronouns are plural: *both, few, many, several.*

The following indefinite pronouns may be either singular or plural: *all, any, most, none, some.* Treat these pronouns as singular when the antecedent is singular.

All of the <u>gold</u> is gone, and we do not know who took *it.*

Treat these pronouns as plural when the antecedent is plural.

Most of my <u>friends</u> are going, and *they* will have a good time.

Exercise B **Making Personal Pronouns Agree With Indefinite Pronouns.** Choose the correct pronoun in each sentence.

1. Many of these visitors to India begin (his, their) vacations in Bombay.

2. All of the students enjoyed (his or her, their) visit to that city.

3. One of Bombay's best features is (its, their) pleasant climate.

4. Some of the city's appeal is (its, their) blend of old and new.

5. Both students knew (his, their) trip would be great.

Using Modifiers

Degrees of Comparison

Most adjectives and adverbs have three different forms to show degrees of comparison—the *positive,* the *comparative,* the *superlative.*

Use *-er* or *more* to form the comparative degree and *-est* or *most* to form the superlative degree of most one- and two-syllable modifiers.

Use *more* and *most* to form the comparative and superlative degrees of all modifiers with three or more syllables.

The irregular comparative and superlative forms of certain adjectives and adverbs must be memorized.

Notice in the chart on page R-46 that the form of some irregular modifiers differs only in the positive degree. The modifiers *bad, badly,* and *ill,* for example, all have the same basic form in the comparative and superlative degrees (*worse, worst*).

IRREGULAR MODIFIERS

Positive	Comparative	Superlative
bad	worse	worst
badly	worse	worst
far (distance)	farther	farthest
far (extent)	further	furthest
good	better	best
ill	worse	worst
late	later	last *or* latest
little (amount)	less	least
many	more	most
much	more	most
well	better	best

Exercise A **Forming the Comparative and Superlative Degrees.** Rewrite the underlined modifier in the degree indicated in parentheses.

1. The stronger the vibrations of the player's lips, the <u>loud</u> the sound from a horn. (comparative)

2. The <u>simple</u> type of horn is made from an animal horn. (superlative)

3. These instruments are <u>commonly</u> used in religious rituals. (superlative)

4. Horns made from shells are <u>little</u> used as musical instruments. (comparative)

5. Adding finger holes on the side gives it a <u>wide</u> range of notes. (comparative)

Capitalization and Punctuation

Capitalization

Capitalize the first word of a sentence and also the first word in a quotation if the quotation is a complete sentence.

> "No matter," he concluded, "I'll go toward the rising sun."   — Leo Tolstoy, p. 308

Capitalize all proper nouns and adjectives.

W. W. Jacobs   Flanders Fields   African writers

Capitalize a person's title when it is followed by the person's name or when it is used in direct address.

Reverend Tallboys   Mrs. Prothero   "Hello, Major."

Capitalize titles showing family relationships when they refer to a specific person and are used with a name or as a name.

Aunt Mae   Let's ask Grandmother.   *but*   his father

Capitalize the first word and all other key words in the titles of books, periodicals, poems, stories, plays, paintings, and other works of art.

Lord of the Flies   "Spring and All"

Exercise A **Capitalizing Proper Nouns, Proper Adjectives, and Titles Correctly.** Copy the following sentences onto your paper, adding the missing capitals. Underline any titles that appear in italics.

1. Throughout history, many influential new yorkers have entertained and educated us and helped us create a better american way of life.

2. james baldwin—author of many essays, plays, and novels, including *go tell it on the mountain*—was born and raised in new york city.

3. The director woody allen has used the city for the setting of many of his films, such as *manhattan, broadway danny rose,* and *annie hall.*

4. Eleanor Roosevelt, wife of president Franklin d. Roosevelt, helped improve conditions for minorities and the poor.

5. Colin Powell, the son of caribbean immigrants, grew up in the south bronx.

End Marks

Use a **period** to end a declarative sentence, an imperative sentence, an indirect question, and most abbreviations.

> The class will meet at noon.

Use a **question mark** to end a direct question, an incomplete question, or a statement that is intended as a question.

> Did you prepare your assignment?

Use an **exclamation mark** after a statement showing strong emotion, an urgent imperative sentence, or an interjection expressing strong emotion.

> Wait until you hear the news!

Exercise B **Using the Period, Question Mark, and Exclamation Mark.** Copy the following items, adding the necessary periods, question marks, or exclamation marks.

1. The moon's diameter is about one fourth the size of the Earth's
2. Is it true that there is no atmosphere on the moon
3. The moon travels around the Earth at approximately 2,300 miles per hour
4. That is really fast
5. Did you see the footage on television of Neil Armstrong's moon landing

Commas

Use a **comma** before the coordinating conjunction to separate two independent clauses in a compound sentence.

> His arms had begun to tremble from the steady strain of clinging to this narrow perch, and he did not know what to do now. . . .
> — Jack Finney, p. 110

Use commas to separate three or more words, phrases, or clauses in a series.

> . . . he produced about fifteen hundred *drawings, prints, pastels,* and *oil paintings* with ballet themes. — Richard Mühlberger, p. 520

Use commas to separate adjectives of equal rank. Do not use commas to separate adjectives that must stay in a specific order.

> With *pink, dimpled* knees, Henri, not yet a year old, sprawls on the lap of his nurse. . . .
> [In Degas's painting], the *creamy white* tones of the passengers stand out.
> — Richard Mühlberger, p. 520

Use a comma after an introductory word, phrase, or clause.

> When Marian Anderson again returned to America, she was a seasoned artist.
> — Langston Hughes, p. 88

Use commas to set off parenthetical and nonessential expressions.

> Now, *yes, now,* it was about to set!
> — Leo Tolstoy, p. 308

Use commas with places, dates, and titles.

> Poe was raised in Richmond, Virginia.
> August 4, 2026
> Alfred, Lord Tennyson

Use a comma to indicate the words left out of an elliptical sentence, to set off a direct quotation, and to prevent a sentence from being misunderstood.

> Vincent Canby writes for *The New York Times;* Roger Ebert, for the *Chicago Sun Times.*

Exercise C **Using Commas Correctly.** Copy the following sentences, adding the necessary commas.

1. On April 21 1836 the Mexicans were defeated by Texans.
2. America had territorial ambitions in Texas and California so in 1846 they declared war on Mexico.
3. In February of 1848 a large part of Mexican territory became part of the United States.
4. "Santa Anna" according to the encyclopedia "was compelled to resign after the war."
5. June 1863 saw French troops reach Mexico and cause the current government officials to flee.

Semicolons

Use a **semicolon** to join independent clauses that are not already joined by a conjunction.

> They could find no buffalo; they had to hang an old hide from the sacred tree.
> — N. Scott Momaday, p. 545

Use a semicolon to join independent clauses separated by either a conjunctive adverb or a transitional expression.

> James Thurber wrote many books; moreover, he was a cartoonist and a journalist.

Use semicolons to avoid confusion when independent clauses or items in a series already contain commas.

> Thurber is remembered for his character Walter Mitty; for his cartoons, many of which illustrated his books; and for his terrifically funny essays.

Colons

Use a **colon** in order to introduce a list of items following an independent clause.

The authors we are reading include a number of poets: Robert Frost, Octavio Paz, and Emily Dickinson.

Use a colon to introduce a formal quotation.

> The next day Howard Taubman wrote enthusiastically in *The New York Times:* "Marian Anderson has returned to her native land one of the great singers of our time. . . . "
> — Langston Hughes, p. 88

Exercise D **Using Semicolons and Colons Correctly.** Copy each of the following sentences, adding semicolons and colons where necessary.

1. Many Americans wish to discover their roots most families can be traced back to the time of their arrival.

2. Tracing the family's country of origin is usually difficult it can also become expensive.

3. My mother gave me a book, *Tracing Your Irish Ancestors A Few Simple Steps.*

4. She would like me to learn more about the place our family came from County Kerry in Ireland.

5. Genealogical research in Britain and Ireland is relatively easy records are well kept and accessible.

Quotation Marks

A **direct quotation** represents a person's exact speech or thoughts and is enclosed in quotation marks.

> "Clara, my mind is made up."

An **indirect quotation** is a restatement or paraphrase of what a person said or thought and does not require quotation marks.

> The cops suggested that it might be a good idea to tie the dog up, but mother said that it mortified him to be tied up. . . .
> — James Thurber, p. 481

Always place a comma or a period inside the final quotation mark.

> "Eh, you're a stranger," she said. "I thought so."
> — Josephina Niggli, p. 246

Place a question mark or an exclamation mark inside the final quotation mark if the end mark is part of the quotation; if it is not part of the quotation, place it outside the final quotation mark.

> He asked, "Which poetry do you like best?"
> Have you ever read the poem "Africa"?

Use single quotation marks for a quotation within a quotation.

Use quotation marks around the titles of short written works, episodes in a series, songs, and titles of works mentioned as parts of a collection.

"Making a Fist"   "These Are Days"

Underline or italicize titles of longer works, such as plays, movies, or novels.

Exercise E **Adding Quotation Marks and Other Punctuation Marks.** Copy the following sentences, adding the necessary quotation marks and punctuation.

1. Does Mary Shelley's *Frankenstein* begin I am by birth a Genevese

2. So soon as the dazzling light vanished says the narrator the oak had disappeared

3. Her immutable laws had decreed my utter and terrible destruction said the Monster

4. He added It is with considerable difficulty that I remember the original era of my being

5. By degrees he said I remember, a stronger light pressed upon my nerves

Dashes

Use **dashes** to indicate an abrupt change of thought, a dramatic interrupting idea, or a summary statement.

> It made her so mad to see Muggs lying there, oblivious of the mice—they came running up to her—that she slapped him and he slashed at her, but didn't make it. — James Thurber, p. 481

Exercise F **Using the Dash.** On your paper, copy the following sentences, adding one or two dashes in each.

1. Basketball which has long been thought to be an urban game is extremely popular in the suburbs.

2. Modern players are much more muscular it's rare to see a lanky player anymore than players from the past.

3. This does not mean that basketball is a game only for giants thank goodness!

4. People of average height less than six feet tall have had basketball careers.

5. Tyrone "Muggsy" Bogues who enjoyed a stellar career at Wake Forest University in the late 1980's and went on to play professionally stands just five feet three inches tall.

Parentheses

Use **parentheses** to set off asides and explanations only when the material is not essential or when it consists of one or more sentences.

> When I finished (What a lot of facts I found out!), I turned in my report.

Exercise G **Using Parentheses.** On your paper, rewrite the following sentences using the necessary parentheses and capitalization.

1. Earvin Johnson did you know that he was called Magic Johnson? was one of the best point guards in basketball.

2. Johnson My dad saw him play was born in 1959 in Lansing, Michigan.

3. He starred as the point guard perhaps the most important position on the team of the Michigan State team.

4. By the time he retired in 1991, he had won numerous All-Star honors 12.

5. I cannot remember when Magic Johnson first led his professional team to a world championship it must have been 1980 or 1982.

Hyphens

Use a **hyphen** with certain numbers, after certain prefixes, with two or more words used as one word, and with a compound modifier coming before a noun.

fifty-two   greenish-blue water

Exercise H Using Hyphens in Numbers, Word Parts, and Words. Rewrite the sentences that need hyphens. Use a dictionary when in doubt. If no hyphen is needed, write *correct*.

1. Wilt Chamberlain was one of the most intimidating players in basketball.

2. He was a perennial allstar during his long professional basketball career.

3. An ex high school standout, he enjoyed a stellar college career at the University of Kansas.

4. Chamberlain played for three seasons with the University of Kansas team—that university had well trained teams.

5. During his long career, he demonstrated great self discipline.

Apostrophes

Add an **apostrophe** and *s* to show the possessive case of most singular nouns.

Prospero's castle   the playwright's craft

Add an apostrophe to show the possessive case of plural nouns ending in -*s* and -*es*.

the sailors' ships   the babies' mothers

Add an apostrophe and -*s* to show the possessive case of plural nouns that do not end in -*s* or -*es*.

the children's games   the people's friend

Use an apostrophe in a contraction to indicate the position of the missing letter or letters.

I *didn't* love any one of you more than any other.

— William Melvin Kelley, p. 220

Exercise I Using Apostrophes for Possessive Nouns. Write the correct possessive for each underlined noun.

1. Also, the <u>Buddhist temples</u> walls are frequently covered in wall paintings.

2. <u>Buddhists</u> attendance at the temples was high.

3. Literature has a strong tradition in India; the <u>Nobel Prize Committee</u> choice in 1913 was Rabindranath Tagore.

4. Many famous <u>folk tales</u> origins can be traced to India.

5. Music is also important in India; recently <u>film music</u> popularity has grown.

Glossary of Common Usage

among, between

Among is usually used with three or more items. *Between* is generally used with only two items.

Among the poems we read this year, Eve Merriam's "Metaphor" was my favorite.

"Like the Sun" tells of the conflict *between* telling the truth and telling white lies.

around

In formal writing, *around* should not be used to mean *approximately* or *about*. These usages are allowable, however, in informal writing or in colloquial dialogue.

Romeo and Juliet had its first performance in *approximately* 1595.

Shakespeare was *about* thirty when he wrote it.

as, because, like, as to

The word *as* has several meanings and can function as several parts of speech. To avoid confusion, use *because* rather than *as* when you want to indicate cause and effect.

Because Cyril was interested in African American poetry, he wrote his report on Langston Hughes.

Do not use the preposition *like* to introduce a clause that requires the conjunction *as*.

James Thurber conversed *as* he wrote—wittily.

The use of *as to* for *about* is awkward and should be avoided.

Rosa has a theory *about* Edgar Allan Poe's style.

beside, besides

Beside is a preposition meaning "at the side of" or "close to." Do not confuse *beside* with *besides,* which means "in addition to." *Besides* can be a preposition or an adverb.

As the men cross the lawn and approach the open window, a brown spaniel trots *beside* them.

There are many other Indian oral epics *besides* the *Ramayana*.

can, may

The verb *can* generally refers to the ability to do something. The verb *may* generally refers to permission to do something.

Dylan Thomas describes his childhood Christmases so vividly that most readers *can* visualize the scenes.

Creon's edict states that no one *may* bury Polyneices.

different from, different than

The preferred usage is *different from*.

The structure and rhyme scheme of a Shakespearean sonnet are *different from* the organization of a Petrarchan sonnet.

farther, further

Use *farther* when you refer to distance. Use *further* when you mean "to a greater degree" or "additional."

The *farther* the ants travel, the more ominous and destructive they seem.

The storm in Act I of *The Tragedy of Julius Caesar further* hints at the ominous deeds to come.

fewer, less

Use *fewer* for things that can be counted. Use *less* for amounts or quantities that cannot be counted.

Poetry often uses *fewer* words than prose to convey ideas and images.

It takes *less* time to perform a Greek tragedy than to perform a Shakespearean play.

good, well

Use the adjective *good* after linking verbs such as *feel, look, smell, taste,* and *seem.* Use *well* whenever you need an adverb or as an adjective describing health.

Caesar remarks that Cassius does not look *good;* on the contrary, his appearance is "lean."

Twain wrote especially *well* when he described eccentric characters.

hopefully

Do not attach this adverb to a sentence loosely, as in "*Hopefully,* the rain will stop by noon." Rewrite the sentence so that *hopefully* modifies a specific verb. Other possible ways of revising such sentences include using the adjective *hopeful* or a phrase such as *everyone hopes that*.

Dr. Martin Luther King, Jr., wrote and spoke *hopefully* about his dream of racial harmony.

Mr. White was *hopeful* that the monkey's paw would bring him good fortune.

Everyone hopes that the class production of *Antigone* will be a big success.

its, it's

Do not confuse the possessive pronoun *its* with the contraction *it's,* used in place of "it is" or "it has."

In *its* very first lines, "The Stolen Child" establishes an eerie mood.

In "The Street of the Cañon," Pepe Gonzalez knows that *it's* dangerous to attend the party.

just, only

When you use *just* as an adverb meaning "no more than," be sure you place it directly before the word it logically modifies. Likewise, be sure you place *only* before the word it logically modifies.

Just one wish changed the Whites' lives forever.

A short story can usually develop *only* a few characters, whereas a novel can include many.

kind of, sort of

In formal writing, you should not use these colloquial expressions. Instead, use a word such as *rather* or *somewhat*.

Poe portrays Prince Prospero as *rather* arrogant.

The tone of the biography is *somewhat* harsh.

lay, lie

Do not confuse these verbs. *Lay* is a transitive verb meaning "to set or put something down." Its principal parts are *lay, laying, laid, laid. Lie* is an intransitive verb meaning "to recline." Its principal parts are *lie, lying, lay, lain.*

They laid the monkey's paw on the table for a while before anyone dared to pick it up.

La Belle Dame sans Merci enchants the knight as he *lies* in her "elfin grot."

leave, let

Be careful not to confuse these verbs. *Leave* means "to go away" or "to allow to remain." *Let* means "to permit."

Threatening Antigone not to disobey his orders, Creon angrily *leaves* the stage.

Creon did not want to *let* Antigone bury her brother.

raise, rise

Raise is a transitive verb that usually takes a direct object. *Rise* is an intransitive verb and never takes a direct object.

In his speech, Antony unexpectedly *raises* the subject of Caesar's will.

When the Cabuliwallah comes to call, Mini *rises* from her chair and runs to greet him.

set, sit

Do not confuse these verbs. *Set* is a transitive verb meaning "to put (something) in a certain place." Its principal parts are *set, setting, set, set*. *Sit* is an intransitive verb meaning "to be seated." Its principal parts are *sit, sitting, sat, sat*.

Antigone's conduct *sets* a high standard for us.

Jerry's mother *sits* in her beach chair while Jerry swims in the ocean.

so, so that

Be careful not to use the coordinating conjunction *so* when your context requires *so that*. *So* means "accordingly" or "with the result that" and expresses a cause-and-effect relationship. *So that* expresses purpose—what someone intends to achieve.

He wanted to do well on the test, *so* he read *The Tragedy of Julius Caesar* again.

Antony uses eloquent rhetoric to stir up the people *so that* they will rebel.

than, then

The conjunction *than* is used to connect the two parts of a comparison. Do not confuse *than* with the adverb *then,* which usually refers to time.

I enjoyed "The Marginal World" more *than* "Flood."

Marian Anderson gave a triumphant singing recital in New York that evening, and she *then* embarked on a coast-to-coast American tour.

that, which, who

Use the relative pronoun *that* to refer to things. Use *which* only for things and *who* only for people.

The poem *that* Cheryl liked the most was "The street."

Haiku, *which* consists of only seventeen syllables, is often built around one or two vivid images.

The assassin *who* strikes Caesar first is Casca.

unique

Because *unique* means "one of a kind," you should not use it carelessly to mean "interesting" or "unusual." Avoid such illogical expressions as "most unique," "very unique," and "extremely unique."

Emily Dickinson's bold experiments with form make her *unique* in the history of nineteenth-century American poetry.

when, where

Do not directly follow a linking verb with *when* or *where*. Be careful not to use *where* when your context requires *that*.

Faulty: The exposition is *when* an author provides the reader with important background information.

Revised: In the exposition, an author provides the reader with important background information.

Faulty: Madras, India, is *where* R. K. Narayan was born.

Revised: R. K. Narayan was born in Madras, India.

Faulty: We read *where* the prizes were worth hundreds of dollars.

Revised: We read *that* the prizes were worth hundreds of dollars.

INDEX OF SKILLS

Note: Page numbers in **boldface** *refer to pages where terms are defined.*

Literary Analysis

Action, rising and falling, **30**, **R13**, R17

Acts of play, **728**, **844**

Address (speech), 409

Age, golden, **964**

Allegory, **338**, **348**, **362**, **R10**

Alliteration, **580**, **680**, **R10**

Allusion, **594**, **R10**

Analogy, **664**, **R10**

Analytic essay, **518**, 521, **524**, 527, 530

Anecdote, **R10**

Antagonist, **203**, 204, 748, 751, 752, 756, 758, 761, 762, 765, 766, **768**, **964**, **R10**

Anthology, **R6**

Anticlimax, **R10**

Antistrophe, **747**

Appeals, logical, ethical, and emotional, **518**. *See also* Persuasion

Archetype, **964–965**, **R10**
archetypal narrative patterns, **1034**, 1037, 1039, 1040, 1042, 1045, 1046, 1049, 1050, **1051**
archetypal themes. *See* Theme, archetypal

Argument, **498**, **502**, **510**

Article
vs. essay, **18**, **406**
feature, **696**
technical, **166**

Aside (in drama), **729**, **868**, **890**, **R10**

Assonance, **580**, **680**, **R10**

Atmosphere, 646, **R10**

Attention-getting hook, **18**

Audience, 18, 410, 730

Author's perspective, **56**, 58, 60, 61, 63, 65, 67, 69, **70**, 74, **78**

Author's purpose, **86**, **97**
in nonfiction, **5**, **18**, **534**, 537, 538, 539, 540, 543, 544, 546, 548, 550, 551, 552, **553**

in essay, **142**, 144, 146, 148, 151, **152**, 156, 158, 161, **162**, **408**
in speech, **408**

Autobiographical essay, 407, **R10**

Autobiography, 407, 410, **R10**

Ballad, **581**, **R10**

Bias, 408

Bibliography, **948**

Biography, **3**, **R10**

Blank verse, **846**, 847, 850, 854, 857, 864, **866**, **R10**

Catastrophe, **820**, **910**

Catharsis, **729**

Character, **R10**
archetypical, **964**
in drama, **728**, 730, 737, **742**, 932, 935, 937
in fiction, **4**, 7, 12, 14
in short story, 200, **203**, 204, 208, **214**, **218**, **230**, **240**
historical, **820**
motivation, **932**, **935**, **937**
in myth, **980**

Character development, **203**, **218**, 230, 240

Characterization, direct and indirect, **203**, **218**, 221, 222, 225, 229, **230**, 235, 237, 238, 239, **240**, **R11**

Choragos, **747**

Chorus, **729**, **747**, 766

Climax, **R11**
in drama, **728**, **820**
in fiction, **4**
in short story, **30**, **202**

Comedy, **729**, 736, **R11**

Comic relief, **820**, **R11**

Conflict, internal and external, **R11**
in drama, **728**, **742**
in Shakespearean tragedy, **820**, 832, 841, **892**, 894, 901, 902, 907, **908**
in fiction, **4**, **26**
in short story, **30**, **108**, 111, 112, 115, 117, 119, 120, 124, 125, **126**, 130, 132, 135, 136, 137, **138**, 200, **202**, 207, 211

Connotation, **R11**

Consonance, **580**, **680**, **R11**

Contemporary interpretation, **R11**

Context, cultural or historical, **964**, 973. *See also Reading Skills and Strategies Index,* Analyzing Cultural Context

Couplet, **626**, **R11**

Crisis, **820**

Cultural context, 973. *See also Reading Skills and Strategies Index,* Analyzing Cultural Context

Cultural details, **956**, **976**

Culturally distinct values, **965**

Culturally specific theme. *See* Theme

Deductive reasoning, **426**, **434**, **444**, 503

Denotation, **R11**

Denouement, **R11**

Description in short story, **244**, **256**, **266**, **R11**

Descriptive essay, **409**, **R11**

Development
character, **218**
plot, R16

Dialect, **604**, **616**, **R12**

Dialogue, **4**, **R12**
in drama, **728**, 732, 735, **742**, 868
in short story, **218**, **230**, **240**

Diction, **86**, **172**, **R12**

Direct characterization, **203**, **R12**

Directions, technical, **448**. *See also* Stage directions

Drama, 726–727, **742**, 746–747, 818–819, **R12**
elements of, 728
types of, 729

Dramatic effect, **728**

Dramatic irony, **274**, **295**, **370**, **R12**

Dramatic monologue, **868**, **R12**

Dramatic poetry, **581**, **R12**

Dramatic speech, **729**, **868**, 869, 875, 876, 877, 878, 880, 881, 882, 883, 888, 890

Origin myth, **980**

Oxymoron, **687, 693, R16**

Paean, **747**

Parados, **747**

Paradox, 370, 375, **381, R16**

Parallel plot, **728,** 730

Parallelism, **498, R16**

Parody, **965, 1096,** 1101, 1102, 1103, 1104, 1106, 1108, 1109, **1110,** 1114, 1117, 1118, 1121, **1122**

Pentameter, **846, 866, R16**

Personification, **580, 664, R16**

Perspective, **5, 408,** 419, **422**

Persuasion, **5, R16**
   persuasive appeals, **518**
   persuasive essays and speeches, **409, 498,** 501, **502,** 506, **510, R16**

Philosophical assumption, **306, 324, 334**

Plagiarism, 947

Plot, **R16**
   in drama, **728,** 730
   in fiction, **4,** 11, 16
      in short story, **30,** 33, 35, 37, 39, 40, 41, **42,** 46, 47, 48, 51, **52,** 200, **202, 214**

Poetry, 578–579, **R16**
   characteristics of, **580**
   and oral tradition, **962**
   poetic forms, **581, 626, 634, 642**
   types of, **581**

Point of view, **4,** 12, **274,** 276, 277, 278, 280, 281, 283, 285, 286, 288, 291, 292, 293, **295, R16**

Position statement, **1126**

Prologue, **747**

Props, **728,** 740

Prose, **R16**
   and oral tradition, **962**

Protagonist, **203, 748,** 751, 752, 756, 758, 761, 762, 765, 766, **768, 964, R16**

Pun, **R16**

Purpose. *See* Author's purpose

Quatrain, **626, R17**

Quest in myth, **980**

Reflective essay, **409, 452,** 456, 459, **460,** 464, 466, 468, **470**

Repetition
   in poetry, 586, 626, 633, 639, **R17**
   in speeches, **498,** 506

Research sources, **622, 1030**

Resolution, **4, R17**
   in drama, **728**
   in short story, **30, 108,** 125, **126, 138, 202**

Review, critical, **366, 794**

Rhetorical devices, **498, 502, 510**

Rhetorical questions, **498**

Rhyme, **580, 626, R17**
   exact rhyme, **R17**
   internal rhyme, **R17**
   rhyme scheme, **580, R17**
   slant rhyme, **R17**

Rhythm, **580,** 582, **R17**

Rising action, **30, 108, R17**

Round character, **R17**

Satire, **474, R17**

Saws, **498**

Scene, **728, R17**

Science fiction, **201,** 204, **R17**

Script, **728**

Sensory language, **580, R17**

Sestet, **R17**

Set of a play, **728, R17**

Setting, **R17**
   in fiction, **4,** 7, **26**
      in short story, 200, **203,** 204, **214, 244,** 247, 252, 255, **256,** 261, 262, 265, **266**

Shakespearean sonnet, **626**

Shakespearean theater, **818–819**

Shakespeare's tragedies, 729, **820,** 829, 832, 834, 841, **844**

Shakespeare's tragic heroes, **910,** 915, 916, 918, 919, 921, 924

Shared values in the oral tradition, **965**

Short story, **4, 214, R18**
   elements of, 200–201, **202–203**

Signs, **928**

Simile, **580, 664, R18**

Situational irony, **370**
   See also Irony

Slogans, **498**

Soliloquy, 729, **868, 890, 910, R18**

Sonnet, **581, 626,** 631, 641, **R18**
   Shakespearean, **626**

Sound devices, **580, 680,** 683, **686,** 690, **692**

Speaker, 582, 583, **588, 592, 606,** 609, 610, **618, R18**

Speech
   characteristics of, **408**
   humorous, **474**
   persuasive, **498,** 501, **502,** 506, **510**
   types of, **409**
   See also Dramatic speech

Stage directions, **728,** 733, 735, 736, **742, R18**

Staging, 730, 746

Stanza, 581, 626, **R18**

Static character, **R18**

Strophe, **747**

Style, **86,** 89, 90, 93, 94, 96, **97, 408,** 420, **R18**

Support, **152, 162**

Supporting role, **820**

Surprise ending, **R18**

Suspense, **108,** 124, **126,** 132, **138, R18**

Symbol, **338, 348,** 362, **R18**

Symbolism, **338,** 347, **348,** 351, 355, 358, 361, **362**

Syntax, **86**

Talk (speech), **409**

Tanka, **581, 626**

Tetrameter, **R18**

Theater
   ancient Greek, 746–747
   Shakespearean, 818–819

Theme, **4, R18**
   archetypal, **R18**
   comparing, **700,** 702, 705, **707, 798**
   cultural context and, 973
   in drama, **728**
   of Greek tragedy, **770, 790**
   oral tradition and, **962, 964–965**
   in poetry, **700,** 702, 705, **707**
   in short story, **203, 214, 306,** 309, 311, 312, 314, 321, 323, **324,** 328, **334**
   stated and implied, **203,** 306
   universal, **4, 798, 807, 964, 1132, R19**
      and culturally specific, **798,** 801, 802, 803, 805, 806, **807**
   worldview and, **1132,** 1134, 1136, 1138, 1140, 1141, 1143, 1144, **1145**

Reading Skills and Strategies

INDEX OF FEATURES

Literature in Context

On Your Own

Reading Informational Materials

Spelling Workshop

Unit Introductions

INDEX OF AUTHORS AND TITLES

Nonfiction selections and informational text appears in red. Page numbers in italic text refer to biographical information.

the Democracy Movement. Translation copyright © 1991 by Donald Finkel.

Norwegian Nobel Institute "Keep Memory Alive" by Elie Wiesel from *Elie Wiesel's Nobel Prize Acceptance Speech.* Copyright © 1986 by the Nobel Foundation. Reprinted with permission from the Norwegian Nobel Institute.

Naomi Shihab Nye "Making a Fist" from *Hugging the Jukebox* by Naomi Shihab Nye. Copyright © 1982 by Dutton: New York. Used by permission of the author, Naomi Shihab Nye, 2004.

Harold Ober Associates, Inc. Excerpt from "Marian Anderson: Famous Concert Singer," by Langston Hughes. Copyright © 1954 by Langston Hughes. Renewed 1982 by George Houston Bass. Text displayed by permission of Harold Ober Associates Incorporated.

Oxford University Press, UK "How Much Land Does a Man Need?" by Leo Tolstoy, translated by Louise and Aylmer Maude from *The Raid and Other Stories.* Copyright © 1935 Oxford University Press UK. Reprinted by permission.

Pantheon Books "The Orphan Boy and the Elk Dog" from *American Indian Myths and Legends* by Richard Erdoes and Alfonso Ortiz. Copyright © 1984 by Richard Erdoes and Alfonso Ortiz. Used by permission of Pantheon Books, a division of Random House, Inc.

Pearson Prentice Hall (formerly Prentice-Hall, Inc.—Secondary) "Tides" from *Prentice Hall Science Explorer: Earth Science.* Copyright © 2001 by Pearson Education, Inc., publishing as Pearson Prentice Hall. Reprinted by permission.

Penguin Group (USA) Inc. From *Places Left Unfinished at the Time of Creation* by John Phillip Santos. Copyright © John Phillip Santos, 1999. All rights reserved. Used by permission of Viking Penguin, a division of Penguin Group (USA) Inc.

G. P. Putnam's Sons "Arthur Becomes King," Part I, Chapter XXII from *The Once and Future King* by T. H. White. Copyright © 1938, 1939, 1940, © 1958 by T. H. White, renewed. Used by permission of G. P. Putnam's Sons, a division of Penguin Group (USA) Inc.

Random House, Inc. from *A Raisin In The Sun,* from Act I, Scene ii, by Lorraine Hansberry. Copyright © 1958 by Robert Nemiroff, as an unpublished work. Copyright © 1959, 1966, 1984 by Robert Nemiroff. "Occupation: Conductorette" by Maya Angelou from *I Know Why the Caged Bird Sings.* Copyright © 1969 and renewed 1997 by Maya Angelou. All rights reserved. Used by permission of Random House, Inc.

Random House Children's Publishing "Ashputtle" from *Grimm's Tales for Young and Old* by Jakob and Wilhelm Grimm, translated by Ralph Manheim, copyright © 1977 by Ralph Manheim. Used by permission of Random House Children's Books, a division of Random House, Inc.

Marian Reiner, Literary Agent "Metaphor" from *It Doesn't Always Have to Rhyme* by Eve Merriam. Copyright © 1964, 1970, 1973, 1986 by Eve Merriam. Copyright renewed 1992 Eve Merriam. Used by permission of Marian Reiner.

Rogers, Coleridge and White, Ltd. "Games at Twilight" from *Games at Twilight and Other Stories* by Anita Desai. Copyright © 1978 by Anita Desai. Reproduced by permission of the author c/o Rogers, Coleridge & White, Ltd., 20 Powis Mews, London W11 1JN.

Scientific American "The Spider and the Wasp" by Alexander Petrunkevitch from *Scientific American,* August 1952. Copyright © 1952 by Scientific American, Inc.

Scribner From *Angela's Ashes* by Frank McCourt. Copyright © 1996 by Frank McCourt. All rights reserved. Reprinted with the permission of Scribner, an imprint of Simon & Schuster Adult Publishing Group.

Elyse Sommer "A Curtain Up Review: *Antigone As Acted and Played by the Three Fates on the Way to Becoming the Three Graces,*" review by Elyse Sommer in *www.curtainup.com,* the online theater magazine. Copyright 2004, Elyse Sommer. Reprinted by permission.

Dr. Nigel Strudwick "Egyptology Resources" by Nigel Strudwick from *www.newton.cam.ac.uk/egypt/index.html.* Copyright © Nigel Strudwick 1994–2001. Reprinted by permission of the author.

Talkin' Broadway "*Antigone* (Theatre Review)" by Matthew Murray from *www.talkinbroadway.com.* Reprinted by permission.

Jeremy P. Tarcher, an imprint of Penguin Group (USA) Inc. "Making History with Vitamin C" (originally titled "Ascorbic Acid") by Penny Le Couteur and Jay Burreson from *Napoleon's Buttons: How 17 Molecules Changed History.* Copyright © 2003 by Micron Geological Ltd. All rights reserved. Used by permission of Jeremy P. Tarcher, an imprint of Penguin Group (USA) Inc.

Anthony Thwaite Tanka: "Was it that I went to sleep" by Ono no Komachi, translated and co-edited by Geoffrey Bownas and Anthony Thwaite from *The Penguin Book Of Japanese Verse.* "When I went to visit" by Ki no Tsurayuki translated by Bownas & Thwaite from *The Penguin Book Of Japanese Verse.* "One cannot ask loneliness" by Priest Jakuren translated by Bownas & Thwaite from *The Penguin Book Of Japanese Verse.* Penguin Books copyright © 1964, revised edition 1998. Translation copyright © Geoffrey Bownas and Anthony Thwaite, 1964, 1998. Reprinted by permission.

David Unger "The Censors," from *Open Doors: Stories by Luisa Valenzuela.* Copyright © translation by David Unger. Reprinted by permission.

University of North Carolina Press "Street of the Cañon" by Josefina Niggli. Copyright © 1945 by the University of North Carolina Press, renewed 1972 by Josefina Niggli. Used by permission of the publisher.

Viking Penguin, a division of Penguin Young Readers Group, a Member of Penguin Group (USA) Inc. From *What Makes a Degas a Degas?* by Richard Mühlberger, copyright © 1993 by The Metropolitan Museum of Art. Used by permission of Viking Penguin, a division of Penguin Young Readers Group, A Member of Penguin Group (USA) Inc., 345 Hudson Street, New York, NY 10014.

Viking Penguin, a division of Penguin Group (USA) Inc. "Like the Sun" from *Under The Banyan Tree* by R. K. Narayan, copyright © 1985 by R. K. Narayan. "My City" by James Weldon Johnson from *Saint Peter Relates an Incident.* Copyright © 1935 by James Weldon Johnson, © renewed 1963 by Grace Nail Johnson. Used by permission of Viking Penguin, a division of Penguin Group (USA) Inc.

Susan Vreeland "Artful Research" from *The Writer,* January 2002, by Susan Vreeland. Copyright © 2001. "Magdalena Looking" by Susan Vreeland. First appeared in *Girl in Hyacinth Blue,* copyright © 1999 by Susan Vreeland. Available in hardback: MacAdam-Cage; paperback: Penguin. Used by permission of the author.

W. W. Norton & Company, Inc. "Don Quixote," excerpt from *Don Quixote: A Norton Critical Edition: The Ormsby Translation, Revised,* by Miguel de Cervantes, edited by Joseph Jones and Kenneth Douglas. Copyright © 1981 by W. W. Norton & Company, Inc. Used by permission of W. W. Norton & Company, Inc.

Walker & Company From *Longitude: The True Story of a Lone Genius Who Solved the Greatest Scientific Problem of His Time* by Dava Sobel. Copyright © Dava Sobel, 1995. All rights reserved. Reprinted by permission.

The Wall Street Journal "The Wall" by Staff from *The Wall Street Journal* (Eastern Edition), November 9, 1999. Reprinted with permission of The Wall Street Journal © 1999 Dow Jones & Company, Inc. All rights reserved.

Wallace Literary Agency "Rama's Initation" by R. K. Narayan. From *The Ramayana* by R. K. Narayan. Published by Penguin Books. Used by permission of the Wallace Literary Agency, Inc.

Wesleyan University Press "Glory" by Yusef Komunyakaa from *Magic City* in *Pleasure Dome: New and Collected Poems* © 2001 by Yusef Komunyakaa and reprinted by permisson of Wesleyan University Press.

Weiser & Elwell, Literary Agents "Auto Wreck" by Karl Shapiro from *Collected Poems, 1940–1978.* Copyright © 1986 Estate of Karl Shapiro by arrangement with Wieser & Elwell, New York. Reprinted by permission.

William Morris Agency "A Visit to Grandmother" by William Melvin Kelley from *Dancers on the Shore.* Copyright © 1964 by William Melvin Kelley.

The Estate of Theodore H. White "The American Idea" by Theodore H. White from *The New York Times Magazine,* July 6, 1986. Copyright © 1986 by Theodore H. White. All rights reserved. Reprinted by permission.

Writers House LLC "Fear" by Gabriela Mistral from *Selected Poems of Gabriela Mistral,* translated by Doris Dana. Copyright 1961, 1964, 1970, 1971 by Doris Dana. Reprinted by permission of The Joan Daves Agency on behalf of the estate of the author.

Note: Every effort has been made to locate the copyright owner of material reproduced in this component. Omissions brought to our attention will be corrected in subsequent editions.

CREDITS

IMAGE CREDITS